FROM MINIATURES BY JEHAN DE GRISE († 1344) IN
BODLEIAN MS. 264 (*Li romans d'Alixandre*)

THE MEDIAEVAL STAGE

E. K. Chambers

TWO VOLUMES BOUND AS ONE

DOVER PUBLICATIONS, INC.

Mineola, New York

Published in Canada by General Publishing Company, Ltd.,
30 Lesmill Road, Don Mills, Toronto, Ontario.
Published in the United Kingdom by Constable and Company,
Ltd., 3 The Lanchesters, 162–164 Fulham Palace Road, London
W6 9ER.

Bibliographical Note

This Dover edition, first published in 1996, is an unabridged
republication in one volume of the work originally published in
two volumes by Oxford University Press, London, in 1903.

Library of Congress Cataloging-in-Publication Data

Chambers, E. K. (Edmund Kerchever), 1866–1954.
    The mediaeval stage / E. K. Chambers.
        p.   cm.
    Originally published: London : Oxford University Press,
1903.
    Includes bibliographical references and index.
    ISBN 0-486-29229-0 (pbk.)
    1. Theater—History—Medieval, 500–1500. 2. Drama,
Medieval—History and criticism.
PN2152.C4   1996
792'.09'02—dc20   96–14913
                                                            CIP

Manufactured in the United States of America
Dover Publications, Inc., 31 East 2nd Street, Mineola, N.Y. 11501

THE MEDIAEVAL STAGE

VOLUME I

TO N. C.

PREFACE

SOME years ago I was thinking of a little book, which now may or may not ever get itself finished, about Shakespeare and the conditions, literary and dramatic, under which Shakespeare wrote. My proper task would have begun with the middle of the sixteenth century. But it seemed natural to put first some short account of the origins of play-acting in England and of its development during the Middle Ages. Unfortunately it soon became apparent that the basis for such a narrative was wanting. The history of the mediaeval theatre had never, from an English point of view, been written. The initial chapter of Collier's *Annals of the Stage* is even less adequate than is usual with this slovenly and dishonest antiquary. It is with some satisfaction that, in spite of the barrier set up by an incorrect reference, I have resolved one dramatic representation elaborately described by Collier into a *soteltie* or sweetmeat. More scholarly writers, such as Dr. A. W. Ward, while dealing excellently with the mediaeval drama as literature, have shown themselves but little curious about the social and economic facts upon which the mediaeval drama rested. Yet from a study of such facts, I am sure, any literary history, which does not confine itself solely to the analysis of genius, must make a start.

An attempt of my own to fill the gap has grown into these two volumes, which have, I fear, been unduly swelled by the inclusion of new interests as, from time to time, they took hold upon me; an interest, for example, in the light-hearted and coloured life of those *poverelli* of letters, the minstrel folk; a very deep interest in the track across the ages of certain customs and symbols of rural gaiety which bear with them the inheritance of a remote and ancestral heathenism. I can only hope that this disproportionate treatment of parts has not wholly destroyed the unity of purpose at which, after all, I aimed. If I may venture to define for myself the formula of my work, I would say that it endeavours to state and explain the pre-existing conditions which, by the latter half of the sixteenth century, made the great Shakespearean stage possible. The story is one of a sudden dissolution and a slow upbuilding. I have arranged the material in four Books. The First Book shows how the organization of the Graeco-Roman theatre broke down before the onslaught of Christianity and the indifference of barbarism, and how the actors became wandering minstrels, merging with the gleemen of their Teutonic conquerors, entertaining all classes of mediaeval society with *spectacula* in which the dramatic element was of the slightest, and in the end, after long endurance, coming to a practical compromise with the hostility of the Church. In the Second Book I pass to *spectacula* of another type, which also had to struggle against ecclesiastical disfavour, and which also made their ultimate peace with all but the most austere forms of the dominant religion. These are the *ludi* of the village feasts, bearing witness, not only to their origin in heathen ritual, but also, by their constant tendency to break out into primitive forms of drama, to the deep-rooted mimetic instinct of the folk. The Third Book is a study of the process by which the Church itself, through the introduction of dramatic elements into its liturgy, came to make its own appeal to this same mimetic instinct ; and of that by which, from such beginnings, grew up the great popular religious drama of the miracle-plays, with its offshoots in the moralities and the dramatic pageants. The Fourth and final Book deals summarily with the transformation of the mediaeval stage, on the literary side under the influence of humanism, on the social and economic side by the emergence from amongst the ruins of minstrelsy of a new class of professional players, in whose hands the theatre was destined to recover a stable organization upon lines which had been departed from since the days of Tertullian.

I am very conscious of the manifold imperfections of these volumes. They are the work, not of a professed student, but of one who only plays at scholarship in the rare intervals of a busy administrative life. They owe much to the long-suffering officials of the British Museum and the London Library, and more recently to the aid and encouragement of the Delegates

of the Clarendon Press and their accomplished staff. The
literary side of the mediaeval drama, about which much
remains to be said, I have almost wholly neglected. I shall
not, I hope, be accused of attaching too much importance in
the first volume to the vague and uncertain results of folk-lore
research. One cannot be always giving expression to the
minuter shades of probability. But in any investigation
the validity of the inferences must be relative to the nature
of the subject-matter; and, whether I qualify it in words or
not, I do not, of course, make a statement about the intention,
say, of primitive sacrifice, with the same confidence which
attaches to one about matters of historic record. The burden
of my notes and appendices sometimes appears to me
intolerable. My excuse is that I wanted to collect, once for
all, as many facts with as precise references as possible.
These may, perhaps, have a value independent of any conclusions which I have founded upon them. And even now
I do not suppose that I have been either exhaustive or accurate.
The remorseless ideal of the historian's duties laid down in the
Introduction aux Études Historiques of MM. Langlois and
Seignobos floats before me like an accusing spirit. I know
how very far I am from having reached that austere standard
of scientific completeness. To begin with, I had not the
necessary training. Oxford, my most kindly nurse, maintained
in my day no *École des Chartes*, and I had to discover the
rules of method as I went along. But the greater difficulty has
been the want of leisure and the spacious life. Shades of Duke
Humphrey's library, how often, as I jostled for my turn at the
crowded catalogue-shelves of the British Museum, have I not
envied those whose lot it is to tread your ample corridors and
to bend over your yellowing folios! Amongst such happy
scholars, the canons of Clio may claim implicit obedience.
A silent company, they 'class' their documents and 'try'
their sources from morn to eve, disturbed in the pleasant ways
of research only by the green flicker of leaves in the Exeter
garden, or by the statutory inconvenience of a terminal lecture.—

'Tanagra! think not I forget!'

E. K. C.

LONDON, *May,* 1903.

CONTENTS

VOLUME I

BOOK I. MINSTRELSY

BOOK II. FOLK DRAMA

VOLUME II

BOOK III. RELIGIOUS DRAMA

BOOK IV. THE INTERLUDE

APPENDICES

CONTENTS

LIST OF AUTHORITIES

[*General Bibliographical Note.* I mention here only a few works of wide range, which may be taken as authorities throughout these two volumes. Others, more limited in their scope, are named in the preliminary notes to the sections of the book on whose subject-matter they bear.—An admirable general history of the modern drama is W. Creizenach's still incomplete *Geschichte des neueren Dramas* (Band i, *Mittelalter und Frührenaissance*, 1893; Bände ii, iii, *Renaissance und Reformation,* 1901–3). R. Prölss, *Geschichte des neueren Dramas* (1881–3), is slighter. The earlier work of J. L. Klein, *Geschichte des Dramas* (13 vols. 1865–76), is diffuse, inconvenient, and now partly obsolete. A valuable study is expected from J. M. Manly in vol. iii of his *Specimens of the Pre-Shakespearean Drama*, of which two volumes, containing selected texts, appeared in 1897. C. Hastings, *Le Théâtre français et anglais* (1900, Eng. trans. 1901), is a compilation of little merit.—Prof. Creizenach may be supplemented for Germany by R. Froning, *Das Drama des Mittelalters* (1891). For France there are the exhaustive and excellent volumes of L. Petit de Julleville's *Histoire du Théâtre en France au Moyen Âge* (*Les Mystères*, 1880; *Les Comédiens en France au Moyen Âge*, 1885; *La Comédie et les Mœurs en France au Moyen Âge*, 1886; *Répertoire du Théâtre comique au Moyen Âge*, 1886). G. Bapst, *Essai sur l'Histoire du Théâtre* (1893), adds some useful material on the history of the stage. For Italy A. d'Ancona, *Origini del Teatro italiano* (2nd ed., 1891), is also excellent.—The best English book is A. W. Ward's *History of English Dramatic Literature to the death of Queen Anne* (2nd ed., 1899). J. P. Collier, *History of English Dramatic Poetry* (new ed., 1879), is full of matter, but, for various reasons, not wholly trustworthy. J. J. Jusserand, *Le Théâtre en Angleterre* (2nd ed., 1881), J. A. Symonds, *Shakespeare's Predecessors in the English Drama* (1884), and G. M. Gayley, *Representative English Comedies* (1903), are of value. Texts will be found in Manly's and Gayley's books, and in A. W. Pollard, *English Miracle Plays, Moralities and Interludes* (3rd ed., 1898); W. C. Hazlitt, *Dodsley's Old Plays* (15 vols. 1874–6); A. Brandl, *Quellen des weltlichen Dramas in England* (1898). F. H. Stoddard, *References for Students of Miracle Plays and Mysteries* (1887), and K. L. Bates and L. B. Godfrey, *English Drama; a Working Basis* (1896), are rough attempts at bibliographies.—In addition the drama of course finds treatment in the general histories of literature. The best are: for Germany, R. Kögel, *Geschichte der deutschen Literatur bis zum Ausgange des Mittelalters* (1894–7, a fragment); K. Gödeke, *Grundriss zur Geschichte der deutschen Dichtung aus den Quellen* (2nd ed., 1884–1900); W. Scherer, *Geschichte der deutschen Litteratur* (8th ed., 1899): for France, L. Petit de Julleville (editor), *Histoire de la Langue et de la Littérature françaises* (1896–1900); G. Paris, *La Littérature française au Moyen Âge* (2nd ed., 1890): for Italy, A. Gaspary, *Geschichte der italienischen Litteratur* (1884–9, Eng. transl. 1901): for England, T. Warton, *History of English Poetry* (ed. W. C. Hazlitt, 1871); B. Ten Brink, *History of English Literature* (Eng. trans. 1893–6); J. J. Jusserand, *Literary History of the English People* (vol. i. 1895); W. J. Courthope, *History of English Poetry* (vols. i, ii. 1895–7); G. Saintsbury, *Short History of English Literature* (1898), and, especially for bibliography, G. Körting, *Grundriss der Geschichte der englischen Litteratur* (3rd ed., 1899). The *Periods of European Literature*, edited by Prof. Saintsbury, especially G. Gregory Smith, *The Transition Period* (1900), and the two great *Grundrisse*, H. Paul, *Grundriss der germanischen Philologie* (2nd ed., 1896–1903), and G. Gröber, *Grundriss der romanischen Philologie* (1888–1903), should also be consulted.—The beginnings of the mediaeval drama are closely bound up with liturgy, and the nature of the liturgical books referred to is explained by W. Maskell, *A Dissertation upon the Ancient Service-Books of the Church of England* (in *Monumenta Ritualia Ecclesiae Anglicanae*, 2nd ed., 1882, vol. iii); H. B. Swete, *Church Services and Service-Books before the Reformation* (1896); Procter-Frere, *New History of the Book of Common Prayer* (1901). The beginnings of Catholic ritual are studied by L. Duchesne, *Origines du Culte chrétien* (3rd ed., 1902, Eng. trans. 1903), and its mediaeval forms described by D. Rock, *The Church of our Fathers* (1849–53), and J. D. Chambers, *Divine Worship in England in the Thirteenth and Fourteenth Centuries* (1877). The following list of books is mainly intended to elucidate the references in the footnotes, and has no claim to bibliographical completeness or accuracy. I have included the titles of a few German and French dissertations of which I have not been able to make use.]

Aberdeen Records. Extracts from the Council Register of the Burgh of Aberdeen. Edited by J. Stuart. 2 vols. 1844–8. [*Spalding Club*, xii, xix.]
Acta SS. Acta Sanctorum quotquot toto orbe coluntur, quas collegit

I. Bollandus.   Operam continuavit G. Henschenius [et alii], 1734–1894. [In progress.]

AHN.   English Mysteries and Miracle Plays.   By Dr. Ahn.   Trier, 1867. [Not consulted.]

ALCUIN.   See DÜMMLER.

ALLARD.   Julien l'Apostat.   Par P. Allard.   3 vols. 1900–3.

ALLEN.   The Evolution of the Idea of God : an Enquiry into the Origins of Religion.   By Grant Allen, 1897.

ALT.   Theater und Kirche in ihrem gegenseitigen Verhältniss.   Von H. Alt, 1846.

Anal. Hymn.   Analecta Hymnica Medii Aevi.   Ediderunt C. Blume et G. M. Dreves.   37 parts, 1886–1901. [In progress.]

ANCONA.   Origini del Teatro italiano.   Per A. d'Ancona, 2nd ed. 2 vols. 1891.

ANCONA, *Sacr. Rappr.*   Sacre Rappresentazioni dei secoli xiv, xv e xvi, raccolte e illustrate per cura di A. d'Ancona, 1872.

Anglia.   Anglia : Zeitschrift für englische Philologie.   24 vols. 1878–1903. [In progress.]

Ann. Arch.   Annales Archéologiques, dirigées par Didron aîné.   28 vols. 1844–81.

Antiquarian Repertory.   The Antiquarian Repertory : A Miscellaneous assemblage of Topography, History, Biography, Customs and Manners. Compiled by F. Grose and T. Astle.   2nd ed. 4 vols. 1807.

ARBOIS DE JUBAINVILLE, *Civ. Celt.*   La Civilisation des Celtes et celle de l'Épopée homérique.   Par H. d'Arbois de Jubainville, 1899. [Vol. vi of *Cours de littérature celtique.*]

ARBOIS DE JUBAINVILLE, *Cycl. Myth.*   Le Cycle mythologique irlandais et la Mythologie celtique.   Par H. d'Arbois de Jubainville, 1884. [Vol. ii of same.]

Archaeologia.   Archaeologia : or Miscellaneous Tracts relating to Antiquity.   Published by the Society of Antiquaries of London.   57 vols. 1770–1901. [In progress.]

ARNOLD.   The Customs of London, otherwise Arnold's Chronicle. Edited by F. Douce, 1811.

ASHTON.   A Righte Merrie Christmasse ! ! !   By J. Ashton, n. d.

BAHLMANN, *Ern.*   Die Erneuerer des antiken Dramas und ihre ersten dramatischen Versuche : 1314–1478.   Von P. Bahlmann, 1896.

BAHLMANN, *L. D.*   Die lateinischen Dramen von Wimpheling's Stylpho bis zur Mitte des sechzehnten Jahrhunderts : 1480–1550.   Von P. Bahlmann, 1893.

BALE.   Scriptorum illustrium maioris Britanniae, quam nunc Angliam et Scotiam vocant, Catalogus.   Autore Ioanne Baleo Sudouolgio Anglo. 2 vols.   Basileae, Oporinus, 1557–9. [Enlarged from the edition in one vol. of 1548.]

BALE, *Index.*   Index Britanniae Scriptorum quos ex variis bibliothecis non parvo labore collegit Ioannes Baleus.   Edited by R. L. Poole and

M. Bateson, 1902. [*Anecdota Oxoniensia, Mediaeval and Modern Series*, ix, from a MS. compiled 1549–1557.]

BAPST. Essai sur l'Histoire du Théâtre. Par G. Bapst, 1893.

BARBAZAN-MÉON. Fabliaux et Contes des Poètes françois des xi, xii, xiii, xiv et xv siècles. Publiés par E. Barbazan. Nouvelle édition, par M. Méon. 4 vols. 1808.

BARRETT. Riding Skimmington and Riding the Stang. By C. R. B. Barrett, 1895. [*Journal of British Archaeological Association*, N. S. vol. i.]

BARTHÉLEMY. Rational ou Manuel des divins Offices de Guillaume Durand, Évêque de Mende au treizième siècle. Traduit par M. C. Barthélemy. 5 vols. 1854.

BARTSCH. Altfranzösische Romanzen und Pastourellen. Par K. Bartsch, 1870.

BATES. The English Religious Drama. By K. L. Bates, 1893.

BATES-GODFREY. English Drama: a Working Basis. By K. L. Bates and L. B. Godfrey, 1896.

BEDE, *D. T. R.* Venerabilis Bedae Opera quae Supersunt Omnia. Edidit J. A. Giles. 12 vols. 1843–4. [The *De Temporum Ratione* forms part of vol. vi.]

BEDE, *E. H.* See PLUMMER.

BÉDIER. Les Fabliaux. Études de Littérature populaire et d'Histoire littéraire du Moyen Âge. Par J. Bédier, 2nd ed. 1895.

BELETHUS. Rationale Divinorum Officiorum Auctore Joanne Beletho Theologo Parisiensi, 1855. [In *P. L.* ccii.]

BELL. Ancient Poems, Ballads, and Songs of the Peasantry of England. Edited by R. Bell, 1857.

BÉRENGER-FÉRAUD. Superstitions et Survivances étudiées au point de vue de leur Origine et de leurs Transformations. Par L. J. B. Bérenger-Féraud. 4 vols. 1896.

BERNHARD. Recherches sur l'Histoire de la Corporation des Ménétriers ou Joueurs d'Instruments de la Ville de Paris. Par B. Bernhard. [*Bibl. de l'École des Chartes*, iii. 377, iv. 525, v. 254, 339.]

BERTRAND. Nos Origines : iv. La Religion des Gaulois ; Les Druides et le Druidisme. Par A. Bertrand, 1897.

Bibl. des Chartes. Bibliothèque de l'Ecole des Chartes. Revue d'Érudition consacrée spécialement à l'étude du Moyen Âge. [I quote the numbers of the annual volumes, without regard to the *Séries.*]

BINGHAM. The Works of Joseph Bingham. Edited by R. Bingham. New ed. 10 vols.

BLOMEFIELD. An Essay towards a Topographical History of the County of Norfolk. By F. Blomefield. 2nd ed. 11 vols. 1805–10.

BÖHCK. Die Anfänge des englischen Dramas. Von Dr. Böhck, 1890. [Not consulted.]

BOLTON. The Counting-Out Rhymes of Children. By H. C. Bolton, 1888.

BORETIUS. Capitularia Regum Francorum. Ediderunt A. Boretius et V. Krause. 2 vols. 1883-7. [*M. G. H. Leges*, Sectio ii.]

BOURQUELOT. Office de la Fête des Fous. Publié par F. Bourquelot, 1858. [*Bulletin de la Société archéologique de Sens*, vol. vi. Not consulted at first hand.]

BOWER. The Elevation and Procession of the Ceri at Gubbio. By H. M. Bower, 1897. [*F. L. S.*]

BRAND. Observations on Popular Antiquities, chiefly illustrating the Origin of our Vulgar Customs, Ceremonies, and Superstitions. By J. Brand. Enlarged by Sir H. Ellis. 3 vols. 1841-2.

BRAND-HAZLITT. Observations on Popular Antiquities. By J. Brand. Edited with additions by W. C. Hazlitt. 3 vols. 1870.

BRANDL. Quellen des weltlichen Dramas in England vor Shakespeare. Ein Ergänzungsband zu Dodsley's Old English Plays. Herausgegeben von A. Brandl, 1898. [*Quellen und Forschungen*, lxxx.]

BREWER. Letters and Papers, Foreign and Domestic, of the Reign of Henry VIII. Arranged and catalogued by J. S. Brewer [and afterwards J. Gairdner and R. H. Brodie]. 18 vols. 1862-1902. [*Calendars of State Papers.*]

BROOKE. The History of Early English Literature : being the History of English Poetry to the Accession of King Alfred. By S. A. Brooke. 2 vols. 1892.

BROOKE, *Eng. Lit.* English Literature from the Beginning to the Norman Conquest. By S. A. Brooke, 1898.

BROTANEK. Die englischen Maskenspiele. Von R. Brotanek, 1902. [*Wiener Beiträge zur englischen Philologie*, xv.]

BROWN. Calendar of State Papers and Manuscripts relating to English Affairs, in the Archives and Collections of Venice and in other Libraries of North Italy. Edited by H. F. Brown and R. Brown. 10 vols. 1864-1900.

BRYLINGER. Comoediae et Tragoediae aliquot ex Novo et Vetere Testamento desumptae. Basileae, Brylinger, 1540.

BURCHARDUS. Burchardi Wormaciencis Ecclesiae Episcopi Decretorum Libri xx, 1853. [In *P. L.* cxl.]

BURNE-JACKSON. Shropshire Folk-lore: A Sheaf of Gleanings. Edited by C. S. Burne, from the collections of G. F. Jackson, 1883.

BURNET. A History of the Reformation of the Church of England. By G. Burnet. Edited by N. Pocock. 7 vols. 1865.

BURTON. Rushbearing. By A. Burton, 1891.

BURY-GIBBON. *See* GIBBON.

CAMPBELL. Materials for a History of the Reign of Henry VII, from documents in the Public Record Office. By W. Campbell. 2 vols. 1873-7. [*R. S.* lx.]

CANEL. Recherches historiques sur les Fous des Rois de France. Par A. Canel, 1873.

Captain Cox. See LANEHAM.

LIST OF AUTHORITIES

Carmina Burana. *See* SCHMELLER.

CASPARI. Eine Augustin fälschlich beilegte Homilia de Sacrilegiis. Herausgegeben von C. P. Caspari, 1886. [*Gesellschaft der Wissenschaften zu Christiania.*]

CASSIODORUS. Cassiodori Senatoris Variae. Recensuit Theodorus Mommsen, 1894. [*M. G. H. Auctores Antiquissimi*, vol. xii.]

Catholicon Anglicum. Catholicon Anglicum : an English-Latin Wordbook (1483). Edited by S. J. Herrtage, 1881. [*C. S. N. S. xxx.*]

CAVENDISH. The Life of Cardinal Wolsey. By J. Cavendish. Edited by S. W. Singer. 2 vols. 1825.

CHAMBERS. Divine Worship in the Thirteenth and Fourteenth Centuries, contrasted with the Nineteenth. By J. D. Chambers, 1877.

CHAMPOLLION-FIGEAC. *See* HILARIUS.

CHAPPELL. Old English Popular Music. By W. Chappell. A new edition by H. E. Wooldridge. 2 vols. 1893.

C. H. B. Corpus Scriptorum Historiae Byzantinae. Editio emendatior, consilio B. G. Niebuhrii instituta, 1828-97.

CHÉREST. Nouvelles Recherches sur la Fête des Innocents et la Fête des Fous. Par A. Chérest, 1853. [*Bulletin de la Société des Sciences de l' Yonne*, vol. vii.]

CHILD. The English and Scottish Popular Ballads. Edited by F. J. Child. 10 vols. 1882-98.

Christmas Prince. *See* HIGGS.

C. I. C. Corpus Iuris Civilis. Editio altera, 1877-95. [Vol. i contains the *Institutiones*, ed. P. Krueger, and the *Digesta*, ed. Th. Mommsen ; vol. ii the *Codex Iustiniani*, ed. P. Krueger ; vol. iii the *Novellae Iustiniani*, ed. Schoell and Kroll.]

C. I. Can. Corpus Iuris Canonici. Editio Lipsiensis secunda : post A. L. Richter curas . . . instruxit A. Friedberg. 2 vols. 1879-81. [Contains the *Decretum* of Gratian (†1139), the *Decretales* of Gregory IX (1234), the *Liber Sextus* of Boniface VIII (1298), the *Decretales* of Clement V and John XXII (1317), and the *Extravagantes* (down to 1484).]

CIVIS. Minutes, collected from the ancient Records and Accounts in the Chamber of Canterbury. [By C. R. Bunce or W. Welfitt. These documents, bound in B. M. under press-mark 10,358, h. i., appear to be reprints or proof-sheets of articles, signed *Civis*, in the *Kentish Chronicle* for 1801-2.]

CLARKE. The Miracle Play in England, an account of the Early Religious Drama. By S. W. Clarke, n. d.

CLÉDAT. Le Théâtre en France au Moyen Âge. Par L. Clédat, 1896. [*Classiques Populaires.*]

CLÉMENT. Histoire générale de la Musique religieuse. Par F. Clément, 1860.

CLÉMENT-HÉMERY. Histoire des Fêtes civiles et religieuses du Département du Nord. Par Mme Clément (née Hémery), 1832.

CLOETTA. Beiträge zur Litteraturgeschichte des Mittelalters und der

Renaissance. Von W. Cloetta. i. Komödie und Tragödie im Mittelalter, 1890. ii. Die Anfänge der Renaissancetragödie, 1892.

Cod. Th. Codex Theodosianus. Edidit G. Haenel, 1844. [*Corpus Iuris Romani Ante-Iustiniani,* vol. ii.]

COLLIER. The History of English Dramatic Poetry to the Time of Shakespeare : and Annals of the Stage to the Restoration. By J. P. Collier. New ed. 1879.

COLLIER, *Five Plays.* Five Miracle Plays, or Scriptural Dramas. Edited by J. P. Collier, 1836.

COLLIER, *P. J.* Punch and Judy, with illustrations by G. Cruikshank. Accompanied by the Dialogue of the Puppet-Show, an account of its Origin, and of Puppet-Plays in England. [By J. P. Collier.] 5th ed. 1870.

CONYBEARE. The History of Christmas. By F. C. Conybeare, 1899 [*Journal of American Theology,* vol. iii.]

CONYBEARE, *Key of Truth.* The Key of Truth : a Manual of the Paulician Church. Edited and translated by F. C. Conybeare, 1898.

CORTET. Essai sur les Fetes religieuses, et les Traditions populaires qui s'y rattachent. Par E. Cortet, 1867.

COTGRAVE. A French-English Dictionary, with another in English and French. By R. Cotgrave, 1650.

County Folk-Lore. Examples of printed Folk-Lore. Vol. i (Gloucestershire, Suffolk, Leicestershire, and Rutland), 1892-5. Vol. ii (North Riding of Yorkshire, York, and the Ainsty), 1901. [*F. L. S.*]

COURTHOPE. A History of English Poetry. By W. J. Courthope. Vols. i, ii. 1895-7. [In progress.]

COUSSEMAKER. Drames liturgiques du Moyen Âge. Par E. de Coussemaker, 1860.

COUSSEMAKER, *Harm.* Histoire de l'Harmonie au Moyen Âge. Par E. de Coussemaker, 1852.

COX. Introduction to Folk-Lore. By M. R. Cox. 2nd ed. 1897.

C. P. B. Corpus Poeticum Boreale : the Poetry of the Old Northern Tongue from the Earliest Times to the Thirteenth Century. Edited by G. Vigfusson and F. Y. Powell. 2 vols. 1883.

CREIZENACH. Geschichte des neueren Dramas. Von W. Creizenach. Vols i–iii, 1893–1903. [In progress.]

CROWEST. The Story of British Music, from the Earliest Times to the Tudor Period. By F. J. Crowest, 1896.

C. S. Camden Society, now incorporated with the Royal Historical Society.

C. S. E. L. Corpus Scriptorum Ecclesiasticorum Latinorum. Editum consilio Academiae Litterarum Caesareae Vindobonensis. 41 vols. 1866–1900. [In progress.]

CUMONT. Textes et Monuments figurés relatifs aux Mystères de Mithra. Par F. Cumont. 2 vols. 1896-9.

CUNLIFFE. The Influence of Seneca on Elizabethan Tragedy. An Essay by J. W. Cunliffe, 1893. [Manchester dissertation.]

CUNNINGHAM. Extracts from the Accounts of Revels at Court in the Reigns of Queen Elizabeth and King James I. By P. Cunningham, 1842. [*Shakespeare Society.*]

CUSHMAN. The Devil and the Vice in the English Dramatic Literature before Shakespeare. By L. W. Cushman, 1900. [*Studien zur englischen Philologie*, vi.]

CUTTS. Parish Priests and their People in the Middle Ages in England. By E. L. Cutts, 1898.

DANKÓ. Die Feier des Osterfestes. Von J. Dankó, 1872. [Not consulted.]

DANKÓ, *Hymn.* Vetus Hymnarium Ecclesiasticum Hungariae. Edidit J. Dankó, 1893.

DAVID. Études historiques sur la Poésie et la Musique dans la Cambrie. Par E. David, 1884.

DAVIDSON. Studies in the English Mystery Plays. By C. Davidson, 1892. [Yale dissertation, in *Transactions of Connecticut Academy*, ix. 1.]

DAVIES. Extracts from the Municipal Records of the City of York during the Reigns of Edward IV, Edward V, and Richard III. By R. Davies, 1843.

DAWSON. Christmas: Its Origin and Associations. By W. F. Dawson, 1902.

D. C. A. A Dictionary of Christian Antiquities. Edited by Sir W. Smith and S. Cheetham. 2 vols. 1875–80.

DEIMLING. The Chester Plays. Re-edited from the MSS. by the late H. Deimling, 1893. [*E. E. T. S.*, Part i, with Plays 1–13, only published.]

DE LA FONS-MELICOCQ. Cérémonies dramatiques et anciens Usages dans les Églises du Nord de la France. Par A. de la Fons-Melicocq, 1850.

DENIFLE. Chartularium Universitatis Parisiensis. Collegit H. Denifle. 4 vols. 1889–97.

DESJARDINS. Histoire de la Cathédrale de Beauvais. Par G. Desjardins, 1865.

DESLYONS. Traitez singuliers et nouveaux contre le Paganisme du Roy Boit. Par J. Deslyons, 1670.

DEVRIENT. Geschichte der deutschen Schauspielkunst. Von E. Devrient. 2 vols. 1848.

DIDRON. See *Annales Archéologiques.*

DIETERICH. Pulcinella; pompejanische Wandbilder und römische Satyrspiele. Von A. Dieterich, 1897.

DIEZ. Die Poesie der Troubadours. Von F. C. Diez, 1826.

DIEZ-BARTSCH. Leben und Werke der Troubadours. Von F. C. Diez. Zweite Auflage, von K. Bartsch, 1882.

Digby Plays. See FURNIVALL ; SHARP.

DILL. Roman Society in the last Century of the Western Empire. By S. Dill. 2nd ed. 1899.

DITCHFIELD. Old English Customs extant at the present Time. By P. H. Ditchfield, 1896.

DIXON. A History of the Church of England from the Abolition of the Roman Jurisdiction. By R. W. Dixon. 6 vols. 1878–1902.

D. N. B. Dictionary of National Biography. Edited by L. Stephen and S. Lee. 66 vols. 1885–1901.

DORAN. A History of Court Fools. By J. Doran, 1858.

DOUCE. Illustrations of Shakspeare, and of Ancient Manners: with Dissertations on the Clowns and Fools of Shakspeare, and on the English Morris Dance. By F. Douce, 1839.

DOUHET. Dictionnaire des Mystères. Par Jules, Comte de Douhet, 1854. [J. P. Migne, Encyclopédie Théologique, Series II, vol. xliii.]

DRAKE. Shakespeare and his Times. By N. Drake. Paris, 1838.

DREUX DE RADIER. Histoire des Fous en titre d'Office. Par J. F. Dreux de Radier, 1768. [In Récréations Historiques.]

DREVES. Zur Geschichte der Fête des Fous. Von G. M. Dreves, 1894. [Stimmen aus Maria-Laach, vol. xlvii.]
See also Analecta Hymnica.

DUCANGE. Glossarium mediae et infimae Latinitatis conditum a Du Cangio, auctum a monachis Ordinis S. Benedicti, cum supplementis Carpenterii suisque digessit G. A. L. Henschel. Editio nova, aucta a L. Favre. 10 vols. 1883–7.

DUCHESNE. Origines du Culte chrétien: Étude sur la Liturgie avant Charlemagne. Par l'Abbé L. Duchesne. 2nd ed. 1898. [A 3rd ed. was published in 1902, and a translation, by M. L. McLure, under the title of Christian Worship: its Origin and Evolution, in 1903.]

DUGDALE. Origines Iuridiciales: or, Historical Memorials of the English Laws ... Inns of Court and Chancery. By W. Dugdale. 2nd ed. 1671.

DUGDALE, Monasticon. Monasticon Anglicanum: or, the History of the Ancient Abbies and other Monasteries, Hospitals, Cathedral and Collegiate Churches in England and Wales. By Sir W. Dugdale. A new edition by J. Caley, Sir H. Ellis, and the Rev. B. Bandinel. 6 vols. 1846.

DU MÉRIL. Origines latines du Théâtre moderne, publiées et annotées par M. Édélestand Du Méril, 1849. [Has also a Latin title-page, Theatri Liturgici quae Latina superstant Monumenta, etc. A facsimile reprint was issued in 1896.]

DU MÉRIL, La Com. Histoire de la Comédie. Par É. du Méril. Période primitive, 1864. [All published.]

DÜMMLER. Epistolae Merowingici et Karolini Aevi. Recensuit E. L. Dümmler. 3 vols. 1892–9. [M. G. H. Epistolae, iii–v. The 2nd vol. contains Alcuin's letters.]

DURANDUS. Rationale Divinorum Officiorum editum per . . . . Gulielmum Duranti. Haec editio a multis erroribus diligenter correcta. [Edidit N. Doard.] Antwerpiae, 1614. See BARTHÉLEMY.

Durham Accounts. Extracts from the Account Rolls of the Abbey of Durham. Edited by Canon Fowler. 3 vols. 1898–1901. [Surtees Soc. xcix, c, ciii.]

DÜRR.   Commentatio Historica de Episcopo Puerorum, vulgo von Schul Bischoff.   Von F. A. Dürr, 1755.   [In J. Schmidt, *Thesaurus Iuris Ecclesiastici* (1774), iii. 58.]

DU TILLIOT.   Mémoires pour servir à l'Histoire de la Fête des Foux. Par M. Du Tilliot, Gentilhomme Ordinaire de S. A. R. Monseigneur le Duc de Berry, 1751.

DYER.   British Popular Customs, Present and Past.   By T. F. Thiselton Dyer, 1876.

EBERT.   Die englischen Mysterien.   Von A. Ebert, 1859.   [*Jahrbuch für romanische und englische Literatur*, vol. i.]

ECKHARDT.   Die lustige Person im älteren englischen Drama (bis 1642).   Von E. Eckhardt, 1903.   [*Palaestra*, xvii; not consulted.]

E. H. Review.   The English Historical Review.   18 vols. 1886–1903. [In progress.]

ELTON.   Origins of English History.   By C. I. Elton.   2nd ed. 1890.

EVANS.   English Masques.   With an introduction by H. A. Evans, 1897.   [*Warwick Library.*]

FABIAN.   The New Chronicles of England and France.   By R. Fabyan. Edited by H. Ellis, 1811.

FAIRHOLT.   Lord Mayor's Pageants.   Edited by F. W. Fairholt. 2 vols. 1843–4.   [*Percy Soc.* xxxviii, xlviii.]

FEASEY.   Ancient English Holy Week Ceremonial.   By H. J. Feasey, 1897.

FISCHER.   Zur Kunstentwickelung der englischen Tragödie von ihren ersten Anfängen bis zu Shakespeare.   Von R. Fischer, 1893.

FITCH.   Norwich Pageants.   The Grocers' Play.   From a manuscript in possession of R. Fitch, 1856.   [Extract from *Norfolk Archaeology*, vol. v.]

F. L.   Folk-Lore: a Quarterly Review of Myth, Tradition, Institution, and Custom.   14 vols. 1890–1903.   [Organ of *F. L. S.*, in progress.]

F. L. Congress.   The International Folk-Lore Congress, 1891.   Papers and Transactions.   Edited by J. Jacobs and A. Nutt, 1892.

F. L. Journal.   The Folk-Lore Journal, 7 vols. 1883–9.   [Organ of *F. L. S.*]

F. L. Record.   The Folk-Lore Record.   5 vols. 1878–82.   [Organ of *F. L. S.*]

FLEAY.   *C. H.*   A Chronicle History of the London Stage, 1559–1642. By F. G. Fleay, 1890.

FLÖGEL.   Geschichte der Hofnarren.   Von C. F. Flögel, 1789.

F. L. S. = Folk-Lore Society.

FOWLER.   The Roman Festivals of the Period of the Republic: an Introduction to the Study of the Religion of the Romans.   By W. W. Fowler, 1899.   [*Handbooks of Archaeology and Antiquities.*]

FOURNIER.   Le Théâtre français avant la Renaissance.   Par E. Fournier, 1872.

FOXE.   The Acts and Monuments of John Foxe.   With a Life of the Martyrologist by G. Townsend.   [Edited by S. R. Cattley.]   8 vols. 1843–9.

FRAZER. The Golden Bough: a Study in Comparative Religion. By J. G. Frazer. 2nd ed. 3 vols. 1900.

FRAZER, *Pausanias*. Pausanias's Description of Greece. Translated with a commentary by J. G. Frazer. 6 vols. 1898.

FRERE. The Winchester Troper. Edited by W. H. Frere, 1894. [*Henry Bradshaw Society*.]

FRERE,*Use of Sarum*. The Use of Sarum. Edited by W. H. Frere. 2 vols. 1898-1901.

See also PROCTER-FRERE.

FREYMOND. Jongleurs und Menestrels. Von E. Freymond, 1883. [Halle dissertation.]

FRIEDLÄNDER. Darstellungen aus der Sittengeschichte Roms in der Zeit von August bis zum Ausgang der Antonine. Von L. Friedländer. 6th ed. 3 vols. 1888-90. [*Das Theater* is in vol. ii.]

FRONING. Das Drama des Mittelalters. Herausgegeben von R. Froning. 3 Parts, 1891. [*Deutsche National-Litteratur*, xiv.]

FROUDE. History of England from the Fall of Wolsey to the Defeat of the Spanish Armada. By J. A. Froude. 2nd ed. 1889-95.

FURNIVALL. The Digby Plays, with an Incomplete Morality of Wisdom, who is Christ. Edited by F. J. Furnivall, 1882. [*N. S. S.* Series vii, 1: re-issue for *E. E. T. S.* 1896.]

See also LANEHAM, MANNYNG, STAFFORD, STUBBES.

Furnivall Miscellany. An English Miscellany Presented to Dr. Furnivall in Honour of his Seventy-fifth Birthday, 1901.

GAIDOZ. Études de Mythologie gauloise. Par H. Gaidoz. I. Le Dieu gaulois du Soleil et le Symbolisme de la Roue, 1886. [Extrait de la *Revue Archéologique*, 1884-85.]

GASPARY. The History of Early Italian Literature to the Death of Dante. Translated from the German of A. Gaspary, by H. Oelsner, 1901.

GASTÉ. Les Drames liturgiques de la Cathédrale de Rouen. Par A. Gasté, 1893. [Extrait de la *Revue Catholique de Normandie*.]

GAUTIER. Les Épopées françaises. Par L. Gautier, vol. ii. 2nd edition, 1892. [Lib. ii. chh. xvii-xxi form the section on *Les Propagateurs des Chansons de Geste*. References to this work may be distinguished from those to *Les Tropaires* by the presence of a volume-number.]

GAUTIER, *Bibl.* Bibliographie des Chansons de Geste. Par L. Gautier, 1897. [A section on *Les Propagateurs des Chansons de Geste*.]

GAUTIER, *Orig.* Origines du Théâtre moderne. Par L. Gautier, 1872. [In *Le Monde*.]

GAUTIER, *Tropaires*. Histoire de la Poésie liturgique au Moyen Âge. Par L. Gautier. Vol. i. *Les Tropaires*, 1886. [All published.]

GAYLEY. Representative English Comedies: from the Beginnings to Shakespeare. Edited by C. M. Gayley, 1903.

GAZEAU. Les Bouffons. Par A. Gazeau, 1882.

GENÉE. Die englischen Mirakelspiele und Moralitäten als Vorläufer des englischen Dramas. Von R. Genée, 1878. [Serie xiii, Heft 305 of

Sammlung gemeinverständlicher wissenschaftlicher Vorträge, herausgegeben von R. Virchow und Fr. v. Holtzendorff.]

GIBBON. The History of the Decline and Fall of the Roman Empire. By E. Gibbon. Edited by J. B. Bury. 7 vols. 1897–1900.

GILPIN. The Beehive of the Romish Church. By G. Gilpin, 1579. [Translated from Isaac Rabbotenu, of Louvain, 1569.]

Gloucester F. L. See *County Folk-Lore.*

GOEDEKE. Grundriss zur Geschichte der deutschen Dichtung, aus den Quellen. Von K. Goedeke. 2nd ed. 7 vols. 1884–1900. [In progress.]

Golden Legend. The Golden Legend: or, Lives of the Saints, as Englished by W. Caxton. Edited by F. S. Ellis, 1900, &c. [*Temple Classics.*]

GÖLTHER. Handbuch der germanischen Mythologie. Von W. Gölther, 1895.

GOMME. Ethnology in Folk-lore. By G. L. Gomme, 1892.

GOMME, *Brit. Ass.* On the Method of determining the Value of Folklore as Ethnological Data. By G. L. Gomme, 1896. [In *Report* of *British Association for the Advancement of Science.*]

GOMME, *Nature.* Christmas Mummers. By G. L. Gomme, 1897. [*Nature*, vol. lvii.]

GOMME, *Vill. Comm.* The Village Community: with special Reference to the Origin and Form of its Survivals in Britain. By G. L. Gomme, 1890. [*Contemporary Science Series.*]

GOMME, MRS. The Traditional Games of England, Scotland, and Ireland, with Tunes. Collected and annotated by A. B. Gomme. 2 vols. 1894–8. [Part i of *Dictionary of British Folk-Lore*, Edited by G. L. Gomme.]

GOOGE. See KIRCHMAYER.

GRACIE. The Presentation in the Temple: A Pageant, as originally represented by the Corporation of Weavers in Coventry, 1836. [Edited by J. B. Gracie for the *Abbotsford Club.*]

GRASS. Das Adamsspiel: anglonormannisches Gedicht des xii. Jahrhunderts. Mit einem Anhang ' Die fünfzehn Zeichen des jüngsten Gerichts.' Herausgegeben von K. Grass, 1891. [*Romanische Bibliothek*, vi.]

GRATIAN. See *C. I. Can.*

GREENIDGE. Infamia: Its Place in Roman Public and Private Law. By A. H. J. Greenidge, 1894.

GREG, *Masques.* A list of Masques, Pageants, &c. Supplementary to a list of English Plays. By W. W. Greg, 1902. [*Bibliographical Society.*]

GREG, *Plays.* A List of English Plays written before 1643, and published before 1700. By W. W. Greg, 1900. [*Bibliographical Society.*]

GREGORY. Gregorii Posthuma: on Certain Learned Tracts written by John Gregory. Published by his Dearest Friend J. G. 1683. [Part II of his *Works*: A separate title-page for *Episcopus Puerorum in Die Innocentium: or, A Discovery of an Ancient Custom in the Church of Sarum, of making an Anniversary Bishop among the Choristers.*]

Gregory's Chronicle. The Historical Collections of a Citizen of London in the Fifteenth Century. Edited by J. Gairdner, III, William Gregory's Chronicle of London. [*C. S. N. S.* xvii.]

GREIN-WÜLCKER. Bibliothek der angelsächsischen Poesie. Herausgegeben von C. W. M. Grein. Neu bearbeitet, vermehrt und herausgegeben von R. P. Wülcker. 3 vols. 1883–98.

GRENIER. Introduction à l'Histoire générale de la Province de Picardie. Par Dom Grenier, 1856. [*Mémoires de la Société des Antiquaires de Picardie. Documents inédits,* iii.]

GRIMM. Teutonic Mythology. By J. Grimm. Translated from the 4th ed. with notes and appendix by J. S. Stallybrass. 4 vols. 1880–8.

GRÖBER. Zur Volkskunde aus Concilbeschlüssen und Capitularien. Von G. Gröber. 1894.

GRÖBER, *Grundriss.* Grundriss der romanischen Philologie. Herausgegeben von G. Gröber. 1888–1902. [In progress. Vol. ii has article by G. Gröber on *Französische Litteratur.*]

GROOS. *Play of Animals.* The Play of Animals : a Study of Animal Life and Instinct. By K. Groos. Translated by E. L. Baldwin, 1898.

GROOS. *Play of Man.* The Play of Man. By K. Gross. Translated by E. L. Baldwin, 1901.

GROSSE. Les Débuts de l'Art. Par E. Grosse. Traduit par E. Dirr. Introduction par L. Marillier. 1902. [*Bibliothèque Scientifique Internationale.*]

GROVE. Dancing. By L. Grove, and other writers. With Musical examples. 1895. [*Badminton Library.*]

GUMMERE, *B. P.* The Beginnings of Poetry. By F. B. Gummere, 1901.

GUMMERE, *G. O.* Germanic Origins : a Study in Primitive Culture. By F. B. Gummere, 1892.

GUTCH. A Lytell Geste of Robin Hood, with other Ballads relative to Robin Hood. Edited by J. M. Gutch. 2 vols. 1847.

GUY. Essai sur la Vie et les Œuvres littéraires du Trouvère Adan de le Hale. Par H. Guy, 1898.

HADDAN-STUBBS. Councils and Ecclesiastical Documents relating to Great Britain and Ireland. Edited, after Spelman and Wilkins, by A. W. Haddan and W. Stubbs. 3 vols. 1869–78.

HADDON. The Study of Man. By A. C. Haddon, 1898. [*Progressive Science Series.*]

HAIGH. The Tragic Drama of the Greeks. By A. E. Haigh, 1896.

HALL. The Union of the Families of Lancaster and York. By E. Hall. Edited by H. Ellis. 1809.

HALLIWELL-PHILLIPPS. Outlines of the Life of Shakespeare. By J. O. Halliwell-Phillipps. 9th ed. 2 vols. 1890.

HALLIWELL-PHILLIPS. *Revels.* A Collection of Ancient Documents respecting the Office of Master of the Revels, and other Papers relating to the Early English Theatre. [By J. O. Halliwell-Phillipps.] 1870.

HAMPSON. Medii Aevi Kalendarium: or Dates. Charters and Customs of the Middle Ages, &c. By R. T. Hampson. 2 vols. 1841.

Handlyng Synne. See MANNYNG.

HARLAND. Lancashire Folk-Lore. By J. Harland and T. T. Wilkinson, 1867.

HARRIS. Life in an Old English Town: a History of Coventry from the Earliest Times. Compiled from Official Records by M. D. Harris, 1898. [*Social England Series.*]

HARTLAND. The Legend of Perseus: a Study of Tradition in Story, Custom and Belief. By E. S. Hartland. 3 vols. 1894-6.

HARTLAND. *Fairy Tales.* The Science of Fairy Tales: an Inquiry into Fairy Mythology. By E. S. Hartland, 1891. [*Contemporary Science Series.*]

HARTZHEIM. See SCHANNAT.

HASE. Miracle Plays and Sacred Dramas. By C. A. Hase. Translated by A. W. Jackson, 1880.

HASTINGS. Le Théâtre français et anglais: ses Origines grecques et latines. Par C. Hastings, 1900.

HASTINGS. The Theatre: its Development in France and England. By C. Hastings. Translated by F. A. Welby, 1901.

HAUCK. Kirchengeschichte Deutschlands. Von A. Hauck. 2nd ed. 3 vols. 1896-1900.

HAVARD. Les Fêtes de nos Pères. Par O. Havard, 1898.

HAZLITT. Remains of the Early Popular Poetry of England. Collected and edited, with introductions and notes, by W. Carew Hazlitt. 4 vols. 1864-6. [*Library of Old Authors.*]

HAZLITT, *E. D. S.* The English Drama and Stage under the Tudor and Stuart Princes, 1543-1664, illustrated by a series of Documents, Treatises, and Poems. Edited by W. C. Hazlitt, 1869. [*Roxburghe Library.*]

HAZLITT, *Liv.* The Livery Companies of London. By W. C. Hazlitt, 1892.

HAZLITT, *Manual.* A Manual for the Collector and Amateur of Old English Plays. By W. C. Hazlitt, 1892.

HAZLITT-DODSLEY. A Select Collection of Old Plays. By R. Dodsley. Chronologically arranged, revised and enlarged by W. C. Hazlitt. 4th ed. 15 vols. 1874-6.

HAZLITT-WARTON. History of English Poetry, from the Twelfth to the close of the Sixteenth Century. By T. Warton. Edited by W. C. Hazlitt. 4 vols. 1871.

H. B. S. = Henry Bradshaw Society.

HEALES. Easter Sepulchres: their Object, Nature, and History. By A. Heales, 1868. [*Archaeologia*, vol. xlii.]

HEINZEL. Beschreibung des geistlichen Schauspiels im deutschen Mittelalter. Von R. Heinzel, 1898. [*Beiträge zur Ästhetik*, iv.]

HENDERSON. Notes on the Folk-Lore of the Northern Counties of England and the Borders. By W. Henderson. 2nd ed. 1879. [*F. L. S.*]

HERBERT. Antiquities of the Inns of Court and Chancery. By W. Herbert, 1804.

HERBERT, *Liv.* History of the Twelve Great Livery Companies of London. By W. Herbert. 2 vols. 1836-7.

Hereford Missal. Missale ad usum percelebris Ecclesiae Herfordensis. Edidit W. G. Henderson, 1874.

HERFORD. The Literary Relations of England and Germany in the Sixteenth Century. By C. H. Herford, 1886.

HERRTRICH. Studien zu den York Plays. Von O. Herrtrich, 1886. [Breslau dissertation ; not consulted.]

HIGGS. The Christmas Prince. By Griffin Higgs, 1607. [In *Miscellanea Antiqua Anglicana*, 1816.]

HILARIUS. Hilarii Versus et Ludi. Edidit J. J. Champollion-Figeac, 1838.

HIRN. The Origins of Art : a Psychological and Sociological Enquiry. By Yrjö Hirn, 1900.

Hist. d'Autun. Histoire de l'Église d'Autun. Autun, 1774.

Hist. Litt. Histoire littéraire de la France. Par des Religieux bénédictins de la Congrégation de S. Maur. Continuée par des Membres de l'Institut. 32 vols. 1733-1898. [In progress.]

Hist. MSS. Reports of the Historical Manuscripts Commission, 1883-1902. [In progress.]

HOBHOUSE. Churchwardens' Accounts of Croscombe, Pilton, Yatton, Tintinhull, Morebath, and St. Michael's, Bath, 1349-1560. Edited by E. Hobhouse, 1890. [*Somerset Record Society*, vol. iv.]

HODGKIN. Italy and her Invaders. By T. Hodgkin. 8 vols. 1892-9.

HOHLFELD. Die altenglischen Kollektivmisterien, unter besonderer Berücksichtigung des Verhältnisses der York- und Towneley-Spiele. Von A. Hohlfeld, 1889. [*Anglia*, vol. xi.]

HOLINSHED. Holinshed's Chronicles of England, Scotland, and Ireland. 6 vols. 1807-8.

HOLTHAUSEN. Noah's Ark : or, the Shipwright's Ancient Play or Dirge. Edited by F. Holthausen, 1897. [Extract from *Göteborg's Högskola's Ärsskrift.*]

HONE. Ancient Mysteries described, especially the English Miracle Plays, founded on Apocryphal New Testament Story, extant among the unpublished Manuscripts in the British Museum. By W. Hone, 1823.

HONE, *E. D. B.* The Every Day Book and Table Book. By W. Hone. 3 vols. 1838.

Household Ordinances. A Collection of Ordinances and Regulations for the Government of the Royal Household, made in divers Reigns from King Edward III to King William and Mary, 1790. [*Society of Antiquaries of London.*]

HROTSVITHA. Hrotsvithae Opera. Recensuit et emendavit P. de Winterfeld, 1902. [In *Scriptores Rerum Germanicarum in usum Scholarum ex Monumentis Germaniae Historicis separatim editi.*]

HUBATSCH. Die lateinischen Vagantenlieder des Mittelalters. Von O. Hubatsch, 1870.

Indiculus. *See* SAUPE.

JAHN. Die deutschen Opfergebräuche bei Ackerbau und Viehzucht. Ein Beitrag von U. Jahn, 1884. [*Germanistische Abhandlungen,* herausgegeben von Karl Weinhold, iii.]

JEANROY. Les Origines de la Poésie lyrique en France au Moyen Âge : Études de Littérature française et comparée, suivies de Textes inédits. Par A. Jeanroy, 1889.

JEVONS. An Introduction to the History of Religion. By F. B. Jevons, 1896.

JEVONS, *Plutarch.* Plutarch's Romane Questions. Translated A.D. 1603 by Philemon Holland. Now again edited by F. B. Jevons. With Dissertations on Italian Cults, 1892.

See also SCHRÄDER.

JONES, *Fasti.* Fasti Ecclesiae Sarisburiensis, or A Calendar of the Bishops, Deans, Archdeacons, and Members of the Cathedral Body at Salisbury, from the Earliest Times to the Present. By W. H. Jones, 1881. [Pages 295–301 contain an account of the Boy Bishop at Salisbury.]

JORDAN. The Creation of the World. By W. Jordan. Edited with a translation by Whitley Stokes, 1863. [*Transactions of Philological Society.*]

JUBINAL. Jongleurs et Trouvères : Choix de Pièces des xiiie et xive Siècles. Par M. L. A. Jubinal, 1835.

JUBINAL, *Myst.* Mystères inédits du xve Siècle. Par M. L. A. Jubinal. 2 vols. 1837.

JUBINAL, *N. R.* Nouveau Recueil de Contes, Dits, Fabliaux, et autres Pièces inédites des xiiie, xive, et xve Siècles. Par M. L. A. JUBINAL. 2 vols. 1839–42.

JULIAN. Iuliani Imperatoris quae supersunt. Recensuit F. C. Hertlein. 2 vols. 1875–6.

JULLEVILLE. *See* PETIT DE JULLEVILLE.

JUSSERAND. Le Théâtre en Angleterre depuis là Conquête jusqu'aux Prédécesseurs immédiats de Shakespeare. Par J. J. Jusserand. 2nd ed. 1881.

JUSSERAND, *E. L.* A Literary History of the English People from the Origins to the Renaissance. By J. J. Jusserand. Vol. i, 1895. [In progress.]

JUSSERAND, *E. W. L.* English Wayfaring Life in the Middle Ages. By J. J. Jusserand. Translated by L. T. Smith. 4th ed. 1892. [The English translation has valuable illustrations.]

KEARY. The Vikings in Western Christendom : A.D. 789 to A.D. 888. By C. F. Keary, 1891.

KELLER. Fastnachtspiele aus dem 15. Jahrhundert. Von A. von Keller, 1853–8.

KELLY. Notices Illustrative of the Drama, and other Popular Amusements, chiefly in the Sixteenth and Seventeenth Centuries, incidentally illustrating Shakespeare and his Contemporaries; extracted from the Chamberlain's Accounts and other Manuscripts of the Borough of Leicester. With an introduction and notes by W. Kelly, 1865.

KEMBLE. The Saxons in England: a History of the English Commonwealth till the Period of the Norman Conquest. By J. M. Kemble. 2 vols. 1849.

KEMPE. Manuscripts and other rare Documents from the Reign of Henry VIII to that of James I, preserved in the Muniment Room at Loseley House. Edited by A. J. Kempe, 1835.

KIRCHMAYER. The Popish Kingdom, or reigne of Antichrist, written in Latine verse by Thomas Naogeorgus (or Kirchmayer), and englyshed by Barnabe Googe, 1570. [See STUBBES.]

KLEIN. Geschichte des Dramas. Von J. L. Klein. 13 vols. 1865–76. Register-Band von T. Ebner, 1886. [Vol. ii contains 'Das Drama der Römer,' vol. iii 'Die lateinischen Schauspiele,' vols. xii, xiii 'Das englische Drama.']

KNAPPERT. Le Christianisme et le Paganisme dans l'Histoire ecclésiastique de Bède le Vénérable. Par L. Knappert, 1897. [In *Revue de l'Histoire des Religions*, vol. xxxv.]

KÖGEL. Geschichte der deutschen Litteratur bis zum Ausgange des Mittelalters. Von R. Kögel. 2 vols. 1894–7. [All published.]

KÖPPEN. Beiträge zur Geschichte der deutschen Weihnachtsspiele. Von W. Köppen, 1893.

KÖRTING. Geschichte des Theaters in seinen Beziehungen zur Kunstentwickelung der dramatischen Dichtkunst. Erster Band: Geschichte des griechischen und römischen Theaters. Von G. Körting, 1897.

KÖRTING, *Grundriss*. Grundriss der Geschichte der englischen Litteratur von ihren Anfängen bis zur Gegenwart. Von G. Körting. 3rd ed. 1899.

KRAMER. Sprache und Heimath der Coventry-Plays. Von M. Kramer. [Not consulted.]

KRUMBACHER. Geschichte der byzantinischen Litteratur von Justinian bis zum Ende des oströmischen Reiches (527–1423). Von K. Krumbacher. 2nd ed. 1897. [Vol. ix. Pt. I of *Handbuch der klassischen Altertumswissenschaft*, herausgegeben von Dr. I. von Müller.]

LABBÉ. Sacrosancta Concilia. Studio Philippi Labbei et Gabrielis Cossartii. 17 vols. 1671–2.

LACROIX. Dissertation sur les Fous des Rois de France. Par P. Lacroix. [*pseud.* P. L. Jacob.]

LANEHAM. Captain Cox, his Ballads and Books: or Robert Laneham's Letter. Re-edited by F. J. Furnivall, 1871. [*Ballad Society*, vii. Reprinted with slight alterations for *N. S. S.*, series vi. 14 in 1890.]

Lang. et Litt. Histoire de la Langue et de la Littérature française, des Origines à 1900. Publiée sous la direction de L. Petit de Julleville, 1896–1900. [Tom. i, in two parts, covers the Moyen Âge: the articles are by various specialists.]

LANG, *M. of R.* The Making of Religion. By A. Lang. 2nd ed. 1900.

LANG, *M.R.R.* Myth, Ritual, and Religion. By A. Lang. 2 vols. 1887. 2nd ed. 1899.

LANGE. Die lateinischen Osterfeiern : Untersuchungen über den Ursprung und die Entwickelung der liturgisch-dramatischen Auferstehungsfeier. Von C. Lange, 1887.

LAVOIX. La Musique au Siècle de Saint-Louis. Par H. Lavoix. [Contributed to G. Raynaud, *Recueil de Motets français,* vol. ii.]

LEACH. The Schoolboys' Feast. By A. F. Leach, 1896. [*Fortnightly Review,* vol. lix.]

LEACH, *Beverley MSS.* Report on the Manuscripts of the Corporation of Beverley. By A. F. Leach, 1900. [*Hist. MSS.*]

LEBER. Collection des meilleures Dissertations, Notices, et Traités particuliers, relatifs à l'Histoire de France. Par C. Leber, J. B. Salgues et J. Cohen. 20 vols. 1826–38.

Leicester F. L. See *Country Folk-Lore.*

LELAND. Iohannis Lelandi de Rebus Britannicis Collectanea. Cum T. Hearnii praefationibus, notis, &c. Accedunt de Rebus Anglicis Opuscula varia. 2nd ed. 6 vols. 1774.

LE ROY. Études sur les Mystères. Par O. Le Roy, 1837.

L. H. T. Accounts. Accounts of the Lord High Treasurer of Scotland. Edited by Thomas Dickson (vol. i, 1473-1498) and Sir J. B. Paul (vols. ii, 1500–1504 ; iii, 1506-1507), 1877-1901.

Lincoln Statutes. Statutes of Lincoln Cathedral. Arranged by H. Bradshaw ; with Illustrative Documents, edited by C. Wordsworth. 2 vols. 1892-7.

LIPENIUS. Martini Lipenii Strenarum Historia, 1699 [in J. G. Graevius. *Thesaurus Antiquitatum Romanarum,* xii. 409.]

LOLIÉE. La Fête des Fous. Par F. Loliée, 1898. [In *Revue des Revues,* vol. xxv.]

London Chronicle. A Chronicle of London, from 1089 to 1483. [Edited by N. H. Nicolas or Edward Tyrrell], 1827.

Ludus Coventriae. Ludus Coventriae. A Collection of Mysteries, formerly represented at Coventry on the Feast of Corpus Christi. Edited by J. O. Halliwell, 1841 [*Shakespeare Society*].

LUICK. Zur Geschichte des englischen Dramas im xvi. Jahrhundert. Von K. Luick, 1898. [In *Forschungen zur neueren Litteraturgeschichte : Festgabe für Richard Heinzel.*]

MAASSEN. Concilia Aevi Merovingici. Recensuit F. Maassen, 1893. [*M. G. H. Leges,* Sectio iii.]

MACHYN. The Diary of Henry Machyn, Citizen and Merchant-Taylor of London, 1550–63. Edited by J. G. Nichols, 1848. [*C. S.* o. s. xlii.]

MACLAGAN. The Games and Diversions of Argyleshire. By R. C. Maclagan, 1901. [*F. L. S.*]

MAGNIN. Les Origines du Théâtre moderne, ou Histoire du Génie dramatique depuis le 1ᵉʳ jusqu'au xviᵉ Siècle. Par C. Magnin, 1838. [Vol. i only published, containing introductory 'Études sur les Origines du Théâtre antique.' Notes of Magnin's lectures in the *Journal général de l'Instruction publique* (1834-6) and reviews in the *Journal des Savants* (1846-7) partly cover the ground of the missing volumes.]

MAGNIN, *Marionnettes*. Histoire des Marionnettes en Europe. Par C. Magnin. 2nd ed. 1862.

MALLESON-TUKER. Handbook to Christian and Ecclesiastical Rome. By H. M[alleson] and M. A. R. T[uker]. 3 vols. 1897-1900.

MANLY. Specimens of the Pre-Shaksperean Drama. With an introduction, notes, and a glossary. By J. M. Manly. 3 vols. 1897. [*Athenæum Press Series*; 2 vols. only yet published.]

MANNHARDT. Wald- und Feld-Kulte. Von W. Mannhardt. 2 vols. 1875-7.

MANNING. Oxfordshire Seasonal Festivals. By P. Manning, 1897. [*Folk-Lore*, vol. viii.]

MANNING. Robert [Mannyng] of Brunne's Handlyng Synne. Edited by F. J. Furnivall, 1862. [*Roxburghe Club*; a new edition promised for E. E. T. S.]

MANSI. Sacrorum Conciliorum Nova et Amplissima Collectio. Editio novissima a patre J. D. Mansi. 30 vols. Florence, 1769-92.

MAP. *See* WRIGHT.

MARKLAND. Chester Mysteries. De deluvio Noe, De occisione innocentium. Edited by J. H. Markland, 1818. [*Roxburghe Club.*]

MARQUARDT-MOMMSEN. Handbuch der römischen Alterthümer. Von J. Marquardt und T. Mommsen. 3rd ed. 7 vols. 1881-8.

MARRIOTT. A Collection of English Miracle-Plays or Mysteries. Edited by W. Marriott. Basle, 1838.

MARTENE. De Antiquis Ecclesiae Ritibus Libri Tres collecti atque exornati ab Edmundo Martene. Editio novissima, 1783. [This edition has a 4th vol., De Monachorum Ritibus.]

MARTIN OF BRAGA. Martin von Bracara's Schrift: De Correctione Rusticorum, herausgegeben von C. P. Caspari, 1883. [*Videnskabs-Selskab* of Christiania.]

MARTINENGO-CESARESCO. Essays in the Study of Folk-Songs. By the Countess E. Martinengo-Cesaresco, 1886.

MARTONNE. La Piété du Moyen Âge. Par A. de Martonne, 1855.

MASKELL. The Ancient Liturgy of the Church of England according to the Uses of Sarum, York, Hereford, Bangor, and the Roman Liturgy. By W. Maskell. 3rd ed. 1882.

MASKELL, *Mon. Rit.* Monumenta Ritualia Ecclesiae Anglicanae. Occasional Offices according to the ancient Use of Salisbury, &c. By W. Maskell. 2nd ed. 3 vols. 1882.

MAUGRAS. Les Comédiens hors la Loi. Par G. Maugras, 1887.

MAYER. Ein deutsches Schwerttanzspiel aus Ungarn. Von F. A. Mayer, 1889. [*Zeitschrift für Völkerpsychologie.*]

Mélusine. Mélusine: Recueil de Mythologie, Littérature populaire, Traditions et Usages, 1878, 1883, &c.

MERBOT. Aesthetìsche Studien zur angelsächsischen Poesie. Von R. Merbot, 1883.

Merc. Fr. Le Mercure de France. 974 vols. 1724–91.

MEYER. Fragmenta Burana. Herausgegeben von W. Meyer aus Speyer, 1901. [Sonderabdruck aus der Festschrift zur Feier des 150-jährigen Bestehens der *Königlichen Gesellschaft der Wissenschaften zu Göttingen.*]

MEYER, *Germ. Myth.* Germanische Mythologie. Par E. H. Meyer, 1891.

M. G. H. Monumenta Germaniae Historica. Auspiciis Societatis Aperiendis Fontibus Rerum Germanicarum Medii Aevi. Edidit G. H. Pertz, T. Mommsen, et alii, 1826–1902. [In progress, under various series, as *Auctores Antiquissimi, Epistolae, Leges, Scriptores,* &c. Indices, 1890.]

MICHELS. Studien über die ältesten deutschen Fastnachtspiele. Von V. Michels, 1896. [*Quellen und Forschungen,* lxxvii.]

MICKLETHWAITE. The Ornaments of the Rubric. By J. T. Micklethwaite, 1897. [*Alcuin Club Tracts,* I.]

MILCHSACK. Die Oster- und Passionsspiele: literar-historische Untersuchungen über den Ursprung und die Entwickelung derselben bis zum siebenzehnten Jahrhundert, vornehmlich in Deutschland. Von G. Milchsack. i, Die lateinischen Osterfeiern, 1880. [All published.]

Miracles de Nostre Dame. Miracles de Nostre Dame par Personnages. Publiés d'après le manuscrit de la Bibliothèque Nationale par G. Paris et U. Robert. 8 vols. 1876–93. [*Société des Anciens Textes Français.*]

MOGK. Mythologie. Von E. Mogk. 2nd ed. 1897–8. [In Paul, *Grundriss,* 2nd ed. vol. iii.]

MOMMSEN, *C. I. L.* Inscriptiones Latinae Antiquissimae. Editio Altera. Pars Prior. Cura Theodori Mommsen [et aliorum], 1893. [*Corpus Inscriptionum Latinarum,* vol. i. part 1.]
See MARQUARDT-MOMMSEN.

MONACI. Appunti per la Storia del Teatro italiano. Per E. Monaci, 1872–5. [*Rivista di Filologia Romanza,* i, ii.]

Monasticon. See DUGDALE.

MONE. Schauspiele des Mittelalters. Herausgegeben und erklärt von F. J. Mone. 2 vols. 1846.

MONE. Altteutsche Schauspiele. Herausgegeben von F. J. Mone, 1835.

MONMERQUÉ-MICHEL. Théâtre français au Moyen Âge. Publié d'après les Manuscrits de la Bibliothèque du Roi par L. J. N. Monmerqué et F. Michel, 1839.

MONTAIGLON-RAYNAUD. Recueil général et complet des Fabliaux des treizième et quatorzième Siècles. Par A. de Montaiglon et G. Raynaud. 6 vols. 1872–90.

MONTAIGLON-ROTHSCHILD. Recueil de Poésies françaises des quinzième et seizième Siècles. Par A. de Montaiglon et J. de Rothschild. 13 vols. 1855–78.

MOREAU. Fous et Bouffons. Étude physiologique, psychologique et historique par P. Moreau, 1885.

MORLEY. Memoirs of Bartholomew Fair. By H. Morley, 1859.

MORLEY, E. W. English Writers : an Attempt towards a History of English Literature. By H. Morley. 11 vols. 1887–95.

MORRIS. Chester in the Plantagenet and Tudor Reigns. By Rupert Morris, 1893.

MORTENSEN, Medeltidsdramat i Frankrike. By Dr. Mortensen, 1899. [Not consulted.]

MÜLLENHOFF. Ueber den Schwerttanz. Von K. Müllenhoff, 1871. [In *Festgaben für Gustav Homeyer, zum* 28. *Juli* 1871 (Berlin). Müllenhoff's essay is contained in pages 111 to 147 ; he published additions to it in *Zeitschrift für deutsches Alterthum*, xviii. 9 ; xx. 10.]

MÜLLER, E. Le Jour de l'An et les Étrennes, chez tous les Peuples dans tous les Temps. Par E. Müller, n. d.

MÜLLER, P. E. Commentatio Historica do Genio, Moribus et Luxu Aevi Theodosiani. By P. E. Müller. 2 parts, 1797–8.

N. E. D. A New English Dictionary on Historical Principles, founded mainly on the Materials collected by the Philological Society. Edited by J. A. H. Murray, H. Bradley, and W. A. Craigie. Vols. 1–6, 1888–1903. [In progress.]

NEWELL. Games and Songs of American Children. By W.W.Newell,1884.

NICHOLS, *Elizabeth*. Progresses and Public Processions of Queen Elizabeth. With historical notes, &c., by J. Nichols. 2nd ed. 3 vols. 1823.

NICHOLS, *James I*. Progresses, Processions, and Festivities of James I, his Court, &c. By J. Nichols. 4 vols. 1828.

NICHOLS, *Pageants*. London Pageants. By J. G. Nichols, 1837.

NICHOLSON. Golspie : Contributions to its Folklore. Edited by E. W. B. Nicholson, 1897.

NICK. Hof- und Volksnarren. Von A. F. Nick, 1861.

Noctes Shaksperianae. Noctes Shaksperianae : Papers edited by C. H. Hawkins, 1887. [*Winchester College Shakespere Society*.]

NÖLDECHEN. Tertullian und das Theater. Von E. Nöldechen, 1894. [*Zeitschrift für Kirchengeschichte*, xv. 161.]

Norf. Arch. Norfolk Archaeology : or, Miscellaneous Tracts relating to the Antiquities of the County of Norfolk, 1847–1903. [In progress : transactions of *Norfolk and Norwich Archaeological Society*.]

NORRIS. The Ancient Cornish Drama. Edited and translated by E. Norris. 2 vols. 1859.

NORTHALL. English Folk-Rhymes: a Collection of Traditional Verses relating to Places and Persons, Customs, Superstitions, &c. By G. F. Northall, 1892.

Northern F. L. See HENDERSON.

N. Q. Notes and Queries: a Medium of Intercommunication for Literary Men and General Readers. 107 vols. 1850–1903. [Ninth decennial series in progress.]

N. S. S. = *New Shakspere Society.*

OLRIK. Middelalderens vandrende Spillemænd. By A. Olrik, 1887. [In *Opuscula Philologica*, Copenhagen; not consulted.]

OPORINUS. Dramata Sacra, Comoediae et Tragoediae aliquot e Veteri Testamento desumptae. 2 vols. Basileae, Oporinus, 1547.

ORDISH. English Folk-Drama. By T. F. Ordish, 1891–3. [*Folk-Lore*, vols. ii, iv.]

OROSIUS. Pauli Orosii Historiarum adversus Paganos libri vii. Recensuit C. Zangemeister, 1882. [*C. S. E. L.* vol. v.]

OWEN-BLAKEWAY. A History of Shrewsbury. [By H. Owen and J. B. Blakeway.] 2 vols. 1825.

PADELFORD. Old English Musical Terms. By F. M. Padelford, 1899.

PARIS. La Littérature française au Moyen Âge. Par G. Paris. 2nd edition, 1890. [A volume of the *Manuel d'ancien Français.*]

PARIS, *Orig.* Les Origines de la Poésie lyrique en France au Moyen Âge. Par G. Paris, 1892. [Extrait du *Journal des Savants.*]

Paston Letters. The Paston Letters; 1422–1509 A.D. Edited by J. Gairdner. 2nd ed. 4 vols. 1900.

PAUL, *Grundriss.* Grundriss der germanischen Philologie. Herausgegeben von H. Paul. 2nd ed. 1896–1902. [In progress.]

PEARSON. The Chances of Death and other Studies in Evolution. By K. Pearson. 2 vols. 1897.

PERCY. Reliques of Ancient English Poetry. By Thomas Percy. Edited by H. B. Wheatley. 3 vols. 1876. [Vol. i contains an *Essay on the Ancient Minstrels in England.*]

PERCY, *N. H. B.* The Regulations and Establishment of the Household of Henry Algernon Percy, the fifth Earl of Northumberland, &c. Edited by T. Percy, 1827.

PERTZ. See *M. G. H.*

PETIT DE JULLEVILLE. Les Mystères. Par L. Petit de Julleville. 2 vols. 1880. [Forms, with three following, the *Histoire du Théâtre en France.*]

PETIT DE JULLEVILLE, *La Com.* La Comédie et les Mœurs en France au Moyen Âge. Par L. Petit de Julleville, 1886.

PETIT DE JULLEVILLE, *Les Com.* Les Comédiens en France au Moyen Âge. Par L. Petit de Julleville, 1889.

PETIT DE JULLEVILLE, *Rép. Com.* Répertoire du Théâtre Comique en France au Moyen Âge. Par L. Petit de Julleville, 1886.

See also *Lang. et Litt.*

PFANNENSCHMIDT. Germanische Erntefeste im heidnischen und christlichen Cultus mit besonderer Beziehung auf Niedersachsen. Von H. Pfannenschmidt, 1878.

P. G. Patrologiae Cursus Completus, seu Bibliotheca Universalis, Integra, Uniformis, Commoda, Oeconomica, Omnium SS. Patrum, Doctorum Scriptorumve Ecclesiasticorum, &c.; Series Graeca. Accurante J. P. Migne. 161 vols. 1857–66.

LIST OF AUTHORITIES

PHILPOT. The Sacred Tree: or the Tree in Religion and Myth. By Mrs. J. H. Philpot, 1897.

PICOT. La Sottie en France. Par E. Picot, 1878. [In *Romania*, vol. vii.]

PILOT DE THOREY. Usages, Fêtes, et Coutumes, existant ou ayant existé en Dauphiné. Par J. J. A. Pilot de Thorey. 2 vols. 1884.

P. L. Patrologiae Cursus Completus, &c. Series Latina. Accurante J. P. Migne. 221 vols. 1844–64.

PLUMMER. *See* BEDE, *E. H.*

POLLARD. English Miracle Plays, Moralities, and Interludes: Specimens of the Pre-Elizabethan Drama. Edited by A. W. Pollard. 3rd ed. 1898.

See also *Towneley Plays.*

PRELLER. Römische Mythologie. Von L. Preller. 3rd ed. by H. Jordan. 2 vols. 1881–3.

PROCTER-FRERE. A New History of the Book of Common Prayer. By F. Procter. Revised and rewritten by W. H. Frere, 1901.

PRÖLSS. Geschichte des neueren Dramas. Von R. Prölss. 3 vols. 1881–3.

Promptorium Parvulorum. Promptorium Parvulorum seu Clericorum: Lexicon Anglo-Latinum Princeps, Auctore Fratre Galfrido Grammatico Dicto, circa 1440. Recensuit A. Way. 3 vols. 1843–65. [*C. S.* O. S. xxv, liv, lxxxix.]

PRYNNE. Histrio-Mastix. The Players Scourge or Actors Tragedie. By W. Prynne, 1633.

PUECH. St. Jean Chrysostome et les Mœurs de son Temps. Par A. Puech, 1891.

RAMSAY, *F. E.* The Foundations of England, or Twelve Centuries of British History; B.C. 55–A.D. 1154. By Sir J. H. Ramsay. 2 vols. 1898.

RAMSAY, *L. Y.* Lancaster and York: 1399–1485. By Sir J. H. Ramsay. 2 vols. 1892.

RASHDALL. The Universities of the Middle Ages. By H. Rashdall. 2 vols. 1895.

RAYNAUD. Recueil de Motets français des douzième et treizième Siècles, avec notes, &c., par G. Raynaud. Suivi d'une Étude sur la Musique au Siècle de S. Louis par H. Lavoix fils. 2 vols. 1881–3.

Regularis Concordia. De Consuetudine Monachorum. Herausgegeben von W. S. Logemann, 1891–3. [*Anglia*, vols. xiii, xv.]

REIDT. Das geistliche Schauspiel des Mittelalters in Deutschland. Von H. Reidt, 1868.

REINERS. Die Tropen-, Prosen- und Präfations-Gesänge des feierlichen Hochamtes im Mittelalter. Von A. Reiners, 1884. [Not consulted.]

Reliquiae Antiquae. See WRIGHT-HALLIWELL.

Rev. Celt. Revue Celtique, dirigée par H. Gaidoz [afterwards H. D'Arbois de Jubainville]. 24 vols. 1890–1903. [In progress.]

Rev. Hist. Rel. Annales du Musée Guimet. Revue de l'Histoire des Religions. 46 vols. 1880-1902. [In progress.]

Rev. T. P. Revue des Traditions populaires, 1886, &c. [Organ of *Société des Traditions populaires.*]

RHYS, C. F. Celtic Folklore: Welsh and Manx. By J. Rhys. 2 vols. 1901.

RHYS, C. H. Lectures on the Origin and Growth of Religion as illustrated by Celtic Heathendom. By J. Rhys, 1888. [The *Hibbert Lectures* for 1886.]

RIBTON-TURNER. A History of Vagrants and Vagrancy. By C. J. Ribton-Turner, 1887.

RIGOLLOT. Monnaies inconnues des Evêques des Innocens, des Fous, et de quelques autres Associations singulières du même Temps. Par M. J. R[igollot] d'Amiens. Avec une introduction par C. L[eber]. 2 vols. (Texte et Planches), 1837.

RILEY. Memorials of London and London Life : a series of Extracts from the Archives of the City of London, 1276–1419. Translated and edited by H. T. Riley, 1868.

RIMBAULT. Two Sermons Preached by the Boy Bishop. Edited by J. G. Nichols. With an introduction giving an account of the Festival of the Boy Bishop in England. By E. F. Rimbault, 1875. [*Camden Miscellany*, vol. vii. *C. S.*]

RITSON. Ancient English Metrical Romanceës. Selected and published by J. Ritson. 2 vols. 1802. [Vol. 1 contains a *Dissertation on Romance and Minstrelsy.*]

RITSON, *Bibl. Poet.* Bibliographia Poetica : a Catalogue of English Poets, from the twelfth to the sixteenth centuries, with an account of their Works. By J. Ritson, 1802.

RITSON, *Robin Hood.* Robin Hood : a Collection of all the Ancient Poems, Songs, and Ballads now extant, relative to that Outlaw. Edited by J. Ritson, 1795.

RITSON, *Songs.* Ancient Songs and Ballads, from Henry II to the Revolution. By J. Ritson. 3rd ed., revised by W. C. Hazlitt, 1877.

Ritual Commission. Second Report of the Commissioners Appointed to Inquire into the Rubrics, Orders, and Directions for Regulating the Course and Conduct of Public Worship, &c., 1868. [A Parliamentary paper. *Appendix E* (pp. 399–685) is a reprint of Injunctions and Visitation Articles from 1561 to 1730.]

ROCK. The Church of our Fathers, in St. Osmund's Rite for Salisbury, &c. By D. Rock. 3 vols. 1849–53.

Romania. Romania : Recueil trimestriel consacré à l'Étude des Langues et des Littératures romanes. 32 vols. 1872–1903. [In progress.]

ROSCHER, *Lexicon.* Ausführliches Lexicon der griechischen und römischen Mythologie. Herausgegeben von W. H. Roscher, 1884-97. [In progress.]

ROVENHAGEN. Alt-englische Dramen. I. Die geistlichen Schauspiele. Von Prof. Dr. Rovenhagen, 1879.

R. S.=Rerum Britannicarum Medii Aevi Scriptores, or, Chronicles and Memorials of Great Britain and Ireland during the Middle Ages. Published under the direction of the Master of the Rolls, 1858-99. [*Rolls Series.*]

RYMER. Foedera, Conventiones, Literae, et cuiuscumque generis Acta Publica. Accurante Thoma Rymer. 20 vols. 1704-35.

SAINTSBURY. A Short History of English Literature. By G. Saintsbury, 1898.

SAINTSBURY, *Ren.* The Earlier Renaissance. By G. Saintsbury, 1901. [*Periods of European Literature*, v.]

SALVIAN. Salviani Presbyteri Massiliensis Opera Omnia. Recensuit Franciscus Pauly, 1883. [*C. S. E. L.* viii. The references in the text are to the *De Gubernatione Dei.*]

SANDYS. Christmastide : its History, Festivities, and Carols. By W. Sandys, n. d.

SANDYS, *Carols.* Christmas Carols, Ancient and Modern, &c. With an introduction and notes by W. Sandys, 1833.

Sarum Breviary. Breviarium ad usum insignis Ecclesiae Sarum. Labore F. Procter et C. Wordsworth. 3 vols. 1882-6.

Sarum Manual. See *York Manual.*

Sarum Missal. Missale ad usum insignis et praeclarae Ecclesiae Sarum. Labore et studio F. H. Dickinson, 1861-83.

Sarum Processional. Processionale ad usum Sarum. Edited by W. G. Henderson, 1882. [From Rouen edition of 1508.] *See* WORDSWORTH, *Proc.*

SATHAS. Ἱστορικὸν δοκίμιον περὶ τοῦ θεάτρου καὶ τῆς μουσικῆς τῶν βυζαντινῶν. By K. N. Sathas, Venice, 1878.

SAUPE. Der Indiculus Superstitionum et Paganiarum : ein Verzeichnis heidnischer und abergläubischer Gebräuche und Meinungen aus der Zeit Karls des Grossen. Von H. A. Saupe, 1891. [Leipziger Programm.]

SCHACK. Geschichte der dramatischen Litteratur und Kunst in Spanien. Von A. F. von Schack. 3 vols. 1845-6.

SCHAFF. History of the Christian Church. By P. Schaff. 2nd ed. 12 vols. 1883-93.

SCHÄFFER. Geschichte des spanischen Nationaldramas. Von A. Schäffer, 1890.

SCHANNAT. Concilia Germaniae, quae J. F. Schannat primum collegit, deinde J. Hartzheim auxit. 11 vols. 1759-90.

SCHELLING. The English Chronicle Play : a Study in the Popular Historical Literature environing Shakespeare. By F. E. Schelling, 1902.

SCHERER. Geschichte der deutschen Litteratur. Von W. Scherer. 8th ed. 1899. [Eng. transl. from 3rd ed. by Mrs. F. C. Conybeare, 1886.]

SCHMELLER. Carmina Burana : lateinische und deutsche Lieder und Gedichte einer Handschrift des xiii. Jahrhunderts aus Benedictbeuern. Herausgegeben von J. A. Schmeller, 3rd edition, 1894.

SCHMIDT. Die Digby-Spiele. Von K. Schmidt, 1884. [Berlin dissertation : continued in *Anglia*, vol. viii.]

SCHMITZ. Die Bussbücher und die Bussdisciplin der Kirche. Von H. J. Schmitz, 1883.

SCHÖNBACH. Über die Marienklagen. Ein Beitrag zur Geschichte der geistlichen Dichtung in Deutschland. Von A. E. Schönbach, 1874.

SCHRÄDER. Reallexicon der indo-germanischen Altertumskunde. Von O. Schräder, 1901.

SCHRÄDER-JEVONS. Prehistoric Antiquities of the Aryan People. Translated from the 'Sprachvergleichung und Urgeschichte' of O. Schräder by F. B. Jevons, 1890.

SCHÜCKING. Studien über die stofflichen Beziehungen der englischen Komödie zur italienischen bis Lilly. Von L. L. Schücking, 1901. [*Studien zur englischen Philologie*, ix.]

SCHULTZ. Das höfische Leben zur Zeit der Minnesinger. Von A. Schultz. 2 vols. 2nd edition, 1889.

SEIFERT. Wit-und-Science Moralitäten. Von J. Seifert, 1892. [Not consulted.]

SEPET. Les Prophètes du Christ. Étude sur les Origines du Théâtre au Moyen Âge. Par Marius Sepet, 1878. [First published in *Bibl. des Chartes*, vols. xxviii, xxix, xxxviii, from which I quote.]

SEPET, *D. C.* Le Drame chrétien au Moyen Âge. Par Marius Sepet, 1878.

SEPET, *Or.* Origines catholiques du Théâtre moderne. Par Marius Sepet, 1901.

SHARP. A Dissertation on the Pageants or Dramatic Mysteries, anciently performed at Coventry. By T. Sharp, 1825.

SHARP. *Digby Plays.* Ancient Mysteries from the Digby Manuscripts in the Bodleian. Edited by T. Sharp, 1835. [*Abbotsford Club.*]

Sh.-Jahrbuch. Jahrbuch der Deutschen Shakespeare-Gesellschaft. 38 vols. 1865–1902.

SIMPSON. The Buddhist Praying-wheel : a Collection of Material bearing upon the Symbolism of the Wheel and Circular Movements in Custom and Religious Ritual. By W. Simpson, 1896.

SITTL. Die Gebärden der Griechen und Römer. Von C. Sittl, 1890.

SMITH, GREGORY. The Transition Period. By G. Gregory Smith, 1900. [*Periods of European Literature.*]

SMITH, ROBERTSON. Lectures on the Religion of the Semites : First Series, The Fundamental Institutions. By W. Robertson Smith. 2nd ed. 1894.

SMITH, TOULMIN. English Gilds : Original Ordinances of more than a Hundred Gilds. Edited with notes by J. T. Smith, 1870. [*E. E. T. S.* xl.]

SÖRGEL. Die englischen Maskenspiele. Von G. Sörgel, 1882. [Halle dissertation.]

S. P. Dom. Calendar of State Papers, Domestic Series, of the Reigns of Edward VI, Mary, Elizabeth, and James I. 12 vols. 1856–72.

SPECHT. Geschichte des Unterrichtswesens in Deutschland. Von F. A. Specht, 1885.

SPENCE. Shetland Folk-Lore. By J. Spence, 1899.

STAFFORD. A Compendious or Brief Examination of Certain Ordinary Complaints. By W. Stafford, 1581. Edited by F. J. Furnivall, 1876. [*N. S. S.* Series vi. 3.]

STEPHENS-HUNT. A History of the English Church. Edited by W. R. W. Stephens and W. Hunt. 4 vols. 1899-1902. [In progress.]

STODDARD. References for Students of Miracle Plays and Mysteries. By F. H. Stoddard, 1887. [*University of California Library Bulletin*, No. viii.]

STOWE, *Annals.* Annales, or a general Chronicle of England. By J. Stowe. Continued to the end of 1631 by E. Howes, 1631.

STOWE, *Survey.* A Survey of London. By J. Stowe. Edited by W. J. Thoms, 1876.

STRUTT. The Sports and Pastimes of the People of England: including the Rural and Domestic Recreations, May Games, Mummeries, Shows, Processions, Pageants, and Pompous Spectacles, from the earliest Period to the present Time. By J. Strutt. New ed. by W. Hone, 1833.

STUBBES. The Anatomie of Abuses. By Phillip Stubbes, 1583. Edited by F. J. Furnivall, 1877-82. [*N. S. S.* Series vi. 4, 6, 12. Part I contains Barnaby Googe's translation (1570) of Kirchmayer's *Regnum Papismi* (1553), Bk. iv.]

Suffolk F. L. See *County Folk-Lore.*

SWETE. Church Services and Service-Books before the Reformation. By H. B. Swete, 1896.

SWOBODA. John Heywood als Dramatiker. Ein Beitrag zur Entwicklungsgeschichte des englischen Dramas. Von W. Swoboda, 1888. [*Wiener Beiträge zur deutschen und englischen Philologie*, iii : not consulted.]

SYMONDS. Shakspere's Predecessors in the English Drama. By J. A. Symonds, 1884.

TABOUROT. Orchésographie; par Thoinot Arbeau [*pseud.* for Jehan Tabourot], 1588. Réimpression précédée d'une notice sur les Danses du xvie Siècle, par Laure Fonta, 1888.

TEN BRINK. History of English Literature. By B. Ten Brink. Translated from the German. 3 vols. 1893-6. [All published ; a 2nd German edition, by A. Brandl, in progress.]

TERTULLIAN. Quinti Septimi Florentis Tertulliani Opera. Ex recensione Augusti Reifferscheid et Georgii Wissowa. Pars i. 1890 [vol. xx of *Corpus Scriptorum Ecclesiasticorum Latinorum.* The *De Spectaculis* and *De Idololatria* are in this vol., and are translated, with the *Apologeticus*, in vol. xi of the *Ante-Nicene Christian Library*, 1869. The complete works of Tertullian are also in *P. L.* vols. i and ii.]

TEUFFEL. Teuffel's History of Roman Literature. Revised and enlarged by L. Schwabe. Authorized translation from the 5th German edition by G. C. W. Warr. 2 vols. 1891.

THIERS. Iohannis Baptistae Thiers, de Festorum Dierum Imminutione Liber, 1668.

THIERS. Traité des Jeux et des Divertissemens qui peuvent être permis. Par J.-B. Thiers, 1686.

TICKNOR. History of Spanish Literature. By G. Ticknor. 6th American ed. 3 vols. 1888.

TIERSOT. Histoire de la Chanson populaire en France. Par J. Tiersot, 1889.

TILLE, *D. W.* Die Geschichte der deutschen Weihnacht. Von A. Tille, 1893.

TILLE, *Y and C.* Yule and Christmas: Their Place in the Germanic Year. By G. Tille, 1899.

TORRACA. Il Teatro italiano dei Secoli xiii, xiv, e xv. Per F. Torraca, 1885.

Towneley Plays. The Towneley Mysteries. Edited by J. Raine, with preface by J. Hunter and glossary by J. Gordon, 1836. [*Surtees Soc.* iii.]

Towneley Plays. Re-edited from the unique MS. by G. England, with side-notes and introduction by A. W. Pollard, 1897. [*E. E. T. S.* E. S. lxxi.]

Trad. La Tradition: Revue générale des Contes, Légendes, Chants, Usages, Traditions et Arts populaires.

UNGEMACHT. Die Quellen der fünf ersten Chester Plays. Von H. Ungemacht, 1890.

USENER. Religionsgeschichtliche Untersuchungen. Von H. Usener. 3 vols. 1889-99.

Use of Sarum. See FRERE.

VACANDARD. L'Idolâtrie dans la Gaule. Par E. Vacandard, 1899. [In *Revue des Questions historiques*, vol. lxv.]

Variorum. The Plays and Poems of William Shakespeare. With a Life of the Poet and an Enlarged History of the Stage. By the late E. Malone. Edited by J. Boswell. 21 vols. 1821.

VAUX. Church Folklore. By the Rev. J. E. Vaux, 1894. [A 2nd ed. was published in 1902.]

Venetian Papers. See BROWN.

Viel Testament. Le Mistère du Viel Testament. Publié avec introduction, notes et glossaire par le Baron J. de Rothschild. 6 vols. 1878-91. [*Société des Anciens Textes Français.*]

VIOLLET-LE-DUC. Ancien Théâtre françois: depuis les Mystères jusqu'à Corneille. Par E. L. N. Viollet-le-Duc. 10 vols. 1854-7.

VOGT. Leben und Dichten der deutschen Spielleute im Mittelalter. Von F. Vogt, 1876.

WACKERNAGEL. Geschichte der deutschen Litteratur. Ein Handbuch von W. Wackernagel. 2nd ed. by E. Martin, 1879.

WACKERNELL. Altdeutsche Passionsspiele aus Tirol. Von J. E. Wackernell, 1897.

WALLASCHEK. Primitive Music: an Inquiry into the Origin and

Development of Music, Songs, Instruments, Dances, and Pantomimes of Savage Races. By R. Wallaschek, 1893.

WALTER. Das Eselsfest. Von A. Walter, 1885. [In *Caecilien-Kalender*, 75.]

WARD. A History of English Dramatic Literature to the Death of Queen Anne. By A. W. Ward. 2nd ed. 3 vols. 1899.

WARTON. *See* HAZLITT-WARTON.

WASSERSCHLEBEN. Die Bussordnungen der abendländischen Kirche. Von F. W. H. Wasserschleben, 1851.

WEBER. Geistliches Schauspiel und kirchliche Kunst in ihrem Verhältnis erläutert an einer Ikonographie der Kirche und Synagoge. Von P. Weber, 1894.

WECHSSLER. Die romanischen Marienklagen. Ein Beitrag zur Geschichte des Dramas im Mittelalter. Von E. Wechssler, 1893.

WESTERMARCK. A History of Human Marriage. By E. Westermarck. 2nd ed. 1894.

WETZER-WELTE. Kirchenlexicon. Von H. J. Wetzer und B. Welte, 2nd ed. by J. Hergenröther and F. Kaulen. 12 vols. 1882-1900. [In progress.]

WIECK. Der Teufel auf der mittelalterlichen Mysterienbühne. Von H. Wieck, 1887. [Marburg dissertation : not consulted.]

WILKEN. Geschichte der geistlichen Spiele in Deutschland. Von E. Wilken, 1872.

WILKINS. Concilia Magnae Britanniae et Hiberniae, 446-1717. Accedunt Constitutiones et alia ad Historiam Ecclesiae Anglicanae Spectantia. 4 vols. 1737.

WILMOTTE. Les Passions allemandes du Rhin dans leur Rapport avec l'ancien Théâtre français. Par M. Wilmotte, 1898. [*Ouvrages couronnés et autres Mémoires publiés par l'Académie Royale de Belgique*, lv.]

Winchester Troper. *See* FRERE.

WIRTH. Die Oster- und Passionsspiele bis zum xvi. Jahrhundert. Von L. Wirth, 1889.

WISSOWA. Religion und Kultus der Römer. Von G. Wissowa, 1902. [Vol. v, Part 4 of I. von Müller's *Handbuch der classischen Altertums-wissenschaft*.]

WOOD, *Athenae.* Athenae Oxonienses, an Exact History of all Writers and Bishops who have had their Education in the University of Oxford. By Anthony à Wood. 2nd ed. by P. Bliss. 4 vols. 1813-20.

WOOD, *Hist. Univ.* History and Antiquities of the University of Oxford. By Anthony à Wood. Now first published in English with continuation by J. Gutch. 2 vols. 1792-6.

WOOD-MARTIN. Traces of the Elder Faiths of Ireland. By W. G. Wood-Martin. 2 vols. 1902.

WORDSWORTH. Notes on Mediaeval Services in England, with an index of Lincoln Ceremonies. By C. Wordsworth, 1898.

WORDSWORTH, *Proc.* Ceremonies and Processions of the Cathedral Church of Salisbury. Edited by C. Wordsworth, 1901. [From *Salisbury Chapter MS*. 148 of †1445, a book for use by the *principalis persona* in the choir, and supplementary to the printed Processional.]

WRIGHT. Early Mysteries and other Latin Poems of the Twelfth and Thirteenth Centuries. By T. Wright, 1838.

WRIGHT, *Chester Plays*. The Chester Plays. Edited by Thomas Wright. 2 vols. 1843. [*Shakespeare Society*.]

WRIGHT, *Map*. The Latin Poems commonly attributed to Walter Mapes. Collected and edited by T. Wright, 1841. [*C. S.* o. s. xvii.]

WRIGHT-HALLIWELL. Reliquiae Antiquae: Scraps from Ancient Manuscripts, illustrating chiefly Early English Literature and the English Language. By T. Wright and J. O. Halliwell. 2 vols. 1841.

WRIGHT-WÜLCKER. Anglo-Saxon and Old English Vocabularies. By T. Wright. Edited and collated by R. P. Wülcker. 2 vols. 1884.

WÜLCKER. Grundriss zur Geschichte der angelsächsischen Litteratur: mit einer Übersicht der angelsächsischen Sprachwissenschaft. Von R. Wülcker, 1885.

WYLIE. A History of England under Henry IV. By J. H. Wylie. 4 vols. 1884-98.

York Breviary. Breviarium ad usum insignis Ecclesiae Eboracensis. Edidit S. W. Lawley. 2 vols. 1880-2. [*Surtees Soc*. lxxi, lxxv.]

York Manual. Manuale et Processionale ad usum insignis Ecclesiae Eboracensis. Edidit W. G. Henderson, 1875. [*Surtees Soc*. lxiii. Contains also *Sarum Manual*.]

York Missal. Missale ad usum insignis Ecclesiae Eboracensis. Edidit W. G. Henderson. 2 vols. 1874. [*Surtees Soc*. lix, lx.]

York Plays. The Plays performed by the Crafts or Mysteries of York on the Day of Corpus Christi. Edited by L. T. Smith, 1885.

Z. f. d. A. Zeitschrift für deutsches Alterthum [*afterwards added* und deutsche Literatur], 1841-1903. [In progress.]

Z. f. rom. Phil. Zeitschrift für romanische Philologie, 1877-1903. [In progress.]

ZSCHECH. Die Anfänge des englischen Dramas. Von Dr. Zschech, 1886. [Not consulted.]

BOOK I

MINSTRELSY

C'est une étrange entreprise que celle de faire rire les honnêtes gens.—J.-B. POQUELIN DE MOLIÈRE.

Molière est un infâme histrion.—J.-B. BOSSUET.

CHAPTER I

THE FALL OF THE THEATRES

[*Bibliographical Note.* — A convenient sketch of the history of the Roman stage will be found in G. Körting, *Geschichte des griechischen und römischen Theaters* (1897). The details given in L. Friedländer, *Sittengeschichte Roms in der Zeit von August bis zum Ausgang der Antonine* (vol. ii, 7th ed. 1901), and the same writer's article on *Die Spiele* in vol. vi of Marquardt and Mommsen's *Handbuch der römischen Alterthümer* (2nd ed. 1885), may be supplemented from E. Nöldechen's article *Tertullian und das Theater* in *Zeitschrift für Kirchengeschichte*, xv (1894), 161, for the *fabulae Atellanae* from A. Dieterich, *Pulcinella* (1897), chs. 4–8, and for the *pantomimi* from C. Sittl, *Die Gebärden der Griechen und Römer* (1890), ch. 13. The account in C. Magnin, *Les Origines du Théâtre moderne* (vol. i, all published, 1838), is by no means obsolete. Teuffel and Schwabe, *History of Latin Literature*, vol. i, §§ 3–18 (trans. G. C. W. Warr, 1891), contains a mass of imperfectly arranged material. The later history of the Greek stage is dealt with by P. E. Müller, *Commentatio historica de genio, moribus et luxu aevi Theodosiani* (1798), vol. ii, and A. E. Haigh, *Tragic Drama of the Greeks* (1896), ch. 6. The ecclesiastical prohibitions are collected by W. Prynne, *Histriomastix* (1633), and J. de Douhet, *Dictionnaire des Mystères* (1854), and their general attitude summarized by H. Alt, *Theater und Kirche in ihrem gegenseitigen Verhältniss* (1846). S. Dill, *Roman Society in the Last Century of the Roman Empire* (2nd ed. 1899), should be consulted for an admirable study of the conditions under which the pre-mediaeval stage came to an end.]

CHRISTIANITY, emerging from Syria with a prejudice against disguisings [1], found the Roman world full of *scenici*. The mimetic instinct, which no race of mankind is wholly without, appears to have been unusually strong amongst the peoples of the Mediterranean stock. A literary drama came into being in Athens during the sixth century, and established itself in city after city. Theatres were built, and tragedies and comedies acted on the Attic model, wherever a Greek foot trod, from Hipola in Spain to Tigranocerta in Armenia. The great capitals of the later Greece, Alexandria,

[1] *Deuteronomy*, xxii. 5, a commonplace of anti-stage controversy from Tertullian (*de Spectaculis*, c. 23) to *Histrio-Mastix*. Tertullian (*loc. cit.*) asserts, 'non amat falsum auctor veritatis; adulterium est apud illum omne quod fingitur.'

Antioch, Pergamum, rivalled Athens itself in their devotion to the stage. Another development of drama, independent of Athens, in Sicily and Magna Graecia, may be distinguished as farcical rather than comic. After receiving literary treatment at the hands of Epicharmus and Sophron in the fifth century, it continued its existence under the name of mime (μῖμος), upon a more popular level. Like many forms of popular drama, it seems to have combined the elements of farce and morality. Its exponents are described as buffoons (γελωτοποιοί, παιγνιογράφοι) and dealers in indecencies (ἀναισχυντογράφοι), and again as concerning themselves with questions of character and manners (ἠθολόγοι, ἀρεταλόγοι). They even produced what sound singularly like problem plays (ὑποθέσεις). Both qualities may have sprung from a common root in the observation and audacious portrayal of contemporary life. The mime was still flourishing in and about Tarentum in the third century[1].

Probably the Romans were not of the Mediterranean stock, and their native *ludi* were athletic rather than mimetic. But the drama gradually filtered in from the neighbouring peoples. Its earliest stirrings in the rude farce of the *satura* are attributed by Livy to Etruscan influence[2]. From Campania came another type of farce, the *Oscum ludicrum* or *fabula Atellana*, with its standing masks of Maccus and Bucco, Pappus and Dossennus, in whom it is hard not to find a kinship to the traditional personages of the Neapolitan *commedia dell' arte*. About 240 B.C. the Greek Livius Andronicus introduced tragedy and comedy. The play now became a regular element in the *spectacula* of the Roman festivals, only subordinate in interest to the chariot-race and the gladiatorial show. Permanent theatres were built in the closing years of the Republic by Pompey and others, and the number of days annually devoted to *ludi scenici* was constantly on the increase. From 48 under Augustus they grew to 101 under Constantius. Throughout the period of

---

[1] J. Denis, *La Comédie grecque* (1886), i. 50, 106; ii. 535. The so-called mimes of Herodas (third cent. B.C.) are literary pieces, based probably on the popular mime but not intended for representation (Croiset, *Hist. de la Litt. grecque,* v. 174).

[2] Livy, vii. 2; Valerius Maximus, ii. 4. 4 (364 B.C.).

the Empire, indeed, the theatre was of no small political importance. On the one hand it was the rallying point of all disturbers of the peace and the last stronghold of a public opinion debarred from the senate and the forum ; on the other it was a potent means for winning the affection of the populace and diverting its attention from dynastic questions. The *scenici* might be thorns in the side of the government, but they were quite indispensable to it. If their perversities drove them from Italy, the clamour of the mob soon brought them back again. Trajan revealed one of the *arcana imperii* when he declared that the *annona* and the *spectacula* controlled Rome[1]. And what was true of Rome was true of Byzantium, and in a lesser degree of the smaller provincial cities. So long as the Empire itself held together, the provision firstly of corn and secondly of novel *ludi* remained one of the chief preoccupations of many a highly placed official.

The vast popular audiences of the period under consideration cared but little for the literary drama. In the theatre of Pompey, thronged with slaves and foreigners of every tongue, the finer histrionic effects must necessarily have been lost[2]. Something more spectacular and sensuous, something appealing to a cruder sense of humour, almost inevitably took their place. There is evidence indeed that, while the theatres stood, tragedy and comedy never wholly disappeared from their boards[3]. But it was probably only the ancient masterpieces that got a hearing. Even in Greece performances of new plays on classical models cannot be traced beyond about the time of Hadrian. And in Rome the tragic poets had long before then learnt to content themselves with recitations and to rely for victims on the good nature, frequently inadequate, of their friends[4]. The stilted dramas of Seneca were the

---

[1] Juvenal, x. 81 ; Dion Chrysostom, *Or.* xxxii. 370, 18 M.; Fronto, *Princip. hist.* v. 13. A fourth-century inscription (*Bull. d. Commis. arch. comun. di Roma*, 1891, 342) contains a list of small Roman *tabernarii* entitled to *locum spectaculis et panem*.

[2] The holding capacity of the theatre of Pompey is variously given at from 17,580 to 40,000, that of the theatre of Balbus at from 11,510 to 30,085, that of the theatre of Marcellus as 20,000.

[3] Friedländer, ii. 100 ; Haigh, 457 ; Krumbacher, 646 ; Welcker, *Die griechischen Tragödien* (1841), iii. 1472.

[4] Juvenal, i. 1 ; Pliny, *Epist.* vi.

delight of the Renaissance, but it is improbable that, until the Renaissance, they were ever dignified with representation. Roughly speaking, for comedy and tragedy the Empire substituted farce and pantomime.

Farce, as has been noticed, was the earliest traffic of the Roman stage. The Atellane, relegated during the brief vogue of comedy and tragedy to the position of an interlude or an afterpiece, now once more asserted its independence. But already during the Republic the Atellane, with its somewhat conventional and limited methods, was beginning to give way to a more flexible and vital type of farce. This was none other than the old mime of Magna Graecia, which now entered on a fresh phase of existence and overran both West and East. That it underwent considerable modifications, and probably absorbed much both of Atellane and of Attic comedy, may be taken for granted. Certainly it extended its scope to mythological themes. But its leading characteristics remained unchanged. The ethical element, one may fear, sank somewhat into the background, although it was by no means absent from the work of the better mime-writers, such as Laberius and Publilius Syrus[1]. But that the note of shamelessness was preserved there is no doubt whatever[2]. The favourite theme, which is common indeed to farce of all ages, was that of conjugal infidelity[3]. Unchaste scenes were represented with an astonishing realism[4].

15; vii. 17; Tacitus, *de Oratoribus*, 9, 11.

[1] The *Sententiae* of Publilius Syrus were collected from his mimes in the first century A.D., and enlarged from other sources during the Middle Ages (Teuffel-Schwabe, § 212). Cf. the edition by W. Meyer, 1880. The other fragments of the mimographs are included in O. Ribbeck, *Comicorum Romanorum Fragmenta* (3rd ed. 1898). Philistion of Bithynia, about the time of Tiberius, gave the mime a literary form once more in his κωμῳδίαι βιολογικαί (J. Denis, *La Com. grecque*, ii. 544; Croiset, *Hist. de la Litt. grecque*, v. 449).

[2] *Incerti* (fourth century) *ad Terentium* (ed. Giles, i. xix) 'mimos ab diuturna imitatione vilium rerum et levium personarum.' Diomedes (fifth century), *Ars Grammatica*, iii. 488 'mimus est sermonis cuiuslibet imitatio et motus sine reverentia, vel factorum et dictorum turpium cum lascivia imitatio.'

[3] Ovid, *Tristia*, ii. 497:
'quid, si scripsissem mimos obscoena iocantes,
qui semper vetiti crimen amoris habent.'

[4] *Hist. Augusta*, *Vita Heliogabali*, 25 'in mimicis adulteriis ea quae solent simulato fieri effici ad verum iussit'; cf. the *pyrrichae*

Contrary to the earlier custom of the classical stage, women took part in the performances, and at the *Floralia*, loosest of Roman festivals, the spectators seem to have claimed it as their right that the *mimae* should play naked[1]. The *mimus*—for the same term designates both piece and actor—was just the kind of entertainer whom a democratic audience loves. Clad in a parti-coloured *centunculus*, with no mask to conceal the play of facial gesture, and *planipes*, with no borrowed dignity of sock or buskin, he rattled through his side-splitting scenes of low life, and eked out his text with an inexhaustible variety of rude dancing, buffoonery and horse-play[2]. Originally the mimes seem to have performed in monologues, and the action of their pieces continued to be generally dominated by a single personage, the *archimimus*, who was provided with certain *stupidi* and *parasiti* to act as foils and butts for his wit. A satirical intention was frequently present in both mimes and Atellanes, and their outspoken allusions are more than once recorded to have wrung the withers of persons of importance and to have brought serious retribution on the actors themselves. Caligula, for instance, with characteristic brutality, had a ribald playwright burnt alive in the amphitheatre[3].

The farce was the diversion of the proletariat and the *bourgeoisie* of Rome. Petronius, with all the insolence of the literary man, makes Trimalchio buy a *troupe* of comedians, and insist on their playing an Atellane[4]. The golden and

described by Suetonius, *Nero*, 12. The Roman taste for bloodshed was sometimes gratified by mimes given in the amphitheatre, and designed to introduce the actual execution of a criminal. Martial, *de Spectaculis*, 7, mentions the worrying and crucifixion of a brigand in the mime *Laureolus*, by order of Domitian:
 'nuda Caledonio sic pectora prae-
  buit urso
  non falsa pendens in cruce Laureolus.'
[1] Martial, i. 1; Ausonius, *Ecl.* xviii. 25; Lactantius (†300), *de Inst. div.* i. 20. 10. Probably the influence of a piece of folk-ritual is

to be traced here.
[2] The 'mimus' type is exactly reproduced by more than one popular performer on the modern 'variety' or 'burlesque' stage.
[3] Macrobius, *Sat.* ii. 7; Cicero, *ad Atticum*, xiv. 3; Suetonius, *Augustus*, 45, 68; *Tiberius*, 45; *Caligula*, 27; *Nero*, 39; *Galba*, 13; *Vespasian*, 19; *Domitian*, 10; *Hist. Augusta, Vita Marc. Aurel.* 8. 29; *Vita Commodi*, 3; *Vita Maximini*, 9.
[4] Petronius, *Satyricon*, liii; cf. *Taming of the Shrew*, i. 1. 258 ''Tis a very excellent piece of work, madam lady; would 'twere done!'

cultured classes preferred the pantomimic dance. This arose
out of the ruins of the literary drama. On the Roman stage
grew up a custom, unknown in Greece, by which the lyric
portions of the text (*cantica*) were entrusted to a singer who
stood with the flute-player at the side of the stage, while
the actor confined himself to dancing in silence with appropriate dumb show. The dialogue (*diverbia*) continued to
be spoken by the actors. The next step was to drop the
diverbia altogether; and thus came the *pantomimus* who
undertook to indicate the whole development of a plot in
a series of dramatic dances, during the course of which he
often represented several distinct *rôles*. Instead of the single
flute-player and singer a full choir now supplied the musical
accompaniment, and great poets—Lucan and Statius among
the number—did not disdain to provide texts for the *fabulae
salticae*. Many of the *pantomimi* attained to an extreme
refinement in their degenerate and sensuous art. They were,
as Lucian said, χειρόσοφοι, erudite of gesture[1]. Their subjects
were, for the most part, mythological and erotic, not to say
lascivious, in character[2]. Pylades the Cilician, who, with
his great rival Bathyllus the Alexandrian, brought the dance
to its first perfection under Augustus, favoured satyric
themes; but this mode does not appear to have endured.
Practically the dancers were the tragedians, and the mimes
were the comedians, of the Empire. The old Etruscan name
for an actor, *histrio*, came to be almost synonymous with
pantomimus[3]. Rome, which could lash itself into a fury
over the contests between the Whites and Reds or the
Blues and Greens in the circus, was not slow to take sides
upon the respective merits of its scenic entertainers. The

---

[1] Lucian, *de Saltatione*, 69.

[2] Juvenal, *Sat.* vi. 63; Zosimus
(450–501 A.D.), i. 6 (*Corp. Script.
Hist. Byz.* xx. 12) ἢ τε γὰρ παντό-
μιμος ὄρχησις ἐν ἐκείνοις εἰσήχθη τοῖς
χρόνοις . . . πολλῶν αἴτια γεγονότα
μέχρι τοῦδε κακῶν.

[3] This is not wholly so, at any
rate in Tacitus, who seems to include the players both of mimes
and of Atellanes amongst *histriones*
(*Ann.* i. 73; iv. 14). For the

origin of the name, cf. Livy, vii. 2
'ister Tusco verbo ludius vocabatur.' Besides *ludius, actor* is good
Latin. But it is generally used in
some such phrase as *actor prima-
rum personarum*, protagonist, and
by itself often means *dominus
gregis*, manager of the *grex* or
company. *Mimus* signifies both
performer and performance, *pantomimus* the performer only. He is
said *saltare fabulas*.

histrionalis favor led again and again to brawls which set the rulers of the city wondering whether after all the *pantomimi* were worth while. Augustus had found it to his advantage that the spirit of partisanship should attach itself to a Pylades or a Bathyllus rather than to more illustrious antagonists[1]. But the personal instincts of Tiberius were not so genial as those of Augustus. Early in his principate he attempted to restrain the undignified court paid by senators and knights to popular dancers, and when this measure failed, he expelled the *histriones* from Italy[2]. The example was followed by more than one of his successors, but Rome clamoured fiercely for its toys, and the period of exile was never a long one[3].

Both *mimi* and *pantomimi* had their vogue in private, at the banquets and weddings of the great, as well as in public. The class of *scenici* further included a heterogeneous variety of lesser performers. There were the rhapsodes who sung the tragic *cantica*, torn from their context, upon the stage. There were musicians and dancers of every order and from every land[4]. There were jugglers (*praestigiatores, acetabuli*), rope-walkers (*funambuli*), stilt-walkers (*grallatores*), tumblers (*cernui, petauristae, petaminarii*), buffoons (*sanniones, scurrae*), beast-tamers and strong men. The pick of them did their 'turns' in the theatre or the amphitheatre; the more humble were content with modest audiences at street corners or in the vestibule of the circus. From Rome the entertainers of the imperial race naturally found their way into the theatres of the provinces. Tragedy and comedy no doubt held their own longer in Greece, but the stage of Constantinople under Justinian does not seem to have differed notably from the stage of Rome under Nero. Marseilles alone distinguished itself by the honourable austerity which forbade the *mimi* its gates[5].

---

[1] Dion Cassius, liv. 17.

[2] Tacitus, *Annales*, i. 77; iv. 14; Dion Cassius, lvii. 21; Suetonius, *Tiberius*, 37.

[3] Tacitus, *Annales*, xiii. 25; xiv. 21; Dion Cassius, lix. 2; lxi. 8; lxviii. 10; Suetonius, *Nero*, 16, 26; *Titus*, 7; *Domitian*, 7; Pliny, *Paneg.* 46; *Hist. Augusta, Vita Hadriani*, 19; *Vita Alex. Severi*, 34.

[4] The *pyrricha*, a Greek concerted dance, probably of folk origin (cf. ch. ix), was often given a mythological *argumentum*. It was danced in the amphitheatre.

[5] Valerius Maximus, ii. 6. 7 'eadem civitas severitatis custos

It must not be supposed that the profession of the *scenici* ever became an honourable one in the eyes of the Roman law. They were for the most part slaves or at best freedmen. They were deliberately branded with *infamia* or incapacity for civil rights. This *infamia* was of two kinds, depending respectively upon the action of the censors as guardians of public dignity and that of the praetors as presidents in the law courts. The censors habitually excluded actors from the *ius suffragii* and the *ius honorum*, the rights of voting and of holding senatorial or equestrian rank ; the praetors refused to allow them, if men, to appear as attorneys, if women, to appoint attorneys, in civil suits [1]. The legislation of Julius Caesar and of Augustus added some statutory disabilities. The *lex Iulia municipalis* forbade actors to hold municipal *honores* [2]: the *lex Iulia de adulteriis* set the example of denying them the right to bring criminal actions [3] ; the *lex Iulia et Papia Poppaea* limited their privileges when freed, and in particular forbade senators or the sons of senators to take to wife women who had been, or whose parents had been, on the stage [4]. On the other hand Augustus confined the *ius virgarum*, which the praetors had formerly had over *scenici*, to the actual place and time of performances [5] ; and so far as the censorian *infamia* was concerned, the whole tendency of the late Republic and early Empire was to relax its application to actors. It came to be possible for senators and knights to appear on the stage without losing caste. It was a grievous insult when Julius Caesar

---

acerrima est: nullum aditum in scenam mimis dando, quorum argumenta maiore in parte stuprorum continent actus ; ne talia spectandi consuetudo etiam imitandi licentiam sumat.'

[1] A. H. J. Greenidge, *Infamia* (*passim*) ; Bouché-Leclercq, *Manuel des Institutions romaines*, 352, 449; *Edictum praetoris* in *C. I. C. Digest*, iii. 2. 1 'infamia notatur qui . . . artis ludicrae pronuntiandive causa in scaenam prodierit.' The jurists limited the application of the rule to professional actors. *Thymelici*, or orchestral musicians, were exempt. Diocletian made a

further exemption for persons appearing in their minority (*C. I. C. Cod. Iust.* ii. 11. 21). The censors, on the other hand, spared the *Atellani*, whose performances had a traditional connexion with religious rites.

[2] *C. I. L.* i. 122.

[3] *C. I. C. Digest*, xlviii. 5. 25. A husband may kill an actor with whom his wife is guilty.

[4] *Ibid.* xxiii. 2. 42, 44 ; xxxviii. 1. 37; Ulpian, *Fragm.* xiii.

[5] Tacitus, *Annales*, i. 77. An attempt to restore the old usage under Tiberius was unsuccessful.

compelled the mimograph Laberius to appear in one of his own pieces. But after all Caesar restored Laberius to his rank of *eques*, a dignity which at a still earlier date Sulla had bestowed on Roscius [1]. Later the restriction broke down altogether, although not without an occasional reforming effort to restore it [2]. Nero himself was not ashamed to take the boards as a singer of *cantica* [3]. And even an *infamis*, if he were the boon companion of a prince, might be appointed to a post directly depending on the imperial dignity. Thus Caracalla sent a *pantomimus* to hold a military command on the frontier, and Heliogabalus made another *praefectus urbi* in Rome itself [4]. Under Constantine a reaction set in, and a new decree formally excluded *scenici* from all *dignitates* [5]. The severe class legislation received only reluctant and piecemeal modification, and the praetorian *infamia* outlived the Empire itself, and left its mark upon Carolingian jurisprudence [6].

The relaxation of the old Roman austerity implied in the popularity of the *mimi* and *histriones* did not pass uncensured by even the pagan moralists of the Empire. The stage has a share in the denunciations of Tacitus and Juvenal, both of whom lament that princes and patricians should condescend to practise arts once relegated to the *infames*. Martial's hypocrite rails at the times and the theatres. Three centuries later the soldierly Ammianus Marcellinus finds in the gyrations of the dancing-girls, three thousand of whom were allowed to remain in Rome when it was starving, a blot upon the fame of the state ; and Macrobius contrasts the sober evenings of Praetextatus and his friends with revels dependent for their mirth on the song and wanton motions of

[1] Caesar was tolerably magnanimous, for Laberius had already taken his revenge in a scurrilous prologue. It had its touch of pathos, too :

'eques Romanus lare egressus meo
domum revertar mimus.'

[2] Cicero, *ad Fam.* x. 32 ; Dion Cassius, xlviii. 33 ; liii. 31 ; liv. 2 ; lvi. 47 ; lvii. 14 ; lix. 10 ; lxi. 9 ; lxv. 6 ; Tacitus, *Ann.* xiv. 20 ; *Hist.* ii. 62 ; Suetonius, *Augustus*, 45 ;
Domitian, 8.

[3] Suetonius, *Nero*, 21 ; Tacitus, *Ann.* xiv. 14 ; Juvenal, viii. 198 ; Pseudo-Lucian, *Nero*, 9.

[4] Dion Cassius, lxxvii. 21 ; *Hist. Augusta, Vita Heliogabali*, 12. Yet in the time of Severus a soldier going on the stage was liable to death (*C. I. C. Digest*, xlviii. 19. 14).

[5] *C. I. C. Cod. Iust.* xii. 1. 2.

[6] Cf. p. 38.

the *psaltria* or the jests of *sabulo* and *planipes*[1]. Policy compelled the emperors to encourage *spectacula*, but even they were not always blind to the ethical questions involved. Tiberius based his expulsion of the *histriones*, at least in part, on moral grounds. Marcus Aurelius, with a philosophic regret that the high lessons of comedy had sunk to mere mimic dexterity, sat publicly in his box and averted his eyes to a state-paper or a book[2]. Julian, weaned by his tutor Mardonius from a boyish love of the stage, issued strict injunctions to the priests of the Sun to avoid a theatre which he despaired of reforming[3]. Christian teachers, unconcerned with the interests of a dynasty, and claiming to represent a higher morality than that either of Marcus Aurelius or of Julian, naturally took even stronger ground. Moreover, they had their special reasons for hostility to the stage. That the actors should mock at the pagan religion, with whose *ludi* their own performances were intimately connected, made a good dialectical point. But the connexion itself was unpardonable, and still more so the part taken by the mimes during the war of creeds, in parodying and holding up to ridicule the most sacred symbols and mysteries of the church. This feeling is reflected in the legends of St. Genesius, St. Pelagia and other holy folk, who are represented as turning from the scenic profession to embrace Christianity, the conversion in some cases taking place on the very boards of the theatre itself[4].

---

[1] Tacitus, *Ann.* xiv. 20; Juvenal, vi. 60; viii. 183; Martial, ix. 28. 9; Ammianus Marcellinus, xiv. 6. 18; xxviii. 4. 32; Macrobius, ii. 1. 5, 9.

[2] M. Aurelius, *Comm.* xi. 6; *Hist. Augusta, Vita M. Aurel.* 15. This refers directly to the *circus*.

[3] Gibbon, ii. 447; Schaff, v. 49; Dill, 34, 100; P. Allard, *Julien l'Apostat*, i. 272; Alice Gardner, *Julian the Apostate*, 201; G. H. Rendall, *The Emperor Julian* (1879), 106. The most interesting passage is a fragmentary 'pastoral letter' to a priest (ed. Hertlein, *Fragm. Ep.* p. 304 B; cf. *Ep.* 49, p. 430 B); Julian requires the priests to abstain even from reading the Old Comedy (*Fragm. Ep.* p. 300 D).

He also thinks that the moral layman should avoid the theatre (*Misopogon*, p. 343 c).

[4] On the critical problem offered by such *vitae* cf. Prof. Bury in Gibbon, i. l. B. von der Lage, *Studien zur Genesius-legende* (1898), attempts to show that the legends of St. Genesius (*Acta SS. Aug.* v. 122), St. Gelasius (*Acta SS. Feb.* iii. 680), St. Ardalio (*Acta SS. Apr.* ii. 213), St. Porphyrius (*Acta SS. Sept.* v. 37), and another St. Porphyrius (*Acta SS. Nov.* ii. 230) are all variants of a Greek story originally told of an anonymous *mimus*. The *Passio* of St. Genesius represents him as a *magister mimithemelae artis*, converted while he

So far as the direct attack upon the stage is concerned, the key-note of patristic eloquence is struck in the characteristic and uncompromising treatise *De Spectaculis* of Tertullian. Here theatre, circus, and amphitheatre are joined in a three-fold condemnation. Tertullian holds that the Christian has explicitly forsworn *spectacula*, when he renounced the devil and all his works and vanities at baptism. What are these but idolatry, and where is idolatry, if not in the *spectacula*, which not only minister to lust, but take place at the festivals and in the holy places of Venus and Bacchus? The story is told of the demon who entered a woman in the theatre and excused himself at exorcism, because he had found her in his own demesne. A fervid exhortation follows. To worldly pleasures Christians have no claim. If they need *spectacula* they can find them in the exercises of their Church. Here are nobler poetry, sweeter voices, maxims more sage, melodies more dulcet, than any comedy can boast, and withal, here is truth instead of fiction. Moreover, for Christians is reserved the last great *spectaculum* of all. 'Then,' says Tertullian, 'will be the time to listen to the tragedians, whose lamentations will be more poignant for their proper pain. Then will the comedians turn and twist, rendered nimbler than ever by the sting of the fire that is not quenched [1].' With Tertullian asceticism is always a passion, but the vivid African rhetoric is no unfair sample of a *catena* of outspoken comment which extends across the third century from Tatian to Lactantius [2].

was mimicking a baptism before Diocletian and martyred. It professes to give part of the dialogue of the mime. The legends of St. Philemon (*Menologium Basilii*, ii. 59; cf. *Acta SS. Mar.* i. 751) and St. Pelagia or Margarita (*Acta SS. Oct.* iv. 248) appear to be distinct. Palladius, *Vita Chrysostomi*, 8, records how the stage of Antioch in the fifth century rang with the scandals caused by the patriarch Severus and other Monophysite heretics.

[1] Tertullian, *De Spect.*, especially cc. 4, 26, 30. Schaff, iv. 833, dates the treatise †200. An earlier Greek writing by Tertullian on the same subject is lost; cf. also his

Apologeticus, 15 (*P. L.* i. 357). The information as to the contemporary stage scattered through Tertullian's works is collected by E. Noldechen, *Tertullian und das Theater* (*Z. f. Kirchengeschichte* (1894), xv. 161). An anonymous *De Spectaculis*, formerly ascribed to St. Cyprian, follows on Tertullian's lines (*P. L.* iv. 779, transl. in *Ante-Nicene Christian Libr.* xiii. 221).

[2] Tatian, *ad Graecos*, 22 (*P. G.* vi. 856); Minucius Felix, *Octavius*, 27 (*P. L.* iii. 352); Cyprian, *Epist.* i. 8 (*P. L.* iv. 207); Lactantius, *de Inst. div.* vi. 20 (*P. L.* vi. 710), 'quid de mimis loquar, corruptelarum praeferentibus disciplinam, qui do-

The judgement of the Fathers finds more cautious expression in the disciplinary regulations of the Church. An early formal condemnation of actors is included in the so-called *Canons* of Hippolytus [1], and the relations of converts to the stage were discussed during the fourth century by the councils of Elvira (306) and of Arles (314) and by the third and fourth councils of Carthage (397–398) [2]. It was hardly possible for practical legislators to take the extreme step of forbidding Christian laymen to enter the theatre at all. No doubt that would be the counsel of perfection, but in dealing with a deep-seated popular instinct something of a compromise was necessary [3]. An absolute prohibition was only established for the clergy: so far as the laity were concerned, it was limited to Sundays and ecclesiastical festivals, and on those days it was enforced by a threat of excommunication [4]. No Christian, however, might be a *scenicus* or a *scenica*, or might marry one ; and if a member of the unhallowed profession sought to be baptized, the preliminary of abandoning his calling was essential [5].

cent adulteria, dum fingunt, et simulatis erudiunt ad vera ? ' ; cf. Du Méril, *Or. Lat.* 6 ; Schaff, iii. 339. A remarkable collection of all conceivable authorities against the stage is given by Prynne, 566, 685, &c.

[1] *Canones Hippolyti*, 67 (Duchesne, 509) ' Quicumque fit θεατρικός vel gladiator et qui currit vel docet voluptates vel [*illegible*] vel [*illegible*] vel κυνηγός vel ἱπποδρόμος [?], vel qui cum bestiis pugnat vel idolorum sacerdos, hi omnes non admittuntur ad sermones sacros nisi prius ab illis immundis operibus purgentur.' This is from an Arabic translation of a lost Greek original. M. Duchesne says ' ce recueil de prescriptions liturgiques et disciplinaires est sûrement antérieur au iv⁰ siècle, et rien ne s'oppose à ce qu'il remonte à la date indiquée par le nom d'Hippolyte ' [†198–236].

[2] *Conc. Illib.* cc. 62, 67 (Mansi, ii. 16) ; *Conc. Arelat.* c. 5 (Mansi, ii. 471) ; 3 *Conc. Carth.* cc. 11, 35 (Mansi, iii. 882, 885) ; 4 *Conc. Carth.* cc. 86, 88 (Mansi, iii. 958).

[3] The strongest pronouncement is that of Augustine and others in 3 *Conc. Carth.* c. 11 ' ut filii episcoporum vel clericorum spectacula saecularia non exhibeant, sed non spectent, quandoquidem ab spectaculo et omnes laici prohibeantur. Semper enim Christianis omnibus hoc interdictum est, ut ubi blasphemi sunt, non accedant.'

[4] 4 *Conc. Carth.* c. 88 ' Qui die solenni, praetermisso solenni ecclesiae conventu, ad spectacula vadit, excommunicetur.'

[5] *D. C. A.* s.vv. *Actor, Theatre* ; Bingham, vi. 212, 373, 439 ; Alt, 310 ; Prynne, 556. Some, however, of the pronouncements of the fathers came to have equal force with the decrees of councils in canon law. The *Code* of Gratian (†1139), besides 3 *Conc. Carth.* c. 35 ' scenicis atque ystrionibus, ceterisque huiusmodi personis, vel apostaticis conversis, vel reversis ad Deum, gratia vel reconciliatio non negetur ' (*C. I. Can.* iii. 2. 96) and 7 *Conc. Carth.* (419) c. 2 (Mansi, iv. 437) ' omnes etiam infamiae maculis aspersi, id est histrio-

It is curious to notice that a certain sympathy with the stage seems to have been characteristic of one of the great heresiarchs. This was none other than Arius, who is said to have had designs of setting up a Christian theatre in rivalry to those of paganism, and his strange work, the *Thaleia*, may perhaps have been intended to further the scheme. At any rate an orthodox controversialist takes occasion to brand his Arian opponents and their works as 'thymelic' or 'stagy'[1]. But it would probably be dangerous to lay undue stress upon what, after all, is as likely as not to be merely a dialectical metaphor.

After the edict of Milan (313), and still more after the end of the pagan reaction with the death of Julian (363), Christian influences began to make themselves felt in the civil legislation of the Empire. But if the councils themselves were chary of utterly forbidding the theatre, a stronger line was not likely to be taken in rescripts from Constantinople or Ravenna. The emperors were, indeed, in a difficult position. They stood between bishops pleading for decency and humanity and populaces now traditionally entitled to their *panem et spectacula*. The theatrical legislation preserved in the *Code* of Theodosius is not without traces of this embarrassment[2]. It

nes ... ab accusatione prohibentur' (*C. I. Can.* ii. 4. 1. 1), includes two patristic citations. One is Cyprian, *Ep.* lxi. (*P. L.* iv. 362), which is 'de ystrione et mago illo, qui apud vos constitutus adhuc in suae artis dedecore perseverat,' and forbids 'sacra communio cum ceteris Christianis dari' (*C. I. Can.* iii. 2. 95); the other Augustine, *Tract. C. ad c.* 16 *Iohannis* (*P. L.* xxxv. 1891) 'donare res suas histrionibus vitium est immane, non virtus' (*C. I. Can.* i. 86. 7). Gratian adds Isidorus Hispalensis, *de Eccl. Off.* ii. 2 (*P. L.* lxxxiii. 778) ' his igitur lege Patrum cavetur, ut a vulgari vita seclusi a mundi voluptatibus sese abstineant ; non spectaculis, non pompis intersint' (*C. I. Can.* i. 23. 3).
[1] Sathas, 7 ; Krumbacher, 644. Anastasius Sinaita (bp. of Antioch, 564) in his tract, *Adversus*

Monophysitas ac Monothelitas (Mai, *Coll. Nov. Script. Vet.* vii. 202), speaks of the συγγράμματα of the Arians as θυμελικὰς βίβλους, and calls the Arian Eunomius πρωτοστάτης τῆς 'Αρείου θυμελικῆς ὀρχήστρας. I doubt if these phrases should be taken too literally ; possibly they are not more than a criticism of the buffoonery and levity which the fragments of the Θάλεια display. Krumbacher mentions an orthodox 'Αντιθάλεια of which no more seems to be known.
[2] Alt, 310 ; Bingham, vi. 273 ; Schaff, v. 106, 125 ; Haigh, 460 ; Dill, 56 ; P. Allard, *Julien l'Apostat.* i. 230. The *Codex Theodosianus*, drawn up and accepted for both empires †435, contains imperial edicts from the time of Constantine onwards.

is rather an interesting study. The views of the Church were met upon two points. One series of rescripts forbade performances on Sundays or during the more sacred periods of the Christian calendar[1]: another relaxed in favour of Christians the strict caste laws which sternly forbade actresses or their daughters to quit the unhappy profession in which they were born[2]. Moreover, certain sumptuary regulations were passed, which must have proved a severe restriction on the popularity as well as the liberty of actors. They were forbidden to wear gold or rich fabrics, or to ape the dress of nuns. They must avoid the company of Christian women and boys. They must not come into the public places or walk the streets attended by slaves with folding chairs[3]. Some of the rescripts contain phrases pointed with the bitterest contempt and detestation of their victims[4]. Theodosius will not have the portraits of *scenici* polluting the neighbourhood of his own *imagines*[5]. It is made very clear that the old court favourites are now to be merely tolerated. But they *are* to be tolerated. The idea of suppressing them is never entertained. On the contrary the provision of *spectacula* and of performers for them remains one of the preoccupations of the government[6]. The praetor is expected to be lavish on this item of his budget[7],

[1] *Spectacula* are forbidden on Sunday, unless it is the emperor's birthday, by *C. Th.* xv. 5. 2 (386), which also forbids judges to rise for them, except on special occasions, and *C. Th.* ii. 8. 23 (399). The exception is removed by *C. Th.* ii. 8. 25 (409) and *C. Iust.* iii. 12. 9 (469). The Christian feasts and fasts, Christmas, Epiphany, the first week in Lent, Passion and Easter weeks are added by *C. Th.* ii. 8. 23 (400) and *C. Th.* xv. 5. 5 (425). According to some MSS. this was done by *C. Th.* ii. 8. 19 (389), but the events of 399 recorded below seem to show that 400 is the right date.

[2] *C. Th.* xv. 7. 1, 2 (371); xv. 7. 4 (380); xv. 7. 9 (381). Historians have seen in some of these rescripts which are dated from Milan the influence of St. Ambrose. *C. Th.* xv. 7. 13 (414) seems to withdraw

the concessions, in the interest of the public *voluptates*, but this may have been only a temporary or local measure.

[3] *C. Th.* xv. 7. 11 (393); xv. 7. 12 (394); xv. 13. 1 (396).

[4] *C. Th.* iv. 6. 3 (336) 'scenicae . . . quarum venenis inficiuntur animi perditorum'; xv. 7. 8 (381), of the relapsing *scenica*, 'permaneat donec anus ridicula, senectute deformis, nec tunc quidem absolutione potiatur, cum aliud quam casta esse non possit.'

[5] *C. Th.* xv. 7. 12 (394).

[6] *C. Th.* xv. 6. 2 (399) is explicit, 'ludicras artes concedimus agitari, ne ex nimia harum restrictione tristitia generetur.'

[7] *C. Th.* vi. 4. 2 (327); vi. 4. 4 (339); vi. 4. 29 (396); vi. 4. 32 (397). It appears from the decree of 396 that the 'theatralis dispensio' of the praetors had been diverted to the

and special municipal officers, the *tribuni voluptatum*, are appointed to superintend the arrangements[1]. Private individuals and rival cities must not deport actors, or withdraw them from the public service[2]. The bonds of caste, except for the few freed by their faith, are drawn as tight as ever[3], and when pagan worship ceases the shrines are preserved from demolition for the sake of the theatres built therein[4].

The love of even professing Christians for *spectacula* proved hard to combat. There are no documents which throw more light on the society of the Eastern Empire at the close of the fourth century than the works of St. Chrysostom; and to St. Chrysostom, both as a priest at Antioch before 397 and as patriarch of Constantinople after that year, the stage is as present a danger as it was to Tertullian two centuries earlier[5]. A sermon preached on Easter-day, 399, is good evidence of this. St. Chrysostom had been attacking the stage for a whole year, and his exhortations had just come to nought. Early in Holy Week there was a great storm, and the people joined the rogatory processions. But it was a week of *ludi*. On Good Friday the circus, and on Holy Saturday the theatre, were thronged and the churches were empty. The Easter sermon was an impassioned harangue, in which the preacher dwelt once more on the inevitable corruption bound up with things theatrical, and ended with a threat to enforce the sentence of excommunication, prescribed only a few months before by the council of Carthage, upon whoever should again venture to defy the Church's law in like fashion on Sunday or holy day[6]. Perhaps one may trace the controversy which

building of an aqueduct; they are now to give 'scenicas voluptates' again. Symmachus, *Ep.* vi. 42, describes his difficulties in getting *scenici* for his son's praetorship, which cost him £80,000. They were lost at sea; cf. Dill, 151.

[1] See Appendix A.

[2] *C. Th.* xv. 7. 5 (380); xv. 7. 10 (385); *C. Iust.* xi. 41. 5 (409).

[3] *C. Th.* xv. 7. 8 (381); xiv. 7. 3 (412).

[4] *C. Th.* xvi. 10. 3 (346). But *C. Th.* xvi. 10. 17 (399) forbids 'voluptates' to be connected with sacrifice or superstition.

[5] A. Puech, *St. Jean Chrysostome et les Mœurs de son Temps* (1891), 266, has an interesting chapter on the *spectacula*. He refers to *Hom. in Matt.* 6, 7, 37, 48; *Hom. in Ioann.* 18; *Hom. in Ep.* 1 *ad Thess.* 5; *Hom. de Dav. et Saul*, 3; *Hom. in Prisc. et Aquil.* 1, &c. Most of these works belong to the Antioch period; cf. also Allard, i. 229. In *de Sacerdotio* 1, Chrysostom, like Augustine, records his own delight in the stage as a young man.

[6] *P. G.* lvi. 263.

St. Chrysostom's deliverance must have awakened, on the one hand in the rescript of the autumn of 399 pointedly laying down that the *ludicrae artes* must be maintained, on the other in the prohibition of the following year against performances in Holy week, and similar solemn tides.

More than a century after the exile and death of St. Chrysostom the theatre was still receiving state recognition at Constantinople. A regulation of Justinian as to the *ludi* to be given by newly elected consuls specified a performance on the stage ominously designated as the 'Harlots'[1]. By this date the *status* of the theatrical profession had at last undergone further and noticeable modification. The ancient Roman prohibition against the marriage of men of noble birth with *scenicae* or other *infames* or the daughters of such, had been re-enacted under Constantine. A partial repeal in 454 had not extended to the *scenicae*[2]. During the first half of the sixth century, however, a series of decrees removed their disability on condition of their quitting the stage, and further made it an offence to compel slaves or freed women to perform against their will[3]. In these humane relaxations of the rigid laws of theatrical caste has often been traced the hand of the empress Theodora, who, according to the contemporary gossip of Procopius, was herself, before her conversion, one of the most shameless of mimes. But it must be noted that the most important of the decrees in question preceded the accession of Justinian, although it may possibly have been intended to facilitate his own marriage[4]. The history of the stage in

---

[1] *C. I. C. Nov. Iust.* cv. 1 (536) 'faciet processum qui ad theatrum ducit, quem pornas vocant, ubi in scena ridiculorum est locus tragoedis et thymelicis choris'; cf. Choricius, *Apology for Mimes*, ed. Ch. Graux, in *R. d. Philologie*, i. 209; Krumbacher, 646.

[2] *C. Th.* iv. 6. 3 (336); *C. Iust.* v. 5. 7 (454).

[3] *C. Iust.* v. 4. 23 (520–3) allows the marriage on condition of an imperial rescript and a *dotale instrumentum. C. Iust.* i. 4. 33 (534) waives the rescript. It also imposes penalties on *fideiussores* or

sureties of actresses who hinder them from conversion and quitting the stage. For similar legislation cf. *Nov.* li; lxxxix. 15; cxvii. 4. By *Nov.* cxvii. 8. 6 a man is permitted to turn his wife out of doors and afterwards repudiate her, if she goes to theatre, circus, or amphitheatre without his knowledge or against his will.

[4] Gibbon, iv. 212, 516 (with Prof. Bury's additions); C. E. Mallet in *E. H. Review*, ii. 1; A. Debidour, *L'Impératrice Théodora*, 59. Neither Prof. Bury nor the editor of the *C. I. C.* accepts M. Debi-

the East cannot be traced much further with any certainty. The canons of the Quinisextine council, which met in the Trullan chamber to codify ecclesiastical discipline in 692, appear to contemplate the possibility of performances still being given [1]. A modern Greek scholar, M. Sathas, has made an ingenious attempt to establish the existence of a Byzantine theatrical tradition right through the Middle Ages; but Dr. Krumbacher, the most learned historian of Byzantine literature, is against him, and holds that, so far as our knowledge goes, the theatre must be considered to have perished during the stress of the Saracen invasions which, in the seventh and eighth centuries, devastated the East [2].

The ending of the theatre in the West was in very similar fashion. Chrysostom's great Latin contemporaries, Augustine and Jerome, are at one with him and with each other in their condemnation of the evils of the public stage as they knew it[3]. Their divergent attitude on a minor point may perhaps be explained by a difference of temperament. The fifth century saw a marked revival of literary interests from which even dignitaries of the Church did not hold themselves wholly aloof. Ausonius urged his grandson to the study of Menander. Sidonius, a bishop and no undevout one, read both Menander and Terence with his son [4]. With this movement Augustine had some sympathy. In a well-known passage of the *Confessions* he records the powerful influence exercised by tragedy,

---

dour's dating of *C. Iust.* v. 4. 23 under Justinian in 534.

[1] Mansi, xi. 943. Canon 3 excludes one who has married a σκηνική from orders. C. 24 forbids priests and monks θυμελικῶν παιγνίων ἀνέχεσθαι, and confirms a decree of the council of Laodicea (cf. p. 24, n. 4) obliging them, if present at a wedding, to leave the room before τὰ παίγνια are introduced. C. 51 condemns, both for clergy and laity, τοὺς λεγομένους μίμους καὶ τὰ τούτων θέατρα and τὰς ἐπὶ σκηνῶν ὀρχήσεις. For clergy the penalty is degradation, for laity excommunication. C. 61 provides a six-years' excommunication for bear-leaders and such. C. 62 deals with

pagan religious festivals of a semi-theatrical character; cf. ch. xiv. C. 66 forbids the circus or any δημώδης θέα in Easter week.

[2] Sathas, *passim*; Krumbacher, 644.

[3] Jerome, *in Ezechiel* (410–15) 'a spectaculis removeamus oculos arenae circi theatri' (*P. L.* xxv. 189); Augustine, *de Fide et Symbolo* (393) 'in theatris labes morum, discere turpia, audire inhonesta, videre perniciosa' (*P. L.* xl. 639; cf. the sermon quoted in Appendix N, N°. x.

[4] Ausonius, *Idyl.* iv. 46; Sidonius, *Ep.* iv. 12 'legebamus, pariter laudabamus, iocabamurque.'

and particularly erotic tragedy, over his tempestuous youth[1]. And in the *City of God* he draws a careful distinction between the higher and the lower forms of drama, and if he does not approve, at least does not condemn, the use of tragedies and comedies in a humane education[2]. Jerome, on the other hand, although himself like Augustine a good scholar, takes a more ascetic line, and a letter of his protesting against the reading of comedies by priests ultimately came to be quoted as an authority in Roman canon law[3].

The references to the stage in the works of two somewhat younger ecclesiastical writers are of exceptional interest. Orosius was a pupil of both Jerome and Augustine ; and Orosius, endeavouring a few years after the sack of Rome by the Goths to prove that that startling disaster was not due to Christianity, lays great and indeed exaggerated importance on the share of the theatre in promoting the decay of the Empire[4]. About the middle of the fifth century the same note is struck by Salvian in his remarkable treatise *De Gubernatione Dei*[5]. The sixth book of his work is almost entirely devoted to the *spectacula*. Like Tertullian, Salvian insists on the definite renunciation of *spectacula* by Christians in their baptismal vow[6]. Like Orosius, he traces to the weakening of

---

[1] Augustine, *Conf.* iii. 2, 3 (*P. L.* xxxii. 683). The whim took him once 'theatrici carminis certamen inire.'

[2] Aug. *de Civ. Dei*, ii. 8 (*P. L.* xli. 53) 'et haec sunt scenicorum tolerabiliora ludorum, comoediae scilicet et tragoediae ; hoc est, fabulae poetarum agendae in spectaculis, multa rerum turpitudine sed nulla saltem sicut alia multa verborum obscoenitate compositae; quas etiam inter studia quae honesta ac liberalia vocantur pueri legere et discere coguntur a senibus.'

[3] Jerome, *Ep.* 21 (*alii* 146) *ad Damasum*, written 383 (*P. L.* xxii. 386) 'at nunc etiam sacerdotes Dei, omissis evangeliis et prophetis, videmus comoedias legere, amatoria bucolicorum versuum verba canere, tenere Vergilium, et id quod in pueris necessitatis est, crimen in se

facere voluptatis' (*C. I. Can.* i. 37. 2).

[4] Orosius, *Hist. adv. Paganos* (417), iv. 21. 5 'theatra incusanda, non tempora.' On the character of the treatise of Orosius cf. Dill, 312; Gibbon, iii. 490. Mr. Dill shows in the third book of his admirable work that bad government and bad finance had much more to do with the breakdown of the Empire than the bad morals of the stage.

[5] Dill, 58, 137 ; Hodgkin, i. 930. Salvian was a priest of Marseilles, and wrote between 439 and 451.

[6] Salvian, vi. 31 'quae est enim in baptismo salutari Christianorum prima confessio ? quae scilicet nisi ut renuntiare se diabolo ac pompis eius et spectaculis atque operibus protestentur ?' The natural interpretation of this is that the word 'spectaculis' actually occurred in

moral fibre by these accursed amusements the failure of the West
to resist the barbarians. *Moritur et ridet* is his epigram on the
Roman world. The citizens of Tréves, three times destroyed,
still called upon their rulers for races and a theatre. With the
Vandals at the very gates of Cirta and of Carthage, *ecclesia
Carthaginiensis insaniebat in circis, luxuriebat in theatris*[1].
Incidentally Salvian gives some valuable information as to
the survival of the stage in his day. Already in 400 Augustine
had been able to say that the theatres were falling on every
side[2]. Salvian, fifty years later, confirms the testimony, but
he adds the reason. It was not because Christians had learnt
to be faithful to their vows and to the teachings of the Church ;
but because the barbarians, who despised *spectacula*, and therein
set a good example to degenerate Romans[3], had sacked half
the cities, while in the rest the impoverished citizens could no
longer pay the bills. He adds that at Rome a circus was still
open and a theatre at Ravenna, and that these were thronged
with delighted travellers from all parts of the Empire[4]. There
must, however, have been a theatre at Rome as well, for
Sidonius found it there when he visited the city, twelve years
after it had been sacked for the second time, in 467. He was
appointed prefect of the city, and in one of his letters expresses
a fear lest, if the corn-supply fail, the thunders of the theatre
may burst upon his head[5]. In a poem written a few years
earlier he describes the *spectacula theatri* of mimes, pantomimes, and acrobats as still flourishing at Narbonne[6].

The next and the latest records of the stage in the West

the *formula abrenuntiationis*. Was
this so ? It was not when Tertullian wrote (†200). He gives the
formula as 'renunciare diabolo et
pompae et angelis eius,' and goes
on to argue that visiting 'spectacula'
amounts to 'idolatria,' or worship of
the ' diabolus' (*de Spectaculis*, c. 4).
Nor is the word used in any of the
numerous versions of the *formula*
given by Schaff, iii. 248 ; Duchesne,
293 ; Martene, i. 44 ; Martin von
Bracara, *de Caeremoniis* (ed. Caspari), c. 15.
    [1] Salvian, vi. 69, 87.
    [2] Augustine, *de Cons. Evang.* i.
33 (*P. L.* xxxiv. 1068) 'per omnes

pene civitates cadunt theatra . . .
cadunt et fora vel moenia, in quibus
demonia colebantur. Unde enim
cadunt, nisi inopia rerum, quarum
lascivo et sacrilego usu constructa
sunt.'
    [3] This point was made also by
Chrysostom in the Easter-day sermon, already cited on p. 15.
    [4] Salvian, vi. 39, 42, 49.
    [5] Sidonius, *Ep.* i. 10. 2 'vereor
autem ne famem Populi Romani
theatralis caveae fragor insonet et
infortunio meo publica deputetur
esuries'; cf. *Ep.* i. 5. 10.
    [6] Sidonius, *Carm.* xxiii. 263
(†460) ; cf. *Ep.* ix. 13. 5.

date from the earlier part of the sixth century, when the Ostrogoths held sway in Italy. They are to be found in the *Variae* of Cassiodorus, who held important official posts under the new lords of Rome, and they go to confirm the inference which the complaint of Salvian already suggests that a greater menace to the continuance of the theatre lay in the taste of the barbarians than even in the ethics of Christianity.

The Ostrogoths had long dwelt within the frontiers of the Empire, and Theodoric, ruling as ' King of the Goths and Romans in Italy,' over a mixed multitude of Italians and Italianate Germans, found it necessary to continue the *spectacula*, which in his heart he despised. There are many indications of this in the state-papers preserved in the *Variae*, which may doubtless be taken to express the policy and temper of the masters of Cassiodorus in the rhetorical trappings of the secretary himself. The *scenici* are rarely mentioned without a sneer, but their performances and those of the *aurigae*, or circus-drivers, who have now come to be included under the all-embracing designation of *histriones*, are carefully regulated [1]. The gladiators have, indeed, at last disappeared, two centuries after Constantine had had the grace to suppress them in the East [2]. There is a letter from Theodoric to an architect, requiring him to repair the theatre of Pompey, and digressing into an historical sketch, imperfectly erudite, of the history of the drama, its invention by the Greeks, and its degradation by the Romans [3]. A number of documents deal with the choice of a *pantomimus* to represent the *prasini* or ' Greens,' and show that the rivalry of the theatre-factions

[1] Cassiodorus, *Variae*, iii. 51 ' quantum histrionibus rara constantia honestumque votum, tanto pretiosior est, cum in eis probabilis monstratur affectus ' ; this is illustrated by the conduct of one ' Thomas Auriga'; *Var.* ii. 8 ' Sabinus auriga . . . quamvis histrio honesta nos supplicatione permovit ' ; *Var.* vi. 4 ' tanta enim est vis gloriosae veritatis, ut etiam in rebus scenicis aequitas desideretur.'

[2] Schaff, v. 122 ; Dill, 55. The rescript of Constantine is *C. Th.*

xv. 12. 1 ' cruenta spectacula in otio civili et domestica quiete non placent; quapropter omnino gladiatores esse prohibemus (325).'

[3] Cassiodorus, *Var.* iv. 51. Of the mime is said ' mimus etiam, qui nunc modo derisui habetur, tanta Philistionis cautela repertus est ut eius actus poneretur in litteris' (cf. p. 4, n. 1) ; of the pantomime, ' orchestrarum loquacissimae manus, linguosi digiti, silentium clamosum, expositio tacita.'

remained as fierce as it had been in the days of Bathyllus and Pylades. Helladius is given the preference over Thorodon, and a special proclamation exhorts the people to keep the peace[1]. Still more interesting is the *formula*, preserved by Cassiodorus, which was used in the appointment of the *tribunus voluptatum*, an official whom we have already come across in the rescripts of the emperors of the fourth century. This is so characteristic, in its contemptuous references to the nature of the functions which it confers, of the whole German attitude in the matter of *spectacula*, that it seems worth while to print it in an appendix[2]. The passages hitherto quoted from the *Variae* all seem to belong to the period between 507 and 511, when Cassiodorus was *quaestor* and secretary to Theodoric at Rome. A single letter written about 533 in the reign of Athalaric shows that the populace was still looking to its Gothic rulers for *spectacula*, and still being gratified[3]. Beyond this the Roman theatre has not been traced. The Goths passed in 553, and Italy was reabsorbed in the Empire. In 568 came the Lombards, raw Germans who had been but little under southern influence, and were far less ready than their predecessors to adopt Roman manners. Rome and Ravenna alone remained as outposts of the older civilization, the latter under an exarch appointed from Constantinople, the former under its bishop. At Ravenna the theatre may conceivably have endured ; at Rome, the Rome of Gregory the Great, it assuredly did not. An alleged mention of a theatre at Barcelona in Spain during the seventh century resolves itself into either a survival of pagan ritual or a bull-fight[4].

---

[1] Cassiodorus, *Var.* i. 20, 31–3.

[2] Cf. Appendix A.

[3] Cassiodorus, *Var.* ix. 21 ' opes nostras scaenicis pro populi oblectatione largimur.'

[4] Du Méril, *Or. Lat.* 13, quotes from Mariana, *Hist. of Spain*, vi. 3, the statement that Sisebut, king of the Visigoths, deposed Eusebius, bishop of Barcelona, in 618, ' quod in theatro quaedam agi concessisset quae ex vana deorum superstitione traducta aures Christianae abhorrere videantur.' Sisebuthus, *Ep.* vi (*P. L.* lxxx. 370), conveys his decision to the bishop. He says, ' obiectum hoc, quod de ludis theatriis taurorum, scilicet, ministerio sis adeptus nulli videtur incertum ; quis non videat quod etiam videre poeniteat.' But I cannot find in Sisebut or in Mariana, who writes Spanish, the words quoted by Du Méril. For ' taurorum ' one MS. has ' phanorum.' I suspect the former is right. A bull-fight sounds so Spanish, and such festivals of heathen origin as the *Kalends* (cf. ch. xi) were not held in theatres. A. Gassier, *Le Théâtre espagnol*

Isidore of Seville has his learned chapters on the stage, but they are written in the imperfect tense, as of what is past and gone [1]. The bishops and the barbarians had triumphed.

(1898), 14, thinks such a festival is intended; if so, 'theatriis' probably means not literally, 'in a theatre,' but merely 'theatrical'; cf. the 'ludi theatrales' of the Feast of Fools (ch. xiii). In any case there is no question of 'scenici.'

[1] Isidorus Hispalensis, *Etymologiarum* (600–636), xviii. 42 (*P. L.* lxxxii. 658).

CHAPTER II

MIMUS AND SCÔP

[*Bibliographical Note* (for chs. ii-iv).—By far the best account of minstrelsy is the section on *Les Propagateurs des Chansons de Gestes* in vol. ii of I., Gautier, *Les Épopées françaises* (2nd ed. 1892), bk. ii, chs. xvii xxi. It may be supplemented by the chapter devoted to the subject in J. Bédier, *Les Fabliaux* (2nd ed. 1895), and by the dissertation of E. Freymond, *Jongleurs und Menestrals* (Halle, 1883). I have not seen A. Olrik, *Middelalderens vandrende Spillemænd* (*Opuscula Philologica*, Copenhagen, 1887). Some German facts are added by F. Vogt, *Leben und Dichten der deutschen Spielleute im Mittelalter* (1876), and A. Schultz, *Das höfische Leben zur Zeit der Minnesinger* (2nd ed. 1889), i. 565, who gives further references. The English books are not good, and probably the most reliable account of English minstrelsy is that in the following pages ; but materials may be found in J. Strutt, *Sports and Pastimes of the People of England* (1801, ed. W. Hone, 1830) ; T. Percy, *Reliques of Ancient English Poetry* (ed. H. B. Wheatley, 1876, ed. Schroer, 1889) ; J. Ritson, *Ancient English Metrical Romances* (1802), *Ancient Songs and Ballads* (1829) ; W. Chappell, *Old English Popular Music* (ed. H. E. Wooldridge, 1893) ; F. J. Crowest, *The Story of British Music, from the Earliest Times to the Tudor Period* (1896); J. J. Jusserand, *English Wayfaring Life in the Middle Ages* (trans. L. T. Smith, 4th ed. 1892). The early English data are discussed by R. Merbot, *Aesthetische Studien zur angelsächsischen Poesie* (1883), and F. M. Padelford, *Old English Musical Terms* (1899). F. B. Gummere, *The Beginnings of Poetry* (1901), should be consulted on the relations of minstrelsy to communal poetry ; and other special points are dealt with by O. Hubatsch, *Die lateinischen Vagantenlieder des Mittelalters* (1870) ; G. Maugras, *Les Comédiens hors la Loi* (1887), and H. Lavoix, *La Musique au Siècle de Saint-Louis* (in G. Raynaud, *Recueil de Motets français*, 1883, vol. ii). To the above list of authorities should of course be added the histories of literature and of the drama enumerated in the *General Bibliographical Note*.]

THE fall of the theatres by no means implied the complete extinction of the *scenici*. They had outlived tragedy and comedy : they were destined to outlive the stage itself. Private performances, especially of *pantomimi* and other dancers, had enjoyed great popularity under the Empire, and had become an invariable adjunct of all banquets and other festivities. At such revels, as at the decadence of the theatre and of public morals generally, the graver pagans had looked askance[1]: the Church naturally included them in its universal condemnation of *spectacula*. Chrysostom in the East[2], Jerome in the West[3], are hostile to them, and a canon of the fourth-century council of Laodicea, requiring the clergy who might be present at weddings and similar rejoicings to rise and leave the room before the actors were introduced, was adopted by council after council and took its place as part of the ecclesiastical law[4]. The permanence of the regulation proves the strength of the habit, which indeed the Church might ban, but was not able to subdue, and which seems to have commended itself, far more than the theatre, to Teutonic manners. Such irregular performances proved a refuge for the dispossessed *scenici*. Driven from their theatres, they had still a vogue, not only at banquets, but at popular merry-makings or wherever in street or country they could gather together the remnant of their old audiences. Adversity and change of masters modified many of their characteristics. The *pantomimi*, in particular, fell upon evil times. Their subtle art had had its origin in an exquisite if corrupt taste, and adapted itself with difficulty to the ruder conditions of the new civilizations[5]. The *mimi* had always appealed to a common and gross humanity. But even they must now rub shoulders and contend for *denarii* with jugglers and with rope-dancers, with out-at-elbows gladiators and beast-tamers. More than ever they learnt to turn their hand to anything that might amuse; learnt to tumble, for instance; learnt to tell the long stories which the Teutons loved. Nevertheless, in essentials they remained the same; still jesters and buffoons,

---

[1] Macrobius, *Saturnalia*, ii. 1. 5, 9.

[2] Chrysostom, *Hom. in Ep. ad Col. cap.* 1, Hom. i. cc. 5, 6 (*P. G.* lxii. 306).

[3] Jerome, *Ep.* 117 (*P. L.* xxii. 957) 'difficile inter epulas servatur pudicitia'; cf. Dill, 110.

[4] *Conc. of Laodicea* (†343–81) can. 54 (Mansi, ii. 574) ὅτι οὐ δεῖ ἱερατικοὺς ἢ κληρικούς τινας θεωρίας θεωρεῖν ἐν γάμοις ἢ δείπνοις, ἀλλὰ πρὸ τοῦ εἰσέρχεσθαι τοὺς θυμελικοὺς ἐγείρεσθαι αὐτοὺς καὶ ἀναχωρεῖν. Cf. *Conc. of Braga* (†572) c. 60 (Mansi, v. 912),

Conc. of Aix-la-Chapelle (816) c. 83 (Mansi, vii. 1361); and finally, *C. I. Can.* iii. 5. 37 'non oportet ministros altaris vel quoslibet clericos spectaculis aliquibus, quae aut in nuptiis aut scenis exhibentur, interesse, sed ante, quam thymelici ingrediantur, surgere eos de convivio et abire.' It is noteworthy that 'scenis' here translates δείπνοις.

[5] Muratori *Antiq. Ital. Med. Aev.* ii. 847, traces the *pantomimi* in the Italian *mattaccini*.

still irrepressible, still obscene. In little companies of two
or three, they padded the hoof along the roads, travelling
from gathering to gathering, making their own welcome in
castle or tavern, or, if need were, sleeping in some grange or
beneath a wayside hedge in the white moonlight. They were,
in fact, absorbed into that vast body of nomad entertainers on
whom so much of the gaiety of the Middle Ages depended.
They became *ioculatores, jougleurs*, minstrels [1].

The features of the minstrels as we trace them obscurely
from the sixth to the eleventh century, and then more clearly
from the eleventh to the sixteenth, are very largely the
features of the Roman *mimi* as they go under, whelmed in
the flood which bore away Latin civilization. But to regard
them as nothing else than *mimi* would be a serious mistake.
On another side they have a very different and a far more
reputable ancestry. Like other factors in mediaeval society,
they represent a merging of Latin and the Teutonic elements.
They inherit the tradition of the *mimus*: they inherit also
the tradition of the German *scôp* [2]. The earliest Teutonic
poetry, so far as can be gathered, knew no *scôp*. As will be
shown in a later chapter, it was communal in character, closely
bound up with the festal dance, or with the rhythmic movements of labour. It was genuine folk-song, the utterance
of no select caste of singers, but of whoever in the ring of
worshippers or workers had the impulse and the gift to link
the common movements to articulate words. At the festivals
such a spokesman would be he who, for whatever reason, took
the lead in the ceremonial rites, the *vates*, germ at once of
priest and bard. The subject-matter of communal song was
naturally determined by the interests ruling on the occasions
when it was made. That of daily life would turn largely on
the activities of labour itself: that of the high days on the
emotions of religion, feasting, and love which were evoked by
the primitive revels of a pastoral or agricultural folk.

Presently the movements of the populations of Europe
brought the Germanic tribes, after separating from their
Scandinavian kinsmen, into contact with Kelts, with Huns,

---

[1] Cf. Appendix B.   *Romania* (1876), 260; G. Paris,
[2] Ten Brink, i. 11; P. Meyer in   36; Gautier, ii. 6; Kögel, i. 2. 191.

with the Roman Empire, and, in the inevitable recoil, with each other. Then for the first time war assumed a prerogative place in their life. To war, the old habits and the old poetry adapted themselves. Tiwaz, once primarily the god of beneficent heaven, became the god of battles. The chant of prayer before the onset, the chant of triumph and thanksgiving after the victory, made themselves heard [1]. From these were disengaged, as a distinct species of poetry, songs in praise of the deeds and deaths of great captains and popular heroes. Tacitus tells us that poetry served the Germans of his day for both chronology and history [2]. Jordanis, four centuries later, has a similar account to give of the Ostrogoths [3]. Arminius, the vanquisher of a Roman army, became the subject of heroic songs [4]: Athalaric has no higher word of praise for Gensimund than *cantabilis* [5]. The glories of Alboin the Lombard [6], of Charlemagne himself[7], found celebration in verse, and Charlemagne was at the pains to collect and record the still earlier *cantilenae* which were the chronicle of his race. Such historical *cantilenae*, mingled with more primitive ones of mythological import, form the basis of the great legendary epics [8]. But the process of epic-making is one of self-conscious and deliberate art, and implies a considerable advance from primitive modes of literary composition. No doubt the earliest heroic *cantilenae* were still communal in character. They were *rondes* footed and sung at festivals by bands of young men and maidens. Nor was such folk-song quick to disappear. Still in the

<hr>

[1] Tacitus, *Ann.* i. 65; iv. 47; *Hist.* ii. 22; iv. 18; v. 15; *Germ.* 3; Ammianus Marcellinus, xvi. 12. 43; xxxi. 7. 11; Vegetius, *de re militari*, iii. 18; cf. Kögel, i. 1. 12, 58, 111; Müllenhoff, *Germania*, ch. 3. The *barditus* or *barritus* of the Germans, whatever the name exactly means, seems to have been articulate, and not a mere noise.

[2] Tacitus, *Germ.* 2 'quod unum apud illos memoriae et annalium genus est.'

[3] Jordanis, *de orig. Getarum* (in *M. G. H.*), c. 4 'in priscis eorum carminibus pene storico ritu in commune recolitur.'

[4] Tacitus, *Ann.* ii. 88 'canitur adhuc barbaras apud gentes.'

[5] Cassiodorus, *Var.* viii. 9.

[6] Kögel, i. 1. 122, quoting Paulus Diaconus, i. 27.

[7] Kögel, i. 1. 122; i. 2. 220; Gautier, i. 72; G. Paris, *Hist. Poét. de Charlemagne*, 50; cf. *Poeta Saxo* (†890) in *M. G. H. Scriptores*, i. 268 'est quoque iam notum; vulgaria carmina magnis laudibus eius avos et proavos celebrant. Pippinos, Karolos, Hludiwicos et Theodricos, et Carlomannos Hlothariosque canunt.'

[8] Gautier, i. 37; Gröber, ii. 1. 447. The shades of opinion on the exact relation of the *cantilenae* to the *chansons de gestes* are numerous.

eleventh century the deeds of St. William of Orange resounded amongst the *chori iuvenum*[1]; and spinning-room and village green were destined to hear similar strains for many centuries more[2]. But long before this the *cantilenae* had entered upon another and more productive course of development: they were in the mouths, not only of the folk, but also of a body of professional singers, the fashioners of the epic that was to be[3]. Like heroic song itself, the professional singers owed

[1] *Vita S. Willelmi* (*Acta SS. Maii*, vi. 801) ' qui chori iuvenum, qui conventus populorum, praecipue militum ac nobilium virorum, quae vigiliae sanctorum dulce non resonant, et modulatis vocibus decantant qualis et quantus fuerit'; cf. Gautier, i. 66. The merest fragments of such folk-song heroic *cantilenae* are left. A German one, the Ludwigslied, on the battle of Saucourt (881) is in Müllenhoff und Scherer, *Denkmäler deutscher Poesie und Prosa* (1892), N°. xi ; cf. Kögel, i. 2. 86; Gautier, i. 62. And a few lines of a (probably) French one on an event in the reign of Clotaire (†620) are translated into Latin in Helgarius (†853–76), *Vita S. Faronis* (*Historiens de France*, iii. 505; Mabillon, *Acta SS. Benedictinorum*, ii. 610). Helgarius calls the song a 'carmen rusticum' and says 'ex qua victoria carmen publicum iuxta rusticitatem per omnium pene volitabat ora ita canentium, feminaeque choros inde plaudendo componebant.' The *Vita S. Faronis* in *Acta SS.* lx. 612, which is possibly an abridgement of Helgarius, says ' carmine rustico . . . suavi cantilena decantabatur'; cf. Gautier, i. 47; Gröber, ii. 1. 446.

[2] Ten Brink, i. 148, quotes from *Hist. Ely*, ii. 27 (†1166), a fragment of a song on Canute, 'quae usque hodie in choris publice cantantur,' and mentions another instance from Wm. of Malmesbury. Cf. *de Gestis Herewardi Saxonis* (Michel, *Chron. Anglo-Norm.* ii. 6) ' mulieres et puellae de eo in choris canebant,' and for Scotland the song on Bannockburn (1314) which, says Fabyan, *Chronicle* (ed. Ellis), 420, 'was after many days sungyn in dances, in carolles of ye maydens and mynstrellys of Scotlande'; cf. also Gummere, *B. P.* 265.

[3] It is important to recognize that the *cantilenae* of the folk and those of the professional singers existed side by side. Both are, I think, implied in the account of the St. William songs quoted above: the folk sung them in choruses and on wake-days, the professional singers in the assemblies of warriors. At any rate, in the next (twelfth) cent. Ordericus Vitalis, vi. 3 (ed. *Soc. de l'Hist. de France*, iii. 5), says of the same Willelmus, 'Vulgo canitur a ioculatoribus de illo cantilena.' M. Gautier (ii. 6) will not admit the filiation of the *ioculatores* to the *scôpas*, and therefore he is led to suppose (i. 78) that the *cantilenae* and *vulgaria carmina* were all folk-song up to the end of the tenth cent. and that then the *ioculatores* got hold of them and lengthened them into *chansons de gestes*. But, as we shall see (p. 34), the Franks certainly had their professional singers as early as Clovis, and these cannot well have sung anything but heroic lays. Therefore the *cantilenae* and *vulgaria carmina* of the Merovingian and Carolingian periods may have been either folk-song, or *scôp*-song, or, more probably, both (Gröber, ii. 1. 449). *Cantilena* really means no more than 'chant' of any kind ; it includes ecclesiastical chant. So Alcuin uses it (e. g. *Ep.* civ in Dümmler, iii. 169); and what Gautier, ii. 65, prints as a folk-song *cantilena* of S. Eulalia is treated by Gröber, ii. 1. 442, as a sequence.

their origin to war, and to the prominence of the individual, the hero, which war entailed. Around the person of a great leader gathered his individual following or *comitatus*, bound to him by ties of mutual loyalty, by interchange of service and reward[1]. Amongst the *comitatus* room was found for one who was no spearman, but who, none the less honoured for that, became the poet of the group and took over from the less gifted *chorus* the duty of celebrating the praises of the chieftain. These he sung to the accompaniment, no longer of flying feet, but of the harp, struck when the meal was over in tent or hall. Such a harper is the characteristically Germanic type of professional entertainer. He has his affinities with the Demodokos of a Homeric king. Rich in dignities and guerdons, sitting at the foot of the leader, consorting on equal terms with the warriors, he differs wholly from the *scenicus infamis*, who was the plaything and the scorn of Rome. Precisely when the shifting of social conditions brought him into being it is hard to say. Tacitus does not mention him, which is no proof, but a presumption, that amongst the tribes on the frontier he had not yet made his appearance in the first century of the Empire. By the fifth century he was thoroughly established, and the earliest records point to his existence at least as early as the fourth. These are not to be found in Latin sources, but in those early English poems which, although probably written in their extant forms after the invasion of these islands, seem to date back in substance to the age when the Angles still dwelt in a continental home around the base of the Jutish peninsula. The English remained to a comparatively late stage of their history remote from Roman influence, and it is in their literature that both the original development of the Teutonic *scôp* and his subsequent contamination by the Roman *mimus* can most easily be studied.

The earliest of all English poems is almost certainly *Widsith*, the 'far-traveller.' This has been edited and interpolated in Christian England, but the kernel of it is heathen and continental[2]. It is an autobiographic sketch of the life of Widsith, who was himself an actual or ideal *scôp*, or rather *gleómon*, for the precise term *scôp* is not used in the

---

[1] Gummere, *G. O.* 260.   [2] Grein, i. 1.

poem. Widsith was of the Myrgings, a small folk who dwelt hard by the Angles. In his youth he went with Ealhhild, the 'weaver of peace,' on a mission to Eormanric the Ostrogoth. Eormanric is the Hermanric of legend, and his death in 375 A.D. gives an approximate date to the events narrated. Then Widsith became a wanderer upon the face of the earth, one who could 'sing and say a story' in the 'mead-hall.' He describes the nations and rulers he has known. Eormanric gave him a collar of beaten gold, and Guthhere the Burgundian a ring. He has been with Caesar, lord of jocund cities, and has seen Franks and Lombards, Finns and Huns, Picts and Scots, Hebrews, Indians, Egyptians, Medes and Persians. At the last he has returned to the land of the Myrgings, and with his fellow Scilling has sung loud to the harp the praises of his lord Eadgils and of Ealhhild the daughter of Eadwine. Eadgils has given him land, the inheritance of his fathers. The poem concludes with an eulogy of the life of gleemen. They wander through realm upon realm, voice their needs, and have but to give thanks. In every land they find a lord to whom songs are dear, and whose bounty is open to the exalters of his name. Of less undeniable antiquity than *Widsith* are the lines known as the *Complaint of Deor*. These touch the seamy side of the singer's life. Deor has been the *scôp* of the Heodenings many winters through. But one more skilled, Heorrenda by name—the Horant of the Gudrun saga—has outdone him in song, and has been granted the land-right that once was Deor's. He finds his consolation in the woes of the heroes of old. 'They have endured: may not I endure [1]?' The outline drawn in *Widsith* and in *Deor* is completed by various passages in the epic of *Beowulf*, which may be taken as representing the social conditions of the sixth or early seventh century. In Heorot, the hall of Hrothgar, there was sound of harp, the gleewood. Sweetly sang the *scôp* after the mead-bench. The lay was sung, the gleeman's *gyd* told. Hrothgar's thanes, even Hrothgar himself, took their turns to unfold the wondrous tale. On the other hand, when a folk is in sorrow, no harp is heard, the glee-beam is silent in the halls [2]. In these three poems, then, is fully

---

[1] Grein, i. 278. [2] *Beowulf*, 89, 499, 869, 1064, 1162, 2106, 2259, 2449.

limned the singer of Teutonic heathenism. He is a man of repute, the equal of thanes. He holds land, even the land of his fathers. He receives gifts of gold from princes for the praise he does them. As yet no distinction appears between *scôp* and *gleómon*. Widsith is at one time the resident singer of a court; at another, as the mood takes him, a wanderer to the ends of the earth. And though the *scôp* leads the song, the warriors and the king himself do not disdain to take part in it. This is noteworthy, because it gives the real measure of the difference between the Teutonic and the Roman entertainer. For a Nero to perform amongst the *scenici* was to descend: for a Hrothgar to touch the harp was a customary and an honourable act.

The singing did not cease when the English came to these islands. The long struggle with the Britons which succeeded the invasions assuredly gave rise to many new lays, both in Northumbria and Wessex. 'England,' says Mr. Stopford Brooke, 'was conquered to the music of verse, and settled to the sound of the harp.' But though Alfred and Dunstan knew such songs, they are nearly all lost, or only dimly discerned as the basis of chronicles. At the end of the sixth century, just as the conquest was completed, came Christianity. The natural development of English poetry was to some extent deflected. A religious literature grew up at the hands of priests. Eadhelm, who, anticipating a notion of St. Francis of Assisi, used to stand on a bridge as if he were a gleeman, and waylay the folk as they hurried back from mass, himself wrote pious songs. One of these, a *carmen triviale*, was still sung in the twelfth century[1]. This was in Wessex. In Northumbria, always the most literary district of early England, the lay brother Cædmon founded a school of divine poetry. But even amongst the disciples of Cædmon, some, such as the author of the very martial *Judith*, seem to have designed their work for the mead-hall as well as the monastery[2]. And the regular *scôp* by no means vanished. The *Wanderer*, a semi-heathen elegiac poem of the early eighth

[1] William of Malmesbury, *de gestis Pontif. Angl.* (R. S.), 336 'quasi artem cantitandi professum, . . . sensim inter ludicra verbis scripturarum insertis.'

[2] Grein, ii. 294.

century, seems to be the lament of a *scôp* driven from his haunts, not by Christianity, but by the tumults of the day[1]. The great poet of the next generation, Cynewulf, himself took treasure of appled gold in the mead-hall. A riddle on 'the wandering singer' is ascribed to him[2], and various poems of his school on the fates or the crafts of man bear witness to the continued existence of the class[3]. With the eighth century, except for the songs of war quoted or paraphrased in the *Anglo-Saxon Chronicle*, the extant Early English poetry reaches a somewhat inexplicable end. But history comes to the rescue, and enables us still to trace the *scôp*. It is in the guise of a harp-player that Alfred is reported to have fooled the Danes, and Anlaf in his turn to have fooled the Saxons[4]: and mythical as these stories may be, they would not have even been plausible, had not the presence of such folk by the camp-fire been a natural and common event.

Certainly the *scôp* survived heathenism, and many Christian bishops and pious laymen, such as Alfred[5], were not ashamed of their sympathy with secular song. Nevertheless, the entertainers of the English folk did not find favour in the eyes of the Church as a whole. The stricter ecclesiastics especially attacked the practice of harbouring them in religious houses. Decrees condemning this were made by the council on English affairs which sat at Rome in 679[6], and by the council of Clovesho in 747[7]. Bede, writing at about the latter date on the

---

[1] Grein, i. 284. A similar poem is *The Sea-farer* (Grein, i. 290).

[2] Cynewulf, *Elene*, 1259 (Grein, ii. 135); *Riddle* lxxxix (Grein, iii. 1. 183). But A. S. Cook, *The Christ* (1900), lv, lxxxiii, thinks that Cynewulf was a thane, and denies him the *Riddle*.

[3] Cynewulf, *Christ* (ed. Gollancz), 668; *Gifts of Men* (Grein, iii. 1. 140); *Fates of Men* (Grein, iii. 1. 148).

[4] William of Malmesbury, *Gesta Reg. Angl.* (R. S.), i. 126, 143.

[5] Asserius, *de rebus gestis Alfredi* (Petrie-Sharp, *Mon. Hist. Brit.* i. 473). Alfred was slow to learn as a boy, but loved 'Saxonica poemata,' and remembered them. His first

book was a 'Saxonicum poematicae artis librum,' and 'Saxonicos libros recitare et maxime carmina Saxonica memoriter discere non desinebat.'

[6] Haddan-Stubbs, iii. 133 'Statuimus atque decernimus ut episcopi vel quicunque ecclesiastici ordinis religiosam vitam professi sunt . . . nec citharoedas habeant, vel quaecunque symphoniaca, nec quoscunque iocos vel ludos ante se permittant, quia omnia haec disciplina sanctae ecclesiae sacerdotes fideles suos habere non sinit.'

[7] *Ibid.* iii. 369 (can. 20) ' ut monasteria . . . non sint ludicrarum artium receptacula, hoc est, poetarum, citharistarum, musico-

condition of church affairs in Northumbria complains of those
who make mirth in the dwellings of bishops [1]; and the complaint is curiously illustrated by a letter of Gutbercht, abbot
of Newcastle, to an episcopal friend on the continent, in which
he asks him for a *citharista* competent to play upon the *cithara*
or *rotta* which he already possesses [2]. At the end of the eighth
century, Alcuin wrote a letter to Higbald, bishop of Lindisfarne,
warning him against the snares of *citharistae* and *histriones* [3]:
and some two hundred years later, when ·Edgar and Dunstan [4]
were setting themselves to reform the religious communities
of the land, the favour shown to such ribald folk was one of
the abuses which called for correction [5]. This hostile attitude
of the rulers of the Church is not quite explained by anything
in the poetry of the *scôpas*, so far as it is left to us. This had
very readily exchanged its pagan for a Christian colouring: it
cannot be fairly accused of immorality or even coarseness, and

rum, scurrorum.' Can. 12 shows
a fear of the influence of the *scôp*
on ritual: 'ut presbyteri saecularium
poetarum modo in ecclesia non
garriant, ne tragico sono sacrorum
verborum compositionem et dis-
tinctionem corrumpant vel con-
fundant.' Cf. the twelfth-century
account of church singers who used
'histrionicis quibusdam gestis,'
quoted by Jusserand, *E.L.* 455, from
the *Speculum Caritatis* of Abbot
Ælred of Rievaulx.

[1] Bede to Egbert in 734 (Haddan-
Stubbs, iii. 315) 'de quibusdam
episcopis fama vulgatum est . . .
quod ipsi . . . secum habeant . . .
illos qui risui, iocis, fabulis . . .
subigantur.'

[2] Gutberchtus to Lullus in 764
(Dümmler, *Epist. Mer. et Car.* in
M. G. H. i. 406).

[3] Alcuin, *Ep.* 124 (797) 'melius
est pauperes edere de mensa tua
quam istriones vel luxuriosos quoslibet . . . verba Dei legantur in
sacerdotali convivio. ibi decet lec-
torem audiri, non citharistam; sermones patrum, non carmina gentium. quid Hinieldus cum Christo?
angusta est domus; utrosque tenere non poterit . . . voces legentium

audire in domibus tuis, non riden-
tium turbam in plateis.' The allusion to a lost epic cycle of Hinieldus (Ingeld) is highly interesting;
on it cf. Haupt in *Z. f. d. A.* xv. 314.

[4] The *Vitae* of Dunstan (Stubbs,
Memorials of Dunstan, R. S. 11, 20,
80, 257) record that he himself
learnt the 'ars citharizandi.' One
day he hung 'citharam suam quam
lingua paterna hearpam vocamus'
on the wall, and it discoursed an
anthem by itself. Anthems, doubtless, were his mature recreation, but
as a young clerk he was accused
'non saluti animae profutura sed
avitae gentilitatis vanissima didi-
cisse carmina, et historiarum frivo-
volas colere incantationum nae-
nias.'

[5] *Anglo-Saxon Canons of Edgar*
(906), can. 58 (Wilkins, i. 228), *sic
Latine*, 'docemus artem, ut nullus
sacerdos sit cerevisarius, nec aliquo
modo scurram agat secum ipso, vel
aliis'; *Oratio Edgari Regis* (969)
pro monachatu propaganda (Wilkins, i. 246) 'ut iam domus clericorum putentur . . . conciliabulum
histrionum . . . mimi cantant et sal-
tant.'

the Christian sentiment of the time is not likely to have been much offended by the prevailing theme of battle and deeds of blood. The probable explanation is a double one. There is the ascetic tendency to regard even harmless forms of secular amusement as barely compatible with the religious life. And there is the fact, which the language of the prohibitions themselves makes plain, that a degeneration of the old Teutonic gleemen had set in. To singing and harping were now added novel and far less desirable arts. Certainly the prohibitions make no exception for *poetae* and *musici*; but the full strength of their condemnation seems to be directed against *scurrae* and their *ioca*, and against the *mimi* and *histriones* who danced as well as sang. These are new figures in English life, and they point to the fact that the merging of the Teutonic with the Latin entertainer had begun. To some extent, the Church itself was responsible for this. The conversion of England opened the remote islands to Latin civilization in general: and it is not to be wondered at, that the *mimi*, no less than the priests, flocked into the new fields of enterprise. If this was the case already in the eighth century, we can hardly doubt that it was still more so during the next two hundred years of which the literary records are so scanty. Such a view is supported by the numerous miniatures of dancers and tumblers, jugglers and bear-leaders, in both Latin and Early English manuscripts of this period [1], and by the glosses which translate such terms as *mimus, iocista, scurra, pantomimus* by *gligmon*, reserving *scôp* for the dignified *poeta* [2].

---

[1] Strutt, 172 and *passim*.

[2] Wright-Wülker, 150, 311, 539. A synonym for *scôp* is *leodwyrhta*. On 188 *lyricus* is glossed *scôp*. But the distinctive use of *scôp* is not in all cases maintained, e.g. *tragicus vel comicus unwurð scôp* (188), *comicus scôp* (283), *comicus id est qui comedia scribit, cantator vel artifex canticorum seculorum, idem satyricus, i. scôp, ioculator, poeta* (206). Other western peoples in contact with Latin civilization came to make the same classification of poet and buffoon. Wackernagel, i. 51, says that the German *liuderi* or poet is opposed to the *skirnun* or *tûmarâ, scurra* or *mimus*. The buffoon is looked askance at by the dignified Scandinavian men of letters (Saxo Grammaticus, *Hist. Danica*, transl. Elton, vi. 186); and Keltic bardism stands equally aloof from the *clerwr* (cf. p. 76). Of course Kelts and Teutons might conceivably have developed their buffoons for themselves, independently of Roman influence, but so far as the Germans go, Tacitus, *Germ.* 24, knows no *spectaculum* but the *sweorda-gelác* or sword-dance (ch. ix).

This distinction I regard as quite a late one, consequent upon the degeneracy introduced by *mimi* from south Europe into the lower ranks of the gleemen. Some writers, indeed, think that it existed from the beginning, and that the *scôp* was always the resident court poet, whereas the *gleómon* was the wandering singer, often a borrower rather than a maker of songs, who appealed to the smaller folk[1]. But the theory is inconsistent with the data of *Widsith*. The poet there described is sometimes a wanderer, sometimes stationary. He is evidently at the height of his profession, and has sung before every crowned head in Europe, but he calls himself a *gleómon*. Nor does the etymology of the words *scôp* and *gleómon* suggest any vital difference of signification[2].

The literary records of the continental Teutons are far scantier than those of the English. But amongst them also Latin and barbaric traditions seem to have merged in the *ioculator*. Ancestral deeds were sung to the harp, and therefore, it may be supposed, by a *scôp*, and not a *chorus*, before the Ostrogoths in Italy, at the beginning of the sixth century[3]. In the year 507 Clovis the Frank sent to Theodoric for a *citharoedus* trained in the musical science of the South, and Boethius was commissioned to make the selection[4]. On the other hand, little as the barbarians loved the theatre, the *mimi* and *scurrae* of the conquered lands seem to have tickled their fancy as they sat over their wine. At the banquet with which Attila entertained the imperial ambassadors in 448, the guests

---

[1] Brooke, i. 12; Merbot, 11. The *gleómon*, according to Merbot, became mixed with the *plegman* or *mimus*. In the glosses *pleʒa=ludus* in the widest sense, including athletics; and *pleʒ-stowe = amphitheatrum* (Wright-Wülker, 342). A synonym of *pleʒa* is the etymological equivalent of *ludus*, *lâc* (cf. ch. viii). *Spil* is not A. S., *spilian*, a loan-word (Kögel, i. 1. 11).

[2] *Scôp*, the O. H. G. *scopf* or *scof* is the 'shaper,' 'maker,' from *skapan*, 'to make'; it is only a West-German word, and is distinct from *scopf*, a 'scoff,' 'mock,' and also from O.N. *skald*. This is not West-German, but both 'sing' and 'say'

are from the same root *seg* (Kögel, i. 1. 140). *Gleómon* is from *gleo*, *gleow*, *gliw*, *glig* = 'glee,' 'mirth.' The harp, in *Beowulf* and elsewhere, is the 'glee-beam,' 'glee-wood.'

[3] Jordanis, *de hist. Get.* (in *M. G. H.*), c. 5 'ante quos etiam cantu maiorum facta modulationibus citharisque cantabant.'

[4] Cassiodorus, *Variae*, ii. 40, 41. Kögel, i. 1. 130, thinks that the professional singer, as distinct from the *chorus*, first became known to the Franks on this occasion. But one may rather infer from Theodoric's letter to Boethius that the *citharoedus* was to replace barbaric by civilized music.

were first moved to martial ardour and to tears by the recital of ancient deeds of prowess, and then stirred to laughter by the antics of a Scythian and a Moorish buffoon[1]. Attila was a Hun and no German; but the Vandals who invaded Africa in 429 are recorded to have taken to the *spectacula* so extravagantly popular there[2], and Sidonius tells how *mimici sales*, chastened in view of barbaric conceptions of decency, found a place in the festivities of another Theodoric, king from 462 to 466 of the Visigoths in Gaul[3]. Three centuries later, under Charlemagne, the blending of both types of entertainer under the common designation of *ioculator* seems to be complete. And, as in contemporary England, the animosity of the Church to the *scenici* is transferred wholesale to the *ioculatores*, without much formal attempt to discriminate between the different grades of the profession. Alcuin may perhaps be taken as representing the position of the more rigid disciplinarians on this point. His letter to the English bishop, Higbald, does not stand alone. In several others he warns his pupils against the dangers lurking in *ludi* and *spectacula*[4], and he shows himself particularly exercised by

---

[1] Priscus, *Hist. Goth.* (ed. Bonn) 205 ἐπιγενομένης δὲ ἑσπέρας δᾷδες ἀνήφθησαν, δύο δὲ ἀντικρὺ τοῦ Ἀττήλα παρελθόντες βάρβαροι ᾄσματα πεποιημένα ἔλεγον, νίκας αὐτοῦ καὶ τὰς κατὰ πόλεμον ᾄδοντες ἀρετάς· ἐς οὓς οἱ τῆς εὐωχίας ἀπέβλεπον, καὶ οἱ μὲν ἥδοντο τοῖς ποιήμασιν, οἱ δὲ τῶν πολέμων ἀναμιμνησκόμενοι διηγείροντο τοῖς φρονήμασιν, ἄλλοι δὲ ἐχώρουν ἐς δάκρυα, ὧν ὑπὸ τοῦ χρόνου ἠσθένει τὸ σῶμα καὶ ἡσυχάζειν ὁ θυμὸς ἠναγκάζετο. μετὰ δὲ τὰ ᾄσματα Σκύθης τις παρελθὼν φρενοβλαβής, ... ἐς γέλωτα πάντας παρεσκεύασε παρελθεῖν. μεθ' ὃν ... Ζέρκων ὁ Μαυρούσιος ... πάντας ... ἐς ἄσβεστον ὁρμῆσαι γέλωτα παρεσκεύασε, πλὴν Ἀττήλα. Cf. Gibbon, iii. 440; Hodgkin, ii. 86; Kögel, i. 1. 114.

[2] Procopius, *de bell. Vandal.* ii. 6; Victor Vitensis, *de persec. Vandal.* i. 15. 47.

[3] Sidonius, *Ep.* i. 2. 9 'sane intromittuntur, quanquam raro, inter coenandum mimici sales, ita ut nullus conviva mordacis linguae felle

teriatur.' There are no musicians, 'rege solum illis fidibus delenito, quibus non minus mulcet virtus animum quam cantus auditum.' In *Carm.* xii Sidonius mentions Gothic songs, without specifying whether they are professional or choric.

[4] Alcuin, *Ep.* cclxxxi (793–804), to a disciple in Italy, 'melius est Deo placere quam histrionibus, pauperum habere curam quam mimorum'; *Ep.* ccl (†801), to the monks of Fulda, 'non sint [adulescentuli] luxuriosi, non ebrietati servientes, non contemptuosi, non inanes sequentes ludos'; *Ep.* ccxliv (†801), to Fredegis, master of the palace school, 'non veniant coronatae columbae ad fenestras tuas, quae volant per cameras palatii, nec equi indomiti inrumpant ostia camerae; nec tibi sit ursorum saltantium cura, sed clericorum psallentium.' The 'coronatae columbae' were Charlemagne's wanton daughters. Dümmler (*Ep. Mer. et Car.* ii. 541)

the favour which they found with Angilbert, the literary and far from strict-lived abbot of St. Richer [1]. The influence of Alcuin with Charlemagne was considerable, and so far as ecclesiastical rule went, he had his way. A capitulary (†787) excluded the Italian clergy from uncanonical sports [2]. In 789 bishops, abbots, and abbesses were forbidden to keep *ioculatores* [3], and in 802 a decree applying to all in orders required abstinence from idle and secular amusements [4]. These prohibitions were confirmed in the last year of Charlemagne's reign (813) by the council of Tours [5]. But as entertainers of the lay folk, the minstrels rather gained than lost status at the hands of Charlemagne. Personally he took a distinct interest in their performances. He treasured up the heroic *cantilenae* of his race [6], and attempted in vain to

prints a *responsio* of Leidradus, Abp. of Lyons, to Charles. This is interesting, because it contrasts the 'mobilitas histrionum' which tempts the eye, with the 'carmina poetarum et comediarum mimorumque urbanitates et strophae,' which tempt the ear. This looks as if *histriones*, in the sense of *pantomimi*, were still known, but the piece also mentions 'teatrorum moles' and 'circenses,' and is, I suspect, quite antiquarian.

[1] *Ep.* clxxv (799), to Adalhart, Bp. of Old Corbey, 'Vereor, ne Homerus [Angilbert] irascatur contra cartam prohibentem spectacula et diabolica figmenta. quae omnes sanctae scripturae prohibent, in tantum ut legebam sanctum dicere Augustinum, "nescit homo, qui histriones et mimos et saltatores introducit in domum suam, quam magna eos immundorum sequitur turba spirituum." sed absit ut in domo christiana diabolus habeat potestatem' (the quotation from Augustine cannot be identified): *Ep.* ccxxxvii (801), also to Adalhart, 'quod de emendatis moribus Homeri mei scripsisti, satis placuit oculis meis ... unum fuit de histrionibus, quorum vanitatibus sciebam non parvum animae sui periculum imminere, quod mihi non placuit, ... mirumque mihi visum est, quomodo

tam sapiens animus non intellexisset reprehensibilia dignitati suae facere et non laudabilia.' Angilbert also seems to have had relations unbecoming an abbot with one of the 'coronatae columbae.'

[2] *Capit. of Mantua* (Boretius, i. 195), can. 6 'neque ulla iocorum genera ante se fieri permittant quae contra canonum auctoritatem eveniunt.'

[3] *Capit. Generale* (Boretius, i. 64; *P. L.* xcvii. 188), c. 31 'ut episcopi et abbates et abbatissae cupplas canum non habeant, nec falcones, nec accipitres, nec ioculatores.' If this is the *carta* of Alcuin's *Ep.* clxxv, and I know of no other which it can be, Dümmler's date for the letter of 799 seems too late. Mabillon's 791 is nearer the mark.

[4] *Capit. Gen.* (Boretius, i. 96), can. 23 'cleri ... non inanis lusibus vel conviviis secularibus vel canticis vel luxuriosis usum habeant.'

[5] *Conc. of Tours* (Mansi, xiv. 84), c. 7 'histrionum quoque turpium et obscoenorum insolentiis iocorum et ipsi [sacerdotes] animo effugere caeterisque sacerdotibus effugienda praedicare debent.'

[6] Einhard, *Vita Caroli Magni*, c. 29 'barbara et antiquissima carmina, quibus veterum regum actus et bella canebantur, scripsit memoriaeque mandavit.'

inspire the *saevitia* of his sons with his own enthusiasm for these[1]. The chroniclers more than once relate how his policy was shaped or modified by the chance words of a *ioculator* or *scurra*[2]. The later tradition of the *jougleurs* looked back to him as the great patron of their order, who had given them all the fair land of Provence in fee[3]: and it is clear that the songs written at his court form the basis not only of the *chansons de gestes*, but also, as we found to be the case with the English war-songs, of many passages in the chronicles themselves[4]. After Charlemagne's death the minstrels fell for a time on evil days. Louis the Pious by no means shared his father's love for them. He attempted to suppress the *cantilenae* on which he had been brought up, and when the *mimi* jested at court would turn away his head and refuse to smile[5]. To his reign may perhaps be ascribed a decree contained in the somewhat dubious collection of Benedictus Levita, forbidding idle dances, songs and tales in public places and at crossways on Sundays[6], and another which continued

---

[1] Alcuin, *Ep.* cxlix (798), to Charlemagne, 'ut puerorum saevitia vestrorum cuiuslibet carminis dulcedine mitigaretur, voluistis'; Alcuin, who doubtless had to *ménager* Charlemagne a little, is apparently to write the poem himself.

[2] Kögel, i. 2. 222. The *Chronicon Novaliciense*, iii. 10, describes how after crossing Mt. Cenis in 773, Charlemagne was guided by a Lombard *ioculator* who sung a 'cantiunculam a se compositam de eadem re rotando in conspectu suorum.' As a reward the *ioculator* had all the land over which his *tuba* sounded on a hill could be heard. The *Monachus S. Galli* (Jaffé, *Bibl. rer. Germ.* iv), i. 13, tells how (†783) a *scurra* brought about a reconciliation between Charlemagne and his brother-in-law Uodalrich. The same writer (i. 33) mentions an 'incomparabilis clericus' of the 'gloriosissimus Karolus,' who 'scientia ... cantilenae ecclesiasticae vel iocularis novaque carminum compositione sive modulatione ... cunctos praecelleret.'

[3] Philippe Mouskes, *de Poetis*

Provincialibus (quoted Ducange, s. v. *leccator*):
'Quar quant li buens Rois Karlemaigne
Ot toute mise à son demaine
Provence, qui mult iert plentive
De vins, de bois, d'aigue, de rive,
As lecours, as menestreus,
Qui sont auques luxurieus,
Le donna toute et departi.'

[4] Kögel, i. 2. 220.

[5] Theganus, *de gestis Ludovici Pii* (*M. G. H. Scriptores*, ii. 594), c. 19 'Poetica carmina gentilia, quae in iuventute didicerat, respuit, nec legere nec audire nec docere voluit,' and 'nunquam in risu exaltavit vocem suam, nec quando in festivitatibus ad laetitiam populi procedebant thymelici, scurrae, et mimi cum choraulis et citharistis ad mensam coram eo, tunc ad mensuram ridebat populus coram eo, ille nunquam vel dentes candidos suos in risu ostendit.' The 'carmina gentilia,' so much disliked by Louis, were probably Frankish and not classic poems.

[6] Benedictus Levita, vi. 205

for the benefit of the minstrels the legal incapacity of the
Roman *scenici*, and excluded *histriones* and *scurrae* from all
privilege of pleading in courts of justice [1].

The ill-will of a Louis the Pious could hardly affect the hold
which the minstrels had established on society. For good or
for bad, they were part of the mediaeval order of things. But
their popularity had to maintain itself against an undying
ecclesiastical prejudice. They had succeeded irrevocably to the
heritage of hate handed down from the *scenici infames*. To be
present at their performances was a sin in a clerk, and merely
tolerated in a layman. Largesse to them was declared tanta-
mount to robbery of the poor [2]. It may be fairly said that
until the eleventh century at least the history of minstrelsy is
written in the attacks of ecclesiastical legislators, and in the
exultant notices of monkish chroniclers when this or that
monarch was austere enough to follow the example of Louis
the Pious, and let the men of sin go empty away [3]. Throughout the Middle Ages proper the same standpoint was officially
maintained [4]. The canon law, as codified by Gratian, treats

---

(*M. G. H. Leges*, ii. 2. 83), 'ne in illo
sancto die vanis fabulis aut locu-
tionibus sive cantationibus vel saltationibus stando in biviis et plateis
ut solet inserviant.' On this collection see Schaff, v. 272.

[1] This capitulary is of doubtful
date, but belongs to the reign either
of Louis the Pious, or Lothair
(Boretius, i. 334; Pertz, i. 324; Ben.
Levita, ii. 49) 'ut in palatiis nostris
ad accusandum et iudicandum et
testimonium faciendum non se exhibeant viles personae et infames,
histriones scilicet, nugatores, man-
zeres, scurrae, concubinarii, . . . aut
servi aut criminosi'; cf. R. Sohm,
*Die fränk. Reichs- und Gerichts-
verfassung*, 354.

[2] For ninth-century prohibitions
see *Statutes* of Haito, Bp. of Basle
(807–23), c. 11 (Boretius, i. 364);
Conc. of Maintz (847), c. 13 (Boretius, ii. 179); *Conc. of Maintz* (852),
c. 6 (Boretius, ii. 187); *Capit.*
of Walter of Orleans (858), c. 17
(Mansi, xv. 507), *Capit.* of Hincmar

of Rheims (*P. L.* cxxv. 776); and
cf. Prynne, 556. Stress is often laid
on the claims of the poor; e. g.
Agobardus (†836), *de Dispens. Eccles. Rer.* 30 (*P. L.* civ. 249) 'satiat
praeterea et inebriat histriones,
mimos, turpissimosque et vanis-
simos ioculares, cum pauperes
ecclesiae fame discruciati inter-
eant.'

[3] Otto Frisingensis, *Chronicon*, vi.
32, records of the Emperor Henry
III in 1045 that 'quumque ex more
regio nuptias Inglinheim celebraret,
omne balatronum et histrionum
collegium, quod, ut assolet, eo con-
fluxerat, vacuum abire permisit,
pauperibusque ea quae membris
diaboli subtraxerat, large distribuit.'
After the death of the Emperor Henry
I of Germany his widow Matilda
'neminem voluit audire carmina saecularia cantantem' (*Vita Machtildis
Antiquior* in *M. G. H. Scriptores*,
iv. 294).

[4] Honorius   Augustodunensis,
Elucidarium (†1092), ii. 18 (*P. L.*

as applicable to minstrels the pronouncements of fathers and
councils against the *scenici*, and adds to them others more
recent, in which clergy who attend *spectacula*, or in any way
by word or deed play the *ioculator*, are uncompromisingly
condemned [1]. This temper of the Church did not fail to find
its expression in post-Conquest England. The council of
Oxford in 1222 adopted for this country the restatement of
the traditional rule by the Lateran council of 1215 [2]; and the
stricter disciplinary authorities at least attempted to enforce
the decision. Bishop Grosseteste of Lincoln, for instance,
pressed it upon his clergy in or about 1238 [3]. The reforming
provisions of Oxford in 1259 laid down that, although minstrels
might receive charitable doles in monasteries, their *spectacula*
must not be given [4]; and a similar prohibition, couched in very

clxxii. 1148) 'Habent spem ioculatores? nullam; tota namque intentione sunt ministri Satanae'; on the vogue of this book cf. *Furnivall Miscellany*, 88.

[1] The following passages of the *Decretum Gratiani*, besides those already quoted, bear on the subject: (*a*) i. 23. 3, *ex Isid. de Eccl. Officiis*, ii. 2 'His igitur lege Patrum cavetur, ut a vulgari vita seclusi a mundi voluptatibus sese abstineant; non spectaculis, non pompis intersint': (*b*) i. 44. 7, *ex Conc. Nannetensi* 'Nullus presbyterorum ... quando ad collectam presbyteri convenerit ... plausus et risus inconditos, et fabulas inanes ibi referre aut cantare praesumat, aut turpia ioca vel urso vel tornatricibus ante se fieri patiatur'; I cannot identify the Council of Nantes referred to : the canon is not amongst those supposed to belong to the Council of 660, and given by Mansi, xviii. 166: (*c*) i. 46. 6, *ex Conc. Carthag.* iv. c. 60 [398. Mansi, iii. 956] 'Clericum scurrilem et verbis turpibus ioculatorem ab officio retrahendum censemus': (*d*) ii. 4. 1. 1, *ex Conc. Carthag.* vii (419) 'Omnes etiam infamiae maculis aspersi, id est histriones ... ab accusatione prohibentur.' The *Decretum Gratiani* was drawn up † 1139. The *Decretales* of Gregory IX (1234) incorporate can. 16 of

the *Lateran Council* (Mansi, xxii. 1003), held in 1215 (*Decr. Greg. IX*, iii. 1. 15) '[Clerici] mimis, ioculatoribus, et histrionibus non intendant'; and the *Liber Sextus* of Boniface VIII (1298) adds the following decree of that Pope (*Sext. Decr.* iii. 1. 1) 'Clerici qui, clericalis ordinis dignitati non modicum detrahentes, se ioculatores seu goliardos faciunt aut bufones, si per annum artem illam ignominiosam exercuerint, ipso iure, si autem tempore breviori, et tertio moniti non resipuerint, careant omni privilegio clericali.'

[2] Wilkins, i. 585. For can. 16 of the Lateran council see last note. The prohibition is again confirmed by can. 17 of the Synod of Exeter in 1287 (Wilkins, ii. 129).

[3] *Constitutiones* of Bp. Grosseteste in his *Epistolae* (R. S.), 159 'ne mimis, ioculatoribus, aut histrionibus intendant.' In 1230, Grosseteste's predecessor, Hugh of Wells, had bid his archdeacons inquire, 'an aliqui intendant histrionibus' (Wilkins, i. 627).

[4] *Annales de Burton* (*Ann. Monast.* R. S. i. 485) 'histrionibus potest dari cibus, quia pauperes sunt, non quia histriones; et eorum ludi non videantur, vel audiantur, vel permittantur fieri coram abbate vel monachis.'

uncomplimentary terms, finds a place in the new statutes
drawn up in 1319 for the cathedral church of Sarum by Roger
de Mortival[1]. A few years later the statutes of St. Albans
follow suit[2], while in 1312 a charge of breaking the canons in
this respect brought against the minor clergy of Ripon minster
had formed the subject of an inquiry by Archbishop Green-
field[3]. Such notices might be multiplied[4]; and the tenor of
them is echoed in the treatises of the more strait-laced amongst
monkish writers. John of Salisbury[5], William Fitz Stephen[6],
Robert Mannyng of Brunne[7], are at one in their disapproval
of *ioculatores*. As the fourteenth century draws to its close,
and the Wyclifite spirit gets abroad, the freer critics of church

[1] *Const.* of Roger de Mortival,
§ 46 (Dayman and Jones, *Sarum
Statutes*, 76) 'licet robustos corpore, laborem ad quem homo nascitur subire contemnentes, et in
delicato otio sibi victum quaerere
sub inepta laetitia saeculi eligentes,
qui "menestralli" et quandoque
"ludorum homines" vulgari eloquio
nuncupantur, non quia tales sunt,
sed quia opus Dei nostramque
naturam conspicimus in eisdem,
nostris domibus refectionis gratia
aliquotiens toleremus,' yet no money
or goods convertible into money
may be given them; 'nec ad fabulas
quas referunt, et quae in detracta-
tionibus, turpiloquio, scurrilitate
consistunt, ullus voluntarium prae-
beat auditum, nec ad eas audiendas
aures habeat prurientes, sed per
obauditionem ab huiusmodi re-
latibus, quin potius latratibus, in
quantum fieri poterit, excludantur,
tamen nemo libenter invito referat
auditori.' They may, if they are not
women, have their dole of bread,
and keep peace from evil words.
'Nec debet de huiusmodi personarum, quae infames sunt, laude,
immo verius fraude, seu obloquio,
aut alias vanae laudis praeconio,
ecclesiasticus vir curare, cum nihil
eo miserius sit praelato, qui luporum
laudibus gloriatur.' The statute is
headed 'De maledicis, adulatoribus,
histrionibus, et detractoribus re-
spuendis.'

[2] Thomas Walsingham, *Gesta
Abbatum S. Albani* (ed. Riley,
R. S. ii. 469) 'illicita spectacula
prorsus evitent' (1326-35).
[3] J. T. Fowler, *Memorials of
Ripon Minster*, ii. 68 (Surtees Soc.);
the charge was that 'vicarii, capellani, et caeteri ministri . . . spectaculis publicis, ludibriis et coreis,
immo teatricalibus ludis inter laicos
frequentius se immiscent.'
[4] The *Statutes*, i. 5. 4, of St. Paul's,
as late as †1450, direct the beadles
'quod menestrallos coram altaribus
Virginis et Crucis indevote strepi-
tantes arceant et eiiciant' (W. S.
Simpson, *Register of St. Paul's*,
72).
[5] John of Salisbury, *Polycraticus*
(†1159), i. 8 (*P.L.* cxcix. 406) 'satius
enim fuerat otiari quam turpiter
occupari. Hinc mimi, salii vel
saliares, balatrones, aemiliani,
gladiatores, palaestritae, gignadii,
praestigiatores, malefici quoque
multi, et tota ioculatorum scena
procedit.'
[6] Cf. *Representations*, s.v. London.
[7] R. Mannyng de Brunne (†1303),
Handlyng Synne (ed. Furnivall),
148. 'Here doyng ys ful perylous'
he translates William of Wadington's
'Qe unt trop perilus mester'; and
tells a tale of divine judgement on
'a mynstralle, a gulardous,' who
disturbed a priest at mass.

and state, such as William Langland [1] or the imagined author of Chaucer's *Parson's Tale* [2], take up the same argument. And they in their turn hand it on to the interminable pamphleteering of the Calvinistic Puritans [3].

[1] *Piers the Plowman, C. text,* viii. 97:

'Clerkus and kny₃tes · welcometh kynges mynstrales,
And for loue of here lordes · lithen hem at festes;
Muche more, me thenketh · riche men auhte
Haue beggars by-fore hem · whiche beth godes mynstrales.'

[2] *Cant. Tales* (ed. Skeat), § 69 'Soothly, what thing that he yeveth for veyne glorie, as to minstrals and to folk, for to beren his renoun in the world, he hath sinne ther-of, and noon almesse.'

[3] e. g. Stubbes, *Anatomy*, i. 169.

CHAPTER III

THE MINSTREL LIFE

THE perpetual *infamia* of the minstrels is variously reflected in the literature of their production. Sometimes they take their condemnation lightly enough, dismissing it with a jest or a touch of bravado. In *Aucassin et Nicolete*, that marvellous romance of the *viel caitif*, when the hero is warned that if he takes a mistress he must go to hell, he replies that, to hell will he go, for thither go all the goodly things of the world. 'Thither go the gold and the silver, and the vair and the grey, and thither too go harpers and minstrels and the kings of the world. With these will I go, so that I have Nicolete, my most sweet friend, with me'[1]. At other times they show a wistful sense of the pathos of their secular lot. They tell little stories in which heaven proves more merciful than the vice-gerents of heaven upon earth, and Virgin or saint bestows upon a minstrel the sign of grace which the priest denies[2]. But often, again, they turn upon their persecutors

---

[1] *Aucassin et Nicolete* († 1150-1200), ed. Bourdillon (1897), 22. The term 'caitif' has puzzled the editors. Surely the minstrel has in mind the abusive epithets with which the clergy bespattered his profession. See Appendix B.

[2] See especially *Le Tombeor de Notre Dame* (*Romania*, ii. 315). Novati (*Rom.* xxv. 591) refers to a passage quoted by Augustine, *de Civ. Dei*, vi. 10, from the lost work of Seneca, *de Superstitionibus*, ' doctus archimimus, senex iam decrepitus, cotidie in Capitolio mimum agebat, quasi dii libenter spectarent quem illi homines desierant.' Somewhat similar are *Don Cierge qui descendi au Jougleour* (Gautier de

Coincy), *Miracles de Nostre Dame* († 1223, ed. Poquet, 1859), and *Le Harpeor de Roncestre* (Michel, *Roms., Contes, Dits, Fabl.* ii. 108). *Saint Pierre et le Jongleur* (Montaiglon Raynaud, v. 117) is a witty tale, in which a minstrel, left in charge of hell, loses so many souls to St. Peter at dice, that no minstrel has been allowed there since. B. Joannes Bonus (*Acta SS. Oct.* ix. 693) was a minstrel in his youth, but the patron saints of the minstrels were always St. Genesius the mime (cf. p. 10), and St. Julian Hospitator (*Acta SS. Jan.* iii. 589), who built a hospital and once entertained an angel unawares.

and rend them with the merciless satire of the *fabliaux*, wherein
it is the clerk, the theologian, who is eternally called upon to
play the indecent or ridiculous part[1].

Under spiritual disabilities the minstrels may have been, but
so far as substantial popularity amongst all classes went, they
had no cause from the eleventh to the fourteenth century to
envy the monks. As a social and literary force they figure
largely both on the continent and in England. The distinctively Anglo-Saxon types of *scôp* and *glebmon* of course disappear at the Conquest. They do not cease to exist; but they
go under ground, singing their defiant lays of Hereward[2]; and
they pursue a more or less subterranean career until the fourteenth century brings the English tongue to its own again.
But minstrelsy was no less popular with the invaders than
with the invaded. Whether the *skald* had yet developed
amongst the Scandinavian pirates who landed with Rollo on
the coasts of France may perhaps be left undetermined[3]: for
a century and a half had sufficed to turn the Northmen into
Norman French, and with the other elements of the borrowed
civilization had certainly come the *ioculator*. In the very van
of William's army at Senlac strutted the minstrel Taillefer,
and went to his death exercising the double arts of his hybrid
profession, juggling with his sword, and chanting an heroic
lay of Roncesvalles[4]. Twenty years later, Domesday Book
records how Berdic the *ioculator regis* held three vills and
five carucates of land in Gloucestershire, and how in Hamp-

[1] Paris, 113; Bédier, 333.
[2] Brooke, *Eng. Lit.* 305; Ten
Brink, i. 149.
[3] Sophus Bugge, in *Bidrag til
den aeldste Skaldedigtnings Historie* (1894; cf. L. Duvau in *Rev.
Celt.* xvii. 113), holds that Skaldic
poetry began in the Viking raids of
the eighth and ninth centuries, under
the influence of the Irish *filid*. The
tenth-century skald as described in
the *Raven-Song* of Hornklofi at the
court of Harold Fair-hair is very
like the *scôp* (*C.P.B.* i. 254), and
here too tumblers and buffoons have
found their way. Cf. Kögel, i. 1. 111;
E. Mogk, in Paul, *Grundriss*[2], iii. 248.

[4] Guy of Amiens, *de Bello Hastin-
gensi* (†1068), 391, 399:
'Histrio, cor audax nimium quem
    nobilitabat . . .
. . . Incisor-ferri mimus cogno-
    mine dictus.'
Wace, *Roman de Rou* (†1170)
(ed. Andresen, iii. 8035):
'Taillefer, ki mult bien chantout,
Sor un cheval ki tost alout,
Devant le duc alout chantant
De Karlemaigne et de Rolant
Et d'Oliver et des vassals
Qui morurent en Rencevals.'
Cf. Freeman, *Norman Conquest*,
iii. 477.

shire Adelinda, a *ioculatrix*, held a virgate, which Earl Roger had given her [1]. During the reigns of the Angevin and Plantagenet kings the minstrels were ubiquitous. They wandered at their will from castle to castle, and in time from borough to borough, sure of their ready welcome alike in the village tavern, the guildhall, and the baron's keep [2]. They sang and jested in the market-places, stopping cunningly at a critical moment in the performance, to gather their harvest of small coin from the bystanders [3]. In the great castles, while lords and ladies supped or sat around the fire, it was theirs to while away many a long bookless evening with courtly *geste* or witty sally. At wedding or betrothal, baptism or knight-dubbing, treaty or tournament, their presence was indispensable. The greater festivities saw them literally in their hundreds [4], and rich was their reward in money and in jewels, in costly garments [5], and in broad acres. They were licensed vagabonds, with free right of entry into the presence-chambers of the land [6]. You might know them from afar by their coats of many colours, gaudier than any knight might respectably wear [7], by the instruments upon their backs and those of their

---

[1] Domesday Book, *Gloc.* f. 162 ; *Hants*, f. 38 (b). Before the Conquest, not to speak of Widsith and Deor, Edmund Ironside had given the hills of Chartham and Walworth 'cuidam ioculatori suo nomine Hitardo' (Somner-Battely, *Antiq. of Canterbury*, app. 39). Hitardus, wishing to visit Rome, gave it to Christ Church, Canterbury.

[2] Bernhard, iii. 378, gives a thirteenth-century regulation for the Petit Pont entry of Paris : ' Et ausi tot li jougleur sunt quite por i ver de chançon.'

[3] Gautier, ii. 124.

[4] There were 426 at the wedding of Margaret of England with John of Brabant in 1290 (Chappell, i. 15, from *Wardrobe Bk.* 18 Edw. I).

[5] Rigordus, *de gestis Philippi Augusti* (1186) 'vidimus quondam quosdam principes qui vestes diu excogitatas et variis florum picturationibus artificiossisimis elaboratas, pro quibus forsan viginti vel triginta marcas argenti consumpserant, vix revolutis septem diebus, histrionibus, ministris scilicet diaboli, ad primam vocem dedisse.'

[6] The *Annales* (†1330) of Johannes de Trokelowe (R. S.), 98, tell *s. a.* 1317, how when Edward II was keeping Pentecost in Westminster 'quaedam mulier, ornatu histrionali redimita, equum bonum, histrionaliter phaleratum, ascensa, dictam aulam intravit, mensas more histrionum circuivit.' She rode to the king, placed an insulting letter in his hands, and retired. The 'ianitores et hostiarii,' when blamed, declared ' non esse moris regii, alicui menestrallo, palatium intrare volenti, in tanta solemnitate aditum denegare '; cf. Walsingham, *Hist. Angl.* (R. S.). i. 149.

[7] Strutt, 189, has a fourteenth-century story of a youth rebuked for coming to a feast in a coat bardy, cut German fashion like a minstrel's;

servants, and by the shaven faces, close-clipped hair and flat shoes proper to their profession [1]. This kenspeckle appearance, together with the privilege of easy access, made the minstrel's dress a favourite disguise in ages when disguise was often imperative. The device attributed by the chroniclers to Alfred and to Anlaf becomes in the romances one of the commonest of *clichés* [2]. The readiness with which the minstrels won the popular ear made them a power in the land. William de Longchamp, the little-loved chancellor of Richard I, found it worth his while to bring a number of them over from France, that they might sing his praises abroad in the public places [3]. Nor were they less in request for satire than for eulogy. The English speaking minstrels, in particular, were responsible for many songs in derision of unpopular causes and personalities [4]; and we need not doubt that 'the lay that Sir Dinadan made by King Mark, which was the worst lay that ever harper sang with harp or with any other instruments,' must have had its precise counterparts in actual life [5]. The Sarum statutes of 1319 lay especial stress on the flattery and the evil speaking with which the minstrels rewarded their

---

cf. the complaint against knights in *A Poem on the times of Edward II* (Percy Soc. lxxxii), 23 :

'Now thei beth disgysed,
So diverselych i-di3t,
That no man may knowe
A mynstrel from a kny3t
Wel ny.'

The miniatures show minstrels in short coats to the knees and sometimes short capes with hoods. The *Act of Apparel* (1463, 3 *Edw. IV*, c. 5) excepts minstrels and 'players in their interludes.' The Franciscan story (p. 57) shows that some of the humbler minstrels went shabby enough.

[1] Klein, iii. 635; Du Méril, *Or. Lat.* 30; Gautier, ii. 104; Geoffrey of Monmouth, *Historia Britonum*, ix. 1 'rasit capillos suos et barbam, cultumque ioculatoris cum cithara cepit.' Cf. the canon quoted on p. 61 requiring Goliardic clerks to be shorn or shaven, to obliterate the tonsure. The flat shoe had been a mark of the *mimi planipedes* at Rome.

[2] Gautier, ii. 105. Thus Nicolete (*Aucassin et Nicolete*, ed. Bourdillon, 120) 'prist une herbe, si en oinst son cief et son visage, si qu'ele fu tote noire et tainte. Et ele fist faire cote et mantel et cemisse et braies, si s'atorna a guise de jogleor'; cf. *King Horn* (ed. Hall, 1901), 1471-2 :

'Hi sede, hi weren harpurs,
And sume were gigours.'

[3] Roger de Hoveden, *Chronicon* (R. S), iii. 143 'De regno Francorum cantores et ioculatores muneribus allexerat, ut de illo canerent in plateis ; et iam dicebatur quod non erat talis in orbe.'

[4] Ten Brink, i. 314.

[5] Malory, *Morte d'Arthur*, x. 27, 31. Even King Mark let the minstrel go quit, because he was a minstrel.

enteÌrtainers[1]. Sometimes, indeed, they over-reached themselves, for Henry I is related to have put out the eyes of Lucas de Barre, a Norman *jougleur*, or perhaps rather *trouvère*, who made and sang songs against him[2]. But Lucas ẗde Barre's rank probably aggravated his offence, and as a rule the minstrels went scot-free. A wiser churchman here and there was not slow to perceive how the unexampled hold of minstrelsy on the popular ear might be turned to the service of religion. Eadhelm, standing in gleeman's attire on an English bridge to mingle words of serious wisdom with his *carmina trivialia*, is one instance[3]. And in the same spirit St. Francis, himself half a troubadour in youth, would call his Minorites *ioculatores Domini*, and send them singing over the world to beg for their fee the repentance and spiritual joy of their hearers[4]. A popular hymn-writer of the present day is alleged to have thought it ' hard that the devil should have all the good tunes'; but already in the Middle Ages religious words were being set to secular music, and graced with the secular imagery of youth and spring[5].

But if the minstrels were on the one hand a force among the people, on the other they had the ear of kings. The

[1] Cf. p. 40.

[2] Ordericus Vitalis, *Hist. Eccles.* xii. 19 ' pro derisoriis cantionibus ... quin etiam indecentes de me cantilenas facetus choraula composuit, ad iniuriam mei palam cantavit, malevolosque mihi hostes ad cachinnos ita saepe provocavit.' Lucas de Barre seems to have been of noble birth, but 'palam cantavit cantilenas.'

[3] Cf. p. 30.

[4] *Speculum Perfectionis* (ed. Sabatier), 197. When Francis had finished his Canticle of the Sun, he thought for a moment of summoning ' frater Pacificus qui in saeculo vocabatur rex versuum et fuit valde curialis doctor cantorum,' and giving him a band of friars who might sing it to the people at the end of their sermons : ' finitis autem laudibus volebat quod praedicator diceret populo : "Nos sumus ioculatores Domini, et pro his volumus remu-

nerari a vobis, videlicet ut stetis in vera paenitentia." Et ait : "Quid enim sunt servi Dei nisi quidam ioculatores eius qui corda hominum erigere debent et movere ad laetitiam spiritualem." ' Cf. Sabatier, *Life of St. Francis*, 9, 51, 307. Perhaps Francis may have heard of Joachim of Flora, his contemporary, who wrote in his *Commentary on the Apocalypse*, f. 183. a. 2 'qui vere monachus est nihil reputat esse suum nisi citharam.'

[5] The MS. of the famous thirteenth-century canon *Sumer is icumen in* has religious words written beneath the profane ones ; cf. Wooldridge, *Oxford Hist. of Music*, i. 326. Several religious adaptations of common motives of profane lyric are amongst the English thirteenth-century poems preserved in Harl. MS. 2253 (*Specimens of Lyrical Poetry* : Percy Soc., 1842, no. 19, and ed. Böddeker, Berlin, 1878).

English court, to judge by the payments recorded in the exchequer books, must have been full of them[1]. The fullest and most curious document on the subject dates from the reign of Edward I. It is a roll of payments made on the occasion of a Whitsuntide feast held in London in the year 1306, and a very large number of the minstrels recorded are mentioned by name[2]. At the head of the list come five minstrels with the high-sounding title of *le roy*[3], and these get five marks apiece. A number of others follow, who received sums varying from one mark upwards. Most of these have French names, and many are said to be in the company of this or that noble or reverend guest at the feast. Finally, two hundred marks were distributed in smaller sums amongst the inferior minstrels, *les autres menestraus de la commune,* and some of these seem to have been of English birth. Below the *roys* rank two minstrels, Adam le Boscu and another, who are dignified with the title of *maistre,* which probably signifies that they were clerks[4]. The other names are mainly descriptive, 'Janin le Lutour,' 'Gillotin le Sautreour,' 'Baudec le Taboureur,' and the like ; a few are jesting stage names, such as the inferior performers of our music halls bear to-day[5]. Such are ' Guillaume sanz Maniere,' ' Reginaldus le Menteur,' ' le Petit Gauteron,' 'Parvus Willielmus,' and those of the attractive comedians Perle in the Eghe, and Matill' Makejoye. The last, by the way, is the only woman performer named. The resources of Edward I could no doubt stand the strain of rewarding with royal magnificence the entertainers of his guests. There is plenty of evidence, however, that even on secular grounds the diatribes of the moralists against the minstrels were often enough justified. To the lavish and unthrifty of purse they became

---

[1] Jusserand, *E. W. L.* 195, 199, 215 ; Strutt, 194-5, 210, 227 ; Hazlitt-Warton, ii. 119 ; Chappell, i. 15 ; Collier, i. 22 ; *Wardrobe Accounts of Edward I* (Soc. Antiq.), 163, 166, 168.

[2] Cf. Appendix C.

[3] Cf. Appendix D.

[4] This cannot be the famous Adan de le Hale (cf. ch. viii), known as ' le Bossu,' if Guy, 178, is right in saying that his nephew, Jean Mados,

wrote a lament for his death in 1288. He quotes *Hist. Litt.* xx. 666, as to this.

[5] Gautier, ii. 103 ; Bédier, 405, quote many similar names ; e.g. Quatre Œufs, Malebouche, Rongefoie, Tourne-en-fuie, Courtebarbe, Porte-Hotte, Mal Quarrel, Songe-Feste a la grant viele, Mal-appareillié, Pelé, Brise-Pot, Simple d'Amour, Chevrete, Passereau.

blood-suckers. Matilda, the wife of Henry I, is said to have squandered most of her revenues upon them[1]; while the unfortunate Robert of Normandy, if no less a chronicler than Ordericus Vitalis may be believed, was stripped by these rapacious gentry to the very skin[2]. Yet for all the days of honour and all the rich gifts the minstrel life must have had its darker side. Easily won, easily parted with ; and the lands and laced mantles did not last long, when the elbow itched for the dice-box. This was the incurable ruin of the minstrel folk[3]. And even that life of the road, so alluring to the fever in the blood, must have been a hard one in the rigours of an English climate. To tramp long miles in wind and rain, to stand wet to the skin and hungry and footsore, making the slow *bourgeois* laugh while the heart was bitter within ; such must have been the daily fate of many amongst the humbler minstrels at least[4]. And at the end to die like a dog in a ditch, under the ban of the Church and with the prospect of eternal damnation before the soul.

Kings and nobles were not accustomed to depend for their entertainment merely upon the stray visits of wandering minstrels. Others more or less domiciled formed a permanent part of the household. These indeed are the minstrels in the stricter sense of that term—*ministri, ministeriales.* In Domesday Book, as we have seen, one Berdic bears the title of the *ioculator regis.* Shortly afterwards Henry I had his *mimus regis,* by name Raherus, who made large sums by his *suavitas iocularis,* and founded the great priory of St. Bartholomew at Smithfield[5]. Laying aside his parti-coloured

---

[1] William of Malmesbury, *Gesta Reg. Angl.* (R. S.), ii. 494.

[2] Ordericus Vitalis, v. 12, &c. On one occasion 'ad ecclesiam, quia nudus erat, non pervenit.'

[3] Bédier, 359.

[4] Gautier, chs. xx, xxi, gives an admirable account of the *jougleur's* daily life, and its seamy side is brought out by Bédier, 399–418. A typical *jougleur* figure is that of the poet Rutebeuf, a man of genius, but often near death's door from starvation. See the editions of his

works by Jubinal and Kressner, and the biography by Clédat in the series of *Grands Écrivains français.*

[5] Morley, *Bartholomew Fair*, 1–25, from *Liber Fundacionis* in *Cott. Vesp. B. ix*; Leland, *Collectanea,* 1, 61, 99 ; Dugdale, *Monasticon,* ii. 166; Stow, *Survey,* 140; C. Knight, *London,* ii. 34; Percy, 406. No minstrels, however, appear in the formal list of Henry I's Norman Household (†1135), which seems to have been the nucleus of the English Royal

coat, he even became himself the first prior of the new community. The old spirit remained with him, however; and it is recorded that the fame of the house was largely magnified by means of some feigned miracles which Raherus put forth. Richard I was a noted lover of song, and the names of more than one minstrel of his are preserved. There was Ambroise, who was present at Richard's coronation in 1189 and at the siege of Acre in 1191, and who wrote a history, still extant, of the third crusade[1]. And there was that Blondiaux or Blondel de Nesle, the story of whose discovery of his captive master, apocryphal though it may be, is in all the history books[2]. Henry III had his *magister Henricus versificator* in 1251[3], and his *magister Ricardus citharista* in 1252[4]. A harper was also amongst the *ministri* of Prince Edward in the Holy War[5], and when the prince became Edward I, he still retained one in his service. He is mentioned as Walter de Stourton, the king's harper, in 1290[6], and as the *citharista regis* in 1300[7]. Edward II had several minstrels, to one of whom, William de Morlee, known as *Roy de North*, he made a grant of land[8]. By this time the royal minstrels seem to have become a regular establishment of no inconsiderable numbers. Under Edward III they received $7\frac{1}{2}d.$ a day[9]. A little later in the reign, between 1344 and 1347, there were nineteen who received $12d.$ a day in war, when they doubtless formed a military band, and $20s.$ a year in peace. These included five trumpeters, one citoler, five pipers, one tabouretter, two clarions, one nakerer, and one fiddler, together with three

Household as it existed up to 1782 (Hall, *Red Book of Exchequer*, R.S., iii. cclxxxvii, 807).

[1] Gautier, ii. 47, 54; G. Paris, § 88; Ambroise, *L'Estoire de la Guerre Sainte*, ed. G. Paris (*Documents inédits sur l'Hist. de France*, 1897).

[2] Percy, 358.

[3] Madox, *Hist. of Exchequer*, 268.

[4] Percy, 365.

[5] Walter Hemmingford, *Chronicon*, c. 35 (*Vet. Hist. Angl. Script.* ii. 591).

[6] Chappell, i. 15, from *Wardrobe Book*, 18 Edw. I.

[7] *Wardrobe Accounts of Edw. I* (Soc. Antiq.), 323.

[8] Anstis, *Register of Order of the Garter*, ii. 303, from *Pat. de terr. forisfact.* 16 Edw. III. Cf. *Gesta Edw. de Carnarvon* in *Chron. of Edw. I and II* (R. S.), ii. 91 'adhaesit cantoribus, tragoedis, aurigis, navigiis et aliis huiuscemodi artificiis mechanicis.'

[9] Strutt, 194; *Issue Roll of Thomas de Brantingham* (ed. Devon), 54–57, 296–8.

additional minstrels, known as waits[1]. The leader of the minstrels bore the title of *rex*, for in 1387 we find a licence given by Richard II to his *rex ministrallorum*, John Caumz, permitting him to pass the seas[2]. Henry V had fifteen minstrels when he invaded France in 1415, and at a later date eighteen, who received 12*d.* a day apiece[3]. At the end of his reign his minstrels received 100*s.* a year, and this annuity was continued under Henry VI, who in 1455 had twelve of them, besides a wait. In the next year this king issued a commission for the impressing of boys to fill vacancies in the body[4]. Edward IV had thirteen minstrels and a wait[5]. By 1469 these had been cut down to eight. At their head was a chief, who was now called, not as in Richard II's time *rex*, but *marescallus*[6]. The eight king's minstrels and their *marescallus* can be traced through the reign of Henry VII, and so on into the sixteenth century[7].

Nor was the royal household singular in the maintenance of a permanent body of minstrels. The *citharista* of Margaret, queen of Edward I, is mentioned in 1300, and her *istrio* in 1302[8]. Philippa, queen of Edward III, had her minstrels in 1337[9], and those of Queen Elizabeth were a regular establishment in the reign of Henry VII[10]. The Scottish court, too, had its recognized troupe, known by the early years of the sixteenth century as the 'minstrels of the chekkar[11].' As with kings and queens so with lesser men. The list of minstrels at court in 1306 includes the harpers and other musicians of several lords, both English and foreign[12]. In 1308 the earl of Lancaster had a body of *menestralli* and an *armiger menestrallorum*[13]. During

---

[1] *Household Ordinances*, 4, 11.
[2] Rymer, vii. 555.
[3] Ibid. ix. 255, 260, 336.
[4] Ibid. x. 287 ; xi. 375.
[5] *Household Ordinances*, 48.
[6] Rymer, xi. 642 ; cf. Appendix D.
[7] Ibid. xiii. 705 ; Collier, i. 45 ; Campbell, i. 407, 516, 570; ii. 100, 224.
[8] *Wardrobe Accounts of Edw. I* (Soc. Antiq.), 7, 95 ; *Calendar of Anc. Deeds*, ii. A, 2050, 2068, 2076.
[9] Strutt, 189.
[10] Collier, i. 46; Campbell, i. 407,

542, 572 ; ii. 68, 84, 176.
[11] The entry 'ad solvendum histrionibus' occurs in 1364 (*Compoti Camerarii Scot.* i. 422). The Exchequer Rolls from 1433–50 contain payments to the 'mimi,' 'histriones,' 'ioculatores regis'; and in 1507–8 for the 'histriones in scaccario' or 'minstrels of the chekkar' (*Accounts of Treasurer of Scotland*, i. xx, cxcix ; ii. lxxi).
[12] Cf. Appendix C.
[13] Collier, i. 21, from *Lansd. MS.* i.

the fourteenth and fifteenth centuries entries of payments to the minstrels of a vast number of *domini*, small and great, are common in the account books[1]. Henry, earl of Derby, took minstrels with him in his expeditions abroad of 1390 and 1392[2]; while the *Household Book* of the earl of Northumberland († 1512) shows that he was accustomed to entertain ' a Taberett, a Luyte, and a Rebecc,' as well as six 'trompettes[3].' Minstrels are also found, from the beginning of the fifteenth century, in the service of the municipal corporations. London, Coventry, Bristol, Shrewsbury, Norwich, Chester, York, Beverley, Leicester, Lynn, Canterbury had them, to name no others. They received fixed fees or dues, wore the town livery and badge of a silver scutcheon, played at all local celebrations and festivities, and were commonly known as *waits*[4]. This term we have already found in use at court, and the ' Black Book,' which contains the household regulations of Edward IV, informs us that the primary duty of a wait was to ' pipe the watch,' summer and winter, at certain fixed hours of the night[5].

It must not be supposed that established minstrels, whether royal, noble, or municipal, were always in constant attendance on their lords. Certain fixed services were required of them,

Two of this lord's *menestriers* were entertained by Robert of Artois, who also had his own (Guy, 154).

[1] Gautier, ii. 51 ; cf. the extracts from various *computi* in Appendix E. There are many entries also in the accounts of King's Lynn (*Hist. MSS.* xi. 3. 213) ; Beverley (Leach, *Beverley MSS.* 171), &c.

[2] L. T. Smith, *Derby Accounts* (C. S.), xcvi.

[3] Percy, *N. H. B.* 42, 344.

[4] Stowe, *Survey*, 39 (London) ; Smith, *English Guilds*, 423, 447 (Bristol, Norwich) ; Davies, 14 (York) ; Kelly, 131 (Leicester); Morris, 348 (Chester) ; Civis, No. xxi (Canterbury) ; Sharpe, 207 (Coventry) ; *Hist. MSS.* xi. 3. 163 (Lynn) ; Leach, *Beverley MSS.* 105, &c. (Beverley) ; for Shrewsbury cf. Appendix E. On *Waits' Badges*, cf. Ll. Jewitt, in *Reliquary*, xii. 145.

Gautier, ii. 57, describes the communal *cantorini* of Perugia, from the fourteenth to the sixteenth century. The usual Latin term for the Beverley waits is *speculatores* ; but they are also called *ministralli*, *histriones* and *mimi*. Apparently waits are intended by the *satrapi* of the Winchester Accounts (App. E. (iv)). Elsewhere *histriones* is the most usual term. The signatories to the 1321 statutes of the Paris guild include several *guètes* (Bernhard, iii. 402).

[5] *Household Ordinances*, 48 'A Wayte, that nyghtly, from Mighelmasse till Shere-Thursday, pipeth the watche within this courte fower tymes, and in the somer nyghtes three tymes.' He is also to attend the new Knights of the Bath when they keep watch in the chapel the night before they are dubbed.

which were not very serious, except in the case of waits[1]; for the rest of their time they were free. This same 'Black Book' of Edward IV is very explicit on the point. The minstrels are to receive a yearly fee and a livery[2]. They must attend at court for the five great feasts of the year. At other times, two or three out of their number, or more if the king desire it, are to be in waiting. The last regulation on the subject is curious. The king forbids his minstrels to be too presumptuous or familiar in asking rewards of any lord of the land; and in support of this he quotes a similar prohibition by the Emperor Henry II[3]. Doubtless, in the intervals of their services, the household minstrels

---

[1] The Lynn waits had to go through the town from All Saints to Candlemas. Those of Coventry had similar duties, and in 1467 were forbidden 'to pass this Cite but to Abbotts and Priors within x myles of this Cite.'

[2] The six minstrels of the Earl of Derby in 1391 had a livery of 'blod ray cloth and tanne facings' (Wylie, iv. 160).

[3] *Household Ordinances*, 48: 'Mynstrelles, xiii, whereof one is verger, that directeth them all in festivall dayes to theyre stations, to bloweings and pipynges, to suche offices as must be warned to prepare for the king and his houshold at metes and soupers, to be the more readie in all servyces ; and all these sittinge in the hall togyder ; whereof sume use trumpettes, sume shalmuse and small pipes, and sume as strengemen, comyng to this courte at five festes of the yere, and then to take theyre wages of houshold after iiij[d] ob. a day, if they be present in courte, and then they to avoyde the next day after the festes be done. Besides eche of them anothyr reward yerely, taking of the king in the resceyte of the chekker, and clothing wynter and somer, or xx[s] a piece, and lyverey in courte, at evyn amonges them all, iiij gallons ale ; and for wynter season, iij candels wax, vj candells peris', iiij talwood, and sufficiaunt logging by the herberger, for them and theyre horses, nygh to the courte. Also havyng into courte ij servauntes honest, to beare theyre trumpettes, pipes, and other instrumentes, and a torche for wynter nyghts, whyles they blowe to souper, and other revelles, delyvered at the chaundrey; and allway ij of these persons to continue in courte in wages, beyng present to warne at the kinge's rydinges, when he goeth to horse-backe, as ofte as it shall require, and by theyre blowinges the houshold meny may follow in the countries. And if any of these two minstrelles be sicke in courte, he taketh ij loves, one messe of grete mete, one gallon ale. They have no part of any rewardes gevyn to the houshold. And if it please the kinge to have ij strenge Minstrelles to contynue in like wise. The kinge wull not for his worshipp that his Minstrelles be too presumptuous, nor too familier to aske any rewardes of the lordes of his londe, remembring De Henrico secundo imperatore [1002 – 24] qui omnes Ioculatores suos et Armaturos monuerit, ut nullus eorum in eius nomine vel dummodo steterint in servicio suo nihil ab aliquo in regno suo deberent petere donandum ; sed quod ipsi domini donatores pro Regis amore citius pauperibus erogarent.'

travelled, like their unattached brethren of the road, but with the added advantage of a letter of recommendation from their lord, which ensured them the hospitality of his friends[1]. Such letters were indeed often given, both to the minstrels of a man's own household and as testimonials to other minstrels who may have especially pleased the giver. Those interesting collections of mediaeval epistolary formulae, the *summae dictaminis*, contain many models for them, and judging by the lavish eulogy which they employ, the minstrels themselves must have had a hand in drawing them up[2]. Many minstrels probably confined themselves to short tours in the vicinity of their head quarters; others, like Widsith, the Anglo-Saxon *scôp*, were far travellers. John Caums received a licence from Richard II to cross the seas, and in 1483 we find Richard III entertaining minstrels of the dukes of Austria and Bavaria[3]. Possibly the object of John Caumz was to visit one of the *scolae ministrallorum* in France, where experiences might be exchanged and new songs learnt. Beauvais, Lyon, Cambrai were famous for these schools, which were held year by year in Lent, when performances were stopped ; and the wardrobe accounts of Edward III record grants of licences and expenses to Barbor and Morlan, two bagpipers, to visit the *scolas ministrallis in partibus trans mare*[4].

---

[1] Percy, *N. H. B.* (†1512), 339. The king's shawms, if they came yearly, got 10s., the king's jugler and the king's or queen's bearward, 6s. 8d. ; a duke's or earl's trumpeters, if they came six together, also got 6s. 8d., an earl's minstrels only 3s. 4d. If the troupe came only once in two or three years, and belonged to a 'speciall Lorde, Friende, or Kynsman' of the earl, the rate was higher.

[2] Gautier, ii. 107, from *Bibl. de l'Arsenal MS.* 854; e.g. '*Deprecatio pro dono instrioni impendendo.* Salutem et amoris perpetui firmitatem. R. latorem praesentium, egregium instrionem qui nuper meis interfuit nuptiis, ubi suum officium exercuit eleganter, ad vos cum magna confidentia destinamus, rogantes precibus, quibus possu-mus, quatinus aliquid subsidium gracie specialis eidem impendere debeatis.' Collier, i. 42, gives a letter of Richard III for his bearward.

[3] Collier, i. 41.

[4] Strutt, 194 ; Gautier, ii. 173–8; H. Lavoix, ii. 198. They are called *Scolae ministrorum, Scolae mimorum.* They can be traced to the fourteenth century. Genève and Bourg-en-Bresse also had them. The Paris statutes of 1407 (cf. Appendix F) require a licence from the *roi des ménestrels* for such an assembly. A Beauvais *computus* (1402) has 'Dati sunt de gratia panes ducenti capitulares mimis in hac civitate de diversis partibus pro cantilenis novis addiscendis confluentibus.'

From the fourteenth century it is possible to trace the growth of the household minstrels as a privileged class at the expense of their less fortunate rivals. The freedom of access enjoyed by the entertainers of earlier days was obviously open to abuse. We have seen that in 1317 it led to the offering of an insult to Edward II by an emissary clad as a minstrel at his own table. It was only two years before that a royal proclamation had considerably restrained the liberty of the minstrels. In view of the number of idle persons who 'under colour of mynstrelsie' claimed food, drink, and gifts in private houses, it was ordered 'that to the houses of prelates earls and barons none resort to meate and drynke, unless he be a mynstrel, and of these mynstrels that there come none except it be three or four minstrels of honour at the most in one day, unlesse he be desired of the lorde of the house.' The houses of meaner men are to be altogether exempt, except at their desire[1]. I think it is probable that by 'minstrels of honour' we must here understand 'household minstrels[2]'; and that the severity of the ordinance must have come upon those irresponsible vagrants who had not the shelter of a great man's name. With the Statutes of Labourers in the middle of the fourteenth century begins a history of legislation against 'vacabonds and valiant beggars,' which put further and serious difficulties in the way of the free movement of the migratory classes through the country[3]. Minstrels, indeed, are not specifically declared to be 'vacabonds' until this legislation was codified by William Cecil in 1572[4]; but there is evidence that they were none

[1] Hearne, *Appendix ad Lelandi Collectanea*, vi. 36; Percy, 367. The proclamation is dated Aug. 6, 9 Edw. II (i. e. 1315).

[2] No technical term seems, however, intended in *Launfal* (ed. Ritson), 668 :
'They hadde menstrales of moch honours,
Fydelers, sytolyrs, and trompours.'

[3] C. J. Ribton-Turner, *Vagrants and Vagrancy*, chs. 3, 4, 5. The proclamation of 1284 against 'Westours, Bards, and Rhymers

and other idlers and vagabonds, who live on the gifts called Cymmortha,' and the Act of 1402 (4 *Hen. IV*, c. 27) in the same sense, seem only to refer to the Welsh bards (cf. p. 77).

[4] Ribton-Turner, 107 (14 *Eliz.* c. 5). Whipping is provided for 'all Fencers Bearewardes Comon Players in Enterludes & Minstrels, not belonging to any Baron of this Realme or towards any other honourable personage of greater Degree; all Juglers Pedlars Tynkers and Petye Chapmen; whiche

the less liable to be treated as such, unless they had some protection in the shape of livery or licence. At Chester from the early thirteenth century, and at Tutbury in Staffordshire from 1380, there existed courts of minstrelsy which claimed to issue licences to all performers within their purview. It is not probable that this jurisdiction was very effective. But a step taken by Edward IV in 1469 had for its avowed object to strengthen the hands of what may be called official minstrelsy. Representation had been made to the king that certain rude husbandmen and artificers had usurped the title and livery of his minstrels, and had thus been enabled to gather an illegitimate harvest of fees. He therefore created or revived a regular guild or fraternity of minstrels, putting his own household performers with their *marescallus* at the head of it, and giving its officers a disciplinary authority over the profession throughout the country, with the exception of Chester. It is not improbable, although it is not distinctly stated, that admission into the guild was practically confined to ' minstrels of honour.' Certainly one of the later local guilds which grew up in the sixteenth century, that of Beverley, limited its membership to such as could claim to be ' mynstrell to some man of honour or worship or waite of some towne corporate or other ancient town, or else of such honestye and conyng as shalbe thought laudable and pleasant to the hearers [1].' In any case the whole drift of social development was to make things difficult for the independent minstrels and to restrict the area of their wanderings.

The widespread popularity of the minstrels amongst the mediaeval laity, whether courtiers, burghers, or peasants, needs no further labouring. It is more curious to find that in spite of the formal anathemas of the Church upon their art, they were not, as a matter of fact, rigorously held at arm's length by the clergy. We find them taking a prominent part in the

said Fencers Bearewardes comon Players in Enterludes Mynstrels Juglers Pedlars Tynkers & Petye Chapmen, shall wander abroade and have not Lycense of two Justices of the Peace at the leaste, whereof one to be of the Quorum, wher and in what Shier they shall happen to wander.' The terms of 39 *Eliz.* c. 4 (1597–8) are very similar, but 1 *Jac. I*, c. 7 (1603–4), took away the exemption for noblemen's servants.

[1] Appendix F.

holyday festivities of religious guilds[1]; we find them solacing the slow progress of the pilgrimages with their ready wit and copious narrative or song[2]; we find them received with favour by bishops, even upon their visitations[3], and not excluded from a welcome in the hall of many a monastery. As early as 1180, one Galfridus, a *citharoedus*, held a 'corrody,' or right to a daily commons of food and drink in the abbey of Hyde at Winchester[4]. And payments for performances are frequent in the accounts of the Augustinian priories at Canterbury[5], Bicester, and Maxtoke, and the great Benedictine houses of Durham, Norwich, Thetford, and St. Swithin's, Winchester[6], and doubtless in those of many another cloistered retreat. The

[1] Gautier, ii. 156; Ducange, s.v. *Ministelli*.

[2] Gautier, ii. 158. Strutt, 195, quotes from *Cott. MS. Nero*, c. viii a payment of Edw. III 'ministrallo facienti ministralsiam suam coram imagine Beatae Mariae in Veltam, rege praesente.'. Chaucer's pilgrims had no professional minstrels, but the miller did as well:

'He was a janglere and a goliardeys, . . .
. . . A baggepype wel koude he blowe and sowne,
And therwithal he broghte us out of towne.'

It was in the absence of regular minstrels that the pilgrims fell to telling one another stories.

[3] Gautier, ii. 160. Richard Swinfield, bishop of Hereford, more than once rewarded minstrels on his episcopal rounds (J. Webb, *Household Expenses of Richard de Swinfield*, C. S. i. 152, 155). The bishops of Durham in 1355, Norwich in 1362, and Winchester in 1374, 1422, and 1481 had 'minstrels of honour,' like any secular noble (see Appendix E, &c.). Even the austere Robert Grosseteste had his private harper, if we may credit Mannyng, 150:

'He louede moche to here the harpe;
For mannys wyt hyt makyth sharpe.
Next hys chaumbre, besyde hys study,

Hys harpers chaumbre was fast therby.'

Mannyng represents Grosseteste as excusing his predilection by a reference to King David.

[4] Madox, *Hist. of Exchequer*, 251.

[5] *Norfolk Archaeology*, xi. 339 (Norwich); Hazlitt-Warton, ii. 97; Kennet, *Parochial Antiq.* ii. 259 (Bicester); *Decem Scriptores*, 2011 (Canterbury); for the rest cf. Appendix E.

[6] Hazlitt-Warton, ii. 97; iii. 118, quotes from the *Register* of St. Swithin's amongst the *Wolvesey MSS.*; in 1338 'cantabat ioculator quidam nomine Herebertus canticum Colbrondi, necdum gestum Emmae reginae a iudicio ignis liberatae, in aula prioris': in 1374 'In festo Alwynis episcopi . . . in aula conventus sex ministralli, cum quatuor citharisatoribus, faciebant ministralcias suas. Et post cenam, in magna camera arcuata domini Prioris, cantabant idem gestum . . . Veniebant autem dicti ioculatores a castello domini regis et ex familia episcopi.' The 'canticum Colbrondi' was doubtless a romance of Guy of Warwick, of which Winchester is the locality. Fragments of early fourteenth-century English versions exist (Ten Brink, i. 246; Jusserand, *E. L.* i. 224; Zupitza, *Guy of Warwick*, E. E. T. S.; G. L. Morrill, *Speculum Gy de Warewyke*, E. E. T. S. lxxxi).

Minorite chroniclers relate, how at the time of the coming of the friars in 1224 two of them were mistaken for minstrels by the porter of a Benedictine grange near Abingdon, received by the prior and brethren with unbecoming glee, and when the error was discovered, turned out with contumely[1]. At such semi-religious foundations also, as the college of St. Mary at Winchester, or Waynflete's great house of St. Mary Magdalen in Oxford, minstrels of all degrees found, at least by the fifteenth century, ready and liberal entertainment[2].

How, then, is one to reconcile this discrepancy between the actual practice of the monasteries and the strict, the uncompromising prohibition of minstrelsy in rule and canon? An incomplete answer readily presents itself. The monks being merely human, fell short of the ideal prescribed for them. We do not now learn for the first time, that the ambitions of the pious founder, the ecclesiastical law-giver, the patristic preacher, were one thing; the effective daily life of churchmen in many respects quite another. Here, as in matters of even more moment, did mediaeval monasticism 'dream from deed dissever'—

> 'The reule of Seint Maure or of Seint Beneit,
> By-cause that it was old and som-del streit
> This ilke monk leet olde thinges pace,
> And held after the newe world the space.'

True enough, but not the whole truth. It doubtless explains the behaviour of the Benedictines of Abingdon; but we can hardly suppose that when Robert de Grosseteste, the sworn enemy of ecclesiastical abuses, kept his harper's chamber next his own, he was surreptitiously allowing himself an illegitimate gratification which he denied to his clergy. The fact is that the condemnations of the Church, transferred, as we have seen, wholesale from the *mimi* and *histriones* of the decaying

---

[1] Bartholomaeus (Albizzi) de Pisis (1385–99), *Liber Conformitatum* (ed. 1590, i. 94[b]); Antoninus Episc. Florentiae (1389–1459), *Chronicon* (ed. 1586, iii. 752) 'alterius linguae ioculatores eos existimans'; cf. A. Wood, *Hist. et Antiq. Univ. Oxon.* (1674), i. 69; *City of Oxford* (O.H.S.), ii. 349.

[2] See Appendix E. At Paris the *Statutes* of Cornouaille College (1380) required abstinence from 'ludis mimorum, ioculatorum, histrionum, goliardorum, et consimilium.' Bulaeus, v. 782, gives another Paris regulation allowing 'mimi, ad summum duo' on Twelfth Night (Rashdall, ii. 674).

Empire, were honestly not applicable without qualification, even from the ecclesiastical point of view, to their successors, the *mimi* and *histriones* of the Middle Ages. The traditions of the Roman stage, its manners, its topics, its ethical code, became indeed a large part of the direct inheritance of minstrelsy. But, as we have seen, they were far from being the whole of that inheritance. The Teutonic as well as the Latin element in the civilization of western Europe must be taken into account. The minstrel derives from the disreputable *planipes*; he derives also from the *scôp*, and has not altogether renounced the very different social and ethical position which the *scôp* enjoyed. After all, nine-tenths of the secular music and literature, something even of the religious literature, of the Middle Ages had its origin in minstrelsy. Practically, if not theoretically, the Church had to look facts in the face, and to draw a distinction between the different elements and tendencies that bore a single name. The formularies, of course, continued to confound all minstrels under the common condemnation of *ioculatores*. The Church has never been good at altering its formularies to suit altered conditions. But it has generally been good at practical compromises. And in the case of minstrelsy, a practical compromise, rough enough, was easily arrived at.

The effective conscience of the thirteenth-century Church had clearly come to recognize degrees in the ethical status of the minstrels. No more authoritative exponent of the official morals of his day can be desired than St. Thomas Aquinas, and St. Thomas Aquinas is very far from pronouncing an unqualified condemnation of all secular entertainment. The profession of an *histrio*, he declares, is by no means in itself unlawful. It was ordained for the reasonable solace of humanity, and the *histrio* who exercises it at a fitting time and in a fitting manner is not on that account to be regarded as a sinner[1]. Another contemporary document is still more

---

[1] Thomas Aquinas, *Summa Theologiae* (†1274), ii. 2, quaest. 168, art. 3 'Sicut dictum est, ludus est necessarius ad conversationem vitae humanae. ad omnia autem, quae sunt utilia conversationi hu- manae, deputari possunt aliqua officia licita. et ideo etiam officium histrionum, quod ordinatur ad solatium hominibus exhibendum, non est secundum se illicitum, nec sunt in statu peccati: dummodo moderate

explicit. This is the *Penitential* written at the close of the thirteenth century by Thomas de Cabham, sub-dean of Salisbury and subsequently archbishop of Canterbury[1]. In the course of his analysis of human frailty, Thomas de Cabham makes a careful classification from the ethical point of view, of minstrels. There are those who wear horrible masks, or entertain by indecent dance and gesture. There are those again who follow the courts of the great, and amuse by satire and by raillery. Both these classes are altogether damnable. Those that remain are distinguished by their use of musical instruments. Some sing wanton songs at banquets. These too are damnable, no less than the satirists and posture-mongers. Others, however, sing of the deeds of princes, and the lives of the saints. To these it is that the name *ioculatores* more strictly belongs, and they, on no less an authority than that of Pope Alexander himself[2], may be tolerated.

Of the three main groups of minstrels distinguished by Thomas de Cabham, two correspond roughly to the two broad types which, from the point of view of racial tradition, we have already differentiated. His musicians correspond to the Teutonic gleemen and their successors ; his posture-mongers and buffoons to the Roman *mimi* and their successors.

ludo utantur, id est, non utendo aliquibus illicitis verbis vel factis ad ludum, et non adhibendo ludum negotiis et temporibus indebitis ... unde illi, qui moderate iis subveniunt, non peccant, sed iusta faciunt, mercedem ministerii eorum iis attribuendo. si qui autem superflue sua in tales consumunt, vel etiam sustentant illos histriones qui illicitis ludis utuntur, peccant, quasi eos in peccatis foventes. unde Augustinus dicit, *super Ioan.* quod *donare res suas histrionibus vitium est immane*,' &c., &c.

[1] Cf. Appendix G.
[2] Another version of this story is given by Petrus Cantor (ob. 1197), *Verbum Abbreviatum*, c. 84 (*P. L.* ccv. 254) 'Ioculatori cuidam papa Alexander (Alex. III) nec concessit vivere de officio suo, nec ei penitus interdixit.' In c. 49 of the same work Petrus Cantor inveighs learnedly *Contra dantes histrionibus*. Doubtless the Alexander in question is Alexander III (1159-81), though the (Alex. III) above may be due to the seventeenth-century editor, Galopinus. A hasty glance at the voluminous and practically unindexed decrees and letters of Alexander III in *P. L.* cc. and Jaffé, *Regesta Pontificum Romanorum* (ed. 2, 1885-8), ii. 145-418, has not revealed the source of the story ; and I doubt whether the Pope's decision, if it was ever given, is to be found in black and white. The two reports of it by Thomas de Cabham and Petrus Cantor are barely consistent. In any case, it never got into the Gregorian Decretals.

Who then are Thomas de Cabham's third and intermediate group, the satirists whose lampoons beset the courts of the great? Well, raillery and invective, as we have seen, were common features of minstrelsy; but Gautier may very likely be right when he surmises that Thomas de Cabham has particularly in mind the *scolares vagantes*, who brought so much scandal upon the Church during the twelfth and thirteenth centuries [1]. Some of these were actually out at elbows and disfrocked clerks; others were scholars drifting from university to university, and making their living meantime by their wits; most of them were probably at least in minor orders. But practically they lived the life of the minstrels, tramping the road with them, sharing the same temptations of wine, women, and dice, and bringing into the profession a trained facility of composition, and at least a flavour of classical learning [2]. They were indeed the main intermediaries between the learned and the vernacular letters of their day; the spilth of their wit and wisdom is to be found in the burlesque Latin verse of such collections as the *Carmina Burana*, riotous lines, by no means devoid of poetry, with their half-humorous half-pathetic burden,

'In taberna quando sumus
Non curamus quid sit humus [3].'

And especially they were satirists, satirists mainly of the hypocrisy, cupidity and evil living of those in the high places of the Church, for whom they conceived a grotesque expression in Bishop Golias, a type of materialistic prelate, in whose name they wrote and whose *pueri* or *discipuli* they declared themselves to be [4]. *Goliardi, goliardenses*, their reputation in

---

[1] Gautier, ii. 42; Bédier, 389; Ten Brink, i. 186; Ducange, s. vv. *Golia*, &c.; O. Hubatsch, *Lat. Vagantenlieder des Mittelalters* (1870).

[2] *Le Département des Livres* (Méon, *N. R.* i. 404):
'A Bouvines delez Dinant
Li perdi-je Ovide le grant . . .
Mon Lucan et mon Juvenal
Oubliai-je a Bonival,
Eustace le grant et Virgile
Perdi aus dez a Abeville.'

[3] The chief collections of goliardic verse are Schmeller, *Carmina Burana* (ed. 3, 1894), and T. Wright, *Latin Poems attributed to Walter Mapes* (C. S. 1841): for others cf. Hubatsch, 16. Latin was not unknown amongst lay minstrels: cf. *Deus Bordeors Ribauz* (Montaiglon-Raynaud, i. 3):
'Mais ge sai aussi bien conter,
Et en roumanz et en latin.'

[4] Hubatsch, 15. The origin, precise meaning, and mutual relations of the terms *Golias, goliardi*

the eyes of the ecclesiastical authorities was of the worst, and their ill practices are coupled with those of the minstrels in many a condemnatory decree [1].

It is not with the *goliardi* then, that Thomas de Cabham's relaxation of the strict ecclesiastical rigours is concerned. Neither is it, naturally enough, with the lower minstrels of the *mimus* tradition. Towards these Thomas de Cabham, like his predecessors, is inexorable. And even of the higher minstrels the musicians and singers, his toleration has its limits. He discriminates. In a sense, a social and professional sense, all these higher minstrels fall into the same class. But from the ethical point of view there is a very marked distinction amongst them. Some there are who haunt taverns and merry-

---

are uncertain. Probably the goliardic literature arose in France, rather than in England with Walter Mapes, the attribution to whom of many of the poems is perhaps due to a confusion of G[olias] with G[ualterus] in the MSS. Giraldus Cambrensis (ob. 1217), *Speculum Ecclesiae*, says 'Parasitus quidam Golias nomine nostris diebus gulositate pariter et leccacitate famosissimus . . . in papam et curiam Romanam carmina famosa . . . evomuit': but the following note points to a much earlier origin for Golias and his *pueri*, and this is upheld by W. Scherer, *Gesch. d. deutsch. Dichtung im* 11. *und* 12. *Jahrh.* 16.

[1] Early decrees forbidding the clergy to be *ioculatores* are given on p. 39. More precise is the order of Gautier of Sens († 913) in his *Constitutiones*, c. 13 (Mansi, xviii. 324) 'Statuimus quod clerici ribaldi, maxime qui dicuntur de familia Goliae, per episcopos, archidiaconos, officiales, et decanos Christianitatis, tonderi praecipiantur vel etiam radi, ita quod eis non remaneat tonsura clericalis: ita tamen quod sine periculo et scandalo ita fiant.' If Mansi's date is right, this precedes by three centuries the almost identical *Conc. of Rouen*, c. 8 (Mansi, xxiii. 215), and *Conc. of Castle Gonther* (Tours), c. 21 (Mansi,

xxiii. 237), both in 1231. Gautier, *Les Tropaires*, i. 186, dwells on the influence of the *goliardi* on the late and ribald development of the tropes, and quotes *Conc. of Treves* (1227), c. 9 (Mansi, xxiii. 33) 'praecipimus ut omnes sacerdotes non permittant trutannos et alios vagos scholares aut goliardos cantare versus super *Sanctus* et *Agnus Dei*.' On their probable share in the Feast of Fools cf. ch. xiv. For later legislation cf. Hubatsch, 14, 95, and the passage from the *Liber Sextus* of Boniface VIII on p. 39. It lasts to the *Conc. Frisingense* (1440) 'statuimus ne clerici mimis, ioculatoribus, histrionibus, buffonibus, galliardis, largiantur' (Labbe, xiii. 1286). By this time 'goliard' seems little more than a synonym for 'minstrel.' The 'mynstralle, a gulardous,' of Mannyng, 148, does not appear to be a clerk, while Chaucer's 'goliardeys' is the Miller (*C. T.* prol. 560). On the other hand, Langland's 'Goliardeys, a glotoun of wordes' (*Piers Plowman*, prol. 139), speaks Latin. Another name for the *goliardi* occurs in an *Epistola Guidonis S. Laurentii in Lucina Cardinalis*, xx (1266, Hartzheim, iii. 807) against 'vagi scolares, qui Eberdini vocantur,' and who 'divinum invertunt officium, unde laici scandalizantur.'

makings with loose songs of love and dalliance. These it is
not to be expected that the holy mother Church should in any
way countenance. Her toleration must be reserved for those
more reputable performers who find material for their verse
either in the life and conversation of the saints and martyrs
themselves, or at least in the noble and inspiring deeds of
national heroes and champions. Legends of the saints and
gests of princes: if the minstrels will confine themselves to
the celebration of these, then, secure in the pronouncement of
a pope, they may claim a hearing even from the devout. It
would be rash to assert that even the comparatively liberal
theory of Thomas de Cabham certainly justified in all cases
the practice of the monasteries. But it is at least noteworthy
that in several instances where the subjects of the minstrelsy
presented for the delectation of a cowled audience remain
upon record, they do fall precisely within the twofold definition which he lays down. At Winchester in 1338 the minstrel
Herbert sang the song of Colbrond (or Guy of Warwick), and
the gest of the miraculous deliverance of Queen Emma;
while at Bicester in 1432 it was the legend of the Seven
Sleepers of Ephesus that made the Epiphany entertainment
of the assembled canons.

If now we set aside the very special class of ribald *galiardi*,
and if we set aside also the distinction drawn by Thomas de
Cabham on purely ethical grounds between the minstrels of
the love-songs and the minstrels of saintly or heroic gest, the
net result is the twofold classification of higher and lower
minstrels already familiar to us. Roughly—it must always be
borne in mind how roughly—it corresponds on the one hand
to the difference between the Teutonic and the Roman tradition, on the other to the distinction between the established
'minstrel of honour' and his unattached rival of the road.
And there is abundant evidence that such a distinction was
generally present, and occasionally became acute, in the consciousness of the minstrels themselves. The aristocrats of
minstrelsy, a Baudouin or a Jean de Condé, or a Watriquet de
Couvin, have very exalted ideas as to the dignity of their
profession. They will not let you, if they can help it, put the
grans menestreus on the same level with every-day *jang-*

leur of poor attainments and still poorer repute[1]. In the *Dit des Taboureurs* again it is a whole class, the *joueurs de vielle*, who arise to vindicate their dignity and to pour scorn upon the humble and uninstructed drummers[2]. But the most instructive and curious evidence comes from Provence. It was in 1273, when the amazing growth of Provençal poetry was approaching its sudden decay, that the last of the great troubadours, Guiraut de Riquier, addressed a verse *Supplicatio* to Alphonso X of Castile on the state of minstrelsy. He points out the confusion caused by the indiscriminate grouping of poets, singers, and entertainers of all degrees under the title of *joglars*, and begs the king, as high patron of letters, to take order for it. A reply from Alphonso, also in verse, and also, one may suspect, due to the fertile pen of Guiraut Riquier, is extant. Herein he establishes or confirms a fourfold hierarchy. At the head come two classes, the *doctors de trobar* and the *trobaires*, who are composers, the former of didactic, the latter of ordinary songs and melodies. Beneath these are the *joglars* proper, instrumentalists and reciters of delightful stories, and beneath these again the *bufos*, the entertainers of common folk, who have really no claim to be considered as *joglars* at all[3]. One of the distinctions here made is new to us. The difference between *doctor de trobar* and *trobaire* is perhaps negligible. But that between the *trobaire*

---

[1] Baudouin de Condé in his *Contes des Hiraus* contrasts the 'grans menestreus,' the
'Maistres de sa menestrandie,
Qui bien viele ou ki bien die
De bouce'
with the 'felons et honteux,' who win pence,
'l'un por faire l'ivre,
L'autre le cat, le tiers le sot,'
while in *Les États du Monde* his son Jean sets up a high standard of behaviour for the true minstrels :
'Soies de cuer nes et polis,
Courtois, envoisiés, et jolis,
Pour les boinnes gens solacier'
(Scheler, *Dits et Contes de Baudouin de Condé et de son fils Jean de Condé*, i. 154; ii. 377). Cf. Watriquet de Couvin, *Dis du fol menestrel* (ed. Scheler, 367) :

'Menestriex se doit maintenir
Plus simplement c'une pucele, . . .
Menestrel qui veut son droit faire
Ne doit le jangleur contrefaire,
Mais en sa bouche avoir tous dis
Douces paroles et biaus dis,
Estre nés, vivre purement.'
These three writers belong to the end of the thirteenth and the beginning of the fourteenth century.

[2] A. Jubinal, *Jongleurs et Trouvères*, 165. Cf. Gautier, ii. 78; Bédier, 418.

[3] F. Diaz, *Poesie der Troubadours* (ed. Bartsch), 63; K. Bartsch, *Grundriss der provenzalischen Literatur*, 25; F. Hueffer, *The Troubadours*, 63. Diaz, *op. cit.* 297, prints the documents.

or composer and the *joglar* or executant of poetry, is an important one. It is not, however, so far as the Teutonic element in minstrelsy goes, primitive. The *scôpas* and the French or Anglo-Norman *ioculatores* up to the twelfth century composed their verses as a class, and sang them as well[1]. In Provence, however, the Teutonic element in minstrelsy must have been of the slightest, and perhaps the Roman tradition, illustrated by the story of Laberius, of a marked barrier between composing and executing, had vaguely lingered. At any rate it is in Provence, in the eleventh century, that the distinction between *trobaire* and *joglar* makes its appearance. It never became a very complete one. The *trobaire* was generally, not always, of gentle or burgess birth ; sometimes actually a king or noble. In the latter case he contented himself with writing his songs, and let the *joglars* spread them abroad. But the bulk of the *trobaires* lived by their art. They wandered from castle to castle, alone with a *vielle*, or with *joglars* in their train, and although they mingled with their hosts on fairly equal terms, they did not disdain to take their rewards of horse or mantle or jewel, just like any common performer. Moreover, they confined themselves to lyric poetry, leaving the writing of epic, so far as epic was abroad in Provence, to the *joglars*[2]. From Provence, the *trobaire* spread to other countries, reappearing in the north of France and England as the *trouvère*. We seem to trace an early *trouvère* in Lucas de Barre in the time of Henry I. But it is Eleanor of Poitiers, daughter of the *trobaire* count William of Poitiers, and mother of the *trouvère* Richard Cœur de Lion, who appears as the chief intermediary between north and south. The intrusion of the *trouvère* was the first step in the degradation of minstrelsy. Amongst the Anglo-Saxons, even apart from the *cantilenae* of the folk, the professional singer had no monopoly of song. Hrothgar and Alfred harped with their *scôpas*. But if there had been a similar tendency amongst the

---

[1] There is nothing to show that Scilling, the companion of Widsith (*Widsith*, 104), was of an inferior grade.

[2] Hueffer, 52 ; G. Paris, 182 : A. Stimming in Grober's *Grundriss*, ii. 2. 15 ; Gautier, ii. 45, 58. The commonest of phrases in troubadour biography is 'cantet et trobet.' The term *trobador* is properly the accusative case of *trobaire*.

continental Teutons who merged in the French and Norman-French, it had been checked by the complete absorption of all literary energies, outside the minstrel class, in neo-Latin. It was not until the twelfth century, and as has been said, under Provençal influence, that secular-minded clerks, and exceptionally educated nobles, merchants, or officials, began to devote themselves to the vernacular, and by so doing to develop the *trouvère* type. The *trouvère* had the advantage of the minstrel in learning and independence, if not in leisure ; and though the latter long held his own by the side of his rival, he was fated in the end to give way, and to content himself with the humbler task of spreading abroad what the *trouvère* wrote [1]. By the second quarter of the fourteenth century, the conquest of literature by the *bourgeoisie* was complete. The interest had shifted from the minstrel on the hall floor to the burgher or clerk in the *puy* ; the prize of a successful poem was no longer a royal mantle, but a laureate crown or the golden violet of the *jeux floraux* ; and its destiny less to be recited at the banquet, than read in the bower. In England the completion of the process perhaps came a little later, and was coincident with the triumph of English, the tongue of the *bourgeois*, over French, the tongue of the noble. The full flower of minstrelsy had been the out-at-elbows vagabond, Rutebeuf. The full flower of the *trouvère* is the comptroller of the customs and subsidies of the port of London, Geoffrey Chaucer.

The first distinction, then, made by Guiraut Riquier, that between *trobaire* and *joglar*, implies a development from within minstrelsy itself that was destined one day to overwhelm it. But the second, that between the *joglar* and the *bufo*, is precisely the one already familiar to us, between the minstrels of the

---

[1] Petrarch, *Epist. Rerum Senil.* v. 3 ' sunt homines non magni ingenii, magnae vero memoriae, magnaeque diligentiae, sed maioris audaciae, qui regum ac potentum aulas frequentant, de proprio nudi, vestiti autem carminibus alienis, dumque quid ab hoc, aut ab illo exquisitius materno praesertim charactere dictum sit, ingenti expressione pronunciant, gratiam sibi nobilium, et pecunias quaerunt, et vestes et munera.' Fulke of Marseilles, afterwards bishop of Toulouse, wrote songs in his youth. He became an austere Cistercian ; but the songs had got abroad, and whenever he heard one of them sung by a *joglar*, he would eat only bread and water (*Sermo* of Robert de Sorbonne in Hauréau, *Man. Fr.* xxiv. 2. 286).

scôp and the minstrels of the *mimus* tradition. And, as has been said, it is partly, if not entirely, identical with that which grew up in course of time between the protected minstrels of the court and of great men's houses, and their vagrant brethren of the road. This general antithesis between the higher and lower mintrelsy may now, perhaps, be regarded as established. It was the neglect of it, surely, that led to that curious and barren logomachy between Percy and Ritson, in which neither of the disputants can be said to have had hold of more than a bare half of the truth[1]. And it runs through the whole history of minstrelsy. It became acute, no doubt, with the growth in importance of the minstrels of honour in the thirteenth and fourteenth centuries. But it had probably been just as acute, if not more so, at the very beginning of things, when the clash of Teutonic and Roman civilization first brought the bard face to face with the serious rivalry of the mime. Bard and mime merged without ever becoming quite identical; and even at the moment when this process was most nearly complete, say in the eleventh century, the *jouglerie seigneuriale*, to use Magnin's happy terms, was never quite the same thing as the *jouglerie foraine et populaire*[2], least of all in a country like England where differences of tongue went to perpetuate and emphasize the breach.

Nevertheless, the antithesis may easily be pushed too far. After all, the minstrels were entertainers, and therefore their business was to entertain. Did the lord yawn over a gest or a saintly legend? the discreet minstrel would be well advised to

---

[1] In the first edition of his *Reliques* (1765), Percy gave the mediaeval minstrel as high a status as the Norse *scald* or Anglo-Saxon *scôp*. This led to an acrid criticism by Ritson who, in his essay *On the ancient English Minstrels* in *Ancient Songs and Ballads* (1829), easily showed the low repute in which many minstrels were held. See also his elaborate *Dissertation on Romance and Minstrelsy* in his *Ancient English Metrical Romances* (1802). The truth really lay between the two, for neither appreciated the wide variety covered by a common name. On the controversy, cf. Minto in *Enc. Brit.* s. v. *Minstrels*, Courthope, i. 426–31, and H. B. Wheatley's Introduction to his edition of Percy's *Reliques*, xiii–xv. Percy in his later editions profited largely by Ritson's criticism; a careful collation of these is given in Schroer's edition (1889).

[2] Magnin, *Journal des Savants* (1846), 545.

drop high art, and to substitute some less exacting, even if less refined fashion of passing the time. The instincts of boor and baron were not then, of course, so far apart as they are nowadays. And as a matter of fact we find many of the most eminent minstrels boasting of the width and variety of their accomplishments. Thus of Baudouin II, count of Guisnes (1169–1206), it is recorded that he might have matched the most celebrated professionals, not only in *chansons de gestes* and *romans d'aventure* but also in the *fabliaux* which formed the delight of the vulgar *bourgeoisie*[1]. Less aristocratic performers descended even lower than Baudouin de Guisnes. If we study the répertoires of such *jougleurs* as the diabolic one in Gautier de Coincy's miracle[2], or Daurel in the romance of *Daurel et Beton*[3], or the disputants who vaunt their respective proficiencies in *Des Deus Bordeors Ribauz*[4], we shall find that they cover not only every conceivable form of minstrel literature proper, but also tricks with knives and strings, sleight of hand, dancing and tumbling. Even in Provence, the *Enseignamens* for *joglars* warn their readers to learn the arts of imitating birds, throwing knives, leaping through hoops, showing off performing asses and dogs, and dangling marionettes[5]. So that

---

[1] Lambertus Ardensis, *Chronicon*, c. 81 (ed. Godefroy Menilglaise, 175) ' quid plura? tot et tantorum ditatus est copia librorum ut Augustinum in theologia, Areopagitam Dionysium in philosophia, Milesium fabularium in naeniis gentium, in cantilenis gestoriis, sive in eventuris nobilium, sive etiam in fabellis ignobilium, ioculatores quosque nominatissimos aequiparare putaretur.'

[2] Freymond, *Jongleurs et Menestrels*, 34:
' Il est de tout bons menesterieux :
Il set peschier, il set chacier,
Il set trop bien genz solacier ;
Il set chançons, sonnez et fables,
Il set d'eschez, il set des tables,
Il set d'arbalestre et d'airon.'

[3] *Daurel et Beton* (ed. Meyer, *Soc. des anc. textes fr.* 1886), 1206:
' El va enant, a lor des jocz mostratz,
Dels us e dels altres, qu'el ne sap pro asatz.

Pueis pres l[a] arpa, a .ij. laisses notatz,
Et ab la viola a los gen deportat[z],
Sauta e tomba ; tuh s'en son alegratz.'

[4] Montaiglon-Raynaud, i. 1 :
' Ge sai contes, ge sai flabeax ;
Ge sai conter beax dix noveax,
Rotruenges viez et noveles,
Et sirventois et pastorels.
Ge sai le flabel du Denier,

.   .   .   .   .

Si sai de Parceval l'estoire,

.   .   .   .   .

Ge sai joer des baasteax,
Et si sai joer des costeax,
Et de la corde et de la fonde,
Et de toz les beax giex du monde,

.   .   .   .   .

De totes les chansons de geste.'

[5] Three of these *Enseignamens*, by Guiraut de Cabreira († 1170), Guiraut de Calanso († 1200), and Bertran de Paris († 1250), are

one discerns the difference between the lower and the higher minstrels to have been not so much that the one did not sink so low, as that the other, for lack of capacity and education, did not rise so high.

The palmy days of minstrelsy were the eleventh, twelfth and thirteenth centuries. The germ of decay, however, which appeared when the separation grew up between *trouvère* and *jougleur*, and when men began to read books instead of listening to recitations, was further developed by the invention of printing. For then, while the *trouvère* could adapt himself readily enough to the new order of things, the *jougleur's* occupation was gone. Like Benedick he might still be talking, but nobody marked him. Eyes cast down over a page of Chaucer or of Caxton had no further glitter or tear for him to win [1]. The fifteenth, and still more the sixteenth century, witness the complete break-up of minstrelsy in its mediaeval form. The mimes of course endured. They survived the overthrow of mediaevalism, as they had survived the overthrow of the Empire [2]. The Tudor kings and nobles had still their jugglers, their bearwards, their domestic buffoons, jesters or fools [3]. Bearbaiting in Elizabethan London rivalled the drama in its vogue. Acrobats and miscellaneous entertainers never ceased to crowd to every fair, and there is applause even to-day in

printed by K. Bartsch, *Denkmäler der provenzalischen Litteratur*, 85–101. Cf. Bartsch, *Grundriss der prov. Lit.* 25 ; Hueffer, *The Troubadours*, 66 ; *Hist. Litt.* xvii. 581.

[1] Bernhard, iii. 397, gives some French references, one dated 1395, for 'menestriers de bouches,' a term signifying minstrels who sang as well as played instruments.

[2] There are numerous payments to jugglers, tumblers and dancers in the Household Accounts of Henry VII (Bentley, *Excerpta Historica*, 85–113 ; Collier, i. 50). A letter to Wolsey of July 6, 1527, from R. Croke, the tutor of Henry VIII's natural son, the Duke of Richmond, complains of difficulties put in his way by R. Cotton, the Clerk-comptroller of the duke's household, and

adds : ' At hic tamen in praeceptore arcendo diligens, libenter patitur scurras et mimos (qui digna lupanari in sacro cubiculo coram principe cantillent)admitti' (Nichols,*Memoir of Henry Fitzroy* in *Camden Miscellany*, iii. xxxviii).

[3] For the *ioculator regis*, cf. Appendix E, and Leach,*Beverley MSS.* 179. He is called 'jugler' in *N.H.B.* 67. Is he distinct from the royal *gestator* (*gestour, jester*) ? Both appear in the Shrewsbury accounts (s. ann. 1521, 1549). In 1554 both *le jugler* and *le gester* were entertained. The *gestator* seems to have merged in the *stultus* or court fool (ch. xvi). The accounts in App. E often mention the royal bearward, who remained an important official under Elizabeth.

circus and music-hall for the old jests and the old somersaults that have already done duty for upwards of twenty centuries. But the *jougleur* as the thirteenth century knew him was by the sixteenth century no more. Professional musicians there were in plenty ; 'Sneak's noise' haunted the taverns of Eastcheap [1], and instrumentalists and vocalists in royal palaces and noble mansions still kept the name and style of minstrels. But they were not minstrels in the old sense, for with the production of literature, except perhaps for a song here and there, they had no longer anything to do. That had passed into other hands, and even the lineaments of the *trouvère* are barely recognizable in the new types of poets and men of letters whom the Renaissance produced. The old fashioned minstrel in his style and habit as he lived, was to be presented before Elizabeth at Kenilworth as an interesting anachronism [2]. Some of the discarded entertainers, as we shall see, were absorbed into the growing profession of stage-players ; others sunk to be ballad singers. For to the illiterate the story-teller still continued to appeal. The ballad indeed, at least on one side of it, was the *detritus*, as the *lai* had been the germ, of romance [3], and at the very moment when Spenser was reviving romance as a conscious archaism, it was still possible for a blind fiddler with a ballad to offend the irritable susceptibilities of a Puritan, or to touch the sensitive heart-strings of a Sidney [4]. But as a social and literary force, the glory of minstrelsy had departed [5].

[1] *2 Hen. IV*, ii. 4. 12.

[2] Cf. Appendix H (i).

[3] Courthope, i. 445 ; A. Lang, s.v. *Ballad* in *Enc. Brit.* and in *A Collection of Ballads*, xi ; *Quarterly Review* (July, 1898) ; Henderson, 335 ; G. Smith, 180. But I think that Gummere, *B.P. passim*, succeeds in showing that the element of folk-poetry in balladry is stronger than some of the above writers recognize.

[4] Sidney, *Apologie for Poetrie* (ed. Arber), 46 'Certainly I must confess my own barbarousness. I never heard the old song of *Percy and Douglas*, that I found not my heart moved more than with a trumpet. And yet is it sung but by some blind Crowder, with no rougher voice than rude style.' For the Puritan view, see Stubbes, i. 169.

[5] Ritson, ccxxiv, quotes the following lines, ascribed to Dr. Bull († 1597), from a *Harl. MS.*, as the epitaph of minstrelsy :

'When Jesus went to Jairus' house
   (Whose daughter was about to dye),
He turned the minstrels out of doors,
   Among the rascal company :
Beggars they are, with one consent,
And rogues, by Act of Parliament.'

CHAPTER IV

THE MINSTREL REPERTORY

THE floor of a mediaeval court, thronged with minstrels of every degree, provided at least as various an entertainment as the Roman stage itself [1]. The performances of the mimes, to the accompaniment of their despised tabor or wry-necked fife, undoubtedly made up in versatility for what they lacked in decorum. There were the *tombeors, tombesteres* or *tumbleres*, acrobats and contortionists, who twisted themselves into incredible attitudes, leapt through hoops, turned somersaults, walked on their heads, balanced themselves in perilous positions. Female tumblers, *tornatrices*, took part in these feats, and several districts had their own characteristic modes of tumbling, such as *le tour français, le tour romain, le tour de Champenois* [2].' Amongst the *tombeors* must be reckoned the rarer *funambuli*

---

[1] *Du Vilain au Buffet* (Mont-aiglon-Raynaud, iii. 202) :
  ' Li quens manda les menestrels,
  Et si a fet crier entr'els
  Qui la meillor truffe sauroit
  Dire ne fere, qu'il auroit
  Sa robe d'escarlate nueve.
  L'uns menestrels a l'autre rueve
  Fere son mestier, tel qu'il sot,
  L'uns fet l'ivre, l'autre le sot ;
  Li uns chante, li autres note,
  Et li autres dit la riote,
  Et li autres la jenglerie ;
  Cil qui sevent de jouglerie
  Vielent par devant le conte ;
  Aucuns i a qui fabliaus conte,
  Où il ot mainte gaberie,
  Et li autres dit l'*Erberie*,
  Là où il ot mainte risée.'
Cf. p. 67 ; also the similar list in Wace, *Brut*, 10823, and *Piers Plowman*, Passus xvi. 205 :
  ' Ich can nat tabre ne trompe · ne
    telle faire gestes,
  Farten, ne fithelen · at festes, ne
    harpen,
  Iapen ne iogelen · ne gentel-
    liche pipe,
  Nother sailen ne sautrien · ne
    singe with the giterne.'
[2] Gautier, ii. 63 ; Strutt, 207. L. T. Smith, *Derby Accounts* (Camden Soc.), 109, records a payment by Henry of Bolingbroke when in Prussia in 1390–1 'cuidam tumblere facienti ministralciam suam.' See miniatures of tumblers (Strutt, 211, 212), stilt-dancing (ibid. 226), hoop-vaulting (ibid. 229), balancing (ibid. 232–4), a contortionist (ibid. 235).

or rope-walkers, such as he whom the Corvei annals record to have met with a sorry accident in the twelfth century[1], or he who created such a *furore* in the thirteenth by his aerial descent from the cathedral at Basle[2]. Nor are they very distinct from the crowd of dancers, male and female, who are variously designated as *saltatores* and *saltatrices*, ' sautours,' ' sailyours,' ' hoppesteres.' Indeed, in many mediaeval miniatures, the daughter of Herodias, dancing before Herod, is represented rather as tumbling or standing on her head than in any more subtle pose[3]. A second group includes the jugglers in the narrower sense, the *jouers des costeax* who tossed and caught knives and balls[4], and the practitioners of sleight of hand, who generally claimed to proceed by *nigremance* or sorcery[5]. The two seem to have shared the names of *prestigiatores* or *tregetours*[6]. Other mimes, the *bastaxi*, or *jouers des basteax*, brought round, like the Punch and Judy men of our own day, little wooden performing puppets or marionettes[7]. Others, to whom Thomas de Cabham more particularly refers, came in masked as animals, and played the dog, the ass or the bird with appropriate noises and behaviour[8].

---

[1] *Annales Corbeienses*, s. a. 1135 (Leibnitz, *Rer. Brunsv. Script.* ii. 307) ' funambulus inter lusus suos in terram deiectus.'

[2] Gautier, ii. 64, quotes *Annales Basilienses*, s.a. 1276 ' Basileam quidam corpore debilis venit, qui funem protensum de campanili maioris ecclesiae ad domum cantoris manibus et pedibus descendebat ' ; for later English examples cf. ch. xxiv.

[3] Strutt, 172, 176, 209; Jusserand, i. 214, and *E. W. L.* 23.

[4] Strutt, 173, 197; Jusserand, *E. W. L.* 212 ; Wright, 33-7.

[5] Gautier, ii. 67, quotes *Joufrois*, 1146:
'Ainz veïssiez toz avant traire
Les jogleors et maint jou faire.
Li uns dançoit . . .
Li autre ovrent de nigremance.'

[6] Strutt, 194, quotes from Cott. MS. *Nero*, c. viii, a payment ' Janins le Cheveretter (bagpiper) called le Tregettour,' for playing

before Edw. II. Collier, i. 30, quotes Lydgate, *Daunce de Macabre* (Harl. 116):
' Maister John Rykell, sometyme tregitoure
Of noble Henry kynge of Englonde,
And of Fraunce the myghty conqueroure,
For all the sleightes and turnyngs of thyne honde,
Thou must come nere this daunce to understonde.

.   .   .   .   .

Lygarde de mayne now helpeth me right nought.'

[7] Ducange, s. v. *bastaxi*; Gautier, ii. 11; C. Magnin, *Hist. des Marionnettes en Europe* (ed. 2, 1862); cf. ch. xxiv. *Bastaxus* seems to be the origin of the modern *bateleur*, used in a wide sense of travelling entertainers.

[8] Du Méril, *Com.* 74; Strutt, 253; Jusserand, *E. W. L.* vi. 218. Amongst the letters commendatory

Others, again, led round real animals ; generally bears or apes, occasionally also horses, cocks, hares, dogs, camels and even lions[1]. Sometimes these beasts did tricks ; too often they were baited[2], and from time to time a man, lineal descendant of the imperial gladiators, would step forward to fight with them[3]. To the gladiatorial shows may perhaps also be traced the fight with wooden swords which often formed a part of the fun.[4] And, finally, whatever the staple of the performance, there was the *parade* or preliminary patter to call the audience together, and throughout the ' carping,' a continuous flow of rough witticism and repartee, such as one is accustomed to hear Joey, the clown, in the pauses of a circus, pass off on Mr. Harris, the ring-master[5]. Here came in the especial talents of the *scurra*, *bordcor* or *japere*, to whom the moralists took such marked exception. ' *L'uns fet l'ivre, l'autre le sot*,' says the *fabliau* ; and indeed we do not need the testimony of Thomas de Cabham or of John of Salisbury to conclude that such buffoonery was likely to be of a ribald type[6].

Even in the high places of minstrelsy there was some measure of variety. A glance at the pay-sheet of Edward I's

of minstrels quoted by Gautier, ii. 109, is one 'De illo qui scit volucrum exprimere cantilenas et voces asininas.' Baudouin de Condé mentions a minstrel who 'fait le cat' (cf. p. 63, n. 1).

[1] See figures of bears (Strutt, 176, 214, 239, 240), apes (ibid. 240, 241 ; Jusserand, *E. W. L.* 218), horses (Strutt, 243, 244), dog (ibid. 246, 249), hare (ibid. 248), cock (ibid. 249). For the *ursarius* and for lion, marmoset, &c., cf. pp. 53, 68, and Appendix E.

[2] Strutt, 256. A horse-baiting is figured in Strutt, 243.

[3] Strutt, 244; figures a combat between man and horse. Gautier, ii. 66, cites *Acta SS. Jan.* iii. 257 for the intervention of St. Poppo when a naked man smeared with honey was to fight bears before the emperor Henry IV († 1048).

[4] Strutt, 260, 262.

[5] *Adam Davie* († 1312):
' Merry it is in halle to here the harpe,

The minstrelles synge, the jogelours carpe.'

[6] John of Salisbury, *Polycraticus*, i. 8 ' Quorum adeo error invaluit, ut a praeclaris domibus non arceantur, etiam illi qui obscenis partibus corporis oculis omnium eam ingerunt turpitudinem, quam erubescat videre vel cynicus. Quodque magis mirere, nec tunc eiiciuntur, quando tumultuantes inferius crebro sonitu aerem foedant, et turpiter inclusum turpius produnt'; Adam of Bremen (*M. G. H.*), iii. 38 'Pantomimi, qui obscoenis corporis motibus oblectare vulgus solent.' Raine, *Hist. Papers from Northern Registers* (R. S.), 398, prints a letter of Archbishop Zouche of York on the indecent behaviour of some clerks of the bishop of Durham in York Minster on Feb. 6, 1349, ' subtus imaginem crucifixi ventositates per posteriora dorsi cum foedo strepitu more ribaldorum emittere fecerunt pluries ac turpiter et sonore.'

Whitsuntide feast will show that the minstrels who aspired to be musicians were habitually distinguished by the name of the musical instrument on which they played. They are *vidulatores, citharistae, trumpatores, vilours, gigours, crouderes, harpours, citolers, lutours, trumpours, taboreurs* and the like. The harp (*cithara*), played by twitching the strings, had been the old instrument of the Teutons, but in the Middle Ages it came second in popularity to the *vielle* (*vidula*), which was also a string instrument, but, like the modern fiddle, was played with a bow. The drum (*tympanum, tabour*) was, as we have seen, somewhat despised, and relegated to the mimes. The trumpeters appear less often singly than in twos and threes, and it is possible that their performances may have been mainly ceremonial and of a purely instrumental order. But the use of music otherwise than to accompany the voice does not seem to have gone, before the end of the thirteenth century, much beyond the signals, flourishes and fanfares required for wars, triumphs and processions. Concerted instrumental music was a later development [1]. The ordinary function of the harp or *vielle* in minstrelsy was to assist the voice of the minstrel in one of the many forms of poetry which the middle ages knew. These were both lyric and narrative. The distinction is roughly parallel to that made by Thomas de Cabham when he subdivides his highest grades of minstrels into those who sing wanton songs at taverns, and those more properly called *ioculatores* who solace the hearts of men with reciting the deeds of the heroes and the lives of the saints. The themes of mediaeval lyric, as of all lyric, are largely wantonness and wine ; but it must be borne in mind that Thomas de Cabham's classification is primarily an ethical one, and does not necessarily imply any marked difference of professional status between the two classes. The haunters of taverns and the solacers of the virtuous were after all the same minstrels, or at least minstrels of the same order. That the *chansons*, in their innumerable varieties, caught up from folk-song, or devised by Provençal ingenuity, were largely in the mouths of the minstrels, may be taken for granted. It was here,

[1] Gautier, ii. 69; Lavoix, *La Musique au Siècle de Saint-Louis*, i. 315; cf. Appendix C.

however, that the competition of *trobaire* and *trouvère* began
earliest, and proved most triumphant, and the supreme minstrel
genre was undoubtedly the narrative. This was, in a sense,
their creation, and in it they held their own, until the laity
learned to read and the *trouvères* became able to eke out the
shortness of their memories by writing down or printing their
stories. With narrative, no doubt, the minstrels of highest
repute mainly occupied themselves. Harp or *vielle* in hand
they beguiled many a long hour for knight and *châtelaine* with
the interminable *chansons de gestes* in honour of Charlemagne
and his heroic band [1], or, when the vogue of these waned, as in
time it did, with the less primitive *romans d'aventure*, of which
those that clustered round the Keltic Arthur were the widest
famed. Even so their repertory was not exhausted. They had
lais, *dits* and *contes* of every kind ; the devout *contes* that
Thomas de Cabham loved, historical *contes*, romantic *contes*
of less alarming proportions than the genuine *romans*. And
for the *bourgeoisie* they had those improper, witty *fabliaux*, so
racy of the French soil, in which the *esprit gaulois*, as we know
it, found its first and not its least characteristic expression.
In most of these types the music of the instrument bore its
part. The shorter *lais* were often accompanied musically
throughout [2]. The longer poems were delivered in a chant or
recitative, the monotony of which was broken at intervals by
a phrase or two of intercalated melody, while during the rest
of the performance a few perfunctory notes served to sustain
the voice [3]. And at times, especially in the later days of
minstrelsy, the harp or *vielle* was laid aside altogether, and the
singer became a mere story-teller. The antithesis, no infrequent
one, between minstrel, and *fabulator, narrator, fableor, conteor,*

---

[1] W. Mapes, *de Nugis Curia-
lium* (Camden Soc.), dist. v. prol.,
' Caesar Lucani, Aeneas Maronis,
multis vivunt in laudibus, plurimum
suis meritis et non minimum vigi-
lantia poetarum ; nobis divinam
Karolorum et Pepinorum nobilita-
tem vulgaribus rithmis sola mimorum concelebrat nugacitas.'
[2] Lavoix, ii. 295.
[3] Ibid. ii. 344. The Paris MS.

(*B. N.* f. fr. 2168) of *Aucassin et
Nicolete* preserves the musical
notation of the verse sections. Only
three musical phrases, with very
slight variations, are used. Two of
these were probably repeated, alternately or at the singer's fancy,
throughout the tirade; the third
provided a cadence for the closing line (Bourdillon, *Aucassin et
Nicolette* (1897), 157).

gestour, disour, segger, though all these are themselves elsewhere classed as minstrels, sufficiently suggests this [1]. It was
principally, one may surmise, the *dits* and *fabliaux* that lent
themselves to unmusical narration ; and when prose crept in,
as in time it did, even before reading became universal, it can
hardly have been sung. An interesting example is afforded
by *Aucassin et Nicolete,* which is what is known as a *cante-
fable.* That is to say, it is written in alternate sections of
verse and prose. The former have, in the Paris manuscript,
a musical accompaniment, and are introduced with the words
' *Or se cante* ' ; the latter have no music, and the introduction
' *Or content et dient et fablent.*'

A further differentiation amongst minstrels was of linguistic
origin. This was especially apparent in England. The mime
is essentially cosmopolitan. In whatever land he finds himself the few sentences of patter needful to introduce his *tour*
or his *nigremance* are readily picked up. It is not so with
any entertainer whose performances claim to rank, however
humbly, as literature. And the Conquest in England brought
into existence a class of minstrels who, though they were by
no means mimes, were yet obliged to compete with mimes,
making their appeal solely to the *bourgeoisie* and the peasants,
because their speech was not that of the Anglo-Norman lords
and ladies who formed the more profitable audiences of the
castles. The native English gleemen were eclipsed at courts
by the Taillefers and Raheres of the invading host. But they
still held the road side by side with their rivals, shorn of their
dignities, and winning a precarious livelihood from the shrunken

---

[1] Chaucer, *House of Fame,* 1197:
' Of alle maner of minstrales,
  And gestiours, that tellen tales,
  Bothe of weping and of game.'
Cf. *Sir Thopas,* 134 ; and Gower,
Confessio Amantis, vii. 2424 :
  ' And every menstral hadde pleid,
  And every disour hadde seid.'
The evidence of Erasmus is late, of
course, for the hey-day of minstrelsy, but in his time there were
certainly English minstrels who
merely recited, without musical
accompaniment; cf. *Ecclesiastes*
(*Opera,* v. col. 958) 'Apud Anglos
est simile genus hominum, quales
apud Italos sunt circulatores, de
quibus modo dictum est; qui irrum-
punt in convivia magnatum, aut in
cauponas vinarias ; et argumentum
aliquod, quod edidicerunt, recitant ;
puta mortem omnibus dominari,
aut laudem matrimonii. Sed quoniam ea lingua monosyllabis fere
constat, quemadmodum Germanica ;
atque illi studio vitant cantum,
nobis latrare videntur verius quam
loqui.'

purses of those of their own blood and tongue [1]. It was they who sang the unavailing heroisms of Hereward, and, if we may judge by the scanty fragments and records that have come down to us, they remained for long the natural focus and mouthpiece of popular discontent and anti-court sentiment. In the reign of Edward III a gleeman of this type, Laurence Minot, comes to the front, voicing the spirit of an England united in its nationalism by the war against France ; the rest are, for the most part, nameless [2]. Naturally the English gleemen did not remain for ever a proscribed and isolated folk. One may suspect that at the outset many of them became bilingual. At any rate they learnt to mingle with their Anglo-Norman *confrères* : they borrowed the themes of continental minstrelsy; translating *roman, fabliau* and *chanson* into the metres and dialects of the vernacular ; and had their share in that gradual fusion of the racial elements of the land, whose completion was the preparation for Chaucer.

Besides the Saxons, there were the Kelts. In the provinces of France that bordered on Armorica, in the English counties that marched with Wales, the Keltic harper is no unusual or negligible figure. Whether such minstrels ranked very high in the bardic hierarchy of their own peoples may be doubted ; but amid alien folk they achieved popularity [3]. Both Giraldus

---

[1] Ten Brink, i. 193, 225, 235, 314, 322 ; Jusserand, i. 219. The Old gleeman tradition was probably less interfered with in the lowlands of Scotland than in England proper ; cf. Henderson, *Scottish Vernacular Literature*, 16.

[2] Ten Brink, i. 322 ; Jusserand, i. 360 ; Courthope, i. 197. Minot's poems have been edited by J. Hall (Oxford, 1887). See also Wright, *Political Songs* (C.S.) and *Political Poems and Songs* (R.S.). Many of these, however, are Latin.

[3] On Welsh bardism see H. d'Arbois de Jubainville, *Intr. à l'Étude de la Litt. celtique*, 63 ; Stephens, *Literature of the Kymry*, 84, 93, 97, 102 ; Ernest David, *Études historiques sur la Poésie et la Musique dans la Cambrie*, 13, 62–103, 147–64. In Wales, an isolated corner of Europe, little touched by Latin influences, the bards long retained the social and national position which it is probable they once had held in all the Aryan peoples. Their status is defined in the laws of Howel Dha († 920) and in those of Gruffyd ab Cynan (1100). The latter code distinguishes three orders of bards proper, the *Pryddyd* or Chair bards, the *Teuluwr* or Palace bards, and the *Arwyddfardd* or heralds, also called *Storiawr*, the *cantores historici* of Giraldus Cambrensis. The *Pryddyd* and *Teuluwr* differ precisely as poets and executants, *trouvères* and *jougleurs*. Below all these come the *Clerwr*, against whom official bardism from the sixth to the thirteenth century showed an inveterate animosity.

Cambrensis and Thomas the author of *Tristan* speak of a certain *famosus fabulator* of this class, Bledhericus or Breri by name [1]. Through Breri and his like the Keltic traditions filtered into Romance literature, and an important body of scholars are prepared to find in *lais* sung to a Welsh or Breton harp the *origines* of Arthurian romance [2]. In England the Welsh, like the English-speaking minstrels, had a political, as well as a literary significance. They were the means by which the spirit of Welsh disaffection under English rule was kept alive, and at times fanned into a blaze. The fable of the massacre of the bards by Edward I is now discredited, but an ordinance of his against Keltic 'bards and rhymers' is upon record, and was subsequently repeated under Henry IV [3].

An important question now presents itself. How far, in this heterogeneous welter of mediaeval minstrelsy, is it possible to distinguish any elements which can properly be called dramatic? The minstrels were entertainers in many *genres*. Were they also actors? An answer may be sought first of all in their literary remains. The first condition of drama is dialogue, and dialogue is found both in lyric and in narrative minstrelsy. Naturally, it is scantiest in lyric. But there is a group of *chansons* common to northern France and to southern France or Provence, which at least tended to develop in this direction. There are the *chansons à danser*, which are frequently a semi-dialogue between a soloist and a chorus, the one singing the verses, the other breaking into

These are an unattached wandering folk, players on flutes, tambourines, and other instruments meaner than the *telyn* or harp, and the *crwth* or viol which alone the bards proper deigned to use. Many of them had also picked up the mime-tricks of the foreigners. It was probably with these *Clerwr* that the English and French neighbours of the Kelts came mainly into contact. Padelford, 5, puts this contact as early as the Anglo-Saxon period.

[1] Giraldus Cambrensis, *Descriptio Cambriae*, i. 17 'famosus ille fabulator Bledhericus, qui tempora nostra paulo praevenit.' Thomas, *Tristan* († 1170, ed. Michel, ii. 847):

' Mès sulum ço que j'ai oy
N'el dient pas sulum Breri,
Ky solt les gestes e les cuntes
De tuz les reis, de tuz les cuntes
Ki orent esté en Bretaingne.'

[2] G. Paris, in *Hist. Litt.* xxx. 1–22 ; *Litt. Fr.* §§ 53–5 ; Nutt, *Legend of the Holy Grail*, 228 ; Rhys, *Arthurian Legend*, 370-90. These views have been vigorously criticized by Prof. Zimmer in *Göttingische gelehrte Anzeigen* (1891), 488, 785, and elsewhere.

[3] David, *op. cit.* 13, 235 ; cf. p. 54.

a burden or refrain. There are the *chansons à personnages* or *chansons de mal mariée*, complaints of unhappy wives, which often take the form of a dialogue between the woman and her husband, her friend or, it may be, the poet, occasionally that of a discussion on courtly love in general. There are the *aubes*, of which the type is the morning dialogue between woman and lover adapted by Shakespeare with such splendid effect in the third act of *Romeo and Juliet*. And finally there are the *pastourelles*, which are generally dialogues between a knight and a shepherdess, in which the knight makes love and, successful or repulsed, rides away. All these *chansons*, like the *chansons d'histoire* or *de toile*, which did not develop into dialogues, are, in the form in which we have them, of minstrel origin. But behind them are probably folk-songs of similar character, and M. Gaston Paris is perhaps right in tracing them to the *fêtes du mai*, those agricultural festivals of immemorial antiquity in which women traditionally took so large a part. A further word will have to be said of their ultimate contribution to drama in a future chapter[1].

Other lyrical dialogues of very different type found their way into the literature of northern France from that of Provence. These were the elaborate disputes about abstract questions, generally of love, so dear to the artistic and scholastic mind of the *trobaire*. There was the *tenso* (Fr. *tençon*) in which two speakers freely discussed a given subject, each taking the point of view which seems good to him. And there was the *joc-partitz* or *partimen* (Fr. *jeu-parti* or *parture*), in which the challenger proposed a theme, indicated two opposed attitudes towards it, and gave his opponent his choice to maintain one or other[2]. Originally, no doubt the *tensons* and the *jocs-partitz* were, as they professed to be, improvised verbal tournaments : afterwards they became little more than academic exercises[3]. To the drama they have nothing to say.

---

[1] Paris, §§ 118, 122, and *Orig.* (*passim*); Jeanroy, 1, 84, 102, 387; *Lang. et Litt.* i. 345; cf. ch. viii. Texts of *chansons à personnages* and *pastourelles* in Bartsch, *Altfranzösische Romanzen und Pastourellen*; of *aubes* in Bartsch, *Chrestomathie de l'ancien français.*

[2] Paris, § 126; *Orig.* (*passim*); Jeanroy, 45, and in *Lang. et Litt.* i. 384; Bartsch, *Grundriss der prov. Lit.* 34; Hueffer, *The Troubadours*, 112; Stimming in Gröber's *Grundriss*, ii. 2. 24.

[3] In 1386 we hear of 'des compaingnons, pour de jeux de parture

The dialogue elements in lyric minstrelsy thus exhausted, we turn to the wider field of narrative. But over the greater space of this field we look in vain. If there is anything of dialogue in the *chansons de gestes* and the *romans* it is merely reported dialogue such as every form of narrative poetry contains, and is not to the purpose. It is not until we come to the humbler branches of narrative, the unimportant *contes* and *dits*, that we find ourselves in the presence of dialogue proper. *Dits* and *fabliaux dialogués* are not rare[1]. There is the already quoted *Deus Bordeors Ribauz* in which two *jougleurs* meet and vaunt in turn their rival proficiencies in the various branches of their common art[2]. There is Rutebeuf's *Charlot et le Barbier*, a similar 'flyting' between two gentlemen of the road[3]. There is *Courtois d'Arras*, a version of the Prodigal Son story[4]. There is *Le Roi d'Angleterre et le Jongleur d'Ely*, a specimen of witty minstrel repartee, of which more will be said immediately. These dialogues naturally tend to become of the nature of disputes, and they merge into that special kind of *dit*, the *débat* or *disputoison* proper. The *débat* is a kind of poetical controversy put into the mouths of two types or two personified abstractions, each of which pleads the cause of its own superiority, while in the end the decision is not infrequently referred to an umpire in the fashion familiar in the eclogues of Theocritus[5]. The *débats* thus bear a strong

juer et esbattre' at Douai (Julleville, *Rép. Com.* 323), which looks as if, by the end of the fourteenth century, the *partures* were being professionally performed.

[1] Paris, § 109; Bédier, 31. A *fabliau* is properly a 'conte à rire en vers'; the term *dit* is applied more generally to a number of short poems which deal, 'souvent avec agrément, des sujets empruntés à la vie quotidienne.' Some *dits* are satirical, others eulogistic of a class or profession, others descriptive. But the distinction is not very well defined, and the *fabliaux* are often called *dits* in the MSS.

[2] Montaiglon-Raynaud, i. 1; ii. 257. The *dit* is also called *La Jengle au Ribaut et la Contrejengle*.

[3] Rutebeuf (ed. Kressner), 99.

[4] Barbazan-Méon, i. 356. Bédier, 33, considers *Courtois d'Arras* as the oldest French comedy, a *jeu dramatique* with intercalated narrative by a *meneur de jeu*. But the fact that it ends with the words *Te Deum* leads one to look upon it as an adaptation of a religious play; cf. ch. xix.

[5] On the *débats* in general, see *Hist. Litt.* xxiii. 216 sqq.; Paris, *Litt. fr.* §§ 110, 155; Arthur Piaget, *Littérature didactique* in *Lang. et Litt.* ii. 208; Jeanroy, 48; R. Hirzel, *Der Dialog*, ii. 382; *Literaturblatt* (1887), 76. A full list is given by Petit, *Rép. Com.* 405-9. The *débats* merge into such allegorical poems as Henri d'Andeli's

resemblance to the lyric *tençons* and *jeux-partis* already mentioned. Like the *chansons*, they probably owe something to the folk festivals with their 'flytings' and seasonal songs. In any case they are common ground to minstrelsy and to the clerkly literature of the Middle Ages. Many of the most famous of them, such as the *Débat de l'Hiver et de l'Été*, the *Débat du Vin et de l'Eau*, the *Débat du Corps et de l'Âme*, exist in neo-Latin forms, the intermediaries being naturally enough those *vagantes* or wandering scholars, to whom so much of the interaction of learned and of popular literature must be due[1]. And in their turn many of the *débats* were translated sooner or later into English. English literature, indeed, had had from Anglo-Saxon days a natural affinity for the dialogue form[2],

---

Bataille des Vins (Barbazon-Méon, i. 152) or *Le Mariage des Sept Arts et des Sept Vertus* (Jubinal, *Œuvres de Rutebeuf*, ii. 415) ; cf. Paris, *Litt. fr.* 158.

[1] Ten Brink, i. 215; Hubatsch, 24; Gummere, *B. P.* 200, 306. The *Débat de l'Yver et de l'Esté* has the nearest folk-lore origin; cf. ch. ix. Paris, *Origines*, 28, mentions several Greek and Latin versions beginning with Aesop (Halm, 414). The most important is the ninth-century *Conflictus Veris et Hiemis* (Riese, *Anth. Lat.* i. 2. 145), variously ascribed to Bede (Wernsdorff, *Poetae Latini Minores*, ii. 239), Alcuin (*Alc. Opera*, ed. Froben, ii. 612) and others. French versions are printed in Montaiglon-Rothschild, *Anc. Poés. fr.* vi. 190, x. 41, and Jubinal, *N. R.* ii. 40. There are imitations in all tongues : cf. M. Émile Picot's note in Mont.-Rothsch. *op. cit.* x. 49; *Hist. Litt.* xxiii. 231 ; Douhet, 1441.—*La Disputoison du Vin et de l'Iaue* is printed in Jubinal, *N. R.* i. 293; Wright, *Lat. Poems of Walter Mapes*, 299 ; *Carmina Burana*, 232. It is based on the *Goliae Dialogus inter Aquam et Vinum* (Wright, *loc. cit.* 87) ; cf. *Hist. Litt.* xxiii. 228; *Romania*, xvi. 366.—On the complicated history of the *Débat du Corps et de l'Âme*, see T. Batiouchkof in *Romania*, xx. 1. 513; G.

Kleinert, *Ueber den Streit von Leib und Seele*; *Hist. Litt.* xxii. 162; P. de Julleville, *Répertoire Comique*, 5, 300, 347 ; Wright, *Latin Poems*, xxiii. 95, 321. Latin, French and other versions are given by Wright, and by Viollet-Leduc, *Anc. Thé.fr.* iii. 325.—*Phillis et Flora*, or *De Phyllis qui aime un chevalier et de Flora qui aime un prêtre*, is also referred by Paris, *Orig.* 28, to a folk-song beginning ; cf. *H. L.* xxii. 138, 165 ; *Romania*, xxii. 536. Latin versions are in *Carmina Burana*, 155 ; Wright, *Latin Poems of W. Mapes*, 258.—A possible influence of the Theocritean and Virgilian eclogues upon these *débats*, through their neo-Latin forms, must be borne in mind.

[2] Wülker, 384; Brooke, i. 139, ii. 93, 221, 268 ; Jusserand, i. 75, 443. The passages of dialogue dwelt on by these writers mostly belong to the work of Cynewulf and his school. It has been suggested that some of them, e.g. the A.-S. *Descent into Hell* (Grein, iii. 175 ; cf. *Anglia*, xix. 137), or the dialogue between Mary and Joseph in Cynewulf's *Christ*, 163 (ed. Gollancz, p. 16), may have been intended for liturgical use by half-choirs ; but of this there is really no proof. Wülker, *loc. cit.*, shows clearly that the notion of a dramatic representation was unfamiliar to the Anglo-Saxons.

and presents side by side with the translated *débats* others—
strifs or *estrifs* is the English term—of native origin [1]. The
thirteenth-century *Harrowing of Hell* is an *estrif* on a subject
familiar in the miracle plays : and for an early miracle play it
has sometimes been mistaken [2]. Two or three other *estrifs*
of English origin are remarkable, because the interlocutors
are not exactly abstractions, but species of birds and
animals [3].

Dialogue then, in one shape or another, was part of the
minstrel's regular stock-in-trade. But dialogue by itself is not
drama. The notion of drama does not, perhaps, necessarily
imply scenery on a regular stage, but it does imply impersonation and a distribution of rôles between at least two performers.
Is there anything to be traced in minstrelsy that satisfies these
conditions? So far as impersonation is concerned, there are
several scattered notices which seem to show that it was not
altogether unknown. In the twelfth century for instance,
Ælred, abbot of Rievaulx, commenting on certain unpleasing
innovations in the church services of the day, complains that
the singers use gestures just like those of *histriones*, fit rather
for a *theatrum* than for a house of prayer [4]. The word *theatrum*

---

[1] Ten Brink, i. 312. Several
English versions of the *Debate be-
tween Body and Soul* are given by
Wright, *loc. cit.* 334. An English
*Debate and Stryfe betwene Somer
and Wynter* is in W. C. Hazlitt,
Early Popular Poetry, iii. 29.

[2] Cf. ch. xx.

[3] Ten Brink, i. 214, 309. *The
Owl and the Nightingale* (c. 1216-
72), was printed by J. Stevenson
(Roxburghe Club) ; *the Thrush and
the Nightingale* and *the Fox and
the Wolf*, by W. C. Hazlitt, *Early
Popular Poetry*, i. 50, 58. There
are also a *Debate of the Carpenter's
Tools* (Hazlitt, i. 79) and an English
version of a Latin *Disputacio inter
Mariam et Crucem* (R. Morris,
Legends of the Holy Rood, 131);
cf. Ten Brink, i. 259, 312. An A.-S.
version of the *Debate between Body
and Soul* is in the *Exeter Book*
(Grein, ii. 92).

[4] Ælred (†1166), *Speculum Cha-*

ritatis, ii. 23 (*P. L.* cxcv. 571) ' Videas aliquando hominem aperto ore
quasi intercluso halitu expirare,
non cantare, ac ridiculosa quadam
vocis interceptione quasi minitari
silentium ; nunc agones morientium,
vel extasim patientium imitari. Interim histrionicis quibusdam gestibus
totum corpus agitatur, torquentur
labia, rotant, ludunt humeri ; et ad
singulas quasque notas digitorum
flexus respondet. Et haec ridiculosa dissolutio vocatur religio ! . . .
Vulgus . . . miratur . . . sed lascivas cantantium gesticulationes, me-
retricias vocum alternationes et
infractiones, non sine cachinno risu-
que intuetur, ut eos non ad oratorium sed ad theatrum, non ad oran-
dum, sed ad spectandum aestimes
convenisse.' Cf. *op. cit.* ii. 17 ' Cum
enim in tragediis vanisve carminibus
quisquam iniuriatus fingitur, vel
oppressus . . . si quis haec, vel cum
canuntur audiens, vel cernens si

is, however, a little suspicious, for an actual theatre in the
twelfth century is hardly thinkable, and with a learned eccle-
siastic one can never be sure that he is not drawing his
illustrations rather from his knowledge of classical literature
than from the real life around him. It is more conclusive,
perhaps, when *fabliaux* or *contes* speak of minstrels as 'doing'
l'ivre, or *le cat*, or *le sot*[1]; or when it appears from contemporary accounts that at a performance in Savoy the
manners of England and Brittany were mimicked [2]. In Provence *contrafazedor* seems to have been a regular name for
a minstrel [3]; and the facts that the minstrels wore masks
'with intent to deceive'[4], and were forbidden to wear ecclesiastical dresses [5], also point to something in the way of rudimentary impersonation.

As for the distribution of rôles, all that can be said, so far
as the *débats* and *dits dialogués* go, is, that while some of them

recitentur . . . moveatur'; and
Johannes de Janua, s.v. *persona*
(cited Creizenach, i. 381) 'Item persona dicitur histrio, repraesentator
comoediarum, qui diversis modis
personat diversas repraesentando
personas.' All these passages, like
the ninth-century *responsio* of archbishop Leidradus referred to on
p. 36, may be suspected of learning
rather than actuality. As for the
epitaph of the mime Vitalis (Riese,
Anth. Lat. i. 2. 143; Baehrens,
P. L. M. iii. 245), sometimes quoted
in this connexion, it appears to be
classical and not mediaeval at all;
cf. Teuffel-Schwabe, §§ 8. 11; 32. 6.
Probably this is also the case with
the lines *De Mimo iam Sene* in
Wright, *Anecdota Literaria*, 100,
where again 'theatra' are mentioned.

¹ Cf. p. 71. The mention of a
'Disare that played the sheppart'
at the English court in 1502 (Nicolas, *Privy Purse Expenses of Elizabeth of York*) is too late to be of
importance here.

² Creizenach, i. 383, citing at
second-hand from fourteenth-century accounts of a Savoy treasurer
'rappresentando i costumi delle

compagnie inglesi e bretoni.'
³ Creizenach, i. 380.
⁴ Thomas de Cabham mentions
the *horribiles larvae* of some
minstrels. A. Lecoy de la Marche,
La Chaire française (ed. 2, 1886),
444, quotes a sermon of Étienne
de Bourbon in *MS. B. N. Lat.*
15970, f. 352 'ad similitudinem
illorum ioculatorum qui ferunt
facies depictas quae dicuntur arti-
ficia gallicè, cum quibus ludunt et
homines deludunt.' Cf. Liudprand,
iii. 15 (Pertz, iii. 310) 'histrionum
mimorumve more incedere, qui, ut
ad risum facile turbas illiciant,
variis sese depingunt coloribus.'
The *monstra larvarum*, however,
of various ecclesiastical prohibitions
I take to refer specifically to the
Feast of Fools (cf. ch. xiii).
⁵ Schack, *Gesch. der dram. Litt.
und Kunst in Spanien*, i. 30, quotes
a Carolingian capitulary, from Hei-
neccius, *Capit.* lib. v. c. 388 'si quis
ex scenicis vestem sacerdotalem aut
monasticam vel mulieris religiosae
vel qualicunque ecclesiastico statu
similem indutus fuerit, corporali
poena subsistat et exilio tradatur.'
This prohibition is as old as the
Codex Theodosianus; cf. p. 14.

may conceivably have been represented by more than one performer, none of them need necessarily have been so, and some of them certainly were not. There is generally a narrative introduction and often a sprinkling of narrative interspersed amongst the dialogue. These parts may have been pronounced by an *auctor* or by one of the interlocutors acting as *auctor*, and some such device must have been occasionally necessitated in the religious drama. But there is really no difficulty in supposing the whole of these pieces to have been recited by a single minstrel with appropriate changes of gesture and intonation, and in *The Harrowing of Hell*, which begins ' A strif will I tellen of,' this was clearly the case. The evidences of impersonation given above are of course quite consistent with such an arrangement ; or, for the matter of that, with sheer monologue. The minstrel who recited Rutebeuf's *Dit de l'Erberie* may readily be supposed to have got himself up in the character of a quack [1].

But the possibilities of secular mediaeval drama are not quite exhausted by the *débats* and *dits dialogués*. For after all, the written literature which the minstrels have left us belongs almost entirely to those higher *strata* of their complex fraternity which derived from the thoroughly undramatic Teutonic *scôp*. But if mediaeval farce there were, it would not be here that we should look for it. It would belong to the inheritance, not of the *scôp*, but of the *mimus*. The Roman *mimus* was essentially a player of farces ; that and little else. It is of course open to any one to suppose that the *mimus* went down in the seventh century playing farces, and that his like appeared in the fifteenth century playing farces, and that not a farce was played between. But is it not more probable on the whole that, while occupying himself largely with other matters, he preserved at least the rudiments of the art of acting, and that when the appointed time came, the despised and forgotten farce, under the stimulus of new conditions, blossomed forth once more as a vital and effective form of literature ? In the absence of data we are reduced to conjecture. But the mere absence of data itself does not render

[1] *Œuvres* de Rutebeuf (ed. Kressner), 115; cf. *Romania*, xvi. 496 ; Julleville, *Les Com.* 24; *Rép. Com.* 407.

the conjecture untenable. For if such rudimentary, or, if you please, degenerate farces as I have in mind, ever existed in the Middle Ages, the chances were all against their literary survival. They were assuredly very brief, very crude, often improvised, and rarely, if ever, written down. They belonged to an order of minstrels far below that which made literature[1]. And one little bit of evidence which has not yet been brought forward seems to point to the existence of something in the way of a secular as well as a religious mediaeval drama. In the well-known Wyclifite sermon against miracle plays, an imaginary opponent of the preacher's argument is made to say that after all it is ' lesse yvels that thei have thyre recreaceon by pleyinge of myraclis than bi pleyinge of other japis'; and again that ' to pley in rebaudye ' is worse than ' to pley in myriclis[2].' Now, there is of course no necessary dramatic connotation either in the word 'pley' or in the word 'japis,' which, like ' bourde' or ' gab ' is frequently used of any kind of rowdy merriment, or of the lower types of minstrelsy in general[3]. But on the other hand the whole tone of the passage seems to draw a very close parallel between the 'japis' and the undeniably dramatic ' myriclis,' and to imply something in the former a little beyond the mere recitation, even with the help of impersonation, of a solitary mime.

Such rude farces or 'japis' as we are considering, if they

---

[1] Creizenach, i. 386, further points out that a stage was not indispensable to the Latin *mimus*, who habitually played before the curtain and probably with very little setting; that the favourite situations of fifteenth-century French farce closely resemble those of the mimes; and that the use of marionettes is a proof of some knowledge of dramatic methods amongst the minstrels.

[2] On this treatise, cf. ch. xx.

[3] A ' japer' is often an idle talker, like a ' jangler' which is clearly sometimes confused with a ' jongleur'; cf. Chaucer, *Parson's Tale*, 89 ' He is a japere and a gabber and no verray repentant that eftsoone dooth thing for which hym oghte repente.' Langland uses the term in a more technical sense. *Activa Vita* in *Piers Plowman*, xvi. 207, is no minstrel, because 'Ich can not . . . japen ne jogelen.' No doubt a ' jape' would include a *fabliau*. It is equivalent etymologically to 'gab,' and Bédier, 33, points out that the *jougleurs* use *gabet*, as well as *bourde*, *trufe*, and *risée* for a *fabliau*.—The use of ' pleye' as ' jest' may be illustrated by Chaucer, *Pardoner's Tale* (*C. T.* 12712) ' My wit is greet, though that I bourde and pleye.'— The ' japis ' of the *Tretise* are probably the ' knakkes ' of the passage on ' japeris ' in *Parson's Tale*, 651 ' right so conforten the vileyns wordes and knakkes of japeris hem that travaillen in the service of the devel.'

formed part of the travelling equipment of the humbler mimes, could only get into literature by an accident; in the event, that is to say, of some minstrel of a higher class taking it into his head to experiment in the form or to adapt it to the purposes of his own art. And this is precisely what appears to have happened. A very natural use of the farce would be in the *parade* or preliminary patter, merely about himself and his proficiency, which at all times has served the itinerant entertainer as a means whereby to attract his audiences. And just as the very similar *boniment* or patter of the mountebank charlatan at a fair became the model for Rutebeuf's *Dit de l'Erberie*, so the *parade* may be traced as the underlying motive of other *dits* or *fabliaux*. The *Deus Bordeors Ribaus* is itself little other than a glorified *parade*, and another, very slightly disguised, may be found in the discomfiture of the king by the characteristic repartees of the wandering minstrel in *Le Roi d'Angleterre et le Jougleur d'Ely* [1]. The *parade*, also, seems to be the origin of a certain familiar type of dramatic prologue in which the author or the presenters of a play appear in their own persons. The earliest example of this is perhaps that enigmatic *Terentius et Delusor* piece which some have thought to point to a representation of Terence somewhere in the dark ages between the seventh and the eleventh century [2]. And there is a later one in the *Jeu du Pèlerin* which was written about 1288 to precede Adan de la Hale's *Jeu de Robin et Marion*.

The renascence of farce in the fifteenth century will call for consideration in a later chapter. It is possible that, as is here suggested, that renascence was but the coming to light again of an earth-bourne of dramatic tradition that had

[1] Montaiglon-Raynaud, ii. 243. Cf. *Hist. Litt.* xxiii. 103; Jusserand, *Lit. Hist.* i. 442. A shorter prose form of the story is found in *La Riote du Monde* (ed. Fr. Michel, 1834), a popular *facétie* of which both French and Anglo-Norman versions exist; cf. Paris, *Litt. fr.* 153. And a Latin form, *De Mimo et Rege Francorum* is in Wright, *Latin Stories*, No. 137. The point consists in the quibbling replies

with which the *jougleur* meets the king's questions. Thus, in *La Riote du Monde* : 'Dont ies tu?—Je suis de no vile.—U est te vile?—Entor le moustier.—U est li moustiers?—En l'atre.—U est li atres?—Sor terre.—U siet cele terre?—Sor l'iaue.—Comment apiel-on l'iaue?—On ne l'apiele nient; ele vient bien sans apieler.'

[2] Cf. Appendix V.

worked its way beneath the ground ever since the theatres of the Empire fell. In any case, rare documents of earlier date survive to show that it was at least no absolutely sudden and unprecedented thing. The *jeux* of Adan de la Hale, indeed, are somewhat irrelevant here. They were not farces, and will fall to be dealt with in the discussion of the popular *fêtes* from which they derive their origin[1]. But the French farce of *Le Garçon et l'Aveugle*, ascribed to the second half of the thirteenth century, is over a hundred years older than any of its extant successors[2]. And even more interesting to us, because it is of English *provenance* and in the English tongue, is a fragment found in an early fourteenth-century manuscript of a dramatic version of the popular mediaeval tale of Dame Siriz[3]. This bears the heading *Hic incipit interludium de Clerico et Puella*. But the significance of this fateful word *interludium* must be left for study at a later period, when the history of the secular drama is resumed from the point at which it must now be dropped.

[1] Cf. ch. viii.

[2] Ed. P. Meyer, in *Jahrbuch für romanische und englische Litera-tur*, vi. 163. The piece was probably written in Flanders, between 1266 and 1290. Cf. Creizenach, i. 398.

[3] See Appendix U. References for the earlier non-dramatic versions in Latin, French, and English of the story are given by Jusserand, *Lit. Hist.* i. 447. A Cornish dramatic fragment of the fourteenth century is printed in the *Athenæum* for Dec. 1, 1877, and *Revue celtique*, iv. 259; cf. Creizenach, i. 401.

BOOK II

FOLK DRAMA

Stultorum infinitus est numerus.

ECCLESIASTES.

CHAPTER V

THE RELIGION OF THE FOLK

[*Bibliographical Note.*—The conversion of heathen England is described in the *Ecclesiastical History* of Bede (C. Plummer, *Baedae Opera Historica*, 1896). Stress is laid on the imperfect character of the process by L. Knappert, *Le Christianisme et le Paganisme dans l'Histoire ecclésiastique de Bède le Vénérable* (in *Revue de l'Histoire des Religions*, 1897, vol. xxxv). A similar study for Gaul is E. Vacandard, *L'Idolatrie dans la Gaule* (in *Revue des Questions historiques*, 1899, vol. lxv). Witness is borne to the continued presence of pre-Christian elements in the folk-civilization of western Europe both by the general results of folk-lore research and by the ecclesiastical documents of the early Middle Ages. Of these the most important in this respect are—(1) the *Decrees* of Councils, collected generally in P. Labbe and G. Cossart, *Sacrosancta Concilia* (1671-2), and J. D. Mansi, *Sacrorum Conciliorum nova et amplissima Collectio* (1759-98), and for England in particular in D. Wilkins, *Concilia Magnae Britanniae et Hiberniae* (1737) and A. W. Haddan and W. Stubbs, *Councils and Ecclesiastical Documents relating to Great Britain and Ireland* (1869-78). An interesting series of extracts is given by G. Gröber, *Zur Volkskunde aus Concilbeschlüssen und Capitularien* (1894) :—(2) the *Penitentials*, or catalogues of sins and their penalties drawn up for the guidance of confessors. The most important English example is the *Penitential of Theodore* (668-90), on which the *Penitentials of Bede* and *of Egbert* are based. Authentic texts are given by Haddan and Stubbs, vol. iii, and, with others of continental origin, in F. W. H. Wasserschleben, *Die Bussordnungen der abendländischen Kirche* (1851), and H. J. Schmitz, *Die Bussbücher und die Bussdisciplin der Kirche* (1883). The most interesting for its heathen survivals is the eleventh-century *Collectio Decretorum* of Burchardus of Worms (Migne, *P. L.* cxl, extracts in J. Grimm, *Teutonic Mythology*, iv. 1740):—(3) *Homilies* or *Sermons*, such as the *Sermo* ascribed to the seventh-century St. Eligius (*P. L.* lxxxvii. 524, transl. Grimm, iv. 1737), and the eighth-century Frankish pseudo-Augustinian *Homilia de Sacrilegiis* (ed. C. P. Caspari, 1886):—(4) the *Vitae* of the apostles of the West, St. Boniface, St. Columban, St. Gall, and others. A critical edition of these is looked for from M. Knappert. The *Epistolae* of Boniface are in *P. L.* lxxxix. 593 :—(5) *Miscellaneous Documents*, including the sixth-century *De correctione Rusticorum* of Bishop Martin of Braga in Spain (ed. C. P. Caspari, 1883) and the so-called *Indiculus Superstitionum et Paganiarum* (ed. H. A. Saupe, 1891), a list of heathen customs probably drawn up in eighth-century Saxony.—The view of primitive religion taken in this book is largely, although not altogether in detail, that of J. G. Frazer, *The Golden Bough* (1890, 2nd ed. 1900), which itself owes much to E. B. Tylor, *Primitive Culture* (1871) ; W. Robertson Smith, *Religion of the Semites* (2nd ed. 1894) ; W. Mannhardt, *Der Baumkultus der Germanen* (1875) ; *Antike Wald- und Feldkulte* (1875-7). A more systematic work on similar lines is F. B. Jevons, *An Introduction to the History of Religion* (1896): and amongst many others may be mentioned A. Lang, *Myth, Ritual, and Religion* (1887, 2nd ed. 1899), the conclusions of which are somewhat modified in the same writer's *The Making of Religion* (1898); Grant Allen, *The Evolution of the Idea of God* (1897); E. S. Hartland, *The Legend of Perseus* (1894-6); J. Rhys, *The Origin and Growth of Religion as illustrated by Celtic Heathendom* (1888). The last of these deals especially with Keltic *data*, which may be further studied in H. D'Arbois de Jubainville, *Le Cycle mythologique irlandais et la Mythologie celtique* (1884), together with the chapter on *La Religion* in the same writer's *La Civilisation des Celtes et celle de l'Épopée homérique* (1899) and A. Bertrand, *La Religion des Gaulois* (1897). Teutonic religion has been more completely investigated. Recent works of authority are E. H. Meyer, *Germanische Mythologie* (1891); W. Golther, *Handbuch der germanischen Mythologie* (1895); and the article by E. Mogk on *Mythologie* in H. Paul's *Grundriss der germanischen Philologie*, vol. iii (2nd ed. 1897). The collection of material in J. Grimm's *Teutonic Mythology* (transl. J. S. Stallybrass, 1880-8) is still of the greatest value. The general facts of early German civilization are given by F. B. Gummere, *Germanic Origins* (1892), and for the Aryan-speaking peoples in general by O. Schräder, *Prehistoric Antiquities of the Aryan Peoples* (transl. F. B. Jevons, 1890), and *Reallexicon der indo-germanischen Altertumskunde* (1901). In dealing with the primitive calendar I have mainly, but not wholly, followed the valuable researches of A. Tille, *Deutsche Weihnacht* (1893) and *Yule and Christmas* (1899), a scholar the loss of whom to this country is one of the lamentable results of the recent war.]

MINSTRELSY was an institution of the folk, no less than of the court and the *bourgeoisie*. At many a village festival, one may be sure, the taberers and buffoons played their conspicuous part, ravishing the souls of Dorcas and Mopsa with merry and doleful ballads, and tumbling through their amazing programme of monkey tricks before the ring of wide-mouthed rustics on the green. Yet the soul and centre of such revels always lay, not in these alien professional *spectacula*, but in other entertainments, home-grown and racy of the soil, wherein the peasants shared, not as onlookers only, but as performers, even as their fathers and mothers, from immemorial antiquity, had done before them. A full consideration of the village *ludi* is important to the scheme of the present book for more than one reason. They shared with the *ludi* of the minstrels the hostility of the Church. They bear witness, at point after point, to the deep-lying dramatic instincts of the folk. And their substantial contribution to mediaeval and Renaissance drama and dramatic *spectacle* is greater than has been fully recognized.

Historically, the *ludi* of the folk come into prominence with the attacks made upon them by the reforming ecclesiastics of the thirteenth century and in particular by Robert Grosseteste, bishop of Lincoln [1]. Between 1236 and 1244 Grosseteste issued a series of disciplinary pronouncements, in which he condemned many customs prevalent in his diocese. Amongst these are included miracle plays, 'scotales' or drinking-bouts, 'ram-raisings' and other contests of athletic prowess, together with ceremonies known respectively as the *festum stultorum* and the *Inductio Maii sivo Autumni*[2]. Very similar are the prohibitions contained in the *Constitutions* (1240) of Walter de Chanteloup, bishop of Worcester [3]. These particularly specify the *ludus de Rege et Regina*, a term which may be taken as generally applicable to the typical English folk-festival, of which the *Inductio Maii sive Autumni*, the 'May-game' and 'mell-supper,' mentioned by Grosseteste, are varieties [4]. Both this *ludus*, in its various forms, and the

---

[1] Stephens-Hunt, ii. 301 ; F. S. Stevenson, *Robert Grosseteste*, 126. The disciplinary attack seems to have begun with Grosseteste's predecessor, Hugh de Wells, in 1230 (Wilkins, i. 627), but he, like Roger Wescham, bishop of Coventry and Lichfield, in 1252 (*Annales Monastici*, R. S. i. 296), merely condemns *ludi*, a term which may mean folk-festivals or minstrelsy, or both. A similar ambiguity attaches to the obligation of the anchoresses of Tarrant Keyneston not to look on at a *ludus* (*pleouwe*) in the church-yard (*Ancren Riwle*, C. S. 318).

[2] In 1236 Grosseteste wrote to his archdeacons forbidding 'arietum super ligna et rotas elevationes, caeterosque ludos consimiles, in quo decertatur pro bravio ; cum huiusmodi ludorum tam actores quam spectatores, sicut evidenter demonstrat Isidorus, immolant daemonibus, ... et cum etiam huiusmodi ludi frequenter dant occasiones irae, odii, pugnae, et homicidii.' His *Constitutiones* of 1238 say 'Praecipimus etiam ut in singulis ecclesiis denuncietur solenniter ne quisquam levet arietes super rotas, vel alios ludos statuat, in quibus decertatur pro bravio : nec huiusmodi ludis quisquam intersit, &c.' About 1244 he

wrote again to the archdeacons : 'Faciunt etiam, ut audivimus, clerici ludos quos vocant miracula : et alios ludos quos vocant Inductionem Maii sive Autumni ; et laici scotales ... miracula etiam et ludos supra nominatos et scotales, quod est in vestra potestate facili, omnino exterminetis' (Luard, *Letters of Robert Grosseteste* (R. S.) *Epp.* xxii, lii, cvii, pp. 74, 162, 317). For his condemnations of the Feast of Fools cf. ch. xiv.

[3] *Const. Walt. de Cantilupo* (Wilkins, i. 673) 'prohibemus clericis ... nec sustineant ludos fieri de Rege et Regina, nec arietas levari, nec palaestras publicas fieri, nec gildales inhonestas.' The clergy must also abstain and dissuade the laity from 'compotationibus quae vocantur scottales' (Wilkins, i. 672). On 'ram-raisings,' &c., cf. ch. vii ; on 'gildales' and 'scotales' ch. viii.

[4] Surely the reference is to the mock kings and queens of the village festivals, and not, as Guy, 521 ; Jusserand, *Litt. Hist.* i. 444, suggest, to the question-and-answer game of *Le Roi qui ne ment* described in Jean de Condé's *Sentier Batu* (Montaiglon-Raynaud, iii. 248), although this is called playing 'as

less strictly popular *festum stultorum*, will find ample illustration in the sequel. Walter de Chanteloup also lays stress upon an aggravation of the *ludi inhonesti* by the performance of them in churchyards and other holy places, and on Sundays or the vigils and days of saints [1].

The decrees of the two bishops already cited do not stand alone. About 1250 the University of Oxford found it necessary to forbid the routs of masked and garlanded students in the churches and open places of the city [2]. These appear to have been held in connexion with the feasts of the 'nations' into which a mediaeval university was divided. Articles of visitation drawn up in connexion with the provisions of Oxford in 1253 made inquiry as to several of the obnoxious *ludi* and as to the measures adopted to check them throughout the country [3]. Prohibitions are upon record by the synod of Exeter in 1287 [4], and during the next century by the synod of York in 1367 [5], and by William of Wykeham, bishop of Winchester, in 1384 [6]; while the denunciations of the rulers of the church

rois et as reines' in Adan de la Hale's *Robin et Marion* (ed. Monmerqué-Michel, 121) and elsewhere (cf. Guy, 222), and possibly grew out of the festival custom. Yet another game of *King and Queen*, of the practical joke order, is described as played at Golspie by Nicholson, 119.

[1] Wilkins, i. 666.

[2] Anstey, *Munimenta Academica* (R. S.), i. 18 'ne quis choreas cum larvis seu strepitu aliquo in ecclesiis vel plateis ducat, vel sertatus, vel coronatus corona ex foliis arborum, vel florum vel aliunde composita alicubi incedat ... prohibemus.'

[3] *Inquisitiones ... de vita et conversatione clericorum et laicorum* in *Annales de Burton* (*Ann. Monast.* R. S. i. 307) 'an aliqui laici mercata, vel ludos, seu placita peculiaria fieri faciant in locis sacris, et an haec fuerint prohibita ex parte episcopi ... An aliqui laici elevaverint arietes, vel fieri faciant schothales, vel decertaverint de praeeundo cum vexillis in visitatione matricis ecclesiae.'

[4] Wilkins, ii. 129 'c. 13 ... Ne quisquam luctas, choreas, vel alios ludos inhonestos in coemeteriis exercere praesumat; praecipue in vigiliis et festis sanctorum, cum huiusmodi ludos theatrales et ludibriorum spectacula introductos per quos ecclesiarum coinquinatur honestas, sacri ordines detestantur.'

[5] Wilkins, iii. 68 'c. 2 ... nec in ipsis [locis sacris] fiant luctationes, sagittationes, vel ludi.' A special caution is given against ludi 'in sanctorum vigiliis' and 'in exequiis defunctorum.'

[6] T. F. Kirby, *Wykeham's Register* (Hampshire Record Soc.), ii. 410, forbids 'ad pilas ludere, iactaciones lapidum facere ... coreas facere dissolutas, et interdum canere cantilenas, ludibriorum spectacula facere, saltaciones et alios ludos inhonestos frequentare, ac multas alias insolencias perpetrare, ex quibus cimeterii huiusmodi execracio seu pollucio frequencius verisimiliter formidetur.'

find an unofficial echo in that handbook of ecclesiastical morality, Robert Mannyng of Brunne's *Handlyng Synne*[1]. There is, however, reason to suppose that the attitude thus taken up hardly represents that of the average ecclesiastical authority, still less that of the average parish priest, towards the *ludi* in question. The condemnatory decrees should probably be looked upon as the individual pronouncements of men of austere or reforming temper against customs which the laxer discipline of their fellows failed to touch ; perhaps it should rather be said, which the wiser discipline of their fellows found it better to regulate than to ban. At any rate there is evidence to show that the village *ludi*, as distinct from the *spectacula* of the minstrels, were accepted, and even to some extent directed, by the Church. They became part of the parochial organization, and were conducted through the parochial machinery. Doubtless this was the course of practical wisdom. But the moralist would find it difficult to deny that Robert Grosseteste and Walter de Chanteloup had, after all, some reason on their side. On the one hand they could point to the ethical lapses of which the *ludi* were undoubtedly the cause—the drunkenness, the quarrels, the wantonings, by which they were disgraced[2]. And on the other they could—if they

---

[1] *Handlyng Synne* (ed. Furnivall), p. 148, l. 4684 :
    'Daunces, karols, somour games,
        Of many swych come many
        shames.'
This poem is a free adaptation (†1303) of the thirteenth-century Anglo-Norman *Manuel de Péché*, which is probably by William de Wadington, but has been ascribed to Bishop Grosseteste himself. The corresponding lines in this are
    ' Muses et tieles musardries,
        Trippes, dances, et teles folies.'
Cf. also *Handlyng Synne*, p. 278, l. 8989 :
    ' Karolles, wrastlynges, or somour
        games,
    Who so euer haunteþ any swyche
        shames,
    Yy cherche, oþer yn cherche-
        ȝerde,
    Of sacrylage he may be a ferde ;

Or entyrludës, or syngynge,
Or tabure bete, or oþer pypynge,
Alle swychë þyng forbodyn es,
Whyle þe prest stondeþ at
    messe' ;
where the *Manuel de Péché* has
    ' Karoles ne lutes nul deit fere,
        En seint eglise qe me veut
        crere ;
    Car en cymiter neis karoler
    Est outrage grant, ou luter :
    Souent lur est mes auenu
    Qe la fet tel maner de iu ;
    Qe grant peche est, desturber
    Le prestre quant deit celebrer.'
[2] The Puritan Fetherston, in his *Dialogue agaynst light, lewde, and lascivious Dancing* (1583), sign. D. 7, says that he has 'hearde of tenne maidens which went to set May, and nine of them came home with childe.' Stubbes, i. 149, has a very similar observation. Cf. the adventures of

were historically minded—recall the origin of the objectionable
rites in some of those obscure survivals of heathenism in the
rustic blood, which half a dozen centuries of Christianity had
failed to purge[1]. For if the comparative study of religions
proves anything it is, that the traditional beliefs and customs
of the mediaeval or modern peasant are in nine cases out of
ten but the *detritus* of heathen mythology and heathen worship,
enduring with but little external change in the shadow of an
hostile creed. This is notably true of the village festivals
and their *ludi*. Their full significance only appears when they
are regarded as fragments of forgotten cults, the naïve cults
addressed by a primitive folk to the beneficent deities of field
and wood and river, or the shadowy populace of its own
dreams. Not that when even the mediaeval peasant set up
his Maypole at the approach of summer or drove his cattle
through the bonfire on Midsummer eve, the real character of
his act was at all explicit in his consciousness. To him, as to
his descendant of to-day, the festival was at once a practice
sanctioned by tradition and the rare amusement of a strenuous
life : it was not, save perhaps in some unplumbed recesses of
his being, anything more definitely sacred. At most it was
held to be ' for luck,' and in some vague general way, to the
interest of a fruitful year in field and fold. The scientific
anthropologist, however, from his very different point of view,
cannot regard the conversion to Christianity as a complete
solution of continuity in the spiritual and social life of western
Europe. This conversion, indeed, was clearly a much slower
and·more incomplete process than the ecclesiastical chroniclers
quite plainly state. It was so even on the shores of the
Mediterranean. But there the triumph of Christianity began
from below. Long before the edict of Milan, the new religion,
in spite of persecutions, had got its firm hold upon the masses
of the great cities of the Empire. And when, less than a

Dr. Fitzpiers and Suke Damson on
Midsummer Eve in Thomas Hardy's
novel, *The Woodlanders*, ch. xx.
    [1] Grosseteste, in 1236, quotes
'Isidorus' as to the pagan origin
of '*ludi, in quo decertatur de bravio.*'
The reference is to Isidore of Seville
(560–636),*Etymologiarum*,xviii.27,
De ludis circensibus (*P. L.* lxxxii.
653). This, of course, refers directly
to the religious associations of
Roman rather than Celto-Teutonic
ludi.

century later, Theodosius made the public profession of any other faith a crime, he was but formally acknowledging a *chose jugée*. But even in these lands of the first ardour the old beliefs and, above all, the old rituals died hard. Lingering unacknowledged in the country, the pagan, districts, they passed silently into the dim realm of folk-lore. How could this but be more so when Christianity came with the missionaries of Rome or of Iona to the peoples of the West? For with them conversion was hardly a spontaneous, an individual thing. As a rule, the baptism of the king was the starting-point and motive for that of his followers: and the bulk of the people adopted wonderingly an alien cult in an alien tongue imposed upon them by the will of their rulers. Such a Christianity could at best be only nominal. Ancient beliefs are not so easily surrendered: nor are habits and instincts, deep-rooted in the lives of a folk, thus lightly laid down for ever, at the word of a king. The churches of the West had, therefore, to dispose somehow of a vast body of practical heathenism surviving in all essentials beneath a new faith which was but skin-deep. The conflict which followed is faintly adumbrated in the pages of Bede: something more may be guessed of its fortunes by a comparison of the customs and superstitions recorded in early documents of church discipline with those which, after all, the peasantry long retained, or even now retain.

Two letters of Gregory the Great, written at the time of the mission of St. Augustine, are a key to the methods adopted by the apostles of the West. In June 601, writing to Ethelbert of Kent by the hands of abbot Mellitus, Gregory bade the new convert show zeal in suppressing the worship of idols, and throwing down their fanes[1]. Having written thus, the pope changed his mind. Before Mellitus could reach England, he received a letter instructing him to expound to Augustine a new policy. 'Do not, after all,' wrote Gregory, 'pull down the fanes. Destroy the idols; purify the buildings with holy water; set relics there; and let them become temples of the true God. So the people will have no need to change their

---

[1] Haddan-Stubbs, iii. 30 'idolorum cultus insequere, fanorum aedificia everate.'

places of concourse, and where of old they were wont to
sacrifice cattle to demons, thither let them continue to resort
on the day of the saint to whom the church is dedicated, and
slay their beasts no longer as a sacrifice, but for a social meal
in honour of Him whom they now worship [1].' There can be
little doubt that the conversion of England proceeded in the
main on the lines thus laid down by Gregory. Tradition has
it that the church of Saint Pancras outside the walls of Canterbury stands on the site of a fane at which Ethelbert himself
once worshipped [2]; and that in London St. Paul's replaced
a temple and grove of Diana, by whom the equivalent
Teutonic wood-goddess, Freyja, is doubtless intended [3].
Gregory's directions were, perhaps, not always carried out
quite so literally as this. When, for instance, the priest Coifi,
on horseback and sword in hand, led the onslaught against
the gods of Northumbria, he bade his followers set fire to the
fane and to all the hedges that girt it round [4]. On the other
hand, Reduald, king of East Anglia, must have kept his fane
standing, and indeed he carried the policy of amalgamation

---

[1] Bede, *Hist. Eccl.* i. 30 ; Haddan-
Stubbs, iii. 37 ' Dicite [Augustino],
quid diu mecum de causa Anglorum
cogitans tractavi : videlicet quia
fana idolorum destrui in eadem
gente minime debeant ; sed ipsa
quae in illis sunt idola destruantur,
aqua benedicta fiat, in eisdem fanis
aspergatur, altaria construantur,
reliquiae ponantur : quia si fana
eadem bene constructa sunt, necesse est ut a cultu daemonum in
obsequium veri Dei debeant com-
mutari, ut dum gens ipsa eadem
fana sua non videt destrui, de corde
errorem deponat, et Deum verum
cognoscens ac adorans, ad loca,
quae consuevit, familiarius con-
currat. Et quia boves solent in
sacrificio daemonum multos occi-
dere, debet eis etiam hac de re
aliqua solemnitas immutari : ut die
dedicationis, vel natalitii sanctorum
martyrum quorum illic reliquiae
ponuntur, tabernacula sibi circa eas-
dem ecclesias quae ex fanis com-
mutatae sunt, de ramis arborum
faciant, et religiosis conviviis sollem-

nitatem celebrent ; nec diabolo iam
animalia immolent, sed ad laudem
Dei in esum suum animalia occidant,
et donatori omnium de satietate sua
gratias referant : ut dum eis aliqua
exterius gaudia reserventur, ad inte-
riora gaudia consentire facilius valeant. Nam duris mentibus simul
omnia abscindere impossibile esse
non dubium est, quia et is qui
summum locum ascendere nititur
gradibus vel passibus non autem
saltibus elevatur '. . .

[2] Stanley, *Memorials of Canterbury*, 37.

[3] H. B. Wheatley, *London, Past
and Present*, iii. 39 ; Donne, *Poems*
(Muses' Library), ii. 23.

[4] Bede, ii. 13 ' iussit sociis de-
struere ac succendere fanum cum
omnibus septis suis.' In Essex in
a time of plague and famine (664),
Sigheri and his people ' coeperunt
fana, quae derelicta sunt, restaurare,
et adorare simulacra.' Bp. Jaruman
induced them to reopen the churches,
' relictis sive destructis fanis aris-
que ' (Bede, iii. 30).

further than its author intended, for he wavered faint-heartedly between the old religion and the new, and. maintained in one building an *altare* for Christian worship and an *arula* for sacrifice to demons [1]. Speaking generally, it would seem to have been the endeavour of the Christian missionaries to effect the change of creed with as little dislocation of popular sentiment as possible. If they could extirpate the essentials, or what they considered as the essentials, of heathenism, they were willing enough to leave the accidentals to be worn away by the slow process of time. They did not, probably, quite realize how long it would take. And what happened in England, happened also, no doubt, on the continent, save perhaps in such districts as Saxony, where Christianity was introduced *vi et armis*, and therefore in a more wholesale, if not in the end a more effectual fashion [2].

The measure of surviving heathenism under Christianity must have varied considerably from district to district. Much would depend on the natural temper of the converts, on the tact of the clergy and on the influence they were able to secure. Roughly speaking, the old worships left their trace upon the new society in two ways. Certain central practices, the deliberate invocation of the discarded gods, the deliberate acknowledgement of their divinity by sacrifice, were bound to be altogether proscribed [3]. And these, if they did not precisely

---

[1] Bede, ii. 15. So too in eighth-century Germany there were priests who were equally ready to sacrifice to Wuotan and to administer the sacrament of baptism (Gummere, 342). See also Grimm, i. 7, and the letter of Gregory the Great to queen Brunichildis in *M. G. H. Epist.* ii. 1. 7 'pervenit ad nos, quod multi Christianorum et ad ecclesias occurrant, et a culturis daemonum non abscedant.'

[2] Willibald (*Gesch.-Schreiber der deutschen Vorzeit*, 27) relates that in Germany, when Boniface felled the sacred oak of Thor (robur Iovis) he built the wood into a church.

[3] A Saxon *formula abrenuntiationis* of the ninth century (Müllenhoff-Scherer, *Denkmäler deutscher Poesie und Prosa aus dem 8.–12. Jahrhundert*, 1892, No. li) specifically renounces 'Thuner ende Uuôden ende Saxnôte ende allum thêm unholdum thê hira genôtas sint.' Anglo-Saxon laws and council decrees contain frequent references to sacrifices and other lingering remnants of heathenism. Cf. *Councils of Pincanhale and Cealcythe* (787), c. 19 (Haddan-Stubbs, iii. 458) 'si quid ex ritu paganorum remansit, avellatur, contemnatur, abiiciatur.' *Council of Gratlea* (928), c. 3 (Wilkins, i. 205) 'diximus. . . de sacrificiis barbaris. . . si quis aliquem occiderit . . . ut vitam suam perdat.' *Council of London* (1075) (Wilkins, i. 363) 'ne offa mortuorum animalium, quasi

vanish, at least went underground, coming to light only as shameful secrets of the confessional [1] or the witch-trial [2], or when the dominant faith received a rude shock in times of especial distress, famine or pestilence [3]. Others again were absorbed into the scheme of Christianity itself. Many of the protective functions, for instance, of the old pantheon were taken over bodily by the Virgin Mary, by St. John, St. Michael, St. Martin, St. Nicholas, and other personages of the new dispensation [4]. And in particular, as we have seen shadowed forth in Pope Gregory's policy, the festal customs of heathenism, purified so far as might be, received a generous amount of toleration. The chief thing required was that the outward and visible signs of the connexion with the hostile religion

pro vitanda animalium peste, alicubi suspendantur; nec sortes, vel aruspicia, seu divinationes, vel aliqua huiusmodi opera diaboli ab aliquo exerceantur.' Also *Leges* of Wihtred of Kent (696), c. 12 (Haddan-Stubbs, iii. 235), and other A.-S. laws quoted by Kemble, i. 523.

[1] *Penitential of Theodore* (Haddan-Stubbs, iii. 189), i. 15, *de Cultura Idolorum*; *Penitential of Egbert* (H.-S. iii. 424), 8, *de Auguriis vel Divinationibus.*

[2] Pearson, ii. 1 (Essay on *Woman as Witch*); cf. A.-S. spells in Kemble, i. 528, and Cockayne, *Leechdoms* (R. S.), iii. 35, 55. Early and mediaeval Christianity did not deny the existence of the heathen gods, but treated them as evil spirits, demons.

[3] An Essex case of 664 has just been quoted. Kemble, i. 358, gives two later ones from the *Chronicle of Lanercost.* In 1268 'cum hoc anno in Laodonia pestis grassaretur in pecudes armenti, quam vocant usitate Lungessouth, quidam bestiales, habitu claustrales non animo, docebant idiotas patriae ignem confrictione de lignis educere et simulachrum Priapi statuere, et per haec bestiis succurrere.' In 1282 'sacerdos parochialis, nomine Johannes, Priapi prophana parans, congregatis ex villa puellulis, cogebat ejs,

choreis factis, Libero patri circuire.' By Priapus-Liber is probably meant Freyr, the only Teutonic god known to have had Priapic characteristics (Adam of Bremen, *Gesta Hammaburgensis Eccles. Pontif.* iv. 26 in *M. G. H. Script.* vii. 267).

[4] Grimm, i. 5, 11, 64, 174; iii. xxxiv–xlv; Keary, 90; Pearson, ii. 16, 32, 42, 243, 285, 350. The Virgin Mary succeeds to the place of the old Teutonic goddess of fertility, Freyja, Nerthus. So elsewhere does St. Walpurg. The toasts or *minni* drunk to Odin and Freyja are transferred to St. John and St. Gertrude. The travels of Odin and Loki become the travels of Christ and St. Peter. Many examples of the adaptation of pre-existing customs to Christianity will be found in the course of this book. A capitulary of Karlmann, drawn up in 742 after the synod of Ratisbon held by Boniface in Germany, speaks of 'hostias immolatitias, quas stulti homines iuxta ecclesias ritu pagano faciunt sub nomine sanctorum martyrum vel confessorum' (Boretius, *Capitularia Reg. Franc.* i. 24 in *M. G. H.*; Mansi, xii. 367). At Kirkcudbright in the twelfth century bulls were killed 'as an alms and oblation to St. Cuthbert (*F. L. x.* 353).

should be abandoned. Nor was this such a difficult matter.
Cult, the sum of what man feels it obligatory upon him to do
in virtue of his relation to the unseen powers, is notoriously
a more enduring thing than belief, the speculative, or mythology,
the imaginative statement of those relations. And it was of
the customs themselves that the people were tenacious, not
of the meaning, so far as there was still a meaning, attached
to them, or of the names which their priests had been wont to
invoke. Leave them but their familiar revels, and the ritual
so indissolubly bound up with their hopes of fertility for their
flocks and crops, they would not stick upon the explicit
consciousness that they drank or danced in the might of
Eostre or of Freyr. And in time, as the Christian interpretation of life became an everyday thing, it passed out of
sight that the customs had been ritual at all. At the most
a general sense of their 'lucky' influence survived. But to
stop doing them ; that was not likely to suggest itself to the
rustic mind. And so the church and the open space around
the church continued to be, what the temple and the temple
precinct had been, the centre, both secular and religious, of the
village life. From the Christian point of view, the arrangement had its obvious advantages. It had also this disadvantage,
that so far as obnoxious elements still clung to the festivals,
so far as the darker practices of heathenism still lingered, it
was precisely the most sacred spot that they defiled. Were
incantations and spells still muttered secretly for the good
will of the deposed divinities? it was the churchyard that
was sure to be selected as the nocturnal scene of the unhallowed
ceremony. Were the clergy unable to cleanse the yearly
wake of wanton dance and song? it was the church itself,
by Gregory's own decree, that became the focus of the
riot.

The partial survival of the village ceremonies under Christianity will appear less surprising when it is borne in mind that
the heathenism which Christianity combated was itself only
the final term of a long process of evolution. The worshippers
of the Keltic or Teutonic deities already practised a traditional
ritual, probably without any very clear conception of the
rationale on which some at least of the acts which they per-

formed were based. These acts had their origin far back in the history of the religious consciousness ; and it must not be supposed, because modern scholarship, with its comparative methods, is able to some extent to reconstruct the mental conditions out of which they arose, that these conditions were still wholly operative in the sixth, any more than in the thirteenth or the twentieth century. Side by side with customs which had still their definite and intelligible significance, religious conservatism had certainly preserved others of a very primitive type, some of which survived as mere fossils, while others had undergone that transformation of intention, that pouring of new wine into old bottles, which is one of the most familiar features in the history of institutions. The heathenism of western Europe must be regarded, therefore, as a group of religious practices originating in very different strata of civilization, and only fused together in the continuity of tradition. Its permanence lay in the law of association through which a piece of ritual originally devised by the folk to secure their practical well-being remained, even after the initial meaning grew obscure, irrevocably bound up with their expectations of that well-being. Its interest to the student is that of a development, rather than that of a system. Only the briefest outline of the direction taken by this development can be here indicated. But it must first be pointed out that, whether from a common derivation, or through a similar intellectual structure reacting upon similar conditions of life, it seems, at least up to the point of emergence of the fully formed village cult, to have proceeded on uniform lines, not only amongst the Teutonic and Keltic tribes who inhabited western and northern Europe and these islands, but also amongst all the Aryan-speaking peoples. In particular, although the Teutonic and the Keltic priests and bards elaborated, probably in comparatively late stages of their history, very different god-names and very different mythologies, yet these are but the superstructure of religion ; and it is possible to infer, both from the results of folk-lore and from the more scanty documentary evidence, a substantial identity throughout the whole Kelto-Teutonic group, of the underlying institutions of ritual and of the fundamental theological conceptions [1]. I am aware that it is no longer permissible to sum up all the facts of European civilization in an Aryan formula. Ethnology has satisfactorily established the existence on the continent of at least two important racial strains besides that of the blonde invader from Latham-land [2]. But I do not think that any of the attempts hitherto made to distinguish Aryan from pre-Aryan elements in folk-lore have met with any measure of success [3]. Nor is it quite clear that any such distinction need have been implied by the difference of blood. Archaeologists speak of a remarkable uniformity of material culture throughout the whole of Europe during the neolithic period; and there appears to be no special reason why this uniformity may not have extended to the comparatively simple notions which man was led to form of the not-man by his early contacts with his environment. In any case the social amalgamation of Aryan and pre-Aryan

[1] In the present state of Gaulish and still more of Irish studies, only a glimmering of possible equations between Teutonic and Keltic gods is apparent.

[2] Recent ethnological research is summed up in G. Vacher de Lapouge, *L'Aryen* (1899); W. Z. Ripley, *The Races of Europe* (1900); A. H. Keane, *Ethnology* (1896); *Man, Past and Present* (1899); J. Deniker, *The Races of Man* (1900); G. Sergi, *The Mediterranean Race* (1901). The three racial types that, in many pure and hybrid forms, mainly compose the population of Europe may be distinguished as (1) *Homo Europaeus*, the tall blonde long-headed (dolichocephalic) race of north Europe, (including Teutons and red-haired 'Kelts'), to which the Aryan speech seems primarily to have belonged; (2) *Homo alpinus*, the medium coloured and sized brachycephalic (round-headed) race of central Europe; (3) *Homo meridionalis* (Lapouge) or *mediterranensis* (Keane), the small dark dolichocephalic race of the Mediterranean basin and the western isles (including dark 'Kelts'). During the formative period of European culture (2) was probably of little importance, and (1) and (3) are possibly of closer racial affinity to each other than either of them is to (2).

[3] Gomme, *Ethnology in Folklore*, 21; *Village Community*, 69; *Report of Brit. Ass.* (1896), 626; *F. L. Congress*, 348; *F. L.* x. 129, ascribes the fire customs of Europe to Aryans and the water customs to the pre-Aryans. A. Bertrand, *Religion des Gaulois*, 68, considers human sacrifice characteristically pre-Aryan. There seems to me more hope of arriving at a knowledge of specific Mediterranean cults, before the Aryan intermixture, from a study of the stone amulets and cup-markings of the megaliths (Bertrand, *op. cit.* 42) or from such investigations into 'Mycenaean' antiquity as that of A. J. Evans, *Mycenaean Tree and Pillar Cult* (1901). The speculations of Nietzsche, in *A Genealogy of Morals* and elsewhere, as to the altruistic 'slave' morality of the pre-Aryan and the self-regarding morality of the conquering Aryan 'blond beast' are amusing or pitiful reading, according to one's mood.

was a process already complete by the Middle Ages ; and for
the purpose of this investigation it seems justifiable, and in
the present state of knowledge even necessary, to treat the
village customs as roughly speaking homogeneous throughout
the whole of the Kelto-Teutonic area.

An analysis of these customs suggests a mental history
somewhat as follows. The first relations of man to the not-
man are, it need hardly be said, of a practical rather than
a sentimental or a philosophic character. They arise out of
an endeavour to procure certain goods which depend, in part
at least, upon natural processes beyond man's own control.
The chief of these goods is, of course, food ; that is to say, in
a primitive state of civilization, success in hunting, whether of
berries, mussels and ' witchetty grubs,' or of more elusive and
difficult game ; and later, when hunting ceases to be the mainstay of existence, the continued fertility of the flocks and
herds, which form the support of a pastoral race, and of the
cornfields and orchards which in their turn come to supplement these, on the appearance of agriculture. Food once
supplied, the little tale of primitive man's limited conception
of the desirable is soon completed. Fire and a roof-tree are
his already. But he asks for physical health, for success in
love and in the begetting of offspring, and for the power to
anticipate by divination that future about which he is always so
childishly curious. In the pursuit, then, of these simple goods
man endeavours to control nature. But his earliest essays in
this direction are, as Dr. Frazer has recently pointed out, not
properly to be called religion [1]. The magical charms by

[1] Frazer, G. B. i. 9 ' The fundamental principles on which it
[savage magic] is based would seem
to be reducible to two : first, that
like produces like, or that an effect
resembles its cause ; and second,
that things which have once been
in contact, but have ceased to be
so, continue to act upon each other
as if the contact still persisted.
From the first of these principles,
the savage infers that he can produce any desired effect merely by
imitating it ; from the second he
concludes that he can influence
at pleasure and at any distance
any person of whom, or any thing
of which, he possesses a particle.
Magic of the latter sort, resting as
it does on the belief in a certain
secret sympathy which unites indissolubly things that have once been
connected with each other may
appropriately be termed sympathetic in the strict sense of the term.
Magic of the former kind, in which
the supposed cause resembles or
simulates the supposed effect, may
conveniently be described as imitative or mimetic.' Cf. Jevons, 31

which he attempts to make the sun burn, and the waters fall, and the wind blow as it pleases him, certainly do not imply that recognition of a quasi-human personality outside himself, which any religious definition may be supposed to require as a minimum. They are rather to be regarded as applications of primitive science, for they depend upon a vague general notion of the relations of cause and effect. To assume that you can influence a thing through what is similar to it, or through what has been in contact with it, which, according to Dr. Frazer, are the postulates of magic in its mimetic and its sympathetic form respectively, may be bad science, but at least it is science of a sort, and not religion.

The magical charms play a large part in the village ritual, and will be illustrated in the following chapter. Presently, however, the scientific spirit is modified by that tendency of animism through which man comes to look upon the external world not as mere more or less resisting matter to be moved hither or thither, but rather as a debateable land peopled with spirits in some sense alive. These spirits are the active forces dimly discerned by human imagination as at work behind the shifting and often mysterious natural phenomena—forces of the moving winds and waters, of the skies now clear, now overcast, of the animal races of hill and plain, of the growth waxing and waning year by year in field and woodland. The control of nature now means the control of these powers, and to this object the charms are directed. In particular, I think,

'The savage makes the generalization that like produces like; and then he is provided with the means of bringing about anything he wishes, for to produce an effect he has only to imitate it. To cause a wind to blow, he flaps a blanket, as the sailor still whistles to bring a whistling gale. . . . If the vegetation requires rain, all that is needed is to dip a branch in water, and with it to sprinkle the ground. Or a spray of water squirted from the mouth will produce a mist sufficiently like the mist required to produce the desired effect; or black clouds of smoke will be followed by black clouds of rain.' I do not feel that magic is altogether a happy term for this sort of savage science. In its ordinary sense (the 'black art'), it certainly contains a large element of what Dr. Frazer distinguishes from magic as religion, 'a propitiation or conciliation of powers superior to man which are believed to direct and control the course of nature and of human life.' True, these powers are not to whom the orthodox religion is directed, but the approach to them is religious in the sense of the above definition. Such magic is in fact an amalgam of charms, which are Dr. Frazer's 'magic,' and spells, which are his 'religion.' But so are many more recognized cults.

at this stage of his development, man conceives a spirit of that food which still remains in the very forefront of his aspirations, of his actual food-plant, or of the animal species which he habitually hunts[1]. Of this spirit he initiates a cult, which rests upon the old magical principle of the mastering efficacy of direct contact. He binds the spirit literally to him by wearing it as a garment, or absorbs it into himself in a solemn meal, hoping by either process to acquire an influence or power over it. Naturally, at this stage, the spirit becomes to the eye of his imagination phytomorphic or theriomorphic in aspect. He may conceive it as especially incarnate in a single sacred plant or animal. But the most critical moment in the history of animism is that at which the elemental spirits come to be looked upon as anthropomorphic, made in the likeness of man himself. This is perhaps due to the identification of them with those other quasi-human spirits, of whose existence man has by an independent line of thought also become aware. These are the ghostly spirits of departed kinsmen, still in some shadowy way inhabiting or revisiting the house-place. The change does not merely mean that the visible phytomorphic and theriomorphic embodiments of mental forces sink into subordination; the plants and animals becoming no more than symbols and appurtenances of the anthropomorphic spirit, or temporary forms with which from time to time he invests himself. A transformation of the whole character of the cult is involved, for man must now approach the spirits, not merely by charms, although conservatism preserves these as an element in ritual, but with modifications of the modes in which he approaches his fellow man. He must beg their favour with submissive speech or buy it with bribes. And here, with prayer and oblation, religion in the stricter sense makes its appearance.

The next step of man is from the crowd of animistic spirits to isolate the god. The notion of a god is much the old notion of an anthropomorphic elemental spirit, widened,

---

[1] Some facts of European animal worship are dealt with in two important recent papers, one by S. Reinach in *Revue celtique*, xxi. 269, the other by N. W. Thomas, in *F. L.* xi. 227. The relation of such worship to the group of savage social institutions classed as totemism is a difficult and far from solved problem, which cannot be touched upon here.

exalted, and further removed from sense. Instead of a local and limited home, the god has his dwelling in the whole expanse of heaven or in some distant region of space. He transcends and as an object of cult supplants the more bounded and more concrete personifications of natural forces out of which he has been evolved. But he does not annul these: they survive in popular credence as his servants and ministers. It is indeed on the analogy of the position of the human chief amongst his *comitatus* that, in all probability, the conception of the god is largely arrived at. Comparative philology seems to show that the belief in gods is common to the Aryan-speaking peoples, and that at the root of all the cognate mythologies there lies a single fundamental divinity. This is the Dyaus of the Indians, the Zeus of the Greeks, the Jupiter of the Romans, the Tiwaz (O.H.G. Zîu, O.N. Týr, A.-S. Tîw) of the Teutons. He is an embodiment of the great clear sunlit heavens, the dispenser of light to the huntsman, and of warmth and moisture to the crops. Side by side with the conception of the heaven-god comes that of his female counterpart, who is also, though less clearly, indicated in all the mythologies. In her earliest aspect she is the lady of the woods and of the blossoming fruitful earth. This primary dualism is an extremely important factor in the explanation of early religion. The all-father, the heaven, and the mother-goddess, the earth, are distinct personalities from the beginning. It does not appear possible to resolve one into a mere doublet or derivative of the other. Certainly the marriage of earth and heaven in the showers that fertilize the crops is one of the oldest and most natural of myths. But it is generally admitted that myth is determined by and does not determine the forms of cult. The heaven-god and the earth-goddess must have already had their separate existence before the priests could hymn their marriage. An explanation of the dualism is probably to be traced in the merging of two cults originally distinct. These will have been sex-cults. Tillage is, of course, little esteemed by primitive man. It was so with the Germans, even up to the point at which they first came into contact with the Romans[1]. Yet all the Aryan languages

[1] Gummere, 39; Caesar, *de B. G.* iv. 1. 7; vi. 22. 2; Tacitus, *Germ.* 26.

show some acquaintance with the use of grains [1]. The analogy with existing savages suggests that European agriculture in its early stages was an affair of the women. While the men hunted or afterwards tended their droves of cattle and horses, the women grubbed for roots, and presently learnt to scratch the surface of the ground, to scatter the seed, and painfully to garner and grind the scanty produce [2]. As the avocations of the sexes were distinct, so would their magic or their religion be. Each would develop rites of its own of a type strictly determined by its practical ambitions, and each would stand apart from the rites of the other. The interest of the men would centre in the boar or stag, that of the women in the fruit-tree or the wheat-sheaf. To the former the stone altar on the open hill-top would be holy; to the latter the dim recesses of the impenetrable grove. Presently when the god concept appeared, the men's divinity would be a personification of the illimitable and mysterious heavens beneath which they hunted and herded, from which the pools were filled with water, and at times the pestilence was darted in the sun rays; the women's of the wooded and deep-bosomed earth out of which their wealth sprang. This would as naturally take a female as that a male form. Agriculture, however, was not for ever left solely to the women. In time pasturage and tillage came to be carried on as two branches of a single pursuit, and the independent sex-cults which had sprung out of them coalesced in the common village worship of later days. Certain features of the primitive differentiation can still be obscurely distinguished. Here and there one or the other sex

---

[1] Schräder-Jevons, 281, says that the Indo-Europeans begin their history 'acquainted with the rudiments of agriculture,' but 'still possessed with nomadic tendencies.' He adds that considerable progress must have been made before the dispersion of the European branches, and points out that agriculture would naturally develop when the migratory hordes from the steppes reached the great forests of central Europe. For this there would be two reasons, the greater fertility of the soil and the narrowed space for pasturage. On the other hand, V. Hehn, *Culturpflanzen und Haustiere*, and Mommsen, *Hist. of Rome*, i. 16, find the traces of agriculture amongst the undivided Indo-Europeans very slight; the word *yáva-ζέα*, which is common to the tongues, need mean nothing more than a wild cereal.

[2] Jevons, 240, 255; Pearson, ii. 42; O. T. Mason, *Woman's Share in Primitive Culture*, 14.

is barred from particular ceremonies, or a male priest must perform his mystic functions in woman's garb. The heaven-god perhaps remains the especial protector of the cattle, and the earth-goddess of the corn. But generally speaking they have all the interests of the farm in a joint tutelage. The stone altar is set up in the sacred grove ; the mystic tree is planted on the hill-top [1]. Theriomorphic and phytomorphic symbols shadow forth a single godhead [2]. The earth-mother becomes a divinity of light. The heaven-father takes up his abode in the spreading oak.

The historic religions of heathenism have not preserved either the primitive dualistic monotheism, if the phrase may be permitted, or the simplicity of divine functions here sketched. With the advance of civilization the objects of worship must necessarily take upon them new responsibilities. If a tribe has its home by the sea, sooner or later it trusts frail barks to the waters, and to its gods is committed the charge of sea-faring. When handicrafts are invented, these also become their care. When the pressure of tribe upon tribe leads to war, they champion the host in battle. Moral ideas emerge and attach themselves to their service: and ultimately they become identified with the rulers of the dead, and reign in the shadowy world beyond the tomb. Another set of processes combine to produce what is known as polytheism. The constant application of fixed epithets to the godhead tends in the long run to break up its unity. Special aspects of it begin to take on an independent existence. Thus amongst the Teutonic peoples Tiwaz-Thunaraz, the thunderous sky, gives rise to Thunar or Thor, and Tiwaz-Frawiaz, the bounteous sky, to Freyr. And so the ancient heaven-god is replaced by distinct gods of rain and sunshine, who, with the mother-goddess, form that triad of divinities so prominent in several European cults [3]. Again as tribes come into contact with each other,

---

[1] Burne-Jackson, 352, 362 ; Rhys, *C. F.* i. 312 ; *F. L.* v. 339 ; Dyer, 133 ; Ditchfield, 70 ; cf. ch. vi. One of the hills so visited is the artificial one of Silbury, and perhaps the custom points to the object with which this and the similar 'mound' at Marlborough were piled up.

[2] Frazer, ii. 261, deals very fully with the theriomorphic corn-spirits of folk belief.

[3] On these triads and others in which three male or three female

there is a borrowing of religious conceptions, and the tribal deities are duplicated by others who are really the same in origin, but have different names. The mythological speculations of priests and bards cause further elaboration. The friendly national gods are contrasted with the dark hostile deities of foreign enemies. A belief in the culture-hero or semi-divine man, who wrests the gifts of civilization from the older gods, makes its appearance. Certain cults, such as that of Druidism, become the starting-point for even more philosophic conceptions. The personal predilection of an important worshipper or group of worshippers for this or that deity extends his vogue. The great event in the later history of Teutonic heathenism is the overshadowing of earlier cults by that of Odin or Wodan, who seems to have been originally a ruler of the dead, or perhaps a culture-hero, and not an elemental god at all [1]. The multiplicity of forms under which essentially the same divinity presents itself in history and in popular belief may be illustrated by the mother-goddess of the Teutons. As Freyja she is the female counterpart of Freyr; as Nerthus of Freyr's northern doublet, Njordr. When Wodan largely absorbs the elemental functions, she becomes his wife, as Frîja or Frigg. Through her association with the heaven-gods, she is herself a heaven- as well as an earth-goddess [2], the Eostre of Bede [3], as well as the Erce of the Anglo-Saxon ploughing charm [4]. She is probably the Tanfana

---

figures appear, cf. Bertrand, 341; A. Maury, *Croyances et Légendes du Moyen Âge* (1896), 6; *Matronen-Kultus* in *Zeitschrift d. Vereins f. Volkskultur*, ii. 24. I have not yet seen L. L. Paine, *The Ethnic Trinities and their Relation to the Christian Trinity* (1901).

[1] Mogk, iii. 333; Golther, 298; Grimm, iv. 1709; Kemble, i. 335; Rhys, *C. H.* 282; H. M. Chadwick, *Cult of Othin* (1899).

[2] Mogk, iii. 366; Golther, 428.

[3] Mogk, iii. 374; Golther, 488; Tille, *Y. and C.* 144; Bede, *de temp. ratione*, c. 15 (*Opera*, ed. Giles, vi. 179) 'Fostur-monath qui nunc paschalis mensis interpretatur, quondam a dea illorum, quae Eostre vocabatur, et cui in illo festa celebrabant, nomen habuit; a cuius nomine nunc paschale tempus cognominant, consueto antiquae observationis vocabulo gaudia novae solemnitatis vocantes.' There seems no reason for thinking with Golther and Tille, that Bede made a mistake. Charlemagne took the name *Ôstarmânoth* for April, perhaps only out of compliment to the English, such as Alcuin, at his court.

[4] *A Charm for unfruitful or bewitched land* (O. Cockayne, *Leechdoms of Early England*, R. S. i. 399); cf. Grimm. i. 253; Golther, 455; Kögel, i. 1. 39. The ceremony has taken on a Christian colouring, but retains many primitive features.

of Tacitus and the Nehellenia of the Romano-Germanic votive stones. If so, she must have become a goddess of mariners, for Nehellenia seems to be the Isis of the *interpretatio Romana.* As earth-goddess she comes naturally into relation with the dead, and like Odin is a leader of the rout of souls. In German peasant-lore she survives under various names, of which Perchta is the most important; in witch-lore, as Diana, and by a curious mediaeval identification, as Herodias [1]. And her more primitive functions are largely inherited by the Virgin, by St. Walpurg and by countless local saints.

Most of the imaginative and mythological superstructure so briefly sketched in the last paragraph must be considered as subsequent in order of development to the typical village cult. Both before and in more fragmentary shape after the death of the old Keltic and Teutonic gods, that continued to be in great measure an amalgam of traditional rites of forgotten magical or pre-religious import. So far as the consciousness of the mediaeval or modern peasant directed it to unseen powers at all, which was but little, it was rather to some of these more local and bounded spirits who remained in the train of the gods, than to the gods themselves. For the purposes of the present discussion, it is sufficient to think of it quite generally as a cult of the spirits of fertilization, without attaching a very precise connotation to that term. Unlike the domestic cult of the ancestral ghosts, conducted for each household by the house-father at the hearth, it was communal in character. Whatever the tenure of land may have been,

Strips of turf are removed, and masses said over them. They are replaced after oil, honey, barm, milk of every kind of cattle, twigs of every tree, and holy water have been put on the spot. Seed is bought at a double price from almsmen and poured into a hole in the plough with salt and herbs. Various invocations are used, including one which calls on ' Erce, Erce, Erce, Eorthan modor,' and implores the Almighty to grant her fertility. Then the plough is driven, and a loaf, made of every kind of corn with milk and holy water, laid under the first furrow. Kögel considers *Erce* to be derived from *ero,* 'earth.' Brooke, i. 217, states on the authority of Montanus that a version of the prayer preserved in a convent at Corvei begins 'Eostar, Eostar, Eordhan modor.' He adds: ' nothing seems to follow from this clerical error.' But why an error? The equation Erce-Eostre is consistent with the fundamental identity of the light-goddess and the earth-goddess.

[1] Tacitus, *Ann.* i. 51 ; Mogk, iii. 373 ; Golther, 458 ; cf. ch. xii.

there seems no doubt that up to a late period 'co-aration,' or co-operative ploughing in open fields, remained the normal method of tillage, while the cattle of the community roamed in charge of a public herd over unenclosed pastures and forest lands [1]. The farm, as a self-sufficing agricultural unit, is a comparatively recent institution, the development of which has done much to render the village festivals obsolete. Originally the critical moments of the agricultural year were the same for the whole village, and the observances which they entailed were shared in by all.

The observances in question, or rather broken fragments of them, have now attached themselves to a number of different outstanding dates in the Christian calendar, and the reconstruction of the original year, with its seasonal feasts, is a matter of some difficulty [2]. The earliest year that can be traced amongst the Aryan-speaking peoples was a bipartite one, made up of only two seasons, winter and summer. For some reason that eludes research, winter preceded summer, just as night, in the primitive reckoning, preceded day. The divisions seem to have been determined by the conditions of a pastoral existence passed in the regularly recurring seasons of central Europe. Winter began when snow blocked the pastures and the cattle had to be brought home to the stall: summer when the grass grew green again and there was once more fodder in the open. Approximately these dates would correspond to mid-November and mid-March [3]. Actually, in the absence of a calendar, they would vary a little from year

---

[1] Gomme, *Village Community*, 157 ; B. C. A. Windle, *Life in Early Britain*, 200 ; F. W. Maitland, *Domesday Book and Beyond*, 142, 337, 346.

[2] I have followed in many points the views on Teutonic chronology of Tille, *Deutsches Weihnacht* (1893) and *Yule and Christmas* (1899), which are accepted in the main by O. Schräder, *Reallexicon der indogermanischen Altertumskunde*, s.vv. Jahr, Jahreszeiten, and partly correct those of Weinhold, *Ueber die deutsche Jahrtheilung* (1862), and Grotefend, *Die Zeitrechnung des*

deutschen Mittelalters (1891).

[3] In Scandinavia the winter naturally began earlier and ended later. Throughout, Scandinavian seasons diverged from those of Germany and the British Isles. In particular the high summer feast and the consequent tripartition of the year do not seem to have established themselves (*C. P. B.* i. 430). Further south the period of stall-feeding was extended when a better supply of fodder made it possible (Tille, *Y. and C.* 56, 62 ; Burne-Jackson, 380).

to year and would perhaps depend on some significant annual event, such as the first snowstorm in the one case[1], in the other the appearance of the first violet, butterfly or cockchafer, or of one of those migratory birds which still in popular belief bring good fortune and the summer, the swallow, cuckoo or stork[2]. Both dates would give occasion for religious ceremonies, together with the natural accompaniment of feasting and revel. More especially would this be the case at mid-November, when a great slaughtering of cattle was rendered economically necessary by the difficulty of stall-feeding the whole herd throughout the winter. Presently, however, new conditions established themselves. Agriculture grew in importance, and the crops rather than the cattle became the central interest of the village life. Fresh feasts sprang up side by side with the primitive ones, one at the beginning of ploughing about mid-February, another at the end of harvest, about mid-September. At the same time the increased supply of dry fodder tended to drive the annual slaughtering farther on into the winter. More or less contemporaneously with these processes, the old bipartite year was changed into a tripartite one by the growth of yet another new feast during that dangerous period when the due succession of rain and sun for the crops becomes a matter of the greatest moment to the farmer. Early summer, or spring, was thus set apart from late summer, or summer proper[3]. This development

[1] Cf. ch. xi, where the winter feasts are discussed in more detail.

[2] Grimm, ii. 675, 693, 762, notes the heralds of summer.

[3] Jahn, 34; Mogk, iii. 387; Golther, 572; Schräder-Jevons, 303. The Germans still knew three seasons only when they came into contact with the Romans; cf. Tacitus, *Germ.* 26 'annum quoque ipsum non in totidem digerunt species: hiems et ver et aestas intellectum ac vocabula habent, autumni perinde nomen ac bona ignorantur.' I do not agree with Tille, *Y. and C.* 6, that the tripartition of the year, in this pre-calendar form, was 'of foreign extraction.' Schräder shows that it is common to the Aryan languages. The Keltic seasons, in particular, seem to be closely parallel to the Teutonic. Of the three great Keltic feasts described by Rhys, *C. H.* 409, 513, 676; *C. F.* i. 308, the Lugnassad was probably the harvest feast, the Samhain the old beginning of winter feast, and the Beltain the high summer feast. The meaning of 'Beltain' (cf. *N. E. D.* s.v. Beltane) seems quite uncertain. A connexion is possible but certainly unproved with the Abelio of the Pyrenean inscriptions, the Belenus-Apollo of those of the eastern Alps, and, more rarely, Provence (Röscher, *Lexicon*, s.v. Belenus; Holder, *Alt-celtischer Sprachschatz*, s.vv. Belenus, Abelio;

also may be traced to the influence of agriculture, whose interest runs in a curve, while that of herding keeps comparatively a straight course. But as too much sun or too much wet not only spoils the crops but brings a murrain on the cattle, the herdsmen fell into line and took their share in the high summer rites. At first, no doubt, this last feast was a sporadic affair, held for propitiation of the unfavourable fertilization spirits when the elders of the village thought it called for. And to the end resort may have been had to exceptional acts of cult in times of especial distress. But gradually the occasional ceremony became an annual one, held as soon as the corn was thick in the green blade and the critical days were at hand.

So far, there has been no need to assume the existence of a calendar. How long the actual climatic conditions continued to determine the dates of the annual feasts can hardly be said. But when a calendar did make its appearance, the five feasts adapted themselves without much difficulty to it. The earliest calendar that can be inferred in central Europe was one, either of Oriental or possibly of Mediterranean *provenance*, which divided the year into six tides of three-score days each [1]. The beginnings of these tides almost certainly fell at about the middle of corresponding months of the Roman calendar [2]. The first would thus be marked by the beginning of winter feast in mid-November; two others by the beginning of summer feast and the harvest feast in mid-March and mid-August respectively. A little accommodation of the seasonal feasts of the farm would be required to adapt them to the remaining three. And here begins a process of dislocation of the original dates of customs, now becoming traditional rather than vital, which

Ausonius, *Professores*, iv. 7), or the Bel of Bohemia mentioned by Allso (ch. xii). The Semitic Baal, although a cult of Belus, found its way into the Roman world (cf. Appendix N, No. xxxii, and Wissowa, 302), is naturally even a less plausible relation. But it is dear to the folk-etymologist; cf. e.g. S. M. Mayhew, *Baalism* in *Trans. of St. Paul's*

Ecclesiological Society, i. 83.
[1] Tille, *Y. and C.* 7, 148, suggests an Egyptian or Babylonian origin, but the equation of the Gothic *Jiuleis* and the Cypriote ἰλαῖος, ἰουλαῖος, ἰουλίηος, ἰούλιος as names for winter periods makes a Mediterranean connexion seem possible.
[2] Cf. ch. xi.

was afterwards extended by successive stages to a bewildering degree. By this time, with the greater permanence of agriculture, the system of autumn ploughing had perhaps been invented. The spring ploughing festival was therefore of less importance, and bore to be shifted back to mid-January instead of mid-February. Four of the six tides are now provided with initial feasts. These are mid-November, mid-January, mid-March, and mid-September. There are, however, still mid-May and mid-July, and only the high summer feast to divide between them. I am inclined to believe that a division is precisely what took place, and that the hitherto fluctuating date of the summer feast was determined in some localities to mid-May, in others to mid July [1].

The European three-score-day-tide calendar is rather an ingenious conjecture than an ascertained fact of history. When the Germano-Keltic peoples came under the influence of Roman civilization, they adopted amongst other things the Roman calendar, first in its primitive form and then in the more scientific one given to it under Julius Caesar. The latter divided the year into four quarters and twelve months, and carried with it a knowledge of the solstices, at which the astronomy neither of Kelts nor of Germans seems to have previously arrived [2]. The feasts again underwent a process of dis-

[1] Grimm, ii. 615, notes that Easter fires are normal in the north, Midsummer fires in the south of Germany. The Beltane fires both of Scotland and Ireland are usually on May 1, but some of the Irish examples collected by J. Jamieson, *Etym. Dict. of the Scottish Language*, s. v., are at midsummer.

[2] Tille, *Y. and C.* 71 ; Rhys, *C. H.* 419. The primitive year was thermometric, not astronomic, its critical moments, not the solstices, a knowledge of which means science, but the sensible increase and diminution of heat in spring and autumn. The solstices came through Rome. The *Sermo Eligii* (Grimm, iv. 1737) has 'nullus in festivitate S. Ioannis vel quibuslibet sanctorum solemnitatibus solstitia ... exerceat,' but Eligius was a seventh-century bishop,

and this *Sermo* may have been interpolated in the eighth century (O. Reich, *Über Audoen's Lebensbeschreibung des heiligen Eligius* (1872), cited in *Rev. celtique*, ix. 433). It is not clear that the un-Romanized Teuton or Kelt made a god of the sun, as distinct from the heaven-god, who of course has solar attributes and emblems. In the same *Sermo* Eligius says 'nullus dominos solem aut lunam vocet, neque per eos iuret.' But the notion of 'domini' may be post-Roman, and the oath is by the permanent, rather than the divine ; cf. A. de Jubainville, *Intr. à l'Étude de la Litt. celt.* 181. It is noticeable that German names for the sun are originally feminine and for the moon masculine.

location in order to harmonize them with the new arrangement.
The ceremonies of the winter feast were pulled back to November 1 or pushed forward to January 1. The high summer feast
was attracted from mid-May and mid-July respectively to
the important Roman dates of the *Floralia* on May 1 and the
summer solstice on June 24. Last of all, to complete the confusion, came, on the top of three-score-day-tide calendar and
Roman calendar alike, the scheme of Christianity with its
host of major and minor ecclesiastical festivals, some of them
fixed, others movable. Inevitably these in their turn began
to absorb the agricultural customs. The present distribution
of the five original feasts, therefore, is somewhat as follows.
The winter feast is spread over all the winter half of the year
from All Souls day to Twelfth night. A later chapter will
illustrate its destiny more in detail. The ploughing feast is
to be sought mainly in Plough Monday, in Candlemas and
in Shrovetide or Carnival[1]; the beginning of summer feast in
Palm Sunday, Easter and St. Mark's day; the early variety
of the high summer feast probably also in Easter, and certainly
in May-day, St. George's day, Ascensiontide with its Rogations, Whitsuntide and Trinity Sunday; the later variety of
the same feast in Midsummer day and Lammastide; and the
harvest feast in Michaelmas. These are days of more or less
general observance. Locally, in strict accordance with the
policy of Gregory the Great as expounded to Mellitus, the
floating customs have often settled upon conveniently neighbouring dates of wakes, rushbearings, kirmesses and other
forms of vigil or dedication festivals[2]; and even, in the utter

---

[1] Mogk, iii. 393; Golther, 584;
Jahn, 84; Caspari, 35; Saupe, 7;
Hauck, ii. 357; Michels, 93. The
ploughing feast is probably the
spurcalia of the *Indiculus* and of
Eadhelm, *de laudibus virginitatis*,
c. 25, and the *dies spurci* of the
Hom. de Sacrilegiis. This term
appears in the later German name
for February, *Sporkele*. It seems
to be founded on Roman analogy
from *spurcus*, 'unclean.' Pearson,
ii. 159, would, however, trace it to an
Aryan root *spherag*, 'swell,' 'burst,'

'shoot.' Bede, *de temp. rat.* c. 15,
calls February *Sol-monath*, which he
explains as 'mensis placentarum.'
September, the month of the harvest-
festival, is *Haleg-monath*, or 'mensis
sacrorum.'

[2] Pfannenschmidt, 244; Brand,
ii. 1; Ditchfield, 130; Burne-Jackson, 439; Burton, *Rushbearing*,
147; Schaff, vi. 544; Duchesne,
385. The dedication of churches
was solemnly carried out from the
fourth century, and the anniversary observed. Gregory the Great

oblivion of their primitive significance, upon the anniversaries of historical events, such as Royal Oak day on May 29 [1], or Gunpowder day. Finally it may be noted, that of the five feasts that of high summer is the one most fully preserved in modern survivals. This is partly because it comes at a convenient time of year for the out-of-door holiday-making which serves as a preservative for the traditional rites; partly also because, while the pastoral element in the feasts of the beginnings of winter and summer soon became comparatively unimportant through the subordination of pasturage to tillage, and the ploughing and harvest feasts tended more and more to become affairs of the individual farm carried out in close connexion with those operations themselves, the summer feast retained its communal character and continued to be celebrated by the whole village for the benefit of everybody's crops and trees, and everybody's flocks and herds [2]. It is therefore mainly, although not wholly, upon the summer feast that the analysis of the agricultural ritual to be given in the next chapter will be based.

ordered 'solemnitates ecclesiarum dedicationum per singulos annos sunt celebrandae.' The A.-S. *Canons* of Edgar (960), c. 28 (Wilkins, i. 227), require them to be kept with sobriety. Originally the anniversary, as well as the actual dedication day, was observed with an all night watch, whence the name *vigilia*, wakes. Belethus, *de rat. offic.* (*P. L.* ccii. 141), c. 137, says that the custom was abolished owing to the immorality to which it led. But the 'eve' of these and other feasts continued to share in the sanctity of the 'day,' a practice in harmony with the European sense of the precedence of night over day (cf. Schräder-Jevons, 311; Bertrand, 267, 354,

413). An Act of Convocation in 1536 (Wilkins, iii. 823) required all wakes to be held on the first Sunday in October, but it does not appear to have been very effectual.

[1] S. O. Addy, in *F. L.* xii. 394, has a full account of 'Garland day' at Castleton, Derbyshire, on May 29; cf. *F. L.* xii. 76 (Wishford, Wilts); Burne-Jackson, 365.

[2] The classification of agricultural feasts in U. Jahn, *Die deutschen Opfergebräuche*, seems throughout to be based less on the facts of primitive communal agriculture, than on those of the more elaborate methods of the later farms with their variety of crops.

CHAPTER VI

VILLAGE FESTIVALS

[*Bibliographical Note.*—A systematic calendar of English festival usages by a competent folk-lorist is much needed. J. Brand, *Observations on Popular Antiquities* (1777), based on H. Bourne, *Antiquitates Vulgares* (1725), and edited, first by Sir Henry Ellis in 1813, 1841-2 and 1849, and then by W. C. Hazlitt in 1870, is full of valuable material, but belongs to the age of pre-scientific antiquarianism. R. T. Hampson, *Medii Aevi Kalendarium* (1841), is no less unsatisfactory. In default of anything better, T. F. T. Dyer, *British Popular Customs* (1891), is a useful compilation from printed sources, and P. H. Ditchfield, *Old English Customs* (1896), a gossipy account of contemporary survivals. These may be supplemented from collections of more limited range, such as H. J. Feasey, *Ancient English Holy Week Ceremonial* (1897), and J. E. Vaux, *Church Folk-Lore* (1894); by treatises on local folk-lore, of which W. Henderson, *Notes on the Folk-Lore of the Northern Counties of England and the Borders* (2nd ed. 1879), C. S. Burne and G. F. Jackson, *Shropshire Folk-Lore* (1883-5), and J. Rhys, *Celtic Folk-Lore, Welsh and Manx* (1901), are the best; and by the various publications of the Folk-Lore Society, especially the series of *County Folk-Lore* (1895-9) and the successive periodicals, *The Folk-Lore Record* (1878-82), *Folk-Lore Journal* (1883-9), and *Folk-Lore* (1890-1903). Popular accounts of French *fêtes* are given by E. Cortet, *Essai sur les Fêtes religieuses* (1867), and O. Havard, *Les Fêtes de nos Pères* (1898). L. J. B. Bérenger-Féraud, *Superstitions et Survivances* (1896), is more pretentious, but not really scholarly. C. Leber, *Dissertations relatives à l'Histoire de France* (1826-38), vol. ix, contains interesting material of an historical character, largely drawn from papers in the eighteenth-century periodical *Le Mercure de France*. Amongst German books, J. Grimm, *Teutonic Mythology* (transl. J. S. Stallybrass, 1880-8), H. Pfannenschmidt, *Germanische Erntefeste* (1878), and U. Jahn, *Die deutschen Opfergebräuche bei Ackerbau und Viehzucht* (1884), are all excellent. Many of the books mentioned in the bibliographical note to the last chapter remain useful for the present and following ones; in particular J. G. Frazer, *The Golden Bough* (2nd ed. 1900), is, of course, invaluable. I have only included in the above list such works of general range as I have actually made most use of. Many others dealing with special points are cited in the notes. A fuller guide to folk-lore literature will be found in M. R. Cox, *Introduction to Folklore* (2nd ed. 1897).]

THE central fact of the agricultural festivals is the presence in the village of the fertilization spirit in the visible and tangible form of flowers and green foliage or of the fruits of the earth. Thus, when the peasants do their 'observaunce to a morn of May,' great boughs of hawthorn are cut before daybreak in the woods, and carried, with other seasonable leafage and blossom, into the village street. Lads plant branches before the doors of their mistresses. The folk deck themselves, their houses, and the church in green. Some of them are clad almost entirely in wreaths and tutties, and become walking bushes, 'Jacks i' the green.' The revel centres in dance and song around a young tree set up in some open space of the village, or a more permanent May-pole adorned for the occasion with fresh garlands. A large garland, often with an anthropomorphic representation of the fertilization spirit in the form of a doll, parades the streets, and is accompanied by a 'king' or 'queen,' or a 'king' and 'queen' together. Such a garland finds its place at all the seasonal feasts; but whereas in spring and summer it is naturally made of the new vegetation, at harvest it as naturally takes the form of a sheaf, often the last sheaf cut, of the corn. Then it is known as the 'harvest-May' or the 'neck,' or if it is anthropomorphic in character, as the 'kern-baby.' Summer and harvest garlands alike are not destroyed when the festival is over, but remain hung up on the May-pole or the church or the barn-door until the season for their annual renewing comes round. And sometimes the grain of the 'harvest-May' is mingled in the spring with the seed-corn [1].

The rationale of such customs is fairly simple. They depend upon a notion of sympathetic magic carried on into the animistic stage of belief. Their object is to secure the beneficent influence of the fertilization spirit by bringing the persons or places to be benefited into direct contact with the physical embodiment of that spirit. In the burgeoning quick set up on the village green is the divine presence. The worshipper clad in leaves and flowers has made himself a garment of the god, and is therefore in a very special sense under his protection. Thus efficacy in folk-belief of physical contact may be illustrated by another set of practices in which recourse is had to the fertilization spirit for the cure of disease. A child suffering from croup, convulsions, rickets,

---

[1] Frazer, i. 193; ii. 96; Brand, i. 125; Dyer, 223; Ditchfield, 95; Philpot, 144; Grimm, ii. 762; &c., &c. A single example of the custom is minutely studied by S. O. Addy, *Garland Day at Castleton*, in *F. L.* xii. 394.

or other ailment, is passed through a hole in a split tree, or beneath a bramble rooted at both ends, or a strip of turf partly raised from the ground. It is the actual touch of earth or stem that works the healing [1].

May-pole or church may represent a focus of the cult at some specially sacred tree or grove in the heathen village. But the ceremony, though it centres at these, is not confined to them, for its whole purpose is to distribute the benign influence over the entire community, every field, fold, pasture, orchard close and homestead thereof. At ploughing, the driving of the first furrow; at harvest, the homecoming of the last wain, is attended with ritual. Probably all the primitive festivals, and certainly that of high summer, included a lustration, in which the image or tree which stood for the fertilization spirit was borne in solemn procession from dwelling to dwelling and round all the boundaries of the village. Tacitus records the progress of the earth-goddess Nerthus amongst the German tribes about the mouth of the Elbe, and the dipping of the goddess and the drowning of her slaves in a lake at the term of the ceremony [2]. So too at Upsala in Sweden the statue of Freyr went round when winter was at an end [3]; while Sozomenes tells how, when Ulfilas was preaching Christianity to the Visigoths, Athanaric sent the image of his god abroad in a wagon, and burnt the houses of all who refused to bow down and sacrifice [4]. Such lustrations continue to be a prominent feature of the folk survivals. They are preserved in a number of processional customs in all parts of England; in the municipal 'ridings,' 'shows,' or 'watches' on St. George's [5] or Midsummer [6]

---

[1] A. B. Gomme, ii. 507; Hartland, *Perseus*, ii. 187; Grimm, iv. 1738, 1747; Gaidoz, *Un vieux rite médical* (1893).

[2] Tacitus, *Germania*, 40.

[3] Vigfusson and Ungar, *Flateyjarbok*, i. 337; Grimm, i. 107; Gummere, *G. O.* 433; Mogk, iii. 321; Golther, 228.

[4] Sozomenes, *Hist. Eccles.* vi. 37. Cf. also *Indiculus* (ed. Saupe, 32) 'de simulacro, quod per campos portant,' the fifth-century *Vita S.*

Martini, c. 12, by Sulpicius Severus (*Opera*, ed. Halm, in *Corp. Script. Eccl. Hist.* i. 122) 'quia esset haec Gallorum rusticis consuetudo, simulacra daemonum, candido tecta velamine, misera per agros suos circumferre dementia,' and Alsso's account of the fifteenth-century *calendisationes* in Bohemia (ch. xii).

[5] Cf. ch. x.

[6] Cf. *Representations* (Chester, London, York). There were similar watches at Nottingham (Deering,

days ; in the 'Godiva' procession at Coventry [1], the 'Bezant' procession at Shaftesbury [2]. Hardly a rural merry-making or wake, indeed, is without its procession ; if it is only in the simple form of the *quête* which the children consider themselves entitled to make, with their May-garland, or on some other traditional pretext, at various seasons of the calendar. Obviously in becoming mere *quêtes*, collections of eggs, cakes and so forth, or even of small coins, as well as in falling entirely into the hands of the children, the processions have to some extent lost their original character. But the notion that the visit is to bring good fortune, or the 'May' or the 'summer' to the household, is not wholly forgotten in the rhymes used [3]. An interesting version of the ceremony is the 'furry' or 'faddy' dance formerly used at Helston wake ; for in this the oak-decked dancers claimed the right to pass in at one door and out at another through every house in the village [4].

Room has been found for the summer lustrations in the scheme of the Church. In Catholic countries the statue of the local saint is commonly carried round the village, either annually on his feast-day or in times of exceptional trouble [5]. The inter-relations of ecclesiastical and folk-ritual in this respect are singularly illustrated by the celebration of St. Ubaldo's eve (May 15) at Gubbio in Umbria. The folk procession of the *Ceri* is a very complete variety of the summer festival. After vespers the clergy also hold a procession in honour of the saint. At a certain point the two companies meet. An interchange of courtesies takes place. The priest elevates the host ; the bearers of the *Ceri* bow them to the ground ; and each procession passes on its way [6]. In England the summer lustrations take an ecclesiastical form in the Roga-

---

Hist. of Nott. 123), Worcester (Smith, *English Gilds*, 408), Lydd and Bristol (Green, *Town Life in the Fifteenth Century*, i. 148), and on St. Thomas's day (July 7) at Canterbury (*Arch. Cant.* xii. 34; *Hist. MSS.* ix. 1. 148).
[1] Harris, 7 ; Hartland, *Fairy Tales*, 71.
[2] Dyer, 205.

[3] Cf. ch. viii.
[4] Dyer, 275 ; Ditchfield, 111 ; cf. the phrase 'in and out the windows' of the singing game *Round and Round the Village* (A. B. Gomme, s. v.).
[5] M. Deloche, *Le Tour de la Lunade*, in *Rev. celtique*, ix. 425 ; Bérenger-Féraud, i. 423 ; iii. 167.
[6] Bower, 13.

tions or 'bannering' of 'Gang-week,' a ceremony which itself appears to be based on very similar folk-customs of southern Europe[1]. Since the Reformation the Rogations have come to be regarded as little more than a 'beating of the bounds.' But the declared intention of them was originally to call for a blessing upon the fruits of the earth ; and it is not difficult to trace folk-elements in the 'gospel oaks' and 'gospel wells' at which station was made and the gospel read, in the peeled willow wands borne by the boys who accompany the procession, in the whipping or 'bumping' of the said boys at the stations, and in the choice of 'Gang-week' for such agricultural rites as 'youling' and 'well-dressing[2].'

Some anthropomorphic representation of the fertilization spirit is a common, though not an invariable element in the lustration. A doll is set on the garland, or some popular 'giant' or other image is carried round[3]. Nor is it surprising that at the early spring festival which survives in

[1] Duchesne, 276; Usener, i. 293; Tille, *Y. and C.* 51 ; W. W. Fowler, 124; Boissier, *La Religion romaine,* i. 323. The Rogations or *litaniae minores* represent in Italy the Ambarvalia on May 29. But they are of Gallican origin, were begun by Mamertus, bishop of Vienne (†470), adapted by the *Council of Orleans* (511), c. 27 (Mansi, viii. 355), and required by the English *Council of Clovesho* (747), c. 16 (Haddan-Stubbs, iii. 368), to be held 'non admixtis vanitatibus, uti mos est plurimis, vel negligentibus, vel imperitis, id est in ludis et equorum cursibus, et epulis maioribus.' Jahn, 147, quotes the German abbess Marcsuith (940), who describes them as 'pro gentilicio Ambarvali,' and adds, 'confido autem de Patroni huius misericordia, quod sic ab eo gyrade terrae semina uberius provenient, et variae aeris inclementiae cessent.' Mediaeval Rogation litanies are in *Sarum Processional,* 103, and York Processional (*York Manual,* 182). The more strictly Roman *litania major* on St. Mark's day (March 25) takes the place of the *Robigalia,* but is not of great importance in English folk-custom.

[2] *Injunctions,* ch. xix, of 1559 (Gee-Hardy, *Docts. illustrative of English Church History,* 426). Thanks are to be given to God 'for the increase and abundance of his fruits upon the face of the earth.' The *Book of Homilies* contains an exhortation to be used on the occasion. The episcopal injunctions and interrogatories in *Ritual Commission,* 404, 409, 416, &c., endeavour to preserve the Rogations, and to eliminate 'superstition' from them ; for the development of the notion of 'beating of bounds,' cf. the eighteenth-century notices in Dyer, *Old English Social Life,* 196.

[3] The image is represented by the doll of the May-garland, which has sometimes, according to Ditchfield, 102, become the Virgin Mary, with a child doll in its arms, and at other times (e. g. Castleton, *F. L.* xii. 469) has disappeared, leaving the name of 'queen' to a particular bunch of flowers ; also by the 'giant' of the midsummer watch. The Salisbury giant, St. Christopher, with his hobby-horse, Hob-nob, is described in *Rev. d. T. P.* iv. 601.

Plough Monday, the plough itself, the central instrument of the opening labour, figures.   A variant of this custom may be traced in certain maritime districts, where the functions of the agricultural deities have been extended to include the oversight of seafaring.   Here it is not a plough but a boat or ship that makes its rounds, when the fishing season is about to begin.   Ship processions are to be found in various parts of Germany[1]; at Minehead, Plymouth, and Devonport in the west of England, and probably also at Hull in the north[2].

The magical notions which, in part at least, explain the garland customs of the agricultural festival, are still more strongly at work in some of its subsidiary rites.   These declare themselves, when understood, to be of an essentially practical character, charms designed to influence the weather, and to secure the proper alternation of moisture and warmth which is needed alike for the growth and ripening of the crops and for the welfare of the cattle.   They are probably even older than the garland-customs, for they do not imply the animistic conception of a fertilization spirit immanent in leaf and blossom; and they depend not only upon the 'sympathetic' principle of influence by direct contact already illustrated, but also upon that other principle of similarity distinguished by Dr. Frazer as the basis of what he calls 'mimetic' magic.   To the primitive mind the obvious way of obtaining a result in nature is to make an imitation of it on a small scale.   To achieve rain, water must be splashed about, or some other characteristic of a storm or shower must be reproduced.   To achieve sunshine, a fire must be lit, or some other representation of the appearance and motion of the sun must be devised.   Both rain-charms and sun-charms are very clearly recognizable in the village ritual.

As rain-charms, conscious or unconscious, must be classified

[1] Grimm, i. 257; Golther, 463; Mogk, iii. 374; Hahn, *Demeter und Baubo*, 38; Usener, *Die Sintfluthsagen*, 115.   There are parallels in south European custom, both classical and modern, and Usener even derives the term 'carnival,' not from *carnem levare*, but from the *currus navalis* used by Roman women.   A modern survival at Fréjus is described in *F. L.* xii. 307.

[2] Ditchfield, 103; *Transactions of Devonshire Association*, xv. 104; cf. the Noah's ship procession at Hull (*Representations*, s. v.).

the many festival customs in which bathing or sprinkling holds an important place. The image or bough which represents the fertilization spirit is solemnly dipped in or drenched with water. Here is the explanation of the ceremonial bathing of the goddess Nerthus recorded by Tacitus. It has its parallels in the dipping of the images of saints in the feast-day processions of many Catholic villages, and in the buckets of water sometimes thrown over May-pole or harvest-May. Nor is the dipping or drenching confined to the fertilization spirit. In order that the beneficent influences of the rite may be spread widely abroad, water is thrown on the fields and on the plough, while the worshippers themselves, or a representative chosen from among them, are sprinkled or immersed. To this practice many survivals bear evidence; the virtues persistently ascribed to dew gathered on May morning, the ceremonial bathing of women annually or in times of drought with the expressed purpose of bringing fruitfulness on man or beast or crop, the 'ducking' customs which play no inconsiderable part in the traditions of many a rural merry-making. Naturally enough, the original sense of the rite has been generally perverted. The 'ducking' has become either mere horse-play or else a rough-and-ready form of punishment for offences, real or imaginary, against the rustic code of conduct. The churl who will not stop working or will not wear green on the feast-day must be 'ducked,' and under the form of the 'cucking-stool,' the ceremony has almost worked its way into formal juris-prudence as an appropriate treatment for feminine offenders. So, too, it has been with the 'ducking' of the divinity. When the modern French peasant throws the image of his saint into the water, he believes himself to be doing it, not as a mimetic rain-charm, but as a punishment to compel a power obdurate to prayer to grant through fear the required boon.

The rain-charms took place, doubtless, at such wells, springs, or brooks as the lustral procession passed in its progress round the village. It is also possible that there may have been, sometimes or always, a well within the sacred grove itself and hard by the sacred tree. The sanctity

derived by such wells and streams from the use of them in
the cult of the fertilization spirit is probably what is really
intended by the water-worship so often ascribed to the
heathen of western Europe, and coupled closely with tree-
worship in the Christian discipline-books. The goddess of
the tree was also the goddess of the well. At the conversion her wells were taken over by the new religion. They
became holy wells, under the protection of the Virgin or one
of the saints. And they continued to be approached with
the same rites as of old, for the purpose of obtaining the
ancient boons for which the fertilization spirit had always
been invoked. It will not be forgotten that, besides the public
cult of the fertilization spirit for the welfare of the crops
and herds, there was also a private cult, which aimed at
such more personal objects of desire as health, success in
love and marriage, and divination of the future. It is this
private cult that is most markedly preserved in modern holy
well customs. These may be briefly summarized as follows [1].
The wells are sought for procuring a husband or children,
for healing diseases, especially eye-ailments or warts, and for
omens, these too most often in relation to wedlock. The
worshipper bathes wholly or in part, or drinks the water.
Silence is often enjoined, or a motion *deasil*, that is, with
the sun's course, round the well. Occasionally cakes are
eaten, or sugar and water drunk, or the well-water is splashed
on a stone. Very commonly rags or bits of wool or hair are
laid under a pebble or hung on a bush near the well, or pins,
more rarely coins or even articles of food, are thrown into it.
The objects so left are not probably to be regarded as offerings ;
the intention is rather to bring the worshipper, through the
medium of his hair or clothes, or some object belonging to
him, into direct contact with the divinity. The close connexion between tree- and well-cult is shown by the use of
the neighbouring bush on which to hang the rags. And the

[1] Brand, ii. 223; Grimm, ii. 584;
Elton, 284; Gomme, *Ethnology*, 73;
Hartland, *Perseus*, ii. 175; Haddon,
362; Vaux, 269; Wood-Martin, ii.
46; Bérenger-Féraud, iii. 291; R. C.
Hope, *Holy Wells*; M.-L. Quiller-
Couch, *Ancient and Holy Wells of
Cornwall* (1894); J. Rhys, *C. F.* i.
332, 354, and in *F. L.* iii. 74, iv. 55;
A. W. Moore, in *F. L.* v. 212; H. C.
March, in *F. L.* x. 479 (Dorset).

practice of dropping pins into the well is almost exactly paralleled by that of driving nails 'for luck' into a sacred tree or its later representative, a cross or saintly image. The theory may be hazarded that originally the sacred well was never found without the sacred tree beside it. This is by no means the case now; but it must be remembered that a tree is much more perishable than a well. The tree once gone, its part in the ceremony would drop out, or be transferred to the well. But the original rite would include them both. The visitant, for instance, would dip in the well, and then creep under or through the tree, a double ritual which seems to survive in the most curious of all the dramatic games of children, 'Draw a Pail of Water[1].'

The private cult of the fertilization spirit is not, of course, tied to fixed seasons. Its occasion is determined by the needs of the worshipper. But it is noteworthy that the efficacy of some holy wells is greatest on particular days, such as Easter or the first three Sundays in May. And in many places the wells, whether ordinarily held 'holy' or not, take an important place in the ceremonies of the village festival. The 'gospel wells' of the Rogation processions, and the well to which the 'Bezant' procession goes at Shaftesbury are cases in point; while in Derbyshire the 'well-dressings' correspond to the 'wakes,' 'rushbearings,' and 'Mayings' of other districts. Palm Sunday and Easter Sunday, as well as the Rogation days, are in a measure Christian versions of the heathen agricultural feasts, and it is not, therefore, surprising to find an extensive use of holy water in ecclesiastical ritual, and a special rite of *Benedictio Fontium* included amongst the Easter ceremonies[2]. But the Christian custom has been moralized, and its avowed aim is purification rather than prosperity.

The ordinary form of heat-charm was to build, in semblance

---

[1] A. B. Gomme, s. v.; Haddon, 362.

[2] Schaff, iii. 247; Duchesne, 281, 385; Rock, iii. 2. 101, 180; Maskell, i. cccxi; Feasey, 235; Wordsworth, 24; Pfannenschmidt, *Das Weihwasser im heidnischen und christ-* *lichen Cultus* (1869). The *Benedictio Fontium* took place on Easter Saturday, in preparation for the baptism which in the earliest times was a characteristic Easter rite. The formulae are in *York Missal*, i. 121; *Sarum Missal*, 350; Maskell, i. 13.

of the sun, the source of heat, a great fire[1]. Just as in the rain-charm the worshippers must be literally sprinkled with water, so, in order that they may receive the full benefits of the heat-charm, they must come into direct physical contact with the fire, by standing in the smoke, or even leaping through the flames, or by smearing their faces with the charred ashes[2]. The cattle too must be driven through the fire, in order that they may be fertile and free from pestilence throughout the summer; and a whole series of observances had for their especial object the distribution of the preserving influence over the farms. The fires were built on high ground, that they might be visible far and wide. Or they were built in a circle round the fields, or to windward, so that the smoke might blow across the corn. Blazing arrows were shot in the air, or blazing torches carried about. Ashes were sprinkled over the fields, or mingled with the seed corn or the fodder in the stall[3]. Charred brands were buried or stuck upright in the furrows. Further, by a simple symbolism, the shape and motion of the sun were mimicked with circular rotating bodies. A fiery barrel or a fiery wheel was rolled down the hill on the top of which the ceremony took place. The lighted torches were whirled in the air, or replaced by lighted disks of wood, flung on high. All these customs still linger in these islands or in other parts of western Europe, and often the popular imagination finds in their successful performance an omen for the fertility of the year.

On *a priori* grounds one might have expected two agricultural festivals during the summer; one in the earlier part of it, when moisture was all-important, accompanied with rain-charms; the other later on, when the crops were well grown

---

[1] Frazer, iii. 237; Gomme, in *Brit. Ass. Rep.* (1896), 626; Simpson, 195; Grenier, 380; Gaidoz, 16; Bertrand, 98; Gummere, *G. O.* 400; Grimm, ii. 601; Jahn, 25; Brand, i. 127, 166; Dyer, 269, 311, 332; Ditchfield, 141; Cortet, 211.

[2] To this custom may possibly be traced the black-a-vised figures who are persistent in the folk *ludi*, and also the curious tradition which makes May-day especially the chimney-sweeps' holiday.

[3] The reasons given are various, 'to keep off hail' (whence the term *Hagelfeuer* mentioned by Pfannenschmidt, 67), 'vermin,' 'caterpillars,' 'blight,' 'to make the fields fertile.' In Bavaria torches are carried round the fields 'to drive away the wicked sower' (of tares?). In Northumberland raids are made on the ashes of neighbouring villages (Dyer, 332).

and heat was required to ripen them, accompanied with sun-charms. But the evidence is rather in favour of a single original festival determined, in the dislocation caused by a calendar, to different dates in different localities[1]. · The Midsummer or St. John's fires are perhaps the most widely spread and best known of surviving heat-charms. But they can be paralleled by others distributed all over the summer cycle of festivals, at Easter[2] and on May-day, and in connexion with the ploughing celebrations on Epiphany, Candlemas, Shrovetide, Quadragesima, and St. Blaize's day. It is indeed at Easter and Candlemas that the *Benedictiones*, which are the ecclesiastical versions of the ceremony, appear in the ritual-books[3]. On the other hand, although, perhaps owing to the later notion of the solstice, the fires are greatly prominent on St. John's day, and are explained with considerable ingenuity by the monkish writers[4], yet this day was never a fire-festival and nothing else. Garland customs are common upon it, and there is even evidence, though slight

---

[1] Cf. p. 113.

[2] I know of no English Easter folk-fires, but St. Patrick is said to have lit one on the hill of Slane, opposite Tara, on Easter Eve, 433 (Feasey, 180).

[3] Schaff, v. 403; Duchesne, 240; Rock, iii. 2. 71, 94, 98, 107, 244; Feasey, 184; Wordsworth, 204; Frazer, iii. 245; Jahn, 129; Grimm, ii. 616; Simpson, 198. The formulae of the *benedictio ignis* and *benedictio cereorum* at Candlemas, and the *benedictio ignis*, *benedictio incensi*, and *benedictio cerei* on Easter Eve, are in *Sarum Missal*, 334, 697; *York Missal*, i. 109; ii. 17. One York MS. has 'Paschae ignis de berillo vel de silice exceptus . . . accenditur.' The correspondence between Pope Zacharias and St. Boniface shows that the lighting of the *ignis* by a crystal instead of from a lamp kept secretly burning distinguished Gallican from Roman ceremonial in the eighth century (Jaffé, 2291). All the lights in the church are previously put out, and this itself has become a ceremony in the *Tenebrae*. Ecclesiastical

symbolism explained the extinction and rekindling of lights as typifying the Resurrection. Sometimes the *ignis* provides a light for the folk-fire outside.

[4] Belethus († 1162), *de Div. Offic.* c. 137 (*P. L.* ccii. 141), gives three customs of St. John's Eve. Bones are burnt, because (1) there are dragons in air, earth, and water, and when these ' in aere ad libidinem concitantur, quod fere fit, saepe ipsum sperma vel in puteos vel in aquas fluviales eiiciunt, ex quo lethalis sequitur annus,' but the smoke of the bonfires drives them away; and (2) because St. John's bones were burnt in Sebasta. Torches are carried, because St. John was a shining light. A wheel is rolled, because of the solstice, which is made appropriate to St. John by *St. John* iii. 30. The account of Belethus is amplified by Durandus, *Rationale Div. Offic.* (ed. corr. Antwerp, 1614) vii. 14, and taken in turn from Durandus by a fifteenth-century monk of Winchelscombe in a sermon preserved in *Harl. MS.* 2345, f. 49 (b).

evidence, for rain-charms[1]. It is perhaps justifiable to infer that the crystallization of the rain- and heat-charms, which doubtless were originally used only when the actual condition of the weather made them necessary, into annual festivals, took place after the exact rationale of them had been lost, and they had both come to be looked upon, rather vaguely, as weather-charms.

Apart from the festival-fires, a superstitious use of sun-charms endured in England to an extraordinarily late date. This was in times of drought and pestilence as a magical remedy against mortality amongst the cattle. A fire was built, and, as on the festivals, the cattle were made to pass through the smoke and flames[2]. On such occasions, and often at the festival-fires themselves, it was held requisite that, just as the water used in the rain charms would be fresh water from the spring, so the fire must be fresh fire. That is to say, it must not be lit from any pre-existing fire, but must be made anew. And, so conservative is cult, this must be done, not with the modern device of matches, or even with flint and steel, but by the primitive method of causing friction in dry work. Such fire is known as 'need-fire' or 'forced fire,' and is produced in various ways, by rubbing two pieces of wood together, by turning a drill in a solid block, or by rapidly rotating a wheel upon an axle. Often certain precautions are observed, as that nine men must work at the job, or chaste boys; and often all the hearth-fires in the village are first extinguished, to be rekindled by the new flame[3].

The custom of rolling a burning wheel downhill from the

[1] Gaidoz, 24, 109; Bertrand, 122; Dyer, 323; Stubbes, i. 339, from Naogeorgos; Usener, ii. 81; and the mediaeval calendar in Brand, i. 179.

[2] Gomme, in *Brit. Ass. Rep.* (1896), 636 (Moray, Mull); *F. L.* ix. 280 (Caithness, with illustration of wood used); Kemble, i. 360 (Perthshire in 1826, Devonshire).

[3] Grimm, ii. 603; Kemble, i. 359; Elton, 293; Frazer, iii. 301; Gaidoz, 22; Jahn, 26; Simpson, 196; Bertrand, 107; Golther, 570. The English term is *needfire*, Scotch *neidfyre*, German *Noth-*

feuer. It is variously derived from *nôt* 'need,' *niuwan* 'rub,' or *hniotan* 'press.' If the last is right, the English form should perhaps be *knead-fire* (Grimm, ii. 607, 609; Golther, 570). Another German term is *Wildfeuer*. The Gaelic *tin-egin* is from *tin* 'fire,' and *egin* 'violence' (Grimm, ii. 609). For ecclesiastical prohibitions cf. *Indiculus* (Saupe, 20) 'de igne fricato de ligno, i. e. *nodfyr*'; *Capit. Karlmanni* (742), c. 5 (Grimm, ii. 604) 'illos sacrilegos ignes quos *niedfyr* vocant.'

festival-fire amongst the vineyards has been noted. The
wheel is, of course, by no means an uncommon solar emblem [1].
Sometimes round bannocks or hard-boiled eggs are similarly
rolled downhill. The use of both of these may be sacrificial
in its nature. But the egg plays such a large part in festival
customs, especially at Easter, when it is reddened, or gilt, or
coloured yellow with furze or broom flowers, and popularly
regarded as a symbol of the Resurrection, that one is tempted
to ask whether it does not stand for the sun itself [2]. And
are we to find the sun in the ' parish top [3],' or in the ball with
which, even in cathedrals, ceremonial games were played [4]?

[1] Gaidoz, 1 ; Bertrand, 109, 140 ;
Simpson, 109, 240 ; Rhys, *C. H.* 54.
The commonest form of the symbol
is the swastika, but others appear to
be found in the ' hammer' of Thor,
and on the altars and statues of
a Gaulish deity equated in the
interpretatio Romana with Jupiter.
There is a wheel decoration on the
barelle or cars of the Gubbio *ceri*
(Bower, 4).

[2] Brand, i. 97 ; Dyer, 159 ; Ditchfield, 78. Eggs are used ceremonially at the Scotch Beltane fires
(Frazer, iii. 261 ; Simpson, 285).
Strings of birds' eggs are hung on
the Lynn May garland (*F. L.* x.
443). In Dauphiné an omelette is
made when the sun rises on St.
John's day (Cortet, 217). In Germany children are sent to look for
the Easter eggs in the nest of a
hare, a very divine animal. Among
the miscellaneous Benedictions in
the *Sarum Manual,* with the *Ben.
Seminis* and the *Ben. Pomorum in
die S[ti] Iacobi* are a *Ben. Carnis
Casei Butyri Ovorum sive Pastil-
larum in Pascha* and a *Ben. Agni
Paschalis, Ovorum et Herbarum in
die Paschae.* These Benedictions
are little more than graces. The
Durham Accounts, i. 71–174, contain entries of fifteenth- and sixteenth-
century payments 'fratribus et soro-
ribus de Wytton pro eorum Egsilver
erga festum pasche.'

[3] *Tw. N.* i. 3. 42 ' He's a coward
and a coystrill, that will not drink to
my niece till his brains turn o' the
toe like a parish-top.' Steevens
says ' a large top was formerly kept
in every village, to be whipt in frosty
weather, that the peasants might be
kept warm by exercise and out of
mischief while they could not work.'
This is evidently a ' fake ' of the
' Puck of commentators.' Hone,
E. D. B. i. 199, says ' According to
a story (whether true or false), in
one of the churches of Paris, a choir
boy used to whip a top marked
with *Alleluia,* written in gold letters,
from one end of the choir to the
other.' The ' burial of Alleluia ' is
shown later on to be a mediaeval
perversion of an agricultural rite.
On the whole question of tops, see
Haddon, 255 ; A. B. Gomme, s. v.

[4] Leber, ix. 391 ; Barthélemy, iv.
447 ; Du Tilliot, 30 ; Grenier, 385 ;
Bérenger-Féraud, iii. 427 ; Belethus,
c. 120 ' Sunt nonnullae ecclesiae
in quibus usitatum est, ut vel etiam
episcopi et archiepiscopi in coenobiis
cum · suis ludant subditis, ita ut
etiam se ad lusum pilae demit-
tant. atque haec quidem libertas
ideo dicta est decembrica. ... quamquam vero magnae ecclesiae, ut
est Remensis, hanc ludendi consuetudinem observent, videtur tamen laudabilius esse non ludere ';
Durandus, vi. 86 ' In quibusdam
locis hac die, in aliis in Natali,
praelati cum suis clericis ludunt,
vel in claustris, vel in domibus epi-
scopalibus ; ita ut etiam descendant

If so, perhaps this game of ball may be connected with the curious belief that if you get up early enough on Easter morning you may see the sun dance [1].

In any case sun-charms, quite independent of the fires, may probably be traced in the circular movements which so often appear invested with a religious significance, and which sometimes form part of the festivals [2]. It would be rash to regard such movements as the basis of every circular dance or *ronde* on such an occasion ; a ring is too obviously the form which a crowd of spectators round any object, sacred or otherwise, must take. But there are many circumambulatory rites in which stress is laid on the necessity for the motion to be *deasil*, or with the right hand to the centre, in accordance with the course of the sun, and not in the opposite direction, *cartuaithaail* or *withershins* [3]. And these, perhaps, may be legitimately considered as of magical origin.

ad ludum pilae, vel etiam ad choreas et cantus, &c.' Often the ball play was outside the church, but the canons of Evreux on their return from the *procession noire* of May 1, played ' ad quillas super voltas ecclesiae '; and the Easter *pilota* of Auxerre which lasted to 1538, took place in the nave before vespers. Full accounts of this ceremony have been preserved. The dean and canons danced and tossed the ball, singing the *Victimae paschali*. For examples of Easter hand-ball or marbles in English folk-custom, cf. Brand, i. 103; Vaux, 240 ; *F. L.* xii. 75 ; Mrs. Gomme, s. v. *Hand-ball*.

[1] Brand, i. 93 ; Burne-Jackson, 335. A Norfolk version (*F. L.* vii. 90) has ' dances as if in agony.' On the Mendips (*F. L.* v. 339) what is expected is ' a lamb in the sun.' The moon, and perhaps the sun also, is sometimes ' wobbly,' ' jumping' or ' skipping,' owing to the presence of strata of air differing in humidity or temperature, and so changing the index of refraction (Nicholson, *Golspie*, 186). At Pontesford Hill in Shropshire (Burne-Jackson, 330) the pilgrimage was on Palm Sunday, actually to pluck a sprig from a haunted yew, traditionally ' to look for the golden arrow,' which must be solar. In the Isle of Man hills, on which are sacred wells, are visited on the Lugnassad, to gather ling-berries. Others say that it is because of Jephthah's daughter, who went up and down on the mountains and bewailed her virginity. And the old folk now stop at home and read *Judges* xi (Rhys, *C. F.* i. 312). On the place of hill-tops in agricultural religion cf. p. 106, and for the use of elevated spots for sun-worship at Rome, ch. xi.

[2] Simpson, *passim* ; cf. *F. L.* vi. 168 ; xi. 220. *Deasil* is from Gaelic *deas*, ' right,' ' south.' Mediaeval ecclesiastical processions went ' contra solis cursum et morem ecclesiasticum ' only in seasons of woe or sadness (Rock, iii. 2. 182).

[3] Dr. Murray kindly informs me that the etymology of *withershins* (A.-S. *wiþersynes*) is uncertain. It is from *wiþer*, ' against,' and either some lost noun, or one derived from *séon*, ' to see,' or *sinþ*, ' course.' The original sense is simply ' backwards,' and the equivalence with *deasil* not earlier than the seventeenth century. A folk-etymology from *shine* may account for the aspirate.

With the growth of animistic or spiritual religion, the mental tendencies, out of which magical practices or charms arise, gradually cease to be operative in the consciousness of the worshippers. The charms themselves, however, are preserved by the conservative instinct of cult. In part they survive as mere bits of traditional ritual, for which no particular reason is given or demanded; in part also they become material for that other instinct, itself no less inveterate in the human mind, by which the relics of the past are constantly in process of being re-explained and brought into new relations with the present. The sprinkling with holy water, for instance, which was originally of the nature of a rain-charm, comes to be regarded as a rite symbolical of spiritual purification and regeneration. An even more striking example of such transformation of intention is to be found in the practice, hardly yet referred to in this account of the agricultural festivals, of sacrifice. In the ordinary acceptation of the term, sacrifice implies not merely an animistic, but an anthropomorphic conception of the object of cult. The offering or oblation with which man approaches his god is an extension of the gift with which, as suppliant, he approaches his fellow men. But the oblational aspect of sacrifice is not the only one. In his remarkable book upon *The Religion of the Semites*, Professor Robertson Smith has formulated another, which may be distinguished as 'sacramental.' In this the sacrifice is regarded as the renewal of a special tie between the god and his worshippers, analogous to the blood-bond which exists amongst those worshippers themselves. The victim is not an offering made to the god; on the contrary, the god himself is, or is present in, the victim. It is his blood which is shed, and by means of the sacrificial banquet and its subsidiary rites, his personality becomes, as it were, incorporated in those of his clansmen [1]. It is not necessary to determine here the general priority of the two types or

---

[1] Robertson Smith, *Religion of the Semites*, 196; Jevons, 130; Frazer, ii. 352; Grant Allen, 318; Hartland, ii. 236; Turnbull, *The Blood Covenant*. Perhaps, as a third type of sacrifice, should be distinguished the 'alimentary' sacrifice of food and other things made to the dead. This rests on the belief in the continuance of the mortal life with its needs and desires after death.

conceptions of sacrifice described. But, while it is probable that the Kelts and Teutons of the time of the conversion consciously looked upon sacrifice as an oblation, there is also reason to believe that, at an earlier period, the notion of a sacrament had been the predominant one. For the sacrificial ritual of these peoples, and especially that used in the agricultural cult, so far as it can be traced, is only explicable as an elaborate process of just that physical incorporation of the deity in the worshippers and their belongings, which it was the precise object of the sacramental sacrifice to bring about. It will be clear that sacrifice, so regarded, enters precisely into that category of ideas which has been defined as magical. It is but one more example of that belief in the efficacy of direct contact which lies at the root of sympathetic magic. As in the case of the garland customs, this belief, originally pre-animistic, has endured into an animistic stage of thought. Through the garland and the posies the worshipper sought contact with the fertilization spirit in its phytomorphic form ; through sacrifice he approaches it in its theriomorphic form also. The earliest sacrificial animals, then, were themselves regarded as divine, and were naturally enough the food animals of the folk. The use made by the Kelto-Teutonic peoples of oxen, sheep, goats, swine, deer, geese, and fowls requires no explanation. A common victim was also the horse, which the Germans seem, up to a late date, to have kept in droves and used for food. The strong opposition of the Church to the sacrificial use of horse-flesh may possibly account for the prejudice against it as a food-stuff in modern Europe[1]. A similar prejudice, however, in the case of the hare, an animal of great importance in folk belief, already existed in the time of Caesar[2]. It is a little more puzzling to find distinct traces of sacrificial

---

[1] Grimm, i. 47 ; Golther, 565; Gummere, *G.O.*40,457. Gregory III wrote (†731) to Boniface (*P.L.*lxxxix. 577) 'inter cetera agrestem caballum aliquantos comedere adiunxisti plerosque et domesticum. hoc nequaquam fieri deinceps sinas,' cf. *Councils of Cealcythe and Pincanhale* (787), c. 19 (Haddan-Stubbs, iii. 458) 'equos etiam plerique in vobis comedunt, quod nullus Christianorum in Orientalibus facit.' The decking of horses is a familiar feature of May-day in London and elsewhere.

[2] C. J. Billson, *The Easter Hare*, in *F. L.* iii. 441.

customs in connexion with animals, such as the dog, cat, wolf, fox, squirrel, owl, wren, and so forth, which are not now food animals[1]. But they may once have been such, or the explanation may lie in an extension of the sacrificial practice after the first rationale of it was lost.

At every agricultural festival, then, animal sacrifice may be assumed as an element. The analogy of the relation between the fertilization spirit and his worshippers to the human blood bond makes it probable that originally the rite was always a bloody one[2]. Some of the blood was poured on the sacred tree. Some was sprinkled upon the worshippers, or smeared over their faces, or solemnly drunk by them[3]. Hides, horns, and entrails were also hung upon the tree[4], or worn as festival trappings[5]. The flesh was, of course, solemnly eaten in the sacrificial meal[6]. The crops, as well as their cultivators, must benefit by the rites; and therefore the fields, and doubtless also the cattle, had their sprinkling of blood, while heads or pieces of flesh were buried in the furrows, or at the threshold of the byre[7]. A fair notion of the whole proceeding may be obtained from the account of the similar Indian worship of the earth-goddess given in Appendix I. The intention of the ceremonies will be obvious by a comparison with those already explained. The wearing of the skins of the victims is precisely parallel to the wearing of the green vegetation, the sprinkling with blood to the sprinkling with lustral water, the burial in the fields of flesh and skulls to the burial of

---

[1] N. W. Thomas in *F. L.* xi. 227.

[2] Grimm, i. 55; Golther, 559, 575; Gummere, *G. O.* 456. The universal Teutonic term for sacrificing is *blôtan.*

[3] Frazer, *Pausanias*, iii. 20; Jevons, 130, 191. Does the modern huntsman know why he 'bloods' a novice?

[4] Grimm, i. 47, 57, 77; Jahn, 24; Gummere, *G. O.* 459. Hence the theriomorphic 'image.'

[5] Robertson Smith, 414, 448; Jevons, 102, 285; Frazer, ii. 448; Lang, *M. R. R.*[1] ii. 73, 80, 106, 214, 226; Grant Allen, 335; Du Méril, *Com.* i. 75. Hence the theriomor-

phic *larva* or mask (Frazer, *Pausanias*, iv. 239).

[6] Grimm, i. 46, 57; Golther, 576; Frazer, ii. 318, 353; Jevons, 144; Grant Allen, 325. Savages believe that by eating an animal they will acquire its bodily and mental qualities.

[7] Jahn, 14, and for classical parallels Frazer, ii. 315; *Pausanias*, iii. 288; Jevons, *Plutarch*, lxix. 143. Grant Allen, 292, was told as a boy in Normandy that at certain lustrations 'a portion of the Host (stolen or concealed, I imagine) was sometimes buried in each field.'

brands from the festival-fire. In each case the belief in the necessity of direct physical contact to convey the beneficent influence is at the bottom of the practice. It need hardly be said that of such physical contact the most complete example is in the sacramental banquet itself.

It is entirely consistent with the view here taken of the primitive nature of sacrifice, that the fertilization spirit was sacrificed at the village festivals in its vegetable as well as in its animal form. There were bread-offerings as well as meat-offerings [1]. Sacramental cakes were prepared with curious rituals which attest their primitive character. Like the *tcharnican* or Beltane cakes, they were kneaded and moulded by hand and not upon a board [2]; like the loaf in the Anglo-Saxon charm, they were compounded of all sorts of grain in order that they might be representative of every crop in the field [3]. At the harvest they would naturally be made, wholly or in part, of the last sheaf cut. The use of them corresponded closely to that made of the flesh of the sacrificial victim. Some were laid on a branch of the sacred tree [4]; others flung into the sacred well or the festival-fire; others again buried in the furrows, or crumbled up and mingled with the seed-corn [5]. And like the flesh they were solemnly eaten by the worshippers themselves at the sacrificial banquet. With the sacrificial cake went the sacrificial draught, also made out of the fruits of the earth, in the southern lands wine, but in the vineless north ale, or cider, or that mead which Pytheas described the Britons as brewing out of honey and wheat [6]. Of this, too, the trees and crops received their share, while it filled the cup for those toasts or *minnes* to the dead and to Odin and Freyja their rulers, which were afterwards transferred by Christian Germany to St. John and St. Gertrude [7].

The animal and the cereal sacrifices seem plausible enough, but they do not exhaust the problem. One has to face the fact that human sacrifice, as Victor Hehn puts it, 'peers

<hr />

[1] Frazer, ii. 318; Grant Allen, 337; Jevons, 206.
[2] *F. L.* vi. 1.
[3] Frazer, ii. 319; Jevons, 214; cf. the πάνσπερμα at the Athenian Pyanepsia.
[4] In the Beltane rite (*F. L.* vi. 2) a bit of the bannock is reserved for the 'cuack' or cuckoo, here doubtless the inheritor of the gods.
[5] Grimm, iii. 1240.
[6] Elton, 428.
[7] Grimm, i. 59; Gummere, *G. O.* 455.

uncannily forth from the dark past of every Aryan race[1].
So far as the Kelts and Teutons go, there is plenty of evidence
to show, that up to the very moment of their contact with
Roman civilization, in some branches even up to the very
moment of their conversion to Christianity, it was not yet
obsolete[2]. An explanation of it is therefore required, which
shall fall in with the general theory of agricultural sacrifice.
The subject is very difficult, but, on the whole, it seems
probable that originally the slaying of a human being at an
annually recurring festival was not of the nature of sacrifice
at all. It is doubtful whether it was ever sacrifice in the
sacramental sense, and although in time it came to be regarded
as an oblation, this was not until the first meaning, both of
the sacrifice and of the human death, had been lost. The
essential facts bearing on the question have been gathered
together by Dr. Frazer in *The Golden Bough*. He brings
out the point that the victim in a human sacrifice was not
originally merely a man, but a very important man, none
other than the king, the priest-king of the tribe. In many
communities, Aryan-speaking and other, it has been the
principal function of such a priest-king to die, annually or
at longer intervals, for the people. His place is taken, as
a rule, by the tribesman who has slain him[3]. Dr. Frazer's
own explanation of this custom is, that the head of the tribe
was looked upon as possessed of great magical powers, as
a big medicine man, and was in fact identified with the god
himself. And his periodical death, says Dr. Frazer, was
necessary, in order to renew the vitality of the god, who
might decay and cease to exist, were he not from time to
time reincarnated by being slain and passing into the body
of his slayer and successor[4].   This is a highly ingenious

[1] V. Hehn, *Culturpflanzen*, 438.

[2] Grimm, i. 44, 48, 53; Golther,
561; Gummere, *G. O.* 459; Schräder,
422; Mogk, iii. 388; Meyer, 199,
and for Keltic evidence Elton, 270.
Many of these examples belong
rather to the war than to the agricultural cult. The latest in the
west are *Capit. de partib. Saxon.* 9
'Si quis hominem diabolo sacrifi-
caverit et in hostiam, more paganorum, daemonibus obtulerit'; *Lex
Frisionum*, additio sup. tit. 42 'qui
fanum effregerit . . . immolatur diis,
quorum templa violavit'; *Epist.
Greg. III*, 1 (*P. L.* lxxxix, 578) 'hoc
quoque inter alia crimina agi in
partibus illis dixisti, quod quidam ex
fidelibus ad immolandum paganis
sua venundent mancipia.'

[3] Frazer, ii. 1; Jevons, 279.

[4] Frazer, ii. 5, 59.

and fascinating theory, but unfortunately there are several difficulties in the way of accepting it. In the first place it is inconsistent with the explanation of the sacramental killing of the god arrived at by Professor Robertson Smith. According to this the sacrifice of the god is for the sake of his worshippers, that the blood-bond with them may be renewed; and we have seen that this view fits in admirably with the minor sacrificial rites, such as the eating and burying of the flesh, as the wearing of the horns and hides. Dr. Frazer, however, obliges us to hold that the god is also sacrificed for his own sake, and leaves us in the position of propounding two quite distinct and independent reasons for the same fact. Secondly, there is no evidence, at least amongst Aryan-speaking peoples, for that breaking down of the very real and obvious distinction between the god and his chief worshipper or priest, which Dr. Frazer's theory implies. And thirdly, if the human victim were slain as being the god, surely this slaughter should have replaced the slaughter of the animal victim previously slain for the same reason, which it did not, and should have been followed by a sacramental meal of a cannibal type, of which also, in western Europe, there is but the slightest trace [1].

Probably, therefore, the alternative explanation of Dr. Frazer's own facts given by Dr. Jevons is preferable. According to this the death of the human victim arises out of the circumstances of the animal sacrifice. The slaying of the divine animal is an act approached by the tribe with mingled feelings. It is necessary, in order to renew the all-essential blood-bond between the god and his worshippers. And at the same time it is an act of sacrilege; it is killing the god. There is some hesitation amongst the assembled worshippers. Who will dare the deed and face its consequences? 'The clansman,' says Dr. Jevons, 'whose religious conviction of the clan's need of communion with the god was deepest, would eventually and after long waiting be the one to strike, and take upon himself the issue, for the sake of

---

[1] Strabo, iv. 5. 4; Bastian, *Oestl. Asien*, v. 272. The Mexican evidence given by Frazer, iii. 134, does not necessarily represent a primitive notion of the nature of the rite.

his fellow men.' This issue would be twofold. The slayer
would be exalted in the eyes of his fellows. He would
naturally be the first to drink the shed blood of the god.
A double portion of the divine spirit would enter into him.
He would become, for a while, the leader, the priest-king, of
the community. At the same time he would incur blood-
guiltiness. And in a year's time, when his sanctity was
exhausted, the penalty would have to be paid. His death
would accompany the renewal of the bond by a fresh sacrifice,
implying in its turn the self-devotion of a fresh annual king [1].

These theories belong to a region of somewhat shadowy
conjecture. If Dr. Jevons is right, it would seem to follow
that, as has already been suggested, the human death at an
annual festival was not initially sacrifice. It accompanied,
but did not replace the sacramental slaughter of a divine
animal. But when the animal sacrifice had itself changed
its character, and was looked upon, no longer as an act of
communion with the god, but as an offering or bribe made
to him, then a new conception of the human death also was
required. When the animal ceased to be recognized as the
god, the need of a punishment for slaying it disappeared.
But the human death could not be left meaningless, and its
meaning was assimilated to that of the animal sacrifice itself.
It also became an oblation, the greatest that could be offered
by the tribe to its protector and its judge. And no doubt
this was the conscious view taken of the matter by Kelts and
Teutons at the time when they appear in history. The human
sacrifice was on the same footing as the animal sacrifice, but it
was a more binding, a more potent, a more solemn appeal.

In whatever way human sacrifice originated, it was obviously destined, with the advance of civilization, to undergo
modification. Not only would the growing moral sense of
mankind learn to hold it a dark and terrible thing, but also
to go on killing the leading man of the tribe, the king-priest,
would have its obvious practical inconveniences. At first,
indeed, these would not be great. The king-priest would be

---

[1] Jevons, 291; *Plutarch,* lxx.
For traces of the blood-guiltiness
incurred by sacrifice, cf. the βουφόνια
at Athens and the *regifugium* at
Rome (Frazer, ii. 294; Robertson
Smith, i. 286).

little more than a rain-maker, a *rex sacrorum*, and one man might perform the ceremonial observances as well as another. But as time went on, and the tribe settled down to a comparatively civilized life, the serious functions of its leader would increase. He would become the arbiter of justice, the adviser in debate; above all, when war grew into importance, the captain in battle. And to spare and replace, year by year, the wisest councillor and the bravest warrior would grow into an intolerable burden. Under some such circumstances, one can hardly doubt, a process of substitution set in. Somebody had to die for the king. At first, perhaps, the substitute was an inferior member of the king's own house, or even an ordinary tribesman, chosen by lot. But the process, once begun, was sure to continue, and presently it was sufficient if a life of little value, that of a prisoner, a slave, a criminal, a stranger within the gates, was sacrificed [1]. The common belief in madness or imbecility as a sign of divine possession may perhaps have contributed to make the village fool or natural seem a particularly suitable victim. But to the very end of Teutonic and Keltic heathenism, the sense that the substitute was, after all, only a substitute can be traced. In times of great stress or danger, indeed, the king might still be called upon to suffer in person [2]. And always a certain pretence that the victim was the king was kept up. Even though a slave or criminal, he was for a few days preceding the sacrifice treated royally. He was a temporary king, was richly dressed and feasted, had a crown set on his head, and was permitted to hold revel with his fellows. The farce was played out in the sight of men and gods [3]. Ultimately, of course, the natural growth of the sanctity of human life in a progressive people, or in an unprogressive people the pressure of outside ideals [4], forbids the sacrifice of a man at all. Perhaps the temporary

---

[1] Frazer, ii. 15, 55, 232; Jevons, 280; Grant Allen, 242, 296, 329.

[2] In three successive years of famine the Swedes sacrificed first oxen, then men, finally their king Dômaldi himself (*Ynglingasaga*, c. 18).

[3] Frazer, ii. 24; Jevons, 280; Grant Allen, 296.

[4] The British rule in India forbids human sacrifice, and the Khonds, a Dravidian race of Bengal, have substituted animal for human victims within the memory of man (Frazer, ii. 245).

king is still chosen, and even some symbolic mimicked slaying
of him takes place; but actually he does not die. An animal
takes his place upon the altar; or more strictly speaking, an
animal remains the last victim, as it had been the first, and in
myth is regarded as a substitute for the human victim which
for a time had shared its fate. Of such a myth the legends
of Abraham and Isaac and of Iphigeneia at Aulis are the
classical examples.

There is another group of myths for which, although they
lack this element of a substituted victim, mythologists find an
origin in a reformation of religious sentiment leading to the
abolition of human sacrifice. The classical legend of Perseus
and Andromeda, the hagiological legend of St. George and
the Dragon, the Teutonic legend of Beowulf and Grendel,
are only types of innumerable tales in which the hero puts
an end to the periodical death of a victim by slaying the
monster who has enforced and profited by it[1]. What is
such a story but the imaginative statement of the fact that
such sacrifices at one time were, and are not? It is, however, noticeable, that in the majority of these stories, although
not in all, the dragon or monster slain has his dwelling in
water, and this leads to the consideration of yet another
sophistication of the primitive notion of sacrifice. According
to this notion sacrifice was necessarily bloody; in the shedding of blood and in the sacrament of blood partaken of by
the worshippers, lay the whole gist of the rite: a bloodless
sacrifice would have no *raison d'être*. On the other hand,
the myths just referred to seem to imply a bloodless sacrifice
by drowning, and this notion is confirmed by an occasional
bit of ritual, and by the common superstition which represents the spirits of certain lakes and rivers as claiming
a periodical victim in the shape of a drowned person[2].
Similarly there are traces of sacrifices, which must have been
equally bloodless, by fire. At the Beltane festival, for
instance, one member of the party is chosen by lot to be

---

[1] Hartland, iii. 1; Frazer, *Pausanias*, iv. 197; v. 44, 143; Bérenger-Féraud, i. 207. Mr. Frazer enumerates forty-one versions of the legend.

[2] Hartland, iii. 81; Grimm, ii. 494; Gummere, *G. O.* 396. The slaves of Nerthus were drowned in the same lake in which the goddess was dipped.

the 'victim,' is made to jump over the flames and is spoken of in jest as ' dead [1].' Various Roman writers, who apparently draw from the second-century B.C. Greek explorer Posidonius, ascribe to the Druids of Gaul a custom of burning human and other victims at quinquennial feasts in colossal images of hollow wickerwork ; and squirrels, cats, snakes and other creatures are frequently burnt in modern festival-fires [2]. The constant practice, indeed, of burning bones in such fires has given them the specific name of bonfires, and it may be taken for granted that the bones are only representatives of more complete victims. I would suggest that such sacrifices by water and fire are really developments of the water- and fire-charms described in the last chapter ; and that just as the original notion of sacrifice has been extended to give a new significance to the death of a human being at a religious festival, when the real reason for that death had been forgotten, so it has been still further extended to cover the primitive water- and fire-charms when they too had become meaningless. I mean that at a festival the victims, like the image and the worshippers, were doubtless habitually flung into water or passed through fire as part of the charm ; and that, at a time when sacrifice had grown into mere oblation and the shedding of blood was therefore no longer essential, these rites were adapted and given new life as alternative methods of effecting the sacrifice.

It is not surprising that there should be but few direct and evident survivals of sacrifice in English village custom. For at the time of the conversion the rite must have borne the whole brunt of the missionary attack. The other elements of the festivals, the sacred garlands, the water- and fire-charms, had already lost much of their original significance. A judgement predisposed to toleration might plausibly look upon

[1] *F. L.* vi. 1.

[2] Frazer, iii. 319 ; Gaidoz, 27 ; Cortet, 213 ; Simpson, 221 ; Bertrand, 68 ; *F. L.* xii. 315. The work of Posidonius does not exist, but was possibly used by Caesar, *B. G.* vi. 15 ; Strabo, iv. 4. 5 ; Diodorus, v. 32. Wicker 'giants' are still burnt in some French festival-fires. But elsewhere, as in the midsummer shows, such 'giants' seem to be images of the agricultural divinities, and it is not clear by what process they came to be burnt and so destroyed. Perhaps they were originally only smoked, just as they were dipped.

them as custom rather than worship. It was not so with sacrifice. This too had had its history, and in divers ways changed its character. But it was still essentially a liturgy. Oblation or sacrament, it could not possibly be dissociated from a recognition of the divine nature of the power in whose honour it took place. And therefore it must necessarily be renounced, as a condition of acceptance in the Church at all, by the most weak-kneed convert. What happened was precisely that to which Gregory the Great looked forward. The sacrificial banquet, the great chines of flesh, and the beakers of ale, cider, and mead, endured, but the central rite of the old festival, the ceremonial slaying of the animal, vanished. The exceptions, however, are not so rare as might at first sight be thought, and naturally they are of singular interest. It has already been pointed out that in times of stress and trouble, the thinly veneered heathenism of the country folk long tended to break out, and in particular that up to a very late date the primitive need-fire was occasionally revived to meet the exigencies of a cattle-plague. Under precisely similar circumstances, and sometimes in immediate connexion with the need-fire, cattle have been known, even during the present century, to be sacrificed [1]. Nor are such sporadic instances the only ones that can be adduced. Here and there sacrifice, in a more or less modified form, remains an incident in the village festival. The alleged custom of annually sacrificing a sheep on May-day at Andreas in the Isle of Man rests on slight evidence [2]; but there is a fairly well authenticated example in the 'ram feast' formerly held on the same day in the village of Holne in Devonshire. A ram was slain at a granite pillar or ancient altar in the village 'ploy-field,' and a struggle took place for slices which were supposed to bring luck [3].

---

[1] Gomme, *Ethnology*, 137; *F. L.* ii. 300; x. 101; xii. 217; Vaux, 287; Rhys, *C. F.* i. 306.

[2] *F. L.* ii. 302; Rhys, *C. F.* i. 307. In 1656, bulls were sacrificed near Dingwall (*F. L.* x. 353). A few additional examples, beyond those here given, are mentioned by N. W. Thomas, in *F. L.* xi. 247.

[3] 1 *N. Q.* vii. 353; Gomme, *Ethnology*, 32; *Village Community*, 113; Grant Allen, 290. The custom was extinct when it was first described in 1853, and some doubt has recently been thrown upon the 'altar,' the 'struggle' and other details; cf. *Trans. of Devonshire Assn.* xxviii. 99; *F. L.* viii. 287.

Still more degenerate survivals are afforded by the Whitsun feast at King's Teignton, also in Devonshire [1], and by the Whitsun 'lamb feast' at Kidlington [2], the Trinity 'lamb ale' at Kirtlington [3], and the 'Whit hunt' in Wychwood Forest [4], all three places lying close together in Oxfordshire. These five cases have been carefully recorded and studied; but they do not stand alone; for the folk-calendar affords numerous examples of days which are marked, either universally or locally, by the ceremonial hunting or killing of some wild or domestic animal, or by the consumption of a particular dish which readily betrays its sacrificial origin [5]. The appearance of animals in ecclesiastical processions in St. Paul's cathedral [6] and at Bury St. Edmunds [7] is especially significant; and it is natural to find an origin for the old English sport of bull-baiting rather in a survival of heathen ritual than in any reminiscence of the Roman amphitheatre [8]. Even where sacrifice itself has vanished, the minor rites which once accompanied it are still perpetuated in the superstitions or the festival customs of the peasantry. The heads and hides of horses or cattle, like the *exuviae* of the sacrificial victims, are worn or carried in dance, procession or *quête* [9]. The dead bodies of animals are suspended by shepherds or gamekeepers upon tree and barn-door, from immemorial habit or from

[1] 1 *N.Q.* vii. 353; Gomme, *Ethnology*, 30; Vaux, 285.

[2] Blount, *Jocular Tenures* (ed. Beckwith), 281; Dyer, 297.

[3] Dunkin, *Hist. of Bicester* (1816), 268; P. Manning, in *F. L.* viii. 313.

[4] P. Manning, in *F. L.* viii. 310; Dyer, 282.

[5] N. W. Thomas, in *F. L.* xi. 227; Dyer, 285, 438, 470; Ditchfield, 85, 131.

[6] Certain lands were held of the chapter for which a fat buck was paid on the Conversion of St. Paul (January 25), and a fat doe on the Commemoration of St. Paul (June 30). They were offered, according to one writer, alive, at the high altar; the flesh was baked, the head and horns carried in festal procession. The custom dated from at least 1274 (Dyer, 49; W.

Sparrow Simpson, *St. Paul's Cath. and Old City Life*, 234).

[7] *F. L.* iv. 9; x. 355. White bulls are said to have been led to the shrine by women desirous of children. F. C. Conybeare, in *R. de l'Hist. des Religions*, xliv. 108, describes some survivals of sacrificial rites in the Armenian church which existed primitively in other Greek churches also.

[8] *F. L.* vii. 346. Bull-baiting often took place on festivals, and in several cases, as at Tutbury, the bull was driven into or over a river. Bear-baiting is possibly a later variant of the sport.

[9] Burton, 165; *Suffolk F. L.* 71; Ditchfield, 227; Dyer, 387; Pfannenschmidt, 279; cf. the Abbots Bromley Horn-dance (ch. viii).

some vague suspicion of the luck they will bring. Although inquiry will perhaps elicit the fallacious explanation that they are there *pour encourager les autres*[1]. In the following chapters an attempt will be made to show how widely sacrifice is represented in popular amusements and *ludi*. Here it will be sufficient to call attention to two personages who figure largely in innumerable village festivals. One is the 'hobby-horse,' not yet, though Shakespeare will have it so, 'forgot[2]': the other the 'fool' or 'squire,' a buffoon with a pendent cow's tail, who is in many places *de rigueur* in Maying or rushbearing[3]. Both of these grotesques seem to be at bottom nothing but worshippers careering in the skins of sacrificed animals.

The cereal or liquor sacrifice is of less importance. Sugar and water, which may be conjectured to represent mead, is occasionally drunk beside a sacred well, and in one instance, at least, bread and cheese are thrown into the depths. Sometimes also a ploughman carries bread and cheese in his pocket when he goes abroad to cut the first furrow[4]. But the original rite is probably most nearly preserved in the custom of 'youling' fruit-trees to secure a good crop. When this is done, at Christmas or Ascension-tide, ale or cider is poured on the roots of the trees, and a cake placed in a fork of the boughs. Here and there a cake is also hung on the horn of an ox in the stall[5]. Doubtless the 'feasten' cake, of traditional

---

[1] *F. L.* iv. 5. The custom of sacrifice at the foundation of a new building has also left traces: cf. Grant Allen, 248; *F. L.* xi. 322, 437; Speth, *Builders' Rites and Ceremonies.*

[2] Douce, 598, gives a cut of a hobby-horse, i. e. a man riding a pasteboard or wicker horse with his legs concealed beneath a foot-cloth. According to Du Méril, *Com.* i. 79, 421, the device is known throughout Europe. In France it is the *chevalet, cheval-mallet, cheval-fol,* &c.; in Germany the *Schimmel.*

[3] Dyer, 182, 266, 271; Ditchfield, 97; Burton, 40; *F. L.* viii. 309, 313, 317; cf. ch. ix on the

'fool' or 'squire' in the sword and morris dances, and ch. xvi on his court and literary congener. The folk-fool wears a cow's tail or fox's brush, or carries a stick with a tail at one end and a bladder and peas at the other. He often wears a mask or has his face blacked. In Lancashire he is sometimes merged with the 'woman' grotesque of the folk-festivals, and called 'owd Bet.'

[4] W. Gregor, *F. L. of N. E. Scotland,* 181, says that bread and cheese were actually laid in the field, and in the plough when it was 'strykit.'

[5] Dyer, 20, 207, 447; Ditchfield, 46; *F. L.* vi. 93. Pirminius v. Reichenau, *Dicta* († 753), c. 22,

shape and composition, which pervades the country, is in its origin sacramental[1]. Commonly enough, it represents an animal or human being, and in such cases it may be held, while retaining its own character of a cereal sacrifice, to be also a substitute for the animal or human sacrifice with which it should by rights be associated[2].

An unauthenticated and somewhat incredible story has been brought from Italy to the effect that the mountaineers of the Abruzzi are still in the habit of offering up a human sacrifice in Holy week[3]. In these islands a reminiscence of the observance is preserved in the 'victim' of the Beltane festival[4], and a transformation of it in the whipping of lads when the bounds are beaten in the Rogations[5]. Some others, less obvious, will be suggested in the sequel. In any case one ceremony which, as has been seen, grew out of human sacrifice, has proved remarkably enduring. This is the election of the temporary king. Originally chosen out of the lowest of the people for death, and fêted as the equivalent or double of the real king-priest of the community, he has survived the tragic event which gave him birth, and plays a great part as the master of the ceremonies in many a village revel. The English 'May-king,' or 'summer-king,' or 'harvest-lord[6],' or 'mock-mayor[7],' is a very familiar personage, and can be even more abundantly paralleled

forbids 'effundere super truncum frugem et vinum.'

[1] *F. L. Congress*, 449, gives a list of about fifty 'feasten' cakes. Some are quite local; others, from the Shrove Tuesday pancake to the Good Friday hot cross bun, widespread.

[2] Grimm, i. 57; Frazer, ii. 344; Grant Allen, 339; Jevons, 215; Dyer, 165; Ditchfield, 81.

[3] *F. L.* vi. 57; viii. 354; ix. 362; x. 111.

[4] *F. L.* vi. 1.

[5] Ditchfield, 116, 227; *Suffolk F. L.* 108; Dyer, *Old English Social Life*, 197. The boys are now said to be whipped in order that they may remember the boundaries; but the custom, which sometimes includes burying them, closely resembles the symbolical sacrifices of the harvest field (p. 158). Grant Allen, 270, suggests that the tears shed are a rain-charm. I hope he is joking.

[6] Brand, ii. 13; *Suffolk F. L.* 69, 71; *Leicester F. L.* 121. A 'harvest-lord' is probably meant by the 'Rex Autumnalis' mentioned in the *Accounts* of St. Michael's, Bath (ed. Somerset Arch. Soc. 88), in 1487, 1490, and 1492. A *corona* was hired by him from the parish. Often the reaper who cuts the last sheaf (i.e. slays the divinity) becomes harvest-lord.

[7] Gomme, *Village Community*, 107; Dyer, 339; Northall, 202; *Gloucester F. L.* 33.

from continental festivals[1]. To the May-king in particular
we shall return. But in concluding this chapter it is worth
while to point out and account for two variants of the custom
under consideration. In many cases, probably in the majority
of cases so far as the English May-day is concerned, the king
is not a king, but a queen. Often, indeed, the part is played
by a lad in woman's clothes, but this seems only to emphasize
the fact that the temporary ruler is traditionally regarded as
a female one[2]. It is probable that we have here no modern
development, but a primitive element in the agricultural
worship. Tacitus records the presence amongst the Germans
of a male priest ' adorned as women use[3],' while the exchange
of garments by the sexes is included amongst festival abuses
in the ecclesiastical discipline-books[4]. Occasionally, moreover, the agricultural festivals, like those of the *Bona Dea* at
Rome, are strictly feminine functions, from which all men are
excluded[5]. Naturally I regard these facts as supporting my
view of the origin of the agricultural worship in a women's
cult, upon which the pastoral cult of the men was afterwards
engrafted. And finally, there are cases in which not a king
alone nor a queen alone is found, but a king and a queen[6].
This also would be a reasonable outcome of the merging of
the two cults. Some districts know the May-queen as the
May-bride, and it is possible that a symbolical wedding of
a priest and priestess may have been one of the regular rites
of the summer festivals. For this there seem to be some
parallels in Greek and Roman custom, while the myth which

---

[1] Frazer, i. 216; E. Pabst, *Die
Volksfeste des Maigrafen* (1865).

[2] Frazer, i. 219; Cortet, 160;
Brand, i. 126; Dyer, 266; Ditchfield, 98.

[3] Tacitus, *Germ.* c. 43 ' apud
Nahanarvalos antiquae religionis
lucus ostenditur. praesidet sacerdos muliebri ornatu.'

[4] *Conc. of Trullo* (692), c. 62
(Mansi, xi. 671) 'Nullus vir deinceps
muliebri veste induatur, vel mulier
veste viro conveniente'; *Conc. of
Braga* (of doubtful date), c. 80
(Mansi, ix. 844) 'Si quis ballationes
ante ecclesias sanctorum fecerit, seu
quis faciem suam transformaverit

in habitu muliebri et mulier in
habitu viri emendatione pollicita
tres annos poeniteat.' The exchange of head-gear between men
and women remains a familiar
feature of the modern bank-
holiday. Some Greek parallels are
collected by Frazer, *Pausanias*, iii.
197. E. Crawley, *The Mystic Rose*
(1902), viii. 371, suggests another
explanation, which would connect
the custom with the amorous side
of the primitive festivals.

[5] Frazer, ii. 93, 109.

[6] Ibid. i. 220; Brand, i. 157;
Dyer, 217; Ditchfield, 97; Kelly,
62: cf. ch. viii.

represents the heaven as the fertilizing husband of the fruitful earth is of hoar antiquity amongst the Aryan-speaking peoples. The forces which make for the fertility of the fields were certainly identified in worship with those which make for human fertility. The waters of the sacred well or the blaze of the festival fire help the growth of the crops; they also help women in their desire for a lover and for motherhood. And it may be taken for granted that the summer festivals knew from the beginning that element of sexual licence which fourteen centuries of Christianity have not wholly been able to banish [1].

[1] Pearson, ii. 24, 407. Cf. the evidence for a primitive human pairing-season in Westermarck, 25.

CHAPTER VII

FESTIVAL PLAY

[*Bibliographical Note.*—A systematic revision of J. Strutt, *The Sports and Pastimes of the People of England* (1801, ed. W. Hone, 1830), is, as in the case of Brand's book, much needed. On the psychology of play should be consulted K. Groos, *Die Spiele der Thiere* (1896, transl. 1898), and *Die Spiele der Menschen* (1899, transl. 1901). Various anthropological aspects of play are discussed by A. C. Haddon, *The Study of Man* (1898), and the elaborate dictionary of *The Traditional Games of England, Scotland and Ireland* by Mrs. A. B. Gomme (1894–8) may be supplemented from W. W. Newell, *Games and Songs of American Children* (1884), H. C. Bolton, *The Counting-Out Rhymes of Children* (1888), E. W. B. Nicholson, *Golspie* (1897), and R. C. Maclagan, *The Games and Diversions of Argyleshire* (F.L.S. 1901). The *charivari* is treated by C. R. B. Barrett, *Riding Skimmington and Riding the Stang* in the *Journal of the British Archaeological Association*, N. S. i. 58, and C. Noirot, *L'Origine des Masques* (1609), reprinted with illustrative matter by C. Leber, *Dissertations relatives à l'Histoire de France*, vol. ix. The account of the Coventry Hox Tuesday Play given in *Robert Laneham's Letter* (1575) will be found in Appendix H.]

THE charms, the prayer, the sacrifice, make up that side of the agricultural festival which may properly be regarded as cult: they do not make up the whole of it. It is natural to ask whether, side by side with the observances of a natural religion, there were any of a more spiritual type; whether the village gods of our Keltic and Teutonic ancestors were approached on festival occasions solely as the givers of the good things of earth, or whether there was also any recognition of the higher character which in time they came to have as the guardians of morality, such as we can trace alike in the ritual of Eleusis and in the tribal mysteries of some existing savage peoples. It is not improbable that this was so; but it may be doubted whether there is much available evidence on the matter, and, in any case, it cannot be gone into here[1]. There is, however, a third element of

---

[1] Purity of life is sometimes required of those who are to kindle the new fire (Frazer, iii. 260, 302).

the village festival which does demand consideration, and that is the element of play. The day of sacrifice was also a day of cessation from the ordinary toil of the fields, a holiday as well as a holy day. Sacred and secular met in the amorous encounters smiled upon by the liberal wood-goddess, and in the sacramental banquet with its collops of flesh and spilth of ale and mead. But the experience of any bank holiday will show that, for those who labour, the suspension of their ordinary avocations does not mean quiescence. When the blood is heated with love and liquor, the nervous energies habitually devoted to wielding the goad and guiding the plough must find vent in new and for the nonce unprofitable activities. But such activities, self-sufficing, and primarily at least serving no end beyond themselves, are, from pushpin to poetry, exactly what is meant by play[1].

The instinct of play found a foothold at the village feast in the débris which ritual, in its gradual transformation, left behind. It has already been noted as a constant feature in the history of institutions that a survival does not always remain merely a survival; it may be its destiny, when it is emptied of its first significance, to be taken up into a different order of ideas, and to receive a new lease of vitality under a fresh interpretation. Sacrifice ceases to be sacrament and becomes oblation. Dipping and smoking customs, originally magical, grow to be regarded as modes of sacrificial death. Other such waifs of the past become the inheritance of play. As the old conception of sacrifice passed into the new one, the subsidiary rites, through which the sacramental influence had of old been distributed over the worshippers and their fields, although by no means disused, lost their primitive meaning. Similarly, when human sacrifice was abolished, that too left traces of itself, only imperfectly intelligible, in mock or symbolical deaths, or in the election of the temporary king. Thus, even before Christianity antiquated the whole structure of the village festivals, there were individual practices kept alive only by the conservatism of

[1] H. Spencer, *Principles of Psychology*, ii. 629; K. Groos, *Play of Man*, 361; Hirn, 25.

tradition, and available as material for the play instinct. These find room in the festivals side by side with other customs which the same instinct not only preserved but initiated. Of course, the antithesis between play and cult must not be pushed too far. The peasant mind is tenacious of acts and forgetful of explanations; and the chapters to come will afford examples of practices which, though they began in play, came in time to have a serious significance of quasi-ritual, and to share in the popular imagination the prestige as fertility charms of the older ceremonies of worship with which they were associated. The *ludi* to be immediately discussed, however, present themselves in the main as sheer play. Several of them have broken loose from the festivals altogether, or, if they still acknowledge their origin by making a special appearance on some fixed day, are also at the service of ordinary amusement, whenever the leisure or the whim of youth may so suggest.

To begin with, it is possible that athletic sports and horse-racing are largely an outcome of sacrificial festivals. Like the Greeks around the pyre of Patroclus, the Teutons celebrated games at the tombs of their dead chieftains[1]. But games were a feature of seasonal, no less than funeral feasts. It will be remembered that the council of Clovesho took pains to forbid the keeping of the Rogation days with horse-races. A bit of wrestling or a bout of quarter-staff is still *de rigueur* at many a wake or rushbearing, while in parts of Germany the winner of a race or of a shooting-match at the popinjay is entitled to light the festival fire, or to hold the desired office of May-king[2]. The reforming bishops of the thirteenth century include public wrestling-bouts and contests for prizes amongst the *ludi* whose performance they condemn; and they lay particular stress upon a custom described as *arietum super ligna et rotas elevationes*. The object of these 'ram-raisings' seems to be explained by the fact that in the days of Chaucer a ram was the traditional reward proposed for a successful wrestler[3]; and this perhaps enables us to push the connexion

---

[1] Gummere, *G. O.* 331.
[2] Frazer, i. 217; iii. 258.
[3] Chaucer says of the Miller

(*C. T.* prol. 548):
'At wrastlynge he wolde have alwey the ram';

with the sacrificial rite a little further. I would suggest that the original object of the man who wrestled for a ram, or climbed a greasy pole for a leg of mutton, or shot for a popinjay, was to win a sacrificial victim or a capital portion thereof, which buried in his field might bring him abundant crops. The orderly competition doubtless evolved itself from such an indiscriminate scrimmage for the fertilizing fragments as marks the rites of the earth-goddess in the Indian village feast[1]. Tug-of-war would seem to be capable of a similar explanation, though here the desired object is not a portion of the victim, but rather a straw rope made out of the corn divinity itself in the form of the harvest-May[2]. An even closer analogy with the Indian rite is afforded by such games as hockey and football. The ball is nothing else than the head of the sacrificial beast, and it is the endeavour of each player to get it into his own possession, or, if sides are taken, to get it over a particular boundary[3]. Originally, of course, this was the player's own boundary; it has come to be regarded as that of his opponents; but this inversion of the point of view is not one on which much stress can be laid. In proof of this theory it may be pointed out that in many places football is still played, traditionally, on certain days of the year. The most notable example is perhaps at Dorking, where the annual Shrove Tuesday scrimmage in the streets

and of Sir Thopas (*C. T.* 13670):
    ' Of wrastlynge was ther noon his
        peer,
    Ther any ram shal stonde.'
Strutt, 82, figures a wrestling from *Royal MS.* 2, B. viii, with a cock set on a pole as the prize.

[1] Cf. Appendix I., and Frazer, ii. 316; Jevons, *Plutarch*, lxix. 143, on the struggle between two wards—the Sacred Way and the Subura—for the head of the October Horse at Rome.

[2] Haddon, 270. The tug-of-war reappears in Korea and Japan as a ceremony intended to secure a good harvest.

[3] Mrs. Gomme, s. vv. *Bandy-ball, Camp, Football, Hockey, Hood, Hurling, Shinty.* These games, in which the ball is fought for, are distinct from those already mentioned as having a ceremonial use, in which it is amicably tossed from player to player (cf. p. 128). If *Golf* belongs to the present category, it is a case in which the endeavour seems to be actually to bury the ball. It is tempting to compare the name *Hockey* with the *Hock-cart* of the harvest festival, and with *Hock-tide*; but it does not really seem to be anything but *Hookey*. The original of both the hockey-stick and the golf-club was probably the shepherd's crook. Mr. Pepys tried to cast stones with a shepherd's crook on those very Epsom downs where the stockbroker now foozles his tee shot.

of the town and the annual efforts of the local authorities to suppress it furnish their regular paragraph to the newspapers. There are several others, in most of which, as at Dorking, the contest is between two wards or districts of the town[1]. This feature is repeated in the Shrove Tuesday tug-of-war at Ludlow, and in annual faction-fights elsewhere[2]. It is probably due to that συνοικισμός of village communities by which towns often came into being. Here and there, moreover, there are to be found rude forms of football in which the primitive character of the proceeding is far more evident than in the sophisticated game. Two of these deserve especial mention. At Hallaton in Leicestershire a feast is held on Easter Monday at a piece of high ground called Hare-pie Bank. A hare—the sacrificial character of the hare has already been dwelt upon—is carried in procession. 'Hare-pies' are scrambled for; and then follows a sport known as 'bottle-kicking.' Hooped wooden field-bottles are thrown down and a scrimmage ensues between the men of Hallaton and the men of the adjoining village of Medbourne. Besides the connexion with the hare sacrifice, it is noticeable that each party tries to drive the bottle towards its own boundary, and not that of its opponents[3]. More interesting still is the Epiphany struggle for the 'Haxey hood' at Haxey in Lincolnshire. The 'hood' is a roll of sacking or leather, and it is the object of each of the players to carry it to a public-house in his own village. The ceremony is connected with the Plough Monday *quête*, and the 'plough-bullocks' or 'boggons' led by their 'lord duke' and their 'fool,' known as 'Billy Buck,' are the presiding officials. On the following day a festival-fire is lit, over which the fool is 'smoked.'

---

[1] *F. L.* vii. 345 ; M. Shearman, *Athletics and Football*, 246 ; Haddon, 271; Gomme, *Vill. Comm.* 240; Ditchfield, 57, 64; W. Fitz-stephen, *Vita S. Thomae* († 1170–82) in *Mat. for Hist. of Becket* (R. S.), iii. 9, speaks of the 'lusum pilae celebrem' in London 'die quae dicitur Carnilevaria.' Riley, 571, has a London proclamation of 1409 forbidding the levy of money for 'foteballe' and 'cok-thresshyng.' At Chester the annual Shrove Tuesday football on the Roodee was commuted for races in 1540 (*Hist. MSS.* viii. 1. 362). At Dublin there was, in 1569, a Shrove Tuesday 'riding' of the 'occupacions' each 'bearing balles' (Gilbert, ii. 54).

[2] Haddon, *loc. cit.*; Gomme, *loc. cit.*; *Gloucester F. L.* 38. Cf. the *conflictus* described in ch. ix, and the classical parallels in Frazer, *Pausanias*, iii. 267.

[3] *F. L.* iii. 441 ; Ditchfield, 85.

The strongest support is given to my theory of the origin of this type of game, by an extraordinary speech which the fool delivers from the steps of an old cross. As usual, the cross has taken the place of a more primitive tree or shrine. The speech runs as follows: 'Now, good folks, this is Haxa' Hood. We've killed two bullocks and a half, *but the other half we had to leave running field*: we can fetch it if it's wanted. Remember it's

> 'Hoose agin hoose, toon agin toon,
> And if you meet a man, knock him doon.'

In this case then, the popular memory has actually preserved the tradition that the 'hood' or ball played with is the half of a bullock, the head that is to say, of the victim decapitated at a sacrifice [1].

Hockey and football and tug-of-war are lusty male sports, but the sacrificial survival recurs in some of the singing games played by girls and children. The most interesting of these is that known as 'Oranges and Lemons.' An arch is formed by two children with raised hands, and under this the rest of the players pass. Meanwhile rhymes are sung naming the bells of various parishes, and ending with some such formula as

> 'Here comes a chopper to chop off your head :
> The last, last, last, last man's head.'

As the last word is sung, the hands forming the arch are lowered, and the child who is then passing is caught, and falls in behind one of the leaders. When all in turn have been so caught, a tug-of-war, only without a rope, follows. The 'chopping' obviously suggests a sacrifice, in this case a human sacrifice. And the bell-rhymes show the connexion of the game with the parish contests just described. There exists indeed a precisely similar set of verses which has the title, *Song of the Bells of Derby on Football Morning.* The set ordinarily used in 'Oranges and Lemons' names London

---

[1] *F. L.* vii. 330 (a very full account); viii. 72, 173; Ditchfield, 50. There is a local aetiological myth about a lady who lost her hood on a windy day, and instituted the contest in memory of the event.

parishes, but here is a Northamptonshire variant, which is particularly valuable because it alludes to another rite of the agricultural festival, the sacramental cake buried in a furrow :

> 'Pancakes and fritters,
> Says the bells of St. Peter's :
> Where must we fry 'em ?
> Says the bells of Cold Higham :
> In yonder land thurrow (furrow)
> Says the bells of Wellingborough, &c.[1]

Other games of the same type are 'How many Miles to Babylon,' 'Through the Needle Eye,' and 'Tower of London.' These add an important incident to 'Oranges and Lemons,' in that a 'king' is said to be passing through the arch. On the other hand, some of them omit the tug-of-war[2]. With all these singing games it is a little difficult to say whether they proceed from children's imitations of the more serious proceedings of their elders, or whether they were originally played at the festivals by grown men and maidens, and have gradually, like the May *quête* itself, fallen into the children's hands. The 'Oranges and Lemons' group has its analogy to the tug-of-war; the use of the arch formation also connects it with the festival 'country' dances which will be mentioned in the next chapter.

The rude punishments by which the far from rigid code of village ethics vindicates itself against offenders, are on the border line between play and jurisprudence. These also appear to be in some cases survivals, diverted from their proper context, of festival usage. It has been pointed out that the ducking which was a form of rain-charm came to be used as a penalty for the churlish or dispirited person, who declined to throw up his work or to wear green on the festival day. In other places this same person has to 'ride the stang.' That is to say, he is set astride a pole and borne about with contumely, until he compounds for his misdemeanour by a fine in coin or liquor[3]. 'Riding the stang,' however, is

---

[1] Mrs. Gomme, s.v. *Oranges and Lemons.*

[2] Mrs. Gomme, s. vv.

[3] Dyer, 6, 481. 'Stang' is a word, of Scandinavian origin, for 'pole' or 'stake.' The Scandinavian *nið-stöng* (scorn-stake) was a horse's head on a pole, with a written

a rural punishment of somewhat wide application[1]. It is common to England and to France, where it can be traced back, under the names of *charivari* and *chevauchée*, to the fifteenth century[2]. The French *sociétés joyeuses*, which will be described in a later chapter, made liberal use of it[3]. The offences to which it is appropriate are various. A miser, a henpecked husband or a wife-beater, especially in May, and, on the other hand, a shrew or an unchaste woman, are liable to visitation, as are the parties to a second or third marriage, or to one perilously long delayed, or one linking May to December. The precise ceremonial varies considerably. Sometimes the victim has to ride on a pole, sometimes on a hobby-horse[4], or on an ass with his face turned to the tail[5]. Sometimes, again, he does not appear at all, but is represented by an effigy or guy, or, in France, by his next-door neighbour[6]. This dramatic version is, according to Mr. Barrett, properly called a 'skimmington riding,' while the term 'riding the stang' is reserved for that in which the offender figures in person. The din of kettles, bones, and cleavers, so frequent an element in rustic ceremonies, is found here also,

curse and a likeness of the man to be ill-wished (Vigfusson, *Icel. Dict.* s.v. *nið*).

[1] Cf. with Mr. Barrett's account, Northall, 253; Ditchfield, 178; *Northern F. L.* 29; Julleville, *Les Com.* 205; also Thomas Hardy's *Mayor of Casterbridge*, and his *The Fire at Tranter Sweatley's* (*Wessex Poems*, 201). The penalty is used by schoolboys (*Northern F. L.* 29) as well as villagers.

[2] Grenier, 375; Ducange, s.v. *Charivarium*, which he defines as 'ludus turpis tinnitibus et clamoribus variis, quibus illudunt iis, qui ad secundas convolant nuptias.' He refers to the statutes of Melun cathedral (1365) in *Instrumenta Hist. Eccl. Melud.* ii. 503. Cf. *Conc. of Langres* (1404) 'ludo quod dicitur Chareuari, in quo utuntur larvis in figura daemonum, et horrenda ibidem committuntur'; *Conc. of Angers* (1448), c. 12 (Labbé, xiii. 1358) 'pulsatione patellarum, pelvium et campanarum, eorum oris

et manibus sibilatione, instrumento aeruginariorum, sive fabricantium, et aliarum rerum sonorosarum, vociferationibus tumultuosis et aliis ludibriis et irrisionibus, in illo damnabili actu (qui cariuarium, vulgariter *charivari*, nuncupatur) circa domos nubentium, et in ipsorum detestationem et opprobrium post eorum secundas nuptias fieri consuetum, &c.'

[3] Cf. ch. xvi, and Leber, ix. 148, 169; Julleville, *Les Com.* 205, 243. In 1579 a regular *jeu* was made by the Dijon *Mère-Folle* of the *chevauchée* of one M. Du Tillet. The text is preserved in *Bibl. Nat. MS.* 24039 and analysed by M. Petit de Julleville.

[4] In Berks a draped horse's head is carried, and the proceeding known as a Hooset Hunt (Ditchfield, 178).

[5] Ducange, s.v. *Asini caudam in manu tenens*.

[6] Julleville, *Les Com.* 207.

and in one locality at least the attendants are accustomed to blacken their faces [1]. It may perhaps be taken for granted that 'riding the stang' is an earlier form of the punishment than the more delicate and symbolical 'skimmington riding'; and it is probable that the rider represents a primitive village criminal haled off to become the literal victim at a sacrificial rite. The fine or forfeit by which in some cases the offence can be purged seems to create an analogy between the custom under consideration and other sacrificial survivals which must now be considered. These are perhaps best treated in connexion with Hock-tide and the curious play proper to that festival at Coventry [2]. This play was revived for the entertainment of Elizabeth when she visited the Earl of Leicester at Kenilworth in July, 1575, and there exists a description of it in a letter written by one Robert Laneham, who accompanied the court, to a friend in London [3]. The men of Coventry, led by one Captain Cox, who presented it called it an 'olld storiall sheaw,' with for argument the massacre of the Danes by Ethelred on Saint Brice's night 1002 [4]. Laneham says that it was 'expressed in actionz and rymez,' and it appears from his account to have been a kind of sham fight or 'barriers' between two parties representing respectively Danish 'launsknights' and English, 'each with allder poll marcially in their hand [5].' In the end the Danes were defeated and 'many led captiue for triumph by our English wéemen.' The presenters also stated that the play was of 'an auncient beginning' and 'woont too bee plaid in oour Citee yeárely.' Of late, however, it had been 'laid dooun,' owing to the importunity of their preachers, and 'they woold make theyr humbl peticion vntoo her highnes, that they myght haue theyr playz vp agayn.' The records of

---

[1] So on Ilchester Meads, where the proceeding is known as Mommets or Mommicks (Barrett, 65).

[2] On Hock-tide and the Hock-play generally see Brand-Ellis, i. 107; Strutt, 349; Sharpe, 125; Dyer, 188; S. Denne, *Memoir on Hokeday* in *Archaeologia*, vii. 244.

[3] Cf. Appendix H. An allusion to the play by Sir R. Morrison († 1542) is quoted in chap. xxv.

[4] Laneham, or his informant, actually said, in error, 1012. On the historical event see Ramsay, i. 353.

[5] There were performers both on horse and on foot. Probably hobby-horses were used, for Jonson brings in Captain Cox 'in his Hobby-horse,' which was 'foaled in Queen Elizabeth's time' in the *Masque of Owls* (ed. Cunningham, iii. 188).

Coventry itself add but little to what Laneham gathered. The local *Annals*, not a very trustworthy chronicle, ascribe the invention of 'Hox Tuesday' to 1416–7, and perhaps confirm the *Letter* by noting that in 1575–6 the 'pageants on Hox Tuesday' were played after eight years[1]. We have seen that, according to the statement made at Kenilworth, the event commemorated by the performance was the Danish massacre of 1002. There was, however, another tradition, preserved by the fifteenth-century writer John Rous, which connected it rather with the sudden death of Hardicanute and the end of the Danish usurpation at the accession of Edward the Confessor[2]. It is, of course, possible that local *cantilenae* on either or both of these events may have existed, and may have been worked into the 'rymez' of the play. But I think it may be taken for granted that, as in the Lady Godiva procession, the historical element is comparatively a late one, which has been grafted upon already existing festival customs. One of these is perhaps the faction-fight just discussed. But it is to be noticed that the performance as described by Laneham ended with the Danes being led away captive by English women; and this episode seems to be clearly a dramatization of a characteristic Hock-tide *ludus* found in many places other than Coventry. On Hock-Monday, the women 'hocked' the men; that is to say, they went abroad with ropes, caught and bound any man they came across, and exacted a forfeit. On Hock-Tuesday, the men retaliated in similar fashion upon the women. Bishop Carpenter of Worcester forbade this practice in his diocese in 1450[3], but like some other festival customs it came

---

[1] Cf. *Representations*, s.v. Coventry.

[2] Rossius, *Hist. Regum Angliae* (ed. Hearne, 1716), 105 'in cuius signum usque hodie illa die vulgariter dicta Hox Tuisday ludunt in villis trahendo cordas partialiter cum aliis iocis.' Rous, who died 1491, is speaking of the death of Hardicanute. On the event see Ramsay, i. 434. Possibly both events were celebrated in the sixteenth century at Coventry. Two of the three plays proposed for municipal performance in 1591 were the 'Conquest of the Danes' and the 'History of Edward the Confessor.' These were to be upon the 'pagens,' and probably they were more regular dramas than the performance witnessed by Elizabeth in 1575 (*Representations*, s.v. Coventry).

[3] Leland, *Collectanea* (ed. Hearne), v. 298 'uno certo die heu usitato (*forsan* Hoc vocitato) hoc solempni festo paschatis transacto, mulieres

to be recognized as a source of parochial revenue, and the
'gaderyngs' at Hock-tide, of which the women's was always
the most productive, figure in many a churchwarden's budget
well into the seventeenth century[1]. At Shrewsbury in 1549
'hocking' led to a tragedy. Two men were 'smothered under
the Castle hill,' hiding themselves from maids, the hill falling
there on them[2].' 'Hockney day' is still kept at Hungerford,
and amongst the old-fashioned officers elected on this occasion, with the hay-ward and the ale-tasters, are the two
'tything men' or 'tutti men,' somewhat doubtfully said to be
so named from their poles wreathed with 'tutties' or nose-
gays, whose function it is to visit the commoners, and to claim
from every man a coin and from every woman a kiss[3]. The
derivation of the term Hock-tide has given rise to some wild
conjectures, and philologists have failed to come to a conclusion on the subject[4]. Hock-tide is properly the Monday
and Tuesday following the Second Sunday after Easter, and
'Hokedaie' or *Quindena Paschae* is a frequent term day in
leases and other legal documents from the thirteenth century
onwards[5].

'Hocking' can be closely paralleled from other customs of
the spring festivals. The household books of Edward I
record in 1290 a payment 'to seven ladies of the queen's
chamber who took the king in bed on the morrow of Easter,
and made him fine himself[6].' This was the *prisio* which at
a later date perturbed the peace of French ecclesiastics.
The council of Nantes, for instance, in 1431, complains that
clergy were hurried out of their beds on Easter Monday,
dragged into church, and sprinkled with water upon the
altar[7]. In this aggravated form the *prisio* hardly survived

---

homines, alioque die homines mulieres ligare, ac cetera media utinam
non inhonesta vel deteriora facere
moliantur et exercere, lucrum
ecclesiae fingentes, set dampnum
animae sub fucato colore lucrantes,
&c.' Riley, 561, 571, gives London
proclamations against 'hokkyng' of
1405 and 1409.
[1] Brand-Ellis, i. 113; Lysons,
Environs of London, i. 229; C.
Kerry, *Accts. of St. Lawrence, Read-*

ing; Hobhouse, 232; *N.E.D.* s.vv.
Hock, &c.
[2] Owen and Blakeway, *Hist. of
Shrewsbury*, i. 559.
[3] Dyer, 191; Ditchfield, 90.
[4] *N.E.D.* s.v. *Hock-day*.
[5] Brand-Ellis, i. 106.
[6] Ibid. i. 109.
[7] Ducange, s.v. *Prisio*; Barthélemy, iv. 463. On Innocents' Day,
the customs of taking in bed and
whipping were united (cf. ch. xii).

the frank manners of the Middle Ages. But it was essentially identical with the ceremonies in which a more modern usage has permitted the levying of forfeits at both Pasque and Pentecost. In the north of England, women were liable to have their shoes taken on one or other of these feasts, and must redeem them by payment. On the following day they were entitled to retaliate on the shoes of the men [1]. A more widely spread method of exacting the *droit* is that of ' heaving.' The unwary wanderer in some of the northern manufacturing towns on Easter Monday is still liable to find himself swung high in the air by the stalwart hands of factory girls, and will be lucky if he can purchase his liberty with nothing more costly than a kiss. If he likes, he may take his revenge on Easter Tuesday [2]. Another mediaeval custom described by Belethus in the twelfth century, which prescribed the whipping of husbands by wives on Easter Monday and of wives by husbands on Easter Tuesday, has also its modern parallel [3]. On Shrove Tuesday a hockey match was played at Leicester, and after it a number of young men took their stand with cart whips in the precincts of the Castle. Any passer-by who did not pay a forfeit was liable to lashes. The ' whipping Toms,' as they were called, were put down by a special Act of Parliament in 1847 [4]. The analogy of these customs with the requirement made of visitors to certain markets or to the roofs of houses in the building to 'pay their footing ' is obvious [5].

In all these cases, even where the significant whipping or sprinkling is absent, the meaning is the same. The binding with ropes, the loss of the shoes, the lifting in the air, are

[1] *Northern F. L.* 84; Brand-Ellis, i. 94, 96 ; Vaux, 242 ; Ditchfield, 80 ; Dyer, 133.

[2] Brand-Ellis, i. 106; Owen and Blakeway, i. 559; Dyer, 173; Ditchfield, 90; Burne-Jackson, 336; *Northern F. L.* 84; Vaux, 242. A dignified H. M. I. is said to have made his first official visit to Warrington on Easter Monday, and to have suffered accordingly. Miss Burne describes sprinkling as an element in Shropshire heaving.

[3] Belethus, c. 120 'notandum quoque est in plerisque regionibus secundo die post Pascha mulieres maritos suos verberare ac vicissim viros eas tertio die.' The spiritually minded Belethus explains the custom as a warning to keep from carnal intercourse.

[4] Dyer, 79; Ditchfield, 83.

[5] Brand-Ellis, i. 114; Ditchfield, 252. Mr. W. Crooke has just studied this and analogous customs in *The Lifting of the Bride* (*F.L.* xiii. 226).

symbols of capture. And the capture is for the purposes of sacrifice, for which no more suitable victim, in substitution for the priest-king, than a stranger, could be found. This will, I think, be clear by comparison with some further parallels from the harvest field and the threshing-floor, in more than one of which the symbolism is such as actually to indicate the sacrifice itself, as well as the preliminary capture. In many parts of England a stranger, and sometimes even the farmer himself, when visiting a harvest field, is liable to be asked for 'largess'[1]. In Scotland, the tribute is called 'head-money,' and he who refuses is seized by the arms and feet and 'dumped' on the ground[2]. Similar customs prevail on the continent, in Germany, Norway, France; and the stranger is often, just as in the 'hocking' ceremony, caught with straw ropes, or swathed in a sheaf of corn. It is mainly in Germany that the still more elaborate rites survive. In various districts of Mecklenburg, and of Pomerania, the reapers form a ring round the stranger, and fiercely whet their scythes, sometimes with traditional rhymest which contain a threat to mow him down. In Schleswig, and again in Sweden, the stranger in a threshing-floor is 'taught the flail-dance' or 'the threshing-song.' The arms of a flail are put round his neck and pressed so tightly that he is nearly choked. When the madder-roots are being dug, a stranger passing the field is caught by the workers, and buried up to his middle in the soil[3].

The central incident of 'hocking' appears therefore to be nothing but a form of that symbolical capture of a human victim of which various other examples are afforded by the village festivals. The development of the custom into a play or mock-fight at Coventry may very well have taken place, as the town annals say, about the beginning of the fifteenth century. Whether it had previously been connected by local tradition with some event in the struggles of Danes and Saxons or not, is a question which one must be content to leave

---

[1] *Suffolk F. L.* 69; *F. L.* v. 167. The use of *largess*, a Norman-French word (*largitio*), is curious. It is also used for the subscriptions to Lancashire gyst-ales (Dyer, 182).
[2] Ditchfield, 155.
[3] Frazer, ii. 233; Pfannenschmidt, 93.

unsolved. A final word is due to the curious arrangement by which in the group of customs here considered the rôles of sacrificers and sacrificed are exchanged between men and women on the second day ; for it lends support to the theory already put forward that a certain stage in the evolution of the village worship was marked by the merging of previously independent sex-cults.

CHAPTER VIII

THE MAY-GAME

[*Bibliographical Note.*—The festal character of primitive dance and song is admirably brought out by R. Wallaschek, *Primitive Music* (1893); E. Grosse, *Die Anfänge der Kunst* (1894, French transl. 1902); Y. Hirn, *The Origins of Art* (1900); F. B. Gummere, *The Beginnings of Poetry* (1901). The popular element in French lyric is illustrated by A. Jeanroy, *Les Origines de la Poésie lyrique en France au Moyen Âge* (1889), and J. Tiersot, *Histoire de la Chanson populaire en France* (1889). Most of such English material as exists is collected in Mrs. Gomme's *Traditional Games* (1896-8) and G. F. Northall, *English Folk-Rhymes* (1892). For comparative study E. Martinengo-Cesaresco, *Essays in the Study of Folk-Songs* (1886), may be consulted. The notices of the May-game are scattered through the works mentioned in the bibliographical note to ch. vi and others.]

THE foregoing chapter has illustrated the remarkable variety of modes in which the instinct of play comes to find expression. But of all such the simplest and most primitive is undoubtedly the dance. Psychology discovers in the dance the most rudimentary and physical of the arts, and traces it to precisely that overflow of nervous energies shut off from their normal practical ends which constitutes play[1]. And the verdict of psychology is confirmed by philology; for in all the Germanic languages the same word signifies both 'dance' and 'play,' and in some of them it is even extended to the cognate ideas of 'sacrifice' or 'festival[2].' The dance must therefore

---

[1] Haddon, 335; Grosse, 167; Herbert Spencer in *Contemp. Review* (1895), 114; Groos, *Play of Man*, 88, 354. Evidence for the wide use of the dance at savage festivals is given by Wallaschek, 163, 187.

[2] Grimm, i. 39; Pearson, ii. 133; Müllenhoff, *Germania*, ch. 24, and *de antiq. Germ. poesi chorica*, 4; Kögel, i. 1. 8. The primitive word form should have been *laikaz*, whence Gothic *laiks*, O. N. *leikr*, O. H. G. *leih*, A.-S. *lác*. The word has, says Müllenhoff, all the senses '*Spiel,*

Tanz, Gesang, Opfer, Aufzug.' From the same root come probably *ludus,* and possibly, through the Celtic, the O. F. *lai.* The A.-S. *lác* is glossed *ludus, sacrificium, victima, munus.* It occurs in the compounds *ecga-gelác* and *sveorða-gelác,* both meaning 'sword-dance,' *sige-lác,* 'victory-dance,' *as-lác,* 'god-dance,' *wine-lác,* 'love-dance' (cf. p. 170), &c. An A.-S. synonym for *lác* is *plega,* 'play,' which gives *sweord-plega* and *ecg-plega. Spil* is not A.-S. and *spilian* is a loan-word from O. H. G.

be thought of as an essential part of all the festivals with which we have to deal. And with the dance comes song: the rhythms of motion seem to have been invariably accompanied by the rhythms of musical instruments, or of the voice, or of both combined [1].

The dance had been from the beginning a subject of contention between Christianity and the Roman world [2]; but whereas the dances of the East and South, so obnoxious to the early Fathers, were mainly those of professional entertainers, upon the stage or at banquets, the missionaries of the West had to face the even more difficult problem of a folk-dance and folk-song which were amongst the most inveterate habits of the freshly converted peoples. As the old worship vanished, these tended to attach themselves to the new. Upon great feasts and wake days, choruses of women invaded with wanton *cantica* and *ballationes* the precincts of the churches and even the sacred buildings themselves, a desecration against which generation after generation of ecclesiastical authorities was fain to protest [3]. Clerkly sentiment in the matter is repre-

[1] Gummere, *B. P.* 328; Kögel, i. 1. 6.

[2] S. Ambrose, *de Elia et Ieiunio*, c. 18 (*P. L.* xiv. 720), *de Poenitentia*, ii. 6 (*P. L.* xvi. 508); S. Augustine, *contra Parmenianum*, iii. 6 (*P. L.* xliii. 107); S. Chrysostom, *Hom.* 47 *in Iulian. mart.* p. 613; *Hom.* 23 *de Novilun.* p. 264; *C. of Laodicea* (†366), c. 53 (Mansi, ii. 571). Cf. *D. C. A.* s. v. Dancing, and ch. i. Barthélemy, ii. 438, and other writers have some rather doubtful theories as to liturgical dancing in early Christian worship; cf. Julian. *Dict. of Hymn.* 206.

[3] Du Méril, *Com.* 67; Pearson, ii. 17, 281; Gröber, ii. 1. 444; Kögel, i. 1. 25; *Indiculus Superstitionum* (ed. Saupe), 10 'de sacrilegiis per ecclesias.' Amongst the prohibitions are Caesarius of Arles (†542), *Sermo* xiii (*P. L.* xxxix. 2325) 'quam multi rustici et quam multae mulieres rusticanae cantica diabolica, amatoria et turpia memoriter retinent et ore decantant'; *Const. Childeberti* (c. 554) *de abol. relig. idololatriae* (Mansi, ix. 738) 'noctes

pervigiles cum ebrietate, scurrilitate, vel canticis, etiam in ipsis sacris diebus, pascha, natale Domini, et reliquis festivitatibus, vel adveniente die Dominico dansatrices per villas ambulare . . . nullatenus fieri permittimus'; *C. of Auxerre* (573–603), c. 9 (Maassen, i. 180) 'non licet in ecclesia choros secularium vel puellarum cantica exercere'; *C. of Chalons* (639–54), c. 19 (Maassen, i. 212) 'Valde omnibus noscetur esse decretum, ne per dedicationes basilicarum aut festivitates martyrum ad ipsa solemnia confluentes obscoena et turpia cantica, dum orare debent aut clericos psallentes audire, cum choris foemineis, turpia quidem decantare videantur. unde convenit, ut sacerdotes loci illos a septa basilicarum vel porticus ipsarum basilicarum etiam et ab ipsis atriis vetare debeant et arcere.' *Sermo Eligii* (Grimm, iv. 1737) 'nullus in festivitate S. Ioannis vel quibuslibet sanctorum solemnitatibus solstitia aut valla-

sented by a pious legend, very popular in the Middle Ages, which told how some reprobate folk of Kölbigk in Anhalt disobeyed the command of a priest to cease their unholy revels before the church of Saint Magnus while he said mass on Christmas day, and for their punishment must dance there the year round without stopping [1]. The struggle was a long one, and in the end the Church never quite succeeded even in expelling the dance from its own doors. The chapter of Wells about 1338 forbade *choreae* and other *ludi* within the cathedral and the cloisters, chiefly on account of the damage

tiones vel saltationes aut caraulas aut cantica diabolica exerceat'; *Iudicium Clementis* († 693), c. 20 (Haddan-Stubbs, iii. 226) 'si quis in quacunque festivitate ad ecclesiam veniens pallat foris, aut saltat, aut cantat orationes amatorias . . . excommunicetur' (apparently a fragment of a penitential composed by Clement or Willibrord, an A.-S. missionary to Frisia, on whom see Bede, *H. E.* v. 9, and the only dance prohibition of possible A.-S. *provenance* of which I know); *Statuta Salisburensia* (Salzburg: † 800; Boretius, i. 229) 'Ut omnis populus . . . absque inlecebroso canticu et lusu saeculari cum laetaniis procedant'; *C. of Mainz* (813), c. 48 (Mansi, xiv. 74) 'canticum turpe atque luxuriosum circa ecclesias agere omnino contradicimus'; *C. of Rome* (826), c. 35 (Mansi, xiv. 1008) 'sunt quidam, et maxime mulieres, qui festis ac sacris diebus atque sanctorum natalitiis non pro eorum quibus debent delectantur desideriis advenire, sed ballando, verba turpia decantando, choros tenendo ac ducendo, similitudinem paganorum peragendo, advenire procurant'; cf. *Dicta abbatis Pirminii* (Caspari, *Kirchenhistorische Anecdota,* 188); *Penitentiale pseudo-Theodorianum* (Wasserschleben, 607); *Leonis IV Homilia* (847, Mansi, xiv. 895); Benedictus Levita, *Capitularia* († 850), vi. 96 (*M. G. H. Script.* iv. 2); and for Spain, *C. of Toledo* (589), c. 23 (Mansi, ix. 999), and the undated *C. of Braga,* c. 80 (quoted on p. 144). Cf. also the

denunciations of the *Kalends* (ch. xi and Appendix N). Nearly four centuries after the *C. of Rome* we find the *C. of Avignon* (1209), c. 17 (Mansi, xxii. 791) 'statuimus, ut in sanctorum vigiliis in ecclesiis historicae saltationes, obscoeni motus, seu choreae non fiant, nec dicantur amatoria carmina, vel cantilenae ibidem . . .' Still later the *C. of Bayeux* (1300), c. 31 (Mansi, xxv. 66) 'ut dicit Augustinus, melius est festivis diebus fodere vel arare, quam choreas ducere'; and so on *ad infinitum.* The pseudo-Augustine *Sermo,* 265, *de Christiano nomine cum operibus non Christianis (P. L.* xxxix. 2237), which is possibly by Caesarius of Arles, asserts explicitly the pagan character of the custom: 'isti enim infelices et miseri homines, qui balationes et saltationes ante ipsas basilicas sanctorum exercere non metuunt nec erubescunt, etsi Christiani ad ecclesiam venerint, pagani de ecclesia revertuntur; quia ista consuetudo balandi de paganorum observatione remansit.' A mediaeval preacher (quoted by A. Lecoy de la Marche, *Chaire française au Moyen Âge,* 447, from *B. N. Lat. MS.* 17509, f. 146) declares, 'chorea enim circulus est cuius centrum est diabolus, et omnes vergunt ad sinistrum.'

[1] Tille, *D. W.* 301; G. Raynaud, in *Études dédiées à Gaston Paris,* 53; E. Schröder, *Die Tänzer von Kölbigk,* in *Z. f. Kirchengeschichte,* xvii. 94; G. Paris, in *Journal des Savants* (1899), 733.

too often done to its property[1]. A seventeenth-century French writer records that he had seen clergy and singing-boys dancing at Easter in the churches of Paris[2]; and even at the present day there are some astounding survivals. At Seville, as is well known, the six boys, called *los Seises*, dance with castanets before the Holy Sacrament in the presence of the archbishop at Shrovetide, and during the feasts of the Immaculate Conception and Corpus Christi[3]. At Echternach in Luxembourg there is an annual dance through the church of pilgrims to the shrine of St. Willibrord[4], while at Barjols in Provence a 'tripe-dance' is danced at mass on St. Marcel's day in honour of the patron[5].

Still less, of course, did dance and song cease to be important features of the secular side of the festivals. We have already seen how *cantilenae* on the great deeds of heroes had their vogue in the mouths of the *chori* of young men and maidens, as well as in those of the minstrels[6]. The *Carmina Burana*

---

[1] H. E. Reynolds, *Wells Cathedral*, 85 'cum ex choreis ludis et spectaculis et lapidum proiectionibus in praefata ecclesia et eius cemeteriis ac claustro dissentiones sanguinis effusiones et violentiae saepius oriantur et in hiis dicta Wellensis ecclesia multa dispendia patiatur.'

[2] Menestrier, *Des Ballets anciens et modernes* (1863), 4; on other French church dances, cf. Du Tilliot, 21; Barthélemy, iv. 447; Leber, ix. 420. The most famous are the *pilota* of Auxerre, which was accompanied with ball-play (cf. ch. vi) and the *bergeretta* of Besançon. Julian, *Dict. of Hymn.* 206, gives some English examples.

[3] Grove, 106. A full account of the ceremony at the feast of the Conception in 1901 is given in the *Church Times* for Jan. 17, 1902.

[4] Grove, 103; Bérenger-Féraud, iii. 430; *Mélusine* (1879), 39; *N. and Q.* for May 17, 1890. The dance is headed by the clergy, and proceeds to a traditional tune from the banks of the Sûre to the church, up sixty-two steps, along the north aisle, round the altar *deasil*, and down the south aisle. It is curious that until the seventeenth century only *men* took part in it. St. Willibrord is famous for curing nervous diseases, and the pilgrimage is done by way of vow for such cures. The local legend asserts that the ceremony had its origin in an eighth-century cattle-plague, which ceased through an invocation of St. Willibrord: it is a little hard on the saint, whose prohibition of dances at the church-door has just been quoted.

[5] Bérenger-Féraud, iii. 409. A similarly named saint, St. Martial, was formerly honoured in the same way. Every psalm on his day ended, not with the *Gloria Patri*, but with a dance, and the chant, 'Saint-Marceau, pregas per nous, et nous epingaren per vous' (Du Méril, *La Com.* 68).

[6] Cf. p. 26. There were 'madinnis that dansit' before James IV of Scotland at Forres, Elgin and Dernway in 1504, but nothing is said of songs (*L. H. T. Accounts*, ii. 463).

describe the dances of girls upon the meadows as amongst the pleasures of spring [1]. William Fitzstephen tells us that such dances were to be seen in London in the twelfth century[2], and we have found the University of Oxford solemnly forbidding them in the thirteenth. The *romans* and *pastourelles* frequently mention *chansons* or *rondets de carole*, which appear to have been the *chansons* used to accompany the choric dances, and to have generally consisted of a series of couplets sung by the leader, and a refrain with which the rest of the band answered him. Occasionally the refrains are quoted [3]. The minstrels borrowed this type of folk *chanson*, and the conjoint dance and song themselves found their way from the village green to the courtly hall. In the twelfth century ladies *carolent*, and more rarely even men condescend to take a part [4]. Still later *carole*, like *tripudium*, seems to become a term for popular rejoicing in general, not necessarily expressed in rhythmical shape [5].

The customs of the village festival gave rise by natural development to two types of dance [6]. There was the processional dance of the band of worshippers in progress round their boundaries and from field to field, from house to house,

---

[1] *Carm. Bur.* 191 :
　‘ludunt super gramina
　　virgines decorae
　　quarum nova carmina
　　　dulci sonant ore.’
Ibid. 195 :
　‘ecce florescunt lilia,
　et virginum dant agmina
　summo deorum carmina.’
[2] W. Fitzstephen, *Descriptio Londin.* (*Mat. for Hist. of Becket*, R. S. iii. 11) ‘puellarum Cytherea ducit choros usque imminente luna, et pede libero pulsatur tellus.’
[3] Jeanroy, 102, 387 ; Guy, 504 ; Paris, *Journal des Savants* (1892), 407. M. Paris points out that dances, other than professional, first appear in the West after the fall of the Empire. The French terms for dancing—*baller, danser, treschier, caroler*—are not Latin. *Caroler*, however, he thinks to be the Greek χοραυλεῖν, ‘to accompany a dance with a flute.’ But the

French *carole* was always accompanied, not with a flute, but with a sung *chanson*.
[4] Paris, *loc. cit.* 410 ; Jeanroy, 391. In Wace’s description of Arthur’s wedding, the women *carolent* and the men *behourdent*. Cf. Bartsch, *Romanzen und Pastourellen*, i. 13 :
　‘Cez damoiseles i vont por caroler,
　cil escuier i vont por behorder,
　cil chevalier i vont por esgarder.’
[5] On the return of Edward II and Isabella of France in 1308, the mayor and other dignitaries of London went ‘coram rege et regina karolantes’ (*Chronicles of Edward I and Edward II*, R. S. i. 152). On the birth of Prince Edward in 1312, they ‘menerent la karole’ in church and street (Riley, 107).
[6] Kögel, i. 1. 6.

from well to well of the village. It is this that survives in the dance of the Echternach pilgrims, or in the 'faddy-dance' in and out the cottage doors at Helston wake. And it is probably this that is at the bottom of the interesting game of 'Thread the Needle.' This is something like 'Oranges and Lemons,' the first part of which, indeed, seems to have been adapted from it. There is, however, no sacrifice or 'tug-of-war,' although there is sometimes a 'king,' or a 'king' and his 'lady' or 'bride' in the accompanying rhymes, and in one instance a 'pancake.' The players stand in two long lines. Those at the end of each line form an arch with uplifted arms, and the rest run in pairs beneath it. Then another pair form an arch, and the process is repeated. In this way long strings of lads and lasses stream up and down the streets or round and about a meadow or green. In many parts of England this game is played annually on Shrove Tuesday or Easter Monday, and the peasants who play it at Châtre in central France say that it is done 'to make the hemp grow.' Its origin in connexion with the agricultural festivals can therefore hardly be doubtful[1]. It is probable that in the beginning the players danced rather than ran under the 'arch'; and it is obvious that the 'figure' of the game is practically identical with one familiar in *Sir Roger de Coverley* and other old English 'country' dances of the same type.

Just as the 'country' dance is derived from the processional dance, so the other type of folk-dance, the *ronde* or 'round,' is derived from the comparatively stationary dance of the group of worshippers around the more especially sacred objects of the festival, such as the tree or the fire[2]. The custom of dancing round the May-pole has been more or less preserved wherever the May-pole is known. But 'Thread the Needle' itself often winds up with a circular dance or *ronde*, either around one of the players, or, on festival occasions, around the representative of the earlier home of the fertilization divinity,

---

[1] Mrs. Gomme, ii. 228; Haddon, 345.

[2] Cf. ch. vi on the motion *deasil* round the sacred object. It is curious that the modern round dances go *withershins* round a room. Grimm, i. 52, quotes Gregory the Great, *Dial.* iii. 28 on a Lombard sacrifice, 'caput caprae, hoc ei, per circuitum currentes, carmine nefando dedicantes.'

the parish church. This custom is popularly known as
'clipping the church[1].'

Naturally the worshippers at a festival would dance in their
festival costume; that is to say, in the garb of leaves and
flowers worn for the sake of the beneficent influence of the
indwelling divinity, or in the hides and horns of sacrificial
animals which served a similar purpose. Travellers describe
elaborate and beautiful beast-dances amongst savage peoples,
and the Greeks had their own bear- and crane-dances, as well
as the dithyrambic goat-dance of the Dionysia. They had
also flower dances[2]. In England the village dancers wear
posies, but I do not know that they ever attempt a more
elaborate representation of flowers. But a good example of
the beast-dance is furnished by the 'horn-dance' at Abbots
Bromley in Staffordshire, held now at a September wake, and
formerly at Christmas. In this six of the performers wear sets
of horns. These are preserved from year to year in the church,
and according to local tradition the dance used at one time
to take place in the churchyard on a Sunday. The horns are
said to be those of the reindeer, and from this it may possibly
be inferred that they were brought to Abbots Bromley by
Scandinavian settlers. The remaining performers represent
a hobby-horse, a clown, a woman, and an archer, who makes
believe to shoot the horned men[3].

The *motifs* of the dances and their *chansons* must also at first
have been determined by the nature of the festivals at which
they took place. There were dances, no doubt, at such domestic

---

[1] At Bradford-on-Avon, Wilts
(which preserves its Anglo-Saxon
church), and at South Petherton,
Somerset, in both cases on Shrove
Tuesday (Mrs. Gomme, ii. 230); cf.
Vaux, 18. The church at Painswick,
Gloucester, is danced round on
wake-day (*F. L.* viii. 392). There
is a group of games, in which the
players wind and unwind in spirals
round a centre. Such are *Eller Tree*,
Wind up the Bush Faggot, and *Bulli-
heisle*. These Mrs. Gomme regards
as survivals of the ritual dance
round a sacred tree. Some obscure
references in the rhymes used to

'dumplings' and 'a bundle of rags'
perhaps connect themselves with
the cereal cake and the rags hung
on the tree for luck. In Cornwall
such a game is played under the
name of 'Snail's Creep' at certain
village feasts in June, and directed
by young men with leafy branches.

[2] Du Méril, *La Com.* 72; Haddon, 346; Grove, 50, 81; Haigh,
14; N. W. Thomas, *La Danse
totémique en Europe*, in *Actes d.
Cong. intern. d. Trad. pop.* (1900).

[3] Plot, *Hist. of Staffs.* (1686);
F. L. iv. 172; vii. 382 (with cuts of
properties); Ditchfield, 139.

festivals as weddings and funerals [1]. In Flanders it is still the custom to dance at the funeral of a young girl, and a very charming *chanson* is used [2]. The development of epic poetry from the *cantilenae* of the war-festival has been noted in a former chapter. At the agricultural festivals, the primary *motif* is, of course, the desire for the fertility of the crops and herds. The song becomes, as in the Anglo-Saxon charm, so often referred to, practically a prayer [3]. With this, and with the use of 'Thread the Needle' at Châtre 'to make the hemp grow,' may be compared the games known to modern children, as to Gargantua, in which the operations of the farmer's year, and in particular his prayer for his crops, are mimicked in a *ronde*[4]. Allusions to the process of the seasons, above all to the delight of the *renouveau* in spring, would naturally also find a place in the festival songs. The words of the famous thirteenth-century lyric were perhaps written to be sung to the twinkling feet of English girls in a round. It has the necessary refrain :

[1] The O. H. G. *hileih*, originally meaning 'sex-dance,' comes to be 'wedding.' The root *hi*, like *wini* (cf. p. 170), has a sexual connotation (Pearson, ii. 132; Kögel, i. 1. 10).

[2] Coussemaker, *Chants populaires des Flamands de France*, 100 :
'In den hemel is eenen dans :
    Alleluia.
Daer dansen all' de maegdekens :
Benedicamus Domino,
Alleluia, Alleluia.
't is voor Amelia :
Alleluia.
Wy dansen naer de maegdekens :
Benedicamus, etc.'

[3] Frazer, i. 35 ; Dyer, 7 ; Northall, 233. A Lancashire song is sung 'to draw you these cold winters away,' and wishes 'peace and plenty' to the household. A favourite French May *chanson* is
'Étrennez notre épousée,
    Voici le mois,
Le joli mois de Mai,
Étrennez notre épousée
    En bonne étrenne.

    Voici le mois,
Le joli mois de Mai,
    Qu'on vous amène.'
If the *quêteurs* come on a churl, they have an ill-wishing variant. The following is characteristic of the French peasantry :
' J'vous souhaitons autant d'enfants,
    Qu'y a des pierrettes dans les champs.'
Often more practical tokens of revenge are shown. The Plough Monday 'bullocks' in some places consider themselves licensed to plough up the ground before a house where they have been rebuffed.'

[4] Mrs. Gomme, ii. 1, 399 ; Haddon, 343 ; Du Méril, *La Com.* 81. Amongst the *jeux* of the young Gargantua (Rabelais, i. 22) was one 'à semer l'avoyne et au laboureur.' This probably resembled the games of *Oats and Beans and Barley*, and *Would you know how doth the Peasant?* which exist in English, French, Catalonian, and Italian versions. On the mimetic character of these games, cf. ch. viii.

'Sumer is icumen in,
    Lhude sing cuccu!
Groweth sed and bloweth med
And springth the wdë nu,
            Sing cuccu!

'Awë bleteth after lomb,
    Lhouth after calvë cu.
Bulloc sterteth, buckë verteth,
    Murie sing cuccu!

'Cuccu, cuccu, wel singës thu, cuccu;
    Ne swik thu naver nu.
Sing cuccu nu. Sing cuccu.
    Sing cuccu. Sing cuccu nu!'[1]

The savour of the spring is still in the English May songs,
the French *maierolles* or *calendes de mai* and the Italian
calen di maggio. But for the rest they have either become
little but mere *quête* songs, or else, under the influence of the
priests, have taken on a Christian colouring[2]. At Oxford
the ' merry ketches ' sung by choristers on the top of Magdalen
tower on May morning were replaced in the seventeenth
century by the hymn now used[3]. Another very popular
Mayers' song would seem to show that the Puritans, in despair
of abolishing the festival, tried to reform it.

---

[1] Text from *Harl. MS.* 978 in
H. E. Wooldridge, *Oxford Hist. of
Music*, i. 326, with full account.
The music, to which religious as
well as the secular words are attached, is technically known as a
rota or *rondel*. It is of the nature
of polyphonic part-song, and of
course more advanced than the
typical mediaeval *rondet* can have
been.

[2] On these songs in general, see
Northall, 233 ; Martinengo-Cesaresco, 249 ; Cortet, 153 ; Tiersot,
191 ; Jeanroy, 88 ; Paris, *J. des
Savants* (1891), 685, (1892), 155,
407.

[3] H. A. Wilson, *Hist. of Magd.
Coll.* (1899), 50. Mr. Wilson dis-
credits the tradition that the per-

formance began as a mass for the
obit of Henry VII. The hymn is
printed in Dyer, 259 ; Ditchfield,
96. It has no relation to the summer festival, having been written in
the seventeenth century by Thomas
Smith and set by Benjamin Rogers
as a grace. In other cases hymns
have been attached to the village
festivals. At Tissington the ' well-
dressing,' on Ascension Day includes a clerical procession in which
' Rock of Ages ' and ' A Living
Stream ' are sung (Ditchfield, 187).
A special ' Rushbearers' Hymn '
was written for the Grasmere Rushbearing in 1835, and a hymn for
St. Oswald has been recently added
(E. G. Fletcher, *The Rushbearing*,
13, 74).

'Remember us poor Mayers all,
   And thus we do begin
To lead our lives in righteousness,
   Or else we die in sin.

' We have been rambling all this night,
   And almost all this day :
And now returned back again,
   We have brought you a branch of May.

' A branch of May we have brought you,
   And at your door it stands ;
It is but a sprout, but it's well budded out,
   By the work of our Lord's hands,' &c.[1]

Another religious element, besides prayer, may have entered
into the pre-Christian festival songs ; and that is myth.
A stage in the evolution of drama from the Dionysiac dithyramb was the introduction of mythical narratives about the
wanderings and victories of the god, to be chanted or recited by
the *choragus.* The relation of the *choragus* to the *chorus* bears
a close analogy to that between the leader of the mediaeval
carole and his companions who sang the refrain. This leader
probably represents the Keltic or Teutonic priest at the head
of his band of worshippers ; and one may suspect that in the
north and west of Europe, as in Greece, the pauses of the
festival dance provided the occasion on which the earliest
strata of stories about the gods, the hieratic as distinguished
from the literary myths, took shape. If so the development of
divine myth was very closely parallel to that of heroic myth[2].

After religion, the commonest *motif* of dance and song at
the village festivals must have been love. This is quite in
keeping with the amorous licence which was one of their
characteristics. The goddess of the fertility of earth was also
the goddess of the fertility of women. The ecclesiastical prohibitions lay particular stress upon the *orationes amatoriae* and
the *cantica turpia et luxuriosa* which the women sang at the
church doors, and only as love-songs can be interpreted the
winileodi forbidden to the inmates of convents by a capitulary

---

[1] Dyer, 240, from Hertfordshire. There are many other versions ; cf.
Northall, 240.   [2] Kögel, i. 1. 32.

of 789 [1]. The love-interest continues to be prominent in the folk-song, or the minstrel song still in close relation to folk-song, of mediaeval and modern France. The beautiful wooing *chanson* of *Transformations*, which savants have found it difficult to believe not to be a *supercherie*, is sung by harvesters and by lace-makers at the pillow [2]. That of *Marion*, an ironic expression of wifely submission, belongs to Shrove Tuesday [3]. These are modern, but the following, from the *Chansonnier de St. Germain*, may be a genuine mediaeval folk-song of Limousin *provenance*:

> ' A l'entrada dal tems clar, eya,
> Per joja recomençar, eya,
> Et per jelos irritar, eya,
> Vol la regina mostrar
> Qu'el' es si amoroza.
> Alavi', alavia jelos,
> Laissaz nos, laissaz nos
> Ballar entre nos, entre nos [4].'

The 'queen' here is, of course, the festival queen or lady of the May, the *regina avrillosa* of the Latin writers, *la reine, la mariée, l'épousée, la trimousette* of popular custom [5]. The defiance of the *jelos*, and the desire of the queen and her maidens to dance alone, recall the conventional freedom of women from restraint in May, the month of their ancient sex-festival, and the month in which the mediaeval wife-beater still ran notable danger of a *chevauchée*.

---

[1] Pertz, *Leges*, i. 68 ' nullatenus ibi uuinileodos scribere vel mittere praesumat.' Kögel, i. 1. 61 : Goedeke, i. 11, quote other uses of the term from eighth-century glosses, e.g. ' *uuiniliod*, cantilenas saeculares, psalmos vulgares, seculares, plebeios psalmos, cantica rustica et inepta.' *Winiliod* is literally ' love-song,' from root *wini* (conn. with *Venus*). Kögel traces an earlier term O. H. G. *winileih*, A.-S. *winelâc = hîleih*. On the erotic motive in savage dances, cf. Grosse, 165, 172 ; Hirn, 229.

[2] *Romania*, vii. 61 ; *Trad. Pop.* i. 98. Mr. Swinburne has adapted

the idea of this poem in *A Match* (*Poems and Ballads*, 1st Series, 116).

[3] *Romania*, ix. 568.

[4] K. Bartsch, *Chrest. Prov.* 111. A similar *chanson* is in G. Raynaud, *Motets*, i. 151, and another is described in the *roman* of *Flamenca* (ed. P. Meyer), 3244. It ends

> ' E, si parla, qu'il li responda :
> Nom sones mot, faitz vos en lai,
> Qu'entre mos bracs mos amics
>   j'ai.
> Kalenda maia. E vai s' en.'

[5] *Trimousette*, from *tri mâ câ*, an unexplained burden in some of the French *maierolles*.

The amorous note recurs in those types of minstrel song which are most directly founded upon folk models. Such are the *chansons à danser* with their refrains, the *chansons de mal-mariées*, in which the '*jalous*' is often introduced, the *aubes* and the *pastourelles*[1]. Common in all of these is the spring setting proper to the *chansons* of our festivals, and of the 'queen' or 'king' there is from time to time mention. The leading theme of the *pastourelles* is the wooing, successful or the reverse, of a shepherdess by a knight. But the shepherdess has generally also a lover of her own degree, and for this pair the names of Robin and Marion seem to have been conventionally appropriated. Robin was perhaps borrowed by the *pastourelles* from the widely spread refrain

> 'Robins m'aime, Robins m'a :
> Robins m'a demandée : si m'ara[2].'

The borrowing may, of course, have been the other way round, but the close relation of the *chanson à danser* with its refrain to the dance suggests that this was the earliest type of lyric minstrelsy to be evolved, as well as the closest to the folk-song pattern. The *pastourelle* forms a link between folk-song and drama, for towards the end of the thirteenth century Adan de la Hale, known as 'le Bossu,' a minstrel of Arras, wrote a *Jeu de Robin et Marion*, which is practically a *pastourelle par personnages*. The familiar theme is preserved. A knight woos Marion, who is faithful to her Robin. Repulsed, he rides away, but returns and beats Robin. All, however, ends happily with dances and *jeux* amongst the peasants. Adan de la Hale was one of the train of Count Robert of Artois in Italy. The play may originally have been written about 1283 for the delectation of the court of Robert's kinsman, Charles, king of Naples, but the extant version was probably produced about 1290 at Arras, when the poet was already dead. Another hand has prefixed a dramatic prologue, the *Jeu du Pèlerin*, glorifying Adan, and has also made some interpolations in the text designed to localize the action near Arras.

---

[1] Guy, 503.

[2] Tiersot, *Robin et Marion*; Guy, 506. See the refrain in Bartsch, 197, 295 ; Raynaud, *Rec. de Motets*, i. 227.

The performers are not likely to have been villagers : they may have been the members of some *puy* or literary society, which had taken over the celebration of the summer festival. In any case the *Jeu de Robin et Marion* is the earliest and not the least charming of pastoral comedies [1].

It is impossible exactly to parallel from the history of English literature this interaction of folk-song and minstrelsy at the French *fête du mai*. For unfortunately no body of English mediaeval lyric exists. Even ' Sumer is icumen in ' only owes its preservation to the happy accident which led some priest to fit sacred words to the secular tune ; while the few pieces recovered from a Harleian manuscript of the reign of Edward I, beautiful as they are, read like adaptations less of English folk-song, than of French lyric itself [2]. Nevertheless, the village summer festival of England seems to have closely resembled that of France, and to have likewise taken in the long run a dramatic turn. A short sketch of it will not be without interest.

I have quoted at the beginning of this discussion of folk-customs the thirteenth-century condemnations of the *Inductio Maii* by Bishop Grosseteste of Lincoln and of the *ludi de Rege et Regina* by Bishop Chanteloup of Worcester. The *ludus de Rege et Regina* is not indeed necessarily to be identified with the *Inductio Maii*, for the harvest feast or *Inductio Autumni* of Bishop Grosseteste had also its ' king' and ' queen,' and so too had some of the feasts in the winter cycle, notably Twelfth night [3]. It is, however, in the summer feast held usually on

---

[1] Langlois, *Robin et Marion* : *Romania*, xxiv. 437 ; H. Guy, *Adan de la Hale*, 177 ; J. Tiersot, *Sur le Jeu de Robin et Marion* (1897) ; Petit de Julleville, *La Comédie*, 27 ; *Rep. Com.* 21, 324. A *jeu* of *Robin et Marion* is recorded also as played at Angers in 1392, but there is no proof that this was Adan de la Hale's play, or a drama at all. There were folk going ' desguiziez, à un jeu que l'en dit Robin et Marion, ainsi qu'il est accoutumé de fere, chacun an, en les foiries de Penthecouste ' (Guy, 197). The best editions of *Robin et Marion* are those by E. Langlois (1896), and by Bartsch in *La Langue et la Littérature françaises* (1887), col. 523. E. de Coussemaker, *Œuvres de Adam de la Halle* (1872), 347, gives the music, and A. Rambeau, *Die dem Trouvère Adam de la Halle zugeschriebenen Dramen* (1886), facsimiles the text. On Adan de la Hale's earlier *sottie* of *La Feuillée*, see ch. xvi.

[2] Thomas Wright, *Lyrical Poems of the Reign of Edward I* (Percy Soc.).

[3] Cf. ch. xvii.

the first of May or at Whitsuntide [1], that these rustic dignitaries are more particularly prominent. Before the middle of the fifteenth century I have not come across many notices of them. That a summer king was familiar in Scotland is implied by the jest of Robert Bruce's wife after his coronation at Scone in 1306 [2]. In 1412 a 'somerkyng' received a reward from the bursar of Winchester College [3]. But from about 1450 onwards they begin to appear frequently in local records. The whole *ludus* is generally known as a 'May-play' or 'May-game,' or as a 'king-play [4],' 'king's revel [5],' or 'king-game [6].' The leading personages are indifferently the 'king' and 'queen,' or 'lord' and 'lady.' But sometimes the king is more specifically the 'somerkyng' or *rex aestivalis*. At other times he is the 'lord of misrule [7],' or takes a local title, such as that of the 'Abbot of Marham,' 'Mardall,' 'Marrall,' 'Marram,' 'Mayvole' or 'Mayvoll' at Shrewsbury [8], and the 'Abbot of Bon-Accord'

---

[1] The May-game is probably intended by the 'Whitsun pastorals' of *Winter's Tale*, iv. 4. 134, and the 'pageants of delight' at Pentecost, where a boy 'trimmed in Madam Julias gown' played 'the woman's part' (i. e. Maid Marian) of *Two Gentlemen of Verona*, iv. 4. 163. Cf. also W. Warner, *Albion's England*, v. 25 :
'At Paske began our Morrise, and ere Penticost our May.'

[2] *Flores Historiarum* (R. S.), iii. 130 'aestimo quod rex aestivalis sis; forsitan hyemalis non eris.'

[3] Cf. Appendix E.

[4] 'King-play' at Reading (*Reading St. Giles Accounts* in Brand-Hazlitt, i. 157; Kerry, *Hist. of St. Lawrence, Reading*, 226).

[5] 'King's revel' at Croscombe, Somerset (*Churchwardens' Accounts* in Hobhouse, 3).

[6] 'King's game' at Leicester (Kelly, 68) and 'King-game' at Kingston (Lysons, *Environs of London*, i. 225). On the other hand the King-game in church at Hascombe in 1578 (*Representations*, s. v. Hascombe), was probably a miracle-play of the Magi or Three Kings of Cologne. This belongs to Twelfth night (cf.

ch. xix), but curiously the accounts of St. Lawrence, Reading, contain a payment for the 'Kyngs of Colen' on *May day*, 1498 (Kerry, *loc. cit.*).

[7] Cf. ch. xvii. Local 'lords of misrule' in the *summer* occur at Montacute in 1447-8 (Hobhouse, 183 'in expensis Regis de Montagu apud Tyntenhull existentis tempore aestivali'), at Meriden in 1565 (Sharpe, 209), at Melton Mowbray in 1558 (Kelly, 65), at Tombland, near Norwich (*Norfolk Archaeology*, iii. 7; xi. 345), at Broseley, near Much Wenlock, as late as 1652 (Burne-Jackson, 480). See the attack on them in Stubbes, i. 146. The term 'lord of misrule' seems to have been borrowed from Christmas (ch. xvii). It does not appear whether the lords of misrule of Old Romney in 1525 (*Archaeologia Cantiana*, xiii. 216) and Braintree in 1531 (Pearson, ii. 413) were in winter or summer.

[8] Owen and Blakeway, i. 331; Jackson and Burne, 480 (cf. Appendix E). Miss Burne suggests several possible derivations of the name; from *mar* 'make mischief,' from Mardoll or Marwell (St. Mary's Well), streets in Shrewsbury, or

at Aberdeen[1]. The use of an ecclesiastical term will be explained in a later chapter[2]. The queen appears to have been sometimes known as a 'whitepot' queen[3]. And finally the king and queen receive, in many widely separated places, the names of Robin Hood and Maid Marian, and are accompanied in their revels by Little John, Friar Tuck, and the whole joyous fellowship of Sherwood Forest[4]. This affiliation of the *ludus de Rege et Regina* to the Robin Hood legend is so curious as to deserve a moment's examination [5].

The earliest recorded mention of Robin Hood is in Langland's *Piers Plowman*, written about 1377. Here he is coupled with another great popular hero of the north as a subject of current songs:

'But I can rymes of Robyn hood, and Randolf erle of Chestre[6].'

In the following century his fame as a great outlaw spread far and wide, especially in the north and the midlands[7]. The Scottish chronicler Bower tells us in 1447 that whether for comedy or tragedy no other subject of romance and minstrelsy

from Muryvale or Meryvalle, a local hamlet. But the form ' Mayvoll' seems to point to ' Maypole.'

[1] *Representations*, s. v. Aberdeen. Here the lord of the summer feast seems to have acted also as presenter of the Corpus Christi plays.

[2] Cf. ch. xvii.

[3] Batman, *Golden Books of the Leaden Gods* (1577), f. 30. The Pope is said to be carried on the backs of four deacons, ' after the maner of carying whytepot queenes in Western May games.' A ' whitepot' is a kind of custard.

[4] Such phrases occur as ' the May - play called Robyn Hod' (Kerry, *Hist. of St. Lawrence, Reading*, 226, s. a. 1502), ' Robin Hood and May game' and ' Kynggam and Robyn Hode' (*Kingston Accounts*, 1505–36, in Lysons, *Environs of London*, i. 225). The accounts of St. Helen's, Abingdon, in 1566, have an entry ' for setting up Robin Hood's bower' (Brand-Hazlitt, i. 144). It is noticeable

that from 1553 Robin Hood succeeds the Abbot of Mayvole in the May-game at Shrewsbury (Appendix E). Similarly, in an Aberdeen order of 1508 we find 'Robert Huyid and Litile Johne, quhilk was callit, in yers bipast, Abbat and Prior of Bonacord' (*Representations*, s. v. Aberdeen). Robin Hood seems, therefore, to have come rather late into the May-games, but to have enjoyed a widening popularity.

[5] The material for the study of the Robin Hood legend is gathered together by S. Lee in *D. N. B.* s. v. Hood ; Child, *Popular Ballads*, v. 39 ; Ritson, *Robin Hood* (1832); J.M. Gutch, *Robin Hood* (1847). Prof. Child gives a critical edition of all the ballads.

[6] *Piers Plowman*, B-text, passus v. 401.

[7] Fabian, *Chronicle*, 687, records in 1502 the capture of ' a felowe whych hadde renewed many of Robin Hode's pagentes, which named himselfe Greneleef.'

had such a hold upon the common folk[1]. The first of the extant ballads of the cycle, *A Gest of Robyn Hode*, was probably printed before 1500, and in composition may be at least a century earlier. A recent investigator of the legend, and a very able one, denies to Robin Hood any traceable historic origin. He is, says Dr. Child, 'absolutely a creation of the ballad muse.' However this may be, the version of the Elizabethan playwright Anthony Munday, who made him an earl of Huntingdon and the lover of Matilda the daughter of Lord Fitzwater, may be taken as merely a fabrication. And whether he is historical or not, it is difficult to see how he got, as by the sixteenth century he did get, into the May-game. One theory is that he was there from the beginning, and that he is in fact a mythological figure, whose name but faintly disguises either Woden in the aspect of a vegetation deity[2], or a minor wood-spirit Hode, who also survives in the Hodeken of German legend[3]. Against this it may be pointed out, firstly that Hood is not an uncommon English name, probably meaning nothing but 'à-Wood' or 'of the wood[4],' and secondly that we have seen no reason to suppose that the mock king, which is the part assigned to Robin Hood in the May-game, was ever regarded as an incarnation of the fertilization spirit at all. He is the priest of that spirit, slain at its festival, but nothing more. I venture to offer a more plausible explanation. It is noticeable that whereas in the May-game Robin Hood and Maid Marian are inseparable, in the early ballads Maid Marian has no part. She is barely mentioned in one or two of the latest ones[5]. Moreover Marian is not an English but a French name, and we have already seen that Robin and Marion are the typical shepherd and shepherdess of the French *pastourelles* and of Adan de

---

[1] Cf. p. 177.
[2] Kühn, in Haupt's *Zeitschrift*, v. 481.
[3] Ramsay, *F. E.* i. 168.
[4] In the Nottingham *Hall-books* (*Hist. MSS.* i. 105), the same locality seems to be described in 1548 as 'Robyn Wood's Well,' and in 1597 as 'Robyn Hood's Well.' Robin Hood is traditionally clad in green.

If he is mythological at all, may he not be a form of the 'wild-man' or 'wood-woz' of certain spring dramatic ceremonies, and the 'Green Knight' of romance? Cf. ch. ix.
[5] The earliest mention of her is (†1500) in A. Barclay, *Eclogue*, 5, 'some may fit of Maide Marian or else of Robin Hood.'

la Hale's dramatic *jeu* founded upon these. I suggest then, that the names were introduced by the minstrels into English and transferred from the French *fêtes du mai* to the 'lord' and 'lady' of the corresponding English May-game. · Robin Hood grew up independently from heroic *cantilenae*, but owing to the similarity of name he was identified with the other Robin, and brought Little John, Friar Tuck and the rest with him into the May-game. On the other hand Maid Marian, who does not properly belong to the heroic legend, was in turn, naturally enough, adopted into the later ballads. This is an hypothesis, but not, I think, an unlikely hypothesis.

Of what, then, did the May-game, as it took shape in the fifteenth and sixteenth centuries, consist? Primarily, no doubt, of a *quête* or 'gaderyng.' In many places this became a parochial, or even a municipal, affair. In 1498 the corporation of Wells possessed moneys '*provenientes ante hoc tempus de Robynhode*[1].' Elsewhere the churchwardens paid the expenses of the feast and accounted for the receipts in the annual parish budget[2]. There are many entries concerning the May-game in the accounts of Kingston-on-Thames during some half a century. In 1506 it is recorded that 'Wylm. Kempe' was 'kenge' and 'Joan Whytebrede' was 'quen.' In 1513 and again in 1536 the game went to Croydon[3]. Similarly the accounts of New Romney note that in 1422 or thereabouts the men of Lydd 'came with their may and ours[4],' and those of Reading St. Lawrence that in 1505 came 'Robyn Hod of Handley and his company' and in 1507 'Robyn Hod and his company from ffynchamsted[5].' In contemporary Scotland James IV gave a present at mid-

---

[1] *Hist. MSS.* i. 107, from *Convocation Book*, 'pecuniae ecclesiae ac communitatis Welliae ... videlicet, provenientes ante hoc tempus de Robynhode, puellis tripudiantibus, communi cervisia ecclesiae, et huiusmodi.'

[2] The accounts of Croscombe, Somerset, contain yearly entries of receipts from 'Roben Hod's recones' from 1476 to 1510, and again in 1525 (Hobhouse, 1 sqq.). At Melton Mowbray the amount raised by the 'lord' was set aside for mending the highways (Kelly, 65).

[3] Lysons, *Environs*, i. 225. Mention is made of 'Robin Hood,' 'the Lady,' 'Maid Marion,' 'Little John,' 'the Frere,' 'the Fool,' 'the Dysard,' 'the Morris-dance.'

[4] *Archaeologia Cantiana*, xiii. 216.

[5] C. Kerry, *History of St. Lawrence, Reading*, 226. 'Made Maryon,' 'the tree' and 'the morris-dance,' are mentioned.

summer in 1503 'to Robin Hude of Perth[1].' It would hardly have been worth while, however, to carry the May-game from one village or town to another, had it been nothing but a procession with a garland and a 'gaderyng'; and as a matter of fact we find that in England as in France dramatic performances came to be associated with the summer folk-festivals. The London 'Maying' included stage plays[2]. At Shrewsbury *lusores* under the Abbot of Marham acted interludes 'for the glee of the town' at Pentecost[3]. The guild of St. Luke at Norwich performed secular as well as miracle plays, and the guild of Holy Cross at Abingdon held its feast on May 3 with 'pageants, plays and May-games,' as early as 1445[4]. Some of these plays were doubtless miracles, but so far as they were secular, the subjects of them were naturally drawn, in the absence of *pastourelles*, from the ballads of the Robin Hood cycle[5]. Amongst the Paston letters is preserved one written in 1473, in which the writer laments the loss of a servant, whom he has kept 'thys iij yer to pleye Seynt Jorge and Robyn Hod and the Shryff off Nottyngham[6].' Moreover, some specimens of the plays themselves are still extant. One of them, unfortunately only a fragment, must be the very play referred to in the letter just quoted, for its subject is 'Robin Hood and the Sheriff of Nottingham,' and it is found on a scrap of paper formerly in the possession of Sir John Fenn, the first editor of the *Paston Letters*[7]. A second

---

[1] *L. H. T. Accounts*, ii. 377.

[2] Stowe, *Survey* (1598), 38. He is speaking mainly of the period before 1517, when there was a riot on 'Black' May-day, and afterwards the May-games were not 'so freely used as before.'

[3] Appendix E (vi).

[4] Cf. *Representations*.

[5] Bower († 1437), *Scotichronicon* (ed. Hearne), iii. 774 'ille famosissimus sicarius Robertus Hode et Litill-Iohanne cum eorum complicibus, de quibus stolidum vulgus hianter in comoediis et tragoediis prurienter festum faciunt, et, prae ceteris romanciis, mimos et bardanos cantitare delectantur.' On the ambiguity of 'comoediae' and 'tragoediae' in the fifteenth century, cf. ch. xxv.

[6] Gairdner, *Paston Letters*, iii. 89; Child, v. 90; 'W. Woode, whyche promysed . . . he wold never goo ffro me, and ther uppon I have kepyd hym thys iij yer to pleye Seynt Jorge and Robyn Hod and the Shryff off Nottyngham, and now, when I wolde have good horse, he is goon into Bernysdale, and I withowt a keeper.' The *Northumberland Household Book*, 60, makes provision for 'liveries for Robin Hood' in the Earl's household.

[7] Printed by Child, v. 90; Manly, i. 279. The MS. of the fragment probably dates before 1475.

play on 'Robin Hood and the Friar' and a fragment of a third on 'Robin Hood and the Potter' were printed by Copland in the edition of the *Gest of Robyn Hode* published by him about 1550 [1]. The Robin Hood plays are, of course, subsequent to the development of religious drama which will be discussed in the next volume. They are of the nature of interludes, and were doubtless written, like the plays of Adan de la Hale, by some clerk or minstrel for the delectation of the villagers. They are, therefore, in a less degree folk-drama, than the examples which we shall have to consider in the next chapter. But it is worthy of notice, that even in the heyday of the stage under Elizabeth and James I, the summer festival continued to supply motives to the dramatists. Anthony Munday's *Downfall and Death of Robert Earl of Huntingdon* [2], Chapman's *May-Day*, and Jonson's delightful fragment *The Sad Shepherd* form an interesting group of pastoral comedies, affinities to which may be traced in the *As You Like It* and *Winter's Tale* of Shakespeare himself.

As has been said, it is impossible to establish any direct affiliation between the Robin Hood plays and earlier *caroles* on the same theme, in the way in which this can be done for the *jeu* of Adan de la Hale, and the Robin and Marion of the *pastourelles*. The extant Robin Hood ballads are certainly not *caroles*; they are probably not folk-song at all, but minstrelsy of a somewhat debased type. The only actual trace of such *caroles* that has been come across is the mention of 'Robene hude' as the name of a dance in the *Complaynt of Scotland*

---

[1] Printed by Child, v. 114, 127; Manly, i. 281, 285. They were originally printed as one play by Copland (†1550).

[2] Printed in Dodsley-Hazlitt, vol. viii. These plays were written for Henslowe about February 1598. In November Chettle 'mended Roben hood for the corte' (*Henslowe's Diary*, 118–20, 139). At Christmas 1600, Henslowe had another play of 'Roben hoodes penerths' by William Haughton (*Diary*, 174–5). An earlier 'pastorall pleasant comedie of Robin Hood and Little John' was entered on the Stationers' Register on May 18, 1594. These

two are lost, as is *The May Lord* which Jonson wrote (*Conversations with Drummond*, 27). Robin Hood also appears in Peele's *Edward I* (†1590), and the anonymous *Look About You* (1600), and is the hero of Greene's *George a Greene the Pinner of Wakefield* (†1593). Anthony Munday introduced him again into his pageant of *Metropolis Coronata* (1615), and a comedy of *Robin Hood and his Crew of Soldiers*, acted at Nottingham on the day of the coronation of Charles II, was published in 1661. On all these plays, cf. F. E. Schelling, *The English Chronicle Play*, 156.

about 1548[1]. Dances, however, of one kind or another, there undoubtedly were at the May-games. The Wells corporation accounts mention *puellae tripudiantes* in close relation with *Robynhode*[2]. And particularly there was the morris-dance, which was so universally in use on May-day, that it borrowed, almost in permanence, for its leading character the name of Maid Marian. The morris-dance, however, is common to nearly all the village feasts, and its origin and nature will be matter for discussion in the next chapter.

In many places, even during the Middle Ages, and still more afterwards, the summer feast dropped out or degenerated. It became a mere beer-swilling, an 'ale[3].' And so we find in the sixteenth century a 'king-ale[4]' or a 'Robin Hood's ale[5],' and in modern times a 'Whitsun-ale[6],' a 'lamb-ale[7]' or a 'gyst-ale[8]' beside the 'church-ales' and 'scot-ales' which the thirteenth-century bishops had already condemned[9]. On the other hand, the village festival found its way to court, and became a sumptuous pageant under the splendour-loving Tudors. For this, indeed, there was Arthurian precedent in the romance of Malory, who records how Guenever was taken

[1] Furnivall, *Robert Laneham's Letter*, clxiii. Chaucer, *Rom. of Rose*, 7455, has 'the daunce Joly Robin,' but this is from his French original 'li biaus Robins.'

[2] Cf. p. 176.

[3] Dyer, 278; Drake, 86; Brand-Ellis, i. 157; Cutts, *Parish Priests*, 317; *Archaeologia*, xii. 11; Stubbes, i. 150; *F. L.* x. 350. At an 'ale' a cask of home-brewed was broached for sale in the church or church-house, and the profits went to some public object; at a church-ale to the parish, at a clerk-ale to the clerk, at a bride-ale or bridal to the bride, at a bid-ale to some poor man in trouble. A love-ale was probably merely social.

[4] At Reading in 1557 (C. Kerry, *Hist. of St.Lawrence, Reading*, 226).

[5] At Tintinhull in 1513 (Hob-house, 200, 'Robine Hood's All').

[6] Brand-Ellis, i. 157; Dyer, 278. A carving on the church of St. John's, Chichester, represents a Whitsun-ale, with a 'lord' and 'lady.'

[7] Cf. p. 141.

[8] At Ashton-under-Lyne, from 1422 to a recent date (Dyer, 181). 'Gyst' appears to be either 'gist' (*gîte*) 'right of pasturage' or a corruption of 'guising'; cf. ch. xvii.

[9] Cf. p. 91. On *Scot-ale*, cf. Ducange, s. v. Scotallum; *Archaeologia*, xii. 11; H. T. Riley, *Munimenta Gildhallae Londin.* (R. S.), ii. 760. The term first appears as the name of a tax, as in a Northampton charter of 1189 (Markham-Cox, *Northampton Borough Records*, i. 26) 'concessimus quod sint quieti de . . . Brudtol et de Childwite et de hieresgiue et de Scottale. ita quod Prepositus Northamptonie ut aliquis alius Ballivus scottale non faciat'; cf. the thirteenth-century examples quoted by Ducange. The *Council of Lambeth* (1206), c. 2, clearly defines the term as 'communes potationes,' and the primary sense is therefore probably that of an *ale* at which a *scot* or tax is raised.

by Sir Meliagraunce, when 'as the queen had mayed and all
her knights, all were bedashed with herbs, mosses, and flowers,
in the best manner and freshest [1].' The chronicler Hall tells
of the Mayings of Henry VIII in 1510, 1511, and 1515. In
the last of these some hundred and thirty persons took part.
Henry was entertained by Robin Hood and the rest with
shooting-matches and a collation of venison in a bower; and
returning was met by a chariot in which rode the Lady May
and the Lady Flora, while on the five horses sat the Ladies
Humidity, Vert, Vegetave, Pleasaunce and Sweet Odour [2].
Obviously the pastime has here degenerated in another
direction. It has become learned, allegorical, and pseudo-
classic. At the Reformation the May-game and the May-
pole were marks for Puritan onslaught. Latimer, in one of
his sermons before Edward VI, complains how, when he had
intended to preach in a certain country town on his way to
London, he was told that he could not be heard, for 'it is
Robyn hoodes daye. The parishe are gone a brode to gather
for Robyn hoode [3].' Machyn's *Diary* mentions the breaking
of a May-pole in Fenchurch by the lord mayor of 1552 [4], and
the revival of elaborate and heterogeneous May-games throughout London during the brief span of Queen Mary [5]. The
Elizabethan Puritans renewed the attack, but though something may have been done by reforming municipalities here
and there to put down the festivals [6], the ecclesiastical authori-

---

[1] Malory, *Morte d'Arthur*, xix.1.2.

[2] Hall, 515, 520, 582; Brewer,
Letters and Papers of Henry VIII,
ii. 1504. In 1510, Henry and his
courtiers visited the queen's chamber in the guise of Robin Hood and
his men on the inappropriate date
of January 18. In Scotland, about
the same time, Dunbar wrote a
'cry' for a maying with Robin
Hood; cf. *Texts*, s.v. Dunbar.

[3] Latimer, *Sermon vi before
Edw. VI* (1549, ed. Arber, 173).
Perhaps the town was Melton Mowbray, where Robin Hood was very
popular, and where Latimer is shown
by the churchwardens' accounts to
have preached several years later in
1553 (Kelly, 67).

[4] Machyn, 20.

[5] Ibid. 89, 137, 196, 201, 283,
373. In 1559, e.g. 'the xxiiij of
June ther was a May-game . . .
and Sant John Sacerys, with a
gyant, and drumes and gunes [and
the] ix wordes (worthies), with
spechys, and a goodly pagant with
a quen . . . and dyvers odur, with
spechys; and then Sant Gorge and
the dragon, the mores dansse, and
after Robyn Hode and lytyll John,
and M[aid Marian] and frere Tuke,
and they had spechys round a-bout
London.'

[6] 'Mr. Tomkys publicke prechar'
in Shrewsbury induced the bailiffs
to 'reform' May-poles in 1588, and
in 1591 some apprentices were com-

ties could not be induced to go much beyond forbidding them to take place in churchyards [1]. William Stafford, indeed, declared in 1581 that 'May-games, wakes, and revels' were 'now laid down [2],' but the violent abuse directed against them only two years later by Philip Stubbes, which may be taken as a fair sample of the Puritan polemic as a whole, shows that this was far from being really the, case [3]. In Scotland the Parliament ordered, as early as 1555, that no one 'be chosen Robert Hude, nor Lytill Johne, Abbot of vnressoun, Quenis of Maij, nor vtherwyse, nouther in Burgh nor to landwart in ony tyme to cum [4].' But the prohibition was not very effective, for in 1577 and 1578 the General Assembly is found petitioning for its renewal [5]. And in England no similar action was taken until 1644 when the Long Parliament decreed the destruction of such May-poles as the municipalities had spared. Naturally this policy was reversed at the Restoration, and a new London pole was erected in the Strand, hard by Somerset House, which endured until 1717 [6].

mitted for disobeying the order. A judicial decision was, however, given in favour of the 'tree' (Burne-Jackson, 358; Hibbert, *English Craft-Gilds*, 121). In London the Cornhill Maypole, which gave its name to St. Andrew Undershaft, was destroyed by persuasion of a preacher as early as 1549 (Dyer, 248); cf. also Stubbes, i. 306, and Morrison's advice to Henry VIII quoted in ch. xxv.

[1] Archbishop Grindal's *Visitation Articles* of 1576 (*Remains*, Parker Soc. 175), 'whether the minister and churchwardens have suffered any lords of misrule or summer lords or ladies, or any disguised persons, or others, in Christmas or at May-games, or any morris-dancers, or at any other times, to come unreverently into the church or churchyard, and there to dance, or play any unseemly parts, with scoffs, jests, wanton gestures, or ribald talk, namely in the time of Common Prayer.' Similarly worded *Injunctions* for Norwich (1569), York (1571), Lichfield (1584), London (1601) and Oxford

(1619) are quoted in the *Second Report* of the Ritual Commission; cf. the eighty-eighth *Canon* of 1604. It is true that the *Visitation Articles* for St. Mary's, Shrewsbury, in 1584 inquire more generally 'whether there have been any lords of mysrule, or somer lords or ladies, or any disguised persons, as morice dancers, maskers, or mum'ers, or such lyke, within the parishe, ether in the nativititide or in som'er, or at any other tyme, and what be their names'; but this church was a 'peculiar' and its 'official' the Puritan Tomkys mentioned in the last note (Owen and Blakeway, i. 333; Burne-Jackson, 481).

[2] Stafford, 16.

[3] Stubbes, i. 146; cf. the further quotations and references there given in the notes.

[4] 6 *Mary*, cap. 61.

[5] Child, v. 45; cf. *Representations*, s.v. Aberdeen, on the breaches of the statute there in 1562 and 1565.

[6] Dyer, 228; Drake, 85. At Cerne Abbas, Dorset, the May-pole was cut down in 1635 and made into a town ladder (*F. L.* x. 481).

CHAPTER IX

THE SWORD-DANCE

[*Bibliographical Note.*—The books mentioned in the bibliographical note to the last chapter should be consulted on the general tendency to μίμησις in festival dance and song. The symbolical dramatic ceremonies of the *renouveau* are collected by Dr. J. G. Frazer in *The Golden Bough*. The sword-dance has been the subject of two elaborate studies: K. Müllenhoff, *Ueber den Schwerttanz*, in *Festgaben für Gustav Homeyer* (1871), iii, with additions in *Zeitschrift für deutsches Alterthum*, xviii. 9, xx. 10; and F. A. Mayer, *Ein deutsches Schwerttanzspiel aus Ungarn* (with full bibliography), in *Zeitschrift für Völkerpsychologie* (1889), 204, 416. The best accounts of the morris-dance are in F. Douce, *Illustrations of Shakespeare* (1807, new ed. 1839), and A. Burton, *Rushbearing* (1891), 95.]

THE last two chapters have afforded more than one example of village festival customs ultimately taking shape as drama. But neither the English Robin Hood plays, nor the French *Jeu de Robin et Marion*, can be regarded as folk-drama in the proper sense of the word. They were written not by the folk themselves, but by *trouvères* or minstrels *for* the folk; and at a period when the independent evolution of the religious play had already set a model of dramatic composition. Probably the same is true of the Hox Tuesday play in the form in which we may conjecture it to have been presented before Elizabeth late in the sixteenth century. Nevertheless it is possible to trace, apart from minstrel intervention and apart from imitation of miracles, the existence of certain embryonic dramatic tendencies in the village ceremonies themselves. Too much must not be made of these. Jacob Grimm was inclined to find in them the first vague beginnings of the whole of modern drama[1]. This is demonstrably wrong. Modern drama arose, by a fairly well defined line of evolution, from a threefold source, the ecclesiastical liturgy, the farce of the mimes, the classical revivals of humanism. Folk-drama contributed but the tiniest rill to the mighty stream. Such as

[1] Grimm, ii. 784; *Kleinere Schriften*, v. 281; Pearson, ii. 281.

it was, however, a couple of further chapters may be not unprofitably spent in its analysis.

The festival customs include a number of dramatic rites which appear to have been originally symbolical expressions of the facts of seasonal recurrence lying at the root of the festivals themselves. The antithesis of winter and summer, the *renouveau* of spring, are mimed in three or four distinct fashions. The first and the most important, as well as the most widespread of these, is the mock representation of a death or burial. Dr. Frazer has collected many instances of the ceremony known as the 'expulsion of Death[1].' This takes place at various dates in spring and early summer, but most often on the fourth Sunday in Lent, one of the many names of which is consequently *Todten-Sonntag*. An effigy is made, generally of straw, but in some cases of birch twigs, a beechen bough, or other such material. This is called Death, is treated with marks of fear, hatred or contempt, and is finally carried in procession, and thrust over the boundary of the village. Or it is torn in pieces, buried, burnt, or thrown into a river or pool. Sometimes the health or other welfare of the folk during the year is held to depend on the rite being duly performed. The fragments of Death have fertilizing efficacy for women and cattle ; they are put in the fields, the mangers, the hens' nests. Here and there women alone take part in the ceremony, but more often it is common to the whole village. The expulsion of Death is found in various parts of Teutonic Germany, but especially in districts such as Thuringia, Bohemia, Silesia, where the population is wholly or mainly Slavonic. A similar custom, known both in Slavonic districts and in Italy, France, and Spain, had the name of ' sawing the old woman.' At Florence, for instance, the effigy of an old woman was placed on a ladder. At Mid Lent it was sawn through, and the nuts and dried fruits with which it was stuffed scrambled for by the crowd. At Palermo there was a still more realistic representation with a real old woman, to whose neck a bladder of blood was fitted [2].

---

[1] Frazer, ii. 82 ; Grant Allen, 293, 315 ; Grimm, ii. 764 ; Pearson, ii. 283.

[2] Frazer, ii. 86 ; Martinengo-Cesaresco, 267. Cf. the use of the bladder of blood in the St. Thomas

The 'Death' of the German and Slavonic form of the custom
has clearly come to be regarded as the personification of the
forces of evil within the village ; and the ceremony of expulsion may be compared with other periodical rites, European
and non-European, in which evil spirits are similarly expelled[1].
The effigy may even be regarded in the light of a scapegoat,
bearing away the sins of the community[2]. But it is doubtful
how far the notion of evil spirits warring against the good
spirits which protect man and his crops is a European, or at
any rate a primitive European one[3] ; and it may perhaps be
taken for granted that what was originally thought to be
expelled in the rite was not so much either 'Death' or 'Sin'
as winter. This view is confirmed by the evidence of an
eighth-century homily, which speaks of the expulsion of
winter in February as a relic of pagan belief[4]. Moreover, the
expulsion of Death is often found in the closest relation to
the more widespread custom of bringing summer, in the shape
of green tree or bough, into the village. The procession
which carries away the dead effigy brings back the summer
tree ; and the rhymes used treat the two events as connected[5].

The homily just quoted suggests that the mock funeral or
expulsion of winter was no new thing in the eighth century.
On the other hand, it can hardly be supposed that customs
which imply such abstract ideas as death, or even as summer
and winter, belong to the earliest stages of the village festival.
What has happened is what happens in other forms of festival
play. The instinct of play, in this case finding vent in
a dramatic representation of the succession of summer to

procession at Canterbury (*Representations*, s. v.).

[1] Frazer, iii. 70. Amongst such
customs are the expulsion of Satan
on New Year's day by the Finns,
the expulsion of Kore at Easter in
Albania, the expulsion of witches
on March 1 in Calabria, and on
May 1 in the Tyrol, the frightening
of the wood-sprites Strudeli and
Strätteli on Twelfth night at Brun-
nen in Switzerland. Such ceremonies are often accompanied with
a horrible noise of horns, cleavers
and the like. Horns are also used

at Oxford (Dyer, 261) and elsewhere
on May 1, and I have heard it said
that the object of the Oxford custom is to drive away evil spirits.
Similar discords are *de rigueur* at
Skimmington Ridings. I very much
doubt whether they are anything
but a degenerate survival of a barbaric type of music.

[2] Frazer, iii. 121.

[3] Tylor, *Anthropology*, 382.

[4] Caspari, 10 'qui in mense februario hibernum credit expellere...
non christianus, sed gentilis est.'

[5] Frazer, ii. 91.

winter, has taken hold of and adapted to its own purposes elements in the celebrations which, once significant, have gradually come to be mere traditional survivals. Such are the ceremonial burial in the ground, the ceremonial burning, the ceremonial plunging into water, of the representative of the fertilization spirit. In particular, the southern term ' the old woman ' suggests that the effigy expelled or destroyed is none other than the 'corn mother' or 'harvest-May,' fashioned to represent the fertilization spirit out of the last sheaf at harvest, and preserved until its place is taken by a new and green representative in the spring.

There are, however, other versions of the mock death in which the central figure of the little drama is not the representative of the fertilization spirit itself, but one of the worshippers. In Bavaria the Whitsuntide *Pfingstl* is dressed in leaves and water-plants with a cap of peonies. He is soused with water, and then, in mimicry, has his head cut off. Similar customs prevail in the Erzgebirge and elsewhere [1]. We have seen this *Pfingstl* before. He is the Jack in the green, the worshipper clad in the god under whose protection he desires to put himself [2]. But how can the killing of him symbolize the spring, for obviously it is the coming summer, not the dying winter, that the leaf-clad figure must represent? The fact is that the Bavarian drama is not complete. The full ceremony is found in other parts of Germany. Thus in Saxony and Thuringia a 'wild man' covered with leaves and moss is hunted in a wood, caught, and executed. Then comes forward a lad dressed as a doctor, who brings the victim to life again by bleeding [3]. Even so annually the summer dies and has its resurrection. In Swabia, again, on Shrove Tuesday, 'Dr. Eisenbart' bleeds a man to death, and afterwards revives him. This same Dr. Eisenbart appears also in the Swabian Whitsuntide execution, although here too the actual resurrection seems to have dropped out of the ceremony [4]. It is

[1] Frazer, ii. 60.

[2] Sometimes the *Pfingstl* is called a ' wild man.' Two ' myghty woordwossys [cf. p. 392] or wyld men' appeared in a revel at the court of Henry VIII in 1513 (*Revels Account* in Brewer, ii. 1499), and similar figures are not uncommon in the sixteenth-century masques and entertainments.

[3] Frazer, ii. 62.

[4] Ibid. ii. 61, 82 ; E. Meier, *Deutsche Sagen, Sitten und Gebräuche aus Schwaben*, 374, 409.

interesting to note that the green man of the peasantry, who dies and lives again, reappears as the Green Knight in one of the most famous divisions of Arthurian romance [1].

The mock death or burial type of folk-drama resolves itself, then, into two varieties. In one, it is winter whose passing is represented, and for this the discarded harvest-May serves as a nucleus. In the other, which is not really complete without a resurrection, it is summer, whose death is mimed merely as a preliminary to its joyful renewal; and this too is built up around a fragment of ancient cult in the person of the leaf-clad worshipper, who is, indeed, none other than the priest-king, once actually, and still in some sort and show, slain at the festival [2]. In the instances so far dealt with, the original significance of the rite is still fairly traceable. But there are others into which new meanings, due to the influence of Christian custom, have been read. In many parts of Germany customs closely analogous to those of the expulsion of winter or Death take place on Shrove Tuesday, and have suffered metamorphosis into 'burial of the Carnival [3].' England affords the 'Jack o' Lent' effigy which is taken to represent Judas Iscariot [4], the Lincoln 'funeral of Alleluia [5],' the Tenby

---

[1] *Syr Gawayne and the Grene Knyghte* (ed. Madden, Bannatyne Club, 1839); cf. J. L. Weston, *The Legend of Sir Gawain,* 85. Arthur was keeping New Year's Day, when a knight dressed in green, with a green beard, riding a green horse, and bearing a holly bough, and an axe of green steel, entered the hall. He challenged any man of the Round Table to deal him a buffet with the axe on condition of receiving one in return after the lapse of a year. Sir Gawain accepts. The stranger's head is cut off, but he picks it up and rides away with it. This is a close parallel to the resurrection of the slain 'wild man.'

[2] Frazer, ii. 105, 115, 163, 219; *Pausanias,* iii. 53; v. 259; Gardner, *New Chapters in Greek History,* 395, give Russian, Greek, and Asiatic parallels.

[3] Frazer, ii. 71; Pfannenschmidt, 302. The victim is sometimes known as the Carnival or Shrovetide 'Fool' or 'Bear.'

[4] Dyer, 93. The Jack o' Lent apparently stood as a cock-shy from Ash Wednesday to Good Friday, and was then burnt. Portuguese sailors in English docks thrash and duck an effigy of Judas Iscariot on Good Friday (Dyer, 155).

[5] Alleluia was not sung during Lent. Fosbrooke, *British Monachism,* 56, describes the Funeral of Alleluia by the choristers of an English cathedral on the Saturday before Septuagesima. A turf was carried in procession with howling to the cloisters. Probably this cathedral was Lincoln, whence Wordsworth, 105, quotes payments 'pro excludend' Alleluya' from 1452 to 1617. Leber, ix. 338; Barthélemy, iii. 481, give French examples of the custom; cf. the Alleluia top, p. 128.

'making Christ's bed[1],' the Monkton 'risin' and buryin' Peter[2].' The truth that the vitality of a folk custom is far greater than that of any single interpretation of it is admirably illustrated.

Two other symbolical representations of the phenomena of the *renouveau* must be very briefly treated. At Briançon in Dauphiné, instead of a death and resurrection, is used a pretty little May-day drama, in which the leaf-clad man falls into sleep upon the ground and is awakened by the kiss of a maiden[3]. Russia has a similar custom; and such a magic kiss, bringing summer with it, lies at the heart of the story of the Sleeping Beauty. Indeed, the marriage of heaven and earth seems to have been a myth very early invented by the Aryan mind to explain the fertility of crops beneath the rain, and it probably received dramatic form in religious ceremonies both in Greece and Italy[4]. Finally, there is a fairly widespread spring custom of holding a dramatic fight between two parties, one clad in green to represent summer, the other in straw or fur to represent winter. Waldron describes this in the Isle of Man[5]; Olaus Magnus in Sweden[6]. Grimm says that it is found in various districts on both sides of the middle Rhine[7]. Perhaps both this dramatic battle and that of the Coventry Hox Tuesday owe their origin to the struggle for the fertilizing head of a sacrificial animal, which also issued in football and similar games. Dr. Frazer quotes several instances from all parts of the world in which a mock fight, or an interchange of abuse and raillery taking the place of an actual fight, serves as a crop-charm[8]. The summer and winter battle gave to literature a famous type of neo-Latin and Romance *débat*[9]. In one of the most interesting forms of

[1] Dyer, 158. Reeds were woven on Good Friday into the shape of a crucifix and left in some hidden part of a field or garden.

[2] Dyer, 333. The village feast was on St. Peter's day, June 29. On the Saturday before an effigy was dug up from under a sycamore on Maypole hill; a week later it was buried again. In this case the order of events seems to have been inverted.

[3] Frazer, i. 221. The French May-queen is often called *la mariée* or *l'épouse*.

[4] Frazer, i. 225; Jevons, *Plutarch R. Q.* lxxxiii. 56.

[5] Waldron, *Hist. of Isle of Man*, 95; Dyer, 246.

[6] Olaus Magnus, *History of Swedes and Goths*, xv. 4, 8, 9; Grimm, ii. 774.

[7] Grimm, ii. 765; Paul, *Grundriss* (ed. 1), i. 836.

[8] Frazer, *Pausanias*, iii. 267.

[9] Cf. ch. iv.

this, the eighth- or ninth-century *Conflictus Veris et Hiemis*, the subject of dispute is the cuckoo, which spring praises and winter chides, while the shepherds declare that he must be drowned or stolen away, because summer cometh not. The cuckoo is everywhere a characteristic bird of spring, and his coming was probably a primitive signal for the high summer festival [1].

The symbolical dramas of the seasons stand alone and independent, but it may safely be asserted that drama first arose at the village feasts in close relation to the dance. That dancing, like all the arts, tends to be mimetic is a fact which did not escape the attention of Aristotle [2]. The pantomimes of the decadent Roman stage are a case in point. Greek tragedy itself had grown out of the Dionysiac dithyramb, and travellers describe how readily the dances of the modern savage take shape as primitive dramas of war, hunting, love, religion, labour, or domestic life [3]. Doubtless this was the case also with the *caroles* of the European festivals. The types of *chanson* most immediately derived from these are full of dialogue, and already on the point of bursting into drama. That they did do this, with the aid of the minstrels, in the *Jeu de Robin et de Marion* we have seen [4]. A curious passage in the *Itinerarium Cambriae* of Giraldus Cambrensis († 1188) describes a dance of peasants in and

[1] Grimm, ii. 675, 763 ; Swainson, *Folk-lore of British Birds* (F.L.S.), 109; Hardy, *Popular History of the Cuckoo*, in *F. L. Record*, ii ; Mannhardt, in *Zeitschrift für deutsche Mythologie*, iii. 209. Cf. ch. v.

[2] Aristotle, *Poetics*, i. 5 αὐτῷ δὲ τῷ ῥυθμῷ [ποιεῖται τὴν μίμησιν] χωρὶς ἁρμονίας ἢ [τέχνη] τῶν ὀρχηστῶν, καὶ γὰρ οὗτοι διὰ τῶν σχηματιζομένων ῥυθμῶν μιμοῦνται καὶ ἤθη καὶ πάθη καὶ πράξεις. Cf. Lucian, *de Saltatione*, xv. 277. Du Méril, 65, puts the thing well : ' La danse n'a été l'invention de personne : elle s'est produite d'elle-même le jour que le corps a subi et dû refléter un état de l'âme . . . On ne tarda pas cependant à la séparer de sa cause première et à la reproduire pour elle-même . . . en simulant la gaieté on parvenait réellement à la sentir.'

[3] Wallaschek, 216 ; Grosse, 165, 201 ; Hirn, 157, 182, 229, 259, 261 ; Du Méril, *Com.* 72 ; Haddon, 346 ; Grove, 52, 81 ; Mrs. Gomme, ii. 518 ; G. Catlin, *On Manners . . . of N. Amer. Indians* (1841), i. 128, 244. Lang, *M. R. R.* i. 272, dwells on the representation of myths in savage mystery-dances, and points out that Lucian (*loc. cit.*) says that the Greeks used to 'dance out' (ἐξορχεῖσθαι) their mysteries.

[4] The *chanson* of *Transformations* (cf. p. 170) is sung by peasant-girls as a semi-dramatic duet (*Romania*, vii. 62) ; and that of *Marion* was performed 'à deux personnages' on Shrove Tuesday in Lorraine (*Romania*, ix. 568).

about the church of St. Elined, near Brecknock on the Gwyl
Awst, in which the ordinary operations of the village life, such
as ploughing, sewing, spinning were mimetically represented [1].
Such dances seem to survive in some of the *rondes* or 'singing-
games,' so frequently dramatic, of children [2]. On the whole,
perhaps, these connect themselves rather with the domestic
than with the strictly agricultural element in village cult.
A large proportion of them are concerned with marriage.
But the domestic and the agricultural cannot be altogether
dissociated. The game of 'Nuts in May,' for instance, seems
to have as its kernel a reminiscence of marriage by capture ;
but the 'nuts' or rather 'knots' or 'posies' 'in May' certainly
suggest a setting at a seasonal festival. So too, with 'Round
the Mulberry Bush.' The mimicry here is of domestic operations, but the 'bush' recalls the sacred tree, the natural centre
of the seasonal dances. The closest parallels to the dance
described by Giraldus Cambrensis are to be found in the
rondes of 'Oats and Beans and Barley' and 'Would you know
how doth the Peasant?', in which the chief, though not always
the only, subjects of mimicry are ploughing, sowing and the
like, and which frequently contain a prayer or aspiration for
the welfare of the crops [3].

---

[1] Giraldus Cambrensis, *Itinerarium Cambriae*, i. 2 (*Opera*, R.S. vi.
32) 'Videas enim hic homines seu
puellas, nunc in ecclesia, nunc in
coemiterio, nunc in chorea, quae
circa coemiterium cum cantilena
circumfertur, subito in terram cor-
ruere, et primo tanquam in extasim
ductos et quietos ; deinde statim
tanquam in phrenesim raptos exsi-
lientes, opera quaecunque festis
diebus illicite perpetrare consueverant, tam manibus quam pedibus,
coram populo repraesentantes. videas hunc aratro manus aptare,
illum quasi stimulo boves excitare ;
et utrumque quasi laborem miti-
gando solitas barbarae modulatio-
nis voces efferre. videas hunc artem
sutoriam, illum pellipariam imitari.
item videas hanc quasi colum ba-
iulando, nunc filum manibus et
brachiis in longum extrahere, nunc

extractum occandum tanquam in
fusum revocare : istam deambu-
lando productis filis quasi telam
ordiri : illam sedendo quasi iam
orditam oppositis lanceolae iactibus
et alternis calamistrae cominus icti-
bus texere mireris. Demum vero
intra ecclesiam cum oblationibus ad
altare perductos tanquam experrec-
tos et ad se redeuntes obstupescas.'
[2] Cf. p. 151 with Mrs. Gomme's
Memoir (ii. 458) *passim*, and
Haddon, 328. Parallel savage
examples are in Wallaschek, 216;
Hirn, 157, 259.
[3] Mrs. Gomme, ii. 399, 494 and
s. vv. ; Haddon, 340. Similar
games are widespread on the continent ; cf. the Rabelais quotation on
p. 167. Haddon quotes a French
formula, ending
  'Aveine, aveine, aveine,
  Que le Bon Dieu t'amène.'

I have treated the mimetic element of budding drama in the agricultural festivals as being primarily a manifestation of the activities of play determined in its direction by the dominant interests of the occasion, and finding its material in the débris of ritual custom left over from forgotten stages of religious thought. It is possible also to hold that the *mimesis* is more closely interwoven with the religious and practical side of the festivals, and is in fact yet another example of that primitive magical notion of causation by the production of the similar, which is at the root of the rain- and sun-charms. Certainly the village dramas, like the other ceremonies which they accompany, are often regarded as influencing the luck of the farmer's year ; just as the hunting- and war-dances of savages are often regarded not merely as amusement or as practice for actual war and hunting, but as charms to secure success in these pursuits[1]. But it does not seem clear to me that in this case the magical efficacy belongs to the drama from the beginning, and I incline to look upon it as merely part of the sanctity of the feast as a whole, which has attached itself in the course of time even to that side of it which began as play.

The evolution of folk-drama out of folk-dance may be most completely studied through a comparison of the various types of European sword-dance with the so-called 'mummers',' 'guisers',' or 'Pace-eggers'' play of Saint George. The history of the sword-dance has received a good deal of attention from German archaeologists, who, however, perhaps from imperfect acquaintance with the English data, have stopped short of the affiliation to it of the play[2]. The dance itself can boast a hoar antiquity. Tacitus describes it as the one form of *spectaculum* to be seen at the gatherings of the Germans with whom he was conversant. The dancers were young men who leapt with much agility amongst menacing

---

[1] Wallaschek, 273 ; Hirn, 285.

[2] The German data here used are chiefly collected by Müllenhoff and F. A. Mayer ; cf. also Creizenach, i. 408 ; Michels, 84 ; J. J. Ammann, *Nachträge zum Schwerttanz*, in *Z. f. d. Alterthum* xxxiv (1890), 178; A. Hartmann, *Volksschauspiele* (1880), 130 ; F. M. Böhme, *Ge-* *schichte des Tanzes in Deutschland* (1886); Sepp, *Die Religion der alten Deutschen, und ihr Fortbestand in Volkssagen, Aufzügen und Festbräuchen bis zur Gegenwart* (1890), 91 ; O. Wittstock, *Ueber den Schwerttanz der Siebenbürger Sachsen*, in *Philologische Studien : Festgabe für Eduard Sievers* (1896), 349.

spear-points and sword-blades[1]. Some centuries later the use of *sweorda-gelac* as a metaphor for battle in *Beowulf* shows that the term was known to the continental ancestors of the Anglo-Saxons[2]. Then follows a long gap in the record, bridged only by a doubtful reference in an eighth-century Frankish homily[3], and a possible representation in a ninth-century Latin and Anglo-Saxon manuscript[4]. The minstrels seem to have adopted the sword-dance into their repertory[5], but the earliest mediaeval notice of it as a popular *ludus* is at Nuremberg in 1350. From that date onwards until quite recent years it crops up frequently, alike at Shrovetide, Christmas and other folk festivals, and as an element in the revels at weddings, royal entries, and the like[6]. It is fairly widespread throughout Germany. It is found in Italy, where it is called the *mattaccino*[7], and in Spain (*matachin*), and under this name or that of the *danse des bouffons* it was known both in France and England at the Renaissance[8]. It is given by Paradin in his *Le Blason des Danses* and, with the music and cuts of the performers, by Tabourot in his *Orchésographie* (1588)[9]. These are the sophisticated versions of courtly halls. But about the same date Olaus Magnus describes it as a folk-dance, to the accompaniment of pipes or *cantilenae*, in Sweden[10]. In England, the main area of the

---

[1] Tacitus, *Germania*, 24 'genus spectaculorum unum atque in omni coetu idem. nudi iuvenes, quibus id ludicrum est, inter gladios se atque infestas frameas saltu iaciunt. exercitatio artem paravit, ars decorem, non in quaestum tamen aut mercedem ; quamvis audacis lasciviae pretium est voluptas spectantium.'

[2] *Beowulf*, 1042. It is in the hall of Hrothgar at Heorot,
'þæt wæs hilde - setl : heah-cyninges,
þonne sweorda - gelác : sunu Healfdenes
efnan wolde : næfre on óre læg
wíd - cúþes wíg : þonne walu féollon.'

[3] Appendix N, no. xxxix; 'arma in campo ostendit.'

[4] Strutt, 215. The tenth-century τὸ γοτθικόν at Byzantium seems to

have been a kind of sword-dance (cf. ch. xii *ad fin.*).

[5] Strutt, 260; Du Méril, *La Com.* 84.

[6] Mayer, 259.

[7] Müllenhoff, 145, quoting *Don Quixote*, ii. 20; *Z.f.d. A.* xviii. 11 ; Du Méril, *La Com.* 86.

[8] Webster, *The White Devil*, v. 6, 'a matachin, it seems by your drawn swords'; the 'buffons' is included in the list of dances in the *Complaynt of Scotland* (†1548); cf. Furnivall, *Laneham's Letter*, clxii.

[9] Tabourot, *Orchésographie*, 97, *Les Bouffons ou Mattachins*. The dancers held bucklers and swords which they clashed together. They also wore bells on their legs.

[10] Cf. Appendix J.

acknowledged sword-dance is in the north. It is found, according to Mr. Henderson, from the Humber to the Cheviots; and it extends as far south as Cheshire and Nottinghamshire [1]. Outlying examples are recorded from Winchester [2] and from Devonshire [3]. In Scotland Sir Walter Scott found it among the farthest Hebrides, and it has also been traced in Fifeshire [4].

The name of *danse des bouffons* sometimes given to the sword-dance may be explained by a very constant feature of the English examples, in which the dancers generally include or are accompanied by one or more comic or grotesque person-ages. The types of these grotesques are not kept very distinct in the descriptions, or, probably, in fact. But they appear to be fundamentally two. There is the ' Tommy ' or ' fool,' who wears the skin and tail of a fox or some other animal, and there is the ' Bessy,' who is a man dressed in a woman's clothes. And they can be paralleled from outside England. A *Narr* or *Fasching* (carnival fool) is a figure in several German sword-dances, and in one from Bohemia he has his female counterpart in a *Mehlweib* [5].

With the *cantilenae* noticed by Olaus Magnus may be com-pared the sets of verses with which several modern sword-dances, both in these islands and in Germany, are provided. They are sung before or during part of the dances, and as a rule are little more than an introduction of the performers, to whom they give distinctive names. If they contain any

[1] Henderson, 67. The sword-dance is also mentioned by W. Hutchinson, *A View of North-umberland* (1778), ii *ad fin.* 18; by J. Wallis, *Hist. of Northumberland* (1779), ii. 28, who describes the leader as having ' a fox's skin, generally serving him for a cover-ing and ornament to his head, the tail hanging down his back '; and as practised in the north Riding of Yorks. by a writer in the *Gentle-man's Magazine* (1811), lxxxi. 1.423. Here it took place from St. Ste-phen's to New Year's Day. There were six lads, a fiddler, Bessy and a Doctor. At Whitby, six dancers went with the ' Plough Stots' on Plough Monday. The figures in-cluded the placing of a hexagon or rose of swords on the head of one of the performers. The dance was accompanied with ' *Toms* or *clowns*' masked or painted, and ' *Madgies* or Madgy-Pegs' in women's clothes. Sometimes a farce, with a king, miller, clown and doctor was added (G. Young, *Hist. of Whitby* (1817), ii. 880).

[2] Cf. Appendix J.

[3] R. Bell, *Ancient Poems, Bal-lads and Songs of the Peasantry of England*, 175.

[4] Cf. Appendix J.

[5] Mayer, 230, 417.

incident, it is generally of the nature of a quarrel, in which one of the dancers or one of the grotesques is killed. To this point it will be necessary to return. The names given to the characters are sometimes extremely nondescript; sometimes, under a more or less literary influence, of an heroic order. Here and there a touch of something more primitive may be detected. Five sets of verses from the north of England are available in print. Two of these are of Durham *provenance*. One, from Houghton-le-Spring, has, besides the skin-clad 'Tommy' and the 'Bessy,' five dancers. These are King George, a Squire's Son also called Alick or Alex, a King of Sicily, Little Foxey, and a Pitman[1]. The other Durham version has a captain called True Blue, a Squire's Son, Mr. Snip a tailor, a Prodigal Son (replaced in later years by a Sailor), a Skipper, a Jolly Dog. There is only one clown, who calls himself a 'fool,' and acts as treasurer. He is named Bessy, but wears a hairy cap with a fox's brush pendent[2]. Two other versions come from Yorkshire. At Wharfdale there are seven dancers, Thomas the clown, his son Tom, Captain Brown, Obadiah Trim a tailor, a Foppish Knight, Love-ale a vintner, and Bridget the clown's wife[3]. At Linton in Craven there are five, the clown, Nelson, Jack Tar, Tosspot, and Miser a woman[4]. The fifth version is of unnamed locality. It has two clowns, Tommy in skin and tail, and Bessy, and amongst the dancers are a Squire's Son

[1] Henderson, 67. The clown introduces each dancer in turn; then there is a dance with raised swords which are tied in a 'knot.' Henderson speaks of a later set of verses also in use, which he does not print.

[2] R. Bell, *Ancient Poems, Ballads and Songs of the Peasantry of England*, 175 (from Sir C. Sharpe's *Bishoprick Garland*). A Christmas dance. The captain began the performance by drawing a circle with his sword. Then the Bessy introduced the captain, who called on the rest in turn, each walking round the circle to music. Then came an elaborate dance with careful formations, which degenerated into a fight. Bell mentions a similar set of verses from Devonshire.

[3] Bell, 172. A Christmas dance. The clown makes the preliminary circle with his sword, and calls on the other dancers.

[4] Bell, 181. The clown calls for 'a room,' after which one of the party introduces the rest. This also is a Christmas dance, but as the words 'we've come a pace-egging' occur, it must have been transferred from Easter. Bell says that a somewhat similar performance is given at Easter in Coniston, and Halliwell, *Popular Rhymes and Nursery Tales*, 244, describes a similar set of rhymes as used near York for pace-egging.

and a Tailor[1]. Such a nomenclature will not repay much analysis. The 'Squire,' whose son figures amongst the dancers, is identical with the 'Tommy,' although why he should have a son I do not know. Similarly, the 'Bridget' at Wharfdale and the 'Miser' at Linton correspond to the 'Bessy' who appears elsewhere.

The Shetland dance, so far as the names go, is far more literary and less of a folk affair than any of the English examples. The grotesques are absent altogether, and the dancers belong wholly to that heroic category which is also represented in a degenerate form at Houghton-le-Spring. They are in fact those 'seven champions of Christendom'— St. George of England, St. James of Spain, St. Denys of France, St. David of Wales, St. Patrick of Ireland, St. Anthony of Italy, and St. Andrew of Scotland—whose legends were first brought together under that designation by Richard Johnson in 1596[2].

Precisely the same divergence between a popular and a literary or heroic type of nomenclature presents itself in such of the German sword-dance rhymes as are in print. Three very similar versions from Styria, Hungary, and Bohemia are traceable to a common 'Austro-Bavarian' archetype[3]. The names of these, so far as they are intelligible at all, appear to be due to the village imagination, working perhaps in one or two instances, such as 'Grünwald' or 'Wilder Waldmann,' upon stock figures of the folk festivals[4]. It is the heroic element, however, which predominates in the two other sets of verses which are available. One is from the Clausthal in the Harz mountains, and here the dancers represent the five kings of England, Saxony, Poland, Denmark, and Moorland, together with a serving-man, Hans, and one Schnortison, who acts as leader and treasurer of the

---

[1] Described by Müllenhoff, 138, from *Ausland* (1857), No. 4, f. 81. The clown gives the prologue, and introduces the rest.

[2] Cf. p. 221.

[3] Mayer prints and compares all three texts.

[4] Cf. p. 185. The original names seem to be best preserved in the Styrian verses: they are Obersteiner (the *Vortänzer*) or Hans Kanix, Fasching (the *Narr*), Obermayer, Jungesgsell, Grünwald, Edlesblut, Springesklee, Schellerfriedl, Wilder Waldmann, Handssupp, Rubendunst, Leberdarm, Rotwein, Höfenstreit.

party[1]. In the other, from Lübeck, the dancers are the 'worthies' Kaiser Karl, Josua, Hector, David, Alexander, and Judas Maccabaeus. They fight with one Sterkader, in whom Müllenhoff finds the Danish hero Stercatherus mentioned by Saxo Grammaticus; and to the Hans of the Clausthal corresponds a Klas Rugebart, who seems to be the red-bearded St. Nicholas[2].

In view of the wide range of the sword-dance in Germany, I do not think it is necessary to attach any importance to the theories advanced by Sir Walter Scott and others that it is, in England and Scotland, of Scandinavian origin. It is true that it appears to be found mainly in those parts of these islands where the influence of Danes and Northmen may be conjectured to have been strongest. But I believe that this is a matter of appearance merely, and that a type of folk-dance far more widely spread in the south of England than the sword-dance proper, is really identical with it. This is the morris-dance, the chief characteristic of which is that the performers wear bells which jingle at every step. Judging by the evidence of account-books, as well as by the allusions of contemporary writers, the morris was remarkably popular in the sixteenth and seventeenth centuries[3]. Frequently, but by no means always, it is mentioned in company with the May-game[4]. In a certain painted window at Betley in Staffordshire are represented six morris-dancers, together with a Maypole, a musician, a fool, a crowned man on a hobby-horse, a crowned lady with a pink in her hand, and a friar. The last three may reasonably be regarded as Robin Hood, Maid Marian, and Friar Tuck[5]. The closeness

[1] H. Pröhle, *Weltliche und geistliche Volkslieder und Volksschauspiele* (1855), 245.

[2] Müllenhoff, *Z. f. d. A.* xx. 10.

[3] Brand-Ellis, i. 142; Douce, 576; Burton, 95; Gutch, *Robin Hood*, i. 301; Drake, 76.

[4] Burton, 117; Warner, *Albion's England*, v. 25 'At Paske begun our Morrise, and ere Penticost our May.' The morris was familiar in the revels of Christmas. Laneham, 23, describes at the Bride-ale

shown before Elizabeth at Kenilworth 'a lively morrisdauns, according too the auncient manner: six daunserz, Mawdmarion, and the fool.'

[5] A good engraving of the window is in *Variorum Shakespeare*, xvi. 419, and small reproductions in Brand, i. 145; Burton, 103; Gutch, i. 349; Mr. Tollet's own account of the window, printed in the *Variorum, loc. cit.*, is interesting, but too ingenious. He dates the window

of the relation between the morris-dance and the May-game is, however, often exaggerated. The Betley figures only accompany the morris-dance ; they do not themselves wear the bells. And besides the window, the only trace of evidence that any member of the Robin Hood *cortège*, with the exception of Maid Marian, was essential to the morris-dance, is a passage in a masque of Ben Jonson's, which so seems to regard the friar[1]. The fact is that the morris-dance was a great deal older, as an element in the May-game, than Robin Hood, and that when Robin Hood's name was forgotten in this connexion, the morris-dance continued to be in vogue, not at May-games only, but at every form of rustic merry-making. On the other hand, it is true that the actual dancers were generally accompanied by grotesque personages, and that one of these was a woman, or a man dressed in woman's clothes, to whom literary writers at least continued to give the name of Maid Marian. The others have nothing whatever to do with Robin Hood. They were a clown or fool, and a hobby-horse, who, if the evidence of an Elizabethan song can be trusted, was already beginning to go out of fashion[2]. A rarer feature was a dragon, and it is possible

in the reign of Henry VIII; Douce, 585, a better authority, ascribes it to that of Edward IV.

[1] Ben Jonson, *The Gipsies Metamorphosed* (ed. Cunningham, iii. 151):

'*Clod.* They should be morris-dancers by their gingle, but they have no napkins.

'*Cockrel.* No, nor a hobby-horse.

'*Clod.* Oh, he's often forgotten, that's no rule; but there is no Maid Marian nor Friar amongst them, which is the surer mark.

'*Cockrel.* Nor a fool that I see.'

[2] The lady, the fool, the hobby-horse are all in Tollet's window, and in a seventeenth-century printing by Vinkenboom from Richmond palace, engraved by Douce, 598; Burton, 105. Cf. the last note and other passages quoted by Douce, Brand, and Burton. In *Two Noble Kinsmen*, iii. 5, 125, a morris of six men and six women is thus presented by Gerrold, the •

schoolmaster :

'I first appear . . .
The next, the Lord of May and
　Lady bright,
The Chambermaid and Serving-
　man, by night
That ·seek out silent hanging :
　then mine Host
And his fat Spouse, that wel-
　comes to their cost
The galled traveller, and with a
　beck'ning
Informs the tapster to inflame
　the reck'ning :
Then the beast-eating Clown,
　and next the Fool,
The Bavian, with long tail and
　eke long tool;
Cum multis aliis, that make a
　dance.'

Evidently some of these *dramatis personae* are not traditional; the ingenuity of the presenter has been at work on them. 'Bavian' as a name for the fool, is the Dutch *baviaan*, 'baboon.' His 'tail' is to

that, when there was a dragon, the rider of the hobby-horse
was supposed to personate St. George [1]. The morris-dance
is by no means extinct, especially in the north and midlands.
Accounts of it are available from Lancashire and Cheshire [2],
Derbyshire [3], Shropshire [4], Leicestershire [5], and Oxford-

be noted; for the phallic shape
sometimes given to the bladder
which he carries, cf. Rigollot, 164.
In the Betley window the fool has
a bauble; in the Vinkenboom picture a staff with a bladder at one
end, and a ladle (to gather money
in) at the other. In the window
the ladle is carried by the hobby-
horse. 'The hobby-horse is forgot'
is a phrase occurring in *L. L. L.* iii.
1. 30; *Hamlet*, iii. 2. 144, and
alluded to by Beaumont and
Fletcher, *Women Pleased*, iv. 1,
and Ben Jonson, in the masque
quoted above, and in *The Satyr*
(Cunningham, ii. 577). Apparently
it is a line from a lost ballad.

[1] Stubbes, i. 147, of the 'devil's
daunce' in the train of the lord of
misrule, evidently a morris, 'then
haue they their Hobby-horses,
dragons & other Antiques.' In
W. Sampson's *Vow-breaker* (1636),
one morris-dancer says 'I'll be a
fiery dragon'; another, 'I'll be
a thund'ring Saint George as ever
rode on horseback.'

[2] Burton, 40, 43, 48, 49, 56, 59,
61, 65, 69, 75, 115, 117, 121, 123,
cites many notices throughout the
century, and gives several figures.
The morris is in request at wakes
and rushbearings. Both men and
women dance, sometimes to the
number of twenty or thirty. Gay
dresses are worn, with white skirts,
knee-breeches and ribbons. Hand-
, kerchiefs are carried or hung on
the arm or wrist, or replaced by
dangling streamers, cords, or
skeins of cotton. Bells are not
worn on the legs, but jingling horse-
collars are sometimes carried on
the body. There is generally a fool,
described in one account as wearing
'a horrid mask.' He is, however,
generally black, and is known as

'King Coffee' (Gorton), 'owd sooty-
face,' 'dirty Bet,' and 'owd molly-
coddle.' This last name, like the
'molly-dancers' of Gorton, seems
to be due to a linguistic corruption.
In 1829 a writer describes the fool
as 'a nondescript, made up of the
ancient fool and Maid Marian.' At
Heaton, in 1830, were two figures,
said to represent Adam and Eve,
as well as the fool. The masked
fool, mentioned above, had as companion a shepherdess with lamb
and crook.

[3] Burton, 115, from *Journal of
Archaeol. Assoc.* vii. 201. The
dancers went on Twelfth-night,
without bells, but with a fool, a
'fool's wife' and sometimes a
hobby-horse.

[4] Jackson and Burne, 402, 410,
477. The morris-dance proper is
mainly in south Shropshire and at
Christmas. At Shrewsbury, in
1885, were ten dancers, with a fool.
Five carried trowels and five short
staves which they clashed. The
fool had a black face, and a bell on
his coat. No other bells are mentioned. Staves or wooden swords
are used at other places in Shropshire, and at Brosely all the faces
are black. The traditional music
is a tabor and pipe. A 1652 account of the Brosely dance with
six sword-bearers, a 'leader or lord
of misrule' and a 'vice' (cf. ch.
xxv) called the 'lord's son' is
quoted. In north-east Shropshire,
the Christmas 'guisers' are often
called 'morris-dancers,' 'murry-
dancers,' or 'merry-dancers.' In
Shetland the name 'merry dancers'
is given to the *aurora borealis*
(J. Spence, *Shetland Folk-Lore*,
116).

[5] *Leicester F. L.* 93. The dance
was on Plough Monday with paper

shire[1]; and there are many other counties in which it makes, or has recently made, an appearance [2]. The hobby-horse, it would seem, is now at last, except in Derbyshire, finally ' forgot ' ; but the two other traditional grotesques are still *de rigueur*. Few morris-dances are complete without the ' fool ' or clown, amongst whose various names that of ' squire ' in Oxfordshire and that of 'dirty Bet' in Lancashire are the most interesting. The woman is less invariable. Her Tudor name of Maid Marian is preserved in Leicestershire alone ; elsewhere she appears as a shepherdess, or Eve, or 'the fool's wife'; and sometimes she is merged with the ' fool ' into a single nondescript personage.

The morris-dance is by no means confined to England. There are records of it from Scotland [3], Germany [4], Flanders [5], Switzerland [6], Italy [7], Spain [8], and France [9]. In the last-named

masks, a plough, the bullocks, men in women's dresses, one called Maid Marian, Curly the fool, and Beelzebub. This is, I think, the only survival of the name Maid Marian, and it may be doubted if even this is really popular and not literary.

[1] P. Manning, *Oxfordshire Seasonal Festivals*, in *F. L.* viii. 317, summarizes accounts from fourteen villages, and gives illustrations. There are always six dancers. A broad garter of bells is worn below the knee. There are two sets of figures : in one handkerchiefs are carried, in the other short staves are swung and clashed. Sometimes the dancers sing to the air, which is that of an old country-dance. There is always a fool, who carries a stick with a bladder and cow's tail, and is called in two places ' Rodney,' elsewhere the ' squire.' The music is that of a pipe and tabor ('whittle' and 'dub') played by one man; a fiddle is now often used. At Bampton there was a solo dance between crossed tobacco-pipes. At Spelsbury and at Chipping Warden the dance used to be on the church-tower. At the Bampton Whit-feast and the Ducklington Whit-hunt, the dancers were accompanied by a sword-bearer, who impaled a cake. A

sword-bearer also appears in a list of Finstock dancers, given me by Mr. T. J. Carter, of Oxford. He also told me that the dance on Spelsbury church-tower, seventy years ago, was by women.

[2] Norfolk, Monmouthshire, Berkshire (Douce, 606); Worcestershire, Northamptonshire, Gloucestershire, Somersetshire, Wiltshire, Warwickshire, and around London (Burton, 114).

[3] *L. H. T. Accounts*, ii. 414 ; iii. 359, 381.

[4] Pfannenschmidt, 582; Michels, 84 ; Creizenach, i. 411. Burton, 102, reproduces, from *Art Journal* (1885), 121, cuts of ten morris-dancers carved in wood at Munich by Erasmus Schnitzer in 1480.

[5] Douce, 585, and Burton, 97, reproduce Israel von Mecheln's engraving (†1470) of a morris with a fool and a lady.

[6] Coquillart,*Œuvres*(†1470), 127.

[7] *Mémoires de Pétrarque*, ii. app. 3, 9 ; Petrarch danced ' en pourpoint une belle et vigoureuse moresque ' to please the Roman ladies on the night of his coronation.

[8] *Somers Tracts*, ii. 81, 87. The Earl of Nottingham, when on an embassy from James I, saw morrice-dancers in a Corpus Christi procession.

[9] Douce, 480 ; Favine, *Theater*

country Tabourot described it about 1588 under the name of *morisque*[1], and the earlier English writers call it the *morisce, morisk,* or *morisco*[2]. This seems to imply a derivation of the name at least from the Spanish *morisco,* a Moor. The dance itself has consequently been held to be of Moorish origin, and the habit of blackening the face has been considered as a proof of this[3]. Such a theory seems to invert the order of facts. The dance is too closely bound up with English village custom to be lightly regarded as a foreign importation; and I would suggest that the faces were not blackened, because the dancers represented Moors, but rather the dancers were thought to represent Moors, because their faces were blackened. The blackened face is common enough in the village festival. Hence, as we have seen, May-day became proper to the chimney-sweeps, and we have found a conjectural reason for the disguise in the primitive custom of smearing the face with the beneficent ashes of the festival fire[4]. Blackened faces are known in the sword-dance as well as in the morris-dance[5]; and there are other reasons which make it probable that the two are only variants of the

---

of Honor, 345: at a feast given by Gaston de Foix at Vendôme, in 1458, ' foure young laddes and a damosell, attired like savages, daunced (by good direction) an excellent *Morisco,* before the assembly.'

[1] Tabourot, *Orchésographie,* 94: in his youth a lad used to come after supper, with his face blackened, his forehead bound with white or yellow taffeta, and bells on his legs, and dance the morris up and down the hall.

[2] Douce, 577; Burton, 95.

[3] A dance certainly of Moorish origin is the fandango, in which castanets were used; cf. the comedy of *Variety* (1649) ' like a Bacchanalian, dancing the Spanish Morisco, with knackers at his fingers' (Strutt, 223). This, however, seems to show that the fandango was considered a variety of morisco. Douce, 602; Burton, 124, figure an African woman from Fez dancing with bells on her ankles. This is taken from Hans Weigel's book of national costumes published at Nuremberg in 1577.

[4] Tabourot's morris-dancing boy had his face blackened, and Junius (F. Du Jon), *Etymologicum Anglicanum* (1743), says of England 'faciem plerumque inficiunt fuligine, et peregrinum vestium cultum assumunt, qui ludicris talibus indulgent, ut Mauri esse videantur, aut e longius remota patria credantur advolasse, atque insolens recreationis genus advexisse.' In *Spousalls of Princess Mary* (1508) ' morisks' is rendered ' ludi Maurei quas morescas dicunt.' In the modern morris the black element is represented, except at Brosely, chiefly by 'owd sooty face,' the fool: in Leicestershire it gives rise to a distinct figure, Beelzebub.

[5] Du Méril, *La Com.* 89, quotes a sixteenth-century French sword-dance of ' Mores, Sauvages, et Satyres.' In parts of Yorkshire the sword-dancers had black faces or masks (Henderson, 70).

same performance. Tabourot, it is true, distinguishes *les bouffons*, or the sword-dance, and *le morisque*; but then Tabourot is dealing with the sophisticated versions of the folk-dances used in society, and Cotgrave, translating *les buffons*, can find no better English term than *morris* for the purpose[1]. The two dances appear at the same festivals, and they have the same grotesques; for the Tommy and Bessy of the English sword-dance, who occasionally merge in one, are obviously identical with the Maid Marian and the 'fool'of the morris-dance, who also nowadays similarly coalesce. There are traces, too, of an association of the hobby-horse with the sword-dance, as well as with the morris-dance[2]. Most conclusive of all, however, is the fact that in Oxford-shire and in Shropshire the morris-dancers still use swords or wooden staves which obviously represent swords, and that the performers of the elaborate Revesby sword-dance or play, to be hereafter described, are called in the eighteenth-century manuscript 'morrice dancers[3].' I do not think that the floating handkerchiefs of the morris-dance are found in its congener, nor do I know what, if any, significance they have. Probably, like the ribbons, they merely represent rustic notions of ornament. Müllenhoff lays stress on the white shirts or smocks which he finds almost universal in the sword-dance[4]. The morris-dancers are often described as dressed in white; but here too, if the ordinary work-a-day costume is a smock, the festal costume is naturally a clean white smock. Finally, there are the bells. These, though they have partially disappeared in the north, seem to be proper to the morris-

---

[1] Cotgrave, '*Dancer les Buffons*, To daunce a morris.' The term 'the madman's morris' appears as the name of the dance in *The Figure of Nine* (temp. Charles II); cf. Furnivall, *Laneham's Letter*, clxii. The *buffon* is presumably the 'fool'; cf. Cotgrave, '*Buffon*: m. A buffoon, jeaster, sycophant, merrie fool, sportfull companion: one that lives by making others merrie.'

[2] Henderson, 70. In Yorkshire the sword-dancers carried the image of a white horse; in Cheshire a horse's head and skin.

[3] Cf. ch. x; also Wise, *Enquiries concerning the Inhabitants, . . . of Europe*, 51 'the common people in many parts of England still practise what they call a Morisco dance, in a wild manner, and as it were in armour, at proper intervals striking upon one another's staves,' &c. Johnson's *Dictionary* (1755) calls the morris 'a dance in which bells are gingled, or staves or swords clashed.'

[4] Müllenhoff, 124; cf. Mayer, 236.

dance, and to differentiate it from the sword-dance[1]. But this is only so when the English examples are alone taken into consideration, for Müllenhoff quotes one Spanish and three German descriptions of sword-dances in which the bells are a feature[2]. Tabourot affords similar evidence for the French version[3]; while Olaus Magnus supplements his account of the Scandinavian sword-dance with one of a similar performance, in which the swords were replaced by bows, and bells were added[4]. The object of the bells was probably to increase or preserve the musical effect of the clashing swords. The performers known to Tacitus were *nudi*, and no bells are mentioned. One other point with regard to the morris-dance is worth noticing before we leave the subject. It is capable of use both as a stationary and a processional dance, and therefore illustrates both of the two types of dancing motion naturally evolved from the circumstances of the village festival[5].

Müllenhoff regards the sword-dance as primarily a rhythmic *Abbild* or mimic representation of war, subsequently modified in character by use at the village feasts[6]. It is true that the notice of Tacitus and the allusion in *Beowulf* suggest that it had a military character ; and it may fairly be inferred that it formed part of that war-cult from which, as pointed out in a previous chapter, heroic poetry sprang. This is confirmed by the fact that some at least of the *dramatis personae* of the modern dances belong to the heroic category. Side by side with local types such as the Pitman or the Sailor, and with doublets of the grotesques such as Little Foxey or the

---

[1] Douce, 602 ; Burton, 123. The bells were usually fastened upon broad garters, as they are still worn in Oxfordshire. But they also appear as anklets or are hung on various parts of the dress. In a cut from Randle Holme's *Academie of Armorie*, iii. 109 (Douce, 603 ; Burton, 127), a morris-dancer holds a pair of bells in his hands. Sometimes the bells were harmonized. In *Pasquil and Marforius* (1589) Penry is described as 'the fore gallant of the Morrice with the treble bells' ; cf. Rowley, *Witch of Edmonton*, i. 2.

[2] Müllenhoff, 123 ; Mayer, 235.

[3] Tabourot, *Orchésographie*, 97.

[4] Cf. Appendix J. A figure with a bow and arrow occurs in the Abbots Bromley horn-dance (p. 166).

[5] W. Kempe's *Nine Days Wonder* (ed. Dyce, Camden Soc.) describes his dancing of the morris in bell-shangles from London to Norwich in 1599.

[6] Müllenhoff, 114.

Squire's Son [1], appear the five kings of the Clausthal dance, the 'worthies' of the Lübeck dance, and the 'champions of Christendom' of the Shetland dance. These particular groups betray a Renaissance rather than a mediaeval imagination; as with the morris-dance of *The Two Noble Kinsmen*, the village schoolmaster, Holophernes or another, has probably been at work upon them [2]. Some of the heterogeneous English *dramatis personae*, Nelson for instance, testify to a still later origin. On the other hand, the Sterkader or Stercatherus of the Lübeck dance suggests that genuine national heroes were occasionally celebrated in this fashion. At the same time I do not believe, with Müllenhoff, that the sword-dance originated in the war-cult. Its essentially agricultural character seems to be shown by the grotesques traditionally associated with it, the man in woman's clothes, the skin or tail-wearing clown and the hobby-horse, all of which seem to find their natural explanation in the facts of agricultural worship [3]. Again, the dance makes its appearance, not like heroic poetry in general as part of the minstrel repertory, but as a purely popular thing at the agricultural festivals. To these festivals, therefore, we may reasonably suppose it to have originally belonged, and to have been borrowed from them by the young warriors who danced before the king. They, however, perhaps gave it the heroic element which, in

---

[1] The 'Squire's Son' of the Durham dances is probably the clown's son of the Wharfdale version; for the term 'squire' is not an uncommon one for the rustic fool. Cf. also the Revesby play described in the next chapter. Why the fool should have a son, I do not know.

[2] The 'Nine Worthies' of *Love's Labour's Lost*, v. 2, are a pageant not a dance, and the two sets of speeches quoted from Bodl. Tanner MS. 407, by Ritson, *Remarks on Shakespeare*, 38, one of which is called by Ashton, 127, the earliest mummers' play that he can find, also probably belong to pageants. The following, also quoted by Ritson *loc. cit.* from *Harl. MS.* 1197, f. 101*

(sixteenth century), looks more like a dance or play :

'I ame a knighte
   And menes to fight
      And armet well ame I
Lo here I stand
   With swerd ine hand
      My manhoud for to try.

Thou marciall wite
   That menes to fight
      And sete vppon me so
Lo heare J stand
   With swrd in hand
      To dubbele eurey blow.'

[3] Mayer, 230, 425, finds in the dance a symbolical drama of the death of winter; but he does not seem to see the actual relic of a sacrificial rite.

its turn, drifted into the popular versions. We have already seen that popular heroic *cantilenae* existed together with those of minstrelsy up to a late date. Nor does Müllenhoff's view find much support from the classical sword-dances which he adduces. As to the origin of the *lusus Troiae* or Pyrrhic dance which the Romans adopted from Doric Greece, I can say nothing[1]; but the native Italian dance of the *Salii* or priests of Mars in March and October is clearly agricultural. It belongs to the cult of Mars, not as war-god, but in his more primitive quality of a fertilization spirit[2].

Further, I believe that the use of swords in the dance was not martial at all ; their object was to suggest not a fight, but a mock or symbolical sacrifice. Several of the dances include figures in which the swords are brought together in a significant manner about the person of one or more of the dancers. Thus in the Scandinavian dance described by Olaus Magnus, a *quadrata rosa* of swords is placed on the head of each performer. A precisely similar figure occurs in the Shetland and in a variety of the Yorkshire dances[3]. In the Siebenbürgen dances there are two figures in which the performers pretend to cut at each other's heads or feet, and a third in which one of them has the swords put in a ring round his neck[4]. This latter evolution occurs also in a variety of the Yorkshire dance[5] and in a Spanish one described by Müllen-

---

[1] Müllenhoff, 114; Du Méril, *La Com.* 82; Plato, *Leges*, 815; Dion Cassius, lx. 23; Suetonius, *Julius*, 39, *Nero*, 12; Servius *ad Aen.* v. 602; cf. p. 7. A Thracian sword-dance, ending in a mimic death, and therefore closely parallel to the west European examples mentioned in the next chapter, is described by Xenophon, *Anabasis*, v. 9.

[2] Müllenhoff, 115; Frazer, iii.122; W. W. Fowler, *The Roman Festivals*, 38, 44. The song of the *Salii* mentioned Saeturnus, god of sowing. It appears also to have been their function to expel the Mamurius Veturius in spring. Servius *ad Aen.* viii. 285, says that the *Salii* were founded by Morrius, king of Veii.

According to Frazer, Morrius is etymologically equivalent to Mamurius—Mars. He even suggests that Morris may possibly belong to the same group of words.

[3] Cf. Appendix J. In other dances a performer stands on a similar 'knot' or *Stern* of swords. Mayer, 230, suggests that this may represent the triumph of summer, which seems a little far-fetched.

[4] Mayer, 243; O. Wittstock, in *Sievers-Festgabe*, 349.

[5] Grimm, i. 304, gives the following as communicated to him by J. M. Kemble, from the mouth of an old Yorkshireman: 'In some parts of northern England, in Yorkshire, especially Hallamshire, popular customs show remnants of the

hoff after a seventeenth-century writer. And here the figure has the significant name of *la degollada*, 'the beheading [1].'

worship of Fricg. In the neighbourhood of Dent, at certain seasons of the year, especially autumn, the country folk hold a procession and perform old dances, one called the giant's dance : the leading giant they name *Woden*, and his wife *Frigga*, the principal action of the play consisting in two swords being swung and clashed together about the neck of a boy without hurting him.' There is nothing about this in the account of Teutonic mythology in J. M. Kemble's own *Saxons in England*. I do not believe that the names of Woden and Frigga were preserved in connexion with this custom continuously from heathen times. Probably some antiquary had introduced them; and in error, for there is no reason to suppose that the 'clown' and 'woman' of the sword-dance were ever thought to represent gods. But the description of the business with the swords is interesting.

[1] Müllenhoff, *Z. f. d. A.* xviii. 11, quoting Covarubias, *Tesoro della lengua castellana* (1611), s.v. *Danza de Espadas* : 'una mudanza que llaman la degollada, porque cercan el cuello del que los guia con las espadas.' With these sword manœuvres should be compared the use of scythes and flails in the mock sacrifices of the harvest-field and threshing-floor (p. 158), the 'Chop off his head' of the 'Oranges and Lemons' game (p. 151), and the ancient tale of Wodan and the Mowers.

CHAPTER X

THE MUMMERS' PLAY

[*Bibliographical Note.*—The subject is treated by T. F. Ordish, *English Folk-Drama* in *Folk-Lore*, ii. 326, iv. 162. The Folk-Lore Society has in preparation a volume on Folk-Drama to be edited by Mr. Ordish (*F. L.* xiii. 296). The following is a list of the twenty-nine printed versions upon which the account of the St. George play in the present chapter is based. The Lutterworth play is given in Appendix K.

NORTHUMBERLAND.
  1. *Newcastle.* Chap-book—W. Sandys, *Christmastide*, 292, from *Alexander and the King of Egypt. A mock Play, as it is acted by the Mummers every Christmas.* Newcastle, 1788. (Divided into Acts and Scenes.)

CUMBERLAND.
  2. *Whitehaven.* Chap-book—Hone, *E. D. B.* ii. 1646. (Practically identical with (1).)

LANCASHIRE.
  3. *Manchester.* Chap-book—*The Peace Egg*, published by J. Wrigley, 30, Miller Street, Manchester. (Brit. Mus. 1077, *g*/27 (37): Acts and Scenes: a coloured cut of each character.)

SHROPSHIRE.
  4. *Newport.* Oral. Jackson and Burne, 484. (Called the Guisers' (gheez'u'rz) play.)

STAFFORDSHIRE.
  5. *Eccleshall.* Oral. *F. L. J.* iv. 350. (Guisers' play: practically identical with (4). I have not seen a version from Stone in W. W. Bladen, *Notes on the Folk-lore of North Staffs.*: cf. *F. L.* xiii. 107.)

LEICESTERSHIRE.
  6. *Lutterworth.* Oral. Kelly, 53; Manly, i. 292; *Leicester F. L.* 130.

WORCESTERSHIRE.
  7. *Leigh.* Oral. 2 *N. Q.* xi. 271.

WARWICKSHIRE.
  8. *Newbold.* Oral. *F. L.* x. 186 (with variants from a similar Rugby version).

OXFORDSHIRE.
  9. *Islip.* Oral. Ditchfield, 316.
  10. *Bampton.* Oral. Ditchfield, 320.
  11. *Thame.* Oral. 5 *N. Q.* ii. 503; Manly, i. 289.
  12. *Uncertain.* Oral. 6 *N. Q.* xii. 489; Ashton, 128.

BERKSHIRE.
  13. *Uncertain.* Oral. Ditchfield, 310.

MIDDLESEX.
  14. *Chiswick.* Oral. 2 *N. Q.* x. 466.

Sussex.
   15. *Selmeston.* Oral. Parish, *Dict. of Sussex Dialect* (2nd ed. 1875), 136.
   16. *Hollington.* Oral. 5 *N. Q.* x. 489.
   17. *Steyning.* Oral. *F. L. J.* ii. 1. (The 'Tipteerers'' play.)
Hampshire.
   18. *St. Mary Bourne.* Oral. Stevens, *Hist. of St. Mary Bourne,* 340.
   19. *Uncertain.* Oral. 2 *N. Q.* xii. 492.
Dorsetshire.
   20. (A) *Uncertain.* Oral. *F. L. R.* iii. 92; Ashton, 129.
   21. (B) *Uncertain.* Oral. *F. L. R.* iii. 102.
Cornwall.
   22. *Uncertain.* Oral. Sandys, *Christmastide,* 298. (Slightly different version in Sandys, *Christmas Carols,* 174; Du Méril, *La Com.* 428.)
Wales.
   23. *Tenby.* Oral. Chambers, *Book of Days,* ii. 740, from *Tales and Traditions of Tenby.*
Ireland.
   24. *Belfast.* Chap-book. 4 *N. Q.* x. 487. ('The Christmas Rhymes.')
   25. *Ballybrennan, Wexford.* Oral. Kennedy, *The Banks of the Boro,* 226.
Uncertain Locality.
   26. *Sharpe's London Magazine,* i. 154. Oral.
   27. *Archaeologist,* i. 176. Chap-book. H. Sleight, *A Christmas Pageant Play or Mysterie of St. George, Alexander and the King of Egypt.* (Said to be 'compiled from and collated with several curious ancient black-letter editions.' I have never seen or heard of a 'black-letter' edition, and I take it the improbable title is Mr. Sleight's own.)
   28. *Halliwell.* Oral. *Popular Rhymes,* 231. (Said to be the best of six versions.)
   29. *F. L. J.* iv. 97. (Fragment, from 'old MS.')]

The *degollada* figures of certain sword-dances preserve with some clearness the memory of an actual sacrifice, abolished and replaced by a mere symbolic dumb show. Even in these, and still more in the other dances, the symbolism is very slight. It is completely subordinated to the rhythmic evolutions of a choric figure. There is an advance, however, in the direction of drama, when in the course of the performance some one is represented as actually slain. In a few dances of the type discussed in the last chapter, such a dramatic episode precedes or follows the regular figures. It is recorded in three or four of the German examples [1]. A writer in the *Gentleman's Magazine* describes a Yorkshire dance in which 'the Bessy interferes while they are making a hexagon with their swords, and is killed.' Amongst the characters of this dance is

---

[1] Mayer, 229.

a Doctor, and although the writer does not say so, it may be
inferred that the function of the Doctor is to bring the Bessy
to life again [1]. It will be remembered that a precisely similar
device is used in the German Shrove Tuesday plays to
symbolize the resurrection of the year in spring after its death
in winter. The Doctor reappears in one of the Durham
dances, and here there is no doubt as to the part he plays.
At a certain point the careful formations of the dance degenerate
into a fight. The parish clergyman rushes in to separate the
combatants. He is accidentally slain. There is general
lamentation, but the Doctor comes forward, and revives the
victim, and the dance proceeds [2].

It is but a step from such dramatic episodes to the more
elaborate performances which remain to be considered in the
present chapter, and which are properly to be called plays
rather than dances. They belong to a stage in the evolution
of drama from dance, in which the dance has been driven into
the background and has sometimes disappeared altogether.
But they have the same characters, and especially the same
grotesques, as the dances, and the general continuity of the
two sets of performances cannot be doubted. Moreover,
though the plays differ in many respects, they have a common
incident, which may reasonably be taken to be the central
incident, in the death and revival, generally by a Doctor, of
one of the characters. And in virtue of this central incident
one is justified in classing them as forms of a folk-drama in
which the resurrection of the year is symbolized.

I take first, on account of the large amount of dancing which
remains in it, the play acted at the end of the eighteenth
century by ' The Plow Boys or Morris Dancers ' of Revesby
in Lincolnshire [3]. There are seven dancers : six men, the Fool

---

[1] *Gentleman's Magazine*, lxxxi
(1811), I. 423. The dance was given
in the north Riding from St.
Stephen's day to the New Year.
Besides the Bessy and the Doctor
there were six lads, one of whom
acted king ' in a kind of farce
which consists of singing and
dancing.'

[2] Bell, 178 ; cf. p. 193. I do not
feel sure whether the actual parish

clergyman took part, or whether
a mere personage in the play is
intended ; but see what Olaus
Magnus (App. J (i)) says about the
propriety of the sword-dances for
clerici. It will be curious if the
Christian priest has succeeded to
the part of the heathen priest slain,
first literally, and then in mimicry,
at the festivals.

[3] Printed by Mr. T. F. Ordish in

and his five sons, Pickle Herring, Blue Breeches, Pepper
Breeches, Ginger Breeches, and Mr. Allspice[1]; and one
woman, Cicely. The somewhat incoherent incidents are as
follows. The Fool acts as presenter and introduces the play.
He fights successively a Hobby-horse and a 'Wild Worm' or
dragon. The dancers 'lock their swords to make the glass,'
which, after some jesting, is broken up again. The sons
determine to kill the Fool. He kneels down and makes his
will, with the swords round his neck[2]; is slain and revived by
Pickle Herring stamping with his foot: This is repeated
with variations. Hitherto, the dancers have 'footed it' round
the room at intervals. Now follow a series of sword-dances.
During and after these the Fool and his sons in turn woo Cicely,
the Fool taking the name of 'Anthony[3],' Pickle Herring that
of 'the Lord of Pool,' and Blue Breeches that of 'the Knight
of Lee.' There is nothing particularly interesting about this
part of the play, obviously written to 'work in' the woman
grotesque. In the course of it a morris-dance is introduced,
and a final sword-dance, with an obeisance to the master of the
house, winds up the whole.

Secondly, there are the Plough Monday plays of the east
Midlands[4]. These appear in Nottinghamshire, Northampton-

F.L.J. vii. 338, and again by Manly,
i. 296. The MS. used appears to be
headed 'October Ye 20, 1779';
but the performers are called 'The
Plow Boys or Morris Dancers' and
the prologue says that they 'takes
delight in Christmas toys.' I do
not doubt that the play belonged
to Plough Monday, which only
falls just outside the Christmas
season.

[1] On the name Pickle Herring,
see W. Creizenach, *Die Schauspiele
der englischen Komödianten*, xciii.
It does not occur in old English
comedy, but was introduced into
Anglo-German and German farce
as a name for the 'fool' or 'clown'
by Robert Reynolds, the 'comic
lead' of a company of English
actors who crossed to Germany in
1618. Probably it was Reynolds'
invention, and suggested by the
sobriquet 'Stockfish' taken by an

earlier Anglo-German actor, John
Spencer. The 'spicy' names of
the other Revesby clowns are
probably imitations of Pickle Herring.

[2] The lines (197-8)
'Our old Fool's bracelet is not
made of gold
But it is made of iron and
good steel'
suggest the vaunt of the champions
in the St. George plays.

[3] Is 'Anthony' a reminiscence of
the Seven Champions? The Fool
says (ll. 247-9), like Beelzebub in
the St. George plays,
'Here comes I that never come
yet, . . .
I have a great head but little
wit.'
He also jests (l. 229) on his 'tool';
cf. p. 196 n.

[4] Brand, i. 278; Dyer, 37; Ditchfield, 47; Drake, 65; Mrs. Chaworth

shire and Lincolnshire. Two printed versions are available. The first comes from Cropwell in Nottinghamshire[1]. The actors are 'the plough-bullocks.' The male characters are Tom the Fool, a Recruiting Sergeant, and a Ribboner or Recruit, three farm-servants, Threshing Blade, Hopper Joe[2], and the Ploughman, a Doctor, and Beelzebub[3]. There are two women, a young Lady and old Dame Jane. Tom Fool is presenter. The Ribboner, rejected by the young Lady, enlists as a recruit. The Lady is consoled by Tom Fool. Then enter successively the three farm-servants, each describing his function on the farm. Dame Jane tries to father a child on

Musters, *A Cavalier Stronghold*, 387. Plough Monday is the Monday after Twelfth night, when the field work begins. A plough is dragged round the village and a *quête* made. The survivals of the custom are mainly in the north, east and east midlands. In the city, a banquet marks the day. A Norfolk name is 'Plowlick Monday,' and a Hunts one 'Plough-Witching.' The plough is called the 'Fool Plough,' 'Fond Plough,' 'Stot Plough' or 'White Plough'; the latter name probably from the white shirts worn (cf. p. 200). At Cropwell, Notts, horses cut out in black or red adorn these. In Lincolnshire, bunches of corn were worn in the hats. Those who draw the plough are called 'Plough Bullocks,' 'Boggons' or 'Stots.' They sometimes dance a morris- or sword-dance, or act a play. At Haxey, they take a leading part in the Twelfth day 'Hood-game' (p. 150). In Northants their faces are blackened or reddled. The plough is generally accompanied by the now familiar grotesques, 'Bessy' and the Fool or 'Captain Cauf-Tail.' In Northants there are two of each; the Fools have humps, and are known as 'Red Jacks'; there is also a 'Master.' In Lincolnshire, reapers, threshers, and carters joined the procession. A contribution to the *quête* is greeted with the cry of 'Largess!' and a churl is liable to have the ground before his door ploughed up. Of old the profits of the *quête* or 'plowgadrin' went into the parish chest, or as in Norfolk kept a 'plow-light' burning in the church. A sixteenth century pamphlet speaks of the 'sensing the Ploughess' on Plough Monday. Jevons, 247, calls the rite a 'worship of the plough'; probably it rather represents an early spring perambulation of the fields in which the divinity rode upon a plough, as elsewhere upon a ship. A ploughing custom of putting a loaf in the furrow has been noted. Plough Monday has also its water rite. The returning ploughman was liable to be soused by the women, like the bearer of the 'neck' at harvest. Elsewhere, the women must get the kettle on before the ploughman can reach the hearth, or pay forfeit.

[1] Printed by Mrs. Chaworth Musters in *A Cavalier Stronghold* (1890), 388, and in a French translation by Mrs. H. G. M. Murray-Aynsley, in *R. d. T. P.* iv. 605.

[2] 'Hopper Joe' also calls himself 'old Sanky-Benny,' which invites interpretation. Is it 'Saint Bennet' or 'Benedict'?

[3] 'In comes I, Beelzebub,
    On my shoulder I carry my club,
    In my hand a wet leather frying-pan;
    Don't you think I'm a funny old man?'
Cf. the St. George play (p. 214).

Tom Fool. Beelzebub knocks her down [1], and kills her. The Doctor comes in, and after some comic business about his travels, his qualifications and his remedies [2], declares Dame Jane to be only in a trance, and raises her up. A country dance and songs follow, and the performance ends with a *quête*. The second version, from Lincolnshire, is very similar [3]. But there are no farm-servants, and instead of Beelzebub is a personage called 'old Esem Esquesem,' who carries a broom. It is he, not an old woman, who is killed and brought to life. There are several dancers, besides the performers; and these include 'Bessy,' a man dressed as a woman, with a cow's tail.

The distinction between a popular and a literary or heroic type of personification which was noticeable in the sword-dances persists in the folk-plays founded upon them. Both in the Revesby play and in the Plough Monday plays, the drama is carried on by personages resembling the 'grotesques' of the sword- and morris-dances [4]. There are no heroic characters. The death is of the nature of an accident or an execution. On the other hand, in the 'mummers' play' of St. George, the heroes take once more the leading part, and the death, or at least one of the deaths, is caused by a fight amongst them. This play is far more widely spread than its rivals. It is found in all parts of England, in Wales, and in Ireland; in Scotland it occurs also, but here some other hero is generally substituted as protagonist for St. George [5]. The

---

[1] 'Dame Jane' says,
'My head is made of iron,
My body made of steel,
My hands and feet of knuckle-bone,
I think nobody can make me feel.'
In the Lincolnshire play Beelzebub has this vaunt. Cf. the St. George play (p. 220).

[2] The Doctor can cure 'the hipsy-pipsy, palsy, and the gout'; cf. the St. George play (p. 213).

[3] Printed in French by Mrs. Murray Aynsley in *R. d. T. P.* iv. 609.

[4] The farce recorded as occasionally introduced at Whitby (cf. p. 192,

n. 1) but not described, probably belonged to the 'popular' type.

[5] Chambers, *Popular Rhymes of Scotland*, 169, prints a Peebles version. Instead of George, a hero called Galatian fights the Black Knight. Judas, with his bag, replaces Beelzebub. But it is the same play. Versions or fragments of it are found all over the Lowlands. The performers are invariably called 'guizards.' In a Falkirk version the hero is Prince George of Ville. Hone, *E. D. B.*, says that the hero is sometimes Galacheus or St. Lawrence. But in another Falkirk version, part of which he prints, the name is Galgacus, and of this

following account is based on the twenty-nine versions, drawn
from chap-books or from oral tradition, enumerated in the
bibliographical note. The list might, doubtless, be almost
indefinitely extended. As will soon be seen, the local variations of the play are numerous. In order to make them
intelligible, I have given in full in an appendix a version from
Lutterworth in Leicestershire. This is chosen, not as a particularly interesting variant, for that it is not, but on the
contrary as being comparatively colourless. It shows very
clearly and briefly the normal structure of the play, and may be
regarded as the type from which the other versions diverge [1].

The whole performance may be divided, for convenience of
analysis, into three parts, the Presentation, the Drama, the
Quête. In the first somebody speaks a prologue, claiming a
welcome from the spectators[2], and then the leading characters
are in turn introduced. The second consists of a fight
followed by the intervention of a doctor to revive the slain.
In the third some supernumerary characters enter, and there
is a collection. It is the dramatic nucleus that first requires
consideration. The leading fighter is generally St. George,
who alone appears in all the versions. Instead of ' St. George,'
he is sometimes called ' Sir George,' and more often ' Prince
George ' or ' King George,' modifications which one may
reasonably suppose to be no older than the present Hanoverian
dynasty. At Whitehaven and at Falkirk he is ' Prince George
of Ville.' George's chief opponent is usually one of two per-

both Galacheus and Galatian are
probably corruptions, for Galgacus
or Calgacus was the leader of the
Picts in their battle with Agricola
at the Mons Graupius (A. D. 84;
Tacitus, *Agricola*, 29).

[1] Appendix K. Other versions
may be conveniently compared in
Manly, i. 289; Ditchfield, 310. The
best discussions of the St. George
plays in general, besides Mr. Ordish's, are J. S. Udall, *Christmas
Mummers in Dorsetshire* (*F. L. R.*
iii. 1. 87); Jackson and Burne, 482;
G. L. Gomme, *Christmas Mummers*
(*Nature*, Dec. 23, 1897). The notes
and introductions to the versions tabulated above give many useful data.

[2] In *F. L.* x. 351, Miss Florence
Grove describes some Christmas
mummers seen at Mullion, Cornwall,
in 1890-1. ' Every one naturally
knows who the actors are, since
there are not more than a few
hundred persons within several
miles; but no one is supposed to
know who they are or where they
come from, nor must any one speak
to them, nor they to those in the
houses they visit. As far as I can
remember the performance is silent
and dramatic; I have no recollection of reciting.' The dumb show
is rare and probably a sign of decadence, but the bit of rural etiquette is
archaic, and recurs in savage drama.

sonages, who are not absolutely distinct from each other[1]. One is the 'Turkish Knight,' of whom a variant appears to be the 'Prince of Paradine' (Manchester), or 'Paradise' (Newport, Eccleshall), perhaps originally 'Palestine.' He is sometimes represented with a blackened face[2]. The other is variously called 'Slasher,' 'Captain Slasher,' 'Bold Slasher,' or, by an obvious corruption, 'Beau Slasher.' Rarer names for him are 'Bold Slaughterer' (Bampton), 'Captain Bluster' (Dorset [A]), and 'Swiff, Swash, and Swagger' (Chiswick). His names fairly express his vaunting disposition, which, however, is largely shared by the other characters in the play. In the place of, or as minor fighters by the side of George, the Turkish Knight and Bold Slasher, there appear, in one version or another, a bewildering variety of personages, of whom only a rough classification can be attempted. Some belong to the heroic cycles. Such are 'Alexander' (Newcastle, Whitehaven), 'Hector' (Manchester), 'St. Guy' (Newport), 'St. Giles' (Eccleshall)[3], 'St. Patrick' (Dorset [A], Wexford), 'King Alfred' and 'King Cole' (Brill), 'Giant Blunderbore' (Brill), 'Giant Turpin' (Cornwall). Others again are moderns who have caught the popular imagination : 'Bold Bonaparte' (Leigh)[4], and 'King of Prussia' (Bampton, Oxford)[5], 'King William' (Brill), the 'Duke of Cumberland' (Oxford) and the 'Duke of Northumberland' (Islip), 'Lord Nelson' (Stoke Gabriel, Devon)[6], 'Wolfe' and 'Wellington' (Cornwall)[7], even the 'Prince Imperial' (Wilts)[8], all have been pressed into the service. In some cases characters have lost their personal names, if they ever had any, and figure merely as 'Knight,' 'Soldier,' 'Valiant Soldier,' 'Noble Captain,' 'Bold Prince,' 'Gracious King.' Others bear names which defy explanation, 'Alonso' (Chiswick), 'Hy Gwyer' (Hollington),

---

[1] In Berkshire and at Eccleshall, Slasher is 'come from Turkish land.' On the other hand, the two often appear in the same version, and even, as at Leigh, fight together.

[2] Burne-Jackson, 483.

[3] Ibid. 483. He appears in the MSS. written by the actors as 'Singuy' or 'Singhiles.' Professor Skeat points out that, as he 'sprang from English ground,' St. Guy (of Warwick) was probably the original form, and St. Giles a corruption.

[4] Here may be traced the influence of the Napoleonic wars. In Berkshire, Slasher is a 'French officer.'

[5] F. L. v. 88.

[6] Ditchfield, 12.

[7] Sandys, 153.

[8] P. Tennant, Village Notes, 179.

'Marshalee' and 'Cutting Star' (Dorset [B]). The significance of 'General Valentine' and 'Colonel Spring' (Dorset
[A]) will be considered presently; and 'Room' (Dorset [B]),
'Little Jack,' the 'Bride' and the 'Fool' (Brill), and the 'King
of Egypt' (Newcastle, Whitehaven) have strayed in amongst
the fighters from the presenters. The fighting generally takes
the form of a duel, or a succession of duels. In the latter case,
George may fight all comers, or he may intervene to subdue
a previously successful champion. But an important point is
that he is not always victorious. On the contrary, the versions
in which he slays and those in which he is slain are about
equal in number. In two versions (Brill, Steyning) the fighting is not a duel or a series of duels, but a *mêlée*. The Brill
play, in particular, is quite unlike the usual type. A prominent
part is taken by the Dragon, with whom fight, all at once,
St. George and a heterogeneous company made up of King
Alfred and his Bride, King Cole, King William, Giant Blunderbore, Little Jack and a morris-dance Fool.

Whatever the nature of the fight, the result is always the
same. One or more of the champions falls, and then appears
upon the scene a Doctor, who brings the dead to life again.
The Doctor is a comic character. He enters, boasting his
universal skill, and works his cure by exhibiting a bolus, or by
drawing out a tooth with a mighty pair of pliers. At Newbold he is 'Dr. Brown,' at Islip 'Dr. Good' (also called 'Jack
Spinney'), at Brill 'Dr. Ball'; in Dorsetshire (A) he is an
Irishman, 'Mr. Martin' (perhaps originally 'Martyr') 'Dennis.'
More often he is nameless. Frequently the revival scene is
duplicated; either the Doctor is called in twice, or one cure
is left to him, and another is effected by some other performer, such as St. George (Dorset [B]), 'Father Christmas'
(Newbold, Steyning), or the Fool (Bampton).

The central action of the play consists, then, in these two
episodes of the fight and the resurrection; and the protagonists, so to speak, are the heroes—a ragged troop of heroes,
certainly—and the Doctor. But just as in the sword-dances,
so in the plays, we find introduced, besides the protagonists,
a number of supernumerary figures. The nature of these, and
the part they take, must now be considered. Some of them

are by this time familiar. They are none other than the grotesques that have haunted this discussion of the village festivals from the very beginning, and that I have attempted to trace to their origin in magical or sacrificial custom. There are the woman, or lad dressed in woman's clothes, the hobby-horse, the fool, and the black-faced man. The woman and the hobby-horse are unmistakable ; the other two are a little more Protean in their modern appearance. The 'Fool' is so called only at Manchester and at Brill, where he brings his morris-dance with him. At Lutterworth he is the 'Clown'; in Cornwall, 'Old Squire'; at Newbold, 'Big Head and Little Wits.' But I think that we may also recognize him in the very commonly occurring figure 'Beelzebub,' also known in Cornwall as 'Hub Bub' and at Chiswick as 'Lord Grubb.' The key to this identification is the fact that in several cases Beelzebub uses the description 'big head and little wit' to announce himself on his arrival. Occasionally, however, the personality of the Fool has been duplicated. At Lutterworth Beelzebub and the Clown, at Newbold Beelzebub and Big Head and Little Wits appear in the same play[1]. The black-faced man has in some cases lost his black face, but he keeps it at Bampton, where he is 'Tom the Tinker,' at Rugby, where he is 'Little Johnny Sweep,' and in a Sussex version, where he is also a sweep[2]. The analogy of the May-day chimney-sweeps is an obvious one. A black face was a feature in the mediaeval representation of devils, and the sweep of some plays is probably in origin identical with the devil, black-faced or not, of others. This is all the more so,

[1] Beelzebub appears also in the Cropwell Plough Monday play ; cf. p. 209. Doubtless he once wore a calf-skin, like other rural 'Fools,' but, as far as I know, this feature has dropped out. Sandys, 154, however, quotes 'Captain Calf-tail' as the name of the 'Fool' in an eighteenth-century Scotch version, and Mr. Gomme (*Nature*, Dec. 23, 1897), says 'some of the mummers, or maskers as the name implies, formerly disguised themselves as animals—goats, oxen, deer, foxes and horses being represented at different places where details of the mumming play have been recorded.' Nowadays, Beelzebub generally carries a club and a ladle or frying-pan, with which he makes the *quête*. At Newport and Eccleshall he has a bell fastened on his back ; at Newbold he has a black face. The 'Fool' figured in the Manchester chap-book resembles Punch.

[2] See notes to Steyning play in *F. L. J.* ii. 1.

as the devil, like the sweep, usually carries a besom [1]. One would expect *his* name, and not the Fool's, to be Beelzebub. He is, however, 'Little Devil Dout' or 'Doubt,' 'Little Jack Doubt' or 'Jack Devil Doubt.' At Leigh Little Devil Doubt also calls himself 'Jack,'

'With my wife and family on my back';

and perhaps we may therefore trace a further avatar of this same personage in the 'John' or 'Johnny Jack' who at Salisbury gives a name to the whole performance [2]. He is also 'Little Jack' (Brill, St. Mary Bourne), 'Fat Jack' (Islip), 'Happy Jack' (Berkshire, Hollington), 'Humpty Jack' (Newbold). He generally makes the remark about his wife and family. What he does carry upon his back is sometimes a hump, sometimes a number of rag-dolls. I take it that the hump came first, and that the dolls arose out of Jack's jocular explanation of his own deformity. But why the hump? Was it originally a bag of soot? Or the *saccus* with which the German *Knechte Ruperte* wander in the Twelve nights? [3] At Hollington and in a Hampshire version Jack has been somewhat incongruously turned into a press-gang. In this capacity he gets at Hollington the additional name of 'Tommy Twing-twang.'

Having got these grotesques, traditional accompaniments of the play, to dispose of somehow, what do the playwrights do with them? The simplest and most primitive method is just to bring them in, to show them to the spectators when the fighting is over. Thus Beelzebub, like the Fool at one point in the Revesby play, often comes in with

'Here come I ; ain't been yit,
Big head and little wit.'

'Ain't been yit!' Could a more naïve explanation of the presence of a 'stock' character on the stage be imagined?

---

[1] Mr. Gomme, in *Nature* for Dec. 23, 1897, finds in this broom 'the magic weapon of the witch' discussed by Pearson, ii. 29. Probably, however, it was introduced into the plays for the purposes of the *quête*; cf. p. 217. It is used also to make a circle for the players, but here it may have merely taken the place of a sword.

[2] Parish, *Dict. of Sussex Dialect*, 136. The mummers are called 'John Jacks.'

[3] Cf. p. 268, n. 4.

Similarly in Cornwall the woman is worked in by making 'Sabra,' a *persona muta*, come forward to join St. George[1]. In the play printed in *Sharpe's London Magazine* the 'Hobbyhorse' is led in. Obviously personages other than the traditional four can be introduced in the same way, at the bidding of the rustic fancy. Thus at Bampton 'Robin Hood' and 'Little John' briefly appear, in both the Irish plays and at Tenby 'Oliver Cromwell,' at Belfast 'St. Patrick,' at Steyning the 'Prince of Peace.'

Secondly, the supernumeraries may be utilized, either as presenters of the main characters or for the purposes of the *quête* at the end. Thus at Leigh the performance is begun by Little Devil Doubt, who enters with his broom and sweeps a 'room' or 'hall' for the actors, just as in the sword-dances a preliminary circle is made with a sword upon the ground[2]. In the Midlands this is the task of the woman, called at Islip and in Berkshire 'Molly,' and at Bright-Walton 'Queen Mary[3].' Elsewhere the business with the broom is omitted; but there is nearly always a short prologue in which an appeal is made to the spectators for 'room.' This prologue may be spoken, as at Manchester by the Fool, or as at Lutterworth by one of the fighters. The commonest presenter, however, is a personification of the festal season at which the plays are usually performed, 'Old Father Christmas.'

> 'Here comes I, Father Christmas, welcome or welcome not,
> I hope Old Father Christmas will never be forgot.'

At St. Mary Bourne Christmas is accompanied by 'Mince-Pie,' and in both the Dorset versions, instead of calling for 'room,' he introduces 'Room' as an actual personage. Similarly, at Newport and Eccleshall, the prologue speaker receives the curious soubriquet of 'Open-the-Door.' After the pro-

---

[1] Sandys, 301.

[2] Cf. Capulet, in *Romeo and Juliet*, i. 5. 28 'A hall, a hall! give room! and foot it, girls'; and Puck who precedes the dance of fairies in *Midsummer Night's Dream*, v. 1. 396 'I am sent with broom before,
To sweep the dust behind the door.'

[3] Ditchfield, 315. 'The play in this village is performed in most approved fashion, as the Rector has taken the matter in hand, coached the actors in their parts, and taught them some elocution.' This sort of thing, of course, is soon fatal to folk-drama.

logue, the fighters are introduced. They stand in a clump
outside the circle, and in turns step forward and strut round
it [1]. Each is announced, by himself or by his predecessor or
by the presenter, with a set of rhymes closely parallel to
those used in the sword-dances. With the fighters generally
comes the 'King of Egypt' (occasionally corrupted into the
'King of England'), and the description of St. George often
contains an allusion to his fight with the dragon and the
rescue of Sabra, the King of Egypt's daughter. In one or
two of the northern versions (Newcastle, Whitehaven) the
King of Egypt is a fighter; generally he stands by. In
one of the Dorset versions (A) he is called 'Anthony.'
Sabra appears only in Cornwall, and keeps silence. The
Dragon fights with St. George in Cornwall, and also, as we
have seen, in the curious Brill *mêlée*.

The performance, naturally, ends with a *quête*. This takes
various forms. Sometimes the presenter, or the whole body
of actors, comes forward, and wishes prosperity to the household. Beelzebub, with his frying-pan or ladle, goes round to
gather in the contributions. In the version preserved in
Sharpe's London Magazine, this is the function of a special
personage, 'Boxholder.' In a considerable number of cases,
however, the *quête* is preceded by a singular action on the
part of Little Devil Dout. He enters with his broom, and
threatens to sweep the whole party out, or 'into their graves,'
if money is not given. In Shropshire and Staffordshire he
sweeps up the hearth, and the custom is probably connected
with the superstition that it is unlucky to remove fire or
ashes from the house on Christmas Day. 'Dout' appears
to be a corruption of 'Do out [2].'

Another way of working in the grotesques and other supernumeraries is to give them minor parts in the drama itself.
Father Christmas or the King of Egypt is utilized as a sort

[1] Burne-Jackson, 484; Manly, i.
289.
[2] Burne-Jackson, 402, 410; *F. L.*
iv. 162; Dyer, 504. The broom is
used in Christmas and New Year
quêtes in Scotland and Yorkshire,
even when there is no drama.
Northall 205, gives a Lancashire
Christmas song, sung by 'Little
David Doubt' with black face, skin
coat and broom. At Bradford they
'sweep out the Old Year'; at
Wakefield they sweep up dirty
hearths. In these cases the notion
of threatening to do the unlucky
thing has gone.

of chorus, to cheer on the fighters, lament the vanquished, and summon the Doctor. At Newbold the woman, called 'Moll Finney,' plays a similar part, as mother of the Turkish Knight. At Stoke Gabriel, Devon, the woman is the Doctor's wife [1]. Finally, in three cases, a complete subordinate dramatic episode is introduced for their sake. At Islip, after the main drama is concluded, the presenter Molly suddenly becomes King George's wife 'Susannah.' She falls ill, and the Doctor's services are requisitioned to cure her. The Doctor rides in, not on a hobby-horse, but on one of the disengaged characters who plays the part of a horse. In Dorsetshire the secondary drama is quite elaborate. In the 'A' version 'Old Bet' calls herself 'Dame Dorothy,' and is the wife of Father Christmas, named, for the nonce, 'Jan.' They quarrel about a Jack hare, which he wants fried and she wants roasted. He kills her, and at the happy moment the Doctor is passing by, and brings her to life again. Version 'B' is very similar, except that the performance closes by Old Bet bringing in the hobby-horse for Father Christmas to mount.

I do not think that I need further labour the affiliation of the St. George plays to the sword-dances. Placed in a series, as I have placed them in these chapters, the two sets of performances show a sufficiently obvious continuity. They are held together by the use of the swords, by their common grotesques, and by the episode of the Doctor, which connects them also with the German Shrovetide and Whitsun folk-ceremonies. They are properly called folk-drama, because they are derived, with the minimum of literary intervention, from the dramatic tendencies latent in folk-festivals of a very primitive type. They are the outcome of the instinct of play, manipulating for its own purposes the mock sacrifice and other débris of extinct ritual. Their central incident symbolizes the *renouveau*, the annual death of the year or the fertilization spirit and its annual resurrection in spring [2]. To this

---

[1] Ditchfield, 12. An 'Old Bet' is mentioned in 5 *N. Q.* iv. 511, as belonging to a Belper version. The woman is worked in with various ingenuity, but several versions have lost her. The prologue to the New- castle chap-book promises a 'Dives' who never appears. Was this the woman? In the Linton in Craven sword-dance, she has the similar name of 'Miser.'

[2] I hardly like to trace a remi-

have become attached some of those heroic *cantilenae* which, as the early mediaeval chroniclers tell us, existed in the mouths of the *chori iuvenum* side by side with the *cantilenae* of the minstrels. The symbolism of the *renouveau* is preserved unmistakably enough in the episode of the Doctor, but the *cantilenae* have been to some extent modified by the comparatively late literary element, due perhaps to that universal go-between of literature and the folk, the village school-master. The genuine national heroes, a Stercatherus or a Galgacus, have given way to the 'worthies' and the 'champions of Christendom,' dear to Holophernes. The literary tradition has also perhaps contributed to the transformation of the *chorus* or semi-dramatic dance into drama pure and simple. In the St. George plays dancing holds a very subordinate place, far more so than in the 'Plow-boys' play of Revesby. Dances and songs are occasionally introduced before the *quête*, but rarely during the main performance. In the eccentric Brill version, however, a complete morris-dance appears. And of course it must be borne in mind that the fighting itself, with its gestures and pacings round the circle and clashing of swords, has much more the effect of a sword-dance than of a regular fight. So far as it is a fight, the question arises whether we ought to see in it, besides the heroic element introduced by the *cantilenae*, any trace of the mimic contest between winter and summer, which is found here and there, alternating with the resurrection drama, as

niscence of the connexion with the *renouveau* in the 'General Valentine' and 'Colonel Spring' who fight and are slain in the Dorset (A) version; but there the names are. Mr. Gomme (*Nature* for Dec. 23, 1897) finds in certain mumming costumes preserved in the Anthropological Museum at Cambridge and made of paper scales, a representation of leaves of trees. Mr. Ordish, I believe, finds in them the scales of the dragon (*F. L.* iv. 163). Some scepticism may be permitted as to these conjectures. In most places the dress represents little but rustic notions of the ornamental.

Cf. Thomas Hardy, *The Return of the Native*, bk. ii. ch. 3 : ' The girls could never be brought to respect tradition in designing and decorating the armour : they insisted on attaching loops and bows of silk and velvet in any situation pleasing to their taste. Gorget, gusset, bassinet, cuirass, gauntlet, sleeve, all alike in the view of these feminine eyes were practicable spaces whereon to sew scraps of fluttering colour.' The usual costume of the sword-dancers, as we have seen (p. 200), was a clean white smock, and probably that of the mummers is based upon this.

a symbolical representation of the *renouveau*. The fight does not, of course, in itself stand in any need of such an explanation; but it is suggested by a singular passage which in several versions is put in the mouth of one or other of the heroes. St. George, or the Slasher, or the Turkish Knight, is made to boast something as follows:

'My arms are made of iron, my body's made of steel,
  My head is made of beaten brass, no man can make me feel.'

It does not much matter who speaks these words in the versions of Holophernes, but there are those who think that they originally belonged to the representative of winter, and contained an allusion to the hardness of the frost-bound earth[1]. Personally I do not see why they should refer to anything but the armour which a champion might reasonably be supposed to wear.

A curious thing about the St. George play is the width of its range. All the versions, with the possible exception of that found at Brill, seem to be derived from a common type. They are spread over England, Wales, Scotland and Ireland, and only in the eastern counties do they give way to the partly, though not wholly, independent Plough Monday type. Unfortunately, the degeneracy of the texts is such that any closer investigation into their inter-relations or into the origin and transmission of the archetype would probably be futile. Something, however, must be said as to the prominence, at any rate outside Scotland, of the character of St. George. As far as I can see, the play owes nothing at all to John Kirke's stage-play of *The Seven Champions of Christendom*, printed in 1638[2]. It is possible, however, that it may be a development of a sword-dance in which, as in the Shetland dance, the 'seven champions' had usurped the place of more primitive heroes. If so the six champions, other than St. George, have

---

[1] T. F. Ordish, in *F. L.* iv. 158.

[2] Printed in *The Old English Drama* (1830), vol. iii. Burne-Jackson, 490, think that 'the masque owes something to the play,' but the resemblances they trace are infinitesimal. A play of *St. George for England*, by William or Wentworth Smith, was amongst the manuscripts destroyed by Warburton's cook, and a Bartholomew Fair 'droll' of *St. George and the Dragon* is alluded to in the *Theatre of Compliments*, 1688 (Fleay, *C. H.* ii. 251; Hazlitt, *Manual*, 201).

singularly vanished [1]. In any case, there can have been no
' seven champions,' either in sword-dance or mummers' play,
before Richard Johnson brought together the scattered legends
of the national heroes in his *History of the Seven Champions*
in 1596 [2]. This fact presents no difficulty, for the archetype
of our texts need certainly not be earlier than the seventeenth
century [3]. By this time the literary dramatic tradition was
fully established, even in the provinces, and it may well have
occurred to Holophernes to convert the sword-dance into the
semblance of a regular play.

On the other hand, the mediaeval period had its dramatic
or semi-dramatic performances in which St. George figured,
and possibly it is to these, and not to the ' seven champions,'
that his introduction into the sword-dance is due. These
performances generally took the form of a ' riding ' or proces-

[1] In the Dorset (A) version, the
king of Egypt is 'Anthony' and the
doctor ' Mr. Martin Dennis.' Conceivably these are reminiscences of
St. Anthony of Padua and St. Denys
of France. The Revesby Plough
Monday play (cf. p. 208) has also
an 'Anthony.' The ' Seven Champions ' do not appear in the English
sword-dances described in ch. ix, but
the morris-dancers at Edgemond
wake used to take that name (Burne-
Jackson, 491). Mrs. Nina Sharp
writes in *F. L. R.* iii. 1. 113 : 'I was
staying at Minety, near Malmesbury, in Wilts (my cousin is the
vicar), when the mummers came
round (1876). They went through
a dancing fight in two lines opposed
to each other—performed by the
Seven Champions of Christendom.
There was no St. George, and they
did not appear to have heard of the
Dragon. When I inquired for him,
they went through the performance
of drawing a tooth—the tooth produced, after great agony, being a
horse's. The mummers then carried
into the hall a bush gaily decorated
with coloured ribbons . . . [They]
were all in white smock frocks and
masks. At Acomb, near York, I
saw very similar mummers a few
years ago, but they distinguished

St. George, and the Dragon was a
prominent person. There was the
same tooth-drawing, and I think the
Dragon was the patient, and was
brought back to life by the operation.' I wonder whether the ' Seven
Champions ' were *named* or whether
Mrs. Sharp *inferred them*. Any-
how, there could not have been
seven at Minety, without St. George.
The ' bush' is an interesting feature. According to C. R. Smith,
Isle of Wight Words (*Eng.Dial.Soc.*
xxxii. 63) the mummers are known
in Kent as the ' Seven Champions.'

[2] Entered on the *Stationers' Registers* in 1596. The first extant
edition is dated 1597. Johnson first
introduced Sabra, princess of Egypt,
into the story; in the mediaeval
versions, the heroine is an unnamed
princess of Silena in Libya. The
mummers' play follows Johnson, and
makes it Egypt. On Johnson was
based Heylin's *History of St. George*
(1631 and 1633), and on one or both
of these Kirke's play.

[3] Jackson and Burne, 489: ' Miss
L. Toulmin Smith . . . considers
that the diction and composition of
the [Shropshire] piece, as we now
have it, date mainly from the seventeenth century.'

sion on St. George's day, April 23. Such ridings may, of
course, have originally, like the Godiva processions or the
midsummer shows, have preserved the memory of the pre-
Christian perambulations of the fields in spring, but during
the period for which records are available they were rather
municipal celebrations of a semi-ecclesiastical type. St. George
was the patron saint of England, and his day was honoured
as one of the greater feasts, notably at court, where the
chivalric order of the Garter was under his protection [1]. The
conduct of the ridings was generally, from the end of the
fourteenth century onwards, in the hands of a guild, founded
not as a trade guild, but as a half social, half religious fraternity,
for the worship of the saint, and the mutual aid and good
fellowship of its members. The fullest accounts preserved
are from Norwich, where the guild or company of St. George
was founded in 1385, received a charter from Henry V in 1416,
and by 1451 had obtained a predominant share in the government of the city [2]. The records of this guild throw a good
deal of light on the riding. The brethren and 'sustren' had
a chapel in the choir of the cathedral, and after the Reformation held their feasts in a chapel of the common hall of the
city, which had formerly been the church of a Dominican
convent. The riding was already established by 1408 when
the court of the guild ordered that 'the George shall go in
procession and make a conflict with the Dragon and keep his
estate both days.' The George was a man in 'coat armour
beaten with silver,' and had his club-bearer, henchmen, minstrels and banners. He was accompanied by the Dragon, the
guild-priest, and the court and brethren of the guild in red
and white capes and gowns. The procession went to 'the
wood' outside the city, and here doubtless the conflict with
the dragon took place. By 1537 there had been added to the

---

[1] Dyer, 193; Anstis, *Register of the Garter* (1724), ii. 38; E. Ashmole, *Hist. of the Garter* (ed. 1672), 188, 467; (ed. 1715), 130, 410.

[2] F. Blomefield, *Hist. of Norfolk* (1805), iv. 6, 347; Mackerell, MS. *Hist. of Norfolk* (1737), quoted in *Norfolk Archaeology*, iii. 315; *No-tices Illustrative of Municipal Pageants and Processions* (with plates, publ. C. Muskett, Norwich, 1850); Toulmin Smith, *English Gilds* (E. E. T. S.), 17, 443; Kelly, 48. Hudson and Tingey, *Cal. of Records of Norwich* (1898), calendar many documents of the guild.

dramatis personae St. Margaret, also called 'the lady,' who apparently aided St. George in his enterprise[1]. Strange to say, the guild survived the Reformation. In 1552, the court ordered, 'there shall be neither George nor Margaret, but for pastime the dragon to come and show himself, as in other years.' But the feast continued, and in spite of an attempt to get rid of him under the Long Parliament, the Dragon endured until 1732 when the guild was dissolved. Eighteenth-century witnesses describe the procession as it then existed. The Dragon was carried by a man concealed in its body. It was of basket work and painted cloth, and could move or spread its wings, and distend or contract its head. The ranks were kept by ' whifflers ' who juggled with their swords, and by ' Dick Fools,' in motley and decked with cats' tails and small bells. There is one more point of interest about the Norwich guild. In the fifteenth century it included many persons of distinction in Norfolk. Sir John Fastolf gave it an 'angell silver and guylt.' And amongst the members in 1496 was Sir John Paston. I have already quoted the lament in the *Paston Letters* over William Woode, the keeper, whom the writer 'kepyd thys iij yer to pleye Seynt Jorge and Robyn Hod and the Shryff off Nottyngham,' and who at a critical moment went off to Bernysdale and left his master in the lurch[2]. I have also identified his Robin Hood play, and now it becomes apparent where he played ' Seynt Jorge.' It is curious how the fragments of the wreckage of time fit into one another. The riding of the George is not peculiar to Norwich. We find it at Leicester[3], at Coventry[4], at Strat-

---

[1] Hartland, iii. 58, citing Jacobus à Voragine, *Legenda Aurea*, xciii, gives the story of St. Margaret, and the appearance of the devil to her in the shape of a dragon. She was in his mouth, but made the sign of the cross, and he burst asunder.

[2] Cf. p. 177.

[3] Kelly, 37. The 'dressyng of the dragon' appears in the town accounts for 1536. The guild had dropped the riding, even before the Reformation.

[4] Harris, 97, 190, 277 ; Kelly, 41. The guild was formed by journey-men in 1424. Probably there was a riding. In any case, at the visit of Prince Edward in 1474, there was a pageant or *mystère mimé* 'upon the Conddite in the Crosse Chepyng' of 'seint George armed and Kynges dought[r] knelyng afore hym w[t] a lambe and the fader and the moder beyng in a toure a boven beholdyng seint George savyng their dought[r] from the dragon.' There was a similar pageant at the visit of Prince Arthur in 1498.

ford[1], at Chester[2], at York, at Dublin[3]. An elaborate programme for the Dublin procession is preserved. It included an emperor and empress with their train, St. George on horseback, the dragon led by a line and the king and queen of·Dele. But no princess is mentioned. The 'may' or maiden figured at York, however, and there was also a St. Christopher. At other places, such as Reading, Aston[4] and Louth[5], an equestrian figure, called a 'George,' is known to have stood on a 'loft' in the church, and here, too, an annual 'riding' may be presumed.

There is no proof that the dramatic element in these 'ridings' was anything more than a *mystère mimé*, or pageant in dumb show. On the other hand, there were places where the performance on St. George's day took the form of a regular miracle-play. The performance described by Collier as taking place before Henry V and the Emperor Sigismund at Windsor in 1416 turns out on examination of Collier's authority to be really a 'soteltie,' a cake or raised pie of elaborate form. But the town of Lydd had its St. George play in 1456, and probably throughout the century; while in 1490 the chaplain of the guild of St. George at New Romney went to see this Lydd play with a view to reproducing it at the sister town. In 1511 again a play of St. George is recorded to have been held at Bassingbourne in Cambridgeshire, not on St. George's, but on St. Margaret's day[6].

Obviously the subject-matter of all these pageants and miracles was provided by the familiar ecclesiastical legend of

[1] Kelly, 42.

[2] Morris, 139, 168; Fenwick, *Hist. of Chester*, 372; Dyer, 195. The Fraternity of St. George was founded for the encouragement of shooting in 1537. They had a chapel with a George in the choir of St. Peter's. St. George's was the great day for races on the Rood-dee. In 1610 was a famous show, wherein St. George was attended by Fame, Mercury, and various allegorical figures.

[3] Cf. *Representations*, s. v. York, Dublin.

[4] Dyer, 194, gives from Coates,

Hist. of Reading, 221, the account for setting-up a 'George' in 1536. Dugdale, *Hist. of Warwickshire*, 928, has a notice of a legacy in 1526 by John Arden to Aston church of his 'white harneis ... for a George to were it, and to stand on his pewe, a place made for it.'

[5] R. W. Goulding, *Louth Records*, quotes from the churchwardens' accounts for 1538 payments for taking down the image of St. George and his horse.

[6] *Representations*, s. v. Windsor, Lydd, New Romney, Bassingbourne.

St. George the dragon-slayer, with which was occasionally interwoven the parallel legend of St. Margaret[1]. Similar performances can be traced on the continent. There was one at Mons called *le lumeçon*[2]. Rabelais describes one at Metz, of which, however, the hero was not St. George, but yet another dragon-slayer, St. Clement[3]. There is no need to ascribe to them a folk origin, although the dragon-slaying champion is a common personage in folk-tale[4]. They belong to the cycle of religious drama, which is dealt with in the second volume of this book. And although in Shropshire at least they seem to have been preserved in a village stage-

[1] For the legend, see *Acta Sanctorum, April*, iii. 101 ; Jacobus à Voragine, *Legenda Aurea* (1280), lviii ; E. A. W. Budge, *The Martyrdom and Miracles of St. George of Cappadocia: the Coptic Texts* (Oriental Text Series, 1888). In Rudder, *Hist. of Gloucestershire*, 461, and *Gloucester F. L.* 47, is printed an English version of the legend, apparently used for reading in church on the Sunday preceding St. George's day, April 23. Cf. also Gibbon (ed. Bury), ii. 472, 568 ; Hartland, *Perseus*, iii. 38 ; Baring-Gould, *Curious Myths of the Middle Ages*, 266 ; Zöckler, s.v. St. Georg, in Herzog and Plitt's *Encyclopedia*; F. Görres, *Ritter St. Georg in Geschichte, Legende und Kunst*, in *Zeitschrift für wissenschaftliche Theologie*, xxx (1887), 54 ; F. Vetter, *Introduction* to Reimbot von Durne's *Der heilige Georg* (1896). Gibbon identified St. George with the Arian bishop George of Cappadocia, and the dragon with Athanasius. This view has been recently revived with much learning by J. Friedrich in *Sitzb. Akad. Wiss. München (phil.-hist.Kl.)*, 1899, ii. 2. Pope Gelasius (†495) condemned the *Passio* as apocryphal and heretical, but he admits the historical existence of the saint, whose cult indeed was well established both in East and West in the fifth century. Budge tries to find an historical basis for him in a young man at Nicomedia who tore down an edict during the persecution of Diocletian (†303), and identifies his torturer Dadianus with the co-emperor Galerius.

[2] Du Méril, *La Com.* 98. He quotes Novidius, *Sacri Fasti* (ed. 1559), bk. vi. f. 48ᵛᵒ :
'perque annos duci monet [rex]
   in spectacula casum
unde datur multis annua
   scena locis.'
A fifteenth-century Augsburg miracle-play of St. George is printed by Keller, *Fastnachtsspiele*, No. 125 ; for other Continental data cf. Creizenach, i. 231, 246 ; Julleville, *Les Myst.* ii. 10, 644 ; D'Ancona, i. 104.

[3] Rabelais, *Gargantua*, iv. 59. The dragon was called Graoully, and snapped its jaws, like the Norwich 'snap-dragons' and the English hobby-horse.

[4] Cf. p. 138. The myth has attached itself to other undoubtedly historical persons besides St. George (Bury, *Gibbon*, ii. 569). In his case it is possibly due to a misunderstood bit of rhetoric. In the Coptic version of the legend edited by Budge (p. 223), Dadianus is called 'the dragon of the abyss.' There is no literal dragon in this version : the princess is perhaps represented by Alexandra, the wife of Dadianus, whom George converts. Cf. Hartland, *Perseus*, iii. 44.

play up to quite a recent date[1], they obviously do not directly survive in the folk-play with which we are concerned. As far as I know, that nowhere takes place on St. George's day. The Dragon is very rarely a character, and though St. George's traditional exploit is generally mentioned, it is, as that very mention shows, not the motive of the action. On the other hand the legend, in its mediaeval form, has no room for the episode of the Doctor[2]. At the same time the Dragon does sometimes occur, and the traditional exploit is mentioned, and therefore if any one chooses to say that the fame of St. George in the guild celebrations as well as the fame of the 'seven champions' romance determined his choice as the hero of the later sword-dance rhymes, I do not see that there is much to urge against the view[3].

With regard to the main drift of this chapter, the criticism presents itself; if the folk-plays are essentially a celebration of the *renouveau* of spring, how is it that the performances generally take place in mid-winter at Christmas? The answer is that, as will be shown in the next chapter, none of the Christmas folk-customs are proper to mid-winter. They have been attracted by the ecclesiastical feast from the seasons which in the old European calendar preceded and followed it, from the beginning of winter and the beginning of summer or spring. The folk-play has come with the rest. But the transference has not invariably taken place. The Norfolk versions belong not to Christmas but to Plough Monday, which lies immediately outside the Christmas season proper, and is indeed, though probably dislocated from its primitive date, the earliest of the spring feasts. The St. George play itself is occasionally performed at Easter, and even perhaps on May-day, whilst versions, which in their present form contain clear allusions to Christmas, yet betray another origin by the title which they bear of the 'Pace-eggers'' or 'Pasque-eggers''

---

[1] Cf. ch. xxiv, as to these plays.

[2] I ought perhaps to say that in one of the Coptic versions of the legend St. George is periodically slain and brought back to life by a miracle during the space of seven years. But I do not think that this episode occurs in any of the European versions of the legend.

[3] 'Sant George and the dragon' are introduced into a London May-game in 1559 (ch. viii).

play[1]. Christmas, however, has given to the play the characteristic figure of Old Father Christmas. And the players are known as 'mummers' and 'guisers,' or, in Cornwall, 'geese-dancers,' because their performance was regarded as a variety of the 'mumming' or 'disguising' which, as we shall see, became a regular name for the Christmas revel or *quête*[2].

[1] See the Manchester *Peace Egg* chap-book. At Manchester, Langdale, and, I believe, Coniston, the play is performed at Easter: cf. Halliwell, *Popular Rhymes*, 231. The Steyning play is believed to have been given at May-day as well as Christmas. Of course, so far as this goes, the transference might have been from Christmas, not to Christmas, but the German analogies point the other way. The Cheshire performance on All Souls' Day (Nov. 2), mentioned by Child, v. 291, is, so far as I know, exceptional.

[2] Cf. ch. xvii: In the Isle of Wight the performers are called the 'Christmas Boys' (C. R. Smith, *Isle of Wight Words*, in *E. D. S.* xxxii. 63). The terms 'Seven Champions' (Kent) and 'John Jacks' (Salisbury) have already been explained. The Steyning 'Tipteers' or 'Tipteerers' may be named from the 'tips' collected in the *quête*. The 'Guisers' of Staffordshire become on the Shropshire border 'Morris dancers,' 'Murry dancers,' or 'Merry-dancers'—a further proof of the essential identity of the morris- or sword-dance with the play.

CHAPTER XI

THE BEGINNING OF WINTER

[*Bibliographical Note.*—I have largely followed the conclusions of A. Tille, *Deutsche Weihnacht* (1893) and *Yule and Christmas* (1899). The Roman winter feasts are well treated by J. Marquardt and T. Mommsen, *Handbuch der römischen Alterthümer* (3rd ed. 1881-8), vol. vii; W. W. Fowler, *The Roman Festivals of the Period of the Republic* (1899); G. Wissowa, *Religion und Kultus der Römer* (1902); and the Christian feasts by L. Duchesne, *Origines du Culte chrétien* (2nd ed. 1898). On the history of Christmas, H. Usener, *Das Weihnachtsfest*, in *Religions-geschichtliche Untersuchungen*, vol. i (1889), and F. C. Conybeare's introduction to *The Key of Truth* (1898) should also be consulted. Much information on the Kalends customs is collected by M. Lipenius, *Strenarum Historia*, in J. G. Graevius, *Thesaurus Antiquitatum Romanarum* (1699), vol. xii. I have brought together a number of ecclesiastical references to the Kalends, from the third to the eleventh century, in Appendix N.]

SO far this study has concerned itself, on the one hand with the general character of the peasant festivals, on the other with the special history of such of these as fall within the summer cycle of the agricultural year, from ploughing to harvest. The remaining chapters will approach the corresponding festivals, centring around Christmas, of winter. These present a somewhat more difficult problem, partly because their elements are not quite so plainly agricultural, partly because of the remarkable dislocations which the development and clash of civilizations have brought about.

It must, I think, be taken as established that the Germano-Keltic tribes had no primitive mid-winter feast, corresponding directly to the modern Christmas[1]. They had no solstitial feast, for they knew nothing of the solstices. And although they had a winter feast of the dead, belonging rather to the domestic than to the elemental side of cult, this probably fell not at the middle, but at the beginning of the season. It was an aspect in the great feast with which not the winter only but the Germano-Keltic year began. This took place

[1] Tille, *Y. and C.* 78, 107; Rhys, *C. H.* 519 : cf. ch. v.

when the advance of snow and frost drove the warriors back
from foray and the cattle from the pastures. The scarcity of
fodder made the stall-feeding of the whole herd an im-
possibility, and there was therefore an economic reason for
a great slaughtering. This in its turn led to a great banquet
on the fresh meat, and to a great sacrifice, accompanied with
the usual perambulations, water-rites and fire-rites which
sacrifice to the deities of field and flock entailed[1]. The
vegetation spirit would again be abroad, no longer, as in
spring or summer, in the form of flowers and fresh green
boughs, but in that of the last sheaf or 'kern-baby' saved
from harvest, or in that of such evergreens or rarer blossoms
as might chance to brave the snows. The particular 'intention' of the festival would be to secure the bounty of the
divine powers for the coming year, and a natural superstition
would find omens for the whole period in the events of the
initial day. The feast, however, would be domestic, as well
as seasonal. The fire on the hearth was made 'new,' and
beside it the fathers, resting from the toils of war, or herding
or tillage, held jollification with their children. Nor were
the dead forgotten. *Minni* were drunk in honour of ancestors and ancestral deities; and a share of the banquet was
laid out for such of these as might be expected, in the whirl
of the wintry storm, to revisit the familiar house-place.

Originally, no doubt, the time of the feast was determined
by the actual closing of the war-ways and the pastures. Just
as the first violet or some migratory bird of March was
hailed for the herald of summer, so the first fall of snow gave
the signal that winter was at hand[2]. In the continental home
of the Germano-Keltic tribes amongst the forests of central
Europe this would take place with some regularity about the
middle of November[3]. A fixed date for the feast could only
arise when, at some undefined time, the first calendar, the
'three-score-day-tide' calendar of unknown origin, was intro-

---

[1] Tille, *Y. and C.* 18; *D. W.* 6.
Bede, *D. T. R.* 15, gives Blot-monath
as the Anglo-Saxon name for November, and explains it as 'mensis
immolationum, quia in ea pecora
quae occisuri erant, Diis suis vove-
rent.'

[2] Burton, 15, notes a tradition at
Disley, in Cheshire, that the local
wake was formerly held after the
first fall of snow.

[3] Tille, *Y. and C.* 18.

duced [1]. Probably it was thenceforward held regularly upon a day corresponding to either November the 11th or the 12th in our reckoning. If it is accurately represented by St. Martin's day, it was the 11th [2], if by the Manx *Samhain*, the 12th [3]. It continued to begin the year, and also the first of the six tides into which that year was divided. As good fortune will have it, the name of that tide is preserved to us in the Gothic term *Iuleis* for November and December [4], in the Anglo-Saxon *Giuli* or *Geola* which, according to Bede, applied both to December and to January [5], and in *Yule*, the popular designation, both in England and Scandinavia, of Christmas itself [6]. The meaning of this name is, however, more doubtful. The older philology, with solstices running in its brain, supposed that it applied primarily to a mid-winter feast, and connected it with the Anglo-Saxon *hwéol*, a wheel [7]. Bede himself, learned in Roman lore, seems to hint at such an explanation [8]. The current modern explanation derives the

[1] Mogk, iii. 391; Tille, *Y. and C.* 24, find the winter feast in the festival of Tanfana which the Marsi were celebrating when Germanicus attacked them in A.D. 14 (Tacitus, *Ann.* i. 51). Winter, though imminent, had not yet actually set in, but this might be the case in any year after the festival had come to be determined by a fixed calendar.

[2] Tille, *Y. and C.* 57.

[3] Rhys, *C. H.* 513, says that the *Samhain* fell on Nov. 1. The preceding night was known as *Nos Galan-geaf*, the 'night of winter calends,' and that following as *Dy' gwyl y Meirw*, 'the feast of the Dead.' In *F. L.* ii. 308 he gives the date of the Manx *Samhain* as Nov. 12, and explains this as being Nov. 1, O. S. But is it not really the original date of the feast which has been shifted elsewhere to the beginning of the month?

[4] Tille, *Y. and C.* 12, citing M. Heyne, *Ulfilas*, 226: 'In a Gothic *calendarium* of the sixth century November, or *Naubaímbaír*, is called *fruma Iuleis*, which presupposes that December was called **aftuma Iuleis*.'

[5] Bede, *de temp. rat.* c. 15. Tille, *Y. and C.* 20, points out that the application of the old tide-name to fit November and December by the Goths and December and January by the Anglo-Saxons is fair evidence for the belief that the tide itself corresponded to a period from mid-November to mid-January.

[6] Tille, *Y. and C.* 147. The terms *gehhol, geóhel, geól, giúl, iúl,* &c. signify the Christmas festival season from the ninth century onwards, and from the eleventh also Christmas Day itself. The fifteenth-century forms are *Yule, Ywle, Yole, Yowle*. In the A.-S. Chronicle the terms used for Christmas are 'midewinter,' 'Cristes mæssa,' 'Cristes tyde,' 'Natiuitedh.' As a single word 'Cristesmesse' appears first in 1131 (Tille, *Y. and C.* 159). The German 'Weihnacht' (M. H. G. *wich*, 'holy') appears † 1000 (Tille, *D. W.* 22).

[7] Pfannenschmidt, 238, 512.

[8] The notion is of a circular course of the sun, passing through the four turning- or wheeling-points of the solstices and equinoxes. Cf. ch. vi for the use of the wheel as a solar symbol.

word from a supposed Germanic *jehwela*, equivalent to the Latin *ioculus*[1]. It would thus mean simply a 'feast' or 'rejoicing,' and some support seems to be lent to this derivation by the occasional use of the English '*yule*' and the Keltic *gwyl* to denote feasts other than that of winter[2]. Other good authorities, however, prefer to trace it to a Germanic root *jeula-* from which is derived the Old Norse *él*, 'a snowstorm'; and this also, so far as its application to the feast and tide of winter is concerned, seems plausible enough[3]. It is possible that to the winter feast originally belonged the term applied by Bede to December 24 of *Modranicht* or *Modraneht*[4]. It would be tempting to interpret this as 'the night which gives birth to the year'; but philologists say that it can only mean 'night of mothers,' and we must therefore explain it as due to some cult of the *Matres* or triad of mother-goddesses, which took place at the feast[5].

[1] Mogk, iii. 391, quoting Kluge, *Englische Studien*, ix. 311, and Bugge, *Ark. f. nord. Filolog.* iv. 135. Tille, *Y. and C.* 8, 148, desirous to establish an Oriental origin for the Three Score Day tides, doubts the equation **jehwela = ioculus*, and suggests a connexion between the Teutonic terms and the old Cypriote names ἰλαῖος, ἰουλαῖος, ἰουλῖνος, ἰούλιος for the period Dec. 22 to Jan. 23 (K. F. Hermann, *Über griech. Monatskunde*, 64), and, more hesitatingly, with the Greek Ἴουλος or hymn to Ceres. Weinhold, *Deutsche Monatsnamen*, 4; *Deutsche Jahrteilung*, 15, thinks that both the Teutonic and Cypriote names are the Roman *Julius* transferred from mid-summer to mid-winter. Northall, 208, makes *yule = ol, oel*, a feast or 'ale,' for which I suppose there is nothing to be said. Skeat, *Etym. Dict.* s.v., makes it 'a time of revelry,' and connects with M.E. *youlen, yollen*, to 'yawl' or 'yell,' and with A.-S. *gýlan*, Dutch *joelen*, to make merry, G. *jolen, jodeln*, to sing out. He thus gets in a different way much the sense given in the text.

[2] At a Cotswold Whitsun ale a lord and lady 'of yule' were chosen (*Gloucester F. L.* 56). Rhys, *C. H.*

412, 421, 515, and in *F. L.* ii. 305, gives *Gwyl* as a Welsh term for 'feast' in general, and in particular mentions, besides the *Gwyl y Meirw* at the *Samhain*, the *Gwyl Aust* (Aug. 1, Lammas or Lugnassad Day). This also appears in Latin as the *Gula Augusti* (Ducange, s.v. temp. Edw. III), and in English as 'the Gule of August' (Hearne, *Robert of Gloucester's Chron.* 679). Tille, *Y. and C.* 56, declares that *Gula* here is only a mutilation of *Vincula*, Aug. 1 being in the ecclesiastical calendar the feast of St. Peter *ad Vincula*.

[3] Kluge and Lutz, *English Etymology*, s.v. Yule.

[4] Bede, *D. T. R.* c. 15 'ipsam noctem nobis sacrosanctam, tunc gentili vocabulo *Modranicht* [v.l. *Modraneht*], id est, matrum noctem appellabant; ob causam ut suspicamur ceremoniarum, quas in ea pervigiles agebant.'

[5] Mogk, iii. 391. Tille, *Y. and C.* 152, gives some earlier explanations, criticizes that of Mogk, and offers as his own a reference to a custom of baking a cake (*placenta*) to represent the physical motherhood of the Virgin. The practice doubtless existed and was con-

The subsequent history of the winter feast consists in its gradual dislocation from the original mid-November position, and dispersion over a large number of dates covering roughly the whole period between Michaelmas and Twelfth night. For this process a variety of causes are responsible. Some of these are economic. As civilization progressed, mid-November came to be, less than of old, a signal turning-point in the year. In certain districts to which the Germano-Keltic tribes penetrated, in Gaul, for instance, or in Britain with its insular climate, the winter tarried, and the regular central European closing of the pastures was no longer a law. Then again tillage came gradually to equal or outstrip pasturage in importance, and the year of tillage closed, even in Germany, at the end of September rather than in mid-November. The harvest feast began to throw the winter feast rather into the shade as a wind-up of the year's agricultural labours. This same development of tillage, together with the more scientific management of pasturage itself, did more. It provided a supply of fodder for the cattle, and by making stall-feeding possible put off further and further into the winter the necessity of the great annual slaughter. The importance in Germany, side by side with St. Martin's day (November 11), of St. Andrew's day (November 30), and still more St. Nicholas' day (December 6)[1], as folk-feasts, seems to suggest a consequent tendency to a gradual shifting of the winter festival.

These economic causes came gradually into operation throughout a number of centuries. In displacing the November feast, they prepared the way for and assisted the action of one still more important. This was the influence of Roman usage. When the Germano-Keltic tribes first came into

demned by Pope Hormisdas (514–23), by the Lateran Council of 649, the Council of Hatfield (680), and the Trullan Council (692). But Bede must have known this as a Christian abuse, and he is quite plainly speaking of a pre-Christian custom. J. M. Neale, *Essays in Liturgiology* (1867), 511, says, ' In most Celtic languages Christmas eve is called the night of Mary,' the Virgin, here as elsewhere, taking over the cult of the mother-goddesses.

[1] Tille, *Y. and C.* 65. In his earlier book *D. W.* 7, 29, Dr. Tille held the view that there had always been a second winter feast about three weeks after the first, when the males held over for breeding were slain.

contact with the Roman world, the beginning of the Roman year was still, nominally at least, upon the Kalends, or first of March. This did not, so far as I know, leave any traces upon the practice of the barbarians[1]. In 45 B.C. the Julian calendar replaced the Kalends of March by those of January. During the century and a half that followed, Gaul became largely and Britain partially Romanized, while there was a steady infiltration of Roman customs and ideas amongst the German tribes about and even far beyond the Rhine. With other elements of the southern civilization came the Roman calendar which largely replaced the older Germanic calendar of three-score-day-tides. The old winter festival fell in the middle of a Roman month, and a tendency set in to transfer the whole or a part of its customs either to the beginning of this month[2] or, more usually, to the beginning of the Roman year, a month and a half later. This process was doubtless helped by the fact that the Roman New Year customs were not in their origin, or even at the period of contact, essentially different from those of their more northerly cousins. It remained, of course, a partial and incomplete one. In Gaul, where the Roman influence was strongest, it probably reached its maximum. But in Germany the days of St. Martin[3] and St. Nicholas[4] have fully maintained their position as folk-feasts by the side of New Year's day, and even Christmas itself; while St. Martin's day at least has never been quite forgotten in our islands[5]. The state of transition is represented by the

[1] According to Bede, *D. T. R.* c. 15, the Anglo-Saxons had adopted the system of intercalary months which belongs to the pre-Julian and not the Julian Roman calendar. But Bede's chapter is full of confusions: cf. Tille, *Y. and C.* 145.

[2] All Saints' day or Hallowmas (November 1) and All Souls' day (November 2) have largely, though not wholly, absorbed the November feast of the Dead.

[3] Pfannenschmidt, 203; Jahn, 229; Tille, *Y. and C.* 21, 28, 36, 42, 57; *D. W.* 23.

[4] Tille, *D. W.* 29; Müller, 239, 248. According to Tille, *D. W.* 63,

Christmas only replaced the days of St. Martin and St. Nicholas as a German children's festival in the sixteenth century.

[5] Tille, *Y. and C.* 34, 65; Pfannenschmidt, 206; Dyer, 418; N. Drake, *Shakespeare and his Times* (1838), 93. Martinmas was a favourite Anglo-Saxon and mediaeval legal term. It survived also as a traditional 'tyme of slaughter' for cattle. 'Martlemas beef' was a common term for salt beef. In Scotland a Mart is a fat cow or bullock, but the derivation of this appears to be from a Celtic word *Mart* = cow.

isolated Keltic district known as the Isle of Man. Here, according to Professor Rhys, the old *Samhain* or Hollan-tide day of November 12 is still regarded by many of the inhabitants as the beginning of the year. Others accept January 1; and there is considerable division of opinion as to which is the day whereon the traditional New Year observances should properly be held [1].

A final factor in the dislocation of the winter feast was the introduction of Christianity, and in especial the establishment of the great ecclesiastical celebration of Christmas. When Christianity first began to claim the allegiance of the Roman world, the rulers of the Church were confronted by a series of southern winter feasts which together made the latter half of December and the beginning of January into one continuous carnival. The nature and position of these feasts claim a brief attention.

To begin with, there were the feasts of the Sun. The *Bruma* (*brevissima*) or *Brumalia* was held on November 24, as the day which ushered in the period of the year during which the sun's light is diminished. This seems to have been a beginning of winter feast, adopted by Rome from Thrace [2]. The term *bruma* was also sometimes applied to the whole period between November 24 and the solstice, and ultimately even to the solstitial day itself, fixed somewhat incorrectly by the Julian calendar on December 25 [3]. On this day also came a festival, which probably owed its origin to the Emperor Aurelian (270–75), whose mother was a semi-Oriental priestess of the Sun, in one of his Syrian forms as Baal or Belus [4], and who instituted an official cult of this divinity at Rome with a temple on the Quirinal, a *collegium* of *pontifices*, and *ludi circenses* held every fourth year [5]. These fell on the day of the solstice, which from the lengthening of the sun's

---

[1] Rhys, in *F. L.* ii. 308.

[2] Mommsen, *C. I. L.* i². 287; Pauly-Wissowa, *Real-Encycl.* s. v. *Bruma*; Tomaschek, in *Sitzb.Akad. Wiss. Wien*, lx (1869), 358.

[3] Ovid, *Fasti*, i. 163 'bruma novi prima est veterisque novissima solis.'

[4] Cf. p. 112.

[5] Preller, ii. 408; P. Allard, *Julien l'Apostat*, i. 16; J. Réville, *La Religion à Rome sous les Sévères* (1885); Wissowa, 306. An earlier cult of the same type introduced by Elagabalus did not survive its founder.

course was known as the 'birthday' of *Sol Novus* or *Sol Invictus*[1]. This cult was practised by Diocletian and by Constantine before his conversion, and was the rallying-point of Julian in his reaction against Christianity[2]. Moreover, the *Sol Invictus* was identified with the central figure of that curious half-Oriental, half-philosophical worship of Mithra, which at one time threatened to become a serious rival to Christianity as the religion of the thinking portion of the Roman world[3]. That an important Mithraic feast also fell on December 25 can hardly be doubted, although there is no direct evidence of the fact[4].

The cult of the *Sol Invictus* was not a part of the ancient Roman religion, and, like the *Brumalia*, the solstitial festival in his honour, however important to the educated and official classes of the empire, was not a folk-festival. It lay, however, exactly between two such festivals. The *Saturnalia* imme-

[1] The earliest reference is probably that in the calendar of the Greek astronomer, of uncertain date, Antiochus, Ἡλίου γενέθλιον· αὔξει φῶς (Cumont, i. 342, from *Cod. Monac. gr.* 287, f. 132). The *Fasti* of Furius Dionysius Philocalus (A.D. 354) have VIII. KAL. IAN. N[atalis] INVICTI C[ircenses] M[issus] XXX' (*C. I. L.* i². 278, 338). Cf. Julian, *Orat.* 4 (p. 156 ed. Spanheim) εὐθέως μετὰ τὸν τελευταῖον τοῦ Κρόνου μῆνα ποιοῦμεν ἡλίῳ τὸν περιφανέστατον ἀγῶνα, τὴν ἑορτὴν Ἡλίῳ καταφημίσαντες Ἀνικήτῳ ; Corippus, *de laud. Iust. min.* i. 314 'Solis honore novi grati spectacula circi'; cf. the Christian references on p. 242. Mommsen's *Scriptor Syrus* quoted *C. I. L.* i². 338 tells us that lights were used ; 'accenderunt lumina festivitatis causa.'

[2] Preller, ii. 410; Gibbon, ii. 446.

[3] On Mithraicism, cf. F. Cumont, *Textes et Monuments relatifs aux Mystères de Mithra* (1896-9) ; also the art. by the same writer in Roscher's *Lexicon*, ii. 3028, and A. Gasquet, *Le Culte de Mithra* (*Revue des Deux Mondes* for April 1, 1899) ; J. Réville, *La Religion à Rome sous les Sévères*, 77; Wis-

sowa, 307; Preller, ii. 410; A. Gardner, *Julian the Apostate*, 175; P. Allard, *Julien l'Apostat*, i. 18 ; ii. 232 ; G. Zippel, *Le Taurobolium*, in *Festschrift f. L. Friedländer* (1895), 498. Mithra was originally a form of the Aryan Sun-god, who though subordinated in the Mazdean system to Ahoura Mazda continued to be worshipped by the Persian folk. His cult made its appearance in Rome about 70 B.C., and was developed during the third and fourth centuries A.D. under philosophic influences. Mithra was regarded as the fount of all life, and the yearly obscuration of the sun's forces in winter became a hint and promise of immortality to his worshippers : cf. *Carm. adv. paganos*, 47 'qui hibernum docuit sub terra quaerere solem.' Mithraic votive stones have been found in all parts of the empire, Britain included. They are inscribed ' Soli Invicto,' ' Deo Soli Invicto Mithrae,' ' Numini Invicto Soli Mithrae,' and the like.

[4] Cumont, *Textes et Mon.* i. 325 ; ii. 66, and in Roscher's *Lexicon*, ii. 3065; Lichtenberger, *Encycl. des Sciences religieuses*, s. v. Mithra.

diately preceded it; a few days later followed the January *Kalends*.

The *Saturnalia*, so far as the religious feast of Saturn was concerned, took place on December 17. Augustus, however, added two days to the *feriae iudiciariae*, during which the law-courts were shut, and popular usage extended the festival to seven. Amongst the customs practised was that of the *sigillariorum celebritas*, a kind of fair, at which the *sigillaria*, little clay dolls or *oscilla*, were bought and given as presents. Originally, perhaps, these *oscilla* were like some of our feasten cakes, figures of dough. Candles (*cerei* or *candelae*) appear also to have been given. On the second and third days it was customary to bathe in the early morning [1]. But the chief characteristic of the feast was the licence allowed to the lower classes, to freedmen and to slaves. During the *libertas Decembris* both moral and social restraints were thrown off [2]. Masters made merry with their servants, and consented for the time to be on a footing of strict equality with them [3]. A *rex Saturnalitius*, chosen by lot, led the revels, and was entitled to claim obedience for the most ludicrous commands [4].

[1] Preller, *R. M.* ii. 15; Mommsen, in *C. I. L.* i². 337; Marquardt and Mommsen, *Handbuch der römischen Alterthümer*, vi. 562; *Dict. of Cl. A.* s.v. Saturnalia; Tille, *Y. and C.* 85; Frazer, iii. 138; W. W. Fowler, 268; C. Dezobry, *Rome au Siècle d'Auguste* (ed. 4, 1875), iii. 140.

[2] Horace, *Satires*, ii. 7. 4:
'age, libertate Decembri,
quando ita maiores voluerunt,
    utere; narra.'

[3] The democratic character of the feast is brought out in the νόμοι put by Lucian (Luc. *Opp.* ed. Jacobitz, iii. 307; *Saturnalia*, p. 393) in the mouth of the divinely instructed νομοθέτης, Chronosolon, and in the 'Letters of Saturn' that follow.

[4] According to Tacitus, *Ann.* xiii. 15, Nero was king of the Saturnalia at the time of the murder of Britannicus. On the nature of this sovereignty, cf. Arrian, *Epictetus*, i. 25; Martial, xi. 6:

'unctis falciferi senis diebus,
regnator quibus imperat fritillus.'

Lucian, *Saturnalia*, p. 385, introduces a dialogue between Saturn and his priests. Saturn says ἑπτὰ μὲν ἡμερῶν ἡ πᾶσα βασιλεία, καὶ ἢν ἐκπρόθεσμος τούτων γένωμαι, ἰδιώτης εὐθύς εἰμι, καὶ τοῦ πολλοῦ δήμου εἷς· ἐν αὐταῖς δὲ ταῖς ἑπτὰ σπουδαῖον μὲν οὐδὲν οὐδὲ ἀγοραῖον διοικήσασθαί μοι συγκεχώρηται, πίνειν δὲ καὶ μεθύειν καὶ βοᾶν καὶ παίζειν καὶ κυβεύειν καὶ ἄρχοντας καθίσταναι καὶ τοὺς οἰκέτας εὐωχεῖν καὶ γυμνὸν ᾄδειν καὶ κροτεῖν ὑποτρέμοντα, ἐνίοτε δὲ καὶ ἐς ὕδωρ ψυχρὸν ἐπὶ κεφαλὴν ὠθεῖσθαι ἀσβόλῳ κεχρισμένον τὸ πρόσωπον, ταῦτα ἐφεῖταί μοι ποιεῖν; and again: εὐωχώμεθα δὲ ἤδη καὶ κροτῶμεν καὶ ἐπὶ τῇ ἑορτῇ ἐλευθεριάζωμεν, εἶτα πεττεύωμεν ἐς τὸ ἀρχαῖον ἐπὶ καρύων καὶ βασιλέας χειροτονῶμεν καὶ πειθαρχῶμεν αὐτοῖς· οὕτω γὰρ ἂν τὴν παροιμίαν ἐπαληθεύσαιμι, ἥ φησι, παλίμπαιδας τοὺς γέροντας γίγνεσθαι. The ducking is curiously suggestive of

The similarity of the *Saturnalia* to the folk-feasts of western Europe will be at once apparent. The name *Saturnus* seems to point to a ploughing and sowing festival, although how such a festival came to be held in mid-December must be matter of conjecture [1]. The *Kalends*, on the other hand, are clearly a New Year festival. They began on January 1, with the solemn induction of the new consuls into office. As in the case of the *Saturnalia*, the *feriae* lasted for more than one day, covering at least a *triduum*. The third day was the day of *vota* or solemn wishes of prosperity for the New Year to the emperor. The houses were decked with lights and greenery, and once more the masters drank and played dice with their slaves. The resemblance in this respect between the *Kalends* and the *Saturnalia* was recognized by a myth which told how when Saturn came bringing the gifts of civilization to Italy he was hospitably received by Janus, who then reigned in the land [2]. Another Kalends custom, the knowledge of which we owe to the denunciations of the Fathers, was the parading of the city by bands of revellers

western festival customs, but I do not feel sure whether it was the image of Saturn that was ducked or the *rex* with whom he appears to half, and only half, identify himself. Frazer, iii. 140, lays stress on the primitive sacrificial character of the 'rex,' who is said still to have been annually slain in Lower Moesia at the beginning of the fourth century A.D.; cf. *Acta S. Dasii*, in *Acta Bollandiana*, xvi. (1897), 5; Parmentier et Cumont, *Le Roi des Saturnales*, in *R. de Philologie*, xxi (1897), 143.

[1] Frazer, iii. 144, suggests that the *Saturnalia* may once have been in February, and have left a trace of themselves in the similar festival of the female slaves, the *Matronalia*, on March 1, which, like the winter feasts, came in for Christian censure; cf. Appendix N. No. (i).

[2] Preller, *R. M.* i. 64, 178; ii. 13; C. Dezobry, *Rome au Siècle d'Auguste* (ed. 4, 1875), ii. 169; Mommsen and Marquardt, vi. 545;

vii. 245; Roscher, *Lexicon*, ii. 37; W. W. Fowler, 278; Tille, *Y. and C.* 84; M. Lipenius, *Strenarum Historia* in J. G. Graevius, *Thesaurus Antiq. Rom.* (1699), xii. 409. The last-named treatise contains a quantity of information set out with some obsolete learning. The most important contemporary account is that of Libanius (314–†95) in his εἰς τὰς καλάνδας and his καλανδῶν ἔκφρασις (ed. Reiske, i. 256; iv. 1053; cf. Sievers, *Das Leben der Libanius*, 170, 204). In the former speech he says ταύτην τὴν ἑορτὴν εὕροι τ' ἂν τεταμένην ἐφ' ἅπαν, ὅσον ἡ Ῥωμαίων ἀρχὴ τέταται, in the latter, μίαν δὲ οἶδα κοινὴν ἁπάντων ὁπόσοι ζῶσιν ὑπὸ τὴν Ῥωμαίων ἀρχήν. Under the emperors, who made much of the *strenae* and *vota*, the importance of the Kalends grew, probably at the expense of the Saturnalia; cf. Macrobius, *Saturnalia*, i. 2. 1 'adsunt feriae quas indulget magna pars mensis Iano dicati.'

dressed in women's clothes or in the skins of animals. And, finally, a series of superstitious observances testified to the belief that the events of the first day of the year were ominous for those of the year itself. A table loaded all night long with viands was to ensure abundance of food ; such necessaries of life as iron and fire must not be given or lent out of the house, lest the future supply of them should fail. To this order of ideas belonged, ultimately at least, if not originally, the central feature of the whole feast, the *strenae* or presents so freely exchanged between all classes of society on the Kalends. Once, so tradition had it, the *strenae* were nothing more than twigs plucked from the grove of the goddess Strenia, associated with Janus in the feast [1] ; but in imperial times men gave honeyed things, that the year of the recipient might be full of sweetness, lamps that it might be full of light, copper and silver and gold that wealth might flow in amain [2].

Naturally, the Fathers were not slow to protest against these feasts, and, in particular, against the participation in them of professing Christians. Tertullian is, as usual, explicit and emphatic in his condemnation [3]. The position was aggravated when, probably in the fourth century, the Christian feast of the Birthday of Christ came to be fixed upon December 25, in the very heart of the pagan rejoicings and upon the actual day hitherto sacred to *Sol Invictus*. The origin of Christmas is wrapped in some obscurity [4]. The earliest notices of a

---

[1] Preller, i. 180; Mommsen and Marquardt, vi. 14; vii. 245 ; W.W. Fowler, 278; Tille, *Y. and C.* 84, 104. *Strenia* was interpreted in the sense of 'strenuous'; cf. Symmachus, *Epist.* x. 15 'ab exortu paene urbis Martiae strenarum usus adolevit auctore Tatio rege, qui verbenas felicis arboris ex luco Streniae anni novi auspices primus accepit. . . . Nomen indicio est viris strenuis haec convenire virtute.' Preller calls Strenia a Sabine *Segensgöttin.*

[2] Mommsen and Marquardt, vii. 245; Lipenius, 489. The gifts were often inscribed 'anno novo faustum felix tibi.' It is probable

that the sweet cakes and the lamps like the *verbenae* had originally a closer connexion with the rites of the feast than of mere omens. The emperors expected liberal *strenae*, and from them the custom passed into mediaeval and Renaissance courts. Queen Elizabeth received sumptuous new year gifts from her subjects. For a money payment the later empire used the term καλανδικόν or *kalendaticum*. *Strenae* survives in the French *étrennes* (Müller, 150, 504).

[3] Appendix N, Nos. (i), (ii).

[4] The most recent authorities are Tille, *Y. and C.* 119; H. Usener, *Religionsgeschichtliche Untersuch-*

celebration of the birth of Christ in the eastern Church attach it to that of his baptism on the Epiphany. This feast is as old as the second century. By the fourth it was widespread in the East, and was known also in Gaul and probably in northern Italy [1]. At Rome it cannot be traced so early; but it was generally adopted there by the beginning of the fifth, and Augustine blames the Donatists for rejecting it, and so cutting themselves off from fellowship with the East [2]. Christmas, on the other hand, made its appearance first at Rome, and the East only gradually and somewhat grudgingly accepted it. The Paulician Christians of Armenia to this day continue to feast the birth and the baptism together on January 6, and to regard the normal Christian practice as heretical. An exact date for the establishment of the Roman feast cannot be given, for the theory which ascribed it to Pope Liberius in 353 has been shown to be baseless [3]. But it appears from a document of 336 that the beginning of the liturgical year then already fell between December 8 and

---

ungen, i, *Das Weihnachtsfest* (1889); L. Duchesne, *Origines du Culte chrétien* (ed. 2, 1898), 247, and in *Bulletin critique* (1890), 41; F. C. Conybeare, *The History of Christmas,* in *American Journal of Theology* (1899), iii. 1, and *Introduction* to *The Key of Truth* (1898); F. Cumont, *Textes et Monuments mithraïques,* i (1899), 342, 355. I have not been able to see an article praised by Mr. Conybeare, in P. de Lagarde, *Mittheilungen* (1890), iv. 241.

[1] Conybeare, *Am. J. Th.* iii. 7, cites, without giving exact references, two 'north Italian homilies' of the fourth century, which seem to show this.

[2] *Sermo* ccii (*P. L.* xxxviii. 1033).

[3] The *depositio martyrum,* attached to the *Fasti* of Philocalus drawn up in 354, opens with the entry 'viii kl. ianu. natus Christus in Bethleem Iudeae.' December 25 was therefore kept as the birthday at least as early as 353. Usener, i. 267, argued that the change must have taken place in this very year, because Liberius, while veiling Mar-

cellina, the sister of St. Ambrose, on the Epiphany, spoke of the day as 'natalem Sponsi tui' (*de Virginibus,* iii. 1, in *P. L.* xvi. 219). But it is not proved either that this event took place in 363, or that it was on Epiphany rather than Christmas day. Liberius refers to the Marriage at Cana and the Feeding of the Five Thousand. But the first allusion is directly led up to by the *sponsalia* of Marcellina, and both events, although at a later date commemorated at Epiphany, may have belonged to Christmas at Rome, before Epiphany made its appearance (Duchesne, *Bulletin critique* (1890), 41). Usener adds that Liberius built the *Basilica Liberii,* also known as *Sta. Maria ad Praesepe* or *Sta. Maria Maggiore,* which is still a great station for the Christmas ceremonies, in honour of the new feast. But Duchesne shows that the dedication to St. Mary only dates from a rebuilding in the fifth century, that the *praesepe* cannot be traced there before the seventh, and that the original Christmas *statio* was at St. Peter's.

27[1]. Christmas may, therefore, be assumed to have been in existence at least by 336.

It would seem, then, that the fourth century witnessed the establishment, both at Rome and elsewhere, of Christmas and Epiphany as two distinct feasts, whereas only one, although probably not everywhere the same one, had been known before. This fact is hardly to be explained by a mere attempt to accommodate varying local uses. The tradition of the Armenian doctors, who stood out against Christmas, asserts that their opponents removed the birthday of Christ from January 6 out of 'disobedience[2].' This points to a doctrinal reason for the separate celebration of the birth and the baptism. And such a reason may perhaps be found in the Adoptionist controversies. The joint feast appeared to lend credence to the view, considered a heresy, but still adhered to by the Armenian Church, that Christ was God, not from his mother's womb, but only from his adoption or spiritual birth at the baptism in Jordan. It was needful that orthodox Christians should celebrate him as divine from the very moment of his carnal birth[3].

The choice of December 25 as the day for the Roman feast cannot be supposed to rest upon any authentic tradition as to the historic date of the Nativity. It is one of several early

---

[1] Duchesne, *Bulletin critique* (1890), 44. This document also belongs to the collection of Philocalus.

[2] Conybeare, *Key of Truth*, cliiclvii, quoting an Armenian bishop Hippolytus in *Bodl. Armen. Marsh* 467, f. 338 [a], 'as many as were disobedient have divided the two feasts.' According to the *Catechism of the Syrian Doctors* in the same MS., Sahak asked Afrem why the churches feast Dec. 25: the teacher replied, 'The Roman world does so from idolatry, because of the worship of the Sun. And on the 25th of Dec., which is the first of Qanûn; when the day made a beginning out of the darkness they feasted the Sun with great joy, and declared that day to be the nuptials [? 'natals,' but cf. p. 241, n. 1] of the Sun. However, when the Son of God was born of the Virgin, they celebrated the same feast, although they had turned from their idols to God. And when their bishops (*or* primates) saw this, they proceeded to take the Feast of the Birth of Christ, which was on the sixth of January, and placed it there (viz. on Dec. 25). And they abrogated the feast of the Sun, because it (the Sun) was nothing, as we said before.' Mommsen, *C. I. L.* i[2]. 338, quotes to the same effect another *Scriptor Syrus* (in Assemanus, *Bibl. Orient.* ii. 164) : cf. p. 235. The early apologists (Tertullian, *Apol.* 16; *ad Nationes*, i. 13; Origen, *contra Celsum*, viii. 67) defend Christianity against pagan charges of Sun-worship.

[3] Conybeare, *J. Am. Th.* iii. 8.

patristic guesses on the subject. It is not at all improbable that it was determined by an attempt to adopt some of the principal Christian festivals to the solstices and equinoxes of the Roman calendar[1]. The enemies of Roman orthodoxy were not slow to assert that it merely continued under another name the pagan celebration of the birthday of *Sol Invictus*[2]. Nor was the suggestion entirely an empty one.

[1] Most of these dates were in the spring (Duchesne, 247). As late as †243 the Pseudo-Cyprianic *de Pascha computus* gives March 28. On the other hand, December 25 is given early in the third century by Hippolytus, *Comm. super Danielem*, iv. 23 (p. 243, ed. Bonwetsch, 1897), although the text has been suspected of interpolation (Hilgenfeld, in *Berlin. phil. Wochenschrift*, 1897, p. 1324, s.). Ananias of Shirak (†600–50), *Hom. de Nat.* (transl. in *Expositor*, Nov. 1890), says that the followers of Cerinthus first separated the birth and baptism: cf. Conybeare, *Key of Truth*, cliv. This is further explained by Paul of Taron (ob. 1123), *adv. Theopistum*, 222 (quoted Conybeare, clvi), who says that Artemon calculated the dates of the Annunciation as March 25 and the Birth as December 25, 'the birth, not however of the Divine Being, but only of the mere man.' Both Cerinthus (end of 1st cent.) and Artemon (†202–17) appear to have held Adoptionist tenets: cf. Schaff, iv. 465, 574. Paul adds that Artemon calculated the dates from those for the conception and nativity of John the Baptist. This implies that St. John Baptist's day was already June 24 by †200. It was traditional on that day by St. Augustine's time, 'Hoc maiorum traditione suscepimus' (*Sermo* ccxcii. 1, in Migne, *P. L.* xxxviii. 1320). The six months' interval between the two nativities may be inferred from *St. Luke* i. 26. St. Augustine refers to the symbolism of their relation to each other, and quotes with regard to their position on the solstices the words ascribed to the Baptist in *St. John* iii. 30 'illum oportet crescere, me autem minui' (*Sermo* cxciv. 2; cclxxxvii. 3; cclxxxviii. 5; Migne, *P. L.* xxxviii. 1016, 1302, 1306). Duchesne, 250, conjectures that the varying dates of West (Dec. 25) and East (Jan. 6) depended on a similar variation in the date assigned to the Passion, it being assumed in each case that the life of Christ must have been a complete circle, and that therefore he must have died on the anniversary of his conception in the womb. Thus St. Augustine (*in Heptat.* ii. 90) upbraids the Jews, 'non coques agnum in lacte matris suae.' March 25 was widely accepted for the Passion from Tertullian onwards, and certain Montanists held to the date of April 6. Astronomy makes it impossible that March 25 can be historically correct, and therefore the whole calculation, if Duchesne is right, probably started from an arbitrary identification of a Christian date with the spring equinox, just as, if Ananias of Shirak is right, it started from a similar identification of another such date with the summer solstice. But it seems just as likely that the birth was fixed first, and the Annunciation and St. John Baptist's day calculated back from that. If the Passion had been the starting-point, would not the feast of Christmas, as distinct from the traditional date for the event, have become a movable one?

[2] The Armenian criticism just quoted only re-echoes that put by St. Augustine in the mouth of the Manichaeans in *Contra Faustum*, xx. 4 (*Corp. Script. Eccl.* xxv) 'Faustus dixit . . . solemnes gentium

The worshippers of *Sol Invictus,* and in particular the Mithraic sect, were not quite on the level of the ordinary pagans by tradition. Mithraism had claims to be a serious and reasonable rival to Christianity, and if its adherents could be induced by argument to merge their worship of the physical sun in that of the 'Sun of Righteousness,' they were well worth winning [1]. On the other hand there were obvious dangers in the Roman policy which were not wholly averted, and we find Leo the Great condemning certain superstitious customs amongst his flock which it is difficult to distinguish from the sun-worship practised alike by pagans and by Saint Augustine's heretical opponents, the Manichaeans [2].

dies cum ipsis celebratis ut Kalendas et solstitia.' Augustine answers other criticisms of the same order in the course of the book, but he does not take up this one.

[1] Augustine, in his sermons, uses a solar symbolism in two ways, besides drawing the parallel with St. John already quoted. Christ is *lux e tenebris*: 'quoniam ipsa infidelitas quae totum mundum vice noctis obtexerat, minuenda fuerat fide crescente; ideo die Natalis Domini nostri Iesu Christi, et nox incipit perpeti detrimenta, et dies sumere augmenta' (*Sermo* i in *P. L.* xxxviii. 1007). He is also *sponsus procedens de thalamo suo* (*Sermo* cxcii. 3; cxcv. 3, in *P. L.* xxxviii. 1013, 1018). Following this Caesarius or another calls Christmas the *dies nuptialis Christi,* on which ' sponsae suae Ecclesiae adiunctus est' (*Serm. Pseudo-Aug.* cxvi. 2, in *P. L.* xxxix. 1975). Cumont, i. 355, gives other examples of *Le Soleil Symbole du Christ* from an early date, and especially of the use of the phrase *Sol Iustitiae* from *Malachi,* iv. 2.

[2] Pseudo-Chrysostom (Italian, 4th cent.), *de solstitiis et aequinoctiis* (*Op.* Chrys. ed. 1588, ii. 118) 'Sed et dominus nascitur mense Decembri, hiemis tempore, viii kal. Ianuarias . . . Sed et invicti natalem appellant. Quis uti-

que tam invictus nisi dominus noster qui Mortem subactam devicit? vel quod dicant Solis esse natalem, ipse est Sol iustitiae de quo Malachias propheta dixit'; St. Augustine, *Sermo* cxc. 1 (*P. L.* xxxviii. 1007) 'habeamus, igitur, fratres, solemnem istum diem; non sicut infideles propter hunc solem, sed propter eum qui fecit hunc solem'; *Tract. in Iohann.* xxxiv. 2 (*P. L.* xxxv. 1652) 'numquid forte Dominus Christus est Sol iste qui ortu et occasu peragit diem? Non enim defuerunt heretici qui ita senserunt . . . (c. 4) ne quis carnaliter sapiens solem istum intelligendum putaret'; Pseudo-Ambrose (perhaps Maximus of Turin, †412–65), *Sermo* vi. (*P. L.* xvii. 614) 'bene quodammodo sanctum hunc diem natalis Domini solem novum vulgus appellat . . . quod libenter nobis amplectendum est; quia oriente Salvatore non solum humani generis salus, sed etiam solis ipsius claritas innovatur'; Leo Magnus, *Sermo* xxii, *in Nativ. Dom.* (*P. L.* liv. 198) 'Ne idem ille tentator, cuius iam a vobis dominationem Christus exclusit, aliquibus vos iterum seducat insidiis, et haec ipsa praesentis diei gaudia suae fallaciae arte corrumpat, illudens simplicioribus animis de quorumdam persuasione pestifera, quibus haec dies solemnitatis nostrae

From Rome the Christmas feast gradually made its way over East and West. It does not seem to have reached Jerusalem until at least the sixth century, and, as we have seen, the outlying Church of Armenia never adopted it. But it was established at Antioch about 375 and at Alexandria about 430 [1]. At Constantinople an edict of 400 included it in the list of holy days upon which *ludi* must not be held [2]. In 506 the council of Agatha recognized the Nativity as one of the great days of the Christian year [3], while fasting on that day was forbidden by the council of Braga in 561 as savouring of Priscillianist heresy [4]. The feast of the Epiphany, meanwhile, was relegated to a secondary place; but it was not forgotten, and served as a celebration, in addition to the baptism, of a number of events in the life of Christ, which included the marriage at Cana and the feeding of the five

non tam de nativitate Christi quam de novi, ut dicunt, solis ortu honorabilis videatur'; *Sermo* xxvii, *in Nat. Dom.* (*P. L.* liv. 218) 'De talibus institutis etiam illa generatur impietas ut sol in inchoatione diurnae lucis exsurgens a quibusdam insipientioribus de locis eminentioribus adoretur; quod nonnulli etiam Christiani adeo se religiose facere putant, ut priusquam ad B. Petri apostoli basilicam, quae uni Deo vivo et vero est dedicata, perveniant, superatis gradibus quibus ad suggestum areae superioris ascenditur, converso corpore ad nascentem se solem reflectant, et curvatis cervicibus, in honorem se splendidi orbis inclinent. Quod fieri partim ignorantiae vitio, partim paganitatis spiritu, multum tabescimus et dolemus.' Eusebius, *Sermo* xxii. περὶ ἀστρονόμων (*P. G.* lxxxvi. 453), also refers to the adoration of the sun by professing Christians. The 'tentator' of Leo and the 'heretici' of Augustine are probably Manichaeus and his followers, against whose sun-worship Augustine argues at length in *Contra Faustum*, xx (*Corp. Script. Eccl.* xxv).

[1] Duchesne, 248.
[2] Cf. p. 14.

[3] *C. Agathense*, c. 21 (Mansi, viii. 328) 'Pascha vero, natale domini, epiphania, ascensionem domini, pentecostem, et natalem S. Ioannis Baptistae, vel si qui maximi dies in festivitatibus habentur, non nisi in civitatibus aut in parochiis teneant.'
[4] *Conc. Bracarense* († 560), Prop. 4 (Mansi, ix. 775) 'Si quis natalem Christi secundum carnem non bene honorat, sed honorare se simulat, ieiunans in eodem die, et in dominico; quia Christum in vera hominis natura natum esse non credit, sicut Cerdon, Marcion, Manichaeus, et Priscillianus, anathema sit.' A similar prohibition is given by Gregory II († 725), *Capitulare*, c. 10 (*P. L.* lxxxix. 534). To failings in the opposite direction the Church was more tender: cf. *Penitentiale Theodori* (Haddan and Stubbs, iii. 177), *de Crapula et Ebrietate* 'Si vero pro infirmitate aut quia longo tempore se abstinuerit, et in consuetudine non erit ei multum bibere vel manducare, aut pro gaudio in Natale Domini aut in Pascha aut pro alicuius Sanctorum commemoratione faciebat, et tunc plus non accipit quam decretum est a senioribus, nihil nocet. Si episcopus iuberit, non nocet illi, nisi ipse similiter faciat.'

thousand, and of which the visit of the *Magi* gradually
became the leading feature. The *Dodecahemeron*, or period
of twelve days, linking together Christmas and Epiphany,
was already known to Ephraim Syrus as a festal tide at the
end of the fourth century[1], and was declared to be such by
the council of Tours in 567[2].

To these islands Christmas came, if not with the Keltic
Church, at least with St. Augustine in 592. On Christmas
day, 598, more than ten thousand English converts were
baptized[3], and by the time of Bede (†734) Christmas was
established, with Epiphany and Easter, as one of the three
leading festivals of the year[4]. The *Laws* of Ethelred (991–
1016) and of Edward the Confessor ordain it a holy tide of
peace and concord[5]. Continental Germany received it from
the synod of Mainz in 813[6], while Norway owed it to King
Hakon the Good in the middle of the tenth century[7].

Side by side with the establishment of Christmas proceeded the ecclesiastical denunciation of those pagan festivals
whose place it was to take. Little is heard in Christian
times of the *Saturnalia*, which do not seem to have shared
the popularity of the Kalends outside the limits of Rome
itself. But these latter, and especially the Kalends, are the
subject of attack in every corner of the empire. Jerome of
Rome, Ambrose of Milan, Maximus of Turin, Chrysologus
of Ravenna, assail them in Italy; Augustine in Africa;
Chrysostom and Asterius and the Trullan council in the
East. In Spain, Bishop Pacian of Barcelona made a treatise
upon one of the most objectionable features of the festival
which, as he says with some humour, probably tended to
increase its vogue. In Gaul, Caesarius of Arles initiated
a vigorous campaign. To cite all the ecclesiastical pro-

[1] Tille, *Y. and C.* 122.
[2] Cf. Appendix N, No. xxii.
[3] *Epist. Gregorii ad Eulogium* (Haddan and Stubbs, iii. 12).
[4] *Epist. Bedae ad Egbertum* (Haddan and Stubbs, iii. 323).
[5] *Leges Ethelredi* (Thorpe, *Ancient Laws*, i. 309) 'Ordâl and âdhar sindon tocweden . . . fram Adventum Domini odh octavas Epiphanie. . . . And beo tham hâl-gum tîdan eal swa hit riht is, eallum cristenum mannum sib and sôm gemæne, and ælc sacu getwæmed.' Cf. *Leges Edwardi* (Thorpe, i. 443).
[6] *C. Moguntiacum*, c. 36 (Mansi, xiv. 73) 'In natali Domini dies quatuor, octavas Domini, epiphaniam Domini.'
[7] Tille, *Y. and C.* 203.

nouncements on the subject would be tedious. Homily followed homily, canon followed canon, capitulary followed capitulary, penitential followed penitential, for half a thousand years. But the Kalends died hard. When Boniface was tackling them amongst the Franks in the middle of the eighth century, he was sorely hampered by the bad example of their continued prevalence at the very gates of the Vatican; and when Burchardus was making his collection of heathen observances in the eleventh century, those of the Kalends were still to be included. In England there is not much heard of them, but a reference in the so-called *Penitential of Egbert* about 766 proves that they were not unknown. It need hardly be said that all formal religious celebration of the Kalends disappeared with the official victory of Christianity. But this element had never been of great importance in the feast; and the terms in which the ecclesiastical references from beginning to end are couched prove that they relate mainly to popular New Year customs common to the Germanic and the more completely Latinized populations [1].

It appears from a decree of the council of Tours in 567 that, *ad calcandam Gentilium consuetudinem*, the fourth-century Fathers established on the first three days of January a *triduum ieiunii*, with litanies, in spite of the fact that these days fell in the very midst of the festal period of the *Dodecahemeron* [2]. At the same time January 1 was kept as the octave of Christmas, and the early Roman ritual-books show two masses for that day, one *in octavis Domini*, the other *ad prohibendum ab idolis*. The Jewish custom by which circumcision took place eight days after birth made it almost inevitable that there should be some celebration of the circumcision of Christ upon the octave of his Nativity. This was the case from the sixth century, and ultimately, about the eighth, the attempt to keep up a fast on January 1 was surrendered, and the festival of the Circumcision took its place [3].

Some tendency was shown by the Church not merely to

---

[1] Cf. the collection of prohibitions in Appendix N.
[2] *C. of Tours*, c. 18 (Appendix N, No. xxii).
[3] R. Sinker, in *D. C. A.* s.v. Circumcision.

set up Christmas as a rival to the pagan winter feasts, but also to substitute it for the Kalends of January as the beginning of the year. But the innovation never affected the civil year, and was not maintained even by ecclesiastical writers with any consistency, for even they prefer in many cases a year dating from the Annunciation, or more rarely from Easter. The so-called Annunciation style found favour even for many civil purposes in Great Britain, and was not finally abandoned until 1753[1]. But although Christmas cannot be said to have ever become a popular New Year's day, yet its festal importance and its propinquity to January 1 naturally led to a result undesired and possibly undreamt of by its founders, namely, the further transference to it of many of the long-suffering Germano-Keltic folk-customs, which had already travelled under Roman influence from the middle of November to the beginning of January[2]. Already in the sixth century it had become necessary to forbid the abuses which had gathered around the celebration of Christmas eve[3]; and the Christmas customs of to-day, even where their name does not testify to their original connexion with the Kalends[4], are in a large number of

---

[1] On this difficult subject see Tille, *Y. and C.* 134; H. Grotefend, *Taschenbuch der Zeitrechnung* (1898), 11; F. Ruhl, *Chronologie des Mittelalters und der Neuzeit* (1897), 23; C. Plummer, *Anglo-Saxon Chronicle*, ii. cxxix; R. L. Poole, in *Eng. Hist. Review* (1901), 719.

[2] The position of Christmas would have made it natural that it should attract observances from the spring festivals also, and, in fact, it did attract the Mummers' play: cf. p. 226. It cannot of course be positively said whether the Epiphany fires and some of the other agricultural rites to be presently mentioned (ch. xii) came from the November or the ploughing festival.

[3] *C. of Auxerre* (573-603), c. 11 (Appendix N. No. xxv).

[4] In the south of France Christmas is *Chalendes*, in Provence *Calendas* or *Calenos*. The log is *calignau*, *chalendau*, *chalendal*, *calignaon*, or *culenos*, and the peasants sang round it 'Calène vient' (Tille, *D. W.* 286; Müller, 475, 478). Thiers, i. 264, speaks of 'le pain de Calende.' Christmas songs used to be known in Silesia as *Kolende-lieder* (Tille, *D. W.* 287). The Lithuanian term for Christmas is *Kalledos* and the Czechic *Koleda* (Polish *Kolenda*, Russian *Koljada*). A verb *colendisare* appears as a Bohemian law term (Tille, *Y. and C.* 84); while in the fourteenth century the Christmas *quête* at Prague was known as the *Koledasammeln* (Tille, *D. W.* 112). The Bohemian Christmas procession described by Alsso (cf. ch. xii) was called *Calendizatio*, and according to tradition St Adalbert (tenth century) transferred it from the Kalends to Christmas, and called it *colendizatio 'a colendo.'*

cases, so far of course as they are not simply ecclesiastical, merely doublets of those of the New Year.

What is true of Christmas is true also of Epiphany or Twelfth night ; and the history of the other modern festivals of the winter cycle is closely parallel. The old Germanic New Year's day on November 11 became the day of St. Martin, a fourth-century bishop of Tours, and the *pervigiliae* of St. Martin, like those of the Nativity itself, already caused a scandal in the sixth century[1]. The observances of the deferred days of slaughter clustered round the feasts of St. Andrew on November 30, and more especially St. Nicholas on December 6. The *Todtenfest*, which had strayed to the beginning of November, was continued in the feasts of All Saints or Hallowmas, the French *Toussaint*, on November 1, and its charitable supplement of All Souls, on November 2. That which had strayed still further to the time of harvest became the *Gemeinwoche* or week-wake, and ultimately St. Michael and All Angels. Nor is this all. Very similar customs attached themselves to the minor feasts of the *Dodecahemeron*, St. Stephen's, St. John the Evangelist's, Innocents' days, to the numerous dedication wakes that fell on days, such as St. Luke's[2], in autumn or early winter, or to the miscellaneous feasts closely approaching the Christmas season, St. Clement's, St. Catherine's, St. Thomas's, with which indeed in many localities that season is popularly supposed to begin[3]. Nor was this process sensibly affected by the establishment in the sixth century of the *ieiunium* known as Advent, which stretched for a *Quadragesima*, or period

[1] *C. of Auxerre* (573–603), c. 5 (Appendix N, No. xxv). Pfannenschmidt, 498, has collected a number of notices of *Martinalia* from the tenth century onwards.

[2] Pfannenschmidt, 279; Dyer, 386, describe the 'Horn Fair' at Charlton, Kent, on St. Luke's Day, Oct. 18. A king and queen were chosen, who went in procession to the church, wearing horns. The visitors wore masks or women's clothes, and played practical jokes with water. Rams' horns were sold at the fair, which lasted three days,

and the gilt on the gingerbread took the same shape. It will be remembered that the symbol of St. Luke in Christian art is a horned ox.

[3] Cf. p. 114. According to Spence, 196, the Shetland Christmas begins on St. Thomas's Day and ends on Jan. 18, known as 'Four and Twenty Day.' Candlemas (Feb. 2) is also often regarded as the end of the Christmas season. The Anglo-Saxon Christmas feast lasted to the Octave of Epiphany (Tille, *Y and C.* 165).

of forty days, from Martinmas onwards. And finally, just as in May village dipping customs attached themselves in the seventeenth century to Royal Oak day, so in the same century we find the winter festival fires turned to new account in the celebration of the escape of King and Parliament from the nefarious machinations of Guy Fawkes.

CHAPTER XII

NEW YEAR CUSTOMS

[*Bibliographical Note.*—The two works of Dr. Tille remain of importance. The compilations specially devoted to the usages of the Christmas season are chiefly of a popular character; W. Sandys, *Christmas Tide* (n.d.), J. Ashton, *A Righte Merrie Christmasse!!!*(n. d.), and, for French data, E. Müller, *Le Jour de l'An* (n. d.), may be mentioned; H. Usener, *Religionsgeschichtliche Untersuchungen*, vol. ii (1889), prints various documents, including the *Largum Sero* of a Bohemian priest named Alsso, on early fifteenth-century Christmas eve customs. Most of the books named in the bibliographical note to chap. v also cover the subject. A *Bibliography of Christmas* runs through *Notes and Queries*, 6th series, vi. 506, viii. 491, x. 492, xii. 489; 7th series, ii. 502, iii. 152, iv. 502, vi. 483, x. 502, xii. 483; 8th series, ii. 505, iv. 502, vi. 483, viii. 483, x. 512, xii. 502; 9th series, ii. 505, iv. 515, vi. 485.]

IT is the outcome of the last chapter that all the folk-customs of the winter half of the year, from Michaelmas to Plough Monday, must be regarded as the flotsam and jetsam of a single original feast. This was a New Year's feast, held by the Germano-Keltic tribes at the beginning of the central European winter when the first snows fell about the middle of November, and subsequently dislocated and dispersed by the successive clash of Germano-Keltic civilization with the rival schemes of Rome and of Christianity. A brief summary of the customs in question will show clearly their common character. For purposes of classification they may be divided into several groups. There are such customs belonging to the agricultural side of the old winter feast as have not been transferred with the growing importance of tillage to the feast of harvest. There are the customs of its domestic side, as a feast of the family hearth and of the dead ancestors. There are the distinctively New Year customs of omen and prognostication for the approaching twelve months. There are the customs of play, common more or less to all the village festivals. And, finally, there are a small number of customs, or perhaps it would be truer to say legends, which

appear to owe their origin not merely to heathenism transformed by Christianity, but to Christianity itself. Each of
these groups may well claim a more thoroughgoing consideration than can here be given to any one of them.

The agricultural customs are just those of the summer
feasts over again. Once more the fertilization spirit is
abroad in the land. The embodiment of it in vegetation
takes several forms. Obviously the last foliage and burgeoning flowers of spring and summer are no longer available. But there is, to begin with, the sheaf of corn or
'harvest-May' in which the spirit appeared at harvest, and
which is called upon once more to play its part in the winter
rites. This, however, is not a very marked part. A Yorkshire custom of hanging a sheaf on the church door at
Christmas is of dubious origin[1]. But Swedish and Danish
peasants use the grain of the 'last sheaf' to bake the
Christmas cake, and both in Scandinavia and Germany the
'Yule straw' serves various superstitious purposes. It is
scattered on barren fields to make them productive. It is
strewed, instead of rushes, upon the house floor and the
church floor. It is laid in the mangers of the cattle. Fruit-
trees are tied together with straw ropes, that they may bear
well and are said to be 'married[2].'

More naturally the fertilization spirit may be discerned at
the approach of winter in such exceptional forms of vegetation as endure the season. In November the apples and the
nuts still hang upon their boughs, and these are traditional
features in the winter celebrations. Then there are the
evergreens. Libanius, Tertullian, and Chrysostom tell how
on the Kalends the doors of houses throughout the Roman
empire were crowned with bay. Martin of Braga forbade
the 'pagan observance' in a degree which found its way into
the canon law. The original *strena* which men gave one
another on the same day for luck was nothing but a twig
plucked from a sacred grove; and still in the fifth century men

[1] Dyer, 451; Ashton, 118, where
the custom is said to have been
'started by the Rev. J. Kenworthy,
Rector of Ackworth, in Yorkshire,
... for the special benefit of the
birds.'

[2] Frazer, i. 177, ii. 172, 286;
Grimm, iv. 1783; Tille, *D. W.* 50,
178; Alsso, in Usener, ii. 61, 65.

returned from their new year auguries laden with *ramusculi* that they might thereafter be laden with wealth[1]. It is not necessary to dwell upon the surviving use of evergreens in the decoration at Christmas of houses and churches[2]. The sacredness of these is reflected in the taboo which enjoins that they shall not be cast out upon the dust-heap, but shall, when some appropriate day, such as Candlemas, arrives, be solemnly committed to the flames[3]. Obviously amongst other evergreens the holly and the ivy, with their clustering pseudo-blossoms of coral and of jet, are the more adequate representatives of the fertilization spirit[4]; most of all the mistletoe, perched an alien visitant, faintly green and white, amongst the bared branches of apple or of oak. The mistletoe has its especial place in Scandinavian myth[5]: Pliny records the ritual use of it by the Druids[6]; it is essential to the winter revels in their amorous aspect; and its vanished dignities still serve, here to bar it from, there to make it imperative in, the edifices of Christian worship[7]. A more artificial embodiment of the fertilization spirit is the 'Christmas tree'

[1] Lipenius, 423; cf. Appendix N, Nos. i, vi, xiii, xxiv.

[2] Tille, *Y. and C.* 103, 174; Philpot, 164; Jackson and Burne, 397; Dyer, 457; Stow, *Survey of London* (ed. 1618), 149 'Against the feast of Christmas, euery mans house, as also their parish Churches, were decked with Holm, Iuy, Bayes, and whatsoever the season of the yeere aforded to be greene. The Conduits and Standards in the streetes were, likewise, garnished.' He gives an example from 1444.

[3] Burne-Jackson, 245, 397, 411; Ashton, 95. Customs vary: here the evergreens must be burnt; there given to the cattle. They should not touch the ground (Grimm, iii. 1207). With this taboo compare that described by ancient writers, probably on the authority of Posidonius, as existing in a cult of a god identified with Dionysus amongst the Namnites on the west coast of Gaul. A temple on an island was unroofed and reroofed by the priestesses annually. Did

one of them drop her materials on the ground, she was torn to pieces by her companions (Rhys, *C. H.* 196). They are replaced on Candlemas by snowdrops, or, according to Herrick, 'the greener box.' In Shropshire a garland made of blackthorn is left hanging from New Year to New Year, and then burnt in a festival fire (*F. L.* x. 489; xii. 349).

[4] The Christmas rivalry between holly and ivy is the subject of carols, some dating from the fifteenth century; cf. Ashton, 92; Burne-Jackson, 245.

[5] Grimm, iii. 1205.

[6] Pliny, *Nat. Hist.* xxi. 95.

[7] Ashton, 81, 92; Ditchfield, 18; Brand, i. 285; Dyer, 458; Philpot, 164. Mistletoe is the chief ingredient of the 'kissing-bunch,' sometimes a very elaborate affair, with apples and dolls hung in it. The ecclesiastical taboo is not universal; in York Minster, e.g., mistletoe was laid on the altar.

par excellence, adorned with lights and apples, and often with a doll or image upon the topmost sprig. The first recorded Christmas tree is at Strassburg in 1604. The custom is familiar enough in modern England, but there can be little doubt that here it is of recent introduction, and came in, in fact, with the Hanoverians [1].

Finally, there can be little wonder that the popular imagination found a special manifestation of the fertilization spirit in the unusual blossoming of particular trees or species of trees in the depths of winter. In mild seasons a crab or cherry might well adorn the old winter feast in November. A favourable climate permits such a thing even at mid-winter. Legend, at any rate, has no doubt of the matter, and connects the event definitely with Christmas. A tenth-century Arabian geographer relates how all the trees of the forest stand in full bloom on the holy night. In the thirteenth-century *Vita* of St. Hadwigis the story is told of a cherry-tree. A fifteenth-century bishop of Bamberg tells it of two apple-trees, and to apple-trees the miracle belongs, in German folk-belief, to this day [2]. In England the stories of Christmas-flowering hawthorns or blackthorns are specific and probably not altogether baseless [3]. The belief found a

[1] Tille, *Y. and C.* 174; *D. W.* 256, and in *F. L.* iii. 166; Philpot, 164; Ashton, 189; Kempe, *Loseley MSS.* 75. The earliest English mention is in 1789.

[2] Tille, *Y. and C.* 170.

[3] Ibid. 172; Ashton, 105, quoting Aubrey, *Natural Hist. of Wilts*, 'Mr. Anthony Hinton, one of the officers of the Earle of Pembroke, did inoculate, not long before the late civill warres (ten yeares or more), a bud of Glastonbury Thorne, on a thorne, at his farm house, at Wilton, which blossoms at Christmas, as the other did. My mother has had branches of them for a flower-pott, several Christmasses, which I have seen. Elias Ashmole, Esq., in his notes upon *Theatrum Chymicum*, saies that in the churchyard at Glastonbury grew a walnutt tree, that did putt out young leaves at Christmas, as doth the King's Oake in the New Forest. In Parham Park, in Suffolk (Mr. Boutele's), is a pretty ancient thorne, that blossomes like that at Glastonbury; the people flock hither to see it on Christmas day. But in the rode that leades from Worcester to Droitwiche is a black thorne hedge at Clayes, half a mile long or more, that blossoms about Christmas-day for a week or more together. Dr. Ezerel Tong sayd that about Rumly-Marsh in Kent, are thornes naturally like that near Glastonbury. The Soldiers did cutt downe that near Glastonbury: the stump remaines.' Specimens are still found about Glastonbury of *Crataegus oxyacantha praecox*, a winter-flowering variety of hawthorn: some of the alleged slips from the Glastonbury thorn appear, however, to be *Prunus communis*, or blackthorn. A writer in the *Gentleman's*

special location at Glastonbury, where the famous thorn is said by William of Malmesbury and other writers to have budded from the staff of Joseph of Arimathea, who there ended his wanderings with the Holy Grail. Where winter-flowering trees are not found, a custom sometimes exists of putting a branch of cherry or of hawthorn in water some weeks before Christmas in order that it may blossom and serve as a substitute [1].

It may fairly be conjectured that at the winter, as at the summer feast, the fertilization spirit, in the form of bush or idol, was borne about the fields. The fifteenth-century writer, Alsso, records the *calendisationes* of the god Bel in Bohemia, suppressed by St. Adalbert [2]. In modern England, a 'holly-bough' or 'wesley-bob,' with or without an image or doll, occasionally goes its rounds [3]. But a definite lustration of the bounds is rare [4], and, for the most part, the winter procession either is merely riotous or else, like too many of the summer processions themselves, has been converted, under the successive influence of the *strenae* and the cash nexus, into little more than a *quête*. Thus children and the poor go 'souling' for apples and 'soul-cakes' on All Souls' day; on November 5 they collect for the 'guy'; on November 11 in Germany, if not in England, for St. Martin; on St. Clement's day (November 23) they go 'clemencing'; on St. Catherine's (November 25) 'catherning.' Wheat is the coveted boon on St. Thomas's day (December 21) or 'doling day,' and the *quête* is variously known as 'thomasing,' 'mumping,' 'corning,' 'gooding,' 'hodening,' or 'hooding [5].' Christmas brings

Magazine for 1753 reports that the opponents of the 'New Style' introduced in 1752 were encouraged by the refusal of the thorns at Glastonbury and Quainton in Buckinghamshire to flower before Old Christmas day. A Somerset woman told a writer in 3 *N. Q.* ix. 33 that the buds of the thorns burst into flower at midnight on Christmas Eve, 'As they comed out, you could hear 'um haffer.'

[1] Tille, *Y. and C.* 175.

[2] Usener, ii. 61. Alsso says that St. Adalbert substituted a crucifix for the idol, and the cry of ' Vele, Vele,' for that of ' Bely, Bely.'

[3] Ashton, 244; Dyer, 483; Ditchfield, 15. The dolls sometimes represent the Virgin and Child. 'Wesley-bob' and the alternative 'vessel-cup' appear to be corruptions of 'wassail.'

[4] Cf., however, the Burghead ceremony (p. 256).

[5] Brand, i. 217; Burne-Jackson, 381; Dyer, 405; Ditchfield, 25, 161; Northall, 216; Henderson, 66; Haddon, 476; Pfannenschmidt, 206. The *N. E. D.* plausibly ex-

'wassailing' with its bowl of lamb's-wool and its bobbing apple, and this is repeated on New Year's day or eve [1]. The New Year *quête* is probably the most widespread and popular of all. Ducange records it at Rome [2]. In France it is known as *l'Aguilaneuf* [3], in Scotland and the north of England as Hogmanay, terms in which the philologists meet problems still unsolved [4]. Other forms of the winter *quête*

plains 'gooding,' which seems to be used of any of these *quêtes* as 'wishing good,' and 'hooding' may be a corruption of this.

[1] Brand, i. 1 ; Dyer, 501 ; Ditchfield, 42 ; Northall, 183. Skeat derives *wassail*, M.E. *wasseyl*, 'a health-drinking,' from N.E. *wæs hæl*, A.-S. *wes hál*, 'be whole.'

[2] Ducange, *Gloss.* s.v. Kalendae Ianuarii, quoting *Cerem. Rom. ad calcem Cod. MS. eccl. Camerac.* 'Hii sunt ludi Romani communes in Kalendis Ianuarii. In vigilia Kalendarum in sero surgunt pueri, et portant scutum. Quidam eorum est larvatus cum maza in collo ; sibilando sonant timpanum, eunt per domos, circumdant scutum, timpanum sonat, larva sibilat. Quo ludo finito, accipiunt munus a domino domus, secundum quod placet ei. Sic faciunt per unamquamque domum. Eo die de omnibus leguminibus comedunt. Mane autem surgunt duo pueri ex illis, accipiunt ramos olivae et sal, et intrant per domos, salutant domum : Gaudium et laetitia sit in hac domo ; tot filii, tot porcelli, tot agni, et de omnibus bonis optant, et antequam sol oriatur, comedunt vel favum mellis, vel aliquid dulce, ut totus annus procedat eis dulcis, sine lite et labore magno.'

[3] Du Tilliot, 67, quoting J. B. Thiers, *Traité des jeux et des divertissemens*, 452 ; Müller, 103. There are some Guillaneu songs in Bujeaud, ii. 153. The *quête* was prohibited by two synods of Angers in 1595 and 1668.

[4] Brand, i. 247 ; Dyer, 505 ; Ditchfield, 44 ; Ashton, 217 ; Northall, 181 ; Henderson, 76 ; Tille, *Y. and C.* 204 ; Nicholson, *Gol-*

spie, 100 ; Rhys, in *F. L.* ii. 308. Properly. speaking, 'Hogmanay' is the gift of an oaten farl asked for in the *quête*. It is also applied to the day on which the *quête* takes place, which is in Scotland generally New Year's Eve. Besides the *quête*, Hogmanay night, like Halloween elsewhere, is the night for horse-play and practical joking. The name appears in many forms, 'Hogmana,' 'Hogomanay,' 'Nog-money' (Scotland), 'Hogmina' (Cumberland), 'Hagmena' (Northumberland), 'Hagman heigh !' 'Hagman ha !' (Yorkshire), 'Agganow' (Lancashire), 'Hob dy naa,' 'Hob ju naa' (Isle of Man). It is generally accepted as equivalent to the French *aguilanneuf, aguilanleu, guillaneu, hagui men lo, hoquinano,* &c., ad infin., the earliest form being *auguilanleu* (1353). With the Scotch

'Hogmanay,
Trollolay,
Give us of your white bread and
none of your grey' !

may be compared the French,

'Tire lire,
Maint de blanc, et point du bis.'

On no word has amateur philology been more riotous. It has been derived from 'au gui menez,' 'à gui l'an neuf,' 'au gueux menez,' 'Hálig monath,' ἁγία μήνη, 'Homme est né,' and the like. Tille thinks that the whole of December was formerly Hogmanay, and derives from *monâth* and either *hoggva,* 'hew,' *hag,* 'witch,' or *hog,* 'pig.' Nicholson tries the other end, and traces *auguilanleu* to the Spanish *aguinaldo* or *aguilando,* 'a New Year's gift.' This in turn he makes the gerund of *aguilar,* an assumed corruption of *alquilar,* 'to hire one-will crop up presently, and the visits of the guisers with their play or song, the carol singers and the waits may be expected at any time during the Christmas season.   As at the summer *quêtes*, some reminiscence of the primitive character of the processions is to be found in the songs sung, with their wish of prosperity to the liberal household and their ill-will to the churl [1].

In the summer festivals both water-rites and fire-rites frequently occur.   In those of winter, water-rites are comparatively rare, as might naturally be expected at a season when snow and ice prevail.   There is some trace, however, of a custom of drawing 'new' water, as of making 'new' fire, for the new year [2].   Festival fires, on the other hand, are widely distributed, and agree in general features with those of summer.   Their relation to the fertility of crop and herd is often plainly enough marked.   They are perhaps most familiar to-day in the comparatively modern form of the Guy Fawkes celebration on November 5 [3], but they are known

self out.' Hogmanay will thus mean properly 'handsel' or 'hiring-money,' and the first Monday in the New Year is actually called in Scotland 'Handsel Monday.' This is plausible, but, although no philologist, I think a case might be made out for regarding the terms as corruptions of the Celtic *Nos Galan-gaeaf,* 'the night of the winter Calends' (Rhys, 514). This is All Saints' eve, while the Manx 'Hob dy naa' *quête* is on Hollantide (November 12 ; cf. p. 230).

[1] A Gloucestershire wassail song in Dixon, *Ancient Poems*, 199, ends,
'Come, butler, come bring us a bowl of the best :
I hope your soul in heaven will rest ;
But if you do bring us a bowl of the small,
Then down fall butler, bowl and all.'

[2] In Herefordshire and the south of Scotland it is lucky to draw 'the cream of the well' or 'the flower of the well,' i.e. the first pail of water after midnight on New Year's eve (Dyer, 7, 17). In Germany

Heilwag similarly drawn at Christmas is medicinal (Grimm, iv. 1810). Pembroke folk sprinkle each other on New Year's Day (*F. L.* iii. 263). St. Martin of Braga condemns amongst Kalends customs 'panem in fontem mittere (Appendix N, No. xxiii), and this form of well-cult survives at Christmas in the Tyrol (Jahn, 283) and in France (Müller, 500). Tertullian chaffs the custom of early bathing at the *Saturnalia* (Appendix N, No. ii). Gervase of Tilbury (ed. Liebrecht, ii. 12) mentions an English belief (†1200) in a wonder-working Christmas dew. This Tille (*Y. and C.* 168) thinks an outgrowth from the Advent chant *Rorate coeli*, but it seems closely parallel to the folk belief in May-dew.

[3] Burne-Jackson, 388 ; Simpson, 202 ; *F. L.* v. 38 ; Dyer, 410. The festival in its present form can only date from the reign of James I, but the Pope used to be burned in bonfires as early as 1570 upon the accession day of Elizabeth, Nov. 17 (Dyer, 422).

also on St. Crispin's day (October 25)[1], Hallow e'en[2], St. Martin's day[3], St. Thomas's day[4], Christmas eve[5], New Year[6], and Twelfth night[7]. An elaborate and typical example is the 'burning of the clavie' at the little fishing village of Burghead on the Moray Firth[8]. This takes place on New Year's eve, or, according to another account[9], Christmas eve (O.S.). Strangers to the village are excluded from any share in the ritual. The 'clavie' is a blazing tar-barrel hoisted on a pole. In making it, a stone must be used instead of a hammer, and must then be thrown away. Similarly, the barrel must be lit with a blazing peat, and not with lucifer matches. The bearers are honoured, and the bridegroom of the year gets the 'first lift.' Should a bearer stumble, it portends death to himself during the year and ill-luck to the town. The procession passes round the boundaries of Burghead, and formerly visited every boat in the harbour. Then it is carried to the top of a hillock called the 'Doorie,' down the sides of which it is finally rolled. Blazing brands are used to kindle the house fires, and the embers are preserved as charms.

The central heathen rite of sacrifice has also left its abundant traces upon winter custom. Bede records the significant name of *blôt-monath*, given to November by the still unconverted Anglo-Saxons[10]. The tradition of solemn slaughter hangs around both Martinmas and Christmas. 'Martlemas beef' in England, St. Martin's swine, hens, and geese in Germany, mark the former day[11]. At Christmas

[1] Dyer, 389 (Sussex).
[2] Brand, i. 210, 215 (Buchan, Perthshire, Aberdeenshire, North Wales).
[3] Pfannenschmidt, 207; Jahn, 240.
[4] Ashton, 47 (Isle of Man, where the day is called ' Fingan's Eve ').
[5] Jahn, 253.
[6] *F. L.* xii. 349; W. Gregor, *Brit. Ass. Rept.* (1896), 620 (Minnigaff, Galloway; bones being saved up for this fire); Gomme, *Brit. Ass. Rept.* (1896), 633 (Biggar, Lanarkshire).
[7] Brand, i. 14; Dyer, 22 (Gloucestershire, Herefordshire). Twelve

small fires and one large one are made out in the wheat-fields.
[8] Dyer, 507; Ashton, 218; Simpson, 205; Gomme, *Brit. Ass. Rept.* (1896), 631 ; *F. L. J.* vii. 12 ; *Trans. Soc. Antiq. Scot.* x. 649.
[9] Simpson, 205, quoting Gordon Cumming, *From the Hebrides to the Himalayas*, i. 245.
[10] Bede, *D. T. R.* c. 17: cf. the A.-S. passage quoted by Pfannenschmidt, 495; Jahn, 252. Other Germanic names for the winter months are 'Schlachtmonat,' ' Gormânaða': cf. Weinhold, *Die deutschen Monatsnamen*, 54.
[11] Jahn, 229; Tille, *Y. and C.*

the outstanding victim seems to be the boar. *Caput apri defero: reddens laudem Domino*, sings the taberdar at Queen's College, Oxford, as the manciple bears in the boar's head to the Christmas banquet. So it was sung in many another mediaeval and Elizabethan hall [1], while the gentlemen of the Inner Temple broke their Christmas fast on 'brawn, mustard, and malmsey [2],' and in the far-off Orkneys each householder of Sandwick must slay his sow on St. Ignace's or 'Sow' day, December 17 [3]. The older mythologists, with the fear of solstices before their eyes, are accustomed to connect the Christmas boar with the light-god, Freyr [4]. If the cult of any one divinity is alone concerned, the analogous use of the pig in the Eleusinian mysteries of Demeter would make the earth-goddess a more probable guess [5]. A few more recondite customs associated with particular winter anniversaries may be briefly named. St. Thomas's day is at Wokingham the day for bull-baiting [6]. On St. Stephen's day, both in England and Germany, horses are let blood [7]. On or about Christmas, boys are accustomed to set on foot a hunt of victims not ordinarily destined to such a fate [8]; owls and squirrels, and especially wrens, the last, be it noted, creatures which at other times of the year a taboo protects. The wren-hunt is found on various dates in France, England, Ireland, and the Isle of Man, and is carried out with various curious rituals. Often the body is borne in a *quête*, and in the Isle of Man the *quêteurs* give a feather as an amulet in return for hospitality. There are other examples of winter *quêtes*, in which the representation of a sacrificial victim is carried round [9]. 'Hoodening' in Kent and other parts of England

28, 65; Pfannenschmidt, 206, 217, 228.

[1] Dyer, 456, 470, 474, 477; Ashton, 171; Karl Blind, *The Boar's Head Dinner at Oxford and an Old Teutonic Sun-God*, in *Saga Book* of Viking Club for 1895.

[2] Dyer, 473.

[3] Hampson, i. 82.

[4] Gummere, *G. O.* 433.

[5] Tacitus, *Germ.* 45, of the Aestii, 'matrem deum venerantur. insigne superstitionis formas aprorum ges-

tant: id pro armis omnique tutela securum deae cultorem etiam inter hostis praestat.'

[6] Dyer, 439.

[7] Dyer, 492; Ashton, 204; Grimm, iv. 1816.

[8] Dyer, 481; N. W. Thomas, in *F. L.* xi. 250. Cf. ch. xvii for the hunt of a cat and a fox at the 'grand Christmas' of the Inner Temple.

[9] Dyer, 494, 497; Frazer, ii. 442; Northall, 229.

is accompanied by a horse's head or hobby-horse[1]. The Welsh 'Mari Lwyd' is a similar feature[2], while at Kingscote, in Gloucestershire, the wassailers drink to a bull's head called 'the Broad[3].'

The hobby-horse is an example of an apparently grotesque element which is found, widespread in folk-processions, and which a previous chapter has traced to its ritual origin. The man clad in a beast-skin is the worshipper putting himself by personal contact under the influence and protection of the sacrificed god. The rite is not a very salient one in modern winter processions, although it has its examples, but its historical importance is great. A glance at the ecclesiastical denunciations of the Kalends collected in an appendix will disclose numerous references to it. These are co-extensive with the western area of the Kalends celebrations. In Italy, in Gaul, in southern Germany, apparently also in Spain and in England, men decked themselves for riot in the heads and skins of cattle and the beasts of the chase, blackened their faces or bedaubed them with filth, or wore masks fit to terrify the demons themselves. The accounts of these proceedings are naturally allusive rather than descriptive; the fullest are given by a certain Severian, whose locality and date are unknown, but who may be conjectured to speak for Italy, by Maximus of Turin and Chrysologus of Ravenna in the fifth century, and by Caesarius of Arles in the beginning of the sixth. Amongst the *portenta* denounced is a certain *cervulus*, which lingers in the *Penitentials* right up to the tenth century, and with which are sometimes associated a *vitula* or *iuvenca*. Caesarius adds a *hinnicula*, and St. Eadhelm, who is my only authority for the presence of the *cervulus* in England, an *ermulus*. These seem to be precisely of the nature of 'hobby-horses.' Men are said *cervulum ambulare, cervulum facere, in cervulo vadere,* and Christians are forbidden to allow these *portenta* to come before their houses. The *Penitential* of the Pseudo-Theodore tells us that the performers were those who wore the skins

---

[1] Ashton, 114 (Reculver); Dyer, 472 (Ramsgate); Ditchfield, 27 (Walmer), 28 (Cheshire: All Souls' day).
[2] Dyer, 486. [3] Ditchfield, 28.

and heads of beasts. Maximus of Turin, and several writers after him, put the objection to the beast-mimicry of the Kalends largely on the ground that man made in the image of God must not transform himself into the image of a beast. But it is clear that the real reason for condemning it was its unforgettable connexion with heathen cult. Caesarius warns the culprit that he is making himself into a *sacrificium daemonum*, and the disguised reveller is more than once spoken of as a living image of the heathen god or demon itself. There is some confusion of thought here, and it must be remembered that the initial significance of the skin-wearing rite was probably buried in oblivion, both for those who practised it and for those who reprobated. But it is obvious that the worshipper wearing a sacrificial skin would bear a close resemblance to the theriomorphic or semi-therio-morphic image developed out of the sacrificial skin nailed on a tree-trunk; and it is impossible not to connect the fact that in the prohibitions a *cervulus* or 'hobby-buck' rather than a 'hobby-horse' is prominent with the widespread worship throughout the districts whence many of these notices come of the mysterious stag-horned deity, the *Cernunnos* of the Gaulish altars[1]. On the whole I incline to think that at least amongst the Germano-Keltic peoples the agricultural gods were not mimed in procession by human representatives. It is true that in the mediaeval German processions which sprang out of those of the Kalends St. Nicholas plays a part, and that the presence of St. Nicholas may be thought to imply that of some heathen precursor. It will, however, be seen shortly that St. Nicholas may have got into these processions through a different train of ideas, equally connected with the Kalends, but not with the strictly agricultural aspect of that festival. But of the continuity of the beast-masks and other horrors of these Christmas processions with those condemned in the prohibitions, there can be no doubt[2]. A few other survivals of the *cervulus* and its revel can be traced in various parts of Europe[3].

---

[1] Bertrand, 314; Arbois de Jubainville, *Cycl. myth.* 385; Rhys, *C. H.* 77.

[2] Tille, *D. W.* 109.

[3] C. de Berger (1723), *Commentatio de personis vulgo larvis seu*

The sacrifices of cereals and of the juice of the vine or the barley are exemplified, the one by the traditional furmenty, plum-porridge, mince-pie, souling-cake, Yule-dough, Twelfth night cake, *pain de calende*, and other forms of 'feasten' cake[1]; the other by the wassail-bowl with its bobbing apple[2]. The summer 'youling' or 'tree-wassailing' is repeated in the orchard[3], and a curious Herefordshire custom represents an extension of the same principle to the ox-byre[4]. A German hen-yard custom requires mixed corn, for the familiar reason that every kind of crop must be included in the sacrifice[5].

Human sacrifice has been preserved in the whipping of boys on Innocents' day, because it could be turned into the symbol of a Christian myth[6]. It is preserved also, as throughout the summer, in the custom, Roman as well as Germano-Keltic, of electing a mock or temporary king. Of such the Epiphany king or 'king of the bean' is, especially in France, the best known[7]. Here again, the association with

---

mascharis, 218 'Vecolo aut cervolo facere; hoc est sub forma vitulae aut cervuli per plateas discurrere, ut apud nos in festis Bacchanalibus vulgo dicitur *correr la tora*'; J. Ihre (†1769), *Gloss. Suio-Gothicum*, s. v. Jul. 'Julbock est ludicrum, quo tempore hoc pellem et formam arietis induunt adolescentuli et ita adstantibus incursant. Credo idem hoc esse quod exteri scriptores cervulum appellant.' In the *Life of Bishop Arni* (nat. 1237) it is recorded how in his youth he once joined in a *scinnleic* or 'hide-play' (*C. P. B.* ii. 385). Frazer, ii. 447, describes the New Year custom of *colluinn* in Scotland and St. Kilda. A man clad in a cowhide is driven *deasil* round each house to bless it. Bits of hide are also burnt for amulets. Probably the favourite Christmas game of Blind Man's Buff was originally a *scinnleic* (N. W. Thomas, in *F. L.* xi. 262).

[1] Brand, i. 210, 217; Jackson and Burne, 381, 392, 407; Ashton, 178; Jahn, 487, 500; Müller, 487, 500. Scandinavian countries bake the Christmas 'Yule-boar.' Often this is made from the last sheaf and the crumbs mixed with the seed-corn (Frazer, ii. 29). Germany has its *Martinshörner* (Jahn, 250; Pfannenschmidt, 215).

[2] Dyer, 501; Ashton, 214.

[3] Brand, i. 19; Dyer, 21, 447; Ashton, 86, 233. Brand, i. 210, describes a Hallow-e'en custom in the Isle of Lewis of pouring a cup of ale in the sea to 'Shony,' a sea god.

[4] Brand, i. 14; Dyer, 22, 448; Northall, 187. A cake with a hole in the middle is hung on the horn of the leading ox.

[5] Grimm, iv. 1808. Hens are fed on New Year's day with mixed corn to make them lay well.

[6] Gregory, *Posthuma*, 113 'It hath been a Custom, and yet is elsewhere, to whip up the Children upon Innocents-Day morning, that the memory of this Murther might stick the closer, and in a moderate proportion to act over the cruelty again in kind.' In Germany, adults are beaten (Grimm, iv. 1820). In mediaeval France 'innocenter,' 'donner les innocents,' was a custom exactly parallel to the Easter *prisio* (Rigollot, 138, 173).

[7] Dyer, 24; Cortet, 32; Frazer,

the three kings or *Magi* has doubtless prolonged his sway. But he is not unparalleled. The *rex autumnalis* of Bath is perhaps a harvest rather than a beginning of winter king[1]. But the shoemakers choose their King Crispin on October 25, the day of their patron saints, Crispin and Crispinian; on St. Clement's (November 23) the Woolwich blacksmiths have their King Clem, and the maidens of Peterborough and elsewhere a queen on St. Catherine's (November 25). Tenby, again, elects its Christmas mock mayor[2]. At York, the proclaiming of Yule by 'Yule' and 'Yule's wife' on St. Thomas's day was once a notable pageant[3]. At Norwich, the riding of a 'kyng of Crestemesse' was the occasion of a serious riot in 1443[4]. These may be regarded as 'folk' versions of the

iii. 143; Deslyons, *Traités contre le Paganisme du Roi boit* (2nd ed. 1670). The accounts of Edward II record a gift to the *rex fabae* on January 1, 1316 (*Archaeologia*, xxvi. 342). Payments to the 'King of Bene' and 'for furnissing his graith' were made by James IV of Scotland between 1490 and 1503 (*L. H. T. Accounts*, i. ccxliii; ii. xxiv, xxxi, &c.). The familiar mode of choosing the king is thus described at Mont St. Michel 'In vigilia Epyphaniae ad prandium habeant fratres gastellos et ponatur faba in uno; et frater qui inveniet fabam, vocabitur rex et sedebit ad magnam mensam, et scilicet sedebit ad vesperas ad matutinam et ad magnam missam in cathedra parata' (Gasté, 53). The pre-eminence of the bean, largest of cereals, in the mixed cereal cake (cf. ch. vi) presents no great difficulty; on the religious significance attached to it in South Europe, cf. W. W. Fowler, 94, 110, 130. Lady Jane Grey was scornfully dubbed a Twelfth-day queen by Noailles (Froude, v. 206), just as the Bruce's wife held her lord a summer king (ch. viii).

[1] *Accts. of St. Michael's, Bath*, s. ann. 1487, 1490, 1492 (*Somerset Arch. Soc. Trans.* 1878, 1879, 1883). One entry is 'pro corona conducta Regi Attumnali.' The learned editor explains this as 'a quest conducted by the King's Attorney'!

[2] Ashton, 119; Dyer, 388, 423, 427.

[3] Brand, i. 261, prints from Leland, *Itinerary* (ed. 1769), iv. 182, a description of the proclamation of Youle by the sheriffs at the 'Youle-Girth' and throughout the city. In Davies, 270, is a letter from Archbp. Grindal and other ecclesiastical commissioners to the Lord Mayor, dated November 13, 1572, blaming 'a very rude and barbarouse custome maynteyned in this citie and in no other citie or towne of this realme to our knowledge, that yerely upon St. Thomas day before Christmas twoo disguysed persons, called Yule and Yule's wife, shoulde ryde throughe the citie very undecently and uncomely ...' Hereupon the council suppressed the riding. Drake, *Eboracum* (1736), 217, says that originally a friar rode backwards and 'painted like a Jew.' He gives an historical legend to account for the origin of the custom. Religious interludes were played on the same day: cf. *Representations*. The 'Yule' of York was perhaps less a 'king' than a symbolical personage like the modern 'Old Father Christmas.'

[4] Ramsay, *Y. and L.* ii. 52; Blomefield, *Hist. of Norfolk*, iii.

mock king. Others, in which the folk were less concerned, will be the subject of chapters to follow.

Before passing to a fresh group of Christmas customs, I must note the presence of one more bit of ritual closely related to sacrificial survivals. That is, the man masquerading in woman's clothes, in whom we have found a last faint reminiscence of the once exclusive supremacy of women in the conduct of agricultural worship. At Rome, musicians dressed as women paraded the city, not on the Kalends, but on the Ides of January[1]. The Fathers, however, know such disguising as a Kalends custom, and a condemnation of it often accompanies that of beast-mimicry, from the fourth to the eighth century[2].

The winter festival is thus, like the summer festivals, a moment in the cycle of agricultural ritual, and is therefore shared in by the whole village in common. It is also, and from the time of the institution of harvest perhaps pre-eminently, a festival of the family and the homestead. This side of it finds various manifestations. There is the solemn renewal of the undying fire upon the hearth, the central symbol and almost condition of the existence of the family as such. This survives in the institution of the 'Yule-log,' which throughout the Germano-Keltic area is lighted on Christmas or more rarely New Year's eve, and must burn,

---

149. The riot was against the Abbot of St. Benet's Holm, and the monks declared that one John Gladman was set up as a king, an act of treason against Henry VI. The city was fined 1,000 marks. In 1448 they set forth their wrongs in a 'Bill' and explained that Gladman 'who was ever, and at thys our is, a man of sad disposition, and trewe and feythfull to God and to the Kyng, of disporte as hath ben acustomed in ony cite or burgh thorowe alle this realme, on Tuesday in the last ende of Cristemesse, viz. Fastyngonge Tuesday, made a disport with hys neyghbours, havyng his hors trappyd with tynnsoyle and other nyse disgisy things, coronned as kyng of Crestemesse, in tokyn that seson should end with the twelve monethes of the yere, aforn hym yche moneth disguysed after the seson requiryd, and Lenton clad in whyte and red heryngs skinns, and his hors trapped with oystyr-shells after him, in token that sadnesse shuld folowe, and an holy tyme, and so rode in diverse stretis of the cite, with other people, with hym disguysed makyng myrth, disportes and plays.'

[1] Jevons, *Plutarch's Romane Questions*, 86. The Ides (Jan. 9) must have practically been included in the Kalends festival. The Agonium, probably a sacrifice to Janus, was on that day (W. W. Fowler, 282).

[2] Appendix N, Nos. ix, xi, xiv, xvii, xviii, xxviii, xxxvi.

as local custom may exact, either until midnight, or for three days, or during the whole of the Twelve-night period, from Christmas to Epiphany [1]. Dr. Tille, intent on magnifying the Roman element in western winter customs, denies any Germano-Keltic origin to the Christmas blaze, and traces it to the Roman practice of hanging lamps upon the house-doors during the *Saturnalia* and the Kalends [2]. It is true that the Yule-log is sometimes supplemented or even replaced by the Christmas candle [3], but I do not think that there can be any doubt which is the primitive form of rite. And the Yule-log enters closely into the Germano-Keltic scheme of festival ideas. The preservation of its brands or ashes to be placed in the mangers or mingled with the seed-corn suggests many and familiar analogies. Moreover, it is essentially con-nected with the festival fire of the village, from which it is still sometimes, and once no doubt was invariably, lit, afford-ing thus an exact parallel to the Germano-Keltic practice on the occasion of summer festival fires, or of those built to stay an epidemic.

Another aspect of the domestic character of the winter festival is to be found in the prominent part which children take in it. As *quêteurs*, they have no doubt gradually replaced the elder folk, during the process through which, even within the historical purview, ritual has been trans-formed into play. But St. Nicholas, the chief mythical figure of the festival, is their patron saint; for their benefit especially, the *strenae* or Christmas and New Year's gifts are main-tained; and in one or two places it is their privilege, on some fixed day during the season, to 'bar out' their parents or masters [4].

Thirdly, the winter festival included a commemoration of

---

[1] G. L. Gomme, in *Brit. Ass. Rep.* (1896), 616 sqq.; Tille, *D. W.* 11, *Y. and C.* 90; Jahn, 253; Dyer, 446, 466; Ashton, 76, 219; Grimm, iv. 1793, 1798, 1812, 1826, 1839, 1841; Bertrand, 111, 404; Müller, 478.

[2] Tille, *Y. and C.* 95.

[3] Dyer, 456; Ashton, 125, 188. A Lombard *Capitulary* (App. N,

No. xxxviii) forbids a Christmas candle to be burnt beneath the kneading-trough.

[4] Müller, 236; Dyer, 430; Ashton, 54; Rigollot, 173; *Records of Aberdeen* (Spalding Club), ii. 39, 45, 66. In Belgium the household keys are entrusted to the youngest child on Innocents' day (Durr, 73).

ancestors. It was a feast, not only of riotous life, but of the dead. For, to the thinking of the Germano-Keltic peoples, the dead kinsmen were not altogether outside the range of human fellowship. They shared with the living in banquets upon the tomb. They could even at times return to the visible world and hover round the familiar precincts of their òwn domestic hearth. The Germans, at least, heard them in the gusts of the storm, and imagined for them a leader who became Odin. From another point of view they were naturally regarded as under the keeping of earth, and the earth-mother, in one aspect a goddess of fertility, was in another the goddess of the dead. As such she was worshipped under various names and forms, amongst others in the triad of the *Matres* or *Matronae*. In mediaeval superstition she is represented by Frau Perchte, Frau Holda and similar personages, by Diana, by Herodias, by St. Gertrude, just as the functions of Odin are transferred to St. Martin, St. Nicholas, St. John, Hellequin. It was not unnatural that the return of the spirits, in the 'wild hunt' or otherwise, to earth should be held to take place especially at the two primitive festivals which respectively began the winter and the summer. Of the summer or spring commemoration but scant traces are to be recovered[1]; that of winter survives, in a dislocated form, in more than one important anniversary. Its observances have been transferred with those of the agricultural side of the feast to the *Gemeinwoche* of harvest[2];

[1] Saupe, 9; Tille, *Y. and C.* 118; Duchesne, 267. A custom of feasting on the tombs of the dead on the day of St. Peter de Cathedra (Feb. 22) is condemned by the *Council of Tours* (567), c. 23 (Maassen, i. 133) 'sunt etiam qui in festivitate cathedrae domui Petri apostoli cibos mortuis offerunt, et post missas redeuntes ad domos proprias, ad gentilium revertuntur errores, et post corpus Domini, sacratas daemoni escas accipiunt.' I do not doubt that the Germano-Keltic tribes had their spring *Todtenfest*, but the date Feb. 22 seems determined by the Roman *Parentalia* extending from Feb. 13 to either Feb. 21 (*Feralia*) or Feb. 22 (*Cara Cognatio*): cf. Fowler, 306. The 'cibi' mentioned by the council of Tours seem to have been offered in the house, like the winter offerings described below; but there is also evidence for similar Germano-Keltic offerings on the tomb or howe itself; and these were often accompanied by *dadsisas* or dirges; cf. Saupe, *Indiculus*, 5–9. Saupe considers the *spurcalia in Februario*, explained above (p. 114) as a ploughing rite, to be funereal.

[2] Pfannenschmidt, 123, 165, 435; Saupe, 9; Golther, 586; *C. P. B.* i. 43; Jahn, 251. The chronicler Widukind, *Res gestae Sax.* (Pertz,

but they are also retained, at or about their original date, on All Saints' and All Souls' days [1]; and, as I proceed to show, they form a marked and interesting part of the Christmas and New Year ritual. I do not, indeed, agree with Dr. Mogk, who thinks that the Germans held their primitive feast of the dead in the blackest time of winter, for it seems to me more economical to suppose that the observances in question have been shifted like others from November to the Kalends. But I still less share the view of Dr. Tille, who denies that any relics of a feast of the dead can be traced in the Christmas season at all [2].

Bede makes the statement that the heathen Anglo-Saxons gave to the eve of the Nativity the name of *Modranicht* or 'night of mothers,' and in it practised certain ceremonies [3]. It is a difficult passage, but the most plausible of various explanations seems to be that which identifies these ceremonies with the cult of those *Matres* or *Matronae*, corresponding with the Scandinavian *disar*, whom we seem justified in regarding as guardians and representatives of the dead. Nor is there any particular difficulty in guessing at the nature of the ceremonies referred to. Amongst all peoples the cult of the dead consists in feeding them; and there is a long catena of evidence for the persistent survival in the Germano-Keltic area of a Christmas and New Year custom closely parallel to the *alfablót* and *disablót* of the northern *jul*. When the household went to bed after the New Year revel, a portion of the banquet was left spread upon the table in the firm belief that during the night the ancestral spirits and their leaders would come and partake thereof. The practice, which was also known on the Mediterranean, does not escape

Mon. SS. iii. 423), describes a Saxon three-days' feast in honour of a victory over the Thuringi in 534. He adds 'acta sunt autem haec omnia, ut maiorum memoria prodit, die Kal. Octobris, qui dies erroris, religiosorum sanctione virorum mutati sunt in ieiunia et orationes, oblationes quoque omnium nos praecedentium christianorum.' This is probably a myth to account for the harvest *Todtenfest*, which may more naturally be thought of as transferred with the agricultural

rites from November. For the mediaeval *Gemeinwoche*, beginning on the Sunday after Michaelmas, was common to Germany, and not confined to Saxony. Michaelmas, the feast of angels, known at Rome in the sixth century, and in Germany by the ninth, also adapts itself to the notion of a *Todtenfest*.

[1] Pfannenschmidt, 168, 443.
[2] Mogk, in Paul, iii. 260; Tille, *Y. and C.* 107.
[3] Cf. p. 231.

the animadversion of the ecclesiastical prohibitions. The earlier writers who speak of it, Jerome, Caesarius, Eligius, Boniface, Zacharias, the author of the *Homilia de Sacrilegiis*, if they give any explanation at all, treat it as a kind of charm[1]. The laden table, like the human over-eating and over-drinking, is to prognosticate or cause a year of plentiful fare. The preachers were more anxious to eradicate heathenism than to study its antiquities. Burchardus, however, had a touch of the anthropologist, and Burchardus says definitely that food, drink, and three knives were laid on the Kalends table for the three *Parcae*, figures of Roman mythology with whom the western *Matres* or 'weird sisters' were identified[2]. Mediaeval notices confirm the statement of Burchardus. Martin of Amberg[3], the *Thesaurus Pauperum*[4] and the Kloster Scheyern manuscript[5] make the recipient of the bounty Frau Perchte. In Alsso's *Largum Sero* it is for the heathen gods or demons[6]; in *Dives and Pauper* for 'Atholde or Gobelyn[7].' In modern survivals it is still often Frau Perchte or the Perchten or Persteln for whom fragments of food are left; in other cases the custom has taken on a Christian colouring, and the ancestors' bit becomes the portion of *le bon Dieu* or the Virgin or Christ or the *Magi*, and is actually given to *quêteurs* or the poor[8].

---

[1] Appendix N, Nos. xii, xvii, xxvii, xxxiii, xxxv, xxxix.

[2] Appendix N, No. xlii.

[3] Martin of Amberg, *Gewissensspiegel* (thirteenth century, quoted Jahn, 282), the food and drink are left for 'Percht mit der eisnen nasen.'

[4] *Thes. Paup.* s. v. Superstitio (fifteenth century, quoted Jahn, 282) 'multi credunt sacris noctibus inter natalem diem Christi et noctem Epiphaniae evenire ad domos suas quasdam mulieres, quibus praeest domina Perchta ... multi in domibus in noctibus praedictis post coenam dimittunt panem et caseum, lac, carnes, ova, vinum, et aquam et huiusmodi super mensas et coclearea, discos, ciphos, cultellos et similia propter visitationem Perhtae cum cohorte sua, ut eis complaceant ... ut inde sint eis propitii ad prosperitatem domus et negotiorum rerum temporalium.'

[5] Usener, ii. 84 'Qui preparant mensam dominae Perthae'(fifteenth century). Schmeller, *Bairisch. Wörterb.* i. 270, gives other references for Perchte in this connexion.

[6] Usener, ii. 58.

[7] *Dives and Pauper* (Pynson, 1493) 'Alle that ... use nyce observances in the ... new yere, as setting of mete or drynke, by nighte on the benche, to fede Atholde or Gobelyn.' In English folk-custom, food is left for the house-spirit or 'brownie' on ordinary as well as festal days; cf. my 'Warwick' edition of *Midsummer Night's Dream*, 145.

[8] Jahn, 283; Brand, i. 18; Bertrand, 405; Cortet, 33, 45.

It is the ancestors, perhaps, who are really had in mind
when libations are made upon the Yule-log, an observance
known to Martin of Braga in the sixth century [1], and still in
use in France [2]. Nor can it be doubted that the healths
drunk to them, and to the first of them, Odin, lived on in the
St. John's *minnes*, no less than in the St. Martin's *minnes*, of
Germany [3]. Apart from eating and drinking, numerous folk-
beliefs testify to the presence of the spirits of the dead on
earth in the Twelve nights of Christmas. During these days,
or some one of them, Frau Holle and Frau Perchte are
abroad [4]. So is the 'wild hunt [5].' Dreams then dreamt
come true [6], and children then born see ghosts [7]. The wer-
wolf, possessed by a human spirit, is to be dreaded [8]. The
devil and his company dance in the Isle of Man [9] : in Brittany
the *korrigans* are unloosed, and the dolmens and menhirs
disclose their hidden treasures [10]. Marcellus in *Hamlet* declares :

'Some say that ever 'gainst that season comes
Wherein our Saviour's birth is celebrated,
The bird of dawning singeth all night long ;
And then, they say, no spirit dare stir abroad ;
The nights are wholesome ; then no planets strike,
No fairy takes, nor witch hath power to charm,
So hallow'd and so gracious is the time [11].'

The folk-lorist can only reply, ' So have I heard, and do not
in the least believe it.'

---

[1] Appendix N, No. xxiii. If the
words 'in foco' are not part of the
text, 'youling' (cf. pp. 142, 260) may
be intended.

[2] Bertrand, 111, 404.

[3] Jahn, 120, 244, 269: the *Ger-
truden-minnes* on St. Gertrude's day
(March 17) perhaps preserve another
fragment of the spring *Todtenfest*,
St. Gertrude here replacing the
mother-goddess; cf. Grimm, iii.
xxxviii.

[4] Grimm, i. 268, 273, 281 ; Mogk,
in Paul, iii. 279. The especial day
of Frau Perchte is Epiphany.

[5] Mogk, in Paul, iii. 260 ; Tille,
D. W. 173.

[6] Grimm, iv. 1798.

[7] Ibid. iv. 1814.

[8] Tille, *D. W.* 163 ; Grimm, iv.
1782.

[9] Ashton, 104.

[10] Müller, 496.

[11] *Hamlet*, i. 1. 158. I do not
know where Shakespeare got the
idea, of which I find no confirmation ; but its origin is probably an
ecclesiastical attempt to parry folk-
belief. Other Kalends notions have
taken on a Christian colouring.
The miraculous events of Christmas
night are rooted in the conception
that the Kalends must abound in
all good things, in order that the

The wanderings of Odin in the winter nights must be at the bottom of the nursery myth that the Christian representatives of this divinity, Saints Martin and Nicholas (the Santa Claus of modern legend), are the nocturnal givers of *strenae* to children. In Italy, the fairy Befana (Epiphania), an equivalent of Diana, has a similar function [1]. It was but a step to the actual representation of such personages for the greater delight of the children. In Anspach the skin-clad *Pelzmarten*, in Holland St. Martin in bishop's robes, make their rounds on St. Martin's day with nuts, apples, and suchlike [2]. St. Nicholas does the same on St. Nicholas' day in Holland and Alsace-Lorraine, at Christmas in Germany [3]. The beneficent saints were incorporated into the Kalends processions already described, which in the sixteenth-century Germany included two distinct groups, a dark one of devils and beast-masks, terrible to children, and a white or kindly one, in which sometimes appeared the *Jesus-Kind* himself [4].

coming year may do so. But allusions to Christian legend have been worked into and have transformed them. On Christmas night bees sing (Brand, i. 3), and water is turned into wine (Grimm, iv. 1779, 1809). While the genealogy is sung at the midnight mass, hidden treasures are revealed (Grimm, iv. 1840). Similarly, the cattle of heathen masters naturally shared in the Kalends good cheer; whence a Christian notion that they, and in particular the ox and the ass, witnesses of the Nativity, can speak on that night, and bear testimony to the good or ill-treatment of the farmers (Grimm, iv. 1809, 1840); cf. the *Speculum Perfectionis*, c. 114, ed. Sabatier, 225 'quod volebat [S. Franciscus] suadere imperatori ut faceret specialem legem quod in Nativitate Domini homines bene providerent avibus et bovi et asino et pauperibus': also p. 250, n. 1.— Ten minutes after writing the above note, I have come on the following passage in Tolstoi, *Résurrection* (trad. franç.), i. 297 'Un proverbe dit que les coqs chantent de bonne heure dans les nuits joyeuses.'

[1] Müller, 272.
[2] Pfannenschmidt, 207.
[3] Müller, 235, 239, 248.
[4] Tille, *D. W.* 107; *Y. and C.* 116; Saupe, 28; Io. Iac. Reiske, *Comm. ad Const. Porph., de Caeremoniis*, ii. 357 (*Corp. Script. Byz.* 1830) 'Vidi puerulus et horrui robustos iuvenes pelliceis indutos, cornutos in fronte, vultus fuligine atratos, intra dentes carbones vivos tenentes, quos reciprocato spiritu animabant, et scintillis quaquaversum sparsis ignem quasi vomebant, cum saccis cursitantes, in quos abdere puerulos occursantes minitabantur, appensis cymbalis et insano clamore frementes.' He calls them 'die Knecht Ruperte,' and says that they performed in the Twelve nights. The *sacci* are interesting, for English nurses frighten children with a threat that the chimney-sweep (here as in the May-game inheriting the tradition on account of his black face) will put them in his sack. The *beneficent* Christmas wanderers use the sack to bring presents in; cf. the development of the sack in the Mummers' play (p. 215).

It is perhaps a relic of the same merging which gives the German and Flemish St. Nicholas a black Moor as companion in his nightly peregrinations[1].

Besides the customs which form part of the agricultural or the domestic observances of the winter feasts, there are others which belong to these in their quality as feasts of the New Year. To the primitive mind the first night and day of the year are full of omen for the nights and days that follow. Their events must be observed as foretelling, nay more, they must as far as possible be regulated as determining, those of the larger period. The eves and days of All Saints, Christmas, and the New Year itself, as well as in some degree the minor feasts, preserve in modern folk-lore this prophetic character. It is but an extension and systematization of the same notion that ascribes to each of the twelve days between Christmas and Epiphany a special influence upon one of the twelve months of the year[2]. This group of customs I can only touch most cursorily. The most interesting are those which, as I have just said, attempt to go beyond foretelling and to determine the arrival of good fortune. Their method is symbolic. In order that the house may be prosperous during the year, wealth during the critical day must flow in and not flow out. Hence the taboos which forbid the carrying out in particular of those two central elements of early civilization, fire[3] and iron[4]. Hence too the belief that a job of work begun on the feast day will succeed, which

---

[1] Müller, 235, 248.

[2] A mince-pie eaten in a different house on each night of the Twelves (*not* twelve mince-pies eaten *before* Christmas) ensures twelve lucky months. The weather of each day in the Twelves determines that of a month (Harland, 99; Jackson and Burne, 408). I have heard of a custom of leaping over twelve lighted candles on New Year's eve. Each that goes out means ill-luck in a corresponding month.

[3] Caesarius; Boniface (App. N, Nos. xvii, xviii, xxxiii); Alsso, in Usener, ii. 65; *F. L.* iii. 253; Jackson and Burne, 400; Ashton, 111; *Brit. Ass. Report* (1896), 620. In

some of the cases quoted under the last reference and elsewhere, *nothing* may be taken out of the house on New Year's Day. Ashes and other refuse which would naturally be taken out in the morning were removed the night before. Ashes, of course, share the sanctity of the fire. Cf. the maskers' threat (p. 217).

[4] Boniface (App. N, No. xxxiii); cf. the Kloster Scheyern (Usener, ii. 84) condemnation of those 'qui vomerem ponunt sub mensa tempore nativitatis Christi.' For other uses of iron as a potent agricultural charm, cf. Grimm, iv. 1795, 1798, 1807, 1816; Burne-Jackson, 164.

conflicts rather curiously in practice with the universal rustic sentiment that to work or make others work on holidays is the act of a churl[1]. Nothing, again, is more important to the welfare of the household during the coming year than the character of the first visitor who may enter the house on New Year's day. The precise requirements of a 'first foot' vary in different localities; but as a rule he must be a boy or man, and not a girl or woman, and he must be dark-haired and not splay-footed[2]. An ingenious conjecture has connected the latter requirements with the racial antagonism of the high-instepped dark pre-Aryan to the flat-footed blonde or red-haired invading Kelt[3]. A Bohemian parallel enables me to explain that of masculinity by the belief in the influence of the sex of the 'first foot' upon that of the cattle to be born during the year[4]. I regret to add that there are traces also of a requirement that the 'first foot' should not be a priest, possibly because in that event the shadow of celibacy would make any births at all improbable[5].

Some of the New Year observances are but prophetic by second intention, having been originally elements of cult. An example is afforded by the all-night table for the leaders of the dead, which, as has been pointed out, was regarded by

[1] Cf. Burchardus (App. N, No. xlii); Grimm, iv. 1793, with many other superstitions in the same appendix to Grimm; Brand, i. 9; Ashton, 222; Jackson and Burne, 403. The practical outcome is to begin jobs for form's sake and then stop. The same is done on Saint Distaff's day, January 7; cf. Brand, i. 15.

[2] Harland, 117; Jackson and Burne, 314; *Brit. Ass. Rep.* (1896), 620; Dyer, 483; Ashton, 112, 119, 224. There is a long discussion in *F. L.* iii. 78, 253. I am tempted to find a very early notice of the 'first foot' in the prohibition 'pedem observare' of Martin of Braga (App. N, No. xxiii).

[3] *F. L.* iii. 253.

[4] *Kloster Scheyern MS.* (fifteenth century) in Usener, ii. 84 'Qui credunt, quando masculi primi intrant domum in die nativitatis, quod omnes vaccae generent masculos et e converso.'

[5] Müller, 269 (Italy). Grimm, iv. 1784, notes 'If the first person you meet in the morning is a virgin or a priest, 'tis a sign of bad luck; if a harlot, of good': cf. Caspari, *Hom. de Sacrilegiis*, § 11 'qui clericum vel monachum de mane aut quacumque hora videns aut o[b]vians, abominosum sibi esse credet, iste non solum paganus, sed demoniacus est, qui christi militem abominatur.' These German examples have no special relation to the New Year, and the 'first foot' superstition is indeed only the ordinary belief in the ominous character of the first thing seen on leaving the house, intensified by the critical season.

the Fathers who condemned it as merely a device, with the festal banquet itself, to ensure carnal well-being. Another is the habit of giving presents. This, though widespread, is apparently of Italian and not Germano-Keltic origin [1]. It has gone through three phases. The original *strena* played a part in the cult of the wood-goddess. It was a twig from a sacred tree and the channel of the divine influence upon the personality of him who held or wore it. The later *strena* had clearly become an omen, as is shown by the tradition which required it to be honeyed or light-bearing or golden [2]. To-day even this notion may be said to have disappeared, and the Christmas-box or *étrenne* is merely a token of goodwill, an amusement for children, or a blackmail levied by satellites.

The number of minor omens by which the curiosity, chiefly of women, strives on the winter nights to get a peep into futurity is legion [3]. Many of them arise out of the ordinary incidents of the festivities, the baking of the Christmas cakes [4], the roasting of the nuts in the Hallow-e'en fire [5]. Some of them preserve ideas of extreme antiquity, as when a girl takes off her shift and sits naked in the belief that the vision of her future husband will restore it to her. Others are based upon the most naïve symbolism, as when the same girl pulls a stick out of the wood-pile to see if her husband will be straight or crooked [6]. But however diversified the methods, the objects of the omens are few and unvarying. What will be the weather and what his crops? How shall he fare in love and the begetting of children? What are his chances of escaping for yet another year the summons of the lord of shadows? Such are the simple questions to which the rustic claims from his gods an answer.

---

[1] Tille, *D. W.* 189; *Y. and C.* 84, 95, 104.

[2] Cf. p. 238.

[3] Brand, i. 3, 209, 226, 257; Spence, *Shetland Folk-Lore,* 189; Grimm, iv. 1777–1848 *passim*; Jackson and Burne, 176, 380, &c., &c. Burchardus (App. N, No. xlii) mentions that the Germans took New Year omens sitting girt with a sword on the housetop or upon a [sacrificial] skin at the crossways. This was called *liodorsâza*, a term which a *glossator* also uses for the kindred custom of *cervulus* (Tille, *Y. and C.* 96). Is the man in *Hom. de Sacr.* (App. N, No. xxxix) 'qui arma in campo ostendit' taking omens like the man on the housetop, or is he conducting a sword-dance?

[4] Burchardus (App. N, No. xlii).

[5] Brand, i. 209.

[6] Grimm, iv. 1781, 1797, 1818.

Finally, the instinct of play proved no less enduring in the Germano-Keltic winter feasts than in those of summer. The priestly protests against the invasion of the churches by folk-dance and folk-song apply just as much to Christmas as to any other festal period. It is, indeed, to Christmas that the monitory legend of the dancers of Kölbigk attaches itself. A similar pious narrative is that in the thirteenth-century *Bonum Universale de Apibus* of Thomas of Cantimpré, which tells how a devil made a famous song of St. Martin, and spread it abroad over France and Germany[1]. Yet a third is solemnly retailed by a fifteenth-century English theologian, who professes to have known a man who once heard an indecent song at Christmas, and not long after died of a melancholy[2]. During the seventeenth century folk still danced and cried 'Yole' in Yorkshire churches after the Christmas services[3]. Hopeless of abolishing such customs, the clergy tried to capture them. The Christmas crib was rocked to the rhythms of a dance, and such great Latin hymns as the *Hic iacet in cunabulis* and the *Resonat in laudibus* became the parents of a long series of festival songs, half sacred, half profane[4]. In Germany these were known as *Wiegenlieder*, in France as *noëls*, in England as carols; and the latter name makes it clear that they are but a specialized development of those *caroles* or *rondes* which of all mediaeval *chansons* came nearest to the type of Germano-Keltic folk-song. A single passage in a Byzantine

---

[1] Quoted Pfannenschmidt, 489 'quod autem obscoena carmina finguntur a daemonibus et perditorum mentibus immittuntur, quidam daemon nequissimus, qui in Nivella urbe Brabantiae puellam nobilem anno domini 1216 prosequebatur, manifeste populis audientibus dixit: cantum hunc celebrem de Martino ego cum collega meo composui et per diversas terras Galliae et Theutoniae promulgavi. Erat autem cantus ille turpissimus et plenus luxuriosis plausibus.' On *Martinslieder* in general cf. Pfannenschmidt, 468, 613.

[2] T. Gascoigne, *Loci e Libro Veritatum* (1403–58), ed. Rogers, 144.

[3] Aubrey, *Gentilisme and Judaisme (F. L. S.)*, 1.

[4] Tille, *D. W.* 55; K. Simrock, *Deutsche Weihnachtslieder* (1854); Cortet, 246; Grove, *Dict. of Music*, s. v. Noël; Julian, *Dict. of Hymn.* s. v. Carol; A. H. Bullen, *Carols and Poems*, 1885; Helmore, *Carols for Christmastide*. The cry 'Noel' appears in the fifteenth century both in France and England as one of general rejoicing without relation to Christmas. It greeted Henry V in London in 1415 and the Marquis of Suffolk in Rouen in 1446 (Ramsay, *Lancaster and York*, i. 226; ii. 60).

writer gives a tantalizing glimpse of such a folk-revel or *laiks* at a much earlier stage. Constantine Porphyrogennetos describes amongst the New Year sports and ceremonies of the court of Byzantium in the tenth century one known as τὸ Γοτθικόν. In this the courtiers were led by two 'Goths' wearing skins and masks, and carrying staves and shields which they clashed together. An intricate dance took place about the hall, which naturally recalls the sword-dance of western Europe. A song followed, of which the words are preserved. They are only partly intelligible, and seem to contain allusions to the sacrificial boar and to the Gothic names of certain deities. From the fact that they are in Latin, the scholars who have studied them infer that the Γοτθικόν drifted to Byzantium from the court of the great sixth-century Ostrogoth, Theodoric [1].

[1] Constantinus Porphyrogenitus, *de Caeremoniis Aulae Byzantinae*, Bk. i. c. 83 (ed. Reiske, in *Corp. Script. Hist. Byz.* i. 381); cf. Bury-Gibbon, vi. 516; Kögel, i. 34; D. Bieliaiev, *Byzantina*, vol. ii; Haupt's *Zeitschrift*, i. 368; C. Kraus, *Gotisches Weihnachtsspiel*, in *Beitr. z. Gesch. d. deutschen Sprache und Litteratur*, xx (1895), 223.

CHAPTER XIII

THE FEAST OF FOOLS

[*Bibliographical Note.*—The best recent accounts of the Feast of Fools as a whole are those of G. M. Dreves in *Stimmen aus Maria-Laach* (1894), xlvii. 571, and Heuser in Wetzer and Welte, *Kirchenlexicon* (ed. 2), iv. 1402, s. v. *Feste* (2), and an article in *Zeitschrift für Philosophie und katholische Theologie* (Bonn, 1850), N. F. xi. 2. 161. There is also a summary by F. Loliée in *Revue des Revues*, xxv (1898), 400. The articles by L. J. B. Bérenger-Féraud in *Superstitions et Survivances* (1896), vol. iv, and in *La Tradition*, viii. 153 ; ix. 1 are unscholarly compilations. A pamphlet by J. X. Carré de Busserolle, published in 1859, I have not been able to see ; another, or a reprint of the same, was promised in his series of *Usages singuliers de Touraine*, but as far as I know never appeared. Of the older learning the interest is mainly polemical in J. Deslyons, *Traitez singuliers et nouveaux contre le Paganisme du Roy-boit* (1670) ; J. B. Thiers, *De Festorum Dierum Imminutione* (1668), c. 48 ; *Traité des Jeux et des Divertissemens* (1686), c. 33 ; and historical in Du Tilliot, *Mémoires pour servir à l'Histoire de la Fête des Foux* (1741 and 1751) ; F. Douce, in *Archaeologia*, xv. 225 ; M. J. R[igollot] et C. L[eber], *Monnaies inconnues des Évêques des Innocens, des Fous, &c.* (1837). Vols. ix and x of C. Leber, *Collection des meilleurs Dissertations, &c., relatifs à l'Histoire de France* (1826 and 1838), contain various treatises on the subject, some of them, by the Abbé Lebeuf and others, from the *Mercure de France*. A. de Martonne, *La Piété du Moyen Age* (1855), 202, gives a useful bibliographical list. The collection of material in Ducange's *Glossary*, s.vv. *Deposuit, Festum Asini, Kalendae*, &c., is invaluable. Authorities of less general range are quoted in the footnotes to this chapter : the most important is A. Chérest's account of the Sens feast in *Bulletin de la Soc. des Sciences de l'Yonne* (1853), vol. vii. Chérest used a collection of notes by E. Baluze (1630–1718) which are in *MS. Bibl. Nat.* 1351 (cf. *Bibl. de l'École des Chartes*, xxxv. 267). Dom. Grenier (1725–89) wrote an account of the Picardy feasts, in his *Introduction à l'Histoire de Picardie* (*Soc. des Antiquaires de Picardie, Documens inédits* (1856), iii. 352). But many of his *probata* remain in his *MSS. Picardie* in the *Bibl. Nat.* (cf. *Bibl. de l'École des Chartes*, xxxii. 275). Some of this material was used by Rigollot for the book named above.]

THE New Year customs, all too briefly summed up in the last chapter, are essentially folk customs. They belong to the ritual of that village community whose primitive organization still, though obscurely, underlies the complex society of western Europe. The remaining chapters of the present volume will deal with certain modifications and developments introduced into those customs by new social classes which gradually differentiated themselves during the Middle Ages from the village folk. The churchman, the *bourgeois*, the courtier, celebrated the New Year, even as the peasant did. But they put their own temper into the observances ; and it is worth while to accord a separate treatment to the shapes which these took in such hands, and to the resulting influence upon the dramatic conditions of the sixteenth century.

The discussion must begin with the somewhat startling New Year revels held by the inferior clergy in mediaeval cathedrals and collegiate churches, which may be known generically as the 'Feast of Fools.' Actually, the feast has different names in different localities. Most commonly it is the *festum stultorum, fatuorum* or *follorum* ; but it is also called the *festum subdiaconorum* from the highest of the *minores ordines* who, originally at least, conducted it, and the *festum baculi* from one of its most characteristic and symbolical ceremonies ; while it shares with certain other rites the suggestive title of the 'Feast of Asses,' *asinaria festa*.

The main area of the feast is in France, and it is in France that it must first of all be considered. I do not find a clear notice of it until the end of the twelfth century[1]. It is mentioned, however, in the *Rationale Divinorum Officium* († 1182–90) of Joannes Belethus, rector of Theology at Paris, and afterwards a cathedral dignitary at Amiens. 'There are four *tripudia*,' Belethus tells us, 'after Christmas. They are those of the deacons, priests, and choir-children, and finally that of the sub-deacons, *quod vocamus stultorum*, which is held according to varying uses, on the Circumcision, or on Epiphany, or on the octave of Epiphany[2].' Almost simultaneously the feast can

---

[1] Fouquier-Cholet, *Hist. des Comtes de Vermandois*, 159, says that Heribert IV (ob. †1081) persuaded the clergy of the Vermandois to suppress the *fête de l'âne*. This would have been a century before Belethus wrote. But he does not give his *probatum*, and I suspect he misread it.

[2] Belethus, c. 72 'Festum hypo-diaconorum, quod vocamus stultorum, a quibusdam perficitur in Circumcisione, a quibusdam vero in Epiphania, vel in eius octavis. Fiunt autem quatuor tripudia post Nativitatem Domini in Ecclesia, levitarum scilicet, sacerdotum, id est minorum aetate et ordine, et hypodiaconorum, qui ordo incertus est. Unde fit ut ille quandoque annumeretur inter sacros ordines, quandoque non, quod expresse ex eo intelligitur quod certum tempus non habeat,

be traced in the cathedral of Notre-Dame at Paris, through an epigram written by one Leonius, a canon of the cathedral, to a friend who was about to pay him a visit for the *festum baculi* at the New Year [1]. The *baculus* was the staff used by the precentor of a cathedral, or whoever might be conducting the choir in his place [2]. Its function in the Feast of Fools may be illustrated from an order for the reformation of the Notre-Dame ceremony issued in 1199. This order was made by Eudes de Sully, bishop of Paris, together with the dean and other chapter officers [3]. It recites a mandate sent to them by cardinal Peter of Capua, then legate in France. The legate had been informed of the improprieties and disorders, even to shedding of blood, which had given to the feast of the Circumcision in the cathedral the appropriate name of the *festum fatuorum*. It was not a time for mirth, for the fourth crusade had failed, and Pope Innocent III was preaching the fifth. Nor could such *spurcitia* be allowed in the sanctuary of God. The bishop

---

et officio celebretur confuso.' Cf. ch. xv on the three other *tripudia*.

[1] Lebeuf, *Hist. de Paris* (1741), ii. 277 ; Grenier, 365 :
Ad amicum venturum ad festum Baculi.
Festa dies aliis Baculus venit et novus annus,
Qua venies, veniet haec mihi festa dies.
Leonius is named as canon of N.-D. in the *Obituary* of the church Guérard, *Cartulaire de N.-D.* in (*Doc. inédits sur l'Hist. de France*, iv. 34), but unfortunately the year of his death is not given.

[2] During the fifteenth century the *Chantre* of N.-D. 'porta le baston' at the chief feasts as ruler of the choir (F. L. Chartier, *L'ancien Chapitre de N.-D. de Paris* (1897), 176). This *baculus* must be distinguished from the *baculus pastoralis* or *episcopi*.

[3] Guérard, *Cartulaire de N.-D.* (*Doc. inéd. sur l'Hist. de France*), i. 73 ; also printed by Ducange, s. v. *Kalendae* ; *P. L.* ccxii. 70. The *charta*, dated 1198, runs in the

names of 'Odo [de Soliaco] episcopus, H. decanus, R. cantor, Mauricius, Heimericus et Odo archidiaconi, Galo, succentor, magister Petrus cancellarius, et magister Petrus de Corbolio, canonicus Parisiensis.' Possibly the real moving spirit in the reform was the dean H[ugo Clemens], to whom the Paris *Obituary* (Guérard, *loc. cit.* iv. 61) assigns a similar reform of the feast of St. John the Evangelist. Petrus de Corbolio we shall meet again. Eudes de Sully was bishop 1196–1208. His *Constitutions* (*P. L.* ccxii. 66) contain a prohibition of 'choreae ... in ecclesiis, in coemeteriis et in processionibus.' In a second decree of 1199 (*P. L.* ccxii. 72) he provided a *solatium* for the loss of the Feast of Fools in a payment of three *deniers* to each clerk below the degree of canon, and two *deniers* to each boy present at Matins on the Circumcision. Should the abuses recur, the payment was to lapse. This donation was confirmed in 1208 by his successor Petrus de Nemore (*P. L.* ccxii. 92).

and his fellows must at once take order for the pruning of the feast. In obedience to the legate they decree as follows. The bells for first Vespers on the eve of the Circumcision are to be rung in the usual way. There are to be no *chansons*, no masks, and no hearse lights, except on the iron wheels or on the *penna* at the will of the functionary who is to surrender the cope [1]. The lord of the feast is not to be led in procession or with singing to the cathedral or back to his house. He is to put on his cope in the choir, and with the precentor's *baculus* in his hand to start the singing of the prose *Laetemur gaudiis* [2]. Vespers, Compline, Matins and Mass are to be sung in the usual festal manner. Certain small functions are reserved for the sub-deacons, and the Epistle at Mass is to be 'farced [3].' At second Vespers *Laetemur gaudiis* is to be again sung, and also *Laetabundus* [4]. Then comes an interesting direction. *Deposuit* is to be sung where it occurs five times at most, and 'if the *baculus* has been taken,' Vespers are to be closed by the ordinary officiant after a *Te Deum*. Throughout the feast canons and clerks are to remain properly in their stalls [5]. The abuses which it was intended

[1] A 'hearse' was a framework of wood or iron bearing spikes for tapers (Wordsworth, *Mediaeval Services*, 156). The *penna* was also a stand for candles (Ducange, s.v.).

[2] A *prosa* is a term given in French liturgies to an additional chant inserted on festal occasions as a gloss upon or interpolation in the text of the office or mass. It covers nearly, though not quite, the same ground as *Sequentia*, and comes under the general head of *Tropus* (ch. xviii). For a more exact differentiation cf. Frere, *Winchester Troper*, ix. *Laetemur gaudiis* is a prose ascribed to Notker Balbulus of St. Gall.

[3] *cum farsia*: a *farsia*, *farsa*, or *farsura* (Lat. *farcire*, 'to stuff'), is a *Tropus* interpolated into the text of certain portions of the office or mass, especially the *Kyrie*, the *Lectiones* and the *Epistola*. Such farces were generally in Latin, but occasionally, especially in the Epistle, in the vernacular (Frere, *Winchester Troper*, ix, xvi).

[4] *Laetabundus*: i.e. St. Bernard's prose beginning *Laetabundus exultet fidelis chorus; Alleluia* (Daniel, *Thesaurus Hymnologicus*, ii. 61), which was widely used in the feasts of the Christmas season.

[5] The document is too long to quote in full. These are the essential passages. The legate says: The Church of Paris is famous, therefore diligence must be used 'ad exstirpandum penitus quod ibidem sub praetextu pravae consuetudinis inolevit . . . Didicimus quod in festo Circumcisionis Dominicae . . . tot consueverunt enormitates et opera flagitiosa committi, quod locum sanctum . . . non solum foeditate verborum, verum etiam sanguinis effusione plerumque contingit inquinari, et . . . ut sacratissima dies . . . festum fatuorum nec immerito generaliter consueverit appellari.' Odo and the rest order:

to eliminate from the feast are implied rather than stated ; but the general character of the ceremony is clear. It consisted in the predominance throughout the services, for this one day in the year, of the despised sub-deacons. Probably they had been accustomed to take the canons' stalls. This Eudes de Sully forbids, but even in the feast as he left it the importance of the *dominus festi*, the sub-deacons' representative, is marked by the transfer to him of the *baculus*, and with it the precentor's control. *Deposuit potentes de sede : et exaltavit humiles* occurs in the *Magnificat*, which is sung at Vespers ; and the symbolical phrase, during which probably the *baculus* was handed over from the *dominus* of one year to the *dominus* of the next, became the keynote of the feast, and was hailed with inordinate repetition by the delighted throng of inferior clergy[1].

'In vigilia festivitatis ad Vesperas campanae ordinate sicut in duplo simplici pulsabuntur. Cantor faciet matriculam (the roll of clergy for the day's services) in omnibus ordinate ; rimos, personas, luminaria herciarum nisi tantum in rotis ferreis, et in penna, si tamen voluerit ille qui capam redditurus est, fieri prohibemus ; statuimus etiam ne dominus festi cum processione vel cantu ad ecclesiam adducatur, vel ad domum suam ab ecclesia reducatur. In choro autem induet capam suam, assistentibus ei duobus canonicis subdiaconis, et tenens baculum cantoris, antequam incipiantur Vesperae, incipiet prosam *Laetemur gaudiis* : qua finita episcopus, si praesens fuerit . . . incipiet Vesperas ordinate et solemniter celebrandas ; . . . a quatuor subdiaconis indutis capis sericis Responsorium cantabitur. . . . Missa similiter cum horis ordinate celebrabitur ab aliquo praedictorum, hoc addito quod Epistola cum farsia dicetur a duobus in capis sericis, et postmodum a subdiacono . . . Vesperae sequentes sicut priores a *Laetemur gaudiis* habebunt initium : et cantabitur *Laetabundus*, loco hymni. *Deposuit* quinquies ad plus dicetur loco suo ; et si

captus fuerit baculus, finito *Te Deum laudamus*, consummabuntur Vesperae ab eo quo fuerint inchoatae. . . . Per totum festum in omnibus horis canonici et clerici in stallis suis ordinate et regulariter se habebunt.'

[1] The feast lasted from Vespers on the vigil to Vespers on the day of the Circumcision. The *Hauptmoment* was evidently the *Magnificat* in the second Vespers. But what exactly took place then ? Did the cathedral precentor hand over the *baculus* to the *dominus festi*, or was it last year's *dominus festi*, who now handed it over to his newly-chosen successor ? Probably the latter. The *dominus festi* is called at first Vespers 'capam redditurus' : doubtless the cope and *baculus* went together. The *dominus festi* may have, as elsewhere, exercised disciplinary and representative functions amongst the inferior clergy during the year. His title I take to have been, as at Sens, *precentor stultorum*. The order says, ' si captus fuerit baculus' ; probably it was left to the chapter to decide whether the formal installation of the *precentor* in church should take place in any particular year.

Shortly after the Paris reformation a greater than Eudes de Sully and a greater than Peter de Capua was stirred into action by the scandal of the Feast of Fools and the cognate *tripudia*. In 1207, Pope Innocent III issued a decretal to the archbishop and bishops of the province of Gnesen in Poland, in which he called attention to the introduction, especially during the Christmas feasts held by deacons, priests and sub-deacons, of *larvae* or masks and *theatrales ludi* into churches, and directed the discontinuance of the practice[1]. This decretal was included as part of the permanent canon law in the *Decretales* of Gregory IX in 1234[2]. But some years before this it found support, so far as France was concerned, in a national council held at Paris by the legate Robert de Courçon in 1212, at which both regular and secular clergy were directed to abstain from the *festa follorum, ubi baculus accipitur*[3].

It was now time for other cathedral chapters besides that of Paris to set their houses in order, and good fortune has preserved to us a singular monument of the attempts which they made to do so. The so-called *Missel des Fous* of Sens may be seen in the municipal library of that city[4]. It is enshrined in a Byzantine ivory diptych of much older date

---

[1] *P. L.* ccxv. 1070 'Interdum ludi fiunt in eisdem ecclesiis theatrales, et non solum ad ludibriorum spectacula introducuntur in eas monstra larvarum, verum etiam in tribus anni festivitatibus, quae continue Natalem Christi sequuntur, diaconi, presbiteri ac subdiaconi vicissim insaniae suae ludibria exercentes, per gesticulationum suarum debacchationes obscoenas in conspectu populi decus faciunt clericale vilescere. . . . Fraternitati vestrae . . . mandamus, quatenus . . . praelibatam vero ludibriorum consuetudinem vel potius corruptelam curetis e vestris ecclesiis . . . exstirpare.' As to the scope of this decretal and the glosses of the canonists upon it, cf. the account of miracle plays (ch. xx).

[2] *Decretales Greg. IX,* lib. iii.tit. i. cap. 12 (*C. I. Can.* ed. Friedberg, ii.

452). I cannot verify an alleged confirmation of the decretal by Innocent IV in 1246.

[3] *C. of Paris* (1212), pars iv. c. 16 (Mansi, xxii. 842) 'A festis vero follorum, ubi baculus accipitur, omnino abstineatur. Idem fortius monachis et monialibus prohibemus.' Can. 18 is a prohibition against 'choreae,' similar to that of Eudes de Sully already referred to. Such general prohibitions are as common during the mediaeval period as during that of the conversion (cf. ch. viii), and probably covered the Feast of Fools. See e.g. *C. of Avignon* (1209), c. 17 (Mansi,xxii. 791), *C. of Rouen* (1231), c. 14 (Mansi,xxiii. 216), *C. of Bayeux* (1300), c. 31 (Mansi, xxv. 66).

[4] *Codex Senonen.* 46 A. There are two copies in the *Bibl. Nat.,* (i) *Cod. Parisin.* 10520 B, con-

than itself[1]. It is not a missal at all. It is headed *Officium Circumcisionis in usum urbis Senonensis,* and is a choir-book containing the words and music of the *Propria* or special chants used in the Hours and Mass at the feast[2]. Local tradition at Sens, as far back as the early sixteenth century, ascribed the compilation of this office to that very Petrus de

taining the text only, dated 1667; (ii) *Cod. Parisin.* 1351 C, containing text and music, made for Baluze (1630–1718). The *Officium* has been printed by F. Bourquelot in *Bulletin de la Soc. arch. de Sens* (1858), vi. 79, and by Clément, 125 sqq. The metrical portions are also in Dreves, *Analecta Hymnica Medii Aevi,* xx. 217, who cites other *Quellen* for many of them. See further on the MS., Dreves, *Stimmen aus Maria-Laach,* xlvii. 575; Desjardins, 126; Chérest, 14; A. L. Millin, *Monuments antiques inédits* (1802–6), ii. 336; Du Tilliot, 13; J. A. Dulaure, *Environs de Paris* (1825), vii. 576; Nisard, in *Archives des Missions scientifiques et littéraires* (1851), 187; Leber, ix. 344 (l'Abbé Lebeuf). Before the *Officium* proper, on f. 1ᵛᵒ of the MS. a fifteenth-century hand (Chérest, 18) has written the following quatrain:

'Festum stultorum de consuetudine
    morum
omnibus urbs Senonis festivat no-
    bilis annis,
quo gaudet precentor, sed tamen
    omnis honor
sit   Christo   circumciso   nunc
    semper et almo':

and the following couplet:

'Tartara Bacchorum non pocula
    sunt fatuorum,
tartara vincentes sic fiunt ut sa-
    pientes.'

Millin, *loc. cit.* 344, cites a MS. dissertation of one Père Laire, which ascribes these lines to one Lubin, an official at Chartres. The last eight pages of the MS. contain epistles for the feasts of St. Stephen, St. John the Evangelist, and the Innocents.

[1] Chérest, 14; Millin, *op. cit.* ii. 336 (plates), and *Voyage dans le Midi,* i. 60 (plates); Clément, 122, 162; Bourquelot, *op. cit.* vi. 79 (plates); A. de Montaiglon, in *Gazette des Beaux-arts* (1880), i. 24 (plates); E. Molinier, *Hist. générale des Arts appliqués,* i; *Les Ivoires* (1896), 47 (plate); A. M. Cust, *Ivory Workers of the Middle Ages* (1902), 34. This last writer says that the diptych is now in the Bibl. Nationale. The leaves of the diptych represent a Triumph of Bacchus, and a Triumph of Artemis or Aphrodite. It has nothing to do with the Feast of Fools, and is of sixth-century workmanship.

[2] Dreves, 575, thinks the MS. was 'für eine Geckenbruderschaft,' as the chants are not in the contemporary Missals, Breviaries, Graduals, and Antiphonals of the church. But if they were, a separate *Officium* book would be superfluous. Such special *festorum libri* were in use elsewhere, e.g. at Amiens. Nisard, *op. cit.,* thinks the *Officium* was an imitation one written by 'notaires' to amuse the choir-boys, and cites a paper of M. Carlier, canon of Sens, before the Historic Congress held at Sens in 1850 in support of this view. Doubtless the *goliardi* wrote such imitations (cf. the *missa lusorum* in Schmeller, *Carmina Burana,* 248; the *missa de potatoribus* in Wright-Halliwell, *Reliquiae Antiquae,* ii. 208; and the *missa potatorum* in F. Novati, *La Parodia sacra nelle Letterature moderne* (*Studi critici e letterari,* 289)); but this is too long to be one, and is not a burlesque at all.

Corbolio who was associated with Eudes de Sully in the Paris reformation [1]. Pierre de Corbeil, whom scholastics called *doctor opinatissimus* and his epitaph *flos et honor cleri,* had a varied ecclesiastical career. As canon of Notre-Dame and reader in the Paris School of Theology he counted amongst his pupils one no less distinguished than the future Pope Innocent III himself. He became archdeacon of Evreux, coadjutor of Lincoln (a fact of some interest in connexion with the scanty traces of the Feast of Fools in England), bishop of Cambrai, and finally archbishop of Sens, where he died in 1222. There is really no reason to doubt his connexion with the *Officium.* The handwriting of the manuscript and the character of the music are consistent with a date early in the thirteenth century [2]. Elaborate and interpolated offices were then still in vogue, and the good bishop enjoyed some reputation for literature as well as for learning. He composed an office for the Assumption, and is even suspected of contributions in his youth to goliardic song [3]. It is unlikely that he actually wrote much of the text of the *Officium Circumcisionis,* very little of which is peculiar to Sens. But he may well have compiled or revised it for his own cathedral, with the intention of pruning the abuses of the feast ; and, in so doing, he evidently admitted proses and *farsurae* with a far more liberal hand than did Eudes de Sully. The whole office, which is quite serious and not in the least burlesque, well repays study. I can only dwell on those parts of it which throw light on the general character of the celebration for which it was intended.

The first Vespers on the eve of the Circumcision are preceded by four lines sung *in ianuis ecclesiae:*

---

[1] Cf. the chapter decree of 1524 'festum Circumcisionis a defuncto Corbolio institutum,' which is doubtless the authority for the statements of Taveau, *Hist. archiep. Senonen.* (1608), 94 ; Saint-Marthe, *Gallia Christiana* (1770), xii. 60; Baluze, note in *B. N. Cod. Parisin.* 1351 C. (quoted Nisard, *op. cit.*).

[2] Dreves, 575 ; Chérest, 15, who quotes an elaborate opinion of M.

Quantin, 'archiviste de l'Yonne.' M. Quantin believes that the hand is that of a charter of Pierre de Corbeil, dated 1201, in the Yonne archives. On the other hand Nisard, *op. cit.*, and Danjou, *Revue de musique religieuse* (1847), 287, think that the MS. is of the fourteenth century.

[3] Chérest, 35 ; Dreves, 576.

'Lux hodie, lux laetitiae, me iudice tristis
quisquis erit, removendus erit solemnibus istis,
sint hodie procul invidiae, procul omnia maesta,
laeta volunt, quicunque colunt asinaria festa.'

These lines are interesting, because they show that the
thirteenth-century name for the feast at Sens was the
asinaria festa, the 'Feast of the Ass.' They are followed
by what is popularly known. as the 'Prose of the Ass,' but
is headed in the manuscript *Conductus ad tabulam.* A *conductus* is a chant sung while the officiant is conducted from
one station to another in the church[1], and the *tabula* is
the *rota* of names and duties *pro cantu et lectura,* with the
reading of which the Vespers began[2]. The text of the Prose
of the Ass, as used at Sens and elsewhere, is given in an
appendix[3]. Next come a trope and a farsed Alleluia, a
long interpolation dividing 'Alle-' and '-luia,' and then
another passage which has given a wrong impression of the
nature of the office:

'Quatuor vel quinque in falso retro altare:
   Haec est clara dies, clararum clara dierum,
   haec est festa dies, festarum festa dierum,
   nobile nobilium rutilans diadema dierum.

Duo vel tres in voce retro altare:
   Salve festa dies, toto venerabilis aevo,
      qua Deus est ortus virginis ex utero[4].'

[1] Liturgically a *conductus* is a
form of *Cantio,* that is, an interpolation in the mass or office, which
stands as an independent unit,
and not, like the Tropes, Proses
and Sequences, as an extension of
the proper liturgical texts. The *Cantiones* are, however, only a further
step in the process which began
with Tropes (Nisard, *op. cit.* 191;
Dreves, *Anal. Hymn.* xx. 6). From
the point of view of musical science
H. E. Wooldridge, *Oxford Hist. of
Music,* i. 308, defines a *conductus*
as 'a composition of equally free
and flowing melodies in all the
parts, in which the words are metrical and given to the lower voice
only.' The term is several times
used in the *Officium.* Clément, 163,
falls foul of Dulaure for taking it
as an adjective throughout, with
asinus understood.

[2] Wordsworth, *Mediaeval Ser-
vices,* 289; Clément, 126, 163.
Dulaure seems to have taken the
tabula for the altar. The English
name for the *tabula* was *wax-brede.*
An example († 1500) is printed by
H. E. Reynolds, *Use of Exeter
Cathedral,* 73.

[3] Appendix L; where the various
versions of the 'Prose' are collated.

[4] There are many hymns begin-

The phrase *in falso* does not really mean ' out of tune.' It means, ' with the harmonized accompaniment known as *en faux bourdon*,' and is opposed to *in voce*, 'in unison[1].' The Vespers, with many further interpolations, then continue, and after them follow Compline, Matins, Lauds [2], Prime, Tierce, the Mass, Sext, and second Vespers. These end with three further pieces of particular interest from our point of view. The first is a *Conductus ad Bacularium*, the name *Bacularius* being doubtless that given at Sens to the *dominus festi*[3]. This opens in a marked festal strain :

'Novus annus hodie
  monet nos laetitiae
    laudes inchoare,
felix est principium,
  finem cuius gaudium
    solet terminare.
celebremus igitur
  festum annuale,
quo peccati solvitur
  vinculum mortale
et infirmis proponitur
  poculum vitale ;
adhuc sanat aegrotantes
  hoc medicinale,

ning *Salve, festa dies*. The model is a couplet of Venantius Fortunatus, *Carmina*, iii. 9, *Ad Felicem episcopum de Pascha*, 39 (M. G. H. *Auct. Antiquiss.* iv. 1. 60) :

'Salve, festa dies, toto venerabilis aevo,
qua Deus infernum vicit et astra tenet.'

[1] Clément, 127, correcting an error of Lebeuf. A still more curious slip is that of M. Bourquelot, who found in the word *euouae*, which occurs frequently in the *Officium*, an echo of the Bacchic cry *évohé*. Now *euouae* represents the vowels of the words *Seculorum amen*, and is noted at the ends of antiphons in most choir-books to give the tone for the following psalm (Clément, 164).

[2] Clément, 138, reads *Conductus ad Ludos*, and inserts before *In Laudibus* the word *Ludarius*. Dreves, *Anal. Hymn.* xx. 221, reads *Conductus ad Laudes*. The section *In Laudibus*, not being metrical, is not printed by him, so I do not know what he makes of *Ludarius*. If Clément is right, I suppose a secular revel divided Matins and Lauds, which seems unlikely.

[3] I follow Dreves, *Anal. Hymn.* xx. 228. Clément, 151, has again *Ludarium*.

unde psallimus laetantes
   ad memoriale.
ha, ha, ha,
qui vult vere psallere,
trino psallat munere,
corde, ore, opere
   debet laborare,
ut sic Deum colere
   possit et placare.'

The *Bacularius* is then, one may assume, led out of the church, with the *Conductus ad Poculum*, which begins,

'Kalendas Ianuarias
solemnes, Christe, facias,
et nos ad tuas nuptias
vocatus rex suscipias.'

The manuscript ends, so far as the Feast of the Circumcision is concerned, with some *Versus ad Prandium*, to be sung in the refectory, taken from a hymn of Prudentius [1].

The Sens *Missel des Fous* has been described again and again. Less well known, however, is the very similar *Officium* of Beauvais, and for the simple reason that although recent writers on the Feast of Fools have been aware of its existence, they have not been aware of its *habitat*. I have been fortunate enough to find it in the British Museum, and only regret that I am not sufficiently acquainted with textual and musical palaeography to print it *in extenso* as an appendix to this chapter [2]. The date of the manuscript is probably

---

[1] Prudentius, *Cathemerinon*, iii.

[2] *Egerton MS.* 2615 (*Catalogue of Additions to MSS. in B. M. 1882–87*, p. 336). On the last page is written 'Iste liber est beati petri beluacensis.' On ff. 78, 110ᵛ are book-plates of the chapter of Beauvais, the former signed 'Vollet f[ecit].' The MS. was bought by the British Museum in 1883, and formerly belonged to Signor Pachia-rotti of Padua. It was described and a facsimile of the harmonized Prose of the Ass given in *Annales archéologiques* (1856), xvi. 259, 300. Dreves, *Anal. Hymn.* xx. 230 (1895), speaks of it as 'vielleicht noch in Italien in Privatbesitz.' This, and not the MS. used by Ducange's editors, is the MS. whose description Desjardins, 127, 168, gives from a 1464 Beauvais inventory: 'N°. 76. Item ung petit volume entre deux ais sans cuir l'ung d'icelx ais rompu à demy contenant plusieurs proses antiennes et commencemens des messes avec orai-sons commençant au iiᵉ feuillet

1227–34 [1]. Like that of Sens it contains the *Propria* for the Feast of the Circumcision from Vespers to Vespers. Unluckily, there is a lacuna of several pages in the middle [2]. The office resembles that of Sens in general character, but is much longer. There are two lines of opening rubric, of which all that remains legible is . . . *medio stantes incipit cantor.* Then comes the quatrain *Lux hodie* similarly used at Sens, but with the notable variant of *praesentia festa* for *asinaria festa.* Then, under the rubric, also barely legible, *Conductus, quando asinus adducitur* [3], comes the ' Prose of the Ass.' At the end of Lauds is the following rubric: *Postea omnes eant ante ianuas ecclesiae clausas. Et quatuor stent foris tenentes singuli urnas vino plenas cum cyfis vitreis. Quorum unus canonicus incipiat* Kalendas Ianuarias. *Tunc aperiantur ianuae.* Here comes the lacuna in the manuscript, which begins again in the Mass. Shortly before the prayer for the pope is a rubric *Quod dicitur, ubi apponatur baculus,* which appears to be a direction for a ceremony not fully described in the *Officium.* The ' Prose of the Ass ' occurs a second time as the *Conductus Subdiaconi ad Epistolam,* and on this occasion the musical accompaniment is harmonized in three parts [4]. I can find nothing about a *Bacularius* at second Vespers, but the office ends with a series of *conductus* and hymns, some of which are also harmonized in parts. The *Officium* is followed in the manuscript by a Latin cloister play of *Daniel* [5].

An earlier manuscript than that just described was formerly preserved in the Beauvais cathedral library. It dated from 1160–80 [6]. It was known to Pierre Louvet, the seventeenth-century historian of Beauvais [7], and apparently to Dom

---

Bellebouche et au pénultième *coopertum stolla candida.'* The broken board was mended, after 420 years, by the British Museum in 1884.

[1] *B. M. Catalogue, loc. cit.,* ' Written in the xiii[th] cent., probably during the pontificate of Gregory IX (1227–41) and before the marriage of Louis IX to Marguerite of Provence in 1234.' There are prayers for Gregorius Papa and Ludovicus Rex on ff. 42, 42[v], but

none for any queen of France.

[2] Between ff. 40vo and 41.

[3] So *B. M. Catalogue, loc. cit.* To me it reads like ' Conductus asi . . . adducitur.'

[4] F. 43.

[5] Cf. ch. xix.

[6] Louis VII married Adèle de Champagne in 1160 and died in 1180.

[7] Pierre Louvet, *Hist. du Dioc. de Beauvais* (1635), ii. 299, quoted

Grenier, who died in 1789 [1]. According to Grenier's account it must have closely resembled that in the British Museum.

'Aux premières vêpres, le chantre commençait par entonner au milieu de la nef : *Lux hodie, lux laetitiae*, etc. . . . À laudes rien de particulier que le *Benedictus* et son répons farcis. Les laudes finies on sortait de l'église pour aller trouver l'âne qui attendait à la grande porte. Elle était fermée. Là, chacun des chanoines s'y trouvant la bouteille et le verre à la main, le chantre entonnait la prose : *Kalendas ianuarias solemne Christe facias*. Voici ce que porte l'ancien cérémonial : *dominus cantor et canonici ante ianuas ecclesiae clausas stent foris tenentes singuli urnas vini plenas cum cyfis vitreis, quorum unus cantor incipiat : Kalendas ianuarias*, etc. Les battants de la porte ouverts, on introduisait l'âne dans l'église, en chantant la prose : *Orientis partibus*. Ici est une lacune dans le manuscrit jusque vers le milieu du *Gloria in excelsis*. . . . On chantait la litanie : *Christus vincit, Christus regnat*, dans laquelle on priait pour le pape Alexandre III, pour Henri de France, évêque de Beauvais, pour le roi Louis VII et pour Alixe ou Adèle de Champagne qui était devenue reine en 1160 ; par quoi on peut juger de l'antiquité de ce cérémonial. L'Évangile était précédé d'une prose et suivi d'une autre. Il est marqué dans le cérémonial de cinq cents ans que les encensements du jour de cette fête se feront avec le boudin et la saucisse : *hac die incensabitur cum boudino et saucita.*'

---

by Desjardins, 124. I am sorry not to have been able to get hold of the original. Nor can I find E. Charvet, *Rech. sur les anciens théâtres de Beauvais* (1881).

[1] Grenier, 362. He says the 'cérémonial' is 'tiré d'un ms. de la cathédrale de Beauvais,' and gives the footnote 'Preuv. part 1, n°.' On the prose *Kalendas Ianuarias* and the censing his footnotes refer to Ducange, s. v. *Kalendae*. The 'Preuves' for his history are scattered through the *MSS. Picardie* in the *Bibl. Nat.* No doubt the reference here is to MSS. 14 and 158 which are copies of the Beauvais office (Dreves, in *Stimmen aus Maria-Laach*, xlvii. 575). These,

or parts of them, are printed by F. Bourquelot, in *Bulletin de la Soc. arch. de Sens* (1854), vi. 171 (which also, unfortunately, I have not seen), and chants from them are in Dreves, *Anal. Hymn.* xx. 229. But here Dreves seems to speak of them as copies of Pacchiarotti's MS. (*Egerton MS.* 2615). And Desjardins, 124, says that Grenier and Bourquelot used extracts from eighteenth-century copies of Pacchiarotti's MS. in the library of M. Borel de Brétizel. Are these writers mistaken, or did Grenier only see the copies, and take his description from Louvet ? And what has become of the twelfth-century MS. ?

Dom Grenier gives as the authority for his last sentence, not the *Officium*, but the *Glossary* of Ducange, or rather the additions thereto made by certain Benedictine editors in 1733-6. They quote the pudding and sausage rubric together with that as to the drinking-bout, which occurs in both the *Officia*, as from a Beauvais manuscript. This they describe as a *codex ann. circiter* 500[1]. It seems probable that this was not an *Officium* at all, but something of the nature of a Processional, and that it was identical with the *codex* 500 *annorum* from which the same Benedictines derived their amazing account of a Beauvais ceremony which took place not on January 1 but on January 14[2]. A pretty girl, with a child in her arms, was set upon an ass, to represent the Flight into Egypt. There was a procession from the cathedral to the church of St. Stephen. The ass and its riders were stationed on the gospel side of the altar. A solemn mass was sung, in which *Introit, Kyrie, Gloria* and *Credo* ended with a bray. To crown all, the rubrics direct that the celebrant, instead of saying *Ite, missa est*, shall bray three times (*ter hinhannabit*) and that the people shall respond in similar fashion. At this ceremony also the 'Prose of the Ass' was used, and the version preserved in the *Glossary* is longer and more ludicrous than that of either the Sens or the Beauvais *Officium*.

On a review of all the facts it would seem that the Beauvais documents represent a stage of the feast unaffected by any such reform as that carried out by Pierre de Corbeil at Sens. And the nature of that reform is fairly clear. Pierre de

---

[1] Ducange, s. v. *Kalendae*, 'MS. codice Bellovac. ann. circiter 500, ubi 1ª haec occurrit rubrica *Dominus . . . ianuae*. Et alibi *Hac . . . saucita*.'

[2] Ducange, s. v. *Festum Asinorum*. Desjardins and other writers give the date of the 'codex' as twelfth century. But 500 years from 1733-6 only bring it to the thirteenth century. The mistake is due to the fact that the *first* edition of Ducange, in which the 'codex' is not mentioned, is of 1678. Clément,

158, appears to have no knowledge of the MS. but what he read in Ducange; and it is not quite clear what he means when he says that it 'd'après nos renseignements, ne renferme pas un office, mais une sorte de *mystère* postérieur d'un siècle au moins à l'office de Sens, et n'ayant aucune autorité historique et encore bien moins religieuse.' The MS. was contemporary with the Sens *Officium*, and although certainly influenced by the religious drama was still liturgic (cf. ch. xx).

Corbeil provided a text of the *Officium* based either on that of Beauvais or on an earlier version already existing at Sens. He probably added very little of his own, for the Sens manuscript only contains a few short passages not to be found in that of Beauvais. And as the twelfth-century Beauvais manuscript seems to have closely resembled the thirteenth-century one still extant, Beauvais cannot well have borrowed from him. At the same time he doubtless suppressed whatever burlesque ceremonies, similar to the Beauvais drinking-bout in the porch and censing with pudding and sausage, may have been in use at Sens. One of these was possibly the actual introduction of an ass into the church. But it must be remembered that the most extravagant of such ceremonies would not be likely at either place to get into the formal service-books[1]. As the Sens *Officium* only includes the actual service of January 1 itself, it is impossible to compare the way in which the semi-dramatic extension of the feast was treated in the two neighbouring cathedrals. But Sens probably had this extension, for as late as 1634 there was an annual procession, in which the leading figures were the Virgin Mary mounted on an ass and a *cortège* of the twelve Apostles. This did not, however, at that time take part in the Mass[2].

The full records of the Feast of Fools at Sens do not begin until the best part of a century after the probable date of its *Officium*. But one isolated notice breaks the interval, and shows that the efforts of Pierre de Corbeil were not for long successful in purging the revel of its abuses. This is a letter written to the chapter in 1245 by Odo, cardinal of Tusculum, who was then papal legate in France. He calls attention to the *antiqua ludibria* of the feasts of Christmas week and of the Circumcision, and requires these

[1] Cf. Appendix L, on an *Officium* (1553) for Jan. 1, without *stulti* or *asinus*, from Puy.

Leber, ix. 238. This is a note by J. B. Salques to the reprint of D'Artigny's memoir on the *Fête des Fous*. The writer calls the ceremony the 'fête des apôtres,' and says that it was held at the same time as the 'fête de l'âne.'

He describes a Rabelaisian *contretemps*, which is said to have put an end to the procession in 1634. No authority is given for this account, which I believe to be the source of all later notices. I may add that Ducange gives the name *Festum Apostolorum* to the feast of St. Philip and St. James on May 1.

to be celebrated, not *iuxta pristinum modum*, but with the proper ecclesiastical ceremonies. He specifically reprobates the use of unclerical dress and the wearing of wreaths of flowers [1].

A little later in date than either the Sens or the Beauvais *Officium* is a *Ritual* of St. Omer, which throws some light on the Feast of Fools as it was celebrated in the northern town on the day of the Circumcision about 1264. It was the feast of the vicars and the choir. A 'bishop' and a 'dean' of Fools took part in the services. The latter was censed in burlesque fashion, and the whole office was recited at the pitch of the voice, and even with howls. There cannot have been much of a reformation here [2].

A few other scattered notices of thirteenth-century Feasts of Fools may be gathered together. The *Roman do Renard* is witness to the existence of such a feast, with *jeux* and tippling, at Bayeux, about 1200 [3]. At Autun, the chapter forbade the *baculus anni novi* in 1230 [4]. Feasts of Fools

[1] *Cod. Senonens.* G. 133, printed by Chérest, 47; Quantin, *Recueil de pièces pour faire suite au Cartulaire général de l'Yonne* (1873), 235 (N°. 504) 'mandamus, quatenus illa festorum antiqua ludibria, quae in contemptum Dei, opprobrium cleri, et derisum populi non est dubium exerceri, videlicet, in festis Sancti Ioannis Evangelistae, Innocentium, et Circumcisionis Domini, iuxta pristinum modum nullatenus faciatis aut fieri permittatis, sed iuxta formam et cultum aliarum festivitatum quae per anni circulum celebrantur, ita volumus et praecipimus celebrari. Ita quod ipso facto sententiam suspensionis incurrat quicumque in mutatione habitus aut in sertis de floribus seu aliis dissolutionibus iuxta praedictum ritum reprobatum adeo in praedictis festivitatibus seu aliis a modo praesumpserit se habere.'

[2] L. Deschamps de Pas, *Les Cérémonies religieuses dans la Collégiale de Saint-Omer au xiii⁰ Siècle* (*Mém. de la Soc. de la Morinie*, xx. 147). The directions for Jan. 1 are fragmentary: 'In quo vicarii

ceterique clerici chorum frequentantes et eorum episcopus se habeant in cantando et officiando sicut superius dictum est in festo Sanctorum Innocentium (cf. p. 370), hoc tamen excepto quod omnia quae ista die fiunt officiando quando est festum fatuorum pro posse fiunt et etiam ullulando . . . domino decano fatuorum ferunt incensum sed prepostere ut dictum est.' *Ululatus* is, however, sometimes a technical term in church music; cf. vol. ii. p. 7.

[3] *R. de Renard*, xii. 469 (ed. Martin, vol. ii. 14):

'Dan prestre, il est la feste as fox.
Si fera len demein des chox
Et grant departie a Baieus :
Ales i, si verres les jeus.'

Branch xii of the *Roman* is the composition of Richart de Lison, who, according to Martin, suppl. 72, wrote in Normandy † 1200. The phrase 'faire les choux' = 'get drunk,' cabbages being regarded as prophylactic of the ill effects of liquor.

[4] *Hist. de l'Église d'Autun* (1774), 469, 631 'Item innovamus,

on Innocents' and New Year's days are forbidden by the statutes of Nevers cathedral in 1246[1]. At Romans, in Dauphiné, an agreement was come to in 1274 between the chapter, the archbishop of Vienne and the municipal authorities, that the choice of an abbot by the cathedral clerks known as *esclaffardi* should cease, on account of the disturbances and scandals to which it had given rise[2]. The earliest mention of the feast at Laon is about 1280[3]; while it is provided for as the sub-deacons' feast by an Amiens *Ordinarium* of 1291[4]. Nor are the ecclesiastical writers oblivious of it. William of Auxerre opens an era of learned speculation in his *De Officiis Ecclesiasticis*, by explaining it as a Christian substitute for the *Parentalia* of the pagans[5]. Towards the end of the century, Durandus, bishop of Mende, who drew upon both William of Auxerre and Belethus for

---

quod ille qui de caetero capiet baculum anni novi nihil penitus habebit de bursa Capituli' (*Registr. Capit.* s. a. 1230).

[1] Martene and Durand, *Thesaurus Anecdotorum*, iv. 1070 'in festo stultorum, scilicet Innocentium et anni novi ... multa fiunt inhonesta ... ne talia festa irrisoria de cetero facere praesumant.'

[2] Ducange, s. v. *abbas esclaffardorum*, quoting *Hist. Delphin.* i. 132 ; J. J. A. Pilot de Thorey, *Usages, Fêtes et Coutumes en Dauphiné*, i. 182. The latter writer says that there was also an *episcopus*, who was not suppressed, that the canons did reverence to him, and that the singing of the *Magnificat* was part of the feast.

[3] C. Hidé, *Bull. de la Soc. acad. de Laon* (1863), xiii. 115.

[4] Grenier, 361 'Si hoc dicitur festum stultorum a subdiaconis fiat, et dominica eveniat, ab ipsis fiat festum in cappis sericis, sicut in libris festorum continetur.' These *libri* possibly resembled those of Sens and Beauvais.

[5] *Summa Gulielmi Autissiodorensis de Off. Eccles.* (quoted by Chérest, 44, from *Bibl. Nat. MS.* 1411) 'Quaeritur quare in hac die fit festum stultorum. ... Ante ad-

ventum Domini celebrabant festa quae vocabant Parentalia ; et in illa die spem ponebant credentes quod si in illa die bene eis accideret, quod similiter in toto anno. Hoc festum voluit removere Ecclesia quod contra fidem est. Et quia extirpare omnino non potuit, festum illud permittit et celebrat illud festum celeberrimum ut aliud demittatur: et ideo in matutinali officio leguntur lectiones quae dehortantur ab huiusmodi quae sunt contra fidem (cf. p. 245). Et si ista die ab ecclesia quaedam fiunt praeter fidem, nulla tamen contra fidem. Et ideo ludos qui sunt contra fidem permutavit in ludos qui non sunt contra fidem.' There is clearly a confusion here between the Roman *Parentalia* (Feb. 13-22) and *Kalendae* (Jan. 1). On William of Auxerre, whose work remains in MS., cf. Lebeuf, in P. Desmolets, *Mémoires*, iii. 339 ; *Nouvelle Biographie universelle*, s. n. He was bishop of Auxerre, translated to Paris in 1220, ob. 1223. He must be distinguished from another William of Auxerre, who was archdeacon of Beauvais (†1230), and wrote a comment on Petrus Lombardus, printed at Paris in 1500 (Gröber, *Grundriss der röm. Philologie*, ii. 1. 239).

his *Rationale Divinorum Officiorum*, gave an account of it which agrees closely with that of Belethus[1]. Neither William of Auxerre nor Durandus shows himself hostile to the Feast of Fools. Its abuses are, however, condemned in more than one contemporary collection of sermons[2].

With the fourteenth century the records of the Feast of Fools become more frequent. In particular, the account-books of the chapter of Sens throw some light on the organization of the feast in that cathedral[3]. The *Compotus Camerarii* has, from 1345 onwards, a yearly entry *pro vino praesentato vicariis ecclesiae die Circumcisionis Domini.* Sometimes the formula is varied to *die festi fatuorum.* In course of time the whole expenses of the feast come to be a charge on the chapter, and in particular, it would appear, upon the sub-deacon canons[4]. In 1376 is mentioned, for the first time, the *dominus festi*, to whom under the title of *precentor et provisor festi stultorum* a payment is made. The *Compotus Nemorum* shows that by 1374 a prebend in the chapter woods had been appropriated to the vicars *pro festo fatuorum.* Similar entries occur to the end of the

---

[1] Gulielmus Durandus, *Rationale Div. Off.* (Antwerp, 1614), vi. 15, *de Circumcisione*, 'In quibusdam ecclesiis subdiaconi fortes et iuvenes faciunt hodie festum ad significandum quod in octava resurgentium, quae significatur per octavam diem, qua circumcisio fiebat, nulla erit debilis aetas, non senectus, non senium, non impotens pueritia . . . &c.' A reference to the heathen Kalends follows; cf. also vii. 42, *de festis SS. Stephani, Ioannis Evang. et Innocentium*, '. . . subdiaconi vero faciunt festum in quibusdam ecclesiis in festo circumcisionis, ut ibi dictum est : in aliis in Epiphania et etiam in aliis in octava Epiphaniae, quod vocant festum stultorum. Quia enim ordo ille antiquitus incertus erat, nam in canonibus antiquis (extra de aetate et qualitate) multis quandoque vocatur sacer et quandoque non, ideo subdiaconi certum ad festandum non habent diem, et eorum festum officio cele-

bratur confuso.' On Durandus cf. the translation of his work by C. Barthélemy (1854). He was born at Puymisson in the diocese of Béziers (1230), finished the *Rationale* (1284), became bishop of Mende (1285), and ob. (1296).

[2] A. Lecoy de la Marche, *La Chaire française au M. A.* 368, citing *Bibl. Nat. MSS. fr.* 13314, f. 18; 16481, N°. 93. The latter MS., which is analysed by Echard, *Script. Ord. Predicatorum*, i. 269, contains Dominican sermons delivered in Paris, 1272-3.

[3] Chérest, 49 sqq., from Sens *Chapter Accounts* in *Archives de l'Yonne*, at Auxerre. The *Compotus Camerarii* begins in 1295-6. The *Chapter Register* is missing before 1662 : some of Baluze's extracts from it are in *Bibl. Nat. Cod. Parisin.* 1351.

[4] Chérest, 55 'pro servitio faciendo die dicti festi quatenus tangit canonicos subdiaconos in ecclesia.'

fourteenth century and during the first quarter of the fifteenth[1]. Then came the war to disturb everything, and from 1420 the account-books rarely show any traces of the feast. Nor were civil commotions alone against it. As in the twelfth and thirteenth centuries, so in the fourteenth and fifteenth the abuses which clung about the Feasts of Fools rendered them everywhere a mark for the eloquence of ecclesiastical reformers. About 1400 the famous theologian and rector of Paris University, Jean-Charlier de Gerson, put himself at the head of a crusade against the *ritus ille impiissimus et insanus qui regnat per totam Franciam*, and denounced it roundly in sermons and *conclusiones*. The indecencies of the feast, he declares, would shame a kitchen or a tavern. The chapters will do nothing to stop them, and if the bishops protest, they are flouted and defied. The scandal can only be ended by the interposition of royal authority[2]. According

---

[1] Towards the end of this period the accounts are in French: 'le précentre de la feste aux fols.'

[2] *Epistola de Reformatione Theologiae* (Gerson, *Opera Omnia*, i. 121), from Bruges, 1st Jan. 1400 'ex sacrilegis paganorum idololatrarumque ritibus reliquiae,' &c.; *Solemnis oratio ex parte Universitatis Paris. in praesentia Regis Caroli Sexti* (1405, *Opera* iv. 620; cf. French version in *Bibl. Nat. anc. f. fr.* 7275, described P. Paris, *Manus. franç. de la Bibl. du Roi*, vii. 266) 'hic commendari potest bona Regis fides et vestrum omnium Dominorum variis modis religiosorum, ... in hoc quod iam dudum litteras dedistis contra abominabiles maledictiones et quasi idolatrias, quae in Francorum fiunt ecclesiis sub umbra Festi fatuorum. Fatui sunt ipsi, et perniciosi fatui, nec sustinendi, opus est executione'; *Rememoratio quorumdam quae per Praelatum quemlibet pro parte sua nunc agenda viderentur* (1407–8, *Opera*, ii. 109) 'sciatur quomodo ritus ille impiissimus et insanus qui regnat per totam Franciam poterit evelli aut saltem temperari. De hoc scilicet quod ecclesiastici faciunt, vel in die Innocentium, vel in die Circumcisionis, vel in Epiphania Domini, vel in Carnisprivio per Ecclesias suas, ubi fit irrisio detestabilis Servitii Domini et Sacramentorum: ubi plura fiunt impudenter et execrabiliter quam fieri deberent, in tabernis vel prostibulis, vel apud Saracenos et Iudaeos; sciunt qui viderunt, quod non sufficit censura Ecclesiastica; quaeratur auxilium potestatis Regiae per edicta sua vehementer urgentia'; *Quinque conclusiones super ludo stultorum communiter fieri solito* (*Opera* iii. 309) 'qui per Regnum Franciae in diversis fiunt Ecclesiis et Abbatiis monachorum et monialium ... hae enim insolentiae non dicerentur cocis in eorum culina absque dedecore aut reprehensione, quae ibi fiunt in Ecclesiis Sacrosanctis, in loco orationis, in praesentia Sancti Sacramenti Altaris, dum divinum cantatur servitium, toto populo Christiano spectante et interdum Iudaeis ... adhuc peius est dicere, festum hoc adeo approbatum esse sicut festum Conceptionis Virginis Mariae, quod paulo ante asseruit quidam in urbe Altissiodorensi secundum quod dicitur et narrari solet, &c.'

to Gerson, Charles the Sixth did on one occasion issue letters against the feast; and the view of the reformers found support in the diocesan council of Langres in 1404 [1], and the provincial council of Tours, held at Nantes in 1431 [2]. It was a more serious matter when, some years after Gerson's death, the great council of Basle included a prohibition of the feast in its reformatory decrees of 1435 [3]. By the Pragmatic Sanction issued by Charles VII at the national council of Bourges in 1438, these decrees became ecclesiastical law in France [4], and it was competent for the *Parlements* to put them into execution [5]. But the chapters were obstinate; the feasts were popular, not only with the inferior clergy themselves, but with the *spectacle*-loving *bourgeois* of the cathedral towns; and it was only gradually that they died out during the course of the next century and a half. The failure of the Pragmatic Sanction to secure immediate obedience in this matter roused the University of Paris, still possessed with the spirit of Gerson, to fresh action. On March 12, 1445, the Faculty of Theology, acting through its dean, Eustace de Mesnil, addressed to the bishops and

[1] *Council of Langres* (1404) 'prohibemus clericis . . . ne intersint . . . in ludis illis inhonestis quae solent fieri in aliquibus Ecclesiis in festo Fatuorum quod faciunt in festivitatibus Natalis Domini.'

[2] *Council of Nantes* (1431), c. 13 (J. Maan, *Sancta et Metrop. Eccl. Turonensis*, ii. 101) 'quia in talibus Ecclesiis Provinciae Turonensis inolevit et servatur usus, . . . quod festis Nativitatis Domini, Sanctorum Stephani, Ioannis et Innocentium, nonnulli Papam, nonnulli Episcopum, alii Ducem vel Comitem aut Principem in suis Ecclesiis ex novitiis praecipuis faciunt et ordinant . . . Et talia . . . vulgari eloquio festum stultorum nuncupatur, quod de residuis Kalendis Ianuariis a multo tempore ortum fuisse creditur.'

[3] *Council of Basle*, sessio xxi (June 9, 1435), can. xi (Mansi, xxix. 108) 'Turpem etiam illum abusum in quibusdam frequentatum Ecclesiis, quo certis anni celebritatibus nonnullis cum mitra, baculo ac vestibus pontificalibus more episcoporum benedicunt, alii ut reges ac duces induti quod festum Fatuorum, vel Innocentum seu Puerorum in quibusdam regionibus nuncupatur, alii larvales et theatrales iocos, alii choreas et tripudia marium et mulierum facientes homines ad spectacula et cachinnationes movent, alii comessationes et convivia ibidem praeparant.'

[4] *Council of Bourges*, July 7, 1438 (*Ordonnances des Rois de France de la Troisième Race*, xiii. 287) 'Item. Acceptat Decretum de spectaculis in Ecclesia non faciendis, quod incipit: *Turpem*, &c.'

[5] F. Aubert, *Le Parlement de Paris, sa Compétence, ses Attributions*, 1314–1422 (1890), 182; *Hist. du Parlement de Paris*, 1250–1515 (1894), i. 163.

chapters of France a letter which, from the minuteness of its indictment, is perhaps the most curious of the many curious documents concerning the feast [1]. It consists of a preamble and no less than fourteen *conclusiones*, some of which are further complicated by *qualificationes*. The preamble sets forth the facts concerning the *festum fatuorum*. It has its clear origin, say the theologians, in the rites of paganism, amongst which this Janus-worship of the Kalends has alone been allowed to survive. They then describe the customs of the feast in a passage which I must translate:

'Priests and clerks may be seen wearing masks and monstrous visages at the hours of office. They dance in the choir dressed as women, panders or minstrels. They sing wanton songs. They eat black puddings at the horn of the altar while the celebrant is saying mass. They play at dice there. They cense with stinking smoke from the soles of old shoes. They run and leap through the church, without a blush at their own shame. Finally they drive about the town and its theatres in shabby traps and carts; and rouse the laughter of their fellows and the bystanders in infamous performances, with indecent gestures and verses scurrilous and unchaste [2].'

There follows a refutation of the argument that such *ludi* are but the relaxation of the bent bow in a fashion sanctioned by antiquity. On the contrary, they are due to original sin, and the snares of devils. The bishops are besought to follow the example of St. Paul and St. Augustine, of bishops Martin,

---

[1] *Epistola et xiv. conclusiones facultatis theologiae Parisiensis ad ecclesiarum praelatos contra festum fatuorum in Octavis Nativitatis Domini vel prima Ianuarii in quibusdam Ecclesiis celebratum* (H. Denifle, *Chartularium Univ. Paris.* iv. 652; *P. L.* ccvii. 1169). The document is too long and too scholastic to quote in full. The date is March 12, 144⅘.

[2] 'Quis, quaeso, Christianorum sensatus non diceret malos illos sacerdotes et clericos, quos divini officii tempore videret larvatos, monstruosis vultibus, aut in vestibus mulierum, aut lenonum, vel histrionum choreas ducere in choro, cantilenas inhonestas cantare, offas pingues supra cornu altaris iuxta celebrantem missam comedere, ludum taxillorum ibidem exercere, thurificare de fumo fetido ex corio veterum sotularium, et per totam ecclesiam currere, saltare, turpitudinem suam non erubescere, ac deinde per villam et theatra in curribus et vehiculis sordidis duci ad infamia spectacula, pro risu astantium et concurrentium turpes gesticulationes sui corporis faciendo, et verba impudicissima ac scurrilia proferendo?'

Hilarius, Chrysostom, Nicholas and Germanus of Auxerre, all of whom made war on sacrilegious practices, not to speak of the canons of popes and general councils, and to stamp out the *ludibria*. It rests with them, for the clergy will not be so besotted as to face the Inquisition and the secular arm [1].

The *conclusiones* thus introduced yield a few further data as to the ceremonies of the feast. It seems to be indifferently called *festum stultorum* and *festum fatuorum*. It takes place in cathedrals and collegiate churches, on Innocents' day, on St. Stephen's, on the Circumcision, or on other dates. 'Bishops' or 'archbishops' of Fools are chosen, who wear mitres and pastoral staffs, and have crosses borne before them, as if they were on visitation. They take the Office, and give Benedictions to the readers of the lessons at Matins, and to the congregations. In exempt churches, subject only to the Holy See, a 'pope' of Fools is naturally chosen instead of a 'bishop' or an 'archbishop.' The clergy wear the garments of the laity or of fools, and the laity put on priestly or monastic robes. *Ludi theatrales* and *personagiorum ludi* are performed.

The manifesto of the Theological Faculty helped in at least one town to bring matters to a crisis. At Troyes the Feast of Fools appears to have been celebrated on the Circumcision in the three great collegiate churches of St. Peter, St. Stephen, and St. Urban, and on Epiphany in the abbey of St. Loup. The earliest records are from St. Peter's. In 1372 the chapter forbade the vicars to celebrate the feast without leave. In 1380 and 1381 there are significant entries of payments for damage done: in the former year Marie-la-Folle broke a *candelabrum*; in the latter a cross had to be repaired and gilded. In 1436, the year after the council of Basle, leave was given to hold the feast without irreverence. In 1439, the year after the Pragmatic Sanction, it was forbidden. In

---

[1] 'Concludimus, quod a vobis praelatis pendet continuatio vel abolitio huius pestiferi ritus; nam ipsos ecclesiasticos ita dementes esse et obstinatos in hac furia non est verisimile, quod si faciem praelati reperirent rigidam et nullatenus flexibilem a punitione cum assistentia inquisitorum fidei, et auxilio brachii saecularis, quam illico cederent aut frangerentur. Timerent namque carceres, timerent perdere beneficia, perdere famam et ab altaribus sacris repelli.'

1443, it was again permitted. But it must be outside the church. The 'archbishop' might wear a rochet, but the supper must take place in the house of one of the canons, and not at a tavern. The experiment was not altogether a success, for a canon had to be fined twenty sous *pour les grandes sottises et les gestes extravagants qu'il s'était permis à la fête des fols*[1]. Towards the end of 1444, when it was proposed to renew the feast, the bishop of Troyes, Jean Leguisé, intervened. The clergy of St. Peter's were apparently willing to submit, but those of St. Stephen's stood out. They told the bishop that they were exempt from his jurisdiction, and subject only to his metropolitan, the archbishop of Sens; and they held an elaborate revel with even more than the usual insolence and riot. On the Sunday before Christmas they publicly consecrated their 'archbishop' in the most public place of the town with a *jeu de personnages* called *le jeu du sacre de leur arcevesque*, which was a burlesque of the *saint mistère de consécration pontificale*. The feast itself took place in St. Stephen's Church. The vicar who was chosen 'archbishop' performed the service on the eve and day of the Circumcision *in pontificalibus*, gave the Benediction to the people, and went in procession through the town. Finally, on Sunday, January 3, the clergy of all three churches joined in another *jeu de personnages*, in which, under the names of *Hypocrisie*, *Faintise* and *Faux-semblant*, the bishop and two canons who had been most active in opposing the feast, were held up to ridicule. Jean Leguisé was not a man to be defied with impunity. On January 23 he wrote a letter to the archbishop of Sens, Louis de Melun, calling his attention to the fact that the rebellious clerks had claimed his authority for their action. He also lodged a complaint with the king himself, and probably incited the Faculty of Theology at Paris to back him up with the protest already described. The upshot of it all was a sharp letter from

---

[1] T. Boutiot, *Hist. de la Ville de Troyes* (1870–80), ii. 264; iii. 19. A chapter decree of 1437 lays down that a vicar who has served as 'archbishop' and has subsequently left the cathedral and returned again, need not serve a second time. It was doubtless an expensive dignity.

Charles VII to the *bailly* and *prévost* of Troyes, setting forth what had taken place, and requiring them to see that no repetition of the scandalous *jeux* was allowed[1]. Shortly afterwards the chapter of St. Peter's sent for their *Ordinarium*, and solemnly erased all that was derogatory to religion and the good name of the clergy in the directions for the feast. What the chapter of St. Stephen's did, we do not know. The canons mainly to blame had already apologized to the bishop. Probably it was thought best to say nothing, and let it blow over. At any rate, it is interesting to note that in 1595, a century and a half later, St. Stephen's was still electing its *archevesque des saulx*, and that *droits* were paid on account of the vicars' feast until all *droits* tumbled in 1789[2].

The proceedings at Troyes seem to have reacted upon the feast at Sens. In December, 1444, the chapter had issued an elaborate order for the regulation of the ceremony, in which they somewhat pointedly avoided any reference to the council of Bâsle or the Pragmatic Sanction, and cited only the legatine statute of Odo of Tusculum in 1245. The order requires that divine service shall be devoutly and decently performed, *prout iacet in libro ipsius servitii*. By this is doubtless meant the *Officium* already described. There must

---

[1] Boutiot, *op. cit.* iii. 20; A. de Jubainville, *Inventaire sommaire des Archives départementales de l'Aube*, i. 244 (G. 1275); P. de Julleville, *Les Com.* 35, *Rép. Com.* 330; A. Vallet de Viriville, in *Bibl. de l'École des Chartes*, iii. 448. The letter of Jean Leguisé to Louis de Melun is printed in *Annales archéologiques*, iv. 209; *Revue des Soc. Savantes* (2nd series), vi. 94; *Journal de Verdun*, Oct. 1751, and partly by Rigollot, 153. It is dated only Jan. 23, but clearly refers to the events of 1444-5. The *Ordonnance* of Charles VII is in Martene and Durand, *Thesaurus Novus Anecdotorum*, i. 1804; H. Denifle, *Chartularium Univ. Paris.* iv. 657. Extracts are given by Ducange, s. v. *Kalendae*. The king speaks of the Troyes affair as leading to

the Theological Faculty's letter. It is permissible to conjecture that he was moved, no doubt by the abstract rights and wrongs of the case, but also by a rumour spread at Troyes that he had revoked the Pragmatic Sanction. For, as a matter of fact, Peter of Brescia, the papal legate, was trying hard to get him to revoke it.

[2] Boutiot, *op. cit.* i. 494, iii. 20. The chapters of St. Stephen's and St. Urban's and the abbey of St. Loup all continued to make payments for their feasts after 1445. They may have been pruned of abuses. In the sixteenth century the Comte de Champagne pays five sous to the 'archevesque des Saulx' at St. Stephen's, and this appears to be the *droit* charged upon the royal demesne up to 1789.

be no mockery or impropriety, no unclerical costume, no dissonant singing. Then comes what, considering that this is a reform, appears a sufficiently remarkable direction. Not more than three buckets of water at most must be poured over the *precentor stultorum* at Vespers. The custom of ducking on St. John's eve, apparently the occasion when the precentor was elected, is also pruned, and a final clause provides that if nobody's rights are infringed the *stulti* may do what they like outside the church[1]. Under these straitened conditions the feast was probably held in 1445. There was, however, the archbishop as well as the chapter to be reckoned with. It was difficult for Louis de Melun, after the direct appeal made to him by his suffragan at Troyes, to avoid taking some action, and in certain statutes promulgated in November, 1445, he required the suppression of the whole *consuetudo* and ordered the directions for it to be erased from the chant-books[2]. There is now no mention of the feast until 1486, from which date an occasional payment for *la*

[1] Chérest, 66, from *Acta Capitularia* (Dec. 4, 1444) in *Bibl. Nat. Cod. Paris.* 1014 and 1351 'De servitio dominicae circumcisionis, viso super hoc statuto per quemdam legatum edito, et consideratis aliis circa hoc considerandis, et ad evitandum scandala, quae super hoc possent exoriri, ordinatum fuit unanimiter et concorditer, nemine discrepante, quod de caetero dictum servitium fiet, prout iacet in libro ipsius servitii, devote et cum reverentia; absque aliqua derisione, tumultu aut turpitudine, prout fiunt alia servitia in aliis festis, in habitibus per dictum statutum ordinatis, et non alias, et voce modulosa, absque dissonantia, et assistant in huiusmodi servitio omnes qui tenentur in eo interesse, et faciant debitum suum absque discursu aut turbatione servitii, potissime in ecclesia; nec proiiciatur aqua in vesperis super praecentorem stultorum ultra quantitatem trium sitularum ad plus; nec adducantur nudi in crastino festi dominicae nativitatis, sine brachis verenda tegentibus, nec etiam adducantur in ecclesia, sed ducantur ad puteum claustri, non hora servitii sed alia, et ibi rigentur sola situla aquae sine lesione. Qui contrarium fecerit occurrit ipso facto suspensionis censuram per dictum statutum latam; attamen extra ecclesiam permissum est quod stulti faciant alias ceremonias sine damno aut iniuria cuiusquam.' The proceedings on the day after the Nativity are probably explained by the election of the precentor on that day (after Vespers). The victims ducked may have failed to be present at the election; but cf. the Easter *prisio* (ch. vii).

[2] Saint-Marthe, *Gallia Christiana*, xii. 96, partly quoted by Ducange, s. v. *Kalendae.* The bishop describes the feast almost in the *ipsissima verba* of the Paris Theologians, but in one passage ('nudos homines sine verendorum tegmine inverecunde ducendo per villam et theatra in curribus et vehiculis sordidis, &c.') he adds a trait from the Sens chapter act just quoted.

feste du premier jour de l'an begins to appear again in the chapter account-books [1]. In 1511, the *servitium divinum* after the old custom is back in the church. But the chapter draws a distinction between the *servitium* and the *festum stultorum*, which is forbidden. The performance of *jeux de personnages* and the public shaving of the precentor's beard on a stage are especially reprobated [2]. The *servitium* was again allowed in 1514, 1516, 1517, and in 1520 with a provision that the *lucerna precentoris fatuorum* must not be brought into the church [3]. In 1522, both *servitium* and *festum* were forbidden on account of the war with Spain; the shaving of the precentor and the ceremony of his election on the feast of St. John the Evangelist again coming in for express prohibition [4]. In 1523 the *servitium* was allowed upon a protest by the vicars, but only with the strict exclusion of the popular elements [5]. In 1524 even the *servitium* was withheld, and though sanctioned again in 1535, 1539 and 1543, it was finally suppressed in 1547 [6]. Some feast, however, would still seem to have been held, probably outside the church, until 1614 [7], and even as late as 1634 there was a trace of it in the annual procession of the Virgin Mary and the Apostles, already referred to.

This later history of the feast at Sens is fairly typical, as the following chapter will show, of what took place all over France. The chapters by no means showed themselves

---

[1] Chérest, 68. The councils of Sens in 1460 and 1485 (p. 300) are for the province. That of 1528 (sometimes called of Sens, but properly of Paris) is national. They are not evidence for the feast at Sens itself.

[2] Ibid. 72 'Insolentias, tam de die quam de nocte, faciendo tondere barbam parte, ut fieri consuevit, in theatro . . . ac ludere personagia, die scilicet circumcisionis Domini.' The shaven face was characteristic of the mediaeval fool, minstrel, or actor (cf. ch. ii). Dreves, 586, adds that Tallinus Bissart, the precentor of this year, was threatened with excommunication.

[3] Ibid. 75.

[4] Ibid. 76 'prohibitum vicariis ne attentent, ultima die anni, in theatro tabulato ante valvas ecclesiae aut alibi in civitate Senonensi, publice barbam illius qui se praecentorem fatuorum nominat, aut alterius, radere, radifacere, permittere, aut procurare; et ne ad electionem dicti praecentoris die festo Sancti Iohannis Evangelistae sub poenis excommunicationis.

[5] Ibid. 77 'honeste, ac devote, sine laternis, sine precentore, sine delatione baculi domini precentoris, nec poterunt facere rasuram in theatro ante ecclesiam.'

[6] Ibid. 78.

[7] Dreves, 586.

universally willing to submit to the decree promulgated in the Pragmatic Sanction. In many of them the struggle between the conservative and the reforming parties was spread over a number of years. Councils, national, provincial and diocesan, continued to find it necessary to condemn the feast, mentioning it either by name or in a common category with other *ludi, spectacula, choreae, tripudia* and *larvationes*[1]. In one or two instances the authority of the *Parlements* was invoked. But in the majority of cases the feast either gradually disappeared, or else passed, first from the *churches into the streets, and then from the clerks to the *bourgeois*, often to receive a new life under quite altered circumstances at the hands of some witty and popular *compagnie des fous*[2].

---

[1] *Prov. C. of Rouen* (1445), c. 11 (Labbé, xiii. 1304) ' prohibet haec sancta synodus ludos qui fatuorum vulgariter nuncupantur cum larvatis faciebus et alias inhoneste fieri in ecclesiis aut cemeteriis'; *Prov. C. of Sens* (1485, repeats decrees of earlier council of 1460), c. 3 (Labbé, xiii. 1728), quoting and adopting Basle decree, with careful exception for *consuetudines* of Nativity and Resurrection; cf. ch. xx; *Dioc. C. of Chartres* (1526, apparently repeated 1550, tit. 16; cf. Du Tilliot, 62) quoted Bochellus, iv. 7. 46 ' denique ab Ecclesia eiiciantur vestes fatuorum personas scenicas agentium'; *Nat. C. of Paris* (1528, held by Abp. of Sens as primate), *Decr. Morum*, c. 16 (Labbé, xiv. 471) ' prohibemus ne fiat deinceps festum fatuorum aut innocentium, neque erigatur decanatus patellae.' The *Prov. C. of Rheims* (1456, held at Soissons) in Labbé, xiii. 1397, mentions only ' larvales et theatrales ioci,' ' choreae,' ' tripudia,' but refers explicitly to the Pragmatic Sanction. This, it may be observed, was suspended for a while in 1461 and finally annulled in 1516. Still more general are the terms of the *C. of Orleans* (1525, repeated 1587; Du Tilliot, 61); *C. of Narbonne* (1551), c. 46 (Labbé, xv. 26); *C. of Beauvais* (1554; E. Fleury, *Cinquante Ans de Laon*, 53); *C. of Cambrai* (1565), vi. 11 (Labbé, xv. 160); *C. of Rheims* (1583), c. 5 (Labbé, xv. 889); *C. of Tours* (1583, quoted Bochellus, iv. 7. 40). See also the councils quoted as to the Boy Bishop, in ch. xv. Finally, the *C. of Trent*, although in its 22nd session (1562) it renewed the decrees of popes and councils ' de choreis, aleis, lusibus' (*Decr. de Reformatione*, c. 1), made no specific mention of ' fatui' (*Can. et Decr. Sacros. Oec. Conc. Tridentini*, (Romae, 1845), 127). Probably the range of the feast was by this time insignificant.

[2] Cf. ch. xvi.

CHAPTER XIV

THE FEAST OF FOOLS (*continued*)

THE history of the Feast of Fools has been so imperfectly written, that it is perhaps worth while to bring together the records of its occurrence, elsewhere than in Troyes and Sens, from the fourteenth century onwards. They could probably be somewhat increased by an exhaustive research amongst French local histories, archives, and the transactions of learned societies. Of the feast in Notre-Dame at Paris nothing is heard after the reformation carried out in 1198 by Eudes de Sully[1]. The *bourgeois* of Tournai were, indeed, able to quote a Paris precedent for the feast of their own city in 1499 ; but this may have been merely the feast of some minor collegiate body, such as that founded in 1303 by cardinal Le Moine[2] ; or of the scholars of the University, or of the *compagnie joyeuse* of the *Enfants-sans-Souci*. At Beauvais, too, there are only the faintest traces of the feast outside the actual twelfth- and thirteenth-century service-books[3]. But there are several other towns in the provinces immediately north and east of the capital, Île de France, Picardy, Champagne, where it is recorded. The provision made for it in the Amiens *Ordinarium* of 1291 has been already quoted. Shortly after this,

---

[1] But there was another revel on Aug. 28. F. L. Chartier, *L'ancien Chapitre de N.-D. de Paris*, 175, quotes *Archives Nationales*, LL. 288, p. 219 'iniunctum est clericis matutinalibus, ne in festo S. Augustini faciant dissolutiones quas facere assueverant annis praeteritis.'

[2] Dulaure, *Hist. de Paris*, iii. 81 ;

Grenier, 370. A 'cardinal' was chosen on Jan. 13, and took part in the office.

[3] Grenier, 362. A model account form has the heading 'in die Circumcisionis, si fiat festum stultorum.' The 'rubriques du luminaire' provide for a distribution of wax to the sub-deacons and choir-clerks.'

bishop William de Maçon, who died in 1303, left his own
pontificalia for the use of the 'bishop of Fools[1].' When,
however, the feast reappears in the fifteenth century the
dominus festi is no longer a 'bishop,' but a 'pope.' In 1438
there was an endowment consisting of a share in the profits
of some lead left by one John le Caron, who had himself been
'pope[2].' In 1520 the feast was held, but no bells were to be
jangled[3]. It was repeated in 1538. Later in the year the
customary election of the 'pope' on the anniversary of Easter
was forbidden, but the canons afterwards repented of their
severity[4]. In 1540 the chapter paid a subsidy towards the
amusements of the 'pope' and his 'cardinals' on the Sunday
called *brioris*[5]. In 1548 the feast was suppressed[6]. At
Noyon the vicars chose a 'king of Fools' on Epiphany eve.
The custom is mentioned in 1366 as '*le gieu des roys*.' By
1419 it was forbidden, and canon John de Gribauval was
punished for an attempt to renew it by taking the sceptre off
the high altar at Compline on Epiphany. In 1497, 1499,
and 1505 it was permitted again, with certain restrictions.
The cavalcade must be over before Nones; there must be no

[1] Martonne, 49, giving no authority.

[2] Grenier, 361 ; Dreves, 583 ;
Rigollot, 15, quoting *Actum Capit.*
Leave was given to John Cornet,
of St. Michael's, John de Nœux of
St. Maurice's, rectors, and Everard
Duirech, *capellanus* of the cathedral, 'pridem electi, instituti et
assumpti in papatum stultorum
villae Ambianensis . . . quod dictus
Cornet . . . et sui praedecessores in
ipso papatu ordinati superstites die
circumcisionis Domini . . . facerent
prandium in quo beneficiati ipsius
villae convocarentur . . . ut inibi
eligere instituere et ordinare vale-
rent papam ac papatum relevarent
absque tamen praeiudicio in aliquo
tangendo servitium divinum . . .
faciendum.' Apparently the parochial clergy of Amiens joined with
the cathedral vicars and chaplains
in the feast.

[3] Grenier, 362 ; Rigollot, 15 'Servitium divinum facient honeste in
choro ecclesiae solemne, absque
faciendo insolentias aut aliquas
irrisiones, nec deferendo aliquas
campanas in dicta ecclesia, aut
alibi, et si dicti vicarii facere voluerint aliqua convivia, erit eorum
sumptibus et non sumptibus Dominorum canonicorum.'

[4] Rigollot, 16 'inhibuerunt capellanis et vicariis . . . facere recrea-
tiones solitas in pascha annotino,
etiam facere electionem de Papa
Stultorum.' Later in the year the
'iocalia Papae, videlicet annulus
aureus, tassara (*sic*) argentea et
sigillum' were put in charge of the
'canonicus vicarialis.'

[5] Rigollot, 17 'licentiam dederunt
. . . ludere die dominica proxima
brioris.' Rigollot and Leber think
that 'brioris' may be for 'burarum,'
the feast of 'buras' or 'brandons'
on the first Sunday in Lent. Can
it be the same as the 'fête des
Braies' of Laon?

[6] Grenier, 414 ; Rigollot, 17.

licentious or scurrilous *chansons*, no dance before the great doors ; the 'king' must wear ecclesiastical dress in the choir. In 1520, however, he was allowed to wear his crown *more antiquo*. The feast finally perished in 1721, owing to *la cherté des vivres*[1]. At Soissons, the feast was held on January 1, with masquing[2]. At Senlis, the *dominus festi* was a 'pope.' In 1403 there was much division of opinion amongst the chapter as to the continuance of the feast, and it was finally decided that it must take place outside the church. In 1523 it came to an end. The vicars of the chapter of Saint-Rieul had in 1501 their separate feast on January 1, with a 'prelate of Fools' and *jeux* in the churchyard[3]. From Laon fuller records are available[4]. A 'patriarch of Fools' was chosen with his 'consorts' on Epiphany eve after Prime, by the vicars, chaplains and choir-clerks. There was a cavalcade through the city and a procession called the *Rabardiaux*, of which the nature is not stated[5]. The chapter bore the expenses of the banquet and the masks. The first notice is about 1280. In 1307 one Pierre Caput was 'patriarch.' In 1454 the bishop upheld the feast against the dean, but it was decided that it should take place outside the church. A similar regulation was

[1] L. Mazière, *Noyon Religieux* in *Comptes-Rendus et Mémoires* of the *Comité arch. et hist. de Noyon* (1895), xi. 92 ; Grenier, 370, 413 ; Rigollot, 28, quoting *Actum Capit.* of 1497 'cavere a cantu carminum infamium et scandalosorum, nec non similiter carminibus indecoris et impudicis verbis in ultimo festo Innocentium per eos fetide decantatis; et si vicarii cum rege vadant ad equitatum solito, nequaquam fiet chorea et tripudia ante magnum portale, saltem ita impudice ut fieri solet.'

[2] Grenier, 365 ; Rigollot, 29, quoting, I think, a ceremonial (1350) of the collegiate church of Saint-Pierre-au-Parvis. The masquers obtained permission from some canons seated on a theatre near the house called *Grosse-Tête*.

[3] Grenier, 365 ; Rigollot, 26 ;

Dreves, 584, quoting cathedral *Actum Capit.* of 19 Dec. 1403, from Grenier's *MS. Picardie*, 158. Five canons said 'quod papa fieret in ecclesia, sed nulla elevatio, et quod, qui vellet venire, in habitu saeculari honesto veniret, et quod nulla dansio ibi fieret' ; but the casting-vote of the dean was against them, 'sed extra possent facere capellani et alii quidquid vellent.'

[4] Grenier, 370 ; Rigollot, 22 ; E. Fleury, *Cinquante Ans de Laon*, 16 ; C. Hidé, in *Bull. de la Soc. académique de Laon* (1863), xiii. 111.

[5] Hidé, *op. cit.* 116, thinks that the Patriarch used *jetons de présence*, similar to those used by the Boy Bishop at Amiens and elsewhere (ch. xv). He figures some, but they may belong to the period of the *confrérie*.

made in 1455, 1456, 1459. In 1462 the *servitium* was allowed, and the *jeu* was to be submitted to censorship. In 1464 and 1465 mysteries were acted before the *Rabardiaux*. In 1486 the *jeu* was given before the church of St.-Martin-au-Parvis. In 1490 the *jeux* and cavalcade were forbidden, and the banquet only allowed. In 1500 a chaplain, Jean Hubreland, was fined for not taking part in the ceremony. In 1518 the worse fate of imprisonment befell Albert Gosselin, another chaplain, who flung fire from above the porch upon the 'patriarch' and his 'consorts.' By 1521 the *servitium* seems to have been conducted by the *curés* of the Laon churches, and the vicars and chaplains merely assisted. The expense now fell on the *curés*, and the chapter subsidy was cut down. In 1522 and 1525 the perquisites of the 'patriarch' were still further reduced by the refusal of a donation from the chapter as well as of the fines formerly imposed on absentees. In 1527 a protest of Laurent Brayart, 'patriarch,' demanding either leave to celebrate the feast *more antiquo* or a dispensation from assisting at the election of his successor, was referred to the ex-'patriarch.' In this same year canons, vicars, chaplains and *habitués* of the cathedral were forbidden to appear at the farces of the *fête des ânes* [1]. In 1531 the 'patriarch' Théobald Bucquet, recovered the right to play comedies and *jeux* and to take the absentee fines; but in 1541 Absalon Bourgeois was refused leave *pour faire semblant de dire la messe à liesse*. The feast was cut down to the bare election of the 'patriarch' in 1560, and seems to have passed into the hands of a *confrérie*; all that was retained in the cathedral being the *Primes folles* on Epiphany eve, in which the laity occupied the high stalls, and all present wore crowns of green leaves.

At Rheims, a Feast of Fools in 1490 was the occasion for a satirical attack by the vicars and choir-boys on the fashion of the hoods worn by the *bourgeoises*. This led to reprisals in the form of some anti-ecclesiastical farces played on the following *dimanche des Brandons* by the law clerks of the

---

[1] *MS. Hist.* of Dom. Bugniatre (eighteenth century) quoted Fleury, *op. cit.* 16. I do not feel sure that the term 'fête des ânes' was really used at Laon.

Rheims *Basoche*[1]. At Châlons-sur-Marne a detailed and curious account is preserved of the way in which the Feast of Fools was celebrated in 1570[2]. It took place on St. Stephen's day. The chapter provided a banquet on a theatre in front of the great porch. To this the 'bishop of Fools' was conducted in procession from the *maîtrise des fous*, with bells and music upon a gaily trapped ass. He was then vested in cope, mitre, pectoral cross, gloves and crozier, and enjoyed a banquet with the canons who formed his 'household.' Meanwhile some of the inferior clergy entered the cathedral, sang gibberish, grimaced and made contortions. After the banquet, Vespers were precipitately sung, followed by a *motet*[3]. Then came a musical cavalcade round the cathedral and through the streets. A game of *la paume* took place in the market; then dancing and further cavalcades. Finally a band gathered before the cathedral, howled and clanged kettles and saucepans, while the bells were rung and the clergy appeared in grotesque costumes.

Flanders also had its Feasts of Fools. That of St. Omer, which existed in the twelfth century, lasted to the sixteenth[4]. An attempt was made to stop it in 1497, when the chapter forbade any one to take the name of 'bishop' or 'abbot' of Fools. But Seraphin Cotinet was 'bishop' of Fools in 1431, and led the *gaude* on St. Nicholas' eve[5]. The 'bishop' is again mentioned in 1490, but in 1515 the feast was suppressed by Francis de Melun, bishop of Arras and provost of St. Omer[6]. Some payments made by the chapter of Béthune

[1] Julleville, *Les Com.* 36; *Rép. Com.* 348; L. Paris, *Remensiana*, 32, *Le Théâtre à Reims*, 30; Coquillart, *Œuvres* (Bibl. Elzév.), i. cxxxv. Coquillart is said to have written verses for the Basoche on this occasion.

[2] Rigollot, 211, from A. Hugo, *La France pittoresque*, ii. 226, on the authority of a register of 1570 in the cathedral archives.

[3] It begins 'Cantemus ad honorem, gloriam et laudem Sancti Stephani.'

[4] L. Deschamps de Pas, in *Mém. de la Soc. des Antiq. de la Morinie*, xx. 104, 107, 133; O. Bled, in *Bull.*

Hist., de la même Soc. (1887), 62.

[5] Deschamps de Pas, *op. cit.* 133 'solitum est fieri gaude in cena ob reverentiam ipsius sancti.'

[6] Ibid. *op. cit.* 107. Grenier, 414, citing Sammarthanus, *Gallia Christiana*, x. 1510, calls Francis de Melun 'bishop of Terouanne.' An earlier reform of the feast seems implied by the undated Chapter Statute in Ducange, s. v. *Episcopus Fatuorum* 'quia temporibus retroactis multi defectus et plura scandala, deordinationes et mala, occasione Episcopi Fatuorum et suorum evenerint, statuimus et ordinamus quod de caetero in festo Circumcisionis

in 1445 and 1474 leave it doubtful how far the feast was really established in that cathedral [1]. At Lille the feast was forbidden by the chapter statutes of 1323 and 1328 [2]. But at the end of the fourteenth century it was in full swing, lasting under its ' bishop ' or ' prelate ' from the vigil to the octave of Epiphany. Amongst the payments made by the chapter on account of it is one to replace a tin can (*kanne stannee*) lost at the banquet. The ' bishop ' was chosen, as elsewhere, by the inferior clergy of the cathedral ; but he also stood in some relation to the municipality of Lille, and superintended the miracle plays performed at the procession of the Holy Sacrament and upon other occasions. In 1393 he received a payment from the duke of Burgundy for the *fête* of the *Trois Rois*. Municipal subsidies were paid to him in the fifteenth century ; he collected additional funds from private sources and offered prizes, by proclamation *soubz nostre seel de fatuité*, for pageants and *histoires de la Sainte Escripture* ; was, in fact, a sort of Master of the Revels for Lille. He was active in 1468, but in 1469 the town itself gave the prizes, in place *de l'evesque des folz, qui à présent est rué jus*. The chapter accounts show that he was re-appointed in 1485 *hoc anno, de gratia speciali*. In 1492 and 1493 the chapter payments were not to him but *sociis domus clericorum*, and from this year onwards he appears neither in the chapter accounts nor in those of the municipality [3]. Nevertheless, he did not yet cease to exist, for a statute was passed by the chapter for his extinction, together with that of the *ludus, quem Deposuit vocant*, in 1531 [4]. Five years before

Domini Vicarii caeterique chorum frequentantes et eorum Episcopus se habeant honeste, cantando et offi-ciando sicut continetur plenius in Ordinario Ecclesiae.'

[1] De la Fons-Melicocq, *Cérémonies dramatiques et Anciens Usages dans les Églises du Nord de la France* (1850), 4. In 1445 is a payment to the 'évêque des fous de Saint-Aldegonde' for a 'jeu'; in 1474, one for the chapter's share of 'le feste du vesque des asnes, par dessus tout ce que ly cœurz paya.'

[2] E. Hautcœur, *Hist. de l'Église collégiale de Saint-Pierre de Lille* (1896–9), ii. 30 ; Id. *Cartulaire de l'Église*, &c. ii. 630, 651 (*Stat. Capit.* of July 7, 1323, confirmed June 23, 1328) ; 'item volumus festum folorum penitus anullari.'

[3] Hautcœur, *Hist.* ii. 215 ; De la Fons-Melicocq, *Archives hist. et litt. du Nord de France* (3rd series), v. 374 ; Flammermont, *Album paléographique du Nord de la France* (1896), No. 45.

[4] Ducange, s. v. *Deposuit* (*Stat. Capit. S. Petri Insul.* July 13, 1531,

this the canons and vicars were still wearing masks and playing comedies in public[1]. The history of the feast at Tournai is only known to me through certain legal proceedings which took place before the *Parlement* of Paris in 1499. It appears that the young *bourgeois* of Tournai were accustomed to require the vicars of Notre-Dame to choose an *évesque des sotz* from amongst themselves on Innocents' day. In 1489 they took one Matthieu de Porta and insulted him in the church itself. The chapter brought an action in the local court against the *prévost et jurez* of the town; and in the meantime obtained provisional letters inhibitory from Charles VIII, forbidding the vicars to hold the feast or the *bourgeois* to enforce it. All went well for some years, but in 1497 the *bourgeois* grumbled greatly, and in 1498, with the connivance of the municipal authorities themselves, they broke out. On the eve of the Holy Innocents, between nine and ten o'clock, Jacques de l'Arcq, mayor of the *Edwardeurs*, and others got into the house of Messire Pasquier le Pamê, a chaplain, and dragged him half naked, through snow and frost, to a *cabaret*. Seven or eight other vicars, one of whom was found saying his Hours in a churchyard, were similarly treated, and as none of them would be made *évesque des sotz* they were all kept prisoners. The chapter protested to the *prévost et jurez*, but in vain. On the following day the *bourgeois* chose one of the vicars *évesque*, baptized him by torchlight with three buckets of water at a fountain, led him about for three days in a surplice, and played scurrilous farces. They then dismissed the vicar,

---

ex Reg. k.) 'Scandala et ludibria quae sub Fatuitatis praetextu per beneficiatos et habituatos dictae nostrae ecclesiae a vigilia usque ad completas octavas Epiphaniae fieri et exerceri consueverunt ... deinceps nullus nominetur, assumatur et creetur praelatus follorum, nec ludus, quem Deposuit vocant, in dicta vigilia, aut alio quocumque tempore, ludatur, exerceatur, aut fiat.' Probably to this date belongs the very similarly worded but undated memorandum in Delobel, *Collectanea*, f. 76, which Hautcœur,

Hist. ii. 220, 224, assigns to 1490. This adds 'de non ... faciendo officio ... per vicarios in octava Epiphaniae.' The municipal duties of the *praelatus* fell to the *confrérie* of the Prince des Foux, afterwards Prince d'Amour, which held revels in 1547 (Du Tilliot, 87), and still later to the 'fou de la ville' who led the procession of the Holy Sacrament, and flung water at the people in the eighteenth century (Leber, ix. 265).

[1] Rigollot, 14.

and elected as *évesque* a clerk from the diocese of Cambrai, who defied the chapter. They drove Jean Parisiz, the *curé* of La Madeleine, who had displeased them, from his church in the midst of Vespers, and on Epiphany day made him too a prisoner. In the following March the chapter and Messire Jean Parisiz brought a joint action before the High Court at Paris against the delinquents and the municipal authorities, who had backed them up. The case came on for hearing in November, when it was pleaded that the custom of electing an *évesque des sotz* upon Innocents' day was an ancient one. The ceremony took place upon a scaffold near the church door; there were *jeux* in the streets for seven or eight days, and a final *convici* in which the canons and others of the town were satirized. The chapter and some of the citizens sent bread and wine. The same thing was done in many dioceses of Picardy, and even in Paris. It was all *ad solacium populi*, and divine service was not disturbed, for nobody entered the church. The vicar who had been chosen *évesque* thought it a great and unexpected honour. There would have been no trouble had not the *évesque* when distributing hoods with ears at the end of the *jeux* unfortunately included certain persons who would rather have been left out, and who consequently stirred up the chapter to take action. The court adjourned the case, and ultimately it appears to have been settled, for one of the documents preserved is endorsed with a note of a *concordat* between the chapter and the town, by which the feast was abolished in 1500 [1].

Of the Feast of Fools in central France I can say but little. At Chartres, the *Papi-Fol* and his cardinals committed many insolences during the first four days of the year, and exacted *droits* from passers-by. They were suppressed in

---

[1] Two documents are preserved, each giving a full account of the event: (*a*) summons of the delinquents before the Parlement, dated March 16, 1498 (J. F. Foppens, *Supplément* (1748), to A. Miraeus, *Opera Diplomatica*, iv. 295). This is endorsed with some notes of further proceedings; (*b*) official notes of the hearing on Nov. 18, 1499 (*Bibl. de l'École des Chartes*, iii. 568); cf. Julleville, *Rép. com.* 355; Cousin, *Hist. de Tournay*, Bk. iv. 261. The Synod of Tournai in 1520 still found it necessary to forbid students to appear in church 'en habits de fous, en représentant des personnages de comédie' on St. Nicholas' day, Innocents' day, or 'la fête de l'évêque' (E. Fleury, *Cinquante Ans de Laon*, 54).

1479 and again in 1504[1]. At Tours a *Ritual* of the fourteenth century contains elaborate directions for the *festum
novi anni, quod non debet remanere, nisi corpora sint humi.*
This is clearly a reformed feast, of which the chief features
are the dramatic procession of the *Prophetae*, including
doubtless Balaam on his ass, in church, and a *miraculum*
in the cloister[2]. The 'Boy Bishop' gives the benediction
at Tierce, and before Vespers there are *chori* (carols, I suppose) also in the cloisters. At Vespers *Deposuit* is sung
three times, and the *baculus* may be taken. If so, the
thesaurarius is beaten with *baculi* by the clergy at Compline,
and the new *cantor* is led home with beating of *baculi* on
the walls[3]. At Bourges, the use of the 'Prose of the Ass'
in Notre-Dame de Sales seems to imply the existence of
the feast, but I know no details[4]. At Avallon the *dominus
festi* seems to have been, as at Laon, a 'patriarch,' and to
have officiated on Innocents' day. A chapter statute regulated the proceedings in 1453, and another abolished them
in 1510[5]. At Auxerre, full accounts of a long chapter
wrangle are preserved in the register[6]. It began in 1395
with an order requiring the decent performance of the
servitium, and imposing a fee upon newly admitted canons

[1] Rigollot, 19, 157.
[2] Cf. ch. xix.
[3] Martene, iii. 41 '[at second Ves-
pers] Cantor . . . dicit ter *Deposuit*
baculum tenens, et si baculus capitur, *Te Deum Laudamus* incipietur
. . . [at Compline] ascendunt duo
clerici super formam thesaurarii et
cantant *Haec est sancta dies*, &c.
et post *Conserva Deus*, et dum
canitur verberant eum clerici baculis, et ante eos cantores festi et
erupitores . . . Post incipit cantor
novus *Verbum caro factum est*, et
hoc cantando ducunt eum in domum
suam per parietes cum baculis
feriendo. Si autem baculus non
accipitur, nihil de iis dicitur, sed
vadunt, et extinguitur luminare.'
[4] Cf. Appendix L.
[5] Chérest, 9, 55, quoting *Acta
Capit.* (1453) 'item circa festum Innocentium ordinatum est quod in

ecclesia nullae fient insolenciae seu
derisiones potissime tempore divini
servitii et quod pulsentur matutinae
non ante quartam horam. Permittimus tamen quod reverenter et in
habitu ecclesiastico per Innocentes
et alios iuvenes de sedibus inferiori-
bus dictum fiat officium, saltem
circa ea quae sine sacris ordinibus
possunt exerceri'; (1510) 'item
turpem illum abusum festi fatuorum
in nostra hactenus ecclesia, proh
dolor, frequentatum quo in celebri-
tate sanctorum Innocentium quidam
sub nomine patriarchali divinum
celebrant officium, penitus detesta-
mus, abolemus et interdicimus.'
[6] Lebeuf, *Mém. concernant l'Histoire . . . d'Auxerre* (ed. Challe et
Quantin, 1848–55), ii. 30; iv. 232
(quoting *Acta Capit.* partly extracted by Ducange, s.v. *Kalendae*);
and in Leber, ix. 358, 375, 385.

towards the feast. In 1396 the feast was not held, owing to the recent defeat of Sigismund of Hungary and the count of Nevers by Bajazet and his Ottomans at Nicopolis [1]. In 1398 the dean entered a protest against a grant of wine made by the chapter to the thirsty revellers. In 1400 a further order was passed to check various abuses, the excessive ringing of bells, the licence of the *sermones fatui*, the impounding of copes in pledge for contributions, the beating of men and women through the streets, and all *derisiones* likely to bring discredit on the church [2]. In the following January, the bishop of Auxerre, Michel de Crency, intervened, forbidding the *fatui* to form a 'chapter,' or to appoint 'proctors,' or *clamare la fête aux fous* after the singing of the Hours in the church. This led to a storm. The bishop brought an action in the secular court, and the chapter appealed to the ecclesiastical court of the Sens province. In June, however, it was agreed as part of a general *concordat* between the parties, that all these proceedings should be *non avenu* [3]. It seems, however, to have been understood that the chapter would reform the feast. On December 2, the abbot of Pontigny preached a sermon before the chapter in favour of the abolition of the feast, and on the following day the dean came down and warned the canons that it was the intention of the University of Paris to take action, even if necessary, by calling in the secular arm [4]. It was better to

---

[1] 'Cum domini nostri rex et alii regales Franciae sint valde dolorosi, propter nova armaturae factae in partibus Ungariae contra Saracenos et inimicos fidei'; cf. Bury-Gibbon, vii. 35.

[2] 'Ordinavit quod de caetero omnes, qui de festo fatuorum fuerint, non pulsent campanam capituli sui post prandium, dempta prima die in qua suum episcopum eligent, et etiam quod in suis sermonibus fatuis non ponant seu dicant aliqua opprobria in vituperium alicuius personae.'

[3] Lebeuf, *Hist. d'Auxerre*, ii. 30.

[4] I suppose the intended action took shape in the *Quinque Conclusiones* of Gerson (p. 292), in which he quotes the dictum of an Auxerre

preacher that the feast of Fools was as *approbatum* as that of the Conception. To this there seems to be a reference in the account of the Abbot of Pontigny's sermon in the *Acta Capit.* 'praedicavit ... quod dictum festum non erat, nec unquam fuerat a Deo nec Ecclesia approbandum seu approbatum.' Lebeuf, in Leber, ix. 385, points out that Gerson was intimate with one member of the Auxerre chapter This was Nicolas de Clamengis, whose *Opera*, 151 (ed. Lydius, 1613), include a treatise *De novis celebritatibus non instituendis*, in which the suppression of feasts in his diocese by Michael of Auxerre is alluded to.

reform themselves than to be reformed. It was then agreed to suppress the abuses of the feast, the sermons and the wearing of unecclesiastical garb, and to hold nothing but a *festum subdiaconorum* on the day of the Circumcision. Outside the church, however, the clergy might dance and promenade (*chorizare ... et ... spatiare*) on the *place* of St. Stephen's. These regulations were disregarded, on the plea that they were intended to apply only to the year in which they were made. In 1407 the chapter declared that they were to be permanent, but strong opposition was offered to this decision by three canons, Jean Piqueron, himself a sub-deacon, Jean Bonat, and Jean Berthome, who maintained that the *concordat* with the bishop was for reform, not for abolition. The matter was before the chapter for the last time, so far as the extant documents go, in 1411. On January 2, the dean reported that in spite of the prohibition certain *canonici tortrarii*[1], chaplains and choir-clerks had held the feast. A committee of investigation was appointed, and in December the prohibition was renewed. Jean Piqueron was once more a protestant, and on this occasion obtained the support of five colleagues[2]. It may be added that in the sixteenth century an *abbas stultorum* was still annually elected on July 18, beneath a great elm at the porch of Auxerre cathedral. He was charged with the maintenance of certain small points of choir discipline[3].

In Franche Comté and Burgundy, the Feast of Fools is also found. At Besançon it was celebrated by all the four great churches. In the cathedrals of St. John and St. Stephen, 'cardinals' were chosen on St. Stephen's day by the deacons

[1] These were canons of inferior rank at Auxerre (Ducange, s. v. *tortarius*).

[2] Canons J. Boileaue, Devisco, Pavionis, Viandi and H. Desnoes. Was Viandi the canon John Vivien who, according to Lebeuf, *Hist. d'Auxerre*, iv. 234, noted on his Breviary (now *Bibl. Nat. Cod. Colbert.* 4227) that at first Vespers on the Circumcision, *Hodie Christus* was sung after each Psalm, 'quia Festum Circumcisionis vocatur in diversis ecclesiis festum Fatuorum'?

[3] Chérest, 76; Julleville, *Les Com.* 234; Lebeuf, in Leber, ix. 358, 373, quoting a *Cry pour l'abbé de l'église d'Ausserre et ses supposts*, from the *Œuvres* of Roger de Collerye (1536). This resembles the productions of the *confréries des fous* (cf. ch. xvi) and begins,

'Sortez, saillez, venez de toutes parts,
Sottes et sots plus prompts que liépars.'

and sub-deacons, on St. John's day by the priests, on the Holy Innocents' day by the choir-clerks and choir-boys. In the collegiate churches of St. Paul and St. Mary Magdalen, 'bishops' or 'abbots' were similarly chosen. All these *domini festorum* seem to have had the generic title of *rois des fous*, and on the choir-feast four cavalcades went about the streets and exchanged railleries (*se chantaient pouille*) when they met. In 1387 the *Statutes* of cardinal Thomas of Naples ordered that the feasts should be held jointly in each church in turn ; and in 1518 the cavalcades were suppressed, owing to a conflict upon the bridge which had a fatal ending. Up to 1710, however, *reges* were still elected in St. Mary Magdalen's ; not, indeed, those for the three feasts of Christmas week, but a *rex capellanorum* and a *rex canonicorum*, who officiated respectively on the Circumcision and on Epiphany [1]. At Autun the feast of the *baculus* in the thirteenth century has already been recorded. In the fifteenth and sixteenth centuries some interesting notices are available in the chapter registers [2]. In 1411 the feast required reforming. The canons were ordered to attend in decent clothes as on the Nativity ; and the custom of leading an ass in procession and singing a *cantilena* thereon was suppressed [3]. In 1412 the abolition of the feast was decreed [4]. But in 1484 it was sanctioned again, and licence was given to punish those who failed to put in an appearance at the Hours by burning at the well [5].

[1] Dunot de Charnage, *Hist. de Besançon*, i. 227 ; Rigollot, 47 ; Leber, ix. 434 ; x. 40.

[2] The anonymous author of the *Histoire de l'Église d'Autun* (1774), 462, 628, gives *probata* from the *Acta Capitularia* for some, but not all of his statements. Du Tilliot, 24 and possibly Ducange, s. v. *Festum Asinorum* appear also to have seen at least one register kept by the *rotarius* which covered the period 1411 to 1416.

[3] Deliberaverunt super festo folorum quod fieri consuevit anno quolibet in festo Circumcisionis Domini, ad resecandum superfluitates et derisiones quae fieri consueverunt ... item quod amodo non adducatur asinus ad processionem dictae diei, ut fuit solitum fieri, nec dicatur cantilena quae dici solebat super dictum asinum, et supra officio quod fieri consuetum est dicta die in Ecclesia dicti Domini postea providebunt.' Ducange says that the ass had a golden foot-cloth of which four of the principal canons held the corners. On the *cantilena* cf. Appendix L.

[4] 'Ordinaverunt quod festum folorum penitus cesset.'

[5] 'Concluserunt ad requestum stultorum quod hoc anno fiat festum folorum ... cum solemnitatibus in dicto festo requisitis in libris dicti festi descriptis ... qui defecerit in matutinis et aliis horis statutis comburatur in fonte.'

This custom, however, was forbidden in 1498[1]. Nothing more is heard of the *asinus*, but it is possible that he figured in the play of *Herod* which was undoubtedly performed at the feast, and which gave a name to the *dominus festi*[2]. Under the general name of *festa fatuorum* was included at Autun, besides the feast of the Circumcision, also that of the 'bishop' and 'dean' of Innocents, and a *missa fatuorum* was sung *ex ore infantium* from the Innocents' day to Epiphany[3]. In 1499 Jean Rolin, abbot of St. Martin's and dean of Autun, led a renewed attack upon the feast. He had armed himself with a letter from Louis XI, and induced the chapter, in virtue of the Basle decree, to suppress both Herod and the 'bishop' of Innocents[4]. In 1514 and 1515 the play of *Herod* was performed ; but in 1518, when application was made to the chapter to sanction the election of both a 'Herod' and the 'bishop' and 'dean' of Innocents, they applied to the king's official for leave, and failed to get it. Finally in 1535 the chapter recurred to the Basle decree, and again forbade the feast, particularly specifying under the name of *Gaigizons* the obnoxious ceremony of 'ducking.[5]' The feast held in the ducal, afterwards royal chapel of Dijon yields documents which are unique, because they are in French verse. The first is a *mandement* of Philip the Good, duke of Burgundy, in 1454, confirming, on the request of the *haut-Bâtonnier*, the privilege of the fête, against those who would abolish it. He declares

> 'Que cette Fête célébrée
>   Soit à jamais un jour l'année,

---

[1] 'In fine Matutinarum nonnulli larvati alii inordinate vestiti choreas, tripudia et saltus in eadem ecclesia faciunt . . . [aliquos] ad fontem deferunt et ibi aqua intinguntur.'

[2] Cf. ch. xix. A representation of the 'Flight into Egypt' might well come into a play of Herod. The *Hist. d'Autun*, 462, says that, before the reform of 1411, the ass appeared as Balaam's ass in connexion with a *Prophetae* on a stage at the church door. There was a procession to church, and the Prose. The *rex* received a cheese from the chapter.

[3] Cf. ch. xv.

[4] 'Regna Herodis et Episcopatus Innocentium, seu fatuorum festa hactenus . . . fieri solita . . . abolentes.'

[5] 'Quod vulgo dicitur *Les Gaigizons* . . . amplius neminem balneare aut . . . pignus aufferre.' It is here only the choice of 'bishop' and 'dean' of Innocents, 'quod festum fatuorum a nonnullis nuncupatur' that is forbidden. Apparently 'Herod' had died out.

Le premier du mois de Janvier ;
Et que joyeux Fous sans dangier,
De l'habit de notre Chapelle,
Fassent la Fête bonne et belle,
Sans outrage ni derision.'

In 1477 Louis XI seized Burgundy, and in 1482 his representatives, Jean d'Amboise, bishop and duke of Langres, lieutenant of the duchy, and Baudricourt the governor, accorded to Guy Baroset

'Protonotaire et Procureur des Foux,'

a fresh confirmation for the privilege of the feast held by

'Le Bâtonnier et tous ses vrais suppôts [1].'

There was a second feast in Dijon at the church of St. Stephen. In 1494 it was the custom here, as at Sens, to shave the 'precentor' of Fools upon a stage before the church. In 1621 the vicars still paraded the streets with music and lanterns in honour of their 'precentor [2].' In 1552, however, the Feasts of Fools throughout Burgundy had been prohibited by an *arrêt* of the *Parlement* of Dijon. This was immediately provoked by the desire of the chapter of St. Vincent's at Châlons-sur-Saône to end the scandal of the feast under their jurisdiction. It was, however, general in its terms, and probably put an end to the *Chapelle* feast at Dijon, since to about this period may be traced the origin of the famous *compagnie* of the *Mère-Folle* in that city [3].

In Dauphiné there was a *rex et festum fatuorum* at St. Apollinaire's in Valence, but I cannot give the date [4]. At Vienne the *Statutes* of St. Maurice, passed in 1385, forbid the *abbas stultorum seu sociorum*, but apparently allow *rois*

---

[1] Du Tilliot, 100; Petit de Julleville, *Les Com.* 194. Amongst Du Tilliot's woodcuts is one of a *bâton* (No. 4) bearing this date 1482. It represents a nest of fools.

[2] Ibid. 21.

[3] Ibid. 74 'Icelle cour a ordonné et ordonne, que defenses seront faites aux Choriaux et habitués de ladite Église Saint-Vincent et de toutes autres Églises de son Ressort, et dorésnavant le jour de la Fête des Innocens, et autres jours faire aucunes insolences et tumultes esdites Églises, vacquer en icelles, et courir parmi les villes avec danses et habits indécens à leur état ecclésiastique.'

[4] Pilot de Thorey, i. 177.

on the Circumcision and Epiphany, as well as in the three post-Nativity feasts. They also forbid certain *ludibria*. No *pasquinades* are to be recited, and no one is to be carried *in Rost* or to have his property put in pawn[1]. More can be said of the feast at Viviers. A *Ceremonial* of 1365 contains minute directions for its conduct[2]. On December 17 the *sclafardi et clericuli* chose an *abbas stultus* to be responsible, as at Auxerre, for the decorum of the choir throughout the year. He was shouldered and borne to a place of honour at a drinking-bout. Here even the bishop, if present, must do him honour. After the drinking, the company divided into two parts, one composed of inferior clergy, the other of dignitaries, and sang a doggerel song, each endeavouring to sing its rival down. They shouted, hissed, howled, cackled, jeered and gesticulated; and the victors mocked and flouted the vanquished. Then the door-keeper made a proclamation on behalf of the 'abbot,' calling on all to follow him, on pain of having their breeches slit, and the whole crew rushed violently out of the church. A progress through the town followed, which was repeated daily until Christmas eve[3]. On the three post-Nativity feasts,

[1] Pilot de Thorey, i. 178 (*Statuta*, c. 40) 'Item statuimus et ordinamus, quod ex nunc cessent abusus qui fieri consueverunt per abbatem vulgariter vocatum stultorum seu sociorum . . . Item statuimus et ordinamus, cum in ecclesia Dei non deceat fieri ludibria vel inhonesta committi, quod, in festis Sanctorum Stephani, Iohannis evangelistae, Innocentium et Epiphaniae, domino de cetero officiatur et desserviatur in divinis, prout in aliis diebus infra fieri statuetur, et quod nullus, de cetero, ut quandoque factum fuisse audivimus, portetur in Rost, et quod, de nulla persona ecclesiastica vel seculari cuiuscumque status existat, inhonesti vel diffamatorii rithmi recitentur, et quod nullus pignoret aut aliena rapiat quovismodo.' A Vienne writer, in Leber, ix. 259, adds that the performance of the office on the three post-Nativity feasts by deacons,

priests, and choir in the high stalls was continued by these Statutes, but suppressed about 1670.

[2] Lancelot, in *Hist. de l'Académie des Inscriptions* (ed. 4to), vii. 255, (ed. 12mo), iv. 397; Ducange, s. v. *Kalendae*; Du Tilliot, 46.

[3] '. . . *Te Deum*, et tunc per consocios subtollitur, et elevatur, ac super humeros ad domum, ubi caeteri pro potu sunt congregati, laetanter deportatur, atque in loco ad hoc specialiter ornato et praeparato ponitur, statuitur et collocatur. Ad eius introitum omnes debent assurgere, etiam dominus Episcopus, si fuerit praesens, ac impensa reverentia consueta per consodales et consocios electo, fructus species et vinum cum credentia ei dentur, &c. Sumpto autem potu idem Abbas vel maior succentor ex eius officio absente Abbate incipit cantando ea quae secuntur; ab ista enim parte sclafardi, clericuli ceterique de

a distinct *dominus festi*, the *episcopus stultus*, apparently elected the previous year, took the place of the *abbas*. On each of these days he presided at Matins, Mass, and Vespers, sat in full pontificals on the bishop's throne, attended by his ' chaplain,' and gave the Benedictions. Both on St. Stephen's and St. John's days these were followed by the recitation of a burlesque formula of indulgence [1]. The whole festivity seems to have concluded on Innocents' day with the election of a new *episcopus*, who, after the shouldering and the drinking-bout, took his stand at a window of the great hall of the bishop's palace, and blessed the people of the city [2]. The *episcopus* was bound to give a supper to his fellows. In 1406 one William Raynoard attempted to evade this obligation. An action was brought against him in the court of the bishop's official, by the then *abbas* and his predecessor.

suptus chorum debent esse simulque canere, ceteri vero desuper chorum ab alia parte simul debent respondere . . . Sed dum eorum cantus saepius et frequentius per partes continuando cantatu tanto amplius ascendendo elevatur in tantum quod una pars cantando, clamando, *è fort cridar*, vincit aliam. Tunc enim inter se ad invicem clamando, sibilando, ululando, cachinnando, deridendo ac cum manibus demonstrando, pars victrix quantum potest partem adversam deridere conatur ac superare, iocosasque trufas sine taedio breviter inferre.

A parte Abbatis. *Heros.*
Alter chorus. *Et nolic. nolierno.*
A parte Abbatis. *Ad fons sancti bacon.*
Alii. *Kyrie Eleison.*
Quo finito illico gachia ex eius officio facit praeconizationem sic dicendo: *De par Mossenhor Labat è sos Cosselliers vos fam assaber que tot homs lo sequa, lay on voura anar, ea quo sus la pena de talhar lo braye.* Tunc Abbas aliique domum exeunt impetum facientes. Iuniores canonici chorarii scutiferique domini Episcopi et canonicorum Abbatem comitantur per urbem, cui transeunti salutem omnes im-

pertiunt. In istis vero visitationibus (quae usque ad vigiliam Natalis Domini quotidie vespere fiunt) Abbas debet semper deportare habitum, sive fuerit manta, sive tabardum, sive cappa una cum capputio de variis folrato.' It is curious how the characteristic meridional love of sheer noise and of gesture comes out.

[1] *De indulgentiis dandis :*
[St. Stephen's Day]
De par Mossenhor l'Evesque,
Que Dieus vos donne gran mal
  al bescle,
Avec una plena balasta de pardos
E dos das de raycha de sot lo
  mento.
[St. John's Day]
Mossenhor ques ayssi presenz
Vos dona xx balastas de mal
  de dens,
Et à vos autras donas atressi
Dona 1^a coa de rossi.
[2] ' Deinde electus per sclafardos subtollitur et campanilla precedente portatur ad domum episcopalem, ad cuius adventum ianuae domus, absente vel praesente ipso domino Episcopo, debent totaliter aperiri, ac in una de fenestris magni tinelli debet deponi, et stans dat ibi iterum benedictionem versus villam.'

It was referred to the arbitration of three canons, who decided that Raynoard must give the supper on St. Bartholomew's next, August 24, at the accustomed place (a tavern, one fears) in the little village of Gras, near Viviers[1].

Finally, there are examples of the Feast of Fools in Provence. At Arles it was held in the church of St. Trophime, and is said to have been presented, out of its due season, it may be supposed, for the amusement of the Emperor Charles IV at his coronation in 1365, to have scandalized him and so to have met its end[2]. Nevertheless in the fifteenth century an 'archbishop of Innocents,' alias stultus, still sang the 'O' on St. Thomas's day, officiated on the days of St. John and the Innocents, and on St. Trophime's day (Dec. 29) paid a visit to the abadesse fole of the convent of Saint-Césaire. The real abbess of this convent was bound to provide chicken, bread and wine for his regaling[3]. At Fréjus in 1558 an attempt to put down the feast led to a riot. The bishop, Léon des Ursins, was threatened with murder, and had to hide while his palace was stormed[4]. At Aix the chapter of St. Saviour's chose on St. Thomas's day, an episcopus fatuus vel Innocentium from the choir-boys. He officiated on Innocents' day, and boys and canons exchanged stalls. The custom lasted until at least 1585[5]. Antibes, as late as 1645, affords a rare example of the feast held by a religious house. It was on Innocents' day in the church of the Franciscans. The choir and office were left to the lay-brothers, the quêteurs, cooks and gardeners. These put on the vestments inside out, held the books upside down, and wore spectacles with rounds of orange peel instead of glasses. They blew the ashes from the censers upon each other's faces and heads, and instead of the proper liturgy chanted confused and inarticulate gibberish. All this is

[1] Ducange, s.v. Kalendae; Bérenger-Féraud, iv. 14.

[2] Papon, Hist. de Provence (1784), iv. 212.

[3] Rigollot, 125.

[4] Bérenger-Féraud, iv. 131, quoting Mireur, Bull. hist. et philos. du Comité des Travaux hist. (1885), Nos. 3, 4.

[5] Rigollot, 171 ; Fauris de Saint-Vincent, in Magasin encyclopédique (1814), i. 24. A chapter inventory mentions a 'mitra episcopi fatuorum.' The Council of Aix in 1585 (Labbé, xv. 1146) ordered the suppression of 'ludibria omnia et pueriles ac theatrales lusus' on Innocents' day.

recorded by the contemporary free-thinker Mathurin de Neuré in a letter to his leader and inspirer, Gassendi[1].

It will be noticed that the range of the Feast of Fools in France, so far as I have come across it, seems markedly to exclude the west and south-west of the country. I have not been able to verify an alleged exception at Bordeaux[2]. Possibly there is some ethnographical reason for this. But on the whole, I am inclined to think that it is an accident, and that a more complete investigation would disclose a sufficiency of examples in this area. Outside France, the Feast of Fools is of much less importance. The Spanish disciplinary councils appear to make no specific mention of it, although they know the cognate feast of the Boy Bishop, and more than once prohibit *ludi, choreae*, and so forth, in general terms[3]. In Germany, again, I do not know of a case in which the term 'Fools' is used. But the feast itself occurs sporadically. As early as the twelfth century, Herrad von Landsberg, abbess of Hohenburg, complained that miracle-plays, such as that of the *Magi*, instituted on Epiphany and its octave by the Fathers of the Church, had given place to

---

[1] Thiers, *Traité des Jeux et des Divertissements*, 449; Du Tilliot, 33, 39, quoting [Mathurin de Neuré] *Querela ad Gassendum, de parum Christianis Provincialium suorum ritibus . . . &c.* (1645) ' Choro cedunt omnes Therapeutae Sacerdotes, et ipse Archimandrita; in quorum omnium locos sufficiuntur Coenobii mediastini viles, quorum aliis manticae explendae cura est, aliis culina, aliis hortus colendus: Fratres Laicos vocant, qui tunc occupatis hinc et inde Initiatorum ac Mystarum sedibus, . . . Sacerdotalibus nempe induuntur vestibus, sed laceris, si quae suppetant, ac praepostere aptatis, inversisque; inversos etiam tenent libros in quibus se fingunt legere, appensis ad nasum perspicillis, quibus detractum vitrum, eiusque loco mali aurati putamen insertum . . . Thuricremi Sanniones in cuiusque faciem cineres exsufflarunt, et favillas ex acerris, quas per ludibrium temere iactantes, stolidis quandoque capitibus affundunt; sic autem instructi non hymnos, non Psalmos, non liturgias de more concinunt, sed confusa ac inarticula verba demurmurant, insanasque prorsus vociferationes derudunt.' The same M. de Neuré (whose real name was Laurent Mesme) says more generally that in many towns of the province on Innocents' day, ' Stolidorum se Divorum celebrare festa putant, quibus stolide litandum sit, nec aliis quam stolidis illius diei sacra ceremoniis peragenda.' He quotes (p. 72) from a *Rituale* a direction for the singing of the *Magnificat* to the tune ' Que ne vous requinquez-vous, vielle? Que ne vous requinquez-vous donc?'

[2] Bérenger-Féraud, iv. 17.

[3] *C. of Toledo*, N°. 38, in 1582 (Aguirre, *Coll. Conc. Hisp.* vi. 12); *C. of Oriolana*, in 1600 (Aguirre, vi. 452): cf. pp. 162, 350.

licence, buffoonery and quarrelling. The priests came into
the churches dressed as knights, to drink and play in the
company of courtesans[1]. A Mosburg *Gradual* of 1360 contains a series of *cantiones* compiled and partly written by
the dean John von Perchausen for use when the *scholarium
episcopus* was chosen at the Nativity[2]. Some of these,
however, are shown by their headings or by internal evidence
to belong rather to a New Year's day feast, than to one on
Innocents' day[3]. A *festum baculi* is mentioned and an *episcopus* or *praesul* who is chosen and enthroned. One carol
has the following refrain[4]:

> 'gaudeamus et psallamus
> novo praesuli
> ad honorem et decorem
> sumpti baculi.'

[1] Pearson, ii. 285 ; C. M. Engelhardt, *H. von Landsberg* (1818),
104 ; C. Schmidt, *H. von Landsberg*, 40. Herrad was abbess of
Hohenburg, near Strasburg, 1167–
95. The MS. of her *Hortus
Deliciarum* was destroyed at Strasburg in 1870, but Engelhardt, and
from him Pearson, translated the
bit about the Epiphany feasts : cf.
ch. xx.

[2] Dreves, *Anal. Hymn.* xx. 22
(from the Gradual, *Cod. Monacens.*
157, f. 231ᵛᵒ); after quoting a decree
against *cantiones* of the *C. of Lyons*
in 1274: 'ne igitur propter scholarium episcopum, cum quo in multis
ecclesiis a iuniore clero ad specialem
laudem et devotionem natalis Domini solet tripudiari, saecularia par-
liamenta nec non strepitus clamorque
et cachitus mundanarum cantionum
in nostro choro invalescant ... ego
Iohannes, cognomine de Perchausen, Decanus ecclesiae Mosburgen-
sis, antequam in decanum essem
assumptus ... infra scriptas cantiones, olim ab antiquis etiam in
maioribus ecclesiis cum scholarium
episcopo decantatas, paucis modernis, etiam aliquibus propriis,
quas olim, cum rector fuissem scholarium, pro laude nativitatis Domini et beatae Virginis composui,

adiunctis, coepi in unum colligere
et praesenti libro adnectere pro
speciali reverentia infantiae Salvatoris, ut sibi tempore suae nativitatis his cantionibus a novellis cleri-
culis quasi ex ore infantium et
lactentium laus et hymnizans devotio postposita vulgarium lasci
possit tam decenter quam reverenter exhiberi.'

[3] The following may all be
for Jan. 1, and I do not think
that there was a *scholarium episcopus* on any other day at Mosburg : *Gregis pastor Tityrus*
(Dreves, *op. cit.* 110), *Ecce novus
annus est* (Dreves, 131, headed in
MS. 'ad novum annum'), *Nostri
festi gaudium* (Dreves, 131, 'in circumcisione Domini'), *Castis psal-
lamus mentibus* (Dreves, 135, 251,
'cum episcopus eligitur'), *Mos
florentis venustatis* (Dreves, 135
'dum itur extra ecclesiam ad choream'), *Anni novi novitas* (Dreves,
136 'cum infulatus et vestitus praesul inthronizatur'). Some other
New Year *cantiones* found elsewhere by Dreves (pp. 130, 131)
have no special reference to the
feast.

[4] Dreves, *op. cit.* 136 (beginning
anni novi novitas), 250, with
musical notation.

Another is so interesting, for its classical turn, and for the names which it gives to the 'bishop' and his crew that I quote it in full [1].

      1. Gregis pastor Tityrus,
          asinorum dominus,
          noster est episcopus.

   R⁰. eia, eia, eia,
          vocant nos ad gaudia
          Tityri cibaria.

      2. ad honorem Tityri,
          festum colant baculi
          satrapae et asini.

   R⁰. eia, eia, eia,
          vocant nos ad gaudia,
          Tityri cibaria.

      3. applaudamus Tityro
          cum melodis organo,
          cum chordis et tympano.

      4. veneremur Tityrum,
          qui nos propter baculum
          invitat ad epulum.

The reforms of the council of Basle were adopted for Germany by the Emperor Albrecht II in the *Instrumentum Acceptationis* of Mainz in 1439. In 1536 the council of Cologne, quoting the decretal of Innocent III, condemned *theatrales ludi* in churches. A Cologne *Ritual* preserves an account of the sub-deacons' feast upon the octave of Epiphany [2]. The sub-deacons were *hederaceo serto coronati.* Tapers were lit, and a *rex* chosen, who acted as *hebdomarius* from first to second Vespers. Carols were sung, as at Mosburg [3].

John Huss, early in the fifteenth century, describes the Feast of Fools as it existed in far-off Bohemia [4]. The revellers,

---

[1] Dreves, *op. cit.* 110, 254, with notation.

[2] Wetzer und Welte, *Kirchenlexicon*, s. v. *Epiphany*, quoting Crombach, *Hist. Trium Regum* (1654), 752; Galenius, *de admir. Coloniae* (1645), 661. The date of the *Ritual* is not given, but the ceremony had disappeared by 1645.

[3] 'Admiscent autem natalitias cantiones, non sine gestientis animi voluptate.'

[4] *Tractatus de precatione Dei,* i. 302 († 1406–15), in F. Palacký,

of whom, to his remorse, Huss had himself been one as a lad, wore masks. A clerk, grotesquely vested, was dubbed 'bishop,' set on an ass with his face to the tail, and led to mass in the church. He was regaled on a platter of broth and a bowl of beer, and Huss recalls the unseemly revel which took place[1]. Torches were borne instead of candles, and the clergy turned their garments inside out, and danced. These *ludi* had been forbidden by one archbishop John of holy memory.

It would be surprising, in view of the close political and ecclesiastical relations between mediaeval France and England, if the Feast of Fools had not found its way across the channel. It did; but apparently it never became so inveterate as successfully to resist the disciplinary zeal of reforming bishops, and the few notices of it are all previous to the end of the fourteenth century. It seems to have lasted longest at Lincoln, and at Beverley. Of Lincoln, it will be remembered, Pierre de Corbeil, the probable compiler of the Sens *Officium*, was at one time coadjutor bishop. Robert Grosseteste, whose attack upon the *Inductio Maii* and other village festivals served as a starting-point for this discussion, was no less intolerant of the Feast of Fools. In 1236 he forbade it to

Documenta Mag. Ioannis Hus vitam illustrantia (1869), 722 : 'Quantam autem quamque manifestam licentiam in ecclesia committant, larvas induentes — sicut ipse quoque adolescens proh dolor larva fui—quis Pragae describat? Namque clericum monstrosis vestibus indutum facientes episcopum, imponunt asinae, facie ad caudam conversa, in ecclesiam eum ad missam ducunt, praeferentes lancem iusculi et cantharum vel amphoram cerevisiae ; atque dum haec praetendunt, ille cibum potionemque in ecclesia capit. Vidi quoque eum aras suffientem et pedem sursum tollentem audivique magna voce clamantem : bú ! Clerici autem magnas faces cereorum loco ei praeferebant, singulas aras obeunti et suffienti. Deinde vidi clericos cucullos pellicios aversa parte induentes et in ecclesia tripudiantes. Spectatores autem rident atque haec omnia religiosa et iusta esse putant ; opinantur enim, hos esse in eorum rubricis, id est institutis. Praeclarum vero institutum : pravitas, foeditas!—Atque quum tenera aetate et mente essem, ipse quoque talium nugarum socius eram ; sed ut primum dei auxilio adiutus sacras literas intelligere coepi, statim hanc rubricam, id est institutum huius insaniae, ex stultitia mea delevi. Ac sanctae memoriae dominus Ioannes archiepiscopus, is quidem excommunicationis poena proposita hanc licentiam ludosque fieri vetuit, idque summo iure, &c.'

[1] The quotation given above is a translation by J. Kvíčala from the Bohemian of Huss. There seems to be a confusion between the 'bishop' and his steed. It was probably the latter who lifted up his leg and cried *bú*.

be held either in the cathedral or elsewhere in the diocese[1];
and two years later he included the prohibition in his formal
Constitutions[2]. But after another century and a half, when
William Courtney, archbishop of Canterbury, made a visitation
of Lincoln in 1390, he found that the vicars were still in the
habit of disturbing divine service on January 1, in the name
of the feast[3]. Probably his strict mandate put a stop to the
custom[4]. At almost precisely the same date the Feast of
Fools was forbidden by the statutes of Beverley minster,
although the sub-deacons and other inferior clergy were still
to receive a special commons on the day of the Circumcision[5].
Outside Lincoln and Beverley, the feast is only known in
England by the mention of paraphernalia for it in thirteenth-

[1] Grosseteste, *Epistolae* (ed. Luard, R. S.), 118 'vobis mandamus in virtute obedientiae firmiter iniungentes, quatenus festum stultorum cum sit vanitate plenum et voluptatibus spurcum, Deo odibile et daemonibus amabile, ne de caetero in ecclesia Lincolniensi die venerandae circumcisionis Domini nullatenus permittatis fieri.'

[2] *Ibid. op. cit.* 161 'execrabilem etiam consuetudinem, quae consuevit in quibusdam ecclesiis observari de faciendo festo stultorum, speciali authoritate rescripti apostolici penitus inhibemus; ne de domo orationis fiat domus ludibrii, et acerbitas circumcisionis Domini Iesu Christi iocis et voluptatibus subsannetur.' The 'rescript' will be Innocent III's decretal of 1207, just republished in Gregory IX's *Decretales* of 1234; cf. p. 279.

[3] *Lincoln Statutes*, ii. 247 'quia in eadem visitacione nostra coram nobis a nonnullis fide dignis delatum extitit quod vicarii et clerici ipsius ecclesiae in die Circumcisionis Domini induti veste laicali per eorum strepitus truffas garulaciones et ludos, quos festa stultorum communiter et convenienter appellant, divinum officium multipliciter et consuete impediunt, tenore presencium Inhibemus ne ipsi vicarii qui nunc sunt, vel erunt pro tempore, talibus uti de caetero non

praesumant nec idem vicarii seu quivis alii ecclesiae ministri publicas potaciones aut insolencias alias in ecclesia, quae domus oracionis existit, contra honestatem eiusdem faciant quouuismodo.' Mr. Leach, in *Furnivall Miscellany*, 222, notes 'a sarcastic vicar has written in the margin, "Harrow barrow. Here goes the Feast of Fools (*hic subducitur festum stultorum*)."'

[4] What was *ly ffolcfeste* of which Canon John Marchall complained in Bishop Alnwick's visitation of 1437 that he was called upon to bear the expense? Cf. *Lincoln Statutes*, ii. 388 'item dicit quod subtrahuntur ab ipso expensae per eum factae pascendo ly ffolcfeste in ultimo Natali, quod non erat in propria, nec in cursu, sed tamen rogatus fecit cum promisso sibi facto de effusione expensarum et non est sibi satisfactum.'

[5] *Statutes* of Thos. abp. of York (1391) in *Monasticon*, vi. 1310 'in die etiam Circumcisionis Domini subdiaconis et clericis de secunda forma de victualibus annis singulis, secundum morem et consuetudinem ecclesiae ab antiquo usitatos, debite ministrabit [praepositus], antiqua consuetudine immo verius corruptela regis stultorum infra ecclesiam et extra hactenus usitata sublata penitus et extirpata.'

century inventories of St. Paul's[1], and Salisbury[2], and by a doubtful allusion in a sophisticated version of the St. George play[3].

A brief summary of the data concerning the Feast of Fools presented in this and the preceding chapter is inevitable. It may be combined with some indication of the relation in which the feast stands with regard to the other feasts dealt with in the present volume. If we look back to Belethus in the twelfth century we find him speaking of the Feast of Fools as held on the Circumcision, on Epiphany or on the octave of Epiphany, and as being specifically a feast of sub-deacons. Later records bear out on the whole the first of these statements. As a rule the feast focussed on the Circumcision, although the rejoicings were often prolonged, and the election of the *dominus festi* in some instances gave rise to a minor celebration on an earlier day. Occasionally (Noyon, Laon) the Epiphany, once at least (Cologne) the octave of the Epiphany, takes the place of the Circumcision. But we also find the term Feast of Fools extended to cover one or more of three feasts, distinguished from it by Belethus, which immediately follow Christmas. Sometimes it includes them all three (Besançon, Viviers, Vienne), sometimes the feast of the Innocents alone (Autun, Avallon, Aix, Antibes, Arles), once the feast of St. Stephen (Châlons-sur-Marne)[4]. On the other hand, the definition of the feast as a sub-deacons' feast is not fully applicable to its later developments. Traces of a connexion with the sub-deacons appear more than once (Amiens, Sens, Auxerre, Beverley); but as a rule the feast is held by the inferior clergy known as vicars, chaplains, and choir-clerks, all of whom are grouped at Viviers and Romans under the general term of *esclaffardi*. At Laon a part is taken in it by the *curés* of the various parishes in the city.

---

[1] *Inventory* of St. Paul's (1245) in *Archaeologia*, l. 472, 480 'Baculus stultorum est de ebore et sine cambuca, cum pomello de ebore subtus indentatus ebore et cornu : ... capa et mantella puerorum ad festum Innocentum et Stultorum sunt xxviij debiles et contritae.'

[2] Sarum *Inventory* of 1222 in

W. H. R. Jones, *Vetus Registr. Sarisb.* (R. S.), ii. 135 'Item baculi ii ad "Festum Folorum."'

[3] Nº. 27 in the list given for ch. x. Father Christmas says 'Here comes in "The Feast of Fools."'

[4] Cf. the further account of these post-Nativity feasts in ch. xv.

The explanation is, I think, fairly obvious. Originally, perhaps, the sub-deacons held the feast, just as the deacons,
priests, and boys held theirs in Christmas week. But it had
its vogue mainly in the great cathedrals served by secular
canons [1], and in these the distinction between the canons in
different orders—for a sub-deacon might be a full canon [2]—
was of less importance than the difference between the canons
as a whole and the minor clergy who made up the rest of
the cathedral body, the hired choir-clerks, the vicars choral
who, originally at least, supplied the place in the choir of
absent canons, and the chaplains who served the chantries
or small foundations attached to the cathedral [3]. The status
of spiritual dignity gave way to the status of material preferment. And so, as the vicars gradually coalesced into
a corporation of their own, the Feast of Fools passed into
their hands, and became a celebration of the annual election
of the head of their body [4]. The vicars and their associates
were probably an ill-educated and an ill-paid class. Certainly
they were difficult to discipline [5] ; and it is not surprising
that their rare holiday, of which the expenses were met
partly by the chapter, partly by dues levied upon themselves
or upon the bystanders [6], was an occasion for popular rather

---

[1] The *C. of Paris* in 1212 (p. 279)
forbids the Feast of Fools in religious houses. But that in the
Franciscan convent at Antibes is
the only actual instance I have
come across.

[2] There were *canonici presbiteri,
diaconi, subdiaconi* and even *pueri*
at Salisbury (W. H. Frere, *Use of
Sarum*, i. 51).

[3] On the nature and growth of
vicars choral, cf. Cutts, 341 ; W. H.
Frere, *Use of Sarum*, i. xvii ; *Lincoln
Statutes*, passim ; A. R. Maddison,
Vicars Choral of Lincoln (1878) ;
H. E. Reynolds, *Wells Cathedral*,
xxix, cvii, clxx. Vicars choral
make their appearance in the
eleventh century as choir substitutes for non-resident canons.
At Lincoln they got benefactions
from about 1190, and in the thirteenth century formed a regularly
organized *communitas*. The *vicarii*

were often at the same time *capellani* or chantry-priests. On chantries see Cutts, 438.

[4] The Lincoln vicars chose two
Provosts yearly (Maddison, *op. cit.*);
the Wells vicars two Principals
(Reynolds, *op. cit.* clxxi).

[5] Reynolds, *op. cit.*, gives numerous and interesting notices of
chapter discipline from the Wells
Liber Ruber.

[6] In Leber, ix. 379, 407, is described
a curious way of raising funds for
choir suppers, known at Auxerre
and in Auvergne, and not quite
extinct in the eighteenth century.
It has a certain analogy to the
Deposuit. From Christmas to Epiphany the Psalm *Memento* was
sung at Vespers, and the anthem
De fructu ventris inserted in it.
When this began the ruler of the
choir advanced and presented a
bouquet to some canon or *bourgeois*

than refined merry-making [1]. That it should perpetuate or absorb folk-customs was also, considering the peasant or small *bourgeois* extraction of such men, quite natural.

The simple psychology of the last two sentences really gives the key to the nature of the feast. It was largely an ebullition of the natural lout beneath the cassock. The vicars hooted and sang improper ditties, and played dice upon the altar, in a reaction from the wonted restraints of choir discipline. Familiarity breeds contempt, and it was almost an obvious sport to burlesque the sacred and tedious ceremonies with which they were only too painfully familiar. Indeed, the reverend founders and reformers of the feast had given a lead to this apishness by the introduction of the symbolical transference of the *baculus* at the *Deposuit* in the *Magnificat*. The ruling idea of the feast is the inversion of status, and the performance, inevitably burlesque, by the inferior clergy of functions properly belonging to their betters. The fools jangle the bells (Paris, Amiens, Auxerre), they take the higher stalls (Paris), sing dissonantly (Sens), repeat meaningless words (Châlons, Antibes), say the *messe liesse* (Laon) or the *missa fatuorum* (Autun), preach the *sermones fatui* (Auxerre), cense *praepostere* (St. Omer) with pudding and sausage (Beauvais) or with old shoes (Paris theologians). They have their chapter and their proctors (Auxerre, Dijon). They install their *dominus festi* with a ceremony of *sacre* (Troyes), or shaving (Sens, Dijon). He is vested in full pontificals, goes in procession, as at the *Rabardiaux* of Laon, gives the benedictions, issues indulgences (Viviers), has his seal (Lille), perhaps his right of coining (Laon). Much in

as a sign that the choir would sup with him. This was called 'annonce en forme d'antienne,' and the suppers *defructus*. The *C. of Narbonne*(1551), c.47,forbade 'parochis ... ne ... ad commessationes quas defructus appellant,ullo modo parochianos suos admittant, nec permittant quempiam canere ut dicunt: Memento, Domine, *David sans truffe*, &c. Nec alia huiusmodi ridenda, quae in contemptum divini officii ac in dedecus et probrum

totius cleri et fiunt et cantantur.'

[1] When, however, Ducange says that the feast was not called *Subdiaconorum*, because the sub-deacons held it, but rather as being 'ebriorum Clericorum seu Diaconorum: id enim evincit vox *Soudiacres*, id est, ad litteram, *Saturi Diaconi*, quasi *Diacres Saouls*,' we must take it for a 'sole joke of Thucydides.' I believe there is also a joke somewhere in Liddell and Scott.

all these proceedings was doubtless the merest horseplay; such ingenuity and humour as they required may have been provided by the wicked wit of the *goliardi*[1].

Now I would point out that this inversion of status so characteristic of the Feast of Fools is equally characteristic of folk-festivals. What is Dr. Frazer's mock king but one of the meanest of the people chosen out to represent the real king as the priest victim of a divine sacrifice, and surrounded, for the period of the feast, in a naïve attempt to outwit heaven, with all the paraphernalia and luxury of kingship? Precisely such a mock king is the *dominus festi* with whom we have to do. His actual titles, indeed, are generally ecclesiastical. Most often he is a 'bishop,' or 'prelate' (Senlis); in metropolitan churches an 'archbishop,' in churches exempt from other authority than that of the Holy See, a 'pope' (Amiens, Senlis, Chartres). More rarely he is a 'patriarch' (Laon, Avallon), a 'cardinal' (Paris, Besançon), an 'abbot' (Vienne, Viviers, Romans, Auxerre)[2], or is even content with the humbler dignity of 'precentor,' '*bacularius*' or '*bâtonnier*' (Sens, Dijon). At Autun he is, quite exceptionally, 'Herod.' Nevertheless the term 'king' is not unknown. It is found at Noyon, at Vienne, at Besançon, at Beverley, and the council of Basle testifies to its use, as well as that of 'duke.' Nor is it, after all, of much importance what the *dominus festi* is called. The point is that his existence and functions in the ecclesiastical festivals afford precise parallels to his existence and functions in folk-festivals all Europe over.

Besides the 'king' many other features of the folk-festivals may readily be traced at the Feast of Fools. Some here, some there, they jot up in the records. There are dance and *chanson*, *tripudium* and *cantilena* (Noyon, Châlons-sur-

---

[1] Cf. p. 60; Gautier, *Les Tropaires*, i. 186; and *C. of Treves* in 1227 (J. F. Schannat, *Conc. Germ.* iii. 532) 'praecipimus ut omnes Sacerdotes non permittant trutannos et alios vagos scolares aut goliardos cantare versus super *Sanctus* et *Agnus Dei*.'

[2] The 'abbot' appears to have been sometimes charged with choir discipline throughout the year, and at Vienne and Viviers exists side by side with another *dominus festi*. Similarly at St. Omer there was a 'dean' as well as a 'bishop.' The vicars of Lincoln and Wells also chose two officers.

Marne, Paris theologians, council of Basle). There is eating and drinking, not merely in the refectory, but within or at the doors of the church itself (Paris theologians, Beauvais, Prague). There is ball-playing (Châlons-sur-Marne). There is the procession or cavalcade through the streets (Laon, Châlons-sur-Marne, &c.). There are torches and lanterns (Sens, Tournai). Men are led *nudi* (Sens); they are whipped (Tours) ; they are ceremonially ducked or roasted (Sens, Tournai, Vienne, *les Gaigizons* at Autun)[1]. A comparison with earlier chapters of the present volume will establish the significance which these points, taken in bulk, possess. Equally characteristic of folk-festivals is the costume considered proper to the feasts. The riotous clergy wear their vestments inside out (Antibes), or exchange dress with the laity (Lincoln, Paris theologians). But they also wear leaves or flowers (Sens, Laon, Cologne) and women's dress (Paris theologians) ; and above all they wear hideous and monstrous masks, *larvae* or *personae* (decretal of 1207, Paris theologians, council of Basle, Paris, Soissons, Laon, Lille). These masks, indeed, are perhaps the one feature of the feast which called down the most unqualified condemnation from the ecclesiastical authorities. We shall not be far wrong if we assume them to have been beast-masks, and to have taken the place of the actual skins and heads of sacrificial animals, here, as so often, worn at the feast by the worshippers.

An attempt has been made to find an oriental origin for the Feast of Fools[2]. Gibbon relates the insults offered to the church at Constantinople by the Emperor Michael III, the 'Drunkard' (842–67)[3]. A noisy crew of courtiers dressed themselves in the sacred vestments. One Theophilus or Grylus, captain of the guard, a mime and buffoon, was chosen as a mock 'patriarch.' The rest were his twelve

[1] I suppose that 'portetur in rost' at Vienne means that the victims were roasted like the fags in *Tom Brown*.

[2] Ducange, s. v. *Kalendae*.

[3] Gibbon - Bury, v. 201. The Byzantine authorities are Genesius, iv. p. 49 B (*Corp. Hist. Byz.* xi. 2. 102); Paphlagon (Migne, *P. G.* cv. 527) ; Theophanes Continuatus, iv. 38 (*Corp. Hist. Byz.* xxii. 200) ; Symeon Magister, p. 437 D (*Corp. Hist. Byz.* xxii. 661), on all of whom see Bury, App. I to tom. cit.

'metropolitans,' Michael himself being entitled 'metropolitan of Cologne.' The 'divine mysteries' were burlesqued with vinegar and mustard in a golden cup set with gems. Theophilus rode about the streets of the city on a white ass, and when he met the real patriarch Ignatius, exposed him to the mockery of the revellers. After the death of Michael, this profanity was solemnly anathematized by the council of Constantinople held under his successor Basil in 869[1]. Theophilus, though he borrowed the vestments for his mummery, seems to have carried it on in the streets and the palace, not in the church. In the tenth century, however, the patriarch Theophylactus won an unenviable reputation by admitting dances and profane songs into the ecclesiastical festivals[2]; while in the twelfth, the patriarch Balsamon describes his own unavailing struggle against proceedings at Christmas and Candlemas, which come uncommonly near the Feast of Fools. The clergy of St. Sophia's, he says, claim as of ancient custom to wear masks, and to enter the church in the guise of soldiers, or of monks, or of four-footed animals. The superintendents snap their fingers like charioteers, or paint their faces and mimic women. The rustics are moved to laughter by the pouring of wine into pitchers, and are allowed to chant *Kyrie eleison* in ludicrous iteration at every verse[3]. Balsamon, who died in 1193, was almost

---

[1] *C. of Constantinople* (869-70), c. 16 (Mansi, xvi. 169, *ex versione Latina, abest in Graeca*) 'fuisse quosdam laicos, qui secundum diversam imperatoriam dignitatem videbantur capillorum comam circumplexam involvere atque reponere, et gradum quasi sacerdotalem per quaedam inducia et vestimenta sacerdotalia sumere, et, ut putabatur, episcopos constituere, superhumeralibus, id est, palliis, circumamictos, et omnem aliam Pontificalem indutos stolam, qui etiam proprium patriarcham adscribentes eum qui in adinventionibus risum moventibus praelatus et princeps erat, et insultabant et illudebant quibusque divinis, modo quidem electiones, promotiones et consecrationes, modo autem acute calum-

nias, damnationes et depositiones episcoporum quasi ab invicem et per invicem miserabiliter et praevaricatorie agentes et patientes. Talis autem actio nec apud gentes a saeculo unquam audita est.'

[2] Cedrenus, *Historiarum Compendium*, p. 639 B (ed. Bekker, in *Corp. Hist. Byz.* xxiv. 2. 333), follows verbatim the still unprinted eleventh-century John Scylitzes (Gibbon-Bury, v. 508). Theophylactus was Patriarch from 933 to 956.

[3] Theodorus Balsamon, *In Can. lxii Conc. in Trullo* (*P. G.* cxxxvii. 727) Σημείωσαι τὸν παρόντα κανόνα, καὶ ζήτησον διόρθωσιν ἐπὶ τοῖς γινομένοις παρὰ τῶν κληρικῶν εἰς τὴν ἑορτὴν ἐπὶ τῆς γεννήσεως τοῦ Χριστοῦ, καὶ τὴν ἑορτὴν τῶν Φώτων [Luminarium, Candlemas] ὑπεναντίως τούτῳ·

precisely a contemporary of Belethus, and the earlier Byzantine notices considerably ante-date any records that we possess of the Feast of Fools in the West. A slight corroboration of this theory of an eastern origin may be derived from the use of the term ' patriarch ' for the *dominus festi* at Laon and Avallon. It would, I think, be far-fetched to find another in the fact that Theophilus, like the western 'bishops' of Fools, rode upon an ass, and that the *Prose de l'Âne* begins :

' Orientis partibus,
adventavit asinus.'

In any case, the oriental example can hardly be responsible for more than the admission of the feast within the doors of the church. One cannot doubt that it was essentially an adaptation of a folk-custom long perfectly well known in the West itself. The question of origin had already presented itself to the learned writers of the thirteenth century. William of Auxerre, by a misunderstanding which I shall hope to explain, traced the Feast of Fools to the Roman *Parentalia*: Durandus, and the Paris theologians after him, to the January Kalends. Certainly Durandus was right. The Kalends, unlike the more specifically Italian feasts, were coextensive with the Roman empire, and were naturally widespread in Gaul. The date corresponds precisely with that by far the most common for the Feast of Fools. A singular history indeed, that of the ecclesiastical celebration of the

καὶ μᾶλλον εἰς τὴν ἁγιωτάτην Μεγάλην ἐκκλησίαν . . . ἀλλὰ καί τινες κληρικοὶ κατά τινας ἑορτὰς πρὸς διάφορα μετασχηματίζονται προσωπεῖα. καὶ ποτὲ μὲν ξιφήρεις ἐν τῷ μεσονάῳ τῆς ἐκκλησίας μετὰ στρατιωτικῶν ἀμφίων εἰσέρχονται, ποτὲ δὲ καὶ ὡς μοναχοὶ προοδεύουσιν, ἢ καὶ ὡς ζῶα τετράποδα. ἐρωτήσας οὖν ὅπως ταῦτα παρεχωρήθησαν γίνεσθαι, οὐδέν τε ἕτερον ἤκουσα ἀλλ' ἢ ἐκ μακρᾶς συνηθείας ταῦτα τελεῖσθαι. τοιαῦτά εἰσιν, ὡς ἐμοὶ δοκεῖ, καὶ τὰ παρά τινων δομεστικευόντων ἐν κλήρῳ γινόμενα, τὸν ἀέρα τοῖς δακτύλοις κατὰ ἡνιόχους τυπτόντων, καὶ φύκη ταῖς γνάθοις δῆθεν περιτιθεμένων καὶ ὑπορρινομένων ἔργα τινὰ γυναικεῖα, καὶ ἕτερα

ἀπρεπῆ, ἵνα πρὸς γέλωτα τοὺς βλέποντας μετακινήσωσι. τὸ δὲ γελᾶν τοὺς ἀγρότας ἐγχευμένους τοῦ οἴνου τοῖς πίθοις, ὡσεί τι παρεπόμενον ἐξ ἀνάγκης ἐστὶ τοῖς ληνοβατοῖσιν· εἰ μήτις εἴπῃ τὴν σατανικὴν ταύτην ἐργασίαν καταργεῖσθαι διὰ τοῦ λέγειν τοὺς ἀγρότας συχνότερον ἐφ' ἑκάστῳ μέτρῳ σχεδὸν τό, Κύριε ἐλέησον. τὰ μέντοι ποτὲ γινόμενα ἀπρεπῆ παρὰ τῶν νοταρίων παιδοδιδασκάλων κατὰ τὴν ἑορτὴν τῶν ἁγίων νοταρίων, μετὰ προσωπείων σκηνικῶν διερχομένων τὴν ἀγοράν, πρὸ χρόνων τινῶν κατηργήθησαν, καθ' ὁρισμὸν τοῦ ἁγιωτάτου ἐκείνου πατριάρχου κυρίου Λουκᾶ.

First of January. Up to the eighth century a fast, with its mass *pro prohibendo ab idolis*, it gradually took on a festal character, and became ultimately the one feast in the year in which paganism made its most startling and persistent recoil upon Christianity. The attacks upon the Kalends in the disciplinary documents form a catena which extends very nearly to the point at which the notices of the Feast of Fools begin. In each alike the masking, in mimicry of beasts and probably of beast-gods or 'demons,' appears to have been a prominent and highly reprobated feature. It is true that we hear nothing of a *dominus festi* at the Kalends ; but much stress must not be laid upon the omission of the disciplinary writers to record any one point in a custom which after all they were not describing as anthropologists, and it would certainly be an exceptional Germano-Keltic folk-feast which had not a *dominus*. As a matter of fact, there is no mention of a *rex* in the accounts of the pre-Christian Kalends in Italy itself. There was a *rex* at the *Saturnalia*, and this, together with an allusion of Belethus in a quite different connexion to the *libertas Decembrica*[1], has led some writers to find in the *Saturnalia*, rather than the Kalends, the origin of the Feast of Fools[2]. This is, I venture to think, wrong. The *Saturnalia* were over well before December 25: there is no evidence that they had a vogue outside Italy: the Kalends, like the *Saturnalia*, were an occasion at which slaves met their masters upon equal terms, and I believe that the existence of a Kalends *rex*, both in Italy and in Gaul, may be taken for granted.

But the parallel between Kalends and the Feast of Fools cannot be held to be quite perfect, unless we can trace in the latter feast that most characteristic of all Kalends customs, the *Cervulus*. Is it possible that a representative of the *Cervulus* is to be found in the Ass, who, whether introduced from Constantinople or not, gave to the Feast of Fools one of its popular names? The Feast of Asses has been the sport of controversialists who had not, and were at no great pains

---

[1] Belethus, c. 120, compares the ecclesiastical ball-play at Easter to the *libertas Decembrica*. He is not speaking here of the Feast of Fools.

[2] e.g. Du Tilliot, 2.

to have, the full facts before them. I do not propose to awake once more these ancient angers[1]. The facts themselves are briefly these. The 'Prose of the Ass' was used at Bourges, at Sens, and at Beauvais. As to the Bourges feast I have no details. At Sens, the use of the Prose by Pierre de Corbeil is indeed no proof that he allowed an ass to appear in the ceremony. But the Prose would not have much point unless it was at least a survival from a time when an ass did appear ; the feast was known as the *asinaria festa*; and even now, three centuries after it was abolished, the Sens choir-boys still play at being *âne* archbishop on Innocents' day[2]. At Beauvais the heading *Conductus quando asinus adducitur* in the thirteenth-century *Officium* seems to show that there at least the ass appeared, and even entered the church. The document, also of the thirteenth century, quoted by the editors of Ducange, certainly brings him, in the ceremony of January 14, into the church and near the altar. An imitation of his braying is introduced into the service itself. At Autun the leading of an ass *ad processionem*, and the *cantilena super dictum asinum* were suppressed in 1411. At Châlons-sur-Marne in 1570 an ass bore the 'bishop' to the theatre at the church door only. At Prague, on the other hand, towards the end of the fourteenth century, an ass was led, as at Beauvais, right into the church. These, with doubtful references to *fêtes des ânes* at St. Quentin about 1081, at Béthune in 1474, and at Laon in 1527, and the Mosburg description of the 'bishop' as *asinorum dominus*, are all the cases I have found in which an ass has anything to do with the feast. But they are enough to prove that an ass was an early and widespread, though not an invariable feature. I may quote here a curious survival in a *ronde* from the west of France, said to have been sung at church doors on January 1[3]. It is called *La Mort de l'Âne*, and begins :

---

[1] S. R. Maitland, *The Dark Ages*, 141, tilts at the Protestant historian Robertson's *History of Charles V*, as do F. Clément, 159, and A. Walter, *Das Eselsfest* in *Caecilien-Kalender* (1885), 75, at Dulaure, *Hist. des Environs de Paris*, iii. 509, and other 'Voltairiens.'

[2] Chérest, 81.

[3] J. Bujeaud, *Chants et Chansons populaires des Provinces de l'Ouest*, i. 63. The *ronde* is known in Poitou, Aunis, Angoumois. P. Tarbé, *Romancero de Champagne* (2ᵉ partie), 257, gives a variant. Bujeaud, i. 61, gives another *ronde*, the *Testament*

' Quand le bonhomme s'en va,
Quand le bonhomme s'en va,
Trouvit la tête à son âne,
Que le loup mangit au bois.

Parlé. O tête, pauvre tête,
Tâ qui chantas si bé
L'Magnificat à Vêpres.

Daux matin à quat' léçons,
La sambredondon, bredondaine,
Daux matin à quat' léçons,
La sambredondon.'

This, like the Sens choir-boys' custom of calling their 'arch-bishop' *âne*, would seem to suggest that the *dominus festi* was himself the ass, with a mask on ; and this may have been sometimes the case. But in most of the mediaeval instances the ass was probably used to ride. At Prague, so far as one can judge from Huss's description, he was a real ass. There is no proof in any of the French examples that he was, or was not, merely a 'hobby-ass.' If he was, he came all the nearer to the *Cervulus.*

It has been pointed out, and will, in the next volume, be pointed out again, that the ecclesiastical authorities attempted to sanctify the spirit of play at the Feast of Fools and similar festivities by diverting the energies of the revellers to *ludi* of the miracle-play order. In such *ludi* they found a place for the ass. He appears for instance as Balaam's ass in the later versions from Laon and Rouen of the *Prophetae*, and at Rouen he gave to the whole of this performance the name of the *festum* or *processio asinorum*[1]. At Hamburg,

de l'Âne, in which the ass has fallen into a ditch, and amongst other legacies leaves his tail to the *curé* for an *aspersoir.* This is known in Poitou, Angoumois, Franche-Comté. He also says that he has heard children of Poitou and Angoumois go through a mock catechism, giving an ecclesiastical significance to each part of the ass. The tail is the *goupillon*, and so forth. Fournier-Verneuil,*Paris, Tableau moral et philosophique* (1826),

522, with the Beauvais *Officium* in his mind, says ' Voulez-vous qu'au lieu de dire, *Ite, missa est,* le prêtre se mette à braire trois fois de toute sa force, et que le peuple réponde en chœur, comme je l'ai vu faire en 1788, dans l'église de Bellai-gues, en Périgord ? '

[1] Cf. ch. xx. Gasté, 20, considers the Rouen *Festum Asinorum* 'l'ori-gine de toutes les Fêtes de l'Âne qui se célébraient dans d'autres diocèses' : but the Rouen MS. in

by a curious combination, he is at once Balaam's ass and the finder of the star in a *ludus Trium Regum*[1]. His use as the mount of the Virgin on January 14 at Beauvais, and on some uncertain day at Sens, seems to suggest another favourite episode in such *ludi*, that of the Flight into Egypt. At Varennes, in Picardy, and at Bayonne, exist carved wooden groups representing this event. That of Varennes is carried in procession; that of Bayonne is the object of pilgrimage on the *fêtes* of the Virgin[2].

Not at the Feast of Fools alone, or at the miracle-plays connected with this feast, did the ass make its appearance in Christian worship. It stood with the ox, on the morning of the Nativity, beside the Christmas crib. On Palm Sunday it again formed part of a procession, in the semblance of the beast on which Christ made his triumphal entry into Jerusalem[3]. A Cambrai *Ordinarium* quoted by Ducange directs that the *asina picta* shall remain behind the altar for four days[4]. Kirchmeyer describes the custom as it

---

which it occurs is only of the fourteenth century, and the Balaam episode does not occur at all in the more primitive forms of the *Prophetae*, while the Sens Feast of Fools is called the *festa asinaria* in the *Officium* of the early thirteenth century.

[1] Tille, *D. W.* 31. In Madrid an ass was led in procession on Jan. 17, with anthems on the Balaam legend (Clément, 181).

[2] Clément, 182; Didron, *Annales archéologiques*, xv. 384.

[3] Dulaure, *Hist. des Environs de Paris*, iii. 509, quotes a legend to the effect that the very ass ridden by Christ came ultimately to Verona, died there, was buried in a wooden effigy at Sta-Maria in Organo, and honoured by a yearly procession. He guesses at this as the origin of the Beauvais and other *fêtes*. Didron, *Annales arch.* xv. 377, xvi. 33, found that nothing was known of this legend at Verona, though such a statue group as is described above apparently existed in the church named. Dulaure gives as his

authorities F. M. Misson, *Nouveau Voyage d'Italie* (1731), i. 164; *Dict. de l'Italie*, i. 56. Misson's visit to Verona was in 1687, although the passage was not printed in the first edition (1691) of his book. It is in the English translation of 1714 (i. 198). His authority was a French merchant (M. Montel) living in Verona, who had often seen the procession. In *Cenni intorno all' origine e descrizione della Festa che annualmente si celebra in Verona l' ultimo Venerdì del Carnovale, comunamente denominata Gnoccolare* (1818), 75, is a mention of the 'asinello del vecchio padre Sileno' which served as a mount for the 'Capo de' Maccheroni.' This is probably Misson's procession, but there is no mention of the legend in any of the eighteenth-century accounts quoted in the pamphlet. Rienzi was likened to an 'Abbate Asinino' (Gibbon, vii. 269).

[4] Ducange, s. v. *Festum Asinorum*; cf. Leber, ix. 270; Molanus, *de Hist. SS. Imaginum et Picturarum* (1594), iv. 18.

existed during the sixteenth century in Germany [1]; and the stray tourist who drops into the wonderful collection of domestic and ecclesiastical antiquities in the Barfüsserkirche at Basle will find there three specimens of the *Palmesel*, including a thirteenth-century one from Bayern and a seventeenth-century one from Elsass. The third is not labelled with its *provenance*, but it is on wheels and has a hole for the rope by which it was dragged round the church. All three are of painted wood, and upon each is a figure representing Christ [2].

The affiliation of the ecclesiastical New Year revelries to the pagan Kalends does not explain why those who took part in them were called 'Fools.' The obvious thing to say is that they were called 'Fools' because they played the fool; and indeed their mediaeval critics were not slow to

---

[1] T. Naogeorgus (Kirchmeyer), *The Popish Kingdom*, iv. 443 (1553, transl. Barnabe Googe, 1570, in New Shakspere Society edition of Stubbes, *Anatomy of Abuses*, i. 332); cf. *Beehive of the Roman Church*, 199. The earliest notice is in Gerardus, *Leben St. Ulrichs von Augsburg* (ob. 973), c. 4. E. Bishop, in *Dublin Review*, cxxiii. 405, traces the custom in a Prague fourteenth-century *Missal* and sixteenth-century *Breviary*; also in the modern Greek Church at Moscow where until recently the Czar held the bridle. But there is no ass, as he says, in the Palm Sunday ceremony described in the *Peregrinatio Silviae* (Duchesne, 486).

[2] A peeress of the realm lately stated that this custom had been introduced in recent years into the Anglican church. Denials were to hand, and an amazing conflict of evidence resulted. Is there any proof that the *Palmesel* was ever an English ceremony at all? The Hereford riding of 1706 (cf. *Representations*) was not in the church. Brand, i. 73, quotes *A Dialogue: the Pilgremage of Pure Devotyon* (1551?), 'Upon Palme Sondaye they play the foles sadely, drawynge after them an Asse in a rope, when

they be not moche distante from the Woden Asse that they drawe.' Clearly this, like Googe's translation of Naogeorgus, is a description of contemporary continental Papistry. W. Fulke, *The Text of the New Testament* (ed. 1633), 76 (*ad Marc.* xi. 8) quotes a note of the Rheims translation to the effect that in memory of the entry into Jerusalem is a procession on Palm Sunday 'with the blessed Sacrament reverently carried as it were Christ upon the Asse,' and comments, 'But it is pretty sport, that you make the Priest that carrieth the idoll, to supply the roome of the Asse on which Christ did ride. . . . Thus you turn the holy mysterie of Christ's riding to Jerusalem to a May-game and Pageant-play.' Fulke, who lived 1538–89, is evidently unaware that there was an ass, as well as the priest, in the procession, from which I infer that the custom was not known in England. Not that this consideration would weigh with the mediaevally-minded curate, who is as a rule only too ready to make up by the ceremonial inaccuracy of his mummeries for the offence which they cause to his congregation.

draw this inference. But it is noteworthy that pagan Rome already had its Feast of Fools, which, indeed, had nothing to do with the Kalends. The *stultorum feriae* on February 17 was the last day on which the *Fornacalia* or ritual sacrifice of the *curiae* was held. Upon it all the *curiae* sacrificed in common, and it therefore afforded an opportunity for any citizen who did not know which his *curia* was to partake in the ceremony[1]. I am not prepared to say that the *stultorum feriae* gave its name to the Feast of Fools; but the identity of the two names certainly seems to explain some of the statements which mediaeval scholars make about that feast. It explains William of Auxerre's derivation of it from the *Parentalia*, for the *stultorum feriae* fell in the midst of the *Parentalia*[2]. And I think it explains the remark of Belethus, and, following him, of Durandus, about the *ordo subdiaconorum* being *incertus*. The sub-deacons were a regular *ordo*, the highest of the *ordines minores* from the third century[3]. But Belethus seems to be struggling with the notion that the sub-deacons' feast, closing the series of post-Nativity feasts held by deacons, priests and choir-boys, was in some way parallel to the *feriae* of the Roman *stulti* who were *incerti* as to their *curia*.

[1] Marquardt-Mommsen, vi. 191; Jevons, *Plutarch's Romane Questions*, 134; Fowler, 304, 322; Ovid, *Fasti*, ii. 531:

'stultaque pars populi, quae sit
    sua curia, nescit;
sed facit extrema sacra relata
    die.'

[2] Fowler, 306.   [3] Schaff, iii. 131.

CHAPTER XV

THE BOY BISHOP

[*Bibliographical Note.*—Most of the authorities for chh. xiii, xiv, are still available, since many writers have not been careful to distinguish between the various feasts of the Twelve nights. The best modern account of the Boy Bishop is Mr. A. F. Leach's paper on *The Schoolboys' Feast* in *The Fortnightly Review*, N. S. lix (1896), 128. The contributions of F. A. Dürr, *Commentatio Historica de Episcopo Puerorum, vulgo vom Schul-Bischoff* (1755); F. A. Specht, *Geschichte des Unterrichtswesens in Deutschland*, 222 sqq. (1885); A. Gasté, *Les Drames liturgiques de la Cathédrale de Rouen*, 35 sqq. (1893); E. F. Rimbault, *The Festival of the Boy Bishop in England* in *The Camden Miscellany*, vol. vii (Camden Soc. 1875), are also valuable. Dr. Rimbault speaks of 'considerable collections for a history of the festival of the Boy Bishop throughout Europe,' made by Mr. J. G. Nichols, but I do not know where these are to be found. Brand (ed. Ellis), i. 227 sqq., has some miscellaneous data, and a notice interesting by reason of its antiquity is that on the *Episcopus Puerorum, in Die Innocentium*, in the *Posthuma*, 95 sqq., of John Gregory (1649).]

JOANNES BELETHUS, the learned theologian of Paris and Amiens, towards the end of the twelfth century, describes, as well as the Feast of Fools, no less than three other *tripudia* falling in Christmas week [1]. Upon the days of St. Stephen, St. John the Evangelist, and the Holy Innocents, the deacons,

---

[1] Belethus, c. 70 'Debent ergo vesperae Natalis primo integre celebrari, ac postea conveniunt diaconi quasi in tripudio, cantantque *Magnificat* cum antiphona de S. Stephano, sed sacerdos recitat collectam. Nocturnos et universum officium crastinum celebrant diaconi, quod Stephanus fuerit diaconus, et ad lectiones concedant benedictiones, ita tamen, ut eius diei missam celebret hebdomarius, hoc est ille cuius tum vices fuerint eam exsequi. Sic eodem modo omne officium perficient sacerdotes ipso die B. Ioannis, quod hic sacerdos fuerit, et pueri in ipso festo Innocentium, quia innocentes pro Christo occisi sunt, . . . in festo itaque Innocentium penitus subticentur caritas laetitiae, quoniam ii ad inferos descenderunt.' Cf. also c. 72, quoted on p. 275. Durandus, *Rat. Div. Off.* (1284), vii. 42, *De festis SS. Stephani, Ioannis Evang. et Innocentium*, gives a similar account. At Vespers on Christmas Day, he says, the deacons 'in tripudio convenientes cantant antiphonam de sancto Stephano, et sacerdos collectam. Nocturnos autem et officium in crastinum celebrant et benedictiones super lectiones dant: quod tamen facere non debent.' So too for the priests and boys on the following days.

the priests, the choir-boys, held their respective revels, each body in turn claiming that pre-eminence in the divine services which in the Feast of Fools was assigned to the sub-deacons. The distinction drawn by Belethus is not wholly observed in the ecclesiastical prohibitions either of the thirteenth or of the fifteenth century. In many of these the term 'Feast of Fools' has a wide meaning. The council of Nevers in 1246 includes under it the feasts of the Innocents and the New Year; that of Langres in 1404 the 'festivals of the Nativity'; that of Nantes in 1431 the Nativity itself, St. Stephen's, St. John's, and the Innocents'. For the council of Basle it is apparently synonymous with the 'Feast of Innocents or Boys'; the Paris theologians speak of its rites as practised on St. Stephen's, the Innocents', the Circumcision, and other dates. The same tendency to group all these *tripudia* together recurs in passages in which the 'Feast of Fools' is not in so many words mentioned. The famous decretal of Pope Innocent III is directed against the *ludibria* practised in turns by deacons, priests, and sub-deacons during the feasts immediately following upon Christmas. The *irrisio servitii* inveighed against in the *Rememoratio* of Gerson took place on Innocents' day, on the Circumcision, on the Epiphany, or at Shrovetide.

Local usage, however, only partly bears out this loose language of the prohibitions. At Châlons-sur-Marne, in 1570, the 'bishop' of Fools sported on St. Stephen's day. At Besançon, in 1387, a distinct *dominus festi* was chosen on each of the three days after Christmas, and all alike were called *rois des fous*. At Autun, during the fifteenth century, the *regna* of the 'bishop' and 'dean' of Innocents and of 'Herod' at the New Year were known together as the *festa folorum*. Further south, the identification is perhaps more common. At Avallon, Aix, Antibes, the Feast of Fools was on Innocents' day; at Arles the *episcopus stultorum* officiated both on the Innocents' and on St. John's, at Viviers on all three of the post-Nativity feasts. But these are exceptions, and, at least outside Provence, the rule seems to have been to apply the name of 'Feast of Fools' to the *tripudium*, originally that of the sub-deacons, on New Year's day or the Epiphany, and to distinguish from this, as does Belethus, the *tripudia* of the deacons, priests, and choir-boys in Christmas week.

We may go further and say, without much hesitation, that the three latter feasts are of older ecclesiastical standing than their riotous rival. Belethus is the first writer to mention the Feast of Fools, but he is by no means the first writer to mention the Christmas *tripudia*. They were known to Honorius of Autun[1], early in the twelfth century, and to John of Avranches[2], late in the eleventh. They can be traced at least from the beginning of the tenth, more than two hundred and fifty years before the Feast of Fools is heard of. The earliest notice I have come across is at the monastery of St. Gall, hard by Constance, in 911. In that year King Conrad I was spending Christmas with Bishop Solomon of Constance. He heard so much of the Vespers processions during the *triduum* at St. Gall that he insisted on visiting the monastery, and arrived there in the midst of the revels. It was all very amusing, and especially the procession of children, so grave and sedate that even when Conrad bade his train roll apples along the aisle they did not budge[3]. That the other Vespers processions of the *triduum* were of deacons and priests may be taken for granted. I do not know whether the *triduum* originated at St. Gall, but the famous song-school of that monastery was all-important in

[1] Honorius Augustodunensis, *Gemma Animae*, iii. 12 (*P. L.* clxxii. 646).

[2] Ioannes Abrincensis (bishop of Rouen †1070), *de Eccl. Offic.* (*P. L.* cxlvii. 41), with fairly full account of the 'officia.'

[3] Ekkehardus IV, *de Casibus S. Galli*, c. 14 (ed. G. Meyer von Knonau, in *Mittheilungen zur vaterländischen Gesch.* of the Hist. Verein in St. Gallen, N. F., v.; *M. G. H. Scriptores*, ii. 84) 'longum est dicere, quibus iocunditatibus dies exegerit et noctes, maxime in processione infantum ; quibus poma in medio ecclesiae pavimento antesterni iubens, cum nec unum parvissimorum moveri nec ad ea adtendere vidisset, miratus est disciplinam.' Ekkehart was master of the song-school, and von Knonau mentions some *cantiones* written by him and others for the feast, e. g. one beginning 'Salve lacteolo decoratum sanguine festum.' He has another story (c. 26) of how Solomon who was abbot of the monastery, as well as bishop of Constance, looking into the song-school on the 'dies scolarium,' when the boys had a 'ius . . . ut hospites intrantes capiant, captos, usque dum se redimant, teneant,' was duly made prisoner, and set on the master's seat. 'Si in magistri solio sedeo,' cried the witty bishop, 'iure eius uti habeo. Omnes exuimini.' After his jest, he paid his footing like a man. The 'Schulabt' of St. Gall is said to have survived until the council of Trent.

the movement towards the greater elaboration of church ceremonial, and even more of chant, which marked the tenth century. This gave rise to the tropes, of which much will be said in the next volume; and it is in a tropary, an English tropary from Winchester, dating from before 980, that the feasts of the *triduum* next occur. The ceremonies of those feasts, as described by Belethus, belong mainly to the Office, and the tropes are mainly chanted elaborations of the text of the Mass: but the Winchester tropes for the days of St. Stephen, St. John, and the Holy Innocents clearly imply the respective connexion of the services, to which they belong, with deacons, priests, and choir-boys [1]. Of the sub-deacons, on Circumcision or Epiphany, there is as yet nothing. John of Avranches, Honorius of Autun, and Belethus bridge a gap, and from the thirteenth century the *triduum* is normal in service-books, both continental and English, throughout the Middle Ages [2]. It is provided for in the Nantes *Ordinarium* of 1263 [3], in the Amiens *Ordinarium* of 1291 [4], and in the Tours *Rituale* of the fourteenth century [5]. It required reforming at Vienne in 1385, but continued to exist there up to 1670 [6]. In the last three cases it is clearly marked side by side with, but other than, the Feast of Fools. In Germany, it

---

[1] Frere, *Winch. Troper*, 6, 8, 10. The deacons' sang ' Eia, conlevitae in protomartyris Stephani natalicio ex persona ipsius cum psalmista ouantes concinnamus'; the priests, ' Hodie candidati sacerdotum chori centeni et milleni coniubilent Christo dilectoque suo Iohanni'; the boys, ' Psallite nunc Christo pueri, dicente propheta.'

[2] Rock, iii. 2. 214; Clément, 118; Grenier, 353; Martene, iii. 38. These writers add several references for the *triduum* or one or other of its feasts to those here given: e. g. Martene quotes on St. Stephen's feast *Ordinarium of Langres*, 'finitis vesperis fiunt tripudia'; *Ordinarium of Limoges*, 'vadunt omnes ad capitulum, ubi Episcopus, sive praesens, sive absens fuerit, dat eis potum ex tribus vinis'; *Ordinarium of Strasburg* (†1364),

' propinatur in refectorio, sicut in vigilia nativitatis.'

[3] Martene, iii. 38 'tria festa, quae sequuntur, fiunt cum magna solemnitate et tripudio. Primum faciunt diaconi, secundum presbiteri, tertium pueri.'

[4] Grenier, 353 ' si festa [S. Stephani] fiant, ut consuetum est, a diaconis in cappis sericis . . . fit statio in medio choro, et ab ipsis regitur chorus . . . et fiant festa sicut docent libri'; and so for the two other feasts.

[5] Martene, iii. 38 ' cum in primis vesperis [in festo S. Stephani] ad illum cantici *Magnificat* versiculum *Deposuit potentes* perventum erat, cantor baculum locumque suum diacono, qui pro eo chorum regeret, cedebat'; and so on the other feasts.

[6] Cf. p. 315.

is contemplated in the *Ritual* of Mainz [1]. In England I trace it at Salisbury [2], at York [3], at Lincoln [4], at St. Albans [5]. These instances could doubtless be multiplied, although there were certainly places where the special devotion of the three feasts to the three bodies dropped out at an early date. The Rheims *Ordinarium* of the fourteenth century, for instance, knows nothing of it [6]. The extent of the ceremonies, again, would naturally be subject to local variation. The germ of them lay in the procession at first Vespers described by Ekkehard at St. Gall. But they often grew to a good deal more than this. The deacons, priests, or choir-boys, as the case might be, took the higher stalls, and the whole conduct of the services; the *Deposuit* was sung; *epistolae farcitae* were read [7]; there was a *dominus festi*.

The main outlines of the feasts of the *triduum* are thus almost exactly parallel, so far as the divine *servitium* is concerned, to those of the Feast of Fools, for which indeed they probably served as a model. And like the Feast of Fools, they had their secular side, which often became riotousness. Occasionally they were absorbed in, or overshadowed by, the more popular and wilder merry-making of the inferior clergy.

---

[1] Durr, 77. Here the sub-deacons shared in the deacons' feast.

[2] The *Consuetudinarium* of †1210 (Frere, *Use of Sarum*, i. 124, 223) mentions the procession of deacons after Vespers on Christmas day, but says nothing of the share of the priests and boys in those of the following days. The *Sarum Breviary* gives all three (Fasc. i. cols. cxcv, ccxiii, ccxxix), and has a note (col. clxxvi) 'nunquam enim dicitur Prosa ad Matutinas per totum annum, sed ad Vesperas, et ad Processionem, excepto die sancti Stephani, cuius servitium committitur voluntati Diaconorum; et excepto die sancti Iohannis, cuius servitium committitur voluntati Sacerdotum; et excepto die sanctorum Innocentium, cuius servitium committitur voluntati Puerorum.'

[3] *York Missal*, i. 20, 22, 23 (from fifteenth-century MS. *D* used in the Minster) '*In die S. Steph.* . . . finita processione, si Dominica fuerit, ut in Processionali continetur, Diaconis et Subdiaconis in choro ordinatim astantibus, unus Diaconus, cui Praecentor imposuerit, incipiat Officium. . . . *In die S. Ioann.* . . . omnibus Personis et Presbyteris civitatis ex antiqua consuetudine ad Ecclesiam Cathedralem convenientibus, et omnibus ordinate ex utraque parte Chori in Capis sericis astantibus, Praecentor incipiat Officium. . . . *In die SS. Innoc.* . . . omnibus pueris in Capis, Praecentor illorum incipiat.' There are responds for the 'turba diaconorum,' 'presbyterorum' or 'puerorum.'

[4] *Lincoln Statutes*, i. 290; ii. ccxxx, 552.

[5] Gasquet, *Old English Bible*, 250.

[6] Martene, iii. 40.

[7] Ibid. iii. 39.

But elsewhere they have their own history of reformations or suppression, or are grouped with the Feast of Fools, as by the decretal of Innocent III, in a common condemnation. The diversity of local practice is well illustrated by the records of such acts of discipline. Sometimes, as at Paris [1], or Soissons [2], it is the deacons' feast alone that has become an abuse ; sometimes, as at Worms, that of the priests' [3] ; sometimes two of them [4], sometimes all three [5], require correction.

[1] In his second decree of 1199 as to the feast of the Circumcision at Paris (cf. p. 276), Bishop Eudes de Sully says (*P. L.* ccxii. 73) ' quoniam festivitas beati protomartyris Stephani eiusdem fere subiacebat dissolutionis et temeritatis incommodo, nec ita solemniter, sicut decebat et martyris merita requirebant, in Ecclesia Parisiensi consueverat celebrari, nos, qui eidem martyri sumus specialiter debitores, quoniam in Ecclesia Bituricensi patronum habuerimus, in cuius gremio ab ineunte aetate fuimus nutriti ; de voluntate et assensu dilectorum nostrorum Hugonis decani et capituli Parisiensis, festivitatem ipsam ad statum reducere regularem, eumque magnis Ecclesiae solemnitatibus adnumerare decrevimus ; statuentes ut in ipso festo tantum celebritatis agatur, quantum in ceteris festis annualibus fieri consuevit.' Eudes de Sully made a donative to the canons and clerks present at Matins on the feast, which his successor Petrus de Nemore confirmed in 1208 (*P. L.* ccxii. 91). Dean Hugo Clemens instigated a similar reform of St. John's day (see p. 276).

[2] Martene, iii. 40 ; Grenier, 353, 412. The *Ritual* of Bishop Nivelon, at the end of the twelfth century, orders St. Stephen's to be kept as a triple feast, ' exclusa antiqua consuetudine diaconorum et ludorum.'

[3] Schannat, iv. 258 (1316) 'illud, quod . . . causa devotionis ordinatum fuerat . . . ut Sacerdotes singulis annis in festivitate Beati Iohannis Evangelistae unum ex se eligant,

qui more episcopi illa die Missam gloriose celebret et festive, nunc in ludibrium vertitur, et in ecclesia ludi fiunt theatrales, et non solum in ecclesia introducuntur monstra larvarum, verum etiam Presbyteri, Diaconi et Subdiaconi insaniae suae ludibria exercere praesumunt, facientes prandia sumptuosa, et cum tympanis et cymbalis ducentes choreas per domos et plateas civitatis.'

[4] At Rouen in 1445 the feast of St. John, held by the *capellani*, was alone in question. The chapter ordered (Gasté, 46) ' ut faciant die festi sancti euangelistae Iohannis servicium divinum bene et honeste, sine derisionibus et fatuitatibus ; et inhibitum fuit eisdem ne habeant vestes difformes, insuper quod fiat mensa et ponantur boni cantores, qui bene sciant cantare, omnibus derisionibus cessantibus.' But in 1446 the feast of St. Stephen needed reforming, as well as that of St. John (A. Chéruel, *Hist. de Rouen sous la Domination anglaise*, 206) ; and in 1451 all three (Gasté, 47) ' praefati Domini capitulantes ordinaverunt quod in festis solemnitatis Nativitatis Domini nostri Ihesu Christi proxime futuris, omnes indecencie et inhonestates consuete fieri in dedecus ecclesie, tam per presbyteros dyaconos quam pueros chori et basse forme, cessent omnino, nec sit aliquis puer in habitu episcopi, sed fiat servicium devote et honorifice prout in aliis festis similis gradus.'

[5] *C. of Toledo* (1473), c. 19 (Labbé, xiii. 1460) ' Quia vero quaedam tam in Metropolitanis quam in

I need only refer more particularly to two interesting English examples. One is at Wells, where a chapter statute of about 1331 condemns the tumult and *ludibrium* with which divine service was celebrated from the Nativity to the octave of the Innocents, and in particular the *ludi theatrales* and *monstra larvarum* introduced into the cathedral by the deacons, priests, sub-deacons, and even vicars during this period [1]. Nor was the abuse easy to check, for about 1338 a second statute was required to reinforce and strengthen the prohibition [2]. So, too, in the neighbouring diocese of Exeter. The register of Bishop Grandisson records the mandates against *ludi inhonesti* addressed by him in 1360 to the chapters of Exeter cathedral, and of the collegiate churches of Ottery,

Cathedralibus et aliis Ecclesiis nostrae próvinciae consuetudo inolevit ut videlicet in festis Nativitatis Domini nostri Iesu Christi et sanctorum Stephani, Ioannis et Innocentium aliisque certis diebus festivis, etiam in solemnitatibus Missarum novarum dum divina aguntur, ludi theatrales, larvae, monstra, spectacula, necnon quamplurima inhonesta et diversa figmenta in Ecclesiis introducuntur . . . huiusmodi larvas, ludos, monstra, spectacula, figmenta et tumultuationes fieri . . . prohibemus . . . Per hoc tam honestas repraesentationes et devotas, quae populum ad devotionem movent, tam in praefatis diebus quam in aliis non intendimus prohibere'; *C. of Lyons* (1566 and 1577), c. 15 (Du Tilliot, 63) 'Es jours de Fête des Innocens et autres, l'on ne doit souffrir ès Églises jouer jeux, tragédies, farces, &c.'; cf. the Cologne statutes (1662) quoted on p. 352.

[1] H.E. Reynolds, *Wells Cathedral*, 75 '*Quod non sint ludi contra honestatem Ecclesiae Wellensis.* Item a festo Nativitatis Domini usque ad octavas Innocentium quod Clerici Subdiaconi Diaconi Presbiteri etiam huius ecclesiae vicarii ludos faciant theatrales in ecclesia Wellensi et monstra larvarum introducentes, in ea insaniae suae

ludibria exercere praesumunt contra honestatem clericalem et sacrorum prohibitionem canonum divinum officium multipliciter impediendo; quod de cetero in ecclesia Wellensi et sub pena canonica fieri prohibentes volumus quod divinum officium in festo dictorum sanctorum Innocentium sicuti in festis sanctorum consimilibus quiete ac pacifice absque quocunque tumultu et ludibrio cum devotione debita celebretur.'

[2] Reynolds, *op. cit.* 87 '*Prohibitio ludorum theatralium et spectaculorum et ostentationum larvarum in Ecclesia.* Item, cum infra septimanam Pentecostes et etiam in aliis festivitatibus fiant a laicis ludi theatrales in ecclesia praedicta et non solum ad ludibriorum spectacula introducantur in ea monstra larvarum, verum etiam in sanctorum Innocentium et aliorum sanctorum festivitatibus quae Natale Christi secuntur, Presbyteri Diaconi et Subdiaconi dictae Wellensis ecclesiae vicissim insaniae suae ludibria exercentes per gesticulationem debacchationes obscenas divinum officium impediant in conspectu populi, decus faciant clericale vilescere quem potius illo tempore deberent praedicatione mulcere. . . .' The statute goes on to threaten offenders with excommunication.

Crediton, and Glasney. These *ludi* were performed by men and boys at Vespers, Matins, and Mass on Christmas and the three following days. They amounted to a mockery of the divine worship, did much damage to the church vestments and ornaments, and brought the clergy into disrepute[1]. These southern prohibitions are shortly before the final suppression of the Feast of Fools in the north at Beverley and Lincoln. The Wells customs, indeed, probably included a regular Feast of Fools, for the part taken by the subdeacons and vicars is specifically mentioned, and the proceedings lasted over the New Year. But it is clear that even where the term 'Feast of Fools' is not known to have been in use, the temper of that revel found a ready vent in other of the winter rejoicings. Nor was it the *triduum* alone which afforded its opportunities. More rarely the performances of the *Pastores* on Christmas day itself[2], or the suppers given by the great officers of cathedrals and monasteries, when they

---

[1] F. C. Hingeston Randolph, *Bishop Grandison's Register*, Part iii, p. 1213; *Inhibicio Episcopi de ludis inhonestis.* The bishop writes to all four bodies in identical terms. He wishes them 'Salutem, et morum clericalium honestatem,' and adds 'Ad nostram, non sine gravi cordis displicencia et stupore, pervenit noticiam quod, annis praeteritis et quibusdam praecedentibus, in Sanctissimis Dominice Nativitatis, ac Sanctorum Stephani, Iohannis, Apostoli et Evangelistae, ac Innocencium Solempniis, quando omnes Christi Fideles Divinis laudibus et Officiis Ecclesiasticis devocius ac quiescius insistere tenentur, aliqui praedicte Ecclesie nostre Ministri, cum pueris, nedum Matutinis et Vesperis ac Horis aliis, set, quod magis detestandum est, inter Missarum Sollempnia, ludos ineptos et noxios, honestatique clericali indecentes, quia verius Cultus Divini ludibria detestanda, infra Ecclesiam ipsam inmiscendo committere, Divino timore postposito, pernicioso quarundam Ecclesiarum exemplo, temere praesumpserunt; Vestimenta et alia Ornamenta Ecclesie, in non modicum eiusdem Ecclesie nostre et nostrum dampnum et dedecus, vilium scilicet scenulentorumque (*or* scev.) sparsione multipliciter deturpando. Ex quorum gestis, seu risibus et cachinnis derisoriis, nedum populus, more Catholico illis potissime temporibus ad Ecclesiam conveniens, a debita devocione abstrahitur, set et in risum incompositum ac oblectamenta illicita dissolvitur; Cultusque Divinus irridetur et Officium perperam impeditur. . . .'

[2] On the *Pastores* cf. ch. xix. Gasté, 33, gives several Rouen chapter acts from 1449 to 1457 requiring them to officiate 'cessantibus stultitiis et insolenciis.' These orders and those quoted on p. 341 above were prompted by the *Letter* of the Paris theologians against the Feast of Fools and similar revels. In 1445 (or 1449) a committee was chosen 'ad videndum et visitandum ordinationem ecclesiae pro festis Nativitatis Domini et deliberationes Facultatis Theologiae super hoc habitas et quod tollantur derisiones in ipsis fieri solitas.'

sang their ' *Oes*,' on the nights between December 16 and Christmas [1], were the occasions for excesses which called for reprehension.

Already, when Conrad visited St. Gall in 911, the third feast of the *triduum* was the most interesting. In after years this reached an importance denied to the other two. The Vespers procession was the germ of an annual rejoicing, secular as well as ritual, which became for the *pueri* attached as choir-boys and servers to the cathedrals and great churches very much what the Feast of Fools became for the adult inferior clergy of the same bodies. Where the two feasts were not merged in one, this distinction of *personnel* was retained. A good example is afforded by Sens. Here, from the middle of the fourteenth century, the chapter accounts show an *archiepiscopus puerorum* side by side with the *dominus* of the Feast of Fools. Each feast got its own grant of wine from the chapter, and had its own prebend in the chapter woods. In the fifteenth century the two fell and rose together. In the sixteenth, the Feast of Boys was the more flourishing, and claimed certain dues from a market in Sens, which were commuted for a small money payment by the chapter. Finally, both feasts are suppressed together in 1547 [2]. It is to be observed that the original celebration of the Holy Innocents' day in the western Church was not of an unmixed festal character. It commemorated a martyrdom which typified and might actually have been that of Christ himself, and it was therefore held *cum tristitia*. As in Lent or on Good Friday itself, the 'joyful chants,' such as the *Te Deum* or the *Alleluia*, were silenced. This characteristic

---

[1] At Sarum a *Constitutio* of Roger de Mortival in 1324 (Dayman and Jones, *Sarum Statutes*, 52) forbade drinking when the antiphon 'O Sapientia' was sung after Compline on Dec. 16. John of Avranches (†1070) allowed for the feast of his ' O ' at Rouen 'unum galonem vini de cellario archiepiscopi,' and the ' vin de l'O ' was still given in 1377 (Gasté, 47). On these ' Oes,' sung by the great functionaries of cathedrals and monasteries, see E.

Green, *On the words ' O Sapientia'* *in the Kalendar* (*Archaeologia*, xlix. 219); Cynewulf, *Christ* (ed. A. S. Cook), xxxv. Payments 'cantoribus ad ludum suum' or 'ad' or 'ante natale' appear in Durham accounts; cf. *Finchale Priory* ccccxxviii (Surtees Soc.,) and *Durham Accounts, passim* (Surtees Soc.). I do not feel sure what feast is here referred to.

[2] Chérest, 49 sqq.

of the day was known to Belethus, but even before his time it had begun to give way to the festal tendencies. Local practice differed widely, as the notices collected by Martene show, but even when John of Avranches wrote, at the end of the eleventh century, the 'modern' custom was to sing the chants[1].

Many interesting details of the Feast of Boys, as it was celebrated in France, are contained in various ceremonial books. The *Officium Infantum* of Rouen may be taken as typical[2]. After second Vespers on St. John's day the boys marched out of the vestry, two by two, with their 'bishop,' singing *Centum quadraginta*. There was a procession to the altar of the Holy Innocents, and *Hi empti sunt* was sung[3]. Then the 'bishop' gave the Benediction. The feast of the following day was 'double,' but the boys might make it 'triple,' if they would. There was a procession, with the *Centum quadraginta*, at Matins. At Mass, the boys led the choir. At Vespers the *baculus* was handed over, while the *Deposuit potentes* was being sung[4]. At Bayeux the feast followed the same general lines, but the procession at first Vespers was to the altar, not of the Holy Innocents, but of St. Nicholas[5]. Precise directions are given as to the functions of the 'bishop.' He is to wear a silk tunic and cope, and to have a mitre and pastoral staff, but not a ring. The boys are to do him the same reverence that is done to the real

---

[1] Ioannes Abrincensis, *de Eccl. Offic.* (*P. L.* cxlvii. 42) 'Licet, ut in morte Domini, *Te Deum* et *Gloria in excelsis* et *Alleluia* in aliquot ecclesiis, ex more antiquo, omittantur; quia ut Christus occideretur tot parvuli occidi iubentur; et illis occisis fit mors Christi secundum aestimationem Herodis; tamen quia placuit modernis, placet et nobis ut cantentur'; cf. the passage from Belethus quoted on p. 336; also Honorius Augustodunensis, *Gemma Animae*, iii. 14 (*P. L.* clxxii. 646), and Martene, iii. 40.

[2] *Ordinarium* of Rouen (fourteenth century) in Ducange, s.v. *Kalendae*; *P. L.* cxlvii. 155; Gasté, 35. On the Rouen feast cf. also Gasté, 48.

[3] These chants are taken from *Revelation*, xiv. 3 'nemo poterat dicere canticum, nisi illa centum quadraginta quatuor millia, qui empti sunt de terra. Hi sunt, qui cum mulieribus non sunt coinquinati, virgines enim sunt. Hi sequuntur Agnum quocumque ierit.' This passage is still read in the 'Epistle' at Mass on Holy Innocents' day. Cf. the use of the same chants at Salisbury (Appendix M).

[4] 'Et tamdiu cantetur *Deposuit potentes* quod baculus accipiatur ab eo qui accipere voluerit.'

[5] *Ordinarium* of Bayeux (undated) in Gasté, 37. On the Bayeux feast and its *parvus episcopus* or *petit évêque* cf. F. Pluquet, *Essai sur Bayeux*, 274.

bishop. There are also to be a boy *cantor* and a boy ' chaplain.' The ' bishop' is to perform the duties of a priest, so long as the feast lasts, except in the Mass. He is to give the benediction after *Benedicamus* at first Vespers. Then the boys are to take the higher stalls, and to keep them throughout the following day, the ' bishop' sitting in the dean's chair. The boys are to say Compline as they will. The ' bishop' is to be solemnly conducted home with the prose *Sedentem,* and on the following day he is to be similarly conducted both to and from service. At Mass he is to cense and be censed like the 'great bishop' on solemn occasions. He is also to give the benediction at Mass. There is a minute description of the ceremony of *Deposuit,* from which it is clear that, at Bayeux at least, the handing over of the *baculus* was from an incoming to an outgoing ' bishop,' to whom the former was in turn to act as ' chaplain[1].' The rubrics of the Coutances feast are even more minute[2]. The proceedings began after Matins on St. John's day, when the boys drew up a *tabula* appointing their superiors to the minor offices of the coming feast. This, however, they were to do without impertinence[3]. The vesting of the ' bishop' and the Vespers procession are exactly described. As at Bayeux the boys take the high stalls for Compline. The canon who holds a particular

---

[1] ' Dum perventum fuerit ad illum : *Deposuit potentes,* vadunt omnes ad medium ecclesiae et ibi qui in processione stant ordinate eumdem versum, episcopo inchoante, plures replicantes. Qui dum sic cantatur, offert ipse episcopus sociis suis de choro baculum pastoralem. Post multas itaque resumptiones dicti versus, revertuntur in chorum, *Te Deum laudamus,* si habent novum episcopum, decantantes, et ita canendo deducunt eum ad altare, et mitra sibi imposita et baculo cum capa serica, revertuntur in chorum, illo qui fuerat episcopus explente officium capellani, creato nihilominus novo cantore. Tunc chorus, si non fuerit ibi novus episcopus, vel novus episcopus qui baculum duxerit capiendum, cum suis sociis resumit a capite psalmum *Magnificat,* et sic cantant vesperas usque ad finem.'

[2] *Novus Ordinarius* of Coutances (undated) in Gasté, 39.

[3] ' Post Matutinas conveniant omnes pueri ad suam tabulam faciendam, quibus licitum est maiores personas Ecclesiae minoribus officiis deputare. Diaconis et subdiaconis ordinatis, thuribula imponantur et candelabra maiora videlicet et minora. Episcopo vero, cantori et aliis canonicis aquam, manutergium, missale, ignem et campanam possunt imponere pro suae libito voluntatis. Nihil tamen inhonestum aut impertinens apponatur; antiquiores primi ponantur in tabula et ultimi iuniores.'

prebend is bound to carry the candle and the *collectarium* for the 'bishop.' After Compline the 'bishop' is led home with *Laetabundus*, but not in pontificals. Throughout the services of the following day the 'bishop' plays his part, and when Vespers comes gives way to a 'bishop'-elect at the *Deposuit*[1]. The 'bishop' of St. Martin of Tours was installed in the neighbouring convent of Beaumont, whither all the *clericuli* rode for the purpose after Prime on St. John's day. He was vested in the church there, blessed the nuns, then returned to Tours, was installed in his own cathedral, and blessed the populace[2]. The secular side of the feast comes out in the Toul *Statutes* of 1497[3]. Here it may be said to have absorbed in its turn the Feast of Fools, for the 'bishop' was a choir-boy chosen by the choir-boys themselves and also by the sub-deacons, who shared with them the name of *Innocentes*[4]. The election took place after Compline on the first Sunday in Advent, and the 'bishop' was enthroned with a *Te Deum*. He officiated in the usual way throughout the Innocents' day services. In the morning he rode at the head of a *cortège* to the monasteries of St. Mansuetus and St. Aper, sang an anthem and said a prayer at the door of each church, and claimed a customary fee[5]. After Vespers he again rode in state with mimes and trumpeters through the city[6]. On the following day, all the 'Innocents' went

[1] 'Quo facto dicat [Episcopus] *Deposuit*. Statimque electus Episcopus, tradito sibi baculo pastorali a pueris ad altare praesentetur, et osculato altari in domum suam a dictis pueris deferatur. Et interim, finito tumultu, eat processio ad altare S. Thomae martyris.'

[2] *Rituale* (fourteenth century) of Tours in Martene, iii. 39. There was a *cantor puerorum* as well as the *episcopus*. At second Vespers 'quando *Magnificat* canitur, veniunt clericuli in choro cum episcopo habentes candelas accensas de proprio et quando *Deposuit* canitur, accipit cantor puerorum baculum, et tunc in stallo ascendunt pueri, et alii descendunt.'

[3] Ducange, s. v. *Kalendae*.

[4] 'Omnes pueri et subdiaconi feriati, qui in numero dictorum Innocentium computantur.'

[5] 'Ipsa autem die de mane equitare habet idem episcopus Innocentium ad monasteria SS. Mansueti et Apri per civitatem transeundo in comitiva suorum aequalium, quibus etiam maiores et digniores personae dignitatum comitantur per se vel suos servitores et equos, et descendentes ad fores ecclesiarum praedictarum intonat unam antiphonam et dicit episcopus orationem, sibique debentur a quolibet monasteriorum eorundem xviij den. Tullenses, qui si illico non solvantur, possunt accipere libros vel vadia.'

[6] 'Cantatis eiusdem diei vesperis, episcopus ipse cum mimis et tubis procedit per civitatem cum sua

masked into the city, where, if it was fine enough, farces and apparently also moralities and miracles were played [1]. On the octave the 'bishop' and his *cortège* went to the church of St. Geneviève. After an anthem and collect they adjourned to the 'church-house,' where they were entertained by the hospital at a dessert of cake, apples and nuts, during which they chose disciplinary officers for the coming year [2]. The expenses of the feast, with the exception of the dinner on the day after Innocents' day which came out of the disciplinary fines, are assigned by the statutes to the canons in the order of their appointment. The responsible canon must give a supper on Innocents' day, and a dessert out of what is over on the following day. He must also provide the 'bishop' with a horse, gloves, and a *biretta* when he rides abroad. At the supper a curious ceremony took place. The canon returned thanks to the 'bishop,' apologized for any short-comings in the preparations, and finally handed the 'bishop' a cap of rosemary or other flowers, which was then conferred upon the canon to whose lot it would fall to provide the feast for the next anniversary [3]. Should the canon disregard his duties the boys and sub-deacons were entitled to hang up a black cope on a candlestick in the middle of the choir *in illius vituperium* for as long as they might choose [4].

comitiva, via qua fiunt generales processiones.'

[1] 'In crastino Innocentium, quo omnes vadunt per civitatem post prandium, faciebus opertis, in diversis habitibus, et si quae farsae practicari valeant, tempore tamen sicco, fiunt in aliquibus locis civitatis, omnia cum honestate.' Another passage, referring more generally to the feast, has 'Fiunt ibi moralitates vel simulacra miraculorum cum farsis et similibus ioculis, semper tamen honestis.'

[2] 'In octavis Innocentium rursus vadit episcopus cum omni comitiva sua in habitibus suis ad ecclesiam B. Genovefae, ubi cantata antiphona de ipsa virgine cum collecta, itur ad domum parochialem eius ecclesiae vel alibi, ubi magister et fratres domus Dei, quibus ipsa

ecclesia est unita, paraverint focapam unam, poma, nuces, &c. ad merendam oportuna; et ibi instituuntur officiarii ad marencias super defectibus aut excessibus in officio divino per totum annum commissis.'

[3] 'Fit ... assignatio post coenam diei Innocentium; ita quod is qui illa die festum peregit, gratias refert episcopo et toti comitivae, ac excusari petit, si in aliquo defecit; et finaliter pileum romarini vel alterius confectionis floreum exhibet ipsi episcopo, ut tradat canonico in receptione sequenti constituto ad futurum annum ipsum festum agendum.' Cf. the bouquets at the 'defructus' (p. 324).

[4] 'Si autem facere contemneret adveniente festo, suspenderetur cappa nigra in raustro medio chori,

I cannot pretend to give a complete account of all the French examples of the Boy Bishop with which I have met, and it is the less necessary, as the feast seems to have been far more popular and enduring in England than the Feast of Fools. I content myself with giving references for its history at Amiens[1], St. Quentin[2], Senlis[3], Soissons[4], Roye[5], Peronne[6], Rheims[7], Brussels[8], Lille[9], Liège[10], Laon[11], Troyes[12], Mans[13], Bourges[14], Châlons-sur-Saône[15], Grenoble[16]. Not unnaturally it proved less of a scandal to ecclesiastical reformers than the Feast of Fools; for the choir-boys must have been more amenable to discipline, even in moments of festivity, than the adult clerks. But it shared in the general condemnation of all such customs, and was specifically arraigned by more than one council, rather perhaps for puerility than for

et tamdiu ibi maneret in illius. vituperium, quamdiu placeret subdiaconis feriatis et pueris chori; et in ea re non tenerentur nobis capitulo obedire.'

[1] Amiens: Rigollot, 13 and passim; cf. p. 339.

[2] St. Quentin: Rigollot, 32; Grenier, 360.

[3] Senlis: Rigollot, 26; Grenier, 360.

[4] Soissons: Matton, *Archives de Soissons*, 75.

[5] Roye: Rigollot, 33; Grenier, 359.

[6] Peronne: Rigollot, 34; Grenier, 359, 413.

[7] Rheims: Rigollot, 50; Petit de Julleville, *Rép. Com.* 348; Marlot, *Hist. de Rheims*, ii. 266. In 1479 the chapter undertook the expense, 'modo fiat sine larvis et strepitu tubicinis, ac sine equitatione per villam.' Martene, iii. 40, says that there is no trace of any of the *triduum* ceremonies in the early thirteenth-century Rheims *Ordinarium*.

[8] Brussels: Laborde, *Ducs de Bourgogne*, ii. 2. 286 '[1378] Item xxi decembris episcopo scholarium sanctae Gudilae profecto Sancti Nycolay quod scholares annuatim faciunt 1½ mut[ones].'

[9] Lille: E. Hautcœur, *Hist. de*

Saint-Pierre de Lille, ii. 217, 223. On June 29, 1501, Guillemot de Lespine 'trépassa évêque des Innocens.' His epitaph is in the cloister gallery (Hautcœur, *Doc. liturg. de S. P. de Lille*, 342).

[10] Liège: Rigollot, 42; Dürr, 82. A statute of 1330 laid the expense on the last admitted canon 'nisi canonicus scholaris sub virga existens ipsum exemerit.'

[11] Laon: Rigollot, 21; Grenier, 356, 413; C. Hidé, *Bull. de la Soc. acad. de Laon*, xiii. 122; E. Fleury, *Cinquante Ans de Laon*, 52. A chapter act of 1546 states that the custom of playing a comedy at the election of the Boy Bishop on St. Eloi's day (Dec. 1) has ceased. The Mass is not to be disturbed, but 'si les escoliers veulent faire un petit discours, il seroit entendu avec plaisir.'

[12] Troyes: T. Boutiot, *Hist. de Troyes*, iii. 20.

[13] Mans: Gasté, 43; Julleville, *Les Com.* 38.

[14] Bourges: Martene, iii. 40.

[15] Châlons-sur-Saône: Du Tilliot, 20; C. Perry, *Hist. de Châlons* (1659), 435.

[16] Grenoble: Pilot de Thorey, *Usages, Fêtes et Coutumes en Dauphiné*, i. 181.

any graver offence [1]. Gradually therefore, it vanished, leaving only a few survivals to recent centuries [2]. As was the case with the Feast of Fools, the question of its suppression sometimes set a chapter by the ears. Notably was this so at Noyon, where the act of his reforming colleagues in 1622 was highly disapproved of by the dean, Jacques Le Vasseur.· In a letter written on the occasion he declares that the Boy Bishop had flourished in Noyon cathedral for four hundred years, and brands the reformers as brute beasts masquerading in the robes and beards of philosophy [3].

I have no special records of the Boy Bishop in Spain except the council decrees already quoted. In Germany he appears to have been more widely popular than his rival of Fools. My first notice, however, is two centuries after the visit of Conrad to the *triduum* at St. Gall. The chronicle of the monastery of St. Petersburg, hard by Halle, mentions an accident *in ludo qui vocatur puerorum*, by which a lad was trodden to death. This was in 1137 [4]. The thirteenth and fourteenth centuries yield

---

[1] *C. of Cognac* (1260), c. 2 (Mansi, xxiii. 1033) 'cum in balleatione quae in festo SS. Innocentium in quibusdam Ecclesiis fieri inolevit, multae rixae, contentiones et turbationes, tam in divinis officiis quam aliis consueverint provenire, praedictas balleationes ulterius sub intimatione anathematis fieri prohibemus; nec non et Episcopos in praedicto festo creari; cum hoc in ecclesia Dei ridiculum existat, et hoc dignitatis episcopalis ludibrio fiat.' *C. of Salzburg* (1274), c. 17 (Labbé, xi. 1004) 'ludi noxii quos vulgaris elocutio Eptus puor. appellat'; *CC. of Chartres* (1526 and 1575; Bochellus, *Decr. Eccl. Gall.* iv. 7. 46; Du Tilliot, 66) 'stultum aut ridiculum in ecclesia' on days of SS. Nicholas and Catharine, and the Innocents; *C. of Toledo* (1565), ii. 21 (Labbé, xv. 764) 'ficta illa et puerilis episcopatus electio'; *C. of Rouen* (1581; Hardouin, *Concilia*, x. 1217) 'in festivitate SS. Innocentium theatralia.'

[2] There are traces of it in the eighteenth century at Lyons (Martene, iii. 40) and Rheims (Barthé-

lemy, v. 334); at Sens, in the nineteenth, the choir-boys still play at being bishops on Innocents' day, and name the 'archbishop' *âne* (Chérest, 81).

[3] Grenier, 358, quoting Le Vasseur, *Epistolae*, Cent. ii. Epist. 68; cf. on the Noyon feast, Leach, 135; Du Tilliot, 17; Rigollot, 27; L. Mazière, *Noyon religieux*, in *Comptes-Rendus et Mémoires*, xi. 91, of *The Comité arch. et hist. de Noyon*. Le Vasseur, an ex-Rector of the University of Paris, writes to François Geuffrin 'ecce ludunt etiam ante ipsas aras; internecionem detestamur, execramur carnificem. Ludunt et placet iste ludus ecclesiae. . . . Tam grandis est natu ritus iste, quem viguisse deprehendo iam ante quadringentos annos in hac aede, magno totius orbis ordinum et aetatum plausu fructuque . . . O miserum saeculum! . . . solo gestu externoque habitu spectabiles, sola barba et pallio philosophi, caetera pecudes!'

[4] *Chronicon Montis Sereni* in Pertz, *Scriptores*, xxiii. 144.

more examples. In 1249 Pope Innocent IV complained to the bishop of Ratisbon that the clerks and scholars of that cathedral, when choosing their anniversary 'bishop,' did violence to the abbey of Pruviningen [1]. In 1357 the Ratisbon feast was stained with homicide, and was consequently suppressed [2]. In 1282 the feast was forbidden at Eichstädt [3]. In 1304 it led to a dispute between the municipality and the chapter of Hamburg, which ended in a promise by the *scholares* to refrain from defamatory songs either in Latin or German [4]. Similarly at Worms in 1307 the *pueri* were forbidden to sing in the streets after Compline, as had been the custom on the feasts of St. Nicholas and St. Lucy, on Christmas and the three following days, and on the octave of the Holy Innocents' [5]. At Lubeck the feast was abolished in 1336 [6]. I have already quoted the long reference to the *scholarium episcopus* in the Mosburg Gradual of 1360 [7]. He may be traced also at Regensburg [8] and at Prague [9]. But the fullest account of him is from Mainz [10]. Here he was called the *Schul-Bischoff*, and in derision *Apffeln-Bischoff*. He was chosen before St. Nicholas' day by the *ludi magister* of the *schola trivialis*. He had his *equites*, his *capellani*, and his *pedelli*. On St. Nicholas' day, and on that of the Holy Innocents', he had a seat near the high altar, and took part in the first and second Vespers. In the interval he paid a visit with his company to the palace of the elector, sang a hymn [11], and claimed a banquet or a donation. The custom

---

[1] *Monum. Boic.* xiii. 214, quoted by Specht, 228 'in festo nativitatis Dominicae annuatim sibi ludendo constituentes episcopum.'

[2] Vitus Arnpekius, *Chron. Baioariorum*, v. 53, cited by Martene, iii. 40.

[3] Specht, 228.

[4] Ibid. 225 ; Creizenach, i. 391 ; both quoting E. Meyer, *Gesch. des hamburgischen Schul- und Unterrichtswesens im Mittelalter*, 197 'praeterea scholares nunquam, sive in electione sive extra, aliquos rhythmos faciant, tam in latino, quam in teutonico, qui famam alicuius valeant maculare.' In the

thirteenth century a child-abbot was chosen in Hamburg on St. Andrew's day (Nov. 30). On St. Nicholas' day (Dec. 6) he gave way to a child-bishop, who remained in office until Dec. 28 (Tille, *D. W.* 31, citing Beneke, *Hamburgische Geschichte und Sagen*, 90).

[5] Specht, 229.

[6] Ibid. 228.

[7] Cf. p. 319.

[8] Tille, *D. W.* 31.

[9] Ibid. 299.

[10] Dürr, 67, quoting a *Ritual* of the cathedral ('tempore Alberti').

[11] It began :

'Iam tuum festum Nicolae dives

was not altogether extinct in Mainz by 1779[1]. In other German towns, also, it well out-lived the Middle Ages. At Cologne, for instance, it was only suppressed by the statutes of Bishop Max Heinrich in 1662[2].

In England, the Boy Bishop weathered the storms of discipline which swept away the Feast of Fools in the thirteenth and fourteenth centuries. He was widely popular in the later Middle Ages, and finally fell before an austerity of the Reformation. The prerogative instance of the custom is in the church f Salisbury. Here the existence of the Boy Bishop is already implied by the notice of a ring for use at the 'Feast of Boys' in an inventory of 1222[3]. A century later, the statutes of Roger de Mortival in 1319 include elaborate regulations for the ceremony. The 'bishop' may perform the *officium* as is the use, but he must hold no banquet, and no visitation either within or without the cathedral. He may be invited to the table of a canon, but otherwise he must remain in the common house, and must return to his duties in church and school immediately after the feast of Innocents. The statute also regulates the behaviour of the crowds which were wont to press upon and impede the boys in their annual procession to the altar of the Holy Trinity, and the rest of their ministry[4]. Two of the

more solemni recolit iuventus,
nec tibi dignus, sacerdotum Caesar,
    promere laudes.'
[1] Tille, *D. W.* 31, citing Nork, *Festkalender*, 783. Dürr's tract was published at Mainz in 1755.
[2] Wetzer und Welte, s. v. *Feste* 'consuetudo seu potius detestabilis corruptela, qua pueri a die S. Nicolai usque ad festum SS. Innocentium personatum Episcopum colunt ... ea puerilibus levitatibus et ineptiis plena coeperit esse multumque gravitatis et decoris divinis detrahat officiis ... ne clerus se pueris die SS. Inn. submittat ac eorum locum occupet, aut illis functiones aliquas in divinis officiis permittat, neque praesentes aliquis Episcopus benedictiones faciat, aliique pueri in cantandis horariis precibus lectioni-

bus et collectis Sacerdotum, Diaconorum aut Subdiaconorum officia quaedam usurpent; multo minus convenit ut Canonici aut Vicarii ex collegarum suorum numero aliquem designent Episcopum qui reliquos omnes magnis impendiis liberali convivio excipiat.'
[3] W. H. R. Jones, *Vetus Registr. Sarisb.* (R. S.), ii. 128; Wordsworth, *Proc.* 170 'Item, annulus unus aureus ad Festum Puerorum.'
[4] *Constitutiones*, § 45 (Jones and Dayman, *Sarum Statutes*, 75; cf. Jones, *Fasti*, 295) 'Electus puer chorista in episcopum modo solito puerili officium in ecclesia, prout fieri consuevit, licenter exequatur, convivium aliquod de caetero, vel visitationem exterius seu interius nullatenus faciendo, sed in domo

great service-books of the Sarum use, the Breviary and the Processional, give ample details as to the 'ministry' of the Boy Bishop and his fellows. The office, as preserved in these, will be found in an appendix [1]. The proceedings differ in some respects from the continental models already described. There is no mention of the *Deposuit*; and the central rite is still the great procession between Vespers and Compline on the eve of the Holy Innocents. This procession went from the choir either to the altar of the Holy Innocents or to that of the Holy Trinity and All Saints in the Lady chapel, and at its return the boys took the higher stalls and kept them until the second Vespers of the feast. For this procession the boys were entitled to assign the functions of carrying the book, the censer, the candles, and so forth to the canons. Some miscellaneous notices of the Salisbury feast are contained in the chapter register between 1387 and 1473. From 1387 the oblations on the feast appear to have been given to the 'bishop.' In 1413 he was allowed a banquet. In 1448 the precentor, Nicholas Upton, proposed that the boys, instead of freely electing a 'bishop,' should be confined to a choice amongst three candidates named by the chapter. But this innovation was successfully resisted [2]. Cathedral documents also give the names of twenty-one boys who held the office [3]. There is in Salisbury cathedral a dwarf effigy of a bishop, dating from the latter part of the thirteenth century. Local

communi cum sociis conversetur, nisi cum ut choristam ad domum canonici causa solatii ad mensam contigerit evocari, ecclesiam et scholas cum caeteris choristis statim post festum Innocentium frequentando. Et quia in processione quam ad altare Sanctae Trinitatis faciunt annuatim pueri supradicti per concurrentium pressuras et alias dissolutiones multiplices nonnulla damna personis et ecclesiae gravia intelleximus priscis temporibus pervenisse, ex parte Dei omnipotentis et sub poena maioris excommunicationis, quam contravenientes utpote libertates dictae ecclesiae nostrae infringentes et illius pacem et quietem temerarie perturbantes declara-

mus incurrere ipso facto, inhibemus ne quis pueros illos in praefata processione vel alias in suo ministerio premat vel impediat quoquomodo, quominus pacifice valeant facere et exequi quod illis imminet faciendum; sed qui eidem processioni devotionis causa voluerint interesse, ita modo maturo se habeant et honeste sicut et in aliis processionibus dictae ecclesiae se habent qui ad honorem Dei frequentant quando que ecclesiam supradictam.'

[1] Appendix M.
[2] Jones, *Fasti*, 299.
[3] Wordsworth, *Proc.* 259. The *oblationes* vary from lvis. viii*d.* in 1448 to as much as lxxxixs. xi*d.* in 1456.

tradition, from at least the beginning of the seventeenth century, has regarded this as the monument of a Boy Bishop who died during his term of office. But modern archaeologists repudiate the theory. Such miniature effigies are not un-common, and possibly indicate that the heart alone of the person commemorated is buried in the spot which they mark[1].

The gradual adoption of the use of Sarum by other dioceses would naturally tend to carry with it that of the Boy Bishop. But he is to be found at Exeter and at St. Paul's before the change of use, as well as at Lincoln and York which retained their own uses up to the Reformation. At Exeter Bishop Grandisson's *Ordinale* of 1337 provides an *Officium puerorum* for the eve and day of the Innocents which, with different detail, is on the same general lines as that of Salisbury[2]. At St. Paul's there was a Boy Bishop about 1225, when a gift was made to him of a mitre by John de Belemains, prebendary of Chiswick. This appears, with other vestments for the feast, in an inventory drawn up some twenty years later[3]. By 1263 abuses had grown up, and the chapter passed a statute to reform them[4]. They required the election of the *praesul* and his chapter and the drawing up of the *tabula* to take place in the chapter-house instead of in the cathedral, on account of the irreverence of the crowds pressing to see. The great dignitaries must not be put down on the *tabula* for the servers' functions, but only the clergy of the second or third 'form.' The procession and all the proceedings in the cathedral must be orderly and creditable to the boys[5].

---

[1] Jones, *Fasti*, 300 ; Rimbault, xxviii ; Planché, in *Journal of Brit. Archaeol. Assoc.* xv. 123. Gregory, 93, gives a cut of the statue.

[2] *Ordinale secundum Usum Exon.* (ed. H. E. Reynolds), f. 30.

[3] *Archaeologia*, l. 446, 472 sqq. (*Invent.* of 1245) 'mitra alia alba addubbata aurifrigio, plana est ; quam dedit J. Belemains episcopo innocentum . . . Mitra episcopi in-nocentum, nullius precii . . . Capa et mantella puerorum ad festum Innocentum et Stultorum [cf. p. 323] sunt xxviij debiles et contritae.' In 1402 there were two little staves

for the Boy Bishop (Simpson, *St. Paul's Cathedral and Old City Life*, 40).

[4] *Statutes*, bk. i, pars vi. c. 9, *De officio puerorum in festo Sanctorum Innocencium* (W. S. Simpson, *Registrum Statutorum et Consuetudinum Ecclesiae Cathedralis Sancti Pauli Londinensis*, 91).

[5] 'Memorandum, quod Anno Domini Millesimo cc lxiij. tempore G. de fferring, Decani, ordinatum fuit de officio Puerorum die Sanctorum Innocencium, prout sequitur. Provida fuit ab antiquis patribus predecessoribus nostris delibera-

Minute directions follow as to the right of the 'bishop' to
claim a supper on the eve from one of the canons, and as to
the train he may take with him, as well as for the dinner and
supper of the feast-day itself. After dinner a cavalcade is to
start from the cathedral for the blessing of the people. The
dean must find a horse for the 'bishop,' and each canon
residentiary one for the lad who personates him [1]. Other
statutes of earlier date make it incumbent on a new residentiary to entertain his own boy-representative *cum daunsa et
chorea et torchiis* on Innocents' day, and to sit up at night for
the 'bishop' and all his *cortège* on the octave. If he is kept
up very late, he may 'cut' Matins next morning [2]. The Boy
Bishop of St Paul's was accustomed to preach a sermon
which, not unnaturally, he did not write himself. William de
Tolleshunte, almoner of St. Paul's in 1329, bequeathed to the
almonry copies of all the sermons preached by the Boy

cione statutum, ut in sollennitate
Sanctorum Innocencium, qui pro
Innocente Christo sanguinem suum
fuderunt, innocens puer Presulatus
officio fungeretur, ut sic puer pueris
preesset, et innocens innocentibus
imperaret, illius tipum tenens in
Ecclesia, quem sequuntur iuvenes,
quocumque ierit. Cum igitur quod
ad laudem lactencium fuit adinven-
tum, conversum sit in dedecus, et
in derisum decoris Domus Dei,
propter insolenciam effrenatae mul-
titudinis subsequentis eundem, et
affluentis improborum turbae pacem
Praesulis exturbantis, statuendum
duximus ut praedicti pueri, tam in
eligendo suo Pontifice et personis
dignitatum Decani, Archidiaco-
norum, et aliorum, necnon et Stacio-
nariorum, antiquum suum ritum
observent, tabulam suam faciant, et
legant in Capitulo. Hoc tamen
adhibito moderamine, ut nullum
decetero de Canonicis Maioribus
vel Minoribus ad candelabra, vel
turribulum, vel ad aliqua obsequia
eiusdem Ecclesiae, vel ipsius Pontificis deputent in futurum, set suos
eligant ministeriales de illis qui sunt
in secunda forma vel in tercia. Processionem suam habeant honestam,
tam in incessu, quam habitu et
cantu, competenti; ita vero se
gerant in omnibus in Ecclesia, quod
clerus et populus illos habeant re-
commendatos.'

[1] 'Die vero solemnitatis post prandium ad mandatum personae Decani
convenient omnes in atrio Ecclesiae,
ibidem equos ascendant ituri ad
populum benedicendum. Tenetur
autem Decanus Presuli presentare
equum, et quilibet Stacionarius sua
personae in equo providere.'

[2] *Statutes*, bk. i, pars vii. c. 6
(Simpson, *op. cit.* 129), a statute
made in the time of Dean Ralph
de Diceto (1181-†1204) 'Debet
eciam novus Residenciarius post
cenam die Sanctorum Innocencium
ducere puerum suum cum daunsa et
chorea et torchiis ad Elemosinariam,
et ibi cum torticiis potum et species
singulis ministrare, et liberatam vini
cervisiae et specierum et candellarum
facere, et ibidem ministri sui expe-
ctare, quousque alius puer Canonici
senioris veniat. Et secundam
cenam in octavis Innocencium tene-
bit, Episcopum cum pueris et eorum
comitiva pascendo, et in recessu
dona dando, et, si diu expectat
adventum illorum nocte illa, ad
matutinos non teneatur venire.'

Bishops in his time. Probably he was himself responsible for them [1]. One such sermon was printed by Wynkyn de Worde before 1500 [2]. Another was written by Erasmus, and exists both in Latin and English [3]. When Dean Colet drew up the statutes of St. Paul's School in 1512 he was careful to enact that the scholars should attend the cathedral on Childermass day, hear the sermon, and mass, and give a penny to the 'bishop [4].'

The earliest notice of the Boy Bishop at York, or for the matter of that, in England, is in a statute (before 1221), which lays on him the duty of finding rushes for the Nativity and Epiphany feasts [5]. After this, there is nothing further until the second half of the fourteenth century, when some interesting documents become available. The chapter register for 1367 requires that in future the 'bishop' shall be the boy who has served longest and proved most useful in the cathedral. A saving clause is added: *dum tamen competenter sit corpore formosus* [6]. This shows a sense of humour in the chapter, for at York, as at Salisbury, *Corpore enim formosus es, O fili* was a respond for the day. In 1390, was added a further qualification that the 'bishop' must be a lad in good voice [7]. Doubtless the office was much coveted, for it was a very remunerative one. The visitation forbidden at

---

[1] Rimbault, xxxii.

[2] Printed in Rimbault, 1. Duff, *Handlists*, ii. 5, notes also a *Sermo pro episcopo puerorum* by J. Alcock, printed, in the fifteenth century by R. Pynson.

[3] *Concio de puero Iesu pronunciata a puero in nova schola Iohannis Coleti per eum instituta Londini in qua praesidet imago Pueri Iesu docentis specie* (Erasmi *Opera* (1704), v. 599). The English version was printed by W. Redman (Lupton, *Life of Colet*, 176). It is not clear that this *Concio* was preached by a boy bishop, for Colet's school (cf. next note) attended the 'bishop' of St. Paul's song-school.

[4] Lupton, *op. cit.* 175 'Alle these Chyldren shall every Chyldremasse day come to paulis Church and here the Chylde Bisshoppis sermon, and after be at the hye masse, and eche

of them offre a 1 [d]. to the Childe Bisshopp; and with theme the Maisters and surveyours of the scole.'

[5] *Lincoln Statutes*, ii. 98 'Inveniet [thesaurarius] stellas cum omnibus ad illas pertinentibus, preter cirpos, quos inveniet Episcopus Puerorum futurorum [?fatuorum], vnam in nocte Natalis Domini pro pastoribus et ·ij[as] in nocte Epiphanie, si debeat fieri presentacio ·iij[um] regum.'

[6] Warton, iv. 224 'Ioannes de Quixly confirmatur Episcopus Puerorum, et Capitulum ordinavit, quod electio Episcopi Puerorum in ecclesia Eboracensi de cetero fieret de eo, qui diutius et magis in dicta ecclesia laboraverit, et magis idoneus repertus fuerit, dum tamen competenter sit corpore formosus, et quod aliter facta electio non valebit.'

[7] Warton, iv. 237 'nisi habuerit claram vocem puerilem.'

Salisbury by Roger de Mortival was permitted at York, and the profits were considerable. Robert de Holme, who was 'bishop' in 1369, received from the choirmaster, John Gisson, who acted as his treasurer, no less a sum than £3 15s. 1½d.[1] In 1396 the amount was only £2 0s. 6½d. But this was only a small portion of the total receipts. The complete *Computus* for this year happens to be preserved, and shows that the Boy Bishop made a *quête* at intervals during the weeks between Christmas and Candlemas, travelling with a 'seneschal,' four singers and a servant to such distant places as Bridlington, Leeds, Beverley, Fountains abbey and Allerton. Their principal journey lasted a fortnight. The oblations on Christmas and Innocents' days and the collection from the dignitaries in the cloister realized £2 15s. 5d. In the city they got 10s. and abroad £5 10s. Out of this there were heavy expenses. The supper given by the 'bishop' cost 15s. 6½d. Purchased meals had to supplement hospitality at home and abroad. Horse hire and stable expenses had to be met. There were the 'bishop's' outfit, candles to be borne in procession, fees to the minor cathedral officials, gloves for presents to the vicars and schoolmasters. There was the 'bishop's' own company to be rewarded for its services. The £2 0s. 6½d. represents the balance available for his private use[2]. The most generous contributor to the *quête* was the countess of Northumberland, who gave 20s. and a gold ring. This is precisely the amount of the reward prescribed about 1522 for the 'barne bishop' of York, as well as for his brother of Beverley in the *Household Book* of the fifth earl of Northumberland[3].

The printed service-books of the use of York do not deal as fully with the Feast of Boys as do those of Sarum; but a manuscript missal of the fifteenth century used in the cathedral itself contains some additional rubrics with regard to the functions of the 'bishop' and his 'precentor' at Mass[4]. The names of some of the York 'bishops' are

---

[1] Warton, iv. 224.
[2] Appendix M. Cf. Rimbault, xi, for further elucidations of the *Computus.*
[3] Percy, *North. H. B.* 340.
[4] *York Missal,* i. 23. The rubric at the beginning of Mass is 'Omni-

bus pueris in Capis, Praecentor illorum incipiat.' There are some responds for the 'Praecentor' and the 'turba puerorum.' After the Kyrie, 'omnibus pueris in medio Chori stantibus et ibi omnia cantantibus, Episcopo eorum interim

preserved, and show that the ceremony prevailed up to the Reformation [1]. And this is confirmed by a list of ornaments for the 'bishop' in a sixteenth-century inventory [2].

I am unable to give such full data for Lincoln as for the cathedrals already named ; but regulations of 1300 and 1527 provide for the supply of candles to the 'bishop' and the rest of the choir at Vespers on the eve and matins on the day of the Innocents [3], and an inventory of 1536 mentions a cope for the 'barne busshop' with a moral 'scriptur' embroidered on it [4]. Nor can I hope to supply any exhaustive list of localities where the Boy Bishop flourished. These include minor cathedrals such as Hereford [5], Lichfield [6], Gloucester [7], and Norwich [8], great collegiate churches such as Beverley minster [9], St. Peter's, Canterbury [10], and Ottery

in cathedra sedente ; et si Dominica fuerit, dicitur ab Episcopo stante in cathedra *Gloria in excelsis Deo* : aliter non.' · The *Sequentia* for the day is

'Celsa pueri concrepent melodia, eia, Innocentum colentes tripudia, &c.'

[1] Rimbault, xvi. The dates are between 1416 and 1537.

[2] Raine, *Fabric Rolls of York Minster* (Surtees Soc.), 213 sqq. (†1500, the additions in brackets being †1510) 'una mitra parva cum petris pro episcopo puerorum . . . [unus annulus pro episcopo puerorum et duo owchys, unus in medio ad modum crucis cum lapidibus in circumferenciis cum alio parvo cum uno lapide in medio vocato turchas] . . . Capae Rubiae . . . Una capa de tyssue pro Episcopo puerili . . . [duae capae veteres olim pro Episcopo puerorum].' Leach, 132, says 'At York, in 1321, the Master of the Works gave "a gold ring with a great stone for the Bishop of the Innocents." In 1491 the Boy Bishop's pontifical was mended with silver-gilt.'

[3] *Lincoln Statutes*, i. 290 (*Black Book*, †1300) ; ii. ccxxxi.

[4] *Archaeologia*, liii. 25, 50 ; *Monasticon*, viii. 1282 'Item, a coope of Rede velvett w[t] Rolles & clowdes ordenyd for the barne busshop w[t]

this scriptur "the hye wey ys best".' The entry is repeated in a later inventory of 1548.

[5] Hereford, *Consuetudines* of thirteenth century (*Lincoln Statutes*, ii. 67) 'Thesaurarius debet invenire . . . in festo Innocencium pueris candelas et ·ij[os] cereos coram parvo Episcopo.'

[6] Lichfield—J. C. Cox, *Sports in Churches*, in W. Andrews, *Curious Church Customs*, 3, quoting inventories of 1345 and of the fifteenth century. The latter uses the term 'Nicholas Bishop.'

[7] Gloucester—Rimbault, 14, prints from *Cotton MSS. Vesp.* A. xxv, f. 173, a *Sermon of the Child Bishop, Pronownysed by John Stubs, Querester, on Childermas Day, at Gloceter*, 1558.

[8] Norwich—a fourteenth-century antiphonal of Sarum Use, probably of Norwich *provenance* (*Lansd. MS.* 463, f. 16[v]), provides for the giving of the *baculus* to the *Episcopus Puerorum* at Vespers on St. John's Day.

[9] Beverley—the fifth earl of Northumberland about 1522 gave xxs. at Christmas to the 'Barne Bishop' of Beverley, as well as to him of York (Percy, *North. H. B.* 340) ; cf. p. 357.

[10] Wordsworth, *Proc.* 52 ; cf. Appendix M (I).

St. Mary's[1], college chapels such as Magdalen[2] and All Souls[3], at Oxford, the private chapels of the king[4] and the earl of Northumberland[5], and many parish churches both in London[6], and throughout the length and breadth of England[7] and Scotland[8].

Nor is this all. Unlike the Feast of Fools, the Feast of Boys enjoyed a considerable vogue in religious houses. When

[1] Ottery—*Statutes* of Bishop Grandisson (1337), quoted by Warton, ii. 229 'Item statuimus, quod nullus canonicus, vicarius, vel secundarius, pueros choristas in festo sanctorum Innocentium extra parochiam de Otery trahant, aut eis licentiam vagandi concedant.'

[2] Magdalen—see Appendix E.

[3] All Souls—An inventory has 'j chem. j cap et mitra pro Episcopo Nicholao' (Rock, iii. 2. 217).

[4] In 1299 Edward I heard vespers said 'de Sancto Nicholao ... in Capella sua apud Heton iuxta Novum Castrum super Tynam' (*Wardrobe Account*, ed. Soc. of Antiq., 25). In 1306 a Boy Bishop officiated before Edward II on St. Nicholas' Day in the king's chapel at Scroby (*Wardrobe Account* in *Archaeologia*, xxvi. 342). In 1339 Edward III gave a gift 'Episcopo puerorum ecclesiae de Andeworp cantanti coram domino rege in camera sua in festo sanctorum Innocentium' (Warton, ii. 229). There was a yearly payment of £1 to the Boy Bishop at St. Stephen's, Westminster, in 1382 (Devon, *Issues of Exchequer*, 222), and about 1528-32 (Brewer, iv. 1939).

[5] The fifth earl of Northumberland (†1512) was wont to 'gyfe yerly upon Saynt Nicolas-Even if he kepe Chapell for Saynt Nicolas to the Master of his Childeren of his Chapell for one of the Childeren of his Chapell yerely vj⁸. viijᵈ. And if Saynt Nicolas com owt of the Towne wher my Lord lyeth and my Lord kepe no Chapell than to have yerely iij⁸. iiijᵈ.' (Percy, *North. H. B.* 343). An elaborate *Contenta de Ornamentis Ep., puer.*, of uncertain provenance, is printed by Percy, *op. cit.* 439.

[6] St. Mary at Hill (Brand, i. 233); St. Mary de Prees (*Monasticon*, iii. 360); St. Peter Cheap (*Journal of Brit. Arch. Ass.* xxiv.156); Hospital of St. Katharine by the Tower (*Reliquary*, iv. 153); Lambeth (Lysons, *Environs of London*, i. 310); cf. p. 367.

[7] Louth (E. Hewlett, *Boy Bishops*, in W. Andrews, *Curious Church Gleanings*, 241)—the payments for the Chyld Bishop include some for 'making his See' (*sedes*); Nottingham (*Archaeologia*, xxvi. 342); Sandwich (Boys, *Hist. of S.* 376); New Romney(*Hist.MSS*.v.517-28), Yorkshire, Derbyshire, Somersetshire (J. C. Cox, *Sports in Churches*, in W. Andrews, *Curious Church Customs*); Bristol—L. T. Smith, *Ricart's Kalendar*, 80 (1479-1506, Camden Soc.). On Nov. 24, the Mayor, Sheriff, and 'worshipfull men' are to 'receyue at theire dores Seynt Kateryn's pleyers, making them to drynk at their dores and rewardyng theym for theire playes.' On Dec. 5 they are 'to walke to Seynt Nicholas churche, there to hire theire even-song: and on the morowe to hire theire masse, and offre, and hire the bishop's sermon, and have his blissyng.' After dinner they are to play dice at the mayor's counter, 'and when the Bishope is come thedir, his chapell there to synge, and the bishope to geve them his blissyng, and then he and all his chapell to be serued there with brede and wyne.' And so to even-song in St. Nicholas' church.

[8] *L. T. Accounts*, i. ccxlvi record annual payments by James IV (†1473-98) to Boy Bishops from Holyrood Abbey and St. Giles's, Edinburgh.

John Peckham, archbishop of Canterbury, was drawing up his constitutions for such communities in 1279, he found it necessary to limit the duration of this feast to the eve and day of the Holy Innocents[1]. Traces of the Boy Bishop are to be found in the archives of more than one great monastery. A Westminster inventory of 1388 gives minute descriptions of vestments and ornaments for his use, many of which appear to have been quite recently provided by the 'westerer' or *vestiarius*, Richard Tonworthe[2]. There was a mitre with silvered and gilt plates and gems, and the inscription *Sancte Nicholae ora pro nobis* set in pearls. There was a *baculus* with images of St. Peter and St. Edward the Confessor upon thrones. There were two pair of cheveril gloves, to match the mitre. There were an amice, a rochet and a surplice. There were two albs and a cope of blood colour worked with gryphons and other beasts and cisterns spouting water. There was another 'principal' cope of ruby and blood-coloured velvet embroidered in gold, and with the 'new arms of England' woven into it. An older mitre and pair of gloves and a ring had been laid aside as old-fashioned or worn out. Evidently the feast was celebrated with some splendour. Several of the vestments are again inventoried in 1540[3]. A payment for the feast is recorded in a *Computus* of 1413–14[4]. The accounts of the obedientiaries of Durham priory show from 1369 onwards many payments by nearly all these officers to a Boy Bishop of the almonry. He also received a gift up to 1528 from the dependent house or 'cell' of Finchale priory. This payment was made at the office of the *feretrarius* or keeper of Saint Cuthbert's shrine. The 'bishop' is called *episcopus puerilis*, *episcopus eleemosynariae*, or the like. In 1405 he was not elected, *propter guerras eo tempore*. In 1423 and 1434 there was also an *episcopus de Elvett* or Elvetham,

---

[1] Wilkins, ii. 38 'Puerilia autem solemnia, quae in festo solent fieri Innocentum post vesperas S. Iohannis, tantum inchoari permittimus, et in crastino in ipsa die Innocentum totaliter terminentur.'

[2] *Archaeologia*, lii. 221 sqq.

[3] *Transactions* of *London and Middlesex Arch. Soc.* vols. iv, v.

[4] *Athenæum* (1900), ii. 655, 692 'data Pueris de Elemosinaria ludentibus coram Domino apud Westmonasterium, iij[s]. iiij[d].' Dr. E. J. L. Scott and Dr. Rutherford found in this entry a proof of the existence of the Westminster Latin play at 'a period anterior to the foundation of Eton'!

a manor of the priory[1]. The abbey of Bury St. Edmunds had its *episcopus sancti Nicolai* in 1418 and for at least a century longer[2]. At Winchester each of the great monasteries held a Feast of Boys; the abbey of Hyde on St. Nicholas' day[3]; the priory of St. Swithin's on that of the Holy Innocents. Here, too, the accounts of the obedientiaries contain evidence of the feast in payments between 1312 and 1536 for beer or wine sent to the *episcopus iuvenum*. Nearly all the officers whose rolls are preserved, the chamberlain, the curtarian, the cellarian, the almoner, the sacristan, the *custos operum*, the hordarian, seem to have contributed[4]. A *Computus* of 1441 contains a payment to the *pueri eleemosynariae* who, with the *pueri* of St. Elizabeth's chapel, visited St. Mary's convent, dressed as girls, and danced, sang and sported before the abbess and the nuns[5]. We have had some French instances in which the Boy Bishop visited a neighbouring convent. But the nuns were not always dependent on outside visitors for their revel. In some places they held their own feast, with an 'abbess' instead of a 'bishop.' Archbishop John Peckham, in addition to his general constitution already quoted, issued a special mandate to Godstow nunnery, forbidding the office and prayers to be said *per parvulas* on Innocents' day[6]. Three centuries later, in 1526, a visitation of Carrow nunnery by Richard Nicke, bishop of Norwich, disclosed a custom of electing a Christmas 'abbess' there, which the bishop condemned[7]. Continental parallels to these

---

[1] Rimbault, xviii; *Finchale Priory* (Surtees Soc.), ccccxxviii; *Durham Accounts* (Surtees Soc.), iii. xliii, and passim.

[2] *Hist. MSS.* xiv. 8. 124, 157.

[3] *Computi* of Cellarer (Warton, ii. 232, iii. 300) '1397, pro epulis Pueri celebrantis in festo S. Nicholai ... 1490, in larvis et aliis indumentis Puerorum visentium Dominum apud Wulsey, et Constabularium Castri Winton, in apparatu suo, necnon subintrantium omnia monasteria civitatis Winton, in festo sancti Nicholai.'

[4] G. W. Kitchin, *Computus Rolls of St. Swithin's* (*Hampshire Rec. Soc.*), passim; G. W. Kitchin and F. T. Madge, *Winchester Chapter*

Documents (*H. R. Soc.*), 24.

[5] Warton, ii. 231 '1441, pro pueris Eleemosynariae una cum pueris Capellae sanctae Elizabethae, ornatis more puellarum, et saltantibus, cantantibus, et ludentibus, coram domina Abbatissa et monialibus Abbathiae beatae Mariae virginis, in aula ibidem in die sanctorum Innocentium.'

[6] Harpsfield, *Hist. Eccl. Angl.* (1622), 441, citing Peckham's *Register*. He says the mandate was in French.

[7] *Visitations of Diocese of Norwich* (Camden Soc.), 209 'Domina Iohanna Botulphe dicit ... quod ... habent in festo Natalis Domini

examples are available. An eighth-century case, indeed, which is quoted by some writers, has probably been the subject of a misinterpretation [1]. But the visitation-books of Odo Rigaud, archbishop of Rouen (1248–69) record that he forbade the *ludibria* of the younger nuns at the Christmas feasts and the feast of St. Mary Magdalen in more than one convent of his diocese. One of these was the convent of the Holy Trinity at Caen, in which an 'abbess' was still chosen by the novices in 1423 [2]. All the monastic examples here quoted come from houses of the older foundations. The *Statutes*, however, of the Observant Franciscans made at Barcelona in 1401, expressly forbid the use of secular garments or the loan of habits of the order for *ludi* on St. Nicholas' or Innocents' days [3]; whence it may be inferred that the irregularities provided against were not unknown.

Mediaeval education began with the song-school: and

iuniorem monialem in abbatissam assumptam, vocandi [? iocandi] gratia; cuius occasione ipsa consumere et dissipare cogitur quae vel elemosina vel aliorum amicorum largitione acquisierit . . . Iniunctum est . . . quod de cetero non observetur assumptio abbatissae vocandi causa.'
[1] Gregory of Tours, x. 16 (*M. G. H. Script. Rerum Meroving.* i. 427), mentions among the complaints laid before the visitors of the convent of St. Radegund in Poitou, that the abbess 'vittam de auro exornatam idem neptae suae superflue fecerit, barbaturias intus eo quod celebraverit.' Ducange, s. v. *Barbatoriae*, finds here a reference to some kind of masquing, and Peter of Blois, *Epist.* 14, certainly uses *barbatores* as a synonym for *mimi*. The *M. G. H.* editors of Gregory, however, explain '*barbatoria*' as '*primam barbam ponere*,' the sense borne by the term in Petronius, *Sat.* lxxiii. 6. The abbess's niece had probably no beard, but may not the reference be to the cutting of the hair of a novice when she takes the vows?
[2] Ducange, s. v. *Kalendae* ('de monialibus Villae-Arcelli'), 'Item inhibemus ne de caetero in festis Innocentum et B. M. Magdalenae

ludibria exerceatis consueta, induendo vos scilicet vestibus saecularium aut inter vos seu cum secularibus choreas ducendo'; and again 'in festo S. Iohannis et Innocentium mimia iocositate et scurrilibus cantibus utebantur, ut pote farsis, conductis, motulis; praecepimus quod honestius et cum maiori devotione alias se haberent'; Gasté, 36 (on Caen) 'iuniores in festo Innocentium cantant lectiones suas cum farsis. Hoc inhibuimus.' In 1423, the real abbess gave place to the little abbess at the *Deposuit*. Gasté, 44, describes a survival of the election of an 'abbess' from amongst the *pensionnaires* on the days of St. Catherine and the Innocents in the Abbaye aux Bois, Faubourg St. Germain, from the *Mémoires* of Hélène Massalska. This was about 1773.
[3] Howlett, *Monumenta Franciscana* (R. S.), ii. 93 'Caveant fratres in festo Sancti Nicolai seu Innocentium, vel quibuscunque aliis festis vestes extraneas religiosas seu seculares aut clericales vel muliebres sub specie devotionis induere; nec habitus fratrum secularibus pro ludis faciendis accommodentur sub poena amotionis confusibilis de conventu.'

although the universities and other great seats of learning came to be much more than glorified choirs, they still retained certain traces of their humble origin. Amongst these was the Boy Bishop. The students of Paris regularly chose their Boy Bishops on St. Nicholas' day. In 1275, indeed, the Faculty of Arts forbade the torchlight processions which took place on that day and on St. Catherine's, the two great common holidays of the clerks [1]. But in 1367 such processions were held as of ancient custom, and it would appear that every little group of students gathered together under the protection and in the house of a master of arts considered itself entitled to choose a 'bishop,' and to lead him in a rout through the streets. In that year the custom led to a tragic brawl which came under the cognizance of the *Parlement* of Paris [2]. The scholars of one Peter de Zippa, dwelling *in vico Bucherie ultra Parvum Pontem*, had chosen as 'bishop' Bartholomew Divitis of Ypres. On St. Nicholas' eve, they were promenading, with a torch but unarmed, to the houses of the rector of the Faculty and others *causa solacii et iocosa*, when they met with the watch. Peter de Zippa was with them, and the watch had a grudge against Peter. On the previous St. Catherine's day they had arrested him, but he had been released by the *préfet*. They now attacked the procession with drawn swords, and wounded Jacobus de Buissono in the leg. As the scholars were remonstrating, up came Philippus de Villaribus, *miles gueti*, and Bernardus Blondelli, his deputy, and cried '*Ad mortem.*' The scholars fled home, but the watch made an attack on the house. Peter de Zippa attempted to appease them from a window, and was wounded four fingers from a mortal spot. As the watch were on the point of breaking in, the scholars surrendered. The house was looted, and

---

[1] Denifle, i. 532. It was forbidden ' in eisdem festis vel aliis paramenta nec coreas duci in vico de die nec de nocte cum torticiis vel sine.' But it was on Innocents' Day that the *béjaunes* or 'freshmen' of the Sorbonne were subjected to rites bearing a close analogy to the feast of fools ; cf. Rigollot, 172 '1476 ... condemnatus fuit in crastino Innocentium capellanus

abbas beiannorum ad octo solidos parisienses, eo quod non explevisset officium suum die Innocentium post prandium, in mundationem beiannorum per aspersionem aquae ut moris est, quanquam solemniter incoepisset exercere suum officium ante prandium inducendo beiannos per vicum super asinum.'

[2] Denifle, iii. 166.

the inmates beaten. One lad was pitched out on his head and driven into the Seine, out of which he was helped by a woman. Peter de Zippa and twenty-four others were rolled in the mud and then carried off to the *Châtelet*, where they were shut up in a dark and malodorous cell. Worst of all, the 'bishop' had disappeared altogether. It was believed that the watch had slain him, and flung the body into the Seine. A complaint was brought before the *Parlement*, and a commission of inquiry appointed. The watch declared that Peter de Zippa was insubordinate to authority and, although warned, as a foreigner, both in French and Latin[1], that they were the king's men, persisted in hurling logs and stones out of his window, with the result of knocking four teeth out of Peter Patou's mouth, and wounding the horse of Philip de Villaribus. This defence was apparently thought unsatisfactory, and a further inquiry was held, with the aid of torture. Finally the court condemned the offending watch to terms of imprisonment and the payment of damages. They had also to offer a humble apology, with bare head and bent knee, to the bishop of Paris, the rector of the Faculty, Peter de Zippa, and the injured scholars, in the cloister or the chapter-house of St. Mathurin's. The case of the alleged murder of the 'bishop,' Bartholomew Divitis, was not to be prejudiced by this judgement, and Peter de Zippa was warned to be more submissive to authority in future. The whole episode is an interesting parallel to the famous 'town and gown' at Oxford on St. Scholastica's day, 1353[2].

Provision is made for a Boy Bishop in the statutes of more than one great English educational foundation. William of Wykeham ordained in 1400 that one should be chosen at Winchester College, and at New College, Oxford, and should recite the office at the Feast of the Innocents[3]. Some notices

---

[1] 'Verbis nedum gallicis sed eciam latinis, ut ipsi qui de partibus alienis oriundi linguam gallicam nequaquam intelligebant plenarie.'

[2] S. F. Hulton, *Rixae Oxonienses*, 68. There had been many earlier brawls.

[3] *Statute* xxix (T. F. Kirby, *Annals of Winchester College*, 503) 'Permittimus tamen quod in festo Innocencium pueri vesperas matutinas et alia divina officia legenda et cantanda dicere et exsequi valeant secundum usum et consuetudinem ecclesiae Sarum.' The same formula is used in *New College Statute* xlii (*Statutes of the Colleges of Oxford*, vol. i).

in the Winchester College accounts during the fifteenth century show that he also presided at secular revels. In 1462 he is called *Episcopus Nicholatensis*, and on St. Nicholas' day he paid a visit of ceremony to the warden, who presented him, out of the college funds, with fourpence[1]. The example of William of Wykeham was followed, forty years later, in the statutes of the royal foundations of Eton College and King's College, Cambridge. But there was one modification. These colleges were dedicated to the Virgin and to St. Nicholas, and it was carefully laid down that the performance of the *officium* by the 'bishop' was to be on St. Nicholas' day, 'and by no means on that of the Innocents[2].' The Eton 'bishop' is said by the Elizabethan schoolmaster Malim, who wrote a *Consuetudinarium* of the college in 1561, to have been called *episcopus Nihilensis*, and to have been chosen on St. Hugh's day (November 17). Probably *Nihilensis* is a scribal mistake for *Nicholatensis*[3]. The custom had been abolished before Malim wrote, but was extant in 1507, for in that year the 'bishop's' rochet was mended[4]. Some Eton historians have thought that the Boy Bishop ceremony was the origin of the famous

[1] Cf. Appendix E. Kirby, *op. cit.* 90, quotes an inventory of 1406 'Baculus pastoralis de cupro deaurato pro Epō puerorum in die Innocencium . . . Mitra de panno aureo ex dono Dñi. Fundatoris hernesiat (mounted) cum argento deaurato ex dono unius socii coll. [Robert Heete] pro Epō puerorum.'

[2] *The Charter of King's College* (1443), c. 42 (*Documents relating to the Univ. of Camb.* ii. 569; Heywood and Wright, *Ancient Laws of the Fifteenth Century for King's Coll. Camb. and Eton Coll.* 112), closely follows Wykeham's formula: 'excepto festo Sᵗⁱ Nicholai praedicto, in quo festo et nullatenus in festo Innocentium, permittimus quod pueri . . . secundum usum in dicto Regali Collegio hactenus usitatum.' The Eton formula (c. 31) in 1444 is slightly different (Heywood and Wright (*op. cit.* 560) 'excepto in festo Sancti Nicholai, in quo, et nullatenus in festo Sanctorum Innocentium, divina officia praeter missae

secreta exequi et dici permittimus per episcopum puerorum scholarium, ad hoc de eisdem annis singulis eligendum.'

[3] Warton, ii. 228; Leach, 133. The passage from the *Consuetudinarium* is given from *Harl. MS.* 7044 f. 167 (apparently a transcript from a *C. C. C. MS.*) by Heywood and Wright, *op. cit.* 632; E. S. Creasy, *Eminent Etonians*, 91 'in die Sᵗⁱ Hugonis pontificis solebat Aetonae fieri electio Episcopi Nihilensis, sed consuetudo obsolevit. Olim episcopus ille puerorum habebatur nobilis, in cuius electione ad literata et laudatissima exercitatio, ad ingeniorum vires et motus excitandos, Aetonae celebris erat.'

[4] *Eton Audit Book*, 1507-8, quoted by H. C. Maxwell-Lyte, *Hist. of Eton* (ed. 1899), 149 'Pro reparatione le rochet pro episcopo puerorum, xjᵈ.' An inventory of Henry VIII's reign says that this rochet was given by James Denton (K. S. 1486) for use at St. Nicholas' time.

' Montem '; but as the ' Montem ' was held on the feast of the Conversion of St. Paul (January 25), and as Malim mentions both customs independently, this is improbable [1].

Smaller schools than Winchester or Eton had none the less their Boy Bishops. Archbishop Rotherham, who founded in 1481 a college at his native place of Rotherham in Yorkshire, left by will in 1500 a mitre for the 'barnebishop [2].' The grammar school at Canterbury had, or should have had, its Boy Bishop in 1464 [3]. Aberdeen was a city of which St. Nicholas was the patron, and at Aberdeen the master of the grammar school was paid by a collection taken when he went the rounds with the 'bishop' on St. Nicholas' day [4]. Dean Colet, on the other hand, when founding St. Paul's school did not provide for a 'bishop' in the school itself, but, as we have seen, directed the scholars to attend the mass and sermon of the 'bishop' in the cathedral.

Naturally the Reformation made war on the Boy Bishop. A royal proclamation of July 22, 1541, forbade the 'gatherings' by children 'decked and apparalid to counterfaite priestes, bysshopps, and women' on 'sainte Nicolas, sainte Catheryne, sainte Clement, the holye Innocentes, and such like,' and also the singing of mass and preaching by boys on these days [5]. Naturally also, during the Marian reaction the Boy

[1] Maxwell-Lyte, *op. cit.* 450.

[2] Hearne, *Liber Niger Scaccarii*, 674 ' Item, unam Mitram de Cloth of goold habentem 2 knoppes arḡ. enameld, dat. ad occupand. per Barnebishop.'

[3] John Stone, a monk of Canterbury, records in his *De Obitibus et aliis Memorabilibus sui Coenobii* (*MS. C. C. C. C.*, Q. 8, quoted Warton, ii. 230) 'Hoc anno, 1464, in festo Sancti Nicolai non erat episcopus puerorum in schola grammatica in civitate Cantuariae ex defectu Magistrorum, viz. I. Sidney et T. Hikson.'

[4] J. Stuart, *Extracts from Council Registers of Aberdeen* (Spalding Club), i. 186. The council ordered on Nov. 27, 1542, 'that the maister of thair grammar scuyll sell haf iiij[s] Scottis, of the sobirest persoun that resauis him and the bischop at Sanct Nicolace day.' This is to be held a legal fee, 'he hes na uder fee to leif on.'

[5] Wilkins, *Concilia*, iii. 860 'And whereas heretofore dyverse and many superstitious and childysshe observations have been usid, and yet to this day are observed and kept in many and sondry parties of this realm, as upon sainte Nicolas, sainte Catheryne, sainte Clement, the holye Innocentes, and such like; children be strangelye decked and apparelid to counterfaite priestes, bysshopps, and women; and so ledde with songes and daunces from house to house, bleasing the people, and gatherynge of monye; and boyes doo singe masse, and preache in the pulpitt, with suche other unfittinge and inconvenyent usages, rather to

Bishop reappeared. On November 13, 1554, Bishop Bonner issued an order permitting all clerks in the diocese of London to have St. Nicholas and to go abroad ; and although this order was annulled on the very eve of the festival, apparently because Cardinal Pole had appointed St. Nicholas' day for a great ceremony of reconciliation at Lambeth, yet the custom was actually revived in several London parishes, including St. Andrew's, Holborn, and St. Nicholas Olave, Bread Street [1]. In 1556 it was still more widely observed [2].

the derision than to any true glory of God, or honour of his saints ; the kyng's majestie therefore mynding nothing so moche, as to avaunce the true glorye of God without vayne superstition, willith and commaundeth, that from henccforth all suche superstitions be loste and clyerlye extinguisshed throughowte all this his realmes and dominions, forasmoche as the same doo resemble rather the unlawfull superstition of gentilitie, than the pure and sincere religion of Christe.' Brand, i. 236, suggests that there was an earlier proclamation of July 22, 1540, to the same effect. Johan Bale in his *Yet a Course at the Romyshe Foxe* (1542), says that if Bonner's censure of those who lay aside certain 'auncyent rytes' is justified, 'then ought my Lorde also to suffer the same selfe ponnyshment, for not goynge abought with Saynt Nycolas clarkes.' Thomas Becon, *Catechism*, 320 (ed. Parker Soc.), compares a bishop who does not preach, a 'dumb dog,' to a 'Nicholas bishop.' The *Articles* put to bishop Gardiner in 1550 required him to declare 'that the counterfeiting St. Nicholas, St. Clement, St. Catherine and St. Edmund, by children, heretofore brought into the church, was a mockery and foolishness' (Froude, iv. 550).

[1] *Machyn's Diary*, 75 'The xij day of November [1554] was commondyd by the bysshope of London to all clarkes in the dyoses of London for to have Sant Necolas and to go a-brod, as mony as wold have ytt . . . [the v day of December, the which was Saint Nicholas' eve, at

evensong time, came a commandment that St. Nicholas should not go abroad, nor about. But, notwithstanding, there went about these Saint Nicholases in divers parishes, as St. Andrew's, Holborn, and St.] Nicolas Olytte in Bredstret.' Warton, iv. 237, says that during Mary's reign Hugh Rhodes, a gentleman or musician of the Chapel royal, printed in black letter quarto a poem of thirty-six octave stanzas, entitled *The Song of the Chyldbyfshop, as it was songe before the queenes maiestie in her privie chamber at her manour of saynt James in the Feeldes on Saynt Nicholas day and Innocents day this yeare nowe present, by the chylde bysshope of Poules churche with his company.*' Warton apparently saw the poem, for he describes it as 'a fulsome panegyric on the queen's devotion, in which she is compared to Judith, Esther, the Queen of Sheba, and the Virgin Mary,' but no copy of it is now known ; cf. F. J. Furnivall, *The Babees Book* (E. E. T. S.), lxxxv.

[2] *Machyn's Diary*, 121 'The v day of Desember [1556] was Sant Necolas evyn, and Sant Necolas whentt a-brod in most partt in London syngyng after the old fassyon, and was reseyvyd with mony good pepulle in-to ther howses, and had myche good chere as ever they had, in mony plasses.' Foxe, *Acts and Monuments*, viii. 726, celebrates the wit of a 'godly matron,' Mrs. Gertrude Crockhay, who shut 'the foolish popish Saint Nicholas' out of her house in this year, and

But upon the accession of Elizabeth it naturally fell again into disuse, and it has left few, if any, traces in modern folk-custom [1].

I need not, after the last two chapters, attempt an elaborate analysis of the customs connected with the Boy Bishop. In the main they are parallel to those of the Feast of Fools. They include the burlesque of divine service, the *quête*, the banquet, the *dominus festi*. Like the Feast of Fools, they probably contain a folk as well as an ecclesiastical element. But the former is chastened and subdued, the strength of ecclesiastical discipline having proved sufficient, in the case of the boys, to bar for the most part such excesses as the adult clerks inherited from the pagan Kalends. On one point, how-ever, a little more must be said. The *dominus festi*, who at the Feast of Fools bears various names, is almost invariably at the Feast of Boys a 'bishop [2].' This term must have been

told her brother-in-law, Dr Mallet, when he remonstrated, that she had heard of men robbed by 'Saint Nicholas's clerks.' This was a slang term for thieves, of whom, as of children, St. Nicholas was the patron; for the reason of which cf. *Golden Legend*, ii. 119. Another procession forbidden by the pro-clamation of 1541 was also revived in 1556; cf. *Machyn's Diary*, 119 '[The xxiv day of November, being the eve of Saint Katharine, at six of the clock at night] sant Katheryn('s) lyght [went about the battlements of Saint Paul's with singing,] and Sant Katheryn gohying a prosses-syon.'

[1] At Exton in Rutlandshire, chil-dren were allowed at the beginning of the nineteenth century to play in the church on Innocents' Day (*Leicester and Rutland Folk-Lore*, 96). Probably a few other examples could be collected.

[2] At Mainz, not only the *pueri*, but also the *diaconi* and the *sacer-dotes*, had their *episcopus* (Dürr, 71). On the other hand at Vienne the term used at all the feasts, of the *triduum* and on January 1 and 6, was *rex* (Pilot de Thorey, *Usages*,

Fêtes et Coutumes en Dauphiné, i. 179). The Boy Bishops received, for their brief day, all the external marks of honour paid to real bishops. They are alleged to have occasionally enjoyed more solid privileges. Louvet (*Hist. et Ant. de Beauvais*, cited Rigollot, 142), says that at Beauvais the right of presentation to chapter benefices falling vacant on Innocents' Day fell to the *pueri*. Jean Van der Muelen or Molanus (*De Canonicis* (1587), ii. 43) makes a similar statement as to Cambrai: 'Immo personatus hic episcopus in quibusdam locis redi-tus, census et capones, annue per-cipit: alibi mitram habet, multis episcoporum mitris sumptuosiorem. In Cameracensi ecclesia visus est vacantem, in mense episcopi, prae-bendam, quasi iure ad se devoluto, conferre; quam collationem bene-ficii vere magnifici, reverendissimus praesul, cum puer grato animo, ma-gistrum suum, bene de ecclesia meritum, nominasset, gratam et ra-ram habuit.' At Mainz lost tradi-tion had it that if an Elector died during the tenure of office by a Boy Bishop, the revenues *sede vacante* would fall to him. Unfortunately

familiar by the end of the eleventh century for it lends a point of sarcasm to the protest made by Yves, bishop of Chartres, in a letter to Pope Urban II against the disgraceful nomination by Philip I of France of a wanton lad to be bishop of Orleans in 1099 [1]. In later documents it appears in various forms, *episcopus puerorum, episcopellus* [2], *episcopus puerilis* or *parvulus*, 'boy bishop,' 'child bishop,' 'barne bishop.' In some English monasteries it is *episcopus eleemosynariae* ('of the almonry'); in Germany, *Schul-Bischof*, or, derisively, *Apfeln-Bischof*. More significant than any of these is the common variant *episcopus Nicholatensis*, 'Nicholas bishop.' For St. Nicholas' day (December 6) was hardly less important in the career of the Boy Bishop than that of the Holy Innocents itself. At this feast he was generally chosen and began his *quête* through the streets. In more than one locality, Mainz for instance in Germany, Eton in England, it was on this day as well as, or in substitution for, that of the Innocents that he made his appearance in divine service [3]. St. Nicholas was, of course, the patron saint

the chapter and verse of history disprove this (Dürr, 67, 79). On the other hand it is certain that the Boy Bishops assumed the episcopal privilege of coinage. Rigollot, 52 sqq., describes and figures a long series of fifteenth- and sixteenth-century coins. or medals mostly struck by 'bishops' of the various churches and monastic houses of Amiens. They are the more interesting, because some of them bear 'fools' as devices, and thus afford another proof of the relations between the feasts of Boys and Fools. Lille *monetae* of the sixteenth century are figured by Vanhende, *Numismatique Lilloise*, 256, and others from Laon by C. Hidé, in *Bull. de la Soc. acad. de Laon*, xiii. 126. Some of Rigollot's specimens seem to have belonged, not to Boy Bishops, but to *confréries*, who struck them as 'jetons de présence' (Chartier, *L'ancien Chapitre de N.-D. de Paris*, 178); and probably this is also the origin of the pieces found at Bury St. Edmunds, which have nothing in their devices to connect them with a Boy Bishop (Rimbault, xxvi).

[1] Ivo Carnotensis, *Epist.* 67, *ad papam Urbanum* (*P. L.* clxii. 87) 'eligimus puerum, puerorum festa colentes, non nostrum morem, sed regis iussa sequentes.' Cf. Rigollot, 143.

[2] Lucas Cusentinus (†1203-24) *Ordinarium* (Martene, iii. 39): ' Puero episcopello pontificalia conceduntur insignia, et ipse dicit orationes.'

[3] The *Ritual* (†1264) of St. Omer (*Mém. de la Soc. des Antiq. de la Morinie*, xx. 186) has the following rubric for St. Nicholas' day 'in secundis vesperis . . . a choristis incipitur prosa *Sospitati dedit egros*, in qua altercando cantatur iste versus *Ergo laudes* novies tantum, ne immoderatum tedium generet vel derisum.' The same rubric recurs on St. Catherine's Day. At St. Omer, as at Paris (cf. p. 363), these were the two winter holidays for scholars. Cf. also p. 289, and A. Legrand, *Réjouissances des écoliers*

of schoolboys and of children generally [1]. His prominence in the winter processions of Germany and the presents which in modern folk-belief he brings to children have been touched upon in an earlier chapter. It now appears that originally he took rather than gave presents, and that where he appeared in person he was represented by the Boy Bishop. And this suggests the possibility that it was this connexion with St. Nicholas, and not the profane mummings of Michael the Drunkard at Constantinople, which led to the use of the term 'bishop' for the *dominus festi*, first at the Feast of Boys, and ultimately at the other Christmas feasts as well. For St. Nicholas was not only the boys' saint *par excellence*; he was also, owing to the legend of his divinely ordered consecration when only a layman as bishop of Myra, the bishop saint *par excellence* [2]. However this may be, I think it is a fair guess that St. Nicholas' day was an older date for a Feast of Boys than that of the Holy Innocents, and that the double date records an instance of the process, generally imperfect, by which, under Roman and Christian influence, the beginning of

de N.-D. de St. Omer, le jour de St.-Nicholas, leur glorieux patron (*Mémoires, ut cit.* vii. 160). The St. Omer *Episcopus puerorum* also officiated on Innocents' Eve and the octave. Dreves, *Anal. Hymn.* xxi. 82, gives various *cantiones* for St. Nicholas' Day; e.g.

'Nicolai praesulis
Festum celebremus,

. . . .

In tanto natalitio
Patrum docet traditio
Ut consonet in gaudio
Fidelium devotio,
Est ergo superstitio
Vacare a tripudio.'

In England it is probable that the Beverley Boy Bishop also officiated on St. Nicholas' Day. A chapter order of Jan. 7, 1313, directs the transfer of the 'servitium sancti Nicholai in festo eiusdem per Magistrum Scholarum Beverlacensium celebrandum' to the altar of St. Blaize during the building of a new nave (A. F. Leach, *Memorials of Beverley Minster*, Surtees Soc. i. 307).

[1] Tille, *D. W.* 32; Leach, 130. The connexion of St. Nicholas with children may be explained by, if it did not rather give rise to, either the legend of his early piety, 'The first day that he was washed and bained, he addressed him right up in the bason, and he wold not take the breast nor the pap but once on the Wednesday and once on the Friday, and in his young age he eschewed the plays and japes of other young children' (*Golden Legend*, ii. 110); or the various other legends which represent him as bringing children out of peril. Cf. *Golden Legend*, ii. 119 sqq., and especially the history of the resurrection of three boys from a pickle-tub narrated by Mr. Leach from Wace. A. Maury, *Croyances et Légendes du Moyen Âge* (ed. 1896), 149) tries to find the origin of this in misunderstood iconographic representations of the missionary saint at the baptismal font.

[2] Leach, 130; *Golden Legend*, ii. 111.

winter customs of the Germano-Keltic peoples were gradually transformed into mid-winter customs [1]. The beginning of winter feast was largely a domestic feast, and the children probably had a special part in it. It is possible also to trace a survival of the corresponding beginning of summer feast in the day of St. Gregory on March 12, which was also sometimes marked by the election of a *Schul-Bischof* [2].

[1] Cf. ch. xi. The position of St. Nicholas' Day in the ceremonies discussed in this chapter is sometimes shared by other feasts of the winter cycle: St. Edmund's (Nov. 20), St. Clement's (Nov. 23), St. Catherine's (Nov. 25), St. Andrew's (Nov. 30), St. Eloi's (Dec. 1), St. Lucy's (Dec. 13). Cf. pp. 349-51, 359, 366-8. The feast of St. Mary Magdalen, kept in a Norman convent (p. 362), was, however, in the summer (July 22).

[2] Specht, 229 ; Tille, *D. W.* 300 ; Wetze and Welte, iv. 1411. Roman schoolmasters expected a present at the *Minervalia* (March 18-23) ; cf. the passage from Tertullian in Appendix N (1).

CHAPTER XVI

GUILD FOOLS AND COURT FOOLS

[*Bibliographical Note.*—The best account of the *Sociétés joyeuses* is that of L. Petit de Julleville, *Les Comédiens en France au Moyen Âge* (1889). Much material is collected in the same writer's *Répertoire du Théâtre comique en France au Moyen Âge* (1886), and in several of the books given as authorities on the Feast of Fools (ch. xiii), especially those of Du Tilliot, Rigollot, Leber, and Grenier. Mme. Clément (née Hémery), *Histoire des Fêtes civiles et religieuses du Département du Nord* (1832), may also be consulted. M. Petit de Julleville's account of the *Sottie* is supplemented by E. Picot, *La Sottie en France*, in *Romania*, vol. vii, and there is a good study of the fool-literature of the Renascence in C. H. Herford, *Literary Relations between England and Germany in the Sixteenth Century* (1886). Amongst writers on the court fool are J. F. Dreux du Radier, *Histoire des Fous en Titre d'Office*, in *Récréations historiques* (1768); C. F. Flögel, *Geschichte der Hofnarren* (1789); F. Douce, *Clowns and Fools of Shakespeare* in *Variorum Shakespeare* (1821), xxi. 420, and *Illustrations of Shakespeare* (1839); C. Leber in Rigollot, xl; J. Doran, *History of Court Fools* (1858); A. F. Nick, *Hof- und Volksnarren* (1861); P. Lacroix (le bibliophile Jacob); *Dissertation sur les Fous des Rois de France*; A. Canel, *Recherches historiques sur les Fous des Rois de France* (1873); A. Gazeau, *Les Bouffons* (1882); P. Moreau, *Fous et Bouffons* (1885). Much of this literature fails to distinguish between the *stultus* and the *ioculator regis* (ch. iii). There is an admirable essay by L. Johnson on *The Fools of Shakespeare* in *Noctes Shakesperianae* (1887).]

THE conclusion of this volume must call attention to certain traces left by the ecclesiastical *ludi* of the New Year, themselves extinct, upon festival custom, and, through this, upon dramatic tradition. The Feast of Fools did not altogether vanish with its suppression in the cathedrals. It had had its origin in the popular celebration of the Kalends. Throughout it did not altogether lack a popular element. The *bourgeois* crowded into the cathedral to see and share in the revel. The Fool Bishop in his turn left the precincts and made his progress through the city streets, while his satellites played their pranks abroad for the entertainment of the mob. The feast was a dash of colour in the civic as well as the ecclesiastical year. The Tournai riots of 1499 show that the *jeunesse* of that city had come to look upon it as a *spectacle* which they were entitled to claim from the cathedral. What happened in Tournai doubtless happened elsewhere. And the upshot of it was that when in chapter after chapter the reforming party got the upper hand and the official celebration was dropped, the city and its *jeunesse* themselves stepped into the breach and took measures to perpetuate the threatened delightful dynasty. It was an easy way to avert the loss of a holiday. And so we find a second tradition of Feasts of Fools, in which the *fous* are no longer vicars but *bourgeois*, and the *dominus festi* is a popular 'king' or 'prince' rather than a clerical 'bishop.' A mid-fifteenth-century writer, Martin Franc, attests the vogue of the *prince des folz* in the towns of northern France:

> 'Va t'en aux festes à Tournay,
> A celles d'Arras et de Lille,
> D'Amiens, de Douay, de Cambray,
> De Valenciennes, d'Abbeville.
> Là verras tu des gens dix mille,
> Plus qu'en la forest de Torfolz,
> Qui servent par sales, par viles,
> A ton dieu, le prince des folz[1].'

The term *Roi* or *Prince des Sots* is perhaps the most common one for the new *dominus festi*, and, like *sots* or *folz* themselves, is generic. But there are many local variants, as the *Prévôt des Étourdis* at Bouchain[2], the *Roi des Braies* at Laon, the *Roi de l'Epinette* at Lille, and the *Prince de la Jeunesse* at St. Quentin[3]. The *dominus festi* was as a rule chosen by one or more local guilds or *confréries* into which the *jeunesse* were organized for the purpose of maintaining the feast. The fifteenth century was an age of guilds in every department of social life, and the *compagnies des fous* or *sociétés joyeuses* are but the frivolous counterparts of religious *confréries* or literary *puys*. The most famous of all such *sociétés*, that of *l'Infanterie Dijonnaise* at Dijon, seems directly trace-

---

[1] Martin Franc, *Champion des dames* (*Bibl. de l'École des Chartes*, v. 58).

[2] Du Tilliot, 87.

[3] Julleville, *Les Com.* 241.

able to the fall of an ecclesiastical Feast of Fools. Such a feast was held, as we have seen, in the ducal, afterwards royal, chapel, and was abolished by the *Parlement* of Dijon in 1552. Before this date nothing is heard of *l'Infanterie*. A quarter of a century later it is in full swing, and the character of its dignitaries and its badges point clearly to a derivation from the chapel feast [1]. The Dijon example is but a late one of a development which had long taken place in many parts of northern France and Flanders. It would be difficult to assert that a *société joyeuse* never made its appearance in any town before the ecclesiastical Feast of Fools had died out therein. Occasionally the two institutions overlap [2]. But, roughly speaking, the one is the inheritor of the other; '*La confrérie des sots, c'est la Fête des Fous sécularisée* [3].' Amongst the chief of these *sociétés* are the *Enfants-sans-Souci* of Paris, the *Cornards* or *Connards* of Rouen and Evreux [4], the *Suppôts du Seigneur de la Coquille*

[1] Julleville, *Les Com.* 193, 256; Du Tilliot, 97. The chief officers of the chapel *fous* were the 'bâtonnier' and the 'protonotaire et procureur des fous.' In the *Infanterie* these are replaced by the emblematical *Mère Folle* and the 'Procureur fiscal' known as 'Fiscal vert' or 'Griffon vert.' Du Tilliot and others have collected a number of documents concerning the *Infanterie*, together with representations of seals, badges, &c., used by them. These may be compared in Du Tilliot with the *bâton* belonging to the Chapel period (1482), which he also gives. The motto of the *Infanterie* is worth noticing. It was *Numerus stultorum infinitus est*, and was taken from *Ecclesiastes*, i. 15. It was used also at Amiens (Julleville, *Les Com.* 234).

[2] At Amiens the 'feste du Prince des Sots' existed in 1450 (Julleville, *Les Com.* 233), but the 'Pope of Fools' was not finally suppressed in the cathedral for another century. But at Amiens there was an immense multiplication of 'fool'-organizations. Each church and

convent had its 'episcopus puerorum,' and several of these show *fous* on their coins. Rigollot, 77, 105, figures a coin with *fous*, which he assigns to a *confrérie* in the parish of St. Remigius; also a coin, dated 1543, of an 'Evesque des Griffons.'

[3] Julleville, *Les Com.* 144.

[4] The term *cornard* seems to be derived from the 'cornes' of the traditional fool headdress. Leber, ix. 353, reprints from the *Mercure de France* for April, 1725, an account of a procession made by the *abbas cornardorum* at Evreux mounted upon an ass, which directly recalls the Feast of Fools. A macaronic *chanson* used on the occasion of one of these processions is preserved:

'*De asino bono nostro,*
    Meliori et optimo,
    Debemus faire fête.
En revenant de Gravignariâ,
Un gros chardon *reperit in viâ*;
Il lui coupa la tête.
Vir monachus, in mense Iulio,
    Egressus est e monasterio,
C'est dom de la Bucaille.

of Lyons [1]. The history of these has been written excellently well by M. Petit de Julleville, and I do not propose to repeat it. A few general points, however, deserve attention.

The ecclesiastical Feast of Fools flourished rather in cathedrals than in monasteries. The *sociétés* however, like some more serious *confréries* [2], seem to have preferred a conventual to a capitular model for their organization [3]. The *Cornards*, both at Rouen and Evreux, were under an *Abbé*. Cambrai had its *Abbaye joyeuse de Lescache-Profit*, Chalons-sur-Saône its *Abbé de la Grande Abbaye*, Arras its *Abbé de Liesse*, Poitiers its *Abbé de Mau Gouverne* [4]. The literary adaptation of this idea by Rabelais in the *Abbaye de Thélème* is familiar. This term *abbaye* is common to the *sociétés*, with some at least of the *Basoches* or associations of law-clerks to the *Parlements* of Paris and the greater provincial towns. The *Basoches* existed for mutual protection, but for mutual amusement also, and on one side at least of their activity they were much of the nature of *sociétés joyeuses* [5]. At Rheims in 1490 a *Basoche* entered into rivalry of dramatic invective with the celebrants of the ecclesiastical Feast of Fools [6]. The *Basoche* of Paris was in the closest relations to, if not actually identical with, the *société* of the *Enfants-sans-Souci* [7]. Just as

Egressus est sine licentiâ,
Pour aller voir donna Venissia,
Et faire la ripaille.'
Research has identified Dom de la Bucaille and Donna Venissia as respectively a prior of St. Taurin, and a prioress of St. Saviour's, in Evreux.

[1] A *coquille* is a misprint, and this *société* was composed of the printers of Lyon.

[2] *Conc. of Avignon* (1326), c. 37, *de societatibus colligationibus et coniurationibus quas confratrias appellant radicitus extirpandis* (Labbé, xi. 1738), forbids both clerks and laymen ' ne se confratres priores abbatas praedictae societatis appellant.' The charges brought against the *confréries* are of perverting justice, not of wanton revelry, and therefore it is probably not ' sociétés joyeuses ' that are in question ; cf. Ducange, s. v. *Abbas*

Confratriae, quoting a Paris example. Grenier, 362, however, mentions a ' confrérie ' in the Hôpital de Rue at Amiens (†1210) which was under an ' évêque ' ; cf. the following note.

[3] I find an ' évesque des folz ' at Béthune, a ' M. le Cardinal ' as head of the ' Joyeux ' at Rheims (Julleville, *Les Com.* 242 ; *Rép. Com.* 340), and an ' évesque des Griffons ' at Amiens (Rigollot, 105). Exceptional is, I believe, the *Société des Foux* founded on the lines of a chivalric order by Adolphe, Comte de Clèves, in 1380 (Du Tilliot, 84).

[4] Julleville, 236 ; Guy, 471.

[5] Julleville, 88, 136. The Paris *Basoche* was a ' royaume ' ; those of Chambéry and Geneva were ' abbayes.'

[6] Cf. p. 304.

[7] Julleville, *Les Com.* 152.

the law-clerks of Paris were banded together in their *Basoche*, so were the students of Paris in their 'university,' 'faculties,' 'nations,' and other groups; and in 1470, long after the regular Feast of Fools had disappeared from the city, the students were still wont to put on the fool habit and elect their *rex fatuorum* on Twelfth night[1]. Yet other guilds of a more serious character, generally speaking, than the *sociétés joyeuses*, none the less occasionally gave themselves over to *joyeuseté*. The *Deposuit* brought rebuke upon religious *confréries* up to a quite late date[2]; and traces of the *fous* are to be found amongst the recreations of no less a body than the famous and highly literary *puy* of Arras. The *sociétés joyeuses*, like the *puys*, were primarily associations of amateur, rather than professional merry-makers, a fact which distinguishes them from the corporations of minstrels described in a previous chapter[3]. But minstrels and *trouvères* were by no means excluded. The poet Gringoire was *Mère-Sotte* of the Paris *Enfants-sans-Souci*. Clément Marot was a member of the same body. In the *puy* of Arras the minstrels traditionally held an important place; and as the literary and dramatic side of the *sociétés* grew, it is evident that the men who were

---

[1] Bulaeus, *Hist. Univ. Paris*, v. 690; Julleville, *Les Com.* 297; Rashdall, *Universities of Europe*, ii. 611. It was probably to this student custom that the Tournai rioters of 1499 appealed (cf. p. 301). In 1470 the Faculty of Arts ordered the suppression of it. Cf. C. Jourdain, *Index Chartarum Paris.* 294 (No. 1369). On Jan. 5 they met 'ad providendum remedium de electione regis fatuorum,' and decreed 'quod nullus scolaris assumeret habitum fatui pro illo anno, nec in collegio, nec extra collegium, nisi forsan duntaxat ludendo farsam vel moralitatem.' Several scholars 'portantes arma et assumentes habitum fatuorum' were corrected on Jan. 24, and it was laid down that 'reges vero fatuorum priventur penitus a gradu quocumque.'

[2] Grenier, 365; Ducange, s. v. *Deposuit*, quoting *Stat. Hosp. S.*

Iacobi Paris. (sixteenth century), 'après le diner, on porte le baton au cueur, et là est le trésorier, qui chante et fait le *Deposuit*.' *Stat. Syn. Petri de Broc. episc. Autiss.* (1642) 'pendant que les bâtons de confrérie seront exposez, pour être enchéris, l'on va chantera *Magnificat*, et n'appliquera-t-on point ces versets *Deposuit* et *Suscepit* à la délivrance d'iceux; ains on chantera quelque antienne et répons avec l'oraison propre en l'honneur du Saint, duquel on célèbre la feste.'

[3] Cf. ch. iii and Appendix F; and on the general character of the *puys*, Julleville, *Les Com.* 42; Guy, xxxiv; Paris, 185. Some documents with regard to a fourteenth-century *puy* in London are in Riley, *Liber Custumarum*, xlviii. 216, 479 (*Munim. Gildh. Lond.* in R. S.); *Memorials of London*, 42.

professionally ready with their pens must everywhere have been in demand.

The primary function of the *sociétés joyeuses* and their congeners was the celebration of the traditional Feast of Fools at or about the New Year. In Paris, Twelfth night was a day of festival for the *Basoche* as well as for the minor association of exchequer clerks known as the *Empire de Galilée*. In mid-January came the *fête des Braies* at Laon, and the *fête* of the *Abbaye de Lescache-Profit* at Cambrai. That of the *Prince des Sots* at Amiens was on the first of January itself[1]. On the same day three *sociétés joyeuses* united in a *fête de l'âne* at Douai[2]. But January was no clement month for the elaborated revels of increasingly luxurious burghers; and it is not surprising to find that many of the *sociétés* transferred their attention to other popular feasts which happened to fall at more genial seasons of the year. To the celebration of these, the spring feast of the carnival or Shrovetide, the summer feasts of May-day or Midsummer, they brought all the wantonness of the Feast of Fools. The *Infanterie Dijonnaise*, the *Cornards* of Rouen and Evreux, the third Parisian law association, that of the *Châtelet*, especially cultivated the carnival. The three obligatory feasts of the *Basoche* included, besides that of Twelfth night, one on May-day and one at the beginning of July[3]. On May-day, too, a guild in the parish of St. Germain at Amiens held its *fête des fous*[4]. It may be noted that

[1] Julleville, *Les Com.* 92, 233, 236, 241.

[2] Clément-Hémery, *Fêtes du Dép. du Nord*, 184, states on the authority of a MS. without title or signature that this *fête* originated in a prose with a bray in it, sung by the canons of St. Peter's. The lay form of the feast can be traced from †1476 to 1668. Leber, x. 135, puts the (clerical) origin before 1282.

[3] Julleville, *Les Com.* 92, 204, 247.

[4] F. Guérard, *Les Fous de Saint-Germain*, in *Mélanges d'Hist. et d'Arch.* (Amiens, 1861), 17. On the Saturday before the first Sunday in May children in the rue St. Germain carry boughs, singing

' Saint Germain, coucou,
Ch'est l'fette d'chés fous, &c.'

In the church they used to place a bottle crowned with yellow primroses, called ' coucous.' The dwellers in the parish are locally known as 'fous,' and an historical myth is told to account for this. Probably May-day has here merged with St. Germain's Day (May 2) in a ' fête des fous.' Payments for decking the church appear in old accounts.

these summer extensions of the reign of folly are not without parallels of a strictly ecclesiastical type. At Châlons-sur-Marne, as late as 1648, a chapter procession went to the woods on St. John's eve to cut boughs for the decking of the church[1]. At Evreux a similar custom grew into a very famous revel[2]. This was the *procession noire*, otherwise known as the *cérémonie de la Saint-Vital*, because the proceedings began on the day of St. Vitalis (April 28) and lasted to the second Vespers on May 1. Originally the canons, afterwards the choir-clerks, chaplains, and vicars, went at day-break on May morning to gather branches in the bishop's woods. Their return was the signal for riotous proceedings. The bells were violently rung. Masks were worn. Bran was thrown in the eyes of passers-by, and they were made to leap over broomsticks. The choir-clerks took the high stalls, and the choir-boys recited the office. In the intervals the canons played at skittles over the vaults; there were dancing and singing and the rest, 'as at the time of the Nativity[3].' The abuses of this festival must have begun at an early date, for two canons of the cathedral, one of whom died in 1206, are recorded to have been hung out of the belfry windows in a vain attempt to stop the bell-ringing. Its extension to St. Vitalis' day is ascribed to another canon, singularly named Bouteille, who is said to have founded about 1270 a very odd *obit*. He desired that a pall should lie on the pavement of the choir, and that on each corner and in the middle of this should stand a bottle of wine, to be drunk by the singing-men. The canon Bouteille may be legendary, but the wine-bottle figured largely in the festival ceremonies. While the branches were distributed in the bishop's wood, which came to be known as the *bois de la Bouteille*, the company drank and ate cakes. Two bottle-shaped holes were dug in the earth and filled with sand. On the day of the *obit* an enormous leather bottle, painted with marmosets, serpents, and other grotesques, was placed in the choir. These rites were still

---

[1] Guérard, *op. cit.* 46.

[2] Leber, x. 125, from *Mercure de France* for April, 1726; Gasté, 46.

[3] 'ludunt ad quillas super voltas ecclesiae . . . faciunt podia, choreas et choros . . . et reliqua sicut in natalibus.'

extant at Evreux in 1462, when a fresh attempt to suppress the bell-jangling led to a fresh riot. No explanation is given of the term *procession noire* as used at Evreux, but a Vienne parallel suggests that, as in some other seasonal festivals, those who took part in the procession had their faces blacked. At Vienne, early on May 1, four men, naked and black, started from the archbishop's palace and paraded the city. They were chosen respectively by the archbishop, the cathedral chapter, and the abbots of St. Peter's and St. John's. Subsequently they formed a *cortège* for a *rex*, also chosen by the archbishop, and a *regina* from the convent of St. Andrew's. A St. Paul, from the hospital dedicated to that saint, also joined in the procession, and carried a cup of ashes which he sprinkled in the faces of those he met. This custom lasted to the seventeenth century [1].

But the seasonal feasts did not exhaust the activities of the *sociétés*. Occasional events, a national triumph, a royal entry, not to speak of local *faits divers*, found them ready with appropriate celebrations [2]. The *Infanterie Dijonnaise* made a solemn function of the admission of new members [3]. And more than one *société* picked up from folk-custom the tradition of the *charivari*, constituting itself thus the somewhat arbitrary guardian of burgess morality [4]. M. Petit de Julleville analyses a curious *jeu* filled with chaff against an unfortunate M. Du Tillet who underwent the penalty at Dijon in 1579 for the crime of beating his wife in the month of May [5]. At Lyon, too, *chevauchées* of a similar type seem to have been much in vogue [6].

In the fifteenth and sixteenth centuries the entertainment of the *sociétés joyeuses* was largely dramatic We find them,

---

[1] Leber, ix. 261.

[2] Julleville, *Les Com.* 233, quotes a decree of the municipality of Amiens in 1450, 'Il a esté dit et declairié qu'il semble que ce sera tres grande recreacion, considéré les bonnes nouvelles que de jour en jour en disoit du Roy nostre sire, et que le ducée de Normendie est du tout reunye en sa main, de fere la feste du Prince des Sots.'

[3] Ibid. 214.

[4] Cf. ch. vii.

[5] Julleville, *Les Com.* 209.

[6] Leber, ix. 150, reprints the *Recueil de la Chevauchée faicte en la Ville de Lyon le dix septiesme de novembre*, 1578. Another Lyon *Recueil* dates from 1566. Cf. Julleville, *Les Com.* 234 (Amiens), 243 (Lyon), 248 (Rouen).

as indeed we find the participants in the strictly clerical feasts of Fools[1] and of Boys[2], during the same period, occupied with the performance both of miracles and of the various forms of contemporary comedy known as farces, moralities, *sotties* and *sermòns joyeux*[3]. Of their share in the miracles the next volume may speak[4]: their relations to the development of comedy require a word or two here. That normal fifteenth-century comedy, that of the farce and the morality, in any way had its origin in the Feast of Fools, whether clerical or lay, can hardly be admitted. It almost certainly arose out of the minstrel tradition, and when already a full-blown art was adapted by the *fous*, as by other groups of amateur performers, from minstrelsy. With the special forms of the *sottie* and the *sermon joyeux* it is otherwise. These may reasonably be regarded as the definite contribution of

---

[1] Cf. chs. xiii, xiv. The *theatrales ludi* of Pope Innocent III's decree in 1207 probably refers only to the burlesque 'offices' of the feasts condemned; and even the terms used by the Theological Faculty in 1445—*spectacula, ludi theatrales, personagiorum ludi*—might mean no more, for at Troyes in the previous year the '*jeu du sacre de leur arcevesque*' was called a 'jeu de personnages,' and this might have been a mere burlesque consecration. However, 'jeu de personnages' generally implies something distinctly dramatic (cf. ch. xxiv). It recurs in the Sens order of 1511. The Beauvais *Daniel* was possibly played at a Feast of Fools: at Tours a *Prophetae* and a *miraculum* appear under similar conditions; at Autun a *Herod* gave a name to the *dominus festi*. At Laon there were 'mysteries' in 1464 and 1465; by 1531 these had given way to 'comedies.' Farces were played at Tournai in 1498 and comedies at Lille in 1526.

[2] Cf. ch. xv. The Toul *Statutes* of 1497 mention the playing of miracles, morals, and farces. At Laon the playing of a comedy had been dropped before 1546.

[3] Julleville, *Rép. Com.* 321 (*Cata-logue des représentations*), and elsewhere, gives many examples. The following decree (†1327) of Dominique Grima, bishop of Pamiers, is quoted by L. Delisle, in *Romania*, xxii. 274: 'Dampnamus autem et anathematizamus ludum cenicum vocatum *Centum Drudorum*, vulgariter *Cent Drutz*, actenus observatum in nostra dyocesi, et specialiter in nostra civitate Appamiensi et villa de Fuxo, per clericos et laycos interdum magni status; in quo ludo effigiabantur prelati et religiosi graduum et ordinum diversorum, facientes processionem cum candelis de cepo, et vexilis in quibus depicta erant membra pudibunda hominis et mulieris. Induebant etiam confratres illius ludi masculos iuvenes habitu muliebri et deducebant eos processionaliter ad quendam quem vocabant priorem dicti ludi, cum carminibus inhonestissima verba continentes...' The *confrates* and the *prior* here look like a *société joyeuse*, but the 'ludus cenicus' was probably less a regular play than a dramatized bit of folk-ritual, like the Troyes *Sacre de l'arcevesque* and the *Charivaris*. The change of sex-costume is to be noted.

[4] Cf. ch. xx.

the Feast of Fools to the types of comedy. The very name of the *sermon joyeux*, indeed, sufficiently declares its derivation. It is parody of a class, the humour of which would particularly appeal to revelling clerks: it finds its place in the general burlesque of divine worship, which is the special note of the feast [1]. The character of the *sotties*, again, does not leave their origin doubtful ; they are, on the face of them, farces in which the actors are *sots* or *fous*. Historically, we know that some at least of the extant *sotties* were played by *sociétés joyeuses* at Paris, Geneva and elsewhere ; and the analysis of their contents lays bare the ruling idea as precisely that expressed in the motto of the *Infanterie Dijonnaise*—' *Stultorum numerus est infinitus.*' It is their humour and their mode of satire to represent the whole world, from king to clown, as wearing the cap and bells, and obeying the lordship of folly. French writers have aptly compared them to the modern dramatic type known as the *revue* [2]. The germ of the *sottie* is to be found as early as the thirteenth century in the work of that Adan de la Hale, whose anticipation of at least one other form of fifteenth-century drama has called for comment [3]. Adan's *Jeu de la Feuillée* seems to have been played before the *puy* of Arras, perhaps, as the name suggests, in the *tonnelle* of a garden, on the eve of the first of May, 1262. It is composed of various elements: the later scenes are a *féerie* in which the author draws upon Hellequin and his *mesnie* and the three *fées*, Morgue, Maglore and Arsile, of peasant tradition. But there is an episode which is sheer *sottie*. The relics of St. Acaire, warranted to cure folly, are

---

[1] Julleville, *Les Com.* 33; *La Com.* 73 'Le premier qui s'avisa, pendant l'ivresse bruyante de la fête, de monter dans la chaire chrétienne et d'y parodier le prédicateur dans une improvisation burlesque, débita le premier sermon joyeux. C'est à l'origine, comme nous avons dit, "une indécente plaisanterie de sacristain en goguette."' A list of extant *sermons joyeux* is given by Julleville, *Rép. Com.* 259.
[2] Julleville, *Les Com.* 32, 145;

La Com. 68 ; E. Picot, *La Sottie en France* (*Romania*, vii. 236). Jean Bouchet, *Épîtres morales et familières du Traverseur* (1545), i. 32, thus defines the *Sottie* :
'En France elle a de *sotie* le nom,
Parce que sotz des gens de grand renom
Et des petits jouent les grands follies
Sur eschaffaux en parolles polies.'
[3] Cf. ch. viii.

tried upon the good burgesses of Arras one by one; and there is a genuine fool or *dervés*, who, like his lineal descendant Touchstone, 'uses his folly as a stalking-horse to shoot his wit' in showers of arrowy satire upon mankind [1]. Of the later and regular *sotties*, the most famous are those written by Pierre Gringoire for the *Enfants-sans-Souci* of Paris. In these, notably the *Jeu du Prince des Sotz*, and in others by less famous writers, the conception of the all-embracing reign of folly finds constant and various expression [2]. Outside France some reflection of the *sottie* is to be found in the *Fastnacht-spiele* or Shrovetide plays of Nuremberg and other German towns. These were performed mainly, but not invariably, at Shrovetide, by students or artisans, not necessarily organized into regular guilds. They are dramatically of the crudest, being little more than processions of figures, each of whom in turn sings his couplets. But in several examples these figures are a string of *Narren*, and the matter of the verses is in the satirical vein of the *sotties* [3]. The *Fastnachtspiele* are probably to be traced, not so much to the Feast of Fools proper, as to the spring sword-dances in which, as we have seen, a *Narr* or 'fool' is *de rigueur*. They share, however, with the *sotties* their fundamental idea of the universal domination of folly.

The extension of this idea may indeed be traced somewhat widely in the satirical and didactic literature of the later Middle Ages and the Renascence. I cannot go at length into this question here, but must content myself with referring to Professor Herford's valuable account of the cycle, which includes the *Speculum Stultorum* of Wireker, Lydgate's *Order*

[1] Creizenach, i. 395; Julleville, *Les Com.* 46; *La Com.* 19; *Rép. Com.* 20; E. Langlois, *Robin et Marion*, 13; Guy, 337; M. Sepet, *Le Jeu de la Feuillée*, in *Études romaines dédiées à G. Paris*, 69. The play is sometimes called *Le Jeu d'Adam*. The text is printed in Monmerque et Michel, *Théâtre français au Moyen Âge*, 55, and E. de Coussemaker, *Œuvres de Adam de la Halle*, 297.

[2] The extant *sotties* are catalogued by Julleville, *Rép. Com.* 104, and E. Picot, in *Romania*, vii. 249.

[3] Creizenach, i. 406; G. Gregory Smith, *Transition Period*, 317; Goedeke, *Deutsche Dichtung*, i. 325; V. Michels, *Studien über die ältesten deutschen Fastnachtspiele*, 101. The latter writer inclines to consider the *Narr* of these plays as substituted by fifteenth century for a more primitive *Teufel*. The plays themselves are collected by A. von Keller, *Fastnachtspiele aus dem* 15. *Jahrhundert* (1853-8).

of Fools, Sebastian Brandt's *Narrenschiff* and its innumerable imitations, the *Encomium Moriae* of Erasmus, and Robert Armin the player's *Nest of Ninnies* [1].

Wireker was an Englishman, and the 'Order' founded in the *Speculum* by Brunellus, the Ass, was clearly suggested by the *sociétés joyeuses*. Traces of such *sociétés* in England are, however, rare. Some of the titles of local lords of misrule, such as the Abbot of Marrall at Shrewsbury or the Abbot of Bon-Accord at Aberdeen, so closely resemble the French nomenclature as to suggest their existence ; but the only certain example I have come across is in a very curious record from Exeter. The register of Bishop Grandisson contains under the date July 11, 1348, a mandate to the archdeacon and dean of Exeter and the rector of St. Paul's, requiring them to prohibit the proceedings of a certain 'sect of malign men' who call themselves the 'Order of Brothelyngham.' These men, says the bishop, wear a monkish habit, choose a lunatic fellow as abbot, set him up in the theatre, blow horns, and for day after day beset in a great company the streets and places of the city, capturing laity and clergy, and exacting ransom from them 'in lieu of a sacrifice.' This they call a *ludus*, but it is sheer rapine [2]. Grandisson's learned editor

[1] C. H. Herford, *Literary Relations of England and Germany*, 323 sqq. ; cf. G. Gregory Smith, *op. cit.* 176. On an actual pseudo-chivalric Order of Fools cf. p. 375.

[2] F. C. Hingeston - Randolph, *Register of Bishop Grandisson*, ii. 1055, *Litera pro iniqua fraternitate de Brothelyngham*. 'Ad nostrum, siquidem, non sine inquietudine gravi, pervenit auditum, quod in Civitate nostra Exonie secta quedam abhominabilis quorundam hominum malignorum, sub nomine Ordinis, quin pocius erroris, de Brothelyngham, procurante satore malorum operum, noviter insurrexit; qui, non Conventum sed conventiculam facientes evidenter illicitam et suspectam, quemdam lunaticum et delirum, ipsorum utique operibus aptissime congruentem, sibi, sub Abbatis nomine, prefecerunt, ipsumque Monachali habitu induentes ac in Theatro constituerunt velut ipsorum idolum adorantes, ad flatum cornu, quod sibi statuerunt pro campana, per Civitatis eiusdem vicos et plateas, aliquibus iam elapsis diebus, cum maxima equitum et peditum multitudine commitarunt [sic] ; clericos eciam laicos ceperunt eis obviam tunc prestantes, ac aliquos de ipsorum domibus extraxerunt, et invitos tam diu ausu temerario et interdum sacrilego tenuerunt, donec certas pecuniarum summas loco sacrificii, quin verius sacrilegii, extorserunt ab eisdem. Et quamvis hec videantur sub colore et velamine ludi, immo ludibrii, attemptari, furtum est, tamen, proculdubio, in eo quod ab invitis capitur et rapina.' There is no such place as Brothelyngham, but 'brethelyng' 'brethel,' 'brothel,' mean 'good-for-nothing' (*N. E. D.*, s.vv.).

thinks that this *secta* was a sect of mediaeval dissenters, but the description clearly points to a *société joyeuse*. And the recognition of the *droits* exacted as being *loco sacrificii* is to a folk-lorist most interesting.

More than one of the records which I have had occasion to quote make mention of an *habit des fous* as of a recognized and familiar type of dress. These records are not of the earliest. The celebrants of the ecclesiastical Feast of Fools wore *larvae* or masks. Laity and clergy exchanged costumes: and the wearing of women's garments by men probably represents one of the most primitive elements in the custom. But there can be little doubt as to the nature of the traditional 'habit des fous' from the fourteenth century onwards. Its most characteristic feature was that hood garnished with ears, the distribution of which to persons of importance gave such offence at Tournai in 1499. A similar hood, fitting closely over the head and cut in scollops upon the shoulders, re-appears in the *bâton*, dated 1482, of the fools in the ducal chapel of Dijon. Besides two large asses' ears, it also bears a central peak or crest[1]. The eared hood became the regular badge of the *sociétés joyeuses*. It is found on most of the seals and other devices of the *Infanterie Dijonnaise*, variously modified, and often with bells hung upon the ears and the points of the scollops[2]. It was used at Amiens[3], and at Rouen and Evreux probably gave a name to the *Cornards*[4]. Marot describes it as appropriate to a *sot de la Basoche* at Paris[5]. It belongs also to the *Narren* of Nuremberg[6], and is to be seen in innumerable figured representations of fools in miniatures, woodcuts, carvings, the Amiens *monetae*, and so forth, during the later Middle Ages and the Renascence[7].

---

[1] Du Tilliot, pl. 4.
[2] Ibid. pll. 1–12 passim.
[3] Julleville, *Les Com.* 234.
[4] Ibid. 246 ; Rigollot, lxxxiv.
[5] Marot, *Epistre du Coq en l'Asne* (ed. Jannet, i. 224 ; ed. Guiffrey, iii. 352) :
'Attachez moy une sonnette
Sur le front d'un moyne crotté,
Une aureille à chaque costé
Du capuchon de sa caboche ;
Voyla un sot de la Basoche,

Aussi bien painct qu'il est possible.'
For other Paris evidence cf. Julleville, *Les Com.* 144, 147 ; E. Picot, in *Romania*, vii. 242.
[6] Picot, in *Romania*, vii. 245 ; Keller, *Fastnachtspiele*, 258.
[7] Rigollot, 73, 166, and passim ; Strutt, 222 ; Douce, 516 ; Julleville, *Les Com.* 147. There are many examples in the literature referred to on p. 382.

Such a close-fitting hood was of course common wear in the fourteenth century. It is said to be of Gaulish origin, and to be retained in the religious cowl. The *differentiae* of the hood of a 'fool' from another must be sought in the grotesque appendages of ears, crest and bells [1]. Already an eared hood, exactly like that of the 'fools,' distinguishes a mask, perhaps Gaulish, of the Roman period [2]. It may therefore have been adopted in the *Kalendae* at an early date. But it is not, I think, unfair to assume that it was originally a sophistication of a more primitive headdress, namely the actual head of a sacrificial animal worn by the worshipper at the New Year festival. That the ears are asses' ears explains itself in view of the prominence of that animal at the Feast of Fools. It must be added that the central crest is developed in some of the examples figured by Douce into the head and neck, in others into the comb only, of a cock [3]. With the hood, in most of the examples quoted above, goes the *marotte*. This is a kind of doll carried by the 'fool,' and presents a replica of his own head and shoulders with their hood upon the end of a short staff. In some of Douce's figures the *marotte* is replaced or supplemented by some other form of bauble, such as a bladder on a stick, stuffed into various shapes, or hollow and containing peas [4]. Naturally the colours of the 'fools' were gay and strikingly contrasted. Those of the Paris *Enfants-sans-Souci* were yellow and green [5]. But it may be doubted whether these colours were invariable, or whether there is much in the symbolical significance attributed to them by

---

[1] Rigollot, lxxix.

[2] F. de Ficoroni, *Le Maschere sceniche e le Figure comiche d' antichi Romani*, 186, pl. 72.

[3] Dieterich, 237, traces the coxcomb to Italian comedy of the Atellane type; cf. ch. xxiii, on 'Punch.'

[4] Douce, pl. 3; cf. Leber, in Rigollot, lxi. 164, quoting the proverb 'pisa in utre perstrepentia' and a statement of Savaron, *Traité contre les Masques* (1611), that at Clermont in Auvergne men disguised 'en Fols' ran through the streets at Christmas 'tenant des masses à la main, farcies de paille ou de bourre,

en forme de braiette, frappant hommes et femmes.' I suppose the bauble, like the hood, was originally part of the sacrificial *exuviae* and the *marotte* a sophistication of it.

[5] Julleville, *Les Com.* 147, quoting *Réponse d'Angoulevent à l'archi-poète des pois pillez* (1603):
'Qu'après, dedans le char de la troupe idiotte
Ayant pour sceptre en main une peinte marotte,
Tu sois parmi Paris pourmené doucement,
Vestu de jaune et vert en ton accoustrement.'

certain writers[1]. The *Infanterie Dijonnaise* in fact added red to their yellow and green[2]. The colours of the Cléves Order of Fools were red and yellow[3].

It will not have escaped notice that the costume just described, the parti-coloured garments, the hood with its ears, bells and coxcomb, and the *marotte*, is precisely that assigned by the custom of the stage to the fools who appear as *dramatis personae* in several of Shakespeare's plays[4]. Yet these fools have nothing to do with *sociétés joyeuses* or the Feast of Fools; they represent the 'set,' 'allowed,' or 'all-licensed' fool[5], the domestic jester of royal courts and noble houses. The great have always found pleasure in that near neighbourhood of folly which meaner men vainly attempt to shun. Rome shared the *stultus* with her eastern subjects and her barbarian invaders alike; and the 'natural,' genuine or assumed, was, like his fellow the dwarf, an institution in every mediaeval and Renascence palace[6]. The question arises how far the *habit* of the *sociétés joyeuses* was also that of the domestic fool. In France there is some evidence that from the end of the fourteenth century it was occasionally at least taken as such. The tomb in Saint Maurice's at Senlis of Thévenin de St. Leger, fool to Charles V, who died in 1374, represents him in a crested hood with a *marotte*[7]. Rabelais describes the fool

---

[1] Leber, in Rigollot, lxviii.

[2] Julleville, *Les Com.* 195, 203.

[3] Du Tilliot, 84.

[4] See e. g. the plate (p. 9) and description (p. xii) of Touchstone in Miss E. Fogerty's 'costume edition' of *As You Like It*.

[5] *Twelfth Night*, i. 5. 95, 101; *Lear*, i. 4. 220.

[6] To the English data given by the historians of court fools may be added *Wardrobe Account* 28 *Edw. I*, 1299-1300 (Soc. Antiq.), 166 'Martinetto de Vasconia fatuo ludenti coram dicto domino Edwardo,' and *Lib. de Comp. Garderobae*, temp. Edw. II (*MS. Cotton, Nero*, C. viii. ff. 83, 85), quoted by Strutt, 194 'twenty shillings paid to Robert le Foll to buy a *boclarium ad ludendum* before the king.' Robert le Foll had also a *garcio*.

For fools at the Scottish court of James IV cf. *L. H. T.* i. cxcix, &c.; iii. xcii, &c.; and on Thomas, the fool of Durham Priory in the fourteenth century, Appendix E (1).

[7] Rigollot, 74; Moreau, 180, quoting a (clearly misdated) letter of Charles V to the municipality of Troyes, which requires the provision of a new 'fol de cour' by that city as a royal *droit*. The king's eulogy of his fool is rather touching: 'savoir faisons à leurs dessus dictes seigneuries que Thévenin nostre fol de cour vient de trespasser de celluy monde dedans l'aultre. Le Seigneur Dieu veuille avoir en gré l'âme de luy qui oncques ne faillit en sa charge et fonction emprès nostre royale Seigneurie et mesmement ne voult si trespasser sans faire quel-

Seigni Joan, apparently intended for a court fool, as having a *marotte* and ears to his hood. On the other hand, he makes Panurge present Triboulet, the fool of Louis XII, with a sword of gilt wood and a bladder [1]. A little later Jean Passerat speaks of the hood, green and yellow, with bells, of another royal fool [2]. In the seventeenth century the green and yellow and an eared hood formed part of the fool's dress which the duke of Nevers imposed upon a peccant treasurer [3]. But in France the influence of the *sociétés joyeuses* was directly present. I do not find that the data quoted by Douce quite bear out his transference of the regular French *habit de fou* to England. Hoods were certainly required as part of the costume for 'fools,' 'disards,' or 'vices' in the court revels of 1551–2, together with 'longe' coats of various gay colours [4]; but these were for masks, and on ordinary occasions the fools of the king and the nobles seem to have worn the usual dress of a courtier or servant [5]. Like Triboulet, they often bore, as part of this, a gilded wooden sword [6]. A coxcomb, however, seems to have been a recognized fool ensign [7], and once, in a tale, the complete *habit* is described [8]. Other fool costumes include a long petticoat [9], the more primitive calf-skin [10],

---

que joyeuseté et gentille farce de son métier.'

[1] Moreau, 177, 197.

[2] Quoted by Julleville, *Les Com.* 148 :

'L'un [le poète] a la teste verte ; et l'autre va couvert D'un joli chapperon, fait de jaune et de vert ; L'un s'amuse aux grelots, et l'autre à des sornettes.'

[3] *Requestes présentées au Roy* . . . *par le S. de Vertau* (1605), quoted by Leber, in Rigollot, lxvi ; Julleville, *Les Com.* 147 'un habit . . . qui estoit faict par bandes de serge, moitié de couleur verte et l'autre de jaune ; et là où il y avoit des bandes jaunes, il y avoit des passemens verts, et sur les vertes des passemens jaunes . . . et un bonnet aussi moitié de jaune et vert, avec des oreilles, &c.'

[4] Kempe, *Loseley MSS*, 35, 47, 85.

[5] Douce, 512 ; Doran, 293.

Lodge, *Wits Miserie* (1599), describes a fool as 'in person comely, in apparell courtly.' The Durham accounts (Appendix E (1)) contain several entries of cloth and shoes purchased for the fool Thomas, but there is no mention of a hood.

[6] Douce, 510.

[7] Ibid. 510, 511. Hence the common derived sense of 'coxcomb' for a foolish, vain fellow.

[8] Douce, 509, quoting 'the second tale of the priests of Peblis,' which, for all I know, may be a translation, 'a man who counterfeits a fool is described "with club and bel and partie cote with eiris"; but it afterwards appears that he had both a club and a bauble.'

[9] Douce, 510.

[10] Douce, 512, quoting *Gesta Grayorum*, 'the scribe claims the manor of Noverinte, by providing sheepskins and calves-skins to wrappe his highness wards and idiotts in';

and a fox-tail hanging from the back [1]. The two latter seem to bring us back to the sacrificial *exuviae*, and form a link between the court fool and the grotesque ' fool,' or ' Captain Cauf Tail' of the morris dances and other village revels.

Whatever may have been the case with the domestic fool of history, it is not improbable that the tradition of the stage rightly interprets the intention of Shakespeare. The actual texts are not very decisive. The point that is most clear is that the fool wears a ' motley' or 'patched' coat [2]. The fool in *Lear* has a ' coxcomb [3] '; Monsieur Lavache in *All's Well* a 'bauble,' not of course necessarily a *marotte* [4] ; Touchstone, in *As You Like It*, is a courtier and has a sword [5]. The sword may perhaps be inherited from the 'vice' of the later moralities [6] ; and, in other respects, it is possible that Shakespeare took his conception of the fool less from contemporary custom, for indeed we hear of no fool at Elizabeth's court, than from the abundant fool-literature, continental and English, above described. The earliest of his fools, Feste in *Twelfth Night*, quotes Rabelais, in whose work, as we have just seen, the fool Triboulet figures [7]. It is noticeable that the appearance of fools as important *dramatis personae* in the plays apparently coincides with the substitution for William Kempe as ' comic lead ' in the Lord Chamberlain's company of Robert Armin [8], whose own *Nest of Ninnies* abounds in reminiscences of the fool-literature [9]. But whatever outward

---

cf. *King John*, iii. 1. 129 'And hang a calf's-skin on those recreant limbs.'

[1] Douce, 511.

[2] *Twelfth Night*, i. 5. 63 ; *As You Like It*, ii. 7. 13, 43 ; *King Lear*, i. 4. 160; *Midsummer Night's Dream*, iv. 1. 215. But the 'long motley coat guarded with yellow' of *Hen. VIII*, prol. 16, does not quite correspond to anything in the ' habit de fou.'

[3] *King Lear*, i. 4. 106. Cf. *Taming of the Shrew*, ii. 1. 226 ' What is your crest? a coxcomb ? '

[4] *All's Well that Ends Well*, iv. 5. 32. There are *double entendre's* here and in the allusion to the ' bauble' of a 'natural' in *Romeo*

and Juliet, ii. 4. 97, which suggest less a 'marotte' than a bauble of the bladder type ; cf. p. 197.

[5] *As You Like It*, ii. 4. 47.

[6] Cf. ch. xxv.

[7] *Twelfth Night*, ii. 3. 22.

[8] Fools appear in *As You Like It* (†1599), *All's Well that Ends Well* (†1601), *Twelfth Night* (†1601), *King Lear* (†1605) ; cf. the allusion to Yorick, the king's jester in *Hamlet*, v. 1. 198 (†1603). Kempe seems to have left the Shakespearian company in 1598 or 1599.

[9] According to Fleay, *Biog. Chron.* i. 25, Armin's *Nest of Ninnies*, of 1608 (ed. Shakes. Soc.), is a revision of his *Fool upon Fool* of 1605.

appearance Shakespeare intended his fools to bear, there can be no doubt that in their dramatic use as vehicles of general social satire they very closely recall the manner of the *sotties.* Touchstone is the type : ' He uses his folly like a stalking-horse, and under the presentation of that he shoots his wit [1].'

[1] *As You Like It,* v. 4. III. Cf. Lionel Johnson, *The Fools of Shake-speare,* in *Noctes Shakespearianae* (Winchester Sh. Soc.) ; J. Thümmel, *Ueber Sh.'s Narren (Sh.-Jahr-buch,* lx. 87).

CHAPTER XVII

MASKS AND MISRULE

[*Bibliographical Note.*—On the history of the English Masque A. Soergel, *Die englischen Maskenspiele* (1882); H. A. Evans, *English Masques* (1897); J. A. Symonds, *Shakespeare's Predecessors*, ch. ix; A. W. Ward, *English Dramatic Literature*, passim; W. W. Greg, *A List of Masques, Pageants, &c.* (1902), may be consulted. Much of the material used by these writers is in Collier, *H. E. D. P.* vol. i, and P. Cunningham, *Extracts from the Accounts of the Revels at Court* (Shakespeare Soc. 1842). For the early Tudor period E. Hall's *History of the Union of Lancaster and York* (1548) and the Revels Accounts in J. S. Brewer and J. Gairdner, *Letters and Papers of the Reign of Henry VIII*, vols. ii, iii, are detailed and valuable. R. Brotanek's very full *Die englischen Maskenspiele* (1902) only reached me when this chapter was in type.]

ALREADY in Saxon England Christmas was becoming a season of secular merry-making as well as of religious devotion[1]. Under the post-Conquest kings this tendency was stimulated by the fixed habit of the court. William the Bastard, like Charlemagne before him, chose the solemn day for his coronation; and from his reign Christmas takes rank, with Easter, Whitsuntide, and, at a much later date, St. George's day, as one of the great courtly festivals of the year. The *Anglo-Saxon Chronicle* is at the pains to record the place of its celebration, twelvemonth after twelvemonth[2]. Among the many forgotten Christmassings of mediaeval kings, history lays a finger on a few of special note: that at which Richard II, with characteristic extravagance and the consumption of '200 tunns of wine and 2,000 oxen with their appurtenances,' entertained the papal legate in 1398; and that, more truly royal, at which Henry V, besieging Rouen in 1418,

---

[1] Tille, *Y. and C.* 162; Sandys, 20. At Christmas, 1065, Edward the Confessor 'curiam tenuit' at London, and dedicated Westminster Abbey on Innocents' day (Florence of Worcester, *Chronicle*, ed. Thorpe, i. 224).

[2] Tille, *Y. and C.* 160; Ramsay, *F. of E.* ii. 43.

'refreshed all the poore people with vittels to their great comfort and his high praise [1].' The Tudors were not behindhand with any opportunity for pageantry and display, nor does the vogue of Christmas throughout the length and breadth of 'merrie England' need demonstration [2]. The Puritans girded at it, as they did at May games, and the rest of the delightful circumstance of life, until in 1644 an ordinance of the Long Parliament required the festival to give place to a monthly fast with the day fixed for which it happened to coincide [3].

The entertainment of a mediaeval Christmas was diverse. There was the banquet. The Boy Bishop came to court. Carols were sung. New Year gifts were exchanged. *Hastiludia*—jousts or tournaments—were popular and splendid. Minstrels and jugglers made music and mirth. A succession of gaieties filled the Twelve nights from the Nativity to the Epiphany, or even the wider space from St. Thomas's day to Candlemas. It is, however, in the custom of masquing that I find the most direct legacy to Christmas of the Kalends celebrations in their *bourgeois* forms. *Larvae* or masks are prominent in the records and prohibitions of the Feast of Fools from the decretal of Innocent III in 1207 to the letter of the Paris theologians in 1445 [4]. I take them as being, like the characteristic hood of the 'fool,' sophistications of the *capita pecudum*, the sacrificial *exuviae* worn by the rout of worshippers at the *Kalendae*. Precisely such *larvae*, under another name, confront us in the detailed records of two fourteenth-century Christmasses. Amongst the documents of the Royal Wardrobe for the reign of Edward III are lists of stuffs issued for

---

[1] Sandys, 23; Ashton, 9.

[2] Sandys, 53; Ashton, 14; Drake, 94.

[3] Ashton, 26; Stubbes, i. 173. Cf. Vaughan's *Poems* (*Muses Library*, i. 107):
'Alas, my God! Thy birth now here
Must not be number'd in the year.'

[4] Cf. ch. xiii. There is much learning on the use of masks in seasonal festivals in C. Noirot, *Traité de l'origine des masques* (1609, reprinted in Leber, ix. 5);

Savaron, *Traité contre les masques* (1611); J. G. Drechssler, *de larvis natalitiis* (1683); C. H. de Berger, *Commentatio de personis vulgo larvis seu mascheratis* (1723); Pfannenschmidt, 617; Fr. Back, *de Graecorum caeremoniis in quibus homines deorum vice fungebantur* (1883); W. H. Dall, *On masks, labrets and certain aboriginal customs* (*Third Annual Report of American Bureau of Ethnology*, 1884, p. 73); Frazer, *Pausanias*, iv. 239.

the *ludi domini regis* in 1347–8 and 1348–9 [1]. For the Christmas of 1347, held at Guildford, were required a number of 'viseres' in the likeness of men, women, and angels, curiously designed 'crestes,' and other costumes representing dragons, peacocks, and swans [2]. The Christmas of 1348 held at Ottford and the following Epiphany at Merton yield similar entries [3]. What were these 'viseres' used for? The term *ludi* must not be pressed. It appears to be distinct from *hastiludia*, which comes frequently in the same documents, although in the *hastiludia* also 'viseres' were used [4]. But it

[1] *Archaeologia*, xxxi, 37, 43, 44, 120, 122.

[2] 'Et ad faciendum ludos domini Regis ad festum Natalis domini celebratum apud Guldefordum anno Regis xxj°, in quo expendebantur iiij. iiij. tunicae de bokeram diversorum colorum, xlij viseres diversorum similitudinum (*specified as* xiiij similitudines facierum mulierum, xiiij similitudines facierum hominum cum barbis, xiiij similitudines capitum angelorum de argento) xxviij crestes (*specified as* xiiij crestes cum tibiis reversatis et calciatis, xiiij crestes cum montibus et cuniculis), xiiij clocae depictae, xiiij capita draconum, xiiij tunicae albae, xiiij capita pavonum cum alis, xiiij tunicae depictae cum oculis pavonum, xiiij capita cygnorum cum suis alis, xiiij tunicae de tela linea depictae, xiiij tunicae depictae cum stellis de auro et argento vapulatis.' The performers seem to have made six groups of fourteen each, representing respectively men, women, angels, dragons, peacocks, and swans. A notion of their appearance is given by the cuts from miniatures (†1343) in Strutt, 160.

[3] 'Et ad faciendum ludos Regis ad festum Natalis domini anno Regis xxij^do celebratum apud Ottefordum ubi expendebantur viseres videlicet xij capita hominum et desuper tot capita leonum, xij capita hominum et tot capita elephantum, xij capita hominum cum alis vespertilionum, xij capita de wodewose

[cf. p. 185], xvij capita virginum, xiiij supertunicae de worsted rubro guttatae cum auro et lineatae et reversatae et totidem tunicae de worsted viridi ... Et ad faciendum ludos Regis in festo Epiphaniae domini celebrato apud Mertonum ubi expendebantur xiij visers cum capitibus draconum et xij visers cum capitibus hominum habentibus diademata, x c^r tepies de bokeram nigro et tela linea Anglica.'

[4] *Archaeologia*, xxxi. 29, 30, 118. The element of semi-dramatic *spectacle* was already getting into the fourteenth-century tournament. In 1331 Edward III and his court rode to the lists in Cheap, 'omnes splendido apparatu vestiti et ad similitudinem Tartarorum larvati' (*Annales Paulini* in *Chron. Edw. I and II*, R. S. i. 354). In 1375 'rood dame Alice Perrers, as lady of the sune, fro the tour of London thorugh Chepe ; and alwey a lady ledynge a lordys brydell. And thanne begun the grete justes in Smythefeld' (*London Chronicle*, 70). These ridings closely resemble the 'mummings' proper. But they were a prelude to *hastiludia*, which from the fourteenth to the sixteenth century constantly grew less actual and more mimetic. In 1343 'fuerunt pulchra hastiludia in Smethfield, ubi papa et duodecim cardinales per tres dies contra quoscumque tirocinium habuerunt' (Murimuth, *Continuatio Chronicarum*, R. S. 146). And so on, through the jousts of Pallas and Diana at the coronation of Henry VIII (Hall, 511)

does not necessarily imply anything dramatic, and the analogies suggest that it is a wide generic term, roughly equivalent to 'disports,' or to the 'revels' of the Tudor vocabulary[1]. It recurs in 1388 when the Wardrobe provided linen coifs for twenty-one counterfeit men of the law in the *ludus regis*[2]. The sets of costumes supplied for all these *ludi* would most naturally be used by groups of performers in something of the nature of a dance; and they point to some primitive form of masque, such as Froissart describes in contemporary France[3], the precursor of the long line of development which, traceable from the end of the following century, culminates in the glories of Ben Jonson. The vernacular name for such a *ludus* in the fourteenth century was 'mumming' or 'disguising'[4].' Orders of the city of London in 1334, 1393, and 1405 forbid a practice of going about the streets at Christmas *ove visere ne faux visage*, and entering the houses of citizens to play at dice

to the regular Elizabethan 'Barriers,' such as the siege of the 'Fortress of Perfect Beauty' by the 'Four Foster Children of Desire,' in which Sidney took part in 1581.

[1] This seems to be clearly the sense of the *ludi Domini Prioris* in the accounts of Durham Priory (cf. Appendix E). The Scottish Exchequer Rolls between 1446 and 1478 contain such entries as 'iocis et ludis,' 'ludis et interludiis,' 'ioculancium et ludencium,' 'ludos et disportus suos,' where all the terms used, except 'interludiis' (cf.ch.xxiv), appear to be more or less equivalent (*Accounts of the Treasurer of Scotland*, i. ccxxxix). The *Liber Niger* of Edward IV declares that in the *Domus* of Henry I were allowed 'ludi honesti,' such as military sports 'cum ceterorum iocorum diversitate' (*Household Ordinances*, 18). 'Ioca' is here exactly the French 'jeux.' Polydore Vergil, *Hist. Anglica* (ed. Thysius), 772, says of the weddings of the children of Henry VII 'utriusque puellae nuptiae omnium generum ludis factae.' For 'disports' cf. Hall, 774, 'enterludes... maskes and disportes,' and *Paston Letters*, iii. 314, where Lady Morley is said to have ordered in 1476 that on account

of her husband's death there should be at Christmas 'non dysgysyngs, ner harpyng, ner lutyng, ner syngyn, ner non lowde dysports, but pleyng at the tabyllys, and schesse, and cards. Sweche dysports sche gave her folkys leve to play, and non odyr.' I find the first use of 'revels' in the Household Books of Henry VII for 1493 (Collier, i. 50). In 1496 the same source gives the Latin 'revelliones' (Collier, i. 46). Sir Thomas Cawarden (1545) was patented 'magister iocorum, revelorum et mascorum' (Rymer, xv. 62). Another synonym is 'triumph,' used in 1511 (Arnold, *Chronicle*, xlv). The latter means properly a royal entry or reception; cf. ch. xxiii.

[2] Warton, ii. 220, from *Compotus Magn. Garderobae*, 14 Ric. II, f. 198[b] 'pro xxi coifs de tela linea pro hominibus de lege contrafactis pro ludo regis tempore natalis domini anno xii.'

[3] Froissart (ed. Buchon, iii. 176), Bk. iv, ch. 32, describes the dance of 1393, in which Charles VI dressed in flax as a wild man was nearly burnt to death.

[4] The English *William of Palerne*, 1620 (†1350, ed. Skeat, E. E. T. S.), has 'daunces disgisi.'

therein [1]. In 1417 'mummyng' is specifically included in a similar prohibition [2]; and in a proclamation of the following year, 'mommyng' is classed with 'playes' and 'enterludes' as a variety of 'disgisyng [3].' But the disport which they denied to less dignified folk the rulers of the city retained for themselves as the traditional way of paying a visit of compliment to a great personage. A fragmentary chronicle amongst Stowe's manuscripts describes such a visit paid to Richard II at the Candlemas preceding his accession in 1377. The 'mummers' were disguised with 'vizards' to represent an emperor and a pope with their *cortèges*. They rode to Kennington, entered the hall on foot, invited the prince and the lords to dice and discreetly lost, drank and danced with the company, and so departed [4]. This is the first of several

[1] H. T. Riley, *Liber Albus* (R. S. xii), i. 644, 645, 647, 673, 676; *Memorials of London*, 193, 534, 561. For similar orders elsewhere cf. L. T. Smith, *Ricart's Calendar*, 85 (Bristol), and *Harl. MS.* 2015, f. 64 (Chester).

[2] Riley, *Memorials*, 658.

[3] Ibid. 669. It was proclaimed 'that no manere persone, of what astate, degre, or condicioun that euere he be, duryng this holy tyme of Cristemes be so hardy in eny wyse to walk by nyght in any manere mommyng, pleyes, enterludes, or eny other disgisynges with eny feynyd berdis, peyntid visers, diffourmyd or colourid visages in eny wyse . . . outake that hit be leful to eche persone for to be honestly mery as he can, with in his owne hous dwellyng.'

[4] Stowe, *Survey* (ed. Thoms), 37, from a fragment of an English chronicle, in a sixteenth-century hand, in *Harl. MS.* 247, f. 172ᵛ (cf. *Archaeologia*, xxii. 208). I print the original text, which Stowe paraphrases, introducing, e.g., the term 'maskers': 'At yᵉ same tyme yᵉ Comons of London made great sporte and solemnity to yᵉ yong prince: for upon yᵉ monday next before yᵉ purification of our lady at night and in yᵉ night were 130 men disguizedly aparailed and well mounted on horsebacke to goe on mumming to yᵉ said prince, riding from Newgate through Cheape whear many people saw them with great noyse of minstralsye, trumpets, cornets and shawmes and great plenty of waxe torches lighted and in the beginning they rid 48 after yᵉ maner of esquiers two and two together clothed in cotes and clokes of red say or sendall and their faces covered with vizards well and handsomely made: after these esquiers came 48 like knightes well arayed after yᵉ same maner: after yᵉ knightes came one excellent arrayed and well mounted as he had bene an emperor: after him some 100 yards came one nobly arayed as a pope and after him came 24 arayed like cardinals and after yᵉ cardinals came 8 or 10 arayed and with black vizardes like deuils appearing nothing amiable seeming like legates, riding through London and ouer London bridge towards Kenyton wher yᵉ yong prince made his aboad with his mother and the D. of Lancaster and yᵉ Earles of Cambridge, Hertford Warrick and Suffolk and many other lordes which were with him to hould the solemnity, and when they were come before yᵉ mansion they alighted on foot and

such mummings upon record. Some chroniclers relate that it was at a mumming that the partisans of Richard II attempted to seize Henry IV on Twelfth night in 1400 [1]. In the following year, when the Emperor Manuel of Constantinople spent Christmas with Henry at Eltham, the 'men of London maden a gret mommyng to hym of xij aldermen and there sons, for whiche they hadde gret thanke [2].' In 1414 Sir John Oldcastle and his Lollards were in their turn accused of using a mumming as a cloak of sedition [3]. Thus the London distrust of false

entered into yᵉ haule and sone after yᵉ prince and his mother and yᵒ other lordes came out of yᵉ chamber into yᵉ haule, and yᵉ said mummers saluted them, shewing a pair of dice upon a table to play with yᵉ prince, which dice were subtilly made that when yᵉ prince shold cast he shold winne and yᵉ said players and mummers set before yᵉ prince three jewels each after other: and first a balle of gould, then a cupp of gould, then a gould ring, yᵉ which yᵉ said prince wonne at thre castes as before it was appointed, and after that they set before the prince's mother, the D. of Lancaster, and yᵉ other earles euery one a gould ringe and yᵉ mother and yᵉ lordes wonne them. And then yᵉ prince caused to bring yᵉ one wyne and they dronk with great joye, commanding yᵉ minstrels to play and yᵉ trompets began to sound and other instruments to pipe &c. And yᵉ prince and yᵉ lordes dansed on yᵉ one syde, and yᵉ mummers on yᵉ other a great while and then they drank and tooke their leaue and so departed toward London.' Collier, i. 26, speaks of earlier mummings recorded by Stowe in 1236 and 1298; but Stowe only names 'pageants' (cf. ch. xxiii). M. Paris, *Chronica Maiora* (R. S. lvii), v. 269, mentions 'vestium transformatarum varietatem' at the wedding of Alexander III of Scotland and Margaret of England in 1251, but this probably means 'a succession of rapidly changed robes.'

[1] *A Chronicle of London* (†1442,

ed. N. H. Nicolas or E. Tyrrell, 1827), 85 'to have sclayn the kyng ... be a mommynge'; *Incerti Scriptoris Chronicon* (before 1455, ed. J. A. Giles), 7 'conduxerunt lusores Londoniam, ad inducendum regi praetextum gaudii et laetitiae iuxta temporis dispositionem, ludum nuncupatum Anglice Mummynge'; Capgrave, *Chronicle of England* (†1464, R.S.), 275 'undir the coloure of mummeris in Cristmasse tyme'; *An English Chronicle* (†1461-71, C. S.), 20 'to make a mommyng to the king ... and in that mommyng they purposid to sle him'; Fabian, *Chronicle*, 567 'a dysguysynge or a mummynge.' But other chroniclers say that the outbreak was to be at a tournament, e. g. *Continuatio Eulogii* (R. S. ix), iii. 385; *Annales Henrici* (R. S. xxviii), 323 'Sub simulatione natalitiorum vel hastiludiorum.' I suppose 'natalitia' is 'Christmas games' and might cover a mumming. Hall, *Chronicle* (ed. 1809), 16, makes it 'justes.' So does Holinshed (ed. 1586), iii. 514, 516, but he knew both versions; 'them that write how the king should have beene made awaie at a justes; and other that testifie, how it should have been at a maske or mummerie'; cf. Wylie, *Henry the Fourth*, i. 93; Ramsay, *L. and Y.* i. 20.

[2] Stowe, *Survey* (ed. Thoms), 37, doubtless from *A Chronicle of London* (†1442, ut supra), 87. I do not find the mumming named in other accounts of the visit.

[3] *Gregory's Chronicle* (before

visages had its justification, and it is noteworthy that so late as 1511 an Act of Parliament forbade the visits of mummers disguised with visors to great houses on account of the disorders so caused. Even the sale of visors was made illegal[1].

So far there is nothing to point to the use of any dialogue or speeches at mummings. The only detailed account is that of 1377, and the passage which describes how the mummers 'saluted' the lords, 'shewing a pair of dice upon a table to play with the prince,' reads rather as if the whole performance were in dumb show. This is confirmed by the explanation of the term 'mummynge' given in a contemporary glossary[2]. The development of the mumming in a literary direction may very likely have been due to the multifarious activity of John Lydgate. Amongst his miscellaneous poems are preserved several which are stated by their collector Shirley to have been written for mummings or disguisings either before the king or before the lord mayor of London[3]. They all seem to belong to the reign of Henry VI and probably to the years

1467, in *Hist. Collections of a Citizen of London*, C. S.), 108 'the whyche Lollers hadde caste to have made a mommynge at Eltham, and undyr coloure of the mommynge to have destryte the Kynge and Hooly Chyrche.'

[1] *Acte against disguysed persons and Wearing of Visours* (3 Hen. VIII, c. 9). The preamble states that 'lately wythin this realme dyvers persons have disgysed and appareld theym, and covert theyr fayces with Vysours and other thynge in such manner that they sholde nott be knowen and divers of theym in a Companye togeder namyng them selfe Mummers have commyn to the dwellyng place of divers men of honor and other substanciall persones; and so departed unknown.' Offenders are to be treated as 'Suspectes or Vacabundes.'

[2] The *Promptorium Parvulorum* (†1440 C. S.), ii. 348, translates 'Mummynge' by 'mussacio vel mussatus' ('murmuring' or 'keeping silence,' conn. *mutus*), and gives

a cognate word 'Mummyn, as they that noȝt speke *Mutio*.' This is of course the ordinary sense of *mum*. But Skeat (*Etym. Dict.* s.v.) derives 'mummer' from the Dutch through Old French, and explains it by the Low German *Mumme*, a 'mask.' He adds 'The word is imitative, from the sound *mum* or *mom*, used by nurses to frighten or amuse children, at the same time pretending to cover their faces.' Whether the fourteenth-century mumming was silent or not, there is no reason to suppose that the primitive folk-procession out of which it arose was unaccompanied by dance and song; and silence is rarely, if ever (cf. p. 211) *de rigueur* in modern 'guisings.'

[3] They are in *Trin. Coll. Camb. MS.* R. iii. 20 (Shirley's; cf. E. P. Hammond, *Lydgate's Mumming at Hertford* in *Anglia*, xxii. 364), and copied by or for Stowe 'out of þe boke of John Sherley' in *B. M. Add. MS.* 29729, f. 132 (cf. E. Sieper, *Lydgate's Reson and Sensuallyte*, E. E. T. S. i. xvi).

1427–30. And they show pretty clearly the way in which verses got into the disguisings. Two of them are 'lettres' introducing mummings presented by the guilds of the mercers and the goldsmiths to lord mayor Eastfield[1]. They were doubtless read aloud in the hall. A *balade* sent to Henry and the queen mother at Eltham is of the same type[2]. Two 'devyses' for mummings at London and Windsor were probably recited by a 'presenter.' The Windsor one is of the nature of a prologue, describing a 'myracle' which the king is 'to see[3].' The London one was meant to accompany the course of the performance, and describes the various personages as they enter[4]. Still more elaborate is a set of verses used at

The Hertford verses have been printed by Miss Hammond (*loc. cit.*) and the others by Brotanek, 306. I do not find any notice of disguisings when Henry VI spent the Christmas of 1433 at Lydgate's own monastery of Bury St. Edmunds (F. A. Gasquet, *A Royal Christmas* in *The Old English Bible*, 226). Devon, *Issues of the Exchequer*, 473, notes a payment for the king's 'plays and recreations' at Christmas, 1449.

[1] 'A lettre made in wyse of balade by daun Johan, brought by a poursuyant in wyse of Mommers desguysed to fore þe Mayre of London, Eestfeld, vpon þe twelffeþe night of Cristmasse, ordeyned Ryallych by þe worthy Merciers, Citeseyns of london' and 'A lettre made in wyse of balade by ledegate daun Johan, of a mommynge, whiche þe Goldesmythes of þe Cite of London mommed in Right fresshc and costele welych desguysing to þeyre Mayre Eestfeld, vpon Candelmasse day at nyght, affter souper; brought and presented vn to þe Mayre by an heraude, cleped ffortune.' The Mercer's pursuivant is sent from Jupiter; the Goldsmiths' mummers are David and the twelve tribes. The Levites were to sing. William Eastfield was mayor 1429–30 and 1437–8. Brotanek, 306, argues that, as a second term is not alluded to, this was probably the first. Fairholt, *Lord Mayors'*

Pageants, ii. 240, prints a similar letter of Lydgate's sent to the Sheriffs at a May-day dinner.

[2] 'A balade made by daun John Lidegate at Eltham in Cristmasse for a momyng tofore þe kyng and þe Qwene.' Bacchus, Juno and Ceres send gifts 'by marchandes þat here be.' The same collections contain a balade, 'gyven vnto þᵉ Kyng Henry and to his moder the quene Kateryne sittyng at þe mete vpon the yeares day in the castell of Hertford.' Some historical allusions make 1427 a likely date (Brotanek, 305).

[3] 'Þe devyse of a momyng to fore þe kyng henry þe sixte, beinge in his Castell of wyndesore, þe fest of his crystmasse holdyng þer, made by lidegate daun John, þe munk of Bury, howe þampull and þe floure delys came first to þe Kynges of ffraunce by myrakle at Reynes.' An allusion to Henry's coming coronation in Paris fixes the date to 1429–30.

[4] 'Þe deuyse of a desguysing to fore þe gret estates of þis lande, þane being at London, made by Lidegate daun Johan, þe Munk of Bury, of dame fortune, dame prudence, dame Rightwysnesse and dame ffortitudo. beholdeþe, for it is moral, plesaunt and notable.' A fifth dame is 'Attemperaunce.' The time is 'Cristmasse.' An elaborate pageant in which Fortune dwelt is described. A song is directed at the close. Henry V is spoken of as dead.

Hertford. The first part of these is certainly spoken by a presenter who points out the 'vpplandishe' complainants to whom he refers. But the reply is in the first person, and apparently put in the mouths of the 'wyues' themselves, while the conclusion is a judgement delivered, again probably by the presenter, in the name of the king[1].

Whether Lydgate was the author of an innovation or not, the introduction of speeches, songs, and dialogues was common enough in the fully-developed mummings. For these we must look to the sumptuous courts of the early Tudors. Lydgate died about 1451, and the Wars of the Roses did not encourage revelry. The *Paston Letters* tell how the Lady Morley forbade 'dysguysyngs' in her house at Christmas after her husband's death in 1476[2]. There were *ludi* in Scotland under James III[3]. But those of his successor, James IV, although numerous and varied[4], probably paled before the elaborate 'plays' and 'disguisings' which the contemporary account-books of Henry VII reveal[5]. Of only one 'disguising,' however, of this period is a full account preserved. It took place in Westminster Hall after the wedding of Prince Arthur with Katharine of Spain on November 18, 1501, and was 'convayed and showed in pageants proper and subtile.' There was a castle, bearing singing children and eight disguised ladies, amongst whom was one 'apparelled like unto the Princesse of Spaine,' a Ship in which came Hope and Desire as

[1] 'Nowe foloweth here the maner of a bille by weye of supplycation put to the kynge holdinge his noble fest of crystmasse in the castell of hartford as in dysguysinge of þe rude vpplandishe people complayninge on their wyues with the boystrus answere of ther wyues deuysed by lidgate at þe requeste of the countrowlore Brys slain at louiers.' Louviers was taken by the French in 1430 and besieged next year (Brotanek, 306). The text has marginal notes, 'demonstrando vj rusticos,' &c.

[2] Cf. p. 393. There is a disguising of 1483 in the Howard Accounts (Appendix E, vii).

[3] *L.H.T.Accounts,* i. ccxl 'Iohanni Rate, pictori, pro le mumre regis' (1465-6); ad le mumre grath' (1466-7).

[4] Ibid. i. lxxix, cxliv, ccxxxix; ii. lxxi, cx; iii. xlvi, lv, and passim, have many payments for dances at court, of which some were morris dances, with 'legharnis,' and also to 'madinnis,' 'gysaris,' or 'dansaris' who 'dansit' or 'playit' to the king in various parts of the country.

[5] Campbell, *Materials for a Hist. of Henry VII* (R.S.), *passim*; Collier, i. 38–64; Bentley, *Excerpta Historica,* 85–133; Leland, *Collectanea,* iii. 256.

Ambassadors, and a Mount of Love, from which issued eight
knights, and assaulted the castle. This allegorical compliment, which was set forth by 'countenance, speeches, and
demeanor,' ended, the knights and ladies danced together and
presently 'avoided.' Thereupon the royal party themselves
fell to dancing[1]. 'Pageants' are mentioned in connexion
with other disguisings of the reign, and on one occasion the
disguising was 'for a moryce[2].' Further light is thrown upon
the nature of a disguising by the regulations contained in
a contemporary book of 'Orders concerning an Earl's House.'
A disguising is to be introduced by torch-bearers and accompanied by minstrels. If there are women disguised, they are
to dance first, and then the men. Then is to come the
morris, 'if any be ordeynid.' Finally men and women are to
dance together and depart in the 'towre, or thing devised for
theim.' The whole performance is to be under the control of
a 'maister of the disguisinges' or 'revills[3].'

It is possible to distinguish a simpler and a more elaborate
type of masked entertainment, side by side, throughout the
splendid festivities of the court of Henry VIII. For the
more or less impromptu 'mumming,' the light-hearted and
riotous king had a great liking. In the first year of his reign
we find him invading the queen's chamber at Westminster 'for
a gladness to the queen's grace' in the guise of Robin Hood,
with his men 'in green coats and hose of Kentish Kendal'
and a Maid Marian[4]. The queen subsequently got left out,
but there were many similar disports throughout the reign.
One of these, in which the king and a party disguised as
shepherds broke in upon a banquet of Wolsey's, has been
immortalized by Shakespeare[5]. Such mummings were com-

[1] Collier, i. 58, from *Harl. MS.*
69. A word which Collier prints
'Maskers' is clearly a misprint for
'Masters,' and misleading.
[2] Ibid. i. 53. The 'morris'
provided a grotesque element,
analogous to the 'antimasque' of
Jonson's day.
[3] Ibid. i. 24, from *Fairfax MSS.*
Of this *Booke of all manner of
Orders concerning an Earle's house*

'some part is dated 16 Henry VII,
although the handwriting appears
to be that of the latter end of the
reign of Henry VIII.'
[4] Hall, 513; Brewer, ii. 1490.
[5] *Hen. VIII*, i. 4; Hall, 719;
Stowe, *Chronicle*, 845; Cavendish,
Life of Wolsey, 112; Boswell-Stone,
Shakespeare's Holinshed, 441;
R. Brown, *Venetian Papers*, iv.
3, 4.

paratively simple, and the Wardrobe was as a rule only called
upon to provide costumes and masks, although on one occasion
a lady in a 'tryke' or 'spell' wagon was drawn in [1]. But the
more formal 'disguisings' of the previous reign were also
continued and set forth with great splendour. In 1527 a
'House of Revel' called the 'Long House' was built for their
performance and decorated by Holbein [2], and there was
constant expenditure on the provision of pageants. 'The
Golldyn Arber in the Arche-yerd of Plesyer,' 'the Dangerus
Fortrees,' 'the Ryche Mount,' the Pavyllon un the Plas
Parlos,' 'the Gardyn de Esperans,' 'the Schatew Vert' [3] are
some of the names given to them, and these well suggest the
kind of allegorical spectacular entertainment, diversified with
dance and song, which the chroniclers describe.

The 'mumming' or 'disguising,' then, as it took shape at
the beginning of the sixteenth century, was a form of court
revel, in which, behind the accretions of literature and pageantry,
can be clearly discerned a nucleus of folk-custom in the entry
of the band of worshippers, with their sacrificial *exuviae*, to
bring the house good luck. The mummers are masked and
disguised folk who come into the hall uninvited and call upon
the company gathered there to dice and dance. It is not
necessary to lay stress upon the distinction between the two
terms, which are used with some indifference. When they
first make their appearance together in the London proclamation of 1418 the masked visit is a 'mumming,' and is included
with the 'enterlude' under the generic term of 'disguising.'
In the Henry VII documents 'mumming' does not occur,
and in those of Henry VIII 'mumming' and 'disguising' are
practically identical, 'disguising,' if anything, being used of
the more elaborate shows, while both are properly distinct
from 'interlude.' But I do not think that 'disguising' ever
quite lost its earlier and widest sense [4]. It must now be added

[1] Brewer, iii. 1552.
[2] Ibid. iv. 1390–3; Hall, 722.
[3] Ibid. ii. 1495, 1497, 1499, 1501,
1509; iii. 1558.
[4] Hall, 597, speaks of a disguising
in 1519, which apparently included
'a goodly commedy of Plautus' and

a mask. Away from court in 1543
four players were committed to the
Counter for 'unlawful disguising'
(*P. C. Acts*, i. 109, 110, 122). They
surely played interludes. It may
be further noted (i) the elaborate
disguisings of Henry VII and

that early in Henry VIII's reign a new term was introduced which ultimately supplanted both the others. The chronicler Hall relates how in 1513 'On the daie of the Epiphanie at night, the kyng with a xi other were disguised, after the maner of Italie, called a maske, a thyng not seen afore in Englande, thei were appareled in garmentes long and brode, wrought all with gold, with visers and cappes of gold & after the banket doen, these Maskers came in, with sixe gentlemen disguised in silke bearyng staffe torches, and desired the ladies to daunce, some were content, and some that knewe the fashion of it refused, because it was not a thyng commonly seen. And after thei dauncced and commoned together, as the fashion of the Maske is, thei tooke their leaue and departed, and so did the Quene, and all the ladies[1].'

The good Hall is not particularly lucid in his descriptions, and historians of the mask have doubted what, beyond the name, was the exact modification introduced 'after the maner of Italie' in 1512. A recent writer on the subject, Dr. H. A. Evans, thinks that it lay in the fact that the maskers danced with the spectators, as well as amongst themselves[2]. But the mummers of 1377 already did this, although of course the custom may have grown obsolete before 1513. I am rather inclined to regard it as a matter of costume. The original Revels Account for this year—and Hall's reports of court revels are so full that he must surely have had access to some such source—mentions provision for '12 nobyll personages, inparylled with

Henry VIII, with much action and speechifying besides the dancing, are difficult to distinguish when merely described from interludes. What Hall, 518, calls in 1511 an interlude, seems from the Revels Accounts (Brewer, ii. 1495) to have been really a disguising. Hall, 641, speaks of a 'disguisyng or play' in 1522, and Cavendish, *Life of Wolsey*, i. 136, of a 'disguising or interlude' in 1527; (ii) a disguising or dance might be introduced, as *entr'acte* or otherwise, into an interlude. In 1514 an interlude 'conteyned a moresk of vj persons and ij ladys' (Collier, i. 68). In 1526

a moral play was 'set forth with straunge deuises of Maskes and Morrishes' (Hall, 719). The interlude of *The Nature of the Four Elements* (early Hen. VIII) has after the *dramatis personae* the direction, 'Also yf ye lyst ye may brynge in a dysgysynge'; cf. Soergel, 21.

[1] Hall, 526.
[2] Evans, xxi. Other not very plausible suggestions are made by Ward, i. 150; Soergel, 13. There is a good account of the Italian *mascherata* from about 1474 in Symonds, *Shakespeare's Predecessors*, 321.

blew damaske and yelow damaske long gowns and hoods with hats after the maner of maskelyng in Etaly[1].' Does not this description suggest that the 'thing not sene afore in England' was of the nature of a domino? In any case from 1513 onwards 'masks,' 'maskelers' or 'maskelings' recur frequently in the notices of the revels[2]. The early masks resembled the simpler type of 'mumming' rather than the more elaborate and spectacular 'disguising,' but by the end of the reign both of the older terms had become obsolete, and all Elizabethan court performances in which the visor and the dance played the leading parts were indifferently known as masks[3]. Outside the court, indeed, the nomenclature was more conservative, and to this day the village performers who claim the right to enter your house at Christmas call themselves 'mummers,' 'guisers' or 'geese-dancers.' Sometimes they merely dance, sing and feast with you, but in most places, as

---

[1] Brewer, ii. 1497. There is a further entry in an account of 1519 (Brewer, iii. 35) of a revel, called a 'masklyne,' after the manner of Italy.

[2] 'Maske' first appears in 1514 (Collier, i. 79 'iocorum larvatorum, vocat. Maskes, Revelles, and Disguysings'); 'masque' is not English until the seventeenth century (Evans, xiii). Skeat derives through the French *masque, masquer, masquerer*, and the Spanish *mascara, mascarada* (Ital. *mascherata*) from the Arabic *maskharat*, a buffoon or droll (root *sakhira*, 'he ridiculed'). The original sense would thus be 'entertainment' and that of 'face-mask' (*larva*, 'vizard,' 'viser') only derivative. But late Latin has already *masca, talamasca* in this sense; e.g. Burchardus of Worms, *Coll. Decretorum* (before 1024), bk. ii. c. 161 'nec larvas daemonum quas vulgo Talamascas dicunt, ibi ante se ferri consentiat'; cf. Ducange, s.v. *Talamasca*; Pfannenschmidt, 617, with some incorrect etymology. And the French *masque* is always the face-mask and never the performance; while *se masquier, masquillier,*

maschurer, are twelfth- to thirteenth-century words for 'blacken,' 'dirty.' I therefore prefer the derivation of Brotanek, 120, from a Germanic root represented by the M.E. *maskel*, 'stain'; and this has the further advantage of explaining 'maskeler,' 'maskeling,' which appear, variously spelt, in documents of †1519-26. Both terms signify the performance, and 'maskeler' the performer also (Brotanek, 122). Face-masks were *de rigueur* in the Mask to a late date. In 1618 John Chamberlain writes 'the gentlemen of Gray's Inn came to court with their show, for I cannot call it a masque, seeing they were not disguised, nor had vizards' (Nichols, *James 1,* iii. 468).

[3] Ben Jonson, iii. 162, *Masque of Augurs* (1623) 'Disguise was the old English word for a masque, sir, before you were an implement belonging to the Revels'; ii. 476, *A Tale of a Tub* (1634), v. 2:
'*Pan.* A masque! what's that?
Scriben. A mumming or a shew,
With vizards and fine clothes.
Clench. A disguise, neighbour,
Is the true word.'

a former chapter has shown, they have adopted from another season of the year its characteristic rite, which in course of time has grown from folk-dance into folk-drama [1].

I now pass from the mask to another point of contact between the Feast of Fools and the Tudor revels. This was the *dominus festi*. A special officer, told off to superintend the revels, pastimes and disports of the Christmas season, is found both in the English and the Scottish court at the end of the fifteenth century. In Scotland he bore the title of Abbot of Unreason [2]; in England he was occasionally the Abbot, but more usually the Lord of Misrule. Away from court, other local designations present themselves: but Lord of Misrule or Christmas Lord are the generic titles known to contemporary literature [3]. The household accounts of Henry VII make mention of a Lord or Abbot of Misrule for nearly every Christmas in the reign [4]. Under Henry VIII a Lord was annually appointed, with one exception, until

---

[1] Cf. ch. x. Less dramatic performances are described for the 'guizards' of the Scottish Lowlands by R. Chambers, *Popular Rhymes of Scotland*, 169, for the 'mummers' of Ireland in *N. and Q.* 3rd series, viii. 495, for the 'mummers' of Yorkshire in *F. L.* iv. 162. The latter sweep the hearth, humming 'mumm-m-m.'

[2] *L. H. T. Accounts*, i. ccxl, 270, 327; ii. cx, 111, 320, 374, 430, 431; iii. 127. In 1504 is a payment 'to the barbour helit Paules hed quhen he wes hurt with the Abbot of Unresoun.' Besides the court Abbot, there was an 'Abbot of Unresone of Linlithgow' in 1501, who 'dansit to the king,' and an 'Abbot of Unresoun of the pynouris of Leith' in 1504. Such entries cease after the Scottish Act of Parliament of 1555 (cf. p. 181).

[3] Stowe, *Survey*, 37 'There was in the feast of Christmas in the King's house, wheresoever he was lodged, a Lord of Misrule or Master of Merry Disports; and the like had ye in the house of every nobleman of honour or good worship, were he

spiritual or temporal. Among the which, the Mayor of London and either of the Sheriffs had their several Lords of Misrule, ever contending, without quarrel or offence, who should make the rarest pastimes to delight the beholders. These Lords beginning their rule on Allhollons eve, continued the same til the morrow after the feast of the Purification, commonly called Candlemas-day. In all which space there were fine and subtle disguisings, masks and mummeries'; Holinshed (ed. 1587), iii. 1067 'What time [at Christmas], of old ordinarie course, there is alwaies one appointed to make sport in the court, called commonlie lord of misrule: whose office is not unknowne to such as haue beene brought up in noble mens houses, & among great house keepers which use liberall feasting in that season.' The sense of 'misrule' in this phrase is 'disorder'; cf. the 'uncivil rule' of *Twelfth Night*, ii. 3. 132.

[4] Collier, i. 48–55; Bentley, *Excerpt. Historica*, 90, 92; Leland,

1520[1]. From that date, the records are not available, but an isolated notice in 1534 gives proof of the continuance of the custom[2]. In 1521 a Lord of Misrule held sway in the separate household of the Princess Mary[3], and there is extant a letter from the Princess's council to Wolsey asking whether it were the royal pleasure that a similar appointment should be made in 1525[4]. Little information can be gleaned as to the functions of the Lord of Misrule during the first two Tudor reigns. It is clear that he was quite distinct from the officer known as the 'Master of the Revels,' in whose hands lay the preparation and oversight of disguisings or masks and similar entertainments. The Master of the Revels also makes his first appearance under Henry VII. Originally he seems to have been appointed only *pro hac vice*, from among the officials, such as the comptroller of the household, already in attendance at court[5]. This practice lasted well into the reign of Henry VIII, who was served in this capacity by such distinguished courtiers, amongst others, as Sir Henry Guildford and Sir Anthony Browne[6]. Under them the preparation of the revels and the custody of the properties were in the hands

Collectanea (ed. Hearne), iv. 255. The 'Lords' named are one Ringley in 1491, 1492, and 1495, and William Wynnesbury in 1508. In this year the terms 'Lordship' and 'Abbot' are both used. The 'Lord' got a fee each year of £6 13s. 4d. Also the queen (1503) gave him £1.

[1] Collier, i. 74, 76; Brewer, i. cxi. Wynnesbury was Lord in 1509, 1511 to 1515, and 1519, Richard Pole in 1516, Edmund Trevor in 1518, William Tolly in 1520. The fees gradually rise to £13 6s. 8d. and a 'rewarde' of £2. Madden, *Expenses of Princess Mary*, xxvi, enters a gift in 1520 'domino mali gubernatoris [? gubernationis] hospicii domini Regis.'

[2] Brewer, vii. 589.

[3] Madden, *op. cit.* xxviii. He was John Thurgood.

[4] Ellis, *Original Letters* (1st series), i. 270.

[5] Campbell, *Materials for Hist. of Hen. VII* (R. S.), i. 337; ii. 60,

83; Collier, i. 50; Yorke, *Hardwicke Papers*, 19. Payments are made for 'revels' or 'disguisings' to Richard Pudsey 'serjeant of the cellar,' Walter Alwyn, Peche, Jaques Haulte, 'my Lord Suff, my Lord Essex, my Lord Will[m], and other,' John Atkinson, Lewes Adam, 'master Wentworth.' In 1501 Jaques Hault and William Pawne are appointed to devise disguisings and morisques for a wedding. The term 'Master of the Revels' is in none of these cases used. But in an 'Order for sitting in the King's great Chamber,' dated Dec. 31, 1494 (*Ordinances and Regulations*, Soc. Antiq. 113), it is laid down that 'if the master of revells be there, he may sit with the chaplains or with the squires or gentlemen ushers.'

[6] *Revels Accounts* (Brewer, ii. 1490; iii. 1548), s. ann. 1510, 1511, 1512, 1513, 1515, 1517, 1522; Brewer, i. 718; ii. 1441; xiv. 2. 284; Kempe, 69; Collier, i. 68.

of a permanent minor official. At first such work was done in the royal Wardrobe, but under Henry VIII it fell to a distinct 'serjeant' who was sometimes, but not always, also 'serjeant' to the king's tents. In 1545, however, a permanent Master of the Revels was appointed in the person of Sir Thomas Cawarden, one of the gentlemen of the privy chamber [1]. Cawarden formed the Revels into a regular office with a clerk comptroller, yeoman, and clerk, and a head quarters, at first in Warwick Inn, and afterwards in the precinct of the dissolved Blackfriars, of which he obtained a grant from the king. This organization of the Revels endured in substance until after the Restoration [2]. Not unnaturally there were some jealousies and conflicts of authority between the permanent Master of the Revels and the annual Lord of Misrule, and this comes out amusingly enough from some of Cawarden's correspondence for 1551-3, preserved in the muniment room at Loseley. For the two Christmases during this period the Lordship of Misrule was held by George Ferrers, one of the authors of the *Mirrour for Magistrates* [3]; and Cawarden seems to have put every possible difficulty in the way of the discharge of his duties. Ferrers appealed to the lords of the council, and it took half a dozen official letters, signed by the great master of the household, Mr. Secretary Cecil, and a number of other dignitaries, to induce the Master of the Revels to provide the hobby horses and fool's coat and what not, that were required [4]. Incidentally this correspondence and the account books kept

---

Guildford is several times called 'master of the revels'; so is Harry Wentworth in 1510. In 1522 Guildford is 'the hy kountrolleler.' It was the 'countrowlore' at whose request Lydgate prepared one of his disguisings (p. 398).

[1] Rymer, xv. 62 'dedimus et concessimus eidem Thomae officium Magistri Iocorum Revelorum & Mascorum omnium & singularium nostrorum vulgariter nuncupatorum Revells & Masks.' The tenure of office was to date from March 16, 1544, and the annual fee was £10.

[2] Collier, i. 79, 131, 139, 153;

Kempe, 69, 73, 93, 101; *Molyneux Papers* (Hist. MS. Comm., seventh Rep.), 603, 614; Brewer, ii. 2. 1517; xiii. 2. 100; xiv. 2. 159, 284; xvi. 603; Halliwell, *A Collection of Ancient Documents respecting the Office of Master of the Revels* (1870); P. Cunningham, *Extracts from the Accounts of Revels at Court* (Sh. Soc. 1842).

[3] Kempe, 19; Collier, i. 147; Holinshed (*ut cit. supra*, p. 403); W. F. Trench, *A Mirror for Magistrates, its Origin and Influence*, 66, 76.

[4] Kempe, 23. One of Ferrers' letters to Cawarden is endorsed

by Cawarden give some notion of the sort of amusement
which the Lord of Misrule was expected to organize. In 1551
he made his entry into court 'out of the mone.' He had his
fool ' John Smith ' in a ' vice's coote' and a ' dissard's hoode,'
a part apparently played by the famous court fool, Will Somers.
He had a 'brigandyne'; he had his 'holds, prisons, and places
of execuc'on, his cannypie, throne, seate, pillory, gibbet,
hedding block, stocks, little ease, and other necessary incydents
to his person'; he had his 'armury' and his stables with
'13 hobby horses, whereof one with 3 heads for his person,
bought of the carver for his justs and challenge at Greenwich.' The masks this year were of apes and bagpipes, of
cats, of Greek worthies, and of 'medyoxes' ('double visaged,
th' one syde lyke a man, th' other lyke death ')[1]. The chief
difficulty with Cawarden arose out of a visit to be paid by the
Lord to London on January 4. The apparel provided for his
' viij counsellors' on that occasion was so 'insufficient ' that
he returned it, and told Cawarden that he had 'mistaken y^e
persons that sholde weere them, as Sr Robt Stafford and Thom^s
Wyndesor, w^h other gentlemen that stande also upon their
reputacõn, and wold not be seen in London, so torche-berer
lyke disgysed, for as moche as they are worthe or hope to be
worthe[2].' After all it took a letter from the council to get the
fresh apparel ready in time. It was ready, for Machyn's *Diary*
records the advent of the Lord and his 'consell' to Tower Wharf,
with a 'mores danse,' and the 'proclamasyon' made of him at the
Cross in Cheap, and his visit to the mayor and the lord treasurer, 'and so to Bysshopgate, and so to Towre warff, and toke
barge to Grenwyche[3].' Before the following Christmas of 1552
Ferrers was careful to send note of his schemes to Cawarden
in good time[4]. This year he would come in in 'blewe' out of
' *vastum vacuum*, the great waste.' The ' serpente with sevin

---

' Ferryrs, the Lorde Myserable, by
the Cunsell's aucketorryte.' Ferrers
solemnly heads his communications
' Qui est et fuit,' and alludes to the
king as ' our Founder.'
    [1] Kempe, 85.
    [2] Ibid. 28.
    [3] Machyn, 13.
    [4] Kempe, 32; Collier, i. 148;

W. F. Trench, *op. cit.* 21 ; D. N. B.
s. v. *William Baldwin*; G[uliel-
mus] B[aldwin] *Beware the Cat*
(1570, reprinted by Halliwell, 1864).
In this pamphlet Baldwin tells a
story heard by him at court 'the
last Christmas,' where he was with
' Maister Ferrers, then maister of
the King's Majesties pastimes.' The

heddes called hidra' was to be his arms, his crest a 'wholme bush' and his 'worde' *semper ferians*. Mr. Windham was to be his admiral, Sir George Howard his master of the horse, and he required six councillors, 'a divine, a philosopher, an astronomer, a poet, a phisician, a potecarie, a m^r of requests, a sivilian, a disard, John Smyth, two gentleman ushers, besides jugglers, tomblers, fooles, friers, and suche other.' Again there was a challenge with hobby horses, and again the Lord of Misrule visited London on January 6, and was met by Sergeant Vauce, Lord of Misrule to 'master Maynard the Shreyff' whom he knighted. He then proceeded to dinner with the Lord Mayor[1]. As he rode his cofferer cast gold and silver abroad, and Cawarden's accounts show that 'coynes' were made for him by a 'wyer-drawer,' after the familiar fashion of the Boy Bishops in France[2]. These accounts also give elaborate details of his dress and that of his retinue, and of a 'Triumph of Venus and Mars'[3]. In the following year Edward was dead, and 'neither Mary nor Elizabeth seems to have revived the appointment of a Lord of Misrule at court[4].

But the reign of the Lord of Misrule extended far beyond the verge of the royal palace. He was especially in vogue at those homes of learning, the Universities and the Inns of Court, where Christmas, though a season of feasting and *ludi*, had not yet become an occasion for general 'going down.' Anthony à Wood records him in several Oxford colleges, especially in Merton and St. John's, and ascribes his downfall, justly, no doubt, in part, to the Puritans[5]. At Merton he

date seems fixed to 1552 by a mention of 'Maister Willott and Maister Stremer, the one his [Ferrers'] Astronomer, the other his Divine' (cf. Kempe, 34). The pamphlet was probably printed in 1553 and suppressed.

[1] Machyn, 28; Stowe, *Annals*, 608. Abraham Fleming in Holinshed (ed. 1587), copying Stowe, transfers the events of this Christmas by mistake to 1551-2.

[2] Kempe, 53; cf. p. 369.

[3] Ibid. 47.

[4] The letter from Ferrers dated in

Kempe, 37 'Saynt John's Daye, ano 1553,' clearly belongs to the Christmas of 1552. The additional garments asked for therein are in the accounts for that year (Kempe, 52).

[5] A. Wood, *Athenae Oxonienses* (ed. Bliss), iii. 480 'The custom was not only observed in that [St. John's] college, but in several other houses, particularly in Merton College, where, from the first foundation, the fellows annually elected, about St. Edmund's day, in November, a Christmas lord, or lord of misrule, styled in their registers *Rex*

bore the title of *Rex fabarum* or *Rex regni fabarum*[1]. He was a fellow of the college, was elected on November 19, and held office until Candlemas, when the winter festivities closed with the *Ignis Regentium* in the hall. The names of various *Reges fabarum* between 1487 and 1557 are preserved in the college registers, and the last holder of the office elected in the latter year was Joseph Heywood, the uncle of John Donne, in his day a famous recusant[2]. At St. John's College a 'Christmas Lord, or Prince of the Revells,' was chosen up to 1577. Thirty years later, in 1607, the practice was for one year revived, and a detailed account of this experiment was committed to manuscript by one Griffin Higgs[3]. The Prince, who was chosen on All Saints' day, was Thomas Tucker. He

Fabarum and *Rex Regni Fabarum*; which custom continued until the reformation of religion, and then, that producing puritanism, and puritanism presbytery, the profession of it looked upon such laudable and ingenious customs as popish, diabolical and antichristian'; *Hist. and Antiq. of the Univ. of Oxford*, ii. 136, 's. a. 1557' mentions an oration 'de ligno et foeno' made by David de la Hyde, in praise of 'Mr. Jasper Heywood, about this time King, or Christmas Lord, of the said Coll. [Merton] being it seems the last that bore that commendable office. That custom hath been as ancient for ought that I know as the College itself, and the election of them after this manner. On the 19th of November, being the vigil of S. Edmund, king and martyr, letters under seal were pretended to have been brought from some place beyond sea, for the election of a king of Christmas, or Misrule, sometimes called with us of the aforesaid college, Rex Fabarum. The said letters being put into the hands of the Bachelaur Fellows, they brought them into the Hall that night, and standing, round the fire, there reading the contents of them, would choose the senior Fellow that had not yet borne that office, whether he was a Doctor of Divin-

ity, Law, or Physic, and being so elected, had power put into his hands of punishing all misdemeanours done in the time of Christmas, either by imposing exercises on the juniors, or putting into the stocks at the end of the Hall any of the servants, with other punishments that were sometimes very ridiculous. He had always a chair provided for him, and would sit in great state when any speeches were spoken, or justice to be executed, and so this his authority would continue till Candlemas, or much about the time that the Ignis Regentium was celebrated in that college'; *Life and Times* (O. H. S.), i. 423 'Fresh nights, carolling in public halls, Christmas sports, vanished, 1661.'

[1] The title is borrowed from the Twelfth - Night King; cf. p. 260. Perhaps 'Rex de Faba' was an early name for the Lord of Misrule at the English court. In 1334 Edward III made a gift to the minstrels 'in nomine Regis Fabae' (Strutt, 344).

[2] G. C. Brodrick, *Memorials of Merton College*, 46 and *passim*; B. W. Henderson, *Merton College*, 267.

[3] *The Christmas Prince* in 1607, printed in *Miscellanea Antiqua Anglicana* (1816); M. L. Lee, *Narcissus: A Twelfth Night Merriment*, xvii.

was installed on November 5, and immediately made a levy upon past and present members of the college to meet the necessary expenses. Amongst the subscribers was 'Mr. Laude.' On St. Andrew's day, the Prince was publicly installed with a dramatic 'deuise' or 'showe' called *Ara Fortunae*. The hall was a great deal too full, a canopy fell down, and the 'fool' broke his staff. On St. Thomas's day, proclamation was made of the style and title of the Prince and of the officers who formed his household [1]. He also ratified the 'Decrees and Statutes' promulgated in 1577 by his predecessor and added some rather pretty satire on the behaviour of spectators at college and other revels. On Christmas day the Prince was attended to prayers, and took the vice-president's chair in hall, where a boar's head was brought in, and a carol sung. After supper was an interlude, called *Saturnalia*. On St. John's day 'some of the Prince's honest neighbours of St. Giles's presented him with a maske or morris'; and the 'twelve daies' were brought in with appropriate speeches. On December 29 was a Latin tragedy of *Philomela*, and the Prince, who played Tereus, accidentally fell. On New Year's day were the Prince's triumphs, introduced by a 'shew' called *Time's Complaint*; and the honest chronicler records that this performance 'in the sight of the whole University' was 'a messe of absurdityes,' and that 'two or three cold plaudites' much discouraged the revellers. However, they went on with their undertaking. On January 10 were two shews, one called *Somnium Fundatoris*, and the other *The Seven Days of the Weeke*. The dearth in the city caused by a six weeks' frost made the President inclined to stop the revels, as in a time of 'generall wo and calamity'; but happily a thaw came, and on January 15 the college retrieved its reputation by a most successful public

---

[1] The Prince's designation was 'The most magnificent and re-nowned THOMAS by the fauour of Fortune, Prince of Alba Fortunata, Lord S^t. Iohn's, high Regent of ye Hall, Duke of S^t. Giles, Marquesse of Magdalens, Landgraue of ye Groue, County Palatine of ye Cloisters, Cheife Bailiffe of ye Beaumonts, high Ruler of Rome, Maister of the Mañor of Waltham, Gouernour of Gloster-greene, Sole Comaunder of all Titles, Turneaments and Triumphes, Superintendent in all Solemnities whatsoeuer.' His seal, a crowned and spotted dog, with the motto *Pro aris et focis*, bears the date 1469. Amongst his officers was a 'M^r of ye Reuells.' His Cofferer was Christopher Wren.

performance of a comedy *Philomathes*. *The Seven Days of the Weeke*, too, though acted in private, had been so good that the vice-chancellor was invited to see a repetition of it, and thus Sunday, January 17, was 'spent in great mirth.' On the Thursday following there was a little *contretemps*. The canons of Christ Church invited the Prince to a comedy called *Yuletide*, and in this 'many things were either ill ment by them, or ill taken by vs.' The play in fact was full of satire of 'Christmas Lords,' and it is not surprising that an apology from the dean, who was vice-chancellor that year, was required to soothe the Prince's offended feelings. Term had now begun, but the revels were renewed about Candlemas. On that day was a *Vigilate* or all-night sitting, with cards, dice, dancing, and a mask. At supper a quarrel arose. A man stabbed his fellow, and the Prince's stocks were requisitioned in deadly earnest. After supper the Prince was entertained in the president's lodging with 'a wassall called the five bells of Magdalen church.' On February 6, 'beeing egge Satterday,' some gentlemen scholars of the town brought a mask of *Penelope's Wooers* to the Prince, which, however, fell through; and finally, on Shrove Tuesday, after a shew called *Ira seu Tumulus Fortunae*, the Prince was conducted to his private chamber in a mourning procession, and his reign ended. Even yet the store of entertainment provided was not exhausted. On the following Saturday, though it was Lent, an English tragedy of *Periander* was given, the press of spectators being so great that '4 or 500' who could not get in caused a tumult. And still there remained 'many other thinges entended,' but unperformed. There was the mask of *Penelope's Wooers*, with the *State of Telemachus* and a *Controversy of Irus and his Ragged Company*. There were an *Embassage from Lubberland*, a *Creation of White Knights of the Order of Aristotle's Well*, a *Triumph of all the Founders of Colleges in Oxford*, not to speak of a lottery 'for matters of mirth and witt' and a court leet and baron to be held by the Prince. So much energy and invention in one small college is astonishing, and it was hard that Mr. Griffin Higgs should have to complain of the treatment meted out to its entertainers by the University at large. 'Wee found ourselves,' he says, '(wee will say justly)

taxed for any the least errour (though ingenious spirits would
have pardoned many things, where all things were entended
for their owne pleasure) but most vnjustly censured, and
envied for that which was done (wee daresay) indifferently
well.'

Amongst other colleges in which the Lord of Misrule was
regularly or occasionally chosen, Anthony à Wood names,
with somewhat vague references, New College and Magdalen[1].
To these may certainly be added Trinity, where the *Princeps
Natalicius* is mentioned in an audit-book of 1559[2]. But the
most singular of all the Oxford documents bearing on the
subject cannot be identified with any particular college. It
consists of a series of three Latin letters[3]. The first is
addressed by *Gloria in excelsis* to all mortals *sub Natalicia
ditione degentibus*. They are bidden keep peace during the
festal season and wished pleasant headaches in the mornings.
The vicegerent of *Gloria in excelsis* upon earth is an annually
constituted *praelatia*, that so a longer term of office may not
beget tyranny. The letter goes on to confirm the election to
the kingly dignity of Robertus Grosteste[4], and enjoins obedience to him *secundum Natalicias leges*. It is *datum in aere
luminoso supra Bethlemeticam regionem ubi nostra magnificentia
fuit pastoribus promulgata*. The second letter is addressed to
R[obert] Regi Natalicio and his *proceres* by *Discretio virtutum
omnium parens pariter ac regina*. It is a long discourse on the
value of moderation, and concludes with a declaration that
a moderate *laetitia* shall rule until Candlemas, and then give
way to a moderate *clerimonia*. The third is more topical and
less didactic in its tone. It parodies a papal letter to a royal

---

[1] Wood, *Hist. of Oxford (ut
supra*, p. 408), ii. 136, has the following note 'New Coll. in Cat. MSS.,
p. 371 . . . Magd. Coll. v. Heylin's
Diary, an. 1617, 1619 et 1620.'

[2] Warton, iii. 304 'pro prandio
Principis Natalicii eodem tempore
xiii[s]. ix[d].'

[3] H. H. Henson, *Letters relating
to Oxford in the fourteenth century*
in the Oxford Hist. Soc.'s *Collectanea*, i. 39. The learned editor
does not give the MS. from which

he takes the letters, but the rest of
his collection is from the fourteenth-
century *Brit. Mus. Royal MS.*
12 D, xi.

[4] 'Quocirca festi praesentis im-
minenti vigilia, vos ut accepimus
in loco potatorio, hora extraordinaria
prout moris est, unanimiter congregati, dominum Robertum Grosteste militem in armis scolasticis
scitis [Ed. satis] providum et ex-
pertum, electione concordi sus-
tulistis ad apicem regiae dignitatis.'

sovereign. *Transaetherius, pater patrum ac totius ecclesiasticae monarchiae pontifex et minister* complains, *R. Regi Natalicio,* of certain abuses of his rule. His *stolidus senescallus, madidus marescallus* and *parliamenti grandiloquus sed nugatorius prolocutor* have *ut plura possent inferre stipendia* assaulted and imprisoned on the very night of the Nativity, *Iohannem Curtibiensem episcopum.* In defence of these proceedings the Rex has pleaded *quasdam antiquas regni tui, non dico consuetudines, sed potius corruptelas.* Transaetherius gives the peccant officials three hours in which to make submission. If they fail, they shall be excommunicated, and Iohannes de Norwico, the warden of Jericho, will have orders to debar them from that place and confine them to their rooms. The letter is *datum in vertice Montis Cancari, pontificatus nostri anni non fluxibili sed aeterno.* I think it is clear that these letters are not a mere political skit, but refer to some actual Christmas revels. The waylaying of *Iohannes Curtibiensis episcopus* to make him 'pay his footing' is exactly the sort of thing that happened at the Feast of Fools, and the *non consuetudines, sed potius corruptelas* is the very language of the decretal of 1207 [1]. But surely they are not twelfth- or early thirteenth-century revels, as they must be if 'Robertus Grosteste' is taken literally as the famous bishop of Lincoln [2]. There was no *parliamenti prolocutor*, for instance, in his day. They are fourteenth-, fifteenth-, or even sixteenth-century fooling, in connexion with some *Rex Natalicius* who adopted, to season his jest, the name of the great mediaeval legislator against all such *ludi.*

At Cambridge an order of the Visitors of Edward VI in 1549 forbade the appointment of a *dominus ludorum* in any college [3]. But the prohibition did not endure, and more than one unsuccessful Puritan endeavour to put down Lords of Misrule is recorded by Fuller [4]. Little, however, is known of

---

[1] Cf. p. 279.

[2] Grosseteste probably became a student at Oxford before 1196. About 1214 he became Chancellor, and it seems hardly likely, as Mr. Stevenson thinks, that he would have been *rex natalicius* as late as †1233 (F. S. Stevenson, *Robert Grosseteste*, 8, 25, 110). There

were of course no colleges †1200; if *rex*, he was *rex* at a hall. But 1200 is an early date even in the history of the Feast of Fools.

[3] Cooper, *Annals of Cambridge,* ii. 32 ; *Stat. Acad. Cantab.* 161.

[4] Fuller, *Good Thoughts in Worse Times* (1646), 193 'Some sixty years since, in the University of Cam-

the Cambridge Lords; their bare existence at St. John's[1] and Christ's Colleges[2]; and at Trinity the fact that they were called *imperatores*, a name on the invention of which one of the original fellows of the college, the astronomer John Dee, plumes himself[3]. At schools such as Winchester and Eton, the functions of Lord of Misrule were naturally supplied by the Boy Bishop. At Westminster there was a *paedonomus*, and Bryan Duppa held the office early in the seventeenth century[4].

The revels of the Inns of Court come into notice in 1422, when the *Black Book* of Lincoln's Inn opens with the announcement *Ceux sont les nouns de ceux qe fuerunt assignes de con-*

bridge it was solemnly debated betwixt the Heads to debarre young schollers of that liberty allowed them in Christmas, as inconsistent with the Discipline of Students. But some grave Governors mentioned the good use thereof, because thereby, in twelve days, they more discover the dispositions of Scholars than in twelve moneths before'; *Hist. of Cambridge* (ed. M Prickett and J. Wright), 301 (s. a. 1610–11), describing a University Sermon by Wm. Ames, Fellow of Christ's, who 'had (to use his own expression) the place of a watchman for an hour in the tower of the University; and took occasion to inveigh against the liberty taken at that time, especially in such colleges who had lords of misrule, a pagan relic which (he said) as Polidore Vergil showeth, remaineth only in England.' W. Ames had, in consequence, to 'forsake his college.' Polydore Vergil, *de Inventoribus Rerum*, v. 2 (transl. Langley, f. 102ᵛ), speaks of 'the Christemass Lordes' of England.

[1] Cooper, *op. cit.* ii. 112; Baker, *St. John's*, ii. 573. Lords in 1545 and 1556.

[2] Ibid. ii. 111. A lord in 1566. Peile, *Christ's College*, 54, quotes payments of the time of Edward VI 'for sedge when the Christenmasse lords came at Candlemas to the Colledge with shewes'; 'for the lordes of S. Andrewes and

his company resorting to the Colledge.' These were perhaps from the city; cf. p. 419.

[3] Dee, *Compendious Rehearsal* (*Chronicle of John of Glastonbury*, ed. T. Hearne, 502), 'in that College also (by my advice and by my endeavors, divers ways used with all the other colleges) was their Christmas Magistrate first named and confirmed an Emperor. The first was one Mr. Thomas Dun, a very goodly man of person, stature and complexion, and well learned also.' Warton, iii. 302, describes a draught of the college statutes in *Rawl. MS.* 233, in which cap. xxiv is headed 'de Praefecto Ludorum qui Imperator dicitur,' and provides for the superintendence by the Imperator of the *Spectacula* at Christmas and Candlemas. But the references to the Imperator have been struck out with a pen, and the title altered to 'de Comoediis Ludisque in natali Christi exhibendis.' This is the title of cap. xxiv as actually issued in 1560 (Mullinger, *University of Cambridge*, 579). The earlier statutes of 1552 have no such chapter.

[4] H. King, *Funeral Sermon of Bishop Duppa* (1662), 34 'Here he had the greatest dignity which the School could afford put upon him, to be the Paedonomus at Christmas, Lord of his fellow scholars: which title was a pledge and presage that, from a Lord in jeast, he

tinuer yci le nowel [1]. They are mentioned in the *Paston Letters*
in 1451 [2], and in Sir Fortescue's *De laudibus Legum Angliae*
about 1463 [3]. Space compels me to be very brief in sum-
marizing the further records for each Inn.

Lincoln's Inn had in 1430 its four revels on All Hallows' day,
St. Erkenwold's (April 30), Candlemas and Midsummer day,
under a 'Master of the Revels.' In 1455 appears a 'marshal,'
who was a Bencher charged to keep order and prevent waste
from the last week of Michaelmas to the first of Hilary term.
Under him were the Master of the Revels, a butler and
steward for Christmas, a constable-marshal, server, and cup-
bearer. In the sixteenth century the 'grand Christmassings'
were additional to the four revels, and those of Candlemas
were called the 'post revels.' Christmas had its 'king.' In
1519 it was ordered that the 'king' should sit on Christmas
day, that on Innocents' day the 'King of Cokneys' [4] should
'sytt and haue due seruice,' and that the marshal should
himself sit as king on New Year's day. In 1517 some doors
had been broken by reason of 'Jake Stray,' apparently a
popular anti-king or pretender, and the order concludes,
'Item, that Jack Strawe and all his adherentes be from hens-
forth uttrely banyshed and no more to be used in Lincolles
Inne.' In 1520 the Bench determine 'that the order of
Christmas shall be broken up'; and from that date a 'solemn
Christmas' was only occasionally kept, by agreement with the
Temples. Both Lincoln's Inn and the Middle Temple had
a 'Prince,' for instance, in 1599. In 1616 the choice of a
'Lieutenant' at Christmas was forbidden by the Bench as
'not accordinge to the auncyant Orders and usages of the
House.' In 1624 the Christmas vacation ceased to be kept.
There were still 'revels' under 'Masters of the Revels' in
Michaelmas and Hilary terms, and there are notices of dis-
order at Christmas in 1660 and 1662. But the last 'Prince'

---

should, in his riper age, become
one in earnest'; cf. J. Sargeaunt,
Annals of Westminster School, 64.

[1] *Records of Lincoln's Inn : Black
Books*, i. 1.

[2] *Paston Letters*, i. 186. The
names of two gentlemen chosen

stewards this year at the Middle
and Inner Temples are mentioned.

[3] Fortescue, *de Laudibus*, cap. xlix.

[4] *N. E. D.* s. v. *Cockney*, supposes
the word to be here used in the
sense of 'cockered child,' 'mother's
darling.'

of Lincoln's Inn, was probably the Prince de la Grange of
1661, who had the honour of entertaining Charles II[1].

The Inner Temple held 'grand Christmasses' as well as
'revels' on All Saints', Candlemas, and Ascension days. The
details of the Christmas ceremonies have been put together from
old account books by Dugdale. They began on St. Thomas's
day and ended on Twelfth night. On Christmas day came in
the boar's head. On St. Stephen's day a cat and a fox were
hunted with nine or ten couple of hounds round the hall[2]. In
the first few days of January a banquet with a play and mask
was given to the other Inns of Court and Chancery. The
Christmas officers included a steward, marshal, butler, constable-marshal, master of the game, lieutenant of the tower,
and one or more masters of the revels. The constable-
marshal was the Lord of Misrule. He held a fantastic court
on St. Stephen's day[3], and came into hall 'on his mule' to
devise sport on the banquetting night. In 1523 the Bench
agreed not to keep Christmas, but to allow minstrels to those
who chose to stay. Soon after 1554 the Masters of Revels
cease to be elected[4]. Nevertheless there was a notable revel

---

[1] *Records of Lincoln's Inn: Black
Books*, i. xxx, 181, 190; ii. xxvii,
191; iii. xxxii, 440; W. Dugdale,
246; W. Herbert, 314; J. A.
Manning, *Memoirs of Rudyerd*, 16;
J. Evelyn, *Diary* (s. ann. 1661-2).
As an appendix to vol. iii of the
Black Book is reprinted Ἐγκυκλο-
χορεία, or *Universal Motion*, Being
part of that Magnificent Entertainment by the noble Prince de la
Grange, Lord Lieutenant of Lincoln's Inn. Presented to the High
and Mighty Charles II' (1662).
Evelyn mentions the 'solemne
foolerie' of the Prince de la Grange.
[2] Cf. p. 257.
[3] 'Supper ended, the Constable-
Marshall presenteth himself with
Drums afore him, mounted upon a
Scaffold, born by four men; and
goeth three times round about the
Harthe, crying out aloud "A Lorde,
a Lorde, &c."—Then he descendeth
and goeth to dance, &c., & after
he calleth his Court, every one by

name, in this manner: "Sir Francis
Flatterer, of Fowleshurst, in the
county of Buckingham. Sir Randle
Rackabite, of Rascall Hall, in the
County of Rakehell. Sir Morgan
Mumchance, of Much Monkery, in
the County of Mad Mopery. Sir
Bartholmew Baldbreech, of But-
tocke-bury, in the County of Breke-
neck"... About Seaven of the
Clocke in the Morning the Lord of
Misrule is abroad, and if he lack any
Officer or attendant, he repaireth
to their Chambers, and compelleth
them to attend in person upon him
after Service in the Church, to
breakfast, with Brawn, Mustard,
and Malmsey. After Breakfast
ended, his Lordship's power is in
suspence, until his personal presence
at night; and then his power is
most potent.'
[4] W. Dugdale, 153; Herbert, 205,
254; F. A. Inderwick, *Calendar of
the I. T. Records*, i. xxxiv, 3, 75,
171, 183.

in 1561 at which Lord Robert Dudley, afterwards earl of Leicester, was constable-marshal. He took the title of 'Palaphilﾑs, prince of Sophie,' and instituted an order of knights of Pegasus in the name of his mistress Pallas [1]. In 1594 the Inner Temple had an emperor,who sent an ambassador to the revels of Gray's Inn [2]. In 1627 the appointment of a Lord of Misrule led to a disturbance between the 'Temple Sparks' and the city authorities. The 'lieutenant' claimed to levy a 'droit' upon dwellers in Ram Alley and Fleet Street. The lord mayor intervened, an action which led to blows and the committal of the lieutenant to the counter, whence he escaped only by obtaining the mediation of the attorney-general, and making submission [3]. A set of orders for Christmas issued by the Bench in 1632 forbade 'any going abroad out of the Circuit of this House, or without any of the Gates, by any Lord or other Gentleman, to break open any House, or Chamber; or to take anything in the name of Rent, or a distress [4].'

The Middle Temple held its 'solemn revels' and 'post revels' on All Saints and Candlemas days, and on the Saturdays between these dates; likewise its 'solemn Christmasses [5].' An account of the Christmas of 1599 was written by Sir Benjamin Rudyerd under the title of *Noctes Templariae: or, A Briefe Chronicle of the Dark Reigne of the Bright Prince of Burning Love.* 'Sur Martino' was the Prince, and one 'Milorsius Stradilax' served as butt and buffoon to the company. A masque and barriers at court, other masques and comedies, a progress, a mock trial, a 'Sacrifice of Love,' visits to the Lord Mayor and to and from Lincoln's Inn, made up the entertainment [6]. In 1631 orders for Christmas

---

[1] G. Legh, *Accedens of Armory* (1562), describes the proceedings; cf. Dugdale, 151; Herbert, 248; Inderwick, *op. cit.* lxiv, 219. Machyn, 273, mentions the riding through London of this 'lord of mysrull' on Dec. 27.

[2] Cf. references for *Gesta Grayorum* in p. 417.

[3] Ashton, 155, quoting *The Reign of King Charles* (1655) 'A Lieutenant, which we country folk call a Lord of Misrule.' In the sixteenth century the lieutenant was only an officer of the constable-marshal.

[4] Dugdale, 149; Herbert, 201.

[5] Dugdale, 202, 205; Herbert, 215, 231, 235.

[6] J. A. Manning, *Memoirs of Rudyerd*, 9. Carleton wrote to Chamberlain on Dec. 29, 1601, that 'Mrs. Nevill, who played her prizes, and bore the belle away in the Prince de Amour's revels, is sworn maid of honour' (*Cal. S. P. Dom. Eliz.* 1601-3, 136).

government were made by the Bench[1]. In 1635 a Cornish gentleman, Francis Vivian, sat as Prince d'Amour. It cost him £2,000, 'but after his deposition he was knighted at Whitehall. His great day was February 24, when he entertained the Princes Palatine, Charles, and Rupert, with Davenant's masque of the *Triumphs of the Prince d'Amour*[2].

There is no very early mention of revels at Gray's Inn, but they were held on Saturdays between All Saints and Candlemas about 1529, and by 1550 the solemn observation of Christmas was occasionally used. In 1585 the Bench forbade that any one should ' in time of Christmas, or any other time, take upon him, or use the name, place, or commandment of *Lord*, or any such other like.[3]' Nevertheless in 1594 one of the most famous of all the legal ' solemn Christmasses ' was held at this Inn. Mr. Henry Helmes, of Norfolk, was ' Prince of Purpoole[4],' and he had the honour of presenting a mask before Elizabeth. This was written by Francis Davison, and Francis Bacon also contributed to the speeches at the revels. But the great glory of this Christmas came to it by accident. On Innocents' day there had been much confusion, and the invited Templarians had retired in dudgeon. To retrieve the evening 'a company of base and common fellows ' was brought in and performed 'a Comedy of Errors, like to Plautus his Menaechmus[5].' In 1617 there was again a Prince of Purpoole, on this occasion for the entertainment of Bacon himself as Lord Chancellor[6]. Orders of 1609 and 1628 mention re-

[1] Dugdale, 191.

[2] G. Garrard to Strafford (*Strafford Letters*, i. 507); Warton, iii. 321; Ward, iii. 173.

[3] Dugdale, 285; Herbert, 333; R. J. Fletcher, *Pension Book of Gray's Inn* (1901), xxviii, xxxix, xlix, 68 and passim.

[4] His full title was ' The High and Mighty Prince Henry, Prince of Purpoole, Arch-duke of Stapulia and Bernardia, Duke of High and Nether Holborn, Marquis of St. Giles and Tottenham, Count Palatine of Bloomsbury and Clerkenwell, Great Lord of the Cantons of Islington, Kentish Town, Paddington and Knightsbridge, Knight of the most heroical Order of the Helmet, and Sovereign of the same.'

[5] Halliwell - Phillipps, i. 122; Ward, ii. 27, 628; Sandys, 93; Spedding, *Works of Bacon*, viii. 235; S. Lee, *Life of Shakespeare*, 70; W. R. Douthwaite, *Gray's Inn*, 227; Fletcher, 107. A full description of the proceedings is in the *Gesta Grayorum* (1688), reprinted in Nichols, *Progresses of Elizabeth*, iii. 262.

[6] Douthwaite, *op. cit.* 234; Fletcher, 72, 299; Nichols, *Progresses of James I*, iii. 466. To this year belong the proceedings of ' Henry

spectively the 'twelve' and the 'twenty' days of Christmas as days of license, when caps may be doffed and cards or dice played in the hall [1]: and the duration of the Gray's Inn revels is marked by notices of Masters of the Revels as late as 1682 and even 1734 [2].

Nobles and even private gentlemen would set up a Lord of Misrule in their houses. The household regulations of the fifth earl of Northumberland include in a list of rewards usually paid about 1522, one of twenty shillings if he had an 'Abbot of Miserewll' at Christmas, and this officer, like his fellow at court, was distinct from the 'Master of the Revells' for whom provision is also made [3]. In 1556 the marquis of Winchester, then lord treasurer, had a 'lord of mysrulle' in London, who came to bid my lord mayor to dinner with 'a grett mene of musysyonars and dyssegyssyd' amongst whom 'a dullvyll shuting of fyre' and one 'lyke Deth with a dart in hand [4].' In 1634 Richard Evelyn of Wotton, high sheriff of Surrey and Sussex, issued 'Articles' appointing Owen Flood his trumpeter 'Lord of Misrule of all good Orders during the twelve dayes [5].' The custom was imitated by more than one municipal ape of gentility. The lord mayor and sheriffs of London had their Lords of Misrule until the court of common council put down the expense in 1554 [6]. Henry Rogers, mayor of Coventry, in 1517, and Richard Dutton, mayor of Chester, in 1567, entertained similar officers [7].

I have regarded the Lord of Misrule, amongst the courtly and wealthy classes of English society, as a direct offshoot from the vanished Feast of Fools. The ecclesiastical suggestion in the alternative title, more than once found, of 'Abbot

the Second,' Prince of Purpoole, printed by Nichols, *Eliz.* iii. 320, as the 'Second Part' of the *Gesta Grayorum*; cf. Hazlitt, *Manual*, 95, 161. 'Henry the Second, Prince of Graya and Purpulia,' was a subscriber to Minsheu's *Dictionary* (1617). An earlier Prince of Purpoole is recorded in 1587 (Fletcher, 78).

[1] Dugdale, 281, 286; Herbert, 334, 336.

[2] Douthwaite, *op. cit.* 243, 245.
[3] Percy, *N. H. B.* 344, 346.
[4] Machyn, 125.
[5] *Archaeologia*, xviii. 333; Ashton, 144. Other passages showing that lords of misrule were appointed in private houses are given by Hazlitt-Brand, i. 272.
[6] Ashton, 144; cf. p. 407.
[7] *Hist. of Cov.* in Fordun, *Scotichronicon*, ed. Hearne, v. 1450; Morris, 353.

of Misrule,' seems to justify this way of looking at the matter. But I do not wish to press it too closely. For after all the Lord of Misrule, like the Bishop of Fools himself, is only a variant of the winter 'king' known to the folk. In some instances it is difficult to say whether it is the folk custom or the courtly custom with which you have to do. Such is the 'kyng of Crestemesse' of Norwich in 1443[1]. Such are the Lords of Misrule whom Machyn records as riding to the city from Westminster in 1557 and Whitechapel in 1561[2]. And there is evidence that the term was freely extended to folk 'kings' set up, not at Christmas only, but at other times in the year[3]. It was a folk and a Christmas Lord whose attempted suppression by Sir Thomas Corthrop, the reforming curate of Harwich, got him into trouble with the government of Henry VIII in 1535[4]. And it was folk rather than courtly Lords which, when the reformers got their own way, were hardest hit by the inhibitions contained in the visitation articles of archbishop Grindal and others[5]. So this discussion, *per ambages atque aequora vectus*, comes round to the point at which it began. It is a far cry from Tertullian to Bishop Grosseteste and a far cry from Bishop Grosseteste to Archbishop Grindal, but each alike voices for his own day the relentless hostility of the austerer clergy during all ages to the ineradicable *ludi* of the pagan inheritance.

[1] Cf. p. 261.

[2] Machyn, 162, 274. The Westminster lord seems to have been treated with scant courtesy, for 'he was browth in-to the contur in the Pultre; and dyver of ys men lay all nyght ther.'

[3] Cf. p. 173.

[4] Brewer, ix. 364. The lord of misrule was chosen in the church 'to solace the parish' at Christmas.

[5] Cf. p. 181.

END OF VOL. I

THE MEDIAEVAL STAGE

VOLUME II

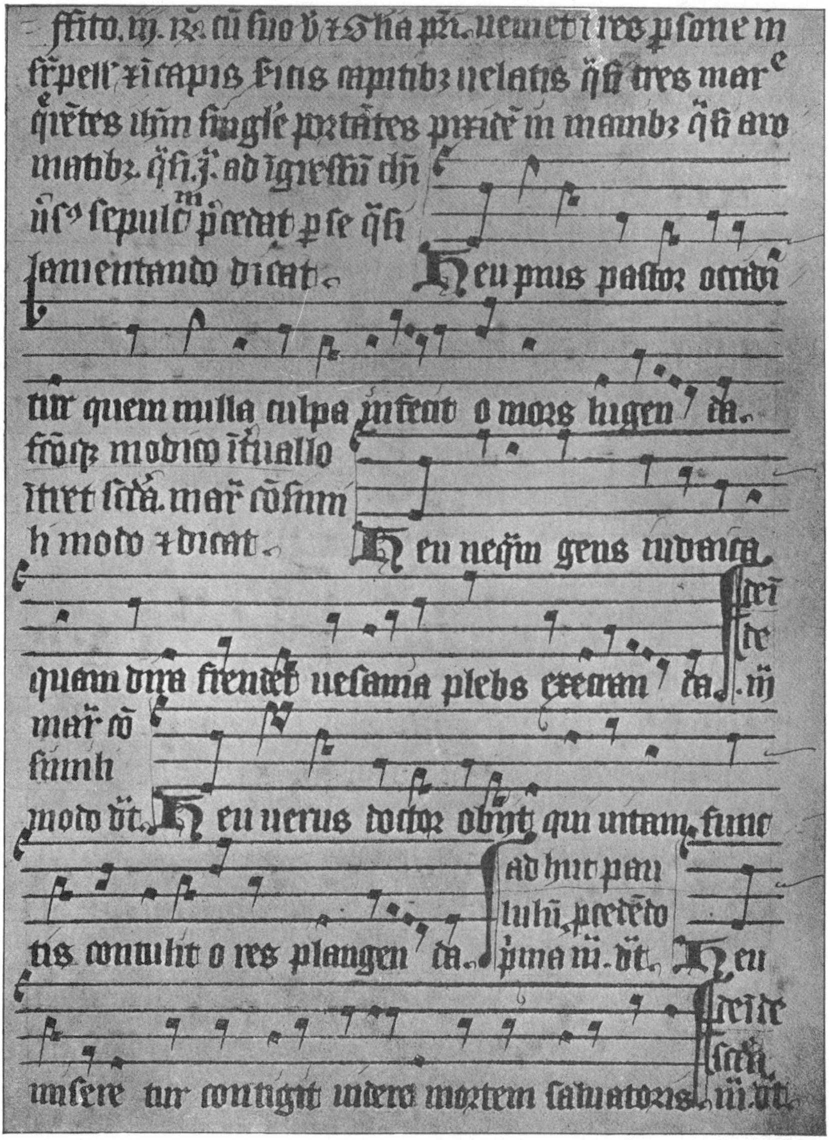

BEGINNING OF DUBLIN *Quem quaeritis*, FROM BODLEIAN RAWLINSON LITURGICAL MS. D. 4 (14TH CENTURY)

CONTENTS

VOLUME I

VOLUME II

BOOK III. RELIGIOUS DRAMA

BOOK IV. THE INTERLUDE

APPENDICES

CONTENTS

BOOK III

RELIGIOUS DRAMA

heʒe vpon a doune,
    þer al folk hit se may,
a mile from þe toune,
    aboute þe midday,
þe rode is vp arered ;
his frendes aren afered,
    ant clyngeþ so þe clay ;
þe rode stond in stone,
marie stont hire one,
    ant seiþ ' weylaway ' !

CHAPTER XVIII

LITURGICAL PLAYS

[*Bibliographical Note.* — The liturgical drama is fully treated by W. Creizenach, *Geschichte des neueren Dramas* (vol. i, 1893), Bk. 2; L. Petit de Julleville, *Les Mystères* (1880), vol. i. ch. 2; A. d'Ancona, *Origini del Teatro Italiano* (2nd ed. 1891), Bk. 1, chh. 3–6; M. Sepet, *Origines catholiques du Théâtre moderne* (1901), and by L. Gautier in *Le Monde* for Aug. and Sept. 1872. The studies of W. Meyer, *Fragmenta Burana* (1901), and C. Davidson, *English Mystery Plays* (1892), are also valuable. A. W. Ward, *History of English Dramatic Literature* (2nd ed. 1899), vol. i. ch. 1 deals very slightly with the subject. A good popular account is M. Sepet, *Le Drame chrétien au Moyen Age* (1878). Of older works, the introduction to E. Du Méril's *Origines latines du Théâtre moderne* (1849, facsimile reprint, 1896) is the best. The material collected for vol. ii of C. Magnin's *Origines du Théâtre* is only available in the form of reviews in the *Journal des Savants* (1846–7), and lecture notes in the *Journal général de l'Instruction publique* (1834–6). Articles by F. Clément, L. Deschamps de Pas, A. de la Fons-Melicocq, and others in A. N. Didron's *Annales archéologiques* (1844–72) are worth consulting; those of F. Clément are reproduced in his *Histoire de la Musique religieuse* (1860). There are also some notices in J. de Douhet, *Dictionnaire des Mystères* (1854). —The texts of the *Quem quaeritis* are to be studied in G. Milchsack, *Die Oster- und Passionsspiele*, vol. i (all published, 1880), and C. Lange, *Die lateinischen Osterfeiern* (1887). The former compares 28, the latter no less than 224 manuscripts. The best general collection of texts is that of Du Méril already named: others are T. Wright, *Early Mysteries and other Latin Poems* (1838); E. de Coussemaker, *Drames liturgiques du Moyen Age* (1860), which is valuable as giving the music as well as the words; and A. Gasté, *Les Drames liturgiques de la Cathédrale de Rouen* (1893). A few, including the important *Antichristus*, are given by R. Froning, *Das Drama des Mittelalters* (1891). The original sources are in most cases the ordinary service-books. But a twelfth-century manuscript from St. Martial of Limoges (*Bibl. Nat. Lat.* 1139) has four plays, a *Quem quaeritis*, a *Rachel*, a *Prophetae*, and the *Sponsus*. Facsimiles are in E. de Coussemaker, *Histoire de l'Harmonie au Moyen Age* (1852). A thirteenth-century manuscript from Fleury (*Orleans MS.* 178) has no less than ten, a *Quem quaeritis*, a *Peregrini*, a *Stella* in two parts, a *Conversio Pauli*, a *Suscitatio Lazari* and four *Miracula S. Nicholai*. Two later plays and fragments of three others are found in the famous thirteenth-century manuscript from Benedictbeuern (*Munich MS.* 19,486, printed in J. A. Schmeller, *Carmina Burana*, 3rd ed. 1894, with additional fragments in W. Meyer, *Fragmenta Burana*, 1901). This is probably the repertory of travelling goliardic clerks. The twelfth-century manuscript which preserves the three plays of Hilarius (*Bibl. Nat. Lat.* 11,331, printed in J. J. Champollion-Figeac, *Hilarii Versus et Ludi*, 1838) is of a similar character.—The tropes are fully dealt with by L. Gautier, *Hist. de la*

Poésie liturgique au Moyen Age, vol. i (all published, 1886), and W. H. Frere, *The Winchester Troper* (1894). I have not been able to see A. Reiners, *Die Tropen-, Prosen- und Präfations-Gesänge des feierlichen Hochamtes im Mittelalter* (1884). Antiquarian data are collected by H. J. Feasey, *Ancient English Holy Week Ceremonial* (1897), and A. Heales, *Easter Sepulchres,* in *Archaeologia,* vol. xlii. I have printed an important passage from the *Regularis Concordia* of St. Ethelwold (965–75) in Appendix O. The *Planctus Mariae* are treated by A. Schönbach, *Die Marienklagen* (1874), and E. Wechssler, *Die romanischen Marienklagen* (1893). W. Köppen, *Beiträge zur Geschichte der deutschen Weihnachtsspiele* (1893), and M. Sepet, *Les Prophètes du Christ* (1878), contain valuable studies of the evolution of the *Stella* and the *Prophetae* respectively. The relation of dramatic to iconic art in the Middle Ages is brought out by P. Weber, *Geistliches Schauspiel und kirchliche Kunst* (1894). A rather primitive bibliography is F. H. Stoddard, *References for Students of Miracle Plays and Mysteries* (1887).—Authorities forEnglish facts given without references in the present volume will be found in Appendices W and X.]

THE discussions of the first volume have often wandered far enough from the history of the stage. But two or three tolerable generalizations emerge. The drama as a living form of art went completely under at the break-up of the Roman world : a process of natural decay was accelerated by the hostility of Christianity, which denied the theatre, and by the indifference of barbarism, which had never imagined it. If anything of a histrionic tradition survived, it took the shape of pitiable farce, one amongst many heterogeneous elements in the *spectacula* of disreputable mimes. For the men of the Middle Ages, however, peasants or burghers, monks or nobles, such *spectacula* had a constant attraction : and the persistence of the deep-rooted mimetic instinct in the folk is proved by the frequent outcrops of primitive drama in the course of those popular observances which are the last sportive stage of ancient heathen ritual. Whether of folk or of minstrel origin, the *ludi* remained to the last alien and distasteful to the Church. The degradation of Rome and Constantinople by the stage was never forgotten ; nor the association with an heathenism that was glossed over rather than extinct: and though a working compromise inevitably tended to establish itself, it remained subject to perpetual protest from the austerer spirit in the counsels of the clergy.

It is the more remarkable that the present volume has to describe a most singular new birth of the drama in the very bosom of the Church's own ritual. One may look at the event as one will, either as an audacious, and at least partly successful, attempt to wrest the pomps of the devil to a spiritual service, or as an inevitable and ironical recoil of a barred human instinct within the hearts of its gaolers themselves. From either point of view it is a fact which the student of European culture cannot afford to neglect. And apart from its sociological implications, apart from the insight which it gives into the temper of the folk and into the appeal of religion, it is of the highest interest as an object lesson in literary evolution. The historian is not often privileged to isolate a definite literary form throughout the whole course of its development, and to trace its rudimentary beginnings, as may here be done, beyond the very borders of articulate speech.

The dramatic tendencies of Christian worship declared themselves at an early period [1]. At least from the fourth century, the central and most solemn rite of that worship was the Mass, an essentially dramatic commemoration of one of the most critical moments in the life of the Founder [2]. It is

---

[1] On these tendencies generally, see Davidson, 130; Ward, i. 32; R. Rosières, *Société française au Moyen Age*, ii. 228; E. King, *Dramatic Art and Church Liturgy* (*Dublin Review*, cxxv. 43). Mediaeval liturgiologists such as Belethus, Durandus, and Honorius of Autun (*P.L.* clxxii), lay great stress on the symbolical aspect of ritual and ceremonial. J. M. Robertson, *The Gospel Mystery-Play* (*The Reformer*, N.S. iii (1901), 657), makes an ingenious attempt to show that the earlier gospel narratives of the Passion, those of Saints Matthew and Mark, are based upon a dramatic version. This, he thinks, to have been on classical lines, and to have been performed liturgically until about the second century, when it was dropped in deference to the ascetic views of the stage then prevalent (cf. vol. i. p. 11). But the narrative, with its short speeches, its crowd of characters and its sufferings 'coram populo' cannot, on the face of it, be derived from a

classical drama. A nearer parallel would be the Graeco-Jewish 'Εξαγωγή of Ezechiel (first century B.C., cf. Ward, i. 3). The Gospel narrative is, no doubt, mainly 'a presentation' of dramatic action and dialogue'; but this may be because it was built up around *Logia*. Of external evidence for Mr. Robertson's view there is none. The ritual of the first two centuries was probably a very simple one; cf. F. E. Warren, *Liturgy of the Ante-Nicene Church*, 54. The earliest liturgical dramas, even in the Greek churches, and those only guessed at, are of the fourth (cf. p. 206). Mr. Robertson claims support from *Galatians*, iii. 1 οἷς κατ' ὀφθαλμοὺς Ἰησοῦς Χριστὸς προεγράφη ἐσταυρωμένος. Lightfoot, however, declares that the meaning of προγράφειν is 'write up in public,' 'placard,' 'proclaim.' If it cannot, as he says, mean 'paint,' still less can it mean 'represent dramatically.'

[2] Duchesne, 47: A. V. G. Allen, *Christian Institutions*, 515.

his very acts and words that day by day throughout the year the officiating priest resumes in the face of the people. And when the conception of the Mass developed until instead of a mere symbolical commemoration it was looked upon as an actual repetition of the initial sacrifice, the dramatic character was only intensified. So far as the Canon of the Mass goes, this point needs no pressing. But the same liturgical principle governs many other episodes in the order of the mediaeval services. Take, for example, the ritual, of Gallican origin, used at the dedication of a church [1]. The bishop and his procession approach the closed doors of the church from without, but one of the clergy, *quasi latens*, is placed inside. Three blows with a staff are given on the doors, and the anthem is raised *Tollite portas, principes, vestras et elevamini, portae aeternales, et introibit Rex gloriae*. From within comes the question *Quis est iste rex gloriae?* and the reply is given *Dominus virtutum ipse est Rex gloriae*. Then the doors are opened, and as the procession sweeps through, he who was concealed within slips out, *quasi fugiens*, to join the train. It is a dramatic expulsion of the spirit of evil. A number of other instances are furnished by the elaborate rites of Holy week. Thus on Palm Sunday, in commemoration of the entry into Jerusalem, the usual procession before Mass was extended, and went outside the church and round the church-yard or close bearing palms, or in their place sprigs of yew, box, or withies, which the priest had previously blessed [2].

[1] Duchesne, 393, 469, with the *Ordo dedicationis Ecclesiae* from a ninth-century Metz *Sacramentary* there printed; Maskell, *Monum. Rit. Eccl. Angl.* (1882) i. cccxxvi, 196, with text from *Sarum Pontifical*. The ceremonies are symbolically explained by Hugo of St. Victor, *de Sacramentis*, ii. 5. 3 (*P. L.* clxxvi, 441), who says, 'Interrogatio inclusi, ignorantia populi.'

[2] Duchesne, 236; Martene, iii. 71; Gasté, 69; Feasey, 53; *Use of Sarum*, i. 59; *Sarum Missal*, 258; *Sarum Processional*, 47; *York Missal*, i. 84; *York Processional*, 148. The custom is described in the *Peregrinatio Silviae* (Du-

chesne, 486) as already in use at Jerusalem in the fourth century. 'Etiam cum coeperit esse hora unde-cima, legitur ille locus de evangelio, ubi infantes cum ramis vel palmis occurrerunt Domino, dicentes: *Benedictus qui venit in nomine Domini*. Et statim levat se epi-scopus et omnis populus porro: inde de summo monte Oliveti totum pedibus itur. Nam totus populus ante ipsum cum ymnis vel anti-phonis, respondentes semper: *Bene-dictus qui venit in nomine Domini*. Et quotquot sunt infantes in hisdem locis, usque etiam qui pedibus ambu-lare non possunt, quia teneri sunt, in collo illos parentes sui tenent,

The introduction of a *Palmesel* might make the ceremony more dramatic still [1]. Some of the texts used were of a prophetic character, and the singer of these was occasionally dressed as a prophet [2]. At the doors of the church the procession was greeted by boys stationed upon the roof of the porch, and certain French uses transferred to the occasion the dedication solemnity of *Tollite portas* just described [3]. The reading of the gospel narratives of the Passion, which on Palm Sunday, on the Monday or Tuesday, and the Wednesday in Holy week and on Good Friday preceded the Gospel proper, was often resolved into a regular oratorio. A tenor voice rendered the narrative of the evangelist, a treble the sayings of Jews and disciples, a bass those of Christ himself [4]. To particular episodes of these Passions special dramatic action was appropriated. On Wednesday, at the words *Velum templi scissum est*, the Lenten veil, which since the first Sunday in Lent had hidden the sanctuary from the sight of the people, was dropped to the ground [5]. On Good Friday the

---

omnes ramos tenentes, alii palmarum, alii olivarum; et sic deducitur episcopus in eo typo quo tunc Dominus deductus est. Et de summo monte usque ad civitatem, et inde ad Anastase per totam civitatem, totum pedibus omnes, sed et si quae matronae sunt aut si qui domini, sic deducant episcopum respondentes, et sic lente et lente, ne lassetur populus; porro iam sera pervenitur ad Anastase.'

[1] Cf. ch. xiv.

[2] Collier, i. 82; Feasey, 68, 75, quoting payments 'for the prophets.' their 'raiment,' 'stages' for them, &c., from sixteenth-century Revels and churchwardens' accounts. The *Sarum Processional*, 50 (from eds. 1508, 1517), has 'finito evangelio, unus puer ad modum prophetae indutus, stans in aliquo eminenti loco, cantat lectionem propheticam modo quo sequitur.' Then come alternating passages between the 'propheta' and 'tres clerici.' Perhaps the latter were also sometimes disguised, but the *Sarum Processional*, as well as the thirteenth-century *Consuetu-*

dinary and the *York Missal* (*MS. D*), all specify that the clergy, other than the prophet, shall be 'habitu non mutato.' Several of the London records given by Mr. Feasey mention an 'angel,' and one of them a 'chylde that playde a messenger.' A Coutances Order of 1573 (Gasté, 74) forbids 'spectacula . . . cum habitibus inhonestis' at the Gospel during Mass on Palm Sunday.

[3] Martene, iii. 72; Gasté, 72; R. Twigge, *Mediaeval Service Bks. of Aquitaine* (*Dublin Review*, cxv. 294; cxvii. 67); Pearson, ii. 296.

[4] *Sarum Missal*, 264. The *York Missal*, i. 102, says, for Good Friday, 'Diaconus legat Passionem,' but *MS. D.* adds 'vel legatur a tribus Presbyteris, si sic ordinatum erit.' Payments for the singers of the Passion are quoted from churchwardens' accounts (1447-1562) by Feasey, 81. The singing was sometimes done from the rood loft.

[5] Feasey, 17; *Use of Sarum*, i. 140 'quarta autem feria ante pascha dum passio domini legitur ad prolacionem ipsius clausulae *Velum*

words *Partiti sunt vestimenta* were a signal for a similar bit of by-play with a linen cloth which lay upon the altar [1]: Maundy Thursday had its commemorative ceremony of the washing of feet [2]; while the *Tenebrae* or solemn extinction, one after another, of lights at the Matins of the last three days of the week, was held to symbolize the grief of the apostles and others whom those lights represented [3].

These, and many other fragments of ceremonial, have the potentiality of dramatic development. Symbolism, mimetic action, are there. The other important factor, of dialogued speech, is latent in the practice of antiphonal singing. The characteristic type of Roman chant is that whereby the two halves of the choir answer one another, or the whole choir answers the single voice of the *cantor*, in alternate versicle and respond [4]. The antiphon was introduced into Italy by St. Ambrose of Milan. It had originated, according to tradition, in Antioch, had been in some relation to the histrionic tendencies of Arianism, and was possibly not altogether uninfluenced by the traditions both of the Greek tragic chorus and of Jewish psalmody [5].

---

templi scissum est: praedictum velum in area presbiterii decidat.' The same rubric is in the Wells *Ordinale* (H. E. Reynolds, *Wells Cathedral*, 42).

[1] J. W. Legg, *Westminster Missal* (H.B.S.), 1469; G. F. Aungier, *Hist. and Antiq. of Syon Monastery*, 350; Lanfranc, *Decreta pro Ord. S. Bened.* (*P.L.* cl. 465) 'Ubi dicitur *Partiti sunt vestimenta mea sibi*, sint duo de indutis iuxta altare, hinc et inde trahentes ad se duos pannos qui ante officium super altare missi fuerant, linteo tamen remanente subtus missale'; *Leofric's Missal* (Exeter, eleventh century), 261 'hac expleta statim duo diaconi nudant altare sindone quae prius fuerit sub evangelio posita in modum furantis. Aliqui vero, antequam legatur passio domini, praeparant sindones duas sibi coherentes et in eo versu ubi legitur: *Partiti sunt vestimenta*, scindunt hinc inde ipsas sindones desuper altare in modum furantis, et secum auferunt';

York Missal, i. 102 'hic distrahantur linteamina super altare connexa'; *Sarum Missal*, 323 'hic accedant duo ministri in superpelliceis, unus ad dextrum et alius ad sinistrum cornu altaris; et inde duo linteamina amoveant quae ad hoc super altare fuerant apposita.' I find the custom in Aquitaine (*Dublin Review* (1897), 366), and in Hungary (Dankó, *Vetus Hymnarium Eccles. Hungariae*, 534).

[2] Martene, iii. 99; Feasey, 107; Wordsworth, 184.

[3] Feasey, 84; Wordsworth, 290.

[4] Strictly speaking the *Antiphon* is begun by one half of the choir and finished by the other; the *Responsorium* is a solo with a short refrain sung by the choir, like the secular *carole*; cf. ch. viii, and *Use of Sarum*, i. 307; Dankó, *Vetus Hymnarium Eccl. Hung.* 11.

[5] Duchesne, 108; Davidson, 134; F. E. Warren, *Liturgy of the Ante-Nicene Church*, 74.

At any rate, it lent itself naturally to dialogue, and it is from the antiphon that the actual evolution of the liturgical drama starts. The course of that evolution must now be followed.

The choral portions of the Mass were stereotyped about the end of the sixth century in the *Antiphonarium* ascribed to Gregory the Great [1]. This compilation, which included a variety of antiphons arranged for the different feasts and seasons of the year, answered the needs of worship for some two hundred years. With the ninth century, however, began a process, which culminated in the eleventh, of liturgical elaboration. Splendid churches, costly vestments, protracted offices, magnificent processions, answered especially in the great monasteries to a heightened sense of the significance of cult in general, and of the Eucharist in particular [2]. Naturally ecclesiastical music did not escape the influence of this movement. The traditional *Antiphonarium* seemed inadequate to the capacities of aspiring choirs. The Gregorian texts were not replaced, but they were supplemented. New melodies were inserted at the beginning or end or even in the middle of the old antiphons. And now I come to the justification of the statement made two or three pages back, that the beginnings of the liturgical drama lie beyond the very borders of articulate speech. For the earliest of such adventitious melodies were sung not to words at all, but to vowel sounds alone. These, for which precedent existed in the Gregorian *Antiphonarium*, are known as *neumae* [3]. Obviously the next stage was to write texts, called generically 'tropes,' to them; and towards the end of the ninth century three more or less independent schools of trope-writers grew up. One, in northern France, produced Adam of St. Victor; of another,

[1] Frere, vi. The Gregorian *Liber Antiphonarius* is in *P.L.* lxxviii. 641.

[2] Radulphus Glaber (+ 1044), iii. 4 (Bouquet, *Rerum Gallic. et Francic. Script.* x. 29) 'Igitur infra supradictum millesimum tertio iam fere imminente anno, contigit in universo pene terrarum orbe, praecipue tamen in Italia et in Galliis, innovari Ecclesiarum Basilicas, licet pleraeque decenter locatae minime indiguissent.' Aemulabatur tamen quaeque gens Christicolarum adversus alteram decentiore frui. Erat enim instar ac si mundus ipse excutiendo semet, reiecta vetustate, passim candidam ecclesiarum vestem induerit.'

[3] Ekkehardus, *Vita B. Notkeri Balbuli,* c. xvi (Goldast, *Rerum Alaman. Script.* i. 235) 'Iubilus, id est neuma ... si autem tristitiae fuerit oratio, ululatus dicitur, si vero gaudii, iubilus.'

at the Benedictine abbey of St. Gall near Constance, Notker
and Tutilo are the greatest names ; the third, in northern
Italy, has hitherto been little studied. The *Troparia* or collections of tropes form choir-books, supplementary to the
Antiphonaria. After the thirteenth century, when trope-
writing fell into comparative desuetude, they become rare ;
and such tropes as were retained find a place in the ordinary
service-books, especially the later successor of the *Antiphonarium*, the *Graduale*. The tropes attached themselves in
varying degrees to most of the choral portions of the Mass.
Perhaps those of the *Alleluia* at the end of the *Graduale* are
in themselves the most important. They received the specific
names, in Germany of *Sequentiae*, and in France of *Prosae*,
and they include, in their later metrical stages, some of the
most remarkable of mediaeval hymns. But more interesting
from our particular point of view are the tropes of the *Officium*
or *Introit,* the antiphon and psalm sung by the choir at the
beginning of Mass, as the celebrant approaches the altar [1].

Several *Introit* tropes take a dialogue form. The following is a
ninth-century Christmas example ascribed to Tutilo of St. Gall [2].

' Hodie cantandus est nobis puer, quem gignebat ineffabiliter
ante tempora pater, et eundem sub tempore generavit inclyta
mater.

[1] Gautier, *Les Tropes*, passim ; *Winchester Troper*, vi ; Dankó, *Vetus Hymnarium Eccles. Hungariae*, 15 ; Julleville, *Myst.* i. 21 ; Creizenach, i. 47. Gautier, i, defines a trope, ' Qu'est-ce qu'un Trope ? C'est l'interpolation d'un texte liturgique,' and M. Gerbert, *de cantu et musica sacra* (1774), i. 340 ' Tropus, in re liturgica, est versiculus quidam aut etiam plures ante inter vel post alios ecclesiasticos cantus appositi.' Of earlier writers, cf. Durandus, iv. 5 ' Est autem proprie tropus quidam versiculus qui in praecipuis festivitatibus cantatur immediate ante introitum quasi quoddam praeambulum et continuatio ipsius introitus.' Gautier, 111, describes a large number of Tropers ; Frere, *Winchester Troper*, xxvii, xxx, those of English uses from Win- chester, Canterbury, Worcester, St. Albans, Dublin ; Pamelius, *Liturgicon* (1609), ii. 611 an English Troper in the library of St. Bavon's, Ghent. Amongst tropes in the wider sense are included the *farsurae* (vol. i. p. 277). Many of the later tropes are trivial, indecent, or profane. They are doubtless the work of *goliardi* (vol. i. p. 60).

[2] *St. Gall MS.* 484, f. 13 (ninth century) ; cf. Gautier, 34, 62, 139, 218 ; *Winchester Troper*, xvi ; Meyer, 34. It is also in the Winchester Tropers (tenth–eleventh century), and the Canterbury Troper (fourth century), and is printed therefrom in *Winchester Troper*, 4, 102. Here it is divided between two groups of *Cantores*, and has the heading ' Versus ante officium canendi in die Natalis Domini.'

Int[errogatio].

quis est iste puer quem tam magnis praeconiis dignum vociferatis ? dicite nobis ut collaudatores esse possimus. *Resp[onsio].*

hic enim est quem praesagus et electus symmista dei ad terram venturum praeuidens longe ante praenotavit, sicque praedixit.'

The nature of this trope is obvious. It was sung by two groups of voices, and its closing words directly introduce the *Introit* for the third mass (*Magna missa*) on Christmas day, which must have followed without a break [1]. It is an example of some half a dozen dialogued *Introit* tropes, which might have, but did not, become the starting-point for further dramatic evolution [2]. Much more significant is another trope of unknown authorship found in the same St. Gall manuscript [3]. This is for Easter, and is briefly known as the *Quem quaeritis.* The text, unlike that of the *Hodie cantandus,* is based closely upon the Gospels. It is an adaptation to the form of dialogue of the interview between the three Maries and the angel at the tomb as told by Saints Matthew and Mark [4].

'Quem quaeritis in sepulchro, [o] Christicolae ?

Iesum Nazarenum crucifixum, o caelicolae.

non est hic, surrexit sicut praedixerat.

ite, nuntiate quia surrexit de sepulchro.

Resurrexi [5].'

This is the earliest and simplest form of the *Quem quaeritis.*

---

[1] The *Introit* is : ' Puer natus est nobis, et filius datus est nobis : cuius imperium super humerum eius, et vocabitur nomen eius magni consilii angelus. *Ps.* Cantate domino canticum novum.'

[2] Gautier, 219, prints a dialogued trope for a feast of St. Peter from an eleventh-century troper of St. Martial of Limoges : the *Winchester Troper,* 6, 103, has one for St. Stephen's day (Winchester) and one for St. John the Evangelist's (Canterbury). Meyer, 35, calls attention to the dialogued Christ-

mas *versus sacerdotales* in Hartker' tenth-century St. Gall *Antiphona-rium* (J. M. Thomasius, *Opera,* i 187).

[3] *St. Gall MS.* 484, f. 11; printed and facsimiled by Gautier, 216, 220.

[4] *S. Matthew* xxviii. 1-7 ; *S. Mark* xvi. 1-7.

[5] The *Introit* is : ' Resurrexi et adhuc tecum sum, alleluia : posuisti super me manum tuam, alleluia ; mirabilis facta est scientia tua, alleluia, alleluia. *Ps.* Domine, probasti me.'

It recurs, almost unaltered, in a tenth-century troper from St. Martial of Limoges [1]. In eleventh-century tropers of the same church it is a little more elaborate [2].

'TROPUS IN DIE.

Quem quaeritis in sepulchro, Christicolae?

Ihesum Nazarenum crucifixum, o caelicole.

non est hic, surrexit sicut praedixerat,
ite, nuntiate quia surrexit. Alleluia.

ad sepulchrum residens angelus nuntiat resurrexisse Christum:

en ecce completum est illud quod olim ipse per pro-
phetam dixerat ad patrem taliter inquiens,

Resurrexi.'

Here the appended portion of narrative makes the trope slightly less dramatic. Yet another addition is made in one of the Limoges manuscripts. Just as the trope introduces the *Introit*, so it is itself introduced by the following words:

'Hora est, psallite. iube, dompnus, canere.
eia, eia, dicite.'

As M. Gautier puts it, the trope is troped [3].

In the Easter *Quem quaeritis* the liturgical drama was born, and to it I shall return. But it must first be noted that it was so popular as to become the model for two very similar tropes belonging to Christmas and to the Ascension. Both of these are found in more than one troper, but not earlier, I believe, than the eleventh century. I quote the Christmas trope from a St. Gall manuscript [4].

---

[1] Lange, 22, from *Bibl. Nat. Lat. MS.* 1240, f. 30b. As to date (923–34) and *provenance* of the MS., I follow H. M. Bannister in *Journal of Theological Studies* (April, 1901). Lange, 4, considers it an eleventh-century *Antiphonar* from Beaune.

[2] Printed by Frere, 176; cf. Gautier, 219. The version in Lange, 20, is incomplete. The Limoges Tropers (*Bibl. Nat.* 887, 909, 1084, 1118, 1119, 1120, 1121),

all of the eleventh century, are described by Gautier, 111; cf. p. 29.

[3] *Bibl. Nat.* 1118, f. 40v; cf. Gautier, 226; Frere, 176.

[4] *Bodl. Douce MS.* 222, f. 6 (eleventh century; cf. Gautier, 136), printed and facsimiled by Gautier, 215, 219. Du Méril, *Or. Lat.* 149, gives it from a Limoges Troper (*B.N.* 909, f. 9): it is also in *B.N.* 1118, f. 8vo, and probably the other

'*In Natale Domini ad Missam sint parati duo diaconi induti dalmaticis, retro altare dicentes*

Quem quaeritis in praesepe, pastores, dicite ?

Respondeant duo cantores in choro

salvatorem Christum Dominum, infantem pannis involutum, secundum sermonem angelicum.

Item diaconi

adest hic parvulus cum Maria, matre sua, de qua, vaticinando, Isaïas Propheta : ecce virgo concipiet et pariet filium. et nuntiantes dicite quia natus est.

Tunc cantor dicat excelsa voce

alleluia, alleluia. iam vere scimus Christum natum in terris, de quo canite, omnes, cum Propheta dicentes :

Puer natus est.'

The Ascension trope is taken from an English troper probably belonging to Christ Church, Canterbury [1].

'Quem cernitis ascendisse super astra, o Christicolae?

Ihesum qui surrexit de sepulchro, o caelicolae.

iam ascendit, ut praedixit, ascendo ad patrem meum et
    patrem vestrum, deum meum et deum vestrum.

alleluia :

regna terrae, gentes, linguae, conlaudate dominum :

quem adorant caeli cives in paterno solio :

deo gratias dicite eia.'

I return now to the Easter *Quem quaeritis.* In a few churches this retained its position at the beginning of Mass, either as an *Introit* trope in the strict sense, or, which comes to much the same thing, as a chant for the procession which

Limoges MSS. Frere, 145, gives it from the twelfth-century St. Magloire Troper (*B.N.* 13,252), and R. Twigge, in *Dublin Review* (1897), 362, from a fifteenth-century breviary of Clermont-Ferrand (*Cl. F. MS.* 67). Here it is sung by two boys, and near the altar after the Te Deum at Matins. According to Gautier, 123, it is also in the late eleventh-century Nevers Troper (*B.N.* 9449).

A. xiv (eleventh century). It comes between an illumination of the Ascension and the heading ' In Die Ascensionis Domini.' It is also in the St. Magloire Troper (*B.N.* 13,252, f. 10ᵛ) under the heading ' In Ascensione Tropi ad Processionem,' and in the St. Martial of Limoges Tropers (Gautier, 219 ; Lange, 20). Martene, iii. 193, describes it as sung in the procession before Mass at Vienne.

[1] Frere, 110, from *Cott. MS. Calig.*

immediately preceded. This was the use of the Benedictine abbey of Monte Cassino at the beginning of the twelfth century, of that of St. Denys in the thirteenth [1], and of the church of St. Martin of Tours in the fifteenth [2]. Even in the seventeenth century the *Quem quaeritis* still appears in a Paris manuscript as a ' *tropus* [3],' and Martene records a practice similar to that of Monte Cassino and St. Denys as surviving at Rheims in his day [4].

But in many tropers, and in most of the later service-books in which it is found, the *Quem quaeritis* no longer appears to be designed for use at the Mass. This is the case in the only two tropers of English use in which, so far as I know, it comes, the Winchester ones printed by Mr. Frere [5]. I reproduce the earlier of these from the Bodleian manuscript used by him [6].

---

[1] Martene, iv. 147 ' " Post processionem," *addunt Dionysianae consuet.* [thirteenth century], " ascendant iuxta Sancta Sanctorum quidam bene cantantes, alii in dextro latere, alii in sinistro latere assistentes, bene et honorifice tropas scilicet : *Quem quaeritis* ; coniubilantes, et sibi invicem respondentes; et cum intonuerint, *Quia surrexi*, dicens, *Patri*, mox Archicantor et duo. socii eius assistentes in choro regias virgas in manibus tenentes, incipiant officium." Hunc ritum accepisse videntur a Cassinensibus, quorum Ordinarium [before 1105] haec habet : " Processione finita, vadat Sacerdos post altare, et versus ad chorum dicat alta voce, *Quem quaeritis ?* et duo alii Clerici stantes in medio chori respondeant : *Iesum Nazarenum ;* et Sacerdos : *Non est hic ;* illi vero conversi ad chorum dicant : *Alleluia*. Post haec alii quatuor cantent tropos, et agatur missa ordine suo." ' As usual in *Ordinaria* (cf. e. g. p. 309) only the opening words of the chants are given. A similar direction is contained in *MS. Casinense*, 199, a twelfth-century breviary (*Bibliotheca Casinensis*, iv. 124) : cf. also Lange, 21, 23.

[2] Martene, iii. 173 ; Lange, 24

(Tours i).

[3] Lange, 26. Cf. the account of the Vienne *Quem quaeritis* (p. 26).

[4] Martene, iv. 148.

[5] Mr. Frere does not print any *Introit* tropes from the Worcester, St. Albans, and Dublin tropers : a leaf is unfortunately missing from the Canterbury troper (Frere, 107) where the *Quem quaeritis* might have come. It is not amongst the few tropes taken by Pamelius, *Liturgicon* (1609), ii. 611, from the English troper at St. Bavon's, Ghent (Frere, 142). As the *Concordia Regularis* was partly based on Ghent customs (cf. p. 307), I should gladly know more of this.

[6] *Bodl. MS.* 775 ; described by Frere, xxvii, as *MS. E* ' Its date lies between 979 and 1016, since Ethelred is mentioned as reigning sovereign in the Litany on f. 18ᵛ, and in consequence it has sometimes been called " The Ethelred Troper." Also, as it has the Dedication Festival on the 24th of November, it is probably anterior to the re-dedication of the Cathedral on Oct. 20, 980, since this day became subsequently the Dedication Festival.' A facsimile from the MS. was published by the *Palaeographical Society* (Series ii. pl. iii), and it was suggested that it

'ANGELICA DE CHRISTI RESURRECTIONE.

Quem quaeritis in sepulchro, Christicolae?

Sanctarum mulierum responsio.

Ihesum Nazarenum crucifixum, o caelicola!

Angelicae voces consolatus.

non est hic, surrexit sicut praedixerat,

ite, nuntiate quia surrexit, dicentes :

Sanctarum mulierum ad omnem clerum modulatio :

allcluia! rcsurrcxit Dominus hodie,

leo fortis, Christus filius Dei! Deo gratias dicite, eia!

Dicat angelus:

venite et videte locum ubi positus erat Dominus,

alleluia! alleluia!

Iterum dicat angelus :

cito euntes dicite discipulis quia surrexit Dominus,

alleluia! alleluia!

Mulieri una voce canant iubilantes :

surrexit Dominus de sepulchro,

qui pro nobis pependit in ligno.'

In this manuscript, which is dated by Mr. Frere in 979 or 980, the text just quoted is altogether detached from the Easter day tropes. Its heading is rubricated and immediately follows the tropes for Palm Sunday. It is followed in its turn, under a fresh rubric, by the ceremonies for Holy Saturday, beginning with the *Benedictio Cerei.* From the second, somewhat later Cambridge manuscript, probably of the early eleventh century, the Holy Saturday ceremonies have disappeared, but the *Quem quaeritis* still precedes and does not follow the regular Easter tropes, which are headed *Tropi in die Christi Resurrectionis* [1]. The precise position which the

is in an early eleventh-century hand, but possibly copied an earlier text. But surely it would have been brought up to date on such a matter as the Dedication Festival.

[1] *C.C.C. Cambridge MS.* 473, of the middle of the eleventh century, described by Frere, xxvii, as *MS. CC.* The text of the *Quem quaeritis* differs slightly from that of the *Bodl.*

MS. and does not appear to be quite complete. It is facsimiled by Frere (pl. 26[a]). The printed text in Frere, 17, represents both versions; that in Manly, i. xxi, follows the *Bodl. MS.* Both Frere and Manly have 'Angelice uocis consolatio' where the *Bodl. MS.*, as I read it, has 'Angelice uoces consolatus' (clearly in error).

Quem quaeritis was intended to take in the Easter services is not evident from these tropers by themselves. Fortunately another document comes to our assistance. This is the *Concordia Regularis*, an appendix to the *Rule* of St. Benedict intended for the use of the Benedictine monasteries in England reformed by Dunstan during the tenth century. The *Concordia Regularis* was drawn up by Ethelwold, bishop of Winchester, as a result of a council of Winchester held at some uncertain date during the reign of Edgar (959–79); it may fairly be taken for granted that it fixed at least the Winchester custom. I translate the account of the *Quem quaeritis* ceremony, which is described as forming part, not of the Mass, but of the third Nocturn at Matins on Easter morning [1].

'While the third lesson is being chanted, let four brethren vest themselves. Let one of these, vested in an alb, enter as though to take part in the service, and let him approach the sepulchre without attracting attention and sit there quietly with a palm in his hand. While the third respond is chanted, let the remaining three follow, and let them all, vested in copes, bearing in their hands thuribles with incense, and stepping delicately as those who seek something, approach the sepulchre. These things are done in imitation of the angel sitting in the monument, and the women with spices coming to anoint the body of Jesus. When therefore he who sits there beholds the three approach him like folk lost and seeking something, let him begin in a dulcet voice of medium pitch to sing *Quem quaeritis*. And when he has sung it to the end, let the three reply in unison *Ihesu Nazarenum*. So he, *Non est hic, surrexit sicut praedixerat. Ite, nuntiate quia surrexit a mortuis*. At the word of this bidding let those three turn to the choir and say *Alleluia! resurrexit Dominus!* This said, let the one, still sitting there and as if recalling them, say the anthem *Venite et videte locum*. And saying this, let him rise, and lift the veil, and show them the place bare of the cross, but only the cloths laid there in which the cross was

---

[1] A full account of the *Concordia Regularis* and extracts from the Latin text are in Appendix O.

wrapped. And when they have seen this, let them set down the thuribles which they bare in that same sepulchre, and take the cloth, and hold it up in the face of the clergy, and as if to demonstrate that the Lord has risen and is no longer wrapped therein, let them sing the anthem *Surrexit Dominus de sepulchro,* and lay the cloth upon the altar. When the anthem is done, let the prior, sharing in their gladness at the triumph of our King, in that, having vanquished death, He rose again, begin the hymn *Te Deum laudamus.* And this begun, all the bells chime out together.'

The liberal *scenario* of the *Concordia Regularis* makes plain the change which has come about in the character of the *Quem quaeritis* since it was first sung by alternating half-choirs as an *Introit* trope [1]. Dialogued chant and mimetic action have come together and the first liturgical drama is, in all its essentials, complete.

I am not quite satisfied as to the relations of date between the *Concordia Regularis* and the Winchester tropers, or as to whether the *Quem quaeritis* was intended in one or both of these manuscripts for use at the Easter Matins [2]. But it is clear that such a use was known in England at any rate before the end of the tenth century. It was also known in France and in Germany: the former fact is testified to by the *Consuetudines* of the monastery of St. Vito of Verdun [3]; the

[1] I cannot understand why Mr. Frere, xvi, thinks that the *Quem quaeritis* was 'a dramatic dialogue which came to be used as a trope to the *Introit* of Easter: but at Winchester it kept its independent place.' It is used as a trope a century before the date of the *Concordia Regularis.*

[2] Why is the *Quem quaeritis* in the *Bodl. MS.* apparently on Good Friday? Perhaps this was an irregular use reformed by Bp. Ethelwold. If so the *C. R.* must be about 980 or later. This is not impossible (cf. App. O). In the later *C.C.C.C. MS.* the *Q. q.* might, I think, from its position be intended for Easter Matins. The version described in the *C. R.* differs slightly from that of the tropers.

[3] Martene, iv. 299 'Saeculo, ut aiunt, x scriptae': cf. Douhet, 849. Martene, iii. 173, cites another Matins version from a 'vetustissimum rituale' of Poitiers. If this is identical with the 'pontificale vetustissimum : annorum circiter 800' mentioned in his list of authorities (i. xxii) it may be earlier than the tenth century. It is certainly not the 'liber sacramentorum annorum 900 circiter' with which Douhet, 848, would identify it. The Pontificale was used by Martene in his edition of 1738; about the first edition of 1700-6, I cannot say. This version is not in Lange, and, as the omission of the usual first line is curious, I print it below (p. 29).

latter by the occurrence of the *Quem quaeritis* in a troper of Bamberg, where it has the heading *Ad visitandum sepulchrum* and is followed by the Matins chant of *Te Deum* [1].

The heading of the Bamberg version and the detailed description of the *Concordia Regularis* bring the *Quem quaeritis* drama into close relations with the Easter 'sepulchre' [2]. They are indeed the first historical notices of the ceremony so widely popular during the Middle Ages. Some account of the Easter sepulchre must accordingly be inserted here, and its basis shall be the admirably full description of St. Ethelwold [3]. He directs that on Good Friday all the monks shall go *discalceati* or shoeless from Prime 'until the cross is adored' [4]. In the principal service of the day, which begins at Nones, the reading of the Passion according to St. John and a long series of prayers are included. Then a cross is made ready and laid upon a cushion a little way in front of the altar. It is unveiled, and the anthem *Ecce lignum crucis* is sung. The abbot advances, prostrates himself, and chants the seven penitential psalms. Then he humbly kisses the cross. His example is followed by the rest of the monks and by the clergy and congregation. St. Ethelwold proceeds :—

'Since on this day we celebrate the laying down of the body of our Saviour, if it seem good or pleasing to any to follow on similar lines the use of certain of the religious, which is worthy of imitation for the strengthening of faith in the unlearned vulgar and in neophytes, we have ordered it on this wise. Let a likeness of a sepulchre be made in a vacant part of the altar, and a veil stretched on a ring which may hang there until the adoration of the cross is over. Let the deacons who previously carried the cross come and wrap it in a cloth

---

[1] Lange, 29; cf. Creizenach, i. 49.

[2] The Verdun *Consuetudines* do not. The burial and resurrection of the cross clearly formed no part of the Good Friday and Easter rites. The dialogue takes place 'in subterraneis specubus,' i.e. the crypt, and the representatives of the Maries return to the choir 'cruce vacua nuntiantes: *Surrexit Dominus*' (Martene, iv. 299).

[3] Appendix O.

[4] Bare feet continued to be the rule for the *Adoratio Crucis*. An exception is at Exeter, where, according to Pearson, ii. 296, they were forbidden, cf. Feasey, 115.

in the place where it was adored [1]. Then let them carry it back, singing anthems, until they come to the place of the monument, and there having laid down the cross as if it were the buried body of our Lord Jesus Christ, let them say an anthem. And here let the holy cross be guarded with all reverence until the night of the Lord's resurrection. By night let two brothers or three, or more if the throng be sufficient, be appointed who may keep faithful wake there chanting psalms.'

The ceremony of the burial or *Depositio Crucis* is followed by the *Missa Praesanctificatorum*, the Good Friday communion with a host not consecrated that day but specially reserved from Maundy Thursday; and there is no further reference to the sepulchre until the order for Easter day itself is reached, when St. Ethelwold directs that 'before the bells are rung for Matins the sacristans are to take the cross and set it in a fitting place.'

In the *Concordia Regularis*, then, the *Depositio Crucis* is a sequel to the *Adoratio Crucis* on Good Friday. The latter ceremony, known familiarly to the sixteenth century as 'creeping to the cross,' was one of great antiquity. It was amongst the Holy week rites practised at Jerusalem in the fourth century [2], and was at an early date adopted in Rome [3]. But the sepulchre was no primitive part of it [4]; nor is it

---

[1] St. Ethelwold's Latin is atrocious, but I think that the sepulchre was made on the altar, not in the hollow of it, and covered from sight until wanted by a veil let down all round it from a circular support above. Cf. the Latin text in Appendix O: perhaps it is corrupt.

[2] *Peregrinatio Silviae* in Duchesne, 490. The object of adoration was a fragment of the true Cross, 'sanctum lignum crucis.' The Invention of the Cross by St. Helena is put by tradition †326. Doubtless many other churches obtained a fragment, and used it for the same purpose: cf. Feasey, 116. Thus the cross used at Rome was 'lignum pretiosae crucis' (Duchesne, 465: cf. his ed. of the *Liber Pontificalis*, i. 374).

[3] Duchesne, 238. For the mediaeval ceremony, cf. Feasey, 114; Pearson, ii. 293; Milchsack, 121; Rock, iii. 2. 241; Martene, iii. 129; iv. 137; *Sarum Missal*, 328; *York Missal*, i. 105; *York Manual*, 156, and the Durham extract in Appendix P: for that of modern Rome, Malleson and Tuker, ii. 271.

[4] The *sepulchrum* is not in the *Sacramentarium Gelasianum* (†seventh century, ed. H. A. Wilson, 77); nor the *Sacramentum Gregorianum* (†eighth century, *P. L.* lxxviii. 86), 'qua salutata et reposita in loco suo'; nor in the Roman *Ordines* collected by Mabillon (*P. L.* lxxviii) nor in those added by Duchesne, 451, 464. The *Ordines* of 954 and 963 repeat the Gregorian formula,

possible to trace either the use which served St. Ethelwold as a model [1], or the home or date of the sepulchre itself. It is unlikely, however, that the latter originated in England, as it appears almost simultaneously on the continent, and English ritual, in the tenth century, was markedly behind and not in advance of that of France and Germany [2]. St. Ethelwold speaks of it as distinctively monastic but certainly not as universal or of obligation amongst the Benedictine communities for whom he wrote. Nor did the *Concordia Regularis* lead to its invariable adoption, for when Ælfric adapted St. Ethelwold's work for the benefit of Eynsham about 1005 he omitted the account of the sepulchre [3], and it is not mentioned in Archbishop Lanfranc's Benedictine *Constitutions* of 1075 [4]. At a later date it was used by many

which is expanded by those of 1215 and 1319 into 'in suo loco super altare.' There is no mention of the *sepulchrum* in the Gallican liturgical books collected by Mabillon (*P. L.* lxxii). Of English books Leofric's *Exeter Missal* (tenth century, ed. F. E. Warren) has no *Sepulchrum*; nor the *Missal* of St. Augustine's Canterbury (†1100, ed. M. Rule), 'reposita in loco solito'; nor the *Missal* of Robert of Jumièges (ninth and tenth century, ed. H. A. Wilson for *H. B. Soc.*). Pearson, ii. 316, suggests that the cross used for adoration was the great rood usually placed in the rood-loft, but sometimes 'super altare.'

[1] Ethelwold's *Concordia Regularis* was largely founded on that of Benedict of Aniane (†817; cf. Miss Bateson in *E. H. Review*, ix. 700), but there is no Easter week *ordo* in this (*P. L.* ciii. 701) nor in the same writer's *Memoriale* or *Ordo Monasticus* (*P. L.* lxvi. 937: cf. his *Vita*, c. viii, in *Acta SS.* Feb. ii. 618). Ethelwold also borrowed customs from Fleury and Ghent (Appendix O). The *sepulchrum* is not mentioned in the *Consuetudines Floriacenses* (tenth century, ed. De Bosco, *Floriac. Vet. Bibl.* (1605), 390); cf. Creizenach, i. 49: nor in the description of a thirteenth-century *coutumier*

in Rocher, *Hist. de l'Abbaye de St.-Benoît-sur-Loire*, 323. The only Fleury *Quem quaeritis* is of a late type in a thirteenth-century MS.; cf. p. 32. At Ghent, however, an inventory of treasures remaining at St. Bavon's after a Norman invasion (1019-24) includes 'tabulas de sepulchro 23,' which appear to be distinct from *reliquiae* 'de sepulchro Domini' and 'de operculo ligneo quod super corpus ipsius positum fuit in sepulchro' (*Neues Archiv*, viii. 374). Did the possession of these 'reliquiae' suggest to the monks of St. Bavon's the construction of an Easter sepulchre?

[2] It is merely a guess to say St. Gall. Schübiger, *Sängerschule St. Gallens*, 69, mentions the sepulchre there, but gives no very early notice. The sepulchre was known in the Eastern, as well as the Western Church, and for all I know may have come from Jerusalem (Feasey, 177). As to date, Weber, 32, suggests that pictorial representations of the Maries at the tomb show the influence of the dramatic *Visitatio Sepulchri* as far back as the ninth century. His chief point is that the Maries carry *turribula* (cf. p. 25, n. 5).

[3] *E. H. Review*, ix. 706.

[4] *P. L.* cl. 465 'adorata ab omni-

Benedictine houses, notably by the great Durham Priory [1] ; but the Cistercians and the Carthusians, who represent two of the most famous reforms of the order, are said never to have adopted it, considering it incompatible with the austerity of their rule [2]. On the other hand it was certainly not, in mediaeval England, confined to monastic churches. The cathedrals of Salisbury [3], York [4], Lincoln [5], Hereford [6], Wells [7], all of which were served by secular canons, had their sepulchres, and the gradual spread of the Sarum use probably brought a sepulchre into the majority of parish churches throughout the land [8].

There are naturally variations and amplifications of the sepulchre ceremonial as described by St. Ethelwold to be recorded. The *Depositio Crucis*, instead of preceding the *Missa Praesanctificatorum*, was often, as in the Sarum use,

---

bus cruce, portitores eius elevantes eam incipiant antiphonam *Super omnia ligna cedrorum*, ct sic vadant ad locum ubi eam collocare debent.' This does not exclude a sepulchre, but probably the *locus* was an altar which might serve as a *statio* for the processions 'ad crucifixum' ordered on Easter Saturday after vespers and thrice a day through Easter week. Such processions continued in later ritual to visit the cross after its *Elevatio* on Easter morning : cf. *York Manual*, 177.

[1] See the description of the ceremony by a sixteenth-century eye-witness in Appendix P. The *sepulchrum* was also used by the Bridgettines of Sion monastery, an order of reformed Benedictine nuns (G. F. Aungier, *Hist. of Syon Monastery*, 350).

[2] J. D. Chambers citing J. B. Thiers, *De Expositione S. Sacramenti*, iii. 19.

[3] See the extracts from Sarum service-books in Appendix Q.

[4] *York Missal*, i. 106; *York Manual*, 163, 170.

[5] Wordsworth, 278.

[6] *Hereford Missal* (ed. Henderson), 96.

[7] H. E. Reynolds, *Wells Cathedral*, 32.

[8] The fullest accounts of the Easter sepulchre in England are those by H. J. Feasey, *Ancient English Holy Week Ceremonial*, 129, and A. Heales, *Easter Sepulchres: their Object, Nature, and History* in *Archaeologia*, xlii. 263 ; cf. also *Monumenta Vetusta* (Soc. of Antiquaries), iii. pll. xxxi, xxxii ; Parker, *Glossary of Architecture*, s.v. Sepulchre; M. E. C. Walcott, *Sacred Archaeology*, s.v. Easter Sepulchre ; T. F. Dyer, *Church Lore Gleanings*, 219; W. Andrews, *Old Church Lore*, iii ; J. D. Chambers, *App.* xxiv ; Micklethwaite, 52; Rock, iii. 2. 92, 240, 251. Continental *ordines* and notices may be found in Martene, iii. 131, 172, 178 ; iv. 141, 145 ; Milchsack, 41, 121 ; Pearson, ii. 295; Wetzer and Welte, *Kirchen-Lexicon*, s.v. Grab ; J. Dankó, *Vetus Hymn. Eccl. Hungariae*, 535, 579. I have not seen this writer's *Die Feier des Osterfestes* (Wien, 1872). On representations of the sepulchre in mediaeval art, cf. P. Weber, 32, and the miniature from Robert of Jumièges' *Missal* (ed. F. E. Warren for *H. B. Soc.* pl. viii).

transferred to the end of Vespers, which on Good Friday followed the *Missa* without a break[1]. The *Elevatio* regularly took place early on Easter morning before Matins. The oldest custom was doubtless that of the *Regularis Concordia*, according to which the cross was removed from the sepulchre secretly by the sacristans, since this is most closely in agreement with the narrative of the gospels. But in time the *Elevatio* became a function. The books of Salisbury and York provide for it a procession with the antiphons *Christus resurgens* and *Surrexit Dominus*. Continental rituals show considerable diversity of custom[2]. Perhaps the most elaborate ceremonials are those of Augsburg and Würzburg, printed by Milchsack. In these the *Tollite portas* procession, which we have already found borrowed from the dedication of churches for Palm Sunday, was adapted to Easter day[3]. But the old tradition was often preserved by the exclusion or only partial admission of the populace to the *Elevatio*. In the Augsburg ritual just quoted, all but a few privileged persons are kept out until the devil has been expelled and the doors solemnly opened[4]. A curious light is thrown upon this by a decree of the synod of Worms in 1316, which orders that the 'mystery of the resurrection' shall be performed before the *plebs* comes

[1] At Exeter on the other hand Vespers on both Good Friday and Easter Eve were sung before the Sepulchre; and so with the Hours at Tours (Feasey, 130).

[2] Martene, iii. 179; Milchsack, 122; Lange, 135. The latter gives a Passau fifteenth-century version which ends 'quibus finitis stantes ante altare, mutua caritate se invicem deosculentur, dicentes: *Surrexit dominus vere. Et apparuit symoni.* Dicatur una oratio de resurrectione. Statim fiat pulsatio.' The Easter greeting and kiss of peace were in use, either before or after Matins at many churches (Martene, iii. 171, 180) and do not depend upon the sepulchre.

[3] Milchsack, 128, 135; cf. Meyer, 64. The *Ordo Augustensis* of 1487 directs that a procession shall go from the sepulchre 'per ambitum vel cimeterium . . . usque ad ultimam ianuam, quae claudatur.' Here the *Tollite portas* dialogue is held with the 'levita iunior, vel alius in figura diaboli grossa voce.' On the other hand, in the *Ordo Wirceburgensis* of 1564 the procession knocks at the door from inside, and the respondent 'loco Sathanae' is without.

[4] 'Sacerdos . . . antequam congregetur chorus, cum processione sibi paucorum adiunctorum . . . foribus ecclesiae clausis, secretius tollat sacramentum de sepulchro'; cf. the fifteenth-century Passau *Breviary* (Lange, 135) 'clam surgitur' and the *Ordo Sepulturae* in the *Missalis Posoniensis* of 1341 (Dankó, 579) 'laicis exclusis.' I have not noticed any such limitation in English rubrics later than the *Concordia Regularis*.

into the church, and gives as a reason the crowds caused by a prevalent superstition that whoever saw the crucifix raised would escape for that year 'the inevitable hour of death'[1].

A widespread if not quite universal innovation on the earlier use was the burial, together with the cross or crucifix, of a host, which was consecrated, like that used in the *Missa Praesanctificatorum*, on Maundy Thursday. This host was laid in a pyx[2], monstrance[3], or cup[4], and sometimes in a special image, representing the risen Christ with the cross or *labarum* in his hands, the breast of which held a cavity covered with beryl or crystal[5]. Within the sepulchre both the host and the crucifix were laid upon or wrapped in a fine linen napkin.

The actual structure of the sepulchre lent itself to considerable variety. St. Ethelwold's *assimilatio quaedam sepulchri* upon a vacant part of the altar may have been formed, like that at Narbonne several centuries later, by laying together some of the silver service-books[6]. There are other examples of a sepulchre at an altar, and it is possible that in some of

[1] Milchsack, 119 'quum a nostris antecessoribus ad nos pervenerit, ut in sacra nocte dominicae resurrectionis ad sustollendam crucifixi imaginem de sepulchro, ubi in parasceve locata fuerat, nimia vilorum et mulierum numerositas, certatim sese comprimendo, ecclesiam simul cum canonicis et vicariis introire nitantur, opinantes erronee, quod si viderent crucifixi imaginem sustolli, evaderent hoc anno inevitabilem mortis horam. His itaque obviantes statuimus, ut resurrectionis mysterium ante ingressum plebis in ecclesiam peragatur': cf. Pearson, ii. 298.

[2] A Finchale inventory of 1481 (J. T. Fowler, *Trans. of Durham and North. Arch. Soc.* iv. 134) includes 'Item 1 pixis argentea cum coopertorio et ymagine crucifixi in summitate coopertorii pro corpore x¹ deferendo in passione x¹.' A pyx was also used in the Sarum rite (Appendix Q).

[3] Feasey, 165; Dankó, *Vet. Hymn. Eccl. Hung.* 535.

[4] *York Manual*, 174 'cuppa in qua est sacramentum.'

[5] At Durham (Appendix P) and at Lincoln (Wordsworth, 278); cf. Feasey, 164; Heales, 307. The image 'cum corona spinea' used at York (*York Manual*, 170) was of course the crucifix. A Reformation record of 1566 at Belton, Lincolnshire, speaks of 'a sepulker with little Jack broken in pieces' (Feasey, 165). Either a mere image or a mechanical puppet (cf. p. 158) may be meant. The *labarum* is the sign of the risen Christ in the later versions of the *Quem quaeritis*; cf. p. 35. It figures in nearly all paintings of the Resurrection.

[6] Narbonne *Ordinarium* (†1400) 'levent cum filo pannum, qui est super libros argenti super altare in figura sepulcri' (Martene, iii. 172; Lange, 65); Le Mans, *Ordinarium* 'Tunc tres clerici accedentes ad altare cum reverentia sublevent palium cum quo sepulchrum fuerit coopertum' (Lange, 66); cf. Pearson, ii. 293.

these the altar itself may have been hollow and have held the
sacred deposit. Sometimes the high altar was used, but
a side-altar was naturally more convenient, and at St. Lawrence's, Reading, the 'sepulchre awlter' was in the rood-loft[1].
The books were a primitive expedient. More often the sepulchre was an elaborate carved shrine of wood, iron, or silver.
If this did not stand upon the altar, it was placed on the north
side of the sanctuary or in a north choir aisle. In large
churches the crypt was sometimes thought an appropriate
site[2]. Often the base of the sepulchre was formed by the
tomb of a founder or benefactor of the church, and legacies
for making a structure to serve this double purpose are not
uncommon in mediaeval wills. Such tombs often have a
canopied recess above them, and in these cases the portable
shrine may have been dispensed with. Many churches have
a niche or recess, designed of sole purpose for the sepulchre[3].
Several of these more elaborate sepulchres are large enough to be
entered, a very convenient arrangement for the *Quem quaeritis*[4];
a few of them are regular chapels, more than one of which is
an exact reproduction of the Holy Sepulchre at Jerusalem, and
is probably due to the piety of some local pilgrim[5]. Wood,
metal, or stone, permanent or movable, the sepulchre was
richly adorned with paintings and carvings of the Passion and
the Resurrection, with Easter texts, with figures of censer-
swinging angels and sleeping knights[6]. A seal was, at least

---

[1] Feasey, 131. In versions of
the *Quem quaeritis* given by Lange,
24, 25, 26, the action is at the altar.
A Senlis *Breviary* (fourteenth century) has 'elevantes palium altaris'
(Lange, 27), and a Sens thirteenth-
century MS. 'Sublevans tapetum
altaris, tamquam respiciens in sepulchrum' (Lange, 64). But I am
not sure that there was a genuine
sepulchre in all these cases: cf.
p. 26.

[2] Würzburg *Breviary* (fourteenth
century) 'descendunt in criptam ad
visitandum sepulcrum' (Lange, 53):
cf. the Verdun *Consuetudines* (p. 16),
where there may or may not have
been a regular sepulchre.

[3] I have seen a beautiful one at

Tarrant Hinton, Dorset, which is
not amongst those mentioned by
Heales or Feasey.

[4] The performers are sometimes
directed to enter the sepulchre;
cf. e. g. Lange, 28.

[5] Feasey, 149. There is such
a chapel beneath the choir of the
Jérusalem church at Bruges. The
Winchester sepulchre is a chapel,
but not of the Jerusalem type. At
St. Gall the sepulchre was (†1583)
in the 'sacellum S. Sebastiani'
(Lange, 69).

[6] J. Britton, *Redcliffe Church*, 47,
prints a contemporary description
of a sepulchre given in 1470 by
'Maister Canynge' to St. Mary
Redcliffe, Bristol, with, amongst

at Hereford and in Hungary, set upon it [1]. A canopy was hung over it and upon it lay a pall, also a favourite object for a pious legacy. Similar legacies might meet the expense of the 'sepulchre light,' which was kept burning from Good Friday to Easter morning, and was only extinguished for a few minutes on Easter Saturday to be re-lit from the freshly blessed 'new fire [2].' Or the light might be provided by one of the innumerable guilds of the Middle Ages, whose members, perhaps, also undertook the devout duty of keeping the two nights' vigil before the sepulchre [3]. This watch was important. The Augsburg ritual already quoted makes the possibility of arranging it a condition of setting up the sepulchre at all [4]. The watchers sang psalms, and it is an example of the irrepressible mediaeval tendency to *mimesis* that they were sometimes accoutred like the knights of Pilate [5]. After the *Elevatio*, the crucifix seems to have been placed upon a side-altar and visited by processions in Easter, while the host was reserved in a tabernacle. The Sarum *Custumary* directs that the empty sepulchre shall be daily censed at Vespers and removed

other adornments, 'Heaven made of timber and stain'd clothes' and 'Hell, made of timber and iron-work thereto, with Divels to the number of 13.' This is apparently not a Chatterton forgery. Feasey, 166, gives a somewhat similar London specification, and also (p. 145) describes a fourteenth-century wooden sepulchre from Kilsby, Northants, believed to be the only one in existence. I have a suspicion that the wooden so-called 'watcher's chamber' to the shrine of St. Frideswide in Christ Church, Oxford, is really a sepulchre. It is in the right place, off the north choir aisle, and why should a watcher of the shrine want to be perched up in a wooden cage on the top of a tomb?

[1] Dankó, 536, 580. Two instances are given. In one the sepulchre was sealed, in the other the pyx, 'sigillo vel clavi ecclesiae.' At Hereford 'episcopus . . . cereo claudat sepulchrum' (Feasey, 159, from *Harl. MS.* 2983).

[2] Cf. vol. i. p. 126.
[3] Wordsworth, 279; Feasey, 161; Heales, 272, 299.
[4] Milchsack, 127.
[5] G. Gilpin, *The Bee-Hive of the Romish Church* (1579) (translated from Isaac Rabbotenu of Louvain, 1569) 'They make the graue in a hie place in the church, where men must goe up manie steppes, which are decked with blacke cloth from aboue to beneath, and upon everie steppe standeth a siluer candlesticke with a waxe candle burning in it, and there doe walke souldiours in harnesse, as bright as Saint George, which keep the graue, till the Priests come and take him up; and then commeth sodenlie a flash of fire, wherwith they are all afraid and fall downe; and then up startes the man, and they begin to sing Alleluia, on all handes, and the clocke striketh eleuen.' Feasey, 168, quotes De Moleon for a statement that the watchers at Orleans were dressed as soldiers.

on the Friday in Easter week before Mass[1]. Naturally there was some division of opinion at the Reformation as to the precise spiritual value of the Easter sepulchre. While Bishop Hooper and his fellow pulpiters were outspoken about the idolatrous cult of a 'dead post[2],' the more conservative views which ruled in the latter years of Henry VIII declared the ceremony to be 'very laudable' and 'not to be contemned and cast away[3].' The Cromwellian *Injunctions* of 1538 sanctioned the continued use of the sepulchre light, and by implication of the sepulchre itself. The Edwardine *Injunctions* of 1547 suppressed the sepulchre light and were certainly interpreted by Cranmer and others as suppressing the sepulchre[4]. The closely related 'creeping to the cross' was forbidden by proclamation in 1548; and in 1549, after the issue of the first Act of Uniformity and the first Prayer Book of Edward VI, the disallowance of both ceremonies was legalized, or renewed by *Articles* for the visitation of that year[5]. Payments for the breaking up of the sepulchre now appear in many churchwardens' accounts, to be complicated before long by payments for setting the sepulchre up again, in consequence of an order by Queen Mary in 1554[6]. In the same year the crucifix and pyx were missing out of the sepulchre at St. Pancras' Church in Cheapside, when the priests came for the *Elevatio* on Easter morning, and one Marsh was committed to the Counter for

[1] Appendix Q.

[2] Hooper, *Early Writings* (Parker Soc.), 45 'The ploughman, be he never so unlearned, shall better be instructed of Christ's death and passion by the corn that he soweth in the field, and likewise of Christ's resurrection, than by all the dead posts that hang in the church, or are pulled out of the sepulchre with *Christus resurgens.* What resemblance hath the taking of the cross out of the sepulchre and going a procession with it, with the resurrection of Christ? None at all: the dead post is as dead when they sing *Iam non moritur,* as it was when they buried it with *In pace factus est locus eius*': cf. Ridley, *Works* (Parker Soc.), 67.

[3] *Articles devised by the King's Majesty,* 1536 (Burnet, i. 1. 435; i. 2. 472; cf. Froude, ii. 486); Strype, *Eccles. Memorials,* i. 1. 546; i. 2. 432.

[4] Dixon, ii. 82, 432, 513, 516; iii. 37; Hardy and Gee, *Doc. illustrative of English Church History,* 278; Cardwell, *Documentary Annals of the Reformation,* i. 7; Froude, iv. 281. There certainly were sepulchres in 1548 (Feasey, 175).

[5] Dixon, iii. 37; Wilkins, iv. 32. The *Act of 2 and 3 Edward VI,* c. 10 (Froude, iv. 495), against images and paintings, was probably also held to require the demolition of many sepulchres: cf. Ridley's *Visitation Articles* of 1550, quoted by Heales, 304.

[6] Dixon, iv. 129.

the sacrilege[1]. The Elizabethan *Injunctions* of 1559, although they do not specifically name the sepulchre, doubtless led to its final disappearance[2]. In many parts of the continent it naturally lasted longer, but the term 'visiting sepulchres' seems in modern times to have been transferred to the devotion paid to the reserved host on Maundy Thursday[3].

I now return to the *Quem quaeritis* in the second stage of its evolution, when it had ceased to be an *Introit* trope and had become attached to the ceremony of the sepulchre. Obviously it is not an essential part of that ceremony. The *Depositio* and *Elevatio* mutually presuppose each other and, together, are complete. For the dramatic performance, as described by St. Ethelwold, the clergy, having removed the cross at the beginning of Matins, revisited the empty sepulchre quite at the close of that service, after the third respond[4], between which and the normal ending of Matins, the *Te Deum*, the *Quem quaeritis* was intercalated. The fact that the Maries bear censers instead of or in addition to the scriptural spices, suggests that this *Visitatio* grew out of a custom of censing the sepulchre at the end of Matins as well as of Evensong[5]. But the *Visitatio* could easily be omitted, and in fact it was omitted in many churches where the *Depositio* and *Elevatio* were in use. The Sarum books, for instance, do not in any way prescribe it. On the other hand, there were probably a few churches

---

[1] Dixon, iv. 157; S. R. Maitland, *Essays on the Reformation* (ed. 1899), 186.

[2] Hardy and Gee, *op. cit.* 428. Art xxiii forbids 'monuments of ... idolatry and superstition.' The Elizabethan *Visitation Articles* collected in the *Second Report* of the *Ritual Commission* make no mention of sepulchres. They generally follow pretty closely the wording of the *Injunctions*. But the *Articles* of Bentham, Bishop of Lichfield and Coventry (1565), specify 'monuments of idolatry and superstition' as including 'Sepulchres which were used on Good Friday' (Heales, 307). Notices of the destruction of sepulchres become numerous, being found, for instance, in the case of 50 out of 153 Lincolnshire churches

(Feasey, 142), and pious legacies begin to direct tombs 'whereas the sepulchre was wonte to stande.'

[3] Davidson, 140; Malleson and Tuker, ii. 263, 267, 272. The latest examples of the *Quem quaeritis* are of the eighteenth century from Cologne and Angers (Lange, 36, 39) and Venice (*Z. f. d. A.* xli. 77).

[4] This respond begins *Dum transisset Sabbatum.*

[5] Cf. p. 18, n. 2. The Sarum *Custumary* provides for censing on feasts (*a*) at the anthem 'super Magnificat' at Vespers, (*b*) during or after the *Te Deum* at Matins (*Use of Sarum*, i. 113, 121). The sepulchre is included only at Vespers (cf. Appendix Q), but the variation I suggest would not be great.

which adopted the *Visitatio* without the more important rite. Bamberg seems to have been one of these, and so possibly were Sens, Senlis, and one or two others in which the *Quem quaeritis* is noted as taking place at an altar [1]. However, whether there was a real sepulchre or not, the regular place of the *Quem quaeritis* was that prescribed for it by St. Ethelwold, between the third respond and the *Te Deum* at Matins. It has been found in a very large number of manuscripts, and in by far the greater part of them it occupies this position [2]. In the rest, with the exception of a completely anomalous example from Vienne [3], it is either a trope [4], or else is merged

[1] Cf. p. 22, n. 1. The Bamberg *Agenda* of †1597 (Lange, 93) has an *Ordo visitandi sepulchrum* which opens with directions for the construction of a sepulchre, which would obviously not be the case if the *Depositio* and *Elevatio* had preceded. Lange rarely prints more than the *Visitatio*, but of one group of texts he notes (p. 135) that the MSS. generally have also the *Elevatio*.

[2] Lange's collection from 224 MSS. supersedes those of Du Méril, Coussemaker, Milchsack, &c. He supplemented it by versions from Meissen, Worms, Venice, and Grau in Hungary in *Z. f. d. A.* (1896), xli. 77; and has not got those from the (*a*) Winchester *Tropers* (cf. p. 12); (*b*) Autun and Nevers *Tropers* of the eleventh century (Gautier, 126, 219); (*c*) St. Magloire, twelfth-century *Troper* (cf. p. 11); (*d*) Dublin *Processionals* (Appendix R); (*e*) Laon twelfth-century *Ordinary* (Chevalier, *Ordinaires de Laon*, 118); (*f*) Clermont-Ferrand fifteenth-century *Breviary* (cf. p. 11); (*g*) Poitiers *Ritual* (Martene, iii. 173); (*h*) Verdun tenth-century *Consuetudinary* (Martene, iv. 299; cf. p. 15). The MSS. extend from the tenth to the eighteenth century. The majority of them are Breviaries; some are Ordinaries, Antiphoners, Processionals; a few are late Tropers, in which, besides the Tropes proper, the Holy week *Ordo* is included (cf.

Gautier, 81); two (*B. N. Lat.* 1139 from Limoges, and *Orleans MS.* 178, from Fleury) are special books of dramatic *repraesentationes*; cf. p. 1.

[3] Martene, iii.180, from an undated *Caeremoniale*. Lange, 26, only gives a portion of the text containing the *Quem quaeritis* proper, which was sung as a processional trope before the *Missa maior*. The procession had immediately before gone to the sepulchre and sung other anthems. But the sepulchre played a part in two other services. Before Matins the clergy had in turn entered the sepulchre, found it empty, came out and given each other the kiss of peace and Easter greeting. No *Elevatio* is described; perhaps it was still earlier 'clam.' After Lauds, the *Missa matutinalis* was sung 'ad sepulchrum' and the *prosa* or Alleluia trope was thus performed: 'Prosa *Victimae Paschali*. Finito ℣ *Dicat nobis Maria*, clericulus stans in sepulcro cum amictu parato et stola, dicat ℣. *Angelicos testes*. Chorus respondeat *Dic nobis Maria*. Clericulus dicat *Angelicos testes*. Clericus dicat *Surrexit Christus*. Chorus *Credendum est magis* usque ad finem.' On this prose and its relation to the *Quem quaeritis* cf. p. 29. At St. Mark's, Venice (*Z.f.d.A.* xli. 77), the position of the *Quem quaeritis* is also abnormal, coming just before Prime, but this version dates from 1736.

[4] Cf. p. 12.

with or immediately follows the *Elevatio* before Matins[1]. The evidence of the texts themselves is borne out by Durandus, who is aware of the variety of custom, and indicates the end of Matins as the *proprior locus*[2].

No less difficult to determine than the place and time at which the Easter sepulchre itself was devised, are those at which the *Quem quaeritis*, attached to it, stood forth as a drama. That the two first appear together can hardly be taken as evidence that they came into being together. The predominance of German and French versions of the *Quem quaeritis* may suggest an origin in the Frankish area: and if the influence of the Sarum use and the havoc of service-books at the Reformation may between them help to account for the comparative rarity of the play in these islands, no such explanation is available for Italy and Spain. The development of the religious drama in the peninsulas, especially in Italy, seems to have followed from the beginning lines somewhat distinct from those of north-western Europe. But between France and Germany, as between France and England, literary influences, so far as clerkly literature goes, moved freely: nor is it possible to isolate the centres and lines of diffusion of that gradual process of accretion and development through which the *Quem quaeritis* gave ever fuller and fuller expression to the dramatic instincts by which it was prompted. The *clerici vagantes* were doubtless busy agents in carrying new motives and amplifications of the text from one church to another. Nor should it be forgotten that, numerous as are the versions preserved, those which have perished must have been more numerous still, so that, if all

---

[1] Lange, 28 (Parma), 30 (Laon), 47 (Constance), 68 (Rheinau), 69 (St. Gall). At Rheinau, the *Elevatio* takes place in the course of the *Quem quaeritis*: at Parma, and probably in the other cases, the 'sacrista pervigil' has already removed the 'Corpus Christi.'

[2] Durandus, lib. vi. c. 87. He describes the normal *Visitatio*, in terms much resembling those of Belethus (cf. p. 31), and adds 'quidam vero hanc presentationem faciunt, antequam matutinum inchoent, sed hic est proprior locus, eo quod *Te deum laudamus* exprimit horam, qua resurrexit. Quidam etiam eam faciunt ad missam, cum dicuntur sequentia illa *Victimae paschali*, cum dicitur versus *Dic nobis* et sequentes.' Ioannes Abrincensis, *de Offic. eccles.* (*P.L.*cxlvii. 54), briefly notes the 'officium sepulchri' as 'post tertium responsorium,' and says no more.

were before us, the apparent anomaly presented by the occurrence of identical features in, for instance, the plays from Dublin and Fleury, and no others, would not improbably be removed. The existence of this or that version in the service-books of any one church must depend on divers conditions ; the accidents of communication in the first place, and in the second the laxity or austerity of governing bodies at various dates in the licensing or pruning of dramatic elaboration. The simplest texts are often found in the latest manuscripts, and it may be that because their simplicity gave no offence they were permitted to remain there. A Strassburg notice suggests that the ordering of the *Quem quaeritis* was a matter for the discretion of each individual parish, in independence of its diocesan use[1] ; while the process of textual growth is illustrated by a Laon *Ordinarium*, in which an earlier version has been erased and one more elaborate substituted[2].

Disregarding, however, in the main the dates of the manuscripts, it is easy so to classify the available versions as to mark the course of a development which was probably complete by the middle of the twelfth and certainly by the thirteenth century. This development affected both the text and the dramatic interest of the play. The former is the slighter matter and may be disposed of first[3].

The kernel of the whole thing is, of course, the old St. Gall trope, itself a free adaptation from the text of the Vulgate, and the few examples in which this does not occur must be regarded as quite exceptional[4]. The earliest additions were taken from anthems, which already had their place

---

[1] Strassburg *Agenda* of 1513 (Lange, 50) 'Haec prescripta visitatio sepulcri observetur secundum consuetudinem cuiuslibet ecclesiae.' Meyer, 33, quotes a passage even more to the point from the Bamberg *Agenda* of 1587 ' Haec dominicae resurrectionis commemoratio celebrioribus servit ecclesiis, unde aliarum ecclesiarum utpote minorum et ruralium rectores et parochi ex ordine hic descripto aliquid saltem desumere possunt, quod pro loci et personarum illic convenientium

qualitate commodum fore iudicaverint.'

[2] Laon *Ordinarium* of twelfth century (U. Chevalier, *Ordinaires de Laon*, 118). The change consisted mainly in the introduction of the *Victimae paschali* : cf. p. 29.

[3] Cf. the full discussion, mainly from the textual point of view, throughout Lange's book, with that of Meyer, and Creizenach, i. 47 ; Froning, 3 ; Wirth, 1.

[4] The Bohemian fourteenth-century version (Lange, 130) is nearly

in the Easter services, and which in some manuscripts of the Gregorian *Antiphonarium* are grouped together as suitable for insertion wherever may be desired [1]. So far the text keeps fairly close to the words of Scripture, and even where the limits of the antiphonary are passed, the same rule holds good. In time, however, a freer dramatic handling partly establishes itself. Proses, and even metrical hymns, beginning as choral introductions, gradually usurp a place in the dialogue, and in the latest versions the metrical character is very marked. By far the most important of these insertions is the famous prose or sequence *Victimae paschali*, the composition of which by the monk Wipo of St. Gall can be pretty safely dated in the second quarter of the eleventh century [2]. It goes as follows:

'Victimae paschali laudes immolant Christiani.

agnus redemit oves, Christus innocens patri reconciliavit peccatores.

mors et vita duello conflixere mirando, dux vitae mortuus regnat vivus.

all narrative sung by the Ebdomarius: the only dialogue is from the *Victimae paschali*. Martene, iii. 173, gives, from a 'vetustissimum Rituale,' this Poitiers version, not in Lange, 'Finitis matutinis, accedunt ad sepulchrum, portantes luminaria. Tunc incipit Maria: *Ubi est Christus meus?* Respondet angelus *Non est hic*. Tunc Maria aperit os sepulchri, et dicit publica voce: *Surrexit Christus*. Et omnes respondent *Deo gratias*.' Possibly Maria here is the Virgin, who is not usually included in the *Visitatio*. But the same anthem opens a twelfth-century Limoges version, headed 'Oc est de mulieribus' in *B. N. Lat. MS*. 1139, a collection of ritual plays. The full text is 'Ubi est Christus meus dominus et filius excelsus?' which is not really appropriate to any other speaker: cf. Milchsack, 38. A frequent variant on 'Quem quaeritis in sepulchro, o Christicolae?' is 'Quem quaeritis, o tremulae mulieres, in hoc tumulo plorantes?'; nor can the two forms be localized (Lange, 84).

[1] Lange, 32. These MSS. are of the eleventh and twelfth centuries. I find no such section in the normal text of the Gregorian *Liber responsalis*, which is the antiphonary for the office (*P. L.* lxxviii. 769). The 'antiphonae de resurrectione domini ubicumque volueris' of the *B. N. Lat. MS*. 17,436 include the 'Cito euntes dicite, &c.,' 'Currebant duo simul, &c.,' 'Ardens est cor meum, &c.,' and others which are regularly introduced into the play. Another commonly used is the *Christus resurgens* with its verse, 'Dicant nunc Iudaei, &c.,' which the Sarum books assign to the *Elevatio* (Appendix Q): cf. Lange, 77.

[2] Text in Daniel, *Thesaurus Hymnologicus*, ii. 95; Kehrein, *Lateinische Sequenzen des Mittelalters*, 81, and with facsimile and setting in A. Schübiger, *Die Sängerschule St. Gallens*, 90, &c.; cf. Lange, 59; Meyer, 49, 76; Milchsack, 34; Chevalier, *Repertorium Hymnologicum*, s. vv.; A. Schübiger, *La Séquence de Pâques Victimae Paschali et son auteur* (1858).

dic nobis, Maria, quid vidisti in via ?
sepulchrum Christi viventis et gloriam vidi resurgentis;
angelicos testes, sudarium et vestes.
surrexit Christus, spes mea, praecedet suos in Galilaeam.
credendum est magis soli Mariae veraci, quam Iudaeo-
    rum turbae fallaci.
scimus Christum surrexisse a mortuis vere: tu nobis,
    victor, rex, miserere.'

Originally written as an *Alleluia* trope or sequence proper,
a place which it still occupies in the reformed Tridentine
liturgy [1], the *Victimae paschali* cannot be shown to have made
its way into the *Quem quaeritis* until the thirteenth century [2].
But it occurs in about a third of the extant versions, sometimes
as a whole, sometimes with the omission of the first three
sentences, which obviously do not lend themselves as well
as the rest to dramatic treatment.   When introduced, these
three sentences are sung either by the choir or by the Maries:
the other six fall naturally into dialogue.

The *Victimae paschali* is an expansion of the text of the
Quem quaeritis, but it does not necessarily introduce any new
dramatic motive.   Of such there were, from the beginning,
at least two.   There was the visit of the Maries to the
sepulchre and their colloquy with the angel ; and there was
the subsequent announcement of the Resurrection made by
them in pursuance of the divine direction.   Each has its
appropriate action : in the one case the lifting of the pall and
discovery of the empty sepulchre, in the other the display by
the Maries of the cast-off grave-clothes, represented by a
linteum, in token of the joyful event.   It is to this second
scene, if the term may be used of anything so rudimentary,
that the *Victimae paschali* attaches itself.   The dialogue of
it is between the Maries and the choir, who stand for the
whole body of disciples, or sometimes two singers, who are
their spokesmen [3].   A new scene is, however, clearly added to

[1] Malleson-Tuker, ii. 27.   It is used throughout Easter week.

[2] Lange, 60.   It was interpolated during the thirteenth century in a twelfth-century Laon version (Chevalier, *Ordinaires de Laon*, 118).

[3] Narbonne, †1400 (Lange, 65) 'duo canonici, tanquam apostoli'; cf. Lange, 75.

the play, when these two singers not only address the Maries, but themselves pay a visit to the sepulchre. Now they represent the apostles Peter and John. In accordance with the gospel narrative John outstrips Peter in going to the sepulchre, but Peter enters first: and the business of taking up the linteum and displaying it to the other disciples is naturally transferred to them from the Maries. The apostle scene first makes its appearance in an Augsburg text of the end of the eleventh century, or the beginning of the twelfth [1]. It occurs in rather more than half the total number of versions. These are mainly German, but the evidence of Belethus is sufficient to show that it was not unknown in twelfth-century France [2]. The addition of the apostle scene completed the evolution of the Easter play for the majority of churches. There were, however, a few in which the very important step was taken of introducing the person of the risen Christ himself ; and this naturally entailed yet another new scene. Of this type there are fifteen extant versions, coming from one Italian, four French, and four German churches [3]. The earliest is of the twelfth century, from a Prague convent. The new scene closely follows the Scripture narrative. Mary

---

[1] Augsburg *liber liturgicus* of eleventh or twelfth century (Lange, 82).

[2] Belethus, c. cxiii (*P. L.* ccii. 119) ' fit enim in plerisque Ecclesiis ut cantato ultimo responso, cum candelis cereis et solemni processione eant ex choro ad locum quemdam, ubi imaginarium sepulcrum compositum est, in quod introducuntur aliquot in personis mulicrum et discipulorum Ioannis et Petri, quorum alter altero citius revertitur, sicut Ioannes velocius cucurrit Petro, atque item alii quidam in personis angelorum qui Christum resurrexisse dixerunt a mortuis. Quo quidem facto personae eae redeunt ad chorum, referuntque ea quae viderint et audierint. Tunc chorus, audita Christi resurrectione, prorumpit in altam vocem, inquiens, *Te Deum laudamus.*' It is to be observed that Belethus knows no *Depositio* and *Elevatio.* After the *Adoratio*, he

has, like the older Roman liturgies, ' crucifixus in suum locum reponi debet' (c. xcviii). Durandus, vi. 87, has an account very similar to that of Belethus, but says ' Si qui autem habent versus de hac representatione compositos, licet non authenticos non improbamus'; cf. also p. 27.

[3] Engelberg (1372), Cividale (fourteenth century), Nuremberg (thirteenth century), Einsiedeln (thirteenth century), Prague (six, twelfth to fourteenth centuries), Rouen (two, thirteenth and fifteenth centuries), Mont St.-Michel (fourteenth century), Coutances (fifteenth century), Fleury (*Orleans MS.* 178, thirteenth century) ; all printed by Lange, 136 sqq. Gasté, 58, 63, also gives the Rouen and Coutances versions, the latter more fully than Lange. Meyer, 80, discusses the interrelations of the texts.

Magdalen remains behind the other Maries at the sepulchre. The Christ appears ; she takes him for the gardener, and he reveals himself with the *Noli me tangere*. Mary returns with the new wonder to the choir. This is the simplest version of the new episode. It occurs in a play of which the text is purely liturgical, and does not even include the *Victimae paschali*. A somewhat longer one is found in a Fleury play, which is in other respects highly elaborate and metrical. Here the Christ appears twice, first disguised *in similitudinem hortolani*, afterwards *in similitudinem domini* with the *labarum* or resurrection banner. The remaining versions do not depart widely from these two types, except that at Rouen and Mont St.-Michel, the Christ scene takes place, not at the sepulchre but at the altar, and at Cividale in a spot described as the *ortus Christi*[1].

The formal classification, then, of the versions of the *Quem quaeritis*, gives three types. In the first, the scenes between the Maries and the angel, and between the Maries and the choir, are alone present ; in the second the apostle scene is added to these ; the third, of which there are only fifteen known examples, is distinguished by the presence of the Christ scene. In any one of these types, the *Victimae paschali* and other proses and hymns may or may not be found [2]. And it must now be added that it is on the presence of these that the greater or less development of lyric feeling, as distinct from dramatic action, in the play depends. The metrical hymns in particular, when they are not merely choral overtures, are often of the nature of *planctus* or laments put in the mouths of the Maries as they approach the sepulchre or at some other appropriate moment. These *planctus* add greatly to the vividness and humanity of the play, and are thus an important step in the dramatic evolution. The use of them

[1] Lange, 138. In this text the Maries have a *locus suus*. The MS. is a *Processional*, and it may be that the play was given not in the church, but in the open square, as was the Annunciation play in the same MS. (Coussemaker, 284 ; cf. p. 67). It is none the less liturgical. Rouen had probably an 'ortus Christi' out of which came the apparition 'in sinistro cornu altaris,' for at Easter, 1570, divine service was performed in a ' paradis dressé avec la plus grande solennité dans la chapelle Notre-Dame, derrière le chœur' (Gasté, 58).

[2] These are of course the 'versus' spoken of with tolerance in the passage just quoted from Durandus.

may be illustrated by that of the hymn *Heu! pius pastor occiditur* in the Dublin version found by Mr. Frere and printed, after a different text from his, in an appendix [1]. This play has not the Christ scene, and belongs, therefore, to the second type of *Quem quaeritis*, but, in other respects, including the *planctus*, it closely resembles the Fleury version described above. Another *planctus*, found in plays of the third type from Engelberg, Nuremberg, Einsiedeln, and Cividale, is the *Heu nobis! internas mentes* [2]; a third, the *Heu! miserae cur contigit*, seems to have been interpolated in the *Heu! pius pastor* at Dublin; a fourth, the *Omnipotens pater altissime*, with a refrain *Heu quantus est dolor noster!* is found at places so far apart as Narbonne and Prague [3]: and a fifth, *Heu dolor, heu quam dira doloris angustia!* is also in the Fleury text [4].

Another advance towards drama is made in four Prague versions of the third type by the introduction of an episode for which there is no Scriptural basis at all. On their way to the sepulchre, the Maries stop and buy the necessary spices of a spice-merchant or *unguentarius*. In three thirteenth-century texts the *unguentarius* is merely a *persona muta*; in one of the fourteenth he is given four lines [5]. The *unguentarius* was destined to become a very popular character, and to afford much comic relief in the vernacular religious drama of Germany. Nor can it be quite confidently said that his appearance in these comparatively late liturgical plays is a natural development and not merely an instance of reaction by the vernacular stage.

---

[1] Appendix R. The *Heu! pius pastor occiditur* does not seem to have been found outside the Fleury and Dublin plays (Chevalier, *Repert. Hymn.* n°. 7741).

[2] Lange, 136, 141; Milchsack, 35, 66.

[3] Lange, 64, 74.

[4] Ibid. 162.

[5] Ibid. 151. The fourteenth-century text runs:

Tres Mariae:
'aromata preciosa querimus,
  Christi corpus ungere volumus,
  holocausta sunt odorifera
  sepulturae Christi memori.'

Ungentarius:
'dabo vobis ungenta optima,
  salvatoris ungere vulnera,
  sepulturae eius ad memoriam
  et nomen eius ad gloriam.'
The earlier texts have 'aromata ... memori,' preceded by 'Mariae cantantes "aromata" procedant ad unguentarium pro accipiendis ungentis' and followed by 'quibus acceptis accedant ad sepulchrum.' Meyer, 58, 91, 106, calls this scene, in which he finds the first introduction of non-liturgical verse, the *Zehnsilberspiel*, and studies it at great length.

The scenic effect of the *Quem quaeritis* can be to some
extent gathered from the rubrics, although these are often absent
and often not very explicit, being content with a general
direction for the performers to be arrayed *in similitudinem
mulierum* or *angelorum* or *apostolorum*, as the case may be.
The setting was obviously simple, and few properties or
costumes beyond what the vestments and ornaments of the
church could supply were used. The Maries had their heads
veiled [1], and wore surplices, copes, chasubles, dalmatics, albs, or
the like. These were either white or coloured. At Fécamp
one, presumably the Magdalen, was in red, the other two in
white [2]. The thuribles which, as already pointed out, they
carried, were sometimes replaced by boxes or vases representing the ointment and spices [3]. Sometimes also they carried,
or had carried before them, candles. Two or three rubrics
direct them to go *pedetemptim*, as sad or searching [4]. They
were generally three in number, occasionally two, or one only.
The angels, or angel, as the case might be, sat within the
sepulchre or at its door. They, too, had vestments, generally
white, and veiled or crowned heads. At Narbonne, and
probably elsewhere, they had wings [5]. They held lights,
a palm, or an ear of corn, symbolizing the Resurrection [6]. The
apostles are rarely described ; the ordinary priestly robes
doubtless sufficed. At Dublin, St. John, in white, held a palm,
and St. Peter, in red, the keys [7]. In the earliest Prague version
of the Christ scene, the Christ seems to be represented by one
of the angels [8]. At Nuremberg the *dominica persona* has
a crown and bare feet [9]. At Rouen he holds a cross, and

[1] Lange, 24, 51, 64 'coopertis
capitibus'(Tours, fifteenth century),
'capita humeralibus velata' (Rheinau),'amictibus in capitibus eorum'
(Narbonne, †1400).
[2] Lange, 36 (fourteenth century).
[3] Ibid. 27, 36, 53, 64, &c. ; Appendix R.
[4] Lange, 51, 160; cf. *Conc. Regularis* (Appendix O).
[5] Lange, 64 'induti albis et amictibus cum stolis violatis et sindone
rubea in facie eorum et alis in
humeris' (Narbonne, †1400).
[6] Lange, 40, 155, 158, 162 'pal-

mam manu tenens, in capite fanu-
lum largum habens'(Toul, thirteenth
century), 'tenens spicam in manu'
(Rouen, fifteenth century), 'tenens
palmam in manu et habens coronam
in capite' (Mont St.-Michel, fourteenth century), 'vestitus alba
deaurata, mitra tectus caput etsi
deinfulatus, palmam in sinistra,
ramum candelarum plenum tenens
in manu dextra' (Fleury, thirteenth
century).
[7] Appendix R.
[8] Lange, 147.
[9] Ibid. 143 'quae sit vestita

though there is a double appearance, there is no hint of any change of costume [1]. But at Coutances and Fleury the first appearance is as *hortulanus*, indicated perhaps by a spade, which is exchanged on the second for the cross [2].

It must be borne in mind that the *Quem quaeritis* remained imperfectly detached from the liturgy, out of which it arose. The performers were priests, or nuns, and choir-boys. The play was always chanted, not spoken [3]. It was not even completely resolved into dialogue. In many quite late versions narrative anthems giving the gist of each scene are retained, and are sung either by the principal actors or by the choir, which thus, as in the hymns or proses which occur as overtures [4], holds a position distinct from the part which it takes as representing the disciples [5]. Finally the whole performance ends in most cases with the *Te Deum laudamus*, and thus becomes a constituent part of Matins, which normally comes to a close with that hymn. The intervention of the congregation, with its Easter hymn *Christ ist erstanden*, seems to lie outside the main period of the evolution of the *Quem quaeritis*. I only find one example so early as the thirteenth century [6].

dalmatica casulamque complicatam super humeros habeat; coronamque capiti superimpositam, nudis pedibus.'

[1] Lange, 156 'albatus cum stola, tenens crucem.'

[2] Ibid. 159, 164 'in habitu ortolani ... redeat, indutus capa serica vel pallio serico, tenens crucem' (Coutances); 'praeparatus in similitudinem hortolani . . . is, qui ante fuit hortulanus, in similitudinem domini veniat, dalmaticatus candida dalmatica, candida infula infulatus, phylacteria pretiosa in capite, crucem cum labaro in dextra, textum auro paratorium in sinistra habens' (Fleury). The *labarum* is the banner of Constantine with the Chi-Ro monogram (cf. Gibbon-Bury, ii. 567): but the banner usually attached to the cross in mediaeval pictures of the Resurrection itself bears simply a large cross; cf. Pearson, ii. 310.

[3] A study of the music might

perhaps throw light on the relation of the versions to each other. I am sorry that it is beyond my powers: moreover Lange does not give the notation; Coussemaker gives it for half a dozen versions.

[4] For such overtures cf. Lange, 36, 62, 64; Milchsack, 37, 38, 40. On the doubtful use of the *Gloriosi et famosi* at Einsiedeln, cf. p. 54.

[5] In the Prague versions (Lange, 151). The choir, or rather 'conventus,' introduces the scenes with the three following anthems: (i) 'Maria Magdalena et alia Maria ferebant diluculo aromata, dominum querentes in monumento,' (ii) 'Maria stabat ad monumentum foris plorans; dum ergo fleret, inclinavit se et prospexit in monumentum,' (iii) 'Currebant duo simul et ille alius discipulus praecucurrit cicius petro et venit prior ad monumentum.'

[6] Lange, 146 (Nuremberg); for later examples cf. Lange, 99 sqq.

It is in quite late texts also that certain other Easter motives have become attached to the play. The commonest of these are the whispered greeting of *Surrexit Christus* and the kiss of peace, which have been noted elsewhere as preceding Matins[1]. At Eichstädt, in 1560, is an amusing direction, which Mr. Collins would have thought very proper, that the *pax* is to be given to the *dominus terrae, si ibi fuerit*, before the priest. The same manuscript shows a curious combination of the *Quem quaeritis* with the irrepressible *Tollite portas* ceremony[2]. Another such is found at Venice[3]. But this is as late as the eighteenth century, to which also belongs the practice at Angers described by De Moleon, according to which the Maries took up from the sepulchre with the *linteum* two large Easter eggs—*deux œufs d'autruche*[4].

Besides the *Quem quaeritis*, Easter week had another liturgical drama in the *Peregrini* or *Peregrinus*[5]. This was established by the twelfth century. It was regularly played at Lichfield[6], but no text is extant from England, except a late transitional one, written partly in the vernacular[7]. France affords four texts, from Saintes[8], Rouen[9],

The hymn generally comes just before the *Te Deum*. A fourteenth-century Bohemian version from Prague (Lange, 131) has a similar Bohemian hymn ' Buoh wssemoh-uczy.' At Bamberg in 1597 'potest chorus populo iterum praecinere cantilenas pascales Germanicas' (Lange, 95). At Rheinau in 1573 it is suggested that the *Quem quaeritis* itself may as an alternative be sung in German (Lange, 68) ' hisce aut Germanicis versibus cantatis.' At Aquileja in 1495 ' Populus cantet *Christus surrexit*,'apparently in Latin (Lange, 106) ; and at Würzburg in 1477, 'Populus incipit Ymnum suum: *Te Deum*' (Lange, 67).

[1] Lange, 39, 119, 122, 124; cf. Martene, iii. 171.

[2] Lange, 41.

[3] *Z. f. d. A.* xli. 77.

[4] Lange, 39.

[5] Creizenach, i. 56 ; Julleville, i. 67.

[6] *Lichfield Statutes of Hugh de Nonant*, 1188-98 (*Lincoln Statutes*, ii. 15, 23) 'Item in nocte Natalis representacio pastorum fieri consuevit et in diluculo Pasche representacio Resurreccionis dominicae et representacio peregrinorum die lune in septimana Pasche sicut in libris super hijs ac alijs compositis continetur . . . De officio succentoris . . . et providere debet quod representacio pastorum in nocte Natalis domini et miraculorum in nocte Pasche et die lune in Pascha congrue et honorifice fiant.'

[7] Cf. p. 90.

[8] Text in *Bibl. de l'École des Chartes*, xxxiv. 314, from *B. N. Lat.* 16,309 (thirteenth-century Saintes *Breviary*), *begins* ' Quando fiunt Peregrini, non dicitur prosa, sed peregrini deforis veniunt canendo ista'; *ends* with *Magnificat* and *Oratio*, ' Deus qui sollempnitate paschali.'

[9] Text in Gasté, 65 ; Du Méril,

Beauvais[1], and Fleury[2]. The play is also recorded at Lille[3]. In Germany it is represented by a recently-discovered fragment of the famous early thirteenth-century repertory of the *scholares vagantes* from the Benedictbeuern monastery[4]. The simplest version is that of Saintes, in which the action is confined to the journey to Emmaus and the supper there. The Rouen play is on the same lines, but at the close the disciples are joined by St. Mary Magdalen, and the *Victimae paschali* is sung. The Benedictbeuern play similarly ends with the introduction of the Virgin and two other Maries to greet the risen Christ. But here, and in the Beauvais and Fleury plays, a distinct scene is added, of which the subject is the incredulity of Thomas and the apparition to him. It is, I think, a reasonable conjecture that the *Peregrini*, in which the risen Christ is a character, was not devised until he had already been introduced into the later versions of the *Quem quaeritis*. Indeed the Fleury *Peregrini*, with its double appearance and change of costume for Christ, seems clearly modelled on the Fleury *Quem quaeritis*. But the lesser play has its own proper and natural place in the Easter week services. It is attached to the *Processio ad fontes*, which is a regular portion, during that season, of Vespers[5]. The Christ with the Resurrection cross is personated by the priest who

117, from Rouen *Ordinarium* (fourteenth century), *begins* 'Officium Peregrinorum debet hic fieri hoc modo'; *ends* 'Et processio, factis memoriis, redeat in choro et ibi finiantur vesperae.' Gasté, 68, quotes an order of 1452 'Domini capitulantes concluserunt quod in istis festis Paschae fiat misterium representans resurrectionem Christi et apparitionem eius suis discipulis, eundo apud castrum de Emaux, amotis et cessantibus indecenciis.'

[1] Text in G. Desjardins, *Hist. de la Cath. de Beauvais* (1865), 115, 269, *begins* 'Ordo ad suscipiendum peregrinum in secunda feria Paschae ad vesperas'; *ends* with *Oratio de Resurrectione*. Meyer, 133, describes the MS. as of the first half of the twelfth century.

[2] Text in Du Méril, 120, from

Orleans MS. 178 (thirteenth century), *begins* 'Ad faciendam similitudinem dominicae apparitionis in specie Peregrini, quae fit in tertia feria Paschae ad Vesperas'; *ends* 'Salve, festa dies.'

[3] E. Hautcœur, *Documents liturgiques de Lille*, 55, from *Ordinarium* of thirteenth century, 'Feria ii. ... in vesperis ... post collectam fit representatio peregrinorum. Qua facta cantatur Christus resurgens, et itur in chorum.'

[4] W. Meyer, *Fragmenta Burana*, 131, with text and facsimile. The play begins 'Incipit exemplum apparicionis domini discipulis suis ⟨iuxta⟩ castellum Emaus, ubi illis apparuit in more peregrini,' &c.

[5] *Use of Sarum*, i. 157; *Sarum Breviary*, i. dcccxxix.

normally accompanies the procession *cum cruce*. At Rouen
the play was a kind of dramatization of the procession itself[1];
at Lille it seems to have had the same position; at Saintes
and Beauvais it preceded the *Magnificat* and *Oratio* or *Collecta*,
after which the procession started. In the remaining cases
there is no indication of the exact time for the *Peregrini*.
The regular day for it appears to have been the Monday in
Easter week, of the Gospel for which the journey to Emmaus
is the subject; but at Fleury it was on the Tuesday, when
the Gospel subject is the incredulity of Thomas. At Saintes,
a curious rubric directs the Christ during the supper at
Emmaus to divide the 'host' among the *Peregrini*. It seems
possible that in this way a final disposal was found for the
host which had previously figured in the *Depositio* and *Elevatio*
of the sepulchre ceremony.

A long play, probably of Norman origin and now preserved
in a manuscript at Tours, represents a merging of the *Elevatio*,
the *Quem quaeritis*, and the *Peregrini*[2]. The beginning is
imperfect, but it may be conjectured from a fragment belonging
to Klosterneuburg in Germany, that only a few lines are
lost[3]. Pilate sets a watch before the sepulchre. An angel
sends lightning, and the soldiers fall as if dead[4]. Then come
the Maries, with *planctus*. There is a scene with the *unguentarius* or *mercator*, much longer than that at Prague,
followed by more *planctus*. After the *Quem quaeritis*, the
soldiers announce the event to Pilate. A *planctus* by the

---

[1] The *Peregrini* start 'a vestiario
. . . per dextram alam ecclesiae
usque ad portas occidentales, et
subsistentes in capite processionis.'
Then the *Sacerdos*, 'nudus pedes,
ferens crucem super dextrum
humerum' comes 'per dextram
alam ecclesiae' to meet them.
They lead him 'usque ad tabernaculum, in medio navis ecclesiae, in
similitudinem castelli Emaux prae-
paratum.'

[2] Text in Milchsack, 97; Coussemaker, 21, from *Tours MS.* 927
(twelfth or thirteenth century); cf.
Creizenach, i. 88; Julleville, i. 62;
Meyer, 95; and on the MS. which

also contains the 'Ordo representa-
cionis Adae,' and is not native to
Tours, cf. p. 71.

[3] Milchsack, 105; Creizenach, i.
90. The beginning and end of the
Klosterneuburg play were printed
from a thirteenth-century MS., now
lost, by B. Pez, *Thesaurus novus
Anecd.* ii. 1. liii. It began 'Primo
producatur Pilatus cum responsorio:
Ingressus Pilatus,' and ended with
'Christ, der ist erstanden'; cf.
Meyer, 126.

[4] 'Modo veniat angelus et iniciat
eis fulgura; milites cadunt in terram velut mortui.'

Magdalen leads up to the apparition to her. The Maries
return to the disciples. Christ appears to the disciples, then
to Thomas, and the *Victimae paschali* and *Te Deum* conclude
the performance. A fragment of a very similar play, breaking
off before the *Quem quaeritis*, belongs to the Benedictbeuern
manuscript already mentioned [1].

It is clear from the rubrics that the Tours play, long as
it is, was still acted in church, and probably, as the *Te Deum*
suggests, at the Easter Matins [2]. Certainly this was the case
with the Benedictbeuern play. In a sense, these plays only
mark a further stage in the process of elaboration by which
the fuller versions of the *Quem quaeritis* proper came into
being. But the introduction at the beginning and end of
motives outside the events of the Easter morning itself points
to possibilities of expansion which were presently realized,
and which ultimately transformed the whole character of the
liturgical drama. All the plays, however, which have so far
been mentioned, are strictly plays of the Resurrection. Their
action begins after the Burial of Christ, and does not stretch
back into the events of the Passion. Nor indeed can the
liturgical drama proper be shown to have advanced beyond
a very rudimentary representation of the Passion. This began
with the *planctus*, akin to those of the *Quem quaeritis*, which
express the sorrows of the Virgin and the Maries and St. John
around the cross [3]. Such *planctus* exist both in Latin and

---

[1] Meyer, 97, 125, with text and
facsimile, ' Incipit ludus immo exemplum Dominice resurrectionis.'
The episode of the Resurrection
with the dismay of the soldiers is
found not only in the Tours and
Benedictbeuern MS., but also in the
simpler Coutances *Quem quaeritis.*
Lange, 157, omits this passage, but
Gasté, 63, gives it; ' Si Mariae
debeant representari, finito responsorio quatuor clerici armati accedentes ad sepulcrum Domini pannis
sericis decenter ornatum et secum
dicant personagia sua. Quo facto,
duo pueri induti roquetis veniant
ad monumentum ferentes duas
virgas decorticatas in quibus sunt
decem candelae ardentes ; et statim
cum appropinquaverint ad sepul-

crum praedicti milites, procidant
quasi mortui, nec surgant donec
incipiatur *Te Deum*, ... &c.' There
is no actual appearance of the
Rising Christ in any of these three
plays as originally written. But a
later hand has inserted in the Benedictbeuern MS. directions for the
Christ to appear, discourse with the
angels, and put on the ' vestem
ortulani.'

[2] Creizenach thinks the play (like
Adam) was outside the church,
because the Maries appear ' ante
ostium ecclesiae.' But ' ante ' may
be inside. Mary Magdalen at one
point is ' in sinistra parte ecclesiae
stans,' and most of the action is
round the *sepulchrum*.

[3] E. Wechssler, *Die romani-*

the vernacular. The earliest are of the twelfth century. Several of them are in dialogue, in which Christ himself occasionally takes part, and they appear to have been sung in church after Matins on Good Friday [1]. The *planctus* must be regarded as the starting-point of a drama of the Passion, which presently established itself beside the drama of the Resurrection. This process was mainly outside the churches, but an early and perhaps still liturgical stage of it is to be seen in the *ludus breviter de passione* which precedes the elaborated *Quem quaeritis* of the Benedictbeuern manuscript, and was probably treated as a sort of prologue to it. The action extends from the preparation for the Last Supper to the Burial. It is mainly in dumb-show, and the slight dialogue introduced is wholly out of the Vulgate. But at one point occurs the rubric *Maria planctum faciat quantum melius potest*, and a later hand has inserted out of its place in the text the most famous of all the laments of the Virgin, the *Planctus ante nescia* [2].

---

schen Marienklagen (1893); A. Schönbach, *Die Marienklagen* (1873); cf. Creizenach, i. 241; Julleville, i. 58; Sepet, 23; Milchsack, 92; Coussemaker, 285, 346; Meyer, 67; Pearson, ii. 384.

[1] A *planctus* ascribed to Bonaventura (thirteenth century) has the titles 'Officium de compassione Mariae' (Wechssler, 14), and 'Officium sanctae crucis' (*Bibl. de l'École des Chartes*, xxxiv. 315). Another, the 'Surgit Christus cum trophaeo,' is headed in thirteenth- and fourteenth-century MSS. 'Sequentia devota antiquorum nostrorum de resurrectionis argumentis. Sanctarum virginum Mariae ac Mariae Magdalene de compassione mortis Christi per modum dyalogi sequentia.' The chorus begins, and 'tres bene vociferati scholares respondent' (text in Milchsack, 92; cf. Wechssler, 14). A third, ' O fratres et sorores,' is headed 'Hic incipit planctus Mariae et aliorum in die Parasceves' (text from fourteenth-century Cividale MS. in Coussemaker, 285; Julleville, i. 58; cf. Wechssler, 17).

Ducange, s. v. *Planctus*, quotes a (thirteenth-century) Toulouse rubric, 'planctum beatissimae Virginis Mariae, qui dicitur a duobus puerulis post Matutinum et debent esse monachi, si possunt reperiri ad hoc apti.' This *planctus* was sung from the 'cathedra praedicatorii.' On the use of vernacular Italian *planctus* by the *laudesi* in churches through Lent, cf. Wechssler, 30. The vernacular German 'ludus passionis' printed by O. Schönemann, *Der Sündenfall und Marienklage* (1855), 129, from a Wolfenbüttel fifteenth-century, MS., seems to have still been meant for liturgical use, as it has the rubric 'debet cantari post *crux fidelis* et sic finiri usque ad vesperam lamentabiliter cum caeteris sicut consuetum est fieri.' It incorporates the *Depositio*.

[2] Meyer, *Fragmenta Burana*, 64, 122, with text and facsimile. The piece ends 'et ita inchoatur ludus de resurrectione. Pontifices: *O domine recte meminimus*,' which is the opening of the Easter play already described.

CHAPTER XIX

LITURGICAL PLAYS (*continued*)

THE 'Twelve days' of the Christmas season are no less important than Easter itself in the evolution of the liturgical drama. I have mentioned in the last chapter a Christmas trope which is evidently based upon the older Easter dialogue. Instead of *Quem quaeritis in sepulchro, o Christicolae?* it begins *Quem quaeritis in praesepe, pastores, dicite?* It occurs in eleventh- and twelfth-century tropers from St. Gall, Limoges, St. Magloire, and Nevers. Originally it was an *Introit* trope for the third or 'great' Mass. In a fifteenth-century breviary from Clermont-Ferrand it has been transferred to Matins, where it follows the *Te Deum*; and this is precisely the place in the Christmas services occupied, at Rouen, by a liturgical drama known as the *Officium Pastorum*, which appears to have grown out of the *Quem quaeritis in praesepe?* by a process analogous to that by which the Easter drama grew out of the *Quem quaeritis in sepulchro*[1]? A *praesepe* or 'crib,' covered by a curtain, was made ready behind the altar, and in it was placed an image of the Virgin. After the *Te Deum* five canons or vicars, representing the shepherds, approached the great west door of the choir. A boy *in similitudinem angeli* perched *in excelso* sang them the 'good tidings,' and a number of others *in voltis ecclesiae* took up the *Gloria in excelsis*. The shepherds, singing a hymn, advanced to the *praesepe*. Here they were met with the *Quem quaeritis* by two priests *quasi obstetrices*[2]. The dia-

---

[1] Printed by Du Méril, 147; Gasté, 25; Davidson, 173, from Rouen *Ordinaria* (*Rouen MSS.* Y. 108 of fifteenth century, Y. 110 of fourteenth century); Coussemaker, 235, with notation, from Rouen *Gradual* (*Bibl. Nat. Lat.*

904); it is also in *B. N. Lat.* 1213 (fifteenth century) and *Bibl. Mazarin.* 216 (Du Méril, 148).

[2] The 'obstetrices' figure in the *Protevangelium Iacobi*, chh. 18 sqq. (Tischendorf, *EvangeliaApocrypha*, 33), and the *Pseudo-Matthaei Evan-*

logue of the trope, expanded by another hymn during which the shepherds adore, follows, and so the drama ends. But the shepherds 'rule the choir' throughout the *Missa in Gallicantu* immediately afterwards, and at Lauds, the anthem for which much resembles the *Quem quaeritis* itself[1]. The *misterium pastorum* was still performed at Rouen in the middle of the fifteenth century, and at this date the shepherds, *cessantibus stultitiis et insolenciis*, so far as this could be ensured by the chapter, took the whole 'service' of the day, just as did the deacons, priests, and choir-boys during the *triduum*[2].

If the central point of the *Quem quaeritis* is the *sepulchrum*, that of the *Pastores* is the *praesepe*. In either case the drama, properly so called, is an addition, and by no means an invariable one, to the symbolical ceremony. The *Pastores* may, in fact, be described, although the term does not occur in the documents, as a *Visitatio praesepis*. The history of the *praesepe* can be more definitely stated than that of the *sepulchrum*. It is by no means extinct. The Christmas 'crib' or *crèche*, a more or less realistic representation of the Nativity, with a Christ-child in the manger, a Joseph and Mary, and very often an ox and an ass, is a common feature in all Catholic countries at Christmas time[3]. At Rome, in particular, the *esposizione del santo bambino* takes place with great ceremony[4]. A tradition ascribes the first *presepio* known in Italy to St. Francis, who is said to have invented it at Greccio in 1223[5]. But this is a mistake. The custom is

---

gelium, ch. 13 (Tischendorf, 77). In the latter they are named Salome and Zelomi.

[1] Gasté, 31 'Archiepiscopus, vel alius sacerdos versus ad Pastores dicat: *Quem vidistis, pastores, dicite; annunciate nobis in terris quis apparuit.* Pastores respondeant: *Natum vidimus et choros angelorum collaudantes Dominum. Alleluia, alleluia,* et totam antiphonam finiant': cf. Meyer, 39; *Sarum Breviary*, clxxxviii; Martene, iii. 36; Durandus, vi. 13, 16 'in laudibus matutinis quasi choream ducimus, unde in prima antiphona dicimus; *Quem vidistis, pastores?*

&c. Et ipsi responderunt: *Natum vidimus.'*

[2] Gasté, 33.

[3] Tille, *D. W.* 309; Pollard, xiii; Durandus - Barthélemy, iii. 411; E. Martinengo - Cesaresco, *Puer Parvulus* in *Contemporary Review*, lxxvii (1900), 117; W. H. D. Rouse, in *F. L.* v. 6; J. Feller, *Le Bethléem Verviétois*, 10. I find a modern English example described in a letter of 1878 written by Mr. Coventry Patmore's son Henry from a Catholic school at Ushaw (*Life of C. Patmore*, i. 308).

[4] Malleson-Tuker, ii. 212.

[5] P. Sabatier, *Life of St. Francis*

many centuries older than St. Francis. Its Roman home
is the church of S. Maria Maggiore or *Ad Praesepe*, otherwise
called the '*basilica* of Liberius.' Here there was in the
eighth century a permanent *praesepe*[1], probably built in imitation of one which had long existed at Bethlehem, and to
which an allusion is traced in the writings of Origen[2]. The
praesepe of S. Maria Maggiore was in the right aisle. When
the Sistine chapel was built in 1585–90 it was moved to the
crypt, where it may now be seen. This church became an
important station for the Papal services at Christmas. The
Pope celebrated Mass here on the vigil, and remained until
he had also celebrated the first Mass on Christmas morning.
The bread was broken on the manger itself, which served as
an altar. At S. Maria Maggiore, moreover, is an important
relic, in some boards from the *culla* or cradle of Christ, which
are exposed on the *presepio* during Christmas[3]. The *presepio*
of S. Maria Maggiore became demonstrably the model for
other similar chapels in Rome[4], and doubtless for the more
temporary structures throughout Italy and western Europe
in general.

In the present state of our knowledge it is a little difficult
to be precise as to the range or date of the *Pastores*. The
only full mediaeval Latin text, other than that of Rouen,
which has come to light, is also of Norman origin, and is still
unprinted[5]. In the eighteenth century the play survived at
Lisieux and Clermont[6]. The earliest Rouen manuscript is of
the thirteenth century, and the absence of any reference to

(Eng. transl.), 285, from Thomas
of Celano, *Vita Prima*, 84, and
Bonaventura, *Vita*, 149; cf. D'Ancona, i. 116.

[1] Usener, i. 280. It is called
'oratorium sanctum quod praesepe
dicitur' (†731–41) and 'camera
praesepii' (†844–7).

[2] Origen, *adv. Celsum*, i. 51; cf.
Usener, i. 283, 287.

[3] Usener, i. 281; Tille, *D. W.*
54; Malleson-Tuker, ii. 210.

[4] Usener, i. 280. Gregory IV
(827–43) 'sanctum fecit praesepe
ad similitudinem praesepii S. dei
genetricis quae appellatur maior,'
in S. Maria in Trastevere.

[5] Gasté, 33, citing *Montpellier
MS.* H. 304. The play occurs, with
an *Officium Stellae*, in an anonymous treatise *De ratione divini
officii*. The Amiens *Ordinarium*
of 1291 (Grenier, 389) gives directions for a *Pastores* during the
procession after the communion at
the midnight mass. In preparation
lights were lit at the *praesepe* during
first vespers 'dum canitur versus
praesepe iam fulget tuum.' At the
end of the first nocturn the figure
of a child was placed there. At the
first lesson of the second nocturn
the cry of *noël* was raised.

[6] Du Méril, 148.

the *Officium Pastorum* by John of Avranches, who writes primarily of Rouen, and who does mention the *Officium Stellae*, makes it probable that it was not there known about 1070[1]. Its existence, however, in England in the twelfth century is shown by the Lichfield *Statutes* of 1188–98, and on the whole it is not likely to have taken shape later than the eleventh. Very likely it never, as a self-contained play, acquired the vogue of the *Quem quaeritis*. As will be seen presently, it was overshadowed and absorbed by rivals. I find no trace of it in Germany, where the *praesepe* became a centre, less for liturgical drama, than for carols, dances, and 'crib-rocking[2].'

Still rarer than the *Pastores* is the drama, presumably belonging to Innocents' day, of *Rachel*. It is found in a primitive form, hardly more than a trope, in a Limoges manuscript of the eleventh century. Here it is called *Lamentatio Rachel*, and consists of a short *planctus* by Rachel herself, and a short reply by a consoling angel. There is nothing to show what place it occupied in the services[3].

The fact is that both the *Pastores* and the *Rachel* were in many churches taken up into a third drama belonging to the Epiphany. This is variously known as the *Tres Reges*, the *Magi*, *Herodes*, and the *Stella*. It exists in a fair number of different but related forms. Like the *Quem quaeritis* and the *Pastores*, it had a material starting-point, in the shape of a star, lit with candles, which hung from the roof of the church, and could sometimes be moved, by a simple mechanical device, from place to place[4]. As with the *Quem quaeritis*,

---

[1] Ioannes Abrincensis, *De officiis ecclesiasticis* (*P. L.* cxlvii. 41, 43). Neither Belethus nor Durandus mentions the *Pastores*.

[2] Cf. vol. i. p. 272. The *praesepe* is of course in the *Stella*, which is found at Strassburg, Bilsen, and Einsiedeln, but even this is more characteristic of France than of Germany.

[3] Text ed. C. Magnin (*Journal des Savants* (1846), 93), from *Bibl. Nat. Lat.* 1139.

[4] Gasté, 50 'Corona ante crucem pendens in modum stellae accendatur' (Rouen); Du Méril,

153 'stellam pendentem in filo, quae antecedit eos' (Limoges). The churchwardens' accounts of St. Nicholas, Yarmouth, from 1462–1512 (*Norfolk Archaeology*, xi. 334), contain payments for 'making a new star,' 'leading the star,' 'a new balk line to the star and ryving the same star.' Pearson, ii. 325, lays stress on the prominence of the star in the German vernacular mysteries. J. T. Micklethwaite, *Ornaments of the Rubric*, 44, says that the 'star' was called a 'trendle' or 'rowell.' Its use does not necessarily imply the presence of a drama.

the development of the *Stella* must be studied without much reference to the relative age of the manuscripts in which it happens to be found. But it was probably complete by the end of the eleventh century, since manuscripts of that date contain the play in its latest forms[1].

The simplest version is from Limoges[2]. The three kings enter by the great door of the choir singing a *prosula*. They show their gifts, the royal gold, the divine incense, the myrrh for funeral. Then they see the star, and follow it to the high altar. Here they offer their gifts, each contained in a gilt cup, or some other *iocale pretiosum*, after which a boy, representing an angel, announces to them the birth of Christ, and they retire singing to the sacristy. The text of this version stands by itself: nearly all the others are derived from a common tradition, which is seen in its simplest form at Rouen[3]. In the Rouen *Officium Stellae*, the three kings, coming respectively from the east, north, and south of the church, meet before the altar. One of them points to the star with his stick, and they sing :

' 1. Stella fulgore nimio rutilat,

2. Quae regem regum natum demonstrat

3. Quem venturum olim prophetiae signaverant.'

---

[1] The account of the *Stella* here given should be supplemented from Creizenach, i. 60; Köppen, 10. The latter studies the verbal relation of the texts much more fully than can be done here. Meyer, 38, argues for their origin in an archetype from Germany. There are doubtless many other texts yet unprinted. Ch. Magnin, *Journal de l'Instruction publique*, Sept. 13, 1835, mentions such in Soleures, Fribourg, and Besançon *Rituals*.

[2] Text in Du Méril, 151 ; Martene, iii. 44, from Limoges *Ordinarium* of unspecified date. The version is partly metrical, and the action took place 'cantato offertorio, antequam eant ad offerendum.

[3] Text in Gasté, 49; Du Méril, 153; Davidson, 176; from *Rouen MS*. Y. 110 (fourteenth-century *Ordinarium*) ; Coussemaker, 242, from

Bibl. Nat. Lat. MS. 904 (thirteenth-century *Gradual*, with notation) ; *P. L.* cxlvii. 135, from *B.N.* 904 and *B.N. Lat.* 1213 (fifteenth-century *Ordinarium*) ; cf. Gasté, 3. The rubric begins 'Officium regum trium secundum usum Rothomagensem. Die epyphaniae, tercia cantata.' John of Avranches (†1070) describing the Epiphany service, probably of Rouen, says, after mentioning the *Evangelium genealogiae*, which follows the ninth *responsorium* of Matins, ' Deinde stellae officium incipiat' (*P. L.* cxlvii. 43). Gasté, 53, quotes some Rouen chapter orders. In 1379 Peter Chopillard, painter, was paid ' pro pingendo baculos quos portant Reges die Apparitionis.' In 1507 the chapter after ' matura deliberatio' ordered the 'representatio trium Regum' to be held. In 1521 they suppressed it.

They kiss each other and sing an anthem, which occurs also in the Limoges version : *Eamus ergo et inquiramus eum, offerentes ei munera ; aurum thus et myrrham.* A procession is now formed, and as it moves towards the nave, the choir chant narrative passages, describing the visit of the *Magi* to Jerusalem and their reception by Herod. Meanwhile a star is lit over the altar of the cross where an image of the Virgin has been placed. The *Magi* approach it, singing the passage which begins *Ecce stella in Oriente.* They are met by two in dalmatics, who appear to be identical with the *obstetrices* of the Rouen *Pastores.* A dialogue follows :

'Qui sunt hi qui, stella duce, nos adeuntes inaudita ferunt.

Magi respondeant :

nos sumus, quos cernitis, reges Tharsis et Arabum et Saba, dona ferentes Christo, regi nato, Domino, quem, stella deducente, adorare venimus.

Tunc duo Dalmaticati aperientes cortinam dicant :

ecce puer adest quem queritis, Iam properate adorate, quia ipse est redemptio mundi.

Tunc procidentes Reges ad terram, simul salutent puerum, ita dicentes :

salve, princeps saeculorum.

Tunc unus a suo famulo aurum accipiat et dicat :

suscipe, rex, aurum.

Et offerat.

Secundus ita dicat et offerat :

tolle thus, tu, vere Deus.

Tercius ita dicat et offerat :

mirram, signum sepulturae.'

Then the congregation make their oblations. Meanwhile the *Magi* pray and fall asleep. In their sleep an angel warns them to return home another way. The procession returns up a side aisle to the choir; and the Mass, in which the *Magi,* like the shepherds on Christmas day, ' rule the choir,' follows.

In spite of the difference of text the incidents of the Rouen and Limoges versions, except for the angelic warning introduced at Rouen, are the same. There was a dramatic advance when the visit to Jerusalem, instead of being merely narrated by the choir, was inserted into the action. In the play performed at Nevers [1], Herod himself, destined in the fullness of time to become the protagonist of the Corpus Christi stage, makes his first appearance. There are two versions of the Nevers play. In the earlier the new scene is confined to a colloquy between Herod and the *Magi*:

'[*Magi.*] Vidimus stellam eius in Oriente, et agnovimus regem regum esse natum.

[*Herodes.*] regem quem queritis natum stella quo signo didicistis? Si illum regnare creditis, dicite nobis.

[*Magi.*] illum natum esse didicimus in Oriente stella monstrante.

[*Herodes.*] Ite et de puero diligenter investigate, et inventum redeuntes mihi renuntiate.'

The later version adds two further episodes. In one a *nuntius* announces the coming of the *Magi*, and is sent to fetch them before Herod: in the other Herod sends his courtiers for the scribes, who find a prophecy of the birth of the Messiah in Bethlehem. Obviously the Herod scene gives point to the words at the end of the Rouen play, in which the angel bids the *Magi* to return home by a different way.

At Compiègne the action closes with yet another scene, in which Herod learns that the *Magi* have escaped him [2].

'*Nuncius.* Delusus es domine, magi viam redierunt aliam.
[*Herodes.* incendium meum ruina extinguam [3].]

---

[1] Texts ed. L. Delisle, in *Romania*, iv (1875), 1. The earlier version is from *Bibl. Nat. Lat.* 9449 (†1060, a *Gradual*, or, according to Gautier, *Les Tropes*, 123, a *Troper*). The text is headed 'Versus ad Stellam faciendam.' The later is from *B. N. Lat.* 1235 (twelfth-century *Gradual*). It is headed 'Ad Comm[unionem].' Of the first part, down to the end of the interview with Herod, there are two alternative forms in this MS. The one, a free revision of the normal text, is headed:
'Sic speciem veteres stellae
    struxere parentes,
quatinus hos pueri versus
    psallant duo regi.'
[2] Text in K. A. M. Hartmann, *Über das altspanische Dreikönigsspiel* (Leipzig Diss. 1879), 43, from eleventh-century *B. N. Lat. MS.* 16,819.
[3] This line is not actually in the Compiègne text. But it is in most

Armiger. decerne, domine, vindicari iram tuam, et stricto mucrone quaerere iube puerum, forte inter occisos occidetur et ipse.

Herodes. indolis eximiae pueros fac ense perire.

Angelus. sinite parvulos venire ad me, talium est enim regnum caelorum.'

In a Norman version which has the same incidents as the Compiègne play, but in parts a different text, the *armiger* is the son of Herod, and the play ends with Herod taking a sword from a bystander and brandishing it in the air [1]. Already he is beginning to tear a passion to tatters in the manner that became traditionally connected with his name. Another peculiarity of this Norman version is that the *Magi* address Herod in an outlandish jargon, which seems to contain fragments of Hebrew and Arabic speech.

The play of the *Stella* must now, perhaps, be considered, except so far as mere amplifications of the text are concerned, strictly complete. But another step was irresistibly suggested by the course it had taken. The massacre of the Innocents, although it lay outside the range of action in which the *Magi* themselves figured, could be not merely threatened but actually represented. This was done at Laon [2]. The cruel suggestion of Archelaus is carried out. The Innocents come in singing and bearing a lamb. They are slain, and the play ends with a dialogue, like that of the distinct Limoges *planctus*, between the lamenting Rachel and an angelic *consolatrix*.

The absorption of the motives proper to other feasts of the Twelve nights into the Epiphany play has clearly begun. A fresh series of examples shows a similar treatment of the *Pastores*. At Strassburg the *Magi*, as they leave Herod, meet the shepherds returning from Bethlehem :

of the later versions of this scene, and is interesting, as being a classical tag from Sallust, *Catilina*, c. 32; cf. Köppen, 21; Creizenach, i. 63. Reminiscences of *Aeneid*, viii. 112; ix. 376, are sometimes put into Herod's mouth in the scene with the *Magi* (Du Méril, 164, 166).

[1] The version is described, but unfortunately not printed by Gasté, 53. It is from the *De ratione divini officii* in *Montpellier MS.* H. 304.

[2] Text, headed 'Ordo Stellae' in U. Chevalier, *Ordinaires de l'église de Laon*, xxxvi, 389 from *Laon MS.* 263 (thirteenth-century *Trophonarium*).

'Pastores, dicite, quidnam vidistis?

infantem vidimus.'

This, however, is not taken from the *Pastores* itself, but from the Christmas Lauds antiphon[1]. Its dramatic use may be compared with that of the *Victimae paschali* in the *Quem quaeritis*. In versions from Bilsen[2] near Liège and from Mans[3], on the other hand, although the meeting of the *Magi* and the shepherds is retained, a complete *Pastores*, with the angelic tidings and the adoration at the *praesepe*, forms the first part of the office, before the *Magi* are introduced at all.

The Strassburg, Bilsen, and Mans plays have not the *Rachel*, although the first two have the scene in which the *nuntius* informs Herod that the *Magi* have deceived him. A further stage is reached when, as at Freising and at Fleury, the *Pastores*, *Stella* and *Rachel* all coalesce in a single, and by this time considerable, drama. The Freising texts, of which there are two, are rather puzzling[4]. The first closely resembles the plays of the group just described. It begins with a short *Pastores*, comprising the angelic tidings only. Then the scenes between the *Magi* and Herod are treated at great length. The meeting of the *Magi* and the shepherds is followed by the oblation, the angelic warning, and the return of the

---

[1] Text printed by Lange in *Zeitsch. f. deutsch. Alterthum*, xxxii. 412, from *B. M. Add. MS.* 23,922 (*Antiphoner* of †1200). The play was 'In octava Epiphaniae' after the *Magnificat* at Vespers.

[2] Text in C. Cahier and A. Martin, *Mélanges d'Archéologie*, i. (1847-9), 258; Clément, 113, from eleventh-century *Evangeliarium*, now in a Bollandist monastery in Brussels (Meyer, 41). It is a revision of the normal text. The author has been so industrious as even to put many of the rubrics in hexameters. The opening is

'*Ordo.* Post Benedicamus puerorum splendida coetus
ad regem pariter debent protendere gressu,
praeclara voce necnon istic resonare.'

The 'rex' who presided and possibly acted Herod (cf. p. 56) was, I suppose, an Epiphany king or 'rex fatuorum.'

[3] Translation only in P. Piolin, *Théâtre chrétien dans le Maine* (1891), 21. The exact source is not given.

[4] The first text in Du Méril, 156; Davidson, 174, from *Munich MS.* 6264[a] (eleventh century). Apparently it begins with a bit of dumb show, 'Rex sedens in solio quaerat consilium: exeat edictum ut pereant continuo qui detrahunt eius imperio.' Then comes 'Angelus, in primis.' Second text, headed 'Ordo Rachaelis' in Du Méril, 171; Froning, 871, from *Munich MS.* 6264 (eleventh century). It is mainly metrical.

messenger to Herod. In the second Freising text, which is almost wholly metrical, the *Pastores* is complete. It is followed by a quite new scene, the dream of Joseph and his flight into Egypt. Then come successively the scene of fury at court, the massacre, the *planctus* and consolation of Rachel. Clearly this second text, as it stands, is incomplete. The *Magi* are omitted, and the whole of the latter part of the play is consequently rendered meaningless. But it is the *Magi* who are alone treated fully in the first Freising text. I suggest, therefore, that the second text is intended to supplement and not to replace the first. It really comprises two fragments : one a revision of the *Pastores*, the other a revision of the closing scene and an expansion of it by a *Rachel*.

As to the Fleury version there can be no doubt whatever [1]. The matter is, indeed, arranged in two plays, a *Herodes* and an *Interfectio Puerorum*, each ending with a *Te Deum* ; and the performance may possibly have extended over two days. But the style is the same throughout and the episodes form one continuous action. It is impossible to regard the *Interfectio Puerorum* as a separate piece from the *Herodes*, acted a week earlier on the feast of the Innocents ; for into it, after the first entry of the children with their lamb, *gaudentes per monasterium*, come the flight into Egypt, the return of the *nuntius*, and the wrath of Herod, which, of course, presuppose the *Magi* scenes. Another new incident is added at the end of the Fleury play. Herod is deposed and Archelaus set up ; the Holy Family return from Egypt, and settle in the parts of Galilee [2].

I have attempted to arrange the dozen or so complete Epiphany plays known to scholars in at least the logical order of their development. There are also three fragments, which fit readily enough into the system. Two, from a Paris manuscript and from Einsiedeln, may be classed respectively with the

---

[1] Texts in Du Méril, 162, 175; Davidson, 175 ; Coussemaker, 143; Wright, 32, from *Orleans MS.* 178. The first part begins with the rubric 'Parato Herode et ceteris personis . . .'; the second with 'Ad interfectionem Puerorum . . .'

[2] Wordsworth, 147, suggests that the name 'Le Galilee,' given at Lincoln to a room over the south porch and also found elsewhere, may be 'derived from some incident in the half-dramatic Paschal ceremonies.' For another liturgical drama in which 'Galilee' is required as a scene, cf. p. 60.

Compiègne and Strassburg texts [1]. The third, from Vienne, is an independent version, in leonine hexameters, of the scene in which the *Magi* first sight the star, a theme common to all the plays except that of Limoges [2]. I do not feel certain that this fragment is from a liturgical drama at all.

The textual development of the *Stella* is closely parallel to that of the *Quem quaeritis*. The more primitive versions consist of antiphons and prose sentences based upon or in the manner of the Scriptures. The later ones, doubtless under the influence of wandering scholars, become increasingly metrical. The classical tags, from Sallust and Virgil, are an obvious note of the scholarly pen. With the exception of that from Limoges, all the texts appear to be derived by successive accretions and modifications from an archetype fairly represented at Rouen. The Bilsen text and the Vienne fragment have been freely rewritten, and the process of re-writing is well illustrated by the alternative versions found side by side in the later Nevers manuscript. With regard to the place occupied by the *Stella* in the Epiphany services, such manuscripts as give any indications at all seem to point to a considerable divergence of local use. At Limoges and Nevers, the play was of the nature of a trope to the Mass, inserted in the former case at the *Offertorium*, in the latter at the *Communio* [3]. At Rouen the *Officium* followed Tierce, and preceded the ordinary procession before Mass. At Fleury the use of the *Te Deum* suggests that it was at Matins; at Strassburg it followed the *Magnificat* at Vespers, but on the octave of Epiphany, not Epiphany itself. Perhaps the second part of the Fleury play was also on the octave. At Bilsen the play followed the *Benedicamus*, but with this versicle nearly all the Hours end [4]. I do not, however, hesitate to

[1] *B.N. Lat.* 1152 (eleventh century) in *Bibl. de l'École des Chartes*, xxxiv. 657. Einsiedeln fragment (eleventh–twelfth century) printed by G. Morel in *Pilger* (1849), 401; cf. Köppen, 13.

[2] Text in Du Méril, 151, from *Vienne MS.* 941 (fourteenth century). It is entitled 'Ad adorandum filium Dei per Stellam invitantur Eoy.' The first three lines, headed 'Stella,' are an address to the 'exotica plebs'; each of the remaining ten lines is divided between three speakers, 'Aureolus,' 'Thureolus,' 'Myrrheolus.'

[3] On the use of tropes at these points in the Mass, cf. Frere, xix.

[4] *Use of Sarum*, i. 280.

say that the Limoges use must have been the most primitive
one. The kernel of the whole performance is a dramatized
Offertorium. It was a custom for Christian kings to offer
gold and frankincense and myrrh at the altar on Epiphany
day[1]; and I take the play to have served as a substitute
for this ceremony, where no king actually regnant was
present.

There is yet one other liturgical play belonging to the
Christmas season, which for the future development of the
drama is the most important of all. This is the *Prophetae*[2].
It differs from the *Quem quaeritis*, the *Peregrini*, the *Pastores*,
and the *Stella* by the large number of performers required,
and by the epical mode of its composition. Its origin, in
fact, is to be sought in a narrative, a *lectio*, not a chant. The
source was the pseudo-Augustinian *Sermo contra Iudaeos,
Paganos et Arianos de Symbolo*, probably written in the sixth
century, but ascribed throughout the Middle Ages to the
great African[3]. A portion of this sermon was used in many
churches as a lesson for some part or other of the Christmas
offices[4]. The passage chosen is in a highly rhetorical vein.
Vos, inquam, convenio, O Iudaei cries the preacher, and calls
upon the Jews to bear witness out of the mouths of their own
prophets to the Christ. Isaiah, Jeremiah, Daniel, Moses,
David, Habakkuk, Simeon, Zacharias and Elisabeth, John
the Baptist;—each in turn is bidden to speak, and each
testimony is triumphantly quoted. Then: *Ecce, convertimur*

---

[1] Martene, iii. 44; in England
the royal offering is still made, by
proxy, at the Chapel Royal, St.
James's (Ashton, 237).

[2] I follow the epoch-making
étude of M. Sepet, *Les Prophètes
du Christ*, in *Bibl. de l'École des
Chartes*, xxviii. (1867), 1, 210, xxix.
(1868), 205, 261, xxxviii. (1877), 397
(I am sorry not to be able to cite
the separate edition printed at Paris,
1878); cf. also Creizenach, i. 67;
Julleville, *Myst.* i. 35; and, especially, Weber, 41. But none of
these writers could make use of the
Laon version discovered by M.
Chevalier. Meyer, 53, suggests that

Sepet has exaggerated the importance of the *Prophetae* in the development of the O.T. dramatic
cycle.

[3] Text in *P.L.* xlii. 1117; on the
date cf. Weber, 41. The *lectio* is
printed by Sepet, xxviii. 3.

[4] At Arles it was the sixth *lectio*
at Matins on Christmas day (Sepet,
xxviii. 2); at Rome the fourth lesson
at Matins on Christmas eve (Martene, iii. 31); at Rouen it was read
at Matins two days earlier (Martene, iii. 34); in the *Sarum Breviary*,
i. cxxxv, it makes the fourth, fifth,
and sixth *lectiones* at Matins on the
fourth Sunday in Advent.

ad gentes. Virgil—*poeta facundissimus*—is pressed into the service, for the famous line of his fourth eclogue:

'iam nova progenies caelo demittitur alto[1],'

Nebuchadnezzar, who saw four walking in the furnace, and finally the Erythraean Sibyl, whose acrostic verses on the 'Signs of Judgement' first appear in the writings of Eusebius[2].

The dramatic form of this *lectio* possibly led to its being chanted instead of read, and distributed between several voices in the manner of the Passions from Palm Sunday to Good Friday[3]. At any rate in the eleventh century there appears in a Limoges manuscript a metrical adaptation in which it has been wholly converted into a dramatic dialogue[4]. This Limoges *Prophetae* follows the sermon pretty closely in its arrangement. A *Precentor* begins:

'Omnes gentes congaudentes, dent cantum laetitiae! deus homo fit, de domo David, natus hodie.'

He addresses a couplet each *Ad Iudaeos, Ad Gentes,* and then calls in turn upon each of the prophets, who reply, Virgil pronouncing his line, the Sibyl the *Iudicii Signum,* and the others a couplet or quatrain apiece. They are nearly identical with the personages of the sermon: Israel is added, Zacharias disappears, and the order is slightly different. Finally the *Precentor* concludes:

'Iudaea incredula, cur manens adhuc inverecunda?'

Two later versions, belonging respectively to Laon[5] and to

---

[1] *Bucol.* iv. 7.

[2] Eusebius, *Orat. Const. Magn. ad Sanctorum Coetum,* c. 18 (*P.G.* xx. 1288). On the *Iudicii Signum* and the *Dit des quinze Signes* (Text in Grass, *Adamsspiel,* 57) derived from it, cf. Sepet, xxviii. 8; Du Méril, 185. According to Martene, iii. 34, the *Versus Sibyllae* were often sung at Matins on Christmas day, apparently apart from the *sermo.* Thus at Limoges they were sung after the sixth *responsorium.*

[3] Sepet, xxviii. 13; cf. p. 5.

[4] Text in Du Méril, 179; Coussemaker, 11; Wright, 60; from *Bibl. Nat. Lat.* 1139 (eleventh or twelfth century). Weber, 51, gives an interesting account of the *Prophetae* in art, and points out that the play seems to have influenced such representations in Italy early in the eleventh century.

[5] Text in U. Chevalier, *Ordinaires de l'Église de Laon,* xxxvi, 385, from *Laon MS.* 263 (thirteenth century *Trophonarium*). It is headed 'Ordo Prophetarum.'

Rouen[1], diverge far more from the model. They are at much the same stage of development. In both the play is ushered in with the hymn *Gloriosi et famosi*, the verses of which are sung by the prophets, and the refrain by the choir[2]. The costumes and symbols of the prophets are carefully indicated in the rubrics. The *Precentor* of Limoges is represented by two singers, called at Laon *Appellatores*, and at Rouen *Vocatores*. The dialogue is amplified beyond that of Limoges. *Sex Iudaei* and *sex Gentiles*, for instance, take parts: and the *Vocatores* comment with the choir in an identical form of words on each prophecy. The Laon text is a good deal the shorter. The prophets are practically the same as at Limoges, with one remarkable exception. At the end is introduced Balaam, and to his prophecy is appended a miniature drama, with the angel and the ass: thus—

'*Hic veniat Angelus cum gladio. Balaam tangit asinam, et illa non praecedente, dicit iratus :*

> quid moraris, asina,
> obstinata bestia?
> iam scindent calcaria
> costas et praecordia.

Puer sub asina respondet:

---

[1] Text in Gasté, 4, from *Rouen MS. Y.* 110 (fourteenth-century *Ordinarium*). The opening is 'Nota, Cantor; si *Festum Asinorum* fiat, processio ordinetur post Terciam. Si non fiat Festum, tunc fiat processio, ut nunc praenotatur. Ordo *Processionis Asinorum* secundum Rothomagensem usum. Tercia cantata, paratis Prophetis iuxta suum ordinem, fornace in medio navis ecclesiae lintheo et stuppis constituta, processio moveat de claustro, et duo clerici de secunda sede, in cappis, processionem regant, hos versus canentes: *Gloriosi et famosi*. ... Tunc processio in medio ecclesiae stet.' At the end the 'Prophetae et ministri' rule the choir. Unfortunately the MS., like other *Ordinaria*, only gives the first words of many of the chants.

[2] The *Gloriosi et famosi* hymn occurs in a twelfth-century Einsiedeln MS. (Milchsack, 36) as an overture to the *Quem quaeritis*. It is arranged for 'chorus' and 'Prophetae,' and was therefore borrowed from Christmas. It is followed by another hymn, more strictly Paschal, the *Hortum praedestinatio*, and this, which is also used with the Sens *Quem quaeritis* (Milchsack, 58), is sung at the end of the Rouen *Prophetae* by 'omnes prophetae et ministri [? = vocatores] in pulpito'—a curious double borrowing between the two feasts. Meyer, 51, argues that the Einsiedeln MS., which is in a fragmentary state, contained a *Prophetae*, to which, and not to the *Quem quaeritis*, the *Gloriosi et famosi* belonged.

> angelus cum gladio,
> quem adstare video,
> prohibet ne transeam;
> timeo ne peream.'

The Rouen text adds quite a number of prophets. The full list includes Moses, Amos, Isaiah, Aaron, Jeremiah, Daniel, Habakkuk, Balaam, Samuel, David, Hosea, Joel, Obadiah, Jonah, Micah, Nahum, Zephaniah, Haggai, Zechariah, Ezekiel, Malachi, Zacharias, Elisabeth, John the Baptist, Simeon, Virgil, Nebuchadnezzar, and the Sibyl. In this version, also, the part of Balaam is expanded into a drama.

'*Duo missi a rege Balac dicant:*
> Balaam, veni et fac.

Tunc Balaam, ornatus, sedens super asinam, habens calcaria, retineat lora et calcaribus percutiat asinam, et quidam iuvenis, habens alas, tenens gladium, obstet asinae. Quidam sub asina dicat:
> cur me cum calcaribus miseram sic laeditis.

Hoc dicto, Angelus ei dicat:
> desine regis Balac praeceptum perficere.'

Here, too, another little drama is similarly introduced. This is the story of Shadrach, Meshach, and Abednego, which, with an *imago* for the brethren to refuse to worship and a *fornax* for them to be cast into, attaches itself to the *vocatio* of Nebuchadnezzar.

In the Limoges manuscript the *Prophetae* is followed by the words *Hic inchoant Benedicamus*[1]. As has been pointed out in the case of the Bilsen *Pastores*, this is not conclusive as to the hour at which the performance took place. The day was probably that of Christmas itself. But even the day would naturally vary with the variable position of the *lectio* out of which the *Prophetae* grew.   At Lincoln it was likewise Christmas day.   But at Rouen the *processio asinorum* was on Christmas eve, and took the place of the ordinary festal procession after Tierce and before Mass[2].   And at St. Martin

[1] Sepet, xxviii. 25.
[2] So says Gasté, 4. But I think he must be wrong, for the *Introit* with which the text concludes is *Puer natus est*, which belongs to the *Magna missa* of the feast-day, and not to the eve.

of Tours the *Prophetae* was on New Year's day, performances being given both at Matins and Vespers[1].

The question naturally suggests itself: What was the relation of these liturgical plays of the Christmas season to the Feast of Fools and other ecclesiastical *ludi* of the Twelve nights, which were discussed in the first volume? At Rouen, the *Prophetae* received the name of *processio asinorum* and took place at a *festum asinorum*, a name which we know to have been elsewhere synonymous with *festum fatuorum*. At Tours, it was played at a reformed *festum novi anni*, with a Boy Bishop and at least traces of expelled disorder. So, too, with the other plays. The Rouen *Pastores* was infected by the fifteenth century with the *stultitiae et insolentiae* of the *triduum*. At Bilsen the *Stella* was performed before a *rex*, who can hardly have been any other than a *rex fatuorum* of Epiphany. At Autun the *regnum Herodis* was considered a Feast of Fools[2]. Probably in both churches the *rex* acted Herod in the play. I think it must be taken for granted that the plays are the older institution of the two. They seem all to have taken shape by the eleventh century, before there is any clear sign that the Kalends had made their way into the churches and become the Feast of Fools. The plays may even have been encouraged as a counter-attraction, for the congregation, to the Kalends outside. On the other hand, I do not hold, as some writers do, that the riotous Feasts of Asses were derived from the pious and instructive ceremony so called at Rouen[3]. On the contrary, Balaam and his ass are an interpolation in the *Prophetae* both at Rouen

---

[1] Martene, iii. 41, from a fourteenth-century *Rituale*: ' dicto versiculo tertii nocturni, accenditur totum luminare, et veniunt Prophetae in capitulo revestiti, et post cantant insimul *Lumen Patris*, et clericus solus dicit *In gaudio*, et post legitur septima lectio. Post nonam lectionem ducunt prophetas de capitulo ad portam Thesaurarii cantilenas cantando, et post in chorum, ubi dicunt cantori prophetias, et duo clericuli in pulpito cantando eos appellant. Post dicitur nonum [responsorium?] in pulpito . . . . . . Post [primam] recitatur miraculum [Martene conjectures *martyrologium*] in claustro . . . [Ad vesperas] dictis psalmis et antiphonis, ducunt ad portam Thesaurarii prophetas, sicut ad matutinum et reducunt in chorum similiter, et habent clerici virgas plenas candelis ardentibus, vocant eos clerici duo sicut ad vesperas [? matutinum].' Presently follows the *Deposuit*: cf. vol. i. p. 309.

[2] Cf. vol. i. p. 313.

[3] Gasté, 20.

and, more obviously, at Laon. Balaam, alone of the Laon performers, is not from the pseudo-Augustine sermon. Is he not, therefore, to be regarded as a reaction of the Feast of Fools upon the *Prophetae*, as an attempt to turn the established presence of the ass in the church to purposes of edification, rather than of ribaldry [1]? I think the explanation is the more plausible one. And I find a parallel reaction of the turbulence of the Feast of Fools upon the *Stella*, in the violence of speech and gesture which permanently associated itself at a very early stage with the character of Herod. The view here taken will be confirmed, when we come to consider certain ecclesiastical criticisms passed upon the liturgical plays in the twelfth century.

Whatever the exact relation of the divine and profane *ludi* at Easter and Christmas may be, it seems to have been, in the main, at these two great seasons of festivity that what may be called the spontaneous growth of drama out of liturgy took place. There are yet a fair number of Latin plays to be spoken of which are in a sense liturgical. That is to say, they were acted, certainly or probably, in churches and during intervals in the services. But of these such a spontaneous growth cannot be asserted, although it cannot also, in the present state of the evidence, be confidently denied. Their metrical and literary style is parallel to that of the Easter and Christmas plays in the latest stages of development ; and, until further data turn up, it is perhaps permissible to conjecture that they were deliberately composed on the model of the *Quem quaeritis* and the *Stella*, when these had become widespread and popular. Indeed, some such derivation of the *Peregrini* from the *Quem quaeritis* and of the *Stella* itself, at least in part, from the *Pastores*, has already appeared probable.

In dealing with this new group of plays, we come, for the first and only time, upon an individual author. As might be expected, this author is a *scholaris vagans*, by name Hilarius.

---

[1] Sepet, xxviii. 219, suggests that Balaam, when first introduced into the *Prophetae*, merely prophesied, as he does in the *Adam* (Grass, 46). Possibly, yet his introduction at the end of the Laon play (unknown to Sepet) looks as if he were an appendix for the sake of his ass.

It would even be doing him no great injustice to call him a goliard. What little is known of Hilarius is gathered from his writings, which exist in a single manuscript. He may have been an Englishman, for a large proportion of his verses are addressed to English folk. He was a pupil, about 1125, of the famous Abelard at his oratory of Paraclete in a desert near Nogent-sur-Seine. Afterwards he made his way to Angers. Many of his verses are of the familiar goliardic type, amorous and jocund; but amongst them are three plays[1]. Two of these are comparatively short, and contain each a few stanzas of French interspersed amongst the Latin. The subject of one is a miracle wrought by St. Nicholas[2]; of the other, the *Suscitatio Lazari*[3]. The third play, wholly in Latin, falls into two parts, and gives at considerable length the story of *Daniel*[4]. I take it that these plays were not written for any church in particular, but represent the repertory of a band of wandering clerks. At the end, both of the *Daniel* and of the *Suscitatio Lazari*, is a rubric or stage-direction, to the effect that, if the performance is given at Matins, the *Te Deum* should follow; if at Vespers, the *Magnificat*. Evidently the connexion with the church service, so organic in the plays of the more primitive type, has become for Hilarius almost accidental. As to the place of the plays in the calendar, the manuscript gives no indication, and probably Hilarius and his friends would be willing enough to act them whenever they got a chance. But the St. Nicholas

---

[1] Champollion - Figeac, *Hilarii Versus et Ludi* (1838), from *B. N. Lat. MS.* 11,331. The plays are also printed by Du Méril, *Or. Lat.* On the life cf. *Hist. Litt. de la France*, xx. 627; *D. N. B.* s.v. Hilary; Morley, *English Writers*, iii. 107.

[2] Du Méril, 272 'Ludus super iconia Sancti Nicolai.' There is a 'persona iconie.' A *Barbarus* speaks partly in French.

[3] Du Méril, 225 'Suscitatio Lazari: ad quam istae personae sunt necessariae: Persona Lazari, duarum Sororum, quatuor Iudaeorum, Iesu Christi, duodecim Apostolorum, vel sex ad minus... (ends).

Quo finito, si factum fuerit ad Matutinas, Lazarus in piat: *Te Deum laudamus*: si vero ad Vesperas: *Magnificat anima mea Dominum.*'

[4] Du Méril, 241 'Historia de Daniel repraesentanda,' with a list of the 'personae necessariae' and a final rubric as in the 'Suscitatio Lazari': cf. Sepet, xxviii. 232, on this and similar plays and their relation to the *Prophetae*. From the names 'Hilarius,' 'Iordanus,' 'Simon,' attached to parts of the *Daniel* in the MS., it would seem that Hilarius had collaborators for this play (Sepet, xxviii. 248).

play would come most naturally on the day of that saint, December 6. The *Suscitatio Lazari* would be appropriate enough as an addition to the *Quem quaeritis* and the *Peregrini* in Easter week. The story is told, indeed, in the Gospel for Friday in the fourth week in Lent; but that does not seem a very likely date for a play. The *Daniel* perhaps grew, as we have seen a *Balaam* and a *Nebuchadnezzar* growing, out of a *Prophetae*; and may have been a substitute for a *Prophetae* at Christmas.

These dates are borne out, or not contradicted, by other similar plays, which have more of a local habitation. For no one of Hilarius' three stands quite alone. Of Latin plays of St. Nicholas, indeed, quite a little group exists; and the great scholastic feast evidently afforded an occasion, less only than Easter and Christmas, for dramatic performances. The earliest texts are from Germany. Two are found in a Hildesheim manuscript of the eleventh century[1]; a third in an Einsiedeln manuscript of the twelfth[2]. The thirteenth-century Fleury playbook contains no less than four, two of which appear to be more developed forms of the Hildesheim plays. The theme is in every case one of the miraculous deeds which so largely make up the widespread legend of the saint[3]. Nicholas restores to life the three clerks

' quos causa discendi literas
apud gentes transmisit exteras,'

and whom the greed of an innkeeper has slain[4]. He provides with a dowry the daughters of a poor gentleman, who are threatened with a life of shame[5]. He brings back from captivity the son of his wealthy adorer[6]. His image preserves

[1] E. Dümmler, in *Z. f. d. Alterthum*, xxxv. 401 ; xxxvi. 238, from *B. M. Addl. MS.* 22,414 (' Liber Sancti Godehardi in Hild[esheim] '). On the group of Nicholas plays cf. Creizenach, i. 105.

[2] G. Morel, in *Anzeiger für Kunde der deutschen Vorzeit*, vi. (1859), 207, from *Einsiedeln MS.* 34.

[3] *Golden Legend*, ii. 109 ; Wace, *Vie de Saint-Nicolas* (ed. Delius, 1850).

[4] Du Méril, 262 ; Coussemaker, 100.

The play ends with the *Te Deum*. The same subject is treated in the Einsiedeln play, and one of those from Hildesheim.

[5] Du Méril, 254 ; Coussemaker, 83. The play ends with the anthem ' O Christi pietas,' used at second Vespers on St. Nicholas' day (*Sarum Breviary*, iii. 38). The same subject is treated in the other Hildesheim play.

[6] Du Méril, 276 ; Coussemaker, 123 ; begins ' Ad repraesentandum

from housebreakers the riches of a Jew[1]. Alone of the extant Latin plays, these of St. Nicholas are drawn from outside the Biblical story. Each of the Fleury versions introduces at the end one of the anthems proper to St. Nicholas' day, and their connexion with the feast is therefore clear.

A second Lazarus play, which includes not only the *Suscitatio* but also the episode of Mary Magdalen in the house of Simon, is likewise in the Fleury playbook[2]. A second *Daniel*, composed by the *iuventus* of Beauvais, occurs in the same manuscript which contains the Office of the Circumcision for that cathedral[3]. It was perhaps intended for performance on the day of the *asinaria festa*. Other plays seem, in the same way as the *Daniel*, to have budded off from the *Prophetae*. A fragment is preserved of an *Isaac and Rebecca* from Kloster Vorau in Styria[4]. A twelfth-century mention of an *Elisaeus*[5] and an eleventh-century one of a *Convivium Herodis*[6], which suggests rather the story of John the Baptist than that of the *Magi*, point to an activity in this direction of which all the traces have possibly not yet been discovered.

quomodo Sanctus Nicolaus, &c....': ends with anthem 'Copiosae caritatis' used at Lauds on St. Nicholas' day (*Sarum Breviary*, iii. 37).

[1] Du Méril, 266; Coussemaker, 109; begins 'Aliud miraculum de Sancto Nicolao, &c. ...': ends with anthem 'Statuit ei Dominus,' not in *Sarum Breviary*, but used at Rome as *Introit* on feasts of Pontiffs. This is the subject of Hilarius' play.

[2] Text in Du Méril, 213; Coussemaker, 220. The play contains a Paschal sequence and ends with a *Te Deum*. Part of the action is in a *platea*; Simon has a *domus*, which afterwards 'efficiatur quasi Bethania.' Other 'loci' represent 'Ierusalem' and 'Galilaea' (cf. p. 50), and the 'Suscitatio' takes place at a 'monumentum' (probably the Easter sepulchre).

[3] Text in Coussemaker, 49, and Danjou, *Revue de la Musique religieuse*, iv. (1848), 65. Cf. Sepet, xxviii. 232, and on the MS., vol. i. p. 284.

As in the Beauvais *Officium Circumcisionis*, there are many processional chants or *conductus*, in one of which are the terms 'celebremus Natalis solempnia' and 'in hoc Natalitio' which attach the play to Christmas, or at least the Christmas season. The text begins 'Incipit Danielis ludus,' and ends with the *Te Deum*. The following quatrain serves as prologue:
'Ad honorem tui, Christe,
Danielis ludus iste
in Belvaco est inventus
et invenit hunc iuventus.'
Meyer, 56, finds relations between the Beauvais *Daniel* and that of *Hilarius*.

[4] Text in *Anzeiger für Kunde d. deutschen Vorzeit* (1877), 169, from late twelfth-century MS.; cf. Creizenach, i. 74.

[5] Cf. p. 99.

[6] Creizenach, i. 6, 71. The unauthentic *Annales* of Corvei mention also a play on *Joseph* under the year 1264 (Creizenach, i. 75).

Three plays, each more or less unique in character, complete the tale. The Fleury playbook has a *Conversio Beati Pauli Apostoli*, doubtless designed for the feast on January 25[1]. The shorter, but highly interesting collection from Limoges, has a play of the wise and foolish virgins, under the title of *Sponsus*[2]. This has attracted much attention from scholars, on account of the fact that it is partly in French, or more strictly in a dialect belonging to the Angoumois, and slightly affected by Provençal. As it is therefore of the nature of a transitional form, it may be well to give a somewhat full account of it. It opens with a Latin chorus beginning

> 'Adest sponsus qui est Christus : vigilate, virgines ! '

The angel Gabriel then addresses the virgins, and warns them in four French stanzas to expect ' un espos, Sauvaire a nom.' Each stanza has a refrain, probably sung chorally :

> 'gaire noi dormet :
> aici 's l'espos que vos or atendet !

Then comes a lyric dialogue, in which the *Fatuae*, who have wasted their oil, attempt in vain to get some, first from the *Prudentes*, and then from some *Mercatores*, whose presence here recalls the *unguentarius* in the Prague versions of the *Quem quaeritis*[3]. This dialogue is in Latin, but with a French refrain :

> ' dolentas, chaitivas, trop i avem (*or* avet) dormit.'

---

[1] Text in Du Méril, 237 ; Coussemaker, 210 ; begins ' Ad repraesentandam conversionem beati Pauli apostoli, &c. . . . ': ends with *Te Deum*. Four ' sedes ' are required, and a ' lectus ' for Ananias.

[2] Latest text, with long introduction, mainly philological, by W. Cloetta, in *Romania*, xxii. (1893), 177 ; others by Du Méril, 233 ; Coussemaker, 1 ; E. Boehmer, in *Romanische Studien*, iv. 99 ; K. Bartsch, *Lang. et Litt. françaises*, 13 ; cf. also Julleville, *Les Myst.* i. 27 ; E. Stengel, *Z. f. rom. Phil.* iii. 233 ; E. Schwan, *Z. f. rom. Phil.* xi. 469 ; H. Morf, *Z. f. rom. Phil.* xx.

385. The manuscript is *Bibl. Nat. Lat.* 1139. MM. Cloetta (p. 221) and G. Paris (*Litt. fr. au moyen âge*[2], 237, 246) assign the *Sponsus* to the earlier half or second third of the twelfth century, and the former, with the delightful diffidence of a philologist, thinks, on linguistic grounds, that it was written at Saint Amant de Boixe (sixteen *kilomètres* north of Angoulême). It only remains for some archivist to find a clerk of St. Martial of Limoges whose native place was this very village.

[3] Cf. p. 33.

Then comes the *Sponsus*, to whom the *Fatuae* finally appeal :

'audi, sponse, voces plangentium :
aperire fac nobis ostium
cum sociis ad dulce prandium ;
nostrae culpae praebe remedium !
dolentas, chaitivas, trop i avem dormit.

Christus.

amen dico, vos ignosco, nam caretis lumine,
quod qui perdunt procul pergunt huius aulae limine.
alet, chaitivas, alet, malaüreias !
a tot jors mais vos son penas livreias,
e en efern ora seret meneias !

Modo accipiant eas daemones et praecipitentur in infernum.'

This stage direction, together with an allusion in the opening lines of the *Sponsus* to the ' second Adam,' link this remarkable, and, I venture to think, finely conceived little piece to the Christmas play of *Adam* to be discussed in the next chapter. It has essentially an Advent theme, and must have been performed either in Advent itself or at the Christmas season, with which Advent is prophetically connected [1].

Finally, there is a play which was almost certainly performed at Advent [2]. This is the Tegernsee play of *Antichristus* [3]. It is founded upon the prophecy in St. Paul's second epistle to the Thessalonians of the *homo peccati, filius perditionis*, who shall sit in the temple of God until the Christ shall slay him with the breath of his mouth, and destroy him with the glory of his advent [4]: and it is an elaborate spectacle, requiring for

[1] H. Morf, *loc. cit.*, considers the *Sponsus* an Easter play.

[2] Creizenach, i. 77. An Italian dramatic *Lauda* on the same subject is headed ' In Dominica de Adventu ' (D'Ancona, i. 141).

[3] Text in Froning, 206, from edition of Zezschwitz, *Vom römischen Kaisertum deutscher Nation* (1877). The earliest edition is by Pez, *Thesaurus Anecd. Noviss.* (1721-9), ii. 3, 187. This writer introduced confusion by giving the play the title *Ludus paschalis de adventu et interitu Antichristi*. It has nothing

to do with Easter. The latest and best edition is that by W. Meyer, in *Sitzungsberichte d. hist.-phil. Classe d. königl. bayr. Akad. d. Wiss.* (Munich), 1882, 1. The unique MS. is *Munich MS.* 19,411 (twelfth-thirteenth century), formerly in Kloster Tegernsee. Both Zezschwitz and Meyer have long and valuable introductions ; cf. also Froning, 199 ; Creizenach, i. 78. T. Wright prints the play from Pez, in *Chester Plays*, ii. 227.

[4] 2 *Thessalonians*, ii. 3-12. According to *York Missal*, i. 10, part

its proper performance a large number of actors and a spacious
stage, with a temple of God and seven royal *sedes*, together
with room for much marching and counter-marching and
warfare[1]. It must have taken up the whole nave of some
great church. It begins with a procession of Emperor, Pope,
and Kings, accompanied by personages emblematic of *Gentilitas*, *Sinagoga* and *Ecclesia* with her attendants *Misericordia*
and *Iustitia*. The first part of the action represents the
conquest of the four corners of Christendom by the Emperor
and his championship of Jerusalem against the King of
Babylon. *Ecclesia*, *Gentilitas*, and *Synagoga* punctuate the
performance with their characteristic chants. Then come the
Hypocrites, *sub silentio et specie humilitatis inclinantes circumquaque et captantes favorem laicorum*. They are followed by
Antichrist himself, who instructs Hypocrisy and Heresy to
prepare the way for his advent. Presently Antichrist is
enthroned in the temple and gradually saps the Empire,
winning over the King of the Greeks by threats, the King of
the Franks by gifts, and the King of the Teutons, who is
incorruptible and invincible, by signs and wonders. He marks
his vassals on the brow with the first letter of his name.
Then the Hypocrites attempt to persuade *Synagoga* that
Antichrist is the Messiah; but are refuted by the prophets
Enoch and Elijah. Antichrist has the rebels slain; but while
he is throned in state, thunder breaks suddenly over his head,
he falls, and *Ecclesia* comes to her own again with a *Laudem
dicite deo nostro*.

The author of the *Antichristus* is not only a skilled crafts-
man in rhyming Latin metres; he is also capable of carrying
a big literary scheme successfully to a close. His immediate
source was probably the tenth-century *Libellus de Antichristo*

---

of this passage is read at Mass on
Saturday in the *Quatuor Tempora*
of Advent.

[1] ' Templum domini et vii sedes
regales primum collocentur in hunc
modum :

Ad orientem templum domini; huic
   collocantur sedes regis Hieroso-
   limorum et sedes Sinagogae.

Ad occidentem sedes imperatoris

Romani ; huic collocantur sedes
regis Theotonicorum et sedes
regis Francorum.

Ad austrum sedes regis Graecorum.

Ad meridiem sedes regis Babiloniae
et Gentilitatis.'

Other than this direction the play
has no heading, but in later stage-
directions it is incidentally called a
' ludus.'

of Adso of Toul[1]. Into this he has worked the central theme of the *Prophetae* and the debating figures from that very popular *débat* or ' estrif,' the *Altercatio Ecclesiae et Synagogae*[2]. His work differs in several obvious respects from the comparatively simple, often naive, liturgical dramas which have been considered. It is ambitious in scope, extending to between four and five hundred lines. It introduces allegorical figures, such as we shall find, long after, in the moralities. It has a purpose other than that of devotion, or even amusement. It is, in fact, a *Tendenzschrift*, a pamphlet. The instinct of the drama, which sways the imaginations of men perhaps more powerfully than any other form of literature, to mix itself up with politics is incorrigible: *Antichristus* is a subtle vindication, on the one hand, of the Empire against the Papacy, on the other of the *rex Teutonicorum* against the *rex Francorum*. It probably dates from about 1160, when Frederick Barbarossa was at the height of his struggle with Alexander III, who enjoyed the sympathies of Louis VII of France. And it is anti-clerical. The Hypocrites who carry out the machinations of Antichrist are the clerical reformers, such as Gerhoh of Reichersberg[3], who were the mainstay of the papacy in Germany.

It is improbable that the few and scattered texts which have come to light represent all the liturgical plays which had made their appearance by the middle of the twelfth century. Besides the lost *Elisaeus* and *Convivium Herodis*, there is evidence, for example, of scholars' plays in honour, not only of St. Nicholas, but of their second patron, the philosophical St. Catharine of Alexandria. Such a *ludus de Sancta Katarina* was prepared at Dunstable in England by one Geoffrey, a Norman clerk who had been invited to England as schoolmaster to the abbey of St. Albans. For it he borrowed certain

---

[1] Printed in *P.L.* ci. 1291.

[2] Pseudo - Augustine, *De altercatione Ecclesiae et Synagogae dialogus* in *P.L.* xlii. 1131. On this theme and the *débats* based thereon cf. *Hist. Litt.* xxiii. 216; G. Paris, § 155 ; Pearson, ii. 376. P. Weber, *Geistliches Schauspiel und kirchliche Kunst* (1894), is mainly occupied with this motive and its place in the religious drama and religious art. It is a most valuable study, but I find no ground for the conjecture (Weber, 31, 36) that the *Altercatio*, like the *Prophetae*, had already, before the *Antichrist*, been semi-dramatically rendered in the liturgy.

[3] Cf. p. 98.

choir copes belonging to the abbey, and had the misfortune to let these be burnt with his house. Deeply repentant, he took the religious habit, and in 1119 became abbot of St. Albans. From this date that of the *ludus* may be judged to be early in the twelfth century[1].

It cannot, of course, be assumed that every play, say in the fifteenth century, which although probably or certainly written in the vernacular was performed in a church, had a Latin prototype[2]. Many such may have been written and acted for the first time on existing models, when the vernacular drama was already well established. But there are certain feasts where it is possible to trace, on the one hand, the element of mimetic ceremony in the services, and on the other, perhaps, some later representation in the dramatic cycles, and where a Latin text might at any time turn up without causing surprise. With a few notes on some of these this chapter must conclude. A highly dramatic trope for Ascension day, closely resembling the *Quem quaeritis*, has already been quoted from the tropers of Limoges[3]. An *Ordinarium* of St. Peter's of Lille directs that, after the respond *Non vos relinquam*, the officiant shall mount a pulpit and thence appear to ascend towards heaven from the top of a mountain[4]. Fifteenth-century *computi* speak of this or of a more elaborate performance as a *mysterium*, and include amongst other items payments for painting the scars on the hands of the performer[5]. On Whit-

---

[1] *Representations*, s.v. Dunstable.

[2] At Rouen, e. g., a confraternity played a *misterium* on the feast of the Assumption in a waxen 'hortus' set up in their chapel; and this between 1446 and 1521 required reformation from various 'derisiones,' especially a 'ludus de marmousetis' (Gasté, 76). But I know of no evidence for a Latin Assumption play, although such may quite well have existed. The Lincoln Assumption play was given in the cathedral, as a wind-up to a cycle (*Representations*, s. v. Lincoln).

[3] Cf. p. 11.

[4] Ducange, s.v. *Festum Ascensionis*, 'qui . . . officio hac die praeerat, cum modicum panis et vini degustasset, cantato responsorio *Non vos relinquam*, ambonem ascendebat, ubi ex monte efficto coelum petere videbatur ; tunc pueri symphoniaci veste angelica induti decantabant *Viri Galilaei*, etc.'

[5] Julleville, *Les Myst.* ii. 9; *Annales archéologiques*, xviii. 173 'pro pingendo cicatrices in manibus D. Iohannis Rosnel, facientis mysterium in die Ascensionis' (1416), 'pro potandum cum discipulis,' 'vicariis representantibus Crucifixum cum suis discipulis et ibidem simul manducantibus et bibentibus vinum,' 'pro pingendo vulnera,' 'pro faciendo novas nubes,' 'pro pictura dictarum nubium,' 'pro cantando non vos.' In Germany (Naogeorgos

Sunday it was the custom at St. Paul's in London and many other churches, during the singing of the hymn *Veni Creator Spiritus* at Tierce, to open a hole in the roof and let down symbols of the Pentecost ; a dove, a globe of fire, bits of burning tow to represent tongues of fire, a censer, flowers, pieces of flaky pastry [1]. This same hole in the roof sometimes served a similar purpose at a mimetic representation of the Annunciation. The Gospel for the day was recited by two clerks dressed as Mary and the angel, and at the words *Spiritus Sanctus supervenit in te* a white dove descended from the roof. This can hardly be called a drama, for, with the exception of a short fifteenth-century text from Cividale, only the words of the Gospel itself seem to have been used ; but obviously it is on the extreme verge of drama. A curious variant in the date of this ceremony is to be noted. In several

in Stubbes, i. 337) the crucifix was drawn up by cords and an image of Satan thrown down. For England, see the end of Lambarde's account, below.

[1] Grenier, 388 (Amiens, 1291, and elsewhere in Picardy) ; Hautcœur, *Documents liturgiques de Lille*, 65 (thirteenth century), and *Histoire de l'Église de Lille*, i. 427 ; Gasté, 75 (Bayeux, thirteenth century, Caen, Coutances) ; D'Ancona, i. 31 (Parma), i. 88 (Vicenza, 1379, a more elaborate out-of-door performance) ; Naogeorgos in Stubbes, i. 337 (Germany) ; Ducange, s. v. *nebulae*. I have three English examples : Hone, *E. D. Book*, i. 685 (*Computus* of St. Patrick's, Dublin, for 1509), 'we have iv^s vii^d paid to those playing with the great and little angel and the dragon ; iii^s paid for little cords employed about the Holy Ghost ; iv^s vi^d for making the angel censing (*thurificantis*), and ii^s ii^d for cords of it—all on the feast of Pentecost' ; *Lincoln Statutes*, i. 335 ; ii. cxviii. 165 (1330) 'in distributione autem Pentecostali percipiet . . . clericus ducens columbam vj denarios' ; W. Lambarde, *Alphabetical Description of the Chief Places in England and Wales* (1730, written in sixteenth century),

459, s. v. Wytney, 'The like Toye I myselfe (beinge then a Chyld) once saw in *Poules* Church at *London*, at a Feast of *Whitsontyde*, wheare the comynge downe of the *Holy Gost* was set forthe by a white Pigion, that was let to fly out of a Hole, that yet is to be sene in the mydst of the Roofe of the great Ile, and by a longe Censer, which descendinge out of the same Place almost to the verie Grounde, was swinged up and downe at suche a Lengthe, that it reached with thone Swepe almost to the West Gate of the Churche, and with the other to the Quyre Staires of the same, breathynge out over the whole Churche and Companie a most pleasant Perfume of suche swete Thinges as burned thearin ; with the like doome Shewes also, they used every wheare to furnishe sondrye Partes of their Churche Service, as by their Spectacles of the Nativitie, Passion, and Ascension of *Christe.*' From further notices in W. S. Simpson, *St. Paul's and Old City Life*, 62, 83, it appears that the censing was on Monday, Tuesday, and Wednesday in Whitweek, that the Lord Mayor attended, and that the ceremony was replaced by sermons in 1548.

Italian examples, of which the earliest dates from 1261, and in one or two from France, it belongs to the feast of the Annunciation proper on March 25[1]. But in later French examples, and apparently also at Lincoln[2], it has been transferred to the Advent season, during which naturally the Annunciation was greatly held in remembrance, and has been attached to the so-called 'golden' Mass celebrated ten days before Christmas during the *Quatuor Tempora*[3]. It thus became absorbed into the Christmas dramatic cycle.

[1] Creizenach, i. 76; D'Ancona, i. 90, 92, 114 (Padua, Venice, Trevigi), and i. 29 (Parma *Ordinarium* of fifteenth century) 'ad inducendum populum ad contritionem, . . . ad confirmandum ipsum in devotione Virginis Mariae . . . fit reverenter et decenter Repraesentatio Virginis Mariae . . . cum prophetis et aliis solemnitatibus opportunis'; Coussemaker, 280 (Cividale *Processionalia* of fourteenth and fifteenth centuries). In the fourteenth century there was a procession to the market-place, where 'diaconus legat evangelium in tono, et fit repraesentatio Angeli ad Mariam.' In the fifteenth century 'In Annuntiatione B. M. Virginis Repraesentatio' was a similar procession and 'cantatur evangelium cum ludo, quo finito, revertendo ad ecclesiam, cantatur Te Deum.' The text goes slightly beyond the words of the Gospel (Luke i. 26-38) having a part for 'Helisabeth.' Gasté, 79, describes the foundation of a *mystère* of the Annunciation during vespers on the eve of the feast at Saint-Lo, in 1521.

[2] I gather this from the *consuetudo* of giving gloves to Mary, the Angel, and the Prophets at Christmas (*Representations*, s. v. Lincoln). Here, as at Parma, the *Prophetae* appear in connexion with the Annunciation ceremony.

[3] See the curious and detailed document in Appendix S as to the Tournai ceremony founded by Peter Cotrel in the sixteenth century. A precisely similar foundation was that of Robert Fabri at Saint Omer in 1543 (*Bull. arch. du Comité des travaux historiques* (1886), 80; *Mém. de la Soc. des Antiquaires de la Morinie*, xx. 207). The inventory of the 'ornementz et parementz' in a 'coffre de cuir boully' includes 'ung colomb de bois revestu de damas blancq.' Alike at Tournai, St. Omer, and Besançon (Martene, iii. 30) the ceremony was on the Wednesday in the *Quatuor Tempora* of Advent. For the 'golden Mass' of this day the Gospel is the same as that of the Annunciation; cf. *York Missal*, i. 6; Pfannenschmidt, 438.

CHAPTER XX

THE SECULARIZATION OF THE PLAYS

[*Bibliographical Note.*—The best general account of the vernacular religious drama of Europe is that of W. Creizenach, *Geschichte des neueren Dramas* (vol. i. 1893), Books 2-4; and this may be supplemented by K. Hase, *Das geistliche Schauspiel* (1858, trans. A. W. Jackson, 1880); R. Proelss, *Geschichte des neueren Dramas* (1880-3), vol. i. ch. 1; C. Davidson, *English Mystery Plays* (1892), and G. Gregory Smith, *The Transition Period* (1900), ch. 7. There is also the cumbrous work of J. L. Klein, *Geschichte des Dramas* (1865-86). The nearest approach to a general bibliography is F. H. Stoddard, *References for Students of Miracle Plays and Mysteries* (1887).—For Germany may be added R. Froning, *Das Drama des Mittelalters* (1890-1); K. Pearson, *The German Passion Play* (in *The Chances of Death and Other Studies in Evolution*, 1897, vol. ii); L. Wirth, *Die Oster- und Passionsspiele bis zum* 16. *Jahrhundert* (1889); J. E. Wackernell, *Altdeutsche Passionsspiele aus Tirol*, 1897; R. Heinzel, *Beschreibung des geistlichen Schauspiels im deutschen Mittelalter* (1898), and the articles by F. Vogt on *Mittelhochdeutsche Literatur*, § 73, and H. Jellinghaus on *Mittelniederdeutsche Literatur*, § 5, in H. Paul, *Grundriss der germanischen Philologie*, vol. ii (2nd ed. 1901). F. Vogt gives a few additional recent references. Older works are F. J. Mone, *Schauspiele des Mittelalters* (1846); H. Reidt, *Das geistliche Schauspiel des Mittelalters in Deutschland* (1868), and E. Wilken, *Geschichte der geistlichen Spiele in Deutschland* (1872). Many of the books named print texts. Lists of others are given by Pearson and by Heinzel, and full bibliographical notices by K. Goedeke, *Grundriss zur Geschichte der deutschen Dichtung* (2nd ed.), vol. i (1884), §§ 67, 92, and vol. ii (1886), § 145.—For France, L. Petit de Julleville, *Les Mystères* (1880), is excellent and exhaustive, and contains many bibliographical references, although the ' Liste des ouvrages à consulter' intended as part of the work seems never to have been printed. M. de Julleville is also the writer of the article on *Théâtre religieux* in the *Hist. de la Langue et de la Littérature françaises*, vol. ii (1896). G. Gröber's article on *Französische Litteratur*, §§ 129, 362 in his *Grundriss der romanischen Philologie*, vol. ii (1901-2),brings the subject uptodate and adds some recent authorities. Mortensen, *Medeltidsdramat i Frankrike* (1899), is beyond my range. G. Paris, *La Littérature française au moyen âge* (2nd ed., 1890), is a brief summary, and L. Clédat, *Le Théâtre au moyen âge* (1897), a useful popular account. G. Bapst, *Essai sur l'Histoire du Théâtre* (1893), is good on matters of stage arrangement. Older works are O. Le Roy, *Études sur les Mystères* (1837), and J. de Douhet, *Dictionnaire des Mystères* (1854). Only fragments of C. Magnin's investigations are available in the *Journal des Savants* (1846-7) and the *Journal général de l'Instruction publique* (1834-6). Texts are in A. Jubinal, *Mystères du* 15ᵉ *siècle* (1837); Monmerqué et Michel, *Théâtre français au moyen âge* (1842); E. Fournier, *Le Théâtre français avant la Renaissance* (1872), and the series published by the *Société des Anciens Textes français.* The most recent text of *Adam* is that by K. Grass, *Das Adamsspiel* (1891). M. Wilmotte, *Les Passions allemandes du Rhin dans leur Rapport avec l'ancien Théâtre français* (1898), deals with the interrelations of the French and German texts. C. Hastings, *Le Théâtre français et anglais* (1900, trans.1901), is a compilation of little merit.—For Italy there is A. D'Ancona, *Origini del Teatro italiano* (2nd ed. 1891), with texts in the same writer's *Sacre Rappresentazioni* (1872), in Monaci, *Appunti per la Storia del Teatro italiano* (*Rivista di Filologia Romana*, vols. i, ii), and in F. Torraca, *Il Teatro italiano dei Secoli xiii, xiv, e xv* (1885).—For Spain, A. F. von Schack, *Geschichte der dramatischen Litteratur und Kunst in Spanien* (1845–54), and G. Baist, *Spanische Litteratur*, §§ 19, 63, in Gröber's *Grundriss*, vol. ii (1897).—For the minor Romance dramatic literatures, Provençal, Catalan, Portuguese, I must be content to refer to the last-named authority, and for that of Holland to the similar *Grundriss* of H. Paul.]

THE evolution of the liturgic play described in the last two chapters may be fairly held to have been complete about the middle of the thirteenth century. The condition of any further advance was that the play should cease to be liturgic. The following hundred years are a transition period. During their course the newly-shaped drama underwent a process which, within the limits imposed by the fact that its subject-matter remained essentially religious, may be called secularization. Already, when Hilarius could write plays to serve indifferently for use at Matins or at Vespers, the primitive relation of *repraesentatio* to liturgy had been sensibly weakened. By the middle of the fourteenth century it was a mere survival. From ecclesiastical the drama had become popular. Out of the hands of the clergy in their naves and choirs, it had passed to those of the laity in their market-places and guild-halls. And to this formal change corresponded a spiritual or literary one, in the reaction of the temper of the folk upon the handling of the plays, the broadening of their human as distinct from their religious aspect. In their origin *officia* for devotion and edification, they came, by an irony familiar to the psychologist, to be primarily *spectacula* for mirth, wonder, and delight.

It is, however, the formal change with which I am here mainly concerned ; and of this it will be the object of the present chapter to trace as briefly as possible the outlines. The principal factor is certainly that tendency to expansion and coalescence in the plays which has been already seen at work in the production of such elaborate pieces as the *Quem quaeritis* of the Tours or that of the Benedictbeuern manuscript, the Fleury *Stella*, the Rouen *Prophetae* and the *Antichristus*. This culminates in the formation of those great dramatic cycles of which the English Corpus Christi plays are perhaps the most complete examples. But before we can approach these, we must consider a little further the independent development of the Easter and Christmas groups.

It is noteworthy that, during the period now under discussion, the importance of Christmas falls markedly into the background when compared with that of Easter ; and a reason for this will presently suggest itself. The *Stella*, indeed, as such, appears to have almost reached its term [1] ; for such further growth as there is we must look chiefly to the *Prophetae*. .The process by which little episodic dramas, as of Balaam and Nebuchadnezzar at Rouen, bud out from the stem of the *Prophetae*, is one capable of infinite extension. By 1204 the play had found its way to Riga, on the extreme border of European civilization, and the *ludus prophetarum ordinatissimus* there performed included scenes from the wars of Gideon, David, and Herod [2]. The text of the Riga play is unfortunately not preserved, but the famous Norman-French *Ordo repraesentationis Adae* is an example of a *Prophetae*, in which the episodes, no longer confined to the stories of the prophets in the stricter sense, have outgrown and cast into the shade the original intention [3]. Most things about the *Adam*

[1] Creizenach, i. 154, 317, 346. A slight addition to the *Stella* is made by two Provençal plays of †13oo (ed. P. Meyer in *Romania*, xiv. 496) and 1333 (*dramatis personae* only in *Revue des Sociétés savantes*, viii. 259) which introduce episodes from the life of the Virgin previous to the Nativity.

[2] Creizenach, i. 70, quoting *Gesta Alberti Livoniensis episcopi* (†1226) in Gruber, *Origines Livoniae* (1740), 34 'Eadem hyeme factus est ludus prophetarum ordinatissimus, quam Latini Comoediam vocant, in media Riga, ut fidei Christianae rudimenta gentilitas fide etiam disceret oculata. Cuius ludi et comoediae materia tam

neophytis, quam paganis, qui aderant, per interpretem diligentissime exponebatur. Ubi autem armati Gedeonis cum Philistaeis pugnabant ; pagani, timentes occidi, fugere coeperunt, sed caute sunt revocati . . . In eodem ludo erant bella, vtpote Dauid, Gedeonis, Herodis. Erat et doctrina Veteris et Novi Testamenti.'

[3] Text edited by V. Luzarche (Tours, 1854) ; L. Palustre (Paris, 1877) ; K. Bartsch, *Chrestomathie*, ed. 1880, 91) ; K. Grass (Halle, 1891) ; cf. the elaborate study by Sepet, xxix, 105, 261, and Julleville, *Les Myst.* i. 81 ; ii. 217 ; Creizenach, i. 130 ; Clédat, 15. The manuscript

are in dispute. Scholars differ as to whether the manuscript belongs to the twelfth or the thirteenth century, and as to whether it is the work of a Norman or of an Anglo-Norman scribe. The piece is manifestly incomplete, but how far incomplete it is hard to say. What we have consists of three sections. There is a long play of nearly six hundred lines on the Fall and Expulsion from Paradise, in which the speakers are Adam and Eve, the *Figura* of God and the *Diabolus*. Then comes a much shorter one of Cain and Abel ; and finally a *Prophetae*, which breaks off after the part of Nebuchadnezzar. Of the general character of this interesting piece something further will be said presently, but the point to notice here is that, although Adam and Abel may of course be regarded as prophetic types of Christ, if not exactly prophets, yet there is a real extension of the dramatic content of the *Prophetae* in the prefixing to it of a treatment of so momentous a subject as the Fall[1]. For with the addition of the Fall to the already dramatized Redemption, the framework of a structural unity was at once provided for the great cosmic drama of the future. And the important motive seems to have been still further emphasized in a lost play performed at Regensburg in 1195, which treated, besides the Prophets and the Creation and Fall of Man, the Creation of the Angels and the Fall of Lucifer[2].

is *Tours MS.* 927, formerly belonging to the Benedictines of Marmoutier. Grass, vi, summarizes the opinions as to its date. In any case the text is probably of the twelfth century, and Grass, 171, after an elaborate grammatical investigation, confirms the opinion of Luzarche, doubted by Littré and others, that it is of Anglo-Norman rather than Norman origin. But, even if the writer was an Anglo-Norman clerk, the play must have been written for performance in France. I doubt if it was ever actually played or finished. It is followed in the MS. by a Norman (not Anglo-Norman) poem on the Fifteen Signs of Judgement (text in Grass, 57), which looks like material collected for an unwritten Sibyl prophecy. The remaining contents of the first part of the MS., which may be of the twelfth century, are some hymns and the Latin Tours *Quem quaeritis* (p. 38).

[1] Sepet, xxix, 112, 128, points out that certain *lectiones* and *responsoria* which accompany the *Adam* and *Cain and Abel* are taken from the office for Septuagesima. Possibly an independent liturgical drama of the Fall arose at Septuagesima and was absorbed by the *Prophetae*. But mention of the 'primus Adam' is not uncommon in the Nativity liturgy ; cf. Sepet, xxix, 107, and the *Sponsus* (p. 61).

[2] *Annales Ratisponenses (M.G.H. Scriptores,* xvii. 590) 'Anno Domini 1194. Celebratus est in Ratispona ordo creacionis angelorum et ruina[e]

Yet another step towards the completion of the Christmas cycle was taken when the *Prophetae* and the *Stella* were brought together in a single drama. Such a merging is represented by two related texts from German sources[1]. One is from a fourteenth-century manuscript now at St. Gall[2]. The structure is of the simplest. The setting of the pseudo-Augustine sermon has altogether disappeared. Eight prophets deliver a speech apiece, announcing their own identities after a naïve fashion—*Ich bin der alte Balaam*, and so forth—which strongly recalls the 'folk' or 'mummers'' plays. Then follows without break a *Stella*, whose scenes range from the Marriage of the Virgin to the Death of Herod. Far more elaborate is the Christmas play found in the famous repertory of the *scholares vagantes* from Benedictbeuern[3]. A peculiarity of this is that for the first time Augustine appears *in propria persona*. He presides over the prophecies, taking the place of the *Precentor* of the Limoges *Prophetae*, and the *Appellatores* or *Vocatores* of Laon and Rouen. The only prophets are Isaiah, Daniel, the Sibyl, Aaron, and Balaam, and there is once more a special episode for Balaam's ass.

' *Quinto loco procedat Balaam sedens in asina et cantans :*
vadam, vadam, ut maledicam populo huic.
Cui occurrat Angelus evaginato gladio dicens :
cave, cave ne quicquam aliud quam tibi dixero loquaris.
Et asinus cui insidet Balaam perterritus retrocedat. Postea recedat angelus et Balaam cantet hoc :
orietur stella ex Iacob, etc.'

A long *disputatio* follows between Augustine, an *Archisynagogus*, and the prophets, in which at one point no less a person intervenes than the *Episcopus Puerorum*, affording an inter-

---

Luciferi et suorum, et creacionis hominis et casus et prophetarum . . . septima Idus Februarii.'
[1] Köppen, 35, discusses the textual relation between the St. Gall and Benedictbeuern plays and their common source, the Freising *Stella*.
[2] Text in Mone, *Schauspiele des Mittelalters*, i. 143; cf. Creizenach, i. 123.

[3] Text in Schmeller, *Carmina Burana*, 80; Du Méril, 187; Froning, 877, from a Munich MS. of thirteenth to fourteenth century formerly in the abbey of Benedictbeuern in Bavaria; cf. Creizenach, i. 96; Sepet, xxxviii, 398. The title 'Ludus scenicus de nativitate Domini' given by Schmeller is not in the MS.

esting example of that interrelation between the religious plays and the festivities of the *triduum* and the Feast of Fools, about which something has already been said[1]. Presently the prophets retire and sit *in locis suis propter honorem ludi*. The *Stella* extends from the Annunciation to the Flight into Egypt. Here the original play seems to have ended; but a later writer has added a scene in Egypt, in which the idols fall at the approach of the Holy Family, and some fragments adapted from the *Antichristus*, and hardly worked up into anything that can be called a scene.

The form of Christmas play, then, characteristic of the transition century, consists of a version of the *Prophetae* extended at the beginning by a dramatic treatment of the Fall, or extended at the end by the absorption of the *Stella*. It so happens that we do not, during the period in question, find examples in which both extensions occur together. But this double amplification would only be the slightest step in advance, and may perhaps be taken for granted. The Rouen *Mystère de l'Incarnation et la Nativité* of 1474 offers, at a much later date, precisely the missing type[2].

The Easter cycle, also, received memorable accretions during the period. The *Quem quaeritis* of the Tours manuscript, it will be remembered, included a series of scenes beginning with the Setting of the Watch before the Sepulchre, and ending with the Incredulity of Thomas. Important additions had still to be made, even within the limits of this *cadre*. One was a more complete treatment of the Resurrection itself through the introduction of the figure of Christ stepping with the *labarum* out of the sepulchre, in place of a mere symbolical indication of the mystery by the presence of angels with lighted candles and the dismay of the soldiers[3]. Another, closely related to the Resurrection, was the scene known as the Harrowing of Hell. This was based upon the account of the *Descensus Christi ad Inferos*, the victory over Satan, and the freeing from limbo of Adam and the other Old

[1] Cf. p. 56. The Balaam in *Adam* is 'sedens super asinam,' but no further notice is taken of the animal.
[2] Text ed. Le Verdier (*Soc. des Bibliophiles normands*); cf. Julleville, *Les Myst.* ii. 36, 430.
[3] Cf. p. 38.

Testament Fathers, which forms part of the apocryphal *Gospel of Nichodemus*[1]. The narrative makes use of that *Tollite portas* passage from the twenty-fourth Psalm, which we have already found adapted to the use of more than one semi-dramatic ceremonial[2], and naturally this found its way into the Harrowing of Hell, together with the so-called *canticum triumphale*, a song of welcome by the imprisoned souls :

' Advenisti, desirabilis, quem exspectabamus in tenebris, ut educeres hac nocte vinculatos de claustris.

    te nostra vocabant suspiria.

    te larga requirebant lamenta.

    tu factus es spes desperatis, magna consolatio in tormentis.'

I cannot share the view of those who look upon the East Midland English *Harrowing of Hell* as intended for dramatic representation. The prologues found in two of the three manuscripts leave it clear that it was for recitation. It is in fact of the nature of an 'estrif' or *débat*, and may be compared with an Anglo-Saxon poem of the eighth or tenth century on the same subject [3]. But there is evidence that the scene had found its way into the Easter cycle at least by the beginning of the thirteenth century, for it occurs amongst the fragments of a play of that date from Kloster Muri ; and in later versions it assumed a considerable prominence [4].

[1] Tischendorf, *Evangelia Apocrypha* (1876), 389.

[2] Cf. pp. 4, 5, 20. One of the anthems for Easter Saturday in the *Sarum Breviary* is *Elevamini, portae*.

[3] Text in Pollard, 166 ; K. Böddeker, *Altenglische Dichtungen des MS. Harl.* 2253 (1878), 264 ; E. Mall, *The Harrowing of Hell* (1871); cf. Ten Brink, ii. 242 ; Ward, i. 90 ; Creizenach, i. 158. There are three MSS.: (*a*) *Bodl. Digby MS.* 86 (late thirteenth century) ; (*b*) *Harl. MS.* 2253 († 1310); (*c*) *Edin. Advoc. Libr.* (*Auchinleck*) *MS.* W. 41 (early fourteenth century). The Digby version has a prologue beginning :

' Hou ihesu crist herewede helle
Of hardegates ich wille telle.'

The Harleian has :

' Alle herkneth to me nou,
A strif will I tellen ou.'

The Auchinleck prologue lacks the beginning, but the end agrees with the Harleian. Böddeker, who accepts the dramatic character of the piece, thinks that the prologues were prefixed later for recitation. In any case this poem became a source for a play in the *Ludus Coventriae* cycle (Pollard, xxxviii).

[4] Text of Muri fragments in Froning, 228 ; cf. Creizenach, i. 114 ; Wirth, 133, 281. A French fragment († 1300–50) also introducing this theme is printed by J. Bédier, in *Romania*, xxiv. (1895), 86. Pez, *Script. rerum austriacarum*, ii. 268, describes a vision of the thirteenth-century recluse

The liturgical drama proper abstained in the main from any strictly dramatic representation of the Passion. The nearest approach to such a thing is in the dialogued versions of the *Planctus Mariae* and in the Benedictbeuern *Ludus breviter de Passione*, which extends very slightly beyond these. The central event of the transition period is, therefore, the growth side by side with the *Quem quaeritis* of a Passion play, which in the end rather absorbs than is absorbed by it. A marked advance in this direction is shown in an Anglo-Norman fragment, probably written in the twelfth century, which includes, not indeed the Crucifixion itself, but the Descent from the Cross, the Healing of Longinus, and the Burial of Christ [1]. The first recorded Passion play is in Italy. It took place at Siena about 1200 [2]. In 1244 the Passion and Resurrection were played together at Padua [3]. The earliest text of a Passion play is contained in the Benedictbeuern manuscript [4]. It opens with the Calling of Andrew and Peter, the Healing of the Blind, Zacchaeus and the Entry into Jerusalem. Then follows a long episode of Mary Magdalen. She is represented with her lover, buying cosmetics of a *Mercator*—we have had the *Mercator* in the *Quem quaeritis* and in the *Sponsus*—and with a profane song upon her lips:

Wilbirgis: 'Item quadam nocte Dominicae Resurrectionis, cum in Monasterio ludus Paschalis tam a Clero quam a populo ageretur, quia eidem non potuit corporaliter interesse, coepit desiderare, ut ei Dominus aliquam specialis consolationis gratiam per Resurrectionis suae gaudia largiretur. Et vidit quasi Dominum ad Inferos descendentem et inde animas eruentem, quae quasi columbae candidissimae circumvolantes ipsum comitabantur, et sequebantur ab inferis redeuntem.' Meyer, 61, 98, deals fully with the development of the Resurrection and Harrowing of Hell themes in the early vernacular plays.

[1] Text in Monmerqué et Michel, *Théâtre fr. au moyen âge*, 10, from *Bibl. Nat. fr.* 902; cf. Creizenach, i. 135; Julleville, *Les Myst.* i. 91; ii. 220; Clédat, 59. The

MS. is of the fourteenth century, but the Norman-French, which some writers, as with the *Adam*, think Anglo-Norman, is assigned to the end of the twelfth century.

[2] D'Ancona, i. 90. The original authority for the statement, taken from a MS. treatise on the *Commedia italiana* by Uberto Benvoglienti, is not given.

[3] D'Ancona, i. 87, quoting several chronicles: 'hoc anno in festo Pascae facta fuit Reppraesentatio Passionis et Resurrectionis Christi solemniter et ordinate in Prato Vallis.'

[4] Text in Schmeller, *Carmina Burana*, 95; Du Méril, 126; Froning, 284; cf. Creizenach, i. 92; Wirth, 131, 278. The only heading to the play in the MS. is 'Sancta Maria assit nostro principio! amen.'

'Mundi delectatio dulcis est et grata,
cuius conversatio suavis et ornata.'

She is converted in a dream, puts on black, buys ointments
from the same *Mercator*, and adores the Lord in the house of
Simon. Then come, far more briefly treated, the Raising of
Lazarus, the Betrayal by Judas, the Last Supper, the Mount
of Olives, the Passion itself, from the Taking in Gethsemane
to the Crucifixion. The introduction here of some *planctus
Mariae* points to the *genesis* of the drama, which closes with
the Begging of the Body of Christ by Joseph of Arimathaea.
And so, at a blow, as it were, the content of the Easter play
is doubled. Certain episodes, such as the Conversion of
Mary Magdalen and the Raising of Lazarus had, as we
know, received an independent dramatic treatment; but in the
main the play before us, or its source, bears the character of
a deliberate composition on the lines of the pre-existing *Quem
quaeritis*. That it was to be followed in representation by
a *Quem quaeritis* may perhaps be taken for granted. Indeed
there is one personage, the wife of the *Mercator*, who is named
in a list at the beginning, but has no part in the text as it
stands[1]. She may have come into the Benedictbeuern *Quem
quaeritis*, of which a fragment only survives, and this may have
been intended for use, as might be convenient, either with the
Ludus breviter de Passione, or with the longer text now under
consideration. At all events, Passion and Resurrection are
treated together in two slightly later texts, one from the south
of France[2], the other from St. Gall[3]. The St. Gall Passion
play takes the action back to the beginning of the missionary
life of Christ, giving the Marriage at Cana, the Baptism,
and the Temptation. It also includes a Harrowing of
Hell.

Certain forms of the Passion play, as the conjoint Passion
and Resurrection may now be termed, show an approximation
to the type of the Christmas play. It is obvious that the

[1] Scenes between the *Mercator*,
his wife, and their lad Rubin play
a large part in the later German
Passion plays; cf. Wirth, 168.
[2] Creizenach, i. 155. Two four-

teenth-century texts exist, one in
Provençal, one in Catalan.
[3] Text in Mone, *Schauspiele des
Mittelalters*, i. 72 ; cf. Creizenach,
i. 121; Wirth, 135, 282.

Fall and the *Prophetae* would be as proper a prologue to the Passion which completes the Atonement as to the Nativity which begins it. And the presence of Adam and other Old Testament characters in the Harrowing of Hell would be the more significant if in some earlier scene they had visibly been haled there. The first trace of these new elements is in the St. Gall play, where the Augustine of the *Prophetae* is introduced to speak a prologue. A long Frankfort play of the fourteenth century, of which unfortunately only the stage directions and actors' cues are preserved, carries the process further [1]. Again Augustine acts as presenter. A *Prophetae* begins the performance, which ends with the Ascension, a *Disputatio Ecclesiae et Synagogae* and the baptizing of the incredulous Jews by Augustine. On the other hand, the Fall forms the first part of an early fourteenth-century Passion play from Vienna [2]. Both the Fall of Lucifer and that of Adam and Eve are included, and there is a supplementary scene in hell, into which the souls of a usurer, a monk, a robber, and a sorceress are successively brought. Lucifer refuses to have anything to do with the monk, an early use of the Tomlinson motive.

The dramatic evolution is now within measurable distance of the ' cosmic ' type finally presented by the English Corpus Christi plays. Two further steps are necessary: the juxtaposition of the Nativity and Passion scenes behind their common Old Testament prologue, and the final winding up of the action by the extension of it from the Ascension to the second coming of the Christ in the Last Judgement. The eschatological scenes of the *Sponsus* and the *Antichristus* are already available for such an epilogue. That the whole of this vast framework was put together by the beginning of the fourteenth century may be inferred from the notices of two performances, in 1298 and 1303 respectively, at Cividale [3]. The

---

[1] Text in Froning, 340 (begins 'Incipit ordo sive registrum de passione domini'); cf. Creizenach, i. 219; Wirth, 137, 295.

[2] Text in Froning, 305 (begins ' Ad materiae reductionem de passione domini. Incipit ludus pascalis '); cf. Creizenach, i. 92, 120; Wirth, 134, 293.

[3] Giuliano da Cividale, *Cronaca Friulana* (D'Ancona, i. 91; Muratori, *Rer. Ital. Script.* xxiv. 1205, 1209): ' Anno domini MCCLXXXXVIII die vii exeunte Maio,

first included the Passion, Resurrection, Ascension, Advent of the Holy Spirit, and Advent of Christ to Judgement: the second added to these the Creation, Annunciation, Nativity, with much else, and the Antichrist. Any further development could now be merely episodic. The text could be amplified at the fancy of the individual writer, or upon the suggestion of the great epic narratives, such as the *Cursor Mundi*, the *Passional*, the *Erlösung*[1]. An infinity of new scenes could be added from the Old Testament[2], from the apocryphal gospels and acts, from the historic narratives of the vengeance of the Crucified One upon Rome and Jewry[3]. But beyond the limits of the fixed *cadre* it was now impossible to go, for these were coincident with the span of time and eternity.

It is now necessary to consider briefly some modifications in the general character of the religious plays which accompanied or resulted from this great expansion of their scope.

videlicet in die Pentecostes et in aliis duobus sequentibus diebus, facta fuit Repraesentatio Ludi Christi, videlicet Passionis, Resurrectionis, Ascensionis, Adventus Spiritus Sancti, Adventus Christi ad iudicium, in curia Domini Patriarchae Austriae civitatis, honorifice et laudabiliter, per Clerum civitatensem . . . Anno MCCCIII facta fuit per Clerum, sive per Capitulum civitatense, Repraesentatio: sive factae fuerunt Repraesentationes infra scriptae : In primis, de Creatione primorum parentum ; deinde de Annunciatione Beatae Virginis, de Partu et aliis multis, et de Passione et Resurrectione, Ascensione et Adventu Spiritus Sancti, et de Antichristo et aliis, et demum de Adventu Christi ad iudicium. Et predicta facta fuerunt solemniter in curia domini Patriarchae in festo Pentecostes cum aliis duobus diebus sequentibus, praesente r. d. Ottobono patriarcha aquileiensi, d. Iacobo q. d. Ottonelli de Civitate episcopo concordiensi, et aliis multis nobilibus de civitatibus et castris Foroiulii, die xv exeunte Maio.' Still earlier, some dramatic fragments not later than the mid-thirteenth

century from Kloster Himmelgarten near Nordhausen, include scenes from both the early and late life of Christ (Text, ed. Sievers, in *Zeitsch. f. d. Phil.* xxi. 393 ; cf. Creizenach, i. 124) ; but these might conceivably belong to a set of plays for different dates, such as those of the Sainte Geneviève MS. (Julleville, *Les Myst.* ii. 379). Besides the English cosmic cycles, there are several fifteenth-century French ones described by Julleville, *Les Myst.* ii. 394 sqq.: in Germany plays of this scope are rare.

[1] Pearson, ii. 312 ; Köppen, 49 ; Ten Brink, i. 287.

[2] Cf. Sepet, xxxviii, 415 ; Creizenach, i. 260 ; G. Smith, 253 ; Julleville, *Les Myst.* ii. 352. *Le Mistère du viel testament*, printed †1510 (ed. Rothschild, 1878–91, for *Soc. des anciens textes français*), is a fifteenth-century compilation of O. T. plays from various sources.

[3] French versions of the *Vengeance de Notre Seigneur*, of which the chief episode is the Siege of Jerusalem, appear in the fifteenth century (Julleville, *Les Myst.* ii. 12, 415, 451). A late Coventry play on the same theme is unfortunately lost.

These all tend towards that process of secularization, that relaxing of the close bonds between the nascent drama and religious worship, which it is the especial object of this chapter to illustrate. Of capital importance is the transference of the plays from the interior of the church to its precincts, to the graveyard or the neighbouring market-place. This must have been primarily a matter of physical necessity. The growing length of the plays, the increasing elaboration of their setting, made it cumbrous and difficult to accommodate them within the walls. It is a big step from the early *Quem quaeritis*, *Pastores* or *Stella*, with their simple *mises-en-scène* of *sepulchrum* and *praesepe* to the complicated requirements, say, of the Fleury group, the *tabernaculum in similitudinem castelli Emaus* for the *Peregrini*, the half-dozen *loca*, *domus*, or *sedes* demanded by the *Suscitatio Lazari* or the *Conversio Pauli*. Still more exigent is the *Antichristus* with its *templum domini* and its seven *sedes regales*, and its space in between for marchings and counter-marchings and the overthrowing of kings. Yet for a long time the church proved sufficient. The Tours *Quem quaeritis* and some, if not all, of the Fleury plays were demonstrably played in the church. So was the Rouen *Prophetae*, and an allusion of Gerhoh of Reichersberg makes it extremely probable that so was the *Antichristus*[1]. One must conceive, I think, of the performances as gradually spreading from choir to nave, with the *domus*, *loca*, or *sedes* set at intervals against the pillars, while the people crowded to watch in the side aisles. It is in the twelfth century that the plays first seek ampler room outside the church. Of the transition plays dealt with in the present chapter, the *Adam*, the Benedict-beuern Christmas play, the Anglo-Norman *Resurrection*, were certainly intended for the open, and the contrary cannot be affirmed in any case with the same assurance. Again, the Riga *Prophetae* of 1204 was *in media Riga*, the Padua Passion play of 1244 was in a meadow, the *Pratum Vallis*, while in England an early thirteenth-century biographer of St. John of Beverley records a miracle wrought at a Resurrection play in the churchyard of the minster.

[1] Cf. p. 99.

Of the type of performance now rendered possible, a very good notion is given by the full stage directions of the *Adam*. These are so valuable a document for the history of stage management that I must take leave to excerpt from them somewhat liberally. The opening rubric recalls at once the minute stage directions of Ibsen and the counsel to the players in *Hamlet*.

'A Paradise is to be made in a raised spot, with curtains and cloths of silk hung round it at such a height that persons in the Paradise may be visible from the shoulders upwards. Fragrant flowers and leaves are to be set round about, and divers trees put therein with hanging fruit, so as to give the likeness of a most delicate spot. Then must come the Saviour clothed in a dalmatic, and Adam and Eve be brought before him. Adam is to wear a red tunic and Eve a woman's robe of white, with a white silk cloak; and they are both to stand before the Figure, Adam the nearer with composed countenance, while Eve appears somewhat more modest. And the Adam must be well trained when to reply and to be neither too quick nor too slow in his replies. And not only he, but all the personages must be trained to speak composedly, and to fit convenient gesture to the matter of their speech. Nor must they foist in a syllable or clip one of the verse, but must enounce firmly and repeat what is set down for them in due order. Whosoever names Paradise is to look and point towards it.'

After a *lectio* and a chant by the choir, the dialogue begins. The *Figura* instructs Adam and Eve as to their duties and inducts them into Paradise.

'Then the Figure must depart to the church and Adam and Eve walk about Paradise in honest delight. Meanwhile the demons are to run about the stage (*per plateas*), with suitable gestures, approaching the Paradise from time to time and pointing out the forbidden fruit to Eve, as though persuading her to eat it. Then the Devil is to come and address Adam.'

The *diabolus* thinks he is prevailing upon Adam. He joins the other demons and make sallies about the *plateae*. Then he returns *hylaris et gaudens* to the charge. But he fails.

'Then, sadly and with downcast countenance, he shall leave Adam, and go to the doors of hell, and hold council with the other demons. Thereafter he shall make a sally amongst the people, and then approach Paradise on Eve's side, addressing her with joyful countenance and insinuating (*blandiens*) manner.'

Eve, too, is hard to persuade, and is scolded by Adam for listening to the *diabolus*. But when a *serpens artificiose compositus* rises hard by the trunk of the forbidden tree, she lends her ear, is won over, takes the apple and gives it to Adam.

'Then Adam is to eat part of the apple; and after eating it he shall immediately recognize his sin and debase himself. He must now be out of sight of the people, and shall put off his solemn raiment, and put on poor raiment sewn together of fig-leaves, and with an air of extreme dolour shall begin his lament.'

When the Figure 'wearing a stole' comes again, Adam and Eve hide in a corner of Paradise, and when called upon stand up, 'not altogether erect, but for shame of their sin somewhat bowed and very sad.' They are driven out, and an angel with a radiant sword is put at the gate of Paradise. The Figure returns to the church.

'Then Adam shall have a spade and Eve a hoe, and they shall begin to till the soil and sow corn therein. And when they have sown, they shall go and sit down a while, as if wearied with toil, and anon look tearfully at Paradise, beating their breasts. Meanwhile shall come the devil and shall plant thorns and thistles in their tillage, and avoid. And when Adam and Eve come to their tillage and see the thorns and thistles sprung up, they shall be smitten with violent grief and shall throw themselves on the earth and sit there, beating their breasts and thighs and betraying grief by their gestures. And Adam shall begin a lament.'

Now the last scene is at hand.

'Then shall come the devil and three or four devils with him, carrying in their hands chains and iron fetters, which they shall put on the necks of Adam and Eve. And some shall push and others pull them to hell; and hard by hell shall be other devils ready to meet them, who shall hold high revel (*tripudium*) at their fall. And certain other devils shall point them out as they come, and shall snatch them up and carry them into hell; and there shall they make a great smoke arise, and call aloud to each other with glee in their hell, and clash their pots and kettles, that they may be heard without. And after a little delay the devils shall come out and run about the stage; but some shall remain in hell.'

The shorter play of Cain and Abel is similarly conceived. The sacrifices are offered on two great stones 'which shall have been made ready for the purpose'; and at the end of the performance the devils hale off Cain and Abel also to hell 'beating Cain often; but Abel they shall lead more gently.' The prophets, who have been prepared in a secret spot, now advance one by one and deliver their prophecies. Their appearance is described much as in the earlier *Prophetae,* and it is noted that each in turn at the finish of his harangue is to be led off to hell by the devils.

Unless the *Adam* extended much beyond the text left to us, a comparatively small number of *loca* would suffice for its representation. The contemporary Anglo-Norman Resurrection play required thirteen, as is set out at length in a versified prologue:

> 'En ceste manere recitom
> La seinte resurreccion.
> Primerement apareillons
> Tus les lius e les mansions:
> Le crucifix primerement
> E puis apres le monument.
> Une jaiole i deit aver
> Pur les prisons emprisoner.
> Enfer seit mis de cele part,
> E mansions de l'altre part,
> E puis le ciel; et as estals
> Primes Pilate od ces vassals.
> Sis u set chivaliers aura.
> Caïphas en l'altre serra;
> Od lui seit la jeuerie,
> Puis Joseph, cil d'Arimachie.
> El quart liu seit danz Nichodemes.

Chescons i ad od sei les soens.
El quint les deciples Crist.
Les treis Maries saient el sist.
Si seit pourvéu que l'om face
Galilée en mi la place;
Jemaüs uncore i seit fait,
U Jhesu fut al hostel trait;
E cum la gent est tute asise,
E la pés de tutez parz mise,
Dan Joseph, cil d'Arimachie,
Venge a Pilate, si lui die.'

I have ventured to arrange these *lius* (*loca*) and *mansions* (*domus*) or *estals* (*sedes*), upon the indications of the prologue, in the following plan :

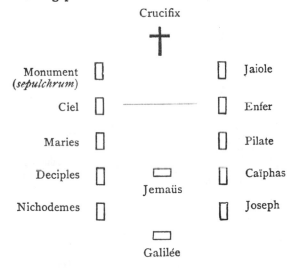

Crucifix

Monument (*sepulchrum*)

Jaiole

Ciel

Enfer

Maries

Pilate

Deciples

Caïphas

Jemaüs

Nichodemes

Joseph

Galilée

And I would point out that such a scheme is simply a continuation of the arrangement down the choir and nave of a church suggested above[1]. The crucifix is where it would stand in the church, above the altar. The place of the monument corresponds to that most usual for the *sepulchrum* on the north side of the chancel. The positions of heaven and hell are those in the former case of the stairs up to the

[1] Cf. p. 79.

rood-loft, in the latter of the stairs down to the crypt; and what, in a church, should serve for hell and heaven but crypt and rood-loft[1]? The Galilee answers to the porch at the west end of the church, which we know to have been so called[2]; and the castle of Emmaus stands in the middle of the nave, just as it did in the Fleury *Peregrini.* With my conjectural

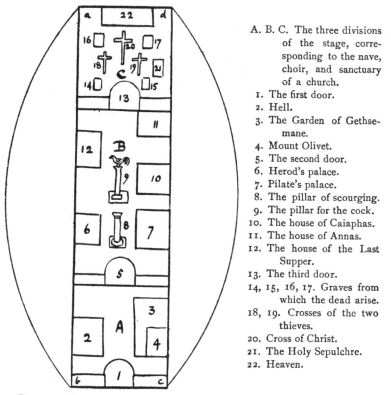

A. B. C. The three divisions of the stage, corresponding to the nave, choir, and sanctuary of a church.

1. The first door.
2. Hell.
3. The Garden of Gethsemane.
4. Mount Olivet.
5. The second door.
6. Herod's palace.
7. Pilate's palace.
8. The pillar of scourging.
9. The pillar for the cock.
10. The house of Caiaphas.
11. The house of Annas.
12. The house of the Last Supper.
13. The third door.
14, 15, 16, 17. Graves from which the dead arise.
18, 19. Crosses of the two thieves.
20. Cross of Christ.
21. The Holy Sepulchre.
22. Heaven.

PLAN OF DONAUESCHINGEN PASSION-PLAY STAGE (*sixteenth century*).

plan may be compared this actual plan of a sixteenth-century stage from Donaueschingen, in which a similar principle is apparent, the three divisions formed by cross-barriers corresponding to the three divisions of a church—sanctuary, choir, nave[3].

---

[1] Pearson, ii. 315; and cf. the angels aloft in the Rouen *Pastores* (p. 41).

[2] Cf. p. 50.
[3] Plan in Mone, ii. 156; Froning, 277; Davidson, 199; Pearson, ii.

The Anglo-Norman Resurrection play was pretty clearly out of doors[1]; and the double line of *sedes* may be thought of as stretching from the west door of the church right across the market-place.   In *Adam* the *Figura* comes and goes from and to the church, which thus serves for a *ciel*; in the Benedictbeuern Christmas play, the chair of Augustine is set *in fronte ecclesiae*.   This arrangement, also, can be paralleled from later plays, both French and German.   At Freiburg in 1504 the stage was built across the cathedral yard from the south door to the Kaufhaus, a space of some 110 feet long[2]. At Rouen, in 1474, the *establies* went across the market-place from the Axe and Crown to the Angel[3].   It must not, however, be supposed that the rectangular stage survived as the invariable type.   In particular a round type was sometimes preferred.   The Cornish guary-plays were given in rounds, and a round is figured in a fifteenth-century miniature by Jean Fouquet, representing a play of Saint Apollonia[4].

I have spoken of a stage, but I am not sure that there was any stage in the sense of a platform.   There is certainly no such scaffold in Fouquet's miniature, and the *plateae* of the Fleury *Suscitatio Lazari* and the *Adam* are probably only the open spaces kept free for the actors between the *sedes*[5].   In the *Adam* the devils are able to make sallies from the *plateae* amongst the spectators.   The latter probably crowded upon barriers between the *sedes*.   In the miniature, however, the *sedes* stand close together and are considerably raised, with

320; Könnecke, *Bilderatlas*, 55: on the play, cf. Creizenach, i. 224; Wirth, 139, 327. Another sixteenth-century plan from Lucerne is given by Leibing, *Die Inscenierung des 2-tägigen Osterspiels*, 1869; cf. Creizenach, i. 168.

[1] See the mention of 'en mi la place' in the prologue; but 'place' might be only the French equivalent of 'platea' as used in the Fleury *Suscitatio Lazari*.

[2] Pearson, ii. 322.

[3] Julleville, *Les Myst.* ii. 37.

[4] Reproduced in Clédat, 4; Bapst, 33, from *Horae* of †1460; cf. Jusse-rand, *Lit. Hist.* i. 470.

[5] D'Ancona, i. 191, however, describes the Italian *devozioni* as taking place on *talami* or platforms in the naves of churches. In France, minor religious plays at least took place on scaffolds, built up sometimes against the wall of a church (Bapst, 23, 29). A raised stage, with *sedes* along the back of it, is shown by the miniatures in the MS. of the Valenciennes *Passion* (reproduced in Jusserand, *Shakespeare in France*, 63; cf. Julleville, *Les Mystères*, ii. 153); but this is as late as 1547.

ladders running up to them. The spectators stand beneath. The prologue to the Anglo-Norman *Resurrection* speaks of *la gent* as seated, and possibly raised scaffolds for the audience were already in use. These were certainly known later, and the descriptions of some of them as no less than nine stories high have given rise to an erroneous theory that the plays were performed upon a many-storied stage [1]. It is clear that this was not really the case. All the *sedes* were on the same level, except that, for greater dignity, the Calvary, the Heaven, the Paradise might be, as in *Adam, loco eminentiore*, and that the *infernum* or hell, conventionally represented by the head and open gullet of a monstrous dragon, was low down, as if in the bowels of the earth [2]. It should be added that, as early as the first quarter of the twelfth century, plays had begun to make their way from the church, if not into the open, at any rate into buildings of domestic use. The authority for this is Gerhoh of Reichersberg, who speaks of performances in the refectory of Augsburg, when he was *magister scholae* there about 1123 [3]. Some of the Fleury or other early plays may conceivably have been intended for the refectory.

The expansion of the cycles caused difficulties of time, as well as of space. Without a compression of manner alien to the long-winded Middle Ages, it was sometimes impossible to get the whole of the matter to be treated within the limits of a single day. The problem was amenable to more than one solution. The performance could be spread over two or more sittings. The first recorded example of such an arrangement is at Cividale in 1298 [4], but it is one that would naturally suggest itself, especially for the Easter cycle, which fell naturally enough into the two dramas of Passion and Resurrection, from which, indeed, it sprang. In the Frankfort cue-book of the fourteenth century, it is carefully noted, that

[1] Julleville, *Les Myst.* i. 386; Bapst, 28.

[2] Cf. p. 137. Amongst the 'establies' required for the Rouen play of 1474 was 'Enfer faict en maniere d'une grande gueulle se cloant et ouvrant quant besoing en est' (Julleville, *Les Myst.* ii. 37). Just such an 'enfer' is represented in the Fouquet and Valenciennes miniatures.

[3] Cf. p. 98.

[4] Cf. p. 77.

if the audience are being kept too long, the *rectores* of the play shall defer the Resurrection to a second day[1]. Another device, which does not occur so early, was to divide the cycle into parts and play them in successive years. This method was adopted with the play of the Seven Joys of Mary at Brussels[2], and English examples will be found in a later chapter[3].

The cycles required in many cases a larger number of actors than the ecclesiastical bodies, even with the aid of wandering clerks and the cloister schools, could supply. It was necessary to press the laity into the service. The Easter play, of which the thirteenth-century anchoress Wilburgis was disappointed, was acted *tam a clero quam a populo*[4]. It was a further step in the same direction when the laity themselves took over the control and financing of plays. For this one must look mainly to that most important element in mediaeval town life, the guilds. Just as the Feast of Fools passed from the hands of the clergy into those of the *sociétés joyeuses*, so did the religious drama into those of more serious confraternities. The *burgenses* of Cahors, who in 1290 and 1302 played a *ludum de miraculis beati Marcialis* in the graveyard of St. Martial of Limoges, not improbably belonged to a guild formed to do honour to the patron[5]. The primary purpose of such guilds as these was devotional, and if they acted plays, it was doubtless with the countenance and assistance of the clergy to whose church they were affiliated. But those more secular and literary guilds, the *puys*, also undertook to act religious plays no less than *sotties* and farces; and in them

[1] Froning, 363 'Et notandum, quod optime congruit, ne populus nimiam moram faciendo gravetur, et ut resurrectio domini gloriosius celebretur, ut ulterior ordo ludi in diem alterum conservetur; quod si apud rectores deliberatum fuerit, Augustinus coram populo proclamet dicens sine rigmo, ut in die crastino revertatur.'

[2] Creizenach, i. 340.

[3] Cf. p. 130.

[4] Cf. p. 74. By the fifteenth century lay performers appear even in the ritual *Quem quaeritis*. An Augsburg version of 1487 (Milchsack, 129) concludes 'Permittitur tamen aliis, qui forsan huiusmodi personas [i.e. 'sacerdotes' et 'cantores'] non habent, ut cum aliis personis et etiam moribus honestis tamen et discretis, huiusmodi visitationem sepulchri exequantur.' See also the jest of Tyll Ulenspiegel with the parson's concubine who played the angel, quoted by Pearson, ii. 308.

[5] Julleville, *Les Myst.* ii. 2. For plays by German guilds cf. Pearson, ii. 364.

it may be suspected that the influence of the clergy would have to contend shrewdly with that of the minstrels[1]. It is not surprising to come in time upon signs of a rivalry between lay and clerical actors. Thus, in 1378, the scholars of St. Paul's are said to have presented a petition to Richard II, praying him to prohibit a play by some 'unexpert people' of the History of the Old Testament, a subject which they themselves had prepared at great expense for the ensuing Christmas. It may have been some similar dispute which led about the same date to the formation of the Parisian *Confrérie de la Passion*, which received from Charles VI a privilege to perform in and about the city, and became a model for many similar *confréries* throughout France. The charter bears the date of 1402. In 1398 the provost of Paris seems to have been moved to forbid dramatic performances without special sanction in the city or suburbs, a prohibition which, by the way, was flouted on the day of its proclamation at Saint-Maur. Exactly what led to this interposition of authority is not clear ; but it probably induced the *confrérie*, who may have had a previous less formal existence, to apply for their privilege[2]. The *confrérie de la Passion* seem to have acted, as a rule, in closed rooms. It is not unlikely that the *puys* did the same.

The altered conditions of representation naturally reacted upon the style and temper of the plays themselves. This is not a subject that can be discussed in detail here, but a few points may be briefly noted. The first is the gradual substitution of vernacular tongues for the Latin of the liturgical drama. This was almost inevitable, where laymen performed to a lay audience. But the liturgical drama itself did not absolutely exclude the vernacular. In the *Sponsus*, and in the *Suscitatio Lazari* and the Nicholas play of Hilarius, fragments of French are inserted, just as they are in the 'farced' epistles used at the feasts of certain saints, notably at that of St. Stephen[3]. It was a step further when in the fourteenth

---

[1] Creizenach, i. 137 ; Julleville, *Les Myst.* i. 115; *Les Com.* 43. Probably the 'Jeu de Nicholas' of Jean Bodel, and the fourteenth-century 'Miracles de Notre Dame,' belong to the *répertoires* of *puys*.

[2] Julleville, *Les Myst.* i. 412 ; *Les Com.* 55.

[3] Du Méril, 410, 414, prints examples of such *épîtres farcies* for

century the nuns of Origny Ste.-Benoîte rewrote their liturgical *Quem quaeritis,* leaving indeed some of the more solemn parts, such as the dialogue of the Maries with the angel, or that of the Magdalen with the risen Christ, in Latin, but turning the rest into French[1]. Such an arrangement as this of Origny Ste.-Benoîte became in the transition plays, intended for out-of-door performance to a popular audience, the rule. There was naturally some local variation. Of the two longer scholars' plays in the Benedictbeuern manuscript, the Christmas play is wholly, the Passion play mainly, in Latin. A large proportion of Latin seems to have been retained in the Frankfort Passion play of the fourteenth century. But on the whole, as the texts grow, and especially as they draw upon the apocryphal books or the great mediaeval vernacular epics for matter not in the liturgical plays, the vernacular steadily gets the upper hand, until in the latest versions the traces of Latin must be regarded as mere survivals.

In some cases where Latin and vernacular appear together, the latter is of the nature of a translation, or rough and often much expanded paraphrase, of the former. This type of mixed and obviously transitional text can, as it happens, be illustrated from French, German, and English sources. It occurs, for instance, in the *Adam.* Here the Adam and Eve and Cain and Abel scenes are wholly, but for the preliminary *lectio* and the interpolated chants by the choir, in Norman-French. The prophecies, however, are given in the double form. Thus Isaiah says:

'Egredietur virga de radice Jesse, et flos de radice eius ascendet, et requiescet super eum spiritus domini.

> 'Or vus dirrai merveillus diz :
> Jessé sera de sa raïz.
> Verge en istra, qui fera flor,
> Qui ert digne de grant unor.

the feasts of St. Stephen and St. Thomas of Canterbury: cf. the numerous references in D'Ancona, i. 66, and vol. i. p. 277.

[1] Text in Coussemaker, 256, from *Bibl. St. Quentin MS.* 75 (fourteenth century); cf. Julleville, *Les Myst.*

i. 64. The *Quem quaeritis* includes the *Hortulanus* scene and has, like the Prague versions, the *Mercator.* It was probably written later than 1286, as the *Ordinarius* of that year (Coussemaker, 337) directs a shorter version in Latin.

Saint espirit l'avra si clos,
Sor ceste flor iert sun repos.'

There are many similar examples in German plays, of which the most complete is a *Quem quaeritis* in a fourteenth-century manuscript at Trèves[1]. In England Professor Skeat discovered at Shrewsbury a fragmentary text of this type in a manuscript of the early fifteenth century[2]. It is written in a northern, probably Yorkshire, dialect, and contains the part, with cues, of a single actor in three plays, a *Pastores*, a *Quem quaeritis*, and a *Peregrini*. In the first he played the Third Shepherd, in the second the Third Mary, in the last probably Cleophas. The fragment shows clearly enough the way in which the Latin text was first sung by a group of performers together, and then expanded by them separately in the vernacular. The two documents last quoted mark not only the transition from Latin to the vernacular, but also that from the sung drama of the liturgies to the spoken drama of the great cycles. In Professor Skeat's Shrewsbury fragments the Latin alone is musically noted. In the Trèves *Quem quaeritis* the Latin and portions of the German are noted, and a careful distinction is made between the lines to be spoken and those to be sung by the use of the terms *cantat* and *dicit* in the rubrics[3].

Again, the laicization of the drama was accompanied by a further development of the secular and even comic elements, of which the germs already existed in the plays. A more human and less distinctively ecclesiastical handling became possible[4]. The figure of Herod offered a melodramatic type of ranting tyrant which the tradition of the stage did not readily forget. The life of the unconverted Magdalen *in gaudio* gave the dramatist his opportunity to paint scenes of wholly secular luxury and romance. Naturally the comic developments attached themselves largely to personalities not

---

[1] Text in Froning, 49, from *Trier MS.* 75 (begins 'incipit ludus de nocte paschae, de tribus Mariis et Maria Magdalena' . . . ends 'explicit ludus'); cf. Creizenach, i. 112; Davidson, 149; Wirth, 120, 235.

[2] Cf. *Academy* for Jan. 4 and 11, 1890, where Prof. Skeat prints the text from *Shrewsbury MS. Mus.* iii. 42 f. 48 (a book of anthems). Manly, i. xxviii, also gives it with some valuable notes of his own.

[3] Creizenach, i. 109.

[4] Ibid. i. 99, 202; Pearson, ii. 271, 302, 394; Wirth, 168, 201, 215; D'Ancona, i. 62.

already defined in the Testament narratives. The *Mercator*,
for instance, whose domesticities with his wife and his
apprentice do so much to enliven the later German plays,
is a thoroughly characteristic production of the mediaeval
folk spirit, for the delectation of which Rutebeuf wrote the
Dit de l'Erberie[1]. It is not, perhaps, altogether unjustifiable
to trace a relation between him and the inveterate quack
doctor of the spring folk drama itself[2]. This would not be
the only point of contact between the *ludi* of the Church and
those of the folk. The significance, from this point of view,
of Balaam's ass has already been touched upon[3]. And in
the growth of the devil scenes, from their first beginnings
in the *Sponsus* or in the devil-deacon of the *Tollite portas*[4],
to their importance in the *Adam* or the various treatments
of the Fall of Lucifer and the Harrowing of Hell, may we not
trace the influence of those masked and blackened demon
figures who from all time had been a dear scandal of the
Kalends and the Feast of Fools[5]? It is certain that the imps
who sallied amongst the spectators and haled the Fathers off
to their limbo of clashed kettles and caldrons must have been
an immensely popular feature of the *Adam*; and it is noteworthy that in more than one place the *compagnies joyeuses*
who inherited the Feast of Fools joined forces with more
serious *confréries* and provided comic actors.for the religious
plays[6].

In yet another way the coming of the vernacular affected
the character of the religious drama. It had been cosmopolitan;
it was to be national: and from the fourteenth century, in
spite of a few lendings and borrowings, and of a certain
uniformity in the general lines of development, it really
requires separate treatment in each of the European countries[7].
In Italy the divergence from the common type was perhaps
most marked of all, although I think that Signor D'Ancona
and others have perhaps pushed the doctrine of the independence and isolation of Italian drama to an extreme. They

[1] Cf. vol. i. p. 83.
[2] Cf. vol. i. pp. 185, 207, 213.
[3] Cf. p. 56.
[4] Cf. p. 4.
[5] Cf. vol. i. pp. 258, 268, 327.

[6] Julleville, *Les Myst.* ii. 412;
Les Com. 149, 237 (Chaumont), 239
(Chauny).
[7] Creizenach, i. 356; cf. p. 146.

consider that it almost began afresh with the religious stirrings of the Umbrian Flagellants in 1260. The *compagnie* or associations of *disciplinati*, who were the outcome of this thoroughly folk movement, were wont, as they lashed themselves, to sing hymns of praise, *laudes*, whence they got the secondary name of *laudesi*. The lauds were mostly sung in the chapels of the *compagnie* after mass and a sermon on Sundays. Several fourteenth-century collections are extant, and contain examples intended for use throughout the circle of the ecclesiastical year. Many of them were dialogued, and appear to have been recited in costume with scenic accessories. The dramatic lauds were specifically known as *devozioni*, and by the end of the fourteenth century were in some cases performed rather elaborately upon a *talamo* or stage in the nave of a church, with *luoghi deputati* for the accommodation of the chief actors. According to Signor D'Ancona, the *devozioni*, which were composed by poor folk, were taken direct from the liturgy and owed little more than the initial hint or impulse to the liturgical drama ; while at the other end of these developments, they became the source of the out-of-door and splendidly-staged *sacre rappresentazioni* which originated in Florence in the fifteenth century and thence spread to other Italian cities [1]. On this theory it must be observed that the *devozioni* have not been shown to be independent of the liturgical drama, and that the derivation of the *sacre rappresentazioni* from the *devozioni* is purely conjectural [3]. The *sacre rappresentazioni* were out of doors and produced by the clergy or laity ; the *devozioni*, which have not been traced to Florence, were produced indoors by religious guilds of a very distinct type. The *sacre rappresentazioni*, moreover, included subjects, such as the *profeti*, which are not within the cycle of the

[1] D'Ancona, i. 87 sqq.; F. Torraca, *Discussioni e ricerche* (1888), 92 ; Creizenach, i. 299 sqq.; J. A. Symonds, *Renaissance in Italy*, iv. 242 sqq.; G. Smith, 297 ; Wechssler, 30 ; Gaspary, i. 138, 357 ; I. S. A. Herford, *The Confraternities of Penance, their Dramas and their Lamentations* in *E. H. Review*, vi. (1891), 646. A first instalment of dramatic Lauds was published by Monaci, *Appunti per la storia del teatro italiano* in *Rivista di Filologia Romana*, i. 235, ii. 29. For other collections cf. D'Ancona, i. 153 ; Gaspary, i. 361. D'Ancona has published *Sacre Rappresentazioni* (1872). A selection of Lauds, Devozioni, and Rappresentazioni is in F. Torraca, *Il teatro italiano dei Secoli xiii, xiv, e xv* (1885).

devozioni, but do belong to the liturgical drama.   It is at least a tenable view, that the *devozioni* were merely a backwater of the drama, and that the *sacre rappresentazioni* were derived, like the fifteenth-century plays of other countries, from the liturgical drama through the medium of such transitional types as those already noted at Padua, Siena, and Cividale.   The fact that the only transitional texts preserved are those of the *devozioni* has perhaps led to an exaggerated estimate of the importance of these.   Even liturgical dramas are rare in Italy, although there are sufficient thoroughly to establish their existence.   The chroniclers, however, mention one or two events which point to another dramatic tradition in Italy than that of the *devozioni.*   At Florence itself, in 1306, there was a show of Heaven and Hell upon the Arno, which though merely pantomimic, may have been based on some dramatic representation of the Last Judgement[1].   At Milan, in 1336, was a *Stella,* in which the *Magi* rode through the streets, and Herod sat by the columns of San Lorenzo[2]. Both of these performances, like those at Padua and Cividale

---

[1] D'Ancona, i. 94.

[2] Galvano Flamma, *de rebus gestis a Vicecomitibus* (D'Ancona, i. 97 ; Muratori, *Rer. Ital. Script.* xii. 1017).   The ceremony was 'in die Epifanie in conventu fratrum Praedicatorum . . . Fuerunt coronati tres Reges in equis magnis, vallati domicellis, vestiti variis, cum somariis multis et familia magna nimis.   Et fuit stella aurea discurrens per aera, quae praecedebat istos tres Reges, et pervenerunt ad columnas Sancti Laurentii, ubi erat rex Herodes effigiatus, cum scribis et sapientibus.   Et visi sunt interrogare regem Herodem, ubi Christus nasceretur, et revolutis multis libris responderunt, quod deberet nasci in civitate Bethleem in distantia quinque milliariorum a Hierusalem. Quo audito, isti tres Reges coronati aureis coronis, tenentes in manibus scyphos aureos cum auro, thure et myrrha, praecedente stella per aera, cum somariis et mirabili famulatu, clangentibus tubis, et bucinis praecedentibus, simiis, babuynis, et diversis generibus animalium, cum mirabili populorum tumultu, pervenerunt ad ecclesiam Sancti Eustorgii. Ubi in latere altaris maioris erat praesepium cum bove et asino, et in praesepio erat Christus parvulus in brachiis Virginis matris.   Et isti Reges obtulerunt Christo munera ; deinde visi sunt dormire, et Angelus alatus ei dixit quod non redirent per contratam Sancti Laurentii, sed per portam Romanam : quod et factum fuit.   Et fuit tantus concursus populi et militum et dominarum et clericorum, quod nunquam similis fere visus fuit.   Et fuit ordinatum, quod omni anno istud festum fieret.' This is precisely the liturgic *Stella* translated into an out - of - door *spectacle,* which in its turn becomes the model for many a Quattrocento painting ; cf., e. g., Botticelli's *Magi* in the Uffizi, or Gentile da Fabriano's, with the baboons done to the life, in the Accademia.

and the *sacre rappresentazioni* themselves, were out of doors. It is true that the *sacre rappresentazioni* fell less into big cycles than did the contemporary plays of. other countries: but cycles were not unknown[1], and it must be borne in mind that the extreme beauty and elaboration of the Florentine *mise-en-scène* made a limited scheme, on grounds both of time and expense, almost imperative.

With out-of-door plays climatic conditions began to be of importance. Even in sunny France, Christmas is not exactly the season to hang about the market-place looking at an interminable drama. It is not to be denied that Christmas plays continued to be occasionally acted well through the fifteenth century[2], but the number of these, compared with the Passions, is small[3]. Even Easter weather is not invariably genial. Nor, as the cycles lengthened, was the attachment of them to any one of the feasts, whose events they commemorated, a matter of first-rate importance. A tendency set in towards playing them as far as possible in the long warm days of the summer months. The first Whitsuntide performances are those at Cividale in 1298 and 1303; and Whitsuntide became a very favourite date[4]. At Florence the great patronal feast and procession of St. John the Baptist on June 24 was a natural occasion for *sacre rappresentazioni* [5].

---

[1] D'Ancona, i. 94, 301, considers, however, that the late fifteenth-century *Passio* of Revello was not a native growth, but modelled on contemporary cyclic plays from France.

[2] The Rouen play of 1474 (Julleville, *Les Myst.* ii. 36) was one, and cf. pp. 119, 122.

[3] Creizenach, i. 242; cf. the lists in Julleville, *Les Myst.* ii. 183.

[4] Julleville, *Les Myst.* ii. 9 sqq.

[5] D'Ancona, i. 218; Guasti, *Le feste di San Giovanni Baptista in Firenze* (1884). *Rappresentazioni* on St. John's day were known to the late fourteenth-century Florentine historian Goro di Stagio Dati. An account of the feast in 1407 makes no mention of them, but they appear in that of 1439, and are elaborately described in the *Storia* of Matteo di Marco Palmieri about 1454 (D'Ancona, i. 228). Early in the morning of June 22 started a procession of clergy, *compagnie, edifizii,* and *cavalleria.* These stopped in the Piazza della Signoria, and *rappresentazioni,* forming a complete cycle from the Fall of Lucifer to the Last Judgement, and lasting sixteen hours, were given upon the *edifizii:* D'Ancona suggests that the dumb show type of *rappresentazioni* preceded the dialogued one, 'come più semplice.' But this seems equally inconsistent with his view that the *rappresentazioni* grew out of *devozioni,* and mine that they were an adaptation of earlier cyclical plays to the conditions of the Florentine feast.

Another high day for the cyclical drama from the fourteenth century onwards, notably in England[1] and Spain[2], and to a much less degree in Germany[3] and France[4], was the recently-established feast of Corpus Christi. This, the most materialistic of all the Church's celebrations, is in honour of the mystery of the transubstantiated sacrament. It originated locally in an alleged revelation to Juliana, a Cistercian religious of Liège. Pope Urban IV designed in 1264 to make it a universal festival, but he died in the same year, and the bull which he had issued remained inoperative until it was confirmed by Clement V at the council of Vienne in 1311. Corpus Christi day was the Thursday after Trinity Sunday. An office was compiled for it by St. Thomas Aquinas, and the leading ceremony was a great procession in which the host, escorted by local dignitaries, religious bodies and guilds, was borne through the streets and displayed successively at out-of-door stations[5]. When the plays were transferred to Corpus Christi day, they became more or less attached to this procession. Sometimes, perhaps, the procession served as a mere preliminary parade for the actors, such as sometimes preceded plays at other times[6]. The play itself would follow on a fixed stage of the ordinary type. But the method of the great English cycles seems to point to a more complete merging of play and procession than this. The *domus, loci,* or *sedes* were set upon wheels, and known as 'pageants[7]'; and the performance was gone through during the procession,

---

[1] Cf. ch. xxi.

[2] D'Ancona, i. 243; Schack, ii. 103; Ticknor, *Hist. of Spanish Lit.* ii. 249. The *Autos Sacramentales* are so named from their connexion with this day.

[3] Creizenach, i. 170, 227. The earliest German mention is at the council of Prague in 1366 (Höfler, *Concilia Pragensia*, 13, in *Abhandl. d. königl. böhmischen Gesellsch. der Wiss.* series v. vol. 12) 'omnibus ... clericis et laicis ... mandatur ut ludos theatrales vel etiam fistulatores vel ioculatores in festo corporis Christi in processionibus ire quovis modo permittant et admittant.' Extant *Frohnleichnamsspiele*

are those of Innsbruck, †1391 (Text in Mone, *Altteutsche Schauspiele,* 145), and of Künzelsau, †1479 (ed. H. Werner, in *Germania,* iv. 338). Cf. the description (†1553) of Naogeorgos (transl. Googe) in Stubbes, i. 337.

[4] Julleville, ii. 208.

[5] Ward, i. 44; Davidson, 215; Malleson-Tuker, ii. 227.

[6] See e.g. the 'Processio huius ludi' at the end of the text of the Alsfeld Passion of 1501 (Froning, 858); cf. Pearson, ii. 365. As to the general relations of processions and plays, cf. p. 160.

[7] Cf. p. 136.

being repeated at the various stations made by the host. If the cycle was a very long one, time could be saved by making an early play at one station coincident with a later play at that in front of it. It is, however, easy to see that with the arrangement here suggested the popularity of the pageants might throw the strictly religious aspect of the procession rather into the shade. The two would then be severed again, but the play might still retain its processional character. This is not, I think, an unreasonable conjecture as to how the type of play found, say at York, may have come into existence[1]. To Chester, where the plays were not on Corpus Christi day, but at Whitsuntide, the method must have been transferred at a later date.

During this brief survey of the critical period for the religious drama between the middle of the thirteenth and the middle of the fourteenth century, I have attempted to bring into relief the tendencies that were at work for its remodelling. But it must not be supposed that either the tendency to expansion or the tendency to secularization acted universally and uniformly. The truth is quite otherwise. To the end of the history of the religious drama, the older types, which it threw out as it evolved, co-existed with the newer ones[2]. The Latin tropes and liturgical dramas held their place in the church services. And in the vernaculars, side by side with the growing Nativities and Passions, there continued to be acted independent plays of more than one sort. There were the original short plays, such as the *Stella*, the *Annunciation*, the *Sponsus*, the *Antichrist*, by the running together of which the cycles came into being. There were plays, on the other hand, which originated as episodes in the cycles, and only subsequently attained to an independent

[1] The closest merging of play and procession is suggested by an order at Draguignan in 1558 (Julleville, *Les Myst.* ii. 209), where it was ordered 'Le dit jeu jora avec la procession comme auparadvant et le plus d'istoeres et plus brieves que puront estre seront et se dira tout en cheminant sans ce que personne du jeu s'areste pour eviter prolixité et confusion tant de ladite prosession que jeu, et que les estrangiers le voient aisement.' Perhaps the short speeches of the Innsbruck play were similarly delivered while the procession was moving. The nearest continental approach to the English type is the Künzelsau play, which was divided into three parts and played at three different stations (Creizenach, i. 227).

[2] Creizenach, i. 218.

existence. The majority of these were Old Testament plays, budded off, like the *Daniel*, from the *Prophetae*. And finally there were numerous plays drawn from hagiological legends, many of which never came into connexion with the cycles at all. Thus in the transition period we find, not only plays on St. Nicholas and St. Catherine for which liturgical models existed, but also the great French series of Miracles of the Virgin, and plays on Saints Theophilus, Dorothy, Martial, and Agnes[1]. The natural tendency of great churches to magnify their own patron saints led to further multiplication of themes. In the same way, long after the lay guilds and corporations had taken up the drama, performances continued to be given or superintended by the clergy and their scholars[2]. Priests and monks supplied texts and lent vestments for the lay plays. To the last, the church served from time to time as a theatre. All these points, as well as the traces of their liturgical origin lingering in the cycles, will be fully illustrated, so far as England is concerned, in the following chapters.

The question presents itself: What was the official attitude of the high ecclesiastical authorities towards the growing religious plays? It is not precisely answered, as the history of the Feast of Fools has shown, by the fact that the chapters and inferior clergy encouraged and took part in them. The liturgical drama had its motive, as St. Ethelwold is careful to point out, in a desire for devotion and the edification of

[1] Creizenach, i. 128, 137 sqq., 156; Julleville, *Les Myst.* i. 95, 107, 115, 185; ii. 2, 4, 5, 221, 226, 345; *Les Com.* 49; Sepet, 202, 242; Clédat, 63, 73, 105.

[2] Creizenach, i. 130, 165, 176; Julleville, *Les Myst.* i. 347; *Les Com.* 291; D'Ancona, i. 57; Pearson, ii. 303; Wirth, 144. A play could be given outside the church without wholly losing its connexion with the liturgy. It became a sort of procession: cf. pp. 32, 67. D'Ancona, i. 59, quotes from *Bibl. de l'École des Chartes*, iii. 450, a licence given by the Bishop of Langres in 1408 'Ut in quadem platea vel plateis congruis et honestis, infra vel extra villam, prope et supra rippariam loci, coram clero et populo, alta et intelligibili voce, lingua latina et materna, cum magna reverentia et honore ac diversis personacium et habituum generibus ad hoc congruis et necessariis, solemniter et publice vitam et miracula egregii confessoris et pontificis Machuti, recitare et exponere, missamque solemnem in pontificalibus, in platea seu plateis supradictis super altare portatili consecrato per alterum vestrum canonicorum vel alium ydoneum sacerdotem celebrare ... licentiam et auctoritatem impertimus per praesentes.' Cf. the examples of plays at the Feasts of Fools and of the Boy Bishop (vol. i. pp. 295, 296, 299, 304, 306, 309, 313, 342, 348, 349, 380).

the vulgar[1]. The hope of affording a counter-attraction to the spring and winter *ludi* of hard-dying paganism probably went for something. Herrad of Landsberg, in the twelfth century, utters a regret that the *Stella* rightly instituted at Epiphany by the Fathers of the Church had given place to a shameless revel[2]. But a contrary opinion to Herrad's arose almost contemporaneously amongst the reforming anti-imperial clergy of Germany. This finds expression more than once in the writings of Gerhoh of Reichersberg[3]. He scoffs at the monks of Augsburg who, when he was *magister scolae* there about 1122, could only be induced to sup in the refectory, when a representation of Herod or the Innocents or some other quasi-theatrical spectacle made an excuse for a feast[4]. And he devotes a chapter of his *De Investigatione Antichristi*, written about 1161, to an argument that clergy who turn the churches into theatres are doing the work of that very Antichrist of whom they make a show[5]. Evidently Gerhoh has

[1] Cf. p. 16.

[2] Cf. vol. i. p. 318. Pearson, ii. 285, translates: 'The old Fathers of the Church, in order to strengthen the belief of the faithful and to attract the unbeliever by this manner of religious service, rightly instituted at the Feast of Epiphany or the Octave religious performances of such a kind as the star guiding the Magi to the new-born Christ, the cruelty of Herod, the dispatch of the soldiers, the lying-in of the Blessed Virgin, the angel warning the Magi not to return to Herod, and other events of the birth of Christ. But what nowadays happens in many churches? Not a customary ritual, not an act of reverence, but one of irreligion and extravagance conducted with all the license of youth. The priests having changed their clothes go forth as a troop of warriors; there is no distinction between priest and warrior to be marked. At an unfitting gathering of priests and laymen the church is desecrated by feasting and drinking, buffoonery, unbecoming jokes, play, the clang of weapons, the presence of shameless wenches,

the vanities of the world, and all sorts of disorder. Rarely does such a gathering break up without quarrelling.'

[3] On Gerhoh (1093–1169) see the article in the 2nd ed. of Wetzer and Welte's *Kirchenlexicon*. He took a strong reforming and anti-imperial line in the controversies of his day.

[4] Gerhohus, *Comm. in Ps. cxxxii* (*P. L.* cxciv. 890) 'Cohaerebat ipsi Ecclesiae claustrum satis honestum, sed a claustrali religione omnino vacuum, cum neque in dormitorio fratres dormirent, neque in refectorio comederent, exceptis rarissimis festis, maxime in quibus Herodem repraesentarent Christi persecutorem, parvulorum interfectorem, seu ludis aliis aut spectaculis quasi theatralibus exhibendis comportaretur symbolum ad faciendum convivium in refectorio aliis pene omnibus temporibus vacuo.'

[5] Gerhohus, *de Inv. Ant.* lib. i. c. 5, *de spectaculis theatricis in ecclesia Dei exhibitis* (*Gerhohi Opera Inedita*, ed. Scheibelberger, i. 25) 'Et sacerdotes, qui dicuntur, iam non ecclesiae vel altaris ministerio dediti

been stung by the lampooning of his party as the *Hypocritae* in the pro-imperialist *Antichristus* which is still extant. But he includes in his condemnation plays of a less special and polemical character, referring especially to the Nativity cycle and to a lost play of *Elisaeus*. He repeats some of the old patristic objections against *larvae* and *spectacula*, and tells tales, such as Prynne will tell after him, of how horrors mimicked by actors have been miraculously converted into verities[1]. Literary historians occasionally commit themselves to the statement that Innocent III forbade the clergy to participate in miracle-plays[2]. It is more than doubtful

cunt, sed exercitiis avaritiae, vanitatum et spectaculorum, adeo ut ecclesias ipsas, videlicet orationum domus, in theatra commutent ac mimicis ludorum spectaculis impleant. Inter quae nimirum spectacula adstantibus ac spectantibus ipsorum feminis interdum et antichristi, de quo nobis sermo est, non ut ipsi aestimant imaginariam similitudinem exhibent sed in veritate, ut credi potest iniquitatis ipsius mysterium pro parte sua implent. Quidni enim diabolus abutatur in serium rebus sibi exhibitis in vanitatis ludicrum, sicut Dominus quoque Iesus convertens in seria ludibria, quibus apud Iudaeos vel Pilatum in passione sua affectus est? ... Quid ergo mirum si et isti nunc antichristum vel Herodem in suis ludis simulantes eosdem non, ut eis intentioni est, ludicro mentiuntur sed in veritate exhibent, utpote quorum vita ab antichristi laxa conversatione non longe abest? ... Contigit, ut comperimus, aliquando apud tales, ut eum quem inter ludicra sua quasi mortuum ab Elisaeo propheta suscitantem exhiberent peracta simulatione mortuum invenirent. Alius item antichristo suo quasi suscitandus oblatus intra septem dies vere mortuus, ut comperimus, et sepultus est. Et quis scire potest an et cetera simulata antichristi scilicet effigiem, daemonum larvas, herodianam insaniem in veritate non exhibeant? ... Exhi-

bent praeterea imaginaliter et salvatoris infantiae cunabula, parvuli vagitum, puerperae virginis matronalem habitum, stellae quasi sidus flammigerum, infantum necem, maternum Rachelis ploratum. Sed divinitas insuper et matura facies ecclesiae abhorret spectacula theatralia, non respicit in vanitates et insanias falsas, immo non falsas sed iam veras insanias, in quibus viri totos se frangunt in feminas quasi pudeat eos, quod viri sunt, clerici in milites, homines se in daemonum larvas transfigurant ...'

[1] Prynne, *Histriomastix*, 556, refers to 'the visible apparition of the Devill on the Stage at the Belsavage Play-house, in Queene Elizabeth's dayes (to the great amazement both of the Actors and Spectators) whiles they were there prophanely playing the History of Faustus (the truth of which I have heard from many now alive, who well remember it), there being some distracted with that fearefull sight.'

[2] Pollard, xxiv. I do not know how Ward, i. 43, gets at the very different theory that in 1210 (*sic* for 1207) Innocent III ordered plays 'to be represented outside the church as well as inside.' Mr. Pollard, by the way, assigns the prohibition to 'Pope Gregory,' a further mistake, due, I suppose, to the fact that it was subsequently included in the Gregorian *Decretals*.

whether this was so. The prohibition in question is familiar to us, and it is clear that the *ludi theatrales* which Innocent barred from the churches were primarily the Feasts of Fools, and the like[1]. And as a matter of fact the *glossa ordinaria* to the decretal by Bernard de Bottone, which itself dates from about 1263, so interprets the words of the Pope as expressly to allow of Christmas and Easter representations calculated to stimulate devotion[2]. Yet there would have been no need for the gloss to have been written had not an opposite interpretation also been current. It was perhaps on the strength of the decree that another reformer, Robert Grosseteste, justified his action when in 1244 he directed his archdeacons to exterminate, so far as they could, the *miracula*, which he put on the same level as May-games and harvest-Mays, or the *scotales* of the folk[3]. And it is certainly appealed to before the end of the thirteenth century in the *Manuel des Péchés* of the Anglo-Norman William of Waddington[4]. Robert

[1] Cf. vol. i. p. 279.

[2] Quoted by Creizenach, i. 101, 'Non tamen hic prohibetur repraesentare praesepe Domini, Herodem, magos et qualiter Rachel ploravit filios suos, etc., quae tangunt festivitates illas, de quibus hic fit mentio, cum talia ad devotionem potius inducant homines quam ad lasciviam vel voluptatem, sicut in pascha sepulcrum Domini et alia repraesentantur ad devotionem excitandam': cf. vol. i. p. 342. J. Aquila, *Opusculum Enchiridion appellatum ferme de omni ludorum genere*, f. 14 (Oppenheim, 1516), after referring to the canon, says, 'Demonstrationes quae fiunt ad honorem dei puta passionis Christi aut vitae alicuius sancti non prohibentur in sacris locis ac temporibus fieri.' Both canon and gloss are cited in *Dives and Pauper*, a book of fifteenth-century English morality (F. A. Gasquet, *Eve of Reformation*, 317): cf. also D'Ancona, i. 54.

[3] Cf. vol. i. p. 91. An anchoress of Tarrant Keynston (*Ancren Riwle*, †1150, C. S. 318) was bound to confess if she 'eode oče pleouwe ine chircheie: biheold hit 't oče wrastlinge 't oč̌er fol gomenes': but 'pleouwe,' like *ludus* (vol. i. p. 393), may have a very general meaning.

[4] Manning, 146:—

Un autre folie apert
Vnt les fols clercs cuntroue,
Qe 'miracles' sunt apele;
Lur faces vnt la deguise
Par visers, li forsene,—
Qe est defendu en decree;
Tant est plus grand lur peche.
Fere poent representement,—
Mes que ceo seit chastement
En office de seint eglise
Quant hom fet la deu servise,—
Cum iesu crist le fiz dee
En sepulcre esteit pose,
Et la resurrectiun,
Pur plus auer deuociun.
Mes, fere foles assemblez
En les rues des citez,
Ou en cymiters apres mangers,
Quant venent les fols volunters,—
Tut dient qe il le funt pur bien,—
Crere ne les deuez pur rien
Qe fet seit pur le honur de dee,
Einz del deable, pur verite,
Seint ysidre me ad testimone
Qe fut si bon clerc lettre;
Il dist qe cil qe funt sepectacles

Grosseteste presumably, and William of Waddington specifically, objected to *miracula* even out of doors, which is surely stretching the words of Innocent III beyond what they will reasonably bear. In any case the austere view of the matter was not that which prevailed. The lax discipline of the 'Babylonish captivity' at Avignon, which allowed the Feast of Fools to grow up unchecked through the fourteenth century, was not likely to boggle at the plays. The alleged indulgence, not without modern parallels [1], of Clement VI to the spectators of the Chester plays and the performance of a *Stella* given by the English bishops in honour of their continental colleagues at the council of Constance in 1417 [2] are two out of

Cume lem fet en miracles,
Or ius qe nus nomames einz —
Burdiz ou turneinens, —
Lur baptesme vnt refusez,
E. deu de ciel reneiez,' &c.
   Robert Mannyng of Brunne
(1303) translates : —
'Hyt ys forbode hym, yn the decre,
Myracles for to make or se ;
For myracles, ȝyf þou begynne,
Hyt ys a gaderyng, a syghtc of synne,
He may yn þe cherche þurghe þys resun
Pley þe resurrecyun,
Þat ys to seye, how Gode ros,
God und man yn myȝt and los,
To make men be yn beleue gode
That he has ros wyþ flesshe and blode :
And he may pleye wyþoutyn plyghte
Howe god was bore yn ȝole nyght,
To make men to beleue stedfastly
Þat he lyghte yn þe vyrgyne Mary.
Ȝuf þou do hyt in weyys or greuys,
A syghte of synne truly hyt semys.
Seynt Ysodre, y take to wytnes,
For he hyt seyþ þat soþ hyt es ;
Þus hyt seyþ yn hys boke,
Þey foresake þat þey toke—
God and here crystendom—
Þat make swyche pleyys to any man
As myracles and bourdys,
Or tournamentys of grete prys,' &c.
The reference to 'Seynt Ysodre' is to Isidore of Seville, *Etymologiarum* xviii. 59, *de horum [ludo-*

rum] exsecratione (*P.L.* lxxxii. 660). The saint is speaking of course of the Roman *spectacula*.

   [1] On the 'pardon' or 'Ablass' given to actors at Oberammergau, and the meaning, or want of meaning, to be attached to it, see an amusing controversy in the *Nineteenth Century* for January and February, 1901.
   [2] L'Enfant, *Hist. du Concile de Constance* (1727), ii. 404 ; Hardt, *Magnum Oecumenicum Constantiense Concilium* (1700), iv. 1089 ; K. Schmidt, *Die Digby-Spiele*, 12. The performance, which was possibly a dumb show, took place at a banquet on Jan. 24, 141⅚, and was repeated on the following Sunday before the emperor, who had arrived in the interval. Hardt quotes the German of one Dacher, an eyewitness : 'Am 24ten tag des Monats Januarii, das vvar auff Timotheus tag, da luden die Bischöff aus Engeland, der Bischoff Salisburgensis, der Bischoff von Londen, der demnach funff Bischoff von Engeland, alle Räht zu Costniz und sonst viel ehrbar Bürger daselbst, in Burchart Walters Haus, das man vorzeiten nennt zu dem Burgthor, itzt zu dem gulden Schvvert, allernächst bey S. Laurenz. Und gab ihnen fast ein köstlich mahl, ie 2. Gericht nach einander, jedes Gericht besonder mit 8 Essen : Die trug man allvveg eins mahl dar, deren allvveg

many proofs that the later mediaeval Church found no difficulty in accommodating itself to the somewhat disconcerting by-product of its own liturgy[1]. Such opposition to the religious drama as can be traced after the thirteenth century came not from the heads of the Church but from its heretics. It is chiefly represented by a curious *Tretise of miraclis pleyinge* which dates from the end of the fourteenth century and may safely be referred to a Wyclifite origin[2]. The burden of it is the sin of making ' oure pleye and bourde of tho myraclis and werkis that God so ernestfully wrou3t to us.' On this note the anonymous preacher harps rather monotonously, and

waren 4 verguld oder versilbert. In dem mahl, zvvischen dem Essen, so machten sie solch bild und geberd, als unser Frau ihr Kind unsern Herrn und auch Gott gebahr, mit fast köstlichen Tüchern und Gevvand. Und Joseph stellten sie zu ihr. Und die heiligen 3 Könige, als die unser Frauen die Opffer brachten. Und hatten gemacht einen lauteren guldnen Stern, der ging vor ihnen, an einem kleinen eisern Drat. Und machten König Herodem, vvie er den drey Königen nachsandt, und vvie er die Kindlein ertodtet. Das machten sie alles mit gar köstlichem Gevvand, und mit grossen guldenen und silbernen Gürteln, und machten das mit grosser Gezierd, und mit grosser Demuht.'

[1] The provincial *C. of Sens* (1460), c. 3 (Labbé, xiii. 1728), while confirming the Basle decree, allowed ' aliquid iuxta consuetudines ecclesiae, in Nativitate Domini, vel Resurrectione ... fiat cum honestate et pace, absque prolongatione, impedimento, vel diminutione servitii, larvatione et sordidatione faciei '; cf. the Toledo decree of 1473 quoted vol. i. p. 342. The *C. of Compostella* (1565), c.c. 9–11 (Aguirra *Conc. Hispan.* v. 450, 460), forbade ' actus sive repraesentationes ' during service in church ; they might take place with leave of the bishop, or in his absence the chapter, before or after service. Devotional ' actus ' were allowed in Passion week on

similar conditions. The Corpus Christi procession ' semel tantum subsistat, causa horum actuum vel representationum in eo loco extra ecclesiam quem Praelatus aut [capitulum] idoneum iudicabit.' On the other hand the *C. of Seville* (1512), c. 21 (Aguirra, v. 370), had forbidden priests or monks to perform or give a ' locus ' for such ' actus ': ' Sumus informati, quod in quibusdam Ecclesiis nostri Archiepiscopatus et Provinciae permittitur fieri nonnullas repraesentationes Passionis Domini nostri Iesu Christi, et alios actus, et memoriam Resurrectionis, Nativitatis Salvatoris nostri, vel alias repraesentationes. Et quia ex talibus actibus orta sunt, et oriuntur plura absurda, et saepe saepius scandala in cordibus illorum qui non sunt bene confirmati in nostra sancta fide Catholica,videntes confusiones, et excessus, qui in hoc committuntur . . .' Cf. also the Langres licence of 1408 (p. 97).

[2] Text in *Reliquiae Antiquae*, ii. 42; Hazlitt,73; from late fourteenth-century volume of homilies formerly in library of St. Martin's-in-the-Fields. There is also in *Rel. Ant.* i. 322 a satirical English poem from *Cott. MS. Cleop.* B. ii (fifteenth century), against the miracle plays of the ' frer mynours,' apparently at Rome. But the Minorite in *Pierce the Ploughman's Crede* (†1394, ed. Skeat), 107, says of his order, ' At marketts & myracles · we medleþ vs nevere.'

adds that 'myraclis pleyinge . . . makith to se veyne siȝtis of degyse, aray of men and wymmen by yvil continaunse, eyther stiryng othere to letcherie and of debatis.' Like Gerhoh of Reichersberg, he thinks the plays 'gynnys of the dyvul to drawen men to the byleve of Anti-Crist.' He elaborately confutes the views that they are for the worship of God, or the more compassion of Christ, or lead to conversion. He will not allow that 'summe recreatioun men moten han, and bettere it is or lesse yvele that thei han theyre recreacoun by pleyinge of myraclis than bi pleyinge of other japis.' The analysis of the piece need not, perhaps, be pushed further. The opinions expressed do not appear to have had any weight either of popular or of ecclesiastical sentiment behind them ; but they curiously antedate the histriomastic tracts of many a sixteenth and seventeenth-century Puritan.

This chapter may be fitly closed by a few words on the subject of nomenclature[1]. The old classical terms of *tragoedia* and *comoedia* are not of course normally used of the religious plays until the Renaissance influences come in towards the end of the fifteenth century. Their mediaeval sense, in fact, implies nothing distinctively dramatic[2]. The liturgical plays have often a purely liturgical heading, such as *Processio Asinorum*[3], or *Officium Sepulchri*[4], or *Ordo Rachaelis*[5]. Perhaps *officium* may be taken to denote the thing itself, the special service or section of a service ; *ordo* rather the book, the written directions for carrying out the *officium*. Or they have

[1] Creizenach, i. 157, 162: Julleville, *Les Myst.* i. 107, 187; G. Smith, 251; Pollard, xix; Ward, i. 41.

[2] Cf. ch. xxv.

[3] Cf. p. 54 (Rouen, *Prophetae*, fourteenth century).

[4] Cf. pp. 37, 41, 45 ; Lange, 130, 155; 'officium sepulchri,' 'officium peregrinorum,' 'officium pastorum,' 'officium regum trium,' 'stellae officium' (Rouen, eleventh century–fifteenth century) ; 'resurrectionis domini aguntur officia' (Prague, fourteenth century). At Melk in 1517, 'acturus officium angeli' (Lange, 110), 'officium' has rather the sense of 'part.'

[5] Cf. pp. 37, 48, 49, 53, 71, 77; Lange, 48, 93, 95, 146; 'Ordo visitationis sepulchri'(Strassburg, 1513), 'Ordo visitandi sepulchrum' (Bamberg, 1597), 'Ordo ad visitandum sepulchrum' (Prague, twelfth century, Haarlem, thirteenth century), 'Ordo sepulchri' (Würzburg, thirteenth century), 'Ordo ad suscipiendum peregrinum' (Beauvais), 'Ordo stellae' (Laon, thirteenth century), 'Ordo [stellae]' (Bilsen, eleventh century), 'Ordo Rachaelis' (Freising, eleventh century), 'Ordo Prophetarum' (Laon, thirteenth century), 'Ordo creacionis, etc.' (Regensburg, 1194), 'Ordo, sive registrum de Passione domini' (Frankfort, fourteenth century).

a title derived from their subject, such as *Visitatio Sepulchri*[1], or *Suscitatio Lazari*[2]. Or they are introduced in terms which cannot be said to have a technical signification at all, *ad faciendam similitudinem*[3], *ad suscipiendum*[4], *ad repraesentandum*[5]. *Similitudo* I do not find outside Fleury, nor the corresponding *exemplum* outside the Benedictbeuern manuscript[6]. From *ad repraesentandum*, however, a technical term does arise, and *repraesentatio* must be considered, more than any other word, as the mediaeval Latin equivalent of 'dramatic performance[7].' This the Italian vernacular preserves as *rappresentazione*. A synonym for *repraesentatio*, which naturally came into use when the intention of recreation began to substitute itself for devotion, is *ludus*, with its vernacular renderings, all in common use, of *jeu*, *Spiel*, 'play.' But *ludus*, as already pointed out[8], is a generic term for 'amusement,' and the special sense of 'dramatic play' is only a secondary one[9]. 'Clerks' play' as a variant for miracle-play is occasionally found[10]. Yet another synonym which makes its appearance in the twelfth century, is *miraculum*; and this, originally a mere convenient shorthand for *repraesentatio miraculi*, came, especially in England, to stand for 'religious play' in general[11]. *Mystère*, or 'mystery,' on the other hand, is not

[1] See last note.

[2] Cf. p. 58.

[3] Cf. pp. 36,37,47; Lange,160 'ad faciendam similitudinem domini sepulchri,' 'ad faciendam similitudinem domini apparitionis' (Fleury, thirteenth century), 'versus ad stellam faciendam' (Nevers, †1060), 'fiunt peregrini' (Saintes, thirteenth century).

[4] Cf. p. 103, n. 5 above.

[5] Cf. pp. 58, 60; Lange, 157; 'ad repraesentandum quomodo sanctus Nicolaus' (Fleury, thirteenth century), 'historia de Daniel repraesentanda' (Hilarius, twelfth century), 'si Mariae debeant repraesentari' (Coutances, fifteenth century).

[6] Cf. pp. 37, 39.

[7] Cf. pp. 45, 107; Lange, 136; 'in resurrectione domini repraesentatio' (Cividale, fourteenth century), 'repraesentatio trium Regum' (Rouen, 1507, 1521), 'repraesentacio pastorum . . . resurreccionis . . . peregrinorum' (Lichfield, †1190).

[8] Cf. vol. i. p. 393.

[9] Cf. pp. 63, 73, 'ludus super iconia Sancti Nicolai' (Hilarius, twelfth century); cf. the Antichrist and Benedictbeuern Nativity, and note 11 below.

[10] Cf. pp. 140, 202.

[11] Cf. vol. i. p. 91; vol. ii. pp. 60, 380; 'miraculum de Sancto Nicolao' (Fleury, thirteenth century), 'repraesentationes miraculorum' (Fitz-Stephen, †1180), 'miraculum in nocte Paschae' (Lichfield, †1190; cf. note 7 above), 'ludum . . . quem Miracula vulgariter appellamus' (Matthew Paris, thirteenth century), 'ludos quos vocant miracula' (Grosseteste, 1244). The vernacular 'miracles,' 'myraclis,' is found in the *Handlyng Synne*, and the *Tretise of miraclis pleyinge*.

English at all, in a dramatic sense [1], and in France first appears as *misterie* in the charter given by Charles VI in 1402 to the Parisian *confrérie de la Passion* [2]. This term also acquires a very general signification by the end of the fifteenth century. Its radical meaning is still matter of dispute. Probably it is derived from *ministerium*, should be spelt *mistère*, and is spelt *mystère* by a natural confusion with the derivative of μυστήριον. Even then the question remains, what sort of *ministerium?* M. Petit de Julleville would explain it as a 'religious function,' and thus equate it precisely with *officium* [3]. Only it does not appear in connexion with the liturgical plays [4], and perhaps it is more plausible to regard it as denoting the 'function' of the guild of actors, just as its doublet *menestrie*, the English 'minstrelsy,' denotes the 'function' of the minstrels [5], or its doublet *métier*, which in English becomes in fact 'mystery,' denotes the 'function' of the craft guilds. Perhaps the theory of M. de Julleville finds a little support from the term *actio*, which appears, besides its meaning in connexion with the Mass [6], to be once at least used for a play [7]. At any rate *actus* is so used as a Latin equivalent of the Spanish *auto* [8].

---

[1] Pollard, xix ; Ward, i. 41. The first English use of the term 'mystery' is in the preface to Dodsley's *Select Collection of Old Plays* (1744). The distinction between 'mysteries' which 'deal with Gospel events only' and 'miracles,' which 'are more especially concerned with incidents derived from the legends of the Saints of the Church' is a not very happy invention of the literary historians.

[2] Julleville, *Les Myst.* i. 417 'Licence de faire et jouer quelque Misterre que ce soit, soit de la dicte Passion, et Résurreccion, ou autre quelconque tant de saincts comme des sainctes.'

[3] Julleville, *Les Myst.* i. 189.

[4] Except after its dramatic sense was already well established ; cf. pp. 42, 65, 'mysterium in die Ascensionis' (Lille, 1416), 'misterium Pastorum' (Rouen, 1457).

[5] Cf. Appendix B.

[6] Walafridus Strabo, *de rebus eccles.*, c. 22, in the ninth century, gives the name 'actio' to the 'canon' or unchangeable portion of the Mass (Maskell, *Ancient Liturgy of the Church of England*, 112).

[7] Cf.*Representations*,s.v. Shipton.

[8] Cf. supra, p. 102, note 1.

CHAPTER XXI

GUILD PLAYS AND PARISH PLAYS

[*Bibliographical Note.* — The English miracle play has been often, fully, and admirably studied from the point of view of dramatic literature ; perhaps less so from that of stage history. The best accounts are those of B. Ten Brink, *History of English Literature*, bk. v, chs. 2-6 (trans. W. C. Robinson, vol. ii, 1893); A. W. Ward, *History of English Dramatic Literature* (2nd ed., 1899), vol. i, ch. 1; W. Creizenach, *Geschichte des neueren Dramas*, vol. i (1893) ; and the introduction to A. W. Pollard, *English Miracle Plays, Moralities and Interludes* (3rd ed., 1898). These supersede J. P. Collier, *History of English Dramatic Poetry* (2nd ed., 1879), vol. ii, and J. L. Klein, *Geschichte des englischen Dramas* (1876), vol. i. Other useful books are J. A. Symonds, *Shakspere's Predecessors in the English Drama* (1884), ch. 3 ; K. L. Bates, *The English Religious Drama* (1893), and J. J. Jusserand, *Le Théâtre en Angleterre* (1881), ch. 2. The substance of this last is incorporated in the same writer's *Literary History of the English People*, vol. i (1895), bk. iii, ch. 6. W. J. Courthope, *History of English Poetry*, vol. i (1895), ch. 10, should also be consulted, as well as the valuable detailed investigations of A. Hohlfeld, *Die altenglischen Kollektivmisterien*, in *Anglia*, vol. xi (1889), and C. Davidson, *Studies in the English Mystery Plays* (1892). I do not think that S. W. Clarke, *The Miracle Play in England* (n.d.), and C. Hastings, *Le Théâtre français et anglais* (1900, trans. 1901), add very much. A. Ebert, *Die englischen Mysterien*, in *Jahrbuch für romanische und englische Literatur*, vol. i (1859), is an early manifestation of German interest in the subject, and the still earlier native learning may be found in T. Warton, *History of English Poetry* (ed. W. C. Hazlitt, 1871), §§ 6, 33 ; E. Malone, *Historical Account of the English Stage*, in *Variorum Shakespeare* (1821), vol. iii; W. Hone, *Ancient Mysteries Described* (1823). The antiquarianism of T. Sharp, *Dissertation on the Pageants or Dramatic Mysteries Anciently Performed at Coventry* (1825), is still a mine of material on the *Realien* of the stage.—The four great cycles have been edited as follows, in most cases with important introductions : the *Chester Plays* by T. Wright (*Shakespeare Society*, 1843-7) and by H. Deimling (*E.E.T.S.*, part only issued in 1893) ; the *York Plays* by L. T. Smith (1885) ; the *Towneley* or *Wakefield Plays* by an uncertain editor (*Surtees Society*, 1836), and by G. England and A. W. Pollard (*E.E.T.S.* 1897) ; the *Ludus Coventriae*, by J. O. Halliwell [-Phillipps] (*Shakespeare Society*, 1841). A miscellaneous collection of late plays from one of the *Bodleian Digby MSS.* has been printed by T. Sharp (*Abbotsford Club*, 1835), and F. J. Furnivall (*New Shakespeare Society*, 1882, *E.E.T.S.* 1896). The Cornish cycle is in E. Norris, *The Ancient Cornish Drama* (1859). Good selections of typical plays are in A. W. Pollard's book, and J. M. Manly, *Specimens of the Pre-Shakespearean Drama* (1897), vol. i. Older books of the same kind are J. P. Collier, *Five Miracle Plays, or Scriptural Dramas* (1836), and W. Marriott, *A Collection of English Miracle Plays or Mysteries*

(Basle, 1838). The bibliographies given by Miss Bates and by F. H. Stoddard, *References for Students of Miracle Plays and Mysteries* (1887), may be supplemented from my *Appendices* of *Representations* and *Texts*, which I have tried to make as complete as possible.]

THERE is no reason to doubt that England had its full share in the earlier development of the religious drama. Texts of the liturgical period are, indeed, rare. The tenth-century version of the *Quem quaeritis* from Winchester and the fourteenth-century version from Dublin stand, at least for the present, alone. But the wholesale destruction of liturgical books at the Reformation is sufficient to account for such a sparseness, and a few stray notices gathered from the wreckage of time bear sufficient witness to the presence in this country of several amongst the more widespread types of liturgical play. The Lichfield statutes (1188 98) pro vide for *repraesentationes* of the *Pastores*, the *Resurrectio*, the *Peregrini*; those of York (†1255) for the *Pastores* and the *Tres Reges*; a Salisbury inventory of 1222 includes 'crowns' or more probably ' stars' (*coronae*) *ad repraesentationes faciendas*; while Lincoln account books of the early fifteenth century appear to add the *Annuntiatio* and the *Prophetae*, a *visus* called *Rubum quem viderat* in 1420 perhaps forming a Moses scene in the latter. So late as 1518 the *Quem quaeritis* was performed in Magdalen College chapel, and plays of the Nativity and the Resurrection by the clerks of the chapel are contemplated at about the same date in the household regulations of the Earl of Northumberland at Leconfield. Nor were dramatic versions of the legends of saints unknown. I do not trace a St. Nicholas cycle in England, although Hilarius, in whose repertory a St. Nicholas play is included, is thought to have been an Englishman by birth. But the memory of a play of St. Catherine prepared by Geoffrey the Norman at Dunstable early in the twelfth century was preserved, owing to the accident which led to Geoffrey ultimately becoming abbot of St. Albans; and towards the close of the same century William Fitzstephen records the representations of the miracles of holy confessors and the passions of martyrs which took the place of minstrelsy in London. For the most part such early plays are found in close connexion with the cathedrals and great monasteries. But a document of about 1220, the interpretation of which must, however, be considered doubtful, would seem to suggest that plays (*actiones*) were habitually given at no less than five chapelries within the single parish of Shipton in Oxfordshire, and that the profits thereof formed an appreciable part of the income derived from that living by the prebendaries of Salisbury cathedral.

Examples of the transitional forms by which the liturgical drama grew into the popular religious drama of the great cycles can also be found in England. At Beverley a Resurrection play is described as taking place in the graveyard of the minster about 1220. The intrusion of the vernacular is represented by the curious bilingual text of a single actor's parts in the *Pastores*, *Quem quaeritis* and *Peregrini*, printed by Professor Skeat from a manuscript found at Shrewsbury. These are probably still liturgical in character, and it is to be observed that their subjects are precisely those of the three plays known to have been used in the neighbouring cathedral of Lichfield. It must remain a moot point whether the religious drama passed directly, in this country, from Latin to English, or whether there was a period during which performances were given in Norman-French. Scholars are inclined to find an Anglo-Norman dialect in that very important monument of the transition, the *Repraesentatio Adae*, as well as in an early example of the expanded Easter play. But even if the authors of these were, like Hilarius, of English birth, it hardly follows that their productions were acted in England. Nor do the probable borrowings of the Chester and other cycles from French texts much affect the question[1]. That the disfavour with which the austerer section of the clergy looked upon the vernacular religious plays had its spokesmen in England, was sufficiently illustrated in the last chapter.

The English miracle-play reaches its full development with the formation of the great processional cycles almost immediately after the establishment of the Corpus Christi festival in 1311. The local tradition of Chester, stripped of a certain

[1] Cf. p. 146.

confusion between the names of two distinct mayors of that city which has clung about it, is found to fix the foundation of the Chester plays in 1328.   The date has the authority of an official municipal document, forms part of a quite consistent story, several points in which can be independently corroborated, and is on *a priori* grounds extremely plausible. Unfortunately, owing to the comparative scarcity of archives during this period, the first fifty years of the history of municipal drama are practically a blank.   A mention, about 1350, of a *ludus filiorum Israelis*, in connexion with a guild of Corpus Christi at Cambridge, spans a wide gulf.   There is no actual record of plays at Chester itself until 1462. Those of Beverley are first mentioned in 1377, those of York in 1378, and those of Coventry in 1392.   But it must be added that the Beverley plays were an *antiqua consuetudo* in 1390, and that those of York were to take place at stations *antiquitus assignatis* in 1394.   It is in 1378 that the earliest notice of plays in London, since the days of William Fitzstephen, comes to light.   The fuller records which are from this time onward available reveal, during the next hundred and fifty years, a vigorous and widespread dramatic activity throughout the length and breadth of the land. It manifests itself at such extreme points as the Cinque Ports in the east, Cornwall in the west, and Newcastle in the north. It penetrates to Aberdeen and to Dublin.   And though naturally it finds its fullest scope in the annually repeated performances of several amongst the greater cities, yet it is curious to observe in what insignificant villages it was from time to time found possible to organize plays.   Performers from thirteen neighbouring places, many of them quite small, made their way to New Romney between 1399 and 1508; whilst the churchwardens of Chelmsford, in the twelve years after their own play in 1562, reaped a profit by hiring out their stock of garments to the men of some seventeen aspiring parishes.   On the other hand, there were several important towns in which, so far as we can judge from documents, such as craft ordinances, which would almost certainly have referred to the plays of the crafts, if these had existed, the normal type of municipal drama failed to establish itself.   London is one, although here the want was supplied in another way; others are Northampton, Nottingham, Bristol, Oxford, and Reading. And occasionally plays, which had once been annual, were allowed to fall into desuetude and decay. The corporation of Canterbury, for instance, called upon the crafts about 1500 to revive a Corpus Christi play which for some time had been 'left and laid apart.' Certainly, by the sixteenth century, if there was still pride and interest taken in many of the municipal plays, signs were not wanting that they were an institution which had almost outlived its day. A reason for this need hardly be sought beyond the *Zeitgeist*. No doubt the plays were a financial burden upon the poorer crafts and the poorer members of crafts. There was much grumbling at Beverley in 1411 because certain well-to-do persons (*generosi*), who did not practise any trade or handicraft, had hitherto escaped the payment of contributions to the civic function; and municipal authorities were constantly called upon to adjust and readjust the responsibility for this and that pageant with the fluctuations of prosperity amongst the various occupations. But on the other hand, the plays were the cause of much and profitable resort to those fortunate towns which possessed them. The mercers' guild at Shrewsbury found it necessary to impose a special fine upon those of its members whose business avocations required them 'to ride or goe to Coventrie Faire' at Corpus Christi tide, and so to miss the procession of guilds at home [1]. And although the mayor of Coventry wrote to Thomas Cromwell, in 1539, that the poor commoners were put to such expense with their plays and pageants that they fared the worse all the year after, yet against this may be set the statement made to Dugdale by 'some old people who had in their younger days been eye-witnesses of these pageants' that 'the confluence of people from farr and neare to see that shew was extraordinary great, and yeilded noe small advantage to this cittye.' Moreover the levy upon individuals was a trifling one; the whole of the company of smiths at Coventry only paid 3s. 4d. amongst them for 'pagent pencys' in 1552. A *leitourgia* is always an unpopular institution, and these

---

[1] *Trans. of Shropshire Antiq. Soc.* viii. 273.

complaints resemble nothing so much as the groans of an opulent London tradesman in the twentieth century over an extra penny on the education rate.   In the smaller places it is clear that plays, far from being a source of expense, were a recognized method of raising funds for public purposes. Even in 1220 the *emolumentum actionum* from the chapelries of Shipton went to swell the purses of the Salisbury prebendaries. In 1505 the churchwardens of Kingston-on-Thames made £4 towards their new steeple by getting up a play for which they secured the patronage of royalty. At Braintree, in Essex, funds were similarly raised by Nicholas Udall and others, between 1523 and 1534, for the repair of the church.   I have little doubt that when the mayor of Coventry said economy he meant Protestantism, just as when, under Elizabeth, the corporation of London wished to make a Puritanic attack upon the theatres, they were always smitten with a terrible dread of the infection of the plague [1].

Certainly the spirit of Protestantism, although it came to be willing to use the religious drama for its own purposes [2], was inclined to see both profanity and superstition in the ordinary miracle-plays [3].   Here, as elsewhere, it inherited the hostile tradition which such reforming clerics as Gerhoh of Reichersberg in the twelfth century and Robert Grosseteste in the thirteenth had handed down to Wyclif and his Lollards. At Bungay in 1514 certain ill-disposed persons 'brake and threw down five pageants' usually borne about the town on Corpus Christi day.   One may fairly suspect, even at this early date, a Lollardist intention in the outrage, and perhaps also in the interposition of the authority of the warden of the Cinque Ports to suppress the play of New Romney in 1518. With the progress of the new ideas the big cycles began to be irregularly performed or to undergo textual modification. The plays of York, for example, were shorn in 1548 of the pageants representing the Death, Assumption, and Coronation

---

[1] *Analytical Index to Remembrancia of City of London*, 330 sqq.; 350 sqq.

[2] Cf. ch. xxv.

[3] For the general Puritan attitude to the stage, see S. Gosson, *Schoole of Abuse*, 1579 (ed. Arber); W. Prynne, *Histriomastix* (1633), with the authorities there quoted; and the tracts in W. C. Hazlitt, *The English Drama and Stage*.

of the Virgin. On the other hand, religious plays sometimes became a rallying-point for those who favoured the old order of things. There is extant a letter from Henry VIII to the justices of York, in which he refers to a riot promoted by certain papists at a play of St. Thomas the Apostle, and warns them not to suffer upon such occasions any language likely to tend to a breach of the peace. The brief Marian reaction led to the resumption of the plays in more than one town which had dropped them. The Lincoln corporation ordered 'St. Anne's Gild with Corpus Cristi play' to be brought forward again in 1554 and 1555. In London Henry Machyn records during 1557 a Passion play at the Grey Friars, and another in the church of St. Olave's, Silver Street, on the festival of the patron. The New Romney play was elaborately revived, after forty-two years' interval, in 1560. But the process of decay soon set in again. Even where the plays survived, they were Protestantized, and as Corpus Christi day was no longer observed, the performances had to be transferred to some other date. At York the text of the Corpus Christi play was 'perused and otherwise amended' in 1568. In 1569 it was acted upon Whit-Tuesday. Then it lay by until 1579, when the book was referred to the archbishop and dean for further revision, and apparently impounded by them. The Creed play was suppressed, by advice of the dean, in 1568, as unsuitable to 'this happie time of the gospell.' The *Paternoster* play was revised and played in 1572. Then this text also fell into the hands of the archbishop, and the corporation seem to have been unable to recover it. So ended the religious drama in York. In Chester the municipal authorities stood out gallantly for their plays. John Hankey and Sir John Savage, mayors in 1572 and 1575 respectively, were called before the privy council for sanctioning performances in spite of inhibitions from the archbishop of York and other persons of authority. They had revised the text, and had a new and Protestant version of the preliminary 'banns' prepared. Copies of the text appear to have been got ready for yet another perform-ance in 1600, but the local annalists record that Henry Hardware, then mayor, 'would not suffer any Playes.' In

one or two cities, new plays, dealing with apocryphal or other
merely semi-religious themes, were substituted for the old
ones.. Thus at Lincoln a 'standing play' of the story of
Tobit was given in 1564 and 1567 ; and in Coventry, where
the old cycle had been 'laid down' in 1580, an Oxford scholar
was hired in 1584 to write a semi-religious semi-historical
drama of the Destruction of Jerusalem. In 1591, the Conquest
of the Danes and the History of King Edward the Confessor
were proposed as alternatives for this. By the end of the
sixteenth century all the cycles of which most is known had
come to an end. The smaller places—Chelmsford in 1574,
Braintree in 1579, Bungay in 1591—had sold off their stock
of playing-garments. For such dramatic entertainment as the
provinces were still to get, they must look to travelling companies taking their summer vacation from the metropolis.
Miracle-plays during the seventeenth century were a mere
survival. They lingered in distant Cornwall and at Kendal in
the hill country of the north ; and had been replaced by morals,
themselves almost equally obsolete, at Manningtree. The
last religious play recorded in England is a quite exceptional
one, given at the end of James I's reign before Gondomar,
the Spanish ambassador, and an audience which numbered
thousands at Ely Place in Holborn.

In giving some account of the distribution of the various
types of religious play throughout England during the
fifteenth and sixteenth centuries, I am dispensed from any
obligation to be exhaustive by the fact that the greater
municipal dramas at least have already been the subject of
more than one fairly adequate discussion. All I shall attempt
will be a brief general summary of the main points which
emerge from the more or less detailed local notices collected
in a lengthy appendix.

The characteristic English type of play was the long cycle
given annually under the superintendence of the corporation
or governing body of an important city and divided into
a number of distinct scenes or 'pageants,' each of which was
the special charge of one or more of the local 'crafts,' 'arts,'
or 'occupations.' Such cycles, organized upon very similar
lines, can be studied in the records available from Chester,

York, Beverley, Coventry, Newcastle, Lincoln, and Norwich ;
and the same general model is known or conjectured—
sometimes, it is true, on the slightest indication—to have
been followed in the plays of Lancaster, Preston, Kendal,
Wakefield, Leicester, Worcester, Louth, Bungay, Canterbury,
Dublin, and Aberdeen. As in all matters of municipal
custom, the relative functions of the corporations and the
crafts were nicely adjusted. The direction and control of
the plays as a whole were in the hands of the corporations.
They decided annually whether the performance should be
given, or whether, for war, pestilence, or other reason, it
should be withheld. They sent round their officers to read
the proclamation or 'banns' of the play. They kept an
official version of the text, at Chester an 'original,' at York
a 'register' copied from the 'originals' belonging to the crafts.
Agreements and disputes as to the liability of this or that
craft to maintain or contribute to a particular pageant were
entered or determined before them. They maintained order
at the time of the play and inflicted fines on the turbulent, or
upon crafts neglectful or unskilful in carrying out their
responsibilities. In particular they required the provision
of properly qualified actors. Thus Robert Greene and others
were admonished before the leet of Coventry in 1440, that
they should play *bene et sufficienter* so as not to cause a
hindrance in any *iocus*. Similarly, Henry Cowper, 'webster,'
was fined by the wardens of Beverley in 1452, *quod nesciebat
ludum suum*. An order at York, in 1476, directed the choice
of a body of 'connyng, discrete, and able players' to test the
quality of all those selected as actors. All 'insufficiant
personnes, either in connyng, voice or personne' they were
to 'discharge, ammove, and avoide '; and no one was to perform
more than twice in the course of the day. Sometimes the
actual oversight of the plays was delegated to specially
appointed officers. At Beverley the wardens themselves
'governed' the Corpus Christi plays, but the Paternoster play
was in the hands of 'aldermen of the pageants.' At Aberdeen
the Haliblude play was undertaken in 1440 by the local lord
of misrule, known as the Abbot of Bon Accord ; for the
Candlemas play 'bailyes' represented the corporation. At

Lincoln the 'graceman' of the guild of St. Anne was responsible, and had the aid of the mayor. At Leicester a number
of 'overseers' with two 'bedalls' were chosen to have the
'gydyng and rule' of the play.

The corporations do not appear to have themselves incurred
much expenditure over the performances. They provided
sitting-room and refreshments for their own members, and for
distinguished guests. Richard II was elaborately entertained
with a special *pagina* when he visited York on Corpus Christi
day, 1397. Sixty years later a collation, including 'ij cofyns
of counfetys and a pot of grene gynger,' was made ready for
Queen Margaret on her visit to Coventry. At York and
Beverley, but not at Coventry, the corporations paid the
minstrels, and occasionally made a special contribution to
the funds of a particularly poor pageant. At York the
corporation could well afford to do this, for they claimed
the right to fix certain 'stations' at which, as well as at two
or three traditional ones, the plays should be given, and
they made a considerable annual profit out of payments by
well-to-do citizens who aspired to have one of these at their
doors. The stations were marked by banners broidered with
the arms of the city. At Leicester the 'playyng germands'
seem to have belonged to the corporation. At Beverley in
1391 they owned all the 'necessaries,' pageant garments and
properties, of the play of Paradise, and lent the same upon
security to the craft charged therewith. The pageants may
also have been originally corporation property in York, for
it was stipulated in 1422 that one of them, like the banners at
the stations, should bear the arms of the city, to the exclusion
of those of the craft.

As a rule, the cost of the plays fell almost wholly upon the
crafts. The ordinances of the craft-guilds provide for their
maintenance as a *leitourgia* or fraternal duty, in the same
way as they often provide for a 'serge' or light to be burnt
in some chapel or carried in the Corpus Christi procession,
or, at Beverley, for the *castellum* in which the craft sat to do
honour to the procession of St. John of Beverley in Rogation
week. At Coventry, where the burden upon the crafts was
perhaps heaviest, they were responsible for the provision,

repairing, ornamenting, cleaning, and strewing with rushes of the pageant, for the 'ferme' or rent of the pageant house, for the payment of actors, minstrels, and prompter, for the revision of play-book and songs and the copying of parts, for the 'drawing' or 'horsing' of the pageant on the day of the performance, for costumes and properties, and above all for copious refreshments before and after the play, at the stations, and during the preliminary rehearsals. The total cost of the smiths' pageant in 1490 was £3 7s. 5½d. In 1453 they had contracted with one Thomas Colclow to have 'the rewle of the pajaunt' for twelve years at an annual payment of £2 6s. 8d., and other examples of 'play lettine' can be traced at Newcastle and elsewhere. But it was more usual for the crafts to retain the management of the pageants in their own hands; at York each guild appointed its 'pageant-masters' for this purpose. The expense to the craft primarily in charge of a pageant was sometimes lightened by fixed contributions from one or more minor bodies affiliated to it for the purpose. Part of it was probably met from the general funds of the craft; the rest was raised by various expedients. A levy, known as 'pagent pencys' at Coventry and as 'pajaunt silver' at York, was made upon every member. The amount varied with the numbers of the craft and the status of the crafts-man. At York it ranged from 1d. to 8d. At Beverley the journeymen paid 8d. to light, play, and castle, and 6d. only in years when there was no play. At Coventry the ordinary members of more than one craft paid 1s.; others apparently less. To the proceeds of the levy might be added fines for the breach of craft ordinances, payments on the taking out of freedom by strangers and the setting up of shop or indenturing of apprentices by freemen. At York, the mercers are found granting free admission to a candidate for their fraternity on condition of his entering into a favourable contract for the supply of a new pageant. At Coventry, in 1517, one William Pisford left a scarlet and a crimson gown to the tanners for their plays, together with 3s. 4d. to every craft charged with the maintenance of a pageant. Besides the levy, certain personal services were binding upon the craftsmen. They had to attend upon the play, to do it honour; the Coventry cappers expected their journeymen to do the 'horsing' of the pageant.

In some cities, the crafts received help from outside. At Coventry, in 1501, the tilers' pageant got a contribution of 5s. from the neighbouring tilers of Stoke. At Chester, vestments were borrowed from the clergy; at Lincoln from the priory and the local gentry. A 'gathering' was also made in the surrounding districts. The only trace of any charge made to the spectators, other than the fees for 'stations' at York, is at Leicester, where, in 1477, the players paid over to the 'pachents' certain sums they had received for playing.

The majority of the crafts in a big city were, of course, already formed into guilds for ordinary trade purposes, and in their case the necessary organization for the plays was to hand. But no citizen could wholly escape his responsibility in so important a civic matter. At Coventry it was ordered in 1494 that every person exercising any craft must become contributory to some pageant or other. At York the innholders, who do not appear to have been a regular guild, were organized in 1483 for the purposes of a pageant on the basis of a yearly contribution of 4d. from each man. The demand at Beverley in 1411 for the appropriation of a play to the *generosi* has already been alluded to. In a Beverley list of 1520 the 'Gentylmen' are put down for the 'Castle of Emaut.' It may be suspected that some of the other crafts named in the same list, such as the 'Husbandmen' and the 'Labourers,' were not regular guilds; not to speak of the 'Prestes,' who played the 'Coronacion of Our Lady.' This participation of religious bodies in the craft plays can be paralleled from other towns. At York the hospital of St. Leonard took the Purification in 1415; at Lincoln the cathedral clergy, like the priests at Beverley, were responsible for the Coronation or Assumption of the Virgin, a play which at Chester was given by the 'worshipfull wyves of this town,' and at York by the innholders. Both at York and Chester this scene was dropped at the Reformation. Possibly its somewhat exceptional position may be accounted for by its having been a comparatively late addition in all four cycles. Some endeavour after dramatic appropriateness is visible in the apportioning of the other plays amongst the crafts. Thus Noah is given to the shipwrights (York, Newcastle), the watermen (Beverley, Chester), the fishers and mariners (York); the *Magi* to the goldsmiths (Beverley, Newcastle, York); the Disputation in the Temple to the scriveners (Beverley), the Last Supper to the bakers (Beverley, Chester, York); the Harrowing of Hell to the cooks (Beverley, Chester).

A somewhat anomalous position is occupied amongst towns in which the plays were in the hands of the crafts by Lincoln. Here the task of supervision was shared with the corporation by a special guild, religious and social rather than industrial in character[1], of St. Anne. Perhaps this guild had at one time been solely responsible for the plays, and there had been a crisis such as took place at Norwich in 1527. Before that date the charge of the plays had been borne, fittingly enough, by the guild of St. Luke, composed of painters and metal-workers. But in 1527 this guild was 'almost fully decayed,' and upon the representation of its members the corporation agreed that in future the pageants should be distributed amongst the various crafts as was customary elsewhere. The Lincoln plays were on St. Anne's day, but one does not find a position comparable to that of the St. Anne's guild held by Corpus Christi guilds in other towns. As a rule such guilds concerned themselves with the Corpus Christi procession, but not with the plays. At Ipswich, indeed, the Corpus Christi guild had the whole conduct of the plays, and the craft-guilds as such were not called upon; but this Ipswich guild arose out of a reorganization of the old merchant-guild, included all the burgesses, and was practically identical with the corporation. Other towns, in which the corporation managed the plays itself, without the intervention of the craft-guilds, are Shrewsbury, New Romney, and Lydd.

On the other hand, where neither the corporation nor the crafts undertook plays, it was no uncommon thing for a guild of the religious or social type to step into the breach. A series of London plays recorded in 1384, 1391, 1409, and 1411 may all be not unreasonably ascribed to a guild of

---

[1] On such guilds cf. Cutts, *Parish Priests*, 476; Rock, ii. 395; F. A. Gasquet, *The Eve of the Reforma-tion*, 351.

St. Nicholas, composed of the 'parish clerks' attached to the
many churches of the city.   At a later date the performances
of this guild seem to have become annual and they are traceable, with no very great certainty, to the beginning of the
sixteenth century.   They were cyclical in character, but not
processional, and took place hard by the well known indifferently as Skinners' well or Clerkenwell, amongst the orchards
to the north of London.   Chaucer says of his 'parish clerk,'
the 'joly Absolon,' that

> 'Somtyme, to shewe his lightnesse and maistrye,
> He pleyeth Heródës, on a scaffold hye[1].'

These London plays may have had some original connexion with the great fair of the neighbouring priory of
St. Bartholomew upon August 24; but they are recorded at
various dates during the summer, and extended over four,
five, or even seven days.   Whether the guild of St. Nicholas
bore any relation to the clerks of St. Paul's, who petitioned
Richard II in 1378 against the rivalry of certain 'unexpert
people' in the production of an Old Testament play, must be
matter for conjecture.   The performance contemplated at
St. Paul's was to be at Christmas.   The Cambridge guild
of Corpus Christi was responsible for a *ludus Filiorum Israelis*
about 1350, and this is more likely to have formed part
of a cycle than to have stood alone.   An unverified extract
of Warton's from a Michael-House *computus* suggests that
some of the Cambridge colleges may have assisted in
dramatic undertakings.   At Abingdon the hospital of Christ
held their feast on Holy Cross day (May 3), 1445, 'with
pageantes and playes, and May games.'   At Sleaford, in 1480,
a play of the Ascension was performed by the guild of the
Holy Trinity.   At Wymondham a guild seems to have
existed in the sixteenth century for the express purpose of
holding a 'watch and play' at Midsummer.   The proceedings
were directed by officers designated 'husbands.'   The one
example of an isolated play under the management of a craft-
guild is at Hull.   Here an annual play of Noah, with a ship
or ark which went in procession, was in the hands of the

[1] *C. Tales*, 3383 (*Miller's Tale*).

Trinity House, a guild of master mariners and pilots. The records extend from 1421 to 1529. There is no sign of a dramatic cycle at Hull. The Noah play was given on Plough Monday, and it is possible that one may trace here a dramatized version of just such a ship procession as may be found elsewhere upon the coasts in spring[1]. After the performance the 'ship' was hung up in the church. The text of the play was perhaps borrowed from that of the watermen of the neighbouring city of Beverley.

Where there were craft-plays, social and religious guilds sometimes gave supplementary performances. The 'schaft' or parochial guild of St. Dunstan's, Canterbury, owned a play of Abraham and Isaac in 1491. This may have been merely a contribution towards the craft-cycle on Corpus Christi day. On the other hand, the play of St. George, contemplated by the guild of that saint at New Romney in 1490, was probably an independent undertaking. The town play here was a Passion play. At York there were two rivals to the Corpus Christi plays. One was the *Paternoster* play, for the production of which a guild of the Lord's Prayer was in existence at least as early as 1378. By 1488 this guild was absorbed into the Holy Trinity guild of the mercers, and in the year named the play was given, apparently at the charges of the mercers, instead of the ordinary cycle. All the crafts contributed to similar performances in 1558 and 1572. But by this time the supervision, under the corporation, of the play had passed to one of the few religious guilds in York which had escaped suppression, that of St. Anthony. The other extraordinary York play was a Creed play, bequeathed to the guild of Corpus Christi in 1446. This was stationary, and was acted decennially about Lammas-tide (August 1) at the common hall. In 1483, it was 'apon the cost of the most onest men of every parish,' who were, it may be supposed, members of the guild. In 1535 the crafts paid for it instead of their usual cycle. Upon the suppression of the guild, the play-book passed into the custody of the hospital of St. Thomas.

In the same way there are instances in which the clergy,

[1] Cf. vol. i. p. 121.

who elsewhere lent help to the craft-plays, gave independent exhibitions of their own. At Chester, before the Reformation, they eked out the Whitsun cycle by a supplementary performance on Corpus Christi day. The priors of St. John of Jerusalem, Holy Trinity, and All Saints contributed their share to the somewhat incongruous blend of religious and secular entertainments provided by the traders of Dublin for the earl of Kildare in 1528. The so-called *Ludus Coventriae* has often been supposed to be the play-book of a cycle acted by the Grey Friars or Franciscans of Coventry. This theory hardly survives critical examination. But in 1557, during the Marian reaction, a Passion play was given at the Grey Friars in London, and the actors were possibly restored brethren. Miracle-plays must often have been performed in choir schools, especially upon their traditional feast-days of St. Nicholas, St. Catherine, and the Holy Innocents. But there are only two examples, besides that of St. Paul's in 1378, actually upon record. In 1430 the *pueri eleemosynae* of Maxstoke acted on Candlemas day in the hall of Lord Clinton's castle; and in 1486 those of St. Swithin's and Hyde abbeys combined to entertain Henry VII with the Harrowing of Hell as he sat at dinner in Winchester.

Many minor plays, both in towns and in country villages, were organized by the clergy and other officials of parish churches, and are mentioned in the account books of churchwardens. At London, Kingston, Oxford, Reading, Salisbury, Bath, Tewkesbury, Leicester, Bungay, and Yarmouth, such parochial plays can be traced, sometimes side by side with those provided by craft or other guilds. The parochial organization was the natural one for the smaller places, where the parish church had remained the centre of the popular life[1]. The *actiones* in the chapelries of Shipton in Oxfordshire during the thirteenth century may have been plays of this type. The municipal records of Lydd and New Romney mention visits of players to the towns between 1399 and 1508 from no less than fourteen neighbouring places in

[1] On the economics of a medi-aeval parish and the functions of the churchwardens cf. Hobhouse, *Churchwardens' Accounts*, xi (Somerset Record Soc.).

Kent and Sussex, many of which must have been then, as they are now, quite insignificant. They are Hythe, Wittersham, Herne, Ruckinge, Folkestone, Appledore, Chart, Rye, Wye, Brookland, Halden, Bethersden, Ham, and Stone. A few other village plays are to be traced in the fifteenth century. In the sixteenth century they are fairly numerous, especially in the eastern counties. In Essex they are found at Chelmsford, Braintree, Halstead, Heybridge, Malden, Saffron Walden, Billericay, Starford, Baddow (by 'children'), Little Baddow, Sabsford, Boreham, Lanchire, Witham, Brentwood, Nayland, Burnham, High Easter, Writtle, Woodham Walter, and Hanningfield; in Cambridgeshire at Bassingbourne; in Lincolnshire at Holbeach; in Norfolk at Harling, Lopham, Garboldisham, Shelfhanger, and Kenninghall; in Suffolk at Boxford, Lavenham, and Mildenhall; in Leicestershire at Foston; in Somersetshire at Morebath; and in Kent once more at Bethersden. The latest instance is a 'Kynge play' at Hascombe in Surrey in 1579.

Parochial plays, whether in town or country, appear to have been in most cases occasional, rather than annual. Sometimes, as at Kingston and Braintree, they became a means of raising money for the church, and even where this object is not apparent, the expenses were lightened in various ways at the cost of neighbouring villages. 'Banns' were sent round to announce the play; or the play itself was carried round on tour. Twenty-seven villages contributed to a play at Bassingbourne in 1511. The Chelmsford play of 1562 and 1563 cost about £50, of which a good proportion was received from the spectators. The play was given at Malden and Braintree as well as at Chelmsford, and for years afterwards the letting out of the stock of garments proved a source of revenue to the parish. This same practice of hiring garments can be traced at Oxford, Leicester, and elsewhere. The parochial plays were always, so far as can be seen, stationary. At Leicester, Braintree, Halstead, and Heybridge they were in the church. That of Harling was 'at the church gate,' that of Bassingbourne in a 'croft'; that of Chelmsford in a 'pightell.' At Reading performances in the market-place and in an open piece of ground called (then and now) the 'Forbury' are mentioned.

There remain a certain number of plays as to the organization of which nothing definite can be said.   Such are the minor plays, on the legends of saints, recorded by the annalists of London, Coventry, and Lincoln; those referred to in the corporation accounts of King's Lynn, as given by unspecified players between 1385 and 1462 ; and those which took place, as late as the seventeenth century, in 'rounds' or amphitheatres at St. Just, Perranzabulo, and elsewhere in Cornwall.

CHAPTER XXII

GUILD PLAYS AND PARISH PLAYS (*continued*)

THE last chapter occupied itself mainly with the diffusion of the vernacular religious plays in England, with their organization, and with their part in municipal and village life. That study must be completed by at least the outline of another, dealing with the content and nature of the performances themselves. Here again it is variety rather than uniformity which requires attention ; for the records and texts of the fifteenth and sixteenth centuries bear witness to the effective survival of all the diverse types of play, to which the evolution of the dramatic instinct gave birth in its progress from liturgical office to cosmic cycle.

The term of the evolution—the cosmic cycle itself—is represented by five complete texts, and one fragment sufficiently substantial to be ranked with these. There are the plays of the York and Chester crafts. The manuscript of the former dates from the middle of the fifteenth century ; those of the latter from the end of the sixteenth and beginning of the seventeenth : but in both cases it may be assumed that we possess the plays, with certain modifications, additions, and omissions, as they were given in the palmy days of their history. There are also, in a fifteenth-century manuscript, the so-called 'Towneley' plays, as to whose origin the most likely theory is that they are the craft-plays of Wakefield. There is the *Ludus Coventriae*, also of the fifteenth century, which has probably nothing to do with Coventry, but is either, as scholars generally hold, the text of a strolling company, or, as seems to me more probable, that of a stationary play at some town in the East Midlands not yet identified. If I am right, the *Ludus Coventriae* occupies a midway position between the three northern craft cycles, which are all processional plays, split up into a number of distinct pageants, and the fifth text, which is Cornish. This is probably of the fourteenth century, although extant in a fifteenth-century manuscript, and doubtless represents a stationary performance in one of the 'rounds' still to be seen about Cornwall. The fragment, also Cornish, is not a wholly independent play, but a sixteenth-century expansion of part of the earlier text.

A study of the table of incidents printed in an appendix will show the general scope of the cyclical plays[1]. My comments thereon must be few and brief. The four northerly cycles have a kernel of common matter, which corresponds very closely with just that dramatic stuff which was handled in the liturgical and the earliest vernacular dramas. It includes the Fall of Lucifer, the Creation, Adam and Eve, Cain and Abel; then the Annunciation and the group of scenes, from the *Pastores* to the Massacre of the Innocents, which went to make up the *Stella*; then the Passion in the narrower sense, centring in the *planctus Mariae* and extending from the Conspiracy of the Jews to the Descent from the Cross; then the Resurrection scenes, centring in the *Quem quaeritis* and ending with the *Peregrini* and Incredulity of Thomas; then the Ascension, the Pentecost, and finally the *Iudicium* or Doomsday. Almost equally invariable is something in the way of a *Prophetae*. But at York this is thrown into narrative instead of dramatic form; and at Chester the typical defile of prophets, each with his harangue, is deferred to almost the close of the cycle (Play xxiii), and in its usual place stand two independent episodes of Balaam and of Octavian and the Sibyl. Two other groups of scenes exhibit a larger measure of diversity between the four cycles. One is that drawn from the history of the Old Testament Fathers, out of which the Deluge and the Sacrifice of Isaac are the only incidents adopted by all four. The other is the series taken from the missionary life of Christ, where the only common scenes are the Raising of Lazarus and the Feast in the House of Simon the Leper, both of which can be traced back to the liturgical drama[2].

---

[1] Cf. Appendix T.   [2] Cf. pp. 58, 60.

The principal source of the plays belonging to this common kernel is, of course, the biblical narrative, which is followed, so far as it goes, with considerable fidelity, the most remarkable divergence being that of the *Ludus Coventriae*, which merges the Last Supper with the scene in the House of Simon. But certain embroideries upon scripture, which found their way into the religious drama at an early stage of its evolution, are preserved and further elaborated. Thus each of the four cycles has its Harrowing of Hell, which links the later scenes with the earlier by introducing, as well as the devils, such personages as Adam and Eve, Enoch and Elijah, John the Baptist and others[1]. Similarly the Suspicion of Joseph and the *obstetrices* at the Virgin Birth finds a place in all four[2], as does the Healing of Longinus, the blind knight, by the blood-drops from the cross[3]. Other apocryphal or legendary elements are confined to one or more of the cycles[4]. The Chester plays, for example, have a marked development of the eschatological scenes. Not only is the *Iudicium* itself extremely long and elaborate, but it is preceded by two distinct plays, one a section of the split-up *Prophetae* ending with the Fifteen Signs, the other an Antichrist, in which, as in the Tegernsee *Antichristus*[5], Enoch and Elijah appear as disputants. The most legendary of the northerly cycles is without doubt the *Ludus Coventriae*. It has the legend of Veronica, which is only hinted at in the corresponding York play. And it has so long a series of scenes drawn from the legends of the Virgin as to make it probable that, like the Lincoln plays and another East Midland cycle of which

[1] Cf. p. 73.
[2] Cf. p. 41.
[3] Cf. p. 75.
[4] I can only give the most general account of the legendary content of the plays. For full treatment of this in relation to its sources cf. the authorities quoted in the bibliographical note to chapter xxi, and especially L. T. Smith, *York Plays*, xlvii; P. Kamann, in *Anglia*, x. 189; A. Hohlfeld, in *Anglia*, xi. 285. Much still remains to be done, especially for the Chester plays and the *Ludus Coventriae*. The

chief earlier sources are probably the *Evangelium Pseudo-Matthaei* and the *Evangelium Nicodemi* (including the *Gesta Pilati* and the *Descensus Christi ad Inferos*), both in Tischendorf, *Evangelia Apocrypha*, and the *Transitus Mariae* in Tischendorf, *Apocalypses Apocryphae*. The later sources include the *Legenda Aurea* of Jacobus de Voragine († 1275) and the *Cursor Mundi* (ed. R. Morris for E.E.T.S.), a Northumbrian poem of the early fourteenth century.
[5] Cf. p. 63.

a fragment is extant, it was performed not on Corpus Christi day but on that of St. Anne. Before the Annunciation it inserts the episodes of Joachim and Anne, Mary in the Temple, and the Betrothal of Mary. To the common episode of the Suspicion of Joseph it adds the Purgation of Mary. In the Resurrection scene is a purely legendary Apparition of Christ to the Virgin; while the Death, Burial, Assumption, and Coronation of Mary intervene between the Pentecost and the *Iudicium*. This matter from the after-history of the Virgin belongs also to the York plays, which add the Apparition to St. Thomas of India.

The Cornish plays, although in many respects they are parallel to those of the north, have yet some very marked features of their own. They have episodes of the miraculous Release of Nicodemus and Joseph of Arimathea from Prison, and of the Death of Pilate and the Interview of Veronica with Tiberius [1]. But their most remarkable legendary addition is an elaborate treatment of the history of the Holy Rood, which provides the motives for the scenes dealing with Seth, Moses, David, Solomon, Maximilla, and the Bridge upon Cedron [2]. On the other hand the Cornish plays close with the Ascension and entirely omit the sub-cycle of the Nativity, passing direct, but for the Holy Rood matter, from the Sacrifice of Isaac to the Temptation.

---

[1] Cf. the *Mors Pilati* in Tischendorf, *Evang. Apocr.* 456.

[2] The 'Holy Rood' episodes are those numbered 6, 13, 14, 16–20, 61 in the table. The fullest accounts of the legend in its varied literary forms are given by W. Meyer, *Die Geschichte des Kreuzholzes vor Christus* (*Abhandlungen der k. bayer. Akad. der Wiss.* I. Cl. xvi. 2. 103, Munich, 1881), and A. S. Napier, *History of the Holy Rood-tree* (E.E.T.S. 1894). Roughly, the story is as follows: Seth went to Paradise to fetch the oil of mercy. An angel gave him three pips from the tree of knowledge. These were laid beneath the tongue of Adam at his burial, and three rods, signifying the Trinity, sprang up. Moses cut the rods, and did miracles with them. At his death they were planted in Mount Tabor. An angel in a dream sent David to fetch them. They grew into one tree, in the shade of which David repented of his sin with Bathsheba. When the Temple was building, a beam was fashioned from the tree, but it would not fit and was placed in the Temple for veneration. The woman Maximilla incautiously sat upon it and her clothes caught fire. She prophesied of Christ, and the Jews made her the first martyr. The beam was cast into the pool of Siloam, to which it gave miraculous properties, and was finally made into a bridge. At the Passion, a portion of it was taken for the Rood.

It is not improbable that the majority of the Corpus Christi and other greater English plays reached the dimensions of a cosmic cycle. But in only a few cases is any definite evidence on the point available. Complete lists are preserved from Beverley and Norwich. The Beverley series seems to have been much on the scale of the four extant cycles. It extended in thirty-six pageants from the Fall of Lucifer to Doomsday. Like the Cornish cycle, it included the episode of Adam and Seth; and it presented an exceptional feature in the insertion of a play of the Children of Israel after the Flight into Egypt. The Norwich cycle, which began with the Creation and ended with Pentecost, was a short one of twelve pageants[1]. The small number is due, partly to the grouping of several episodes in a single play, partly to the omission of the Passion proper. The Resurrection followed immediately upon the Baptism. Of other plays, the chroniclers record that in 1391 the London performance covered both the Old and New Testament, that in 1409 it went from the Creation to the Day of Judgement, and that in 1411 it was 'from the begynnyng of the worlde.' The fragmentary indications of the records preserved show that the Chelmsford play stretched at least from the Creation to the Crucifixion, the Newcastle play at least from the Creation to the Burial of the Virgin[2], the Lincoln play at least from the Deluge to the Coronation of the Virgin. On the other hand the range of the Coventry plays can only be shown to have been from the Annunciation to Doomsday, although it may be by a mere accident that no Old Testament scenes are here to be identified[3].

Examples, though unfortunately no full texts, can also be traced of the separate Nativity and Easter cycles, the merging of which was the most important step in the formation of the complete Corpus Christi play. Both, if I read the evidence aright, existed at Aberdeen. There was a 'Haliblude' play

---

[1] The Norwich play of the Fall is extant in two sixteenth-century versions.

[2] The Newcastle play of the Building of the Ark is extant.

[3] Two Coventry plays are extant, the Shearmen and Taylors' play, extending from the Annunciation to the Massacre of the Innocents, and the Weavers' play of the Purification and Christ in the Temple.

on Corpus Christi day, which I conceive to have been essentially a Passion and Resurrection, and a play at Candlemas, which seems to have included, as well as the Purification, a *Stella*, a Presentation in the Temple, and something in the way of a *Prophetae*. There were performances of Passions in Reading in 1508, in Dublin in 1528, at Shrewsbury in 1567, and in London in 1557 and as late as between 1613 and 1622. I do not suppose that in any of these cases ' Passion' excludes ' Resurrection.' The New Romney town play, also, seems to have been a Passion in the wider sense. The records of Easter plays at Bath (1482), Leicester (1504–7), Morebath (1520–74), Reading (1507, 1533–5), and Kingston (1513–65), are too slight to bear much comment. They may relate to almost anything from a mere Latin *Quem quaeritis* to a full vernacular Passion and Resurrection.

One interesting text falls to be considered at this point. This is a fifteenth-century Burial and Resurrection of 'northern *provenance*. It is very lyrical in character, and apparently the author set out to write a 'treyte' to be read, and shortly after the beginning changed his mind and made a play of it. There are two scenes. The first is an elaborate *planctus*, ' to be playede on gud-friday after-none.' The second, intended for ' Esterday after the resurrectione, In the morowe' is a *Quem quaeritis*. An Ascension play was performed by the Holy Trinity guild at Sleaford in 1480. A ' Christmasse play' is recorded at Tintinhull in 1451. How much it included can hardly be guessed. But the *Stella* maintained its independent position, and is found at Yarmouth (1462–1512), Reading (1499, 1539), Leicester (1547), Canterbury (1503), Holbeach (1548), and Hascombe (1579)[1].

The plays just enumerated may be regarded as of precyclical types. But there are a few others which, although they occur independently, would have their more natural position in cycles of less or greater range. In some of these cases it is probable that the independence is only apparent,

---

[1] Probably these smaller plays, chiefly Paschal, were in English. The Nativity and Resurrection plays in Lord Northumberland's chapel and the Resurrection play in Magdalen College chapel may have been in Latin (cf. p. 107).

a mere matter of incomplete evidence. There are two fifteenth-century plays, both on the subject of Abraham and Isaac, one of which is preserved in the 'Book of Brome' from Suffolk, the other in a manuscript now at Dublin, but probably of South Midland *provenance*. It is of course not impossible that these represent isolated performances, but it is on the whole more likely that they are fragments of lost cycles. A third play, of Midland origin, preserved in the Digby manuscript, occupies an exceptional position. It deals with the Massacre of the Innocents and the Purification, and allusions in a prologue and epilogue make it clear that it belonged to a cycle in which it was preceded by a *Pastores* and a *Magi*, and followed by a Christ in the Temple. This cycle, however, was not played all at once, but a portion was given year by year on St. Anne's day. One of the groups of plays brought together in the *Ludus Coventriae* was evidently intended for performance under similar conditions. It is probable that the *ludus Filiorum Israelis* of the Cambridge Corpus Christi guild about 1350, the Abraham and Isaac of the 'schaft' of St. Dunstan's, Canterbury, between 1491 and 1520, and the Adam and Eve (1507) and 'Cayme's pageaunt' 1512–5) of St. Lawrence's, Reading, formed parts of Corpus Christi cycles given in those towns.

Isolated performances of plays picked out of a cycle, or upon subjects usually treated in a cycle, are, however, not unknown. One or more of the Chester plays occasionally formed part of the civic entertainment of a royal or noble personage. When Henry VII visited Winchester in 1486, the schoolboys of the two great abbeys of Hyde and St. Swithin's gave a *Christi Descensus ad Inferos* before him at dinner. At York the acting of an 'interlude of St. Thomas the Apostle' on a St. Bartholomew's eve towards the end of the reign of Henry VIII became the occasion for a papist demonstration. This might have been either the Incredulity of Thomas (Play xlii) or the Apparition of the Virgin to St. Thomas in India (Play xlvi) from the Corpus Christi cycle. At York, also, there was, in the hands of a Corpus Christi guild, a distinct play, frequently performed between 1446 and the Reformation, called the Creed play. This was apparently an expansion of a motive found in the Pentecost scene at Chester and probably at Coventry, but not at York itself, wherein, after the coming of the Holy Ghost, each of the apostles in turn enunciates one of the articles of the so-called Apostles' creed. At Hull, where I find no trace of a cycle, the Trinity guild of sea-faring men had their play of Noah. At Lincoln, a play of Tobit, which does not actually, so far as I know, form part of the Old Testament section of any English cycle [1], was substituted for the regular Corpus Christi play after the Reformation. Naturally such exceptional performances became more common in the decadence of the religious drama [2]. Thus the very scratch series of plays shown before the earl of Kildare at Dublin, in the Christmas of 1528, included, besides other contributions both sacred, and secular, an Adam and Eve by the tailors and a Joseph and Mary by the carpenters. The choice of these subjects was evidently motived by their appropriateness to the craft representing them. Similarly, when John Bale was bishop of Ossory in 1553, he had performed at the market-cross of Kilkenny, on the day of the proclamation of Queen Mary, a short fragment of a cycle consisting of a *Prophetae*, a Baptism, and a Temptation. One fancies that this strange protagonist of the Reformation must have had in his mind some quaint verbal analogy between 'John Bale' and 'John Baptist,' for he states that he also wrote a dramatic *Vita D. Ioannis Baptistae* in fourteen books. Nor is this the only example of the treatment of a subject, merely episodic in the Corpus Christi cycles, in a distinct and elaborate play. The invaluable Digby manuscript contains a similar expansion, from the East or West Midlands, of the story of Mary Magdalen. It follows the narrative of the *Golden Legend*, and introduces the familiar scenes of the Raising of Lazarus, the Feast in the House of Simon the Leper, the *Quem quaeritis*, and the *Hortulanus*, preceding these with episodes of the life of the Magdalen *in gaudio*, and following them with the Conversion of the

---

[1] 'Thobie' is included in the French collection of mysteries known as the *Viel Testament* (Julleville, *Les Myst.* ii. 354, 370).

[2] On the way in which the later local miracle-play and the scriptural interlude merge into each other, cf. p. 191.

King and Queen of Marseilles, and of Mary's Life in the Wilderness and Death. As offshoots from the Corpus Christi cycle may also be regarded the Deaths of the Apostles played in the Dublin series of 1528, Thomas Ashton's *Julian the Apostate* at Shrewsbury in 1565, and the *Destruction of Jerusalem*, written by John Smith in 1584 to take the place of the traditional plays at Coventry [1].

The Mary Magdalen and the rest of the group just described may be considered as standing halfway between the plays of and akin to the Corpus Christi cycle and those founded on the legends of saints. Of regular saint-plays there are unfortunately only two texts available from these islands. The Digby manuscript contains an East Midland Conversion of St. Paul, which, however, is almost wholly biblical and not legendary. It will be remembered that the subject was one known even to the liturgical drama [2]. There is also a Cornish play of St. Meriasek or Mereadocus, the patron saint of Camborne, written at the beginning of the sixteenth century. Other such plays are, however, upon record. It is perhaps curious that no mention should be found of any English parallel to either the Saint Nicholas plays or the *Miracles de Nostre Dame* of France. It can hardly be doubted that the former at least existed in connexion with the widespread revel of the Boy Bishop [3]. The most popular English saint for dramatic purposes appears to have been St. George. A play of St. George was maintained by the town of Lydd, and was probably copied by a neighbouring guild at New Romney. Another, on an elaborate scale, was given by a group of villages at Bassingbourne in 1511. These seem to have been genuine dramas, and not mere ' ridings ' or folk-plays such as occur elsewhere [4]. A St. George play, described by Collier at Windsor in 1416, can be resolved into a cake.

---

[1] The Destruction of Jerusalem, together with the Visit of Veronica to Tiberius and the Death of Pilate, which are scenes in the Cornish cycle, forms the subject-matter of a French *Vengeance de Nostre Seigneur*, printed in 1491. Another *Vengeance de Nostre Seigneur* is attached to the Passion of Eustache Mercadé (†1414). A representation of a Vengeance, following close on one of a Passion, is recorded at Metz in 1437, and there are several later examples (Julleville, *Les Myst.* ii. 12, 175, 415, 451).

[2] Cf. p. 61.

[3] Cf. p. 97.

[4] Cf. vol. i. p. 221.

St. Thomas of Canterbury was only honoured with a dumb show in his own city, but there was a play upon him at King's Lynn in 1385. Of quite a number of other saint-plays the barest notices exist. London had hers on St. Catherine; Windsor on St. Clotilda; Coventry on St. Catherine and St. Crytyan; Lincoln on St. Laurence, St. Susanna, St. Clara, and St. James; Shrewsbury on St. Feliciana and St. Sabina; Bethersden in Kent on St. Christina; Braintree in Essex on St. Swithin, St. Andrew, and St. Eustace. The Dublin shoe-makers contributed a play on their patron saints Crispin and Crispinian to the Dublin festival of 1528. In London, the plays on the days of St. Lucy and St. Margaret at St. Margaret's, Southwark, may have been on the stories of those saints; and during the Marian reaction a 'goodly' stage-play was given at St. Olave's church on St. Olave's day.

Quite unique, as dealing with a contemporary 'miracle,' is the play of the Blessed Sacrament, performed at one of the many places bearing the name of Croxton, in the latter half of the fifteenth century. According to the manuscript, the event upon which it was based, the marvellous conversion of a Jew who attempted an outrage upon a host, took place at Heraclea in Spain, in 1461. There is, curiously enough, a late French play, quite independent of the English one, upon an exactly parallel miracle assigned to Paris and the thirteenth century [1].

The variation in the types of English miracle-plays naturally implies some variation also in the manner of representation. The normal craft cycles of the greater towns were processional in character. They were not played throughout by a single body of actors and upon a single stage; but the action was divided into a number of independent scenes, to each of which was assigned its own group of performers and its own small movable stage or 'pageant.' And each scene was repeated at several 'stations' in different parts of the city, pageant succeeding pageant in regular order, with the general effect of a vast procession slowly unrolling itself along the streets [2]

---

[1] Julleville, *Les Myst.* ii. 574.

[2] Archdeacon Rogers thus describes the Chester plays (*Digby Plays*, xix) 'They first beganne at ye Abbaye gates; & when the firste pagiente was played at ye Abbaye

This method of playing was convenient to the distribution of the *leitourgia* among the guilds, and was adopted in all those places, Chester, York, Beverley, and Coventry, from which our records happen to be the fullest. But it was not the primitive method and, as has been pointed out in a previous chapter, it probably arose from an attempt about the beginning of the fourteenth century to adapt the already existing miracle-plays to the distinctive feature of the festival of Corpus Christi. To this point it will be necessary to recur [1]. The processional play was rare outside England, and even in England it at no period became universal. Two at least of the great cycles that survive, the Cornish one and the *Ludus Coventriae*, as well as several smaller plays, can be clearly shown from internal evidence to have been intended for stationary performance. They do not naturally cleave asunder into distinct scenes. The same personages appear and reappear : the same properties and bits of scenery are left and returned to, often at considerable intervals. Moreover stationary performances are frequently implied by the records. At Lincoln, after the suppression of the old *visus* of St. Anne's processional play, the corporation ordered the performance of a ' standing ' play ' of some story of the Bible.' At Newcastle, although pageants of the plays went in the procession, the actual performance seems to have been given in a ' stead.' This arrangement is exactly parallel to that of the Florentine *rappresentazioni* on St. John's day in 1454 [2]. Elsewhere there was commonly enough no ' pageant ' at all. The ' standing ' plays may be traced at various removes from their original scene, the floor of the church [3]. Indeed, the examples of Braintree in 1523 and 1525, of Halstead in 1529, of Heybridge in 1532, seem to show that, quite apart from the survival of ritual plays proper, the miracle-play, even at the very moment of its extinction, had not been always and everywhere excluded from the church itself. The Beverley

gates, then it was wheeled from thence to the pentice at yᵉ highe crosse before yᵉ Mayor ; and before that was donne, the seconde came, and yᵉ firste wente in-to the water-gate streete, and from thence vnto yᵉ Bridge-streete, and soe all, one after an other, tell all yᵉ pagiantes weare played.'

[1] Cf. pp. 95, 160.
[2] D'Ancona, i. 228.
[3] Cf. p. 83.

repraesentatio dominicae resurrectionis about 1220 had got as far as the churchyard. At Bungay in 1566 they played in the churchyard, and at Harling in 1452 'at the cherch gate.' The latest of all the village plays, that of Hascombe in 1579, was at, but perhaps not in the church. The next step brought the plays to the market-place, which itself in many towns lay just outside the church door. At Louth the Corpus Christi play was in the 'markit-stede,' and so were some at least of the Reading plays. A neighbouring field might be convenient ; the Bassingbourne play was in a 'croft,' that of Chelmsford in a 'pightell.' Certain places had a bit of waste ground traditionally devoted to the entertainment of the citizens. Such were the 'Forbury' at Reading and the 'Quarry' at Shrewsbury. The Aberdeen Halibludc play took place *apud ly Wyndmylhill.* Edinburgh constructed its 'playfield' in the Greenside at considerable cost in 1554, while in Cornwall permanent amphitheatres were in use. A writer contemporary with the later performances describes these as made of earth in open fields with an enclosed 'playne' of some fifty feet in diameter. If they are correctly identified with the 'rounds' of St. Just and Perranzabulo, these examples at least were much larger. The St. Just round is of stone, with seven tiers of seats, and measures 126 feet in diameter ; the earthen one at Perranzabulo is 130 feet, and has a curious pit in the centre, joined to the edge by a trench. The disposition of these rounds at the time of performance can be studied in the diagrams reproduced from the fifteenth-century manuscript of the plays by Mr. Norris. Within a circular area is arranged a ring of eight spots which probably represent structures elevated above the general surface of the 'playne.' They have labels assigning them to the principal actors. Thus for the *Origo Mundi* the labels are *Celum, Tortores, Infernum, Rex Pharao, Rex Dauid, Rex Sal[omon], Abraham, Ortus.* From the stage directions it would appear that the raised portions were called *pulpita* or *tenti,* and by Jordan at a later date 'rooms'; that the 'playne' was the *platea* ; and that the action went on partly on the *pulpita,* partly on the *platea* between them. Except that it is circular instead of oblong, the scheme corresponds exactly to that

of the continental plays shown in an earlier chapter to have
been determined by the conditions of performance within
a church [1]. Those plays also had their *platea*; and their
domus, loca, or *sedes* answer to the *pulpita* and *tenti* of Cornwall. Judging by the somewhat scanty indications available,
the disposition of other English 'standing' plays must have
been on very similar lines. In some cases there is evidence
that the level *platea* was replaced by a raised 'platform,'
'scaffold,' or 'stage.' Thus Chaucer's 'joly Absolon' played
Herod ' on a scaffold hye [2].' But the 'stages' or 'scaffolds'
mentioned in accounts are sometimes merely for the spectators
and sometimes equivalent to the *loca* of leading actors. In
the Digby play of St. Mary Magdalen, a practicable ship
moves about the *platea*. Possibly a similar bit of realism was
used elsewhere for the ever popular ' Noy schippe,' and, if so,
this may explain the pit and trench of the Perranzabulo 'round [3].'

As to the ' pageant' or movable stage of the processional
plays, a good deal of information is preserved. Dugdale
describes it at Coventry as a 'Theater . . . very large and
high, placed upon wheels'; Rogers at Chester as ' a highe
place made like a howse with ij rowmes, beinge open on
y[e] tope : the lower rowme they apparelled and dressed them
selues ; and in the higher rowme they played ; and they
stood vpon 6 (*v.l.* 4) wheeles.' According to an inventory
of 1565 the grocers' pageant at Norwich was 'a Howse of
Waynskott paynted and buylded on a Carte w[t] fowre
whelys.' It had a square top or canopy ; on it were placed
a gilt griffin and two large and eighty-three small vanes ; and
about it were hung three painted cloths. Similar adornments
of the pageant were in use at Coventry. At York it bore
the arms of the city or of the guild. M. Jusserand has
unearthed from a Bodleian manuscript two fourteenth-century
miniatures which apparently represent pageants. These have
draperies covering the whole of the lower ' room' down to the

---

[1] Cf. p. 83.

[2] *C. T.* 3384 (*Miller's Tale*).
This 'scaffold' may have been
merely a throne or *sedes* for Herod.
But plays on platforms or scaffolds
are found at Chelmsford, Kingston,
Reading, Dublin.

[3] Cf. M. Jusserand, in *Furnivall
Miscellany*, 186, and the pit for *La
Mer* on the 1547 Valenciennes Passion play stage figured in his *Shakespeare in France*, 63.

ground and resemble nothing so much as the ambulant theatre of a Punch and Judy show [1]. The pageants were probably arranged so that the action might be visible from every side. The scenery would therefore be simple—a throne, a house. Certain plays, however, necessitate a divided scene, such as the inside and outside of a temple [2]. For the 'hell,' the traditional monstrous head on a lower level, with practicable chains and fire, was required [3]. The pageant used for the Flood scene was doubtless shaped like an ark. The ' shipp ' belonging to the Trinity guild of Hull cost £5 8s. 4d. The ordinary pageant may have been less expensive. That of the Doom at York was made ' of newe substanciale ' for seven marks, the old pageant and a free admission into the guild. At Lincoln three times as much was charged for housing the ship as for any other pageant.

The origin of the pageant is capable of a very easy explanation [4]. Like the *edifizio* of the Italian *rappresentazioni*, it

---

[1] *Furnivall Miscellany*, 192, 194, from *Bodl. MS.* 264, ff. 54[b], 76[a].

[2] The directions to the Coventry Weavers' play refer to the ' for pagand ' and the ' upper part '; those of the Grocers' play at Norwich to the 'nether parte of y[e] pageant.' For the purposes of the dramas these are distinct localities.

[3] Cf. p. 86. The Digby St. Mary Magdalen play has the stage direction, ' a stage, and Helle ondyrneth that stage.' At Coventry the Cappers had a ' hell-mouth ' for the Harrowing of Hell and the Weavers another for Doomsday.

[4] Every conceivable spelling of the word ' pageant ' appears in the records. The *Promptorium Parvulorum*, ii. 377 († 1440, ed. A. Way for Camd. Soc.), has ' Pagent, *Pagina*,' and this is the usual Latin spelling, although *pagenda* and *pagentes* (acc. pl.) occur at Beverley. The derivation is from *pagina* ' a plank.' The *Catholicon Anglicum* (1483, ed. S. J. H. Herrtage for E. E. T. S.) has ' A Paiande ; *lusorium*,' and there can be little doubt that ' playing-place,' ' stage ' is the primary sense of the word, although

as a matter of fact the derivative sense of ' scene ' or ' episode ' is the first to appear. Wyclif so uses it, speaking of Christmas in his *Ave Maria* (*English Works*, E. E. T. S. 206) ' he that kan best pleie a pagyn of the deuyl, syngynge songis of lecherie, of batailis and of lesyngis ... is holden most merie mon.' In *Of Prelates* (*loc. cit.* 99) he says that false teachers ' comen in viserid deuelis ' and ' pleien the pagyn of scottis,' masking under St. George's ' skochen.' The elaborate pageants used in masks and receptions (cf. p. 176, and vol. i. p. 398) led to a further derivative sense of 'mechanical device.' This, as well as the others, is illustrated in the passages quoted by the editors of the *Prompt. Parv.* and the *Cath. Angl.* from W. Horman, author of *Vulgaria* (1519) ' Alexander played a payante more worthy to be wondred vpon for his rasshe aduenture than for his manhede ... There were v coursis in the feest and as many paiantis in the pley. I wyll haue made v stag3 or bouthis in this playe (*scenas*). I wolde haue a place in the middyl of the pley (*orchestra*) that I myght

is simply the raised *locus*, *sedes*, or *domus* of the stationary play put upon wheels. Just as the action of the stationary play took place partly on the various *sedes*, partly in the *platea*, so Coventry actors come and go to and from the pageant in the street. ' Here Erode ragis in the pagond & in the strete also,' says a stage direction. It should be observed that the plays at Coventry were exceptionally long, and that scaffolds seem to have been attached to the pageant proper in order to get sufficient space.

The number of ' stations ' at which the plays were given varied in the different towns. At York there were from twelve to sixteen ; at Beverley six ; at Coventry not more than three or four can be identified. The many scenes and frequent repetitions naturally made the processional plays very lengthy affairs. At Chester they were spread over three days ; at York they were got through in one, but playing began at half-past four in the morning. At Newcastle, on the other hand, the plays were in the afternoon. The banns of the *Ludus Coventriae* promise a performance 'at vj of the belle,' but whether in the morning or evening is not stated.

The normal occasion for the greater plays was the feast of Corpus Christi on the Thursday after Trinity Sunday. A few exceptions are, however, to be noted. At Chester, Norwich, New Romney, and apparently Leicester, the date chosen was Whitsuntide. Yet at Chester the play is called the ' Corpus Christi play ' in craft documents of the fifteenth century, and even in the municipal ' White Book ' of the sixteenth ; from which it must be inferred either that the term was used of all cyclical plays without regard to their date, or, more probably, that at Chester a performance originally given on Corpus Christi day had been for some reason transferred to Whitsuntide. The motive may have been a desire to. avoid clashing between the plays and the great Corpus Christi procession in which the crafts everywhere

se euery paiaunt. Of all the crafty and subtyle paiantis and pecis of warke made by mannys wyt, to go or moue by them selfe, the clocke is one of the beste.' Synonyms for ' pageant ' in the sense of ' stage ' are ' cariadge ' (Chester) and ' karre ' (Beverley) ; in the sense of ' scene,' *iocus* (Coventry), *visus* (Lincoln), *processus* or ' processe ' (Towneley and Digby plays, Croxton *Sacrament* and Medwall's morality of *Nature*).

took a prominent part. A difficulty arose on this score at York in 1426, and a Franciscan preacher, one William Melton, tried to induce the citizens to have the plays on the day before Corpus Christi. Ultimately the alternative was adopted of having the procession on the day after. At Lincoln the plays were on St. Anne's day (July 26) and the last pageant was acted by the clergy in the nave of the cathedral. At Aberdeen there appear to have been two cycles, a processional Nativity at Candlemas and a Haliblude play on Windmill Hill at Corpus Christi.

The oversight of the actors was, as pointed out in the last chapter, an important element in the civic control of the craft-plays. The mention at York of a commission of 'connyng, discrete and able players' must not be taken to imply that these were in any sense professionals. All the actors received fees, on a scale proportionate to the dignity of their parts. Thus at Coventry one Fawston got 4*d*. 'for hangyng Judas,' and 4*d*. more 'for coc croyng.' The payment to the performer of God was 3*s*. 4*d*. A 'sowle,' whether 'savyd' or 'dampnyd,' got 20*d*., and a 'worme of conscyence' only 8*d*. At Hull, Noah was generally paid 1*s*., God and Noah's wife a trifle less. But there is nothing to show that the performers were drawn from the minstrel class : they were probably, like 'joly Absolon,' members of the guilds undertaking the plays. The Chester men describe themselves in their banns as not 'playeres of price' but 'Craftes men and meane men.' The epilogue to the Conversion of St. Paul in the Digby manuscript similarly deprecates unkindly criticism of folk 'lackyng lytturall scyens . . . that of Retoryk haue non intellygens.' A characteristic of the acting which greatly impressed the imagination of the audience seems to have been the rant and bombast put from very early times in the mouths of such royal or pseudo-royal personages as Herod and Pilate.[1]   In the Chester

---

[1] Cf. p. 90, and *Hamlet*, iii. 2. 9 'O, it offends me to the soul to hear a robustious periwig-pated fellow tear a passion to tatters, to very rags, to split the ears of the groundlings, who for the most part are capable of nothing but inexplic- able dumb-shows and noise: I would have such a fellow whipped for o'erdoing Termagant; it out-herods Herod.' The Miller in *Cant. Tales*, 3124, cries out 'in Pilates vois.' The torturers also seem to have been favourite performers ;

plays fragments of French, as in a liturgical play fragments of gibberish [1], are used to enhance this effect. In the
Cornish plays, as in the modern music hall, each performer
at his first appearance displays himself in a preliminary strut
about the stage. *Hic pompabit Abraham,* or *Moses,* or *David,*
say the stage directions. As is usually the case with
amateurs, the function of the prompter became an exceedingly important one. If the Cornish writer Richard Carew
may be trusted, the local players did not learn their parts
at all, but simply repeated them aloud after the whispers of
the ' ordinary [2].' Probably this was exceptional ; it certainly
was not the practice at Beverley, where there is a record of
an actor being fined *quod nesciebat ludum suum.* But it may
be taken for granted that the ' beryng of the boke,' which is
so frequently paid for in the accounts, was never a sinecure.
Another functionary who occasionally appears is the stage-
manager. In the later Cornish plays he is called the ' conveyour.' The great Chelmsford performance of 1562 was
superintended by one Burles who was paid, with others, for
' suing ' it, and who probably came from a distance, as he and
his boy were boarded for three weeks.

The professional assistance of the minstrels, although not
called in for the acting, was welcome for the music. This
was a usual and a considerable item in the expenses. At the
Chelmsford performance just mentioned the waits of Bristol
and no less than forty other minstrels were employed. There
is no sign of a musical accompaniment to the dialogue of
the existing plays, which was spoken, and not, like that of
their liturgical forerunners, chanted. But the York and
Coventry texts contain some noted songs, and several plays
have invitations to the minstrels to strike up at the conclusion
or between the scenes. Minstrels are also found accompanying the proclaimers of the banns or preliminary
announcements of plays. These banns seem to have been

cf. the *Poem on the Evil Times of
Edward II* (T. Wright, *Political
Songs,* C. S. 336) :
' Hii ben degised as turmentours
  that comen from clerkes plei.'
  [1] Cf. p. 48.

[2] In Jean Fouquet's miniature
representing the French mystery of
St. Apollonia (cf. p. 85) a priest,
with a book in one hand and a wand
in the other, appears to be conducting the play.

versified, like the plays themselves.   They are often mentioned, and several copies exist.   Those of Chester were
proclaimed by the city crier on St. George's day; those of
the Croxton play and the *Ludus Coventriae* were carried round
the country-side by *vexillatores* or banner-bearers.   Minstrelsy
was not the only form of lighter solace provided for the
spectators of the plays.   Two of those in the Digby manuscript were accompanied with dances.   At Bungay a 'vyce'
was paid ' for his pastyme before the plaie, and after the
plaie.'   There were ' vices' too at Chelmsford, and ' fools,'
by which is meant the same thing[1], at Heybridge and New
Romney.   But these examples are taken from the decadence
of the miracle-play, rather than from its heyday.

The accounts of the Bassingbourne play in 1511 include
a payment to 'the garnement man for garnements and
propyrts and playbooks.'   This was an occasional and not
an annual play, and apparently at the beginning of the sixteenth century such plays were sufficiently frequent to render
the occupation of theatrical outfitter a possible one.   Certainly
those lucky parishes, such as Chelmsford or St. Peter's, Oxford,
which possessed a stock of ' game gear,' found a profit in
letting it out to less favoured places.   The guilds responsible for the greater plays naturally preserved their own
costumes and properties from year to year, supplementing
these where necessary by loans from the neighbouring gentry
and clergy.   The Middle Ages were not purists about
anachronism, and what was good enough for an English
bishop was good enough for Annas and Caiaphas.   The
hands of the craftsmen who acted were discreetly cased
in the gloves, without which no ceremonial occasion was
complete, and sometimes, at least, vizors or masks were
worn.   But, as a rule, the stage setting left a good deal to
the imagination.   The necessaries for the play of Paradise
at Beverley in 1391 consisted of the ' karre' or pageant,
eight hasps, eighteen staples, two vizors, a pair of wings for
the angel, a fir-spar (the tree of knowledge), a worm (the
serpent), two pairs of linen breeches, two pairs of shifts, and
one sword.   For a similar play the Norwich grocers possessed

[1] Cf. p. 203.

in 1565, besides the pageant and its fittings, sufficient 'cotes and hosen' for all the characters, that of the serpent being fitted with a tail, a 'face' and hair for the Father, hair for Adam and Eve, and—'a Rybbe colleryd Red.' A few other interesting details can be gathered from various records. ' At Canterbury the steeds of the *Magi* were made of hoops and laths and painted canvas. In the Doomsday scene at Coventry the 'savyd ' and ' dampnyd ' souls were distinguished by their white or black colour [1]. The hell mouth was provided with fire, a windlass, and a barrel for the earthquake. There were also three worlds to be set afire, one, it may be supposed, at each station. The stage directions to Jordan's Cornish Creation of the World are full of curious information. The Father appears in a cloud and when he speaks out of heaven, ' let ye levys open.' Lucifer goes down to hell ' apareled fowle wth fyre about hem ' and the plain is filled with ' every degre of devylls of lether and spirytis on cordis.' In Paradise a fountain and ' fyne flowers ' suddenly spring up, and a little later ' let fyshe of dyuers sortis apeare & serten beastis.' Lucifer becomes 'a fyne serpent made wth a virgyn face & yolowe heare upon her head.' Adam and Eve departing from Paradise ' shewe a spyndell and a dystaff.' For the murder of Abel, according to old tradition, a 'chawbone ' is needed [2], and for the ark, timber and tools, including ' a mallet, a calkyn yren, ropes, masstes, pyche and tarr.' I have not space to dwell further on these archaeological *minutiae*. One point, however, seems to deserve another word. Many writers have followed Warton in asserting that Adam and Eve were represented on the stage in actual nakedness [3].

---

[1] *Hen. V*, ii. 3. 42 ' Do you not remember, a' saw a flea stick upon Bardolph's nose, and a' said it was a black soul burning in hellfire?'

[2] *Hamlet*, v. 1. 85 ' Cain's jawbone, that did the first murder.'

[3] Warton, ii. 223 ' In these Mysteries I have sometimes seen gross and open obscenities. In a play of *The Old and New Testament*, Adam and Eve are both exhibited on the stage naked, and conversing about their nakedness: this very pertinently introduces the next scene, in which they have coverings of figleaves. This extraordinary spectacle was beheld by a numerous assembly of both sexes with great composure: they had the authority of scripture for such a representation, and they gave matters just as they found them in the third chapter of Genesis. It would have been absolute heresy to have departed from the sacred text in personating

The statement is chiefly based upon a too literal interpretation of the stage directions of the Chester plays[1]. There is a fine *a priori* improbability about it, and as a matter of fact there can be very little doubt that the parts were played, as they would have been on any other stage in any other period of the world's history, except possibly at the Roman *Floralia*[2], in fleshings. Jordan is quite explicit. Adam and Eve are to be 'aparlet in whytt lether,' and although Jordan's play is a late one, I think it may be taken for granted that white leather was sufficient to meet the exigencies even of mediaeval realism.

The accounts of miracle-plays frequently contain entries of payments for providing copies of the text used. When the stock of the Chelmsford play was dispersed in 1574, the copies were valued at £4. Such copies were naturally of more than one kind. There was the authoritative text kept for reference by the guild or other body of presenters. This is sometimes called the 'play-book' or 'game-book.' The Cornish term is *ordinale*, a derivative from the *ordo* of the liturgical drama[3]. That in use elsewhere is more commonly 'original,' which appears in a variety of quaint spellings[4]. In the great towns where plays were given by the crafts under the general supervision of the corporation, each craft held the 'original' of its own play, but approved transcripts of these were also in the hands of the corporation officers. At Chester this transcript was itself called the 'original'; at York it was the *registrum*. Most of the extant manuscripts of plays appear to be of the nature of 'originals.' From York and probably from Wakefield we have *registra*. The Chester texts are, however, late transcripts due to the zeal of local antiquaries, perhaps in view of some frustrated revival. Specimens exist also of two other kinds of copy. There are single plays from both Chester and York which have all the appearance of having been folded up for the pocket of a

the primitive appearance of our first parents, whom the spectators so nearly resembled in simplicity.'
[1] Deimling, i. 30 'Statim nudi sunt ... Tunc Adam et Eva cooperiant genitalia sua cum foliis.'
[2] Cf. vol. i. p. 5.
[3] Cf. p. 103. So the 'ordinary' or prompter (p. 140) is the man in charge of the *ordinale*.
[4] 'Oreginale de S. Maria Magdalena' (*Digby MS.*); 'originall booke,' 'regenall,' 'rygynall,' 'orraginall' (Chester); 'orygynall,' 'rygenale' (Coventry); 'regenell' (Louth); 'ryginall' (Sleaford).

prompter. And the nature of the 'parts' prepared for individual actors may be seen from the transition example edited by Professor Skeat from a manuscript found at Shrewsbury. They contained the actors' own speeches, with the 'cues' or closing words of the preceding speeches which signalled to him that his turn was at hand [1].

Indications of the authorship of plays are very scanty. John Bale has preserved a list of his own plays, some at least of which were acted in mediaeval fashion. It may perhaps be assumed that Nicholas Udall, afterwards author of *Ralph Roister Doister*, wrote the play performed at Braintree in 1534, while he was vicar there. At Bassingbourne in 1511 one John Hobarde, 'brotherhood priest,' was paid ' for the play-book.' In this and in several of the following cases it is impossible to determine whether an author or merely a copying scribe is in question. The corporation of Beverley employed Master Thomas Bynham, a friar preacher, to write 'banis' for their plays in 1423. At Reading we find Mr. Laborne 'reforming' the Resurrection play about 1533. The later Cornish play of the Creation of the World was 'wryten' by William Jordan in 1611, and that of St. Meriasek by 'dominus Hadton' in 1504. At Bungay William Ellys was paid in 1558 'for the interlude and game-book [2], and Stephen Prewett, a priest at Norwich, for some labour about the matter of a game-book in 1526. This same Stephen Prewett had a fee from the Norwich grocers 'for makyng of a new ballet' in 1534. One of the extant Coventry plays was 'nexly correcte' and the other 'nevly translate' by Robert Croo in 1535. The name 'Thomas Mawdycke' and the date 1591 are written at the head of some songs belonging to the former. In 1566 Thomas Nycles set a song for the drapers. Robert Croo or Crowe seems to have made himself generally useful in connexion with the Coventry plays. In 1563 the smiths paid him for 'ij leves of our pley boke.' In 1557 he wrote the 'boke' for the drapers, and between 1556 and 1562 further assisted them by playing God, mending the 'devell's cottes,'

---

[1] Cf. p. 90.

[2] As the price paid was only 'iiij^d' a *printed* play was probably bought, from which the 'partes,' at a cost of 'ij^s,' were written; cf. p. 192.

and supplying 'iij worldys' for burning and a hat for the
Pharisee. A later Coventry playwright was John Smith of
St. John's College, Oxford, who wrote the 'new play' of the
Destruction of Jerusalem in 1584 for a sum of £13 6s. 8d.
The fifteenth-century Croxton play has the initials 'R. C.'
One of the plays in the Digby manuscript 'Ihon Parfre ded
wryte.' The three others have the initials 'M. B.,' and against
the *Poeta* of the prologue to one of them a later hand has
written in the margin 'Myles Blomfylde.' I repeat the caution
that some at least of these names may be those of mere
copyists. Miles Blomfield has been identified with a monk
of Bury of that name. As he was born in 1525 he obviously
was not the original author of the Digby plays, which are
probably of the fifteenth century. A much greater monk of
Bury, John Lydgate, has been claimed as the author of the *Ludus
Coventriae*, but there does not seem to be any real evidence
for this [1]. On the other hand I see no reason to doubt the
old Chester tradition which connects the plays of that city
with the name of Randulph Higden, author of the *Polychronicon*.
The story is very fairly coherent, and the date (1328) which
it assigns for the plays falls within the period of Higden's
monastic life at St. Werburgh's abbey.

It must, of course, be borne in mind that the notion of authorship is only imperfectly applicable to the miracle-plays. The
task of the playwrights was one less of original composition
than of adaptation, of rewriting and rearranging existing
texts so as to meet the needs of the particular performances
in which they were interested. Obviously this was a process
that could be carried out with more or with less individuality.
There were slavish adapters and there were liberal adapters.
But on the whole the literary problem of the plays lies in
tracing the evolution of a form rather than in appreciating
individual work. Even when written, the plays, if periodically
performed, were subject to frequent revision, motived partly
by the literary instinct for furbishing up, partly by changing
conditions, such as the existence of a varying number of craft-

[1] Ritson, *Bibl. Poet.* 79, included in his list of Lydgate's works
a 'Procession of pageants from the
creation' which has not been identified. On the 'Procession of Corpus Christi,' which follows in the
list, cf. p. 161.

guilds ready to undertake the responsibility for a scene[1]. Further alterations, on theological rather than literary grounds, were naturally called for at the Reformation. Thus Jordan's Cornish *Creation of the World* is clearly based upon the older play printed by Mr. Norris. The book of the Norwich grocers contains two versions of their play of Paradise, the later of which, ' newely renvid accordynge unto ye Skrypture,' was substituted for the earlier in 1565. The Towneley manuscript has two alternative versions of the *Pastores*. That of York has a fragmentary second version of the Coronation of the Virgin, and when read with the records affords much evidence of the dropping, insertion, and rearrangement of scenes, and of doctrinal revision during the sixteenth century. At Coventry the local annals mention ' new playes ' in 1520, fifteen years before the existing texts were ' nevly correcte' and ' translate' by Robert Crowe.

The determination of the relations in which the plays stand towards one another is a field in which literary scholars, delayed by the want of trustworthy critical texts, are only just beginning to set foot. The question lies outside the scope of these pages. But I may call attention to Mr. Pollard's analysis of the various *strata* in the Towneley plays[2], and to the studies by Professor Hohlfeld[3] and Professor Davidson[4] upon the greater cycles in general and especially upon the influence exercised by York over the Towneley and other plays, as excellent examples of what may be looked for. The *Ludus Coventriae* will afford a good subject for investigation, when the manuscript has been properly re-edited. It is evidently a patchwork cycle, roughly put together and in parts easy to break up into its constituent elements. The problem is not confined to English literature. The Chester tradition represents Higden's work as an affair rather of translation than of anything else. It is not quite clear whether translation from the Latin or from the Norman-French is intended. In any case it is probable that the earlier English playwrights made use of French models, and certain parallels

---

[1] Ten Brink, ii. 235 'An incessant process of separating and uniting, of extending and curtailing, marks the history of the liturgical drama, and indeed of the mediaeval drama generally.'

[2] *Towneley Plays* (E. E. T. S.), xiv.

[3] *Anglia*, xi. 253.

[4] Davidson, 252.

have already been traced between English plays and others
to be found in the French collection known as the *Viel
Testament*. Here, as elsewhere, the international solidarity of
mediaeval literature is to be taken into account.

Two chapters back I defined the change which took place
in the character of the religious drama of western Europe
during the thirteenth century as being, to a large extent,
a process of secularization. ' Out of the hands of the clergy,'
I said, ' in their naves and choirs, the drama passed to those
of the laity in their market-places and guild-halls.' And
I pointed to the natural result of these altered conditions in
' the reaction of the temper of the folk upon the handling of
the plays, the broadening of their human as distinct from their
religious aspect [1].' A study of the texts and records of the
fully developed miracle-play as it existed in these islands from
the fourteenth to the sixteenth century can only confirm this
view. I have indeed shown, I hope, in the course of this
imperfect summary, that the variety of mediaeval theatrical
organization was somewhat greater than a too exclusive
attention to the craft-cycles of the great towns has always
allowed scholars to recognize. But, with all qualifications and
exceptions, it is none the less true that what began as a mere
spectacle, devised by ecclesiastics for the edification of the
laity, came in time to appeal to a deep-rooted native instinct
of drama in the folk and to continue as an essentially popular
thing, a *ludus* maintained by the people itself for its own
inexhaustible wonder and delight [2]. Literary critics have laid
stress upon the emergence of the rude humour of the folk,
with its love of farce and realism, in somewhat quaint juxtaposition to the general subject-matter of the plays. I only
desire to add here that the instinct which made the miracle-
plays a joy to the mediaeval burgher is the same instinct
which the more primitive peasant satisfied in a score of modes
of rudimentary folk-drama [3]. The popularity and elaboration

[1] Cf. p. 69.
[2] Thus at York, the Corpus
Christi procession which the plays
were originally designed to magnify,
had become by 1426 a hindrance to
them; cf. p. 139.

[3] There is but little of direct
merging of the plays with folk-customs. At Aberdeen the ' Haliblude '
play was under the local lord of
misrule. At Norwich the play was
on Whit-Monday; the lord of misrule

of the devil scenes in the plays is the most striking manifestation of this identity [1]. For your horned and blackened devil is the same personage, with the same vague tradition of the ancient heathen festival about him, whether he riots it through the cathedral aisles in the Feast of Fools, or hales the Fathers to limbo and harries the forward spectators in the marketplace of Beverley or Wakefield.

One must not look for absolute breaches of continuity, even in a literary evolution. That the liturgical types of religious drama continued to exist side by side with their popular offshoots, that here the clergy continued to present plays, and in spite of a certain adverse current of ascetic feeling, to assist the lay guilds in divers ways, has already been there shown. It is to be added that the texts of the plays bear traces to the end of their liturgical origin. The music used is reminiscent of church melodies [2]. The dialogue at critical moments follows the traditional lines and occasionally even reverts to the actual Latin of the *repraesentationes*. More than one play— the Towneley *Iuditium*, the Croxton *Sacrament*, the Digby *St. Mary Magdalen*—closes with the *Te Deum* which habitually ended Matins when the dramatic interpolation of the office was over. And what are the *Expositor* of the *Ludus Coventriae*, the *Doctor* of the Brome play, or even *Balaeus Prolocutor* himself, but the lineal descendants, through the dramatized St. Augustine, of certain German plays and the *appellatores* or *vocatores* of the *Prophetae*, of the priest who read the pseudo-Augustinian Christmas *lectio* from which the *Prophetae* sprang? Survivals such as these impress upon the student the unity of the whole religious drama of the Middle Ages, from trope to Corpus Christi cycle.

held revel on Whit-Tuesday. At Reading there were plays on May-day. At Chelmsford and Wymondham they were attached to the Midsummer 'watch' or 'show.' Typically 'folk' personages, the 'wodmen' (cf. vol. i. p. 185), appear in the Aberdeen Candlemas procession, and at Hull the 'hobby-ship' (cf. vol. i. p. 121) becomes the centre of a play.

[1] Richard Carew lays stress on the delight taken by the spectators in the devils of the Cornish plays. Collier, ii. 187, quotes a jest about the devil in a Suffolk stage-play from *C. Mery Talys* (⊦ 1533). In the *Conversion of St. Paul* of the Digby MS., a later hand has carefully inserted a devil scene. On the whole subject of the representation of devils in the plays, cf. Cushman, 16; Eckhardt, 53.

[2] *York Plays*, 524.

CHAPTER XXIII

MORALITIES, PUPPET-PLAYS, AND PAGEANTS

[*Bibliographical Note.*—The English moralities are well treated from a literary point of view in the books by Ten Brink, Ward, Creizenach, Pollard, Collier, Klein, Symonds, Bates, Jusserand, and Courthope, named in the bibliographical note to Chapter xxi, and also in the Introduction to A. Brandl, *Quellen des weltlichen Dramas in England vor Shakespeare* (1898). Some texts not easily available elsewhere are given in the same book; others are in Dodsley's *A Select Collection of Old English Plays* (ed. W. C. Hazlitt, 1874-6), vol. i, and J. M. Manly, *Specimens of the Pre-Shakespearean Drama* (1897), vol. i. Extracts are given by Pollard. Lists both of popular moralities and of moral interludes will be found in Appendix X. The French plays of a similar type are dealt with by L. Petit de Julleville, *La Comédie et les Mœurs en France au Moyen Age* (1886) and *Répertoire du Théâtre comique en France au Moyen Age* (1886).—On puppet-plays, C. Magnin, *Histoire des Marionnettes en Europe* (1852), and A. Dieterich, *Pulcinella* (1897), may be consulted. The traditional text of the stock English play is printed, with illustrations by G. Cruikshank, in J. P. Collier, *Punch and Judy* (1870). English pageants at the Corpus Christi feast and at royal entries are discussed by C. Davidson, *English Mystery Plays* (1892), § xvii, and Sir J. B. Paul, in *Scottish Review*, xxx (1897), 217, and the corresponding French *mystères mimés* by L. Petit de Julleville, *Les Mystères* (1880).]

I HAVE endeavoured to trace from its ritual origins the full development of that leading and characteristic type of mediaeval drama, the miracle-play. I now propose to deal, very briefly, with certain further outgrowths which, in the autumn of the Middle Ages, sprang from the miracle-play stock; and a final book will endeavour to bring together the scattered threads of this discursive inquiry, and to touch upon that transformation of the mediaeval into the humanist type of drama, which prepared the way for the great Elizabethan stage.

The miracle-play lent itself to modification in two directions: firstly, by an extension of its subject-matter; and secondly, by an adaptation of its themes and the methods to other forms of entertainment which, although mimetic, were not, in the full sense of the term, dramatic. There are a few plays upon record which were apparently represented after the traditional manner of miracles, but differ from these in that they treat subjects not religious, but secular. Extant examples must be sought in the relics, not of the English, but of the continental drama. The earliest is the French *Estoire de Griselidis*, a version of the story familiar in Chaucer's *Clerkes Tale*, which was written and acted, according to the manuscript, in 1395 [1]. Slightly later is a Dutch manuscript which contains, amongst other things, probably the *répertoire* of some *compagnie joyeuse*, three plays on the subjects respectively of Esmoreit, Gloriant of Brunswick, and Lanseloet and Sanderijn [2]. Both the French and Dutch plays belong to what may be called the wider circle of chivalric romance. An obvious link between such pieces and the ordinary miracle-play is to be found in those of the *Miracles de Nostre Dame* which, like *Amis et Amiles* or *Robert le Diable*, also handle topics of chivalric romance, but only such as are brought technically within the scope of the miracle-play by the intervention of the Virgin at some point of the action [3]. Similarly, another French play, dating from about 1439, on the subject, drawn not from romance but from contemporary history, of the Siege of Orleans, may be explained by the sanctity already attributed in the national imagination to Joan of Arc, who is naturally its leading figure [4]. But the usual range

[1] Ed. Groeneveld (1888); cf. Creizenach, i. 362; Julleville, *Les Myst.* i. 180, ii. 342.

[2] I do not think that these Dutch plays have been printed. The MS., in the Royal Library at Brussels, is described by Hoffmann von Fallersleben, *Horae Belgicae*, vi, xxix; cf. Creizenach, i. 366. Besides the three chivalric plays, it contains a dramatized *estrif* of Summer and Winter (cf. vol. i. p. 187) included with them under the general title of 'abele Spelen,' and also a long farce or 'Boerd.' To each of the five plays, moreover, is attached a short farcical after-piece. A few notices of other fifteenth-century Dutch chivalric plays are preserved. The subjects are Ar-

noute, Ronchevale, Florys und Blancheflor, Gryselle (Griseldis); cf. Creizenach, i. 372.

[3] Julleville, *Les Myst.* ii. 284, 310.

[4] Ed. F. Guessard et E. de Certain (1862) in *Collection des documents historiques*; cf. Creizenach, i. 372; Julleville, *Les Myst.* ii. 576; H. Tivier, *Étude sur le Myst. du Siège d'O.* (1868). The play may have been designed for performance at the festival held at Orleans in memory of the siege on May 8. The passage quoted from Sir Richard Morrison on p. 221, suggests that a similar commemoration was held in the sixteenth century by the English at Calais of the battle of Agincourt in 1415.

of subject was certainly departed from when Jacques Millet, a student at Orleans, compiled, between 1450 and 1452, an immense *mystère* in 30,000 lines on the *Istoire de la destruction de Troye la grant*[1]. In England, the few examples of the mingling of secular elements with the miracle-plays which present themselves during the sixteenth century can hardly be regarded as mediaeval[2]. The only theme which need be noticed here is that of King Robert of Sicily. A play on this hero, revived at the High Cross at Chester in 1529, is stated in a contemporary letter to have been originally written in the reign of Henry VII. But a still earlier *ludus de Kyng Robert of Cesill* is recorded in the Lincoln *Annales* under the year 1453.

Far more important than this slight secular extension of miracle-plays is another development in the direction of allegory, giving rise to the 'moral plays' or 'moralities,' as they came to be indifferently called[3], in which the characters are no longer scriptural or legendary persons, but wholly, or almost wholly, abstractions, and which, although still religious in intention, aim rather at ethical cultivation than the stablishing of faith. The earliest notices of morals are found about the end of the fourteenth century, at a time when the influence of the *Roman de la Rose* and other widely popular works was bringing every department of literature under the sway of allegory[4]. That the drama also should be touched with the spirit of the age was so inevitable as hardly to call for comment. But it will be interesting to point out some at least of the special channels through which the new tendency established itself. In the first place there is the twelfth-century Latin play of *Antichristus*. In a sense the whole content of this may be called allegorical, and the allegory becomes formal in such figures as *Heresis* and *Ypocrisis*,

[1] Ed. Stengel (1883); cf. Creizenach, i. 374; Julleville, *Les Myst.* ii. 569.
[2] Cf. *Representations*, s.v. Dublin.
[3] Collier, ii. 183, thinks the term 'morality' a 'recent' one, but it was used in 1503: cf. p. 201.
[4] There is not much direct imitation of the *Roman de la Rose* in the moralities. Perhaps the French *Honneur des Dames* of Andrieu de la Vigne (Julleville, *Rép. com.* 73) comes nearest. But its leading episode, the siege of the fortress of Danger, is reflected in the siege of the Castle of Perseverance and that of the Castle of Maudleyn in the *Mary Magdalen* of the Digby MS. On the general place of allegory in contemporary literature cf. Courthope, i. 341.

Iustitia and *Misericordia*, and in those of *Ecclesia, Synagoga,* and *Gentilitas,* suggested to the clerkly author by a well-known *disputatio.* The same theme recurs in more than one later play [1]. Secondly, there is the theme of the Reconciliation of the Heavenly Virtues, which is suggested by the words of the eighty-fifth Psalm : 'Mercy and Truth are met together : Righteousness and Peace have kissed each other.' This is treated in two unprinted and little known French plays, also of the twelfth century, which I have not as yet had occasion to mention and of which I borrow the following analysis from Dr. Ward : 'These four virtues appear personified as four sisters, who meet together after the Fall of Man before the throne of God to conduct one of those disputations which were so much in accordance with the literary tastes of the age ; Truth and Righteousness speak against the guilty Adam, while Mercy and Peace plead in his favour. Concord is restored among the four sisters by the promise of a Saviour, who shall atone to Divine Justice on behalf of man.' One of these pieces is ascribed to the Anglo-Norman poet, Guillaume Herman (1127–70), the other to Stephen Langton, afterwards archbishop of Canterbury. They are generally spoken of as literary exercises, not intended for representation [2]. But it is obvious that they might very well find their places in miracle-play cycles, as links between the scenes dealing respectively with the Fall and the Redemption. Further, precisely such an episode, in precisely such a position, does occur, three hundred years later, in the English cycle known as the *Ludus Coventriae.* Nor is this the only allegorical element which distinguishes a certain part of this patchwork cycle from nearly all the other English plays [3]. It is not, perhaps, of great importance that in the Assumption scene the

---

[1] Cf. pp. 63, 77.

[2] Ward, i. 105; *Archaeologia,* xiii. 232. A *débat* on precisely this theme is introduced into the *Chasteau d'Amour,* a theological work in the form of a romance, ascribed to Robert Grosseteste (1175–1253), on which cf. F. S. Stevenson, *Life of Grosseteste,* 38 ; Jusserand, *Eng. Lit.* i. 214. In the English version

of the fourteenth century (R. F. Weymouth, *The Castel of Love,* 273) the passage begins—

'For now I chul tellen of þe stryf
Þat a-mong þe foure sustren liþ.'

[3] No stress is of course to be laid upon the late introduction of Dolor and Myserye into the Grocers' play at Norwich, when the text was rewritten in 1565.

risen Christ receives the name of *Sapientia*, or that *Contemplatio* is the 'exposytour in doctorys wede,' by whom several other scenes are introduced. But there is a striking passage at the end of the Slaughter of the Innocents, where 'Dethe, Goddys masangere,' intervenes to make an end of the tyrannic Herod[1], and here, I think, may clearly be traced yet a third stream of allegorical tendency making its way into the drama from that singular *danse macabre* or 'Dance of Death,' which exercised so powerful a fascination on the art of the Middle Ages. Death hobnobbing with pope and king and clown, with lord and lady, with priest and merchant, with beggar and fool, the irony is familiar in many a long series of frescoes and engravings. Nor are cases lacking in which it was directly adapted for scenic representation. An alleged example at Paris in 1424 was probably only a painting. But in 1449 a *certain jeu, histoire et moralité sur le fait de la danse macabre* was acted before Philip the Good at Bruges, and a similar performance is recorded at Besancon in 1453[2].

The process of introducing abstractions into the miracle-plays themselves does not seem to have been carried very far. On the other hand, the moralities, if God and the Devil may be regarded as abstractions, admit of nothing else. Two at least of the motives just enumerated, the Dance of Death and the Reconciliation of the Heavenly Virtues, recur in them. But both are subordinate to a third, which may be called the Conflict of Vice and Virtue. This *débat*-like theme is of course familiar in every branch of allegorical literature. Prof. Creizenach traces one type of it, in which the conflict is conceived under the symbols of siege or battle, to the *Psychomachia* of Prudentius[3], and perhaps even further to the passage about the 'whole armour of God' in St. Paul's epistle to the Ephesians[4]. For the purposes of the stage it

[1] *Ludus Cov.* 106 (play xi, *Virtutes*), 70, 79, 89, 105, 124, 129, 289 (plays viii–xiii, xxix, *Contemplacio*), 184 (play xix, *Mors*), 386 (play xli, *Sapientia*); cf. Hohlfeld, in *Anglia*, xi. 278.

[2] Jusserand, *Théâtre*, 123; Pearson, i. 2; Creizenach, i. 461; *Captain Cox*, clxvi; W. Seelmann, *Die*

Totentänze des Mittelalters (Jahrb. d. Vereins f. niederdeutsche Sprachforschung, xvii. 1). A bibliography of the Dance of Death is given by Goedeke, i. 322 (bk. iii. § 92).

[3] Prudentius, *Psychomachia* († 400 *P. L.* lx. 11); cf. Creizenach, i. 463.

[4] *Ephesians*, vi. 11.

is eminently suitable, both because it lends itself to many and various modes of representation, and because conflict is the very stuff out of which drama is wrought.

As the earliest notices of moralities are found in English records and as this particular development of the drama is thoroughly well represented in English texts, I may save space by confining my attention to these, merely noting as I pass the contemporary existence of precisely parallel records and texts on the continent and particularly in France [1]. The first English moralities seem to have been known as *Paternoster* plays. Such a play is mentioned by Wyclif about 1378 as existing at York, and at some date previous to 1389 a special guild *Orationis Domini* was founded in that city for its maintenance. The play, however, survived the guild, and was acted from time to time as a substitute for the ordinary Corpus Christi plays up to 1572. Similarly, at Beverley a *Paternoster* play was acted by the crafts, probably in emulation of that of York, in 1469, while a third is mentioned in Lincoln documents as played at various dates from 1397 to 1521. Although all these *Paternoster* plays are lost, their general character can be made clear. In that of York 'all manner of vices and sins were held up to scorn and the virtues were held up to praise,' while an incidental entry in a *computus* shows that one division of it was known as the *ludus accidiae*. The information to be derived from Beverley is even more explicit. There were eight pageants. One was assigned to 'Vicious,' probably a typical representative of frail humanity, the other seven to the seven deadly sins which beset him, 'Pryde: Invy: Ire: Avaryce: Sleweth (or Accidie): Glotony: Luxuria.' The *Paternoster* play seems, therefore, to have been in some fashion a dramatization of the struggle of the vices and the corresponding virtues for the soul of man,

---

[1] Creizenach, i. 470; Julleville, *La Com.* 44, 78. The earliest French notice is that of the 'Gieux des sept vertuz et des sept pechiez mortelz' at Tours in 1390. A 'mystère de Bien-Avisé et Mal-avisé' is said to have been played in 1396 (Julleville, *Rép. com.* 324). The extant play of that name, somewhat later in date, is a morality. Other early French morals on a large scale are *L'Homme juste et l'Homme mondain* (1508) and *L'Homme pécheur* († 1494) (Julleville, *Rép. com.* 39, 67, 72). All these are on variants of the Contrast of Vice and Virtue theme.

and the name given to it may be explained by the mediaeval notion that each clause of the Lord's Prayer was of specific merit against one of the deadly sins[1]. Here then is one version of just that theme of the Conflict of Vice and Virtue noted as dominant in the moralities.

Of the half dozen extant English moralities which can with any plausibility be assigned to the fifteenth century, two are based upon a motive akin to that of the Dance of Death. These are the fragmentary *Pride of Life*, which is the earliest of the group, and *Everyman*, which is by far the finest[2]. In the former Death and Life contend for the soul of *Rex Vivus*, the representative of humanity, who is only saved from the fiends by the intervention of the Virgin. In the latter, God sends Death to summon Everyman, who finds to his dismay that of all his earthly friends only Good Deeds is willing to accompany him. The Conflict of Vice and Virtue is resumed in the moral of *Mundus et Infans* and in the three morals of the Macro manuscript, the *Castle of Perseverance, Mind, Will and Understanding*, and *Mankind*. In all four plays the representative of humanity, *Infans* or *Humanum Genus* or *Anima* or Mankind, is beset by the compulsion or swayed this way and that by the persuasion of allegorized good and bad qualities. At the end of the *Castle of Perseverance* the motive of the Reconciliation of the Heavenly Virtues is introduced in a scene closely resembling that of the *Ludus Coventriae* or the earlier essays of Guillaume Herman and Stephen Langton.

A somewhat unique position between miracle-play and morality is occupied by the Mary Magdalen drama contained in the Digby manuscript. The action of this, so far as it is scriptural or legendary, has already been summarized[3]; but it must now be added that the episodes of the secular life of the Magdalen *in gaudio* are conceived in a wholly allegorical vein. The 'kyngs of the world and the flesch' and the 'prynse of dylles' are introduced with the seven

---

[1] Creizenach, i. 465, quoting a thirteenth-century German sermon.
[2] Cf. p. 201 and *Texts* (ii). It is not quite clear whether the English play of *Everyman* is the original or a translation of the Dutch *Elckerlijk*, or whether the two plays have a common source.
[3] Cf. p. 131.

deadly sins and a good and a bad angel. The castle of Magdala, like the castle of Perseverance, is besieged. The Magdalen is led into a tavern by *Luxuria* and there betrayed by Curiosity, a gallant. We have to do less with a mystery beginning to show morality elements than with a deliberate combination effected by a writer familiar with both forms of drama.

The manner of presentation of the fifteenth-century moralities did not differ from that of the contemporary miracle-plays. The manuscript of the *Castle of Perseverance* contains a prologue delivered by *vexillatores* after the fashion of the *Ludus Coventriae* and the Croxton *Sacrament*. There is also, as in the Cornish mysteries published by Mr. Norris, a diagram showing a circular 'place' bounded by a ditch or fence, with a central 'castel' and five 'skaffoldys' for the principal performers. Under the castle is 'Mankynde, is bed' and near it 'Coveytyse cepbord.' The scaffolds are the now familiar *loca* or *sedes*. The scantier indications of more than one of the other moralities proper suggest that they also were performed in an outdoor 'place' with *sedes*, and a similar arrangement is pointed to by the stage directions of the *Mary Magdalen*. Nor could the moralities dispense with those attractions of devils and hell-fire which had been so popular in their predecessors. Belial, in the *Castle of Perseverance*, is to have gunpowder burning in pipes in his hands and ears and other convenient parts of his body; *Anima*, in *Mind, Will and Understanding*, has little devils running in and out beneath her skirts; and in *Mary Magdalen*, the 'prynse of dylles' enters in 'a stage, and Helle ondyr-neth that stage.' The later moralities, of which the sixteenth century affords several examples, were presented under somewhat different conditions, which will be discussed in another chapter [1]. Allusions to the 'morals at Manningtree,' however, in the beginning of the seventeenth century, suggest that moralities may have continued in out-of-the-way places to hold the open-air stage, just as miracle-plays here and there did, to a comparatively late date. Actual examples of the more popular type of morality from the sixteenth century

[1] Cf. p. 199.

are afforded by Skelton's *Magnificence* and by Sir David Lyndsay's *Satyre of the Thrie Estaitis*, shown successively at Linlithgow in 1540, on the Castle-hill at Cupar of Fife in 1552, and in the Greenside at Edinburgh about 1554. This remarkable piece differs in many ways from the English moralities. The theme consists of the arraignment of the estates of the realm before *Rex Humanitas*. Various 'vycis' and allegorical personages appear and plead, and the action is enlivened by farcical interludes for the amusement of the vulgar, and wound up by a sermon of 'Folie,' which points rather to French than to English models[1]. The flight of time is also shown by the fact that the *Satyre* aims less at the moral edification with which the fifteenth-century plays contented themselves, than at the introduction of a sharp polemic against abuses in church and state. Skelton's *Magnificence* had also, not improbably, some political bearing. To this matter also I return in another chapter[2].

Miracle-plays and moralities ranked amongst the most widespread and coloured elements, century after century, of burgher and even of village life. It is not surprising that their subjects and their methods exercised a powerful influence upon other manifestations of the mediaeval spirit. The share which their vivid and sensuous presentations of religious ideas had in shaping the conceptions of artists and handicraftsmen is a fascinating topic of far too wide a scope to be even touched upon here[3]. But a few pages must be devoted to indicating the nature of their overflow into various pseudo-dramatic, rather than strictly dramatic, forms of entertainment.

One of these is the puppet-show. It has been pointed out, in speaking of the liturgical drama, that the use of puppets to provide a figured representation of the mystery of the Nativity, seems to have preceded the use for the same purpose of living and speaking persons; and further, that the puppet-show, in the form of the 'Christmas crib,' has outlived the drama founded upon it, and is still in use in all Catholic

---

[1] Cf. vol. i. p. 381.
[2] Cf. p. 218.
[3] See Pearson, ii. 260, and the interesting study of P. Weber, *Geistliches Schauspiel und kirchliche Kunst* (1894).

countries[1]. An analogous custom is the laying of the crucifix in the 'sepulchre' during the Easter ceremonies, and there is one English example of a complete performance of a Resurrection play by 'certain smalle puppets, representinge the Persons of Christe, the Watchmen, Marie and others.' This is described by a seventeenth-century writer as taking place at Witney in Oxfordshire 'in the dayes of ceremonial religion,' and one of the watchmen, which made a clacking noise, was 'comonly called Jack Snacker of Wytney[2].' This points to the use of some simple mechanical device by which motion was imparted to some at least of the puppets. A similar contrivance was produced by Bishop Barlow to point a sermon against idolatry at Paul's Cross in 1547 and was given afterwards to the boys to break into pieces[3]. More elaborate representations of miracle-plays by means of moving puppets or *marionnettes* make their appearance in all parts of Europe at a period when the regular dramatic performances of similar subjects were already becoming antiquated, nor can they be said to be even yet quite extinct[4]. Most of them belong to the repertory of the professional showmen, and it will be remembered that some form or other of *marionnette* seems to have been handed down continuously amongst the minstrel class from Roman times[5]. In England the puppet-shows were much in vogue at such places as Bartholomew Fair, where they became serious rivals of the living actors[6]. The earliest name for them was 'motions[7].' Italian players brought 'an instrument of strange motions' to London in 1574[8]. Autolycus, in *The Winter's Tale*, amongst his other shifts for a living,

---

[1] Cf. p. 42.

[2] W. Lambarde, *Alphabetical Description of the Chief Places in England and Wales* (1730, written in the sixteenth century), 459, s. v. Wytney.

[3] Gairdner, 253, quoting an unnamed chronicler, 'a picture of the Resurrection of Our Lord made with vices, which put out his legs of sepulchre, and blessed with his hand and turned his head.'

[4] Magnin, *Marionnettes*; J. Feller, *Le Bethléem vervietois* (*Bull. de la Soc. verviétoise d'Arch. et d'Hist.*

1900).

[5] Cf. vol. i. p. 71.

[6] Morley, *passim*; Hone, 229; Strutt, 164; T. Frost, *Old Showmen and Old London Fairs* (1874); W.B. Boulton, *Amusements of Old London*, ii. 49, 224.

[7] The term 'motion' is not, however, confined to puppet-plays. Bacon, Essay xxxvii, uses it of the dumb-shows of masquers, and Jonson, *Tale of a Tub*, v. 1, of shadow-plays.

[8] *P. C. Acts*, viii. 131.

'compassed a motion of the Prodigal Son[1].' Ben Jonson, in *Bartholomew Fair*, introduces one Lanthorn Leatherhead, a puppet-showman, who presents in his booth a curious rigmarole of a motion in which Hero and Leander, Damon and Pythias, and Dionysius are all mixed up[2]. It would appear to have been customary for the showman, like his brethren of the modern Punch and Judy, to 'interpret' for the puppets by reciting a suitable dialogue as an accompaniment to their gestures[3]. The repertory of Lanthorn Leatherhead contained a large proportion of 'motions' on subjects borrowed from the miracle-play. Similar titles occur in the notices of later performances at Bartholomew Fair[4] and of those given by the popular London showman, Robert Powell, during the reign of Queen Anne[5]. In more recent times all other puppet-shows have been outdone by the unique vogue of Punch and Judy[6]. The derivation of these personages from the Pontius Pilate and Judas Iscariot of the miracle-plays is the merest philological whimsy. Punch is doubtless the Pulcinella[7], who makes

---

[1] *Winter's Tale*, iv. 3. 102.

[2] *Bartholomew Fair*, v. 3; cf. v. 1. 8 'O, the motions that I, Lanthorn Leatherhead, have given light to in my time, since my master Pod died! Jerusalem was a stately thing, and so was Nineveh, and the City of Norwich, and Sodom and Gomorrah, with the rising of the prentices and pulling down the bawdy-houses there upon Shrove-Tuesday; but the Gunpowder Plot, there was a get-penny! I have presented that to an eighteen or twenty pence audience, nine times in an afternoon'; also *Every Man out of His Humour*, Induction:
'Will show more several motions in his face
Than the new London, Rome, or Nineveh.'

[3] Lanthorn Leatherhead says of his puppets, 'I am the mouth of them all'; cf. *Hamlet*, iii. 2. 256 'I could interpret between you and your love, if I could see the puppets dallying'; *Two Gentlemen of Verona*, ii. 1. 100 'O excellent motion! O exceeding puppet! Now

will he interpret to her.'

[4] Morley, 179, 187, 190, 247, 261, 273, 304, 321, records 'Patient Grisel' (1655, 1677), 'Susanna' (1655), 'Sodom and Gomorrah' (1656), 'Judith and Holophernes' (1664), 'Jephtha's Rash Vow' (1697, 1698, 1701, 1704, 1733), 'The Creation of the World' (1701).

[5] Powell's performances of the 'Creation of the World' at Bath and 'Susanna' at Covent Garden are referred to in the *Tatler* for May 14, 1709, and the *Spectator* for March 16, 1711.

[6] Hone, 230, describes a 'gallantee show' of the Prodigal Son and of Noah's Ark with a scene of 'Pull Devil, Pull Baker,' showing the judgement upon a baker who gave short weight (cf. the cut in Morley, 356), seen by him in London in 1818. This was an exhibition of *ombres chinoises* rather than a puppet-play proper.

[7] A. Dieterich, *Pulcinella*, 234, considers Pulcinella a descendant of Maccus, derives the name from *pullicenus*, *pulcinus*, *pullus*, and

his appearance about 1600 as a stock figure in the impromptu comedy of Naples. Under other names his traditions may, for all one knows, go back far beyond the miracle-plays to the *fabulae Atellanae*. But the particular drama in which alone he now takes the stage, although certainly not a miracle-play, follows closely upon the traditional lines of the moralities [1].

Another kind of religious dumb-show, at once more ancient and more important than that of the puppets, was presented by living persons in the 'ridings' or processions which formed an integral part of so many mediaeval festivals. Like the miracle-plays themselves, these *tableaux* reached their highest point of elaboration in connexion with the ceremonies of Corpus Christi day; and, in order to understand their relation to the regular dramas, it is necessary to return for a moment to the early history of the great feast. It has already been suggested that the processional character of the great English craft-cycles, with their movable pageants and their 'stations,' may be explained on the hypothesis, that the performances were at one time actually given during the 'stations' or pauses before temporary street altars of the Corpus Christi procession itself. The obvious inconveniences of such a custom, if it really existed, might not unnaturally lead to its modification. Except at Draguignan, where the dialogue was reduced to the briefest limits, no actual traces of it are left [2]. In England the difficulty seems to have been solved at Newcastle by sending the pageants round with the pro-

---

connects the fowl-masks of Italian comedy with the cockscomb of the English fool (cf. vol. i. p. 385).

[1] Collier, *Punch and Judy* (1870), 11 sqq.; Frost, *The Old Showmen and the Old London Fairs*, 29. The earliest English notice of Punch in England is in the overseers' books of St. Martin's-in-the-Fields for 1666 and 1667, 'Rec⁴ of Punchinello, yᵉ Italian popet player, for his booth at Charing Cross.' In a Bartholomew Fair playbill of the early eighteenth century, 'the merry conceits of Squire Punch and Sir John Spendall' were attached to the puppet-show of the Crea-

tion of the World. Punch was also amongst the *dramatis personae* of Robert Powell. The nature of these earlier Punch plays is unknown. That now traditional in England is implied by the ballad of *Punch's Pranks* (†1790). Collier, who prints it as given by one Piccini in Drury Lane, with cuts by Cruikshank, considers it to be derived from *Don Juan*. But it seems to me to come still nearer to the morality plays. French Punch plays have many other themes.

[2] Julleville, *Les Myst.* ii. 208; cf. p. 95.

cession in the early morning and deferring the actual plays until the afternoon. At Coventry representatives of the *dramatis personae* appear to have ridden in the procession, the cumbrous pageants being left behind until they were needed. Herod, for instance, rode on behalf of the smiths. At other places, again, the separation between procession and play was even more complete. The crafts which produced the plays were as a rule also burdened by their ordinances with the duties of providing a light and of walking or riding in honour of the host ; but the two ceremonies took place at different hours on the same day, and there was no external relation, so far as the evidence goes, between them. Even so there was still some clashing, and at York, after an unsuccessful attempt on the part of the clergy in 1426 to get the plays put off, the procession itself appears to have been transferred to the following day.

On the other hand the difficulty seems to have been met in certain towns by suppressing the plays and reducing them to dumb-show 'pageants' carried in the procession. Lists are extant of such pageants as they were assigned to the crafts at Dublin in 1498 and at Hereford in 1503, and although it is not of course impossible that there were to be plays later in the day, there is no proof that this was the case. For a similar procession of *tableaux* held in London, in the earlier part of the fifteenth century, a set of descriptive verses was written by John Lydgate, and the adoption of this method of 'interpreting' the dumb-show seems to put the possibility of a regular dramatic performance out of court [1].

[1] Printed by Halliwell, *Minor Poems of Lydgate* (Percy Soc.), 95, from Shirley's *Harl.* 2251, f. 293, as a *Processioune of Corpus Cristi*, with a note at the end that 'Shirley kowde fynde no more.' It is also, with the same note, in Shirley's *Trin. Coll. Camb. MS.* R. 3. 20, f. 348, with the heading, 'Ordenaunce of a p'cessyoun of the feste of Corpus Cristi, made in London by Daun John Lydegate' (E. P. Hammond, in *Anglia*, xxii. 364), and is copied thence by John Stowe in *B. M. Add. MS.* 29,729, f. 166. The piece is nᵒ. 153 in the list of Lydgate's works given by Ritson, *Bibl. Poet.* 79. It may be doubted whether Ritson's nᵒ. 152 'A Procession of pageants from the creation' is really distinct. Lydgate describes to his hearers 'figures shewed in your presence' which embody 'gracious mysteries grounded in Scripture.' Of course 'mysteries' has no technical dramatic sense here. Lydgate's method of 'interpreting' may have been based on the incorrect mediaeval notion of the methods of the classical stage,

There were pageants also in the Corpus Christi processions at Bungay and at Bury St. Edmunds, but the notices are too fragmentary to permit of more than a conjecture as to whether they were accompanied by plays. The *tableaux* shown at Dublin, Hereford, and London were of a continuous and cyclical character, although at Hereford St. Catherine, and at Dublin King Arthur, the Nine Worthies, and St. George's dragon were tacked on at the tail of the procession[1]. A continental parallel is afforded by the twenty-eight *remontrances*, making a complete cycle from the Annunciation to the Last Judgement, shown at Béthune in 1549[2]. But elsewhere, both in England and abroad, the shows of the Corpus Christi procession were of a much less systematic character, and Dublin was not the only place where secular elements crept in[3]. At Coventry, in addition to the representative figures from the craft-plays, the guild of Corpus Christi and St. Nicholas, to which, as to special Corpus Christi guilds elsewhere, the general supervision of the procession fell, provided in 1539 a Mary and a Gabriel with the lily, Saints Catherine and Margaret, eight Virgins and twelve Apostles.

which he adopts in his *Troy Book* (cf. p. 208). The 'figures' represented twenty-seven persons whose utterances revealed the mystery of the Mass. There were eight patriarchs, the Ecclesiast, four prophets, the Baptist, four evangelists, St. Paul, and seven Christian doctors.

[1] Sharp, 172, quotes from a contemporary writer a passage showing that the Dublin procession, like those of Coventry and Shrewsbury, lasted to a recent date: 'The Fringes was a procession of the trades and corporations, performed in Ireland on Corpus Christi day, even within the author's recollection. King Solomon, Queen of Sheba, with Vulcan, Venus, and Cupid, were leading persons upon this occasion.'

[2] Julleville, *Les Myst.* ii. 211; Davidson, 219.

[3] The following is from an account of a continental Corpus Christi procession in Barnabe Googe's translation of Naogeorgos' *Popish Kingdom* (1553), iv. 699 (Stubbes, i. 337):

'Christes passion here derided is, with sundrie maskes and playes;
Faire Ursley with hir maydens all, doth passe amid the wayes:
And valiant George, with speare thou killest the dreadfull dragon here;
The deuil's house is drawne about, wherein there doth appere
A wondrous sort of damned sprites, with foule and fearefull looke;
Great Christopher doth wade and passe with Christ amid the brooke:
Sebastian full of feathred shaftes, the dint of dart doth feele;
There walketh Kathren with hir sworde in hande, and cruell wheele:
The Challis and the singing Cake, with Barbara is led,
And sundrie other Pageants playde in worship of this bred, &c.'

The Coventry procession, it may be added, outlived the Corpus Christi feast. In the seventeenth century Godiva had been placed in it and became the most important feature. By the nineteenth century the wool-combers had a shepherd and shepherdess, their patron saint Bishop Blaize, and Jason with the Golden Fleece [1]. At the Shrewsbury 'Show,' which also until a recent date continued the tradition of an older Corpus Christi procession, Saints Crispin and Crispinian rode for the shoemakers. At Norwich the grocers sent the 'griffin' from the top of their pageant and a 'tree' which may have been the tree of knowledge from their Whitsun play of Paradise, but which was converted by festoons of fruit and spicery into an emblem of their trade [2].

Aberdeen seems to have been distinguished by having two great mimetic processions maintained by the guilds. The interpretation of the data is rather difficult, but apparently the 'Haliblude' play, which existed in 1440 and 1479, had given way by 1531 to a procession in which pageants of the Crucifixion, the Resurrection, and the Coronation of the Virgin were eked out by others of Saints Sebastian, Laurence, Stephen, Martin, Nicholas, John, and George. The other procession seems originally to have been introduced as an episode in a play of the Presentation in the Temple on Candlemas day. Its 'personnes' or 'pageants' are such as might furnish out the action of a short Nativity cycle, together with 'honest squiares' from each craft, 'wodmen,' and minstrels. But in this case also the play seems to have vanished early in the sixteenth century, while the procession certainly endured until a much later date.

There are no other English religious dumb-shows, outside those of Corpus Christi day, so elaborate as the Aberdeen Candlemas procession. On the same day at Beverley the guild of St. Mary carried a pageant of the Virgin and Child with Saints Joseph and Simon and two angels holding a great

---

[1] Sharp, 217, records a play of the *Golden Fleece* provided by Robert Crowe for the Cappers' Candlemas Dinner in 1525 ; the London drapers had a pageant with the same title in 1522 (cf. p. 165).

[2] Cf. the Paradise show at the London reception of Henry VI in 1432 (p. 170).

candlestick[1]. The guild of St. Helen, on the day of the
Invention of the Cross (May 3), had a procession with a boy
to represent the saint, and two men bearing a cross and a
shovel[2]. The guild of St. William of Norwich paraded
a knave-child between two men holding candles in honour
of the youthful martyr[3]. In the Whitsuntide procession at
Leicester walked the Virgin and Saint Martin, with the twelve
Apostles[4]. More interesting is the pageant of St. Thomas
the Martyr on December 29 at Canterbury, with the saint
on a cart and knights played by children and an altar and
a device of an angel and a 'leder bag for the blode[5].'
Probably this list could be largely increased were it worth
while[6]. The comparatively modern elements in the Corpus
Christi pageantry of Coventry, Shrewsbury, and Dublin may
be paralleled from the eighteenth-century festival of the
Preston guild merchant on or near St. John Baptist's day
with its Crispin and Crispinian, Bishop Blaize, Adam and
Eve, Vulcan, and so forth[7], or the nineteenth-century wool
trade procession on St. Blasius' day (February 3), at Bradford,
in which once more Bishop Blaize, with the Jason and Medea
of the Golden Fleece, appears[8]. It is noticeable how, as such
functions grow more civic and less religious, the pageants
tend to become distinctively emblematic of the trades
concerned. The same feature is to be observed in the choice
of subjects for the plays given by way of entertainment to
the earl of Kildare at Dublin in 1528.

The dumb-show pageants, which in many cities glorified
the 'ridings' on the day of St. George (April 23), have been

[1] Toulmin Smith, *English Guilds*,
149.
[2] Ibid. 148.   [3] Ibid. 30.
[4] Kelly, 7, 11.
[5] Cf. *Representations*, s. v. Canterbury.
[6] The 'pagent's paynted and
lemenyd with gold' of the Holy
Trinity, Saints Fabian, Sebastian,
and Botulph, 'and the last pagent
of the terement, & gen'all obyte, of
the brether'n and suster'n, that be
passed to God,' which the London
guild of the Holy Trinity had on a
' rolle of velom, cou'ed with a golde-
skyn' in 1463 (Hone, 81), were
probably not, as Davidson, 224,
thinks, 'a description and representation of the pageants which were
carried in procession by the guild,'
but illuminated pages (*paginae*).
For a similar misunderstanding cf.
p. 401, n. 1. Abp. Thoresby († 1357)
circulated a 'tretys in Englisce . . .
in smale pagynes' (Shirley, *Fasci-
culi Zizaniorum*, xiii).
[7] *Representations*, s. v. Preston.
[8] Dyer, 60.

described in an earlier chapter[1]. These 'ridings,' of curiously mingled religious and folk origin, stand midway between the processions just mentioned and such seasonal perambulations as the 'shows' and 'watches' of Midsummer. Even in the latter, elements borrowed from the pageants of the miracle-plays occasionally form an odd blend with the 'giants' and other figures of the 'folk' tradition[2]. The 'wache and playe' went together at Wymondham, and also apparently at Chelms-ford, in the sixteenth century. At York we find the pageants of some of the crafts borrowed for a play, though apparently a classical and not a religious one, at the Midsummer show of 1585. At Chester, when the Whitsun plays were beginning to fall into desuetude, the crafts were regularly represented in the Midsummer show by some of their *dramatis personae*, who, however, rode without their pageants. The smiths sent 'the Doctors and little God,' the butchers sent 'the divill in his fethers,' the barbers sent Abraham and Isaac, the brick-layers sent Balaam and the Ass, and so forth. These with the giants, a dragon, a man in woman's clothes, naked boys, morris-dancers and other folk elements, made up a singular cavalcade.

In London, pageants were provided for the Midsummer show by the guilds to which the lord mayor and sheriffs for the year belonged. Thus the drapers had a pageant of the Golden Fleece in 1522, and pageants of the Assumption and Saint Ursula in 1523[3]. To a modern imagination the type of civic pageantry is the annual procession at the installation of the lord mayor in November, known familiarly as the lord mayor's show. This show was important enough from the middle of the sixteenth century, and the pens of many goodly poets, Peele, Dekker, Munday, Middleton, and others, were employed in its service[4]. But its history cannot be taken much further back, and it is exceedingly probable that when the Midsummer show came to an end in 1538, the pageants were transferred to the installation procession. The earliest

[1] Cf. vol. i. p. 221.
[2] Cf. vol. i. pp. 118, 120.
[3] Cf. *Representations*, s.v. London.
[4] J. G. Nichols, *London Pageants*

(1837); F. W. Fairholt, *Lord Mayor's Pageants* (1843–4, Percy Soc. nos. 38, 43), and *The Civic Garland* (Percy Soc. 1845).

clear notice is in 1540, when a pageant of the Assumption, perhaps that which had already figured at the Midsummer show of 1523, was used[1]. The ironmongers had a pageant when the lord mayor was chosen from their body in 1566. It was arranged by James Peele, father of the dramatist, and there were two 'wodmen' in it, but unfortunately it is not further described[2]. In 1568, Sir Thomas Roe, merchant tailor, had a pageant of John the Baptist[3]. William Smith, writing an account of city customs in 1575, mentions, as a regular feature of the procession, 'the Pagent of Triumph richly decked, whereupon, by certain figures and writings, some matter touching Justice and the office of a Magistrate is represented[4].' And about ten years later the series of printed 'Devices' of the pageants begins.

The influence of miracle-plays and moralities is also to be looked for in the municipal 'shows' of welcome provided at the state entries of royal and other illustrious visitors. A large number of these, chiefly at coronations, royal marriages and the like, are recorded in chronicles of London origin, and with the London examples in their chronological order I will briefly deal. The earlier features of such ceremonies include the riding of the mayor and corporation to meet the king at some place outside the gates, such as Blackheath, or, in the case of a coronation, at the Tower, and the escorting of him with joyous *tripudium* or *carole* to the palace of Westminster, the reading of loyal addresses and the giving of golden gifts, the decking of walls and balconies with costly robes and tapestries, the filling of the conduits with wine, white and red, in place of the accustomed water[5]. The first example

---

[1] Herbert, i. 457. The same writer quotes a payment from the drapers' accounts of 1516 of £13 4s.7d. for 'Sir Laurens Aylmer's Pageant.' But this cannot have been intended for a lord mayor's show, for Aylmer's only mayoralty was in 1507–8, and a grocer, not a draper, was mayor in 1515–6 and in 1516–7.

[2] Malcolm, *Londinium Redivivum*, ii. 42; W. C. Hazlitt, *Livery Companies* (1892), 310.

[3] Herbert, i. 199.

[4] W. Smith, *A breffe description of the Royall Citie of London* (1575), quoted by Nichols, 95.

[5] The *Annales Londonienses* record at the visit of the Emperor Otho to King John in 1207 'tota civitas Londoniae induit solempnitatem pallis et aliis ornamentis circumornata,' and at the entry of Edward II after his marriage in 1308 'tapeti aurei' and the city dignitaries 'coram rege et regina

of pageantry in the proper sense occurs about the middle of
the thirteenth century, in certain 'devices and marvels' shown
at the wedding of Henry III to Eleanor of Provence in
1236[1]. These are not described in detail; but when Edward I
returned to London after the defeat of William Wallace at
Falkirk in 1298, it is recorded by a chronicler, quoted in
Stowe's *Annals*, that the crafts made 'great and solemne
triumph' and that the fishmongers in particular 'amongst
other pageantes and shewes' had, as it was St. Magnus's day,
one of the saint accompanied by a thousand horsemen, and
preceded by four gilded sturgeons, four salmons on horseback
and 'sixe and fourtie knights armed, riding on horses made
like luces of the sea[2].' It was the fishmongers again who on
the birth of Edward III in 1313 went in a *chorea* to Westminster with an ingeniously contrived ship in full sail, and
escorted the queen on her way to Eltham[3]. At the coronation
of Richard II in 1377 an elaborate castle was put up at the
head of Cheapside. On the four towers of this stood four
white-robed damsels, who wafted golden leaves in the king's
face, dropped gilt models of coin upon him and his steed, and
offered him wine from pipes laid on to the structure. Between
the towers was a golden angel, which by a mechanical device
bent forward and held out a crown as Richard drew near[4].
Similar stages, with a *coelicus ordo* of singers and boys and
maidens offering wine and golden crowns, stood in Cheapside
when Richard again rode through the city in 1392, in token

karolantes' (*Chronicles of the
Reigns of Edw. I and Edw. II*,
R. S. i. 13, 152). At the coronation of Henry IV in 1399 was an
'equitatio magnifica' (*Annales
Hen. IV*, R. S. 291), and the streets
were hung with 'paremens,' and
there were 'nœuf broucherons a
manière de fontaines en Cep a
Londres, courans par plusieurs
conduits, jettans vin blanc et ver-
meil' (Froissart, *Chroniques*, ed.
Kervyn de Lettynhove, xvi. 205).

[1] M. Paris, *Chronica Maiora*
(R. S.), iii. 336 'quibusdam pro-
digiosis ingeniis et portentis.'

[2] Stowe, *Annals*, 207. The authority quoted in the margin is 'Chro.
Dun.,' which I cannot identify. It
is not the Dunstable Annals in the
Annales monastici (R. S.), vol. iii.

[3] *Annales Londonienses* (*Chron.
of Edw. I and Edw. II*, R. S.), i.
221 'quaedam navis, quodam
mirabili ingenio operata, cum malo
et velo erectis, et depictis de supradictis armis [of England and
France] et varietate plurima'; cf.
H. T. Riley, *Memorials of London*,
107, from *Corporation Letter Book
D*. f. 168.

[4] T. Walsingham, *Hist. Anglica*
(R. S.), i. 331.

of reconciliation with the rebellious Londoners. And at St. Paul's was a youth enthroned amongst a triple circle of singing angels; and at Temple Bar St. John Baptist in the desert surrounded by all kinds of trees and a menagerie of strange beasts [1]. No similar details of pageantry are recorded at the coronations of Henry IV or Henry V. But when the latter king returned to London after the battle of Agincourt in 1415 there was a very fine show indeed. The procession came to the city from Eltham and Blackheath by way of London Bridge. Upon the tower masking the bridge stood two gigantic figures, one a man with an axe in his right hand and the city keys in his left, the other a woman in a scarlet mantle. Beyond this were two columns painted to resemble white marble and green jasper, on which were a lion and an antelope bearing the royal arms and banner. Over the foot of the bridge was a tower with a figure of St. George, and on a house hard by a number of boys representing the heavenly host, who sang the anthem *Benedictus qui venit in nomine Dei.* The tower upon the Cornhill conduit was decked with red and had on it a company of prophets, who sent a flight of sparrows and other birds fluttering round the king as he passed, while the prophets chanted *Cantate Domino canticum novum.* The tower of the great Cheapside conduit was green, and here were twelve Apostles and twelve Kings, Martyrs and Confessors of England, whose anthem was *Benedic, anima, Domino,* and who, even as Melchisedek received Abraham with bread and wine, offered the king thin wafers mixed with silver leaves, and a cup filled from the conduit pipes. On Cheapside, the cross was completely hidden by a great castle, in imitation white marble and green and red jasper, out of the door of which issued a bevy of virgins, with timbrel and dance and songs of 'Nowell, Nowell,' like unto the daughters of Israel who danced before David after the slaying of Goliath. On the castle stood boys feathered like angels, who sang *Te Deum* and flung down gold coins and boughs of laurel. Finally, on the tower of the little conduit near St. Paul's, all blue as the sky,

---

[1] Fabyan, 538; H. Knighton, *Chronicon* (R. S.), ii. 320; Richard Maydiston, *De concordia inter* *regem Ricardum II et civitatem London* (*Political Poems,* R. S. i. 282).

were more virgins who, as when Richard II was crowned, wafted golden leaves out of golden cups, while above were wrought angels in gold and colours, and an image of the sun enthroned [1]. The details of the reception of Henry and Catherine of France, six years later, are not preserved [2]. Nor are those of the London coronation of Henry VI in 1429. But there was a grand dumb-show at the Paris coronation in 1431 [3], and it was perhaps in emulation of this that on his return to London in the following year the king was received with a splendour equal to that lavished on the victor of Agincourt. There is a contemporary account of the proceedings by John Carpenter, the town clerk of London [4]. As in 1415 a giant greeted the king at the foot of London Bridge. On the same 'pageant [5]' two antelopes upbore the arms of England and France. On the bridge stood a magnificent 'fabric,' occupied by Nature, Grace, and Fortune, who gave the king presents as he passed. To the right were the seven heavenly Virtues, who signified the seven gifts of the Holy Ghost, by letting fly seven white doves. To the left, seven other virgins offered the regalia. Then all fourteen, clapping their hands and rejoicing in *tripudia*, broke into songs of welcome. In Cornhill was the Tabernacle of Lady Wisdom, set upon seven columns. Here stood Wisdom, and here the seven liberal Sciences were represented by Priscian, Aristotle, Tully, Boethius, Pythagoras, Euclid, and Albumazar. On the conduit was the Throne of Justice, on which sat a king surrounded by Truth, Mercy, and Clemency, with two Judges and eight Lawyers. In Cheapside was a Paradise with a grove full of all manner of foreign fruits, and three wells from which

[1] Full contemporary accounts in *Gesta Henrici Quinti* (Eng. Hist. Soc.), 61, and a set of verses by John Lydgate printed in *London Chronicle*, 214, and H. Nicolas, *Hist. of Agincourt* (1833), 326; more briefly in *London Chronicle*, 103; T. Walsingham, *Hist. Anglic.* (R. S.), ii. 314; cf. C. L. Kingsford, *Henry V*, 156.

[2] T. Walsingham, *Hist. Anglica* (R. S.), ii. 336 'ludicis et vario apparatu.'

[3] Cf. p. 174.

[4] Printed from *Corp. Letter Book K.* f. 103[v], by H. T. Riley, *Liber Albus* (R.S.), iii. 457; cf. descriptive verses by Lydgate, *Minor Works* (Percy Soc.), 2; *London Chronicle*, 119; Fabyan, 603; Gregory, 173.

[5] Carpenter uses the term *pagina*, which here occurs for the first time in connexion with these London receptions. Mr. Riley quite unnecessarily proposes to read *machina.*

gushed out wine, served by Mercy, Grace, and Pity. Here the
king was greeted by Enoch and Elijah [1]. At the cross was
a castle of jasper with a Tree of Jesse, and another of the
royal descent ; and at St. Paul's conduit a representation of
the Trinity amongst a host of ministering angels. In 1445
Margaret of Anjou came to London to be crowned. Stowe
records ' a few only ' of the pageants. She entered by South-
wark bridge foot where were Peace and Plenty. On the
bridge was Noah's ship ; in Leadenhall, ' madam Grace
Chancelor de Dieu ' ; on the Tun in Cornhill, St. Margaret ;
on the conduit in Cheapside, the Wise and Foolish Virgins ;
at the Cross, the Heavenly Jerusalem ; and at Paul's Gate,
the General Resurrection and Judgement [2].

The rapid kingings and unkingings of the wars of the Roses
left little time and little heart for pageantries, but with the
advent of Henry VII they begin again, and continue with
growing splendour throughout the Tudor century. Space
only permits a brief enumeration of the subjects chosen for
set pageants on a few of the more important occasions.
Singing angels and precious gifts, wells of wine and other
minor delights may be taken for granted [3]. As to the details
of Henry VII's coronation in 1485 and marriage in 1486
the chroniclers are provokingly silent, and of the many
' gentlemanlie pageants ' at the coronation of the queen in
1487 the only one specified is ' a great redde dragon spouting
flames of fyer into the Thames,' from the ' bachelors' barge '

---

[1] A pun was concealed here, for
John de *Welles*, grocer, was mayor,
and the ' oranges, almonds, and the
pomegranade ' on the trees were
the grocers' wares. Cf. the tree of
the Norwich grocers in the Corpus
Christi procession (p. 163).

[2] Stowe, *Annals*, 385 ; cf. *London
Chronicle*, 134 ' goodly sights
ayenst her coming ' ; Fabyan, 617
' sumptuous and costly pagentes,
and resemblaunce of dyuerse olde
hystoryes ' ; Gregory, 186 ' many
notabylle devysys in the cytte.'
According to Stowe, Lydgate wrote
verses for these pageants.

[3] A memorandum of ceremonial
As ffor the ressaunge off a Quene and

her Crownacion of the reign of
Henry VII (*Antiquarian Repertory*,
i. 302) has the following direction
for the riding from the Tower to
Westminster, ' at the condit in
Cornylle ther must be ordined a
sight w[t] angelles singinge and
freche balettes y[ron] in latene,
engliche and ffrenche, mad by the
wyseste docturs of this realme ; and
the condyt of Chepe in the same
wyse ; and the condit must ryn
bothe red wyn and whit wyne ; and
the crosse in Chepe muste be araid
in y[e] most rialle wyse that might
be thought ; and the condit next
Poules in the same wyse.'

of the lord mayor's company as she passed up the river from Greenwich to the Tower[1]. At the wedding of Prince Arthur to Katharine of Aragon in 1501, 'vi goodly beutiful pageauntes' lined the way from London Bridge to St. Paul's. The contriver is said to have been none other than Bishop Foxe the great chancellor and the founder of Corpus Christi College in Oxford. The subject of the first pageant was the Trinity with Saints Ursula and Katharine; of the second, the Castle of Portcullis, with Policy, Nobleness, and Virtue; of the third, Raphael, the angel of marriage, with Alphonso, Job, and Boethius; of the fourth, the Sphere of the Sun; of the fifth, the Temple of God; and of the sixth, Honour with the seven Virtues[2]. As to Henry VIII's coronation and marriage there is, once more, little recorded. In 1522 came Charles V, Emperor of Germany, to visit the king, and the city provided eleven pageants 'very faire and excellent to behold[3].' The 'great red dragon' of 1487 reappeared in 1533 when yet another queen, Anne Boleyn, came up from Greenwich to enjoy her brief triumph. It stood on a 'foist' near the lord mayor's barge, and in another 'foist' was a mount, and on the mount Anne's device, a falcon on a root of gold with white roses and red. The pageants for the progress by land on the following day were of children 'apparelled like merchants,' of Mount Parnassus, of the falcon and mount once more, with Saint Anne and her children, of the three Graces, of Pallas, Juno, Venus, and Mercury with the golden apple, of three ladies, and of the Cardinal Virtues[4]. The next great show was at the coronation of Edward VI in 1547, and included Valentine and Orson, Grace, Nature, Fortune and Charity, Sapience and the seven Liberal Sciences, Regality enthroned with Justice, Mercy and Truth, the Golden Fleece, Edward the Confessor and St. George, Truth, Faith, and

---

[1] Contemporary account in Leland, *Collectanea* (ed. Hearne), iv. 218, and J. Ives, *Select Papers* (1773), 127.
[2] Minutely detailed contemporary account in *Antiquarian Repertory*, ii. 248; cf. Stowe, *Annals*, 483; Hazlitt-Warton, iii. 160.

[3] Stowe, *Annals*, 517; Hall, 638; cf. *Representations* (London).
[4] Minutely detailed contemporary account in *Antiquarian Repertory*, ii. 232; Hall, 801; Collier, ii. 353. Leland's and Udall's verses for the pageants are in *Ballads from MSS.*, i. 378 (Ballad Soc.).

Justice. There was also a cunning Spanish rope-dancer, who performed marvels on a cord stretched to the ground from the tower of St. George's church in St. Paul's churchyard[1]. Mary, in 1553, enjoyed an even more thrilling spectacle in 'one Peter a Dutchman,' who stood and waved a streamer on the weathercock of St. Paul's steeple. She had eight pageants, of which three were contributed by the Genoese, Easterlings, and Florentines. The subjects are unknown, but that of the Florentines was in the form of a triple arch and had on the top a trumpeting angel in green, who moved his trumpet to the wonder of the crowd[2]. There were pageants again when Mary brought her Spanish husband to London in 1554. At the conduit in Gracechurch Street were painted the Nine Worthies. One of these was Henry VIII, who was represented as handing a bible to Edward; and the unfortunate painter was dubbed a knave and a rank traitor and villain by Bishop Gardiner, because the bible was not put in the hands of Mary[3]. At the coronation of Elizabeth in 1559, with which this list must close, it was Time and Truth who offered the English bible to the queen. The same pageant had representations of a Decayed Commonwealth and a Flourishing Commonwealth, while others figured the Union of York and Lancaster, the Seat of Worthy Governance, the Eight Beatitudes, and Deborah the Judge. At Temple Bar, those ancient *palladia* of London city, the giants Gotmagot and Corineus, once more made their appearance[4].

I do not wish to exaggerate the influence exercised by the miracle-plays and moralities over these London shows. London was not, in the Middle Ages, one of the most dramatic of English cities, and such plays as there were were not in the hands of those trade- and craft-guilds to whom the glorifying of the receptions naturally fell. The functions carried out by the fishmongers in 1298 and 1313 are much of the nature of masked ridings or 'disguisings,' and must be held to have a folk origin. The ship of 1313 suggests a 'hobby ship[5].'

---

[1] Contemporary account in Leland, *Collectanea* (ed. Hearne), iv. 313.
[2] Stowe, *Annals*, 616; cf. *Texts*, s. v. John Heywood.
[3] Holinshed, iii. 1121.
[4] Contemporary account in Nichols, *Progresses of Elizabeth*, i. 38.
[5] Cf. vol. i. p. 121.

Throughout the shows draw notions from many heterogeneous sources. The giants afford yet another ' folk ' element. The gifts of gold and wine and the speeches of welcome [1] need no explanation. Devices of heraldry are worked in. The choirs of boys and girls dressed as angels recall the choirs perched on the battlements of churches in such ecclesiastical ceremonies as the Palm Sunday procession [2]. The term ' pageant ' (*pagina*), which first appears in this connexion in 1432 and is in regular use by the end of the century, is perhaps a loan from the plays, but the structures themselves appear to have arisen naturally out of attempts to decorate such obvious architectural features of the city as London Bridge, the prison known as the Tun, and the conduits which stood in Cornhill and Cheapside [3]. It is chiefly in the selection of themes for the more elaborate mimetic pageants that the reflection of the regular contemporary drama must be traced. Such scriptural subjects as John the Baptist of 1392 or the Prophets and Apostles of 1415 pretty obviously come from the miracle-plays. The groups of allegorical figures which greeted Henry VI in 1432 are in no less close a relation to the moralities, which were at that very moment beginning to outstrip the miracle-plays in popularity. And in the reign of Henry VII the humanist tendencies begin to suggest subjects for the pageants as well as to transform the drama itself.

Certainly one does not find in London or in any English city those *mystères mimés* or cyclical dumb-shows, with which the good people of Paris were wont to welcome kings, and which are clearly an adaptation of the ordinary miracle-play to the conditions of a royal entry with its scant time for long drawn-out dialogue. The earliest of these upon record was in 1313 when Philip IV entertained Edward II and Isabella. It is not quite clear whether this was

---

[1] Warton, iii. 158, says that ' Speakers seem to have been admitted into our pageants about the reign of Henry VI.' But there were songs, and for all we know, speeches also in 1377 and 1415. Verses such as Lydgate wrote for pageants were often fastened on them, and read or not read aloud when the visitor approached, as might be convenient.

[2] Cf. p. 5.

[3] Wheatley-Cunningham, *London Past and Present*, i. 373, 458 ; iii. 409.

a procession like the disguising called the *procession du renard* which accompanied it, or a stationary dumb-show on pageants. But there is no doubt about the *moult piteux mystere de la Passion de Nostre Seigneur au vif* given before Charles VI and Henry V after the treaty of Troyes in 1420, for this is said to have been on *eschaffaulx* and to have been modelled on the bas-reliefs around the choir of Notre-Dame. Very similar must have been the *moult bel mystere du Vieil testament et du Nouvel* which welcomed the duke of Bedford in 1424 and which *fut fait sans parler ne sans signer, comme ce feussent ymaiges enlevez contre ung mur*. *Sans parler*, again, was the *mystère* which stood on an *eschaffault* before the church of the Trinity when Henry VI was crowned, only a few weeks before the London reception already mentioned [1].

It may be added that in many provincial towns the pageants used at royal entries had a far closer affinity to the miracle-plays proper than was the case in London. The place most often honoured in this sort was Coventry. In 1456 came Queen Margaret and poor mad Henry VI. One John Wedurley of Leicester seems to have been employed to organize a magnificent entertainment. At Bablake gate, where stood a Jesse, the royal visitors were greeted by Isaiah and Jeremiah. Within the gate was a 'pagent' with Saint Edward the Confessor and St. John the Evangelist. On the conduit in Smithford Street were the four Cardinal Virtues. In the Cheaping were nine pageants for the Nine Worthies. At the cross there were angels, and wine flowed, and at another conduit hard by was St. Margaret 'sleyng' her dragon and a company of angels. The queen was so pleased that she returned next year for Corpus Christi day. It appears from the smiths' accounts that the pageants used at the reception were those kept by the crafts for the plays. The smiths' pageant was had out again in 1461, with Samson upon it, when Edward IV came after his coronation, and in 1474 when the young prince Edward came for St. George's feast. The shows then represented King Richard II and his court, Patriarchs and Prophets, St. Edward the Confessor, the Three Kings of Cologne and St. George slaying

[1] Julleville, *Les Myst.* i. 196; ii. 186.

the dragon. Prince Arthur, in 1498, saw the Nine Worthies, the Queen of Fortune, and, once more, Saint George. For Henry VIII and Katharine of Aragon in 1511 there were three pageants: on one the ninefold hierarchy of angels, on another 'divers beautiful damsels,' on the third 'a goodly stage play.' The mercers' pageant 'stood' at the visit of the Princess Mary in 1525, and the tanners', drapers', smiths', and weavers' pageants at that of Queen Elizabeth in 1565. I do not know whether it is legitimate to infer that the subjects represented on these occasions were those of the Corpus Christi plays belonging to the crafts named [1].

York was visited by Richard III in 1483, and there were pageants, the details of which have not been preserved, as well as a performance of the Creed play [2]. It was also visited by Henry VII in 1486, and there exists a civic order prescribing the pageants for that occasion. The first of these was a most ingenious piece of symbolism. There was a heaven and beneath it 'a world desolaite, full of treys and floures.' Out of this sprang 'a roiall, rich, rede rose' and 'an othre rich white rose,' to whom all the other flowers did 'lowte and evidently yeve suffrantie.' Then appeared out of a cloud a crown over the roses, and then a city with citizens with 'Ebrauk' the founder, who offered the keys to the king. The other pageants represented Solomon and the six Henries, the Castle of David, and Our Lady. There were also devices by which a rain of rose-water and a hailstorm of comfits fell before the king [3]. During the same progress which took Henry to York, he also visited Worcester, where there were pageants and speeches, 'whiche his Grace at that Tyme harde not' but which should have represented Henry VI and a *Ianitor ad Ianuam*. Thence he went to Hereford, and was greeted by St. George, King Ethelbert, and Our Lady; thence to Gloucester, where the chronicler remarks with some surprise that 'ther was no Pageant nor Speche ordeynede'; and finally to Bristol, where were King Bremmius, Prudence, Justice, 'the Shipwrights Pageannt,' without any speech,

[1] Sharp, 145.
[2] Davies, 162, 171, 282.
[3] J. Raine, *English Miscellanies* (Surtees Soc., vol. lxxxv), 53, from *Corporation House Book*, vi. 15.

and a 'Pageannte of an Olifaunte, with a Castell on his Bakk' and 'The Resurrection of our Lorde in the highest Tower of the same, with certeyne Imagerye smytyng Bellis, and all wente by Veights, merveolously wele done [1].' In 1503 Henry VII's daughter Margaret married James IV of Scotland, and was received into Edinburgh with pageants of the Judgement of Paris, the Annunciation, the Marriage of Joseph and Mary, and the Four Virtues [2]. Eight years later, in 1511, she visited Aberdeen, and the 'pleasant padgeanes' included Adam and Eve, the Salutation of the Virgin, the *Magi*, and the Bruce [3].

The facts brought together in the present chapter show how 'pageant' came to have its ordinary modern sense of a spectacular procession. How it was replaced by other terms in the sense of 'play' will be matter for the sequel. It may be added that the name is also given to the elaborate structures of carpenters' and painters' work used in the early Tudor masks [4]. These the masks probably took over from the processions and receptions. On the other hand, the receptions, by an elaboration of the spoken element, developed into the Elizabethan 'Entertainments,' which are often classified as a sub-variety of the mask itself. This action and reaction of one form of show upon another need not at this stage cause any surprise. A sixteenth-century synonym for 'pageant' is 'triumph,' which is doubtless a translation of the Italian *trionfo*, a name given to the *edifizio* by the early Renascence, in deliberate reminiscence of classical terminology [5].

[1] Contemporary account in Leland, *Collectanea* (ed. Hearne), iv. 185. A description of an earlier reception of Edward IV at Bristol with 'Wylliam conquerour,' 'a greet Gyaunt delyueryng the Keyes,' and St. George is in Furnivall, *Political, Religious, and Love Poems* (E.E. T.S.), 5.

[2] Leland, *Collectanea*, iv. 263.

[3] Cf. *Representations*, s.v. Aberdeen.

[4] Cf. vol. i. p. 398.

[5] Symonds, *Renaissance in Italy*, iv. 338.

BOOK IV

THE INTERLUDE

Patronage cannot kill art : even in kings' palaces the sudden flower blooms serene.

MODERN PLAY.

CHAPTER XXIV

PLAYERS OF INTERLUDES

[*Bibliographical Note.*—The *Annals of the Stage* in J. P. Collier. *History of English Dramatic Poetry* (new ed. 1879), although ill arranged and by no means trustworthy, now become of value. They may be supplemented from the full notices of Tudor *spectacula* in E. Hall, *The Union of Lancaster and York,* 1548, ed. 1809, and from the various calendars of State papers, of which J. S. Brewer and J. Gairdner, *Letters and Papers of the Reign of Henry VIII* (1862-1903), including the *Revels Accounts* and the *Kings Books of Payments,* is the most important. Some useful documents are in W. C. Hazlitt, *The English Drama and Stage* (1869). The French facts are given by L. Petit de Julleville, *Les Comédiens en France au Moyen Âge* (1889).]

THE closing section of this essay may fitly be introduced by a brief retrospect of the conclusions already arrived at. The investigation, however it may have lingered by the way, has not been altogether without its *logos* or rational framework. The first book began with a study of the conditions under which the degenerate stage of the Roman Empire ceased to exist. The most important of these were the indifference of the barbarians and the direct hostility of the Church. A fairly clean sweep was made. Scarcely a thread of dramatic tradition is to be traced amongst the many and diverse forms of entertainment provided by mediaeval minstrelsy. But the very existence of minstrelsy, itself a singular blend of Latin and barbaric elements, is a proof of the enduring desire of the western European peoples for something in the nature of *spectacula*. In the strength of this the minstrels braved the ban of the Church, and finally won their way to at least a partial measure of toleration from their hereditary foes. In the second book it was shown that the instinct for *spectacula* had its definitely dramatic side. The *ludi* of the folk, based upon ancient observances of a forgotten natural religion, and surviving side by side with minstrelsy, broke out at point after point into *mimesis*. Amongst the villages they developed into dramatic May-games and dramatic sword-dances: in their *bourgeois* forms they overran city and cathedral with the mimicries of the Feast of Fools and the Boy Bishop; they gave birth to a special type of drama in the mask; and they further enriched Tudor revels with the characteristic figures of the domestic fool or jester and the lord of misrule. Upon the folk *ludi*, as upon the *spectacula* of the minstrels, the Church looked doubtfully. But the mimetic instinct was irresistible, and in the end it was neither minstrels nor folk, but the Church itself, which did most for its satisfaction. The subject of the third book is a remarkable growth of drama within the heart of the ecclesiastical liturgy, which began in the tenth century, and became, consciously or unconsciously, a powerful counterpoise to the attraction of *ludi* and *spectacula*. So popular, indeed, did it prove that it broke the bonds of ecclesiastical control; and about the thirteenth century a process of laicization set in, which culminated during the fourteenth in the great Corpus Christi cycles of the municipal guilds. The subject-matter, however, remained religious to the end, an end which, in spite of the marked critical attitude adopted by the austerer schools of churchmen, did not arrive until that attitude was confirmed by successive waves of Lollard and Protestant sentiment. Nor was the system substantially affected by certain innovations of the fifteenth century, a tendency to substitute mere spectacular pageantry for the spoken drama, and a tendency to add to the visible presentment of the scriptural history an allegorical exposition of theological and moral doctrine.

   It is the object of the present book briefly to record the rise, also in the fifteenth century, of new dramatic conditions which, after existing for a while side by side with those of mediaevalism, were destined ultimately to become a substitute for these and to lead up directly to the magic stage of Shakespeare. The change to be sketched is primarily a social rather than a literary one. The drama which had already migrated from the church to the market-place, was to migrate still further, to the banqueting-hall. And having passed from the hands of the clergy to those of the folk, it was now to pass, after an interval of a thousand years, not immediately but ultimately, into those of a professional class of actors. Simultaneously it was to put off its exclusively religious character, and enter upon a new heritage of interests and methods, beneath the revivifying breath of humanism.

A characteristic note of the new phase is the rise of the term *interludium* or 'interlude.' This we have already come across in the title of that fragmentary *Interludium de Clerico et Puella* which alone amongst English documents seemed to bear witness to a scanty dramatic element in the repertory of minstrelsy [1]. The primary meaning of the name is a matter of some perplexity. The learned editors of the *New English Dictionary* define it as 'a dramatic or mimic representation, usually of a light or humorous character, such as was commonly introduced between the acts of the long mystery-plays or moralities, or exhibited as part of an elaborate entertainment.' Another recognized authority, Dr. Ward, says [2]: 'It seems to have been applied to plays performed by professional actors from the time of Edward IV onwards. Its origin is doubtless to be found in the fact that such plays were occasionally performed in the intervals of banquets and entertainments, which of course would have been out of the question in the case of religious plays proper.' I cannot say that I find either of these explanations at all satisfactory. In the first place, none of the limitations of sense which they suggest are really borne out by the history of the word. So far as its rare use in the fourteenth century goes, it is not confined to professional plays and it does not exclude religious plays. The *Interludium de Clerico et Puella* is, no doubt, a farce, and something of the same sort appears to be in the mind of Huchown, or whoever else was the author of *Sir Gawain and the Green Knight,* when he speaks of laughter and song as a substitute for 'enterludez' at Christmas [3].

---

[1] Cf. vol. i. p. 86.
[2] Ward, i. 108. The limitation by Collier, ii. 299, of 'what may be properly, and strictly, called *Interludes*' to farces of the type affected by John Heywood has introduced a most inconvenient semi-technical term into literary nomenclature. I do not so limit the word.

[3] *Gawain and the G. K.* 472:
'Wel bycommes such craft vpon, cristmasse,
Laykyng of enterludez, to laȝe & to syng.'

But on the other hand, Robert Mannyng of Brunne, at the very beginning of the century, classes 'entyrludes' with 'somour games' and other forbidden delights of the folk[1], while the Wyclifite author of the *Tretise on Miriclis* at its close, definitely uses 'entirlodies' as a name for the religious plays which he is condemning[2]. In the fifteenth century, again, although 'interlude' is of course not one of the commonest terms for a miracle-play, yet I find it used for performances probably of the miracle-play type at New Romney in 1426 and at Harling in 1452, while the jurats of the former place paid in 1463 for 'the play of the interlude of our Lord's Passion[3].' The term, then, appears to be equally applicable to every kind of drama known to the Middle Ages. As to its philological derivation, both the *New English Dictionary* and Dr. Ward treat it as a *ludus* performed in the intervals of (*inter*) something else, although they do not agree as to what that something else was. For the performance of farces 'between the acts of the long miracle-plays' there is no English evidence whatever[4]. The farcical episodes which find a place in the Towneley plays and elsewhere are in no way structurally differentiated from the rest of the text. There are some French examples of combined performances of farces and miracles, but they do not go far enough back to explain the origin of the word[5]. A certain support is no doubt

---

[1] Cf. vol. i. p. 93.

[2] Hazlitt, *E. D. S.* 80 'How thanne may a prist pleyn in entirlodies?' In Barbour, *Bruce* († 1375), x. 145 'now may ȝe heir ... Interludys and iuperdys, þat men assayit on mony vis Castellis and pelis for till ta,' the sense is metaphorical, as in 'ioculando et talia verba asserendo interludia fuisse vanitatis' quoted by Ducange from *Vit. Abb. S. Alb.*', i.e. probably Thomas Walsingham († 1422), not Matthew Paris († 1249). The reading is doubtful in Anastasius Bibliothecarius (9th cent.), *Hist. Pontif.* (*P. L.* lxxx. 1352), 'quem iussit sibi praesentari in interludo noctu ante templum Palladis.'

[3] For probable 1385 cases, cf.

Representations, s.v. King's Lynn.

[4] A 'vyce' made pastime before and after a play at Bungay, but this was not until 1566.

[5] Julleville, *Les Com.* 97. These performances were known as *les pois pilés* and began about the middle of the fourteenth century. The Anglo - French *entrelude*, asterisked by the *N. E. D.*, is found in 1427 (cf. p. 186). Collier's theory receives some support from the Spanish use of the term *entremes* for a comic piece played in conjunction with a serious *auto*. But the earlier sense of *entremes* itself appears to be for an independent farce played at banquets (Ticknor, *Hist. of Span. Lit.* (ed. 1888), i. 231 ; ii. 449).

given to the theory of the *New English Dictionary* by the 'mirry interludes' inserted in Sir David Lyndsay's morality *Ane Satyre of the Thrie Estaits*, but, once more, it is difficult to elucidate a term which appears at the beginning of the fourteenth century from an isolated use in the middle of the sixteenth. Dr. Ward's hypothesis is perhaps rather more plausible. No doubt plays were performed at court and elsewhere between the banquet and the 'void' or cup of spiced drink which followed later in the evening, and possibly also between the courses of the banquet itself[1]. But this fact would not differentiate dramatic *ludi* from other forms of minstrelsy coming in the same intervals, and the fact that miracle-plays are called interludes, quite as early as anything else, remains to be accounted for. I am inclined myself to think that the force of *inter* in the combination has been misunderstood, and that an *interludium* is not a *ludus* in the intervals of something else, but a *ludus* carried on between (*inter*) two or more performers; in fact, a *ludus* in dialogue. The term would then apply primarily to any kind of dramatic performance whatever.

In any case it is clear that while 'interlude' was only a subordinate name for plays of the miracle-type, it was the normal name, varied chiefly by 'play' and 'disguising,' for plays given in the banqueting-halls of the great[2]. These

[1] Cf. the accounts in Leland, *Collectanea*, iv. 228, 236, of the court of Henry VII. Douglas, *Palace of Honour*, ii. 410 'At eis they eit with interludis betwene,' dates from 1501. Horman, *Vulgaria* (1519), quoted on p. 137, speaks of the 'paiantis' of a play as corresponding in number to the courses of a feast. Much earlier Raoul de Presles (†1374) in his *Exposicion* to Augustine, *de Civ. Dei*, ii. 8 (Abbeville, 1486), says that comedies 'sont proprement apellez interludia, pour ce quilz se font entre les deux mengiers.' But the use of *interludere* by Ausonius, *Idyll*, x. 76, 'interludentes, examina lubrica, pisces,' and Ambrose, *Epist.* xlvii. 4, 'interludamus epistolis,' supports my view.

[2] For a curious distinction, probably neither original nor permanent, drawn about 1530 between 'stage playes' (presumably out of doors) in the summer and 'interludes' (presumably indoors) in the winter, cf. the documents printed by H. R. Plomer, in *Trans. of Bibliographical Society*, iv (1898), 153, and A. W. Pollard in *Fifteenth Century Prose and Verse*, 305, about a suit between John Rastell, lawyer, printer, and playwright, and one Henry Walton. Rastell, going on a visit to France about 1525, had left with Walton a number of players' garments. These are fully described. They were mostly of say or sarcenet, and the tailor, who with the help of Rastell's wife had made them, valued them at 20s. apiece. Walton failed to restore them, and for some

begin to claim attention during the fifteenth century. Dr. Ward's statement that religious plays could not have been the subject of such performances does not bear the test of comparison with the facts. A miracle of St. Clotilda was played before Henry the Sixth at Windsor Castle in 1429, a *Christi Descensus ad Inferos* before Henry the Seventh during dinner at Winchester in 1486; nor is it probable that the play performed by the boys of Maxstoke Priory in the hall of Lord Clinton at Candlemas, 1430, was other than religious in character[1]. The records of the miracle-plays themselves show that they were often carried far from home. There was much coming and going amongst the villages and little towns round about Lydd and New Romney from 1399 to 1508. One at least of the existing texts, that of the Croxton *Sacrament*, appears to be intended for the use of a travelling troupe, and that such troupes showed their plays not only in market-places and on village greens but also in the houses of individual patrons, is suggested by entries of payments to players of this and that locality in more than one *computus*[2].

years let them on hire, to his own profit. Evidence to this effect was given by John Redman, stationer, and by George Mayler, merchant tailor, and George Birche, coriar, two of the king's players. These men had played in the garments themselves and had seen them used in 'stage pleyes' when the king's banquet was at Greenwich [in 1527; cf. vol. i. p. 400]. They had been used at least twenty times in stage plays every summer and twenty times in interludes every winter, and Walton had taken, as the 'common custume' was, at a stage play 'sumtyme xl^d., sometyme ij^s., as they couth agree, and at an interlude viij^d for every tyme.' Rastell had brought a previous suit in the mayor's court, but could only receive 35s. 9d., at which the goods had been officially appraised. But they were then 'rotten and torne,' whereas Rastell alleged that they were nearly new when delivered to Walton and worth 20 marks. Walton relied on the official appraise-ment, and had a counter-claim for 40s. balance of a bill for 50s. costs 'in making of stage for player in Restall's grounde beside Fyndesbury, in tymbre, bourde, nayle, lath, sprigge and other thyngs.' He held the clothes against payment of this amount, which Rastell challenged.

[1] In 1503 a *Magi* was given in Canterbury guildhall. Some of the crafts of Coventry (1478–1568) and Newcastle (1536) had plays at their guild feasts. The indoor performances of Chester plays in 1567 and 1576 are late and exceptional.

[2] Cf. Appendix E, ii (Maxstoke), iii (Thetford), vii (Howard), viii (Tudor Court). 'Moleyn's wedding' attended by Lord Howard, is the first of many at which the players are recorded to have made the mirth. Some of the entries may imply visits *to* the plays, rather than *of* the plays, and this I suppose to be the case with Henry VII's payment 'to the players *at* Myles End.' It is perhaps a little arbitrary to

Thus Maxstoke Priory, between 1422 and 1461, entertained *lusores*[1] from Nuneaton, Coventry, Daventry, and Coleshill ; while Henry the Seventh, between 1492 and 1509, gave largess, either at court or abroad, to 'pleyers' from Essex, Wimborne Minster, Wycombe, London, and Kingston. The accounts of the last-named place record an ordinary parochial play in the very year of the royal 'almasse.'

It is obvious that this practice of travelling must have brought the local players into rivalry with those hereditary gentlemen of the road, the minstrels. Possibly they had something to do with provoking that *querelosa insinuatio* against the *rudes agricolae et artifices diversarum misterarum* which led to the formation of the royal guild of minstrels in 1469. If so, the measure does not seem to have been wholly successful in suppressing them. But the minstrels had a better move to make. Their own profession had fallen, with the emergence of the *trouvère* and the spread of printing, upon evil days. And here were the scanty remnants of their audiences being filched from them by unskilled rustics who had hit upon just the one form of literary entertainment which, unlike poetry and romance in general, could not dis-

assume, as I have done, that players locally named are never professional. Thus the *lusores de Writhill* paid by the duke of Buckingham on Jan. 6, 1508, are almost certainly identical with the *lusores Dñi de Wrisell* (his brother-in-law, the earl of Northumberland) paid by him at Xmas, 1507 (*Archaeologia*, xxv. 318, 324), although it happens curiously enough that the Chelmsford wardrobe was drawn upon by players of Writtle in 1571-2. The local designation of members of the minstrel class is exceptional ; but cf. the York example in the next note. The locally named *lusores* may, however, sometimes have acted not a miracle, but a May-game or sword-dance ; e.g., at Winchester College in 1400 when they came 'cum tripudio suo' (App. E, iv).

[1] I have taken *lusores* in the *computi* as always meaning performers of a dramatic *ludus*. This is often demonstrably correct and never demonstrably incorrect, except that when Colet in his *Oratio ad Clerum* of 1511 quotes the canon 'ne sit publicus lusor' he seems to use the term in its canonical sense of 'gambler.' The English version (1661) has 'common gamer or player.' A similar ambiguity is, I think, the only one which attaches itself to 'player' where it is a technical term after the middle of the fourteenth century. Lydgate in his *Interpretacyon of the names of Goddys and Goddesses* (quoted by Collier, i. 31) uses it of an actor, although an older sense is preserved by the *Promptorium Parvulorum* (1440), 'Bordyoure or pleyere, *ioculator.*' The sense of *ludentes*, I think, is wide. The *ludentes* 'de Donyngton' and 'de Wakefield' paid by the York corporation in 1446 (*York Plays*, xxxviii) are more likely to have been minstrels

pense with the living interpreter [1]. What could they do
better than develop a neglected side of their own art and
become players themselves? So there appear in the *computi*,
side by side with the local *lusores*, others whose methods and
status are precisely those of minstrels [2]. The generosity
of Henry the Sixth at the Christmas of 1427 is called forth
equally by the *entreludes* of the *jeweis de Abyndon* and the
jeuues et entreludes of *Jakke Travail et ses compaignons*. By
1464 'players in their enterludes' were sufficiently recognized
to be included with minstrels in the exceptions of the Act of
Apparel [3]. Like other minstrels, the players put themselves
under the protection of nobles and persons of honour. The
earliest upon record are those of Henry Bourchier, earl of
Essex, and those of Richard, duke of Gloucester, afterwards
Richard the Third. Both companies were rewarded by Lord
Howard in 1482. The earls of Northumberland, Oxford,
Derby, and Shrewsbury, and Lord Arundel, all had their
players before the end of the century [4]. The regulations of
the *Northumberland Household Book*, as well as entries in

whom the corporation did provide
for the plays than actors whom
they did not. On the other hand
about *interludentes* and *interlusores*,
neither of them very common terms,
there can be no doubt. *Lusiatores*
occurs as a synonym for *lusores* at
Shrewsbury only. *Mimi* and *histriones* I have uniformly treated as
merely minstrels. At a late date
they might, I suppose, be actors,
but it is impossible to differentiate.

[1] Plays were sometimes read,
even in the fifteenth century. The
prologue of *The Burial and Resurrection* has 'Rede this treyte,' although it was also converted into
'a play to be playede'; and the
epilogue of the Digby *St. Mary
Magdalen* has 'I desyer the redars
to be my frynd.' Thomas Wylley in
1537 describes some of his plays to
Cromwell as 'never to be seen, but
of your Lordshyp's eye.' Prynne,
834, asserts that 'Bernardinus
Ochin his Tragedy of Freewil,
Plessie Morney his Tragedie of

Jeptha his daughter, Edward the
6 his Comedie de meretrice Ba-
bilonica, Iohn Bale his Comedies
de Christo et de Lazaro, Skelton's
Comedies, de Virtute, de Magnificentia, et de bono Ordine, Nicholaus Grimoaldus, de Archiprophetae
Tragedia . . . were penned only
to be read, not acted'; but this is
incorrect as regards Bale and Skelton and probably as regards others.
The earliest printed plays are perhaps *Mundus et Infans* (1522) and
Hickscorner (n. d.) both by Wynkyn
de Worde (1501–35), *Everyman*
(n. d.) by Richard Pynson (1509–
27). If a *Nigramansir*, by Skelton,
was really, as Warton asserts,
printed by Wynkyn de Worde in
1504, it might take precedence.

[2] Cf. Appendix E.

[3] 3 *Edw. IV*, c. 5; cf. vol. i. p. 45.
This was continued by 1 *Hen. VIII*,
c. 14, 6 *Hen. VIII*, c. 1, and 24
Hen. VIII, c. 13.

[4] Cf. Appendix E; *Hist. MSS.*
v. 548.

many *computi*, show that by the reign of Henry the Eighth the practice was widespread [1]. Naturally it received a stimulus when a body of players came to form a regular part of the royal household. Whether Richard the Third retained his company in his service during his brief reign is not upon record. But Henry the Seventh had four *lusores regis, alias, in lingua Anglicana, les pleyars of the Kyngs enterluds* at least as early as 1494. These men received an annual fee of five marks apiece, together with special rewards when they played before the king. When their services were not required at court, they took to the road, just as did the minstrels, *ioculator*, and *ursarius* of the royal establishment. In 1503 they were sent, under their leader John English, in the train of Margaret of Scotland to her wedding with James the Fourth at Edinburgh, and here they 'did their devoir' before the Scottish court [2]. Henry the Eighth increased their number to eight, and they can be traced on the books of the royal household through the reigns of Edward the Sixth and Mary, and well into that of Elizabeth [3].

[1] Percy, *N. H. B.* 22, 158, 339. An estimate for 1511–12 includes 'for rewardes to Players for Playes playd in Christynmas by Stranegers in my house after xxᵈ every play by estimacion. Somme xxxiijˢ iiijᵈ.' Another of 1514–15 has 'for Rewards to Players in Cristynmas lxxijˢ.' By 1522–3 the customary fee had largely grown, for a list of 'Al maner of Rewardis' of about that date has 'Item. My Lorde usith and accustometh to gif yerely when his Lordshipp is at home to every Erlis Players that comes to his Lordshipe bitwixt Cristynmas ande Candelmas If he be his speciall Lorde and Frende ande Kynsman, xxˢ . . . to every Lordis Players, xˢ.'

[2] Leland, *Collectanea* (ed. Hearne), iv. 265. The *computi* of James IV (*L. H. T. Accts.* ii. 131, 387; iii. 361) contain entries for plays before him by 'gysaris' including one at this wedding; but there is no evidence of a regular royal company at the Scottish court.

In 1488 occurs a payment to 'Patrik Johnson and the playaris of Lythgow that playt to the King,' and in 1489 one to 'Patrick Johnson and his fallowis that playt a play to the kyng in Lythqow.' This Johnson or Johnstone, celebrated in Dunbar's *Lament for the Makaris*, seems to have held some post, possibly as a minstrel, at court (*L. H. T. Accts.* i. c, cxcviii, ccxliv, 91, 118; ii. 131; Dunbar, *Poems* (ed. S. T. S.), i. ccxxxvii).

[3] Collier, i. 44 and passim; Henry, *Hist. of Britain*, 454; cf. Appendix E, viii. The *Transactions of the New Shakspere Soc.* (1877–9), 425, contain papers about a dispute in 1529 between one of the company George Maller, glazier, and his apprentice, who left him and went travelling on his own account. From these it appears that 'the Kinge's plaierz' wore 'the Kinge's bage.' George Maller is the same player who appeared as a witness in the Rastell suit (cf. p. 184). There he is described as a merchant

The new conditions under which plays were now given naturally reacted upon the structure of the plays themselves. The many scenes of the long cyclical miracles, with their multitudinous performers, must be replaced by something more easy of representation. The typical interlude deals with a short episode in about a thousand lines, and could be handled in the hour or so which the lord might reasonably be expected to spare from his horse and his hounds [1]. Economy in travelling and the inconvenience of crowding the hall both went to put a limit on the number of actors. Four men and a boy, probably in apprenticeship to one of them, for the women's parts, may be taken as a normal troupe. In many of the extant interludes the list of *dramatis personae* is accompanied by an indication as to how, by the doubling of parts, the caste may be brought within reasonable compass [2]. The simplest of scenic apparatus and a few boards on trestles for a stage had of course to suffice. But some sort of a stage there probably was, as a rule, although doubtless the players were prepared, if necessary, to perform, like masquers, on the floor in front of the screen, or at best upon the dais where the lord sat at meals [3]. The pleasure-loving monks of Durham seem as far back as 1465 to have built at their cell of Finchale a special player-chamber for the

tailor; here as a glazier. That a king's player should have a handicraft, even if it were only nominal, at all, looks as if the professional actors were not invariably of the minstrel type. Perhaps the glamour of a royal 'bage' made even minstrelsy respectable. Arthur, prince of Wales, had his own company in 1498 (*Black Book of Lincoln's Inn*, i. 119), and Henry, prince of Wales, his by 1506.

[1] Medwall's *Nature* is divided into two parts, for performance on different days. But Medwall was a tedious person. Another interlude of his played in 1514 was so long and dull that Henry VIII went out before the end. *The Four Elements* was intended to take an hour and a half 'but if you list you may leave out much of the said matter

... and then it will not be past three quarters of an hour of length.'

[2] This method begins with the Croxton *Sacrament*, which has twelve parts, but 'ix may play it at ease.' Bale's *Three Laws* claims to require five players and *Lusty Juventus* four. Several of the early Elizabethan interludes have similar indications.

[3] A Winchester *computus* of 1579 (Hazlitt-Warton, ii. 234) has 'pro diversis expensis circa Scaffoldam erigendam et deponendam, et pro domunculis de novo compositis cum carriagio et recarriagio ly joystes et aliorum mutuatorum ad eandem Scaffoldam, cum vj linckes et jᵒ duodeno candelarum, pro lumine expensis, tribus noctibus in ludis comediarum et tragediarum xxvˢ viijᵈ.'

purposes of such entertainments [1]. Henry the Eighth, too, in 1527 had a 'banket-house' or 'place of plesyer,' called the 'Long house,' built in the tiltyard at Greenwich, and decorated by none other than Hans Holbein [2]. But this was designed rather for a special type of disguising, half masque half interlude, and set out with the elaborate pageants which the king loved, than for ordinary plays. A similar banqueting-house 'like a theatre' had been set up at Calais in 1520, but unfortunately burnt down before it could be used [3]. Another characteristic of the interlude is the prayer for the sovereign and sometimes the estates of the realm with which it concludes, and which often helps to fix the date of representation of the extant texts [4].

Like the minstrels, the interlude players found a welcome not only in the halls of the great, but amongst the *bourgeois* and the village folk. In the towns they would give their first performance before the municipality in the guild-hall and take a reward [5]. Then they would find a profitable pitch in the courtyard of some old-fashioned inn, with its convenient

---

[1] Appendix E (i).

[2] Brewer, iv. 1390, 1393, 1394; Hall, 723; Collier, i. 98.

[3] Stowe, *Annals*, 511.

[4] The miracle-plays and popular morals have a more general prayer for the spiritual welfare of the 'sofereyns,' 'lordinges,' and the rest of their audience.

[5] Willis, *Mount Tabor* (1639, quoted Collier, ii. 196), describing the morality of *The Castle of Security* seen by him as a child, says 'In the city of Gloucester the manner is (as I think it is in other like corporations) that when Players of Enterludes come to towne, they first attend the Mayor, to enforme him what noble-mans servants they are and so to get licence for their publike playing: and if the Mayor like the Actors, or would show respect to their Lord and Master, he appoints them to play their first play before himselfe and the Aldermen and Common Counsell of the City; and that is called the Mayor's play, where every one that will comes in without money, the Mayor giving the players a reward as hee thinks fit, to show respect unto them. At such a play, my father tooke me with him, and made mee stand betweene his leggs, as he sate upon one of the benches, where we saw and heard very well.' In *Histriomastix*, a play of 1590–1610 (Simpson, *School of Shakespeare*, ii. 1), a crew of tippling mechanicals call themselves 'Sir Oliver Owlet's men and proclaim at the Cross a play to be given in the townhouse at 3 o'clock. They afterwards throw the town over to play in the hall of Lord Mavortius. In *Sir Thomas More* († 1590, ed. A. Dyce, for Shakespeare Society, 1844) 'my Lord Cardinall's players,' four men and a boy, play in the Chancellor's hall and receive ten angels. For similar scenes cf. the *Induction* to *The Taming of the Shrew*, and *Hamlet*, ii. 2; iii. 2.

range of outside galleries[1]. It is, however, rather surprising to find that Exeter, like Paris itself[2], had its regular theatre as early as 1348, more than two centuries before anything of the kind is heard of in London. This fact emerges from two mandates of Bishop Grandisson; one, already quoted in the previous volume, directed against the *secta* or *ordo*, probably a *société joyeuse*, of Brothelyngham[3], the other inhibiting a satirical performance designed by the youth of the city, in disparagement of the trade and mystery of the cloth-dressers. In both cases the 'theatre' of the city was to be the locality of the revels[4]. Much later, in 1538, but still well in anticipation of London, the corporation of Yarmouth

---

[1] The earliest record of plays at inns which I have noticed is in 1557, when some Protestants were arrested and their minister burnt for holding a communion service in English on pretence of attending a play at the Saracen's Head, Islington (Foxe, *Acts and Monuments*, ed. Cattley, viii. 444).

[2] Eustace Deschamps (†1415), *Miroir de Mariage* (*Œuvres*, in *Anc. Textes franç.* vol. ix), 3109 (cf. Julleville, *La Com.* 40):

Mais assez d'autres femmes voy,
Qui vont par tout sanz nul convoy
Aux festes, aux champs, au theatre,
Pour soulacier et pour esbatre :

.   .   .   .   .   .

Elles desirent les cités,
Les douls mos a euls recités,
Festes, marchiés, et le theatre,
Lieux de delis pour euls esbatre.

This theatre was probably one established towards the end of the fourteenth century by the *confrérie de la Passion*. From about 1402 they performed in the *Hôpital de la Trinité*; cf. Julleville, *Les Com.* 61, *La Com.* 40.

[3] Cf. vol. i. p. 383.

[4] *Register of Bishop Grandisson* (ed. Hingeston-Randolph), ii. 1120. The letter, unfortunately too long-winded to quote in full, was written on Aug. 9, 1352, to the archdeacon of Exeter or his official. Grandisson says :—' Sane, licet artes mechani-cas, ut rerum experiencia continue nos informat, mutuo, necessitate quadam, oporteat se iuvare; pridem, tamen, intelleximus quod nonnulli nostrae Civitatis Exoniae inpruden-tes filii, inordinate lasciviae dediti, fatue contempnentes quae ad ipsorum et universalis populi indigenciam fuerunt utiliter adinventa, quendam Ludum noxium qui culpa non caret, immo verius ludibrium, in contumeliam et opprobrium allutariorum, necnon eorum artificii, hac instanti Die Dominica, in Theatro nostrae Civitatis predictae publice peragere proponunt, ut inter se statuerunt et intendunt ; ex quo, ut didicimus, inter praefatos artifices et dicti Ludi participes, auctores pariter et fautores, graves discordiae, rancores, et rixae, cooperante satore tam exe-crabilis irae et invidiae, vehementer pululant et insurgunt.' The *ludus* is to be forbidden under pain of the greater excommunication. At the same time the *allutarii* are to be admonished, since they them-selves, 'in mercibus suis distra-hendis plus iusto precio, modernis temporibus,' have brought about the trouble, 'ne exnunc, in vendendo quae ad eos pertinent, precium per Excellentissimum Principem et Do-minum nostrum, Angliae et Franciae Regem illustrem, et Consilium suum, pro utilitate publica limitatum, exi-gant quovis modo.'

appear to have built a 'game-house' upon the garden of the recently surrendered priory[1].

In the villages the players probably had to content themselves with a stage upon the green ; unless indeed they could make good a footing in the church. This they sometimes did by way of inheritance from the local actors of miracles. For while the great craft-cycles long remained unaffected by the professional competition and ultimately came to their end through quite different causes, it was otherwise in the smaller places. If the parson and the churchwardens wanted a miracle in honour of their patron saint and could readily hire the services of a body of trained actors, they were not likely to put themselves to the trouble of drilling bookless rustics in their parts. And so the companies got into the churches for the purpose of playing religious interludes, but, if the diatribes of Elizabethan Puritans may be trusted, remained there to play secular ones [2]. The rulers of the Church condemned the abuse[3], but it proved difficult to abolish, and even in 1602 the authorities of Syston in Leicestershire had to buy players off from performing in the church [4].

Even where the old local plays survived they were probably

[1] L. G. Bolingbroke, *Pre-Elizabethan Plays and Players in Norfolk* (*Norfolk Archaeology*, xi. 336). The corporation gave a lease of the 'game-house' on condition that it should be available 'at all such times as any interludes or plays should be ministered or played.' John Rastell's 50s. stage in Finsbury about 1520-5 (cf. p. 184), although not improbably used for public representations, is not known to have been permanent.

[2] At Rayleigh, Essex (1550), 20s. from the produce of church goods was paid to stage-players on Trinity Sunday (*Archaeologia*, xlii. 287). *An Answer to a Certain Libel* (1572, quoted Collier, ii. 72) accuses the clergy of hurrying the service, because there is 'an enterlude to be played, and if no place else can be gotten, it must be doone in the church'; cf. S. Gosson, *Third Blast of Retrait from Plaies and Theaters*, 1580 (Hazlitt, *E. D. S.*

134) 'Such like men, vnder the title of their maisters or as reteiners, are priuiledged to roaue abroad, and permitted to publish their mametree in euerie Temple of God, and that through England, vnto the horrible contempt of praier. So that now the Sanctuarie is become a plaiers stage, and a den of theeues and adulterers.' Possibly only the publication of the *banns* of plays in church is here complained of. Cf. also Fuller, *Church History* (1655), 391.

[3] Bonner's *Injunctions*, 17, of April, 1542 (Wilkins, iii. 864), forbade 'common plays games or interludes' in churches or chapels. Violent enforcers of them were to be reported to the bishop's officers ; cf. the various injunctions of Elizabethan bishops in *Ritual Commission*, 409, 411, 417, 424, 436, and the 88th *Canon* of 1604.

[4] Kelly, 16 'Paid to Lord Morden's players because they should not play in the church, xij^d.'

more or less assimilated to the interlude type. It was certainly so with those written by John Bale and played at
Kilkenny. It was probably so with the play of *Placidas* or *St.
Eustace* given at Braintree in 1534, if, as is most likely, it was
written by Nicholas Udall, who was vicar of Braintree at the
time. And when we find the wardens of Bungay Holy
Trinity in 1558 paying fourpence for an 'interlude and game-
booke' and two shillings for writing out the parts, the conjecture seems obvious that what they had done was to obtain
a copy of one of the printed interludes which by that time
the London stationers had issued in some numbers. On the
other hand the example of the travelling companies sometimes
stirred up the folk, with the help, no doubt, of Holophernes
the schoolmaster, to attempt performances of secular as well
as religious plays on their own account. The rendering of
Pyramus and Thisbe by the mechanicals of Athens, which
is Stratford-upon-Avon, is the classical instance. But in
Shropshire the folk are said to have gone on playing debased
versions of *Dr. Faustus* and other Elizabethan masterpieces,
upon out-of-door stages, until quite an incredibly late date [1].

I return to the atmosphere of courts. It must not be
supposed that, under the early Tudors, the professional players
had a monopoly of interludes. On the contrary, throughout
nearly the whole of the sixteenth century, it remained doubtful whether the future of the drama was to rest in professional
or amateur hands. The question was not settled until the
genius of Marlowe and of Shakespeare came to the help of
the players. Under the pleasure-loving Henries accomplish-

---

[1] Jackson-Burne, 493, citing Sir
Offley Wakeman in *Shropshire
Archaeological Transactions*, vii.
383. Such plays were performed
on wagons at Shropshire wakes
within the last century. The
'book' seems to have been adapted
from the literary drama, if one may
judge by the subjects which included 'St. George,' 'Prince Muci-
dorus,' 'Valentine and Orson,' and
'Dr. Forster' or 'Faustus.' But
a part was always found for a Fool
in a hareskin cap, with balls at his
knees. He is described as a sort

of presenter or chorus, playing 'all
manner of megrims' and 'going on
with his manœuvres all the time.'
I have not been able to see a paper
on *Shropshire Folk-plays* by J. F. M.
Dovaston. G. Borrow, *Wild Wales*,
chh. lix, lx (ed. 1901, p. 393), describes similar Welsh interludes
which lasted to the beginning of
the nineteenth century. The titles
named suggest moralities. He
analyses the *Riches and Poverty*
of Thomas Edwards. This, like
the Shropshire interludes, has its
'fool.'

ment in the arts of social diversion was as likely a road to preferment as another. Sir Thomas More won a reputation as a page by his skill in improvising a scene [1]. John Kite stepped almost straight from the boards to the bishopric of Armagh. His performances, not perhaps without some scandal to churchmen, were given when he was subdean of the Chapel Royal [2]. This ancient establishment, with its thirty-two gentlemen and its school of children, proved itself the most serious rival of the regular company. Both gentlemen and children, sometimes together and sometimes separately, took part in the performances, the records of which begin in 1506 [3]. The rather exceptional nature of the repertory will be considered presently. Few noblemen, of course, kept a chapel on the scale of the royal one. But that of the earl of Northumberland was of considerable size, and was accustomed about 1523 to give, not only a Resurrection play at Easter and a Nativity play at Christmas, but also a play on the night of Shrove-Tuesday. The functionary to whom it looked for a supply of interludes was the almoner [4].

[1] Roper, *Life and Death of Sir Thomas More* († 1577, J. R. Lumby, *More's Utopia*, vi) 'would he at Christmas .tyd sodenly sometymes stepp in among the players, and never studinge for the matter, make a parte of his owne there presently amonge them'; Erasmus, *Epist.* ccccxlvii 'adolescens comoediolas et scripsit et egit.' Bale, *Scriptores* (1557), i. 655, ascribes to him 'comoedias iuveniles. Lib. I.' In the play of *Sir Thomas More* (cf. p. 189) he is represented, even when Chancellor, as supplying the place of a missing actor with an improvised speech. Bale, ii. 103, says that Henry Parker, Lord Morley (1476–1556) 'in Anglica sermone edidit comoedias et tragoedias, libros plures.'

[2] The *Revels Account* for 1511 (Brewer, ii. 1496) notes an interlude in which 'Mr. Subdean, now my Lord of Armykan' took part. In his *Oratio ad Clerum* of the same year Colet criticizes the clerics who 'se ludis et iocis tradunt' (Collier,

i. 64). A *Sermo exhortatorius cancellarii Eboracensis his qui ad sacros ordines petunt promoveri* printed by Wynkyn de Worde about 1525 also calls attention to the canonical requirement that the clergy should abstain 'a ludis theatralibus' (Hazlitt, *Bibl. Coll. and Notes*, 3rd series (1887), 274).

[3] Collier, i. 46 and *passim*; Bernard Andrew, *Annales Hen. VII* in Gairdner, *Memorials of Henry VII* (R. S.), 103; Hall, 518, 583, 723; Kempe, 62; *Revels Accounts*, &c., in Brewer, *passim*; cf. Appendix E (viii). The Chapel formed part of the household of Henry I about 1135 (*Red Book of Exchequer*, R. S. iii. cclxxxvii, 807); for its history cf. *Household Ordinances*, 10, 17, 35, 49; E. F. Rimbault, *The Old Cheque Book of the Chapel Royal* (C. S.); F. J. Furnivall, *Babees Book* (E. E. T. S.), lxxv.

[4] Percy, *N. H. B.* 44, 254, 345. In household lists for 1511 and 1520 comes the entry 'The Almonar, and if he be a maker of

The gentlemen of the Inns of Courts were always ready to follow in the wake of courtly fashion. Their interludes were famous and important in the days of Elizabeth, but, although Lincoln's Inn entertained external *lusores* in 1494 and 1498 [1], Gray's Inn is the only one in which amateur performances are recorded before 1556. A 'disguising' or 'plaie' by one John Roo was shown here in 1526, and got the actors into trouble with Wolsey, who found, or thought that he found, in it reflections on his own administration [2]. All 'comedies called enterludes' were stopped by an order of the bench in 1550, except during times of solemn Christmas [3]. In 1556 an elaborate piece for performance by all the Inns was in preparation by William Baldwin [4].

There were interludes, moreover, at universities and in schools. The earliest I have noted are at Magdalen College, Oxford, where they occur pretty frequently from 1486 onwards. They were given in the hall at Christmas, and overlap in point of time the performances of the *Quem quaeritis* in the chapel [5]. There was a play at Cardinal's College in 1530 [6]. Nicholas Grimald's *Christus Redivivus* was given at Brasenose about 1542. Possibly his *Archipropheta* was similarly given about 1546 at Christ Church, of which he had then become a member. Beyond these I do not know of any other Oxford representations before 1558. But in 1512 the University granted one Edward Watson a degree in grammar on condition of his composing a comedy [7]. At Cambridge

Interludys than he to have a Servaunt to the intent for Writynge of the Parts and ells to have non.' There were nine gentlemen and six children of the chapel. The 1522–3 list of 'Rewardes' has 'them of his Lordship Chappell and other his Lordshipis Servaunts that doith play the Play befor his Lordship uppon Shroftewsday at night, x[s],' and again, ' Master of the Revells . . . yerly for the overseyinge and orderinge of his Lordschip's playes interludes and Dresinge [? disguisinges] that is plaid befor his Lordship in his Hous in the xij days of Xmas, xx[s].' This latter officer seems to have been, as at court, distinct from the ' Abbot of Miserewll ' (vol. i. p. 418).

[1] *Black Books of Lincoln's Inn*, i. 104, 119.

[2] Hall, 719 ; Collier, i. 103.

[3] R. J. Fletcher, *Pension Book of Gray's Inn*, xxxix, 496.

[4] *Hist. MSS.* vii. 613. The play was to comprehend a ' discourse of the world,' to be called *Love and Life*, and to last three hours. There were to be sixty-two *dramatis personae*, each bearing a name beginning with L.

[5] Cf. Appendix E (v).

[6] Brewer, iv. 6788.

[7] Boase, *Register of the University of Oxford* (O. H. S.), i. 298.

the pioneer college was St. John's, where the *Plutus* of Aristophanes was given in Greek in 1536[1]. Christ's College is noteworthy for a performance of the antipapal *Pammachius* in 1545[2]; and also for a series of plays under the management of one William Stevenson in 1550–3, amongst which it is exceedingly probable that *Gammer Gurton's Needle* was included[3]. Most of these university plays were however, probably, in Latin. The Elizabethan statutes of Trinity College[4] and Queens' College[5] both provide for plays, and in both cases the performances really date back to the reign of Henry VIII. At Trinity John Dee seems to have produced the *Pax* of Aristophanes, with an ingenious contrivance for the flight of the Scarabaeus to Zeus, shortly upon his appointment as an original fellow in 1546[6].

The Westminster Latin play cannot be clearly shown to be pre-Elizabethan[7], and the Westminster dramatic tradition is,

[1] Mullinger, *Hist. of Cambridge*, ii. 73. Ascham, *Epist.* (1581), f. 126[v], writing †1550 (quoted Hazlitt-Warton, iii. 304) says that Antwerp excels all other cities 'quemadmodum aula Iohannis, theatrali more ornata, seipsam post Natalem superat.' Speaking in *The Scholemaster* (ed. Mayor, 1863), 168, of his contemporaries at St. John's (†1530–54), Ascham highly praises the *Absalom* of Thomas Watson, which he puts on a level with Buchanan's *Jephthah*. Watson, however, 'would never suffer it to go abroad.' This play apparently exists in manuscript; cf. *Texts* (iv). Ascham himself, according to his *Epistles*, translated the *Philoktetes* into Latin (Hazlitt, *Manual*, 179). In *The Scholemaster*, he further says, 'One man in Cambrige, well liked of many, but best liked of him selfe, was many tymes bold and busie to bryng matters upon stages which he called Tragedies.' Ascham did not approve of his Latin metre. Possibly he refers to John Christopherson, afterwards bishop of Chichester, to whom Warton, iii. 303; Cooper, *Athenae Cantab.* i. 188; *D. N. B.* attribute a tragedy in Greek and Latin of *Jepthes*

(1546). I can find no trace of this. It is not mentioned by Bahlmann.

[2] Cf. p. 220.

[3] J. Peile, *Christ's College*, 54; cf. p. 216.

[4] Mullinger, *Hist. of Cambridge*, ii. 627. *Statute* 24 of 1560, *De comoediis ludisque in Natali Christi exhibendis*, requires that 'novem domestici lectores ... bini ac bini singulas comoedias tragoediasve exhibeant, excepto primario lectore quem per se solum unam comoediam aut tragoediam exhibere volumus.' A fine is imposed on defaulters, and the performances are to be in the hall 'privatim vel publice' during or about the twelve nights of Christmas. On an earlier draft of this statute cf. vol. i. p. 413.

[5] *Statute* 36 (*Documents relating to Cambridge*, iii. 54); cf. Mullinger, *op. cit.* ii. 73.

[6] Dee, *Compendious Rehearsall* (app. to Hearne, *Ioh. Glastoniensis Chronicon*, 501), after mentioning his election, says 'Hereupon I did sett forth a Greek comedy of Aristophanes' play named in Greek Εἰρήνη, in Latin *Pax*.'

[7] J. Sargeaunt, *Annals of Westminster*, 49; *Athenæum* (1903), i. 220.

therefore, less old than that of either Eton or St. Paul's. Professor Hales has, indeed, made it seem plausible that Udall's *Ralph Roister Doister* dates from his Westminster (? 1553–6) and not his Eton mastership (1534–41). But the Eton plays can be traced back to 1525–6[1], and were a recognized institution when Malim wrote his *Consuetudinary* about 1561[2]. In 1538 the Eton boys played, under Udall, before Cromwell[3]. A decade earlier, in 1527, John Ritwise had brought the boys of Colet's new foundation at St. Paul's to court. They acted an anti-Lutheran play before Henry and probably also the *Menaechmi* before Wolsey. Certainly they acted the *Phormio* before him in the following year[4]. The dramatic history of this school is a little difficult to disentangle from that of its near neighbour, the song-school of St. Paul's cathedral[5]. The song-school probably provided the children whom Heywood brought before the princess Mary in 1538[6] and to court in 1553. But some doubt has been cast upon the *bona fides* of the account which Warton gives of further performances by them before the princess Elizabeth at Hatfield in 1554[7]. Plays,

---

[1] Maxwell-Lyte, *Hist. of Eton* (3rd ed. 1899), 118 'pro expensis circa ornamenta ad duos lusus in aula tempore natalis Domini, x[8].'

[2] Printed in E. S. Creasy, *Memoirs of Eminent Etonians*, 91 'circiter festum D. Andreae ludimagister eligere solet pro suo arbitrio scaenicas fabulas optimas et quam accommodatissimas, quas pueri feriis natalitiis subsequentibus, non sine ludorum elegantia, populo spectante, publice aliquando peragant. Histrionum levis ars est, ad actionem tamen oratorum et gestum motumque corporis decentem tantopere facit, ut nihil magis. Interdum etiam exhibet Anglico sermone contextas fabulas, quae habeant acumen et leporem.'

[3] Brewer, xiv. 2. 334 'Woodall, the schoolmaster of Eton, for playing before my Lord, £5.'

[4] Brown, *Cat. of Venetian Papers*, iv. 3. 208, 225 ; Brewer, iv. 3563 ; Hall, 735 ; Cavendish, *Life of Wolsey* (ed. Singer), 201; Collier, i. 104.

[5] Lupton, *Life of Colet*, 154.

[6] *Texts*, s. v. Heywood.

[7] Warton speaks of a play by the 'children' or 'choirboys' of St. Paul's at a visit to Elizabeth by Mary and of another play of *Holophernes* 'perhaps' by the same children later in the year. But the dates given in his *Hist. of Poetry* (ed. Hazlitt), ii. 234, iii. 312, and his *Life of Sir Thomas Pope* (ed. 1780), 46, do not agree together, and the authority to which he refers (*Machyn's Diary*, then in MS.) does not bear him out. On his *bona fides* cf. H. E. D. Blakiston, in *E. H. Review*, for April, 1896. Ward, i. 153, rather complicates the matter by adding to *Holophernes* a second play called *The Hanging of Antioch*, but even in Warton's account this 'hanging' was only a curtain.

either in English or in Latin, of which Bale preserves a list, were also acted in the private school set up in 1538 by one Ralph Radclif in the surrendered Carmelite convent of Hitchin [1].

It will be seen that the non-professional dramatic activities of England, outside the miracle-plays, although of some importance in the sixteenth century, came late and hardly extended beyond courtly and scholastic circles. There is nothing corresponding to the plentiful production of farces by amateur associations of every kind which characterized fifteenth-century France. Besides the scholars and the *Basoche*, which corresponded roughly to the Inns of Court, but was infinitely more lively and fertile, there were the *Enfants sans Soucis* in Paris, and in the province a host of *puys* and *sociétés joyeuses*. All of these played both morals and farces, particularly the latter, for which they claimed a very free licence of satirical comment [2]. As a result,

---

[1] Bale, *Scriptores* (1557), i. 700 'Radulphus Radclif, patria Cestriensis, Huchiniae in agro Hartfordiensi, & in coenobio, quod paulo ante Carmelitarum erat, ludum litcrarium anno Domini 1538 aperuit, docuitque Latinas literas. Mihi quidem aliquot dies in unis & eisdem aedibus commoranti, multa arriserunt: eaque etiam laude dignissima. Potissimum vero theatrum, quod in inferiori aedium parte longe pulcherrimum extruxit. Ibi solitus est quotannis simul iucunda & honesta plebi edere spectacula, cum ob iuventutis, suae fidei & institutioni commissae, inutilem pudorem exuendum, tum ad formandum os tenerum & balbutiens, quo clare, eleganter, & distincte verba eloqui & effari consuesceret. Plurimas in eius museo vidi ac legi tragoedias & comoedias . . . Scripsit de Nominis ac Verbi, potentissimorum regum in regno Grammatico, calamitosa &

Exitiali pugna, Lib. 2 . . .
De patientia Grisilidis, Com. 1 . . .
De Melibaeo Chauceriano, Com. 1 . . .
De Titi & Gisippi amicitia,

Com. 1 . . .
De Sodomae incendio, Tra. 1 . . .
De Io. Hussi damnatione, Tra. 1 . . .
De Ionae defectione, Com. 1 . . .
De Lazaro ac diuite, Com. 1 . . .
De Iudith fortitudine, Com. 1 . . .
De Iobi afflictionibus, Com. 1 . . .
De Susannae liberatione, Tra. 1 . . .
Claruit Radclifus, anno a Christi servatoris ortu 1552 . . . Nescioque an sub Antichristi tyrannide adhuc vivat.' Bale, *Index*, 333, has fuller titles. Some of Radclif's plays were almost certainly in Latin, for Bale gives in Latin the opening words of each, and as Herford, 113, points out, those of the *Lazarus* and the *Griselda* clearly form parts of Latin verses. But he showed them 'plebi.' Professor Herford learnt 'that no old MSS. in any way connected with Radclif now remain at Hitchin, where his family still occupies the site of his school.'

[2] Julleville, *Les Com., passim*. A collection of farces is in E. L. N. Viollet-le-Duc, *Ancien Théâtre français* (1854–7). For morals

although salaried *joueurs de personnages* begin to make their appearance in the account books of the nobles as early as 1392–3 [1], the professional actors were unable to hold their own against the unequal competition, and do not really become of importance until quite the end of the sixteenth century [2]. In England it was otherwise. The early suppression of the Feast of Fools and the strict control kept over the Boy Bishop afforded no starting-point for *sociétés joyeuses*, while the late development of English as a literary language did not lend itself to the formation of *puys*. We hear indeed of satirical performances by the guild of Brothelyngham at Exeter in 1348, and again by the *filii civitatis* in 1352 [3], but Bishop Grandisson apparently succeeded in checking this development which, so far as the information at present available goes, does not seem to have permanently established itself either at Exeter or elsewhere.

and farces at the Feasts of Fools and of the Boy Bishop abroad, and for the satirical tendency of such entertainments, cf. vol. i. p. 380. In 1427, after the feast of St. Laurent, Jean Bussières, chaplain of St. Remi de Troyes, 'emendavit quod fecerat certum perconnagium rimarum in cimiterio dicte ecclesie Sancti Remigii; de quibus rimis fuerat dyabolus et dixerat plura verba contra viros ecclesiasticos' (*Inv. des Arch. de l'Aube*, sér. G, i. 243). The fifteenth-century Dutch farces appear to have been played at the meetings of the *Rederijkerkammern*, and the German *Fastnachtsspiele*, which derive largely from folk *ludi*, by associations of handicraftsmen (Creizenach, i. 404, 407).

[1] Julleville, *Les Com.* 325.

[2] Ibid. 342. There is nothing to show the character of the French players who visited the English court in 1494 and 1495 (Appendix E, viii).

[3] Cf. p. 190 and vol. i. p. 383. The only known English *puy* is that of London (vol. i. p. 376).

CHAPTER XXV

HUMANISM AND MEDIAEVALISM

[*Bibliographical Note.*—The literary discussions and collections of texts named in the bibliographical note to chap. xxiii and the material on the annals of the stage in that to chap. xxiv remain available. W. Creizenach, *Geschichte des neueren Dramas,* vols. i–iii (1893–1903), is the best general guide on the classical drama and its imitations during the Middle Ages and the Renascence. W. Cloetta, *Beiträge zur Litteraturgeschichte des Mittelalters und der Renaissance* : i. *Komödie und Tragödie im Mittelalter* (1890) ; ii. *Die Anfänge der Renaissancetragödie* (1892), deals very fully with certain points. C. H. Herford, *Studies in the Literary Relations of England and Germany in the Sixteenth Century* (1886), has an admirable chapter on *The Latin Drama.* G. Saintsbury, *The Earlier Renaissance* (1901), chap. vi, may also be consulted. Useful books on the beginnings of the Elizabethan forms of drama are R. Fischer, *Zur Kunstentwicklung der englischen Tragödie von ihren ersten Anfängen bis zu Shakespeare* (1893) ; J. W. Cunliffe, *The Influence of Seneca on Elizabethan Tragedy* (1893); L. L. Schücking, *Studien über die stofflichen Beziehungen der englischen Komödie zur italienischen bis Lilly* (1901) ; F. E. Schelling, *The English Chronicle Play* (1902). The best bibliographies are, for the Latin plays, P. Bahlmann, *Die Erneuerer des antiken Dramas und ihre ersten dramatischen Versuche,* 1314–1478 (1896), and *Die lateinischen Dramen von Wimpheling's Stylpho bis zur Mitte des sechzehnten Jahrhunderts,* 1480–1550 (1893) ; and for English plays, W. W. Greg, *A List of English Plays written before 1643 and printed before 1700* (1900). This may be supplemented from W. C. Hazlitt, *A Manual for the Collector and Amateur of Old English Plays* (1892). A list of early Tudor interludes will be found in Appendix X.]

THE dramatic material upon which the interlude was able to draw had naturally its points of relation to and of divergence from that of the popular stage, whose last days it overlapped. It continued to occupy itself largely with the morality. The 'moral interludes' of the early Tudor period are in fact distinguished with some difficulty from the popular moralities by their comparative brevity, and by indications of the *mise en scène* as a 'room' or 'hall' rather than an open 'place[1].' The only clearly popular texts later than those

---

[1] The titles of the printed plays do not help, as they were probably added by the printers, and in any case 'enterlude' does not exclude a popular play.

of the fifteenth century, discussed in a previous chapter, are Sir David Lyndsay's Scottish *Satyre of the Thrie Estaitis*, and the *Magnificence*, which alone survives of several plays from the prolific pen of the 'laureate' poet, John Skelton. A somewhat intermediate type is presented by the *Nature* of Cardinal Morton's chaplain, Henry Medwall. This was certainly intended for performance as an interlude, but it is on the scale of the popular moralities, needing division into two parts to bring it within the limits of courtly patience ; and like them it is sufficiently wide in its scope to embrace the whole moral problem of humanity. The conditions of the interlude, however, enforced themselves, and the later morals have, as a rule, a more restricted theme. They make their selection from amongst the battalions of sins and virtues which were wont to invade the stage together, and set themselves the task of expounding the dangers of a particular temperament or the advantages of a particular form of moral discipline. *Hickscorner* shows man led into irreligion by imagination and freewill. *Youth* concerns itself with pride, lechery, and riot, the specific temptations of the young. *The Nature of the Four Elements* and John Redford's somewhat later *Wit and Science* preach the importance of devotion to study. The distinction between the episodic and the more comprehensive moralities was in the consciousness of the writers themselves ; and the older fashion did not wholly disappear. William Baldwin describes his play for the Inns of Court in 1556 as 'comprehending a discourse of the worlde[1]'; and mention is more than once made of an interesting piece called *The Cradle of Security*, which seems to have had a motive of death and the judgement akin to that found in *The Pride of Life* and in *Everyman*[2].

[1] *Hist. MSS.* vii. 613.

[2] Collier, ii. 196, quotes the description by Willis, *Mount Tabor* (1639), and refers to other notices of the play. In *Sir Thomas More* († 1590, ed. A. Dyce, from *Harl. MS.* 7368 for Shakes. Soc. 1844) 'my lord Cardinall's players' visit More's house and offer the following repertory :

'The Cradle of Securitie, Hit nayle o' th' head, Impacient Pouertie, The play of Foure Pees, Diues and Lazarus, Lustie Iuuentus, and the Mariage of Witt and Wisedom.'

The ascription of these plays to Wolsey's lifetime must not be pressed too literally. Of *Hit Nayle o' th' Head* nothing is known. Radclif (p. 197) wrote a *Dives and*

The morality was not, perhaps, quite such an arid type of drama as might be supposed, especially after the dramatists learnt, instead of leaving humanity as a dry bone of contention between the good and evil powers, to adopt a biographic mode of treatment, and thus to introduce the interest of growth and development[1]. But by the sixteenth century allegory had had its day, and the light-hearted court of Henry VIII and Katharine of Aragon might be excused some weariness at the constant presentation before it of argumentative abstractions which occasionally yielded nothing more entertaining than a personified *débat*[2]. Certainly it is upon record that Medwall's moral of ' the fyndyng of Troth,' played at the Christmas of 1513, appeared to Henry so long, that he got up and 'departyd to hys chambre[3].' The offenders on this occasion were English and his company of household players. They seem to have been unwisely wedded to the old methods. They pursued the princess Margaret to Scotland with a 'Moralite' in 1503, and in the reign of Edward VI they were still playing the play of *Self-Love*[4]. Perhaps this explains why they make distinctly

Lazarus. For the rest cf. p. 189; *Texts* (iv). The piece actually performed in *Sir Thomas More* is called *Wit and Wisdom*, but is really an adaptation of part of *Lusty Juventus.* A play of *Old Custome*, probably a morality, was amongst the effects of John, earl of Warwick, in 1545–50 (*Hist. MSS.* ii. 102).

[1] Cf. Brandl, xl. The performances of *Everyman* given in the courtyard of the Charterhouse in 1901, and subsequently in more than one London theatre, have proved quite unexpectedly impressive.

[2] John Rastell printed † 1536 *Of gentylnes and nobylyte, A dyalogue ... compilit in maner of an enterlude with divers toys and gestis addyd thereto to make mery pastyme and disport;* cf. *Bibliographica,* ii. 446. Heywood's *Witty and Witless* is a similar piece, and a later one, *Robin Conscience,* is in W. C. Hazlitt, *Early Popular Poetry,* iii. 221. In 1527 Rastell seems to have provided for the court a pageant of 'The Father of Hevin' in which a dialogue, both in English and Latin, of riches and love, written by John Redman, and also a 'barriers' were introduced (Brewer, iv. 1394; Collier, i. 98; Hall, 723; Brown, *Venetian Papers,* iv. 105). A dialogue of Riches and Youth, issuing in a 'barriers,' is described by Edward VI in 1552 (*Remains,* ii. 386). On the vogue during the Renascence of this dialogue literature, which derives from the mediaeval *débats,* cf. Herford, ch. 2.

[3] Collier, i. 69. This notice is said by Collier to be from a slip of paper folded up in the *Revels Account* for 1513–4. It is not mentioned in Brewer's *Calendar.*

[4] Leland, *Collectanea* (ed. Hearne), iv. 265; *Computus* for 1551–6 of Sir Thos. Chaloner (*Lansd. MS.* 824, f. 24) 'Gevyn on Shrove monday to the king's players who playd the play of Self-love ... xxˢ.'

less show in the accounts of Tudor revels than do their competitors of the Chapel. Unfortunately none of the pieces given by this latter body have been preserved. But, to judge by the descriptions of Hall, many of them could only be called interludes by a somewhat liberal extension of the sense of the term. There was perhaps some slight allegorical or mythological framework of spoken dialogue. But the real amusement lay in an abundance of singing, which of course the Chapel was well qualified to provide, and of dancing, in which the guests often joined, and in an elaborately designed pageant, which was wheeled into the hall and from which the performers descended. They were in fact masques rather than dramas in the strict sense, and in connexion with the origin of the masque they have already been considered[1].

The popular stage, as has been said, had its farcical elements, but did not, in England, arrive at any notable development of the farce. Nor is any marked influence of the overseas habit even now to be traced. The name is not used in England, although it is in Scotland, where at the beginning of the sixteenth century the relations with France were much closer[2]. Whether directly or indirectly through French channels, the farce is perhaps the contribution of minstrelsy to the nascent interlude. That some dramatic tradition was handed down from the *mimi* of the Empire to the *mimi* of the Middle Ages, although not susceptible of demonstration, is exceedingly likely[3]. That solitary mediaeval survival, the *Interludium de Clerico et Puella*, hardly declares its origin. But the farce, in its free handling of contemporary life, in the outspokenness, which often becomes indecency, of its language, in its note of satire, especially towards the priest and other institutions deserving of reverence, is the exact counter-

---

[1] Cf. ch. xvi.

[2] There was a 'farsche' at Edinburgh in 1554 (*Representations*, s. v.). In 1558 the Scottish General Assembly forbade 'farseis and clerke playis' (Christie, *Account of Parish Clerks*, 64). Julleville, *La Com.* 51, explains the term. *Farsa* is the L. L. past part. of *farcire* ' to stuff.' Besides its liturgical use (vol. i. p. 277) ' on appela *farce* au

théâtre une petite pièce, une courte et vive satire formée d'éléments variés et souvent mêlée de divers langages et de différents dialectes. . . . Plus tard, ce sens premier s'effaça ; le mot de farce n'éveilla plus d'autre idée que celle de comédie très réjouissante.' *Farce* is, therefore, in its origin, precisely equivalent to the Latin *Satura*.

[3] Cf. vol. i. p. 83.

part of one of the most characteristic forms of minstrel literature, the *fabliau*. These qualities are reproduced in the interludes of John Heywood, who, though possibly an Oxford man, began life as a singer and player of the virginals at court, and belonged therefore to the minstrel class. He grew quite respectable, married into the family of Sir Thomas More and John Rastell the printer, and had for grandson John Donne. He was put in charge of the singing-school of St. Paul's, the boys of which probably performed his plays. Of the six extant, *Wit and Folly* is a mere dialogue, and *Love* a more elaborate disputation, although both are presented 'in maner of an enterlude.' But the others, *The Pardoner and the Friar, The Four P's, The Weather*, and *John, Tib and Sir John* are regular farces. And with them the farce makes good its footing in the English drama.

Those congeners of the French farce which took their origin from the Feast of Fools, the *Sottie* and the *Sermon joyeux*, are only represented in these islands by the Sermon of 'Folie' in Sir David Lyndsay's *Satyre of the Thrie Estaitis*[1]. But the 'fool' himself, as a dramatic character, is in Shakespeare's and other Elizabethan plays, and it must now be pointed out that he is in some of the earliest Tudor interludes. Here he has the not altogether intelligible name of the 'vice.' A recent writer, Professor Cushman of the Nevada State University, has endeavoured to show that the vice came into the interludes through the avenue of the moralities. Originally 'an allegorical representation of human weaknesses and vices, in short the summation of the Deadly Sins,' he lost in course of time this serious quality, and 'the term Vice came to be simply a synonym for buffoon[2].' This theory has no doubt the advantage of

---

[1] *Texts*, s. v. Lyndsay. The only other fragment of the Scottish drama under James IV is that ascribed to Dunbar (*Works*, ed. Scot. Text Soc., ii. 314). In one MS. this is headed '*Ane Littill Interlud of the Droichis Part of the* [*Play*] but in another *Heir followis the maner of the crying of ane playe*. Both have the colophon. *Finis*

off the Droichis Pairt of the Play. From internal evidence the piece is a *cry* or *banes*. Ll. 138–41 show that it was for a May-game:
'ʒe noble merchandis ever ilkane
Address ʒow furth with bow and flane
    In lusty grene lufraye,
And follow furth on Robyn Hude.'
[2] Cushman, 63, 68.

explaining the name. Unfortunately it proceeds by disregarding several plays in which the vice does occur, and
reading him into many where there is none [1]. 'Vicious' had
his pageant in the Beverley *Paternoster* play, and vices in the
ordinary sense of the word are of course familiar personages
in the morals, which generally moreover have some one
character who can be regarded as the representative or the
chief representative of human frailty. But the vice is not
found under that name in the text, list of *dramatis personae*,
or stage directions of any popular morality or of any pre-
Elizabethan moral interlude except the Marian *Respublica*.
The majority of plays in which he does occur are not morals,
even of the modified Elizabethan type; and although in those
which are he generally plays a bad part, even this is not an
invariable rule. In *The Tide Tarrieth for No Man*, as in the
tragedy of *Horestes*, he is Courage. Moreover, as a matter
of fact, he comes into the interludes through the avenue of
the farce. The earliest vices, by some thirty years, are those
of Heywood's *Love*, in which he is 'Neither Loving nor Loved,'
who mocks the other disputants, and plays a practical joke
with fireworks upon them, and *The Weather*, in which he is
'Merry Report,' the jesting official of Jupiter. And in the
later plays, even if he has some other dramatic function,
he always adds to it that of a riotous buffoon. Frequently
enough he has no other. It must be concluded then that,
whatever the name may mean—and irresponsible philology
has made some amazing attempts at explanation [2]—the
character of the vice is derived from that of the domestic
fool or jester. Oddly enough he is rarely called a fool,
although the description of Medwall's *Finding of Truth*
mentions 'the foolys part [3].' But the Elizabethan writers

---

[1] No play in the first two sections
of the 'vice-dramas' tabulated by
Cushman, 55, has a vice. Of the
eleven plays (excluding *King John*,
which has none) that remain, eight
can be called morals. But to these
must be added Heywood's *Love*
and *Weather*, Grimald's *Archipropheta*, *Jack Juggler*, *Hester*, *Tom
Tiler and His Wife*, none of which
are morals, unless the first can be

so called.

[2] Cushman, 68. It has been derived from *vis d'âne*, and from
vis, 'a mask'; from the Latin *vice*,
because the vice is the devil's representative; from *device*, 'a puppet moved by machinery,' and
finally, by the ingenious Theobald,
from 'O. E. *jeck*—Gk. εἰκαῖ, i.e.
Ϝικαῖ = Ϝεικ = formal character.'

[3] Cf. *Texts*, s.v. Medwall. In

speak of his long coat and lathen sword, common trappings of the domestic fool[1]. Whether he ever had a cockscomb, a bauble, or an eared hood is not apparent. A vice seems to have been introduced into one or two of the later miracle-plays[2]. At Bungay in 1566 he 'made pastime' before and after the play, as Tarleton or Kempe were in time to do with their 'jigs' upon the London boards. And probably this was his normal function on such occasions.

From the moral the interlude drew abstractions; from the farce social types. The possibility of vital drama lay in an advance to the portraiture of individualities. The natural way to attain to this was by the introduction of historical, mythical, or romantic personages. The miracle-play had, of course, afforded these; but there is little to show that the miracle-play, during the first half of the sixteenth century, had much influence on the interlude[3]. The local players brought it to court, but, for the present, it was *démodé*. It was, however, to have its brief revival. The quarry of romantic narrative had hardly been opened by the Middle Ages. An old theme of Robert of Sicily, once used at Lincoln, was now remembered at Chester. Robin Hood had yielded dramatic May-games, and his revels were popular at Henry VIII's court[4]. New motives, however, now begin to assert themselves. Some at least of these were suggested by the study of Chaucer. Ralph Radclif's school plays at Hitchin included one on *Griselda* and one on *Meliboeus*[5]. Nicholas Grimald wrote one on *Troilus*, and another had been acted by the Chapel at court in 1516[6]. Radclif was also responsible for a *Titus and Gisippus*, while the king's players, shaking off their devotion to the moral, prepared in 1552 'a play of *Aesop's Crow*, wherein the most part of the actors were birds[7].' An extant piece on 'the

Misogonos († 1560) Cacurgus, the *Morio*, is a character, and is called 'foole' and 'nodye' but not 'vice.'
  [1] Collier, ii. 191; Cushman, 69; cf. ch. xvi.
  [2] Cf. *Representations*, s. vv. Bungay, Chelmsford.
  [3] The 'pleyers with Marvells' at court in 1498 are conjectured to

have played miracles. But they may have been merely *praestigia-tores.*
  [4] Cf. vol. i. p. 180.
  [5] Cf. p. 197, n. 1.
  [6] Cf. *Texts*, s. v. Grimald.
  [7] W. B[aldwin], *Bell the Cat* (1553).

beauty and good properties of women' and 'their vices and evil conditions' is really a version through the Italian of the Spanish *Celestina*, one of the first of many English dramatic borrowings from South European sources.

So far I have written only of developments which were at least latent in mediaevalism. But the interlude had its rise in the very midst of the great intellectual and spiritual movement throughout Europe which is known as humanism ; and hardly any branch of human activities was destined to be more completely transformed by the new forces than the drama. The history of this transformation is not, however, a simple one. Between humanism and mediaevalism there is no rigid barrier. As at all periods of transition, a constant action and reaction established themselves between the old and new order of ideas. Moreover, humanism itself held elements in solution that were not wholly reconcilable with each other. Many things, and perhaps particularly the drama, presented themselves in very different lights, according as they were viewed from the literary or the religious side of the great movement. Some brief indication of the in-and-out play of the forces of humanism as they affected the history of the interlude during the first half of the sixteenth century is, therefore, desirable.

The chief of these forces is, of course, the influence of classical comedy and tragedy. These, as vital forms of literature, did not long survive the fall of the theatres, with which, indeed, their connexion had long been of the slightest. In the East, a certain tradition of Christian book dramas begins with the anti-Gnostic dialogues of St. Methodius in the fourth century and ends with the much disputed Χριστὸς Πάσχων in the eleventh or twelfth[1]. It is the merest conjecture that some of these may have been given some kind of representation in the churches[2]. In the West the *Aulu-*

---

[1] Krumbacher, 534, 644, 653, 717, 746, 751, 766, 775. The Χριστὸς Πάσχων (ed. by J. G. Brambs, 1885 ; and in *P. G.* xxxviii. 131) was long ascribed to the fourth-century Gregory Nazianzen. Later scholars have suggested Joannes Tzetzes or Theodorus Prodromus, but Krumbacher thinks the author unidentified. A third of the text is a cento from extant plays, mainly of Euripides.

[2] Krumbacher, 645.

laria of Plautus was rehandled under the title of *Querolus* at the end of the fourth century, and possibly also the *Amphitruo* under that of *Geta*[1]. In the fifth, Magnus, the father of Consentius, is said by Sidonius, as Shakespeare is said by Ben Jonson, to have ' outdone insolent Greece, or haughty Rome[2].' Further the production of plays cannot be traced. Soon afterwards most of the classical dramatists pass into oblivion. A knowledge of Seneca or of Plautus, not to speak of the Greeks, is the rarest of things from the tenth century to the fourteenth. The marked exception is Terence who, as Dr. Ward puts it, led 'a charmed life in the darkest ages of learning.' This he owed, doubtless, to his unrivalled gift of packing up the most impeccable sentiments in the neatest of phrases. His vogue as a school author was early and enduring, and the whole of mediaevalism, a few of the stricter moralists alone dissenting, hailed him as a master of the wisdom of life[3]. At the beginning of the eleventh century, Notker Labeo, a monk of St. Gall, writes that he has been invited to turn the *Andria* into German[4]. Not long before, Hrotsvitha, a Benedictine nun of Gandersheim in Saxony, had taken Terence as her model for half a dozen plays in Latin prose, designed to glorify chastity and to celebrate the constancy of the martyrs. The dramaturgy of Hrotsvitha appears to have been an isolated experiment and the merest literary exercise. Her plays abound in delicate situations, and are not likely to have been intended even for cloister representation[5]. Nor is there much evidence for any representation of the Terentian

---

[1] Teuffel, ii. 372; Cloetta, i. 3, 70; Creizenach, i. 4, 20. The *Querolus* (ed. L. Havet, 1880) was ascribed by the Middle Ages to Plautus himself. The *Geta*, if it existed, is lost.

[2] Sidonius, *Carm.* xxiii. 134.

[3] Cloetta, i. 14; ii. 1; Creizenach, i. 1, 486; Bahlmann, *Ern.* 4; M. Manitius, in *Philologus*, suppl. vii. 758; Ward, i. 7, quoting Hrotsvitha, ' sunt etiam . . . qui, licet alia gentilium spernant, Terentii tamen fragmenta frequentius lectitant.'

[4] Creizenach, i. 2; Ward, i. 8;

Göttinger gelehrte Anzeigen (1835), 911.

[5] Creizenach, i. 17; Cloetta, i. 127; Ward, i. 6; Pollard, xii; A. Ebert, *Gesch. d. Litt. d. Mittelalters* (1887), iii. 314; W. H. Hudson in *E. H. R.* iii. 431. The plays of Hrotsvitha (ed. K. A. Barack, 1858; ed. P. L. Winterfeld, 1901) are the *Gallicanus, Dulcitius, Callimachus, Abraham, Paphnutius, Sapientia.* They were discovered by Conrad Celtes and edited in 1501. It is not probable that he forged them.

comedies themselves. A curious fragment known as *Terentius et Delusor* contains a dialogue between the *vetus poeta* and a *persona delusoris* or mime. The nature of this is somewhat enigmatic, but it certainly reads as if it might be a prologue or *parade* written for a Terentian representation. In any case, it is wholly unparalleled [1]. In fact, although the Middle Ages continued to read Terence, the most extraordinary ideas prevailed as to how his dramas were originally produced. Vague reminiscences of the pantomimic art of later Rome led to the mistāken supposition that the poet himself, or a *recitator*, declaimed the text from a *pulpitum* above the stage, while the actors gesticulated voicelessly below [2]. By a further confusion the name of Calliopius, a third- or fourth-century grammarian through whose hands the text of Terence has passed, was taken for that of a *recitator* contemporary with the poet, and the *Vita Oxoniensis* goes so far as to describe him as a powerful and learned man, who read the comedies aloud in the senate [3]. The same complete ignorance of things scenic declares itself in the notions attached to the terms *tragoedia* and *comoedia*,

---

[1] Printed in Appendix U.

[2] Creizenach, i. 5; Cloetta, i. 38. One of the exceptionally learned men who really knew something about the classical drama was John of Salisbury († 1159), *Polycraticus*, i. 8 'comicis et tragoedis abeuntibus, cum omnia levitas occupaverit, clientes eorum, comoedi videlicet et tragoedi, exterminati sunt'; iii. 8 'comoedia est vita hominis super terram, ubi quisque sui oblitus personam exprimit alienam' (*P. L.* cxcix. 405, 488). For the popular notion cf. Lydgate, *Troy Book* (ed. 1555), ii. 11, perhaps translating Guido delle Colonne:

'In the theatre there was a smale aulter,
Amyddes sette that was half Circuler,
Which into East of custome was directe,
Upon the whiche a Pulpet was erecte,
And therin stode an auncient poete,
For to reherse by rethorykes swete,

The noble dedes that were hystoryall,
Of kynges & prynces for memoryall . . .
All this was tolde and red of the Poete,
And whyle that he in the pulpet stode,
With deadly face all deuoyde of blode,
Synging his ditees with muses all to rent,
Amyd the theatre shrowded in a tent,
There came out men gastfull of their cheres,
Disfygured their faces with viseres,
Playing by sygnes in the peoples syght,
That the Poet songe hath on heyght, . . .
And this was done in Apryll and in May.'

[3] Creizenach, i. 6; Cloetta, i. 35. See the miniature reproduced from a fifteenth-century MS. of Terence in P. Lacroix, *Sciences et Lettres au Moyen Âge* (1877), 534.

not only vulgarly, but in the formal definitions of lexico-
graphers and encyclopaedists [1].

The characteristics which really differentiate the drama
from other forms of literature, dialogue and scenic representation, drop out of account, the latter entirely, the former very
nearly so.   Both tragedy and comedy are regarded as forms
of narrative.   Tragedy is narrative which concerns persons of
high degree, is written in a lofty style, and beginning happily
comes to a sad conclusion.   Comedy, on the other hand, concerns itself with ordinary persons, uses humble and everyday
language, and resolves its complications in a fortunate ending [2].
Even these distinctions are not all consistently maintained, and
the sad or happy event becomes the only fixed and invariable
criterion [3].   The origin of such conceptions is to be found
partly in the common derived classical use of *tragoedia* and
comoedia to describe tragic and comic events as well as the
species of drama in which these are respectively represented;
partly in a misunderstanding of grammarians who, assuming
the dialogue and the representation, gave definitions of tragedy
and comedy in relation to each other [4]; and partly in the
solecism of the fifth-century epic writer Dracontius, who

---

[1] Cloetta, i. 14, has accumulated
a fund of learning on this subject;
cf. Creizenach, i. 9.

[2] Johannes Januensis, *Catholicon*
(1286), quoted by Cloetta, i. 28
'differunt tragoedia et comoedia,
quia comedia privatorum hominum
continet facta, tragoedia regum et
magnatum. Item comoedia humili
stilo describitur, tragoedia alto.
Item comoedia a tristibus incipit
sed cum laetis desinit, tragoedia e
contrario.'

[3] Vincent of Beauvais, *Speculum
maius triplex* († 1250), i. 109
'Comoedia poesis exordium triste
laeto fine commutans. Tragoedia
vero poesis a laeto principio in
tristem finem desinens.' The Dante-
commentator Francesco da Buti,
quoted by Cloetta i. 48, illustrates
this notion with an extraordinary
explanation of the derivation of
tragedia from τράγος; 'come il
becco ha dinanzi aspetto di prin-

cipe per le corna e per la barba,
e dietro è sozzo mostrando le na-
tiche nude e non avendo con che
coprirle, così la tragedia incomincia
dal principio con felicità e poi ter-
mina in miseria.' Krumbacher,
646, describes the very similar history of the terms τραγῳδία and
κωμῳδία in Byzantine Greek.

[4] Boethius, who of course understood the nature of comedy and
tragedy, says (*Cons. Philosoph.*
ii. pr. 2. 36) 'quid tragoediarum
clamor aliud deflet, nisi indiscreto
ictu fortunam felicia regna verten-
tem?' This becomes in the paraphrase of his eleventh-century commentator Notker Labeo (ed. Hat-
temar, 52b) 'tragoediae sínt luctuosa
carmina. álso díu sínt. díu sophocles scréib apud grecos. de euer-
sionibus regnorum et urbium. únde sínt uuideruuártig tien comoediis.
án dîen uuir ío gehórên laetum
únde iocundum exitum.'

seems to have called his *Orestes* a tragedy, merely because it was from tragedies that the material he used was drawn [1]. The *comoedia* and *tragoedia* of the Latin writers, thus defined, was extended to all the varieties of narrative, in the widest sense of the word. The epics of Lucan and Statius, the elegies of Ovid, are *tragoediae*; the epistles of Ovid, the pastoral dialogues of Virgil, are *comoediae*; the satires of Horace, Persius, Juvenal, are one or the other, according to the point of view [2]. It is curious that, with all this wide extension of the terms, they were not applied to the one form of mediaeval Latin composition which really had some analogy to the ancient drama; namely to the liturgical plays out of which the vernacular mysteries grew. These must have been written by learned writers: some of them were probably acted by schoolboys trained in Terence; and yet, if Hrosvitha, as she should be, is put out of the reckoning, no inward or outward trace of the influence of classical tragedy or comedy can be found in any one of them. In the manuscripts, they are called *officium, ordo, ludus, miraculum, repraesentatio* and the like, but very rarely *comoedia* or *tragoedia*, and never before 1204 [3]. From the Latin the mediaeval notions of tragedy and comedy were transferred to similar compositions in the vernaculars. Dante's *Divina Commedia* is just a story which begins in Hell and ends in Paradise [4].

[1] Cloetta, i. 4; Teuffel, ii. 506. Blossius Aemilius Dracontius was a Carthaginian poet. The *Orestes* is printed in L. Baehrens, *Poet. Lat. Min.* (*Bibl. Teub.*), v. 218. There seems a little doubt whether the title *Orestis tragoedia* in the Berne MS. is due to the author or to a scribe. The Ambrosian MS. has *Horestis fabula*.

[2] Creizenach, i. 12.

[3] Ibid. i. 7; Cloetta, i. 49. The *ludus prophetarum* played at Riga in 1204 (p. 70) is called 'ludus ... quam Latini comoediam vocant.' Probably this is a bit of learning on the part of the chronicler; cf. the Michael-House instance (p. 344). For scraps from non-dramatic classical authors in liturgical plays, cf. p. 48. The 'theatricales ludi' of Innocent III and others (vol. i. p. 40; vol. ii. p. 99) seem to be not miracle-plays, but the Feast of Fools and similar mummings.

[4] Dante, *Dedicatio* of *Paradiso* to Can Grande (*Opere Latine*, ed. Giuliani, ii. 44) 'est comoedia genus quoddam poeticae narrationis ... Differt ergo a tragoedia in materia per hoc quod tragoedia in principio est admirabilis et quieta, in fine sive exitu est foetida et horribilis ... comoedia vero inchoat asperitatem alicuius rei, sed eius materia prospere terminatur.' P. Toynbee (*Romania*, xxvi. 542) shows that Dante substantially owed these definitions to the *Magnae Derivationes* of the late twelfth-century writer, Uguccione da Pisa.

Boccaccio [1], Chaucer [2], and Lydgate [3] use precisely similar language. And, right up to the end of the sixteenth century, 'tragedy' continues to stand for 'tragical legend' with the authors of the *Mirror for Magistrates* and their numerous successors [4]. Long before this, of course, humanistic research, without destroying their mediaeval sense, had restored to the wronged terms their proper connotation. There is a period during which it is a little difficult to say what, in certain instances, they do mean. When Robert Bower, in 1447, speaks of *comoediae* and *tragoediae* on the theme of Robin Hood and Little John, it is a matter for conjecture whether he is referring to dramatized May-games or merely to ballads [5]. Bale, in writing of his contemporaries, certainly applies the words to plays; but when he ascribes *tragoedias vulgares* to Robert Baston, a Carmelite friar of the time of Edward II, it is probable that he is using, or quoting a record which used, an obsolescent terminology [6]. What the *comoediae* of John Scogan, under Edward IV, may have been, must remain quite doubtful [7].

It is in the early fourteenth century and in Italy that a renewed interest in the Latin dramatists, other than Terence, can first be traced. Seneca became the subject of a commentary by the English Dominican Nicholas Treveth, and also attracted the attention of Lovato de' Lovati and the scholarly circle which gathered round him at Padua. The chief of these was Albertino Mussato, who about 1314 was moved by indignation at the intrigues of Can Grande of Verona to write his *Ecerinis* on the fate of that Ezzelino who, some eighty

---

[1] Boccaccio's *Ameto* bears the sub-title *Comedia delle Ninfe fiorentine*.

[2] Chaucer, *Monk's Prologue*, (*C. T.* 13,999):
'Or elles first Tragedies wol I telle
Of whiche I have an hundred in my celle.
Tragedie is to seyn a certeyn storie,
As olde bokes maken us memorie,
Of him that stood in greet prosperite
And is y-fallen out of heigh degree
Into miserie, and endeth wrecchedly.'
Cf. the gloss in his *Boethius*, ii. pr.

2, 78, to the passage already quoted on p. 20¹; and the description of *Troilus* in *T. C.* v. 1786.

[3] Lydgate, *Fall of Princes*, prol.:
'My maister Chaucer with his fressh commedies,
Is deed, alas, chefe poete of Bretayne:
That sometyme made full pitous tragedies.'

[4] W. F. Trench, *A Mirror for Magistrates; its Origin and Influence* (1898), 18, 76, 82, 120, 125.

[5] Cf. vol. i. p. 177.

[6] Bale, i. 370.

[7] Ibid. ii. 68.

years before, had tyrannized over Padua. This first of the Senecan tragedies of the Renascence stirred enthusiasm amongst the growing number of the *literati*. It was read aloud and Mussato was laureated before the assembled university. Two learned professors paid it the tribute of a commentary. The example of Mussato was followed in the *Achilleis* (1390) of Antonio de' Loschi of Vicenza and the *Progne* (†1428) of Gregorio Corraro of Mantua. Petrarch was familiar not only with Terence, but also with Seneca and Plautus, and his *Philologia*, written before 1331 and then suppressed, may claim to take rank with the *Ecerinis* as the first Renascence comedy. It was modelled, says Boccaccio, upon Terence. A fresh impulse was given to the study and imitation of Latin comedy in 1427 by the discovery of twelve hitherto unknown Plautine plays, including the *Menaechmi* and the *Miles Gloriosus*, and various attempts were made to complete the imperfect plays. In 1441 Leonardo Dati of Florence introduced a motive from the *Trinummus* into his, not comedy, but tragedy of *Hiempsal*[1].

It must be borne in mind that during these early stages of humanism classical models and neo-Latin imitations alike were merely read and not acted. There is no sign whatever that as yet the mediaeval misconception as to the nature of Roman scenic representation had come to an end. It was certainly shared by Nicolas Treveth and probably by both Petrarch and Boccaccio[2]. It was not indeed in these regular dramas that the habit of acting Latin first re-established itself, but in a mixed and far less classical type of play. It is probable that in schools the exercise of reciting verse, and amongst other verse dialogue, had never died out since the time of the Empire. In the fourth century the *Ludus Septem Sapientum* of the Bordeaux schoolmaster Ausonius, which consists of no more than a set of verses and a '*Plaudite!*' for each sage, was doubtless written for some such purpose[3]. Such also may have been the destiny of the 'elegiac' and

[1] Cloetta, ii. 4, 11, 91, 147; Creizenach, i. 487, 529, 572; Bahlmann, *Ern.* 9, 13, 15, 30, 40.

[2] Cloetta, ii. 69, 221; Creizenach, i. 490, 510, 580.

[3] The earliest printed text (†1473) of Claudian's *De Raptu Proserpinae* is from a version arranged as two pseudo-dramas (Cloetta, i. 135).

'epic' comedies and tragedies of which a fair number were produced, from the eleventh century to the thirteenth. These are comedies and tragedies, primarily, in the mediaeval sense. They are narrative poems in form. But in all of them a good deal of dialogue is introduced, and in some there is hardly anything else. Their subject-matter is derived partly from Terence and partly from the stock of motives common to all forms of mediaeval light literature. Their most careful student, Dr. Cloetta, suggests that they were intended for a half-dramatic declamation by minstrels. This may sometimes have been the case, but the capacity and the audience of the minstrels for Latin were alike limited, and I do not see why at any rate the more edifying of them may not have been school pieces [1]. By the fifteenth century it will be remembered, students, who had long been in the habit of performing miracle-plays, had also taken to producing farces, morals, and those miscellaneous comic and satiric pieces which had their origin in the folk-festivals. Many of these were in the vernaculars; but it is difficult to avoid classing with them a group of Latin dialogues and loosely constructed comedies, written in Terentian metres and presenting a curious amalgam of classical and mediaeval themes. Of hardly any of these can it be said positively that they were intended to be acted. This is, however, not unlikely in the case of the anonymous *Columpnarium*, which goes back to the fourteenth century. Pavia probably saw a performance of Ugolini Pisani's *Confabulatio coquinaria* (1435), which has all the characteristics of a carnival drollery, and certainly of Ranzio Mercurino's *De Falso Hypocrita*, which is stated in the manuscript to have been 'acta' there on April 15, 1437. The *Admiranda* of Alberto Carrara was similarly 'acta' at Padua about 1456. The exact way in which these pieces and others like them were performed must remain doubtful. Acting in the strict sense can only be distinctly asserted

---

[1] Cloetta, i, *passim*; Creizenach, i. 20; Peiper, *Die profane Komödie des Mittelalters*, in *Archiv f. Litteraturgeschichte*, v. 497. Some of the texts are in Müllenbach, *Comoe-*diae *Elegiacae* (1885), and T. Wright, *Early Mysteries and other Latin Poems* (1844). Cloetta gives references for the rest.

of Francesco Ariosto's dialogue of *Isis* which was given '*per personatos*' at the Ferrara carnival of 1444 [1].

All this pseudo-classic comedy was looked upon with scorn by the purists of humanism. But it made its way over the Alps and had a considerable vogue in Germany. In France it found an exponent in Jean Tissier de Ravisy (Ravisius Textor), professor of rhetoric in the College of Navarre at Paris, and afterwards rector of the Paris University, who wrote, in good enough Latin, but wholly in the mediaeval manner, a large number of morals, farces, and dialogues for representation by his pupils [2]. Two at least of these were turned into English interludes. The classical element predominates in the pseudo-Homeric *Thersites*, the production of which can be fixed to between October 12 and 24, 1537; the mediaeval in Thomas Ingelend's *The Disobedient Child*, which belongs to the very beginning of the reign of Elizabeth.

It was doubtless the study of Vitruvius which awakened the humanists to the fact that their beloved comedies had after all been acted after very much the fashion so long familiar in farces and miracle-plays. Exactly when the knowledge came is not clear. Polydore Vergil is still ignorant, and even Erasmus, at the date of the *Adagia*, uncertain. Alberti put a *theatrum* in the palace built on the Vatican for Nicholas V about 1452, but there is no record of its use for dramatic performances at that time, and the immediate successors of Nicholas did not love humanism. Such performances seem to have been first undertaken by the pupils of a Roman professor, Pomponius Laetus. Amongst these was Inghirami, who was protagonist in revivals of the *Asinaria* of Plautus and the *Phaedra* of Seneca. These took place about 1485. Several other representations both of classical plays and of neo-Latin imitations occurred in Italy before the end of the century; and the practice spread to other countries affected by the humanist wave, soon establishing itself as part of the regular sixteenth-century scheme of education. By this time, of course, Greek as well as Latin dramatic models were avail-

---

[1] Creizenach, i. 533, 548, 563, 581; Bahlmann, *Ern.* 13, 36, 38, 44, 48.
[2] Creizenach, i. 569; ii. 23, 43, 59; Bahlmann, *L. D.* 31; Julleville, *Les Com.* 298; J. Bolte, in *Vahlen-Festschrift* (1900), 589.

able. The Latin translation of the *Plutus* of Aristophanes by Leonardo Bruni (†1427) found several successors, and the play was acted at Zwickau in 1521. The study of Sophocles and Euripides began with Francesco Filelfo (†1481), but no representations of these authors are mentioned [1].

The outburst of dramatic activity in English schools and universities during the first half of the sixteenth century has already been noted. Wolsey may claim credit for an early encouragement of classical comedy in virtue of the performances of the *Menaechmi* and the *Phormio* given in his house by the boys of St. Paul's in 1527 and 1528 [2]. The master of St. Paul's from 1522 to 1531 was John Ritwise, who himself wrote a Latin play of *Dido*, which also appears to have been acted before Wolsey [3]. The *Plutus* was given at St. John's College, Cambridge, in 1536; the *Pax* at Trinity about a decade later [4]. A long series of English translations of classical plays begins with one of the *Andria* printed, possibly by John Rastell, under the title of *Terens in Englysh* [5].

A more important matter is the influence exercised by classical models upon the vernacular interludes. This naturally showed itself in school dramas, and only gradually filtered down to the professional players. Two plays compete for the honour of ranking as 'the first regular English comedy,' a term which is misleading, as it implies a far more complete break with the past than is to be discerned in either of them. One is Nicholas Udall's *Ralph Roister Doister*, the per-

[1] Creizenach, ii. 1, 71, 88, 370, 374; Heiland, *Dramatische Aufführungen*, in K. A. Schmid, *Enc.. d. gesammten Erziehungs- und Unterrichtswesens* (2nd ed. 1876-87).

[2] Cf. p. 196.

[3] A. Wood, *Athenae* (ed. Bliss), i. 35, s. v. *Lilly*, says that Ritwise 'made the Tragedy of Dido out of Virgil; and acted the same with the scholars of his school before cardinal Wolsey with great applause.' The date of this performance is given in the *D. N. B.*, through a confusion with the anti-Lutheran play at court (cf. p. 196), as 1527. It is often identified with

the *Dido* played before Elizabeth at Cambridge in 1564. But there is no reason to doubt the statement of Hatcher's sixteenth-century MS. account of King's College (transcript in *Bodl.* 11,614) that the author of this was Edward Halliwell, who, like Ritwise, was a fellow of the college.

[4] Cf. p. 195.

[5] For the translation of the *Philoktetes* of Sophocles by Roger Ascham, cf. p. 195. Bale, *Scriptores* (1557), i. 720, mentions a translation from Greek into Latin of *tragoedias quasdam Euripidis* by Thomas Keye or Caius († 1550).

formance of which can be dated with some confidence in
1553, by which time its author may already have been
head master of Westminster ; the other is *Gammer Gurton's
Needle*, which was put on the stage at Christ's College,
Cambridge, has been ascribed to John Still, afterwards
bishop of Bath and Wells, and to John Bridges, afterwards
bishop of Oxford, but is more probably the work of one
William Stevenson, who was certainly superintending plays
at Christ's College in 1550–3. Both plays adopt the classical
arrangement by acts and scenes. But of the two *Gammer
Gurton's Needle* is far closer to the mediaeval farce in its
choice and treatment of subject. *Ralph Roister Doister*,
although by no means devoid of mediaeval elements, is in
the main an adaptation of the *Miles Gloriosus* of Plautus.
A slighter and rather later piece of work, *Jack Juggler*, was
also intended for performance by schoolboys, and is based
upon the *Amphitruo*. The earliest ' regular English tragedy '
on Senecan lines, or at least the earliest which oblivion has
spared, is the *Gorboduc* or *Ferrex and Porrex* of 1561. This
falls outside the strict scope of this chapter. But a fragment of a play from the press of John Rastell (1516–33)
which introduces 'Lucres' and Publius Cornelius, suggests
that, here as elsewhere, the Elizabethan writers were merely
resuming the history of the earlier English Renascence,
which religious and political disturbances had so wofully
interrupted.

Towards the end of Henry VIII's reign, the course of
the developing interlude was further diverted by a fresh
wave of humanist influence. This came from the wing of
the movement which had occupied itself, not only with
erudition, but also with the spiritual stirrings that issued
in the Reformation. It must be borne in mind that the
attitude of mere negation which the English Puritans, no
doubt with their justification in 'antiquity,' came to adopt
towards the stage, was by no means characteristic of the
earlier Protestantism. The Lutheran reformers were humanists as well as theologians, and it was natural to them to
shape a literary weapon to their own purposes, rather than
to cast it aside as unfit for furbishing. About 1530 a new

school of neo-Latin drama arose in Holland, which stood in much closer relations to mediaevalism than that which had had its origin in Italy.   It aimed at applying the structure and the style of Terence to an edifying subject-matter drawn from the tradition of the religious drama. The English *Everyman* belongs to a group of related plays, both in Latin and in the vernaculars, on its moral theme. The *Acolastus* (1530, acted 1529) of William Gnaphaeus and the *Asotus* (1537, written †1507) of George Macropedius began a cycle of 'Prodigal Son' plays which had many branches.   The movement began uncontroversially, but developed Protestant tendencies.   It spread to Basle, where Sixt Birck, who called himself Xystus Betuleius, wrote a *Susanna* (1537), an *Eva* (1539), a *Judith* (1540), and to France, where the Scotchman George Buchanan added to the 'Christian Terence' a 'Christian Seneca' in the *Jephthes* (1554) and *Baptistes* (1564) performed, between 1540 and 1543, by his students at Bordeaux.   In these, which are but a few out of many similar plays produced at this period, the humanists drew in the main upon such scriptural subjects, many of them apocryphal or parabolic, as were calculated, while no doubt making for edification, at the same time to afford scope for a free portrayal of human life.   This on the whole, in spite of the treatment of such episodes as the Magdalen *in gaudio*, was a departure from the normal mediaeval usage[1].

A new note, of acute and even violent controversy, was introduced into the Protestant drama by the fiery heretic, Thomas Kirchmayer, or Naogeorgos.   Kirchmayer wrote several plays, but the most important from the present point of view is that of *Pammachius* (1538), written during his pastorate of Sulza in Thuringia before his extreme views had led, not merely to exile from the Empire, but also to a quarrel with Luther.   The *Pammachius* goes back to one of the most interesting, although of course not one of the

---

[1] Creizenach, ii. 74 ; Herford, 84; Ward, i. 120; Bahlmann, *L. D.* 39, 53, 66, 82.   Many plays of this school are in *Comoediae et Tragoe-diae aliquot ex Novo et Vetere Testamento desumptae* (Brylinger, Basle, 1540) and *Dramata Sacra* (Oporinus, Basle, 1547).

most usual, themes of mediaeval drama, that of Antichrist; and it will readily be conceived that, for Kirchmayer, the Antichrist is none other than the Pope. It is interesting to observe that the play was dedicated to Archbishop Cranmer, whose reforming *Articles* of 1536 had roused the expectations of Protestant Germany. It was translated into English by John Bale, and was certainly not without influence in this country[1].

Both the merely edifying and the controversial type of Lutheran drama, indeed, found its English representatives. To the former belong the *Christus Redivivus* (1543) and the *Archipropheta* (1548) of the Oxford lecturer, Nicholas Grimald, one of which deals, somewhat exceptionally at this period, with the Resurrection, the other with John the Baptist. The *Absalon* of Thomas Watson, the *Jephthes* of John Christopherson (1546)[2], and the *Sodom, Jonah, Judith, Job, Susanna,* and *Lazarus and Dives* of Ralph Radclif (1546–56)[3], can only conjecturally be put in this class; and Nicholas Udall, who wrote an *Ezechias* in English, certainly did not commit himself irrecoverably in the eyes of good Catholics. John Palsgrave's *Ecphrasis* or paraphrase of *Acolastus* (1540) is supplied with grammatical notes, and is conceived wholly in the academic interest. On the other hand controversy is suggested in the titles of Radclif's *De Iohannis Hussi Damnatione,* and of the *De Meretrice Babylonica* ascribed by Bale to Edward VI[4], and is undeniably present in the *Christus Triumphans* (1551) of John Foxe, the martyrologist. This, like *Pammachius,* to which it owes much, belongs to the Antichrist cycle.

Nor was controversy confined to the learned language. As Protestantism, coquetted with by Henry VIII, and en-

---

[1] Creizenach, ii.76; Herford, 119; Bahlmann, *L. D.* 71. The play is in Brylinger, 314. A recent edition is that by Bolte and Schmidt (1891).

[2] Cf. p. 195. Both Thomas Artour, of Cambridge (ob. 1532), who wrote a *Microcosmum, tragoediam,* and a *Mundum plumbeum, tragoediam* (Bale, i. 709), and John Hooker (ob. †1543), of Magdalen College, Oxford, who wrote a *comoe-*diam, scilicet Piscatorem . . . alio titulo Fraus illusa vocatur* (Bale, i. 712), seem to have been Protestants, but nothing is known of the character of their plays, which may have been either English or Latin.

[3] Cf. p. 197.

[4] Bale, *Scriptores,* i. 674. It was written in his eleventh year (1547–8): cf. his *Remains,* i. xvi.

couraged by Cromwell, became gradually vocal in England and awakened an equally resonant reply, the vernacular drama, like every other form of literary expression, was swept into the war of creeds. This phase, dominating even the professional players, endured through the reigns of Edward VI and Mary, and still colours the early Elizabethan interludes. Its beginnings were independent of the Lutheran influences that so profoundly affected its progress. The morality already contained within itself that tendency to criticism which was perhaps the easiest way to correct its insipidity. Historically it was politics rather than religion with which the interlude first claimed to interfere. The story begins, harmlessly enough, at court, with an allegorical 'disguising' during the visit of the Emperor Charles V to London in 1523, in which the French king, typified by an unruly horse, was tamed by Amitie, who stood for the alliance between Charles and Henry[1]. In 1526 John Roo's morality, played at Gray's Inn, of 'Lord Governaunce' and 'Lady Publike-Wele' wrung Wolsey's withers, although as a matter of fact it was twenty years old[2]. Religion was first touched in 1527 in a piece of which one would gladly know more. It was played, as it seems, in Latin and French by the St. Paul's boys under John Ritwise, before ambassadors from France. The subject was the captivity of the Pope, and amongst the singular medley of characters named are found 'the herretyke, Lewtar' and 'Lewtar's wyfe, like a frowe of Spyers in Almayn[3].' This was, no doubt, all in the interests of orthodoxy ; and a similar tone may be assumed in the comedies acted before Wolsey in the

[1] Hall, 641.
[2] Hall, 719; Collier, i. 103.
[3] Hall, 735; Collier, i. 104; Brewer, iv. 1603; Brown, *Venetian Papers*, iv. 208; Cavendish, *Life of Wolsey*, i. 136. The characters further included 'an oratur,' a Poet, Religion, Ecclesia, Veritas, Heresy, False Interpretation, 'Corrupcio Scriptoris,' St. Peter, St. Paul, St. James, a Cardinal, two Serjeants, the Dauphin and his brother, a Messenger, three 'Almayns,' 'Lady Pees,' 'Lady Quyetnes,' 'Dame Tranquylyte.' Brandl, lvi suggests that the play might have been related to the *Ludus ludentem Luderum ludens* of Johannes Hasenberg (1530), and the analysis of this piece given by Bahlmann, *L. D.* 48, shows that the two had several characters in common. Another anti-Luther play, the *Monachopornomachia* (1538) of Simon Lemnius (Bahlmann, *L. D.* 70), appears to be distinct.

following year on the release of the Pope[1]. But much water passed under the mill in the next few years, and in 1533 there was a comedy at court ' to the no little defamation of certain cardinals[2].' In the same year, however, a proclamation forbade 'playing of enterludes' 'concerning doctrines in matters now in question and controversie[3].' This is a kind of regulation which it is easier to make than to enforce. Its effect, if it had any, was not of long duration. In 1537 much offence was given to Bishop Gardiner, the Chancellor of Cambridge University, by the performance amongst the youth of Christ's College of a ' tragedie,' part at least of which was ' soo pestiferous as were intolerable.' This ' tragedie' was none other than the redoubtable *Pammachius* itself[4]. In the same year, strict orders were issued to stay games and unlawful assemblies in Suffolk, on account of a 'seditious May-game' which was ' of a king, how he should rule his realm,' and in which ' one played Husbandry, and said many things against gentlemen more than was in the book of the play[5].' These were exceptional cases. Both the students of Christ's and the Suffolk rustics had in their various ways overstepped the permitted mark. Certainly Henry was not going to have kingship called in question on a village green. But it is notorious that, in matters of religion, he secretly encouraged many obstinate questionings which he openly condemned. And there is evidence that Cromwell at least found the interlude a very convenient instrument for the encouragement of Protestantism. Bale tells us that he himself won the minister's favour *ob editas comedias*[6] ; and there is extant amongst his papers a singular letter of this same year 1537, from Thomas Wylley, the vicar of Yoxford in Suffolk, in which he calls attention to three plays he has written, and asks that he may

---

[1] Brown, *Venetian Papers*, iv. 229.

[2] Herbert of Cherbury, *Life of Henry VIII* (Kennet, *Hist. of England*, ii. 173).

[3] Collier, i. 119, quoting Foxe, *Martyrologie* (1576), 1339.

[4] Herford, 129; Mullinger, *Hist. of Cambridge*, ii. 74; Cooper, *Annals of Cambridge*, i. 422 ; J. Peile,

Christ's College, 48. The correspondence about the play between Gardiner and Parker is printed in full in J. Lamb, *Collection of Documents from C. C. C.* (1838), 49.

[5] Brewer, xii. 1. 557, 585.

[6] Bale, *Scriptores*, i. 702. Cf. also S. R. Maitland, *Essays on the Reformation*, 182.

have 'fre lyberty to preche the trewthe[1].' Cranmer, too, seems to have been in sympathy with Cromwell's policy, for in 1539 there was an enterlude at his house which a Protestant described as 'one of the best matiers that ever he sawe towching King John,' and which may quite possibly have been John Bale's famous play[2].

The position was altered after 1540, when Cromwell had fallen and the pendulum of Henry's conscience had swung back to orthodoxy. Foxe records how under the *Act Abolishing Diversity in Opinions* (1539), known as the *Act of the Six Articles*, one Spencer, an ex-priest who had become an interlude-player, was burned at Salisbury for 'matter concerning the sacrament of the altar'; and how, in London, one Shermons, keeper of the Carpenters' Hall in Shoreditch, 'was presented for procuring an interlude to be openly played, wherein priests were railed on and called knaves[3].' But the stage was by now growing difficult to silence. In 1542 the bishops petitioned the king to correct the acting of plays 'to the contempt of God's Word[4]'; and in 1543 their desire

---

[1] Brewer, xii. 1. 244; Collier, i. 128. 'The Lorde make you the instrument of my helpe, Lorde Cromwell, that I may have fre lyberty to preche the trewthe.

I dedycat and offer to your Lordeshype A Reverent Receyving of the Sacrament, as a Lenton matter, declaryd by vj chyldren, representyng Chryst, the worde of God, Paule, Austyn, a Chylde, a Nonne callyd Ignorancy; as a secret thyng that shall have hys ende ons rehersyd afore your eye by the sayd chyldren.

The most part of the prystes of Suff. wyll not reseyve me ynto ther chyrchys to preche, but have dysdaynyd me ever synns I made a play agaynst the popys Conselerrs, Error, Colle Clogger of Conscyens, and Incredulyte. That, and the Act of Parlyament had not folowyd after, I had be countyd a gret lyar.

I have made a playe caulyd A Rude Commynawlte. I am a makyng of a nother caulyd The Woman on the Rokke, yn the fyer of faythe a fynyng, and a purgyng in the

trewe purgatory; never to be seen but of your Lordshyp's eye.

Ayde me for Chrystys sake that I may preche chryst.

Thomas Wylley
of Yoxforthe Vykar
fatherlesse and forsaken.'

[2] Brewer, xiv. 1. 22; Collier, i. 124.

[3] Foxe, *Acts and Monuments* (ed. Cattley), v. 443, 446.

[4] Brewer, xvii. 79; Wilkins, iii. 860. About the same date a *Discourse* (*Cotton MSS. Faustina*, C. ii. 5) addressed by Sir Richard Morison to Henry VIII is described by Brewer xvii. 707 as proposing 'a yearly memorial of the destruction of the bishop of Rome out of the realm, as the victory of Agincourt is annually celebrated at Calais, and the destruction of the Danes at Hoptide (*sic*: cf. vol. i. p. 154). It would be better that the plays of Robin Hood and Maid Marian should be forbidden, and others devised to set forth and declare lively before the people's

was met by the *Act for the Advauncement of true Religion and for the Abolishment of the Contrary*, which permitted of 'plays and enterludes for the rebukyng and reproching of vices and the setting forth of vertue'; but forbade such as meddled with 'interpretacions of scripture, contrary to the doctryne set forth or to be set forth by the kynges maiestie[1].' This led to a vigorous protest from John Bale, writing under the pseudonym of Henry Stalbridge, in his *Epistel Exhortatorye of an Inglyshe Christian*. Its repeal was one of the first measures passed under Edward VI[2].

Lord Oxford's men were playing in Southwark at the very hour of the dirge for Henry in the church of St. Saviour's[3]. Almost immediately 'the Poope in play' and 'prests in play' make their appearance once more[4]. Edward himself wrote his comedy *De Meretrice Babylonica*. In 1551 the English comedies ' in demonstration of contempt for the Pope ' were reported by the Venetian ambassador to his government[5]. But the players were not to have quite a free hand. It was now the Catholic interludes that needed suppression. A proclamation of August 6, 1549, inhibited performances until the following November in view of some ' tendyng to sedicion[6].' The *Act of Uniformity* of the same year forbade interludes

eyes the abomination and wickedness of the bishop of Rome, the monks, friars, nuns and such like, and to declare the obedience due to the King.' In 1543 the Lord Mayor complained to the Privy Council of the 'licentious manner of players.' Certain joiners, who were the Lord Warden's players, were imprisoned and reprimanded for playing on Sunday (*P. C. Acts*, i. 103, 109, 110, 122).

[1] 34, 35 *Hen. VIII*, c. 1; Hazlitt, *E. D. S.* 3; Collier, i. 127. A proclamation of May 26, 1545 (Hazlitt, *E. D. S.* 6), states an intention to employ in the fleet ' all such ruffyns, Vagabonds, Masterles men, Comon players and euill disposed persons ' as haunt ' the Banke, and such like naughtie places,' and forbids the retaining of servants, other than household servants or others allowed by law or royal licence. I have

already (p. 185) called attention to the ambiguity of the term 'comon player,' and on the whole, in view of a reference in the proclamation to 'theft and falsehood in play' I think that gamblers are here in question. In any case the protected players were not suppressed.

[2] 1 *Edw. VI*, c. 12.

[3] *S. P. Dom. Edw. VI*, i. 5; Collier, i. 135.

[4] Kempe, 64, 74, with a list of personages for precisely such a play. W. Baldwin, on whom cf. pp. 194, 200, and *Modern Quarterly*, i. 259, was probably a dramatist of this temper.

[5] Brown, *Venetian Papers*, v. 347; cf. the letters between Gardiner and Somerset, quoted by Maitland, *Essays on the Reformation*, 228, from Foxe, vi. 31, 57.

[6] Hazlitt, *E. D. S.* 8; Collier, i. 142; Fuller, *Ch. Hist.* (1655), 391.

'depraving and despising' the *Book of Common Prayer*[1]. A more effective measure came later in a proclamation of 1551, requiring either for the printing or the acting of plays a licence by the king or the privy council[2]. Mary, at whose own marriage with Philip in 1554 there were Catholic interludes and pageants[3], issued a similar regulation in 1553, though naturally with a different intention[4]. But this was not wholly effectual, and further orders and much vigilance by the Privy Council in the oversight of players were required in the course of the reign[5].

Only a few texts from this long period of controversial drama have come down to us. On the Catholic side there is but one, the play of *Respublica* (1553). In this, and in the Protestant fragment of *Somebody, Avarice and Minister*, the ruling literary influence is that of Lyndsay's *Satyre of the Thre Estaitis*. Of the remaining Protestant plays, *Nice Wanton* (1560) and Thomas Ingelend's *The Disobedient Child* (n. d.) derive from the Dutch school of Latin drama and its offshoots. *Nice Wanton* is an adaptation of the *Rebelles* (1535) of Macropedius. *The Disobedient Child* has its relations, not only to the play of Ravisius Textor already mentioned, but also to the *Studentes* (1549) of Christopher Stymmelius. More distinctly combative in tendency is the *Lusty Juventus* (n. d.) of R. Wever, who may be reckoned as a disciple of John Bale. The activity of Bale himself can be somewhat obscurely discerned as the strongest impelling

[1] 2, 3 *Edw. VI*, c. 1.
[2] Hazlitt, *E. D. S.* 9; Collier, i. 144. In 1550 'il plaiers' were sought for in Sussex (*Remains* of Edward VI, ii. 280). In 1551 the council gave Lord Dorset a licence for his players to play in his presence only (*P. C. Acts*, iii. 307). In 1552 Ogle sent to Cecil a forged licence taken from some players (*S. P. Dom. Edw. VI*, xv. 33).
[3] Holinshed (1808), iv. 61.
[4] Hazlitt, *E. D. S.* 15; Collier, i. 155; *P. C. Acts*, iv. 426.
[5] *S. P. Dom. Mary*, viii. 50; *P. C. Acts*, v. 234, 237; vi. 102, 110, 118, 148, 168, 169. In Feb. 1556 the council sent Lord Rich to

inquire into a stage-play to be given at Shrovetide at Hatfield Bradock, Essex, and directed him to stop such assemblies. An order against strolling players who spread sedition and heresy came in May. In June, 1557, performers of 'naughty' and 'lewd' plays were arrested in London and Canterbury. An order forbade plays throughout the country during the summer. In August a 'lewd' play called a 'Sackfull of News' was suppressed at the Boar's Head, Aldgate; and in September plays were forbidden in the city except, after licence by the ordinary, between All Saints and Shrovetide.

force on the Protestant side. He had his debts both to
Lyndsay and to Kirchmayer, whose *Pammachius*, if not
his other plays, he translated. But he is very largely original,
and he is set apart from the other great figures of ·the
Lutheran drama by the fact that all his plays were written
in idiomate materno. Moreover, though not without classical
elements, they were probably intended for popular performance, and approach more closely to the mediaeval structure
than to that of the contemporary interlude. In his *Scriptores*
he enumerates, under twenty-two titles, some forty-six of
them. The five extant ones were probably all 'compiled'
about 1538 while he was vicar of Thorndon in Suffolk. But
some of them were acted at the market-cross of Kilkenny
in 1553, and the others show signs of revision under Edward
VI or even Elizabeth. In *God's Promises, John Baptist,*
and *The Temptation*, Bale was simply adapting and Pro-
testantizing the miracle-play. The first is practically a
Prophetae, and they are all 'actes,' or as the Middle Ages
would have said 'processes' or 'pageants,' from a scriptural
cycle. Of similar character were probably a series of eleven
plays extending from Christ in the Temple to the Resurrection. A *Vita D. Joannis Baptistae* in fourteen *libri* perhaps
treated this favourite sixteenth-century theme in freer style.
The polemics are more marked in *Three Laws*, which is
a morality ; and in *King John*, which is a morality varied
by the introduction of the king himself as a champion against
the Pope and of certain other historical figures. It thus
marks an important step in the advance of the drama towards
the treatment of individualities. With the *Three Laws* and
King John may be grouped another set of lost plays whose
Latinized titles point unmistakably to controversy. An
Amoris Imago might be merely edifying ; but it would be
difficult to avoid meddling in matters of doctrine with such
themes to handle as *De Sectis Papisticis, Erga Momos et
Zoilos, Perditiones Papistarum, Contra Adulterantes Dei
Verbum, De Imposturis Thomae Becketi*. A pair of plays
Super utroque Regis Coniugio, must have been, if they were
ever acted, a climax of audacity even for John Bale.

What then, in sum, was the heritage which the early

Elizabethan writers and players of interludes received from their immediate predecessors? For the writers there were the stimulus of classical method and a widened range both of intention and of material. Their claim was established to dispute, to edify, or merely to amuse. They stood on the verge of more than one field of enterprise which had been barely entered upon and justly appeared inexhaustible. ' Tragedy, comedy, history, pastoral, pastoral-comical, historical-pastoral, tragical-historical, tragical-comical-historical-pastoral'; they possessed at least the keys to them all. Their own work is a heterogeneous welter of all the dramatic elements of the past and the future. Belated morals and miracle-plays jostle with adaptations of Seneca and Plautus. The *dramatis personae* of a single play will afford the abstractions of the allegory and the types of the farce side by side with real living individualities ; and the latter are drawn indifferently from contemporary society, from romance, from classical and from national history. These are precisely the dry bones which one day, beneath the breath of genius, should spring up into the wanton life of the Shakespearean drama. The players had made good their footing both in courts and amongst the folk. But their meddlings with controversy had brought upon them the hand of authority, which was not to be lightly shaken off. Elizabeth, like her brother, signalized the opening of her reign by a temporary inhibition of plays[1] ; and her privy council assumed a jurisdiction, by no means nominal, over things theatrical. In their censorship they had the assistance of the bishop of London, as 'ordinary.' The lesser companies may have suffered from the statute of 1572 which confined the privilege of maintaining either minstrels or players of interludes to barons and personages of higher degree[2]. But the greater ones which had succeeded in establishing themselves in London, grew and flourished.

---

[1] The proclamation of 16 May 1559 is printed in Hazlitt, *E. D. S.* 19 ; Collier, i. 166 ; *N. S. S. Trans.* 1880-5, 17 †. I do not think the proclamation loosely referred to by Holinshed (1587), iii. 1184, as at 'the same time' as another proclamation of 7 April is distinct from this. By 1 *Eliz.* c. 2 (the *Act of Uniformity*) the provision of 2, 3 *Edw. VI*, c. 1, against 'derogation, depraving or despising' the *Book of Common Prayer* in interludes was re-enacted with a penalty of 100 marks.

[2] Cf. vol. i. p. 54.

They lived down the competition of the amateurs which during the greater part of the century threatened to become dangerous, by their profitable system of double performances, at court and in the inn yards. Thus they secured the future of the drama by making it economically independent ; and the copestone of their edifice was the building of the permanent theatres. But for courtesy and a legal fiction, they were vagabonds and liable to whipping : yet the time was at hand when one player was to claim coat armour and entertain preachers to sack and supper at New Place, while another was to marry the daughter of a dean and to endow an irony for all time in the splendid College of God's Gift at Dulwich.

APPENDICES

APPENDICES

A

THE TRIBUNUS VOLUPTATUM

[The *tribunus voluptatum* was a municipal officer of the later Empire charged with the superintendence of the *spectacula*. He seems to have been appointed for life by the Emperor, and to have taken over functions formerly discharged by the praetors and quaestors. Mommsen, *Ostgothische Studien* (*Neues Archiv*, xiv. 495), says that he first appears in the fifth century. Possibly, therefore, Suetonius, *Tiberius*, 42, 'novum denique officium instituit a voluptatibus, praeposito equite R. T. Caesonio Prisco' refers to some other post. A *titulus*, 'de officio tribuni voluptatū qd a temelicis et scenariis,' which should be *C. Th.* i. 19, is missing from the text. *C. Th.* xv. 7, 13 (413), is addressed to the *tribunus voluptatum* of Carthage. The office was maintained in Italy under Theodoric (493–526). The *formula* of appointment here given is preserved by Cassiodorus, *Variae*, vii. 10; cf. *Var.* vi. 19 'cum lascivae voluptates recipiant tribunum.' The Senate is informed by *Var.* i. 43 (†509) of the promotion of Artemidorus, who had held the office, to be *praefectus urbanus*. The *tribunus voluptatum* of Rome is referred to in two inscriptions of 522 and 526 (Rossi, *Inscr. Christ.* i. Nos. 989, 1005). One Bacauda is appointed *tribunus voluptatum* in Milan by *Var.* v. 25 (523–6). Constantine Porphyrogenitus *de Caer.* i. 83 mentions an ἄρχων τῆς θυμέλης in the tenth-century court of Byzantium, who may be the same officer.]

Formula Tribuni Voluptatum.

Quamvis artes lubricae honestis moribus sint remotae et histrionum vita vaga videatur efferri posse licentia, tamen moderatrix providit antiquitas, ut in totum non effluerent, cum et ipsae iudicem sustinerent. amministranda est enim sub quadam disciplina exhibitio voluptatum. teneat scaenicos si non verus, vel umbratilis ordo iudicii. temperentur et haec legum qualitate negotia, quasi honestas imperet inhonestis, et quibusdam regulis vivant, qui viam rectae conversationis ignorant. student enim illi non tantum iucunditati suae, quantum alienae laetitiae et condicione perversa cum dominatum suis corporibus tradunt, servire potius animos compulerunt. Dignum fuit ergo moderatorem suscipere, qui se nesciunt iuridica conversatione tractare. locus quippe tuus his gregibus hominum veluti quidam tutor est positus. nam sicut illi aetates teneras adhibita cautela custodiunt, sic a te voluptates fervidae impensa maturitate frenandae sunt. age bonis institutis quod nimia prudentia constat invenisse maiores. leve desiderium etsi verecundia non cohibet, districtio praenuntiata modificat. agantur spectacula suis consuetudinibus ordinata, quia nec illi possunt invenire gratiam, nisi imitati fuerint aliquam disciplinam. Quapropter tribunum te voluptatum per illam indictionem nostra fecit electio, ut omnia sic agas, quemadmodum tibi vota civitatis adiungas, ne quod ad laetitiam constat inventum, tuis temporibus ad culpas videatur fuisse transmissum. cum fama diminutis salva tua opinione versare. castitatem dilige, cui subiacent prostitutae : ut magna laude dicatur: ' virtutibus studuit, qui voluptatibus miscebatur.' optamus enim ut per ludicram amministrationem ad seriam pervenias dignitatem.

B

TOTA IOCULATORUM SCENA

John of Salisbury, *Polycraticus* i. 8 (†1159, *P. L.* cxcix, 406), says, Satius enim fuerat otiari quam turpiter occupari. Hinc mimi, salii vel saliare⸗, balatrones, aemiliani, gladiatores, palaestritae, gignadii, praestigiatores, malefici quoque multi, et tota ioculatorum scena procedit.' The specific terms belong to John of Salisbury's classical learning rather than to contemporary use ; but his generic *ioculator* is the normal mediaeval Latin term for the minstrel in the widest sense. Classically the word, like its synonym *iocularis*, is an adjective, ' given to ioca,' ' merry.' Thus Cicero, *ad Att.* iv. 16. 3 ' huic ioculatorem senem illum interesse sane nolui.' Similarly Firmicus Maternus (fourth century), *Mathesis*, viii. 22 ' histriones faciat, pantomimos, ac scaenicos ioculatores,' and 4 *Conc. Carthag.* (398), c. 60 (*C. I. C. Decr. Gratiani*, i. 46. 6) ' clericum scurrilem et verbis turpibus ioculatorem ab officio retrahendum censemus.' Here the technical meaning is approached, which Gautier, ii. 12, declares to be complete in Salvian (fifth century), *de gubernatione Dei*. I cannot, however, find the word in Salvian, though I do find *iugulator*, ' cut-throat.' I have not come across *ioculator* as a noun before the eighth century (vol. i. p. 37), but thenceforward it is widely used for minstrels of both the *scóp* and the *mimus* type. A rarer form is *iocista*. *Ioculator* gives rise to the equally wide French term *jouglere, jougleur*, which seems to merge with the doublet *jogeler, jougler*, from *iocularis*. Similarly *ioca* becomes *jeu*, the equivalent of the classical and mediaeval Latin *ludus*, also in the widest sense. In Provençal *ioculator* becómes *joglar*, in English *jugelour, jugelere, jogeler*, &c. Thus *S. Eng. Leg.* i. 271 († 1290) 'Is iugelour a day bifore him pleide faste And nemde in his ryme and in is song þene deuel atþe laste'; King Horn (ed. Ritson), 1494 (†1300) ' Men seide hit were harperis, Jogelers, ant fythelers.' The incorrect modern French form *jongleur* seems due to a confusion between *jougleur* and *jangleur*, ' babbler,' and the English *jangler* has a similar use ; cf. *Piers the Plowman*, B. Text, *passus* x. 31 (ed. Skeat, i. 286) ' Iaperes and Iogeloures, and Iangelers of gestes.' Here both words appear side by side. The English *jogelour* sometimes has the full sense of the French *jougleur*, as in the instances just given, but as a term for minstrels of the higher or *scóp* type it has to compete, firstly, with the native *gleeman*, from O. E. *gleoman, gligman*, and secondly, with *minstrel*; and as a matter of fact its commoner use is for the lower type of minstrel or buffoon, and in particular, in the exact sense of the modern *juggler*, for a conjuror, *tregetour* or *prestigiator*. The latter is the usual meaning of *jogelour*, with the cognate *jogelrye*, in Chaucer ; for the former, cf. Adam Davie (†1312) 'the minstrels sing, the jogelours carpe.' In English documents the Latin *ioculator* itself to some extent follows suit ; the *ioculator regis* of late fifteenth or early sixteenth-century accounts is not a minstrel or musician, but the royal *juggler* (cf. vol. i. p. 68). On the other hand the Provençal *joglar* is differentiated in the opposite sense, to denote a grade of minstrelsy raised above the mere *bufos* (vol. i. p. 63).

A street in Paris known at the end of the thirteenth century as the ' *rue aus Jugléeurs*,' came later to be known as the *rue des Ménétriers* (Bernhard, iii. 378). This is significant of a new tendency in nomenclature which appears with the growth during the fourteenth century of the household entertainers at the expense of their unattached brethren of the road. *Minister* is classical Latin for ' inferior ' and so ' personal attendant.' The *ministeriales* of the later Empire are officers personally appointed by the Emperor. Towards the end of the thirteenth century *minister*, with its diminutives *ministellus* and *ministrallus* (French *menestrel*), can be seen passing from the general sense of ' household attendant ' to the special sense of ' household *ioculator*.' A harper was one of the *ministri* of Prince Edward in 1270 (vol. i. p. 49). Gautier, ii. 13, 51, quotes *li famles* (*famuli*) as a synonym for such *ioculatores*, and such doublets as 'menestrel et serviteur,' 'menestrel et varlet de chambre.' The *ministeralli* of Philip IV in 1288 include, with the musicians, the *rex heraudum* and the *rex ribaldorum*. From the beginning of the fourteenth century, however, *ministrallus*, with French *menestrel, menestrier*, and English *menestrel, mynstral*, is firmly established in the special sense. The antithesis between the *ministrallus* and the unattached *ioculator* appears in the terminology of the 1321 statutes of the Paris guild, 'menestreus et menestrelles, jougleurs et jougleresses'; but even this disappears, and the new group of terms becomes equivalent to the *ioculator* group in its widest sense. So too, *ministralcia, menestrardie, minstralcie*, although chiefly used, as by Chaucer, for music, are not confined to that; e. g. *Derby Accounts*, 109, 'cuidam tumblere facienti ministralciam suam.' The word is here approaching very near its kinsman *métier* (vol. ii. p. 105). Wright-Wülcker, 596, 693, quotes from the fifteenth-century glossaries, '*simphonia*, mynstrylsy,' and '*mimilogium*, mynstrisye.'

Ioculator and *ministrallus* are in their technical sense post-classical. But it is to be noted that the classical *histrio* and *mimus*, widened in connotation to an exact equivalent with these, remain in full use throughout the Middle Ages. They are indeed the more literary and learned words, as may be seen from the fact that they did not give rise to Romance or English forms; but they are not differentiated as to meaning. In particular, I do not find that *mimus* is used, as I have occasionally for convenience used it, to denote the lower minstrel of classical origin, as against the higher minstrel or *scóp*. Here are a few of many passages which go to establish this complete fourfold equivalence of *ioculator, ministrallus, mimus* and *histrio*; *Gloss.* in *B.N. MS.* 4883ᵃ, f. 67ᵇ (Du Méril, *Or. Lat.* 23) 'istriones sunt ioculatores'; *Constit. regis Minorcae* (1337, Mabillon, *Acta SS. Bened. Ian.* iii. 27) 'In domibus principum, ut tradit antiquitas, mimi seu ioculatores licite possunt esse'; *Conc. Lateran.* (1215), c. 16 'mimis, ioculatoribus et histrionibus non intendant.' This triple formula, often repeated by ecclesiastics, is of course conjunctive, like 'rogues and vagabonds.' Guy of Amiens (†1068) calls Taillefer both *histrio* and *mimus* (vol. i. p. 43). At the beginning of the sixteenth century the royal minstrels are *histriones* in the accounts of Shrewsbury, *ministralli* in those of Winchester College (*App. E. (iv)*), *mimi* in those of Beverley (Leach, *Beverley MSS.* 171). The *ioculator regis*, as already said, is by this time distinct. The Scottish royal minstrels appear in the Exchequer

Rolls for 1433–50 as *mimi, histriones, ioculatores* (*L.H.T. Accounts,* i, cxcix). The town musicians of Beverley, besides their specific names of *waits* and *spiculatores*, have indifferently those of *histriones, ministralli, mimi* (Leach, *Beverley MSS. passim*). It is largely a matter of the personal taste of the scribe. Thus the Shrewsbury accounts have both *histriones* and *menstralles* in 1401, *histriones* in 1442, *ministralli* regularly from 1457 to 1479, and *histriones* regularly from 1483 onwards.

Many other names for minstrels, besides these dominant four, have been collected by scholars (Gautier, ii. 10; Julleville, *Les Com.* 17; Gröber, ii. 489; Bédier, 366). From the compliments exchanged in the *fabliau* of *Des Deux Bordeors Ribaux* (Montaiglon-Raynaud, i. 1) one may extract the equivalence of *menestrel, trouvère, ribaud, bordeor, jougleur, chanteur, lecheor, pantonnier.* Of such subordinate names many are specific, and have been dealt with in their turn in chh. iii, iv. Others, again, are abusive, and found chiefly in the mouths of ecclesiastics, or as distinctive of the lower orders of minstrels. There are *garcio, nebulo, delusor, saccularius, bufo, ribaud, harlot.* There are *bourdyour, japer, gabber, jangler* (vol. i. p. 84). There is *scurra,* an early and favourite term of this class; cf. Ælfric's gloss (Ducange, s.v. *Iocista*), '*Mimus, iocista, scurra,* gligmon'; Wright-Wülcker, 693 (fifteenth-century gloss), '*scurra,* harlot'; and vol. i. p. 32. There is *leccator, leccour* (cf. above and *App. F.* s.v. *Chester*). And finally, there are a few terms of general, but not very common, application. *Scenici* and *thymelici* come from the early Christian prohibitions (vol. i. pp. 12, 17, 24). More important are a group derived from *ludus,* which like *jeu* has itself the widest possible sense, covering every possible kind of amusement. The *Sarum Statutes* of 1319, in a *titulus* dealing with *histriones,* speak of those ' qui " menestralli" et quandoque "ludorum homines" vulgari eloquio nuncupantur' (vol. i. p. 40). In the fifteenth and sixteenth centuries appear such terms as *lusor, lusiator, ludens, interlusor, interludens.* The two latter of these are always specific, meaning ' actor '; the three former are usually so, although they may occasionally have the more general sense, and this is probably also true of the English *player.* This question is more fully discussed in vol. i. pp. 84, 393, and vol. ii. p. 185.

C

COURT MINSTRELSY IN 1306

[From *Manners and Household Expenses of England in the Thirteenth and Fifteenth Centuries*, 141 (Roxburghe Club, 1841), from Exchequer Roll (King's Remembrancer's Dept.) in Rolls Office. The Pentecost feast of 1306 was that at which Prince Edward, who became in the next year Edward II, was knighted. It is described in the *Annales Londonienses* (*Chronicles of Edward I and Edward II*, R. S. i. 146).]

Solutio facta diversis Menestrallis die Pentecostes anno xxxiiij^to.

[A.D. 1306.]

Le Roy de Champaigne
Le Roy Capenny   cuilibet v.*marc.* ;
Le Roy Baisescue   summa, xvj.*li.*
Le Roy Marchis   i.*marc.*
Le Roy Robert

Phelippe de Caumbereye   lx.*s.* ; summa, lx.*s.*

Robert le Boistous   cuilibet iiij.*marc.* ;
Gerard de Boloigne   summa, c. vj.*s.* viij.*d.*

Bruant   cuilibet xl.*s.* ;
Northfolke   summa, iiij.*li.*

Carltone
Maistre Adam le Boscu   cuilibet xx.*s.* ;
Devenays   summa, lx.*s.*

Artisien   cuilibet xxx.*s.* ;
Lucat.   summa, iiij.*li.*
Henuer   [x.*s.*]

Le menestral Mons. de Montmaranci
Le Roy Druet
Janin le Lutour
Gillotin le Sautreour
Gillet de Roos
Ricard de Haleford
Le Petit Gauteron   cuilibet xl.*s.* ;
Baudec le Tabourer   summa, xxvj.*li.*
Ernolet
Mahu qui est ove la dammoisele de Baar
Janin de Brebant
Martinet qui est ove le Conte de Warwike
Gauteron le Grant

Le Harpour Levesque de Duresme   x.*s.*

Guillaume le Harpour qui est ove le Patriarke

Robert de Clou

Maistre Adam de Reve

Henri le Gigour

Corraud son compaignon

Le tierz Gigour

Gillot le Harpour

Johan de Newentone   cuilibet ij.*marc.* ;

Hugethun le Harpour lour compaignon   summa,

Adekin son compaignon   xxj.*li.* di.*marc.*

Adam de Werintone

Adam de Grimmeshawe

Hamond Lestivoun

Mahuet qui est ove Mons. de Tounny

Johan de Mochelneye

Janin Lorganistre

Simond le Messager

Les ij. Trumpours Mons. Thomas de Brother-
tone

Martinet le Taborour

Richard Rounlo

Richard Hendclck

Janin de La Tour son compaignon

Johan le Waffrer le Roy

Pilk

Januche } Trumpours Mons. le Prince
Gillot

Le Nakarier

Le Gitarer   cuilibet j.*marc.* ;

Merlin   summa, xl.*marc.*

Tomasin, Vilour Mons. Le Prince

Raulin qui est ove le Conte Mareschal

Esvillie qui est ove Mons. Pierres de Maule

Grendone

Le Taborer La Dame de Audham

Gaunsaillie

Guillaume sanz maniere

Lambyn Clay

Jaques Le Mascun

Son compaignon

Mahu du North
Le menestral ove les cloches
Les iij. menestraus Mons. de Hastinges
Thomelin de Thounleie
Les ij. Trompours le Comte de Hereforde
Perle in the eghe
Son compaignon
Janyn le Sautreour qui est ove Mons. de Percy
Les ij. Trumpours le Comte de Lancastre
Mellet
Henri de Nushom
Janyn le Citoler
Gilliame
Fairfax　　　　　　　　　　　　cuilibet xx.*s.* ;
Monet　　　　　　　　　　　　summa, iiij.*li.*
Hanecocke de Blithe

Summa totalis,—cxiiij.*li.* x.*s.*—Et issi demoerent des cc.*marc.*, pur partir entre les autres menestraus de la commune,—xviij.*li.* xvj.*s.* viij.*d.*— Et a ceste partie faire sunt assigne Le Roy Baisescu, Le Roy Marchis, Le Roy Robert, et Le Roy Druet, Gauteron le Graunt, Gauteron le Petit, Martinet le Vilour qui est ove le Conte de Warewike, et del hostiel Mons. le Prince, ij. serjantz darmes . . . clerke.

[Five lines of which only a few words are legible.]

Richard le Harpour qui est ove le Conte de Gloucestre.
Wauter Bracon Trounpour
Wauter le Trounpour
Johan le Croudere
Tegwaret Croudere
Geffrai le Estiveur
Guillot le Taborer
Guillot le Vileur
Robert le Vilour
Jake de Vescy
Richard Whetacre

A ceux xj., por toute la commune, xvii.*li.* iiii.*s.* viii.*d.*

Denarii dati Menestrallis.

Vidulatori Dominae de Wak'	v.*s.*
Laurentio Citharistae	di.*marc.*
Johanni du Chat cum Domino J. de Bur' . .	di.*marc.*

Mellers	v.*s.*
Parvo Willielmo, Organistae Comtissae Herefordiae	v.*s.*
Ricardo de Quitacre, Citharistae	di.*marc.*
Ricardo de Leylonde, Citharistae	di.*marc.*
Carleton Haralde	v.*s.*
Gilloto Vidulatori Comitis Arundelliae	di.*marc.*
Amakyn Citharistae Principis	v.*s.*
Bolthede	v.*s.*
Nagary le Crouder Principis	v.*s.*
Matheu le Harpour	v.*s.*
Johanni le Barber	v.*s.*
ij. Trumpatoribus J. de Segrave	di.*marc.*
Ricardo Vidulatori Comitis Lancastriae	v.*s.*
Johanni Waffrarario Comitis Lancastriae	xl. *d.*
Sagard Crouther	xl. *d.*
William de Grymesar', Harpour	xl.*d.*
Citharistae Comitissae Lancastriae	xl.*d.*
ij. Menestrallis J. de Ber[wyke]	xl.*d.*
Henrico de Blida	xl.*d.*
Ricardo Citharistae	xl.*d.*
William de Duffelde	xl.*d.*
v. Trumpatoribus Principis, pueris, cuilibet ij.*s.*	x.*s.* in toto.
iiijᵒʳ. Vigil' Regis, cuilibet di.*marc.*	xx.*s.*
Adinet le Harpour	
Perote le Taborer	
Adae de Swylingtone Citharistae	ij.*s.*
David le Crouther	xij.*d.*
Lion de Normanville	ij.*s.*
Gerardo	xij.*d.*
Ricardo Citharistae	ij.*s.*
Roberto de Colecestria	iij.*s.*
Johanni le Crouther de Salopia	xij.*d.*
Johanni le Vilour domini J. Renaude	xij.*d.*
Johanni de Trenham, Citharistae	ij.*s.*
Willielmo Woderove, Trumpatori	ij.*s.*
Johanni Citharistae J. de Clyntone	ij.*s.*
Waltero de Brayles	xij.*d.*
Roberto Citharistae Abbatis de Abbyndone	xij.*d.*
Galfredo Trumpatori domini R. de Monte Alto	
Richero socio suo	ij.*s.*
Thomae le Croudere	ij.*s.*

Rogero de Corleye, Trumpatori	ij.*s.*
Audoeno le Crouther	xij.*d.*
Hugoni Daa Citharistae	ij.*s.*
Andreae Vidulatori de Hor'	ij.*s.*
Roberto de Scardeburghe	xij.*d.*
Guilloto le Taborer Comitis Warrewici . . .	iij.*s.*
Paul' Menestrallo Comitis Marescalli	iij.*s.*
Matheo Waffraris domini R. de Monte Alto . . .	ij.*s.*
iij. diversis menestrallis, cuilibet iij.*s.*	ix.*s.*
Galfrido Citharistae Comitis Warrenniae . . .	ij.*s.*
Matill' Makejoye	xij.*d.*
Johanni Trumpatori domini R. de Filii Pagani . .	xij.*d.*
Adae Citharistae domini J. Lestraunge. . . .	xij.*d.*
Reginaldo le Menteur, Menestrallo domini J. de Buteturt	xij.*d.*
Perle in the Eghe	xij.*d.*
Gilloto Citharistae Domini P. de Malo Lacu . .	x.*s.*
Roberto Gaunsillie	xl.*d.* Item. xl.*d.*
Jacke de Vescy	di.*marc.*
Magistro Waltero Leskirmissour et fratri suo, cuilibet iij.*s.*	vj.*s.*

D

THE MINSTREL HIERARCHY

The term *rex* is not seldom applied as a distinction amongst minstrels. At the wedding of Joan of England in 1290 were present King Grey of England and King Caupenny of Scotland, together with Poveret, minstrel of the Marshal of Champagne (Chappell, i. 15). Poveret is perhaps the 'roy de Champaigne' of the 1306 list, which also includes the 'roys' Capenny, Baisescue, Marchis, Robert, and Druet (*Appendix C*). A 'rex Robertus,' together with 'rex Pagius de Hollandia,' reappears in accounts of the reign of Edward II (1307–27), while one of the minstrels of the king was William de Morlee, 'roy de North' (Percy, 416–8; cf. vol. i. p. 49). In France a list of the 'ministeralli' of Philip IV in 1288 includes the 'rex Flaiolatus,' 'rex Heraudum,' and 'rex Ribaldorum.' A certain Pariset, who was minstrel to the Comte de Poitiers in 1314, signs the statutes of the Paris guild in 1321 as 'Pariset, menestrel le roy,' and the various 'roys des menestreuls du royaume de France' who appear in and after 1338 may have been heads at once of the king's household minstrels and of the guild (*Appendix F*; cf. Bernhard, iii. 380). Further, the title is claimed by the authors of various pieces of minstrel literature. 'Adenet le roi' is the author of *Cleomadès* (Paris, 84; Percy, 416–8), and 'Huon le roi,' perhaps identical with ' Huon de Cambrai' and 'Huon Paucele,' of the *fabliau* of *Du Vair Palefroi* (Bedier, 438; Montaiglon-Raynaud, i. 3). The term *rex* is of course common enough in connexion with temporary or permanent associations of all sorts, and is probably of folk origin (vol. i. chaps. iv, viii). It is possible that some of these 'rois' may have been crowned by 'puis' (Lavoix, ii. 377), but it is more probable that they had some official pre-eminence amongst their fellows, and perhaps some jurisdiction, territorial or otherwise. Clearly this was the case with the 'roy des ministralx' at Tutbury. The appearance of the 'rex Flaiolatus' with the 'rex Heraudum' and the 'rex Ribaldorum' in the French list of 1288 is thus significant, for the latter had just such a jurisdiction over the riff-raff of the court (Ducange, s.v.), and I conceive the relation of the minstrel 'roys' to their fellows to have been much that of the 'Kings at arms' to the ordinary heralds. It seems that minstrels and heralds belonged to the same class of *ministri*. The order of the Emperor Henry II (vol. i. p. 52) couples 'ioculatores et armaturi' and 'Carleton Haralde' is actually rewarded in the 1306 list (*App. C*, p. 237). If one may quote a Celtic parallel, the *Arwyddfardd* or heralds formed a regular division (†1100) of Welsh minstrelsy (E. David, *La Poésie et la Musique dans la Cambrie*, 72–91). Under Richard II the head of the English royal minstrels was a *rex*, but from 1464 onwards the term used is *marescallus* (Rymer, xi. 512), and this again may be paralleled from the supreme position of the Earl Marshal in heraldry. At the head of the Earl of Lancaster's minstrels in 1308 was an *armiger*. I only find this term again in the burlesque account of the 'auncient minstrell' shown before Elizabeth at Kenilworth (*Appendix H*). He was 'a squier minstrel of Middilsex' and, as he bore the arms of Islington, presumably a 'wait.'

E

EXTRACTS FROM ACCOUNT BOOKS

I. Durham Priory.

[The entries, unless otherwise specified, are amongst the extracts
(generally of *Dona Prioris*) from the Bursars' Rolls between 1278 and
1371, printed by Canon Fowler in vols. ii, iii of the *Durham Account
Rolls* (Surtees Soc.). *D. H. B.* = *Durham Household Book* (Surtees Soc.),
F. P. = *Inventories and Account Rolls of Finchale Priory* (Surtees Soc.).
This was a cell of Durham Priory. The minstrelsy often took place at
the *ludi Domini Prioris*, either in his *camera* (*D. A.* ii. 424) or at
Beaurepaire, Witton, or other *maneria* of the Priory. There seem to
have been in most years four *ludi ordinarii* (*D. A.* ii. 296), though
occasionally only two or three are mentioned. These were at the feasts
of Candlemas, Easter, St. John Baptist, and All Saints (*D. A.* i. 242,
iii. 932). But the Prior, Sub-Prior, and brethren seem often to have been
ludentes, spatiantes, or *in recreacione* (*D. A.* i. 118, 235), without much
regard to fixed dates. In 1438–9 they were *ludentes* for as much as
eleven weeks and four days at Beaurepaire (*D. A.* i. 71). See also *D. A.*
i. 16, 116, 120, 129, 137, 138, 142, 166, 207, 263; ii. 287, 419, 456, 515;
iii. 810, s.vv. *Ludi*, &c.; *D. H. B.* 9, 13, 54, 141, 240, 339; *F. P.* 30,
ccxcv, ccccxxxvi.]

1278 Menestrallo Regis Scociae.
Menestrallo de Novo Castro.

1299. Roberto le Taburer.

1300–1. Cuidam hystrioni Regis.

1302–3. Histrionibus domini Regis.

1310–11. Hugoni de Helmeslaye stulto domini Regis.
Cuidam Iugulatori d'ni Regis.
Cuidam Cytharistae.

†1310. Histrionibus d'ni H. de Bello Monte.
In scissura tunicae stulti.

†1315. Histrionibus ad Natale.

1330–1. In uno garniamento pro Thoma fatuo empto.
Histrionibus ad Natale.
„   in fest. S. Cuthberti in Marcio.
„   ad fest. S. Cuthberti in Sept.
„   d'ni Henrici de Beaumond.
Citharistae (in another roll 'citharatori') d'ni Roberti de
Horneclyff ex precepto Prioris.

1333–4. Duobus histrionibus in die Veneris proximo post octavam
beati Martini.

Histrionibus d'ni Regis quando d'nus noster Rex rediit de Novo Castro.

Stulto d'ni Episcopi.

Histrionibus comitis Warenne.

Histrionibus Regis Scociae.

1334-5. Histrionibus ad Natale.

1335-6. Histrionibus d'ni Regis Scociae.

Duobus histrionibus die Sci. Cuthberti.

Duobus histrionibus ex precepto Prioris.

Histrionibus Novi Castri ad fest. S. Cuthberti.

Histrionibus d'ni R. de Nevill, per Priorem.

In 1 Cythara empta pro Thom. Harpour.   3^s.

Cuidam histrioni apud Beaurepaire per R. de Cotam ex dono Prioris.

Thomae fatuo ex precepto eiusdem.

†1335. Istrionibus d'ni Regis.

Istrionibus Reginae apud Pytingdon.

Istrionibus [die Dominica proxima post festum Epiphaniae, quo die d'nus Episcopus epulabatur cum Priore].

Will'o de Sutton, Citharaedo d'ni Galfridi Lescrop eodem die.

Istrionibus die Natalis Domini.

†1336. Duobus istrionibus d'ni Regis.

Edmundo de Kendall, Cytharaeto, de dono Prioris ad Pascha.

Menestrallis de dono [quando Episcopus epulabatur cum Priore].

†1337. In 1 pari sotularium pro Thoma fatuo.

1338-9. Several payments to 'istriones' and 'menestralli.'

In 4 ulnis burelli scacciati emptis pro garniamento Thomae Fole per preceptum Prioris.

1339-40. In panno empto in foro Dunelm. pro uno garniamento pro Thoma fatuo.

Willelmo Piper istrioni d'ni Radulphi de Nevill die Circumcisionis.

1341. Pelidod et duobus sociis suis histrionibus d'ni Regis post Natale Domini.

1341-42. In garniamentis emptis pro . . . Thoma fatuo (and similar entries, or for 'Russet,' 'pannus,' 'Candelwykstret' in other years).

†1343. Various payment to 'Istriones.'

1347-8. 'Istrionibus,' &c.

1350–51. Istrionibus ad Natale.

    ,, ad S. Cuthbertum in Sept.

1355–6. Will'o Pyper et aliis istrionibus ad Natale.

  Item duobus istrionibus d'ni Episcopi et duobus istrionibus Comitis de Norhamton in festo Sci. Cuthberti in Marcio.

  Item istrionibus d'ni Episcopi ad festum Paschae.

  Item istrionibus in festo Sci. Cuthberti in Sept.

1356–7. In sepultura Thomae fatui et necessariis expensis circa corpus eius, per manus d'ni Prioris (similar entry in miscellaneous roll, ' Thomae Fole,' *D. A.* iii. 719).

  Diversis ministrallis (*D. A.* iii. 718).

†1357. Et Will'o Blyndharpour ad Natale.

  Et Ioh'i Harpour d'ni Ioh'is de Streuelyn et Will'o Blyndharpour de Novo Castro.

  Et duobus Trompours Comitis de Norhamton apud Wyuestow.

  Et cuidam Harpour vocato Rygeway.

  Istrionibus d'ni Episcopi (and Harpers, &c.).

†1360. Petro Crouder apud Pityngton, per Capellanum.

  Item eidem Petro pro uno quarterio ordii sibi dato per Priorem.

  Duobus Istrionibus Episcopi in festo Assensionis Domini.

  Et cuidam Istrioni Maioris villae Novi Castri per Capellanum.

1360–61. Will'o Pyper et aliis istrionibus ad Natale per manus Ioh'is del Sayles.

  Cuidam Welsharpour d'ni Will'i de Dalton.

  Item histrionibus aliorum dominorum.

1361–2. In uno viro ludenti in uno loyt et uxori eius cantanti apud Bewrpayr (*D. A.* i. 127, *Hostiller's Accounts*).

1362. Item cuidam histrioni harper episcopi Norwychiae in festo Transl. S^{ci}. Cuthberti.

  Cuidam Istrioni Jestour Jawdewyne in festo Natalis Domini.

  Will'o ye kakeharpour ad idem festum.

  Et Barry similem sibi ad id. festum.

  Et cuidam ystrioni caecò franco cum uno puero fratre suo.

  Barry harper ex precepto Prioris in una tunica empta.

1363–4. Item cantoribus in Adventu Domini cum histrionibus ibidem ex dono Prioris.

  Item cuidam histrioni die Dominica *Quasimodo geniti.*

1364–5. To two players of the Lord Duke at the said feast (of St. Cuthbert) (Raine, *St. Cuthbert,* 109, *Surtees Soc.*).

1365–6. Barry Harpour, ystrionibus, &c.

1366–8. Ministrallis, Istrionibus.

1368–9. Rob'o Trompour et Will'o Fergos ministrallo in die Sci. Cuthberti.

1373–4. Duobus Ministrallis cum uno Weyng.

1374. 12 ministrallis in festo S^{ci}. Cuthb.

1375–6. Ministrall. in die S. Cuthb. in Mar.

Cuidam ministrallo ludenti coram domino Priori in camera sua.

Tribus ministrallis Comitis del Marchie ludentibus coram domino Priore.

Cuidam ministrallo domini Regis veniente cum domino de Neuill.

12 ministrallis in festo Sci. Cuthb. in Sept.

4 ministrallis domini Principis in festo exaltacionis S^{ce}. Crucis.

Cuidam ministrallo in festo S^{ci}. Mathaei.

Ministrallis in festo S^{ci}. Cuthb. in Marcio anno Domini, &c. lxxv^{to}.

Duobus ministrallis in die Pasche.

1376–7. Willielmo Fergos et Rogero Harpour caeco ad Natale Domini.

Aliis ministrallis domini de Percy in eadem fest.

1377–8. Haraldis, histrionibus et nunciis, ut patet per cedulam.

1378–9. Histrionibus . . . dominorum Regis, Ducis, et aliorum dominorum.

1380–1. Iohanni Momford ministrallo domini Regis.

1381–2. Ministrallis domini de Neuill apud Beaurepaire cum domina de Lomly.

Ministrallo domini Ducis cum uno saltante in camera domini Prioris.

(and others.)

1384–5. Ministrallis domini Regis.

1394–5. Ministrallis in festo S. Cuthb., Henrici Percy, domini Ducis Lancastr., domini de Neuill, Ducis Eborac., de Scocia, comitis Canciae, ad Nat. Domini, de Hilton, Ric. Brome ministrallo, in fest. S. Cuthb. in Marc.

Uni Trompet domini Regis.

Uni Rotour de Scocia.

1395. Item, in vino, speciebus, in donis datis Confratribus, ministrallis et aliis diversis, ex curialitate (*F. P.* cxv).

1399–1400. Ministrallis.

1401–2. Ministrallis.

1416–7. Ministrallis.

Diversis pueris ludentibus coram eodem priore in festo S^{ci.} Stephani hoc anno.

1441–2. Per . . . capellanum [et] . . . per bursarium ministrallis domini Regis et aliorum dominorum supervenientibus.

1446–7. Ministrallis.

1449–50. Ministrallis.

1464–5. Et solvit Iohanni Andrewson et sociis suis operantibus pro nova tectura unius camerae vocatae le Playerchambre (*F. P.* ccxcv).

1465. Item j por de ferro in camera Prioris, j in le plaer cha . . . (*F. P.* ccxcviii).

1496. Paid to Robert Walssch for two days playing John Gibson of Elvet 'herper' (*D. H. B.* 340).

1532–3. . . . bus lusoribus . . . Regis, in regardis, in auro, 15ˢ.

Et custodi ursorum et cimearum dominae Principis.

Et capellano, per bursarium, pro 4 lusoribus domini Comitis de Darby, in auro, 7ˢ. 6ᵈ. (*D. H. B.* 143, the last two items crossed out).

1536–7. In diversis donis datis ministrallis diversorum dominorum.

1538. Paid to the ministrels (*ministrallis*) at 'le musters' upon 'le Gelymore.'

1539–40. Paid to the players (*lusoribus*) of Auklande at Christmas before Master Hyndley, as a present (*D. H. B.* 340).

1554–5. [Cathedral Account.] Paid for two mynstralles.

II. Maxstoke Priory.

[Printed by Hazlitt-Warton, ii. 97, '*ex orig. penes me.*']

'In the Prior's accounts of the Augustine canons of Maxstoke in Warwickshire, of various years in the reign of Henry VI (1422–61), one of the styles or regular heads is *De Ioculatoribus et Mimis* . . . .

Ioculatori in septimana S. Michaelis, ivᵈ.

Citharistae tempore natalis domini et aliis iocatoribus, ivᵈ.

Mimis de Solihull, viᵈ.

Mimis de Coventry, xxᵈ.

Mimo domini Ferrers, viᵈ.

Lusoribus de Eton, viii^d.

Lusoribus de Coventry, viii^d.

Lusoribus de Daventry, xii^d.

Mimis de Coventry, xii^d.

Mimis domini de Asteley, xii^d.

Item iiij mimis domini de Warewyck, x^d.

Mimo caeco, ii^d.

Sex mimis domini de Clynton.

Duobus mimis de Rugeby, x^d.

Cuidam citharistae, vi^d.

Mimis domini de Asteley, xx^d.

Cuidam citharistae, vi^d.

Citharistae de Coventry, vi^d.

Duobus citharistis de Coventry, viii^d.

Mimis de Rugeby, viii^d.

Mimis domini de Buckeridge,. xx^d.

Mimis domini de Stafford, ii^s.

Lusoribus de Coleshille, viij^d. . . .

[1432] Dat. duobus mimis de Coventry in die consecrationis Prioris, xii^d.'

III. THETFORD PRIORY.

[From Collier, i. 55, 84, on the authority of a 'MS. of the expenses of the Priory of Thetford, from 1461 to 1540, lately in the collection of Mr. Craven Orde, and now of the Duke of Newcastle.']

'The mention of "plays" and "players" does not begin until the 13th of Henry VII; but "Minstrels" and "Waytes" are often spoken of there as receiving rewards from the convent. The following entries, regarding "plays" and "players," occur between the 13th and 23rd of Henry VII:—

13 Henry VII [1497–8].   It^m. sol. in regard 12 capital plays, 4^s.

   It^m. sol. to menstrell and players in festo Epiphaniae, 2^s.

19 Henry VII [1503–4].   It^m. sol. to the play of Mydenale, 12^d.

21 Henry VII [1505–6].   It^m. sol. in regard lusoribus et menstrall, 17^d.

23 Henry VII [1507–8].   It^m. sol. in regard lusoribus div. vices, 3^s 4^d.

   It^m. sol. in regard to Ixworth play, 16^d.

   It^m. sol. in regard to Schelfanger play, 4^d.

. . . From the 1st to the 31st Henry VIII, the King's players, the King's jugglers, the King's minstrels, and the King's bearwards were visitors of Thetford, and were paid various sums, from 4d to 6s 8d, by the Prior of the convent there, as appears by the entries in the account-book during that period. On one occasion, 16 Henry VIII, Cornyshe, "the master of the King's chapel," was paid 3s 4d by the prior; but he was then, probably, attendant upon the King, who is not unfrequently spoken of as having arrived, and being lodged at the Priory. Mr. Brandon and Mr. Smith are more than once rewarded as " Jugglers of the King." The Queen's players, the Prince's players, and the players of the Queen of France, also experienced the liberality of the Prior, as well as those of the Duke of Norfolk, the Duke of Suffolk, the Earl and Countess of Derby, Lord and Lady Fitzwater, the Lord Privy Seal, the Lord Chancellor, Sir Thomas Challoner and two gentlemen who are called Marks and Barney.'

IV. WINCHESTER COLLEGE.

[Extracts from *computi* partly by Hazlitt-Warton, ii. 98, and partly by M. E. C. Walcott, *William of Wykeham and his Colleges*, 206. The *satrapae* of 1466 and 1479 are said by Mr. Walcott to have been local notables, but a collation to them would not cost so little or be grouped with rewards to minstrels in the *computus*. Ducange says that the word is used 'pro quodam ministro vel satellite.' The Magdalen accounts use it for the ' serjeants ' of the mayor of Oxford (Macray, *Register*, i. 15).]

1400. In dono lusoribus civitatis Wynton venient. ad collegium cum suo tripudio ex curialitate, xijd.

1412. In dat. Rico. Kent bochier tempore regno suo vocat. Somer-kyng, xijd.

1415. In dat. diversis hominibus de Ropley venientibus ad coll. diè Sanct. Innoc. et tripudiantibus et cantantibus in aula coram Epō. scholarium, xxd.

1422. Dat. histrioni dni epi Wynton et ioculatori ejusdem 5ti die Ianuarii, cuilibet, xxd.

1425. Dat. Gloucester ioculatori ludenti coram custode et sociis penultimo die Iulii, ob reverentiam ducis Exon. xijd.

1426. Dat. ministrellis d. epi Wynton tempore Nat. Dni. ex curialitate et honestate, ijs viiid.

Dat. ij ministrallis comitissae de Westmorland venient' ad coll. xxd.

1433. In dat. mimis dni cardinalis venient' ad collegium erga festum natale Dni iiijs.

1462. Dat' Epo Nicholatensi visitanti Dominum custodem in hospitio suo de nocte Sti. Nicholai, iiijd.

1464. Et in dat. ministrallis comitis Kanciae venient. ad coll. in mense Iulii, iiijs iiijd.

1466. Et in dat. satrapis Wynton venientibus ad coll. festo Epiphaniae, cum ijs dat. iiij. interludentibus et J. Meke citharistae eodem festo, iiijs.

1467. Et in datis iiijor mimis dom. de Arundell venient. ad coll. xiij. die Febr. ex curialitate dom. custodis, ijs.

In dat. Ioh. Pontisbery et socio ludentibus in aula in die circumcisionis, ijs.

1471. In dat. uni famulo dni regis Angliae venienti ad collegium cum Leone mense Ianuarii, xxd.

1472. Et in dat. ministrallis dom. Regis cum viijd. dat. duobus Berewardis ducis Clarentiae, xxd.

Et in dat. Iohanni Stulto quondam dom. de Warewyco, cum iiijd dat. Thomae Nevyle taborario.

Et in datis duobus ministrallis ducis Glocestriae, cum iiijd. dat. uni ministrallo ducis de Northumberland, viijd.

Et in datis duobus citharatoribus ad vices venient. ad collegium viijd.

1477. Et in dat. ministrallis dom. Principis venient. ad coll. festo Ascensionis Domini, cum xxd. dat. ministrallis dom. Regis, vs.

1479. Et in datis satrapis Wynton venientibus ad coll. festo Epiphaniae, cum xijd dat. ministrallis dom. episcopi venient. ad coll. infra octavas epiphaniae, iiis.

Dat. lusoribus de civitate Winton. venientibus ad collegium in apparatu suo mens. Iulii, vs vijd.

1481. Et in sol. ministrallis dom. regis venientibus ad collegium xv die Aprilis cum xijd solut. ministrallis dom. episcopi Wynton venientibus ad collegium io die Iunii, iiijs iiijd.

Et in dat. ministrallis dom. Arundell ven. ad coll. cum viijd dat. ministrallis dom. de la Warr, ijs iijd.

1483. Sol. ministrallis dom. regis, ven. ad coll. ijs iiijd.

1484. Et in dat. uni ministrallo dom. principis et in aliis ministrallis ducis Glocestriae v die Iulii, xxd.

1536. In dat. ministrallis dni regis venientibus ad coll. xiij die April pro regardo, ijs.

1573. In regardis dat' tibicinis dominae reginae cum vino, vijs iiijd.

In regardis dat. lusoribus dominae reginae, vjs viijd.

V. Magdalen College, Oxford.

[Extracts from account books made by J. R. Bloxam and W. D. Macray, *A Register of the Members of St. Mary Magdalen College, Oxford*, First Series, ii. 235; New Series, i. 3; ii. 3. The dates given below are for the year in which the account begins.]

1481. pro cerothecis pro chorustis, iiij^d.

1482. v^o die Decembris pro cerothecis episcopi in festo S. Nicholai iiij^d.

1483. pro cerothecis datis ad honorem Sancti Nicolai duobus choristis, viij^d.

1484. pro cerothecis Episcopi in festo Sancti Nicholai et eius crucem ferentis, viij^d.

1485. 'Ursarii' of Lord Stanley dined with the Fellows.

1486. pro factura sepulturae erga pascham, xij^d.

'Sex vagatores' dined with the servants.

Solut. vi^o die Ian. citharistis et mimis tempore ludi in aula in regardo, in tempore Nativitatis Domini, viij^d.

Solut. pro quodam ornamento lusorum vocato *ly Cape mayntenawnce*, ix^d.

1487. pro vestimentis lusorum tempore Nativ. Domini, consilio unius decani, ii^s ij^d.

pro clavis ad pannos in ornatum aulae pendendos, j^d.

1488. Sol. Iohanni Wynman pro scriptura unius libri de servicio episcopi pro die Innocencium, v^d.

1490. Singers from Abingdon, London and Hereford entertained.

1494. Sol. Pescode servanti quandam bestiam vocatam *ly merumsytt* ex consilio seniorum, quia Rex erat apud Woodstocke, xij^d.

1495. Sol. Henrico Mertyn pro lino, *alyn*, et aliis emptis pro ludo in die Paschae, xvij^d ob.

Sol. Pescod ducenti duo animalia nuncupata *mermosettes*.

1502. Sol. in expensis factis tempore Nativitatis Domini, in biberiis post interludia et alia, xiij^s iiij^d.

1506. To John Burgess, B.A., ... x^d were paid for writing out a miracle-play ('scriptura lusi') of S^t. Mary Magd., and v^s. for some music; and viij^d to a man who brought some songs from Edward Martyn, M.A. For his diligence with regard to the above miracle-play, Kendall, a clerk, was rewarded with i^s.

pro expensis mimi, iiij^s, at Christmas.

1507. in quatuor refectionibus citharistae, at Epiphany.

1508. Sol. famulo Regis ducenti ursam ad collegium, ex mandato Vice-presidentis, xij^d.

1509. Sol. pane, cibo et aliis datis pueris ludentibus in die Paschae, mandato Vicepr. xvij^d ob.

1510. Sol. pro expensis factis in aula tempore Nativitatis Domini, xiij^s iiij^d.

Sol. cuidam mimo tempore Nativitatis Domini in regardo, viij^d.

1512. Sol. Petro Pyper pro pypyng in interludio nocte Sancti Iohannis, vj^d.

Sol. Iohanni Tabourner pro lusione in interludio Octavis Epiphaniae, vj^d.

Sol. Roberto Johnson pro una tunica pro interludiis, iiij^s.

1514. pro carnibus [? carbonibus] consumptis in capella tribus noctibus ante Pascha et in tempore Nativitatis, ij^s.

1518. To Perrot, the Master of the choristers, 'pro tinctura et factura tunicae eius qui ageret partem Christi et pro crinibus mulieribus, ij^s vj^d.'

1520. pro pane . . . datis clericis in vigiliis S^{ti}. Nicolai.

pro cerothecis puerorum in festo Sancti Nicolai.

1526. pro merendis datis episcopo capellanis clericis et aliis in vigilia S^t. Nicolai.

1529. pro . . . episcopo Nicholai.

1530. pro pueris in festo Sancti Nicholai.

1531. Solut. mimis dominae principisshae, xx^d.

Pro biberio dato sociis et scolaribus post interludia in tempore Natalis Domini, vj^s viij^d.

1532. To the Queen's players, by the President's order, xii^d.

pro biberio dato sociis post ludum baccalaureorum in magna aula, vj^s viij^d.

1535. pro merenda facta in vigilia Sancti Nicolai.

Actors at Christmas, iiij^s iiij^d.

pro merenda facta post comediam actam, ix^s iij^d.

'ioculatoribus Regis,' by the President's order, xx^d.

1536. pro biberio in nocte Sancti Nicholai.

Sol. mimo pro solatiis factis sociis et scholasticis tempore Nativitatis Domini, viij^s.

1537. pro carbonibus consumptis in sacrario, per custodes sepulchri, et per pueros in festis hiemalibus, ij^s [and in other years].

1539. pro bellariis datis sociis cum ageretur comedia, viij^s.

1540. pro epulis datis sociis eo tempore quo agebatur tragedia, viij^s iiij^d.

pro bellariis datis sociis et clericis vigilia divi Nicolai, iiij^s viij^d.

pro pane et potu datis semicommunariis dum curabant publicam exhibere comediam, xx^d.

1541. A 'tympanista' was hired at Christmas and comedies acted.

1554. 30 Ian. in adventu [dom. Matravers] ad tragedias per duas noctes, xlij⁸ viij^d ob.

Pro epulis datis sociis post exactas tragedias, x⁸ ix^d.

The only Elizabethan entry I need note is :—

1561. Sol. Joyner, pictori, depingenti portenta religiosorum in spectaculo Baulino, iij⁸ iiij^d . . . depingenti nomina haeresium in spectaculo (in aula) quod choristarum moderator [Richard Baull] ordinavit.

VI. Shrewsbury Corporation.

[Extracts from the Bailiffs' accounts by Owen and Blakeway, *Hist. of Shrewsbury* (1825), i. 262, 267, 275, 284, 290, 292, 325 sqq.; and by W. D. Macray in *Hist. MSS.* xv. 10. 25. It is not always clear to which calendar year an entry belongs. The accounts run from Michaelmas to Michaelmas, but Owen and Blakeway generally quote entries under one calendar year and sometimes under one regnal year.]

1401. 'Histriones' of the Prince and the Earl of Stafford.
'Menstralles' of the Earls of Worcester and Stafford.

1409. Players [i. e. in these early accounts, 'histriones,' not 'lusores'] of the countess and earl of Arundel, of Lord Powis, Lord Talbot, and Lord Furnivall.
Players 'in honorem villae' at the marriage of a cousin of David Holbache.

1437. Minstrels' of earl of Stafford.

1438. Livery to two town minstrels, 'voc. *waytes.*'

1442. Some town minstrels called 'histriones.' In same year, 'histrionibus regis,' and in subsequent years 'histrionibus' of earl of Shrewsbury and others, including one 'voc. Trumpet.'

1450. Players and minstrels at coming of duke of York from Ireland.

1457. Denaria soluta uni ministrallo domini principis [Edward] pro honestate villae.
Quatuor ministrallis domini ducis de Bukyngham.
Duobus ministrallis d'ni de Powys.
1 lagenae vini de Ruyn dictis ministrallis.
Denaria data uni ministrallo d'ni principis et suo puero.
iiij. ministrallis d'ni ducis de Eboraco.
iv. ministrellis d'ni ducis de Excestro.

1474. Regardo ministrallis d'ni ducis de Clarence.

1478. Waltero Harper ministrallo d'ni principis.
Regardo dato uni ministrallo ducis Gloucestris vocato le Taborer.

Regardo sex ministrallis d'ni Regis.

1479. Soluta pro liberata ministrallorum vocatorum Wayts, quilibet eorum.

Soluta pro conductu unius ministralli vocati Wayt a villa de Norhampton usque Salop.

Soluta pro quodam regardo dato uni ministrallo d'ni Regis via elemosinaria causa eius paupertatis et aetatis.

[From this point *histriones* replaces *ministralli* in the accounts.]

1483. Soluta pro quodam regardo dato sex histrionibus domini Regis pro honestate villae.

Pro vino dato dictis histrionibus in praesencia ballivorum et aliorum proborum hominum pro honestate villae.

Pro liberatura communium histrionum vocatorum le Wayts villae.

Soluta ursenario domini Regis pro honestate villae

1495. Pro vino dato domino Principi [Arthur] ad ludum in quarell.

1496. Wine given to the minstrels of our Lord the King.

To the King's minstrels.

To the Queen's minstrels.

To the Prince's players.

To the Earl of Derby's players.

To the Earl of Shrewsbury's players.

1503. In regardo dato ij Walicis histrionibus domini Regis.

1510. 'Lusoribus' in feast of Pentecost.

'Histrionibus' of Earl of Shrewsbury and King.

1516. In vino, pomis, waffers, et aliis novellis datis et expenditis super abbatem Salop et famulos suos ad ludum et demonstrationem martiriorum Felicianae et Sabinae in quarera post muros.

In regardo dato lusoris eiusdem martirii tunc temporis hoc anno.

1517. Regardo ursinario comitis Oxoniae.

In regardo dato ursinario domini Regis pro agitacione bestiarum suarum ultra denarios tunc ibidem collectos.

1518. In vino expendito super tres reges Coloniae equitantibus in interludio pro solacio villae Salop in festo Pentecost.

1520. Ralph Hubard, minstrel of Lord de 'Mountegyle.'

In regardo dato iiij^{or} interlusoribus comitis Arundele ostendentibus ballivis et comparibus suis diversa interludia.

Et in vino dato eis et aliis extraneis personis intuentibus interludia, ultra denarios collectos.

In regardo dato histrionibus Iohannis Talbot militis pro melodia eorum facta in presencia ballivorum.

In regardo dato iij histrionibus comitis Arundelle pro honestate villae Salop.

In regardo dato Benet & Welles histrionibus comitis Salop.

In regardo ij histrionibus comitissae de Derby pro honestate villae Salop.

Et in vino expendito per ballivos et compares suos audientes melodiam eorum.

Histrionibus domini Regis ex consuetudine.

In regardo dato et vino expendito super Willelmum More histrionem domini Regis eo quod est caecus et principalis citherator Angliae.

1521. Regardo dato M. Brandon · ioculatori domini Regis pro honestate villae

Et in vino expendito par ballivos & compares suos videntes lusum et ioculationem dicti ioculatoris ultra ij denarios collectos de qualibet persona villae extraneis exceptis.

Soluta pro una roba nova depicta, sotularibus & aliis necessariis regardis & expensis factis super Ricardum Glasyer, abbatem de Marham, pro honestate & iocunditate villae.

In regardo dato portitori communis campanae circa villam pro proclamacione facta pro attendencia facienda super abbatem de Marham tempore Maii hoc anno.

In regardo dato iiijᵒʳ histrionibus domini Regis de consuetudine.

Histrionibus comitis Derby.

Regardo dato ursinario ducis Suffolke ultra 2ˢ. 3ᵈ. de pecuniis collectis de circumstantibus ad agitacionem ursarum suarum.

Pro ursinario domini marchionis Dorsett.

1522. 'Ursenarius' of duke of Suffolk.

In regardo dato ioculatori domini Regis.

1524. 'Histrio' of Henry Knight.

'Histriones' of Earl of Derby.

'Histriones' of Lord Mount Egle.

1525. In regardo dato iiij histrionibus comitis Arundell.

Et in vino expendito super ballivos & compares suos audientes melodiam et ludentes inspicientes.

In regardo dato iiijᵒʳ interlusoribus ducis Suffolk.

Interluders of the Lady Princess, and wine spent at hearing their interludes.

1526. In regardo dato custodi cameli domini Regis ostendenti ballivis et comparibus suis ioca illius cameli.

Interlusoribus dominae principissae.

Ralph Hubard, minstrel of Lord de 'Mountegyle,' with one Lokkett.

1527. In regardo dato lusoribus villae tempore veris et mensis Maii pro iocunditate villae.

Interlusoribus dominae principissae.

Interluders of our Lord the King.

'Histriones,' of Sir John Talbot, Arthur Neuton and Sir John Lyngen.

1528. 'Ursenarius' of marquis of Exeter.

1530. 'Histrio' of baron of Burford.

1531. Data interlusoribus dominae principissae.

1533. Soluta Thomae Eton pro factura unius mansionis de duobus stagiis pro domino presidenti [Bishop of Exeter] et ballivis tempore ludi septimana Pentecostes.

Et in regardo dato lusoribus ad dictum lusum et pro reparacione ornamentorum suorum.

In vino dato domino presidenti & ballivis in mansione sua tempore lusi in Quarrera pone muros.

In regardo dato lusoribus & interlusoribus domini Regis ostendentibus & offerentibus ioca sua.

Et in vino expendito super eos et comitivam ballivorum & comparium suorum audientium & supervidentium lusum & melodiam eorum.

In expensis factis in garniamentis, liberatis et histrion[ibus] pro domino abbate de Marham tempore mensis Maii pro honestate villae hoc anno.

1535. In regardo m[agistro] Brandon, ioculatori domini Regis.

In regardo dato histrionibus extraneis melodiam et cantilenas eorum coram ballivis et comparibus pronunciantibus.

1538. Data in regardo lusoribus domini privati sigilli.

Data in regarda lusoribus domini principis [Edward].

Expendita super lusores domini principis, domini privati sigilli, domini visitatoris . . . pro honestate villae.

'Histriones' of Sir Thomas Cornewall and of Thomas Newport.

Rogero Philipps, goldsmyth, pro argento et emendacione colarium histrionum villae.

'Ursenarius' of marquis of Exeter.

1540. Data in regardo quibusdam interlusoribus de Wrexam ludentibus coram ballivis et comparibus suis in vino tunc
expendito.

'Item, Mr. Bayleffes left on p^d more the same day at aft^r
the play.

'Item, the vj men spend appon the kyng's pleyers in wyne.

'Item, there was left on p^d by Mr. Bayleffs w^t my Lorde
Prinssys plears on Sonday after Seint Bartlaumew day.

'Item, there was sent them the nyght to supper a po^l of red
and a po^l of claret.

'Item, Mr. Bayleffs left on p^d on Sonday after owre Lade day
wyth my Lord Prinsys plears.'

Cuidam iugulatori ludenti coram ballivis.

1541. 'Ursenario ducis Norfoxiae.'

1542. In vino dato interlusoribus post interlusum in cimitirio sancti
Cedde coram commissariis domini Regis ballivis et aliis.

Cuidem ursuario de la Northewiche.

Ursiatori praepotentis viri comitis Derby ad ij tempora.

Pro reparacione et pictura ornamentorum abbatis de Mayvole.

Et soluta pro una toga de nova facta dicto abbati de Mayvole.

Soluta Ricardo Glasier pro labore suo in ludendo abbatem
de Mardall.

1548. Interlusoribus ludentibus cum domino abbate de Marall.

Soluta Iohanni Mason, peynter, pro pictura togae pro dicto
domino de Marrall.

In regardo istrionibus ludentibus ante viros armatos.

Cuidam istrioni ludenti ante viros equiles equitantes ad
Scociam.

1549. James Lockwood ' servienti et gestatori domini Regis.'

Interluders of Sir John Bridges and of Sir Edward Braye.

William Taylor, and others, interluders of the town of Salop,
playing there in the month of May.

'Histriones' of William Sheldon and of Lord Ferrers [last use
of term histrio].

1552. Interluders of Lord Russell.

Soluta domino de abbott Marram et pro apparatu eorum
videlicet pro calciamentis tunicis et aliis vestibus.

1553. Expendita per ballivos et associatos suos die lunae in le
Whitson wuck post visum lusum.

Pro tunicis et aliis vestimentis ac pistura eorundem pro
Robyn Hood.

In vino dato eisdem interlusoribus.

In regardo le tomlers.

1554. In regardo Thomae Staney le jugler.

Wyett le gester.

1559. Regardo lusiatoribus domini Stafford.

1561. Item, gyvyn unto my lord Wyllybe's playarys in reward.

Item, spent at the gullet on the saem playarys.

1565. To Master Baly Pursell with the Quenes players.

1566. Yeven Mr. Justes Throgmerton's mynstrell.

1574. Paid and geven to my L. Sandwayes man, the berwart.

The players of noblemen and others and ber-wards of noblemen and mynstrells of noblemen, this yere, viii^{li} x^8 viij^d.

1576. Leid out to my lord of Derby and my lord Staffart's musicions.

1582. Bestowed on her Majesty's players this yere.

1591. To my lord of Derby's musysyons, and to the erle of Woster's players . . . to my L. Beachem men, beinge players.

[From *Books of Council Orders* in *Hist. MSS.* xv. 13, 16, 18.]

1556. 16 May. The bailiffs to set forward the stage play this next Whitsontide for the worship of the town and not to disburse above £5 about the furniture of the play.

1570. 8 July. Lease of pasture 'behind the walles, exceptinge the Quarrell where the plases have bine accustomyd to be usyd.'

1575. 17 July. Five marks to be given to Mr. Churchyard for his pains taken in setting forth the show against the Queen's coming, being sent hither by the Lord President.

VII. THE HOWARDS OF STOKE-BY-NAYLAND, ESSEX.

[From accounts of Sir John Howard, in *Manners and Household Expenses* (Roxburghe Club, 1841), 325, 511.]

2 May, 1465. Item that he [my master] delyverd the pleyers at Moleyns [a servant of Sir John's] weddynge, ij^s.

12 Jan. 1466. And the sonday nexte after the xij day, I ʒafe to the pleyeres of Stoke, ij^s.

[From accounts of John, Lord Howard, afterwards Duke of Norfolk, in *Household Books of John, Duke of Norfolk, and Thomas, Earl of Surrey* (ed. Collier, Roxburghe Club, 1844), 104, 145, 146, 148, 149, 202, 336, 339.]

29 Aug. 1481. I paid to the pleirs of Turton [Thorington] Strete, xx^d.

26 Dec. 1481. Item, the xxvj day of December, my Lord toke the Plaiers of Kokesale [Coggeshall], iij^s iiij^d.

27 Dec. 1481. Item, to the Plaiers of Hadley [Hadleigh], and the olde man and ij. children, vj^s viij^d.

7 Jan. 1482. Item, to the Plaiers of Esterforde, iij^s iiij^d.

9 Jan. 1482. Item, to Senclowe, that he paid to my Lord of Essex [Henry Bourchier] men, plaiers, xx^d.
Thei are of Canans.

22 May, 1482. Item, that my Lord yaffe to the cherche on Whitson Monday at the pley, x^s.

25 Dec. 1482. Item, on Crystemas day, my Lord gaff to iiij pleyers of my lord of Gloucestres, iij^s iiij^d.
Item, the same day, my Lord gaff to iiij pleyers of Coksale, iij^s iiij^d.

9 Jan. 1483. Item, the same day, my Lord paid to Garard, of Sudbury, for all suche stoffe as folewyth, that he bought for the Dysgysing [a schedule of paper, gunpowder, ' arsowde,' packthread, &c., follows]. Summe totall, xxj^s ob.

[From accounts of Thomas, Earl of Surrey, in *Household Books* (*ut supra*), 515, 517, 519.]

20 Dec. 1490. Payd for xviij yardes of lynen cloth, that M. Leynthorpe had for dysgysyng, at iiij^d the yard, . . . vj^s iiij^d.
[Other expenses for the disguising follow.]

27 Dec. 1490. Item, payd to the playars of Chemsford, vj^s. viij^d.

2 Jan. 1491. Item, the said day, in reward to the panget [pageant (?)], iij^s iiij^d.
Item, payd to ——, when he went to Bury to fach stuff for dygysers on Saynt Stevens day, xvj^d.

8 Jan. 1492. Item, in reward to the players of Lanam [Lavenham], xl^s.

[The Howard accounts also include many payments for minstrelsy, &c. The Duke of Norfolk kept singers, a harper, children of the chapel, and two fools, ' Tom Fool' and Richard, ' the fool of the kitchen.']

VIII. The English Court.

[From Rymer, *Foedera*, x. 387. A memorandum *de strenis, liberatis et expensis*, at Christmas, 1427.]

A Jakke Travail et ses compaignons feisans diverses jeuues et entreludes dedeins le feste de Noell devant notre dit sire le roi, 4 lib.

Et as autres jeweis de Abyndon feisantz autres entreludes dedeins le
dit feste de Noel, 20 sol.

[Extracted by Collier, i. 50, from the *Household Book* of Henry VII,
1491-1505, and the *Book of King's Payments*, 1506-9. I cannot identify
the former; the latter appears to be vol. 214 of the *Miscellanea of the
Treasury of the Receipt of the Exchequer* (Scargill-Bird, *Guide to the
Public Records*, 228). I omit, here and below, entries referring to minstrelsy, disguisings, and plays by the King's players and the Chapel.
Probably some of the performances were given at London; others before
the King on progress. I have corrected some of Collier's dates from the
similar entries in Bentley, *Excerpta Historica*, 85, taken from a transcript
in *B. M. Add. MS.* 7099.]

1 Jan. 1492.   To my Lorde of Oxon pleyers, in rewarde, £1.

7 Jan. 1493.   To my Lorde of Northumberlande Pleyers, in
               rewarde, £1.

1 Jan. 1494.   To four Pleyers of Essex in rewarde, £1.
               To the Pleyers of Wymborne Minster, £1.

6 Jan. 1494.   To the Frenche Pleyers for a rewarde, £1.

31 Dec. 1494. To 3 Pleyers of Wycombe in rewarde, 13ˢ 4ᵈ.

4 Jan. 1495.   To the Frenshe Pleyers in rewarde, £2.

20 July, 1498. To the pleyers of London in rewarde, 10ˢ.

14 June, 1499. To the pleyers with Marvells, £4.

6 Aug. 1501.   To the Pleyers at Myles End, 3ˢ 4ᵈ.

2 Jan. 1503.   To the Pleyers of Essex in rewarde, £1.

20 May, 1505. To the Players of Kingeston toward the bilding of
               the churche steple, in almasse, 3ˢ 4ᵈ.

1 Jan. 1506.   To the players that played afore the Lord Stewarde in
               the Hall upon Sonday nyght, 6ˢ 8ᵈ.
               To my lorde Princes players that played in hall on
               new-yeres even, 10ˢ.

25 Dec. 1506. To the Players that played affore the Lord Stewarde
               in the Hall upon Tewesday nyght, 10ˢ.

2 Jan. 1509.   To my lord of Buckingham's pleyers that playd in
               the Hall at Grenewich, 6ˢ 8ᵈ.

[Extracted by Collier, i. 76, from the *Book of King's Payments* for
1509-17, now vol. 215 of the *Miscellanea of the Treasury of the Receipt
of the Exchequer*. The document is more fully analysed in Brewer, ii.
1441. It is an account of the Treasurer of the Chamber.]

6 Jan. 1512.   To the Players that cam out of Suffolke, that playd
               affore the Lorde Stewarde in the Kings Hall upon Monday
               nyght, 13ˢ 4ᵈ.

1 Jan. 1515. To the Erle of Wiltyshires playres, that shulde have played in the Kings Hall oppon Thursday at nyght, in rewarde, 13ˢ 4ᵈ.

1 Jan. 1516. To the Erle of Wilshire's players, 13ˢ 4ᵈ.

[From *Accounts of Treasurer of Chamber* in *Trevelyan Papers* (C.S.), i. 146, 161, 174.]

1 Jan. 1530. To the Prince's plaiers.

1 Jan. 1531. To the Princes pleyers.

Item, paid to certain Players of Coventrye, as in wey of the Kinges rewarde, for playnge in the Corte this last Cristmas.

1 Jan. 1532. To the Princesse plaiers.

F

MINSTREL GUILDS

A. FRANCE.

1. *Arras*, †1105.

The famous *Pui d'Arras* (vols. i. p. 376, ii. p. 88) was in a sense a minstrel guild. According to tradition a plague was stayed by a simultaneous apparition of the Virgin in a dream to two minstrels, which led to the acquisition of 'le joyel d'Arras,' the miraculous 'cierge de notre Dame.' This was about 1105, and the result was the foundation of the *Confrérie* or *Carité de N. D. des Ardents*, which afterwards developed into the *pui*. This was not confined to minstrels, but they were predominant. The *Statutes* say, 'Ceste carité est estorée des jogleors, et les jogleors en sont signors[1].' The objects of the *pui*, however, were religious, social, and literary. It was not a craft guild, such as grew up two centuries later.

2. *Paris*, 1321.

Ordinances were made in 1321 'à l'acort du commun des menestreus et menestrelles, jougleurs et jougleresses' of Paris for the reformation of their 'mestier,' and registered with the provost of Paris in 1341. They chiefly regulate the employment of minstrels within the city. The 'mestres du dit mestier' are to be 'ii ou iii preudes hommes' appointed by the provost on behalf of the King. A number of 'guètes' and other minstrels sign, beginning with 'Pariset, menestrel le roy,' and ending with 'Jaque le Jougleur.' As a possible head of the 'mestier' is named 'li prevost de Saint-Julian.' This seems to contemplate the foundation of the *hospice et confrérie* under the

---

[1] Guy, xxvii.

patronage of SS. Julian and Genesius, and in close connexion with the 'mestier,' which actually took place 1328–35. But in the later Statutes of 1407 the head of the guild is called the 'roy des ménestriers,' and as by this time the guild seems to claim some authority over the whole of France, it is probable that this 'roy' was identical with the 'roy des menestreuls du royaume de France,' a title which occurs in various documents from 1338 onwards. He may also have been identical with the 'roy' of the King's household minstrels (cf. p. 239). The Paris guild lasted until the suppression of all such privileged bodies in 1776[1].

3. *Chauny.*

The corporation of 'les Trompettes jougleurs' of Chauny was founded during the fifteenth century. This town claimed to provide *bateleurs* for all the north of France[2].

B. ENGLAND.

There are two early jurisdictions over minstrelsy, which are not strictly of the nature of guilds.

1. *Chester.*

Tradition has it that † 1210 Randal Blundeville, Earl of Chester, besieged by the Welsh in Rhuddlan Castle, was relieved by Roger Lacy, constable of Cheshire, with a mob of riff-raff from Chester Midsummer fair. Randal gave to Lacy, and Lacy's son John gave to his steward Hugh de Dutton and his heirs the 'magistratum omnium leccatorum et meretricum totius Cestriae.' The fact of the jurisdiction is undoubted. It was reserved by the charter to the London guild in 1469, claimed by Laurence de Dutton in 1499, admitted upon an action of *quo warranto* as a right 'from time immemorial,' further reserved in the first Vagrant Act (1572) which specifically included minstrels, and in the successive Acts of 1597, 1603, 1628, 1641, 1713, 1740, 1744. It lapsed when this last Act was repealed in 1822. Up to 1756 the heir of Dutton regularly held his *curia Minstralciae* at Chester Midsummer fair, and issued licences to fiddlers in the city and county for a fee of 4½d., afterwards raised to 2s. 6d. Thomas Dutton (1569–1614), under puritan influences, inserted a proviso against piping and dancing on Sundays[3].

---

[1] B. Bernhard, *Rech. sur l'Hist. de la Corp. des Ménétriers ou Joueurs d'Instruments de la Ville de Paris* (*Bibl. de l'École des Chartes*, iii. 377; iv. 525; v. 254, 339).
[2] Julleville, *Les Com.* 238.

[3] Morris, 12, 346; Rymer, xi. 642; Ribton-Turner, 109, 129, 133, 148, 182, 201; Ormerod, *Hist. of Cheshire*, i. 36; *Memorials of the Duttons* (1901), 9, 209.

2. *Tutbury.*

Letters patent of John of Gaunt dated 1380 and confirmed by an
'inspeximus' of Henry VI in 1443 assigned 'le roy des ministralx'
in the honour of Tutbury to arrest all minstrels within the honour
not doing service on the feast of the Assumption. It was a custom
that the prior of Tutbury should provide a bull for a bull-running by
the assembled minstrels on this feast. The court was still held by
an annual 'king of the fiddlers,' with the steward and bailiff of the
honour (including Staffs., Derby, Notts., Leicester, and Warwick), at
the end of the seventeenth century, and the minstrels claimed to be
exempt, like those of Chester, from vagrancy legislation. But their
rights were not reserved, either by the Charter of 1469 or the Vagrant
Acts [1].

The first English craft guild of minstrels is later by a century and
a half than that of Paris.

3. *London.*

A charter of Edward IV (1469), 'ex querelosa insinuatione
dilectorum nobis Walteri Haliday, marescalli [and seven others]
ministrallorum nostrorum,' declares that 'nonnulli rudes Agricolae
et Artifices diversarum Misterarum Regni nostri Angliae finxerunt
se fore Ministrallos. Quorum aliqui Liberatam nostram, eis minime
datam, portarunt, seipsos etiam fingentes esse Ministrallos nostros
proprios. Cuius quidem Liberatae ac dictae Artis sive Occupationis
Ministrallorum colore in diversis Partibus Regni nostri praedicti
grandes Pecuniarum Exactiones de Ligeis nostris deceptive colligunt
et recipiunt.' Hence illegitimate competition with the real minstrels,
decay of the art, and neglect of agriculture. The charter then does
two things. It makes the royal minstrels a corporation with a
marshall elected by themselves, and it puts them at the head of
a 'Fraternitatem sive Gildam' of minstrels already existing in the
chapel of the Virgin in St. Paul's, and in the royal free chapel of
St. Anthony. All minstrels in the country are to join this guild
or be suppressed. It is to have two *custodes* and to make statutes
and ordinances. The jurisdiction of Dutton over Chester minstrels
is, as already stated, reserved [2]. A 'serviens' or 'serjeant' seems to
have been an officer of the guild [3]. With this exception nothing more
is heard of it until 1594, when a dispute as to the office of the Master

---

[1] *Carta le Roy de Ministralx*, in
Dugdale, *Monasticon* (1822), iii. 397,
from *Tutbury Register* in Coll. of
Arms; Plot, *Hist. of Staffs.* (1686), ch.
x. § 69.
[2] Rymer (1710), xi. 642, (1741) v. 2.
169.
[3] Percy, 372.

of the Musicians' Company called for the intervention of the Lord Keeper[1].' In 1604 the Company received a new charter, which gave it jurisdiction within the city and a radius of three miles from its boundaries. It was further restricted to the city itself under Charles I. It still exists as the Corporation of the Master, Wardens, and Commonalty of the Art or Science of the Musicians of London[2].

The London guild would appear, from its peculiar relation to the royal household minstrels, and its claim to jurisdiction throughout the country, to have been modelled upon that of Paris. This claim was evidently not maintained, and in fact at least three other local guilds can be shown to have existed in the sixteenth century. A search, which I have not undertaken, would probably readily discover more.

4. Canterbury.

Ordinances, dated 1526, of the 'felowshyp of the craft and mystery of mynstrells' give the prerogative right to perform in the city to the members of this body, saving the privileges of the city waits, and 'the King's mynstrells, the Queane's, my Lord Prince's, or any honorable or wurshipfull mann's mynstrells of thys realme[3].'

5. Beverley.

An order of the Governors of the city (1555) recites an old custom 'since Athelstan' of the choice by minstrels between Trent and Tweed of aldermen of their fraternities during Rogation days, and renews orders for the 'fraternity of our Lady of the read arke in Beverley.' The statutes deal with the employment of minstrels in Beverley, and with their 'castells' at the Rogation-day procession. A new member must be 'mynstrell to some man of honour or worship or waite of some towne corporate or other ancient town or else of such honestye and conyng as shalbe thought laudable and pleasant to the hearers.' It is claimed that such are excluded from the 'Kyng's acts where they speake of vacabonds and valiant beggers.' Quite in the spirit of the London charter of 1469 it is ordered that 'no myler shepherd or of other occupation or husbandman or husbandman servant' shall assume the functions of a minstrel outside his own parish[4]. The earliest notice of this guild in the Beverley archives seems to be in 1557[5], but the terms of the order and the existence of pillars put up

---

[1] *Analytical Index to Remembrancia of the City of London*, 92.
[2] Grove, *Dict. of Music*, s.v. Musicians; W. C. Hazlitt, *Livery Companies of London*.

[3] Civis, No. xxi.
[4] Poulson, *Beverlac*, i. 302 (probably from *Lansd. MS*. 896, f. 180).
[5] Leach, *Beverley MSS*. 179.

by the minstrels in fifteenth-century churches in Beverley[1] point to some informal earlier association.

6. *York.*

A craft of Mynstrells certainly existed by 1561, in which year they undertook the pageant of Herod at the Corpus Christi plays[2].

G

THOMAS DE CABHAM

[The following extract from a *Penitential* formerly ascribed to John of Salisbury, but now to Thomas de Cabham, Bishop of Salisbury (†1313), is printed by B. Haurèau, *Notices et Extraits de Manuscrits*, xxiv. 2, 284, from *B. N. MSS. Lat.* 3218 and 3529ᵃ, and by F. Guessard and C. Grandmaison, *Huon de Bordeaux*, vi, from *B. N. Sorbonne MS.* 1552, f. 71. The two texts differ in several points. According to Gautier, ii. 22, there are several similar thirteenth-century *Penitentials*, and it is difficult to say which was the original. The doctrine laid down about minstrels is often repeated in later treatises. See e.g. a passage from the fifteenth-century *Le Jardin des Nobles* in P. Paris, *Manuscrits français*, ii. 144.]

Tria sunt histrionum genera. Quidam transformant et transfigurant corpora sua per turpes saltus et per turpes gestus, vel denudando se turpiter, vel induendo horribiles larvas, et omnes tales damnabiles sunt, nisi reliquerint officia sua. Sunt etiam alii qui nihil operantur, sed criminose agunt, non habentes certum domicilium, sed sequuntur curias magnatum et dicunt opprobria et ignominias de absentibus ut placeant aliis. Tales etiam damnabiles sunt, quia prohibet Apostolus cum talibus cibum sumere, et dicuntur tales scurrae vagi, quia ad nihil utiles sunt, nisi ad devorandum et maledicendum. Est etiam tertium genus histrionum qui habent instrumenta musica ad delectandum homines, et talium sunt duo genera. Quidam enim frequentant publicas potationes et lascivas congregationes, et cantant ibi diversas cantilenas ut moveant homines ad lasciviam, et tales sunt damnabiles sicut alii. Sunt autem alii, qui dicuntur ioculatores, qui cantant gesta principum et vitam sanctorum, et faciunt solatia hominibus vel in aegritudinibus suis vel in angustiis, et non faciunt innumeras turpitudines sicut faciunt saltatores et saltatrices et alii qui ludunt in imaginibus inhonestis et faciunt videri quasi quaedam fantasmata per incantationes vel alio modo. Si autem non faciunt talia, sed cantant in instrumentis suis gesta principum et alia

---

[1] Crowest, 244.
[2] *York Plays*, xxxviii, 125; M. Sellers in *Eng. Hist. Review*, ix. 284.

talia utilia ut faciant solatia hominibus, sicut supradictum est, bene possunt sustineri tales, sicut ait Alexander papa. Cum quidam ioculator quaereret ab eo utrum posset salvare animam suam in officio suo, quaesivit Papa ab eo utrum sciret aliquod aliud opus unde vivere posset: respondit ioculator quod non. Permisit igitur Papa quod ipse viveret de officio suo, dummodo abstineret a praedictis lasciviis et turpitudinibus. Notandum est quod omnes peccant mortaliter qui dant scurris vel leccatoribus vel praedictis histrionibus aliquid de suo. Histrionibus dare nichil aliud est quam perdere.

H

PRINCELY PLEASURES AT KENILWORTH

[From *Robert Laneham's Letter* (ed. F. J. Furnivall for New Shakspere Society (1890) ; and in Nichols, *Progresses of Elizabeth*, i. 420) describing the entertainment of Elizabeth by the Earl of Leicester at Kenilworth, in July, 1575. G. Gascoigne, *The Princelye Pleasures at the Courte at Kenelworth* (1576, in Nichols, i. 502), leaves undescribed what he calls the 'Coventrie' (ed. 2, 'Countrie') shows.]

I. A SQUIRE MINSTREL.

Mary, syr, I must tell yoo : Az all endeuoour waz too mooue mirth & pastime (az I tolld ye): éeuen so a ridiculoous deuise of an auncient minstrell & hiz song waz prepared to haue been profferd, if méet time & place had béen foound for it. Ons in a woorshipfull company, whear, full appointed, he recoounted his matter in sort az it should haue been vttred, I chaunsed too be: what I noted, heer thus I tel yoo: A parson very méet séemed he for the purpoze, of a xlv. yéers olld, apparelled partly as he woold himself. Hiz cap of: his hed séemly roounded tonster wyze: fayr kemb, *that* with a spoonge deintly dipt in a littl capons greaz was finely smoothed too make it shine like a Mallard's wing. Hiz beard smugly shauen : and yet hiz shyrt after the nu trink, with ruffs fayr starched, sléeked, and glistening like a payr of nu shooz: marshalld in good order : wyth a stetting stick, and stoout, that euery ruff stood vp like a wafer : a side gooun of kendall green, after the freshnes of the yéer noow, gathered at the neck with a narro gorget, fastened afore with a white clasp and a keepar close vp to the chin : but easily for heat too vndoo when he list : Séemly begyrt in a red caddiz gyrdl : from that a payr of capped Sheffield kniuez hanging a to side : Out of hiz bozome drawne forth a lappet of his napkin, edged with a blu lace, & marked with a trulooue, a hart, and A. D. for Damian : for he was but a bachelar yet.

Hiz gooun had syde sleeuez dooun to midlegge, slit from the shooulder too the hand, & lined with white cotten. Hiz doobled sleeuez of blak woorsted, vpon them a payr of poynets of towny Chamblet laced a long the wreast wyth blu threeden points, a wealt toward the hand of fustian anapes : a payr of red neatherstocks : a pair of pumps on hiz féet, with a cross cut at the toze for cornz : not nu indéede, yet cleanly blakt with soot, & shining az a shoing horn.

Aboout hiz nek a red rebond sutable too hiz girdl : hiz harp in good grace dependaunt before him : hiz wreast tyed to a gréen lace, and hanging by : vnder the gorget of hiz gooun a fair flagon cheyn, (pewter, for) siluer, as a squier minstrel of Middilsex, that trauaild the cuntrée this soommer seazon vnto fairz & worshipfull mens hoousez : from hiz chein hoong a Schoochion, with mettall & cooller resplendant vpon hiz breast, of the auncient armez of Islington :

[Apparently the minstrel was got ready ; but not shown. He was to have recited an Arthurian romance in verse.]

II. The Coventry Hock-Tuesday Show.

And héertoo folloed az good a sport (me thooght) prezented in an historicall ku, by certain good harted men of Couentrée, my Lordes neighboors thear : who, vnderstanding amoong them *the* thing that coold not bee hidden from ony, hoow carefull and studious hiz honor waz, that by all pleazaunt recreasions her highnes might best fynd her self wellcom, & bee made gladsum and mery, (the ground-worke indeede, and foundacion, of hiz Lordship's myrth and gladnesse of vs all), made petition that they mooought renu noow their olld storiall sheaw : Of argument, how the Danez whylom héere in a troublous seazon wear for quietnesse born withall, & suffeard in peas, that anon, by outrage & importabl insolency, abuzing both Ethelred, the king then, and all estates euerie whear beside : at the greuoous complaint & coounsell of Huna, the king's chieftain in warz, on Saint Brices night, Ann. Dom. 1012 (Az the book sayz) that falleth yéerely on the thirtéenth of Nouember, wear all dispatcht, and the Ream rid. And for becauz the matter mencioneth how valiantly our English women for looue of their cuntrée behaued themseluez : expressed in actionz & rymez after their maner, they thought it mooought mooue sum myrth to her Maiestie the rather.

The thing, said they, iz grounded on story, and for pastime woont too bee plaid in oour Citee yéerely: without ill exampl of mannerz, papistry, or ony superstition: and elz did so occupy the heads of a number, that likely inoough woold haue had woorz meditationz: had an auncient beginning, and a long continuauns: tyll noow of late laid dooun, they knu no cauz why, onless it wear by the zeal of certain theyr Preacherz: men very commendabl for their behauiour and learning, & swéet in their sermons, but sumwhat too sour in preaching awey theyr pastime: wisht therefore, that az they shoold continu their good doctrine in pulpet, so, for matters of pollicy & gouernauns of the Citie, they woold permit them to the Mair and Magistratez: and seyed, by my feyth, Master Martyn, they woold make theyr humbl peticion vntoo her highnes, that they might haue theyr playz vp agayn.

But aware, kéep bak, make room noow, heer they cum! And fyrst, . . . Captain Cox cam marching on valiantly before, cléen trust, & gartered aboue the knée, all fresh in a veluet cap (master Goldingham lent it him) floorishing with hiz tonswoord, and another fensmaster with him: thus in the foreward making room for the rest. After them proudly prickt on formost, the Danish launsknights on horobak, and then the English: each with their alldei poll marcially in their hand. Eeuen at the first entrée the méeting waxt sumwhat warm: that by and by kindled with corage a both sidez, gru from a hot skirmish vnto a blazing battail: first by speare and shield, outragious in their racez az ramz at their rut, with furious encoounterz, that togyther they tumbl too the dust, sumtime hors and man: and after fall too it with sworde & target, good bangz a both sidez: the fight so ceassing; but the battail not so ended: folloed the footmen, both the hostez, ton after toother: first marching in ranks: then warlik turning, then from ranks into squadrons, then in too trianglz; from that intoo rings, & so winding oout again: A valiant captain of great prowez, az fiers az a fox assauting a gooz, waz so hardy to giue the first stroke: then get they grisly togyther: that great waz the actiuitée that day too be séen thear a both sidez: ton very eager for purchaz of pray, toother vtterly stoout for redemption of libertie: thus, quarrell enflamed fury a both sidez. Twise the Danes had the better; but at the last conflict, beaten doun, ouercom, and many led captiue for triumph by our English wéemen.

This waz the effect of this sheaw, that, az it waz handled, made mooch matter of good pastime: brought all indéed intoo the great court, een vnder her highnes windo too haue been séen: but (az vnhappy it waz for the bride) that cam thither too soon, (and yet waz it a four a clok). For her highnes beholding in the chamber delectabl .daúncing indéed : and héerwith the great throng and vnrulines of the people, waz' cauz that this solemnitee of Brideale & daúncing, had not the full muster waz hoped for : and but a littl of the Couentrée plea her highnes also saw : commaunded thearfore on the Tuisday folloing to haue it ful oout : az accordingly it waz prezented, whearat her Maiestie laught well : they wear the iocunder, and so mooch the more becauz her highnes had giuen them too buckes, and fiue marke in mony, to make mery togyther : they prayed for her Maiesty, long, happily to reign, & oft to cum thither, that oft they moought sée héer : & what, reioycing vpon their ampl reward, and what, triumphing vpon the good acceptauns, they vaunted their play waz neuer so dignified, nor euer any players afore so beatified. . . .

Tuisday, according to commandement, cam oour Couentrée men : what their matter waz, of her highnes myrth and good acceptauns, and rewarde vntoo them, and of their reioysing thearat, I sheawd you afore, and so say the less noow.

I

THE INDIAN VILLAGE FEAST

[From Sir Walter Elliot, *On the Characteristics of the Population of Central India*, in *Journal of the Ethnological Society of London*, N. S. i. 94 (1869).]

In the north-east corner of the central mountainous region repre-sented on the map, between the Mahanadi and Godavery rivers, is found a tribe which has preserved its normal character remarkably free from change and from external influence. The Konds, or, as they call themselves, the Kuingas, although only discovered within the last thirty-five years, are better known than most of the other barbarous tribes from the fact that for ages they have been in the habit of sacri-ficing human victims in great numbers to secure the favour of the deities presiding over their dwellings, fields, hills, &c., but especially of the earth-goddess.

The successful efforts employed to abolish this barbarous rite have made the subject familiar to all, and it is remarkable that such know-ledge should have failed to attract attention to a practice precisely similar in its objects and in its details, which is observed in every village of Southern India, with this single difference, that a buffalo is substituted for a human victim. My attention was early drawn to this practice, which is called the festival of the village goddess (*Devi*, or *Grama Devati*), the descriptions of which led me to believe it might throw light on the early condition of the servile classes, and resolving to witness its celebrations, I repaired to the village of Serúr, in the Southern Mahratta country, in March, 1829. It would occupy too much time to describe the ceremony in full, which is the less necessary as the details vary in different places; but the general features are always the same.

The temple of the goddess is a mean structure outside the village. The officiating priests are the Parias, who, on this occasion, and on it alone, are exempt from the degrading condition which excludes them from the village, and from contact with the inhabitants. With them are included the Mangs or workers in leather, the Asádis or Dásaris, *paria* dancing-girls devoted to the service of the temple, the musician in attendance on them called Rániga, who acts also as a sort of jester or buffoon, and a functionary called Pót-raj, who officiates as *pujári* to a rural god named also Pót-raj, to whom a small altar is erected behind the temple of the village goddess. He is armed with a long whip, which he cracks with great dexterity, and to which also at various parts of the ceremony divine honours are paid.

All the members of the village community take part in the festival with the hereditary district officers, many of them Brahmans. The shepherds or *Dhangars* of the neighbouring villages are also invited, and they attend with their priests called *Virgars* or *Irgars*, accompanied by the *dhol* or big drum peculiar to their caste. But the whole is under the guidance and management of the Parias.

The festival commences always on a Tuesday, the day of rest among the agricultural classes, both for man and beast. The most important and essential ceremonies take place on the second and fifth days. On the former, the sacred buffalo, which had been purchased by the Parias, an animal without a blemish, is thrown down before the goddess, its head struck off by a single blow and placed in front of the shrine with one fore-leg thrust into its mouth. Around are placed vessels containing the different cereals, and hard by a heap of mixed grains, with a drill plough in the centre. The carcase is then cut up into small pieces, and each cultivator receives a portion to bury in his field. The blood and offal are collected into a large basket, over which some pots of the cooked food which had been presented as a meat offering (*naivedya*) had previously been broken, and Pót-raj taking a live kid called the *hari-mariah*, hews it in pieces over the whole. The mess (*cheraga*) is then mixed together, and the basket being placed on the head of a naked Mang, he runs off with it, flinging the contents into the air, and scattering them right and left, as an offering (*bhut-bali*) to the evil spirits, and followed by the other Parias, and the village Paiks, with drawn swords. Sometimes the demons arrest the progress of the party, when more of the mess is thrown about, and fowls and sheep are sacrificed, till the spirits are appeased.

During the whole time of the sacrifice the armed paiks keep vigilant guard, lest any intruder should secrete a morsel of flesh or a drop of blood, which, if carried off successfully, after declaring the purpose, would transfer the merit of the offering to the strangers' village.

On the return of the party from making the circuit of the village another buffalo, seized by force wherever it can be found (*zulmi-khulga*), is sacrificed by decapitating it in the same manner as the former ; but no particular importance is attached to it, and the flesh is distributed to be eaten.

The third and fourth days are devoted to private offerings. On the former all the inhabitants of caste, who had vowed animals to the goddess during the preceding three years for the welfare of their families, or the fertility of their fields, brought the buffaloes or sheep to the *paria pujári*, who struck off their heads. The fourth day was appropriated exclusively to the offerings of the Parias. In this way, some fifty or sixty buffaloes and several hundred sheep were slain, and the heads piled up in two great heaps. Many women on these days walked naked to the temple in fulfilment of vows, but they were covered with leaves and boughs of trees and surrounded by their female relations and friends.

On the fifth and last day (Saturday) the whole community marched in procession, with music, to the temple, and offered a concluding sacrifice at the Pót-raj altar. A lamb was concealed close by. The Pót-raj having found it after a pretended search, struck it simply with his whip, which he then placed upon it, and, making several passes with his hands, rendered it insensible ; in fact, mesmerised it. When it became rigid and stiff he lifted it up and carried it about on the palm of his hand, to the amazement of the spectators, and then laid it down on the ground. His hands were then tied behind his back by the *pujári*, and the whole party began to dance round him with noisy shouts, the music and the shepherd's drum making a deafening noise. Pót-raj joined in the excitement, his eyes began to roll, his long hair fell loose over his shoulders, and he soon came fully under the influence of the *numen*. He was now led up, still bound, to the place where the lamb lay motionless. He rushed at it, seized it with his teeth, tore through the skin, and ate into its throat. When it was quite dead, he was lifted up, a dishful of the meat offering was presented to him ; he thrust his bloody face into it, and it was then, with the remains of the lamb, buried beside the altar. Meantime his hands were untied, and he fled the place, and did not appear for three days. The rest of the party now adjourned to the front of the temple, where the heap of grain deposited the first day was divided among the cultivators, to be buried by each one in his field with the bit of flesh. After this a distribution of the piled-up heads was made by the hand of the Ràniga. About forty sheep's heads were given to certain privileged persons, among which two were allotted to the Sircar ! For the rest a general scramble took place, paiks, shepherds, Parias, and many boys and men of good caste, were soon rolling in the mass of putrid gore. The heads were flung about in all directions, without regard to rank or caste, the Brahmans coming in for an ample share of the filth. The scramble for the buffalo heads was confined to the Parias. Whoever was fortunate enough to secure one of either kind carried it off and buried it in his field. The proceedings terminated by a procession round the boundaries of the village lands, preceded by the goddess, and the head of the sacred buffalo carried on the head of one of the Mangs. All order and propriety now ceased. Ràniga began to abuse the goddess in the foulest terms; he then turned his fury against the government, the head man of the village, and every one who fell in his way. The Parias and Asàdis attacked the most respectable and gravest citizens, and laid hold of the Brahmans, Lingayats, and Zamindars without scruple. The dancing-women jumped on their shoulders, the shepherds beat the big drum, with deafening clangor, and universal license reigned.

On reaching a little temple, sacred to the goddess of boundaries (*polimera-amma*), they halted to make some offerings, and bury the sacred head. As soon as it was covered, the uproar began again. Ràniga became more foul-mouthed than ever. In vain the head-men, the government officers, and others tried to pacify him by giving him small copper coins. He only broke out with worse imprecations and grosser abuse, till the circuit being completed, all dispersed ; the Parias retired to their hamlet outside the town, resuming their humble, servile character, and the village reverted to its wonted peaceful appearance.

Next day (Sunday) the whole population turned out to a great hunting-party.

I found this remarkable institution existing in every part of India where I have been, and I have descriptions of it corresponding in all essential points, from the Dekhan, the Nizam's country, Mysore, the Carnatic, and the Northern Circars. The details vary in different places, but the main features agree in all, and correspond remarkably with the *Mariah* sacrifice of the Konds, which also varies considerably on minor points in different places.

J

SWORD-DANCES

I. Sweden (*Sixteenth Century*).

[From Olaus Magnus, *Historia de gentibus septentrionalibus* (1555), Bk. xv. chh. 23, 24.]

Ch. 23, *de chorea gladiatoria vel armifera saltatione.*

Habent septentrionales Gothi et Sueci pro exercenda iuventute alium ludum, quod inter nudos enses et infestos gladios seu frameas sese exerceant saltu, idque quodam gymnastico ritu et disciplina, aetate successiva, a peritis et praesultare sub cantu addiscunt: et ostendunt hunc ludum praecipue tempore carnisprivii, maschararum Italico verbo dicto. Ante etenim tempus eiusdem carnisprivii octo diebus continua saltatione sese adolescentes numerose exercent, elevatis scilicet gladiis sed vagina reclusis, ad triplicem gyrum. Deinde evaginatis itidemque elevatis ensibus, postmodo manuatim extensis, modestius gyrando alterutrius cuspidem capulumque receptantes, sese mutato ordine in modum figurae hexagoni fingendi subiiciunt, quam rosam dicunt: et illico eam gladios retrahendo elevandoque resolvunt ut super uniuscuiusque caput quadrata rosa resultet: et tandem vehementissima gladiorum laterali collisione, celerrime retrograda saltatione determinant ludum, quem tibiis vel cantilenis, aut utrisque simul, primum per graviorem, demum vehementiorem saltum et ultimo impetuosissimum moderantur. Sed haec speculatio sine oculari inspectione vix apprehenditur quam pulchra honestaque sit, dum unius parcissimo praecepto etiam armata multitudo quadam alacritate dirigitur ad certamen: eoque ludo clericis sese exercere et immiscere licet, quia totus deducitur honestissima ratione.

Ch. 24. Alia etiam iuvenum exercitatio est, ut certa lege arcualem choream ducant et reducant, aliis quidam instrumentis, sed eadem ut gladiatorum saltantium disciplina reducta. Arcubus enim seu circulis inclusis [inclusi ?], primum modesto cantu heroum gesta referente vel tibiis aut tympanis excitati, gyrando incedunt seque dirigentis, qui rex dicitur, sola voçe reducunt, tandem solutis arcubus aliquantulum celerius properantes mutua inclinatione conficiunt, veluti alias per gladios, rosam, ut formam sexangularem efficere videantur. Utque id festivius sonoriusque fiat, tintinnabula seu aereas campanulas genu tenus ligant.

II. SHETLAND (*Eighteenth Century*).

[From Sir Walter Scott's *Diary* for August 7, 1814, printed in Lockhart, *Life of Scott* (1837), iii. 162 ; (1878) i. 265.

At Scalloway my curiosity was gratified by an account of the sword-dance, now almost lost, but still practised in the Island of Papa, belong-ing to Mr. Scott. There are eight performers, seven of whom represent the seven Champions of Christendom, who enter one by one with their swords drawn, and are presented to the eighth personage, who is not named. Some rude couplets are spoken (in *English*, not *Norse*), containing a sort of panegyric upon each champion as he is presented. They then dance a sort of cotillion, as the ladies described it, going through a number of evolutions with their swords. One of my three Mʳˢ. Scotts readily promised to procure me the lines, the rhymes, and the form of the dance. . . . A few years since a party of Papa-men came to dance the sword-dance at Lerwick as a public exhibition with great applause. . . . In a stall pamphlet, called the history of Bucks-haven [Fifeshire], it is said those fishers sprung from Danes, and brought with them their *war-dance* or *sword-dance*, and a rude wooden cut of it is given.

[A footnote by Lockhart adds :—]

Mr. W. S. Rose informs me that, when he was at school at Winchester, the morris-dancers there used to exhibit a sword-dance resembling that described at Camacho's wedding in *Don Quixote* ; and Mr. Morritt adds that similar dances are even yet performed in the villages about Rokeby [Yorks, N.R.] every Christmas.

[The following account was inserted in a note to Scott's *The Pirate* (1821).]

To the Primate's account of the sword-dance, I am able to add the words sung or chanted, on occasion of this dance, as it is still per-formed in Papa Stour, a remote island of Zetland, where alone the custom keeps its ground. It is, it will be observed by antiquaries, a species of play or mystery, in which the Seven Champions of Christendom make their appearance, as in the interlude presented in *All's Well that ends Well*. This dramatic curiosity was most kindly procured for my use by Dr. Scott of Haslar Hospital [died 1875], son of my friend Mr. Scott of Melbie, Zetland. Dr. Hibbert has, in his *Description of the Zetland Islands*, given an account of the sword-dance, but somewhat less full than the following :—

'WORDS USED AS A PRELUDE TO THE SWORD-DANCE, A DANISH OR NORWEGIAN BALLET, COMPOSED SOME CENTURIES AGO, AND PRESERVED IN PAPA STOUR, ZETLAND.

PERSONÆ DRAMATIS [1].

(*Enter* MASTER, *in the character of* SAINT GEORGE.)
Brave gentles all within this boor [2],
If ye delight in any sport,
Come see me dance upon this floor,
Which to you all shall yield comfort.
Then shall I dance in such a sort,
As possible I may or can;
You, minstrel man, play me a Porte [3],
That I on this floor may prove a man.
          [*He bows, and dances in a line.*
Now have I danced with heart and hand,
Brave gentles all, as you may see,
For I have been tried in many a land,
As yet the truth can testify;
In England, Scotland, Ireland, France, Italy, and Spain,
Have I been tried with that good sword of steel.
          [*Draws, and flourishes.*
Yet I deny that ever a man did make me yield;
For in my body there is strength,
As by my manhood may be seen;
And I, with that good sword of length,
Have oftentimes in perils been,
And over champions I was king.
And by the strength of this right hand, ·
Once on a day I kill'd fifteen,
And left them dead upon the land.

---

[1] So placed in the old MS.
[2] *Boor*—so spelt to accord with the vulgar pronunciation of the word *bower*.
[3] *Porte*—so spelt in the original. The word is known as indicating a piece of music on the bagpipe, to which ancient instrument, which is of Scandinavian origin, the sword-dance may have been originally composed.

Therefore, brave minstrel, do not care,
But play to me a Porte most light,
That I no longer do forbear,
But dance in all these gentles' sight.
Although my strength makes you abased,
Brave gentles all, be not afraid,
For here are six champions, with me, staid,
All by my manhood I have raised.   [*He dances.*
Since I have danced, I think it best
To call my brethren in your sight,
That I may have a little rest,
And they may dance with all their might;
With heart and hand as they are knights,
And shake their swords of steel so bright,
And show their main strength on this floor,
For we shall have another bout
Before we pass out of this boor.
Therefore, brave minstrel, do not care
To play to me a Porte most light,
That I no longer do forbear,
But dance in all these gentles' sight.
        [*He dances, and then introduces his knights as under.*
Stout James of Spain, both tried and stour[1],
Thine acts are known full well indeed;
And champion Dennis, a French knight,
Who stout and bold is to be seen;
And David, a Welshman born,
Who is come of noble blood;
And Patrick also, who blew the horn,
An Irish knight amongst the wood.
Of Italy, brave Anthony the good,
And Andrew of Scotland King;
Saint George of England, brave indeed,
Who to the Jews wrought muckle tinte[2].
Away with this!—Let us come to sport,
Since that ye have a mind to war.
Since that ye have this bargain sought,
Come let us fight and do not fear.
Therefore, brave minstrel, do not care

---

[1] *Stour*—great.   [2] *Muckle tinte*—much loss or harm; so in MS.

To play to me a Porte most light,
That I no longer do forbear,
But dance in all these gentles' sight.

   [He dances, and advances to JAMES *of Spain.*

Stout James of Spain, both tried and stour,
Thine acts are known full well indeed,
Present thyself within our sight,
Without either fear or dread.
Count not for favour or for feid,
Since of thy acts thou hast been sure;
Brave James of Spain, I will thee lead,
To prove thy manhood on this floor.   *[*JAMES *dances.*
Brave champion Dennis, a French knight,
Who stout and bold is to be seen,
Present thyself here in our sight,
Thou brave French knight,
Who bold hast been;
Since thou such valiant acts hast done,
Come let us see some of them now
With courtesy, thou brave French knight,
Draw out thy sword of noble hue.

   *[*DENNIS *dances, while the others retire to a side.*

Brave David a bow must string, and with awe
Set up a wand upon a stand,
And that brave David will cleave in twa [1]. *[*DAVID *dances solus.*
Here is, I think, an Irish knight,
Who does not fear, or does not fright,
To prove thyself a valiant man,
As thou hast done full often bright;
Brave Patrick, dance, if that thou can.   *[He dances.*
Thou stout Italian, come thou here;
Thy name is Anthony, most stout;
Draw out thy sword that is most clear,
And do thou fight without any doubt;
Thy leg thou shake, thy neck thou lout [2],
And show some courtesy on this floor,
For we shall have another bout,
Before we pass out of this boor.

---

[1] Something is evidently amiss or omitted here. David probably exhibited some feat of archery.

[2] *Lout*—to bend or bow down, pronounced *loot*, as *doubt* is *doot* in Scotland.

Thou kindly Scotsman, come thou here;
Thy name is Andrew of Fair Scotland;
Draw out thy sword that is most clear,
Fight for thy king with thy right hand;
And aye as long as thou canst stand,
Fight for thy king with all thy heart;
And then, for to confirm his band,
Make all his enemies for to smart.

⌊*He dances.—Music begins.'*

'FIGUIR[1].

' The six stand in rank with their swords reclining on their shoulders. The Master (Saint George) dances, and then strikes the sword of James of Spain, who follows George, then dances, strikes the sword of Dennis, who follows behind James. In like manner the rest—the music playing—swords as before. After the six are brought out of rank, they and the Master form a circle, and hold the swords point and hilt. This circle is danced round twice. The whole, headed by the Master, pass under the swords held in a vaulted manner. They jump over the swords. This naturally places the swords across, which they disentangle by passing under their right sword. They take up the seven swords, and form a circle, in which they dance round.

' The Master runs under the sword opposite, which he jumps over backwards. The others do the same. He then passes under the right-hand sword, which the others follow, in which position they dance, until commanded by the Master, when they form into a circle, and dance round as before. They then jump over the right-hand sword, by which means their backs are to the circle, and their hands across their backs. They dance round in that form until the Master calls "Loose," when they pass under the right sword, and are in a perfect circle.

' The Master lays down his sword, and lays hold of the point of James's sword. He then turns himself, James, and the others, into a clew. When so formed, he passes under out of the midst of the circle; the others follow; they vault as before. After several other evolutions, they throw themselves into a circle, with their arms across the breast. They afterwards form such figures as to form a shield of their swords, and the shield is so compact that the Master and his knights dance alternately with this shield upon their heads. It is then

---

[1] *Figuir*—so spelt in MS.

laid down upon the floor. Each knight lays hold of their former points and hilts with their hands across, which disentangle by figuirs directly contrary to those that formed the shield. This finishes the ballet.

'Epilogue.

' Mars does rule, he bends his brows,
He makes us all agast[1];
After the few hours that we stay here,
Venus will rule at last.
Farewell, farewell, brave gentles all,
That herein do remain,
I wish you health and happiness
Till we return again.   [*Exeunt.*'

The manuscript from which the above was copied was transcribed from *a very old one*, by Mr. William Henderson, jun., of Papa Stour, in Zetland. Mr. Henderson's copy is not dated, but bears his own signature, and, from various circumstances, it is known to have been written about the year 1788.

K

THE LUTTERWORTH ST. GEORGE PLAY

[From W. Kelly, *Notices Illustrative of the Drama, &c., . . . from . . . Manuscripts of the Borough of Leicester* (1865), 53. The version is that ' performed in some of the villages near Lutterworth, at Christmas 1863.']

THE CHRISTMAS MUMMERS' PLAY.

Dramatis Personae.

1. Captain Slasher, *in military costume, with sword and pistol.*
2. King of England, *in robes, wearing the crown.*
3. Prince George, *King's Son, in robes, and sword by his side.*
4. Turkish Champion, *in military attire, with sword and pistol.*
5. A Noble Doctor.
6. Beelzebub.
7. A Clown.

 Enter Captain Slasher. I beg your pardon for being so bold,
I enter your house, the weather 's so cold,
Room, a room! brave gallants, give us room to sport;
For in this house we do resort,—

---

[1] *Agast*—so spelt in MS.

Resort, resort, for many a day;
Step in, the King of England,
And boldly clear the way.

Enter King of England. I am the King of England, that
boldly does appear;
I come to seek my only son,—my only son is here.

Enter Prince George. I am Prince George, a worthy knight;
I'll spend my blood for England's right.
England's right I will maintain;
I'll fight for old England once again.

Enter Turkish Knight. I am the Turkish Champion;
From Turkey's land I come.
I come to fight the King of England
And all his noble men.

Captain Slasher. In comes Captain Slasher,
Captain Slasher is my name;
With sword and pistol by my side,
I hope to win the game.

King of England. I am the King of England,
As you may plainly see,
These are my soldiers standing by me;
They stand by me your life to end,
On them doth my life depend.

Prince George. I am Prince George, the Champion bold,
And with my sword I won three crowns of gold;
I slew the fiery dragon and brought him to the slaughter,
And won the King of Egypt's only daughter.

Turkish Champion. As I was going by St. Francis' School,
I heard a lady cry 'A fool, a fool!'
'A fool,' was every word,
'That man's a fool,
Who wears a wooden sword.'

Prince George. A wooden sword, you dirty dog!
My sword is made of the best of metal free.
If you would like to taste of it,
I'll give it unto thee.
Stand off, stand off, you dirty dog!
Or by my sword you'll die.
I'll cut you down the middle,
And make your blood to fly.

[*They fight; Prince George falls, mortally wounded.*

Enter King of England.   Oh, horrible ! terrible ! what hast
  thou done ?
Thou hast ruin'd me, ruin'd me,
By killing of my only son !
Oh, is there ever a noble doctor to be found,
To cure this English champion
Of his deep and deadly wound?
  Enter Noble Doctor.   Oh yes, there is a noble doctor to
    be found,
To cure this English champion
Of his deep and deadly wound.
   King of England.   And pray what is your practice?
   Noble Doctor.   I boast not of my practice, neither do I study
     in the practice of physic.
   King of England.   What can you cure?
   Noble Doctor.   All sorts of diseases,
Whatever you pleases :
I can cure the itch, the pitch,
The phthisic, the palsy and the gout;
And if the devil's in the man,
I can fetch him out.
My wisdom lies in my wig,
I torture not my patients with excations,
Such as pills, boluses, solutions, and embrocations;
But by the word of command
I can make this mighty prince to stand.
   King.   What is your fee ?
   Doctor.   Ten pounds is true.
   King.   Proceed, Noble Doctor;
You shall have your due.
   Doctor.   Arise, arise ! most noble prince, arise,
And no more dormant lay ;
And with thy sword
Make all thy foes obey.   [*The Prince arises.*
   Prince George.   My head is made of iron,
My body is made of steel,
My legs are made of crooked bones
To force you all to yield.
   Enter Beelzebub.   In comes I, old Beelzebub,
Over my shoulder I carry my club,
And in my hand a frying-pan,

Pleased to get all the money I can.

Enter Clown. In come I, who's never been yet,
With my great head and little wit:
My head is great, my wit is small,
I'll do my best to please you all.

Song (all join). And now we are done and must be gone,
No longer will we stay here;
But if you please, before we go,
We'll taste your Christmas beer.   [*Exeunt omnes.*

L

THE PROSE OF THE ASS

[The text is taken from the following sources :—
i. *Beauvais, thirteenth century.*—(*a*) [Duc.]—Ducange, *Glossarium* (ed.
1733–6), s.v. *Festum*, from a lost MS.; copied incorrectly by Gasté, 23, and
apparently also by Clément, 158: (*b*) [B¹]—*Brit. Mus. Egerton MS.*
2615, f. 1, with music for singing in unison : (*c*) [B²]—Same *MS.* f. 43,
with music harmonized in three parts; partly facsimiled in *Annales
Archéologiques* (1856), xvi. 259, 300.
ii. *Sens, thirteenth century.*—[S]—*MS. Senonense*, 46 ᴬ, as printed by
G. M. Dreves, *Analecta Hymnica*, xx. 217. The text has also been given
from the MS. by F. Bourquelot, in *Bull. de la Soc. Arch. de Sens* (1858),
vi. 79, and others. The version of Clément, 126 is probably, like the
facsimile given by him in *Ann. Arch.* vii. 26, based on one 'calqué' from
the MS. by a M. Amé, and, where it differs from that of Dreves, is the
less trustworthy. Dreves, xx. 257 (cf. *infra*) and Millin, *Monum. Ant.
Inédits*, ii. 348, also give the music of the opening lines. Modern settings
are provided by B. De la Borde, *Essai sur la Musique* (1780), and Clément,
in *Ann. Arch.* vii. 26, and *Chantes de la Sainte Chapelle.* An old French
translation of the text is printed in Leber, ix. 368.
On these Beauvais and Sens MSS. cf. ch. xiii.
iii. *Bourges.*—[Bo.]—The first verse with the music and variants in the
later verses are given by A. Gachet d'Artigny, *Nouveaux Mémoires* (1756),
vii. 77, from a copy of a book given to Bourges cathedral by a canon
named Jean Pastoris. Part of the Bourges music is also given by Millin,
loc. cit.
I print the fullest version from Ducange, italicizing the lines not found
elsewhere, and giving all variants, except of spelling, for the rest.
Outside Beauvais, Sens, and Bourges the only localized allusion to the
prose that I have found is the Autun order of 1411 (vol. i. p. 312) 'nec
dicatur cantilena quae dici solebat super dictum asinum.' It is not in
the Puy *officium* for the Circumcision, which, though in a MS. of 1553,
represents a ceremony as old as 1327 (U. Chevalier, *Prosolarium Ecclesiae Aniciensis*, 1894). The *officium* is full of *conductus* and *farsumina*,
and the *clericuli* at second Vespers *tripudiant firmiter.* The *sanctum
Praepucium* was a relic at Puy.
The following passage is from Theoph. Raynaudus, *Iudicium de puer-*

orum symphoniacorum processione in festo SS. Innocentium (Opera Omnia, 1665, xv. 209): 'Legi prosam quandam *de asino* e Metropolitanae cuiusdam Ecclesiae rituali exscriptam ; quae super sacrum concinebatur in die S. Stephani, et dicebatur *prosa fatuorum*, qua nihil insulsius aut asino convenientius. Similis prosa *de bove*, quae canebatur in die S. Ioannis, intercidisse dicitur, haud magno sane dispendio. Itaque hae prosae erant particulae festi fatuorum, occoepti a die S. Stephani.' I have never come across the 'Prose of the Ox,' or any notice of it which appears to be independent of Raynaud's.]

L

Orientis partibus
Adventavit Asinus,
Pulcher et fortissimus,
4 Sarcinis aptissimus.
Hez, Sire Asnes, car chantez,
Belle bouche rechignez,
Vous aurez du foin assez
8 *Et de l'avoine a plantez.*

II.

Lentus erat pedibus,
Nisi foret baculus,
Et eum in clunibus
12 *Pungeret aculeus.*
Hez, Sire Asnes, etc.

III.

Hic in collibus Sichen
Iam nutritus sub Ruben,
Transiit per Iordanem,
20 Saliit in Bethleem.
Hez, Sire Asnes, etc.

IV.

Ecce magnis auribus
Subiugalis filius
Asinus egregius
28 *Asinorum dominus.*
Hez, Sire Asnes, etc.

B[1] has heading *Conductus asi⟨ni ubi⟩ adducitur*; S, *Conductus ad tabulam.*

5-8 B[1,2] *Hez, hez, sire Asnes, hez*; S. *Hez, Sir asne, hez*; Bo. *He, he, he, Sire Ane. He.*

18. B[1,2]; S, *Enutritus.*

21-4. B[1] *Hez, hez* (and so in all verses but last); B[2] *Hez* (and so in all verses); S, *Hez, Sir asne, hez* (and so in all verses).

V.

Saltu vincit hinnulos,
Dammas et capreolos,
Super dromedarios
36 Velox Madianeos.
Hez, Sire Asnes, etc.

VI.

Aurum de Arabia,
Thus et myrrham de Saba
Tulit in Ecclesia
44 Virtus Asinaria.
Hez, Sire Asnes, etc.

VII.

Dum trahit vehicula,
Multa cum sarcinula,
Illius mandibula
52 Dura terit pabula.
Hez, Sire Asnes, etc.

VIII.

Cum aristis hordeum
Comedit et carduum:
Triticum e palea
60 Segregat in area.
Hez, Sire Asnes, etc.

IX.

Amen dicas, Asine,
Iam satur de gramine,
Amen, Amen, itera,
68 Aspernare vetera.
Hez va, hez va! hez va, hez!
Bialx Sire Asnes, car allez:
71 *Belle bouche, car chantez.*

vi. B¹,² omit ; Bo. places after viii.
59. Duc. *a palea.*
65. Duc. adds (*hic genuflectebatur*).
66. Bo. *Iam satis de carmine.*

69-71. B² *Hez* ; Clément,
Hez va! hez va! hez va! hez!
Bialx, sir asnes, car chantez,
Vous aurez du foin assez
Et de l'avoine a plantez.

I append the air of the Sens prose, as given by Dreves, *Analecta Hymnica*, xx. 257.

O ... ri ... en...tis par...ti ... bus   Ad..ven...ta...vit   A ... si ... nus,

Pul...cher et for...tis...si ... mus,   Sar.;. ci...nis ap...tis...si.,.mus.

Hez, Sir As...ne, hez.

M

THE BOY BISHOP

I. The Sarum Office.

[From C. Wordsworth, *Ceremonies and Processions of the Cathedral Church of Salisbury* (1901), 52, which follows the practically identical texts of the printed *Processionals* of 1508 (ed. Henderson, 1882, 17) and 1555 and the printed *Breviary* (ed. Procter-Wordsworth, I. ccxxix). Mr. Wordsworth also found the office in two MS. breviaries (*Sarum Chapter MS.* 152 and *Peterhouse, Cambridge, MS.* 270). In the MS. († 1445) processional from Salisbury Cathedral (*Chapter MS.* 148), on which his book is mainly based, there is a *lacuna*, probably due to intentional mutilation, where the office should come. I find no allusion to the Boy Bishop in the printed *Sarum Missal* (ed. Dickinson, 67), or in the *Sarum Consuetudinary, Custumary,* or *Ordinal* (Frere, *Use of Sarum*).]

❡ *In die sancti Johannis.*

[De Episcopo Puerorum.]

Ad uesperas, post memoriam de S. Stephano eat processio Puerorum ad altare Innocencium, uel Sancte Trinitatis et Omnium Sanctorum quod dicitur Salue, *in capis sericis, cum cereis illuminatis et ardentibus in manibus, cantando, Episcopo Puerorum pontificalibus induto* (*executore officij, siue Episcopo presente*) *incipiente hoc responsorium.*

Solus Episcopus Innocencium, si assit, Christum Puerum, uerum et eternum, Pontificem designans, incipiat:

R. Centum quadraginta quattuor millia qui empti sunt de terra: hij sunt qui cum mulieribus non sunt coinquinati, uirgines enim permanserunt. Ideo regnant cum Deo et Agno, et Agnus Dei cum illis.

Tres pueri dicant hunc uersum.

V. Hij empti sunt ex omnibus, primicie Deo et Agno, et in ore illorum non est inventum mendacium. Ideo.

Omnes pueri dicant cantando simul hanc prosam
Sedentem in superne.

Chorus post vnumquemque uersum respondeat cantum prose super vltimam literam E.

V. Sedentem in superne maiestatis arce–e.

V. Adorant humillime proclamantes ad te–e.

V. Sancte · Sancte · Sancte · Sabaoth rex–e.

V. Plena sunt omnia glorie tue–e.

V. Cum illis vndeuiginti quinque–e.

V. Atque cum innocentissimo grege–e.

V. Qui sunt sine vlla labe–e.

V. Dicentes excelsa uoce–e.

V. Laus Tibi, Domine–e.

Rex eterne glorie–e.

Chorus respondeat Ideo regnant.

Ad hanc processionem non dicatur Gloria Patri *sed dum prosa canitur tunc Episcopus Puerorum thurificet altare: deinde ymaginem Sancte Trinitatis.*

Et postea dicat Sacerdos, modesta uoce, hunc uersum.

V. Letamini in Domino, et exvltate iusti.

R. Et gloriamini omnes recti corde.

Deinde dicat Episcopus Puerorum, sine Dominus uobiscum, *sed cum* Oremus, *oracionem.*

Deus, cuius hodierna die preconium innocentes martires non loquendo sed moriendo confessi sunt: omnia in nobis uitiorum mala mortifica, vt fidem tuam, quam lingua nostra loquitur, eciam moribus uita fateatur. Qui cum Deo Patre.

In redeundo precentor puerorum incipiat responsorium de S. Maria, uel aliquam antiphonam de eadem.

R. Felix namque es, sacra uirgo Maria, et omni laude dignissima. Quia ex te ortus est Sol iusticie, Christus Deus noster.

Et, si necesse fuerit, dicatur uersus:

V. Ora pro populo, interueni pro clero, intercede pro deuoto femineo sexu: senciant omnes tuum leuamen, quicumque celebrant tuam solempnitatem. Quia ex te Gloria · Quia ·

Et sic processio chorum intret, per ostium occidentale, vt supra. Et omnes pueri, ex vtraque parte chori, in superiori gradu se recipiant; et ab hac hora vsque post processionem diei proximi succedentis nullus clericorum solet gradum superiorem ascendere, cuiuscumque condicionis fuerit.

Ad'istam processionem pro disposicione puerorum scribuntur canonici, ad ministrandum eisdem, maiores ad thuribulandum, et ad librum deferendum, minores ad candelabra deferenda.

Responsorio finito, cum suo uersu, Episcopus Puerorum in sede sua dicat uersum modesta uoce:

V. Speciosus forma pre filijs hominum:

R. Diffusa est gracia in labijs tuis.

Oracio. Deus qui salutis eterne beate Marie uirginitate fecunda humano generi premia prestitisti; tribue, quesumus, vt ipsam pro nobis intercedere senciamus, per quam meruimus Auctorem uite suscipere, Dominum nostrum Jesum Christum Filium tuum. *Que sic terminetur:* Qui Tecum uiuit et regnat in vnitate Spiritus Sancti Deus. Per omnia secula seculorum. Amen.

Pax uobis.

R. Et cum spiritu tuo.

Sequatur Benedicamus Domino, *a duobus uicarijs, uel a tribus, extra regulam.*

Tunc Episcopus Puerorum intret stallum suum, et in sede sua, benedicat populum.

Et interim cruciferarius accipiat baculum episcopi, conuersus ad Episcopum, et cum uenerit ad istum versum Cum mansuetudine *conuertat se ad populum et incipiat hanc antiphonam sequentem (que non dicatur Episcopo absente): et cantet totam antiphonam vsque ad finem.*

Ant. Princeps ecclesie, pastor ouilis, cunctam plebem tuam benedicere digneris. *Hic conuertat se ad populum sic dicendo:*

Cum mansuetudine et caritate, humilitate uos ad benediccionem.

Chorus respondeat: Deo gracias.

Deinde retradat baculum Episcopo, et tunc Episcopus Puerorum, primo signando se in fronte, dicat, hoc modo incipiens:

Adiutorium nostrum in nomine Domini:

Chorus respondeat sic: Qui fecit celum et terram.

Item Episcopus, signando se in pectore, dicat sic:

Sit nomen Dei benedictum:

Chorus respondeat: Ex hoc nunc, et vsque in seculum.

Deinde Episcopus Puerorum, conuersus ad clerum, eleuet brachium suum, et dicat hanc benediccionem:

Crucis signo uos consigno:

Hic conuertat se ad populum, sic dicendo:

Nostra sit tuicio.

Deinde conuertat se ad altare, dicens :

Qui nos emit et redemit,

*Postea ad seipsum reuersus ponat manum suam super pectus suum
dicendo :*

Sue carnis precio,

Chorus respondeat, vt sequitur, Amen.

His itaque peractis incipiat Episcopus Puerorum COMPLETORIUM *de
die, more solito, post* Pater Noster *et* Aue Maria.

*Et post Completorium dicat Episcopus Puerorum ad chorum conuersus
sub tono supradicto.*

Adiutorium nostrum in nomine Domini,

Chorus respondeat : Qui fecit celum et terram.

Episcopus Puerorum dicat :

Sit nomen Domini benedictum :

Chorus. Ex hoc nunc, et vsque in seculum.

Deinde dicat Episcopus :

Benedicat nos omnipotens Deus, Pater, et Filius, et Spiritus Sanctus.

Chorus : Amen.

¶ *In die SS. Innocencium*

si in DOMINICA euenerit :

*Eodem modo processio fiat vt in die S. Stephani, excepto quod hac die
tres pueri prosam in eundo dicant, in medio procedentes : que in ipsa
stacione ante crucem ab eisdem terminetur.*

In eundo, R. Centum quadraginta.

V. Hij empti.

Prosa. Sedentem in superne.

Sequatur. Gloria Patri, et Filio.

Ideo.

In introitu chori, de Natiuitate, vt supra.

AD MATUTINAS *in Die Innocencium :*

*In tercio Nocturno, post lecciones et cetera, ad gradum altaris omnes
pueri incipiant nonum Responsorium.*

R. Centum quadraginta, *ut supra.*

Omnes simul dicant uersum :

V. Hij empti. Gloria Patri. Ideo.

V. Justi autem.

IN LAUDIBUS, *post Ps.* Laudate, *Episcopus Puerorum dicat modesta
uoce, quasi legendo, Capitulum, loco nec habitu mutato, quia per totum
diem capa serica vtitur* (Apoc. xix.)

Cap. Vidi supra montem Syon Agnum stantem, &c.

Ympnus. Rex glóriose martirum. *De Communi plurimorum marti-rorum* (Brev. Sarum, ii. 406).

V. Mirabilis Deus.

Ant. Hij sunt qui cum mulieribus, *et cetera, quam precentor dabit Episcopo.*

Ps. Benedictus.

Oracio. Deus, cuius hodierna, &c. Qui tecum uiuit.

Tunc omnes pueri dicant, loco Benedicamus, Verbum Patris (Brev. Sarum, i. p. cxc).

Chorus respondeat.

Consequenter dicat Episcopus Puerorum benediccionem super populum eodem modo quo ad uesperas precedentes.

Post tres Memorias (scilicet de Natiuitate Domini, de S. Stephano, et de S. Johanne) dicat Episcopus Puerorum benediccionem super populum, sicut et post Completorium supra dictum est.

Deinde tres de secunda forma dicant Benedicamus Domino, *more solito.*

AD VESPERAS. *Episcopus Puerorum incipiat* Deus in adiutorium meum intende.

Ant. Tecum principium.

Ps. Dixit Dominus (*cix*).

Capitulum. Vidi supra montem.

R. Centum quadraginta.

Hoc Responsorium ab vno solo Puero, scilicet Cancellario, incipiatur ad gradum chori, in capa serica, et suus versus ab omnibus pueris cantetur in superpelliceis in stacione puerorum, cum prosa, si placet, et eciam cum Gloria Patri.

V. Hij empti sunt.

Ympnus. Rex gloriose martirum. *De Communi.*

V. Mirabilis Deus.

Episcopus Puerorum incipiat antiphonam :

Ant. Ecce vidi Agnum stantem.

Ps. Magnificat.

Oracio. Deus, cuius hodierna.

Dicta oracione, omnes pueri loco Benedicamus *dicant* Verbum Patris.

Ant. ad gradum altaris.

Et chorus totum respondeant.

⁋ IN DIE S. THOMAE ARCHIEPISCOPI MARTYRIS.

Ad Vesperas, post memoriam de S. Johanne, accipiat cruciferarius baculum Episcopi Puerorum, et cantet antiphonam Princeps ecclesie, *sicut ad primas uesperas.*

Similiter Episcopus Puerorum benedicat populum supradicto modo.

Et sic compleatur seruicium (*officium Puerorum*) *huius diei.*

II. THE YORK COMPUTUS.

[I have expanded the following document from the copy printed with all the contractions by Dr. E. F. Rimbault in *The Camden Miscellany* (C.S.), vii (1875), 31. The original roll was in the possession of the late Canon Raine.]

Compotus Nicholay de Newerk custodis bonorum Johannis de Cave Episcopi Innocencium Anno domini etc. nonagesimo sexto.

In primis receptum de xij denariis receptis in oblacione die Nativi- *Clausura.* tatis domini. Et de xxiiij solidis j denario receptis in oblacione die Innocentium et j cochleare argenteum ponderis xx*d.* et j annulum argenteum cum bursa cerica eodem die ad missam. Et de xx*d.* rec. de Magistro Willelmo de Kexby precentore. Et de ij*s.* rec. de Magistro Johanne de Schirburne cancellario. Et de vj*s.* viij*d.* rec. de Magistro Johanne de Newton thesaurario ad Novam. Et de vj*s.* viij*d.* rec. de Magistro Thoma Dalby archidiacono Richmunde. Et de vj*s.* viij*d.* rec. de Magistro Nicholao de Feriby. Et de vj*s.* viij*d.* rec. de Magistro Thoma de Wallworthe. *Summa* lv*s.* v*d.*

Item rec. de vj*s.* viij*d.* rec. de Domino Abbate Monasterii beatae *Villa.* Mariae virginis extra Muros Eboraci. Et de iij*s.* iiij*d.* rec. de Magistro Willelmo de Feriby Archidiacono Estridinge.

Summa x*s.*

Item de iij*s.* iiij*d.* rec. de domino Thoma Ugtreht milite. Et de *Patria.* ij*s.* rec. de priore de Kyrkham. Et de vj*s.* viij*d.* rec. de priore de Malton. Et de xx*s.* rec. de comitissa de Northumbria et j anulum aureum. Et de vj*s.* viij*d.* de priore de Bridlyngtone. Et de iij*s.* iiij*d.* de priore de Watton. Et de iij*s.* iiij*d.* de rectore de Baynton. Et de iij*s.* iiij*d.* de Abbate de Melsa. Et de xx*d.* rec. de priore de Feriby. Et de vj*s.* viij*d.* rec. de domino Stephano de Scrope. Et de ij*s.* de priore de Drax. Et de vj*s.* viij*d.* de Abbate de Selby. Et de iij*s.* iiij*d.* rec. de priore de Pontefracte. Et de vj*s.* viij*d.* rec. de priore Sancti Oswaldi. Et de iij*s.* iiij*d.* rec. de priore de Munkbretton. Et de vj*s.* viij*d.* rec. de domino Johanne Depdene. Et de vj*s.* viij*d.* rec. de domina de Marmeon et j anulum aureum cum bursa cerica. Et de iij*s.* iiij*d.* de domina de Harsay. Et de vj*s.* viij*d.* de domina de Rosse. Et de ij*s.* rec. de Abbate Ryavalli. Et de ij*s.* rec. de Abbate

Bellalandi. Et de ij s. rec. de priore de Novoburgo. Et de xx d. rec. de priore de Marton. *Summa* v lib. x s.

Summa totalis Receptorum viij lib. xv s. v d.

De quibus dictus Nicholaus compotat.

Ad 'O virgo virginum.' In pane pro speciebus j d. In cervisia vj d. Item in sua Cena. In pane vij d. Et in pane dominico iiij d. In cervisia xxj d. In carne vitulorum et mutulorum ix d. obolus. In sawcetiis iiij d. In ij anatibus iiij d. In xij gallinis ij s. vj d. In viij wodkoks et j pluver ij s. ij d. In iij doŝ et x feldfars xix d. In parvis avibus iij d. In vino ij s. iij d. In diversis speciebus xj d. In lx wardons v d. ob. In melle ij d. ob. In cenapio j d. In ij libris candelorum ij d. ob. In floure ij d. In focali j d. ob. Item coco vj d.

Summa xv s. vj d. ob.

Item die Innocentium ad cenam. In pane iij d. In cervisia v d. In carne vitulorum et mutulorum vij d. In pipere et croco j d.

Diebus veneris et sabbati nichil quia non visitarunt.

Item dominica prima sequentibus diebus lunae Martis Mercurii nichil quia non visitarunt.

Die Jovis seu die Octavarum Innocentium inierunt versus Kexby ad dominum de Ugtrehte et revenerunt ad cenam. In pane ij d. In cervisia iiij d. In carne v d.

Diebus veneris et sabbati nichil quia non visitarunt.

Dominica ija seu die Sancti Willelmi devillaverunt. In pane ad Jantaculum ij d. In cervisia iij d. In carne v d.

Die lunae cum ebdomade sequente nichil quia extra villam.

Dominica iija cum ebdomade sequente extra villam.

Die sabbati revenerunt ad cenam. In pane j d. ob. In cervisia iij d. In lacte et piscibus iij d.

Dominica iiija nichil.

Die lunae inierunt ad scolas et post Jantaculum devillaverunt. In pane ij d. In cervisia iij d. ob. In carne vij d.

Die sabbati revenerunt ad cenam. In pane ij d. ob. In cervisia ij d. In piscibus vj d.

Dominica va usque ad finem Purificationis nichil.

Summa v s. vij d. ob.

In primis. In zona empta pro episcopo iij d. In emendacione pilii sui j d. In pane equino ante arreptum itineris ij d. In oblacione apud Bridlyngtone ij d. In elemosina ibidem j d. In ferilay apud Melsam iiij d. In ferilay apud Drax iiij d. In pane equino apud Selby iiij d. Item barbitonsori j d. In j garth apud Bridlyngton j d. In emendacione j garth ibidem ob. In ij pectinibus equinis emptis apud

Bridlyngtone et Eboracum iiij*d*. In j garth apud Beverlacum j*d*. In ferracione equorum apud Feriby viij*d*. ob. In emendacione j garth ob. In cena apud Ledes xvij*d*. In feno et avena ibidem xiij*d*. Item in cena apud Riplay xvj*d*. In feno et avena ibidem xij*d*. ob. In ferracione equorum apud Fontans iiij*d*. In ferilay versus Harlsay iiij*d*. In bayting apud Allertone vj*d*. In vino pro episcopo viij*d*. In pane et feno equorum apud Helmslay vj*d*. In ferracione equorum apud Novumburgum iij*d*. *Summa* x*s*. vij*d*.

In primis, In j torchio empto ponderis xij lib. iiij*s*. iij*d*. In j pilio *Variae* ix*d*. In j pari cirothecarum linearum iij*d*. In j pari manicarum iij*d*. *expensae ad usum* In j pari cultellorum xiiij*d*. In j pari calcarium v*d*. Item pro factura *episcopi* robae xviij*d*. In furura agnina empta pro supertunica ij*s*. vj*d*. In *infra civi tatem.* fururis ex convencione vj*s*. In tortricidiis per totum tempus viij*d*. In carbone marino vij*d*. In carbone ligneo x*d*. In paris candelorum iiij*d*. ob. In xxviij paribus cirothecarum emptis pro vicariis et magistris scolarum iij*s*. iiij*d*. ob. Item pro emendacione capae cericae ij*d*.

Summa xxiij*s*. j*d*.

In primis Nicholao de Newsome tenori suo xij*s*. iiij*d*. Et eidem *Stipendia* pro suo equo conducto ij*s*. Item Roberto Dawtry senescallo vj*s*. viij*d*. *servien-tium et* Et pro predicationibus ejusdem in capella ij*s*. j*d*. ob. Item Johanni *equorum.* Baynton cantanti medium x*s*. Item Johanni Grene v*s*. Item Johanni Ellay iij*s*. iiij*d*. Item Johanni Schaptone servienti eidem cum ij equis suis x*s*. ij*d*. Item Thomae Marschale pro j equo iij*s*. iiij*d*. Item j sellare pro j equo iij*s*. vj*d*. Item pistori pro j equo iij*s*. vj*d*. Item Ricardo Fowler pro ij equis v*s*. *Summa* lxvij*s*. xj*d*. ob.

In primis succentori vicariorum ij*s*. Subcancellario xij*d*. Item *Feoda mi-* cerae puerorum xij*d*. Item clericis de vestibus xij*d*. Item sacristis *nistrorum in ecclesia* xij*d*. Item pro ornacione cathedrae episcopalis iiij*d*. Item in ligno *ministran-* pro stallis iiij*d*. Item in denariis communibus xviij*d*. Item custodi *cium.* choristarum iij*s*. iiij*d*. *Summa* xj*s*. vj*d*.

Summa totalis Expensarum vj lib. xiiij*s*. x*d*. ob. Et sic Recepta excedunt expensas xl*s*. vj*d*. ob. ad usum Episcopi.

N

WINTER PROHIBITIONS

I. 190–200. TERTULLIAN.

[From *De Idololatria* (*Tertulliani Opera*, ed. A. Reifferscheid and G. Wissowa, in *Corpus Script. Eccles.* xx; *P. L.* i. 674). Part of the argument of c. 15 is repeated in *De Corona Militari*, c. 13 (*P. L.* ii. 97). In *De Fuga in Persecutione*, c. 13 (*P. L.* ii. 119), bribes given by Christians to avoid persecution are called 'saturnalitia' given to soldiers.]

c. 10. [de ludimagistris]. Ipsam primam novi discipvli stipem Minervae et honori et nomini consecrat ... quam Minervalia Minervae, quam Saturnalia Saturni, quae etiam serviculis sub tempore Saturnalium celebrari necesse est. Etiam strenuae captandae et septimontium, et Brumae et carae cognationis honoraria exigenda omnia, Florae scholae coronandae : flaminicea et aediles sacrificant creati ; schola honoratur feriis ; idem fit idolo natali : omnis diaboli pompa frequentatur. Quis haec competere Christiano existimabit, nisi qui putabit convenire etiam non magistris ?

c. 14. *Quemadmodum*, inquit, *omnibus per omnia placeo*, nimirum Saturnalia et Kalendas Ianuarias celebrans hominibus placebat ? ... *Sabbata*, inquit, *vestra et numenias et ceremonias odit anima mea;* nobis, quibus sabbata extranea sunt et numeniae et feriae a deo aliquando dilectae, Saturnalia et Ianuariae et Brumae et Matronales frequentantur, munera commeant et strenae, consonant lusus, convivia constrepunt.

c. 15. Sed luceant, inquit, opera vestra ; at nunc lucent tabernae et ianuae nostrae, plures iam invenias ethnicorum fores sine lucernis et laureis, quam Christianorum ... ergo, inquis, honor dei est lucernae pro foribus et laurus in postibus ? ... certi enim esse debemus, si quos latet per ignorantiam litteraturae saecularis, etiam ostiorum deos apud Romanos, Cardeam a cardinibus appellatam et Forculum a foribus, et Limentinum a limine et ipsum Ianum a ianua ... si autem sunt qui in ostiis adorantur, ad eos et lucernae et laureae pertinebunt ; idolo feceris, quicquid ostio feceris ... scis fratrem per visionem eadem nocte castigatum graviter, quod ianuam eius subito adnuntiatis gaudiis publicis servi coronassent. Et tamen non ipse coronaverat aut prae-ceperat ; nam ante processerat et regressus reprehenderat factum ... accendant igitur quotidie lucernas, quibus lux nulla est ; affigant postibus lauros postmodum arsuras, quibus ignes imminent ; illis competunt et testimonia tenebrarum et auspicia poenarum. Tu lumen es mundi et arbor virens semper ; si templis renuntiasti, ne feceris templum ianuam tuam, minus dixi; si lupanaribus renuntiasti, ne induaris domui tuae faciem novi lupanaris.

II. 190–200. TERTULLIAN.

[*Apologeticus*, c. 42 in *P. L.* i. 492.]

Sed si ceremonias tuas non frequento, attamen et illa die homo sum. Non lavo sub noctem Saturnalibus, ne et noctem et diem perdam: attamen lavo et debita hora et salubri.

III. † 348. PRUDENTIUS.

[*Contra Symmachum*, i. 237 in *P. L.* lx. 139.]

Iano etiam celebri de mense litatur
auspiciis epulisque sacris, quas inveterato
heu! miseri sub honore agitant, et gaudia ducunt
festa Kalendarum.

IV. † 370. PACIANUS, BISHOP OF BARCELONA.

[Pacianus, *Paraenesis ad Poenitentiam* (*P. L.* xiii. 1081). Jerome, *de Viris illustribus*, c. 106 (*P. L.* xxiii. 703), says of Pacianus, 'scripsit varia opuscula, de quibus est Cervus.']

Hoc enim, puto, proximus Cervulus ille profecit, ut eo diligentius fieret, quo impressius notabatur. . . . Puto, nescierant Cervulum facere, nisi illis reprehendendo monstrassem.

V. 374–397. ST. AMBROSE.

[From *De Interpellatione Job et David*, ii. 1 (*P. L.* xiv. 813), concluding a passage on the *cervus* as a type of David and of Christ. The Benedictine editors think that if the allusion were to the *Cervulus*, St. Ambrose would have reprobated it. But in any case it is only a passing allusion.]

Sed iam satis nobis in exordio tractatus, sicut in principio anni, more vulgi, cervus allusit.

VI. 380–397. ST. CHRYSOSTOM.

[*Oratio Kalendis Habita* (*P. G.* xlviii. 953). A sermon preached at Antioch.]

'Αλλὰ πρὸς ἕτερα κατεπείγοντα ἡμῖν ὁ λόγος ὥρμηται, τὰ σήμερον ὑπὸ τῆς πόλεως ἁπάσης ἁμαρτηθέντα . . . καὶ γὰρ καὶ ἡμῖν πόλεμος συνέστηκε νῦν . . . δαιμόνων πομπευσάντων ἐπὶ τῆς ἀγορᾶς. αἱ γὰρ διαβολικαὶ παννυχίδες αἱ γινόμεναι τήμερον, καὶ τὰ σκώμματα, καὶ αἱ λοιδορίαι, καὶ αἱ χορεῖαι αἱ νυκτεριναί, καὶ ἡ καταγέλαστος αὕτη κωμῳδία, παντὸς πολεμίου χαλεπώτερον τὴν πόλιν ἡμῶν ἐξηχμαλώ- τισαν . . . περιχαρὴς ἡμῖν ἡ πόλις γέγονε καὶ φαιδρά, καὶ ἐστεφάνωται, καὶ καθάπερ γυνὴ φιλόκοσμος καὶ πολυτελής, οὕτως ἡ ἀγορὰ φιλο- τίμως ἐκαλλωπίσατο σήμερον, χρυσία περιτιθεμένη, καὶ ἱμάτια πολυτελῆ, καὶ ὑποδήματα, καὶ ἔτερά τινα τοιαῦτα, τῶν ἐν τοῖς ἐργαστηρίοις ἑκάστου τῇ τῶν οἰκείων ἔργων ἐπιδείξει τὸν ὁμότεχνον παραδραμεῖν φιλονεικοῦντος. Ἀλλ᾽ αὕτη μὲν ἡ φιλοτιμία, εἰ καὶ παιδικῆς ἐστι διανοίας, καὶ ψυχῆς οὐδὲν μέγα οὐδὲ ὑψηλὸν φανταζομένης, ἀλλ᾽ ὅμως οὐ τοσαύτην ἐπισύρεται βλάβην. ... Ἀλλ᾽, ὅπερ ἔφην, οὐ τοσούτων ἐγκλημάτων ἀξία αὕτη ἡ φιλοτιμία· οἱ δὲ ἐν τοῖς καπηλείοις ἀγῶνες γινόμενοι τήμερον, οὗτοι μὲν μάλιστα ὀδυνῶσι, καὶ ἀσωτίας καὶ ἀσεβείας ἐμπεπλημένοι πολλῆς· ἀσεβείας μέν, ὅτι παρατηροῦσιν ἡμέρας οἱ ταῦτα ποιοῦντες, καὶ οἰωνίζονται, καὶ νομίζουσιν, εἰ τὴν νουμηνίαν τοῦ μηνὸς τούτου μεθ᾽ ἡδονῆς καὶ εὐφροσύνης ἐπιτελέσαιεν, καὶ τὸν ἅπαντα τοιοῦτον ἔξειν ἐνιαυτόν· ἀσωτίας δέ, ὅτι ὑπὸ τὴν ἕω γυναῖκες καὶ ἄνδρες φιάλας καὶ ποτήρια πληρώσαντες μετὰ πολλῆς τῆς ἀσωτίας τὸν ἄκρατον πίνουσι. ... Ταῦτα ἀπὸ νουμηνίας φιλοσόφει, ταῦτα ἀπὸ τῆς περιόδου τῶν ἐνιαυτῶν ἀναμιμνήσκου ... Τὸ παρατηρεῖν ἡμέρας οὐ Χριστιανικῆς φιλοσοφίας, ἀλλ᾽ Ἑλληνικῆς πλάνης ἐστίν. ... Οὐδὲν ἔχεις κοινὸν πρὸς τὴν γῆν, ἔνθα ἡλίου δρόμοι, καὶ περίοδοι, καὶ ἡμέραι ... Τὸ πρὸς ἡμέρας ἐπτοῆσθαι τοιαύτας, καὶ πλείονα ἐν αὐταῖς δέχεσθαι ἡδονήν, καὶ λύχνους ἅπτειν ἐπὶ τῆς ἀγορᾶς, καὶ στεφανώματα πλέκειν, παιδικῆς ἀνοίας ἐστίν. ... Μὴ τοίνυν ἐπὶ τῆς ἀγορᾶς ἀνακαύσῃς πῦρ αἰσθητόν, ἀλλ᾽ ἐπὶ τῆς διανοίας ἄναψον φῶς πνευματικόν ... Μὴ τὴν θύραν τῆς οἰκίας στεφανώσῃς, ἀλλὰ τοιαύτην ἐπίδειξαι πολιτείαν, ὥστε τὸν τῆς δικαιοσύνης στέφανον σῇ κεφαλῇ παρὰ τῆς τοῦ Χριστοῦ δέξασθαι χειρός ... Ὅταν ἀκούσῃς θορύβους, ἀταξίας καὶ πομπὰς διαβολικάς, πονηρῶν ἀνθρώπων καὶ ἀκολάστων τὴν ἀγορὰν πεπληρωμένην, οἴκοι μένε, καὶ τῆς ταραχῆς ἀπαλλάττου ταύτης, καὶ ἔμεινας εἰς δόξαν Θεοῦ.

VII. 380–397. St. Chrysostom.

[*Concio de Lazaro* I (*P. L.*, xlviii. 963). Preached at Antioch on the day after No. vi.]

Τὴν χθὲς ἡμέραν, ἑορτὴν οὖσαν σατανικήν, ἐποιήσατε ὑμεῖς ἑορτὴν πνευματικήν ... Διπλοῦν τοίνυν οὕτω τὸ κέρδος ὑμῖν γέγονεν, ὅτι καὶ τῆς ἀτάκτου τῶν μεθυόντων ἀπηλλάγητε χορείας, καὶ σκιρτήματα ἐσκιρτήσατε πνευματικά, πολλὴν εὐταξίαν ἔχοντα· καὶ μετέσχετε κρατῆρος, οὐκ ἄκρατον ἐκχέοντος, ἀλλὰ διδασκαλίας πεπληρωμένου πνευματικῆς· καὶ αὐλὸς ἐγένεσθε καὶ κιθάρα τῷ Πνεύματι τῷ ἁγίῳ· καὶ τῶν ἄλλων τῷ διαβόλῳ χορευόντων, ὑμεῖς ... ἐδώκατε τῷ Πνεύματι κροῦσαι τὰς ὑμετέρας ψυχάς.

VIII. 388. St. Jerome.

[*Comm. in Ephes.* vi. 4 in *P. L.* xxvi. 540.]

Legant episcopi atque presbyteri, qui filios suos saecularibus litteris erudiunt, et faciunt comoedias legere, et mimorum turpia scripta cantare, de ecclesiasticis forsitan sumptibus eruditos; et quod in corbonam pro peccato virgo aut vidua, vel totam substantiam suam effundens quilibet pauper obtulerat, hoc kalendariam strenam, et Saturnalitiam sportulam et Minervale munus grammaticus, et orator, aut in sumptus domesticos, aut in templi stipes, aut in sordida scorta convertit.

IX. †396. Asterius of Amasea.

[*Sermo adv. Kal. Festum*, in *P. G.* xl. 215.]

Δύο κατὰ ταυτὸν ἑορταὶ συνέδραμον ἐπὶ τῆς χθιζῆς καὶ τῆς ἐνεστώσης ἡμέρας, οὐ σύμφωνοί τε καὶ ἀδελφοί, πᾶν δὲ τοὐναντίον ἐχθρῶς τε καὶ ἐναντίως ἔχουσαι πρὸς ἀλλήλας. Ἡ μὲν γάρ ἐστι τοῦ ἔξωθεν συρφετοῦ, πολὺ συνάγουσα τοῦ μαμωνᾶ τὸ ἀργύριον . . . φιλεῖται μὲν τὸ στόμα, ἀγαπᾶται δὲ τὸ νόμισμα· τὸ σχῆμα διαθέσεως, καὶ τὸ ἔργον πλεονεξίας . . . τὰ δὲ ἄλλα πῶς ἄν τις εἴποι; μὴ καὶ ἐκκαλυψάμενος γυναικίζεται ὁ ἀριστεύς; κ.τ.λ.

X. 387–430. St. Augustine.

[*Sermo* cxcviii in *P. L.* xxxviii. 1024. In *Sermones* cxcvi and cxcvii Augustine also attacks the Calends, but in more general terms.]

Et modo si solemnitas gentium, quae fit hodierno die in laetitia saeculi atque carnali, in strepitu vanissimarum et turpissimarum cantionum, in conviviis et saltationibus turpibus, in celebratione ipsius falsae festivitatis, si ea quae agunt gentes non vos delectent, congregabimini ex gentibus. . . . Qui ergo aliud credit, aliud sperat, aliud amat, vita probet, factis ostendat. Acturus es celebrationem strenarum, sicut paganus, lusurus alea, et inebriaturus te : quomodo aliud credis, aliud speras, aliud amas? . . . Noli te miscere gentibus similitudine morum atque factorum. Dant illi strenas, date vos eleemosynas. Avocantur illi cantionibus luxuriarum, avocate vos sermonibus scripturarum : currunt illi ad theatrum, vos ad ecclesiam ; inebriantur illi, vos ieiunate. Si hodie non potestis ieiunare, saltem cum sobrietate prandete. . . . Sed dicis mihi ; quando strenas do, mihi accipio et ego. Quid ergo, quando das pauperi, nihil accipis? . . . Etenim illa daemonia delectantur canticis vanitatis, delectantur nugatorio spectaculo, et turpitudinibus variis theatrorum, insania circi, crudelitate amphitheatri, certaminibus animosis eorum qui pro pestilentibus hominibus lites et contentiones usque ad inimicitias suscipiunt, pro mimo, pro histrione, pro pantomimo, pro auriga, pro venatore. Ista facientes, quasi thura ponunt daemoniis de cordibus suis.

XI. †400. SEVERIAN.

[*Homilia de Pythonibus et Maleficis* (Mai, *Spicilegium Romanum*, x. 222). The author's name is given as Severian. A Severian was bishop of Gabala in Syria †400, a prolific preacher and an opponent of St. Chrysostom in Constantinople. It seems, however, a little hazardous to ascribe to him a Latin homily.]

Ecce veniunt dies, ecce kalendae veniunt, et tota daemonum pompa procedit, idolorum tota producitur officina, et sacrilegio vetusto anni novitas consecratur. Figurant Saturnum, faciunt Iovem, formant Herculem, exponunt cum venantibus suis Dianam, circumducunt Vulcanum verbis haletantem turpitudines suas, et plura, quorum, quia portenta sunt, nomina sunt tacenda ; quorum deformitates quia natura non habet, creatura nescit, fingere ars laborat. Praeterea vestiuntur homines in pecudes, et in feminas viros vertunt, honestatem rident, violant iudicia, censuram publicam rident, inludunt saeculo teste, et dicunt se facientes ista iocari. Non sunt ioca, sed sunt crimina. In idola transfiguratur homo. Et, si ire ad idola crimen est, esse idolum quid videtur? . . . Namque talium deorum facies ut pernigrari possint, carbo deficit ; et ut eorum habitus pleno cumuletur horrore, paleae, pelles, panni, stercora, toto saeculo perquiruntur, et quidquid est confusionis humanae, in eorum facie collocatur.

XII. 408–410. ST. JEROME.

[*Comm. in Isaiam*, lxv. 11 (*P. L.* xxiv. 638).]

Et vos qui dereliquistis Dominum, et obliti estis montem sanctum meum. Qui ponitis fortunae mensam et libatis super eam. . . . Est autem in cunctis urbibus, et maxime in Aegypto, et in Alexandria idololatriae vetus consuetudo, ut ultimo die anni et mensis eorum qui extremus est, ponant mensam refertam varii generis epulis, et poculum mulso mixtum, vel praeteriti anni, vel futuri fertilitatem auspicantes. Hoc autem faciebant Israelitae, omnium simulacrorum portenta venerantes : et nequaquam altari victimas, sed huiusce modi mensae liba fundebant.

XIII. †412–†465. MAXIMUS OF TURIN.

[*Homilia* ciii, *de Calendis Gentilium* (*P. L.* lvii. 491).]

Bene quodammodo Deo providente dispositum est, ut inter medias gentilium festivitates Christus Dominus oriretur, et inter ipsas tenebrosas superstitiones errorum veri luminis splendor effulgeret. . . . Quis enim sapiens, qui dominici Natalis sacramentum colit, non ebrietatem condemnet Saturnalium, non declinet lasciviam calendarum? . . . Sunt plerique, qui trahentes consuetudinem de veteri superstitione vanitatis, calendarum diem pro summa festivitate procurent; et sic laetitiam habere velint, ut sit magis illis tristitia. Nam ita lasciviunt, ita vino et epulis satiantur, ut qui toto anno castus et temperans fuerit, illa die sit temulentus atque pollutus; et quod nisi ita fecerit, putet perdidisse se ferias; quia non intelligit per tales se ferias perdidisse salutem. Illud autem quale est, quod surgentes mature ad publicum cum munusculo, hoc est, cum strenis unusquisque procedit; et salutaturus amicos, salutat praemio antequam osculo? . . . Adhuc et ipsam munificentiam strenas vocant, cum magis strenuum, quod——cogitur. . . . Hoc autem quale est quod, interposita die, tali inani exordio, velut incipientes vivere, aut auspicia colligant, omniaque perquirant; et exinde totius anni sibi vel prosperitatem, vel tristitiam metiuntur? . . . Hoc autem malis suis addunt, ut quasi de auspicatione domum redeuntes ramusculos gestent in manibus, scilicet pro omine, ut vel onusti ad hospitium redeant.

XIV. †412-†465. Maximus of Turin.

[*Homilia* xvi, *de Cal. Ian.* (*P. L.* lvii. 255).]

Quamquam non dubitem vos . . . universas calendarum supervenientium vanitates declinare penitus et horrere . . . necessarium, nec superfluum reor . . . precedentium patrum vobis repetantur alloquia. . . . Et illorum gravior atque immedicabilis languor est, qui superstitionum furore et ludorum suavitate decepti sub specie sanitatis insaniunt. An non omnia quae a ministris daemonum illis aguntur diebus falsa sunt et insana, cum vir, virium suarum vigore mollito, totum se frangit in feminam, tantoque illud ambitu atque arte agit, quasi poeniteat illum esse, quod vir est? Numquid non universa ibi falsa sunt et insana, cum se a Deo formati homines, aut in pecudes, aut in feras, aut in portenta transformant? Numquid non omnem excedit insaniam, cum decorem vultus humani Dei specialiter manibus in omnem pulchritudinem figuratum, squalore sordium et adulterina foeditate deturpant? . . . Post omnia, ad offensionis plenitudinem, dies ipsos annum novum vocant. . . . Novum annum Ianuarias appellant calendas, cum vetusto semper errore et horrore sordescant. Auspicia etiam vanissimi colligere se dicunt, ac statum vitae suae inanibus indiciis aestimantes, per incerta avium ferarumque signa imminentis anni futura rimantur.

XV. †412-†465. Maximus of Turin?

[*Sermo* vi, *de Cal. Ian.* (*P. L.* lvii. 543). The *Sermo* is ascribed to Maximus in three good MSS. and the style agrees with his. Other MSS. give it to St. Augustine or St. Ambrose, and it is printed in the Benedictine edition of the latter's works (*Sermo* vii. in *P. L.* xvii. 617). The editors, however, do not think it his.]

Est mihi adversus plerosque vestrum, fratres, querela non modica: de iis loquor qui nobiscum natale Domini celebrantes gentilium se feriis dediderunt, et post illud coeleste convivium superstitionis sibi prandium praepararunt. . . . Quomodo igitur potestis religiose Epiphaniam Domini procurare, qui Iani calendas quantum in vobis est devotissime celebratis? Ianus enim homo fuit unius conditor civitatis, quae Ianiculum nuncupatur, in cuius honore a gentibus calendae sunt Ianuariae nuncupatae; unde qui calendas Ianuarias colit peccat, quoniam homini mortuo defert divinitatis obsequium. Inde est quod ait Apostolus: *Dies observastis, et menses, et tempora, et annos; timeo ne sine causa laboraverim in vobis.* Observavit enim diem et mensem qui his diebus aut non ieiunavit, aut ad Ecclesiam non processit. Observavit diem qui hesterna die non processit ad ecclesiam, processit ad campum. Ergo, fratres, omni studio gentilium festivitatem et ferias declinemus, ut quando illi epulantur et laeti sunt, nunc nos simus sobrii, atque ieiuni, quo intelligant laetitiam suam nostra abstinentia condemnari.

XVI. *Fifth century.* St. Peter Chrysologus.

[Sermo clv in *P. L.* lii. 609.]

Ubi nostram Christus pie natus est ad salutem, mox diabolus divinae bonitati numerosa genuit et perniciosa portenta, ut ridiculum de religione componeret, in sacrilegium verteret sanctitatem. . . . Quorum formant adulteria in simulacris, quorum fornicationes imaginibus mandant, quorum titulant incesta picturis, quorum crudelitates commendant libris, quorum parricidia tradunt saeculis, quorum impietates personant tragoediis, quorum obscaena ludunt, hos qua dementia deos crederent, nisi quia criminum desiderio, amore scelerum possidentur, deos exoptant habere criminosos? . . . Haec diximus, quare gentiles hodie faciant deos suos talia committere, quae sustinemus, et faciant tales qui videntibus et horrori sunt et pudori; faciant ut eos aliquando et ipsi qui faciunt horreant et relinquant, et Christiani glorientur a talibus se liberatos esse per Christum: si modo non eorum ex spectaculis polluantur. . . . Et si tanta est de assensione damnatio, quis satis lugeat eos qui simulacra faciunt semetipsos? . . . Qui se deum facit, Deo vero contradictor existit; imaginem Dei portare noluit, qui idoli voluerit portare personam; qui iocari voluerit cum diabolo, non poterit gaudere cum Christo. . . . Abstrahat ergo pater filium, servum dominus, parens parentem, civem civis, homo hominem, Christianus omnes qui se bestiis compararunt, exaequarunt iumentis, aptaverunt pecudibus, daemonibus formaverunt.

XVII. 470–542. Caesarius of Arles?

[*Sermo Pseud.-Augustin.* cxxix *de Kal. Ian.* in *P. L.* xxxix. 2001. Parts of this sermon are reproduced ' mutatis mutandis' in the eighth-century Frankish *Homilia de Sacrilegiis* (§§ 23-26), edited by Caspari (cf. No. xxxix, below), and also in a MS. homily, *De Kalendis Ianuariis*, in *Cod Lat. Monac.* 6108 (tenth century), f. 48ᵛ. The rest of that homily is mainly from Maximus Taurinensis, *Hom.* 16 (No. xiv, above). And nearly the whole of the present *Sermo* is included in the *Homiliarium* of Burchardus of Würzburg and printed from his MS. by Eckart, *Francia Orientalis*, i. 837.

On the date and authorship of the *Sermo*, cf. Caspari, 67. It is ascribed to Augustine by a *Codex Colbertinus*. His editors, Blancpain and Coutant, treat it as not his (*a*) on account of the difference of style, (*b*) on account of the reference to the *ieiunium* prescribed by the *sancti antiqui patres* (i. e. amongst others, Augustine himself: cf. No. x). A *Codex Aceiensis* ascribes it to Faustinus (i.e. Faustus of Raji), and this is accepted by the Bollandists (*Acta SS. Ian.* i. 2), and by Eckart, *op. cit.* i. 433. Finally a *codex Navarricus* assigns it to Maxentius. This can hardly be the Scythian monk of that name (†520). Caspari suggests that there has been a scribal error. The *sermo* is headed 'De natali Domini. In calendis ianuariis.' There is nothing about the Nativity in it, and possibly a Nativity sermon and the author's name of the Kalends sermon which followed it have dropped out. He also thinks Maximus Taurinensis may be meant. However Caspari finally agrees with Blancpain and Coutant, that the style and the allusion to the *triduum ieiunii* so closely resembling that of the Council of Tours (No. xxii) point to a writer of the first half of the sixth century, and that he may very likely be Caesarius of Arles, who, as his *Vita* (cf. No. xx) states, did preach against the Kalends.]

Dies calendarum istarum, fratres carissimi, quas Ianuarias vocant, a quodam Iano homine perdito ac sacrilego nomen accepit. Ianus autem iste dux quidam et princeps hominum paganorum fuit: quem imperiti homines et rustici dum quasi regem metuunt, colere velut Deum coeperunt. . . . Diem ergo calendarum hodiernarum de nomine Iani, sicut iam dictum est, nuncuparunt: atque ut ei homini divinos honores conferre cupiebant, et finem unius anni et alterius initium deputarunt. Et quia apud illos Ianuariae calendae unum annum implere, et alterum incipere dicebantur, istum Ianum quasi in principio ac termino posuerunt, ut unum annum implere, alterum incipere diceretur. Et hinc est, quod idolorum cultores ipsi Iano duas facies figurarunt. . . . Hinc itaque est quod istis diebus pagani homines perverso omnium rerum ordine obscenis deformitatibus teguntur; ut tales utique se faciant qui colunt, qualis est iste qui colitur. In istis enim diebus miseri homines, et, quod peius est, aliqui baptizati, sumunt formas adulteras, species monstrosas, in quibus quidem sunt quae primum pudenda, aut potius dolenda sunt. Quis enim sapiens poterit credere, inveniri aliquos sanae mentis qui cervulum facientes, in ferarum se velint habitum commutare? Alii vestiuntur pellibus pecudum; alii assumunt capita bestiarum, gaudentes et exsultantes, si taliter se in ferinas species transformaverint, ut homines non esse videantur. . . . Iamvero illud quale et quam turpe est, quod viri nati tunicis muliebribus vestiuntur, et turpissima demum demutatione puellaribus figuris virile robur effeminant, non erubescentes tunicis muliebribus inserere militares lacertos : barbatas facies praeferunt, et videri feminae volunt. . . . Sunt enim qui calendis ianuariis auguria observant, ut focum de domo sua, vel aliud quodcumque beneficium, cuicumque petenti non tribuant.   Diabolicas etiam strenas, et ab aliis accipiunt, et ipsi aliis tradunt.   Aliqui etiam rustici, mensulas in ista nocte quae praeteriit, plenas multis rebus, quae ad manducandum sunt necessariae, componentes, tota nocte sic compositas esse volunt, credentes quod hoc illis calendae ianuariae praestare possint, ut per totum annum convivia illorum in tali abundantia perseverent. . . . Qui enim aliquid de paganorum consuetudine in istis diebus observare voluerint, timendum est ne eis nomen christianum prodesse non possit. Et ideo sancti antiqui patres nostri considerantes maximam partem hominum diebus istis gulae vel luxuriae deservire, et ebrietatibus et sacrilegis saltationibus insanire, statuerunt in universum mundum, ut per omnes Ecclesias publicum indiceretur ieiunium. . . . Ieiunemus ergo, fratres carissimi, in istis diebus. . . . Qui etiam in istis calendis stultis hominibus luxuriose ludentibus aliquam humanitatem impenderit, peccati eorum participem se esse non dubitet.

XVIII. ? 470–542. Caesarius of Arles ?

[*Sermo Pseud.-Augustin.* cxxx in *P.L.* xxxix. 2003.   The authorship is generally taken to follow that of No. xvii, although a Fleury MS. ascribes it to Bp. Sedatus of Besiers † 589.]

Sic enim fit ut stultae laetitiae causa, dum observantur calendarum dies aut aliarum superstitionum vanitas, per licentiam ebrietatis et ludorum turpem cantum, velut ad sacrificia sua daemones invitentur. . . . Quid enim est tam demens quam virilem sexum in formam mulieris, turpi habitu commutare ?   Quid tam demens quam deformare faciem, et vultus induere, quos ipsi etiam daemones expavescunt ?   Quid tam demens quam incompositis motibus et impudicis carminibus vitiorum laudes inverecunda delectatione cantare ?   indui ferino habitu, et capreae aut cervo similem fieri, ut homo ad imaginem Dei et similitudinem factus sacrificium daemonum fiat ? . . . Quicunque ergo in calendis ianuariis quibuscunque miseris hominibus sacrilego ritu insanientibus, potius quam ludentibus, aliquam humanitatem dederint, non hominibus, sed daemonibus se dedisse cognoscant.   Et ideo si in

peccatis eorum participes esse non vultis, cervulum sive iuvencam [1],
aut alia quaelibet portenta, ante domos vestras venire non permittatis.
. . . Sunt enim aliqui, quod peius est, quos ita observatio inimica sub-
vertit, ut in diem calendarum si forte aut vicinis aut peregrinantibus opus
sit, etiam focum dare dissimulent. Multi praeterea strenas et ipsi
offerre, et ab aliis accipere solent. Ante omnia, fratres, ad confun-
dendam paganorum carnalem et luxuriosam laetitiam, exceptis illis qui
prae infirmitate abstinere non praevalent, omnes auxiliante Deo ieiunemus ; et pro illis miseris qui calendas istas, pro gula et ebrietate,
sacrilega consuetudine colunt, Deo, quantum possumus, supplicemus.

XIX. 470–542. CAESARIUS OF ARLES ?

[*Sermo Pseud.-Augustin.* 265, *De Christiano Nomine cum Operibus non
Christianis*, in *P. L.* xxxix. 2239.]

Licet credam quod illa infelix consuetudo . . . iam . . . fuerit . . .
sublata ; tamen, si adhuc agnoscatis aliquos illam sordidissimam turpitudinem de hinnicula vel cervula exercere . . . castigate.

XX. 470–542. CAESARIUS OF ARLES.

[Episcopi Cyprianus, Firminus et Viventius, *Vita S. Caesarii Arela-
tensis*, i. 5. 42 ; *P. L.* lxvii. 1021.]

Predicationes . . . contra calendarum quoque paganissimos ritus . . .
fecit.

XXI. †554. CHILDEBERT.

[*Constitutio Childeberti, De Abolendis Reliquiis Idolatriae*, in Mansi,
ix. 738 ; Boretius, i. 2.]

Noctes pervigiles cum ebrietate, scurrilitate, vel canticis, etiam in
ipsis sacris diebus, pascha, natale Domini, et reliquis festivitatibus, vel
adveniente die Dominico dansatrices per villas ambulare. Haec omnia,
unde Deus agnoscitur laedi, nullatenus fieri permittimus.

XXII. 567. COUNCIL OF TOURS.

[Maassen, i. 121 ; Mansi, ix. 803.]

c. 18. [De ieiuniis monachorum]
Quia inter natale Domini et epyfania omni die festivitates sunt,
idemque prandebunt excepto triduum illud, quod ad calcandam gentilium consuetudinem patris nostri statuerunt, privatas in kalendis
Ianuarii fieri letanias, ut in ecclesia psalletur et ora octava in ipsis
kalendis circumcisionis missa Deo propitio celebretur.

---

[1] *var. lect. anulas, agniculam, anniculam.*

c. 23. Enimvero quoniam cognovimus nonnullos inveniri sequi-
pedes erroris antiqui, qui Kalendas Ianuarii colunt, cum Ianus homo
gentilis fuerit, rex quidam, sed esse Deus non potuit; quisquis ergo
unum Deum Patrem regnantem cum Filio et Spiritu Sancto credit, non
potest integer Christianus dici, qui super hoc aliqua custodit.

XXIII. 572–574. MARTIN OF BRAGA.

[Martin von Bracara, *De Correctione Rusticorum*, ed. C. P. Caspari,
Christiania, 1883.]

c. 10. Similiter et ille error ignorantibus et rusticis hominibus
subrepit, ut Kalendas Ianuarias putent anni esse initium, quod omnino
falsissimum est. Nam, sicut scriptura dicit, viii. kal. Aprilis in ipso
aequinoctio initium primi anni est factum.

c. 11. . . . Sine causa autem miser homo sibi istas praefigurationes
ipse facit, ut, quasi sicut in introitu anni satur est et laetus ex omnibus,
ita illi et in toto anno contingat. Observationes istae omnes paganorum sunt per adinventiones daemonum exquisitae.

c. 16. . . . Vulcanalia et Kalendas observare, menses ornare, lauros
ponere, pedem observare, effundere [in foco] super truncum frugem et
vinum, et panem in fontem mittere, quid est aliud nisi cultura diaboli?

XXIV. †560. MARTIN, BISHOP OF BRAGA.

[Quoted in the *Decretum Gratiani*, Pars ii, Causa 26, Quaestio 7, c. 13
(*C. I. Can.* ed. Friedberg, i. 1044), as from 'Martinus Papa,' or 'Martinus
Bracarensis' [c. 74]. Mansi, ix. 857, gives the canon with a reference to
C. of Laodicea, c. 39, which is a more general decree against taking part in
Gentile feasts. Burchardus, x. 15, quotes it 'ex decreto Martialis papae.'
Martin of Braga ob. 580. His *Capitula* are collected from the councils
of Braga and the Great Councils. Caspari, *Martin von Bracara's De
Con. Rusticorum*, xl, thinks that several of them, including c. 74, were his
own additions.]

Non licet iniquas observationes agere calendarum, et otiis vacare
gentilibus, neque lauro aut viriditate arborum cingere domos: omnis
enim haec observatio paganismi est.

XXV. 573–603. COUNCIL OF AUXERRE.

[Maassen, i. 179.]

c. 1. Non licet kalendis Ianuarii vetolo aut cervolo facere vel streneas
diabolicas observare, sed in ipsa die sic omnia beneficia tribuantur,
sicut in reliquis diebus.

c. 5. Omnino inter supra dictis conditionibus pervigilias, quos in
honore domini Martini observant, omnimodis prohibite.

c. 11. Non licet vigilia paschae ante ora secunda noctis vigilias per-expedire, quia ipsa nocte non licet post media nocte bibere, nec natale Domini nec reliquas sollemnitates.

XXVI. 6th cent. St. Samson, Bishop of Dôle.

[Anonymi *Vita S. Samsonis*, ii. 13 (*Acta S. S. Iulii*, vi. 590).]

Nam cum quodam tempore in Resia insula praedicaret, veniente per annuam vertiginem Kalenda Ianuaria, qua homines supradictae insulae hanc nequam solemnem inepte iuxta patrum abominabilem consuetudinem prae ceteris sane celebrare consueverant, ille providus spiritu ob duritiam eorum mitigandam, convenire eos omnes in unum fecit, ut, Deo revelante, sermo ad detestanda tam gravia mala sit. Tum hi omnes verum de eo amantes, pravos ritus anathematizaverunt, ac verum iuxta praecepta tenus sine suscipere spoponderunt. Ille nihilominus in Domino secundum Apostolos gaudens, omnes parvulos qui per insulam illam ob hanc nefariam diem discurrebant, vocavit ad se, eisque singulis per sobriam vocem mercedem nummismunculi auro quod est mensura domuit, praecipiens in nomine Domini, ne ulterius ab illis haec sacrilega consuetudo servaretur. Quod ita Deo operante factum est, ut usque hodie ibidem spiritales ioci eius solide et catholice remanserint.

XXVII. 588–659. St. Eligius of Rouen?

[*Sermo* in *Vita Eligii* of Audoënus of Rouen (*P. L.* lxxxvii. 524). According to E. Vacandard in *R. des Questions historiques*, lxiv. 471, this is largely a compilation from the sermons of St. Caesarius of Arles.]

Nullus in Kalendis Ianuarii nefanda et ridiculosa, vetulas aut cervulos, aut iotticos [1] faciat, neque mensas supra noctem componat, neque strenas aut bibitiones superfluas exerceat.

XXVIII. †636. St. Isidore of Seville.

[*De Ecclesiasticis Officiis*, i. 41 ; *De Ieiunio Kalendarum Ianuariarum* (*P. L.* lxxxiii. 774). This is the chief source of the similar passage in the ninth-century Pseudo-Alcuin, *De Div. Offic.* c. 4 (*P. L.* ci. 1177).]

1. Ieiunium Kalendarum Ianuariarum propter errorem gentilitatis instituit Ecclesia. Ianus enim quidam princeps paganorum fuit, a quo nomen mensis Ianuarii nuncupatur, quem imperiti homines veluti Deum colentes, in religione honoris posteris tradiderunt, diemque ipsam scenis et luxuriae sacraverunt.

2. Tunc enim miseri homines, et, quod peius est, etiam fideles,

---

[1] *var. lect.* ulerioticos. Ducange explains *jotticos* as ' *ludi*, Gall. *jeux*.'

sumentes species monstruosas, in ferarum habitu transformantur:
alii, femineo gestu demutati, virilem vultum effeminant. Nonnulli
etiam de fanatica adhuc consuetudine quibusdam ipso die obser-
vationum auguriis profanantur; perstrepunt omnia saltantium pedibus,
tripudiantium plausibus, quodque est turpius nefas, nexis inter se
utriusque sexus choris, inops animi, furens vino, turba miscetur.

3. Proinde ergo sancti Patres considerantes maximam partem
generis humani eodem die huiusmodi sacrilegiis ac luxuriis inservire,
statuerunt in universo mundo per omnes Ecclesias publicum ieiunium,
per quod agnoscerent homines in tantum se prave agere, ut pro eorum
peccatis necesse esset omnibus Ecclesiis ieiunare.

XXIX. †685. St. Aldhelm.

[*Epist.* iii *in Eahfridum* (*P. L.* lxxxix. 93).]

Et ubi pridem eiusdem nefandae natriçis ermuli[1] cervulique cruda
fanis colebantur stoliditate in profanis, versa vice discipulorum gur-
gustia (imo almae oraminum aedes) architecti ingenio fabre conduntur.

XXX. 692. Quinisextine Council.

[*Conc. Quinisextinum* or *in Trullo*, held at Constantinople, *versio
Latina*, c. 62 (Mansi, xi. 971).]

Kalendas quae dicuntur, et vota [Gk. βότα], et brumalia quae
vocantur; et qui in primo Martii mensis die fit conventum ex fidelium
universitate omnino tolli volumus: sed et publicas mulierum saltationes multam noxam exitiumque afferentes: quin etiam eas, quae
nomine eorum, qui falso apud gentiles dii nominati sunt, vel nomine
virorum ac mulierum fiunt, saltationes ac mysteria more antiquo et
a vita Christianorum alieno, amandamus et expellimus; statuentes,
ut nullus vir deinceps muliebri veste induatur, vel mulier veste viro
conveniente. Sed neque comicas vel satyricas, vel tragicas personas
induat; neque execrati Bacchi nomen, uvam in torcularibus expri-
mentes, invocent; neque vinum in doliis effundentes risum moveant,
ignorantia vel vanitate ea, quae ab insaniae impostura procedunt,
exercentes.

XXXI. 714. Gregory II.

[Gregorius II. *Capitulare datum episcopo et aliis in Bavariam
ablegatis*, c. 9 (Mansi, xii. 260).]

Ut incantationes, et fastidiationes, sive diversae observationes dierum
Kalendarum, quas error tradidit paganorum, prohibeantur.

---

[1] *Ermuli.* Ducange, s. v., would read *hinnuli.* He says that Archbishop Ussher thought that the passage referred to the Saxon god Irminsul.

WINTER PROHIBITIONS 303

XXXII. 731–741. GREGORY III.

[*Iudicia*, c. 23 (*P. L.* lxxxix. 594). In *Epist.* 3 sent to Germany on the return of Boniface from Rome in 739, Gregory gives the more general direction 'abstinete et prohibete vosmetipsos ab omni cultu paganorum' (*P. L.* lxxxix. 579).]

Si quis ... ut frater in honore Iovis vel Beli aut Iani, secundum paganam consuetudinem, honorare praesumpserit, placuit secundum antiquam constitutionem sex annos poeniteant. Humanius tres annos iudicaverunt.

XXXIII. † 742. ST. BONIFACE (*alias* WINFRID).

[Bonifatius, *Epistola* xlix (*P. L.* lxxxix. 746). *Epistola* xlii (Jaffé, *Monumenta Moguntina*), *Epistola* l (Dummler, *Epistolae Merowingici et Karolini Aevi*, i. 301): cf. Kögel, i. 28 ; Tille, *Y. ad C.* 88. The letter is *Ad Zachariam Papam.*]

Quia carnales homines idiotae Alamanni, vel Bagoarii, vel Franci, si iuxta Romanam urbem aliquid fieri viderint ex his peccatis quae nos prohibemus, licitum et concessum a sacerdotibus esse putant ; et dum nobis improperium deputant, sibi scandalum vitae accipiunt. Sicut affirmant se vidisse annis singulis in Romana urbe, et iuxta ecclesiam sancti Petri, in die vel nocte quando Kalendae Ianuariae intrant, paganorum consuetudine choros ducere per plateas, et acclamationes ritu gentilium, et cantationes sacrilegas celebrare, et mensas illa die vel nocte dapibus onerare, et nullum de domo sua vel ignem, vel ferramentum, vel aliquid commodi vicino suo praestare velle. Dicunt quoque se ibi vidisse mulieres pagano ritu phylacteria et ligaturas in brachiis et in cruribus ligatas habere, et publice ad vendendum venales ad comparandum aliis offerre. Quae omnia eo quod ibi a carnalibus et insipientibus videntur, nobis hic improperium et impedimentum praedicationis et doctrinae faciunt.

XXXIV. † 742. POPE ZACHARY.

[Zacharias Papa, *Epistola* ii (*P. L.* lxxxix. 918), *Epistola* li (Dümmler, *Epist. Merow. et Karol. Aevi*, i. 301). Written *Ad Bonifatium* in reply to No. xxxiii. The *constitutio* of Pope Gregory referred to appears to be No. xxxii.]

De Kalendis vero Ianuariis, vel ceteris auguriis, vel phylacteriis, et incantationibus, vel aliis diversis observationibus, quae gentili more observari dixisti apud beatum Petrum apostolum, vel in urbe Roma ; hoc et nobis et omnibus Christianis detestabile et perniciosum esse iudicamus.... Nam et sanctae recordationis praedecessoris atque nutritoris nostri domini Gregorii papae constitutione omnia haec pie ac fideliter amputata sunt et alia diversa quam plura.

XXXV. 743. COUNCIL OF ROME.

[Conc. Romanum, c. 9: Mansi, xii. 384. A slightly different version, headed 'Zacharias Papa in Conc. Rom. c. 9,' is in *Decretum Gratiani*, ii. 26. 7, c. 14 (*C. I. Can.* ed. Friedberg, i. 1045). This seems to be a result of Nos. xxxiii, xxxiv.]

Ut nullus Kalendas Ianuarias et broma ritu paganorum colere praesumpserit, aut mensas cum dapibus in domibus praeparare, aut per vicos et plateas cantiones et choreas ducere, quod maxima iniquitas est coram Deo: anathema sit.

XXXVI. † 750. PRIMINIUS.

[*Dicta Abbatis Priminii*, c. 22 (Caspari, *Kirchenhistorische Anecdota*, i. 172).
Priminius was a German contemporary of Boniface.]

Nam Vulcanalia et Kalendas observare . . . quid aliut nisi cultura diabuli est? . . . Cervulos et vetulas in Kalendas vel aliud tempus nolite anbulare. Viri vestes femineas, femine vestes virilis in ipsis Kalandis vel in alia lusa quam plurima nolite vestire.

XXXVII. † 766. EGBERT.

[*Penitentiale Egberti*, viii. 4 (Haddan and Stubbs, iii. 424).]

Kalendas Ianuarias secundum paganam causam honorare, si non desinit, v annos poeniteat clericus, si laicus, iii annos poeniteat.

XXXVIII. † 790–800. LOMBARD CAPITULARY.

[*Capit. Langobardicum*, c. 3; Boretius, i. 202; Gröber, *Zur Volkskunde aus Concilbeschlüssen und Capitularien* (1893), No. 11.]

De pravos homines qui brunaticus colunt et de hominibus suis subtus maida[1] cerias incendunt et votos vovent: ad tale vero iniquitas eos removere faciant unusquisque.

XXXIX. †*Eighth century*. HOMILIA DE SACRILEGIIS.

[C. P. Caspari, *Eine Augustin fälschlich beilegte Homilia de Sacrilegiis* (1886), § 17. Caspari (pp. 71, 73) assigns the homily to a Frankish clerk, probably of the eighth century. Later on (§§ 23–26) is another passage on the Kalends taken from the pseud-Augustine, *Sermo* cxxix, which is No. xvii, above.]

Quicumque in kalendas ienuarias mensas panibus et aliis cybis ornat et per noctem ponet et diem ipsum colit et [in eo] auguria aspicet vel arma in campo ostendit et feclum[2] et cervulum et alias miserias vel lusa

---

[1] *maida* G. explains as *Backtrog*, i. e. 'kneading-trough' (Gk. μάκτρα); cf. Diez, *Etym. Wörterbuch*, s. v. madia;

Körting, *Lat.-Rom. Wörterbuch*, No. 4980.
[2] MS. *fectum.*

[facit] quę in ipso die insipientes solent facere, vel qui in mense februario hibernum credit expellere, vel qui in ipso mense dies spurcos ostendit, [et qui in kalendis ianuariis] aliquid auguriatur, quod in ipso anno futurum sit, non christianus, sed gentilis est.

XL. *Ninth century.* Pseudo-Theodore.

[*Penit. Pseudo-Theod.* c. xii (Wasserschleben, *ut infra*, 597 ; cf. Haddan and Stubbs, iii. 173). This *Penitential*, quoted by Tille, *Y. and C.* 98, and others as Theodore's, and therefore English, is really a Frankish one, partly based, but not so far as these sections are concerned, on the genuine *Penitential* of Theodore. I do not quote all the many Penitentials which copy from each other, often *totidem verbis*, prohibitions of the *Cervulus* and *Vetula.* They may be found in F. W. H. Wasserschleben, *Bussordnungen der abendländ. Kirche*, 368, 382, 395, 414, 424, 428, 480, 517 ; H. J. Schmitz, *Die Bussbücher und die Bussdisciplin der Kirche*, 311, 379, 479, 633. On the general character of these compilations and their filiation, see Schaff, vii. 371. Their ultimate authority for the particular prohibition of *cervulus* and *vetula*, under these names, is probably No. xxv.]

§ 19. Si quis in Kalendas ianuarii in cervolo aut vetula vadit, id est, in ferarum habitus se communicant et vestiuntur pellibus pecudum, et assumunt capita bestiarum : qui vero taliter in ferinas species se transformant, iii annos poeniteant, quia hoc daemoniacum est.

§ 24. Qui . . . kalendas Ianuarii, more paganorum, honorat, si clericus est, v annos poeniteat, laicus iii annos poeniteat.

XLI. †915. Regino of Prüm.

[Regino von Prüm, *De synodalibus causis et disciplina ecclesiastica* (ed. Wasserschleben, 1840), i. 304.]

Fecisti aliquid quod pagani faciunt in Kalendis januariis in cervulo vel vetula tres annos poeniteas.

XLII. Before 1024. Burchardus of Worms.

[*Collectio Decretorum*, xix. 5 (Grimm, iv. 1743; *P. L.* cxl. 960). The larger part of the book is from earlier Penitentials, &c., but the long chapter from which these extracts are taken appears to be based upon the writer's own knowledge of contemporary superstition. On the collection generally, cf. A. Hauck, in *Sitzb. Akad. Leipzig, phil.-hist. Kl.*, xlvi (1894), 65.]

Observasti Kalendas Ianuarias ritu paganorum, ut vel aliquid plus faceres propter novum annum, quam antea vel post soleres facere, ita dico, ut aut mensam tuam cum lapidibus vel epulis in domo tua praeparares eo tempore, aut per vicos et per plateas cantores et choros duceres, aut supra tectum domus tuae sederes ense tuo circumsignatus, ut ibi videres et intelligeres, quid tibi in sequenti anno futurum esset?

vel in bivio sedisti supra taurinam cutem, ut et ibi futura tibi intelligeres? vel si panes praedicta nocte coquere fecisti tuo nomine, ut, si bene elevarentur et spissi et alti fierent, inde prosperitatem tuae vitae eo anno praevideres?

Credidisti ut aliqua femina sit quae hoc facere possit, quod quaedam a diabolo deceptae se affirmant necessario et ex praecepto facere debere, id est, cum daemonum turba in similitudinem mulierum transformatam, quam vulgaris stultitia holdam [1] vocat, certis noctibus equitare debere super quasdam bestias, et in eorum se consortio annumeratam esse?

Fecisti quod quidam faciunt in Kalendis Ianuarii, i.e. in octava Natalis Domini; qui ea sancta nocte filant, nent, consuunt, et omne opus quodcunque incipere possunt, diabolo instigante propter novum annum incipiunt?

Fecisti ut quaedam mulieres in quibusdam temporibus anni facere solent, ut in domo tuo mensam praeparares, et tuos cibos et potum cum tribus cultellis supra mensam poneres, ut si venissent tres illae sorores quas antiqua posteritas et antiqua stultitia parcas nominavit, ibi reficerentur; et tulisti divinae pietati potestatem suam et nomen suum, et diabolo tradidisti, ita dico, ut crederes illas quas tu dicis esse sorores tibi posse aut hic aut in futuro prodesse?

O

THE REGULARIS CONCORDIA OF ST. ETHELWOLD

[The following extracts are taken from the text printed by W. S. Logemann in *Anglia*, xiii (1891), 365, from *Cotton MS. Tiberius A. III*, † 1020–1030. This MS. has Anglo-Saxon glosses. Other MSS. are in *Cotton MS. Faustina B. III*, and *Bodleian MS. Junius*, 52, ii. Earlier editions of the text are in Reyner, *De Antiquitate Ordinis Benedictinorum in Anglia*, App. iii. p. 77, and Dugdale, *Monasticum Anglicanum*, i. xxvii. The literary history is discussed by W. S. Logemann in *Anglia*, xv (1893), 20; M. Bateson, *Rules for Monks and Canons* in *English Hist. Review*, ix (1894), 700; and F. Tupper, *History and Texts of the Benedictine Reform of the Tenth Century*, in *Modern Language Notes*, viii. 344. The *Prooemium* of the document states that it was drawn up by the bishops, abbots, and abbesses of England upon the suggestion of King Edgar at a Council of Winchester, and that certain additions were made to it by Dunstan. The traditional ascription by Cotton's librarian and others of the authorship of the *Regularis Concordia* to Dunstan is probably based on this record of the revision which, as archbishop, he naturally gave it. The actual author is thought by Dr. Logemann, and by

---

[1] *Cod. Madrid*, Friga holdam; *var. lect.* unholdam.

Dr. Stubbs (*Memorials of Dunstan*, R. S. cx) to have been Ælfric, a monk, first of Abingdon and then of Winchester, who became abbot of Cerne, and in 1005 of Eynsham, and was a considerable writer in Anglo-Saxon. Dr. Logemann's view is based on a theory that the *Concordia* is the 'Regula Aluricii, glossata Anglice' which occurs amongst the titles of some tracts once in the library of Christ Church, Canterbury (*Anglia*, xv. 25). But the *Concordia* is more likely to have been the 'Consuetudines de faciendo servitio divino per annum, glossatae Anglice,' which is in the same list, and in fact the Canterbury copy is probably that in *Cotton MS. Faustina, B. III* (*E. H. R.* ix. 708). Perhaps the 'Regula Aluricii' was a copy of the letter to the monks of Eynsham, which Ælfric at some date after 1005 based upon the *Concordia* and the *De Ecclesiasticis Officiis* of Amalarius of Metz. This is printed, from *C. C. C. C. MS.* 265, by Miss Bateson, in Dean Kitchin's *Obedientiary Rolls of St. Swithin's, Winchester*, 173 (*Hampshire Record Soc.*). It omits the *Sepulchrum* and its *Visitatio*. In any case this letter makes it clear that Ælfric was not the author of the *Concordia*, for he says 'haec pauca de libro consuetudinum quem sanctus Aethelwoldus Wintoniensis episcopus cum coepiscopis et abbatibus tempore Eadgari felicissimi regis Anglorum undique collegit ac monachis instituit observandum.' The author, therefore, so far as there was a single author, was Ethelwold, whom I take to be the 'abbas quidam' of the *Prooemium*. He became Abbot of Abingdon about 954, and Bishop of Winchester in 963. In 965 Elfrida, who is also mentioned in the *Prooemium*, became queen. The date of the *Concordia* probably falls, therefore, between 965 and the death of Edgar in 975. There were Councils of Winchester in 969 and 975 (Wilkins, i. 247, 261) : but the Council at which the *Concordia* was undertaken may be an earlier one, not otherwise recorded. The *Concordia* is said in the *Prooemium* to have been based in part upon customs of Fleury and of Ghent. It is worth pointing out that Ethelwold had already reformed Abingdon after the model of Fleury, and that Dunstan, during his banishment, had found refuge in St. Peter's at Ghent (Stephens-Hunt, *Hist. of the English Church*, i. 347, 349). Miss Bateson suggests that another source is to be found in the writings of an earlier Benedictine reformer, Benedict of Aniane (*E. H. R.* ix. 700).]

De Consuetudine Monachorum.

Prohemum Regularis Concordiae Anglicae Nationis Monachorum Sanctimonialiumque Orditur.

[The *Prooemium* opens with an account of the piety of King Edgar 'abbate quodam assiduo monente' and the purification of the English monasteries.]

. . . Regulari itaque sancti patris Benedicti norma honestissime suscepta, tam abbates perplurimi quam abbatissae cum sibi subiectis fratrum sororumque collegiis sanctorum sequi vestigia una fide non tamen uno consuetudinis usu certatim cum magna studuerunt hilaritate. Tali igitur ac tanto studio praefatus rex magnopere delectatus arcana quaeque diligenti cura examinans synoda le concilium Wintoniae fieri decrevit . . . cunctosque . . . monuit ut concordes aequali consuetudinis usu . . . nullo modo dissentiendo discordarent . . . Huius praecellentissimi regis sagaci monitu spiritualiter conpuncti non tantum episcopi verum etiam abbates et abbatissae . . . eius imperiis toto mentis conamine alacriter obtemperantes, sanctique patroni nostri Gregorii documenta quibus beatum Augustinum monere studuit, ut non solum Romanae verum etiam Galliarum honestos ecclesiarum usus rudi Anglorum ecclesia decorando constitueret, recolentes, accitis Floriacensibus beati Benedicti nec non praecipui coenobii quod celebri Gent nuncupatur vocabulo monachis quaeque ex dignis eorum moribus honesta colligentes, . . . has morum consuetudines ad vitae honestatem et regularis observantiae dulcedinem . . . hoc exiguo apposuerunt codicello . . . Hoc etenim Dunstanus egregius huius patriae archiepiscopus praesago afflatus spiritu ad corroborandum praefati sinodalis conventus conciliabulum provide ac sapienter addidit, ut videlicet

. . . .

[On Maundy Thursday] In qua missa sicut in sequentium dierum communicatio prebetur tam fratribus quam cunctis fidelibus reservata nihilominus ea die eucharistia quae sufficit ad communicandum cunctis altera die . . . .

In die Parascevae agatur nocturna laus [i. e. the *Tenebrae*] sicut supra dictum est. Post haec venientes ad primam discalceati omnes incedant quousque crux adoretur. Eadem enim die hora nona abbas cum fratribus accedat ad ecclesiam. . . . Postea legitur passio domini nostri Ihesu Christi secundum Iohannem . . . Post haec celebrentur orationes . . . Quibus expletis per ordinem statim preparetur crux ante altare interposito spatio inter ipsam et altare sustentata hinc et inde a duobus diaconibus. Tunc cantent . . . Deferatur tunc ab ipsis diaconibus ante altare, et eos acolitus cum pulvillo sequatur super quem sancta crux ponatur . . . Post haec vertentes se ad clerum nudata cruce dicant antiphonam *Ecce lignum crucis* . . . Ilico ea nudatâ veniat abbas ante crucem sanctam ac tribus vicibus se prosternat cum omnibus fratribus dexterioris chori scilicet senioribus et iunioribus et cum magno cordis suspirio viim poenitentiae psalmos cum orationibus sanctae cruci competentibus decantando peroret . . . Et eam humiliter deosculans surgat. Dehinc sinisterioris chori omnes fratres eadem mente devota peragant. Nam salutata ab abbate vel omnibus cruce redeat ipse abbas ad sedem suam usque dum omnis clerus ac populus hoc idem faciat. Nam quia ea die depositionem corporis salvatoris nostri celebramus usum quorundam religiosorum imitabilem ad fidem indocti vulgi ac neofitorum corroborandam equiparando sequi si ita cui visum fuerit vel sibi taliter placuerit hoc modo decrevimus. Sit autem in una parte altaris qua vacuum fuerit quaedam assimilatio sepulchri velamenque quoddam in gyro tensum quod dum sancta crux adorata fuerit deponatur hoc ordine. Veniant diaconi qui prius portaverunt eam et involvant eam sindone in loco ubi adorata est. Tunc reportent eam canentes antiphonas . . . donec veniant ad locum monumenti depositaque cruce ac si domini nostri Ihesu Christi corpore sepulto dicant antiphonam . . . In eodem loco sancta crux cum omni reverentia custodiatur usque dominicae noctem resurrectionis. Nocte vero ordinentur duo fratres aut tres aut plures si tanta fuerit congregatio, qui ibidem psalmos decantando excubias fideles exerceant. . . . [The *Missa de Praesanctificatorum* follows] . . . Sabbato sancto hora nona veniente abbate in ecclesiam cum fratribus novus ut supra dictum est afferatur ignis. Posito vero cereo ante altare ex illo accendatur igne. Quem diaconus more solito benedicens hanc orationem quasi voce legentis proferens dicat . . .

In die sancto paschae. . . eiusdem tempore noctis antequam matutinorum signa moveantur sumant editui crucem et ponant in loco sibi congruo. . . . Dum tertia recitatur lectio quatuor fratres induant se, quorum unus alba indutus ac si ad aliud agendum ingrediatur atque latenter sepulchri locum adeat, ibique manu tenens palmam quietus sedeat. Dumque tertium percelebratur responsorium residui tres succedant, omnes quidem cappis induti turribula cum incensu manibus gestantes ac pedetemptim ad similitudinem querentium quid veriant ante locum sepulchri. Aguntur enim haec ad imitationem angeli sedentis in monumento atque mulierum cum aromatibus venientium ut ungerent corpus Ihesu. Cum ergo ille residens tres velut erraneos ac aliquid querentes viderit sibi adproximare incipiat mediocri voce dulcisono cantare *Quem quaeritis*: quo decantato fine tenus respondeant hi tres uno ore *Ihesum Nazarenum*. Quibus ille, *Non est hic : surrexit sicut praedixerat. Ite nuntiate quia surrexit a mortuis.* Cuius iussionis voce vertant se illi tres ad chorum dicentes *Alleluia : resurrexit dominus.* Dicto hoc rursus ille residens velut revocans illos dicat antiphonam *Venite et videte locum*: haec vero dicens surgat et erigat velum ostendatque eis locum cruce nudatum sed tantum linteamina posita quibus crux involuta erat. Quo viso deponant turribula quae gestaverunt in eodem sepulchro sumantque linteum et extendant contra clerum, ac veluti ostendentes quod surrexerit dominus, etiam non sit illo involutus, hanc canant antiphonam, *Surrexit dominus de sepulchro,* superponantque linteum altari. Finita antiphona Prior, congaudens pro triumpho regis nostri quod devicta morte surrexit, incipiat hymnum *Te deum laudamus*: quo incepto una pulsantur omnia signa.

THE DURHAM SEPULCHRUM

[From *A Description or Breife Declaration of all the Ancient Monuments, Rites and Customes belonginge or beinge within the Monastical Church of Durham before the Suppression* (ed. J. Raine, Surtees Soc. xv). This anonymous tract was written in 1593. A new edition is in course of preparation for the Surtees Society.]

p. 9. THE QUIRE—THE PASSION.

Within the Abbye Church of Durham, uppon Good Friday theire was marvelous solemne service, in the which service time, after the PASSION was sung, two of the eldest Monkes did take a goodly large CRUCIFIX, all of gold, of the picture of our Saviour Christ nailed uppon the crosse, lyinge uppon a velvett cushion, havinge St. Cuthbert's armes uppon it all imbroydered with gold, bringinge that betwixt them uppon the said cushion to the lowest greeces in the Quire; and there betwixt them did hold the said picture of our Saviour, sittinge of every side, on ther knees, of that, and then one of the said Monkes did rise and went a pretty way from it, sittinge downe uppon his knees, with his shooes put of, and verye reverently did creepe away uppon his knees unto the said Crosse, and most reverently did kisse it. And after him the other Monke did so likewise, and then they did sitt them downe on every side of the Crosse, and holdinge it betwixt them, and after that the Prior came forth of his stall, and did sitt him downe of his knees, with his shooes off, and in like sort did creepe also unto the said Crosse, and all the Monkes after him one after another, in the same order, and in the mean time all the whole quire singinge an himne. The seruice beinge ended, the two Monkes did carrye it to the SEPULCHRE with great reverence, which Sepulchre was sett upp in the morninge, on the north side of the Quire, nigh to the High Altar, before the service time; and there lay it within the said SEPULCHRE with great devotion, with another picture of our Saviour Christ, in whose breast they did enclose, with great reverence, the most holy and blessed Sacrament of the Altar, senceinge it and prayinge unto it upon theire knees, a great space, settinge two tapers lighted before it, which tapers did burne unto Easter day in the morninge, that it was taken forth.

THE QUIRE—THE RESURRECTION.

There was in the Abbye Church of Duresme verye solemne service uppon Easter Day, betweene three and four of the clocke in the morninge, in honour of the RESURRECTION, where two of the oldest

Monkes of the Quire came to the Sepulchre, being sett upp upon Good Friday, after the Passion, all covered with red velvett and embrodered with gold, and then did sence it, either Monke with a pair of silver sencers sittinge on theire knees before the Sepulchre. Then they both rising came to the Sepulchre, out of which, with great devotion and reverence, they tooke a marvelous beautifull IMAGE OF OUR SAVIOUR, representing the resurrection, with a crosse in his hand, in the breast wherof was enclosed in bright christall the holy Sacrament of the Altar, throughe the which christall the Blessed Host was conspicuous to the beholders. Then, after the elevation of the said picture, carryed by the said two Monkes uppon a faire velvett cushion, all embrodered, singinge the anthem of *Christus resurgens*, they brought it to the High Altar, settinge that on the midst therof, whereon it stood, the two Monkes kneelinge on theire knees before the Altar, and senceing it all the time that the rest of the whole quire was in singinge the foresaid anthem of *Christus resurgens*. The which anthem beinge ended, the two Monkes tooke up the cushions and the picture from the Altar, supportinge it betwixt them, proceeding, in procession, from the High Altar to the south Quire dore, where there was four antient Gentlemen, belonginge to the Prior, appointed to attend theire cominge, holdinge upp a most rich CANNOPYE of purple velvett, tached round about with redd silke and gold fringe; and at everye corner did stand one of theise ancient Gentlemen, to beare it over the said image, with the Holy Sacrament, carried by two Monkes round about the church, the whole quire waitinge uppon it with goodly torches and great store of other lights, all singinge, rejoyceinge, and praising God most devoutly, till they came to the High Altar againe, whereon they did place the said image there to remaine untill the Ascension day.

p. 26. THE SOUTH ALLEY OF THE LANTERN.

Over the [second of the iij Alters in that plage] was a merveylous lyvelye and bewtiful Immage of the picture of our Ladie, so called the LADY OF BOULTONE, which picture was maide to open with gymmers from her breaste downdward. And within the said immage was wrowghte and pictured the immage of our Saviour, merveylouse fynlie gilted, houldinge uppe his handes, and houlding betwixt his handes a fair large CRUCIFIX OF CHRIST, all of gold, the which crucifix was to be taiken fourthe every Good Fridaie, and every man did crepe unto it that was in that church at that daye. And ther after yt was houng upe againe within the said immage.

Q

THE SARUM SEPULCHRUM

[I give the various directions and rubrics referring to the sepulchre from the *Consuetudinary* (†1210), *Ordinal* (†1270), *Customary* (first half of fourteenth century), *Processional* (1508, &c.), *Missal* (1526, &c.), and *Breviary* (1531). The printed sixteenth-century rubrics practically reproduce the later *Ordinal* of the middle of the fourteenth century.]

The Depositio.

[From the *Processional*, with which the *Missal* practically agrees.]

Finitis vesperis, exuat sacerdos casulam, et sumens secum unum de praelatis in superpelliceis discalceati reponant crucem cum corpore dominico [scilicet in pixide, *Missal*] in sepulcrum incipiens ipse solus hoc responsorium *Aestimatus sum*, genuflectendo cum socio suo, quo incepto statim surgat. Similiter fiat in responsorio *Sepulto Domino*. Chorus totum responsorium prosequatur cum suo versu, genuflectendo per totum tempus usque ad finem servitii. Responsoria ut sic: *Aestimatus sum.* Chorus prosequatur *cum descendentibus in lacum* . . . Dum praedictum responsorium canitur cum suo versu, praedicti duo sacerdotes thurificent sepulcrum, quo facto et clauso ostio, incipiet idem sacerdos responsorium *Sepulto Domino.* . . . Item praedicti duo sacerdotes dicant istas tres antiphonas sequentes genuflectendo continue: *In pace . . . In pace factus est . . . Caro mea . . .* His finitis, et dictis prius orationibus ad placitum secrete ab omnibus cum genuflexione, omnibus aliis ad libitum recedentibus, ordine [non, *Missal*] servato, reinduat sacerdos casulam, et eodem modo quo accessit in principio servitii, cum diacono et subdiacono et ceteris ministris abscedat.

The Sepulchre Light.

[From the *Consuetudinary*.]

In die parasceues post repositum corpus domini in sepulcro, duo cerei dimidie libre ad minus in thesauraria tota die ante sepulcrum ardebunt. In nocte sequente et exinde usque ad processionem quae fit in die pasche ante matutinas, unus illorum tan-

[From the *Processional*, with which the *Missal* and *Customary* practically agree.]

Exinde [i. e. from the *Depositio*] continue ardebit unus cereus ad minus ante sepulcrum usque ad processionem quae fit in Resurrectione Dominica in die Paschae: ita tamen quod dum Psalmus *Benedictus* canitur et cetera quae sequuntur, in sequenti

tum, magnum eciam cereum pa-
schalem.

nocte extinguatur: similiter et
extinguatur in Vigilia Paschae,
dum benedicitur novus ignis,
usque accendatur cereus paschalis.

The Elevatio.

[From the *Consuetu-
dinary.*]

[From the *Ordinal.*]

[From the *Breviary*,
with which the *Pro-
cessional*, although less
full, practically agrees.]

In die pasche ante
matutinas conueniant
clerici ed ecclesiam
accensis cunctis cereis
per ecclesiam : duo
excellenciores presbi-
teri in superpelliceis
ad sepulchrum acce-
dant prius incensato
ostio sepulchri cum
magna ueneratione,
corpus dominicum
super altare deponant:
deinde crucem de se-
pulchro tollant, ex-
cellenciore presbitero
inchoante antiphonam
Christus resurgens et
sic eant, per ostium
australe presbiterii in-
cedentes, per medium
chori regredientes,
cum thuribulario et
ceroferariis precedent-
ibus, ad altare sancti
martini canentes prae-
dictam antiphonam
cum uersu suo. Deinde
dicto uersiculo *Surre-
xit dominus de sepul-
chro,* et dicta oracione

*In Die Pasche
Ad Processionem
ante Matutinas* con-
uchiant omnes clerici
ad ecclesiam ac accen-
dantur luminaria per
ecclesiam. Episcopus
uel decanus in super-
pelliceo cum cerofe-
rariis thuribulariis et
clero in sepulcrum
accedant, et incensato
prius sepulcro cum
magna ueneracione
corpus domini assu-
mant et super altare
ponant. Iterum ac-
cipientes crucem de
sepulcro inchoet epi-
scopus uel decanus
Ant. *Christus resur-
gens.* Tunc omnes cum
gaudio genua flectant
et ipsam crucem ado-
rent, idipsum canentes
cum ℣. *Dicant nunc.*
Tunc omnes cam-
pane in classicum
pulsentur, et cum
magna ueneracione
deportetur crux ad

In die sancto Paschae
ante Matutinas et ante
campanarum pulsati-
onem conveniant Cle-
rici ad ecclesiam, et
accendantur lumin-
aria per totam eccle-
siam. Tunc duo ex-
cellentiores Presbyteri
in superpelliceis cum
duobus Ceroferariis, et
duobus thuribulis, et
clero ad sepulchrum
accedant: et incensato
a praedictis duobus
Presbyteris prius se-
pulchro cum magna
veneratione, videlicet
genuflectendo, statim
post thurificationem
corpus Dominicum
super altare privatim
deponant: iterum ac-
cipientes crucem de
sepulchro, choro et
populo interim genu-
flectente incipiat ex-
cellentior persona
Ant. *Christus resur-
gens.* Et Chorus pro-
sequatur totam anti-

ab excellenciore sacerdote post debitam campanarum pulsacionem inchoentur matutine. locum ubi prouisum sit, clero canente predictam antiphonam. Quo facto dicat Sacerdos ℣. *Surrexit dominus de sepulcro.* Or. *Deus qui pro nobis.* Que terminetur sic, *Per eundem christum dominum nostrum.* phonam sic, *ex mortuis . . . Alleluya.*

Et tunc dum canitur Antiphona, eat processio per ostium australe presbyterii incedens et per medium chori regrediens [per ostium presbyterii australe incedendo per medium chori, et ingrediens, *Processional*] cum praedicta cruce de sepulchro inter praedictos duos Sacerdotes super eorum brachia venerabiliter portata, cum thuribulis et Ceroferariis praecedentibus, per ostium presbyterii boreale exeundo, ad unum altare ex parte boreali ecclesiae, Choro sequente, habitu non mutato, minoribus [excellentioribus, *Processional*] praecedentibus: ita tamen quod praedicti duo excellentiores in fine processionis subsequantur, corpore Dominico super altare in pixide dimisso et sub Thesaurarii custodia [in subthesaurarii custodia, *Processional*], qui illud statim in praedicta pixide in tabernaculo deponat [dependat ut potest in ista statione praecedente, *Processional*]: et tunc pulsentur omnes campanae in classicum.

Finito Antiphona praedicta, sequatur a toto Choro

V. *Dicant nunc Iudei . . . Alleluya.*

Finita autem Antiphona cum suo Versu a toto Choro, dicat excellentior persona in sua statione ad altare conversus hunc Versum.

V. *Surrexit Dominus de sepulchro.*

R. *Qui pro nobis pependit in ligno. Alleluya.*

Oremus.

Oratio. *Deus, qui pro nobis . . . Per Christum Dominum nostrum.*

Et terminetur sub Dominicali tono ad processionem: nec praecedat nec subsequatur *Dominus vobiscum.*

Finita Oratione omnes cum gaudio genuflectent ibidem et ipsam crucem adorent, in primis digniores, et tunc secrete sine processione in chorum redeant.

His itaque gestis discooperiantur ẏmagines et cruces per totam ecclesiam: et interim pulsentur campanae, sicut in Festis principalibus, ad Matutinas more solito.

The Censing in Easter Week.

[From the *Customary*.]

Ad primas uesperas . . . post inchoacionem antiphone super psal-

mum *Magnificat* procedat executor officii cum alio sacerdote . . . ad
thurificandum altare . . . In die tamen pasche et per ebdomadam
thurificetur sepulchrum domini post primam thurificacionem altaris,
scilicet antequam thurificator altaris circumeat.

The Removal of the Sepulchre.

[From the *Customary*.]

Die ueneris in ebdomada pasche ante missam amoueatur sepulchrum.

R

THE DUBLIN QUEM QUAERITIS

[From *Bodleian MS*. 15,846 (*Rawlinson Liturg*. D. 4), f. 130, a Sarum
processional written in the fourteenth century and belonging in the fifteenth
to the church of St. John the Evangelist, Dublin. A less good text from
Dublin, Abp. Marsh's Library, MS. V. 3, 2, 10, another fourteenth
century processional from the same church, is facsimiled by W. H. Frere,
Winchester Troper, pl. 26[b], and printed therefrom by Manly, i. xxii.
I give all the important variants of this version.]

[1]Finito iij R⁰ cum suo ℣ et G*lo*ria pa*t*ri uenient tres p*er*sone in
sup*er*pell*ic*eis et i*n* capis[1] *se*ricis capit*ibus* uclatis quasi tres M*a*rie
querentes Ih*es*um[2], si*n*gule portantes pixidem in man*ibus* q*ua*si aroma-
t*ibus*, qua*rum* prima ad ingressu*m* chori usque sepulcru*m* procedat
p*er* se[3] quasi lam*en*tando dic*n*t :

Heu! pius pastor occiditur,

Quem nulla culpa infecit:

O mors lugenda!

Factoq*ue* modico int*er*uallo, i*n*tret sec*un*da Maria co*n*simili[4] modo
et dicat :

Heu! nequam gens Iudaica,

Quam dira frendet uesania,

Plebs execranda!

Deinde iij Maria consimili m*od*o d*i*cat[5] :

Heu! uerus doctor obijt,

Qui uita*m* fu*n*ctis contulit:

O res plangenda!

[1–1] *Omitted by Frere, probably because
it was inconvenient to facsimile part
only of a page.*

[2] *Christu*m.
[3] *et.*
[5] *Omitted.*

[4] *Sim*i*li.*

Ad huc paululum procedendo prima Maria dicat [1]:

>Heu! misere cur contigit [2]
>Uidere mortem Saluatoris?

Deinde secunda Maria dicat [3]:

>Heu! Consolacio nostra,
>Ut quid mortem sustinuit!

Tunc [4] iij Maria:

>Heu! Redempcio nostra,
>Ut quid taliter ágere uoluit!

Tunc se coniungant et procedant ad gradum chori ante altare simul [5] dicentes:

>Iam, iam, ecce, iam properemus ad tumulum
>Unguentes [6] Delecti [7] corpus sanctissimum

[8] Deinde procedant similiter prope sepulchrum et prima Maria dicat per se

>Condumentis aromatum
>Ungamus corpus sanctissimum
>Quo preciosa [8].

Tunc secunda Maria dicat per se:

>Nardi uetet commixtio,
>Ne putrescat in tumulo
>Caro beata!

Deinde iij Maria [9] dicat per se [9]:

>Sed nequimus hoc patrare sine adiutorio.
>Quis nam saxum reuoluet [10] a monumenti ostio?

Facto interuallo, angelus nixus sepulcrum apparuit [11] eis et dicat hoc modo:

>Quem queritis ad sepulcrum, o Cristicole?

Deinde respondeant tres Marie simul dicentes [12]:

>Ihesum Nazarenum crucifixum, o celicola!

Tunc angelus dicet [13]:

>Surrexit, non est hic, sicut dixit;
>Uenite et uidete locum ubi positus fuerat.

Deinde predicte Marie sepulcrum intrent et [14] inclinantes se et prospicientes undique intra sepulcrum, alta uoce quasi gaudentes [15] et admirantes et parum a sepulcro recedentes simul dicant [16]:

---

[1] dicat hoc modo.
[2] contingit.
[3] Omitted.
[4] Deinde.
[5] Omitted.
[6] Ungentes.
[7] Dilecti.
[8—8]. Omitted: but a later hand has written on a margin of the manuscript, Condimentis aromatum vnguentes corpus sanctissimum quo preciosa.
[9—9] Omitted.
[10] reuoluit.
[11] appariat.
[12] Omitted.
[13] dicat sic.
[14] Omitted.
[15] gaudendo.
[16] dicant simul.

Alleluya! resurrexit Dominus!

Alleluya! resurrexit Dominus hodie!

Resurrexit potens, fortis, *Christus*, Filius Dei!

Deinde angelus ad eas[1]:

Et euntes dicite discipulis eius et Petro quia surrexit.

In quo reuertant ad angelum quasi mandatum suum ad implendum parate simul dicentes[2]:

Eya! pergamus propere

Mandatum hoc perficere!

Interim ueniant ad ingressum chori due persone nude pedes sub personis apostolorum Iohannis *et* Petri indute albis sine paruris cum tunicis, quorum Iohannes amictus tunica alba palmam in manu gestans, Petrus uero rubea tunica indutus claues in manu ferens[3]; *et* predicte mulieres de sepulcro reuertentes *et* quasi de choro simul exeuntes, dicat prima Maria [4] *per* se [4] sequentiam:

Victime paschali laudes

Immolant *Christ*iani.

Agnus redemit oues:

Christus innocens Patri

Reconsiliauit peccatores.

Mors et uita duello

Conflixere mirando:

Dux uite mortuis [5]

Regnat uiuus.

Tunc obuiantes eis in medio chori predicti discipuli, interrogantes simul dicant:

Dic nobis, Maria,

Quid uidisti in uia?

Tunc *pri*ma Maria respondeat quasi monstrando:

Sepulcrum *Christi* uiuentis

Et gloriam uidi resurgentis.

Tunc ij Maria respondet similiter [6] monstrando:

Angelicos testes,

Sudarium et uestes.

Tunc iij [7] Maria respondeat:

Surrexit *Christus*, spes nostra,

Precedet uos in Galileam.

Et sic procedant simul ad ostium chori; interim [8] currant duo ad

---

[1] eas dicens.
[2] dicentes simul.   [3] deferens.
[4]—[4] *Omitted. Lines 3–5 of the sequence are preceded by* Secunda Maria, *and*

lines 6–9 by Tercia Maria *dicat.*
[5] *Manly suggests* mortuus.
[6] respondeat quasi.
[7] Tercia.   [8] et interim.

monumentu*m*; ueru*m*ptamen ille discip*ulus* que*m* diligebat Ih*esus*
uenit pr*i*or ad monume*n*tum, iuxta eu*a*ngelium : ' Currebant au*tem* duo
sim*ul et* ille alius discipulus p*re*cucurrit cicius Petro *et* uenit pr*i*or ad
monume*n*tum, non *tam*en introiuit.' Uidentes discipuli p*redi*cti [1]
sepulcru*m* uacuu*m et* uerbis Marie credentes reu*ert*a*n*t se ad chorum
dicentes [2] :

> Credendum est magis soli Marie ueraci
>
> Q*uam* Iudeo*rum* turbe fallaci!

Tunc audita [3] *Christ*i resurreccione, chorus p*ro*seq*uatur* alta uoce
quasi gaude*n*tes *et* exultantes si*c* dicentes [4] :

> Scimus *Christu*m surrexisse,
>
> A mortuis uere.
>
> Tu nobis, uictor Rex, miserere!

Qua fi*ni*ta, executor officii incipiat :

> Te Deum laudamus.

[5] Tu*n*c receda*n*t sa*n*c*tae* Mar*i*e ap*ostol*i *et* angelus [5].

S

THE AUREA MISSA OF TOURNAI

[Communicated from *Lille Bibl. Munic. MS.* 62 (sixteenth century) by
L. Deschamps de Pas to the *Annales archéologiques*, xvii (1857), 167.]

Sequuntur ceremonie et modus observandus pro celebratione misse
Missus est Gabriel Angelus, &c., vulgariter dicte Auree Misse
quolibet anno in choro ecclesie Tornacensis decantande feria x[a] ante
festum nativitatis Domini nostri Iesu-Christi, ex fundatione venerabilis
viri magistri Petri Cotrel, canonici dicti ecclesie Tornacensis et in
eadem archidiaconi Brugensis, de licentia et permissione dominorum
suorum decani et capituli predicte ecclesie Tornacensis.—Primo, feria
tercia, post decantationem vesperum, disponentur per carpentatorem
ecclesie in sacrario chori dicte ecclesie Tornacensis, in locis iam ad
hoc ordinatis et sibi oppositis, duo stallagia, propter hoc appropriata,
que etiam ornabuntur cortinis et pannis cericeis ad hoc ordinatis per
casularium iam dicte ecclesie, quorum alterum, videlicet quod erit de
latere episcopi, serviet ad recipiendam beatam virginem Mariam, et
alterum stallagium ab illo oratorio oppositum, quod erit de latere
decani, serviat ad recipiendum et recludendum Angelum.— Item

---

[1] *Omitted.* [2] dicentes hoc modo. [3] audito. [4] dicant.
[5]—[5] *Omitted.*

similiter eodem die deputatus ad descendendum die sequenti columbam, visitabit tabernaculum in altis carolis dispositum, disponet cordas, et parabit instrumentum candelis suis munitum, per quod descendet Spiritus Sanctus in specie columbe, tempore decantationis ewangelii, prout postea dicetur, et erit sollicitus descendere cordulam campanule, et illam disponere ad stallagium Angeli, ad illam campanulam pulsandam suo tempore, die sequenti, prout post dicetur.—Item in crastinum durantibus matutinis, magistri cantus erunt solliciti quod duo iuvenes, habentes voces dulces et altas, preparentur in thesauraria, hostio clauso, unus ad modum virginis seu regine, et alter ad modum angeli, quibus providebitur de ornamentis et aliis necessariis propter hoc per fundatorem datis et ordinatis.—Item post decantationem septime lectionis matutinarum, accedent duo iuvenes, Mariam videlicet et Angelum representantes, sic parati de predicta thesauraria, ad chorum intrando per maius hostium dicti chori, duabus thedis ardentibus precedentibus: Maria videlicet per latus domini episcopi, in manibus portans horas pulchras, et Angelus per latus domini decani, portans in manu dextra sceptrum argenteum deauratum, et sic morose progredientur, cum suis magistris directoribus, usque ad summum altare, ubi, genibus flexis, fundent ad Dominum orationem. Qua facta, progredientur dicti iuvenes quilibet ad locum suum, Maria videlicet ad stallagium, de parte episcopi preparatum, cum suo magistro directore, et Angelus ad aliud stallagium de parte decani similiter preparatum, etiam cum suo alio magistro directore, et ubique cortinis clausis. Coram quibus stallagiis remanebunt predicte thede, ardentes usque ad finem misse.—Item clerici thesaurarie, durantibus octava et nona lectionibus matutinarum, preparabunt maius altare solemniter, ut in triplicibus festis, et omnes candele circumquaque chorum sacrarum de rokemes, et in corona nova existentes accendentur. Et clerici revestiarii providebunt quod presbyter, dyaconus, subdiaconus, choriste, cum pueris revestitis, sint parati, in fine hymni TE DEUM, pro missa decantanda, ita quod nulla sit pausa inter finem dicti himpni TE DEUM et missam. Et in fine praedicte misse sit paratus presbiter ebdomarius cantandi versum *Ora pro nobis*, et deinde, *Deus in adiutorium*, de laudibus illas perficiendo per chorum, et in fine psalmi *De profundis* dicendi, in fine matutinarum, more consueto, adiungetur collecta *Adiuva nos* pro fundatore ultra collectam ordinariam.—Item, cum celebrans accesserit ad maius altare, pro incipienda missa, et ante *Confiteor* immediate cortine circumquaque oratorium Virginis solum aperientur, ipsa Virgine attente orante et ad genua existente suo libro aperto, super pulvinari ad hoc ordinato, Angelo adhuc semper clauso in suo stallagio remanente.—Item cum cantabitur *Gloria in Excelsis Deo* tunc cortine stallagii, in quo erit Angelus, aperientur. In quo stallagio stabit dictus Angelus erectus, tenens in manibus suis suum sceptrum argenteum, et nichil aliud faciens, quousque fuerit tempus cantandi ewangelium, nec interim faciet Virgo aliquod signum videndi dictum angelum, sed, submissis oculis, erit semper intenta ad orationem.—Item cum appropinquarit tempus cantandi dictum ewangelium, diaconus cum subdiacono, pueris cum candelis et cruce precedentibus, progredientur ad locum in sacrario sibi preparatum, et cantabit ewangelium *Missus est Gabriel,* et etiam cantabunt partes suas Maria et Angelus, prout ordinatum et notatum est in libro ad hoc ordinato. —Item cum Angelus cantabit hec verba ewangelii, *Ave, gratia plena, Dominus tecum,* faciet tres ad Virginem salutationes ; primo ad illud verbum *Ave,* humiliabit se tam capite quam corpore, post morose se elevando ; et ad illa verba, *gratia plena,* faciet secundam humiliationem, flectendo mediocriter genua sua, se postea relevando ; et ad illa verba, *Dominus tecum,* quae cantabit cum gravitate et morose, tunc faciet terciam humiliationem ponendo genua usque ad terram et finita clausula assurget, Virgine interim se non movente. Sed dum Maria virgo cantabit *Quomodo fiet istud,* assurget et vertet modicum faciem suam ad Angelum cum gravitate et modestia, non aliter se movendo. Et dum cantabit Angelus *Spiritus Sanctus superveniet in te,* etc., tunc Angelus vertet faciem suam versus columbam illam ostendendo, et subito descendet ex loco in altis carolis ordinato, cum candelis in circuitu ipsius ardentibus, ante stallagium sive oratorium Virginis, ubi remanebit, usque post ultimum *Agnus Dei,* quo decantato, revertetur ad locum unde descenderat.—Item magister cantus, qui erit in stallagio Angeli, sit valde sollicitus pro propria vice pulsare campanam in altis carolis, respondente in initio ewangelii, ut tunc ille qui illic erit ordinatus ad descendendum columbam sit preadvisatus et preparet omnia necessaria et candelas accendat. Et secunda vice sit valde sollicitus pulsare dictam campanulam, ita quod precise ad illud verbum *Spiritus Sanctus* descendat ad Virginem columbam ornatam candelis accensis, et remaneat ubi descenderit, usque ad ultimum *Agnus Dei* decantatum, prout dictum est. Et tunc idem magister cantus iterum pulsabit pro tercia vice eamdem campanulam, ut revertatur columba unde descenderit. Et sit ille disponendus vel deputandus ad descendendum dictam columbam bene preadvisatus de supra dicta triplici pulsatione et quid quilibet significabit ne sit in aliquo defectus.—Item predicti, diaconus, Maria, et Angelus complebunt totum ewangelium in eodem tono prout cuilibet sibi competit, et ewangelio finito reponet se Maria ad genua et orationem, et Angelus remanebit rectus, usque in finem misse, hoc excepto, quod in elevatione corporis Christi ponet se ad genua.—Item postea proficietur missa, Maria et Angelo in suis stallagiis usque in fine permanentibus.—Item missa finita, post *Ite, missa est*, Maria et Angelus descendent de suis stallagiis et revertentur cum reliquiis et revestitis usque ad revestiarium predictum eorum, flambellis precedentibus. In quo revestiario presbiter celebrans cum predictis revestitis Maria et Angelo dicet psalmum *De profundis*, prout in choro cum adiectione collecte *Adiuva* pro fundatore.—Item fiet missa per omnia, ut in die Annunciationis dominice cum sequentia sive prosa *Mittit ad virginem*, cum organis et discantu prout in triplicibus.

T

SUBJECTS OF THE CYCLICAL MIRACLES

[This comparative table is based on that drawn up by Prof. Hohlfeld in *Anglia*, xi. 241. The episodes are taken in their scriptural order, which is not always that of the plays. I have added the Cornish data, using O. P. R. to indicate the *Origo Mundi, Passio Domini*, and *Resurrectio Domini* of the older text, and J. for William Jordan's *Creation of the World*. I have quoted Halliwell's divisions of the *Ludus Coventriae*, really a continuous text, for convenience sake.]

Episodes.	*York.*	*Town-ley.*	*Ches-ter.*	*Ludus Cov.*	*Cornwall.*
1. Fall of Lucifer . .	i	i	i	i	O. 48[1]: J. 114–334.
2. Creation and Fall of Man	ii–vi	i [2]	ii	i, ii	O. 1–437: J. 1–113, 335–1055.
3. Cain and Abel . .	vii	ii	ii	iii	O. 438–633: J. 1056–1317.
4. Wanderings of Cain	—	—	—	—	J. 1332–1393.
5. Death of Cain . .	—	—	—	iv	J. 1431–1726.
6. Seth in Paradise and Death of Adam	—	—	—	—	O. 634–916: J. 1318–1331,1394–1430, 1727–2093, 2146–2210.
7. Enoch . . .	—	—	—	—	J. 2094–2145.
8. Noah and the Flood	viii, ix	iii	iii	iv	O. 917–1258: J. 2211–2530[3].
9. Abraham and Melchisedec . .	—	—	iv	—	
10. Abraham and Isaac.	x	iv	iv	v	O. 1259–1394.
11. Jacob's Blessing .	—	v [2]	—	—	
12. Jacob's Wanderings .	—	vi	—	—	

[1] Only a stage-direction, *Hic ludit* [? *cadit*] *Lucifer de celo.*
[2] Imperfect.

[3] Jordan closes with an invitation to a *Redemptio* on the morrow.

Episodes.	York.	Town-ley.	Ches-ter.	Ludus Cov.	Cornwall.
13. Moses and the Exodus	xi	viii	—	vi	O. 1395–1714.
14. Moses in the Wilderness	—	vii	v	vi	O. 1715–1898.
15. Balaam	—	—	v	—	
16. David and the Rods	—	—	—	—	O. 1899–2104.
17. David and Bathsheba	—	—	—	—	O. 2105–2376.
18. Building of the Temple	—	—	—	—	O. 2377–2628.
19. Prophecy of Maximilla	—	—	—	—	O. 2629–2778.
20. Bridge over Cedron	—	—	—	—	O. 2779–2824.
21. *Prophetae*	xii[1]	vii	—	vii	
22. Joachim and Anna	—	—	—	viii	
23. Mary in the Temple	—	—	—	ix	
24. Betrothal of Mary	—	x[1]	—	x	
25. Annunciation	xii	x	vi	xi	
26. Salutation of Elizabeth	xii	xi	vi	xiii	
27. Suspicion of Joseph	xiii	x	vi	xii	
28. Purgation of Mary	—	—	—	xiv	
29. Augustus and Cyrenius	—	ix	—	—	
30. Nativity	xiv	—	vi	xv	
31. Conversion of Octavian	—	—	vi	—	
32. *Pastores*	xv	xii,xiii[2]	vii	xvi	
33. Purification	xli[3]	xvii[4]	xi	xviii	
34. *Magi* before Herod	xvi, xvii[2]	xiv	viii	xvii	
35. Offering of *Magi*	xvii	xiv	ix	xvii	
36. Flight into Egypt	xviii	xv	x	xix	
37. Massacre of Innocents	xix	xvi	x	xix	
38. Death of Herod	—	—	—	xix	
39. Presentation in Temple	xx	xviii[4]	—	xx	
40. Baptism	xxi	xix	—	xxi	
41. Temptation	xxii	—	xii	xxii	P. 1–172.
42. Marriage in Cana	[lost]	—	—	—	
43. Transfiguration	xxiii				
44. Woman in Adultery	xxiv	—	xii	xxiii	
45. Healing of Blind in Siloam	—	—	xiii	—	
46. Raising of Lazarus	xxiv	xxxi[3]	xiii	xxiv	
47. Healing of Bartimaeus	—	—	—	—	P. 393–454.
48. Entry into Jerusalem	xxv	—	xiv	xxvi	P. 173–330.
49. Cleansing of Temple	—	—	xiv	—	P. 331–392.
50. Jesus in House of Simon the Leper	[lost]	xx[1]	xiv	xxvii	P. 455–552.
51. Conspiracy of Jews	xxvi	xx	xiv	xxv	P. 553–584.

[1] Narrated.   [2] Duplicates.   [3] Misplaced.   [4] Imperfect.

Episodes.	York.	Town-ley.	Ches-ter.	Ludus Cov.	Cornwall.
52. Treachery of Judas .	xxvi	xx	xiv	xxvii	P. 585–616.
53. Last Supper . .	xxvii	xx	xv	xxvii	P. 617–930.
54. Gethsemane . .	xxviii	xx	xv	xxviii	P. 931–1200.
55. Jesus beforeCaiaphas	xxix	xxi	xvi	xxx	P. 1200–1504.
56. Jesus before Pilate .	xxx	—	xvi	xxx	P. 1567–1616.
57. Jesus before Herod .	xxxi	—	xvi	xxix, xxx	P. 1617–1816.
58. Dream ofPilate'sWife	xxx	—	—	xxxi	P. 1907–1968, 2193–2212.
59. Remorse and Death of Judas . .	xxxii	xxxii [1]	—	xxxii	P. 1505–1566.
60. Condemnation .	xxxiii	xxii	xvi	xxxii	P. 1817–2533.
61. Cross Brought from Cedron . .	—	—	—	—	P. 2534–2584.
62. Bearing of the Cross	xxxiv	xxii	xvii	xxxii	P. 2585–2662.
63. Veronica . . .	xxxiv	—	—	xxxii	—
64. Crucifixion .	xxxv	xxiii	xvii	xxxii	P. 2663–2840.
65. Casting of Lots .	xxxv	xxiii, xxiv	xvii	—	P. 2841–2860.
66. *Planctus Mariae* [cf. p. 39] . .	xxxvi	xxiii	xvii	xxxii	P. 2925–2954.
67. Death of Jesus. .	xxxvi	xxiii	xvii	xxxii	P. 2861–3098.
68. Longinus . .	xxxvi	xxiii	xvii	xxxiv	P. 3003–3030.
69. Descent from Cross.	xxxvi	xxiii	xvii	xxxiv	P. 3099–3201.
70. Burial . . .	xxxvi	—	—	xxxiv	P. 3202–3216.
71. Harrowing of Hell .	xxxvii	xxv	xviii	xxxiii, xxxv	P. 3031–3078 : R. 97–306.
72. Release ofJoseph and Nicodemus	—	—	—	—	R. 1–96, 307–334, 625–662.
73. Setting of Watch .	xxxviii	xxvi	xix	xxxv	R. 335–422.
74. Resurrection .	xxxviii	xxvi	xix	xxxv	R. 423–678.
75. *Quem Quaeritis* .	xxxviii	xxvi	xix	xxxvi	R. 679–834.
76. *Hortulanus* . .	xxxix	xxvi	xix [2]	xxxvii	R. 835–892.
77. *Peregrini* . .	xl	xxvii	xx	xxxviii	R. 1231–1344.
78. Incredulity ofThomas	xlii	xxviii	xx	xxxviii	R. 893–1230, 1345–1586.
79. Death of Pilate .	—	—	—	—	R. 1587–2360.
80. Veronica and Tiberius . . .	—	—	—	—	R. 1587–2360.
81. Ascension . .	xliii	xxix	xxi	xxxix	R. 2361–2630.
82. Pentecost . .	xliv	[? lost]	xxii	xl	
83. Death of Mary. .	xlv	—	—	xli	
84. Burial of Mary .	[lost]	—	—	xli	
85. Apparition of Mary to Thomas . .	xlvi	—	—	—	
86. Assumption andCoronation . . .	xlvii [3]	—	[lost]	xli	
87. Signs of Judgement [cf. p. 53] . .	—	—	xxiii	—	
88. Antichrist [cf. p. 62].	—	—	xxiv	—	
89. Doomsday . .	xlviii	xxx	xxv	xlii [4]	

[1] Late addition.   [2] Imperfect?   [3] And later fragment.   [4] Imperfect.

U

INTERLUDIUM DE CLERICO ET PUELLA

[Printed by Wright and Halliwell, *Reliquiae Antiquae* (1841), i. 145, from an early fourteenth-century MS., then belonging to the Rev. R. Yerburgh, of Sleaford. On the piece and its sources in the Latin, French, and English *fabliaux* of *Dame Siriz*, cf. Ten Brink, i. 255; ii. 295; Jusserand, *Lit. Hist.* i. 446. Ten Brink assigns the dramatic text, which is in the South Northumbrian dialect, to the reign of Edward I (1272–1307).]

Hic incipit Interludium de Clerico et Puella.

[Scene 1.]

Clericus. Damishel, reste wel.

Puella. Sir, welcum, by Saynt Michel!

Clericus. Wer esty sire, wer esty dame?

Puella. By Gode, es noner her at hame.

Clericus. Wel wor suilc a man to life,
That suilc a may mithe have to wyfe!

Puella. Do way, by Crist and Leonard,
No wily lufe, na clerc fayllard,
Na kepi herbherg, clerc, in huse no y flore
Bot his hers ly wit-uten dore.
Go forth thi way, god sire,
For her hastu losye al thi wile.

Clericus. Nu, nu, by Crist and by sant Jhon,
In al this land ne wis hi none,
Mayden, that hi luf mor than the,
Hif me mithe ever the bether be.
For the hy sory nicht and day,
Y may say, hay wayleuay!
Y luf the mar than mi lif,
Thu hates me mar than gayt dos chuief.
That es noute for mys-gilt,
Certhes, for thi luf ham hi spilt.
A, suythe mayden, reu ef me
That es ty luf, hand ay salbe.
For the luf of [the] y mod of efne;
Thu mend thi mode, and her my stevene.

Puella. By Crist of heven and sant Jone!
Clerc of scole ne kepi non;

For many god wymman haf thai don scam.
By Crist, thu michtis haf be at hame.
    Clericus. Synt it nothir gat may be,
Jhesu Crist, by-tethy the,
And send neulit bot thar inne,
That thi be lesit of al my pyne.
    Puella. Go nu, truan, go nu, go,
For mikel thu canstu of sory and wo.

[Scene 2.]

    Clericus. God te blis, Mome Helwis.
    Mome Helwis. Son, welcum, by san Dinis!
    Clericus. Hic am comin to the, Mome,
Thu hel me noth, thu say me sone.
Hic am a clerc that hauntes scole,
Y hidy my lif wyt mikel dole;
Me wor lever to be dedh,
Than led the lif that hyc ledh,
For ay mayden with and schen,
Fayrer ho lond hawy non syen.
Tho hat mayden Malkyn, y wene;
Nu thu wost quam y mene,
Tho wonys at the tounes ende,
That suyt lif, so fayr and hende.
Bot if tho wil hir mod amende,
Neuly Crist my ded me send.
Men send me hyder, vyt uten fayle,
To haf thi help anty cunsayle.
Thar for amy cummen here,
That thu salt be my herand-bere,
To mac me and that mayden sayct,
And hi sal gef the of my nayct,
So that hever al thi lyf
Saltu be the better wyf.
So help me Crist! and hy may spede,
Rithe saltu haf thi mede.
    Mome Ellwis. A, son, wat saystu? benedicite,
Lift hup thi hand, and blis the.
For it es boyt syn and scam,
That thu on me hafs layt thys blam.
For hic am an ald quyne and a lam.

Y led my lyf wit Godis love.
Wit my roc y me fede,
Cani do non othir dede,'
Bot my pater noster and my crede,
Tho say Crist for missedede,
And my navy Mary,
For my scynne hic am sory,
And my de profundis,
For al that yn sin lys.
For cani me non othir think,
That wot Crist, of heven kync.
Ihesu Crist, of heven hey,
Gef that hay may heng hey,
And gef that hy may se,
That thay be henge on a tre,
That this ley as leyit onne me.
For aly wymam (*sic*) ami on.

V

TERENTIUS ET DELUSOR

[I follow the text of P. de Winterfeld, *Hrotsvithae Opera* (1902), xx ; the piece was previously edited by C. Magnin in *Bibliothèque de l'École des Chartes*, i (1840), 517 ; A. de Montaiglon in *L'Amateur des Livres* (1849) ; A. Riese, in *Zeits. f. d. österreich. Gymn.* xviii. 442 ; R. Sabbadini (1894). The only manuscript is *B. N. Lat. MS.* 8069 of the late tenth or early eleventh century. Various scholars have dated the poem from the seventh to the tenth century; Winterfeld declares for the ninth. It might have been intended as a prologue to a Terentian revival or to a mime. The homage paid to the *vetus poeta* by the *delusor* in his asides rather suggests the former ; cf. Cloetta, i. 2 ; Creizenach, i. 8.]

[DELUSOR.]

Mitte recordari monimenta vetusta, Terenti ;
    cesses ulterius : vade, poeta vetus.
vade, poeta vetus, quia non tua carmina curo ;
    iam retice fabulas, dico, vetus veteres.
dico, vetus veteres iamiam depone camenas,
    quae nil, credo, iuvant, pedere ni doceant.
tale decens carmen, quod sic volet ut valet istud ;
    qui cupit exemplum, captet hic egregium.
huc ego cum recubo, me taedia multa capescunt :
    an sit prosaicum, nescio, an metricum.

dic mihi, dic, quid hoc est? an latras corde sinistro?
dic, vetus auctor, in hoc quae iacet utilitas?

Nunc TERENTIUS *exit foras audiens haec et ait*:

quis fuit, hercle, pudens, rogo, qui mihi tela lacessens
turbida contorsit? quis talia verba sonavit?
hic quibus externis scelerosus venit ab oris,
qui mihi tam durum iecit ridendo cachinnum?
quam graviter iaculo mea viscera laesit acuto!
hunc ubi repperiam, contemplor, et hunc ubi quaeram?
si mihi cum tantis nunc se offerat obvius iris,
debita iudicio persolvam dona librato.

Ecce persona DELUSORIS *praesentatur et hoc audiens inquit*:

quem rogitas ego sum: quid vis persolvere? cedo;
huc praesens adero, non dona probare recuso.

TERENTIUS.

tune, sceleste, meas conrodis dente Camenas?
tu quis es? unde venis, temerarie latro? quid istis
vocibus et dictis procerum me, a! perdite, caedis?
tene, superbe, meas decuit corrumpere Musas?

PERSONA DELUSORIS.

si rogitas, quis sum, respondeo: te melior sum:
tu vetus atque senex, ego tyro valens adulescens;
tu sterilis truncus, ego fertilis arbor, opimus.
si taceas, vetule, lucrum tibi quaeris enorme.

TERENTIUS.

quis tibi sensus inest? numquid melior me es?...
nunc, vetus atque senex quae fecero, fac adolescens.
si bonus arbor ades, qua fertilitate redundas?
cum sim truncus iners, fructu meliore redundo.

PERSONA *secum*.

nunc mihi vera sonat; set huic contraria dicam—
quid magis instigas? quid talia dicere certas?
haec sunt verba senum, qui cum post multa senescunt
tempora, tunc mentes in se capiunt pueriles.

TERENTIUS.

hactenus antiquis sapiens venerandus ab annis
inter et egregios ostentor et inter honestos.

sed mihi felicem sapientis tollis honorem,
qui mihi verba iacis et vis contendere verbis.

PERSONA.

si sapiens esses, non te mea verba cierent.
o bone vir, sapiens ut stultum ferre libenter,
obsecro, me sapias; tua me sapientia firmet.

TERENTIUS.

cur, furiose, tuis lacerasti carmina verbis?
me retinet pietas, quin haec manus arma cerebro
implicet ista tuo: pessumdare te miseresco.

PERSONA *secum.*

quam bene ridiculum mihi personat iste veternus.—
te retinet pietas? nam fas est credere, credo.
me, peto, ne tangas, ne sanguine tela putrescant.

TERENTIUS.

cur, rogo, me sequeris? cur me ludendo lacessis?

[PERSONA.]

sic fugit horrendum praecurrens damna leonem.

[TERENTIUS.]

vix ego pro superum teneor pietate deorum,
ad tua colla meam graviter lentescere palmam.

PERSONA.

vae tibi, pone minas: nescis quem certe minaris.
verba latrando, senex cum sis vetus, irrita profers.
i, rogo, ne vapules et, quod minitare, reportes;
nunc ego sum iuvenis: patiarne ego verba vetusti?

TERENTIUS.

o iuvenis, tumidae nimium ne crede iuventae:
saepe superba cadunt, et humillima saepe resurgunt.
o mihi si veteres essent in pectore vires,
de te supplicium caperem quam grande nefandum.
si mihi plura iacis et tali voce lacessis,
p. . . . .

W

REPRESENTATIONS OF MEDIAEVAL PLAYS

[I have attempted to bring together, under a topographical arrangement, the records of such local plays of the mediaeval type as I am acquainted with. Probably the number could be increased by systematic search in local histories and transactions of learned societies. But my list is a good deal longer than those of L. T. Smith, *York Plays*, lxiv; Stoddard, 53; or Davidson, 219. For convenience I have also noted here a few records of Corpus Christi processions, and of folk 'ridings' and other institutions. The following index-table shows the geographical distribution of the plays. The names italicized are those of places where plays have been reported in error or are merely conjectural.]

INDEX.

NORFOLK.

Croxton, 363.
Garboldisham, 367.
Harling, 368.
Kenninghall, 374.
King's Lynn, 374.
Lopham, 383.
Middleton, 384.
Norwich, 386.
Shelfhanger, 393.
Wymondham, 398.
Yarmouth, 399.

NORTHAMPTONSHIRE.

Daventry, 363.
Northampton, 386.

NORTHUMBERLAND.

Newcastle, 385.

OXFORDSHIRE.

Fyfield, 367.
Idbury, 371.
Langley, 375.
Lyneham, 383.
Milton, 384.
Oxford, 389.
Shipton, 394.

SHROPSHIRE.

Shrewsbury, 394.

SOMERSETSHIRE.

Bath, 338.
Tintinhull, 396.

STAFFORDSHIRE.

Lichfield, 377.

SUFFOLK.

Boxford, 342.
Bury St. Edmunds,
   343.
Bungay, 343.
Ipswich, 371.
Ixworth, 373.
Lavenham, 375.
Mildenhall, 384.

SURREY.

Hascombe, 368.
Kingston, 374.

SUSSEX.

Rye, 393.

WARWICKSHIRE.

Coleshill, 357.
Coventry, 357.
Maxstoke, 384.
Nuneaton, 389.

WESTMORELAND.

Kendal, 373.

WILTSHIRE.

Salisbury, 393.

WORCESTERSHIRE.

Worcester, 398.

YORKSHIRE.

Beverley, 338.
Hull, 370.
Leconfield, 375.
Leeds, 375.
Wakefield, 396.
Woodkirk, 398.
York, 399.

SCOTLAND.

Aberdeen, 330.
Edinburgh, 366.

IRELAND.

Dublin, 363.
Kilkenny, 374.

ABERDEEN, SCOTLAND.

I summarize the references to plays and pageants in the Burgh Records [1].

May 13, 1440. Richard Kintor, abbot of Boneacord, was granted ' unus burgensis futurus faciendus' (i.e. the fees on taking up the freedom), 'pro expensis suis factis et faciendis in quodam ludo de ly Haliblude ludendo apud ly Wyndmylhill.'

Sept. 5, 1442. 'Thir craftes vndirwritten sal fynd yerly in the offerand of our Lady at Candilmes thir personnes vnderwrittin ; that is to say,

           The littistares sal fynd,

The empriour and twa doctoures, and alsmony honeste squiares as thai may.

           The smythes and hammermen sal fynd,

The three kingis of Culane, and alsmony honeste squiares as thai may.

---

[1] J. Stuart, *Extracts from the Council Register of the Burgh of Aberdeen,*   vol. i. 1398–1570 (Spalding Club, 1844).

The talzoures sal fynd,
Our lady Sancte Bride, Sancte Helone, Joseph, and alsmony
squiares as thai may.
The skynnares sal fynd,
Two bischopes, four angeles, and alsmony honeste squiares as
thai may.
The webstares and walkares sal fynd,
Symon and his disciples, and alsmony honeste squiares, etc.
The cordinares sal fynd,
The messyngear and Moyses, and alsmony honeste squiares, etc.
The fleschowares sal fynd,
Twa or four wodmen, and alsmony honest squiares, etc.
The brethir of the gilde sall fynd,
The knyghtes in harnace, and squiares honestely araiit, etc.
The baxsteiris sal fynd,
'The menstralis, and alsmony honest squyares as thai may.'

May 21, 1479. Order for the alderman 'to mak the expensis and
costis of the comon gude apon the arayment, and uthris necessaris, of
the play to be plait in the fest of Corpos Xristi nixttocum.'

Feb. 1, 148⅘. Order for all craftsmen to 'beyr thare takyinis of
thare craft apon thare beristis, and thare best aray on Canddilmes
day at the Offerand.'

Feb. 3, 150⅔. Fine imposed upon certain websters, because 'thai
did nocht it that accordit thame to do one Candilmese day, in the
Passioun [? Pr'ssioun, "Procession"],' owing to a dispute as to
precedence with the tailors.

Jan. 30, 150⅝. Order for continuance of 'the ald lovabile consuetud and ryt of the burgh' that the craftsmen 'kepit and decorit
the procession one Candilmes day yerlie; . . . and thai sale, in order
to the Offering in the Play, pass tua and ij togidr socialie; in the
first the flesshoris, barbouris, baxturis, cordinaris, skineris, couparis,
wrichtis, hat makars [and] bonat makars togidr, walcaris, litstaris,
wobstaris, tailyeouris, goldsmiths, blaksmithis and hammermen; and
the craftsmen sal furnyss the Pageants; the cordinaris, the Messing[er];
wobstaris and walcaris, Symeon; the smyths [and] goldsmiths, iij Kingis
of Cullane; the litstaris, the Emperour; the masons, the Thrie
Knichtis; the talyors, our Lady, Sanct Brid, and Sanct Elene; and
the skynners, the Tua Bischopis; and tua of ilke craft to pass with
the pageant that thai furnyss to keip thair geir.'

May 28, 1507. Order for precedence 'in ale processiounis, baitht
in Candilmes play and utheris processionis.'

Jan. 30, 151$\frac{0}{1}$. The order of Jan. 30, 150$\frac{5}{6}$ repeated *verbatim*.

Feb. 3, 151$\frac{0}{1}$. Citizens fined 'becauss thai passt not in the procession of Candilmes day to decoir the samyn.'

Feb. 5, 152$\frac{3}{4}$. Johne Pill, tailor, to do penance, 'for the disobeing of David Anderson, bailze, becaus he refusit to pas in the Candilmess processioun with his taikin and sing of his craft in the place lemit to his craft, and in likewise for the mispersoning of the said Dauid Andersoun, the merchandis of the said guid town, in calling of thame Coffeis, and bidding of thame to tak the salt pork and herboiss in thair handis.'

May 22, 1531. Order for the craftsmen to 'keipe and decoir the processioun on Corpus Cristi dais, and Candilmes day . . . every craft with thair awin baner . . . And euery ane of the said craftis, in the Candilmes processioun, sall furneiss thair pageane, conforme to the auld statut, maid in the yeir of God jai v^c and x yeris . . .

The craftis ar chargit to furneiss thair panzeanis vnder writtin.

The flescharis, Sanct Bestian and his Tourmentouris.

The barbouris, Sanct Lowrance and his Tourmentouris.

The skynnaris, Sanct Stewin and his Tourmentouris.

The cordinaris, Sanct Martyne.

The tailzeouris, the Coronatioun of Our Lady.

Litstaris, Sanct Nicholes.

Wobstaris, walcaris, and bonet makaris, Sanct John.

Baxstaris, Sanct Georg.

Wrichtis, messonis, sclateris, and cuparis, The Resurrectioun.

The smithis and hemmirmen to furneiss The Bearmen of the Croce.'

June 13, 1533. A very similar order, but without the list of pageants, and so worded as to extend the obligation of furnishing pageants to the Corpus Christi, as well as the Candlemas procession:—
'The craftismen . . . sall . . . keip and decoir the processionis on XXi day and Candelmes day . . . euery craft with thair avin banar . . . with thair pegane . . . And euery craft in the said processionis sall furneiss thair pegane and banar honestlie as effers, conforme to the auld statut maid in the yeir of God jaj v^c and tene yers.'

June 21, 1538. Dispute between goldsmiths and hammermen as to precedence 'in the processioun of Corpus Xri.'

June 25, 1546. Litsters ordered to 'haue thar banar and Pagane, as uther craftis of the said Burgh hes, ilk yeir, on Corpus Xhri day, and Candilmess dayis processiounis.'

June 4, 1553. Disputes as to ordering of Corpus Christi procession.

May 21, 1554. Similar disputes. A 'Pagane' in procession mentioned.

May 29, 1556. Order for observance of statute as to Corpus Christi procession.

The interpretation of these notices is not quite clear. Davidson, 220, seems to think that there was never more than a *mystère mimé* at Candlemas. But the 'play' is mentioned in 1506, 1507, and 1510. I conjecture that the Passion and Nativity cycles were not merged in Aberdeen. The Passion (Haliblude play) was performed, perhaps only occasionally, on Corpus Christi day; the Nativity annually, at Candlemas. The 'persones' of 1442 and the 'Pageants' of 150$\frac{5}{6}$ are practically identical, and would furnish a short play, with Moses and Octavian to represent the *Prophetae*, a *Stella*, and a *Presentation in the Temple*. But there was certainly also a procession in which the 'honest squiares' of 1442 figured. This may have preceded the play, but it may have been in some way introduced into it at 'the offerand' (of the Virgin in the Temple, or of the Magi?). The pageants in the list of 1531 are such as cannot all have formed part of a connected cycle. But some of them might come from the 'Haliblude' play, and I take it that this list was meant for the Corpus Christi procession only, the Candlemas procession being still regulated by the order of 1507.

Bon Accord.

The Haliblude play of 1440 was directed by the Abbot of Bon Accord. This was the Aberdeen name for the Lord of Misrule. There are many notices of him.

April 30, 1445. Order 'for letting and stanching of diuerse enormyteis done in time bygane be the abbotis of this burgh, callit of bone acorde, that in time to cum thai will giue na feis to na sic abbotis. Item, it is sene speidful to thame that for the instant yher thai will haue na sic abbot; but thai will that the alderman for the tyme, and a balyhe quhom that he will tak til him, sall supple that faute.'

August 17, 1491. Dispute as to fee of 'Abbat of Bonacord.'

May 8, 1496. Choice, 'for vphaldin of the auld lovable consuetud, honour, consolacioun, and pleasour of this burgh,' of two 'coniunctlie abbotis and priour of Bonacord,' with fee of five marks.

Nov. 30, 1504. All 'personis burges nichtbours, and burgyes sonnys' to ride with 'Abbot and Prior of Bonaccord' on St. Nicholas day annually when called on by them.

[In 1511 and 1515 this function of the Abbot has passed to the provost and baillies.]

May 16, 1507. 'All manere of youthis, burgeis and burges sonnys salbe redy everie halyday to pass with the Abbat and Prior of Bonacord.'

May 8, 1508. 'All personis that are abill within this burghe sall be ready with thair arrayment maid in grene and yallow, bowis, arrowis, brass, and all uther convenient thingis according thairto, to pass with Robyne Huyd and Litile Johnne, all tymes convenient tharto, quhen thai be requirit be the saidis Robyne and Litile Johnne.'

Nov. 17, 1508. Order for St. Nicholas riding 'with Robert Huyid and Litile Johne, quhilk was callit, in yers bipast, Abbat and Prior of Bonacord.'

April 13, 1523. Choice of 'Lordis of Bonaccord,' young men 'to rise and obey to thame.' They are also to be 'Mastris of Artuilyery.'

April 30, 1527. Grant of 'x marks of the fyrst fremen that hapynnis to be frathinfurht' to 'the Lord of Bonnacord and his fellow.'

Aug. 3, 1528. Similar grant to 'thair lovits, Jhone Ratray and Gilbert Malisoun, thair Abbatis out of ressoun.'

April 16, 1531. One of those chosen to be 'lords of Bonacord, to do plesour and blythnes to the toune in this sessoun of symmir incumming' protests against his appointment.

Oct. 11, 1533. Grant of fee to 'lordis of Bonaccord.'

April 30, 1535. Order 'that all the zoung abil men within this guid [toune] haue thair grene cottis, and agit men honest cottis, efferand to thame, and obey and decor the lordis of Bonaccord.'

April 4, 1539. 'The lordis of Bonacordis desyr' for their fee, and for 'all the yong able men within this guid towne to conwey ws euery Sunday and halyday, and wther neidfull tymes, aboulzeit as your M. has deuisit, and agit men to meit us at the crabstane or kirkyard' is granted.

June 23, 1539. Fee to 'lordis of Bonacord.'

April 17, 1541. Similar fee 'to help to the decoration and plesour to be done be thaim to this guid towne.'

April 17, 1542. Similar fee.

April 24, 1542. 'Alex. Kayn, accusit in gugment for his wyff . . . for the hawy strublens and vile mispersoning of Alex. Gray and Dauid Kintoir, lordis of Bonacord, and thair company present with thame for the tyme, sayand common beggaris and skafferis, thair meltyd was but small for all thair cuttit out hoyss, with moy oder inurious wordis, unleful to be expremit.'

July 24, 1545. Grant of 'compositioun siluer' as fee.

April 20, 1548. Similar fee.

April 14, 1552. 'The said day, the counsell, all in ane voce, havand respect and consideratioune that the lordis of Bonnacord in tymes bygane hase maid our mony grit, sumpteous, and superfleous banketing induring the tyme of thair regnn, and specialie in May, quhilks wes thocht nother profitabill nor godlie, and did hurt to sundry young men that wer elekit in the said office, becaus the last elekit did aye pretent to surmont in thair predecessouris in thair ryetouss and sumpteous banketing, and the causs principal and gud institutiounn thairof, quhilk wes in halding of the gud toun in glaidnes and blythtnes, witht danssis, farsiis, playis, and gamis, in tymes convenient, necleckit and abusit; and thairfor ordinis that in tyme cummin all sic sumpteous banketing be laid doun aluterlie except thre sobir and honest, vizt., upoun the senze day, the first Sonday of May, and ane [   ] upoun Tuisday eftcr Paschc day, and na honest man to pass to ony of thair banketis except on the said thre dais allanerlie; and in ane place of the forsaid superfleouss banketing to be had and maid yeirly to generall plais, or ane at the lest, with danssis and gammes usit and wont; and quha souer refuisis to accept the said office in tyme cumming, beand elekit thairto be the toun, to tyne his fredome, priuelege, takis, and profit he hes or ma haf of the toun, and neuer to be admittit frathinfurtht to office, honour, nor dingnete.'

May 27, 1552. Grant of fee, larger than usual, 'be ressoune that thai ar put to grytar coist this yeir nor utheris that bar office before thaim hes bene put to, and that be ressoune of cummyng of the quenis grace, my lord governor, and the maist of the lordis and grit men of this realme, presently to this toun.'

[1555. Parliament 'statute and ordanit that in all tymes cumming na maner of persoun be chosin Robert Hude nor Lytill Johne, Abbot of vnressoun, Quenis of Maij, nor vtherwyse, nouther in Burgh nor to landwart in ony tyme to cum, and gif ony Prouest, Baillies, counsall, and communitie, chesis sic ane Personage as Robert Hude, Lytill Johne, Abbottis of vnressoun, or Quenis of Maij within Burgh, the chesaris of sic sall tyne thair fredome for the space of fyve zeiris, and vtherwyse salbe punist at the Quenis grace will, and the acceptar of sicklyke office salbe banist furth of the Realme. And gif ony sic persounis sic as Robert Hude, Lytill Johne, Abbottis of vnresson, Quenis of Maij, beis chosin outwith Burgh and vthers landwart townis, the chesars sall pay to our Souerane Lady x pundis, and thair persounis put in waird, thair to remane during the Quenis grace plesoure. And gif ony wemen or vthers about simmer treis singand makis perturbatioun to the Quenis liegis in the passage throw Burrows and vthers landwart townis, the wemen perturbatouris for skafrie of money or vtherwyse salbe takin handellit and put upon the Cukstulis of everie Burgh or towne.]

May 4, 1562. ' John Kelo, belman, wes accusit in jugement for the passing throw the rewis of the toune with the hand bell, be oppin voce, to convene the haill communitie, or sa mony thairof as wald convene, to pass to the wood to bring in symmer upoun the first Sonday of Maii, contravinand the actis and statutis of the quenis grace, and lordis of consell, eppeirandlie to raise tumult and ingener discord betuix the craftismen and the fre burgessis of gild, and the saidis craftismen to dissobey and adtempt aganis the superioris of the toun, gif it stuid in thair power, as the saidis prowest and baillies ar informit, the said Johnne hawing na command of the saidis prowest and baillies to do the same ; and inlykwyise, Alexander Burnat *alias* Potter wes accusit for passing throw the toun with ane swech, to the effect and occasioun aboun wryttin.'

May 14 *and* 18, 1565. Several citizens disfranchised for disobeying the proclamation made by ' Johnne Kelo, belman,' forbidding any persons 'to mak ony conventione, with taburne plaing, or pype, or fedill, or have anseinges, to convene the quenis legis, in chusing of Robin Huid, Litill Johnne, Abbot of Ressoune, Queyne of Maii, or sicklyk contraveyne the statutis of parliament, or mak ony tumult, scism, or conventione.'

Royal Entry.

The entertainment of Queen Margaret, wife of James IV, in May, 1511, seems to have included some of the pageants from the Nativity cycle. The following extract is from Dunbar's *The Quenis Reception at Aberdein*[1] :—

> ' Ane fair processioun mett hir at the Port,
>   In a cap of gold and silk, full pleasantlie,
> Syne at hir entrie, with many fair disport,
>   Ressauet hir on streittis lustilie ;
>   Quhair first the salutatioun honorabilly
> Of the sweitt Virgin, guidlie mycht be seine ;
>   The sound of menstrallis blawing to the sky ;
> Be blyth and blisfull, burgh of Aberdein.
>
> And syne thow gart the orient kingis thrie
>   Offer to Chryst, with benyng reuerence,
> Gold, sence, and mir, with all humilitie,
>   Schawand him king with most magnificence ;

---

[1] Dunbar, *Works* (ed. J. Small, for Scottish Text Soc.), ii. 251.

Syne quhow the angill, with sword of violence,
Furth of the joy of paradice putt clein
Adame and Eve for innobedience;
Be blyth and blisfull, burgh of Aberdein.

And syne the Bruce, that euir was bold in stour,
Thow gart as roy cum rydand vnder croun,
Richt awfull, strang, and large of portratour,
As nobill, dreidfull, michtie campioun;
The [nobill Stewarts] syne, of great renoun,
Thow gart upspring, with branches new and greine,
Sa gloriouslie, quhill glaided all the toun:
Be blyth and blisfull, burgh of Aberdein.

Syne come thair four and twentie madinis jing,
All claid in greine of mervelous hewtie,
With hair detressit, as threidis of gold did hing,
With quhyt hattis all browderit rycht bravelie,
Playand on timberallis, and syngand rycht sweitlie;
That seimlie sort, in ordour weill besein,
Did meit the quein, hir saluand reverentlie:
Be blyth and blisfull, burgh of Aberdein.

The streittis war all hung with tapestrie,
Great was the press of peopill dwelt about,
And pleasant padgeanes playit prattelie;
The legeiss all did to thair lady loutt,
Quha was convoyed with ane royall routt
Off gryt barrounes and lustie ladyis [schene];
Welcum, our quein! the commoness gaif ane schout:
Be blyth and blisfull, burgh of Aberdein.

ABINGDON, BERKSHIRE.

Certain 'jeweis de Abyndon' were at Court at Xmas 1427 (Appendix E, viii).

A seventeenth-century account of the Hospital of Christ says that the fraternity held their feast on May 3 (Holy Cross day), 1445, with 'pageantes and playes and May games.' They employed twelve minstrels [1].

APPLEDORE, KENT.

Appledore players were at New Romney in 1488.

---

[1] Hearne, *Liber Niger Scaccarii* (ed. 2), ii. 598.

Baddow, Essex.

The Chelmsford (q.v.) wardrobe was hired by 'children of Badow' during 1564–6.

Bassingbourne, Cambridgeshire.

A play 'of the holy martyr St. George' was held in a field at Bassingbourne on the feast of St. Margaret, July 20, 1511. The churchwardens' accounts for the play show, besides payments for refreshments:—

'First paid to the garnement man for garnements and propyrts and playbooks, xx[s].

To a minstrel and three waits of Cambridge . . .

Item . . . for setting up the stages.

Item to John Beecher for painting of three Fanchoms and four Tormentors.

Item to Giles Ashwell for easement of his croft to play in, i[s].

Item to John Hobarde, Brotherhood Priest, for the play book, ii[s]. viii[d].'

Twenty-seven neighbouring villages contributed to these expenses[1].

Bath, Somersetshire.

The accounts of St. Michael's, Bath, for 1482, include 'pro potatione le players in recordacione ['rehearsing'?] ludorum diversis vicibus,' with other expenditure on players and properties. As one item is 'et Iohī Fowler pro cariando le tymbe a cimiterio dicto tempore ludi,' the play was perhaps a *Quem quaeritis*[2].

Chaucer's Wife of Bath, in her husband's absence at London during Lent, would make her 'visitaciouns '—

'To pleyes of miracles and mariages[3].'

Bethersden, Kent.

The churchwardens' accounts record *ludi beatae Christinae*, in 1522. St. Christina's day was July 24[4]. Bethersden players were at New Romney in 1508.

Beverley, Yorkshire.

A thirteenth-century *continuator* of the *Vita* of St. John of Beverley records a recent (†1220) miracle done in the Minster:—

[1] B. H. Wortham, *Churchwardens' Accounts of Bassingbourne (Antiquary,* vii. 25); Lysons, *Magna Britannia, Cambridgeshire,* 89; Dyer, 343, from *Antiquarian Repertory* (1808), iii. 320.

[2] C. B. Pearson, *Accounts of St. Michael's, Bath (R. Hist. Soc. Trans.* vii. 309).
[3] *Cant. Tales,* 6140 (*W. of B.'s Prol.* 558).
[4] L. T. Smith, *York Plays,* lxv.

'Contigit, ut tempore quodam aestivo intra saepta polyandri ecclesiae B. Ioannis, ex parte aquilonari, larvatorum, ut assolet, et verbis et actu fieret repraesentatio Dominicae resurrectionis. Confluebat ibi copiosa utriusque sexus multitudo, variis inducta votis, delectationis videlicet, seu admirationis causa, vel sancto proposito excitandae devotionis. Cum vero, prae densa vulgi adstante corona, pluribus, et praecipue statura pusillis, desideratus minime pateret accessus, introierunt plurimi in ecclesiam; ut vel orarent, vel picturas inspicerent, vel per aliquod genus recreationis et solatii pro hoc die taedium evitarent.' Some boys climbed into the *triforium*, in order that, through the windows, 'liberius personarum et habitus et gestus respicerent, et earundem dialogos auditu faciliori adverterent.' One of these fell into the church, but was miraculously preserved[1].

The Corpus Christi play is first mentioned in 1377. It was 'antiqua consuetudo' in 1390, when an 'ordinacio ludi Corporis Christi cum pena' was entered in the Great Guild Book, requiring the crafts or 'artes' to produce 'ludos suos et pagentes' under a penalty of 40s. The plays were held annually, subject to an order by the oligarchical town council of twelve *custodes* or *gubernatores* on St. Mark's day. The *custodes* 'governed' the play, and met certain general expenses. In 1423 they paid Master Thomas Bynham, a friar preacher, for writing 'banis'; also the waits ('*spiculatores*') who accompanied the 'banis.' In the same year they gave a breakfast to the Earl of Northumberland. In 1460 they put up a scaffold for their own use. Apparently the pageants and properties belonged to them, for in 1391 they handed over to John of Arras, on behalf of the 'hairers,' for his life and under surety, the necessaries for the play of Paradise; 'viz. j karre, viij hespis, xviij stapels, ij visers, ij wenges angeli, j fir-sparr, j worme, ij paria caligarum linearum, ij paria camisarum, j gladius.' Otherwise the expenses were met by the crafts, whose members paid a fixed levy towards the play, the 'serge' or light maintained by the craft in some chapel, and the wooden 'castle' erected at the procession of St. John of Beverley on Monday in Rogation week. Thus the Barbers' *Ordinances* in 1414 require their members to pay 2s. and a pound of wax on setting up shop, and 2s. on taking an apprentice. Certain fines also were in this company appropriated to the same purposes. In 1469 journeymen cappers paid 8d. for any year when there was a play, and 6d. when there was not. The town *Ordinances* of 1467 contemplate annual payments by all craftsmen. In 1449 the

---

[1] *Acta Sanctorum*, Maii, ii. 189; 328 (Rolls Series, lxxi); Rock, ii. 430; *Historians of the Church of York*, i. A. F. Leach in *Furnivall Miscellany*, 206.

custodes contributed 4*s.* to the Skinners' play as 'alms of the community.' If a craft failed to produce its play, the *custodes* exacted the whole or a part of the fine of 40*s.* specified in the *Ordinacio* of 1390. They also levied other disciplinary fines; as on John 'cordewainer' in 1423, for hindering the play, on Henry Cowper, 'webster,' in 1452, 'quod nesciebat ludum suum'; on the alderman of the 'paynetors,' in 1520–1 'because their play was badly and confusedly played, in contempt of the whole community, before many strangers'; and so forth. The order of 1390 specified thirty-eight crafts to play; 'viz. mercers et drapers, tannatores, masons, skynners, taillors, goldsmyths, smyths, plummers, bollers, turnors, girdelers, cutlers, latoners, broche-makers, horners, sponers, ladilers, furburs, websters, walkers, coverlid-wevers, cartwrightes, coupars, fletchers, bowers, cordewaners, baksters, flesshewers, fysshers, chaundelers, barburs, vynters, sadilers, rapers, hayrers, shipmen, glovers, and workmen.' As elsewhere, changing conditions of social life led to alterations in this list, and consequent divisions and mergings of the plays. Thus in 1411 it seems to have been felt as a grievance that certain well-to-do inhabitants of Beverley, who belonged to no craft, escaped all charge for the plays, and it was agreed that in future the 'digniores villae' should appoint four representatives and contribute a play. In 1493 the Drapers formed a craft of their own apart from the Mercers, and consequently a play was divided, the Drapers taking 'Demyng Pylate,' and leaving to the Mercers 'Blak Herod.' On the fly-leaf of the *Great Guild Book* is a list of crafts and their plays, dated by Mr. Leach †1520, which differs considerably from that of 1390. It is as follows :—

'Gubernacio Ludi Corporis Christi.

Tylers: the fallinge of Lucifer.
Saddelers: the makinge of the World.
Walkers: makinge of Adam and eve.
Ropers: the brekinge of the Comaundments of God.
Crelers: gravinge and Spynnynge.
Glovers: Cayn.
Shermen: Adam and Seth.
Wattermen: Noe Shipp.
Bowers and Fletshers: Abraham and Isaak.
Musterdmakers and Chanlers: Salutation of Our Lady.

Husbandmen: Bedleem.
Vynteners: Sheipherds.
Goldsmyths: Kyngs of Colan.
Fyshers: Symeon.
Cowpers: fleyinge to Egippe.
Shomakers: Children of Ysraell.
Scryveners: Disputacion in the Temple.
Barbours: Sent John Baptyste.
Laborers: the Pynnacle.
The Mylners: rasynge of Lazar.
Skynners: ierusalem.
Bakers: the Mawndy.

Litsters: prainge at the Mownte.

Tailyours: Slepinge Pilate.

Marchaunts [i. e. *Mercers*]: Blak Herod.

Drapers: Demynge Pylate.

Bocheours: Scorgynge.

Cutlers and Potters: the Stedynynge.

Wevers: the Stanginge.

Barkers: the Takinge of the Crose.

Cooks: Haryinge of hell.

Wrights: the Resurrection.

Gentylmen: Castle of Emaut.

Smyths: Ascencion.

Prestes: Coronacion of Our Lady.

Marchaunts: Domesday.

The thirty-eight pageants of 1390 have become thirty-six in 1520. Besides the 'Gentylmen,' dating from 1411, the 'Prestes' are noticeable. These are probably the 'clerus Gildae Corporis Christi,' who in 1430 led the Corpus Christi procession in which many of the crafts with their lights took part. Procession and play, though on the same day, seem to have been in 1430 quite distinct. The play lasted only one day, and was given in 1449 at six stations; viz. at the North Bar, by the Bull-ring, between John Skipworth and Robert Couke in Highgate, at the Cross Bridge, at the Fishmarket (now called Wednesday Market), at the Minster Bow, and at the Beck. Poulson stated that the performances lasted into the reign of James I. Mr. Leach could find no trace of them in the municipal archives after 1520[1]. But the *Ordinances*, dated 1555, of the Minstrels' guild 'of our Lady of the read arke' provide that certain forfeits shall go to the 'comon place' (which I take to be 'common plays') of Beverley.

A second craft-play appears in 1469, when a number of crafts, thirty-nine in all, gave a Pater Noster play on the Sunday after St. Peter and Vincula (August 1). Copies of the text (*registra*) were made for the crafts. The stations were those of the Corpus Christi play. There were eight 'pagends' named after the eight principal 'lusores,' viz. 'Pryde: Invy: Ire: Avaryce: Sleweth (also called 'Accidie'): Glotony: Luxuria: Vicious.' A number of crafts united to furnish each of these; apparently the most important was that of 'Vicious,' provided by the 'gentilmen, merchands, clerks and valets.' Aldermen of the pageants were appointed[2].

BILLERICAY, ESSEX.

The Chelmsford (q.v.) wardrobe was twice hired by men of 'Beleryca,' or 'Belyrica' during 1564-6.

[1] A. F. Leach, *Beverley Town Documents* (Selden Soc. xiv), l. lix. 33, 45, 75, 99, 109, 117; and in *Furnivall Miscellany*, 208; Poulson, *Beverlac*, i. 268 sqq., 302; *Lansdowne MS.* 896, f. 133 (Warburton's eighteenth-century collections for a history of Yorkshire).

[2] A. F. Leach, in *Furnivall Miscellany*, 220.

BISHOP AUCKLAND, DURHAM.

The *lusores* of 'Auklande' received a present from Durham Priory for playing before Master Hyndley, at Christmas, 1539. (App. E, i.)

BOREHAM, ESSEX.

'Casse of Boreham' hired the Chelmsford (q.v.) wardrobe in 1566 and 1573, and the 'players of Boreham,' at Twelfth Night, 1574.

BOXFORD, SUFFOLK.

A play appears in the churchwardens' accounts for 1535 [1].

BRAINTREE, ESSEX.

The churchwardens' accounts of St. Michael's include the following :—

'*Anno* 1523.   A Play of St Swythyn, acted in the Church on a Wednesday, for which was gathered 6 : 14 : $11\frac{1}{2}$; P^d at the said Play, 3 : 1 : 4 ; due to the Church, 3 : 13 : $7\frac{1}{2}$.

Anno 1525.   There was a Play of St Andrew acted in the Church the Sunday before Relique Sunday; Rc^d, 8 : 9 : 6; P^d, 4 : 9 : 9; Due to the Church, 3 : 19 : 8.

Anno 1529.   A Play in Halstead Church.

Anno 1534.   A Play of Placidas *alias* St Eustace. R^d, 14 : 17 : $6\frac{1}{2}$; P^d, 6 : 13 : $7\frac{1}{2}$; due, 8 : 2 : $8\frac{1}{2}$.

Anno 1567. R^d of the Play money, 5 : 0 : 0.

Anno 1570. Rec^d of the Play money, 9 : 7 : 7 ; and for letting the Playing garments, 0 : 1 : 8.

Anno 1571. Rc^d for a Playbook, 20^d ; and for lending the Play gere, 8 : 7^d.

Anno 1579.   For the Players Apparel, 50^s [2].'

Nicholas Udall was vicar of Braintree, 1533–1537. The plays were probably in aid of the large expenditure on the fabric of the church between 1522 and 1535.

The Chelmsford (q.v.) play was given at Braintree in 1562.

BRENTWOOD, ESSEX.

'Mr. Johnston of Brentwoode' hired the Chelmsford (q.v.) wardrobe in 1566.

BRISTOL, GLOUCESTERSHIRE.

A town-clerk's account of municipal customs, after describing the banquet on St. Katharine's Eve (Nov. 24), concludes :—

[1] Corrie, *Boxford Parish Accounts* (*Cambridge Antiq. Soc. Trans.* i. 266).

[2] Pearson, ii. 413; Morant, *History of Essex* (1768), ii. 399.

'And then to depart, euery man home: the Maire, Shiref, and the worshipfull men redy to receyue at theire dores Seynt Kateryns players, makyng them to drynk at their dores, and rewardyng theym for theire plays[1].' Were these plays more than a 'catternyng' *quête* (vol. i. p. 253)?

There is no mention of plays amongst the records, including several craft-guild ordinances, in the *Little Red Book of Bristol* (ed. W. B. Bickley, 1901). But 'the Shipwrights Pageannt' was used at the reception of Henry VII in 1486 (p. 175).

BROOKLAND, KENT.

Brookland players were at New Romney in 1494.

BUNGAY, SUFFOLK.

On the night after Corpus Christi day, June 16, 1514, certain persons 'brake and threw down five pageants of the said inhabitants, that is to saye, hevyn pagent, the pagent of all the world, Paradyse pagent, Bethelem pagent, and helle pagent, the whyche wer ever wont tofore to be caryed abowt the seyd town upon the seyd daye in the honor of the blissyd Sacrement.'

The churchwardens' accounts of St. Mary's show payments in 1526 for copying the game-book, and to Stephen Prewett, a Norwich priest, for his labour in the matter.

The accounts of Holy Trinity show payments: in 1558, to a man riding to Yarmouth for the 'game gear,' 'to William Ellys for the interlude and game booke, iiij^d,' 'for writing the partes, ij^s'; in 1566, on occasion of 'the interlude in the churchyarde,' for apparel borrowed from Lord Surrey, 'for visors,' and 'to Kelsaye, the vyce, for his pastyme before the plaie, and after the playe, both daies, ij^s.' In 1577, a churchwarden gave a receipt to his predecessor for 'game pleyers gownes and coats, that were made of certayne peces of olld copes.' In 1591, 5s. was received for 'players cootes[2].'

BURNHAM, ESSEX.

'Wm Crayford of Burnam' hired the Chelmsford (q.v.) wardrobe in 1568.

BURY ST. EDMUND'S, SUFFOLK.

The *Ordinances* of the Weavers (1477) assign half of certain fines to 'the sustentacione and mayntenaunce of the payent of the

---

[1] L. Toulmin Smith, *Ricart's Kalendar* (Camden Soc.), 80.
[2] L. G. Bolingbroke, in *Norfolk Archaeology*, xi. 336; *Eastern Counties Collectanea*, 272.

Assencione of oure Lord God and of the yiftys of the Holy Gost, as yt hath be customed of olde tyme owte of mynde yeerly to be had to the wurschepe of God, amongge other payenttes in the processione in the feste of Corpus Xp̄i.'

Journeymen weavers are to pay 'iiijᵈ' yearly to the 'payent' and all 'foreyne' as well as 'deyzin' weavers are to be contributory to it[1].

It is not clear whether the 'payent' had a *ludus* or was a dumb-show.

CAMBORNE, CORNWALL.

See Texts (i), *Cornish Plays, St. Meriasek.*

CAMBRIDGE, CAMBRIDGESHIRE.

William de Lenne and Isabel his wife, joining the guild of Corpus Christi (†1350), spent half a mark '*in ludo Filiorum Israelis*[2].'

Warton says:—

'The oldest notice I can recover of this sort of spectacle [Latin plays] in an English University is in the fragment of an ancient accompt-roll of the dissolved college of Michael-House in Cambridge; in which, under 1386, the following expense is entered: 'Pro ly pallio brusdato et pro sex larvis et barbis in comedia[3].'

CANTERBURY, KENT.

A Burghmote order (†1500) directed 'a play called Corpus Christi play . . . maintained and played at the costs of the Crafts and Mysteries,' although 'of late days it hath been left and laid apart,' to be revived at Michaelmas[4].

A book of the play of Abraham and Isaac, belonging to the 'schaft' or parochial guild of St. Dunstan's, lay in the keeping of the church-wardens of that church from 1491 to 1520[5].

On Jan. 6, 1503, the corporation paid for a play of the *Three Kyngs of Coleyn* in the guildhall. The account mentions three 'bests' made of hoops and laths and painted canvas, 'heddyng of the Hensshemen,' a castle in the courthall, and a gilt star.

Annual accounts for 'the pagent of St. Thomas' on the day of his

---

[1] *Hist. MSS.* xiv. 8, 133; Arnold, *Memorials of St. Edmund's Abbey* (R. S.), iii. 361.
[2] Masters, *Hist. of C.C.C. Cambridge* (ed. 1753), i. 5.
[3] Hazlitt-Warton, iii. 302. The only reference given is 'MSS. Rawlins. Bibl.

Bodl. Oxon.' Mr. F. Madan kindly informs me that the document cannot now be identified amongst the Rawlinson MSS.
[4] *Arch. Cantiana*, xvii. 147.
[5] *Ibid.* xvii. 80.

martyrdom (Dec. 29), appear amongst the financial records of the corporation from 1504–5 until 'far on in the reign of Queen Elizabeth.' I select some items:—

'1504–5.

Paied to Sampson Carpenter and hys man hewyng and squeryng of tymber for the Pagent.

For makyng St Thomas Carte with a peyer of whyles.

To iiij men to helpe to cary the Pagent.

For a newe myghter.

For two bagges of leder.

For payntyng of the awbe and the hedde.

For gunpowder.

For lynnen cloth bought for St Thomas garment.

For forgyng and makyng the knyghts harnes.

For the hyre of a sworde.

For wasshynge of an albe and an amys.'

In later years.

' Pro le yettyng sanguynem.

Pro le payntyng capitis Sci Thomae.

For them that holpe to dress the Pagent and for standyng of the same in the barne.

For a payer of new gloves for Seynt Thomas.

For payntyng of the hede and the Aungell of the pagent.

Paied to hym that turned the vyce.

Paied for wyre for the vyce of the Angell.

For 1 quarter of lambe and brede and drynke gevyn to the children that played the knyghtes, and for them that holpe to convey the Pagent abowte.

For a new leder bag for the blode.

For wasshyng of the albe and other clothys abowte the Auter, and settyng on agayn the apparell.'

Until 1529 the pageant stood in the barn of St. Sepulchre's convent; thenceforward in the archbishop's palace. In 1536–7 'Seynt Thomas' became 'Bysshop Bekket,' and the show was suppressed, to be revived with some added ' gyaunts' under Mary[1].

This pageant was probably a dumb-show of the martyrdom of Becket.

CHELMSFORD, ESSEX.

The Earl of Surrey rewarded the players of ' Chemsford' on Dec. 27, 1490 (Appendix E, vii).

[1] *Hist. MSS. Comm.* ix. 1, 147.

The churchwardens' accounts give minute details of a play held in 1562 and 1563. The following are the chief items :—

'Inprms paid unto the Mynstrolls for the Show day and for the play day.

Unto Willm. Hewet for makinge the vices coote, a fornet of borders, and a Jerken of borders.

To John Lockyer for making iiij shep hoks and for iron work that Burle occupied for the hell.

Item paide to Robt Mathews for a pair of wombes.

to Lawrence for watching in the Churche when the temple was a-dryenge.

for carrying of plonk for the stages.

for . . . the scaffold.

to M. Browne for the waightes of Bristowe.

for makyng the conysants.

forty Mynstrells meate and drinke.

to William Withers for making the frame for the heaven stage and tymber for the same.

for writtinge.

to William Withers for makynge the last temple, the waies, and his paynnes.

to John Wryght for makynge a cotte of lether for Christ.

to Solomon of Hatfild for parchmente.

to Mother Dale and her company for reaping flagges for the scaffold.

to Polter and Rosse for watching in the pightell on the play show.

for fyftie fadam of lyne for the cloudes.

for tenn men to beare the pagiante.

to Browne for keapinge the cornehill on the showe daye.

to Roistone for payntenge the Jeiants, the pagiante, and writing the plaiers names.

for paper to wright the Bookes.'

There are many other payments to workmen and for refreshments, and large sums to various people 'for suinge the play.' Is this 'showing,' 'stage-managing'? One Burles, who was twice paid for 'suinge,' was also boarded with his boy for three weeks.

An inventory of garments made in February, 1564, includes, with many velvet gowns and jerkins, &c. :—

'ij vyces coates, and ij scalpes, ij daggers (j dagger wanted).

v prophets cappes (one wantinge).

iij flappes for devils.

iiij shepehoks, iiij whyppes (but one gone).'

I infer that the play was a cyclical one, extending at least from Creation to Crucifixion. The temple, which required renewing, was probably rent in twain. There were heaven, hell, *Prophetae, Pastores.* The performance was not in the church, although the temple was put to dry there, but in a 'pightell' or enclosure, upon a scaffold, with stages for the spectators. It was held in connexion with a 'showe,' which was on Cornhill, and to which I assign the 'pagiante' and 'jeiantes.' The time was therefore probably Midsummer.

The accounts seem to cover two years and at least four performances. In 1562, Midsummer day with its show fell on a Saturday. The play was on Monday. On Tuesday it was repeated at Braintree, and later on at Malden, and possibly elsewhere. Then in 1563 it was again given in Chelmsford at Midsummer.

The total expenditure was over £50, although, unless the forty minstrels acted, nothing was paid to actors. Against this was received 'at the seconde play' £17 11s. 3d., and 'at the ij last plaies' £19 19s. 4d., and £2 19s. was realized by letting out the garments to the men of Sabsford in 1562 and 1563, and 16s. more for letting them to 'Mr William Peter, Knyght.' Nor did this source of income soon close. A second inventory of 1573 shows that the garments were carefully preserved. They became a valuable stock. In 1564–6 alone the hire of them brought in £10 14s. 3d. They were let to men of Colchester, Walden, Beleryca, Starford, Little Badow, and to 'children of Badow.' Further loans are noted as follows in later years:—

'Receipts, June 3, 1566.
> Sabsforde men.
> Casse of Boreham.
> Somers of Lanchire.
> Barnaby Riche of Witham.
> Willm Monnteyne of Colchester.
> Mr. Johnston of Brentwoode, the 10th Dec.
> Richard More of Nayland.
> Frauncis Medcalfe, the iiij of June, 1568.
> Wm Crayford of Burnam, the ij of June, 1568.

1570–1572.
> High Ester men.
> Parker of Writtell.
> Mrs Higham of Woodham Walter.

1572.
> Parker of Writtell, Aprill.

The Earle of Sussex players.

John Walker of Hanfild.

1573.

Casse of Boreham.

1574.

Players of Boreham, till the mondaye after twelfe day.

In 1574 the 'playe books' were valued at £4, and in the same year all the garments, &c., included in the inventory of 1573 were sold to George Studley and others for £6 12s. 4d. In 1575 one Mr. Knott was paid 8d. 'for the makinge of two oblijacyons for the assurance of the players garments belonginge to the Pyshe [1].'

CHESTER, CHESHIRE.

[*Authorities.*—(i) Editions of the plays by Wright and Deimling, described on p. 408. (ii) Notices in Furnivall, *Digby Plays*, xviii, from (*a*) *Harl. MSS.* 1944, 1948, which are versions of a *Breviary of the City of Chester*, compiled in 1609 by David Rogers from the collections of his father, Robert Rogers, Archdeacon of Chester, who died in 1595; (*b*) local *Annales* in *Harl.* 2125 (Randle Holme's *Collections*), and Daniel King's *Vale-Royall* (1656). (iii) Notices in R. H. Morris, *Chester in the Plantagenet and Tudor Reigns* (1894), from (*a*) Corporation archives,(*b*) accounts of the Smiths' Company in *Harl.* 2054, (*c*) a copy in *Harl.* 2150 (cited in error as *Harl.* 2050) of part or all of the contents of a record known as the *White Book of the Pentice*. This was bound with other documents by Randle Holme, and indexed by him in 1669. I do not find any mention of such a 'White Book' in the calendar of extant Corporation archives by Mr. J. C. Jeaffreson, in *Hist. MSS.* viii. 1. 355, unless it is identical with the *Pentice Chartulary* compiled in 1575-6 on the basis, partly of an older 'Black Book,' 'translated oute of Laten and Frenche' in 1540, and partly of loose 'sceduls, papers and books' in the Treasure House.]

The Whitsun Plays : The Tradition.

The Chester plays are traditionally ascribed to the mayoralty of one John Arneway. As 'John Arneway,' 'de Arnewey,' 'Hernwey,' or 'Harnwey' served continuously as mayor from 1268 to 1277 [2], and as no other of the great English cycles of municipal plays can claim anything like this antiquity, it is worth while to examine the evidence pretty closely. I therefore put the versions of the tradition in chronological order.

(*a*) 1544. The following document is headed 'The proclamation for the Plaies, newly made by William Newhall, clarke of the Pentice, the first yere of his entre.' It is dated 'tempore Willi Sneyde, draper, secundo tempore sui maioritatis' [Oct. 9, 1543-1544], endorsed as made 'opon the rode ee' [Rood-eye], and stated on an accompanying

---

[1] Pearson, ii. 414; *Freemasons' Magazine and Magic Mirror*, Sept. 1861.
[2] Morris, 575.

sheet to be 'of laten into Englishe translated and made by the said William Newhall the yere aforesaid [1].'

'For as moche as of old tyme, not only for the Augmentacon and increase of [the holy and catholick] faith of our Savyour, Jhu' Crist, and to exort the mynds of the co'mon people to [good devotion and holsome] doctryne thereof, but also for the co'men Welth and prosperitie of this Citie a plaie [and declaration—] and diverse stories of the bible, begynnyng with the creacon and fall of Lucifer, and [ending with the general] jugement of the World to be declared and plaied in the Witson wek, was devised [and made by one Sir] Henry Fraunces, somtyme monk of this dissolved monastery, who obtayned and gate of Clement, then beyng [bushop of Rome, a thousand] daies of pardon, and of the Busshop of Chester at that time beyng xl[ti] daies of pardon graunted from thenseforth to every person resortyng in pecible maner with good devocon to here and se the sayd [plaies] from tyme to tyme as oft as they shalbe plaied within this Citie [*and that every person disturbing the same plaies in any manner wise to be accursed by thauctoritie of the said Pope Clement bulls unto such tyme as he or they be absolved therof* (*erased*)], which plaies were devised to the honour of God by John Arneway, then maire of this Citie of Chester, and his brethren, and holl cominalty therof to be brought forthe, declared and plead at the cost and charges of the craftsmen and occupacons of the said Citie, whiche hitherunto have frome tyme to tyme used and performed the same accordingly.

Wherfore Maister Maire, in the Kynges name, straitly chargeth and co'mandeth that every person and persons of what estate, degre or condicion soever he or they be, resortyng to the said plaics, do use [themselves] pecible without makyng eny assault, affrey, or other disturbance whereby the same plaies shalbe disturbed, and that no maner person or persons who soever he or they be do use or weare eny unlaufull wepons within the precynct of the said Citie duryng the tyme of the said plaies [*not only upon payn of cursyng by thauctoritie*

[1] Morris, 317. Canon Morris does not say where he found the document. He dates it in '24 Hen. VIII, 1531.' [The regnal year, 24 Hen. VIII, by the way, is 1532–3.] But the monastery is called 'dissolved,' which it was not until 1541. The list of Mayors (Morris, 582) gives William Snead (1516–7), William Sneyde (1531–2), William Sneyde, jun. (1543–4). Obviously two generations are concerned. The second mayoralty of the younger man was 1543–4. And the appointment of Newhall as clerk of the Pentice was in 1543 (Morris, 204). Oddly, Canon Morris's error was anticipated in a copy of the proclamation made on the fly-leaf of *Harl. MS.* 2013 of the plays (Deimling, 1), which states that it was 'made by W[m] newall, Clarke of the pentice [in R]udio 24, H. 8 [1532–3].'

of the said Pope Clement Bulls, but also (erased)] opon payn of enprisonment of their bodies and makyng fyne to the Kyng at Maister Maires pleasure. And God save the Kyng and Mr. Maire, &c.[1]'

(*b*) †1544–7[2]. The documents concerning the plays copied for •Randle Holme out of the 'White Book of the Pentice[3]' are (1) a list of the plays and the crafts producing them (cf. p. 408); (2) a note that 'On Corpus Xρi day the colliges and prestys bryng forth a play at the assentement of the Maire'; (3) a note that all the arrangements detailed are subject to alteration by the Mayor and his brethren; (4) a version, without heading, of Newhall's proclamation which entirely omits the allusions to Sir Henry Fraunces and the pardons, while retaining that to Arneway; (5) verses headed 'The comen bannes to be proclaymed and Ryddon with the Stewardys of every occupacon.' These are printed in Morris, 307. They give a list of the plays (cf. p. 408), and add that there will be a 'solempne procession' with the sacrament on Corpus Christi day from 'Saynt Maries on the Hill' to 'Saynt Johns,' together with 'a play sett forth by the clergye In honor of the fest.' The passage referring to Corpus Christi is marked by Randle Holme's copyist as 'Erased in the Booke[4].' The only historical statement in the Banns is that

'Sir John Arnway was maire of this citie
When these playes were begon truly.'

(*c*) †1551–1572. The later Banns, given most fully in Rogers's *Breauarye of Chester* (cf. Furnivall, xx), but also more or less imperfectly in MSS. *h* and *B* of the plays (Deimling, i. 2), were probably written for one or other of the post-Reformation performances, but not that of 1575, as they contemplate a Whitsun performance, while that of 1575 was after Midsummer. They state that

'some tymes there was mayor of this Citie
Sir John Arnway, Knyght, who most worthilye
contented hym selfe to sett out in playe
The devise of one done Rondall, moonke of Chester abbe.'

(*d*) 1609. The *Breauarye* itself, in an account probably due to

---

[1] I reproduce Canon Morris's text *literatim*. But he does not explain the square brackets, and I do not understand them.

[2] The 'proclamation' in the White Book is clearly a revision of the 1544 version. On the other hand, the Corpus Christi procession was suppressed in 1547. The 'Banns,' which include a pageant 'of our lady thassumpcon' not in the list of plays, are perhaps rather earlier.

[3] *Harl. MS.* 2150, ff. 85ᵇ–88ᵇ.

[4] It is this entry which shows that *Harl. MS.* 2150 is not the 'White Book,' but a copy. The official catalogue of the Harleian collection is in doubt on this point.

the elder Rogers, who may have himself seen some of the later performances, says (Furnivall, xviii) :—'Heare note that these playes of Chester called yᵉ whitson playes weare the woorke of one Rondoll, a monke of yᵉ Abbaye of Sᵗ Warburge in Chester, who redused yᵉ whole history of the byble into Englishe storyes in metter, in yᵉ englishe tounge ; and this moncke, in a good desire to doe good, published yᵉ same, then the firste mayor of Chester, namely Sir Iohn Arneway, Knighte, he caused the same to be played ["anno domini, 1329"]¹.' In a list of Mayors contained in the same MS. is given (Furnivall, xxv), under the year 1328 and the mayoralty of Sir John Arneway, 'The whitson playes Inuented, in Chester, by one Rondoll Higden, a monke in Chester abbaye.'

(e) 1628. On the cover of MS. H of the plays (*Harl. MS.* 2124) is this note :—'The Whitsun playes first made by one Don Randle Heggenet, a Monke of Chester Abbey, who was thrise at Rome, before he could obtain leaue of the Pope to haue them in the English tongue.

The Whitsun playes were playd openly in pageants by the Cittizens of Chester in the Whitsun Weeke.

Nicholas the fift Then was Pope in the year of our Lord 1447.

Ano 1628.

Sir Henry ffrancis, sometyme a Monke of the Monestery of Chester, obtained of Pope Clemens a thousand daies of pardon, and of the Bishop of Chester 40 dayes pardon for every person that resorted peaceably to see the same playes, and that every person that disturbed the same, to be accursed by the said Pope untill such tyme as they should be absolued therof.'

(f) 1669. Randle Holme made a note upon his copy of the 'White Book of the Pentice' (*Harl.* 2150, f. 86 ᵇ), of the 'Whitson plaies . . . being first presented and putt into English by Rand. Higden, a monck of Chester Abbey.'

(g) *Seventeenth century.* A 'later hand' added to the copy of Newhall's proclamation on the fly-leaf of MS. h (1600) of the plays:

'Sir Io Arnway, maior 1327 and 1328, at which tyme these playes were written by Randall Higgenett, a monk of chester abby, and played openly in the witson weeke.'

(h) *Seventeenth century.* An account of the plays amongst Lord De Tabley's MSS.² assigns them to 'Randall Higden, a monk of Chester Abbey, A. D. 1269.'

---

¹ So printed by Furnivall, possibly as an addition to the text of *Harl.* 1944, from the shorter copy of the *Breauarye*   in *Harl.* 1948.   ² *Hist. MSS.* i. 49.

Up to a certain point these fragments of tradition are consistent and, *a priori*, not improbable. About 1328 is just the sort of date to which one would look for the formation of a craft-cycle. Randall or Randulf Higden[1], the author of the *Polychronicon*, took the vows at St. Werburgh's in 1299 and died in 1364. An accident makes it possible also to identify Sir Henry Francis, for he is mentioned as senior monk of Chester Abbey in two documents of May 5, 1377, and April 17, 1382. The occurrence of the name of this quite obscure person in a tradition of some 200 years later is, I think, evidence that it is not wholly an unfounded one. It is true that Newhall's proclamation states that Francis 'devised and made' the plays, whereas the Banns of 1575 and the later accounts assign the 'devise' to 'done Rondall.' But this discrepancy seems to have afforded no difficulty to the writer of 1628, who clearly thought that Heggenet 'made' the plays, and Francis obtained the 'pardon' for them. The Pope Clement concerned is probably Clement VI (1342–52), but might be the Antipope Clement VII (1378–94). The one point which will not harmonize with the rest is that about which, unfortunately, the tradition is most uniform, namely, the connexion of the plays with the mayoralty of Sir John Arneway. For neither Higden nor Francis could have worked for a mayor whose terms of office extended from 1268 to 1277. But even this difficulty does not appear to be insoluble. I find from Canon Morris's invaluable volume that a later mayor bearing a name very similar to Arneway's, one Richard Erneis or Herneys, was in office from 1327 to 1329, precisely at the date to which the tradition, in some of its forms, ascribes the plays. Is it not then probable that to this Richard Herneys the establishment of the plays is really due, and that he has been confused in the memory of Chester with his greater predecessor, the 'Dick Whittington' of the city, John Arneway or Hernwey? I am glad to be the means of restoring to him his long withheld tribute of esteem.

The Records.

If the plays were actually established in 1327–9, the first hundred years of their history is a blank. The earliest notice in any record is in 1462, when the Bakers' charter refers to their 'play and light of

---

[1] C. L. Kingsford in *D. N. B.* s.v. Higden. Mr. Kingsford does not think that 'Randle Heggenett,' the author of the *Chester Plays*, can be identified with Higden. But 'Higden,' which occurs in Rogers's list of Mayors, is an earlier form in the tradition than 'Heggenett.'

[2] Ormerod, *Hist. of Cheshire* (ed. Helsby), iii. 651 ; Morris, 315.

Corpus Christi.' The Saddlers' charter of 1471 similarly speaks of their 'paginae luminis et ludi corporis Christi[1].' It will be observed that the play is here called a Corpus Christi play. The term 'Whitson Playe' first occurs in a record of 1520[2], but there is no doubt that during the sixteenth century the regular season for the performances was Whitsuntide. As the 'White Book' (†1544) still speaks of 'pagyns in play of Corpus Χρι[3],' it is possible that a cyclical play was so called, whether actually given on Corpus Christi day or not. It is also, I think, possible that the Chester plays may have been transferred from Corpus Christi to Whitsuntide in order to avoid clashing with the procession, without quite losing their old name; and this may be what is meant by the statement on the cover of MS. 'H' of the plays that they were 'playd openly . . . in the Whitsun Weeke' in 1447. It was in 1426 that a question as to the clashing of procession and plays arose in York (cf. p. 400).

Nearly all the extant notices of the plays belong to the sixteenth century. Originally annual, they became occasional at the Reformation. They can be traced in 1546, 1551, 1554, 1561, 1567 (at Christmas), 1568, 1569, 1572, and 1575. The two last performances aroused considerable opposition. In 1572 Mayor John Hankey 'would needs have the playes go forward, against the wills of the Bishops of Canterbury, York and Chester.' Apparently an inhibition was sent by Archbishop Grindal; 'but it came too late.' In 1575, under Mayor Sir John Savage, the plays were subjected to revision, and such of them as were thought suitable given 'at the cost of the inhabitants' on Sunday, Monday, Tuesday, and Wednesday after Midsummer. This performance was 'to the great dislike of many, because the playe was in on parte of the Citty.' It was also in direct contravention of inhibitions from the Archbishop and the Earl of Huntingdon. As a result both Hankey and Savage were cited before the Privy Council, but the aldermen and common council took the responsibility upon themselves, and apparently nothing further came of the matter[4].

Probably 1575 was the last year in which the plays were given as a whole. A performance in 1600 has been alleged[5], but this date is probably taken from the heading of the Banns in MS. 'h' of the plays, which runs:—

[1] Morris, 316. The Painters and Glaziers' charter is quoted as calling them 'tyme out of minde one brotherhood for the . . . plaie of the Shepperds' Wach,' but no date is given.

[2] Ibid.
[3] *Harl. MS.* 2150, f. 85 [b].
[4] Morris, 318; Furnivall, xxv; *Hist. MSS.* viii. 1. 363, 366.
[5] Pennant, *Wales*, i. 145.

'The reading of the banes, 1600.

The banes which are reade Beefore the beginning of the playes of Chester 1600.

4 June 1600.'

Doubtless 1600 is the date of the transcript, as it is repeated after the signature to several of the plays. It is quite possible that this manuscript was made in view of an intended performance. George Bellin, the scribe, seems to have been of a Chester family. But if so, the intention was frustrated, for the annalists declare that Henry Hardware, mayor in 1600 'would not suffer any Playes.'...It is to be noted also that David Rogers, whose *Breauarye* was completed in 1609 and certainly contains matter subsequent to the death of his father in 1595, states that 1575 was the last time the plays were played[1].

Mode of Performance.

The Banns were proclaimed on St. George's day by the city crier, with whom rode the Stewards of each craft. The Mayor's proclamation against disturbers of the peace was read upon the Roodee. The plays themselves lasted through the first three week-days of Whitsuntide. Nine were given on the Monday, nine on the Tuesday, and seven on the Wednesday. The first station was at the Abbey gates, the next by the pentice at the high cross before the Mayor, others in Watergate Street, Bridge Street, and so on to Eastgate Street. Scaffolds and stages were put up to accommodate the spectators, and in 1528 a law-suit is recorded about the right to a 'mansion, Rowme, or Place for the Whydson plaies.' Rogers describes the 'pagiente' or 'cariage' as

'a highe place made like a howse with ij rowmes, being open on yᵉ tope: the lower rowme they apparrelled & dressed them selues; and ⁱn the higher rowme they played; and they stood vpon 6 wheeles [*Harl.* 1944. It is "4 wheeles" in *Harl.* 1948].'

The term 'pageant' is used at Chester both for the vehicle and for the play performed on it; but, contrary to the custom elsewhere, more usually for the latter. The vehicle is generally called a 'carriage.' It was kept in a 'caryadghouse' and occasionally served two crafts on different days. The expenses of carriage, porters, refreshments, actors, and rehearsals fell, as shown by the extant *Accounts* of the Smiths' company, on the crafts. They were met by a levy upon each member and journeyman. Vestments were hired from the clergy; both minstrels and choristers were in request for songs and music.

---

[1] Furnivall, xxiii, xxviii.

The Corporation supervised the performances, questions as to the incidence of the burden upon this or that craft coming before the Pentice court. In 1575 the Smiths submitted two alternative plays for the choice of the aldermen. The authoritative copy or 'originall booke' of the plays seems to have belonged to the city. The Smiths paid for reading the 'Regenall,' 'an Rygynall' or 'orraginall.' In 1568 one 'Randall Trevor, gent.' seems to have lost the book. There is an interesting allusion to the unprofessional quality of the actors, in the copy of the later Banns preserved by Rogers. The plays are not

'contryued
In such sorte & cunninge, & by such playeres of price,
As at this day good players & fine wittes coulde devise,

.   .   .   .

By Craftes men & meane men these Pageauntes are played
And to Commons and Contryemen acustomablye before.
If better men & finer heades now come, what canne be saide?
But of common and contrye players take thou the storye;
And if any disdaine, then open is ye doore
That lett him in to heare; packe awaye at his pleasure;
Oure playeinge is not to gett fame or treasure [1].'

Exceptional Performances.

In 1567 'Richard Dutton, mayor, kept a very worthy house for all comers all the tyme of Christmas with a Lorde of Misrule and other pastymes in this city as the Whitson Plays.'

Single plays from the cycle were similarly used for purposes of special entertainment. In 1488 was the *Assumption* before Lord Strange at the High Cross; in 1497 the *Assumption* before Prince Arthur at the Abbey gates and the High Cross; in 1515 the *Assumption* again together with the *Shepherds*' play in St. John's churchyard. In 1576, the Smiths had 'our plas' (the *Purification*) 'at Alderman Mountford's on Midsomer Eve.' Finally, in 1578, Thomas Bellin, mayor, caused the Shepherds' play 'and other triumphs' to be played at the high cross on the Roodee before the Earl of Derby, Lord Strange, and others [2].

Other plays.

The play by the 'colliges and prestys' on Corpus Christi day mentioned in the 'White Book' and in the 'Banes' preserved therein has already been noted.

---

[1] D. Rogers, *Breauarye*, in Furnivall, xviii; Morris, 303.
[2] Morris, 322, 353; Furnivall, xxvi.

In 1529 *King Robert of Sicily* was shown at the High Cross. This is doubtless the play on the same subject referred to in a fragmentary letter to some 'Lordshypp' among the State Papers as to be played on St. Peter's day at the cost of some of the companies. It was said to be 'not newe at thys time, but hath bin before shewen, evyn as longe agoe as the reygne of his highnes most gratious father of blyssyd memorye, and yt was penned by a godly clerke.'

In 1563 'upon the Sunday after Midsommer day, the History of *Æneas* and Queen *Dido* was play'd in the *Roods Eye*. And were set out by one *William Croston*, gent. and one Mr. *Man*, on which Triumph there was made two Forts, and shipping on the Water, besides many horsemen well armed and appointed.'

The entertainment of Lords Derby and Strange by Thomas Bellin in 1578 included a 'comedy' by the 'scollers of the freescole' at the mayor's house. Was this theatrical mayor a relative of George Bellin, the scribe of MSS. 'W' and 'h' of the Chester plays?

In 1589 *King Ebranke with all his Sons* was shown before the Earl of Derby at the High Cross [1].

The Midsummer Show.

This was doubtless in its origin a folk procession. Traditionally, it was founded in 1498 and only went in years when there were no Whitsun plays. The crafts were represented by personages out of their plays, 'the Doctors and little God' riding for the Smiths, the Devil for the Butchers, Abraham and Isaac for the Barbers, Balaam and his Ass for the Bricklayers, and so forth. It does not appear that the 'carriages' were had out. Other features of the 'Show' were four giants, an elephant and castle, an unicorn, a camel, a luce, an antelope, a dragon with six naked boys beating at it, morris-dancers, the 'Mayor's Mount' and the 'Merchants' Mount,' the latter being of the nature of a hobby-ship. In 1600, Mayor Henry Hardware, a 'godly zealous man,' would not let the 'Graull' go at Midsummer Watch, but instead a man in white armour. He suppressed also 'the divill in his fethers,' a man in woman's clothes with another devil called 'cuppes and cans,' 'god in stringes,' the dragon and the naked boys, and had the giants broken up. But next year the old customs were restored. The Midsummer Show again suffered eclipse under the Commonwealth, but was revived at the Restoration and endured until 1678 [2].

---

[1] Morris, 322; Furnivall, xxvi; Collier, i. 112.

[2] Morris, 324; Furnivall, xxiii; Fenwick, *Hist. of Chester*, 370.

COGGESHALL, ESSEX.

Lord Howard rewarded the players of 'Kokesale' or 'Coksale' on Dec. 26, 1481, and Dec. 25, 1482 (Appendix E, vii).

COLCHESTER, ESSEX.

The Chelmsford (q.v.) wardrobe was twice hired by Colchester men during 1564–6; also by William Monnteyne of Colchester in 1566.

COLESHILL, WARWICKSHIRE.

The 'lusores de Coleshille' played at Maxstoke Priory between 1422 and 1461 (Appendix E, ii).

COVENTRY, WARWICKSHIRE.

[*Authorities.* The facts are taken, where no other reference is given, from T. Sharp, *A Dissertation on the Pageants or Dramatic Mysteries Anciently Performed at Coventry* (1825), and J. B. Gracie, *The Weavers' Pageant* (1836: Abbotsford Club). The latter accounts of J. O. Halliwell-Phillipps, *Outlines of the Life of Shakespeare* (ninth edition, 1890), i. 335, ii. 289, and M. D. Harris, *Life in an Old English Town*, 319, add a little. The *Leet-Book* and other municipal archives used by Sharp are described by Harris, 377; his private collection passed into that of Mr. Staunton at Longbridge House, and thence into the Shakespeare Memorial Library at Birmingham, where it was burnt in 1879. It included two craft-plays, the account-books of the Smiths, Cappers, Drapers, and Weavers, and one or two MSS. (one of which is referred to as 'Codex Hales') of a set of brief local seventeenth-century *Annales*, of which other texts are printed by Dugdale, *Hist. of Warwickshire*, i. 147, and Hearne, *Fordun's Scotichronicon*, v. 1438. Several versions of these *Annales* are amongst the manuscripts of the Coventry Corporation (cf. E. S. Hartland, *Science of Fairy Tales*, 75). On their nature, cf. C. Gross, *Bibl. of Municipal History*, xviii.]

Corpus ·Christi Craft-Plays.

The earliest notice is a mention of the 'domum pro le pagent pannarum' in a deed of 1392. There must therefore be an error, so far as the pageants go, in the statement of the *Annals*, under the mayoral year 1416–7, 'The pageants and Hox tuesday invented, wherein the king and nobles took great delight[1].' Henry V was more than once at Coventry as prince, in 1404 for example, and in 1411. His only recorded visit as king was in 1421, too early for Corpus Christi or even Hox Tuesday[2]. There is frequent reference to the plays in corporation and craft documents of the fifteenth century. In

---

[1] Sharp, 8.

[2] C. L. Kingsford, *Henry V*, 346, says that he reached Coventry alone on March 15, and joined Katharine at Leicester on March 19. Ramsay, *Y. and L.* i. 290, quoting J. E. Tyler, *Henry of Monmouth*, ii. 28, gives the same dates. The entry in the *Leet Book* (Harris, 139) brings him to Coventry on March 21 and with the queen. But this was Good Friday. If the *Leet Book* is right, he might have remained for Hox Tuesday, April 1.

1457 they were seen by Queen Margaret, who 'lodged at Richard Wodes, the grocer,' whither the corporation sent an elegant collation, including ' ij cofyns of counfetys and a pot of grene gynger.' With her were the Duke and Duchess of Buckingham, Lord and Lady Rivers, the elder and younger Lady of Shrewsbury, and ' other mony moo lordes and ladyes.' They were seen also by Richard III in 1485 and twice by Henry VII. The first occasion was on St. Peter's day (June 29) in 1486, and the second in 1493, when say the *Annals*, rather oddly (cf. p. 420), ' This yeare the King came to se the playes acted by the Gray Friers, and much commended them.' In 1520 the *Annals* record ' New playes at Corpus Christi-tyde, which were greatly commended.' In 1539 the mayor of Coventry, writing to Cromwell, told him that the poor commoners were at such expense with their plays and pageants that they fared the worse all the year after[1]. In the sixteenth century the Coventry plays were probably the most famous in England. The *C. Mery Talys* (1526) has a story of a preacher, who wound up a sermon on the Creed with ' Yf you beleue not me then for a more suerte & suffycyent auctoryte go your way to Couentre and there ye shall se them all playd in Corpus Cristi playe[2].' And John Heywood, in his *Foure PP*, speaks of one who

' Oft in the play of Corpus Cristi
He had played the deuyll at Couentry[3].'

Foxe, the martyrologist, records that in 1553 John Careless, in Coventry gaol for conscience sake, was let out to play in the pageant about the city. There is some confusion here, as Careless was only in gaol in Coventry for a short time in November before he was sent to London[4].

When the *Annals* say that in 1575–6 ' the Pageants on Hox Tuesday that had been laid down eight years were played again,' there is probably some confusion between 'Hox Tuesday' and 'the Pageants,' for the account-books show that the latter were played regularly, except in 1575, until 1580, when the *Annals* report them as 'again laid down.' In 1584 a different play was given (cf. *infra*), and possibly also in 1591, although the fact that the songs of the Taylors and Shearmen's pageant are dated 1591 rather suggests that after all the regular plays may have been revived that year. Some of the pageants were sold in 1586 and 1587, but the Cappers preserved

---

[1] Brewer, xiv (1), 77.
[2] *C. Mery Talys*, lvi (ed. Oesterley, 100).
[3] Heywood, *The Foure PP*, 831

(Manly, i. 510).
[4] Foxe, vi. 411; viii. 170; Maitland, *Essays on the Reformation*, 24.

the properties of their play in 1597, and the Weavers had still players' apparel to lend in 1607. According to the *Annals*, by 1628 the pageants had 'bine put downe many yeares since.'

The plays were given annually and in one day at the feast of Corpus Christi. Contrary to the custom of the northern towns, there were only some ten or twelve pageants, each covering a fairly wide range of incident (cf. p. 423). Nor can the performances be shown to have been repeated at more than three or four stations. 'Gosford Street,' 'Mikel' or 'Much Park Street end' and 'Newgate' are recorded, and in one of these may have been the house of Richard Wodes, where Queen Margaret lay. The Drapers only provided three 'worlds' for their pageant, and probably one was burnt at each station. According to the *Annals*, part of the charges of the plays was met by the enclosure of a piece of common land (possibly to build pageant houses upon). Otherwise they fell wholly upon the crafts, to some one of which every artisan in the town was bound to become contributory for the purpose. The principal crafts were appointed by the Leet to produce the pageants, and with each were grouped minor bodies liable only for fixed sums, varying from 3s. 4d. to 16s. 8d. In 1501 an outside craft, the Tilemakers of Stoke, is found contributing 5s. to a pageant. These combinations of crafts varied considerably from time to time. Within the craft the necessary funds were raised, in part at least, by special levies. Strangers taking out their freedom were sometimes called upon for a contribution. Every member of the craft paid his 'pagent pencys.' In several crafts the levy was 1s. Amongst the Smiths it must have been less, as they only got from 2s. 2d. to 3s. 4d. in this way, whereas the Cappers in 1562 collected 22s. 4d. In 1517 William Pisford left a scarlet and a crimson gown to the Tanners for their play, together with 3s. 4d. to each craft that found a pageant. The total cost of the Smiths' play in 1490 was £3 7s. 5½d. In 1453 we find the Smiths contracting with one Thomas Colclow to have 'the rewle of the pajaunt' for twelve years, and to produce the play for a payment of 46s. 8d. A similar contract was made in 1481. But as a rule, the crafts undertook the management themselves, and the account-books studied by Sharp afford more detailed information as to the mode of production than happens to be available for any other of the great cycles.

It is therefore worth while to give some account of the chief objects of expenditure. First of all there was the pageant itself. The name appears in every possible variety of spelling in Coventry documents. Dugdale, on the authority of eye-witnesses, describes the pageants as

'Theaters for the severall Scenes, very large and high, placed upon wheels.' Painted cloths were used 'to lap aboubt the pajent,' and there was a carved and painted top, adorned with a crest, with vanes, pencils, or streamers. On the platform of the pageant such simple scenic apparatus as a seat for Pilate, a pillar for the scourging, a 'sepulchre,' and the like, was fixed. The Weavers' pageant seems to have had an 'upper part' representing the Temple; also divisions described in the stage directions as 'the for pagand' and 'the tempull warde.' The Cappers' pageant was fitted up with a 'hell-mouth.' The Drapers also had a 'hell-mouth,' with a windlass, and fire at the mouth, and a barrel for the earthquake, and three worlds to be set afire. 'Scaffolds,' distinct from the pageant itself, were drawn round with it. These, according to Sharp, were for spectators, but they may have been supplementary stages, made necessary by the number of episodes in each play at Coventry. Certainly the action was not wholly confined to the pageant, for in the Shearmen and Taylors' play, 'Here Erode ragis in the pagond & in the strete also'; and again, 'the iij Kyngis speykyth in the strete.' The pageant was constantly in need of repairs. A pageant-house had to be built or hired for it. On the day of the feast it was cleaned, strewn with rushes; and the axle was greased with soap. Men were paid to 'drive' or 'horse' it, and the Cappers expected their journeymen to undertake this job.

The players received payments varying with the importance of their parts. The sums allowed by the Weavers in 1525 ranged from 10d. to 2s. 4d. Minstrels, both vocalists and instrumentalists, were also hired, and in 1573 one Fawston, evidently an artist of exceptional talent, received from the Smiths, besides 4d. 'for hangyng Judas,' another 4d. 'for Coc croyng.' The Drapers paid as much as 3s. 4d. 'for pleayng God,' and 5s. 'to iij whyte sollys' or 'savyd sowles,' 5s. 'to iij blake sollys,' or 'dampnyd sowles,' 16d. 'to ij wormes of conscyence,' and the like. Payments also occur for speaking the prologue, preface, or 'protestacyon.'

The corporation exercised control over the players, and in 1440 ordered under a penalty of 20s. 'quod Robertus Gñe et omnes alii qui ludunt in festo Corporis Christi bene et sufficienter ludant ita quod nulla impedicio fiat in aliquo ioco.' In 1443, an order forbade members of certain crafts to play in any pageant except their own without the mayor's licence.

The players required refreshment at intervals during the day, and probably the craftsmen who attended the pageant took their share. Further expenses, both for refreshment, and for the hire of a room or hall, were incurred at rehearsals. The Smiths in 1490 had their first 'reherse' in Easter week, and their second in Whitsun week.

Each craft had its own 'orygynall' or 'play-boke,' and paid for making the necessary copies, for setting or 'pricking' songs, for 'beryng of ye Orygynall' or prompting, and occasionally for bringing the text up to date. Thus the Smiths had a 'new rygenale' in 1491, and in 1573 a 'new play,' by which is apparently meant an additional scene to their existing play (cf. p. 423). The Drapers added 'the matter of the castell of Emaus' in 1540. The Weavers paid 5s. 'for makyng of the play boke' in 1535, and the colophon of their extant text shows it to have been 'newly translate' in that year by Robert Croo. This was a regular theatrical man of all work. The matter of the Shearmen and Taylors' play was 'nevly correcte' by him in the same year. In 1557 he got 20s. from the Drapers 'for makyng of the boke for the paggen.' The Smiths paid him in 1563 'for ij leves of our pley boke.' And between 1556 and 1562 he further assisted the Drapers, by playing God, mending the 'devells cottes,' supplying a hat for the Pharisee, and manufacturing the requisite 'iij worldys.'

Finally, there was the not inconsiderable cost of costumes and properties, including the gloves for the performers which figure so invariably in mediaeval balance sheets. Further details as to these and all other objects of expenditure than I have here room for will be found in the invaluable volumes of Mr. Sharp.

The Destruction of Jerusalem.

In 1584, four years after the ordinary Corpus Christi plays were laid down, the *Annals* record 'This year the new Play of the Destruction of Jerusalem was first played.' This is confirmed by the accounts of the corporation, which include a sum of £13 6s. 8d. 'paid to Mr. Smythe of Oxford the xv^th daye of Aprill 1584 for hys paynes for writing of the tragedye.' This was one John Smythe, a scholar of the Free School in Coventry and afterwards of St. John's College, Oxford. The play was produced at considerable expense upon the pageants of the crafts, but the day of performance is not stated. From the detailed accounts of the Smiths and the Cappers, Mr. Sharp infers that it was based upon the narrative of Josephus.

In 1591, the old Corpus Christi plays seem to have been proposed for exhibition, as the MS. of the Shearmen and Taylors' songs bears the date of May 13 in that year. But on May 19 the corporation resolved 'that the destruction of Jerusalem, the Conquest of the Danes, or the historie of K[ing] E[dward] the X [Confessor], at the request of the Comons of this Cittie shal be plaied on the pagens on Midsomer daye & St. Peters daye next in this Cittie & non other playes.' The two last-named plays may have been inspired by the traditional interpretations of the Hox Tuesday custom (cf. vol. i. p. 154). Which was chosen does not appear ; but some performance or other was given. Several of the crafts had by this time sold their pageants. Those who had not lent them ; and all compounded for the production of a scene by the payment of a sum down. This appears to have gone to one Thomas Massey, who contracted for the production. He had already supplied properties in 1584. In 1603 he quarrelled with the corporation about certain devices shown on the visit of the Princess Elizabeth to Coventry. In 1606 he hired some acting-apparel from the Weavers' company [1].

Miscellaneous Plays.

The *Annals* record :—

1490–1. ' This year was the play of St. Katherine in the little Park.
1504–5. 'This yeare they played the play of St. Crytyan in the little parke [2].'
In 1511, one of the pageants at the entry of Henry VIII had a 'goodly Stage Play' upon it [3].

The Dyers in 1478, the Cappers in 1525, and the Drapers in 1556, 1566, and 1568 appear to have had plays at their dinners. Probably ' the Golden Fleece,' for which the Cappers paid the inevitable Robert Crowe and two others, was a play [4].

The ' lusores de Coventry' played at Maxstoke Priory between 1422 and 1461 (Appendix E, ii). ' Certain Players of Coventrye' were at court in 1530 (Appendix E, viii).

Towards the end of the sixteenth century occur notices of travelling ' players of Coventrie.' They were at Bristol and Abingdon in 1570, and at Leicester in 1569 and 1571. At Abingdon they are described as ' Mr. Smythes players of Coventree.' John Smythe, the writer of the Destruction of Jerusalem, was only seven years old in 1570. Mr. Halliwell-Phillipps would read ' *the* Smythes' players [5].'

The Corpus Christi Procession.

The procession or ' Ridyng' on Corpus Christi day is first mentioned in the *Leet Book* in 1444, and in 1446 is an order ' quod le Ruydyng in festo Corporis Christi fiat prout ex antiquo tempore consueverint.'

---

[1] Sharp, 12, 39, 64, 75, 78 ; *Weavers' Play,* 21.
[2] Sharp, 9 ; Hearne, *Fordun's Scotichronicon,* v. 1450.
[3] Sharp, 157 ; Hearne, loc. cit.
[4] Sharp, 216.
[5] Sharp, 209 ; Halliwell-Phillipps, *Outlines,* ii. 296.

It took place early in the day after a 'breakfast.' The craft-guilds rode in it, and provided minstrels and torchbearers. The Trinity Guild seems to have borne a crucifix, and the Guild of Corpus Christi and St. Nicholas the host under a canopy. The accounts of the Smiths include the following items :—

'1476. Item ffor hors hyre to Herod, iij^d.

1489. Item payd for Aroddes garment peynttyng that he went a prossasyon in, xx^d.'

The other extant guild accounts throw no light on the presence of representatives of the plays in the procession; but the Corpus Christi guild itself provided dramatic personages.

'1501. payd for a Crown of sylver & gyld for the Mare on Corpus Christi day, xliij^s ix^d.

1539. peny bred for the appostells, vj^d.

boiff for tho appootloo, viij^d.

to the Marie for hir gloves and wages, ij^s.

the Marie to offer, j^d.

Kateryne & Margaret, iiij^d.

viij virgyns, viij^d.

to Gabriell for beryng the lilly, iiij^d.

to James & Thomas of Inde, viij^d.

to x other apostells, xx^d.

1540. for makyng the lilly, iij^s iiij^d.

1541. to Gabryel for beryng the light [lilly?] iiij^d.

xij torches of wax for the apostles.

1544. a new coat & a peir of hoes for Gabriell, iij^s. iiij.[1] '

CROXTON, NORFOLK (?).

See s. v. *Texts* (i), *Croxton Play*, *The Sacrament*.

DAVENTRY, NORTHAMPTONSHIRE.

The 'lusores de Daventry' played at Maxstoke Priory between 1422 and 1461 (Appendix E, ii).

DUBLIN, IRELAND.

The version of the *Quem quaeritis* used at the Church of St. John the Evangelist in the fourteenth century is printed in Appendix R.

The Chain Book of the City contains the following memorandum, apparently entered in 1498.

Corpus Christi day a pagentis :—

'The pagentis of Corpus Christi day, made by an olde law and

---

[1] Sharp, 159.

confermed by a semble befor Thomas Collier, Maire of the Citte of Divelin, and Juries, Baliffes and commones, the iiiith Friday next after midsomer, the xiii. yere of the reign of King Henri the VIIth [1498]:

'Glovers: Adam and Eve, with an angill followyng berryng a swerde. Peyn, xl. s.

'Corvisers: Caym and Abell, with an auter and the ofference. Peyn, xl. s.

'Maryners, Vynters, Shipcarpynderis, and Samountakers: Noe, with his shipp, apparalid acordyng. Peyn, xl. s.

'Wevers: Abraham [and] Ysack, with ther auter and a lambe and ther offerance. Peyn, xl. s.

'Smythis, Shermen, Bakers, Sclateris, Cokis and Masonys: Pharo, with his hoste. Peyn, xl. s.

'Skynners, House-Carpynders, and Tanners, and Browders: for the body of the camell, and Oure Lady and hir chil[d]e well aperelid, with Joseph to lede the camell, and Moyses with the children of Israell, and the Portors to berr the camell. Peyn, xl. s. and Steyners and Peyntors to peynte the hede of the camell. [Peyn,] xl. s.

'[Goldsmy]this: The three kynges of Collynn, ridyng worshupfully, with the offerance, with a sterr afor them. Peyn, xl. s.

'[Hoopers]: The shep[er]dis, with an Angill syngyng Gloria in excelsis Deo. Peyn, xl. s.

'Corpus Christi yild: Criste in his Passioun, with three Maries, and angilis berring serges of wex in ther hands. [Peyn,] xl. s.

'Taylors: Pilate, with his fellaship, and his lady and his knyghtes, well beseyne. Peyn, xl. s.

'Barbors: An[nas] and Caiphas, well araied acordyng. [Peyn,] xl. s.

'Courteours: Arthure, with [his] knightes. Peyn, xl. s.

'Fisshers: The Twelve Apostelis. Peyn, xl. s.

'Marchauntes: The Prophetis. Peyn, xl. s.

'Bouchers: tormentours, with ther garmentis well and clenly peynted. [Peyn,] xl. s.

'The Maire of the Bulring and bachelers of the same: The Nine Worthies ridyng worshupfully, with ther followers accordyng. Peyn, xl. s.

'The Hagardmen and the husbandmen to berr the dragoun and to repaire the dragoun a Seint Georges day and Corpus Christi day. Peyn, xl. s.'

This list is immediately followed by a second, practically identical with it, of 'The Pagentys of Corpus Christi Processioun.'

These pageants, though the subjects are drawn from the usual Corpus Christi play-cycle (with the addition of King Arthur and the nine Worthies), appear, from their irregular order, to be only dumb-show accompaniments of a procession. In 1569 the crafts were directed to keep the same order in the Shrove Tuesday ball riding (cf. vol. i. p. 150), 'as they are appointed to go with their pageants on Corpus Christi daye by the Chayne Boke [1].'

The same intermixture of profane and sacred elements marks the late and scanty records of actual plays in Dublin.

'Tho. Fitzgerald, Earl of Kildare and Lord Lieutenant of Ireland in the year 1528, was invited to a new play every day in Christmas, Arland Usher being then mayor, and Francis Herbert and John Squire bayliffs, wherein the taylors acted the part of Adam and Eve; the shoemakers represented the story of Crispin and Crispinianus; the vintners acted Bacchus and his story; the Carpenters that of Joseph and Mary; Vulcan, and what related to him, was acted by the Smiths; and the comedy of Ceres, the goddess of corn, by the Bakers. Their stage was erected on Hoggin Green (now called College Green), and on it the priors of St. John of Jerusalem, of the blessed Trinity, and All Hallows caused two plays to be acted, the one representing the passion of our Saviour, and the other the several deaths which the apostles suffered [2].' In 1541 there were 'epulae, comoediae, et certamina ludicra' when Henry VIII was proclaimed King of Ireland. These included 'the nine Worthies.' On the return of Lord Sussex from an expedition against James MacConnell in 1557, 'the Six Worthies was played by the city [3].'

A seventeenth-century transcript of a lost leaf of the Chain Book has the following order for the St. George's day procession:—

'The Pageant of St. George's day, to be ordered and kept as hereafter followeth:

'The Mayor of the yeare before to finde the Emperour and Empress with their followers, well apparelled, that is to say, the Emperor, with two Doctors, and the Empress, with two knights, and two maydens to beare the traynes of their gownes, well apparelled, and [the Guild of] St. George to pay their wages.

[1] J. T. Gilbert, *Calendar of Ancient Records of Dublin*, i. 239; ii. 54. Cf. Davidson, 222, and in *Modern Language Notes*, vii. 339.

[2] Harris, *Hist. of Dublin*, 147; J. C. Walker, *Hist. Essay on the Irish Stage* (*Trans. Roy. Irish Acad.* ii (1788), 2. 75), from MS. of Robert Ware.

[3] Walker, loc. cit.; Sir James Ware, *Annales Rerum Hibern.* (1664), 161; *Variorum*, iii. 30, from MS. in Trin. Coll. Dublin. W. F. Dawson, *Christmas: its Origin and Associations*, 52, says that Henry II kept Christmas at Hogges in 1171 with 'miracle plays.' But I cannot find the authority for this.

'Item: Mr. Mayor for the time being to find St. George a-horseback, and the wardens to pay three shillings and four pence for his wages that day. And the Bailives for the time being to find four horses, with men upon them, well apparelled, to beare the pole-axe, the standard, and the Emperor and St. George's sword.

'Item: The elder master of the yeald to find a mayd well aparelled to lead the dragon; and the Clerk of the Market to find a good line for the dragon.

'Item: The elder warden to find St. George, with four trumpettors, and St. George's [Guild] to pay their wages.

'Item: the yonger warden to finde the king of Dele and the queene of Dele, and two knightes to lead the queene of Dele, with two maydens to beare the trayne of her goune, all wholy in black apparell, and to have St. George's chappell well hanged and apparelled to every purpose with cushins . . . russhes and other necessaries belonging for said St. George's day [1].'

DUNSTABLE, BEDFORDSHIRE.

One Geoffrey, a Norman, was 'apud Dunestapliam, expectans scholam S. Albani sibi repromissam; ubi quendam ludum de S. Katerina (quem Miracula vulgariter appellamus) fecit; ad quae decoranda petiit a Sacrista S. Albani, ut sibi capae chorales accommodarentur, et obtinuit.' Unfortunately the 'capae' were burnt. This must have been early in the twelfth century, as Geoffrey in grief became a monk, and was Abbot of St. Albans by 1119 [2].

EDINBURGH, SCOTLAND.

The civic records show traces of municipal plays in 1554, but it is not clear that they were miracle-plays proper or of long standing. Sir David Lyndsay's *Satyre of the Thrie Estaitis* was played in the Greenside between 1550 and 1559 (cf. p. 442). On June 15, 1554, a payment was made to Sir William Makdougall, 'maister of werk,' for those 'that furneist the grayth to the convoy of the moris to the Abbay and of the play maid that samyn day the tent day of Junii instant.' Makdougall was to deliver to the dean of guild the 'hand-scenye [ensign] and canves specifiit in the said tikkit to be kepit to the behuif of the town.' Sums were also paid this summer for 'the playing place' or 'the play field now biggand in the Grenesid.'

---

[1] Gilbert, op. cit. i. 242.
[2] Matthew Paris, *Gesta Abbat. S. Albani*, ap. H. T. Riley, *Gesta Abbatum*

S. Albani (R. S.), i. 73; Bulaeus, *Historia Universitatis Parisiensis*, ii. 226; Collier, i. 13.

On Oct. 12 Walter Bynnyng was paid for 'the making of the play graith' and for painting the 'handsenye' and 'playariss facis.' He was to 'mak the play geir vnderwrittin furthcumand to the town, quhen thai haif ado thairwith, quhilkis he has now ressauit; viz. viij play hattis, ane kingis crown, ane myter, ane fulis hude, ane septour, ane pair angell wingis, twa angell hair, ane chaplet of tryvmphe.'

On Dec. 28 'the prouest, baillies and counsale findis it necessar and expedient that the litill farsche and play maid be William Lauder be playit afoir the Quenis grace [1].' I trace a note of regret for the doubtful morals and certain expense of the entertainments which the presence in Edinburgh of the newly-made Regent, Mary of Lorraine, imposed upon the burghers.

EASTERFORD, ESSEX.

Lord Howard rewarded the players of 'Esterforde' on Jan. 7, 1482 (Appendix E, vii). This place is now known as Kelvedon.

FOLKESTONE, KENT.

Folkestone players were at New Romney in 1474, and at Lydd in 1479.

FOSTON, LEICESTERSHIRE.

In 1561 the players of 'Fosson' borrowed 'serten stufe' from the churchwardens of St. Martin's, Leicester [2].

FYFIELD, OXFORDSHIRE.

See s. v. SHIPTON.

GARBOLDISHAM, NORFOLK.

'Garblesham game' was at Harling (q. v.) in 1457.

GREAT CHART, KENT.

'Chart' players were at New Romney in 1489.

HADLEIGH, ESSEX.

Lord Howard rewarded the 'Plaiers of Hadley' on Dec. 27, 1481 (Appendix E, vii).

HALSTEAD, ESSEX.

There was a play in the church in 1529 [3].

HAM STREET, KENT.

Ham players were at Lydd in 1454.

---

[1] J. D. Marwick, *Records of Edinburgh* (Scottish Burghs Record Soc.), ii. 193 sqq.

[2] Kelly, 19.
[3] Pearson, ii. 413.

HANNINGFIELD, ESSEX.

'John Walker of Hanfild' hired the Chelmsford (q. v.) wardrobe in 1572.

HARLING, NORFOLK.

In 1452 the wardens paid for the 'original of an Interlude pleyed at the Cherch gate.' In 1457 payments were made for 'Lopham game,' and 'Garblesham game,' in 1463 for 'Kenningale game,' in 1467 to the 'Kenyngale players[1].'

HASCOMBE, SURREY.

Amongst the *Loseley MSS.* is a deposition of $157\frac{8}{9}$:

'Coram me Henr. Goringe, ar. xij° die Januar. 1578. George Longherst and John Mill ex^d sayeth, that on Sondaye last they were together at widow Michelles house, in the parish of Hascombe, and there delyvered their mares to kepe till they came agayne, and sayde that they wold goo to Hascombe Churche, to a kynge playe wch then was there. And sayeth y^t they went thither and there contynued about an houre, at which tyme the sonne was then downe[2].'

The date suggests a performance on Jan. 6. Evidently a May 'kynge playe' is out of the question; but a Twelfth Night King, or a 'Stella' belated in the afternoon, are both possible.

HEREFORD, HEREFORDSHIRE.

On April 30, 1440, John Hauler and John Pewte sued Thomas Sporyour in the city court 'de placito detencionis unius libri de lusionibus, prec. iis. iiij*d*.[3]'

The Register of the Corporation for 1503 contains a list of 'The paiants for the procession of Corpus Christi:

Furst, Glovers. Adam, Eve, *Cayne and Abell* (erased).
Eldest seriant. Cayne, Abell, and Moysey, Aron.
Carpenters. Noye ship.
Chaundelers. Abram, Isack, Moysey cum iiij^or pueris.
Skynners. Jesse.
Flacchers. Salutaçon of our Lady.
Vynteners. Nativite of our Lord.
Taillours. The iii Kings of Colen.
The belman. The purificaçon of our Lady, with Symyon.

[1] L. G. Bolingbroke, *Pre-Eliz. Plays and Players in Norfolk* (*Norfolk Archaeology*, xi. 338).

[2] *N. and Q.* xii. 210; Kelly, 68.
[3] *Hist. MSS.* xiii. 4. 300.

Drapers. The . . . (*blank*) deitours, goyng with the good Lord.

Sadlers. Fleme Jordan.

Cardeners. The castell of Israell.

Walkers. The good Lord ridyng on an asse ("judging at an assize," in Johnson!) with xii Appostelles.

The tanners. The story of Shore Thursday.

Bochours. The takyng of our Lord.

The eldest seriant. The tormentyng of our Lord with iiii tormentoures, with the lamentacõn of our Lady [and Seynt John the evaungelist: *faintly added by another hand*].

[Cappers. Portacio crucis usque montem Oilverii: *added*.]

Dyers. Iesus pendens in cruce [*altered by the second hand from* Portacio crucis et Iohanne evangelista portante Mariam].

Smythes. Longys with his knyghtes.

The eldest seriant. Maria and Iohannes evangelista (*interlined*).

Barbours. Joseth Abarmathia.

Dyers. Sepultura Christi.

The eldest seriant. Tres Mariae.

Porters. Milites armati custodes sepulcri.

Mercers. Pilate, Cayfes, Annas, and Mahounde. [*This last name has been partly erased*.]

Bakers. Knyghtes in harnes.

Journeymen cappers. Seynt Keterina with tres (?) tormentors[1].'

At a law day held on Dec. 10, 1548, it was agreed that the crafts who were 'bound by the grantes of their corporacions yerely to bring forthe and set forward dyvers pageaunttes of ancient history in the processions of the cytey upon the day and fest of Corpus Xpi, which now is and are omitted and surceased' should instead make an annual payment towards the expense of repairing walls, causeways, &c.[2] The 1503 list seems to concern a dumb-show only, and it cannot be positively assumed that the *lusiones* of 1440 were a Corpus Christi play.

In 1706 a labourer went through the city in the week before Easter, being Passion week, clothed in a long coat with a large periwig, with a great multitude following him, sitting upon an ass, to the derision of our Saviour Jesus Christ's riding into Jerusalem, to the great scandal of the Christian religion, to the contempt of our Lord and his doctrine, and to the ill and pernicious example of others[3].

---

[1] *Hist. MSS.* xiii. 4. 288.
[2] R. Johnson, *Ancient Customs of Hereford* (ed. 2. 1882), 119.
[3] *Hist. MSS.* xiii. 4. 352.

HERNE, KENT.

Herne players were at New Romney in 1429.

HEYBRIDGE, ESSEX.

The churchwardens' accounts for 1532 show a play, with 'a fool' and 'pagent players,' apparently in the church[1].

HIGH EASTER, ESSEX.

High Easter men hired the Chelmsford (q. v.) wardrobe in 1570–2.

HIGH HALDEN, KENT.

'Haldene' players were at New Romney in 1499.

HOLBEACH, LINCOLNSHIRE.

In 1548 the churchwardens paid v^s viij^d for the 'costs of the iij kyngs of Coloyne[2].'

HULL, YORKSHIRE.

The accounts of the Trinity House, a guild of master mariners and pilots, contain entries concerning a play of Noah.

' 1483. To the minstrels, vj^d.

>To Noah and his wife, j^s vj^d.
>To Robert Brown playing God, vj^d.
>To the Ship-child, j^d.
>To a shipwright for clinking Noah's ship, one day, vij^d.
>22 kids for shoring Noah's ship, ij^d.
>To a man clearing away the snow, j^d.
>Straw, for Noah and his children, ij^d.
>Mass, bellman, torches, minstrels, garland, &c., vj^s.
>For mending the ship, ij^d.
>To Noah for playing, j^s.
>To straw and grease for wheels, ¼^d.
>To the waits for going about with the ship, vj^d.

1494. To Thomas Sawyr playing God, x^d.

>To Jenkin Smith playing Noah, j^s.
>To Noah's wife, viij^d.
>The clerk and his children, j^s vj^d.
>To the players of Barton, viij^d.
>For a gallon of wine, viij^d.
>For three skins for Noah's coat, making it, and a rope to hang the ship in the kirk, vij^s.

[1] Nichols, *Extracts from Churchwardens' Accounts*, 175.
[2] W. Sandys, *Christmas Carols*, xc.

> To dighting and gilding St. John's head, painting two
> tabernacles, beautifying the boat and over the table,
> vij^s ij^d.
> Making Noah's ship, v^{li} viij^s.
> Two wrights a day and a half, j^s vj^d.
> A halfer (rope) 4 stone weight, iiij^s viij^d.
> Rigging Noah's ship, viij^d.'

Hadley, the historian of Hull, extracts these items 'from the
expences on Plough-day,' and says, 'This being a maritime society,
it was celebrated by a procession adapted to the circumstance[1].'
There are continental parallels for ship-processions at spring feasts
(vol. i. p. 121); but evidently that at Hull had been assimilated,
perhaps under the influence of Beverley, to a miracle-play or
pageant. A recent writer, apparently from some source other than
Hadley, says that the entries in the accounts run from before 1421 to
1529. Amongst his additional extracts are:—

> 'A payr of new mytens to Noye, iiij^d.
> Amending Noye Pyleh, iiij^d.
> Nicholas Helpby for wryt^g the pley, vij^d.
> A rope to hyng the shipp in ye kyrk, ij^d.
> Takyng down shype and hyngyng up agayn, ij^s.
> Wyn when the shype went about, ij^d.

1421. New shype, v^{li} viij^s iiij^d[2].'

Hythe, Kent.

Hythe players were at New Romney in 1399 and at Lydd in 1467.

Idbury, Oxfordshire.

See s. v. Shipton.

Ipswich, Suffolk.

In 1325 the former Guild Merchant was reconstituted as a Guild
of Corpus Christi. The Constitution provides for a procession, on
Corpus Christi day, unless it is hindered 'pro qualitate temporis[3].'

The notices in the seventeenth-century Annals of the town point to
a play as well as a procession[4]. The Guild included all the burgesses;

[1] G. Hadley, *Hist. of Kingston upon Hull* (1788), 823.
[2] W. Andrews, *Historic Yorkshire*, 43; *Curiosities of the Church*, 19.
[3] J. Wodderspoon, *Memorials of the Ancient Town of Ipswich* (1850), 161;

Hist. MSS. ix. 1. 245.
[4] Nathaniel Bacon, *The Annalls of Ipswich*, 1654 (ed. W. H. Richardson, 1884), 102 and *passim*. Some additional notices are in *Hist. MSS.* ix. 1. 241 sqq.

each paying 16*d.* a year and attending the dinner on Corpus Christi day.

In 1443 the common marsh was devised ' to maintaine and repaire the pageants of the Guilde.'

In 1445 J. Causton was admitted burgess on condition of maintaining for seven years 'the ornaments belonging to Corpus X^i pageant and the stages, receiving the Charges thereof from the farmers of the Common Marshe and the Portmen's medow, as the Bayliffs for the time being shall think meete.' Arrears were paid to J. Caldwell for his charge of ' Corpus Chr. pageant.'

In 1491 an order was made, laying down, ' Howe euery occupacion of craftsmen schuld order themselves in the goyng with their pageantes in the procession of Corpus Christi.' The list closes with the ' Friers Carmelites,' ' Friers Minors,' and ' Friers Prechors.' The subjects of the pageants are unfortunately not given. The pageant cost 45*s.* 1*d.*

In 1492 ' areres of ye Pageant ' were paid, and ' kepers of the Ornaments and utensiles of Corpus Christi appointed.'

In 1493, 1494, 1495, 1496 orders were made for the provision of the ' pageant.' In 1495 there was a grant of £3 11. 0 for it. In 1496 it was ' at the charge of such as have been used.'

In 1502 ' Corpus Christi pageant shall hereafter be observed, and a convenient artificer shall be intertained to that end, and shall have 40*s.*' Each Portman was to pay 1*s.* 4*d.*, each of the ' twenty-four ' 8*d.* ; the other 6*s.* 8*d.* to be levied. ' Noe Bayliff shall interrupt or hinder the pageant, unless by order of the great court or uppon special cause.' Collectors for the pageant were chosen.

In 1504 the ' collectors for the play of Corpus Christi ' were ' to make a free burgess for their expences at Corpus Christi play.' These collectors are again mentioned in 1505 and 1506, and in the latter year ' ornaments ' and ' stageing for Corpus Christi play.'

In 1509 all inhabitants are to have ' their Tabernas and attendance at the ffeast of Corpus Christi ' and ' everyone shall hold by the order of their procession, according to the Constitutions.'

In 1511 a contribution is ordered to a pageant of St. George, and the Corpus Christi dinner and pageant are laid aside.

From 1513 to 1519 the play is ordered to be laid aside in every year except 1517. In 1520 it ' shall hold this yere,' and the pageant is ordered to be ready. It is laid aside in 1521 until further order, and the master of the pageant called ' the shipp ' is to have the same ready under forfeiture of £10. It is ' deferred ' in 1522 and ' laid aside for ever ' in 1531.

Probably it was never revived. But there is an order for the procession with the Sacrament in 1540, and in 1542 this had its 'pageants' to which each householder was rated at 1*d.*

In 1552 the guild is held on the Sunday after Trinity Sunday, and similar meetings continue until 1644.

On a possible performance of Bale's *King John* at the visit of Elizabeth to Ipswich in 1561 see *Texts* (iii), s. v. *Bale.*

IXWORTH, SUFFOLK.

Thetford Priory made a payment 'in regard to Ixworth play,' in 1507-8 (Appendix E, iii).

KELVEDON, ESSEX.

See s.v. EASTERFORD.

KENDAL, WESTMORELAND.

The 'Boke of Record,' a municipal register begun at the incorporation in 1575, refers to the Corpus Christi play by the crafts as established at that date. On Feb. 14, 1575, the corporation forbade feasts of more than twelve guests ;

'Such lyke ... as have bene comonlye used at ... metyings of men off Occupacyons aboute orders for their severall pagiands off Corpus xpi playe ... exceptyd and reserved.'

An order 'ffor the playe' of Sept. 22, 1586, forbade the alderman to give permission for the acting of the play in any year without the consent of his brethren[1].'

The plays lasted into the seventeenth century. Thomas Heywood says in 1612, that, 'to this day,' Kendall holds the privilege of its fairs and other charters by yearly stage-plays[2]. And Weever, about 1631, speaks of—

'Corpus Christi play in my countrey, which I have seene acted at Preston, and Lancaster, and last of all at Kendall, in the beginning of the raigne of King James; for which the Townesmen were sore troubled; and upon good reasons the Play finally suppresst, not onely there, but in all other Townes of the Kingdome[3].'

In the MS. life of the Puritan vicar of Rotherham, John Shaw, is a description of how he spoke to an old man at Cartmel of salvation by Christ :—

'Oh Sir,' said he, 'I think I heard of that man you speak of once in a play at Kendall, called Corpus Christ's play, where there was a man

---

[1] R. S. Ferguson, *A Boke of Record ... of Kirkbie Kendall* (Cumb. and Westm. Arch. and Ant. Soc.), 91, 136.

[2] See s. v. Manningtree.

[3] Weever, *Funeral Monuments,* 405.

on a tree, and blood ran down, &c. And afterwards he professed he could not remember that he ever heard of salvation by Jesus, but in that play [1].'

KENNINGHALL, NORFOLK.

'Kenningale game' was at Harling (q.v.) in 1463, and the 'Kenyngale players' in 1467.

KILKENNY, IRELAND.

John Bale, in his description of his brief episcopate of Ossory, gives an account of the proclamation of Queen Mary, at Kilkenny, on August 20, 1553, 'The yonge men, in the Forenone, played a Tragedye of God's Promyses in the olde Lawe, at the Market Crosse, with Organe, Plainges, and Songes very aptely. In the Afternone agayne they played a Commedie of Sanct Johan Baptistes Preachinges, of Christes Baptisynge, and of his Temptacion in the Wildernesse, to the small contentacion of the Prestes and other Papistes there [2].'

These plays are extant; cf. *Texts* (iii), s.v. *Bale.*

KING'S LYNN, NORFOLK.

There was a Corpus Christi guild as early as 1400, and the Tailors' *Ordinances* of 1449 require them to take part in the Corpus Christi procession; but I do not find evidence of regular annual plays. The Chamberlains' Accounts for 1385, however, include:—

'iij[s] iiij[d] to certain players, playing an interlude on Corpus Christi day.'

'iij[s] iiij[d] paid by the Mayor's gift to persons playing the interlude of St. Thomas the Martyr.'

And those for 1462—

'iij[s] paid for two flagons of red wine, spent in the house of Arnulph Tixonye, by the Mayor and most of his brethren, being there to see a certain play at the Feast of Corpus Christi.' In the same year the Skinners and Sailors 'of the town' received rewards 'for their labour about the procession of Corpus Christi this year [3].'

In 1409–10 Lady de Beaufort came to see a play [4].

See also s.v. MIDDLETON.

KINGSTON-ON-THAMES, SURREY.

On May 20, 1505, Henry VII made a payment

'To the Players of Kingeston toward the bilding of the churche steple, in almasse, iij[s] iiij[d] [5].'

---

[1] I. Disraeli, *Curiosities of Literature,* Second Series, iii. 343.

[2] Bale, *Vocacyon to Ossory* (1553), in *Harleian Miscellany* (ed. 1745), vi. 402; (ed. 1808), i. 345.

[3] *Hist. MSS.* xi. 3. 165, 223, 224. The original documents appear to be in Latin.

[4] Harrod, *King's Lynn Records,* 87.

[5] Cf. Appendix E (viii).

The churchwardens' accounts for 1505-6 include

'That we, Adam Backhous and Harry Nycol, amountyd of a play, 4^{li}.'

A few later items relate to plays at Easter.

'1513-4. For thred for the resurrection, j^d.

> For 3 yards of dorneck for a player's cote, and the makyng, xv^d.

1520-1. Paid for a skin of parchment and gunpowder for the play on Ester-day, viij^d.

> For bred and ale for them that made the stage and other thinges belonginge to the play, j^s ij^d.

1565. Rec^d. of the players of the stage at Easter, j^s ij^d ob.[1]'

LANCASTER.

A Corpus Christi play was acted within the lifetime of Weever, who was born 1576, and wrote 1631 [2].

LANCHIRE (?), ESSEX.

'Somers of Lanchire' hired the Chelmsford (q.v.) wardrobe in 1566. But I can find no such place.

LANGLEY, OXFORDSHIRE.

See s. v. SHIPTON.

LAVENHAM, SUFFOLK.

The Earl of Surrey rewarded the players of 'Lanam' on Jan. 8, 1492 (Appendix F., vii).

LECONFIELD, YORKSHIRE.

The list of customary rewards given by the fifth Earl of Northumberland to his servants, drawn up †1522, includes :—

'Them of his Lordschipes Chapell if they doo play the Play of the Nativite uppon Cristynmes-Day in the mornynge in my Lords Chapell befor his Lordship, xx^s.

... Them of his Lordship Chappell and other, if they doo play the play of Resurrection upon Esturday in the morning in my Lords Chapell, xx^s [3].'

LEEDS, YORKSHIRE.

Ten Brink, ii. 256, says that Leeds formed a centre 'for the art of the cyclic plays, which were represented yearly'; and Ward, i. 55,

---

[1] Lysons, *Environs of London*, i. 229.

[2] See s. v. Kendal.

[3] Percy, *N.H.B.* 343, 345.

that at Leeds 'the religious drama was assiduously cultivated by the citizens.' I cannot find any authority for this, and can only suggest that it is a misapprehension of an entry in the *Catalogue* of Ralph Thoresby's manuscripts appended to his *Ducatus Leodensis* (1715), 517. This was copied by Sharp, 141. But it refers to the *York Plays*, then in Thoresby's possession.

LEICESTER.

The Hall book of the Corporation contains the following entries :—

1477, March 26. 'The pleyers the which pleed the passion play the yere next afore brought yne a byll the whiche was of serten devties of mony and whed^r the passion shulbe put to crafts to be bounden or nay. And at y^t tyme the seid pleyers gaff to the pachents y^r mony which that thei had getten yn playng of the seid play euer fore to that day and all y^r Rayments w^h al oth^r maner of stuff y^t they had at that tyme. And at the same Common Halle be the advyse of all the Comons was chosen thies persones after named for to have the gydyng and Rule of the said play' [19 persons with 2 'bedalls' named] [1].

1495, Friday after xij^{te} day. 'Y^t ys ordent agreyt stabelechyd & acte for the comon well of the towne and of seche guds as ys yn a store hows in the Setterday marcat y^t ys to say wodde tymber and vdyr playyng germands yf ther be ony her hys chosyn to be ouersears thereof' [6 names] [2].

It is not clear on what day the Passion play took place. There were great processions on Whit Monday from the churches of St. Martin and St. Mary to that of St. Margaret, and in these the Twelve Apostles figured [3].

The accounts of the same churches show plays apparently distinct from the Passion play.

St. Mary's.

1491. Paid to the Players on New-year's day at even in the church, vj^d.

1499. Paid for a play in the church, in Dominica infra Octavam Epiphaniae, ij^s.

1504. Paid for mending the garment of Jesus and the cross painting, j^s iij^d.
  Paid for a pound of hemp to mend the angels heads, iiij^d.
  Paid for linen cloth for the angels heads, and Jesus hoose, making in all, ix^d.

[1] Kelly, 27, 187. M. Bateson, *Records of Leicester*, ii. 297; J. Nichols, *History of Leicestershire*, iv. i. App. 378, 9.   [2] Kelly, 188.   [3] Kelly, 7.

1507. Paid for a pound of hemp for the heads of the angels, iij^d.

Paid for painting the wings and scaff, &c., viij^d [1].

These entries suggest a *Quem quaeritis*, but perhaps only a puppet-show.

St. Martin's.

1492. Paid to the players on New-year's day at even in the church, vj^d.

1516-7. P^d, for makynge of a sworde & payntynge of the same for Harroode.

1555-6. P^d. to the iij shepperds at Whytsontyde, vj^d.

1559-60. P^d. to ye plears for ther paynes.

1561. R^d. for serten stufe lent to the players of Fosson [2].

In 1551 the Corporation came not to a feast ' because of the play that was in the church [3].'

LICHFIELD, STAFFORDSHIRE.

The Cathedral Statutes of Bishop Hugh de Nonant (1188-98) provide for the *Pastores* at Christmas and the *Quem quaeritis* and *Peregrini* at Easter.

' Item in nocte Natalis representacio pastorum fieri consueuit et in diluculo Paschae representacio Resurreccionis dominicae et representacio peregrinorum die lunae in septimana Paschae sicut in libris super hijs ac alijs compositis continetur.'

Similarly in the account of the *officium* of the *Succentor* it is provided:

' Et prouidere debet quod representacio pastorum in nocte Natalis domini et miraculorum in nocte Paschae et die lunae in Pascha congrue et honorifice fiant [4].'

LINCOLN.

About 1244 Bishop Grosseteste names ' miracula' amongst other ' ludi' which the archdeacons, so far as possible, are to exterminate in the diocese [5].

Chapter *computi* for 1406, 1452, and 1531 include entries of payments, 'In serothecis emptis pro Maria et Angelo et Prophetis ex consuetudine in Aurora Natalis Dñi hoc anno [6].'

' In 1420 tithes to the amount of 8^s 8^d were assigned to Thomas Chamberleyn for getting up a spectacle or pageant (" cuiusdam ex-

---

[1] Kelly, 14, 16.
[2] Kelly, 15, 18, 19, 20; T. North, *Accounts of Churchwardens of St. Martin's*, 2, 21, 74, 86, 87.
[3] Kelly, 193.

[4] *Lincoln Statutes*, ii. 15, 23.
[5] Cf. vol. i. p. 91.
[6] Wordsworth, 126, and in *Lincoln Statutes*, ii. lv. The entry given for 1452 in the latter omits ' et Prophetis.'

cellentis visus ") called *Rubum quem viderat* at Christmas . . . An anthem sung at Lauds on New Year's day . . . begins thus [1]' (cf. *Sarum Breviary*, ccxciii). Was this spectacle a Moses play forming part of, or detached from, an *Ordo Prophetarum*?

A set of local annals (1361–1515) compiled in the sixteenth century records the following plays :—

1397–8. Ludus de Pater Noster lvi anno.
1410–11. Ludus Pater Noster.
1424–5. Ludus Pater Noster.
1441–2. Ludus Sancti Laurentii.
1447–8. Ludus Sanctae Susannae.
1452–3. Ludus de Kyng Robert of Cesill.
1455–6. Ludus de Sancta Clara.
1456–7. Ludus de Pater Noster.
1471–2. Ludus Corporis Christi.
1473–4. Ludus de Corporis Christi.

Canon Rock, apparently quoting the same document, also mentions a ' Ludus de Sancto Iacobo[2].'

On Dec. 13, 1521, the Corporation 'agreed that Paternoster Play shall be played this year [3].'

In 1478–80 the Chapter *Curialitates* include ' In commun' canonicorum existent' ad videndum ludum Corporis Christi in camera Iohannis Sharpe infra clausum, 17ˢ 11ᵈ [4].'

But the Corpus Christi play, although so called, would appear not to have been played upon Corpus Christi day, but to be identical with the *visus* or ' sights' of St. Anne's day (July 26). These are mentioned almost yearly in the city minute-books of the early sixteenth century, and appear to have been cyclic and processional. They certainly included Noah's Ship, the Three Kings of Cologne, the Ascension, and the Coronation of the Virgin. The Corporation ordered them to be played ; the mayor and the 'graceman,' or chief officer of the guild of Saint Anne, directed them ; the guild priest gave his assistance in the preparations. In 1517 Sir Robert Denyer was appointed on condition of doing this. Garments were often borrowed from the priory and the local magnates. In 1521 Lady Powys lent a gown for one of the Maries, and the other had a crimson gown of velvet belonging to the guild. Each craft was bound under penalty to provide a pageant. In 1540 some of the crafts had broken their

---

[1] Wordsworth, 126.
[2] A. F. Leach, in *Furnivall Miscellany*, 223 ; Rock, ii. 430.
[3] Leach, loc. cit. 224.
[4] Wordsworth, 139.

pageants and were ordered to restore them. In the same year a large door was made at the late school-house that the pageants might be sent in, and 4d. was charged for housing every pageant, 'and Noy schippe 12d.' In 1547 the valuables of the procession were sold, but the 'gear' (i.e. the theatrical properties) still existed in 1569. During the Marian reaction in 1554 and 1555 'it was ordered that St. Anne's Gild with Corpus Christi Play shall be brought forth and played this year[1].'

The friendly relations of the Cathedral Chapter to the civic play are noteworthy. In 1469 the chapter paid the expenses of the *visus* of the Assumption given on St. Anne's day in the nave of the church. In 1483 it was similarly agreed to have 'Ludum, sive Serimonium, de Coronatione, sive Assumptione, beatae Mariae, prout consuetum fuerat, in navi dictae Ecclesiae.' This was to be played and shown in the procession to be made by the citizens on St. Anne's day. Apparently the crafts played the earlier plays of the cycle during the progress of the St. Anne's procession through the streets, and the Chapter gave the Assumption as a finale to the whole in the cathedral itself. But their interest extended beyond their own *visus*. In 1488 Robert Clarke received an appointment, because 'he is so ingenious in the show and play called the Ascension, given every year on St. Anne's Day[2].'

Under Elizabeth a new play appears. In 1564 the Corporation ordered 'that a standing [i.e. non-processional?] play of some story of the Bible shall be played two days this summertime.' The subject chosen was Tobias, and the place the Broadgate. Some of the properties, e.g. 'Hell mouth, with a nether chap,' were possibly the old 'gear' of St. Anne's guild. In 1567 'the stage-play of the story of Toby' was again played at Whitsuntide[3].

LITTLE BADDOW, ESSEX.

Little Baddow men hired the Chelmsford (q.v.) wardrobe during 1564–6.

LONDON.

William Fitzstephen (†1170–82), in a description of London prefatory to his *Vita* of St. Thomas à Becket, says:—

'Lundonia pro spectaculis theatralibus, pro ludis scenicis, ludos habet

[1] Leach, loc. cit. 224; *Lincoln Statutes*, ii. ccliv; *Hist. MSS.* xiv. 8. 25.
[2] Wordsworth, 141; Leach, loc. cit. 223, from *Chapter Act Book*, A. 31, f. 18; *Shaks. Soc. Papers*, iii. 40, from copy of same document in *Harl. MS.*

6954, p. 152. The latter has 'Serenomium' (for Ceremonium). Mr. Leach reads 'Sermonium' and translates 'speech.'
[3] Leach, loc. cit. 227; *Gentleman's Magazine*, liv. 103.

sanctiores, representationes miraculorum quae sancti confessores operati sunt, seu representationes passionum quibus claruit constantia martyrum[1].'

Nothing more is heard of plays in London until 1378, when the scholars of St. Paul's petitioned Richard II,

' to prohibit some unexpert people from representing the History of the Old Testament, to the great prejudice of the said Clergy, who have been at great expence in order to represent it publickly at Christmas[2].'

The chronicler Malvern records that in 1384,—

' Vicesimo nono die Augusti clerici Londoniae apud Skynnereswelle fecerunt quendam ludum valde sumptuosum, duravitque quinque diebus[3].'

In 1391 Malvern again records,—

' Item xviij⁰ die Iulii clerici Londonienses fecerunt ludum satis curiosum apud Skynnereswell per dies quatuor duraturum, in quo tam vetus quam novum testamentum oculariter ludendo monstrabant[4].'

In 1393, according to the *London Chronicle*, 'was the pley of seynt Katerine[5].'

Other chronicles record a play in 1409 :—

' This yere was the play at Skynners Welle, whiche endured Wednesday, Thorsday, Friday, and on Soneday it was ended[6].'

The accounts of the royal wardrobe show that a scaffold of timber was built for the King (Henry IV), prince, barons, knights, and ladies on this occasion, and that the play showed,—

' how God created Heaven and Earth out of nothing, and how he created Adam and so on to the Day of Judgment[7].'

Finally, the Grey Friars Chronicle mentions a yet longer play in 1411 :—

---

[1] J. C. Robertson, *Materials for the Hist. of Becket* (R. S.), iii. 9.

[2] Dodsley, *Collection of Old Plays* (1744), i. xii. I cannot trace the original authority.

[3] Malvern, *Continuator* to Higden's *Polychronicon* (ed. J. R. Lumby in R.S.), ix. 47.

[4] Malvern, loc. cit. ix. 259. Probably this is the play for which the Issue Roll of the Exchequer for Easter—Michaelmas, 1391 (F. Devon, *Issues of the Exchequer, Hen. III–Hen. VI*, 244), records on July 11, 1391, a payment 'to the Clerkes of the Parish Churches and to divers other clerkes of the City of London, in money paid to them in discharge of £10 which the Lord and King commanded

to be paid them of his gift on account of the play of the Passion of our Lord and the Creation of the World by them performed at Skynner Well, after the Feast of Bartholomew last past.' But the dates do not quite agree, and there may have been a play at Bartholomewtide 1390 as well as that of July, 1391.

[5] *London Chronicle*, 80.

[6] *London Chronicle*, 91. The *Cott. MS.* reads ' Clerkenwelle' for the ' Skynners Welle' of the *Harl. MS. Gregory's Chronicle* (*Hist. Coll. of a Citizen of London*, Camden Soc.), 105, also mentions 'the grette playe at Skynners Welle' in 1409.

[7] J. H. Wylie, *Hist. of Henry IV*, iv. 213.

'This year beganne a gret pley from the begynnyng of the worlde at the skynners' welle, that lastyd vij dayes contynually; and there ware the moste parte of the lordes and gentylles of Ynglond[1].'

The performers in most, if not all, of this group of plays were the clerks in minor orders who naturally abounded in London. The Guild of St. Nicholas of Parish Clerks had existed since 1233. In 1442 they received a charter, which refers to 'diversis charitatis et pietatis operibus per ipsos annuatim exhibitis et inventis[2].' These *opera* possibly include the plays, which may have become annual between 1411 and 1442. They seem to have been given at various times of year, and hard by the well, variously described as Skinners Well or Clerkenwell. The Priory of St. Bartholomew is not far, and the plays may have had some connexion, at one time or another, with the famous Bartholomew Fair[3]. It was probably the double name of the well that led Stowe to say that 'the skinners of London held there certain plays yearly, played of Holy Scripture[4].'

There is another gap of a century in the history of these greater London plays. But on July 20, 1498, Henry VII rewarded 'the pleyers of London' (Appendix E, viii), and of 1508 the annalist of Henry VII, Bernard Andrew, says :—

'Spectacula vero natalis divi Iohannis vespere longe praeclarissima hoc anno ostensa fuerunt, quemadmodum superioris mensis huiusque aliquot festis diebus pone Christi ecclesiam circa urbis pomaria divinae recitatae fuere historiae[5].'

Some of the London churches had their own plays, as may be seen from their churchwardens' accounts. Those of St. Margaret's, South-wark, have the following entries :—

'1444–5. Peid for a play vpon Seynt Lucy day [Dec. 13], and for a pley vpon Seynt Margrete day [July 20], xiij⁸ iiij^d.

1445–6. [Similar entry.]

1447–8. Also peid for a pley vpon Seynt Margrete day, vij⁸.

1449–50. Item, peyd vpon Seynt Lucy day to the Clerkes for a play, vj⁸ viij^d.

1450–1. [Similar entry.]

1451–2. Fyrste, peyd to the Pleyrs vpon Seynt Margretes day, vij⁸.

---

[1] J. G. Nichols, *Grey Friars Chronicle* (Camden Soc.), 12 ; R. Howlett, *Monumenta Franciscana* (R.S.), ii. 164.
[2] J. Christie, *Some Account of Parish Clerks*, 24, 71.

[3] H. Morley, *Memoirs of Bartholomew Fair*, 15.
[4] Stowe, *Survey*, 7.
[5] Andrew, *Annales Henr. VII* (R.S.), 121.

Also peyd for hyryng of Germentes xiiij^d.

1453–7 and 1459 [a play on St. Margaret's day in each year [1]].'

Towards the end of Henry VIII's reign the Revels office was able to borrow 'frames for pageants' from the wardens of St. Sepulchre's[2]. Probably the guild of Parish Clerks made it a profession to supply such church plays as these for a regular fee. They were employed also at the feasts of the city guilds. The Brewers, for instance, had plays in 1425 and 1433, and in 1435 paid '4 clerkis of London, for a play[3].' The Carpenters paid iiij^s iiij^d for a play in 1490[4]. London players occasionally performed before Henry VII. Besides 'the players of London' in 1498, he rewarded in 1501 the players at 'Myles ende[5].'

Attempts were made to revive religious plays during the Marian reaction. On June 7, 1557, 'be-gane a stage play at the Grey freers of the Passyon of Cryst[6].' On St. Olave's day, July 29, in the same year 'was the church holiday in Silver street; and at eight of the clock at night began a stage play of a goodly matter, that continued until xij at mydnyght, and then they mad an end with a good song[7].'

The last such play in London was 'the acting of Christ's Passion at Elie house in Holborne when Gundemore [Gondomar] lay there, on Good-Friday at night, at which there were thousands present[8].' This would be between 1613 and 1622.

Midsummer Watch.

A 'marching watch' was kept on the eves of Midsummer and SS. Peter and Paul (June 29) until 1538, and revived, for one year only, in 1548. Some 2,000 men went in armour; lamps and bonfires were lit in the streets, and 'every man's door shadowed with green birch, long fennel, St. John's wort; orpine, white lilies and such like, garnished upon with garlands of beautiful flowers.' It seems to have been customary for the guilds to which the Lord Mayor and Sheriffs for the year belonged to furnish pageants. Stowe says that 'where the mayor had besides his giant three pageants, each of the sheriffs had besides their giants but two pageants, each their morris dance.' In

[1] Collier, in *Shakesp. Soc. Papers*, iii. 40. The 'pagents' on a roll of vellum belonging to the Holy Trinity Guild in St. Botolph's, Bishopsgate (†1463), were probably only paintings with descriptive verses (Hone, 81).

[2] Kempe, 71. The date given, Shrovetide, 38 Hen. VIII, must be wrong, as the king died before Shrovetide (Feb. 20–2) in the thirty-eighth year of his reign.

[3] Herbert, *Hist. of Livery Companies*, i. 80.

[4] E. B. Jupp, *Hist. of Carpenters' Company*, 198.

[5] Collier, i. 51.

[6] Machyn, 138.

[7] Machyn, 145.

[8] Prynne, 117.

1505 the Grocers had 'a pageant for the maire [Sir John Wyngar] at Midsomer.' In 1510 Henry VIII, disguised as a groom, came to see the Midsummer Watch, and on St. Peter's eve came openly with the queen. There were 'diverse goodlie shewes, as had beene accustomed.' In 1522 the Drapers resolved 'that there shall be no Mydsom^r pageant becaus there was so many pageants redy standyng for the Emperors coming into London,' and 'for divers considerations' to 'surcease the said pageants and find xxx men in harness instead.' But later they decided to 'renew all the old pageants for the house; including our newe pageant of the Goldyn Flees for the mayr against mydsom^r; also the gyant, lord Moryspyks, and a morys daunce, as was used the last year.' The account-books mention Lord Moryspyks or 'Marlingspikes,' and a 'king of the Moors,' with a 'stage' and 'wyld fire.' In 1523, the King of Denmark being in London, the Drapers allowed the Sheriff two pageants, 'but to be no precedent hereafter.' They paid 'for garnyshyng and newe repayring of th' Assumpcion, and also for making a new pageant of St. Ursula.' The King of Denmark was duly brought to see the watch. In 1524 they again had a pageant, the nature of which is not specified [1].

LOPHAM, NORFOLK.

'Lopham game' was at Harling (q. v.) in 1457.

LOUTH, LINCOLNSHIRE.

An inventory of documents in the rood-loft in 1516 includes the 'hole Regenall of corpus xr̄i play.' In 1558 the corporation paid for a play 'in the markit-stede on corpus xr̄i day.'

LYDD, KENT.

The town accounts show a play of St. George on July 4, 1456, and payment to the 'bane cryars' of 'our play' in 1468. In 1422 the Lydd players acted at New Romney, and in 1490 the chaplain of the guild of St. George at New Romney went to see a play at Lydd, with a view to reproducing it. Between 1429 and 1490 the New Romney players acted often at Lydd, and also players of Ruckinge (1431), Wytesham (1441), Ham (1454), Hythe (1467), Folkestone (1479), Rye (1480), Stone (1490). Unnamed players were in the high street in 1485 [3].

LYNEHAM, OXFORDSHIRE.

See s. v. SHIPTON.

---

[1] Stowe, *Annales*, 489; *Survey*, 38; Herbert, i. 197, 454; Brand-Ellis, i. 166.

[2] R. W. Goulding, *Louth Records*.
[3] *Hist. MSS.* v. 517.

MALDEN, ESSEX.

The Chelmsford (q. v.) play was shown at Malden in 1562.

MANNINGTREE, ESSEX.

John Manningham, of the Middle Temple, wrote in his Diary, on Feb. 8, 1602, 'The towne of Manitree in Essex holds by stage plays [1].' So Heywood, in his *Apology for Actors* (1612), ' To this day there be townes that hold the priviledge of their fairs and other charters by yearly stage-plays, as at Manningtree in Suffolke, Kendall in the North, and others [2].' There are further allusions to these plays in T. Nash, *The Choosing of Valentines*,

'a play of strange moralitie,
Showen by bachelrie of Manning-tree,
Whereto the countrie franklins flock-meale swarme [3] ';

and in Dekker, *Seven Deadly Sins of London* (1607), ' Cruelty has got another part to play ; it is acted like the old morals at Manning-tree [4].'

MAXSTOKE, WARWICKSHIRE.

The accounts of Maxstoke Priory (a house of Augustinian canons) for 1430 include, 'pro ientaculis puerorum eleemosynae exeuntium ad aulam in castro ut ibi ludum peragerent in die Purificationis, xiv[d]. Unde nihil a domini [Clinton] thesaurario, quia saepius hoc anno ministralli castri fecerunt ministralsiam in aula conventus et Prioris ad festa plurima sine ullo regardo [5].'

MIDDLETON, NORFOLK.

In 1444 the corporation of Lynn (q. v.) showed a play with Mary and Gabriel before Lord Scales [6].

MILDENHALL, SUFFOLK.

Thetford Priory made a payment to ' the play of Mydenale ' in 1503–4 (Appendix E, iii).

MILE END, MIDDLESEX.

Henry VII rewarded ' the Pleyers at Myles End ' on Aug. 6, 1501 (Appendix E, viii).

MILTON, OXFORDSHIRE.

See s. v. SHIPTON.

MOREBATH, DEVONSHIRE.

The churchwardens' accounts record an Easter play at some date between 1520 and 1574 [7].

---

[1] *Manningham's Diary* (Camden Soc.), 130.
[2] Heywood, *Apology for Actors* (Shakespeare Soc.), 61.
[3] Quoted in *Variorum*, xvi. 295.
[4] Dekker's *Plays* (ed. Pearson).
[5] Hazlitt-Warton, iii. 312.
[6] Harrod, *King's Lynn Records*, 88.
[7] W. Hobhouse, *Churchwardens' Accounts* (Somerset Record Soc.), 209.

NAYLAND, ESSEX.

Richard More, of Nayland, hired the Chelmsford (q.v.) wardrobe in 1566.

NEWCASTLE-ON-TYNE, NORTHUMBERLAND.

The craft-plays on Corpus Christi day are mentioned in several fifteenth-century ordinaries, the earliest being that of the Coopers in 142⁶₇. The last years in which performances can be proved to have been given are 1561 and 1562. Ordinaries dated from 1578 to 1589 stipulate for a performance by the crafts 'whensoever the generall plaies of the town of Newcastle, antiently called the Corpus Christi plays, shall be plaied,' or the like. The determination of this point rested with the Corporation. The Goldsmiths drew up an 'invoic of all the players apperell pertainyng to' them in 159⁰₉. The cost of the plays fell on the crafts, who took fixed contributions from their members. The Taylors in 1536 required iij^d from each hireling, and vij^d from each newly admitted member. The Fullers and Dyers paid 9s. in 1561 for 'the play lettine' to four persons.

The mentions of 'bearers of the care and baneres' of them 'that wated of the paient' and of 'the carynge of the trowt and wyn about the town' seem to show that the plays were processional. On the other hand the one extant play (cf. p. 424) ends with a remark of the *Diabolus* to 'All that is gathered in this stead.' Perhaps the pageants first took part in the Corpus Christi procession proper and afterwards gathered in a field. The Mercers' ordinary of 1480 shows that the procession was 'by vij in morning,' and the plays were certainly in the evening, for it was deposed in a law-suit at Durham in 1569 that Sir Robert Brandling of Newcastle said on Corpus Christi day, 1562, that 'he would after his dinner draw his will, and after the plays would send for his consell, and make it up' (*Norfolk Archaeology*, iii. 18).

For the list of plays, so far as it can be recovered, see p. 424. The ordinary of the Goldsmiths (1536) requires their play (Kynges of Coleyn) to be given at their feast[1].

NEW ROMNEY, KENT.

There are many notices of a play in the town accounts between 1428 and 1560. In 1456 the wardens of the play of the *Resurrection* are mentioned. In 1463 the jurats paid Agnes Ford 6s. 8d. 'for the

---

[1] F. Holthausen, *Das Noahspiel von N. upon T.* (1897), 11; H. Bourne, *Hist. of N.* (1736), 139; J. Brand, *Hist. of N.* (1789), ii. 369; E. Mackenzie, *Hist. of N.* (1827), ii. 664, 707; F. W. Dendy, *Newcastle Gilds* (Surtees Soc.), i. 4; ii. 161, 164, 171.

play of the Interlude of our *Lord's Passion.*' From 1474 the banns of the play are mentioned. In 1477 the play was on Whit-Tuesday. In 1518 the Lord Warden of the Cinque Ports forbade the play, but it was revived elaborately in 1560. The accounts mention the purchase of copes and vestures from the corporation of Lydd, and refer to 'a fool,' 'the Cytye of Samarye,' 'our last play,' 'the iij^th play,' 'the iiij^th play,' and the 'bane cryers.' No crafts are mentioned : perhaps the play was produced by the corporation itself. The performances may have been on Crockhill or Crockley Green. 'Playstool' is a common name for a bit of land in Kent. Performances were often given in other towns: see s.v. LYDD. The play seems to have been only a *Passion* and *Resurrection* play, and not a complete cycle. 'Le Playboke' is mentioned from 1516. It is in an Elizabethan inventory of town records. A second play of *St. George* was probably started in 1490 when a chaplain of the guild of St. George went to see the Lydd *St. George* play, with a view to reproducing it. In 1497 the chaplains received the profits of the play. Players from the following towns are found acting at New Romney : Hythe (1399), Lydd (1422), Wittersham (1426, they 'shewed th' interlude'), Herne (1429), Ruckinge (1430), Folkestone (1474), Appledore (1488), Chart (1489), Rye (1489), Wye (1491), Brookland (1494), Halden (1499), Bethersden (1508) [1].

NORTHAMPTON, NORTHAMPTONSHIRE.

Brotanek (*Anglia*, xxi. 21) conjectures that the *Abraham and Isaac* of the Dublin MS. may come from Northampton (cf. p. 427), and hints at an explanation of the 'N. towne' in the prologue to the *Ludus Coventriae* as 'N[orthampton] towne' (cf. p. 421).

But the only allusion even remotely suggesting miracle-plays that I can find in the printed civic records is in 1581, in which year some interrogatories as to St. George's Hall contain a deposition by an old man to the effect that he had known the hall fifty years, and that the mayor and chamberlains had been wont to lay therein pageants, &c.[2]

NORWICH, NORFOLK.

Whitsun Plays.

J. Whetley writes from Norwich on Corpus Christi even (May 20), 1478, to Sir John Paston in London, of a visit of Lord Suffolk to Hellesden, 'at hys beyng ther that daye ther was never no man that

---

[1] W. A. Scott-Robertson, *The Passion Play and Interludes at New Romney* (*Archaeologia Cantiana*, xiii. 216); *Hist. MSS.* v. 533 ; *Arch. Cantiana*, xvii. 28.
[2] C. A. Markham and J. C. Cox, *Northampton Borough Records*, ii. 184.

playd Herrod in Corpus Crysty play better and more agreable to hys pageaunt than he dud [1].'

I do not know whether it is fair to infer from this that in 1478 the Norwich plays were not at Whitsuntide, but at Corpus Christi; but this would account for J. Whetley's trope.

On Sept. 21, 1527, the guild of St. Luke, composed of painters, braziers, plumbers, &c., made a presentment to the Assembly of the town that,—

'where of longtime paste the said Guylde of Seynt Luke yerly till nowe hath ben used to be kept and holden within the citie aforesaid upon the Mundaye in pentecoste weke at which daye and the daye next ensuyng many and divers disgisyngs and pageaunts, as well of the lieffs and martyrdoms of divers and many hooly Saynts, as also many other light and feyned figurs and picturs of other persones and bests; the sight of which disgisings and pageaunts, as well yerly on the said Mondaye in pentecoste weke in the time of procession then goyng about a grett circuitte of the forsaid citie, as yerly the Tuysday in the same weke [serving] the lord named the Lord of Misrule at Tumlond within the same citie, hath ben and yet is sore coveted, specially by the people of the countre.'

The presentment goes on to show that much resort and profit have accrued to the city, but all the cost has fallen on the guild, which 'is almost fully decayed'; and urges an order,—

'that every occupacion wythyn the seyd Citye maye yerly at the said procession upon the Mondaye in Pentecost weke sette forth one pageaunt.'

It was agreed that each craft should play,—

'one such pageaunt as shalbe assigned and appoynted by Master Mair and his brethern aldermen, as more playnly appereth in a boke thereof made.'

In the same hand is a list of crafts and plays (cf. p. 425) [2].

Some extracts made in the eighteenth century from the, now lost, books of the Grocers' Company, contain (a) two versions of their play on *The Fall*, dating from 1533 and 1565 respectively (cf. p. 425), and (b) various notices of the same from the Assembly Book.

The latter begin in 1534, when '4 Surveyors of yᵉ Pageant' with a 'Bedell' were chosen, and an assessment of 22s. 10d. made for the pageant and the Corpus Christi procession. The expenses include, besides repairs to the pageant, fees to actors, refreshments, &c.,—

[1] *Paston Letters*, iii. 227.
[2] H. Harrod, *Particulars concerning* *Early Norwich Pageants* (*Norfolk Archaeology*, iii. 3).

'It. to Sr Stephen Prowet for makyng of a newe ballet, 12^d.

House ferme for ye Pageant, 2^s.'

The pageant went in 1535 and 1536. In 1537 it 'went not at Wytsontyde,' but went in October 'in ye Processyon for ye Byrthe of Prynce Edward.' From 1538 to 1546 it went, the assessment for pageant and procession being about 20s. to 30s. As to 1547 the record is not clear. Then there is a gap in the extracts, and from 1556 onwards the 'Gryffon,' 'Angell,' and 'Pendon' of the Corpus Christi procession, with flowers, grocery, and fruit 'to garnish ye tre wth,' &c., appear alone in the accounts. In 1559 was 'no solemnite' at all. In 1563 it was agreed that the pageant should be 'preparyd ageynst ye daye of Mr Davy his takyng of his charge of ye Mayralltye,' with a 'devyce' to be prepared by the surveyors at a cost of 6s. 8d. The play cannot have quite lapsed, for in 1565 a new version was written (cf. p. 425). It was apparently contemplated that it might be played either alone or in a cycle. To the same year belongs the following

'*Inventory of ye p'ticulars appartaynyng to ye Company of ye Grocers, a.d. 1565.*

A Pageant, y^t is to saye, a Howse of Waynskott paynted and buylded on a Carte w^t fowre whelys.

A square topp to sett over ye sayde Howse.

A Gryffon, gylte, w^t a fane to sette on ye sayde toppe.

A bygger Iron fane to sett on ye ende of ye Pageante.

iiij^{xx} iij small Fanes belongyng to ye same Pageante.

A Rybbe colleryd Red.

A cote & hosen w^t a bagg & capp for dolo^r, steyned.

2 cotes & a payre hosen for Eve, stayned.

A cote & hosen for Adam, Steyned.

A cote w^t hosen & tayle for ye serpente, steyned, w^t a w^t heare.

A cote of yellow buckram w^t ye Grocers' arms for ye Pendon bearer.

An Angell's Cote & over hoses of Apis Skynns.

3 paynted clothes to hang abowte ye Pageant.

A face & heare for ye Father.

2 hearys for Adam & Eve.

4 head stallis of brode Inkle wth knopps & tassells.

6 Horsse Clothes, stayned, w^t knopps & tassells.

Item, Weights, &c.'

There is a final memorandum that in 1570 the pageant was broken to pieces for six years 'howse ferm' due. There had been no 'semblye nor metynge' of the Company for eight years. The pageant had stood for six years in a 'Gate howse,' and then 'at ye Black Fryers brydge in open strete,' where it became 'so weather beaten, y^t ye cheife parte was rotton[1].'

Processions.

There were three notable annual processions at Norwich.

(a) The *Corpus Christi* Procession, in which the crafts were held to take part in 1489, and which appears, as above stated, in the Grocers' records until 1558. They seem to have been represented by the 'griffon' from the top of their pageant, a banner with their arms, a crowned angel, and an emblematic 'tree' of fruit and grocery (possibly the 'tree of knowledge')[2].

(b) The Procession of the Guild of *S. Thomas à Becket* on the day of his Translation (July 7) to his chapel in the wood. Here interludes were played[3].

(c) The Riding of the Guild of *St. George* on his day (April 23). This dates from at least 1408, and a good many details as to it are preserved[4].

NUNEATON, WARWICKSHIRE.

The 'lusores de Eaton' played at Maxstoke Priory between 1422 and 1461 (Appendix E, ii).

OXFORD, OXFORDSHIRE.

The following extracts from the Bursars' *computi* of Magdalen College point to a *Quem quaeritis* of the longer type, with the 'Noli me tangere' episode.

1486–7. 'pro factura sepulturae erga pascham. xij^d.'

1506–7. 'pro scriptura lusi' of St. Mary Magdalen. x^d.'

[There were further payments in connexion with this play, and for music.]

1509–10. 'pro pane, cibo et aliis datis pueris ludentibus in die Paschae . . . xvij^d ob.'

1514–5. 'pro carnibus consumptis in capella tribus noctibus ante Pascha et in tempore Nativitatis. ij^s.'

1518–9. 'pro tinctura et factura tunicae eius qui ageret partem Christi et pro crinibus mulieribus. ij^s vj^d.'

1536–7. 'pro carbonibus consumptis in sacrario per custodes sepulchri, et per pueros in festis hiemalibus.'

[Repeated in other years.]

---

[1] R. Fitch, *Norwich Pageants : The Grocers' Play*, in *Norfolk Archaeology*, v. 8, and separately.
[2] Fitch, op. cit.; Blomfield, *Hist. of Norfolk*, iii. 176.
[3] Blomfield, iv. 426.
[4] Cf. vol. i. p. 222.

A chapel inventory of 1495 includes 'unum frontale . . . et unum dorsale cum quibus solet sepulcrum ornari.'

The same accounts (cf. p. 248) show items for plays in the hall at various seasons, and for the Boy Bishop at Christmas [1].

The churchwardens of St. Peter's in the East kept between 1444 and 1600 a stock of players' garments, and let them out on hire [2].

PENRHYN, CORNWALL.

See *Texts* (i), *Cornish Plays, Origo Mundi.*

PERRANZABULO, CORNWALL.

The earliest historical notice of plays in Cornwall is by Richard Carew in 1602 :—

'The Guary miracle, in English, a miracle-play, is a kinde of Enterlude, compiled in *Cornish* out of some Scripture history, with that grossenes which accompanied the Romanes *vetus Comoedia.* For representing it they raise an earthen Amphitheatre in some open field, hauing the Diameter of his enclosed playne some 40 or 50 foot. The Country people flock from all sides, many miles off, to hear and see it : for they haue therein, deuils and deuices, to delight as well the eye as the eare; the players conne not their parts without booke, but are prompted by one called the Ordinary, who followeth at their back with the book in his hand, and telleth them softly what they must pronounce aloud.'

Whereupon Carew has a story of a 'pleasant conceyted gentleman' who raised laughter by repeating aloud all the Ordinary's asides to himself.

One Mr. Scawen (†1660) describes the Guirremears as—

'solemnized not without shew of devotion in open and spacious downs, of great capacity, encompassed about with earthen banks, and in some part stonework of largeness to contain thousands, the shapes of which remain in many places to this day, though the use of them long since gone.'

Bp. Nicholson, writing in 1700, says that the plays were :—

'called Guirimir, which Mr Llhuyd supposes a corruption of Guari-mirkle, and in the Cornish dialect to signify a miraculous play or interlude. They were composed for begetting in the common people a right notion of the Scriptures, and were acted in the memory of some not long since deceased.'

The eighteenth-century antiquary, Borlase, identifies the places in

---

[1] Cf. Appendix E (v).
[2] W. Hobhouse, *Churchwardens' Accounts* (Somerset Record Soc.), 232.

which the miracle-plays were given with those known as 'rounds,' or, in Cornish, *plân an guare.* Of these he describes and figures two. That of St. Just was of stone, 126 feet in diameter, with seven rows of seats inside. It was much decayed when Norris wrote in 1859. That of Perranzabulo, or Piran-sand, was of earth, 130 feet in diameter, with a curious pit in the centre, joined to the outer ring by a narrow trench. Borlase thought that this was used for a Hell[1]. It was more likely filled with water for Noah's ship to float upon.

The *Ordinalia* printed by Mr. Norris take the Cornish plays back to at least the fourteenth, if not the thirteenth century. The circular diagrams in the manuscript exactly fall in with the round *plân an guare* described by Borlase and others. They show a ring of eight *loci* or *sedes* (cf. p. 83), for which the terms used in the stage-directions are *pulpita* or *tenti*, with an open circular space in the middle, which the stage-directions call the *platea.* The action is partly at the *pulpita*, partly in the *platea.* A new character often marks his appearance by strutting about his *pulpitum*, or perhaps around the ring—*Hic pompabit Abraham*, &c.

In the English stage-directions to the later (before 1611) *Creation of the World*, the *platea* becomes the *playne*, and for *pulpitum* the term *room* is used. The manager of the play is the 'conveyour.' Some of the directions are curious and minute. At the opening, 'The father must be in a clowde, and when he speakethe of heaven let yᵉ levys open.' Within is a 'trone,' which Lucifer tries to ascend. After the fight, 'Lucifer voydeth & goeth downe to hell apareled fowle wᵗʰ fyre about hem turning to hell and every degre of devylls of lether & spirytis on cordis runing into yᵉ playne and so remayne ther.' Meanwhile are got ready 'Adam and Eva aparlet in whytt lether in a place apoynted by the conveyour & not to be sene tyll they be called & thei knell & ryse.' Paradise has 'ii fayre trees in yt' and a 'fowntaine' and 'fyne flowers,' which appear suddenly. Similarly, a little later, ' Let fyshe of dyuers sortis apeare & serten beastis as oxen kyne shepe & such like.' Lucifer incarnates as 'a fyne serpent made wᵗʰ a virgyn face & yolowe heare vpon her head.' Presently comes the warning, 'ffig leaves redy to cover ther members,' and at the expulsion, 'The garmentis of skynnes to be geven to adam and eva by the angell. Receave the garmentis. Let them depart out of paradice and adam and eva following them. Let them put on the garmentis and shewe a spyndell and a dystaff.' The Cain and Abel scene requires 'a

[1] Norris, ii. 452; E. H. Pedler in Norris, ii. 507; Carew, *Survey of Cornwall*; D. Gilbert, *History of Cornwall*; Borlase, *Antiquities of Cornwall* (ed. 2), 207; *Nat. Hist. of Cornwall*, 295; T. F. Ordish, *Early London Theatres*, 15.

chawbone' ('Cain's jawbone, that did the first murder'). Seth is led
to Paradise and 'Ther he vyseth all thingis, and seeth ij trees and in
the one tree sytteth mary the virgyn & in her lappe her son jesus
in the tope of the tree of lyf, and in the other tree ye serpent w^{ch}
caused Eva to eat the appell.' When Adam dies, his soul is taken
'to lymbo,' and he is buried 'in a fayre tombe wth som churche
songis at hys buryall.' The Noah scene requires 'tooles and tymber
redy, wth planckis to make the arcke, a beam a mallet a calkyn yre[n]
ropes mass[t]es pyche and tarr.' Presently 'let rayne appeare' and
'a raven & a culver ready.' When the flood ends, 'An alter redy
veary fayre,' at which 'som good church songes' are sung, and
'a Rayne bowe to appeare.' Like the earlier plays, this ends with a
call on the minstrels to pipe for a dance.

A study of the place names in the *Ordinalia* led Mr. Pedler to
suggest that they probably belonged to the neighbourhood of Penrhyn,
and may have been composed at the collegiate house of Glasney. The
St. Meriasek play is assigned by Mr. Stokes to Camborne, of which
that saint was patron. It ends with an invocation of St. Meriasek,
St. Mary of Camborne, and the Apostles.

Preston, Lancashire.

A Corpus Christi play was acted within the lifetime of Weever, who
was born 1576 and wrote 1631 [1].

I find no trace of plays at the meetings of the Guild Merchant,
although there was always a great procession, which from 1762 or
earlier included such allegorical figures as Adam and Eve for the
Tailors, Vulcan for the Smiths, &c. [2]

Reading, Berkshire.

The churchwardens' accounts of St. Lawrence's record 'a gaderyng
of a stage-play' in 1498.

In 1507 a play of *Adam and Eve* was held on 'the Sunday afore
Bartylmastyde' 'in the Forbury.' There was a 'schapfold,' but
'pagentts' were also used. A Corpus Christi procession is also
mentioned in 1509, 1512, and 1539.

In 1512 also was the 'play of Kayme,' and in 1515, 'Cayme's
pageaunt' in the market-place.

On May 1, 1499, and again in 1539, was the *Kings of Cologne*.
This was distinct, no doubt, from the 'king play,' with its 'tree,' 'king

---

[1] See s. v. Kendal.
[2] W. A. Abram, *Memorials of the Preston Guilds*, 18, 21, 61, 99.

game,' or 'kyng ale,' which took place at Whitsuntide (cf. vol. i. p. 173). But the date, May 1 (for which cf. Abingdon), is curious for a miracle-play, and must have been influenced by the folk feast.

A payment for 'rosyn to the resurrecyon pley' (possibly for making a blaze: cf. p. 23, note 5) occurs in 1507, and in 1533–5 payments to 'Mr Laborne' 'for reforming the Resurrecon pley,' and 'for a boke' of it.

In 1508 was a 'pageaunt of the Passion on Easter Monday [1].'

RUCKINGE, KENT.

Ruckinge players were at New Romney in 1430, and Lydd in 1431.

RYE, SUSSEX.

Rye players were at Lydd in 1480, and at New Romney in 1489.

SABSFORD (?), ESSEX.

'Sabsforde men' hired the Chelmsford (q. v.) wardrobe in 1562, 1563, and 1566. But I can find no such place.

SAFFRON WALDEN, ESSEX.

'Men of Waldyne' hired the Chelmsford (q. v.) wardrobe during 1564–6.

ST. JUST, CORNWALL.

See s. v. PERRANZABULO.

SALISBURY, WILTSHIRE.

A cathedral inventory of 1222 includes :—

'Coronae ij de latone ad representationes faciendas.'

These latten 'coronae' may, I suppose, have been either crowns for the Magi, or 'stellae [2].'

The churchwardens' accounts of St. Edmund's for 1461 include an item 'for all apparel and furniture of players at the Corpus Christi [3].'

SHELFHANGER, NORFOLK.

Thetford Priory made a payment 'in regard to Schelfanger play' in 1507–8 (Appendix E, iii).

---

[1] C. Kerry, *History of St. Lawrence, Reading*, 233. Extracts only from the accounts are given; a full transcript would probably yield more information.

[2] W. H. R. Jones, *Vetus Registrum Sarisburiense* (R.S.), ii. 129.

[3] *Cal. State Papers, Dom. Addl.* (1580–1625), 101.

SHIPTON, OXFORDSHIRE.

It was decided († 1220–28), as part of an award concerning the rights of collation to the churches of Shipton and Bricklesworth, both being prebends in Sarum cathedral, as follows :—

'Actiones autem, si quae competant, in villa de Fifhide et de Idebire cedant canonico de Brikeleswrth. Actiones vero, si quae competant, in villa de Mideltone et de Langele, cedant canonico de Schiptone. Emolumentum vero actionum, si quae competant, in villa de Linham aequaliter inter se dividant[1].'

The editor of the *Sarum Charters* can only explain *actiones* as 'plays.' Ducange gives the word in the sense of *spectacula*.

All the places named, Fyfield, Idbury, Milton, Langley, and Lyneham, are in Wychwood, and may have formed in the thirteenth century, if they do not all now, part of the parish of Shipton-under-Wychwood.

SHREWSBURY, SHROPSHIRE.

The civic orders and accounts refer occasionally to plays. The first on record was given before Prince Arthur in 1495. In 1516 the abbot of Shrewsbury, in 1533 the bishop of Exeter, and in 1542 the royal commissioners were present. The subject in 1516 was the martyrdoms of Saints Feliciana and Sabina. In 1518 it was the Three Kings of Cologne. In 1510, 1518, 1533, 1553, and 1556 the performances were at Whitsuntide. The bailiffs, according to a notice in 1556, 'set forward' the plays, and the 'lusores' belonging to the town, who are mentioned in 1527 and 1549, were perhaps the performers. The locality was, in 1542, the churchyard of St. Chad's. In 1495, 1516, and 1533 it was the quarry outside the walls, where it is stated in 1570 that 'the plases have bin accustomyd to be usyd[2].' Here there were traces of a seated amphitheatre as late as 1779[3]. Thomas Ashton became master of the free school in 1561, and he produced plays in the quarry. Elizabeth was to have been at his *Julian the Apostate* in 1565, but came too late. In 1567 he gave the *Passion of Christ*[4]. An undated list of Costs for the Play includes 'a desert's (*disard's*) hed and berd,' 'vi dossen belles' for a morris, 'gonne poudor' and other attractions for a devil[5].

Shrewsbury Show.

The craft-guilds took part in the Corpus Christi procession, and

---

[1] Jones and Macray, *Salisbury Charters* (R.S.), xi, 102.
[2] Cf. Appendix E (vi).
[3] Phillips, *Hist. of Shrewsbury*, 201.
[4] Phillips, 201.
[5] Owen and Blakeway, *Hist. of Shrewsbury*, i. 328.

the guild of Mercers inflicted a penalty of 12*d.* on brethren who on that feast should 'happen to ride or goe to Coventre Faire or elleswhere out of the town of Shrewesburye to by or sell[1].' Until about 1880 Shrewsbury Show was held on the Monday after Corpus Christi day. The crafts had tableaux which, after the Reformation at least, were emblematic rather than religious[2]; thus—

Tailors. Adam and Eve or Elizabeth.	Painters. Rubens.
Shearmen. St. Blasius or Edward IV.	Bricklayers. King Henry VIII.
Skinners and Glovers. King of Morocco.	Shoemakers. SS. Crispin and Crispinian.
Smiths. Vulcan.	Barbers. St. Katharine.
	Bakers. Venus and Ceres.

SLEAFORD, LINCOLNSHIRE.

The accounts of the guild of Holy Trinity for 1480 include :—

'It. payd for the Ryginall of ye play for ye Ascencon & the wrytyng of spechys & payntyng of a garmet for god, iij^s. viij^d.[3]'

Miss Toulmin Smith finds in the same accounts for 1477, a 'kyngyng,' i. e. *Three Kings of Cologne* on Corpus Christi day[4]; but I read the entry :—

'It. payd for the ryngyng of ye same day, ij^d.'

Oliver, the historian of the guild, reads 'hymnall' for 'Ryginall' in the 1480 entry. He also asserts that there was a regular Corpus Christi play by the crafts. This seems improbable in a place of the size of Sleaford, and in fact Oliver's elaborate description is entirely based upon data from elsewhere, especially the *Gubernacio Ludi* of Beverley (cf. p. 340)[5].

STAPLEFORD, ESSEX.

'Men of Starford' hired the Chelmsford (q.v.) wardrobe during 1564–6. I find no Starford, but a Stapleford Tawney and a Stapleford Abbots in Essex.

STOKE BY NAYLAND, ESSEX.

Sir John Howard 'зafe to the pleyeres of Stoke, ij^s' on Jan. 12, 1466. Lord Howard 'paid to the pleirs of Turton Strete xx^d' on Aug. 29,

[1] *Shropshire Arch. Soc. Trans.* viii. 273.

[2] F. A. Hibbert, *Influence and Development of English Craft Guilds* (1891), 113.

[3] *Add. MS.* 28,533, ff. 1^v, 2. *Computi* from 1477 to 1545 are in this MS.; but most of them are very summary.

[4] *York Plays*, lxv.

[5] G. Oliver, *Hist. of Holy Trinity Guild at Sleaford* (1837), 50, 68, 73, 82.

1481. Thorington is still the name given to part of Stoke. There is also an independent township so named in Essex.

On May 22, 1482, Lord Howard 'yaff to the cherche on Whitson Monday at the pley x⁸.'

On Jan. 2, 1491, the Earl of Surrey paid iij⁸ iiijᵈ 'in reward to the panget' [? pageant] [1].

STONE, KENT.

Stone players were at Lydd in 1490.

TEWKESBURY, GLOUCESTERSHIRE.

The churchwardens' accounts in 1578 mention payments for 'the players' geers, six sheep-skins for Christ's garments'; and an inventory of 1585 includes 'eight heads of hair for the Apostles, and ten beards, and a face or vizier for the Devil [2].'

TINTINHULL, SOMERSET.

The churchwardens' accounts for 1451–2 include a receipt :—
'de incremento unius ludi vocati Christmasse play [3].'

WAKEFIELD, YORKSHIRE.

See *Texts* (i), *Towneley Plays*.

WIMBORNE MINSTER, DORSETSHIRE.

Players of 'Wymborne Minster' were rewarded by Henry VII on Jan. 1, 1494 (Appendix E, viii).

WINCHESTER, HAMPSHIRE.

The early use of the *Quem quaeritis* in the liturgy of the cathedral served by the Benedictines of St. Swithin's Priory has been fully discussed in Chapter xviii and Appendix O.

In 1486, Henry VII was entertained at dinner on a Sunday in the castle with a performance of *Christi descensus ad inferos* by the 'pueri eleemosynarii' of the monasteries of St. Swithin's and Hyde [4].

WINDSOR, BERKS.

On May 24, 1416, Henry V invested the Emperor Sigismund with the Garter, the annual feast being deferred from April 23 for that purpose. Mr. John Payne Collier says, 'A chronicle in the Cottonian

---

[1] Cf. Appendix E (vii).
[2] Collier, ii. 67.
[3] Hobhouse, 184.
[4] Hazlitt-Warton, iii. 163, from *Register* of St. Swithin's. This is amongst the *Wulvesey MSS.*, now in

the possession of the Ecclesiastical Commissioners (*York Plays*, lxv). The date is given as 1487 by Hazlitt-Warton, but the visit is said to be that 'on occasion of the birth of Prince Arthur,' which took place in the autumn of 1486.

collection gives a description of a performance before him and Henry V, on the incidents of the life of St. George. The representation seems to have been divided into three parts, and to have been accomplished by certain artificial contrivances, exhibiting, first, "the armyng of Seint George, and an Angel doyng on his spores [spurs]"; secondly, "Seint George riding and fightyng with the dragon, with his spere in his hand"; and, thirdly, "a castel, and Seint George and the Kynges daughter ledyng the lambe in at the castel gates." Here we have clearly the outline of the history of St. George of Cappadocia, which often formed the subject of a miracle-play; but whether, in this instance, it was accompanied with dialogue, or was (as is most probable) merely a splendid dumb show, assisted by temporary erections of castles, &c., we are not informed.' This performance is accepted from Collier, i. 29, by Ward, i. 50, Pollard, xx, and other distinguished writers. They ought to have known him better. The authority he quotes, *Cotton. MS. Calig. B. II*, is wrong. But in *Cotton. MS. Julius B. I*, one of the MSS. of the *London Chronicle*, is the following passage, 'And the first sotelte was our lady armyng seint George, and an angel doyng on his spores; the ij[de] sotelte was seint George ridyng and fightyng with the dragon, with his spere in his hand; the iij[de] sotelte was a castel, and seint George, and the kynges doughter ledynge the lambe in at the castel gates. And all these sotelties were served to the emperor, and to the kyng, and no ferther: and other lordes were served with other sotelties after theire degrees[1].' The representation, then, was in cake or marchpane. The term 'soteltie' is surely not uncommon". But it has led a French scholar into another curious mistake. According to M. E. Picot 'La sotelty paraît n'avoir été qu'une simple farce, comme la sotternie néerlandaise[3].' A mumming by Lydgate in 1429–30 seems to have introduced a 'miracle' of St. Clotilda and the Holy Ampulla (cf. vol. i. p. 397).

WITHAM, ESSEX.

'Barnaby Riche of Witham' hired the Chelmsford (q. v.) wardrobe in 1566.

WITTERSHAM, KENT.

Wittersham players were at New Romney in 1426 and Lydd in 1441.

WOODHAM WALTER, ESSEX.

'Mrs. Higham of Woodham Walter' hired the Chelmsford (q.v.) wardrobe in 1570–2.

[1] *London Chronicle*, 159.
[2] Cf. e. g. *Durham Accounts*, i. 95, 101, 105 'Soteltez . . . Sutiltez . . .
Suttelties erga Natale.'
[3] E. Picot, in *Romania*, vii. 245.

Woodkirk, Yorkshire.

See *Texts*, (i) *Towneley Plays*.

Worcester, Worcestershire.

A cathedral inventory of 1576 includes:—

'players gere

A gowne of freres gyrdles.   A woman's gowne.   A K⁸ cloke of Tysshew.   A Jerkyn and a payer of breches.   A lytill cloke of tysshew.   A gowne of silk.   A Jerkyn of greene, 2 cappes, and the devils apparell ¹.'

There was a Corpus Christi play, mentioned ĩn 1467 and 1559.   It consisted of five pageants, maintained by the crafts, and was held yearly, if the corporation so decided.   In 1584 a lease of the 'vacant place where the pagantes do stand' was granted for building, and there was a building known as the 'Pageant House' until 1738².

Wrexham, Denbighshire.

The corporation of Shrewsbury saw a play by 'quibusdam interlusoribus de Wrexam' in 1540 (Appendix E, vi).

Writtle, Essex.

'Parker of Writtell' twice hired the Chelmsford (q. v.) wardrobe during 1570–2.   See also p. 184, n. 2.

Wycombe, Buckinghamshire.

Henry VII rewarded players of Wycombe on Dec. 31, 1494 (Appendix E, viii).

Wye, Kent.

Wye players were at New Romney in 1491.

Wymondham, Norfolk.

An account of the 'husbands for the wache and play of Wymondham,' made up to June, 1538, includes payments for 'the play,' 'devyls shoes,' 'the giant,' a man 'in armour,' 'the revels and dances³.'   It was at this play on July 1, 1549, that Kett's rebellion broke out.   According to Alexander Neville, the 'ludi ac spectacula ... antiquitus ita instituta' lasted two days and nights; according to Holinshed, 'one day and one night at least⁴.'

---

¹ *Hist. MSS.* xiv. 8, 187.
² Halliwell-Phillipps, i. 342; Toulmin Smith, *Ordinances of Worcester* in *English Guilds*, 385, 407 (E. E. T. S.).

³ *Norfolk Archaeology*, ix. 145; xi. 346.
⁴ A. Nevyllus, *De furoribus Norfolciensium Ketto Duce* (1575), i. 18; Holinshed (1587), iii. 1028.

Yarmouth, Norfolk.

The churchwardens' accounts of St. Nicholas's contain items between 1462 and 1512 for 'making a new star,' 'leading the star,' 'a new balk line to the star and ryving the same star.' In 1473 and 1486 are mentioned plays on Corpus Christi day; in 1489, a play at Bartholomew tide; in 1493, a game played on Christmas day[1].

York, Yorkshire.

[*Authorities.*—The chief are R. Davies, *Municipal Records of the City of York* (1843); L. Toulmin Smith, *York Plays* (1885). From one or other of these all statements below, of which the authority is not given, are taken. The municipal documents used are enumerated in *York Plays*, ix. The earliest date from 1371. F. Drake, *Eboracum* (1736); R. H. Skaife, *Guild of Corpus Christi* (Surtees Soc.); H. T. Riley, in *Hist. MSS. Comm.* i. 109; M. Sellers, *City of York in the Sixteenth Century*, in *Eng. Hist. Rev.* ix. 275; and some craft-guild documents in *Archaeological Review*, i. 221; *Antiquary*, xi. 107; xxii. 266; xxiii. 27, may also be consulted.]

Liturgical Plays.

The traditional *Statutes* of York Cathedral, supposed to date in their present form from about 1255, provide for the *Pastores* and the *Stella*.

'Item inueniet [thesaurarius] stellas cum omnibus ad illas pertinentibus, praeter cirpos, quos inueniet Episcopus Puerorum futurorum [? fatuorum], vnam in nocte natalis Domini pro pastoribus, et ij[as] in nocte Epiphaniae, si debeat fieri presentacio iij[um] regum[2].'

Corpus Christi Plays.

The first mention is in 1378, when part of a fine levied on the Bakers is assigned 'a la pagine des ditz Pestours de corpore cristi.' In 1394 a civic order required all the pageants to play in the places 'antiquitus assignatis,' in accordance with the proclamation, and under penalty of a fine. In 1397 Richard II was present to view the plays. In 1415 the town clerk, Roger Burton, entered in the *Liber Memorandorum* a copy of the *Ordo paginarum ludi Corporis Christi*, which was a schedule of the crafts and their plays, together with the *Proclamacio ludi corporis cristi facienda in vigilia corporis cristi*. At this date the plays were given *annuatim*. About 1440 the existing manuscript of the plays was probably written. It was a 'register,' drawn up from the 'regynalls' or 'origenalls' in the possession of the several crafts, and kept by the city[3]. Halfway

[1] L. G. Bolingbroke, in *Norfolk Archaeology*, xi. 334.
[2] *Lincoln Statutes*, ii. 98; cf. *Use of Sarum*, i. xxii*.
[3] Cf. p. 409.

through the sixteenth century performances become irregular. In 1535 the Creed play, in 1558 the Paternoster play was given instead. In 1548 'certen pagyauntes ... that is to say, the deyng of our lady, the assumption of our lady, and the coronacion of our lady,' were cast out. In 1550 and 1552 the play was suppressed on account of the plague, half the 'pageant silver' in 1552 being given to the sick. In 1562 the corporation attempted in vain to defer it to St. Barnabas day. In 1564, 1565, and 1566 it was not given, on account of war and sickness. In 1568 there was a dispute as to whether it should be played, and it was ordered that it must be 'perused and otherwaise amended' first. In 1569 it was given on Whit-Tuesday. It then seems to have lain dormant until 1579, when the Council made an order that it should be played but 'first the booke shalbe caried to my Lord Archebisshop [Edwin Sandys] and Mr. Deane [Mathew Hutton] to correcte, if that my Lord Archebisshop doo well like theron.' Various notes upon the 'register,' addressed to a 'Doctor,' and indicating that this or that play had been revised, were probably written at this time. In 1580 the citizens petitioned for the play, and the mayor replied that the request would be considered. There is no proof that any performance took place after this date; although the Bakers were still choosing 'pageant-masters' in 1656[1].

The ordering of the plays about 1415 was as follows: Yearly in the first or second week in Lent, the town clerk copied the 'sedulae paginarum' from the *Ordo* in the *Liber Memorandorum* and delivered it to the crafts 'per vj servientes maioris ad clavam.' On the eve of Corpus Christi a proclamation of mayor and sheriffs forbade 'distorbaunce of the kynges pees, and ye play, or hynderyng of ye processioun of Corpore Christi.' It went on to direct that the pageants must be played at the assigned places, that the men of the crafts are to come forth in customary array and manner, 'careynge tapers of ye pagentz,' that there shall be provided 'good players, well arayed and openly spekyng,' and that all shall be ready to start 'at the mydhowre betwix iiij[th] and v[th] of the cloke in the mornynge, and then all oyer pageantz fast followyng ilk one after oyer as yer course is, without tarieng.' Fines are imposed for any neglect or failure. At this date the play and the Corpus Christi procession were on the same day. In 1426 it is recorded that a Franciscan preacher, William Melton, while commending the play, 'affirmando quod bonus erat in se et laudabilis valde,' urged that it should be put on the day

---

[1] *York Plays*, xxxv, xli; *Arch. Review*, i. 221.

before Corpus Christi, so as not to interfere with the ecclesiastical feast [1]. This seems to have been agreed to, but the arrangement did not last. The procession was under the management of a Corpus Christi guild, founded in 1408, and the statutes of this guild dated in 1477 show that it was then the procession which was displaced, falling on the Friday after Corpus Christi day [2].

Thus the plays were essentially the affair of the whole community, and the control of them by the mayor and council may be further illustrated. In 1476 the council made an order regulating the choice of actors, and laid down—

'That yerely in the tyme of lentyn there shall be called afore the maire for the tyme beyng iiij of the moste connyng discrete and able players within this Citie, to serche, here, and examen all the plaiers and plaies and pagentes thrughoute all the artificers belonging to Corpus X^ti Plaie. And all suche as thay shall fynde sufficiant in personne and connyng, to the honour of the Citie and worship of the saide Craftes, for to admitte and able; and all other insufficiant personnes, either in connyng, voice, or personne to discharge, ammove, and avoide. And that no plaier that shall plaie in the saide Corpus X^ti plaie be conducte and reteyned to plaie but twise on the day of the saide playe; and that he or thay so plaing plaie not ouere twise the saide day, vpon payne of xl^s to forfet vnto the chaumbre as often tymes as he or thay shall be founden defautie in the same.'

By 'twise' is probably meant 'in two distinct pageants'; for each pageant repeated its performance at several stations. In 1394 these stations were 'antiquitus assignatis.' In 1399 the commons petitioned the council to the effect that 'le juer et les pagentz de la jour de corpore cristi' were not properly performed on account of the number of stations, and these were limited to twelve. In later years there were from twelve to sixteen, and from 1417 the corporation made a profit by letting to prominent citizens the right to have stations opposite their houses. A list of 'Leases for Corpuscrysty Play' in 1554, for instance, shows twelve stations bringing in from xiij^d to iij^s iiij^d each, while nothing was charged for the places 'at the Trinitie yaits where the clerke kepys the register,' 'at the comon Hall to my Lord Maior and his bredren,' 'at Mr. Bekwyth's at

[1] Drake, *Eboracum*, App. xxix; Davies, 243; *York Plays*, xxxiv. Melton is called 'sacrae paginae professor,' which Drake and many light-hearted scholars after him, down to

A. W. Ward (ed. 2, 1899), i. 53, translate 'professor of holy pageantry.' The 'sacred page,' however, is the Bible, and the title = S.T.P., or D.D.

[2] Davies, 245.

Hosyerlane end, where as my Lady Mayres and her systers lay' and 'uppon the Payment.'

Outward signs of the civic control were the 'vexilla ludi cum armis civitatis,' which were set up at the stations by order of the mayor on Corpus Christi eve. Apparently the city claimed also to put its mark on the pageants themselves, for in an agreement of 1422 merging the pageants of the Shoemakers, Tilemakers, Hayresters, and Millers it was declared, 'quod nulla quatuor artium praedictarum ponet aliqua signa, arma, vel insignia super paginam praedictam, nisi tantum arma huius honorabilis civitatis.' But the more important crafts, who had a pageant to themselves, may not have been subject to this restriction.

Although the corporation profited from the 'dimissio locorum ludi Corporis Christi,' they did not meet many of the expenses. They paid for the services of the minstrels employed, and for refreshments for themselves and for important visitors to the town. They occasionally helped out the resources of a poor craft. The following extract from the Chamberlains' accounts for 1397 seems to be quite exceptional :—

'Expens' in festo de Corpore Xp' i.

Item : pro steyning de iiij^{or} pannos ad opus paginae, iiij^s.

Et pro pictura paginae, ij^s.

Et pro vexillo novo cum apparatu, xij^s ij^d.

Et in portacione et reportacione meremii ad barras coram Rege, ij^s j^d.

Et pro xx fursperres ad barras praedictas coram Rege, v^s x^d.

Et pro xix sapplynges emptis de Iohanne de Craven pro barris praedictis, vj^s viij^d.

Et viij portitoribus ducentibus et moventibus paginam, v^s iiij^d.

Et Ianitori Sanctae Trinitatis pro pagina hospitanda, iiij^d.

Et ludentibus, iiij^d.

Et ministrallis in festo de Corpore Xp'i, xiij^s iiij^d.

Et in pane, cervisiis, vino, et carnibus, et focalibus pro maiore et probis hominibus in die ad ludum, xviij^s viij^d.

Et in ministrallis domini Regis ac aliorum dominorum supervenientibus, vj^{li} vij^s iiij^d.

Et ministris camerae in albo panno et rubeo pro adventu Regis, lviij^s x^d.'

Certainly the corporation did not themselves provide a 'pagina' in 1415 or later years. I think that in 1397 they prepared one for some allegorical performance of welcome, distinct from the play itself, to Richard II. The king was evidently placed at the gate of Trinity Priory, where was the first station as late as 1569.

But the bulk of the cost fell upon the crafts. They had to build, repair, decorate, and draw the pageant (Latin, *pagina*; English, *pagiaunt, paiaunt, pachent, pagende, pagyant, padgin, padgion, paidgion, padzhand*, &c., &c.). They had to house it in one of the 'pageant howses' which until recently gave a name to 'Pageant green,' and for each of which a yearly rent of xij^d seems to have been the usual charge. They had also doubtless to provide dress and refresh the actors ; and some of their members were bound personally to conduct the pageant on its journey. The fully organized craft-guilds appointed annual 'pageant-masters,' and met the ordinary charges by a levy of 'pageant-silver' upon each member according to his status. The amounts varied from 1*d.* to 8*d.*, and were supplemented by the proceeds of fines and payments on admissions and on setting up shop. Smaller guilds were often grouped together, and produced one pageant amongst three or four of them. Even the unincorporated trades did not escape. In 1483 four Innholders undertook the responsibility of producing a pageant for eight years on condition of a fixed payment of 4*d.* from each innholder in the city. Exceptional expenses were sometimes met in exceptional ways. The Mercers gave free admission into their fraternity to one Thomas Drawswerd, on condition that he should 'mak the Pagiant of the Dome . . . of newe substanciale for vij marks and the old pageant.' In 1501 the Cartwrights made four new wheels to a pageant, and were thereupon discharged from further charges for 6*d.* a year. Evidently the obligation of producing a pageant was considered an onerous one, and as trades rose and fell in York, the incidence of it upon this or that trade or trades was frequently altered. All such rearrangements came before the civic authorities, and many of them are upon record. Naturally they involved some corresponding revision, piecing together, or splitting up of plays (cf. p. 412). I only find one example of a play produced by any other body than a craft. The Hospital of St. Leonard produced the play of the Purification in 1415, but had ceased to do so some time before 1477. It is to be noted that in 1561 the Minstrels took their place with the other crafts, and became responsible for the Herod play[2].

Pater-Noster Play.

Wyclif in his *De Officio Pastorali*, cap. 15 (1378), says that,—

'herfore freris han tauȝt in Englond þe Paternoster in Engliȝcsh tunge, as men seyen in þe pleye of Yorke[3].'

---

[1] *Antiquary*, xxiii. 29.
[2] *York Plays*, xxi, 125 ; *E.H.R.* ix. 285.
[3] Wyclif, *English Works*, ed. Mathew (E. E. T. S.), 429.

The reference here is to a performance distinct from the Corpus Christi play. The preamble to a return of the ordinances and so forth of the guild 'Orationis Domini,' made in 1389, states that

'Once upon a time, a Play setting forth the goodness of the Lord's Prayer was played in the city of York; in which play all manner of vices and sins were held up to scorn, and the virtues were held up to praise.'

The guild was formed to perpetuate this play, and the members were bound to produce it and accompany it through the streets. In 1389 they had no possessions beyond the properties of the play and a chest. A *computus* of the guild for 1399 contains an entry of an old debt of 2s. 2d., owed by John Downom and his wife for entrance fee :—

'Sed dictus Iohannes dicit se expendisse in diuersis expensis circa ludum Accidiae ex parte Ric. Walker ij^s j^d, ideo de praedicto petit allocari[1].'

It would appear that by 1488 the guild had been converted to or absorbed in a guild of the Holy Trinity, which was moreover the craft-guild of the Merchants or Mercers. Certainly in that year this guild chose four pageant-masters to bring forth the Paternoster play. They were to bring in the pageants ' within iiij days next after Corpus Christi Day[2].' In 1488 the Paternoster play was presumably a variant for the usual Corpus Christi plays. It was similarly played on Corpus Christi day in 1558. The management was in the hands of one of the few unsuppressed guilds, that of St. Anthony; but the corporation gathered 'pageant silver' from the crafts and met the charges. A 'bayn,' or messenger, rode to proclaim the play on St. George's day, and another on Whit Monday. Another performance took place on Corpus Christi day (now called ' Thursday next after Trinitie Sonday'), 1572. The book was 'perused, amended and corrected.' Nevertheless, on July 30 the council sent a 'trewe copie' of it, at his request, to the Archbishop [Grindal] of York, and although in 1575 they sent a deputation to urge him to appoint a commission to reform ' all suche the play bookes as perteyne this cittie now in his grace's custodie,' there is no proof that his grace complied.

Creed Play.

As already stated, the guild of Corpus Christi had nothing to do with the regular craft-plays. But in 1446, William Revetor, a chantry priest and warden of the guild, bequeathed to it a 'ludus incompara-

---

[1] *York Plays*, xxix; Toulmin, *English Gilds* (E. E. T. S.), 137.
[2] *Antiquary*, xxii. 265.

bilis' called the 'Crede play,' to be performed every tenth year 'in variis locis dictae civitatis.' An inventory of 1465 includes:—

'Liber vocatus Originale continens Articulos Fidei Catholicae in lingua anglicana, nuper scriptum, appreciatum x^{li}.

Et alius liber inveteratus de eodem ludo, c^s.

Et alius liber de eodem anglice vocatus *Crede Play* continens xxij quaternos.'

There were also many banners and properties, amongst which

'Et xij rotulae nuper scriptae cum articulis fidei catholicae, apprec' iij^s iiij^d.

Et una clavis pro sancto Petro cum ij peciis unius tunicae depictae, apprec' xij^d.

Et x diademata pro Xp'o et apostolis cum una larva et aliis novem chevcrons, vj^s.'

Various performances of the Creed play are recorded. In 1483 it was given on Sunday, September 7, before Richard III, by order of the Council, 'apon the cost of the most onest men of every parish in thyo Cite.' From 1495 decennial performances can be traced, generally about Lammas (August 1), and 'at the common hall.' In 1535 the Corpus Christi play proper was omitted, and the crafts contributed 'pageant silver' to the Creed play at Lammas. But they refused to give way to it again in 1545. The guild was suppressed in 1547, and the 'original or regestre' passed into the hands of the hospital of St. Thomas. In 1562 the corporation proposed the Creed play as a possible alternative for 'th' ystories of the old and new testament' on St. Barnabas day; and in 1568 they again designed to replace the regular Corpus Christi play by it. But first they submitted it to the Dean of York, Matthew Hutton, who, in a letter still extant, advised that—

'thogh it was plawsible to yeares ago, and wold now also of the ignorant sort be well liked, yet now in this happie time of the gospell, I knowe the learned will mislike it, and how the state will beare with it, I knowe not.'

Consequently the book was 'delyveryd in agayn,' and no more is heard of it.

Mr. Davies suggests that the play probably fell into twelve scenes, in each of which one of the apostles figured. If so, there is perhaps an allusion to a performance of it in a letter of Henry VIII to the justices of York in which he speaks of a riot which took place—

'at the acting of a religious interlude of St. Thomas the Apostle made in the said city on the 23rd of August now last past . . . owing to the seditious conduct of certain papists who took a part in preparing for the said interlude.'

He requires them to imprison any who in 'performing interludes which are founded on any portions of the Old or New Testament' use language tending to a breach of the peace[1].

St. George Riding.

In April, 1554, the Council made an order for ' Seynt George to be brought forth and ryde as hath been accustomed,' and the following items in the accounts show that the personages in the procession were much the same as at Dublin (q. v.) :—

' to the waites for rydyng and playing before St. George and the play.'

'to the porters for beryng of the pagyant, the dragon and St. Xp'ofer.'

' to the King and Quene [of Dele] that playd.'

' to the May [the Maid].'

''to John Stamper for playing St. George[2].'

Midsummer Show.

As the regular plays waned, the 'show' or ' watch' of armed men on Midsummer eve became important. There is an ordinance for it in 1581. In 1584 it took place in the morning, and in the afternoon John Grafton, a schoolmaster, gave at seven stations a play with 'certaine compiled speaches,' for which the council allowed him to have 'a pageant frame.' Apparently the Baker's pageant was repaired for the purpose. In 1585 Grafton borrowed the pageants of the Skinners, Cooks, Tailors, Innholders, Bakers, and Dyers, and gave another play. Grafton's account for 1585 mentions ' the hearse,' ' the angell,' 'the Queene's crowne,' ' the childe one of the furyes bare.' He got iij[s], vj[s], viij[d] for his pains[3].

---

[1] Halliwell, *Letters of the Kings of England*, i. 354, from a Latin original in the *Bodl. Rawlinson MSS.*

[2] Davies, 263.

[3] Davies, 273; *Arch. Review*, i. 221.

X

TEXTS OF MEDIAEVAL PLAYS AND EARLY TUDOR INTERLUDES

I. MIRACLE-PLAYS.

CHESTER PLAYS.

Manuscripts.

(i) Hg. †1475–1500. *Hengwrt MS.* 229, in the library of Mr. Wynne of Peniarth, containing Play xxiv (*Antichrist*) only. Probably a prompter's copy, as some one has 'doubled it up and carried it about in his pocket, used it with hot hands, and faded its ink.'

(ii) D. 1591. *Devonshire MS.,* in the library of the Duke of Devonshire, written by 'Edward Gregorie, a scholar of Bunbury.'

(iii) W. 1592. *Brit. Mus. Addl. MS.* 10,305. Signed at the end of each play 'George Bellin.'

(iv) h. 1600. *Brit. Mus. Harl. MS.* 2013, also signed after some of the plays by 'George Bellin.' or 'Billinges.' A verse proclamation or 'banes' is prefixed, and on a separate leaf a copy of the prose proclamation made by the clerk of the pentice in 1544 (cf. p. 349) with a note, in another hand.

(v) B. 1604. *Bodl. MS.* 175, written by 'Gulielmus Bedford,' with an incomplete copy of the 'banes.'

(vi) H. 1607. *Brit. Mus. Harl. MS.* 2124, in two hands, the second being that of 'Jacobus Miller.' An historical note, dated 1628, is on the cover.

(vii) M. MS. in Manchester Free Library, containing fragment of Play xix (*Resurrection*) only.

[The MSS. D, W, h, B are derived from a common source, best represented by B. MS. H varies a good deal from this group, and is the better text. MS. Hg is probably related to H.]

Editions.

(a) 1818. Plays iii, x (*Noah, Innocents*) and Banes; J. H. Markland, for Roxburghe Club (No. 11).

(b) 1836. Play xxiv (*Antichrist*); J. P. Collier, *Five Miracle-Plays.*

(c) 1838. Plays iii, xxiv (*Noah, Antichrist*); W. Marriott, *English Miracle-Plays.*

(d) 1843–7, 1853. Cycle; Thomas Wright, from MS. W, for Shakespeare Society.

(e) 1883. Part of Play xix (*Resurrection*), from MS. M, in *Manchester Guardian*, for May 19, 1883.

(f) 1890. Plays iii, part of iv (*Noah, Isaac*); Pollard, 8.

(g) 1893–. Cycle (vol. i with Introduction, Banes and Plays i–xiii only issued by 1902); H. Deimling, from MS. H (with collation), for E. E. T. S. (Extra Series, lxii).

(h) 1897. Plays v, xxiv (*Prophetae, Antichrist*); Manly, i. 66, 170, from (g) and MS. Hg respectively.

[F. J. Furnivall, *Digby Plays*, xx, prints eighteen additional lines to the Banns as given by Deimling from MSS. h, B. These are from a copy in Rogers's *Breviary of Chester* (cf. p. 350), *Harl. MS.* 1944. A distinct and earlier (pre-Reformation) Banns is printed by Morris, 307, from *Harl. MS.* 2150 (cited in error as 2050), which is a copy of the White Book of the Pentice belonging to the City of Chester.]

The Cycle.

The list of ' pagyns in play of Corpus Xρi ' contained in the ' White Book of the Pentice ' (*Harl. MS.* 2150, f. 85 b), and given apparently from this source, by Rogers (Furnivall, xxi), makes them twenty-five in number, as follows :—

i. The fallinge of Lucifer.
ii. The creation of yᵉ worlde.
iii. Noah & his shipp.
iv. Abraham & Isacke.
v. Kinge Balack & Balaam with Moyses.
vi. Natiuytie of our Lord.
vii. The shepperdes offeringe.
viii. Kinge Harrald & yᵉ mounte victoriall.
ix. Yᵉ 3 Kinges of Collen.
x. The destroyeinge of the Childeren by Herod.
xi. Purification of our Ladye.
xii. The pinackle, with yᵉ woman of Canan.
xiii. The risinge of Lazarus from death to liffe.

xiv. The cominge of Christe to Ierusalem.
xv. Christs maundy with his desiples.
xvi. The scourginge of Christe.
xvii. The Crusifienge of Christ.
xviii. The harrowinge of hell.
xix. The Resurrection.
xx. The Castle of Emaus & the Apostles.
xxi. The Ascension of Christe.
xxii. Whitsonday yᵉ makeinge of the Creede.
xxiii. Prophetes before yᵉ day of Dome.
xxiv. Antecriste.
xxv. Domes Daye.

The list of plays contained in the pre-Reformation Banns is the same as this, with one exception. Instead of twenty-five plays it has twenty-six. After *Wyt Sonday* is inserted the play 'of our lady thassumpcon,' to be brought forth by 'the worshipfull wyves of this towne.' This play of *The Assumption* was given in 1477, and as a separate performance in 1488, 1497, and 1515 (Morris, 308, 322, 323). Doubtless it was dropped, as at York, out of Protestantism. The post-Reformation Banns and the extant MSS. of the cycle have it not. Further, they reduce the twenty-five plays of the 'White Book' list to twenty-four, by merging the plays of the *Scourging* and *Crucifixion* into one. In MSS. B, W, h, the junction is plainly apparent (see Deimling, i. ix; Wright, ii. 50). In MS. H there is no break (Deimling, i. xxiv).

Literary Relations.

Wright, i. xiv, and Hohlfeld, in *Anglia*, xi. 223, call attention to the parallels between the Chester plays and the French *Mystère du Viel Testament* and to the occurrence in them of scraps and fragments of French speech. The chief of these are put into the mouths of Octavian, the *Magi*, Herod, and Pilate, and may have been thought appropriate to kings and lordings. They may also point to translation from French originals. Davidson, 254, suggests that the earliest performances at Chester were in Anglo-Norman, and points to the tradition of MS. II (cf. p. 351) as confirming this. There are slight traces of influence upon some of the Chester plays by the York cycle (Hohlfeld, loc. cit. 260; Davidson, 287). Hohlfeld, in *M.L.N.* v. 222, regards Chester play iv as derived from a common original with the Brome *Abraham and Isaac*. H. Ungemacht, *Die Quellen der fünf ersten Chester Plays*, discusses the relation of the plays to the Brome play and the French *mystères*, and also to the *Vulgate*, the Fathers, Josephus, and the *Cursor Mundi*.

York Plays.

Manuscripts.

(i) *Brit. Mus. Addl. MS.* 35,290, recently *Ashburnham MS.* 137, fully described by L. T. Smith, *York Plays*, xiii. The MS. dates from about 1430–40, and appears to be a 'register' or transcript made for the corporation of the 'origenalls' in the hands of the crafts. In 1554 the 'register' was kept by the clerk at the gates of the dissolved Holy Trinity Priory. After the plays ceased to be performed it got into the hands of the Fairfaxes of Denton. In 1695 it belonged to Henry Fairfax, and its ownership can be traced thence to the present day.

(ii) *Sykes MS.* in possession of the York Philosophical Society, fully described in *York Plays*, 455. This is of the early sixteenth century. It contains only the Scriveners' play, of 'The Incredulity of Thomas,' is not a copy from the Ashburnham MS., and may be an 'origenall,' or a transcript for the prompter's use. It has a cover with a flap, and has been folded lengthwise, as if for the pocket.

Editions.

(a) 1797. Play xlii (*Incredulity of Thomas*), from *Sykes MS.*, in J. Croft, *Excerpta Antiqua*, 105.

(b) 1859. Play xlii (*Incredulity of Thomas*), from *Sykes MS.*, ed. J. P. Collier, in *Camden Miscellany*, vol. iv.

(c) 1885. Cycle, from *Ashburnham MS.*, in L. Toulmin Smith, *York Plays*.

(d) 1890. Play i (*Creation and the Fall of Lucifer*), from *York Plays*, in Pollard, 1.

(e) 1897. Plays xxxviii, xlviii (*Resurrection, Judgment Day*), from *York Plays*, in Manly, i. 153, 198.

The Cycle.

The subjects of the forty-eight plays and one fragment contained in the *Ashburnham MS.* are as follows :—

i. *The Barkers.* The Creation, Fall of Lucifer.
ii. *Playsterers.* The Creation to the Fifth Day.
iii. *Cardmakers.* God creates Adam and Eve.
iv. *Fullers.* Adam and Eve in the Garden of Eden.
v. *Cowpers.* Man's disobedience and Fall.
vi. *Armourers.* Adam and Eve driven from Eden.
vii. *Glovers.* Sacrificium Cayme et Abell.
viii. *Shipwrites.* Building of the Ark.
ix. *Fysshers and Marynars.* Noah and the Flood.
x. *Parchmyners and Bokebynders.* Abraham's Sacrifice.
xi. *The Hoseers.* The Israelites in Egypt, the Ten Plagues, and Passage of the Red Sea.
xii. *Spicers.* Annunciation, and visit of Elizabeth to Mary.
xiii. *Pewtereres and Foundours.* Joseph's trouble about Mary.
xiv. *Tille-thekers.* Journey to Bethlehem : Birth of Jesus.
xv. *Chaundelers.* The Angels and the Shepherds.
xvi. *Masonns.* Coming of the three Kings to Herod.
xvii. *Goldsmyths.* Coming of the three Kings, the Adoration.
xviii. *Marchallis.* Flight into Egypt.

xix. *Gyrdillers and Naylers.* Massacre of the Innocents.

xx. *Sporiers and Lorimers.* Christ with the Doctors in the Temple.

xxi. *Barbours.* Baptism of Jesus.

xxii. *Smythis.* Temptation of Jesus.

xxiii. *Coriours.* The Transfiguration.

xxiv. *Cappemakers.* Woman taken in Adultery. Raising of Lazarus.

xxv. *Skynners.* Entry into Jerusalem.

xxvi. *Cutteleres.* Conspiracy to take Jesus.

xxvii. *Baxteres.* The Last Supper.

xxviii. *Cordewaners.* The Agony and Betrayal.

xxix. *Bowers and Flecchers.* Peter denies Jesus: Jesus examined by Caiaphas.

xxx. *Tapiterers and Couchers.* Dream of Pilate's Wife: Jesus before Pilate.

xxxi. *Lytsteres.* Trial before Herod.

xxxii. *Cokis and Waterlederes.* Second accusation before Pilate: Remorse of Judas: Purchase of Field of Blood.

xxxiii. *Tyllemakers.* Second trial continued: Judgment on Jesus.

xxxiv. *Shermen.* Christ led up to Calvary.

xxxv. *Pynneres and Paynters.* Crucifixio Christi.

xxxvi. *Bocheres.* Mortificacio Christi.

xxxvii. *Sadilleres.* Harrowing of Hell.

xxxviii. *Carpenteres.* Resurrection: Fright of the Jews.

xxxix. *Wyne drawers.* Jesus appears to Mary Magdalen after the Resurrection.

xl. *The Sledmen.* Travellers to Emmaus.

xli. *Hatmakers, Masons, and Laborers.* Purification of Mary: Simeon and Anna prophesy.

xlii. *Escreueneres.* Incredulity of Thomas.

xliii. *Tailoures.* The Ascension.

xliv. *Potteres.* Descent of the Holy Spirit.

xlv. *Draperes.* The Death of Mary.

xlvi. *Wefferes.* Appearance of our Lady to Thomas.

xlvii. *Osteleres.* Assumption and Coronation of the Virgin.

xlviii. *Merceres.* The Judgement Day.

(Fragment.) *Inholders.* Coronation of our Lady.

The majority of these plays were entered in the register about 1440. The fragment of a later play on *The Coronation of Our Lady* was added at the end of the fifteenth century. It was doubtless intended to supersede xlvii. *Adam and Eve in the Garden of Eden* (iv) and *The Purification of Mary, Simeon and Anna prophesy* (xli) were inserted in 1558. The former is probably of the same date as the rest; the latter is thought by the editor to be later. It is misplaced both in the MS. and the printed text. It should follow xvii, but there was no room for it in the MS. Some notes, probably written when the plays were submitted to the Dean of York in 1579, state that xii, xviii, xxi, xxviii had been rewritten since the register was compiled.

The register does not represent quite all the plays ever performed at York. Spaces are left for *The Marriage at Cana* and *Christ in the House of Simon the Leper*, which were never written in; and the corporation archives refer to a play of *Fergus* or *Portacio Corporis Mariae*, which came between xlv and xlvi and was 'laid apart' in 1485; and to a scene of *Suspencio Iudae*, which was in 1422 an episode of xxxiii. In other respects the contents of the register agree substantially with the fifty-one plays of the *Ordo paginarum* entered by the Town Clerk in the *Liber Memorandorum* in 1415[1] and with the fifty-seven plays of a second *Ordo* of uncertain date which comes a little later in the same *Liber*[2]. The three lists show some variations in the grouping of the subject-matter into pageants, due to the constant shifting of responsibility amongst the crafts.

Literary Relations.

Davidson, 252 sqq., attempts to trace the growth of the York plays out of a parent cycle, from which the Towneley and Coventry plays borrowed. The biblical and apocryphal sources are discussed by L. Toulmin Smith, *York Plays*, xlvii; A. R. Hohlfeld, in *Anglia*, xi. 285; P. Kamann, *Die Quellen der York-Spiele*, in *Anglia*, x. 189; F. Holthausen, in *Arch. f. d. Studium d. neueren Sprachen und Litteratur*, lxxxv. 425; lxxxvi. 280; W. A. Craigie, in *Furnivall Miscellany*, 52. I have not been able to see O. Herrtrich, *Studien zu den York Plays* (Breslau Diss. 1886). There are textual studies by F. Holthausen as above, and in *Philologische Studien* (Sievers-Festgabe), 1896; E. Kölbing, in *Englische Studien*, xvi. 279; xx. 179; J. Hall, in *Eng. Stud.* ix. 448; Zupitza, in *Deutsche Litteraturzeitung*, vi. 1304; K. Luick, in *Anglia*, xxii. 384.

TOWNELEY PLAYS.

Manuscript.

Written in the second half of the fifteenth century, formerly in the

---

[1] Printed in *York Plays*, xix.   [2] Printed in Davies, 233.

library of Towneley Hall, long in the possession of Mr. Quaritch, the bookseller, and now in that of Major Coates, of Ewell, Surrey. There are thirty-two plays in all, but twenty-six leaves are missing.

Editions.

(a) 1822. Play xxx (*Iudicium*); F. Douce, for Roxburghe Club (*Publications*, No. 16).

(b) 1836. Play xiii (*Secunda Pastorum*); J. P. Collier, in *Five Miracle-Plays*.

(c) 1836. Complete cycle; for *Surtees Soc.* (It is uncertain whether the editor was J. Raine, J. Hunter, or J. S. Stevenson.)

(d) 1838. Plays viii, xiii, xxiii, xxv, xxx (*Pharao, Secunda Pastorum, Crucifixio, Extractio Animarum ab Inferno, Iudicium*); W. Marriott, *English Miracle-Plays*.

(e) 1867. Play iii (*Processus Noe cum filiis*), E. Mätzner, *Altenglische Sprachproben*, 360.

(f) 1875. Play ii (*Mactacio Abel*); T. Valke, *Der Tod des Abel* (Leipzig).

(g) 1885. Plays viii, xviii, xxv, xxvi, xxx (*Pharao, Pagina Doctorum, Extraccio Animarum, Resurreccio Domini, Iudicium*); L. Toulmin Smith, *York Plays*, 68, 158, 372, 397, 501 (not quite in full, for comparison with corresponding York plays).

(h) 1890. Play xiii (*Secunda Pastorum*), abridged; Pollard, 31.

(i) 1897. Cycle, G. England and A. W. Pollard, for E. E. T. S. (Extra Series, lxxi).

(k) 1897. Plays iii, v, vi, xiii (*Processus Noe, Isaac, Iacob, Secunda Pastorum*) from (i); Manly, i. 13, 58, 94.

The Cycle.

There are thirty-two extant plays, as follows:—

i. The Creation (The Barkers, Wakefeld).

ii. Mactacio Abel (The Glovers).

iii. Processus Noe cum filiis (Wakefeld).

iv. Abraham (incomplete).

v. [Isaac].

vi. Iacob.

vii. Processus Prophetarum (incomplete).

viii. Pharao (the Litsters or Dyers).

ix. Cesar Augustus.

x. Annunciacio.

xi. Salutacio Elezabeth.

xii. Una pagina Pastorum (Prima).

xiii. Alia eorundem (Secunda).

xiv. Oblacio Magorum.

xv. Fugacio Iosep & Mariae in Egyptum.

xvi. Magnus Herodes.

xvii. Purificacio Mariae (incomplete at end).

xviii. Pagina Doctorum (incomplete at beginning).

xix. Iohannes Baptista.

xx. Conspiracio (et Capcio).

xxi. Coliphizacio.

xxii. Fflagellacio.

xxiii. Processus Crucis (et Crucifixio).

xxiv. Processus Talentorum.

xxv. Extraccio Animarum.

xxvi. Resurreccio Domini.

xxvii. Peregrini (the Fishers).

xxviii. Thomas Indiae (et Resurreccio Domini).

xxix. Ascencio Domini (incomplete).

xxx. Iudicium.

xxxi. Lazarus.

xxxii. Suspencio Iudae (incomplete).

Plays xxxi and xxxii (a fragment) are obviously misplaced. The former should come between xix and xx; the latter, which is added to the MS. in an early sixteenth-century hand, between xxii and xxiii. Probably two plays at least are lost. Twelve leaves are missing after Play i, and twelve more after Play xxix. These doubtless contained plays of *The Fall* and *Pentecost*.

Literary Relations.

The Towneley Cycle is a composite one (Ten Brink, ii. 257; iii. 274; Davidson, 253; England-Pollard, xxi). Mr. Pollard distinguishes three fairly well-marked strata, and this classification is probably not exhaustive. There are (a) a group of plays of the ordinary didactico-religious type; (b) a group derived from the York plays in an earlier form than the extant text; (c) a group written by a single writer of marked power and a bold sense of humour. The plays of this group include iii, xii, xiii, xiv, xxi, and are, for literary quality, the pick of the vernacular religious drama. Mr. Pollard considers the cycle practically complete by about 1420. The horned female headdress (xxx. 269) which led the Surtees editor to put the composition in 1388, is found in miniatures of the later date. The relation of the cycle to that of York is also studied by Davidson, 271 sqq., and A. R. Hohlfeld, in *Anglia*, xi. 253, 285. Ten Brink, ii. 244; iii. 274, thinks that a much earlier (late thirteenth century) play is preserved in Plays v and vi (*Isaac* and *Iacob*). I agree with Mr. Pollard that this conjecture lacks proof.

A. Ebert has a study, *Die englischen Mysterien, mit besonderer Berücksichtigung der Townley-Sammlung*, in *Jahrbuch f. rom. u. engl. Lit.* i. 44, 131. The folk-lore incident of the *Secunda Pastorum* is supplied with parallels by E. Kölbing, in England-Pollard, xxxi, and by H. A. Eaton, in *M.L.N.* xiv. 265, from *The Merry Tales of Gotham* (H. Oesterley, *A Hundred Merry Tales* (1526), No. xxiv; Hazlitt, *Shakespeare's Jest-Books*, iii. 4). There is an allusion to the 'foles of Gotham,' in Play xii. 180. J. Hugienen, in *M.L.N.* xiv. 255, finds in Play iv. 49 an adaptation of the French *Viel Testament*, 9511.

The Locality.

Douce described the manuscript for the sale of Towneley MSS. in 1814 as supposed to have 'belonged to the Abbey of Widkirk, near Wakefield, in the county of York.' In his Roxburghe Club edition of the *Iudicium* he substitutes the name of the Abbey of Whalley, near Towneley Hall. How far either of these statements or conjectures rests upon Towneley family tradition is unknown. Widkirk is merely another form (cf. Prof. Skeat, in *Athenæum* for Dec. 2, 1893) of Wood-kirk, also called West Ardsley, a small place four milles north of Wakefield. There was not, strictly speaking, an abbey at Woodkirk, but a small cell of Augustinian canons, dependent upon the great house of St. Oswald at Nostel.

The MS. itself seems to bear witness to a connexion of the plays with the crafts of Wakefield. Play i is headed ' Assit Principio, Sancta Maria, Meo. Wakefeld.' In the margin of Play ii is written 'Glover Pag.' in a later hand. Play iii is headed ' Processus Noe cum filiis. Wakefeld.' In the margin of Play viii is ' Litsters Pagonn ' in a later hand, and further down, in a third hand, is ' lyster play.' Under the title of Play xxvii is ' fysher pagent' in a later hand. Further in Play xiii is a mention of ' Horbury Shroges,' Horbury being a village two or three miles from Wakefield, and a ' crokyd thorne' which may be a ' Shepherd's Thorn' near Horbury in Mapplewell. These indications are spread over the three groups of plays distinguished by Mr. Pollard, and certainly suggest that the whole cycle belonged to the Wakefield crafts. On the other hand, I find no hint of any plays in the local histories of Wakefield. The evidence for a connexion with Wakefield is strengthened by M. H. Peacock, *The Wakefield Mysteries*, in *Anglia*, xxiv. 509, from which it appears that there are places called Thornhill and Thornes to the E. and W. respectively of Horbury. Play ii, line 367 ' bery me in gudeboure at the quarell hede' points to Goodybower Close in Wakefield, which once had a quarry. Play xxiv, line 155 ' from this towne vnto lyn' suggests at least a borrowing from East Anglia.

Perhaps we may combine the data of the manuscript and of tradition by supposing that the plays were acted by the crafts of Wakefield, not in the town at Corpus Christi or Whitsuntide, but at one of the great fairs which the canons of Nostel held under charter at Woodkirk about the feasts of the Assumption (Aug. 15) and the Nativity (Sept. 8) of the Virgin. These fairs, run into one continuous horse fair, and known from a local family of Legh, as Lee fair, lasted until quite recently [1].

Ludus Coventriae.

Manuscript.

Brit. Mus. Cotton MS. Vespasian D. viii. Forty-two plays, the last incomplete. On f. 100ᵛ is the date 1468. At the beginning is written 'Robert Hegge, Dunelmensis' and before the twenty-ninth play 'Ego R. H. Dunelmensis, Possideo: Ου κτησις αλλα χρησις.' On the fly-leaf, in an Elizabethan hand, is 'The plaie called Corpus Christi,' and in the hand of Cotton's librarian, Richard James, 'Contenta Novi Testamenti scenice expressa et actitata olim per monachos sive fratres mendicantes: vulgo dicitur hic liber Ludus Coventriae, sive ludus Corporis Christi: scribitur metris Anglicanis.' The following account was given by a later librarian, Dr. Smith, in his printed catalogue (1696) of the Cottonian MSS.: 'A collection of plays, in Old English metre: h.e. Dramata sacra, in quibus exhibentur historiae veteris & N. Testamenti, introductis quasi in scenam personis illic memoratis quas secum invicem colloquentes pro ingenio finget Poeta. Videntur olim coram populo, sive ad instruendum sive ad placendum, a Fratribus mendicantibus representata.'

Editions.

(a) 1830. Plays i–v (*Fall of Lucifer, Days of Creation and Fall of Adam, Cain and Abel, Noah's Flood, Abraham and Isaac*) in Dugdale, *Monasticon Anglicanum* (ed. 2). vi, pt. 3, 1534.

(b) 1836. Play x (*Betrothal of Mary*), Collier, *Five Miracle-Plays.*

(c) 1838. Plays xii, xiv (*Doubt of Joseph, Trial of Mary*), William Marriott, *English Miracle-Plays.*

(d) 1841. Cycle: J. O. Halliwell[-Phillipps] for Shakespeare Society.

(e) 1890. Play xi (*Annunciation*), Pollard, 44.

(f) 1897. Plays iv, xi (*Noah's Flood, Annunciation*), Manly, i. 31, 82.

(g) A new edition of the complete cycle is promised in the 'Extra Series' of the Early English Text Society.

---

[1] W. Andrews, *Yorkshire in Olden Times,* 105, 146.

The Cycle.

The text is not definitely divided up into plays in the MS., although some such indication as an *Explicit* occasionally helps. Probably the following division is correct. Halliwell's is clearly wrong, but for convenience of reference I give his numbers in brackets.

i. Fall of Lucifer (Halli-well, i).	iv. Noah's Flood (H. iv).
ii. Days of Creation. Fall of Adam (H. i, ii).	v. Abraham and Isaac (H. v).
iii. Cain and Abel (H. iii).	vi. Moses (H. vi).
	vii. Prophets (H. vii).

Then a prologue by Contemplacio, promising a 'matere' of 'the modyr of mercy' from her conception to the meeting with Elizabeth, and a 'conclusyon.'

viii. Joachim and Anna (II. viii).	x. Betrothal of Mary (H. x).
ix. Mary in the Temple (H. ix).	xi. Annunciation (H. xi).

Opens with scene between Contemplacio, Virtutes, Pater, Veritas, Misericordia, Iusticia, Pax, Filius.

xii. Doubt of Joseph (H. xii).	xiii. Visit to Elizabeth (H. xiii).

This group of plays closes with the promised 'conclusyon,' namely 'Ave regina coelorum,' and Contemplacio disappears.

xiv. Trial of Mary (H. xiv).	xxiii. Temptation (H. xxii).
xv. Nativity (H. xv).	xxiv. Woman Taken in Adul-tery (H. xxiii).
xvi. *Pastores* (H. xvi).	
xvii. *Magi* (H. xvii).	xxv. Lazarus (H. xxiv).
xviii. Purification (H. xviii).	xxvi. Conspiracy of Jews (H. xxv).
xix. Slaughter of Innocents (H. xix).	
	xxvii. Entry into Jerusalem (H. xxvi).
xx. Death of Herod (H. xix).	
xxi. Dispute in Temple (H. xx).	xxviii. Last Supper (H. xxvii).
	xxix. Mount of Olives (H. xxviii).
xxii. Baptism (H. xxi).	

Another group of scenes begins. Contemplacio, called in the stage direction 'an exposytour, in doctorys wede,' reappears; and after a procession has 'enteryd into the place, and the Herowdys taken his schaffalde and Pylat and Annas and Cayphas here schaffaldys,' says :—

'Be the leve and soferauns of allemythty God,
   We intendyn to procede the matere that we lefte the last ȝere;

. . . .

The last ȝere we shewyd here how oure Lord for love of man
Cam to the cety of Jherusalem mekely his deth to take;
And how he made his mawndé.

. . . .

Now wold we procede, how he was browth than
Beforn Annas and Cayphas, and sythe beforn Pylate :
And so forth in his passyon how mekely he toke it for man.'

This group does not well bear splitting up into plays.   The action is
continuous, although it takes place now at one scaffold, now at another.

xxx. Herod desires to see Christ.
   Trial before Caiaphas
   (H. xxix, xxx).
xxxi. Death of Judas, Christ before Pilate and Herod
   (H. xxx).
xxxii. Pilate's Wife's Dream.

Here, possibly, the group ends.

xxxvi. *Quem quaeritis* (H. xxxvi).
xxxvii. *Hortulanus* (H. xxxvii).
xxxviii. *Peregrini* (H. xxxviii).
xxxix. Incredulity of Thomas
   (H. xxxviii).

   The Condemnation (H.
   xxxi, xxxii).
xxxiii. Crucifixion (H. xxxii, xxxiii).
xxxiv. Longinus. Burial of Christ
   (H. xxxiv).
xxxv. Harrowing of Hell. Resurrection (H. xxxv).

Then follow :—

xl. Ascension (H. xxxix).
xli. Pentecost (H. xl).
xlii. Assumption of Virgin
   (H. xli).

The Assumption play, according to Halliwell, is inserted in a hand
of the time of Henry VIII.

   xliii. Doomsday (H. xlii).

A few lines appear to be missing at the end.

In dividing the plays, I have been helped by a prologue which
is put in the mouths of three *Vexillatores*. Says *Primus* :—

   'We purpose us pertly stylle in this prese,
      The pepyl to plese with pleys full glad.
   Now lystenyth us, lovely, bothe more and lesse,
      Gentyllys and ȝemanry of goodly lyff lad,
         This tyde.'

The *Vexillatores* then take turns to describe the 'ffyrst pagent,'
'secunde pagent,' and so on, up to 'the xl^ti pagent.'   This should be
'xlii,' but by a slip two numbers are used twice.   The prologue ends :—

   'A Sunday next, yf that we may,
      At vj of the belle we gynne oure play,
   In N. towne, wherfore we pray,
         That God now be ȝoure spede. *Amen.*'

The prologue so far agrees with the plays that it must have been written for them; but it was not written for them as they stand. It gives some of the incidents, especially of the trial scenes, in a different order from the text. Plays viii, xiii, xviii, xxvi, and xlii are omitted altogether. Of these xlii is a late interpolation in the text; but the fact that the numbers viii and xiii are skipped over in the enumeration, although the order in which the *Vexillatores* speak proceeds regularly, shows that the prologue is later in date than the text, and contemplates the omission of existing plays.

The Problem.

The exact nature of the *Ludus Coventriae* is a nice literary point. It is much doubted whether they have anything to do with Coventry at all. Cotton's librarians regarded them as Coventry plays, acted not by craft-guilds, but by monks or begging friars. But what was their authority? The earliest possessor of the MS. who can be traced is Robert Hegge, a Durham man by birth, and a Fellow of C. C. C., Oxford. Hegge died in 1629, and probably the MS. then passed into Sir Robert Cotton's collection through Richard James, who happened to be also a C. C. C. man, and was in the habit of picking up finds for Cotton in Oxford[1]. The note on the MS. may represent a tradition as to its origin gathered by James from Hegge.

With this ·note should be compared the following passage in Dugdale's *History of Warwickshire*, referring to the house of Franciscans or Grey Friars at Coventry :—

'Before the suppression of the monasteries, this city was very famous for the *Pageants* that were play'd therein, upon *Corpus-Christi*-day; which occasioning very great confluence of people thither from far and near, was of no small benefit thereto; which *Pageants* being acted with mighty state and reverence by the Friers of this House, had Theaters for the severall Scenes, very large and high, placed upon wheels, and drawn to all the eminent parts of the City, for the better advantage of Spectators: And contain'd the story of the New-Testament, composed into Old English Rithme, as appeareth by an antient MS. intituled *Ludus Corporis Christi* or *Ludus Coventriae*' [*in bibl.* Cotton, *sub effigie Vesp.* D. 9].

'I have been told by some old people, who in their younger years were eye-witnesses of these Pageants so acted, that the yearly con-

---

[1] *D. N. B.* s.v. Hegge. *Poems of Richard James* (ed. Grosart, xxii);   T. Fowler, *Hist. of C. C. C.* 175, 183, 394.

fluence of people to see that shew was extraordinary great, and yielded no small advantage to this City[1].'

Dugdale, it is to be observed, has the MS. as one of his authorities, but he goes further than the librarians by ascribing the plays to a particular house of friars. Unfortunately his account will not hold water. He was born in 1605, and educated for five years in Coventry. Now there could have been no plays performed by the Grey Friars after 1538, for they were suppressed in that year. But the craft-plays survived, with great *éclat*, until 1580, and it is manifest that it is these plays which his informants described to him. They were acted on Corpus Christi day, obviously leaving no room for Grey Friars plays on the same day. The craft-plays seem to have been confined to the history of the New Testament (cf. p. 423), but the *Ludus Coventriae* is not. There is, however, a not very trustworthy bit of evidence which makes it just possible that the Grey Friars did act, not at Corpus Christi, but at Whitsuntide. This is the statement of the Coventry *Annals* that in 1492–3, Henry VII came to see the plays acted by the Grey Friars[2]. But the *Annals* only date from the seventeenth century, and they are not trustworthy (cf. p. 358) as to the history of the plays. I incline to think that the Grey Friars connexion is an Oxford guess of Hegge or his friends, which has found its way alike into the accounts of Richard James and Dugdale, and into the *Annals*. But is the connexion of the plays with Coventry also part of the guess, inspired by the fact that the Coventry mysteries, and these alone, obtained literary notice in the sixteenth century? Or have we Coventry guild-plays to deal with? The *Ludus Coventriae* is quite distinct from the two extant Coventry plays (p. 422); but those are of the sixteenth century, and appear to represent a recension in 1535 of 'new plays' produced, according to the *Annals*, in 1520 (p. 358). So far as this goes, the *Ludus Coventriae* might be the

[1] Dugdale, *Hist. of W.* (1656), 116. A not materially different version, from Dugdale's MSS., is given by Sharp, *Dissertation*, 218. Nor does Sharp, in the account of the Grey Friars in his *Hist. and Antiq. of Coventry* (1817), add any information as to their plays.

[2] Hearne, *Fordun's Scotichronicon*, v. 1493 (from MS. of *Annals*, penes Thomas Jesson of Ch. Ch.) 'This yeare the King came to se the playes acted by the Gray Friers and much commended them.' The mayoral list in this text of the *Annals* goes to 1675. It is probably another that Sharp, *Diss.* 5, quotes as making the same

statement and describes as 'not older than the *beginning* of Charles I's reign.' He does not give the full entry. Is it the basis of Mr. Fretton's addition to the 1871 ed. of Sharp's *Hist. and Antiq. of Cov.* 202 '1492. Henry 7th and his Queen saw the Plays at Whitsuntide'? Can 'by the Gray Friers' mean 'at a station by the convent'? In the Carpenters' accounts for 1453 is an item 'for the mynstrell at the frer[s].' This, says Sharp, *Diss.* 213, relates to the craft's annual dinner held at the White Friars. There is no other possible allusion to friars' plays in Mr. Sharp's extracts.

discarded fifteenth-century cycle of the Coventry crafts. Ten Brink points out certain features in the *Ludus* which seem, from the Cappers' accounts extracted by Sharp, to have existed also at Coventry [1]. On the other hand, the Coventry plays, unlike the *Ludus*, seem to have been confined to the New Testament. The *Ludus* does not give those opportunities for showing off artisanship which are characteristic of other craft-cycles [2]. And, strongest of all, while the Coventry plays were processional, a study of the *Ludus* will make it quite clear that it was intended for a stationary performance. The 'pagents' contemplated by the prologue can only be episodes artificially distinguished in a practically continuous action. Often there is no well-marked break between pageant and pageant. The same personages appear and reappear in more than one; and the whole performance evidently takes place in and around a 'place' or *locus interludii* (Halliwell, 44) upon which are situated various 'scaffolds' or 'stages [3],' a heaven, a hell, a temple, a *sepulchrum*, and so forth. The *navis* for Noah is practicable, and can come and go.

If the plays are not from Coventry, can they be located elsewhere? They have been ascribed to Durham, but merely I think, because Robert Hegge was 'Dunelmensis.' Mr. Pollard follows Ten Brink in assigning their dialect and scribal peculiarities to the North-East Midlands, and in ascribing them to a strolling company [4]. They regard 'N. towne' in the prologue as a common form (N = 'nomen,' as in the Church Catechism and Marriage Service). As to the dialect I offer no opinion; I am sorry not to have been able to see M. Kramer, *Sprache und Heimath der Coventry-Plays*. But I do not think that the strolling company is proved. The *vexillatores* may be merely proclaimers of banns sent round the villages hard by the town where the play was given. And 'N.' may be an abbreviation for a definite town name. Northampton (q.v.) has been suggested; but would not scan. Norwich (q.v.) would; and these might conceivably be a cycle played by the guild of St. Luke at Norwich before the crafts took the responsibility for the Whitsun plays from it. But the elaborate treatment of the legends of the Virgin suggests a performance, like that of the Lincoln plays, and of the *Massacre of the Innocents* in the *Digby MS.*, on St. Anne's day (July 26). It is to be

[1] Ten Brink, iii. 276; Sharp, 45.

[2] Hohlfeld, in *Anglia*, xi. 228.

[3] The term 'pageant' is once used in the stage-directions (Halliwell, 132) 'Hic intrabit pagentum de purgatione Mariae et Joseph.'

[4] Ten Brink, ii. 283; Pollard, xxxvii. Hohlfeld (*Anglia*, xi. 228) combines two theories by suggesting that the Coventry Grey Friars were driven by the popularity of the rival craft-plays to travel.

observed that both these examples are in the E. Midland area to which philologists assign the text of the *Ludus Coventriae*.

Literary Relations.

Ten Brink, ii. 283, calls attention to the composite character of the cycle, in which groups of various origin are placed side by side without much attempt at imposing a literary unity upon them. He thinks, however, that all the plays received their form in the same part of England, and considers the dialect to be that of the North-East Midlands. In a note (iii. 276) he finds an analogy in the treatment of certain themes between the *Ludus Coventriae* and the Coventry plays proper. Davidson, 259, thinks that the author might have been 'connected with one of the great religious houses of the Fen District.' Hohlfeld (*Anglia*, xi. 219) has some interesting remarks on the cycle. It may be observed that Plays xxx–xxxv in my grouping are evidently taken from a cycle of which only a part was given in each year. The *Purification and Presentation in the Temple* of the Digby MS. affords a parallel example. Possibly Plays viii–xiii in which, as in Plays xxx–xxxv, Contemplacio appears, have the same source.

COVENTRY PLAYS.

[See also account of *Ludus Coventriae*.]

Manuscripts.

A copy, probably the 'original' of the Shearmen and Tailors' play, was in the possession of Thomas Sharp. It is descr᎑᎑᎑ in a colophon as 'T[h]ys matter nevly correcte by Robert Croo the xiiijth day of marche fenysschid in the yere of owre lorde god mccccc & xxxiiij^{te} [153⅘].' At the end are three songs, with the date 1591. A similar copy of the Weavers' play 'nevly translate be Robert Croo in the yere of oure Lorde God Mlv^c xxxiiij^{te} . . . yendide the seycond day of Marche in yere above sayde,' was 'unexpectedly discovered in 1832,' and a transcript made by Sharp. This also has songs at the end, but no date. The collections of Sharp passed into the Staunton collection at Longbridge House, and thence into the Shakespeare Memorial Library at Birmingham, where they were burnt in 1879.

Editions.

(a) 1817. *Shearmen and Tailors' Play.* Thos. Sharp in a series, separately paged, of *Illustrative Papers of the History and Antiquities of the City of Coventry*. [Reprinted 1871 under editorship of W. G. Fretton.]

(b) 1825. *Shearmen and Tailors' Play*. Reprinted from (a) by Thomas Sharp, with full illustrative matter, in *A Dissertation on the Coventry Mysteries*, 83.

(c) 1836. *Weavers' Play*. J. B. Gracie for the Abbotsford Club.

(d) 1838. *Shearmen and Tailors' Play*. William Marriott, *English Miracle-Plays*.

(e) 1897. *Shearmen and Tailors' Play*. Manly, i. 120, from (b).

(f) 1902. *Weavers' Play*. Edited from (c) by F. Holthausen, in *Anglia*, xxv. 209.

(g) 1903. *Shearmen and Tailors' Play*. A. W. Pollard, in *Fifteenth Century Prose and Verse* (*English Garner*), 245.

(h) Both plays are being edited by H. Craig for the E. E. T. S.

The Cycle.

The *Shearmen and Tailors' Play* has a prologue by 'Isaye the profet.' Then follow in order, the Annunciation, the Doubt of Joseph, the Journey to Bethlehem, the Nativity and Shepherds, a dialogue of two 'Profettis,' Herod and the Magi, the Flight to Egypt, the Massacre of the Innocents. The *Weavers' Play* must have followed next in the cycle. It opens with a dialogue of two '*Profetae*.' Then come the Presentation in the Temple and the Dispute with the Elders. The subjects of four of the other plays can be pretty clearly identified. The Smiths' accounts show them to have played the Trial and Crucifixion, to which was added in 1573 the 'new play' of the Death of Judas; the Descent from the Cross passed through various hands from the Pinners and Needlers in 1414 to the Coopers in 1547; the Cappers' accounts point to the Resurrection, Harrowing of Hell, and *Quem quaeritis*, with from 1540 the 'Castell of Emaus'; and those of the Drapers to Doomsday. It is difficult to say how many plays remain unidentified. The crafts were grouped and regrouped, and the total number of plays may have varied. But it would seem that besides the crafts already named, the Mercers, Whittawers, Girdlers, Cardmakers, and Tanners were playing in the middle of the fifteenth century. The 'jest' quoted on p. 358 points to a Pentecost play with the 'xij Articles of the Creed,' similar to that of Chester. It is noticeable that no Old Testament play can be established at Coventry.

Literary Relations.

These plays, of which the *Weavers' Play* was, until recently, difficult to procure, have been but little studied. Two communications by C. Davidson and A. R. Hohlfeld in *Modern Language Notes*, vii. 184,

308, call attention to the fact that the larger part of the dialogue in the *Dispute in the Temple* scene is practically the same as that common to the York, Towneley, and Chester plays (cf. *York Plays*, 158, and A. R. Hohlfeld in *Anglia*, xi. 260),

NEWCASTLE-UPON-TYNE.

Manuscript.

The Shipwrights' Play of *Noah's Ark* was in the hands of its first editor, Henry Bourne; but is not known to be now preserved (Holthausen, 32).

Editions.

(a) 1736. *Noah's Ark; or, The Shipwrights' Ancient Play or Dirge;* in H. Bourne, *Hist. of Newcastle*, 139.

(b) 1789. Reprint of (a) in J. Brand, *Hist. of Newcastle*, ii. 373.

(c) 1825. Reprint of (a) in T. Sharp, *Dissertation on Coventry Mysteries*, 223.

(d) 1897. F. Holthausen, in *Göteborg's Högskola's Årsskrift*, and separately:

(e) 1899. R. Brotanek, in *Anglia*, xxi. 165.

Both (d) and (e) are founded on Bourne's text; but Brotanek has endeavoured to restore what he considers to have been the probable MS. text. This he dates, conjecturally, at about 1425–50.

The Cycle.

The Shipwrights' play deals with the Making of the Ark, but stops short of the Deluge. The personages are Deus, Angelus, Diabolus, Noah, Uxor Noah. The subjects of most of the plays of the other crafts can be recovered, as follows:—

Creation of Adam.	Baptism.
Noah's Ark.	Last Supper.
Offering of Isaac.	Bearing of Cross.
Israel in Egypt.	Burial of Christ.
Kings of Cologne.	Descent into Hell.
Flight into Egypt.	Burial of Our Lady.

Of these, two, the Creation of Adam and the Flight into Egypt, were maintained, in 1454, by one craft, the Bricklayers and Plasterers. The Merchant Adventurers, in 1552, paid for 'fyve playes, whereof the towne must pay for the ostmen playe.' There are six guilds whose plays are not known; so that the total number may have been as many as twenty-three [1].

---

[1] Holthausen, 16.

The accounts of the Merchant Adventurers also include in 1554 and 1558 charges in and about 'Hoggmaygowyk' or 'Hogmagoge[1].' I do not think, with Holthausen, that this was one of the Corpus Christi plays. I think it was a spring or summer folk-feast. One of the London 'giants' is Gogmagog.

NORWICH.

Manuscript.

The extracts, made early in the seventeenth century from the Grocers' Book, and in the possession (1856) of Mr. Fitch, included two versions of the play of the *Fall*. The first was copied into the Book in 1533. It is headed *The Story of y^e Creačon of Eve, $w^t y^e$ expellyng of Adam & Eve out of Paradyce*. It ends with a 'dullfull song,' perhaps the 'newe ballet' paid for in 1534 (cf. p. 388). It appears to have a *lacuna*. The second version is 'newely renvid & accordynge unto y^e Skrypture, begon thys yere A⁰ 1565. A⁰ 7 Eliz.' It is quite a new text. It is provided with two speeches by a Prolocutor, one to be used 'when ye Grocers Pageant is played w^t owte eny other goenge befor y^t,' the other for use 'yf ther goeth eny other Pageants before y^t.' The former speaks of the 'Pageants apparellyd in Wittson dayes' that 'lately be fallen into decayes.'

Editions.

(a) 1856. Robert Fitch in *Norfolk Archaeology*, v. 8, and separately.
(b) 1897. Manly, i. 1, from (a).

The Cycle.

The Grocers' play begins in both versions with the creation of Eve. The first ends with the expulsion from Paradise. The *dramatis personae* are *Pater, Adam, Eva, Serpens*. In the second is added an *Angel*, and after the expulsion Adam and Eve depart 'to ye nether parte of ye Pageants,' are threatened by *Dolor* and *Myserye*, and comforted by the *Holy Ghost*.

A list, dating probably from 1527, makes it possible to complete the outline of the cycle [2]:—

Creation off the world.	Abraham & Isaak.
Paradyse [*Grocers' play*].	Moises & Aaron, with the
Helle Carte.	Children of Israel & Pharo
Abell & Cain.	with his Knyghts.
Noyse Shipp.	Conflict off David and Golias.

---

[1] F. W. Denby, *Newcastle Gilds* (Surtees Soc.), ii. 165, 168.
[2] *Norfolk Archaeology*, iii. 3.

The Birth off Christ with Shep-   The Resurrection.
herds and iij Kyngs of Colen.   The Holy Gost.
The Baptysme of Criste.

ABRAHAM AND ISAAC (Dublin MS.).

Manuscript.

Trinity College, Dublin, MS. D. iv. 18, f. 16ᵛ. In the same hand are a list of mayors and bailiffs of North[ampton] up to 1458 and a brief chronicle, in which N[orthampton] recurs.

Editions.

(a) 1836. J. P. Collier, in *Five Miracle-Plays.*
(b) 1899. R. Brotanek, in *Anglia,* xxi. 21.

Literary Relations.

The play has probably no connexion with Dublin, beyond the fact that the MS. is there. Brotanek conjectures from the character of the MS. that it belongs to Northampton (cf. p. 386). The dialect appears to be South Midland of about the first half of the fifteenth century, and the text to be based on the corresponding play (xi) in the *Viel Testament* (Julleville, *Les Myst.* ii. 363).

ABRAHAM AND ISAAC (Brome MS.).

Manuscript.

'The Book of Brome,' a commonplace book of 1470–80 in the possession of Sir Edward Kerrison of Brome Manor, Norfolk.

Editions.

(a) 1884. L. T. Smith, in *Anglia,* vii. 316.
(b) 1886. L. T. Smith, in *A Commonplace Book of the Fifteenth Century.*
(c) 1887. W. Rye, in *Norfolk Antiquarian Miscellany,* iii. 1.
(d) 1897. Manly, i. 41, from (a) and (b).

Literary Relations.

The play is 465 lines long. There is an epilogue by a *Doctor,* but no title or prologue, and nothing to show that it was, or was not, part of a cycle. The text is probably derived from a common source with that of the corresponding Chester play: cf. Pollard, 185; A. R. Hohlfeld, in *M. L. N.* v. 222.

F. Holthausen has some critical notes on the text in *Anglia,* xiii. 361.

CROXTON PLAY: THE SACRAMENT.

Manuscript.

Trinity College, Dublin, MS. F. 4. 20, of the latter half of the fifteenth century.

Editions.

(a) 1861. Whitley Stokes, in *Transactions of Philological Society,* 1860–1 (Appendix).

(b) 1897. Manly, i. 239.

There is a prologue by two *Vexillatores,* ending—

> 'And y^t place yow, thys gaderyng that here y^s,
> At Croxston on Monday y^t shall be sen ;
> To see the conclusyon of this lytell processe
> Hertely welcum shall yow bene.
>
> .   .   .   .
>
> Now, mynstrell, blow vp with a mery stevyn !'

Then comes a title : ' Here after foloweth the Play of the Conversyon of Ser Jonathas the Jewe by Myracle of the Blyssed Sacrament.' The play is 927 lines long, with occasional lines in Latin. It ends with a *Te Deum.* The colophon runs : ' Thus endyth the Play of the Blyssyd Sacrament, whyche myracle was don in the forest of Aragon, in the famous cite Eraclea, the yere of ower Lord God M^{l}ccc.lxi, to whom be honower. Amen !' This account of the event on which the play is founded is confirmed by ll. 56–60 of the prologue. The date of composition cannot therefore be earlier than 1461, and probably is not much later. After the colophon is a list of the *dramatis personae,* who are twelve in all, and the note 'IX may play it at ease,' signed 'R.C.' The name Croxton is common to places in Norfolk, Cambridgeshire, Leicestershire, and other counties. Further identification may perhaps be helped by ll. 540–1—

> 'Inquyre to the Colkote, for ther ys hys loggyng,
> A lytylle besyde Babwelle Mylle.'

The stage-directions imply a ' place,' with ' stages' for the chief players, a 'tabyll,' and a 'chyrche' (ll. 149, 288, 305, 445).

F. Holthausen has some textual criticism on the play in *Englische Studien,* xvi. 150, and *Anglia,* xv. 198.

SHREWSBURY FRAGMENTS.

On these, which are transitional between the liturgical play and the miracle-play proper, cf. p. 90.

DIGBY PLAYS.

[*Authorities.*—The best edition is that of Dr. Furnivall. The careful study by K. Schmidt, published partly as a Berlin dissertation (1884), partly in *Anglia*, viii (1885), 371, should be consulted.]

Manuscript.

Bodleian Digby MS. 133. The dramatic contents of this composite manuscript are as follows:—(i) f. 37. *The Conversion of St. Paul.* This is written in a single hand, except that a second has inserted on f. 45 a scene between two devils, Belial and Mercury. At the end (f. 50ᵛ), is ' ffinis conuercionis sancti pauli.' There is a prologue, headed *Poeta*, against which has been written in a later hand ' Myles Blomefylde.' Schmidt, *Diss.* 6, identifies a Miles Blomefylde as a monk of Bury born in 1525. (ii) f. 95. *St. Mary Magdalen,* written in the second hand of (i). At the beginning are the initials M. B.; at the end (f. 145) 'Explycit oreginale de sancta Maria magdalena.' (iii) f. 146. *Massacre of Innocents* and *Purification,* written in the first hand of (i). At the beginning is ' candelmes day & the kyllynge of the children of Israell, anno domini 1512 '; at the end ' Anno domini Millesimo, cccccxij,' and after a list of ' The Namys of the Pleyers ' the entry ' Ihon Parfre ded wryte thys booke.' None of these notes seem to be in the hand of the text. (iv) f. 158. Fragment of morality of *Mind, Will, and Understanding,* found complete in the *Macro MS.* (cf. p. 437), in a hand apparently distinct from those of (i), (ii), (iii). This also has ' M. B.' at the beginning.—The texts in the MS. are probably early sixteenth-century copies of late fifteenth-century plays. There is nothing to show that Parfre or Blomfield was concerned in the authorship. They may have been the copyists. If Blomfield was really the monk of Bury born in 1525, he was probably only an owner of the MS.

Editions.

(a) 1773. *Massacre of Innocents,* in T. Hawkins, *Origin of the English Drama.*

(b) 1835. *Massacre of Innocents, Conversion of St. Paul, St. Mary Magdalen,* in T. Sharp, *Ancient Mysteries from the Digby Manuscripts* (Abbotsford Club).

(c) 1838. *Massacre of Innocents,* in W. Marriott, *English Miracle-Plays.*

(d) 1882. Complete series in F. J. Furnivall, *The Digby Mysteries* (New Shakspere Soc., reprinted in 1896 for E. E. T. S.).

(e) 1890. *St. Mary Magdalen* (part only), from (d), in Pollard, 49.

(f) 1897. *Conversion of St. Paul,* from (d), in Manly, i. 215.

The Plays.

The plays appear to have been accidentally brought together in one MS., and should be treated separately for the purposes of literary history.

A. Conversion of St. Paul.

Schmidt, *Diss.* 28, assigns this to an East Midland author, and a Southern scribe. The play opens with a prologue by the *Poeta* who speaks of 'owr processe.' In the first scene or 'station,' Saul starts for Damascus and 'rydyth forth with hys seruantes a-bout the place & owt of the place.' There is a 'conclusyon' by the 'Poeta—si placet,'—

> 'ffynally of this stacon we mak a conclusyon,
> besechyng thys audyens to folow and succede
> with all your delygens this generall processyon.'

After a stage-direction ' ffinis Istius stacionis, et altera sequitur,' the *Poeta* introduces another ' prosses,'—

> ' Here shalbe brefly shewyd with all our besynes
> At thys pagent saynt poullys conuercyon.'

This scene takes place outside and in Damascus. There is a tempest, and ' godhed spekyth in heuyn.' Saul meets Ananias, and 'thys stacion' is concluded by the *Poeta*, and ' ffinis Istius secunde stacionis et sequitur tarcia.'

Again the *Poeta* calls on the audience ' To vnderstond thys pagent at thys lytyll stacion.' Saul returns to Jerusalem, preaches and plans to escape over the wall in a basket. Here the later hand inserted the devil scene. The *Poeta* has his ' Conclusyo,' which ends :—

> ' Thys lytyll pagent thus conclud we
> as we can, lackyng lytturall scyens ;
> besechyng yow all of hye and low degre,
> owr sympylnes to hold excusyd, and lycens,
> That of Retoryk haue non intellygens ;
> Commyttyng yow all to owr lord Ihesus,
> To whoys lawd ye syng,—Exultet celum laudibus.'

The play, but for the devil scene, follows closely the biblical narrative. It was probably written for a small village, and for scene had a *platea*, and two *loca*, for Damascus and Jerusalem (with possibly a third for heaven). The audience moved with the actors from one ' station ' or ' pageant ' to the other, and back again. A later hand has inserted marginal directions for a ' Daunce ' at various points in the speeches of the *Poeta*.

B. *St. Mary Magdalen.*

Schmidt, *Anglia*, viii. 385, assigns this to a West Midland author and Kentish scribe. Furnivall, 53, thinks the dialect East Midland. The plot covers the whole legendary life of the Magdalen, as it appears in the *Golden Legend.* The characters are very numerous, and include Satan and other devils, with allegorical figures such as the 'Kyngs of the World and the Flesch' and the 'Seven Dedly Synnes.' The action is not in any way divided in the manuscript, and implies an elaborate stationary *mise en scène* with various *loca.* These include the 'castell of Maudleyn' or Magdalum, thrones for the *Imperator*, who opens the play by calling for silence, Herod and Pilate, 'a stage, and Helle ondyr-neth that stage' for 'the prynse of dylles,' Jerusalem with a 'place,' an 'erbyr' or arbour, a tavern, the 'howse of symont leprovs,' a *sepulchrum* for Lazarus, and another for the *Quem quaeritis* and *Hortulanus* scenes which are introduced, a palace for the King of 'Marcylle' (Marseilles), a heathen temple, a 'hevyne' able to open, a lodge for the Magdalen in Marcylle, another castle, a rock, and a wilderness. There is also a practicable ship which goes to and from Marcylle (l. 1395 'Here xall entyre a shyp with a mery song'; l. 1445 'Her goth the shep owt of the place'; l. 1717 'Ett tunc navis venit in placeam'; l. 1797 'tunc remigat a montem'; l. 1879 'et tunc navis venit adcirca plateam'; l. 1915 'et tunc remigant a monte'; l. 1923 'Here goth the shep owȝt ofe the place'). The play ends with a *Te Deum*; but the following lines, added after the *Explicit*, suggest that the author had readers as well as spectators in mind:—

> 'yff Ony thyng Amysse be,
> blame connyng, and nat me :
> I desyer the redars to be my frynd,
> yff ther be ony amysse, that to amend.'

C. *Massacre of the Innocents.*

Assigned by Schmidt, *Diss.* 18, to a Midland author and Southern scribe. Against the title of the play has been written, in a hand identified as that of the chronicler Stowe, 'the vij booke.' Evidently the play was one of a series, spread over successive years, and given on Saint Anne's day (July 26). This is shown by the opening speech of a *Poeta*, from which I extract:—

> 'This solenne fest to be had in remembraunce
> Of blissed seynt Anne moder to our lady,
>
> .   .   .   .
>
> The last yeer we shewid you in this place

how the shepherdes of Cristes birth made letificacion,
And thre kynges that came fro ther Cuntrees be grace
To worshipe Iesu, with enteer deuocion ;
And now we purpose with hooll affeccion
To procede in oure mater as we can,
And to shew you of our ladies purificacion
That she made in the temple, as the vsage was than.
. . . .
ffrendes, this processe we purpose to pley as we can
before you all, here in your presens,
To the honour of god, our lady, & seynt Anne,
besechyng you to geve vs peseable Audiens.
And ye menstrallis, doth your diligens,
& ye virgyncs, shcwc cumme sport & plesure,
These people to solas, & to do god reuerens,
As ye be appoynted, doth your besy curo !
    ¶ Et tripident.'

The action includes the Wrath of Herod, with a comic knight, Watkin,
the Flight into Egypt, the Massacre of the Innocents, the Death of
Herod, the Purification. The stage-directions mention a ' place' and
a 'tempill.' In the latter are the virgins, who 'tripident' with Anne
at the end. The *Poeta* excuses the ' rude eloquens ' and ' sympyll
cunnyng' of his company, promises 'the disputacion of the doctours '
for next year, and calls on the minstrels and virgins for a final dance.

D. *Morality of Wisdom.*
See *Texts* (ii), s. v. *Macro Morals.*

BURIAL AND RESURRECTION.

Manuscript.

Bodleian MS. e Museo, 160, f. 140. Furnivall, vii. 166, asserts
that this once formed part of the *Digby MS.* 133, but offers no proof.
The copy seems to date from the early fifteenth century. After the
Explicit, in a later hand, is ' written by me . . .'; unfortunately the
name is torn off. Lines here and there in the earlier part of the piece
have been crossed out.

Editions.

(a) 1843. Wright and Halliwell, *Reliquiae Antiquae,* ii. 124.
(b) 1882. F. J. Furnivall, *The Digby Plays,* 171 (New Shakspere
Soc., reprinted 1896 for E. E. T. S.).
See study by K. Schmidt in *Anglia,* viii. 393.

The Play.

Schmidt assigns the play to a writer whose dialect was a mixture of Northern and East Midland forms; Morris to a Northern author and West Midland scribe. Ten Brink, ii. 287, also thinks it to be Northern, and to date from 1430–60. Apparently the author set out to write, not a drama, but a narrative poem, mainly in dialogue. The first fifteen lines are headed 'The prologe of this treyte or meditatione off the buryalle of Criste & mowrnynge therat,' and contain a request to 'Rede this treyte.' The first 419 lines have a few narrative phrases introducing the speeches, such as 'Said Maudleyn,' 'Said Joseph.' At this point the writer seems to have stopped these, crossed out such as he had already written, and inserted in the margin of his second page,—

'This is a play to be playede, on part on gudfriday after-none, & the other part opon Esterday after the resurrectione, In the morowe, but at the begynnynge ar certene lynes [the prologue] which must not be saide if it be plaiede, which (. . . *a line cut off*).'

The Good Friday scene is an elaborate *planctus*. It is opened by Joseph of Arimathea, and the three Maries. Then comes Nicodemus, and the body of Christ is taken from the cross. The Virgin Mary enters with St. John, and the *planctus* is resumed. The body is laid in the sepulchre, and the scene is closed with—

> 'Thus her endes the most holy
> Beriall of the body of Crist Iesu.'

The Easter morning scene begins with—

> 'Her begynnes his resurrection
> On pashe daye at Morn.'

It contains a *Quem quaeritis*, a scene of lamentation between Peter, Andrew, and John, a *Hortulanus*, with a second apparition to all three Maries. They sing the first part of the *Victimae paschali*, 'in cantifracto vel saltem in pallinodio,' and the Apostles come in for the dialogue part. Then the tidings are announced, and Peter and John visit the sepulchre; after which, 'Tunc cantant omnes simul *Scimus Christum* vell aliam sequentiam aut ympnum de resurrectione.'

UNIDENTIFIED PLAYS.

(i) C. Hastings, *Le Théâtre Français et Anglais*, 167, says:—

'Il existe, en plus des quatre cycles de Mystères dont nous avons parlé dans les chapitres précédents, une cinquième collection (manuscrit), propriété d'un simple particulier, M. Nicholls.'

(ii) W. C. Hazlitt, *Manual for the Collector and Amateur of Old English Plays*, 274, says:—

'Mr..F. S. Ellis told me (Dec. 10, 1864) that a gentleman at Leipsic then had a fragment of a large sheet on which was printed in types formed from a block and of a very large size an English Miracle-Play. In its perfect state it seems to have been intended to attach to a church door or any other suitable place.'

CORNWALL

i. *Origo Mundi: Passio Domini: Resurrexio Domini.*

Manuscripts.

(i) *Bodl. MS.* 791. Fifteenth century, with some alterations and additional stage-directions in a later hand. The text is Cornish, not earlier in date than the fourteenth century. Mr. Pedler (Norris, ii. 506) puts it, not very convincingly, at the end of the thirteenth.

(ii) *Bodl. MS.* 28,556. Seventeenth-century copy of (i), with an' English translation of the larger part of the text by John Keigwyn, of Mousehole, 1695.

Edition.

1859. In Edwin Norris, *The Ancient Cornish Drama*, from (i), with modern translation by the editor.

Analysis.

The text forms three dramas, intended, as the closing words of the first two show, for performance on three consecutive days. At the end of each is a diagram of the disposition of the *pulpita* or *tenti* (cf. p. 391) for the day. The action on each day is continuous, but for the sake of comparison I divide it into scenes. These are sometimes indicated by a *Hic incipit* or similar formula.

(1) *Hic Incipit Ordinale de Origine Mundi.*

Fall of Lucifer (line 48).

Creation and Fall of Man (1–437).

Cain and Abel (438–633).

Seth in Paradise, and Death of Adam (634–916).

Noah and the Flood (917–1258).

Abraham and Isaac (1259–1394).

Moses and the Exodus (1395–1708).

Moses in the Wilderness (1709–1898).

David and the Rods (1899–2104).

David and Bathsheba (2105–2376).

Building of the Temple (2377–2628).

Prophecy of Maximilla (2629–2778).

Bridge over Cedron (2779–2824).

The diagram gives *Celum, Tortores, Infernum, Rex Pharao, Rex Dauid, Rex Sal[omon], Abraham, Ortus.*

(2) *Hic Incipit Passio Domini Nostri Jhesu Christi.*

Temptation (1–172).

Entry into Jerusalem (173–330).

Cleansing of the Temple (331–392).

Healing of Bartimaeus (393–454).

Jesus in House of Simon the Leper (455–552).

Conspiracy of Jews (533–584).

Treachery of Judas (585–616).

Last Supper (617–930).

Gethsemane (931–1200).

Jesus before Caiaphas (1200–1504).

Remorse and Death of Judas (1505–1566).

Jesus before Pilate (1567–1616).

Jesus before Herod (1617–1816).

Condemnation (1817–2533), including—

Dream of Pilate's Wife (1907–1968, 2193–2212).

Cross brought from Cedron (2534–2584).

Bearing of the Cross (2585–2662).

Crucifixion (2663–2840).

Casting of Lots (2841–2860).

Death of Jesus (2861–3098), including—

Planctus Mariae (2925–2954).

Longinus (3003–3030).

Harrowing of Hell (3031–3078).

Descent from Cross (3099–3201).

Burial (3202–3216).

The diagram gives *Celum, Tortores, Doctores, Pilatus, Herodes, Princeps Annas, Cayaphas, Centurio.*

(3) *Hic Incipit Ordinale de Resurrexione Domini Nostri Jhesu Christi.*

Release of Joseph and Nicodemus (1–96, 307–334, 625–662).

Harrowing of Hell, resumed (97–306).

Setting of Watch (335–422).

Resurrection (423–678).

Quem quaeritis (679–834).

Hortulanus (835–892).

Incredulity of Thomas (893–1230, 1345–1586).

Peregrini (1231–1344).

Death of Pilate (1587–2360), including—

Veronica and Tiberius 1587–2360).

Ascension (2361–2630).

The diagram gives *Celum, Tortores, Infernum, Pilatus, Imperator, Josep Abar[imat], Nichodemus, Milites.*

At the end of (1) and (3) the minstrels are directed to pipe for a dance.

Locality.

Mr. Norris prints an opinion of Mr. Pedler that the place-names suggest the neighbourhood of Penrhyn, and that the plays may have been composed in the collegiate house, hard by, of Glasney.

ii. *Creation of the World.*

Manuscripts.

(i) *Bodl.* 219, with colophon 'Heare endeth the Creacion of the worlde wth noyes flude wryten by William Jordan: the xiith of August, 1611.' The text is Cornish, with English stage-directions containing forms earlier than 1611.

(ii) *Bodl.* 31,504 (MS. Corn. C. 1). Copy of (i), with English translation by John Keigwyn, 1693, written by ' H. Usticke.'

iii) *Harl.* 1867. Similar copy of (i), with Keigwyn's translation.

(iv) MS. belonging (in 1864) to J. C. Hotten the bookseller, containing also a copy of the narrative *Passion* or *Mount Calvary.*'

Editions.

(a) 1827. *The Creation of the World, with Noah's Flood.* Edited from (iii) by Davies Gilbert (with Keigwyn's translation).

(b) 1864. *Gwreans an Bys. The Creation of the World.* Edited from (i), with a [new] translation by Whitley Stokes, as appendix to *Transactions of Philological Society* (1863).

The Play.

The text is headed ' The first daie [of] ye playe ' and ends with a direction to minstrels to pipe for dancing, and an invitation to return on the morrow to see the Redemption. It is, therefore, probably unfinished. It appears to be based, with certain additions, on the *Origo Mundi.* It is continuous, but may be divided as follows :—

Creation and Fall of Lucifer (1–334).	Death of Cain (1431–1726).
Temptation and Fall (335–1055).	Visit of Seth to Paradise (1727–1964).
Cain and Abel. Birth of Seth (1056–1430).	Death of Adam (1965–2093).
	Seth and Enoch (2094–2210).
	Noah's Flood (2211–2530).

iii. *St. Meriasek.*

Manuscript.

In *Hengwrt MSS.* of Mr. Wynne at Peniarth. Cornish *Ordinale de Vita Sancti Mereadoci Episcopi et Confessoris,* written by ' dominus Hadton ' in 1504. At the end is a circular diagram.

Edition.

1872. *Beunans Meriasek: The Life of Saint Meriasek.* Edited and translated by Whitley Stokes.

Locality.

Mr. Stokes suggests Camborne, of which place St. Meriasek was patron. The play invokes St. Meriasek and St. Mary of Camborne at the close.

II. POPULAR MORALITIES.

THE PRIDE OF LIFE.

Manuscript.

Written in two hands of the first half of the fifteenth century on blank spaces of a *Computus* of Holy Trinity Priory, Dublin, for 1343, preserved in the Irish Record Office, Dublin (Christ Church collection).

Editions.

1891. J. Mills in *Proceedings of Royal Soc. of Antiquaries of Ireland.*

1898. Brandl, 2.

Cf. H. Morley, *English Writers*, vii. 1730.

The play was probably written early in the fifteenth century. The dialect is that of the South of England, not far from London, modified by Northern scribes.

Only a fragment (502 ll.) is preserved, but a prologue gives the plot. There is no title; but ' [A mens]ke gam schal gyn & ende' (l. 7), and '[Of Kyng of] lif I wol ȝou telle' (l. 17). The extant characters are *Rex Vivus, Primus Miles Fortitudo, Secundus Miles Sanitas, Regina, Nuntius Mirth, Episcopus.* The King rejoices with Mirth and his soldiers, and Queen and Bishop vainly call on him to repent. Later in the play Death and Life strove for the King, and Death took him. He was claimed by the 'ffendis,' but 'oure lady mylde' prayed to have him.

The play was out of doors (l. 10); the King had a *tentorium* which could be closed (l. 306); the Bishop sat on his 'se' (*sedes*); and so probably with the other actors, except Mirth, who perhaps came in 'oure þe lake' (l. 269); cf. Brandl, xix.

MACRO MORALS.

Manuscripts.

(a) *Macro MS.*, formerly in the possession of Mr. Cox Macro, now in that of Mr. Gurney, of Keswick Hall, Norfolk. The MS. appears from a gloss in *Mankind* (l. 674; cf. Brandl, xxvi), naming King Edward, to have been written during the reign of Edward IV (1461–1483). At the end of two of the plays is the name of Hyngham, a monk, to whom the MS. belonged.

(b) *Digby MS.* 133, on which cf. p. 428, has on f. 158 the first 754 lines of *Mind, Will, and Understanding.* The handwriting is said to be the same as that of the *Macro MS.* (Collier, ii. 207).

[A complete edition of the three moralities of the *Macro MS.* has long been contemplated by the E. E. T. S.]

i. *The Castle of Perseverance.*

Edition. 1890. Pollard, 64 (408 lines only).

Pollard dates the play not later than the middle of the reign of Henry VI. It contains about 3,500 lines.

The subject is the struggle of good and bad qualities for *Humanum Genus.* On the one side are *Malus Angelus* and *Mundus, Belial,* and *Caro,* aided by the Seven Deadly Sins and *Voluptas, Stultitia, Detractio*: on the other *Bonus Angelus,* with *Confessio, Schrift, Penitencia,* and the Six Divine Graces. Amongst other episodes *Humanum Genus* is besieged in the *Castle of Perseverance.* At the end *Misericordia, Iustitia, Pax, Veritas,* dispute in heaven, and *Pater sedens in trono* inclines to mercy.

The indications of *mise en scène* are very valuable. On the first leaf of the MS. is a diagram of the playing place, reproduced by Sharp, 23. There is a large circle with a double circumference, in which is written, 'This is the watyr a bowte the place, if any dyche may be mad ther it schal be pleyed; or ellys that it be stronglye barryd al a bowte : & lete nowth ower many stytelerys be withinne the plase.' Within the circle is a rude representation of a castle, and above, 'This is the castel of perseveranse that stondyth in the myddys of the place ; but lete no men sytte ther for lettynge of syt, for ther schal be the best of all.' Beneath the castle is a small bed, with the legend, 'Mankynde is bed schal be under the castel, & ther schal the sowle lye under the bed tyl he schal ryse & pleye.' At the side is a further direction, 'Coveytyse cepbord schal be at the ende of the castel, be the beddys feet.' Outside the circle are written five directions for scaffolds, 'Sowth, Caro skaffold — West, Mundus skaffold — Northe, Belial skaffold—North Est, Coveytyse skaffold—Est, deus skaffold.' At the foot of the page are some notes for costume : '& he that schal pley belyal, loke that he have gunne powder brennyng in pypys in his

hands and in his ers, and in his ars whanne he gothe to batayle. The
iiij dowters schul be clad in mentelys, Mercy in wyth, rythwysnesse
in red al togedyr, Trewthe in sad grene, & Pes al in blake, and they
schul pleye in the place al to gedyr tyl they brynge up the sowle.'

There is a prologue by two *vexillatores*, who declare—

> 'These percell in propyrtes we spose us to playe,
> This day sevenenyt before you in syth,
> At N on the grene in ryal aray.'

They add that they will 'be onward be underne of the day' (9 a.m.).

ii. *Mind, Will, and Understanding.*
Editions.

1835. T. Sharp, *Ancient Mysteries* (Abbotsford Club, 754 lines from
Digby MS.).

1837. W. B. D. D. Turnbull (Abbotsford Club, the rest from
Macro MS.).

1882. F. J. Furnivall, *Digby Plays*, 139 (754 lines only).

Lucifer seduces Mind, Will, and Understanding. These are the
three parts of Anima, who enters with devils running from under her
skirts. Everlasting Wisdom effects a re-conversion. There are a
number of mute persons attendant on the chief characters, whose
coming and going, 'dysgysyde,' create scenic effects, as in a masque.
There are minstrels and a hornpipe, songs and dances. At one point
Lucifer snatches up 'a shrewde boy' (perhaps from the audience),
and carries him off. An allusion to the Holborn quest suggests
a London origin, but Schmidt (*Anglia*, viii. 390) thinks the dialect to
be that of the north border of the West Midlands.

iii. *Mankind.*
Editions.

1897. Manly, i. 315.

1898. Brandl, 37.

The text is 901 lines long. A list of place-names (l. 491) makes it
probable that it belongs to the borders of Norfolk and Cambridgeshire.

Mercy and Mischief, the latter helped by Nought, New Gyse,
Nowadays, and the devil Titivillus, essay in turns to win the soul
of Mankind.

The scene is divided. Part represents a tavern, of which Titivillus
is host; part a 'deambulatorye' outside. A reference to the spectators
(l. 29) runs, 'O ʒe souerens, þat sytt, and ʒe brotherne, þat stonde
ryghte wppe': cf. Brandl, xxxii.

The Summoning of Everyman.

Editions.

[1509–1530.] Richard Pynson (fragment in B. M.).
[1509–1530.] Richard Pynson (fragment in Bodl.).
[1521–1537.] John Skot. 'Here begynneth a treatyse how the hye fader of heuen sendeth dethe to somon euery creature to come and gyue a counte of theyr lyues in this Worlde, and is in maner of a morall playe' (B. M. and Huth Library).
[1529–1537.] John Skot (in St. Paul's Churchyard).

There are modern editions by Hawkins (1773, vol. i), Gödeke (1865), Hazlitt-Dodsley (1874, vol. i), Pollard (1890, part only, and in full in *Fifteenth Century Prose and Verse*, 1903), H. Logeman, *Elckerlijk and Everyman* (1892), F. Sidgwick (1902). Another is announced in a series edited by I. Gollancz.

There are about 900 lines. Pollard, 202, assigns the text to the end of the fifteenth century; Ten Brink, ii. 302, to the reign of Edward IV. Prof. H. Logeman, *Elckerlijk* (1892), argues the play to be an English version of the closely similar Dutch *Elckerlijk*, attributed to Petrus Dorlandus of Diest, but K. H. de Raaf, *Spyeghel der Salicheyt van Elckerlijk* (1897), would invert the relation: cf. Brandl, xiv. The characters are Messenger, God, Death, Everyman, Fellowship, Kindred, Goods, Good Deeds, Knowledge, Confession, Beauty, Strength, Discretion, Five Wits, Angel, Doctor. The Messenger prologizes. God sends Death for Everyman, who finds that no one will accompany him save Good Deeds. The Doctor epilogizes. There are no indications of the *mise en scène*, except that there was a central scaffold for the 'House of Salvation' (Gödeke, 174, 200, cf. Brandl, xx).

The World and the Child.

Editions.

An Oxford bookseller, John Dorne, had a copy of 'mundus, a play' in 1520[1].

1522. Wynkyn de Worde. 'Here begynneth a propre newe Interlude of the Worlde and the chylde, otherwyse called (Mundus & Infans) . . .'

1523. Wynkyn de Worde.

There are a reprint by Lord Althorp (Roxburghe Club, 1817) and modern editions in Hazlitt-Dodsley, vol. i; Manly, i. 353.

[1] *Collectanea* (Oxf. Hist. Soc.), i. 130.

The *dramatis personae* are Mundus or the World, Infans or Dalliance or Wanton or Love-Lust and Liking or Manhood or Shame or Age or Repentance, Conscience, Folly, Perseverance. The representative of Man in various ages is alternately won over to good and evil. There are 979 lines. Collier, ii. 224; Pollard, li, assign the play to the reign of Henry VII; Brandl, xlii, thinks that the use of the *Narrenmotif* points to a date of composition not long before that of publication. Mundus says, 'Here I sette semely in se' (l. 22), and Manhood 'Here in this sete sytte I' (l. 285).

John Skelton. (*Magnificence.*)

Skelton was born, probably in Norfolk, about 1460. He studied at Cambridge and acquired fame as a scholar. Both universities honoured him with the degree of *poeta laureatus*. He was tutor to Henry VIII as a boy, and became rector of Diss in Norfolk. But he died in sanctuary at Westminster (1529), driven there on account of his bitter satires against Wolsey. In his *Garland of Laurell* (pr. 1523), a late work, he has a list of his writings, including—

> ' Of Vertu also the souerayne enterlude:
>
> . . . .
>
> His commedy, Achademios callyd by name:
>
> . . . .
>
> And of Soueraynte a noble pamphelet;
> And of Magnyfycence a notable mater.'

Bale, *Scriptores*, i. 652, ascribes to him *Comoediam de uirtute*, Lib. 1; *De magnificentia comoediam*, Lib. 1; *Theatrales ludos*, Lib. 1; *De bono ordine comoediam*, Lib. 1. *Magnificence* is, however, his only extant play.

Warton (Hazlitt-Warton, iii. 287) describes a piece shown him by William Collins, the poet, at Chichester, about 1759. He says:—

'It is the Nigramansir, a morall *Enterlude* and a pithie, written by Maister Skelton laureate, and plaid before the King and other estatys at Woodstoke on Palme Sunday. It was printed by Wynkyn de Worde in a thin quarto, in the year 1504. It must have been presented before Henry VII, at the royal manor or palace at Woodstock in Oxfordshire, now destroyed. The characters are a Necromancer or conjurer, the devil, a notary public, Simony, and Philargyria or Avarice. It is partly a satire on some abuses in the church . . . The story, or plot, is the trial of Simony and Avarice.'

Warton proceeds to describe the action at some length. Nothing further is known of the play. Ritson, *Bibliographia Poetica*, 106, said 'it is utterly incredible that the *Nigramansir* . . . ever existed,' and Mr. H. E. D. Blakiston (*Eng. Hist. Rev.* for April, 1896) has called attention to several cases in which Warton showed *mala fides* as a literary historian. In another place (iii. 310) Warton incidentally calls the piece ' Skelton's *The Trial of Simonie.*' E. G. Duff, *Hand Lists of English Printers*, Part i, knows of no extant copy.

Magnificence.

Editions.

[1529–1533.] John Rastell. ' Magnyfycence, a goodly interlude and a mery, deuysed and made by mayster Skelton, poet laureate, late deceasyd.' Folio.

1533. John Rastell. Quarto.

1821. J. Littledale (Roxburghe Club).

1843. A. Dyce, *Poetical Works of Skelton*, i. 225.

1890. Pollard, 106 (extract).

The characters are Felicity, Liberty, Measure, Magnificence, Fancy, Counterfeit Countenance, Crafty Countenance, Cloked Collusion, Courtly Abusion, Folly, Adversity, Poverty, Despair, Mischief, Good Hope, Redress, Sad Circumspection, Perseverance. The plot shows Magnificence brought low by evil counsellors, and restored by good ones. The players come in and out of 'the place.' There are 2,596 lines. The play was written later than 1515, as a reference to the liberality of the dead Louis of France (l. 283) must intend Louis XII who died in that year, not the niggard Louis XI.

Sir David Lyndsay. (*Ane Satyre of the Thrie Estaitis.*)

Sir David Lyndsay ' of the Mount' in Fifeshire was born in 1490. By 1511 he was employed in the royal household, first as an actor or musician, then as ' Keeper of the Kingis Grace's person.' In 1529 he became Lyon King at Arms, a post which included the charge of court entertainments. His satire did not spare the church, and he seems to have been in sympathy with Knox and other reformers, but he did not so far commit himself as to endanger his office, which he held until his death in 1555.

The Thrie Estaitis.

Performances.

(i) *Jan.* 6, 1540, *Linlithgow*, before James V. This performance, the first of which there is any satisfactory evidence, was described by Sir W. Eure in a letter to Cromwell (Ellis, *Original Letters*, 3rd Series,

iii. 275 ; Brewer-Gairdner, xv. 36), enclosing a ' Copie of the Nootes of the Interluyde.' The version seems to have been different from that now extant. ' Solaice ' figured as the presenter. Eure mentions the 'scaffald ' and ' the interluyds of the Play.' He adds that, as a result, James V admonished the Bishops to reform their ways.

(ii) *June 7 (Whit-Tuesday)*, 1552, *Cupar of Fife*. The Bannatyne MS. (see below) has the 'Proclamation maid at Cowpar of Fyffe, upon the Castell-hill, 7 June, beginning at seven.' This was therefore the extant version. The year is fixed by an incidental reference to the day (June 7) as Whit-Tuesday.

(iii) 1554 (?), *Edinburgh*. Henry Charteris, in his preface to Lyndsay's *Warkis* of 1568 (Laing, iii. 231), says of the ' makar's ' relations to the clergy, ' Sic ane spring he gaif thame in the Play, playit besyde Edinburgh, in presence of the Quene Regent, and ane greit part of the Nobilitie, with ane exceding greit nowmer of pepill, lestand fra ix houris afoir none till vj houris at evin.' The Bannatyne MS. gives the play as ' maid in the Grenesyd besyd Edinburgh,' and ' in anno 155– 3eiris.' Cf. Appendix W, p. 366.

Editions.

(*a*) 1602. Robert Charteris. ' Ane satyre of the thrie estaits, in commendation of vertew in vituperation of vyce. Maid be Sir Dauid Lindesay of the Mont, alias, Lyon King of Armes.'

Diligence, as presenter, summons the three estates before Rex Humanitas. Many ' Vycis' and other allegorical personages appear before the Rex on his ' royall sait.' In ll. 1288–1411 comes the first interlude (although the term is not used in the text) of ' The Sowtar and Tailor.' At l. 1931 is the ' End of the First Part of the Satyre,' with the direction, ' Now sall the Pepill mak collatioun : then beginnis the Interlude : the Kings, Bischops, and principal Players being out of their seats.' This interlude introduces the Pauper, Pardoner, Sowtar, and others. Part ii begins at l. 2298. At l. 4283, ' Heir sall enter Folie,' and at l. 4483, ' Heir sall Folie begin his Sermon, as followis.' The theme is, of course, *Stultorum numerus infinitus*, and at the close the preacher names recipients of his ' Follie Hattis or Hudes' (cf. ch. xvi). At l. 4629, the people are finally dismissed to dance and drink, Diligence calling on a minstrel.

(*b*) † 1568. Bannatyne MS. (ed. Hunterian Club, 1873–1896, Part iv).

George Bannatyne included in his collection of pieces by the Scots ' makaris ' (*a*) the ' Proclamation ' at Cupar of Fife (see above), (*b*) a preliminary interlude, not in Charteris's edition, of a Cottar, an Auld Man and his Wife, a 'Fuill,' &c.; (*c*) seven extracts from the play, headed, 'Heir begynnis Schir Dauid Lyndsay Play maid in the Grenesyd besyd Edinburgh, quhilk I writtin bot schortly be Interludis, levand the grave mater thereof, becaws the samyne abuse is weill reformit in Scotland, praysit be God, quhairthrow I omittit that principall mater and writtin only Sertane mirry Interludis thairof verry pleasand, begynnyng at the first part of the Play.'

1869. F. Hall, *Works of Lindsay*, Pt. iv (E. E. T. S. o. s. 37).

1879. D. Laing, *Works of Lindsay*, vol. ii.

[Other editions are enumerated by Laing, iii. 259. There is an analysis of the play in T. F. Henderson, *Scottish Vernacular Literature*, 219.]

III. TUDOR MAKERS OF INTERLUDES.

HENRY MEDWALL.

Medwall was chaplain to John Morton, cardinal and Archbishop of Canterbury (1486–1500), who is probably the 'my lord' of *Nature*, i. 1438. Besides *Nature*, he wrote an interlude 'of the fyndyng of Troth, who was carried away by ygnoraunce and ypocresy,' played by the King's players before Henry VIII at Richmond on Jan. 6, 1514. The 'foolys part' was the best, but the play was too long to please the King (cf. p. 201). See also s. v. *Lucrece* (p. 458).

Nature.

Editions.

[1530–4.] William Rastell. 'A goodly interlude of Nature compyled by mayster Henry Medwall,' &c.

1898. Brandl, 73.

There are two 'partes' of the 'processe' (i. 1434). The first (1439 ll.) has Mundus, Worldly Affection, Man, Nature, Innocency, Reason, Sensuality, Privy Council, Pride, a Boy, Shamefastness. In the second (1421 ll.), on a different day, some of these recur, with Bodily Lust, Wrath, Envy, Sloth, Gluttony, Humility, Charity, Abstinence, Liberality, Chastity, Good Occupation, and Patience. The personages come in and out at 'dorys' (i. 728) and sit down on 'stole' or 'chayr.' There was also a fire (ii. 518 sqq.). Probably the scene was in a room. At the end 'they syng some goodly ballet.'

JOHN HEYWOOD.

John Heywood was born either in London or at North Mimms in Hertfordshire, about 1497. He is claimed as a member of Broadgates

Hall, afterwards Pembroke College, Oxford. From about 1515 he was employed at Court ; in 1519 he is called a 'singer,' later a 'player at virginals,' and finally he was master of a company of children, possibly the singing-school of St. Paul's. His advancement with Henry VIII and the Princess Mary is ascribed to Sir Thomas More, whose kinsman he became. More's sister Elizabeth married John Rastell, lawyer and printer. John Heywood's wife was their granddaughter, Elizabeth. It may be added that their daughter, another Elizabeth, was the mother of John Donne. Heywood took More's line in Church matters, but conformed to the Act of Supremacy. He was in high favour under Mary, and at her death retired to Malines. He was alive in 1577, but dead in 1587.

Heywood's extant interludes are all early work; although Bale, writing in 1557 (*Scriptores*, ed. 2, ii. 110), only ascribes to him *De Aura, comoediam ; De Amore, tragoediam ; De quadruplici P*. The *Pardoner and Friar*, which mentions Leo X as alive, must be before 1521. *Love* and the *Four Ps* may be about as early : the rest may belong to the following decade (Brandl, li). In 1538 Heywood showed a play of children before Mary (Madden, 62). In 1539, Wolsey paid him for a masque of Arthur's Knights, or Divine Providence, at court (Brewer, xiv. (2) 782). In 1553 he set out a play of children at court (*Loseley MSS*. 89). At Mary's coronation he sat in a pageant under a vine against the school in St. Paul's Churchyard and made speeches (Holinshed (1808), iv. 6).

See W. Swododa, *J. Heywood als Dramatiker* (1888).

Plays.

i. *The Pardoner and the Friar*.

Editions.

1533. Wyllyam Rastell. 'A mery Play betwene the pardoner and the frere, the curate and neybour Pratte.'

There are modern editions in F. J. Child, *Four Old Plays* (1848); Hazlitt-Dodsley, vol. i ; Pollard, 114 (extract).

The scene of the action is supposed to be a church. About 1,000 lines. The date of composition was under Leo X (1513–1521).

ii. *Love*.

Editions.

1533. William Rastell. 'A play of loue, A newe and mery enterlude concerning pleasure and payne in loue, made by Ihoñ Heywood.'

[Unique copy in Magd. Coll., Camb. See Greg, *Plays*, 143.]

[1546-1586.] John Waley.

[Unique copy, without title-page, in Bodl., bound with *Weather* and *Four Ps.* (Bodl. 4°, P. 33, Jur.). Copies of these three plays, with one now lost, of 'Old Custom,' are mentioned in an inventory of the effects of John, Earl of Warwick, 1545-1550 (*Hist. MSS.* ii. 102).]

1898. Brandl, 159.

Little more than a series of disputations between Lover Loved, Lover not Loved, Loved not Loving, and No Lover nor Loved. There are 1,573 lines. Towards the end, 'Here the vyse cometh in ronnynge sodenly aboute the place among the audiens with a hye copyn tank on his hed full of squybs fyred.'

iii. *Four Ps.*

Editions.

[1541-1547.] William Myddleton. 'The playe called the foure P, P. A newe and very mery enterlude of A palmer. A pardoner. A poticary. A pedler. Made by Iohn Heewood.'

[1549-1569.] William Copland.

1569. John Allde.

There are modern editions in W. Scott, *Ancient British Drama,* vol. i (1810): Hazlitt-Dodsley, vol. i; Manly, i. 483.

[Copyright, with that of *Love* and *Weather* transferred, Jan. 15, 1582, from late Sampson Awdeley to John Charlwood (Arber, ii. 405). The *Four Pees* is mentioned with other early plays in *Sir Thomas More* (Shakes. Soc. 1844).]

There are no indications of *mise en scène.* There are 1,236 lines.

iv. *Weather.*

Editions.

1533. William Rastell. 'The Play of the wether. A new and very mery enterlude of all maner wethers made by Iohn̄ Heywood.'

[1564-1576.] Anthony Kytson.

1898. Brandl, 211.   1903. Gayley, 19.

The characters are Jupiter, Merry Report, 'the vyce,' Gentleman, Merchant, Ranger, Water Miller, Wind Miller, Gentlewoman, Launder, A Boy ('the lest that can play'). All in turn petition different weather from Jupiter. The piece is 1,255 lines long. Jupiter has his 'thron' (l. 179).

v. *John, Tib and Sir John.*

Editions.

153¾. William Rastell. 'A mery play between Iohan Iohan the husbande, Tyb his wyfe and Syr Ihān the preest.'

1819. Chiswick Press.   1898. Brandl, 259.   1903. Gayley, 61.

The action proceeds in the 'place' (l. 667), which represents Johan's house with a fire (ll. 399, 460). The door of the priest's chamber is also visible (ll. 316, 673). There are 680 lines.

vi. *Witty and Witless.*

Manuscript.

Harl. MS. 367.

Edition.

1846. F. W. Fairholt (Percy Soc.). 'A dialogue concerning witty and witless.'

Thomas Hacket entered the 'pleye of wytles' on S. R. in 1560–1 (Arber, i. 154). This piece is a mere dialogued *débat* or *estrif.*

vii. *Gentleness and Nobility.*

[1516–1533.] John Rastell. 'Of Gentylnes and Nobylyte. A dyaloge ... compilid in maner of an enterlude with diuers toys and gestis addyt therto to make mery pastyme and disport.'

1829. J. H. Burn.

This resembles *Witty and Witless* in character. It is only conjecturally assigned to Heywood. The copy in the British Museum of Rastell's edition (C. 40, i. 16) has a mounted woodcut portrait with the initials I. H., but I do not know whether that really belongs to it.

JOHN BALE.

[*Authorities.*—Collier, i. 123; ii. 159; Ward, i. 173; Lives of Bale in *D. N. B.* (article by Mandell Creighton) and Cooper, *Athenae Cantabrigienses*; his own works, especially *Illustrium Maioris Britanniae Scriptorum Catalogus* (1548, ed. 2, 1557–9, i. 704) and *Vocacyon to Ossory* (*Harl. Miscellany*, ed. 1808, i. 328); editions of plays named below, especially that of Schröer.]

John Bale was born in 1495 at Cove, near Dunwich, in Suffolk. He was placed as a boy in the Carmelite convent of Norwich, thence went to that of Holn, or Holm, in Northumberland, and finally to Jesus College, Cambridge. He took orders, but was converted to Protestantism by Lord Wentworth, and married a 'faithful Dorothy.' He became vicar of Thorndon, in Suffolk, and earned the protection of Thomas Cromwell *ob editas comoedias.* Cromwell's accounts (Brewer, xiv. 2. 337) show payments to him for plays on Sept. 8, 1538, at St. Stephen's, Canterbury, and on Jan. 31, 1539. At his patron's fall in 1540 he fled to Germany, and joined vigorously in polemic. In his *Epistel Exhortatorye of an Inglyshe Christian* (1544), written under the pseudonym of Henry Stalbridge, he says: 'None leave ye unvexed and untrobled—no, not so much as the poore minstrels, and players of enterludes, but ye are doing with them. So long as they played lyes, and sange baudy songes, blasphemed God, and corrupted men's consciences, ye never blamed them, but were verye well contented. But sens they persuaded the people to worship theyr Lorde God aryght, accordyng to hys holie lawes and not yours, and to acknolêdge Jesus Chryst for their onely redeemer and saviour, without your lowsie legerdemains, ye never were pleased with them.' He returned in 1547, and in 1548 printed in his *Scriptores* the following list of his 'in idiomate materno, comedias sub vario metrorum genere.'

1. 'Lib. 14. Vitam D. Ioannis Baptistae.
2. Com. 1. de Christo duodenni.
3. Com. 2. de baptismo & tentatione.
4. Com. 1. de Lazaro resuscitato.
5. Com. 1. de consilio pontificum.
6. Com. 1. de Simone leproso.
7. Com. 1. de coena Domini & pedum lotione.
8. Com. 2. de passione Christi.
9. Com. 2. de sepultura & resurrectione.
10. Lib. 2. super utroque regis coniugio.
11. Lib. 2. de sectis Papisticis.
12. Lib. 2. erga Momos et Zoilos.
13. Lib. 2. Proditiones Papistarum.
14. Lib. 1. contra adulterantes Dei verbum.
15. Lib. 2. *de Ioanne Anglorum rege.*
16. Lib. 1. de imposturis Thomae Becketi.
17. Lib. 1. *de magnis Dei promissionibus.*
18. Lib. 1. *de predicatione Ioannis.*
19. Lib. 1. *de Christi tentatione.*
20. Lib. 1. *Corruptiones legum divinarum.*
21. Lib. 1. Amoris imaginem.
22. Lib. 4. Pammachii tragoedias transtuli.'

As Bale gives a Latin translation of the opening words of each piece, his five extant plays can be identified with those I have italicized. It is to be noted that Nos. 18 and 19 have the same subject as No. 3, which seems to form part of a complete Passion cycle (Nos. 2–9).

In 1547 Bale was made rector of Bishopstoke, Hants, in 1551 of Swaffham, Norfolk, and in 1553 Bishop of Ossory, in Ireland. On the day of the proclamation of Queen Mary he had some of his plays performed at the market-cross of Kilkenny (cf. p. 374). But he had to take refuge at Basle, and on the accession of Elizabeth found himself too old to resume his see, and retired on a prebend in Canterbury Cathedral, where he died in 1563.

Plays.

i. *God's Promises.*

Editions.

(i) 1577. 'A Tragedye or enterlude manyfestyng the chefe promyses of God vnto man by all ages in the olde lawe, from the fall of Adam to the incarnacyon of the lorde Jesus Christ. Compyled by John Bale, An. Do. 1538, and now fyrst imprynted 1577. [List of characters.] *Iohn Charlwood for Stephen Peele, 1577.*'

(ii) n.d. [Another edition]. 'Compyled by Johan Bale, Anno Domini M.D.XVXXVIII.' *B. L.*

(iii) 1874. Hazlitt-Dodsley, i. 277 (and in all earlier editions of Dodsley, from 1744).

A prologue by *Baleus prolocutor* is followed by seven 'Actes,' in which *Adam, Noah, Abraham, Moses, David, Esaias, Iohannes Baptista* discourse in turn with *Pater Coelestis.* Each Act ends with one of the pre-Christmas antiphons known as the seven Oes (cf. vol. i. p. 344), to be sung by a 'Chorus cum organis' in Latin or English. *Baleus Prolocutor* epilogizes, ending 'More of thys matter conclude hereafter we shall.' This play is practically a *Prophetae.*

ii. *John Baptist.*

Editions.

(i) n.d. 'A Brefe Comedy or Enterlude of Johan Baptystes preach-ynge in the Wyldernesse; openynge the craftye assaultes of the hypocrytes, with the gloryouse Baptyme of the Lorde Jesus Christ. Compyled by Johan Bale, Anno M.D.XXXVIII.'

(ii) 1744. *Harleian Miscellany,* i. 97.

Praefatio by *Baleus Prolocutor.* Then *Incipit Comoedia.* Bale has a final speech. The *Interlocutores* are *Pater Coelestis, Ioannes Baptista, Publicanus, Pharisaeus, Iesus Christus, Turba vulgaris, Miles armatus, Sadducaeus.*

iii. *Temptation.*

Editions.

(i) n.d. 'A brefe Comedy or enterlude concernynge the temptacyon of our Lorde and sauer Iesus Christ, by Sathan in the desart. Com-pyled by Iohan Bale, Anno M.D.XXXVIII.'

(ii) 1870. A. B. Grosart, *Miscellanies of Fuller Worthies Library,* vol. i.

Praefatio by *Baleus Prolocutor.* Then *Incipit Comoedia.* Bale has a final speech. The other *Interlocutores* are *Iesus Christus, Satan tentator, Angelus primus, Angelus alter*. The play calls itself an ' Acte.'

[These three plays closely resemble each other. They were all written at Thorndon in 1538, and are markedly Protestant in tone. They were also all performed at Kilkenny, on Aug. 20, 1553.]

iv. *Three Laws.*

Editions.

(i) n.d.   A Comedy concernynge thre lawes, of nature, Moscs, and Christ, corrupted by the Sodomytes Pharysees and Papystes. Compyled by Johan Bale. Anno M.D.XXXVIII.

Colophon: Thus endeth thys Comedy [&c.]. Compyled by Johan Bale. Anno M.D. XXXVIII, and lately inprented per Nicolaum Bamburgensem.

(ii) 1562. Edition by Thomas Colwell.

(iii) A. Schröer, in *Anglia*, v. 137.

The play may have been written in 1538, but the allusions (ll. 2073, 2080) to King Edward and the Lord Protector show that it was revised after 1547.   It is not, like (i), (ii), and (iii), a miracle-play, but a morality, and its Protestantism is far more advanced and polemical than theirs.   It is 2,081 lines long, and has five *Actus*, with the usual *Praefatio* by *Baleus Prolocutor*. The other *Interlocutores* are *Deus pater, Natura lex, Moseh lex, Christi lex vel Euangelium, Infidelitas, Idololatria, Sodomismus, Ambitio, Auaricia, Pseudodoctrina, Hypocrisis, Vindicta Dei, Fides Christiana*.   At the end is a note how ' Into fyue personages maye the partes of thys Comedy be deuyded,' and another for ' The aparellynge of the six vyces or frutes of Infydelyte.'

v. *King John.*

Manuscript.

In possession of the Duke of Devonshire, found amongst papers probably belonging to the Corporation of Ipswich.   Written in two hands, of which one is believed to be Bale's.

Editions.

(i)   1838. Ed. J. P. Collier for Camden Soc.

(ii)   1890. Extract in Pollard, 146.

(iii)   1897. Manly, i. 525, from (i).

' Kynge Johan ' contains 2,656 lines, but is divided into ' ij playes,' i. e. Acts.   At l. 1119 is a reference to ' the seconde acte ' and a ' Finit

Actus Primus.' There are nineteen personages—*Kynge Johan, Ynglond, Clargy, Sedycyon, Cyvyle Order, Stevyn Langton, Commynalte, Nobylyte, Cardynall Pandulphus, Pryvat Welth, Dissimulacyon, Raymundus, Symon of Swynsett, Usurpyd Power, The Pope, Interpretour* (a presenter), *Treasor, Veryte, Imperyall Majestye*—but these are marked with brackets to show that they can be taken by nine actors. The play is strongly Protestant. It was doubtless written before 1548, as 'Lib. 2. de Ioanne Anglorum Rege' are included in Bale's *Scriptores* list of that year. Collier, i. 123, quotes a deposition as to 'an enterlude concernyng King John' performed 'in Christmas tyme [1538–9] at my Lorde of Canterbury's' which was certainly anti-Papal, and was probably Bale's. But the extant text has undergone a later revision, for the prayer at the end is for Elizabeth. Fleay, *Hist. of Stage*, 62, conjectures that it was performed upon her visit to Ipswich in August, 1561. There was probably a single stage or pageant. The characters enter and go out. At l. 1377 Sedycyon speaks 'extra locum'; at l. 785 is the phrase 'Ye may perseyve yt in pagent here this hower.'

Nicholas Grimald.

Grimald was the son of a Genoese clerk in the service of Henry VII. He migrated from Christ's College, Cambridge, to Oxford, where, after a short stay at Brasenose, he became Fellow and Lecturer first of Merton in 1540, then of Christ Church in 1547. To this period belong his Latin plays, and the bulk of his lyrics and other poems in *Tottel's Miscellany*. He was widely read in theology and scholarship, and was chosen chaplain to Bishop Ridley, for whom he did much controversial work. Under Mary in 1555 he was imprisoned, but escaped by a recantation. He was dead before 1562. Bale, *Scriptores* (1557), i. 701, ascribes to him amongst other writings:—

Archiprophetae tragoediam.	*Protomartyrem.*
Famae comoediam.	*Athanasium, seu infamiam.*
Christum nascentem.	*Troilum ex Chaucero, comoediam.*
Christum redivivum.	

Of these the first and fourth survive; of the others some can only be conjecturally put down as plays.

†1540. *Christus Redivivus.*

Editions.

1543. Gymnicus, Cologne. Christus redivivus. Comoedia tragica, sacra et nova. Authore Nicolao Grimaoldo.

1899. J. M. Hart, in *Publications of the Modern Language Association of America*, xiv. No. 3.

The dedication is dated, 'Oxoniae, e Collegio Martonensi. Anno 1543'; but according to the account of the play given therein by the author, it was performed by the *pubes* of B.N.C. before he joined Merton.

1547. *Archipropheta.*
Manuscript.

Brit. Mus. Royal MS. 12 A. 46.

Edition.

1548. Gymnicus, Cologne. Archipropheta, Tragoedia iam recens in lucem edita. Autore Nicolao Grimoaldo.

The dedication is dated 1547. The play is divided into Acts and Scenes, and has choruses. It deals with the story of John the Baptist. Herford, 116, suggests a possible influence from the *Iohannes Decollatus* (1546) of Jakob Schöpper of Dortmund (Bahlmann, *Lat. Dr.* 93).

NICHOLAS UDALL.

[*Authorities.*—Bale, *Scriptores* (1557), i. 717; Ward, i. 254; Pearson, ii. 413; Kempe, 63, 90; S. L. Lee, s.v. Udall in *D. N. B.*; T. Fowler, *Hist. of C.C.C.* 370; Maxwell-Lyte, *Hist. of Eton* (3rd ed. 1899), 117; J. W. Hales, *The Date of the First English Comedy*, in *Englische Studien*, xviii (1893), 408; E. Flügel, *Nicholas Udall's Dialogues and Interludes*, in *Furnivall Miscellany* (1901), 81.]

Life.

Nicholas Udall, Uvedale, Owdall, Woodall, or Yevedall, was born in Hampshire in 1505, and educated at Winchester and Corpus Christi College, Oxford, where he held an informal lectureship in 1526–8. He was an early Oxford exponent of Lutheran views. In 1532 he assisted Leland in preparing verses for the London pageants at the coronation of Anne Boleyn. From 1533–7 he was vicar of Braintree, Essex, and not improbably wrote the play of *Placidas*, alias *Sir Eustace*, recorded in 1534 in the churchwardens' accounts. But from 1534 he was also head master of Eton. Thomas Cromwell's accounts for 1538 include 'Woodall, the schoolmaster of Eton, for playing before my Lord, £5' (Brewer, xiv. 2. 334). In 1541 he left Eton, under an accusation of theft and other misbehaviour. But he found favour with Katharine Parr, Somerset, and Edward VI through literary and theological work, was made tutor to Edward Courtenay and obtained in 1551 a prebend at Windsor, and in 1553 the living of Calborne, Isle of Wight. He had not, however, so far committed himself on the Protestant side as to make it impossible to conform under Mary. He was tutor to Bishop Gardiner's household, and either in 1553 or 1554 became head master of Westminster. Here he remained to his death in 1556. A letter of Mary in 1554 states that he had 'at soondrie seasons' shown 'dialogues and enterludes' before her, and requires the Revels office to provide him with 'apparell' for his 'devises' at the coming Christmas. The Revels accounts for the year mention 'certen plaies' made by him, but the items referring to them cannot be disentangled from those for masks given at the same Christmas. Bale does not mention Udall in the 1548 edition of his *Scriptores*, but in that of 1557 he gives a list of works 'Latine et Anglice,' including ' Comoedias plures, Lib. 1,' and adds that he 'transtulit' for Katherine Parr, 'tragoediam de papatu.' When Elizabeth was at Cambridge on Aug. 8, 1564, 'an English play called Ezekias made by Mr. Udal' was given before her by King's College men (Nichols, *Progr. of Eliz.* i. 186).

Roister Doister.

Editions.

[1566–7. In this year the play was entered on the Stationers' Registers to Thomas Hacket, and to this edition the unique copy, without title-page or colophon, presented in 1818 to the Eton College library, probably belongs.]

1818. Briggs.

1821. F. Marshall.

1830. Thomas White, in *Old English Drama*, vol. i.

1847. W. D. Cooper, for Shakespeare Society.

1869. E. Arber, in *English Reprints*.

1874. Hazlitt-Dodsley, iii. 53.

1897. J. M. Manly, ii. 3 (based on Arber).

1903. E. Flügel, in C. M. Gayley, *Representative English Comedies*, 105.

The play is divided into *Actus* and *Scenae*, and is called in a prologue, which refers to Plautus and Terence, a 'comedie, or enterlude.' The prayer at the end is for a 'queene' who protects the 'Gospell.' Probably Elizabeth is meant. This, however, must be later in date than that of the play itself, which has been fixed by Prof. Hales to 1553–4, on the ground that a passage in it is quoted in the third edition (1553 or 1554) of T. Wilson's *Rule of Reason*, but not in the earlier editions of 1550–1 and 1552. Prof. Hales thinks that Udall was master of Westminster as early as 1553, and wrote it for the boys there. If Wilson's date is 1554, the play may have been one of those given at court in the Christmas of 1553.

IV. LIST OF EARLY TUDOR INTERLUDES.

Pre-Controversial Moralities.

The *dramatis personae* are all abstractions, with an occasional moral type, such as Hickscorner, or a social type, such as a Taverner.

1. †1486–1501. *Henry Medwall. Nature.*
See s. v. Medwall.

2. †1513. *Hickscorner.*
[1501–35.] W. de Worde.   Hyckescorner.
[1546–86.] J. Waley.
Fragments of unidentified editions are described by Greg, *Plays*, 139.
On Jan. 15, 1582, the copyright was transferred from the late Sampson Awdeley to John Charlwood (Arber, ii. 405). Modern reprints are in Hawkins, vol. i; Hazlitt-Dodsley, vol. i; Manly, vol. i. There are 1,026 lines. Ten Brink, iii. 125, dates the play at about the beginning of the sixteenth century.   Collier, ii. 227, and Ward, i. 119, place it in the reign of Henry VII, whose ship, the Regent, is named.   Brandl, xxviii, notes that this is spoken of (l. 356) as sunk, which occurred in 1513.   This is one of the 'auncient Plays' in *Captain Cox*, cxviii.

3. †1513–29. *Youth.*
[1546–86.] J. Waley.   Thēterlude of Youth.
[1549–69.] W. Copland.
Greg, *Plays*, 141, mentions a fragment of a third edition. The play is printed in Hazlitt-Dodsley, vol. ii.   There are about 1,200 lines. Collier, ii. 230; Ward, i. 126; Pollard, liv, put the date in Mary's reign; Brandl, xxviii, early in that of Henry VIII.   Passages are borrowed from *Hickscorner*.   This is named in *Captain Cox*, cxviii.

4. †1517. *John Rastell. The Nature of the Four Elements.*
[1516–33.] John Rastell.   A new interlude and a mery of the nature of the .iiii. elements declarynge many proper poynts of phylosophy naturall and of dyuers strange landys and of dyuers strannge effect and causis, which interlude, if the whole matter be played, will contain the space of an hour and a half; but if you list you may leave out much of the said matter, as . . . and then it will not be past three quarters of an hour of length.

There are modern editions by Halliwell (Percy Soc. lxxiv), and in Hazlitt-Dodsley, vol. i, and extracts in Pollard, 97.   There are about 900 lines.   A note says 'also, yf ye lyst, ye may brynge in a Dysguysinge,' and a direction for the 'dance' or disguising shows that the stage was a 'hall.'   The date is fixed by Collier, ii. 238; Ward,

i. 126; Pollard, 205, on the ground that the discovery of America is said to be ' within this twenty years' and by 'Americus' (i. e. Amerigo Vespucci, 1497). The authorship has been doubted, apparently in ignorance of the ascription of it to Rastell by Bale, *Scriptores* (1557), i. 660 'Insignis hic Cosmographus, de trium mundi partium, Asiae, Africae, et Europae descriptione, ingeniosissimam ac longissimam comoediam primum edidit, cum instrumentis & figuris, quam uocabat *Naturam naturatam. Lib.* i. *Exuberans diuinae potentiae gratia.*' The opening words quoted by Bale translate those of the play 'Thaboundant grace of the power devyne.' Probably Rastell was also the printer, although the unique and imperfect copy (*B.M.* 643, b. 45) has only a manuscript imprint.

5. †1541–8. *John Redford. Wit and Science.*

Printed by Halliwell (Shakespeare Soc., 1848) and Manly, vol. i, from *Brit. Mus. Addl. MS.* 15,233, which is imperfect at the beginning, but has the colophon 'Thus endyth the Play of Wyt and Science, made by Master Jhon Redford.'

There are 1,059 lines. The final prayer is for the 'Kyng and Quene.' Brandl, lxxii, dates the play between 1541, when the 'gaillard,' which is mentioned, was first danced in England, and the death of Katharine Parr in 1548. It was adapted in more than one Elizabethan interlude; cf. Brandl, loc. cit.; J. Seifert, *Wit- und Science-Moralitäten* (1892); and p. 200, n. 2. Redford was at one time Master of the St. Paul's song-school. The MS. also contains songs and fragments of other moralities by him.

Pseudo-Interludes : Disputations.

6. †1521. *John Heywood. Love.*

7. †1521–31. *John Heywood. Witty and Witless.*

8. †1521–31. *John Heywood* (?). *Gentleness and Nobility.*

See s. v. Heywood.

Pseudo-Interlude : Banns.

9. †1503. *W. Dunbar. The Droichis Part of the Play.* Printed in Dunbar's *Works* (ed. J. Small, for Scottish Text Soc.), ii. 314.

One MS. is headed ' Ane Littill Interlud of the Droichis Part of the [Play] '; another, and the fuller, 'Heir followis the maner of the crying of ane playe.' Both have at the end 'Finis off the Droichis Pairt of the Play.'

There are 176 lines. The Droich (dwarf) enters to an 'amyable audiens' in Edinburgh, 'to cry a cry.' He calls himself ' Welth,' and bids

' ȝe noble merchandis ever ilkane
Address ȝow furth with bow and flane
  In lusty grene lufraye,
And follow furth on Robyn Hude.'

The piece is clearly a ' banns ' for a May-game ; cf. vol. i. p. 174. The
S. T. S. editors (i. ccxxxiii), think it was written for the reception of
Princess Margaret in 1503.

Pseudo-Interlude : Translation.

10. *Necromantia.*

[1516–33.] John Rastell. Necromantia. A dialog of the poet
Lucyan, for his fantesye faynyd for a mery pastyme. And furst by
hym compylyd in the Greke tonge. And after translated owt of the
Greke into Latyn, and now lately translated out of Laten into Englissh
for the erudicion of them, which be diopocyd to lerne the tongis.
Inter locutores, Menippus and Philonides.

R. G. C. Proctor, in *Hand Lists of English Printers*, Pt. ii, distinguishes
two editions, one certainly, the other probably, printed by Rastell.
Hazlitt, *Manual*, 164, describes the translation as ' after the manner of
an interlude.' The Latin and English are in parallel columns, and
Collier, ii. 280, who saw a fragment in the Douce collection, thought
that it was ' a modern Latin play, possibly by Rightwise.' Bale,
Scriptores (1557), i. 656, says that More translated Lucian's '*Menippum,
seu Necromantiam, Dial.* 1. *Salue atrium, domusque uesti[bulum]* ' ; but
the reference is probably to the Latin version of this and other dialogues
published in 1506.

Farces of Mediaeval Type.

11. †1521. *John Heywood. The Pardoner and the Friar.*
12. †1521. *John Heywood. The Four Ps.*
13. †1521–31. *John Heywood. The Weather.*
14. †1521–31. *John Heywood. John, Tib and Sir John.*
See s. v. Heywood.

Translation from Spanish.

15. *Calisto and Melibaea.*

[1516–33.] John Rastell. A new cōmodye in englysh in maner Of
an enterlude ryght elygant & full of craft of rethoryk wherein is shewd
& dyscrybyd as well the bewte & good propertes of women as theyr
vycys & euyll cōdiciōs with a morall cōclusion & exhortacyon to
vertew.

A modern reprint is in Hazlitt-Dodsley, vol. i. The *dramatis personae* are Calisto, Melibaea, Sempronio, Celestina, Parmeno. The play is a partial English version through the Italian of the Spanish *Celestina* (1492) of Fernando Rojas de Montalvan and Rodrigo Costa. A later translation is J. Mabbe, *Celestina* (1630), ed. J. Fitzmaurice Kelly in *Tudor Translations*; cf. J. G. Underhill, *Spanish Literature in the England of the Tudors*, 65, 375.

Translation from Classical Latin.

16. *Terence. Andria.*

[1516–33.] John Rastell (?). Terens in englyssh. The translacyon out of Latin into englysh of the furst comedy of tyrens callyd Andria.

Translations from Neo-Latin.

17. 1537. *Thersites.*

[1558–63.] John Tysdale. A new Enterlude called Thersytes. This Enterlude Folowynge Dothe Declare howe that the greatest boesters are not the greatest doers.

There are modern editions in J. Haslewood, *Two Interludes* (Roxburghe Club, 1820); F. J. Child, *Four Old Plays* (1848); Hazlitt-Dodsley, vol. i; also a facsimile by H. S. Ashbee (1876) and extracts in Pollard, 126. There are 915 lines. The *dramatis personae* are Thersites, Mulciber, Miles, Mater, Telemachus. Mulciber has 'a sharp sword made in the place,' and Mater 'the place which is prepared for her.' The date is fixed by a prayer for Prince Edward, born Oct. 12, 1537, and Queen Jane Seymour, who died Oct. 24, 1537. Bolte, in *Vahlen-Festschrift*, 594, says that the piece is translated from the *Thersites* of J. Ravisius Textor, printed in his *Dialogi* (1651), 239. The first edition of the *Dialogi* was in 1530 (Bahlmann, *Lat. Dr.* 31).

18. †1560. *Thomas Ingelend. The Disobedient Child.*

[Probably an Elizabethan play, but included here on account of its relation to *Thersites.*]

[1561–75.] Thomas Colwell. A pretie and Mery new Enterlude: called the Disobedient Child. Compiled by Thomas Ingelend late Student in Cambridge.

There are modern editions by Halliwell (Percy Soc. xxiii) and in Hazlitt-Dodsley, vol. ii. The closing prayer is for Elizabeth. Bolte, loc. cit., considers this a translation of the *Iuvenis, Pater, Uxor* of Ravisius Textor (*Dialogi*, 71). Brandl, lxxiii, finds in it the influence of the *Studentes* (1549) of Christopherus Stymmelius (Bahlmann, *Lat. Dr.* 98).

Farces on Classical Models.

19. †1550–3. *W. Stevenson* (?). *Gammer Gurton's Needle.*

1575. Thomas Colwell. A Ryght Pithy, Pleasaunt anp merie Comedie: Intytuled Gammer gurton's Nedle: Played on Stage, not longe ago in Christes Colledge in Cambridge. Made by Mʳ S. Mʳ of Art.

1661. Thomas Johnson.

There are modern editions in Hawkins, vol. i; W. Scott, *Ancient British Drama* (1810), vol. i; *Old English Drama* (1830), vol. i; Hazlitt-Dodsley, vol. iii; Manly, vol. ii. The latest is by H. Bradley in C. M. Gayley, *Representative English Comedies* (1903).

The play is divided into Acts and Scenes, has a prologue and a *plaudite*; but the subject is not taken from Latin comedy. It is probably identical with the *Dyccon of Bedlam* entered by Colwell on the Stationers' Register in 1562–3, since 'Diccon, the bedlem' is a character. The 1575 edition may, therefore, not have been the first. Jusserand, *Théâtre*, 181, thinks that the satire is even pre-Reformation in tone. The authorship is much in dispute. I. Reed, *Biographia Dramatica* (1782), suggested John Still, afterwards bishop of Bath and Wells, who was a M.A. of Christ's in 1565. C. H. Ross, in *Modern Language Notes*, vii (1892), no. 6, and *Anglia*, xix. 297, accepts John Bridges, afterwards bishop of Oxford, who is spoken of, but with doubtful seriousness, as the author, in *Martin Marprelate's Epistle* (1588). But Bridges' initial is not S, nor was he a Christ's man. H. Bradley, in *Athenæum* for August 6, 1898, and J. Peile, *Christ's College* (1900), 54, 73, point out that one William Stevenson, a Bachelor Fellow of Christ's, is shown by college accounts to have been in charge of plays there between 1550 and 1553. His seems to me by far the strongest claim yet made.

20. †1553–4. *Nicholas Udall.* *Roister Doister.*
See s. v. Udall.

21. †1553–8. *Jack Juggler.*
[1562–9.] W. Copland, A new Enterlude for Chyldren to playe, named Jacke Jugeler, both wytte, and very playsent Newly Imprentid.

According to Grosart, two leaves of another edition are bound with the Duke of Devonshire's copy.

The play was entered by Copland on the Stationers' Register in 1562–3. There are modern reprints in J. Haslewood, *Two Interludes* (Roxburghe Club, 1820); F. J. Child, *Four Old Plays* (1848); A. B. Grosart, *Fuller Worthies Library Miscellanies* (1873), vol. iv; Hazlitt-

Dodsley, vol. ii, and a facsimile by E. W. Ashbee (1876). The piece is an imitation of the *Amphitruo* of Plautus. Brandl, lxxi, assigns it to the reign of Mary on the strength of a Catholic sentiment.

Tragedy on Classical Model (?).

22. †1516–33. *Lucrece.*

A fragment of a 'Play concerning Lucretia' is attributed by R. G. C. Proctor, in *Hand Lists of English Printers* (1896), Part ii, to the press of John Rastell (1516–33). It is in the Bagford collection of fragments, *Harl. MS.* 5919, f. 20 (no. 98), and consists of two pages, containing a scene in which Publius Cornelius instructs a confidential friend with the initial B to sound the feeling of 'Lucres' towards him, and the beginning of a scene between B. and 'Lucres.' Halliwell-Phillipps, ii. 340, says that the play was written by Medwall, †1490, and gives the title as 'A godely interlude of Fulgeus, Cenatoure of Rome, Lucres his daughter, Gayus Flaminius and Publius Cornelius, of the Disputacyon of Noblenes.' The 'Fulgius and Lucrelle' of seventeenth-century play-lists (Hazlitt, *Manual*, s.v.; Greg, *Masques*, lxx, may be related to this. The heroine is not Shakespeare's Lucrece.

Latin Neo-Mysteries.

23. †1535–45. *Thomas Watson (?).* *Absolon.*

Ascham, *Scholemaster* (ed. Mayor, 1869), highly praises, together with Buchanan's *Jephthes*, the *Absolon* of Thomas Watson 'in St John's College Cambridge' which he never would publish because an anapaest sometimes stood where he thought, incorrectly, that there should have been an iambus. Watson became bishop of Lincoln. Fleay, *Biog. Chron.* ii. 267, and others ascribe the play in error to John Watson, bishop of Winchester, and speak of a manuscript at Penshurst, which, however, is not mentioned in the account of the Penshurst MSS. in *Hist. MSS.* iii. app. 227. Probably the play is identical with the *Absolon* preserved in *Brit. Mus. Stowe MS.* 957, described by G. B. Churchill and W. Keller, *Die lat. Universitäts-Dramen Englands in der Zeit der Königin Elisabeth* (*Shakespeare-Jahrbuch*, xxxiv (1898), 229). An eighteenth-century ascription on the first leaf to John Bale is of no authority. The play is of a Senecan type, with acts and scenes and a chorus. The first line was originally 'Adhuc animus vexatur excusso metu,' but in the MS., which has many corrections, 'Animus adhuc' has been substituted.

24. †1540. *Nicholas Grimald.* *Christus Redivivus.*

25. †1547. *Nicholas Grimald.* *Archipropheta.*

See s. v. Grimald.

26. †1550. *John Foxe. Christus Triumphans.*

1551. Christus triumphans, Comoedia apocalyptica. Autore Ioanne Foxo Anglo. London 1551. 8º.

1556. Oporinus, Basle.

1590. Nuremberg, Gerlach.

In 1672 and 1677 the Latin text was edited by Thomas Comber for school use. A French translation by Jacques Bienvenu appeared in 1562. There is also

1579. John and Richard Day. Christ Jesus Triumphant, A fruitefull Treatise, wherein is described the most glorious Triumph, and Conquest of Christ Iesus our Saviour . . . Made to be read for spiritual comfort by Iohn Foxe, and from Latin translated intoo English by the Printer. . . .

There are later editions of 1581 and 1607. This is generally regarded as a translation of the *Christus Triumphans*, but Greg, *Masques*, cxxiii, doubts this, and notes that 'a modern reprint [1828] in the B.M. is not dramatic.' The reprint is in fact a translation of the *De Christo Triumphante, Eiusdem Autoris Panegyricon* appended to the Basle edition of the play. But possibly it does not represent the whole of Day's work. The 1551 edition is given by Bahlmann, *Lat. Dr.* 107. According to S. L. Lee, in *D. N. B.*, it only rests on the authority of Tanner. In 1551 Foxe was tutor to the children of Lord Surrey, who had been executed some years before. In 1555 he entered the printing office of Oporinus at Basle, and in 1564 that of John Day in London. The MS. of the play is *Lansd. MS.* 1073. It is an 'Antichrist' play, written under the influence of the *Pammachius* (1538) of Thomas Kirchmaier or Naogeorgus (Bahlmann, *op. cit.* 71). A full analysis is given by Herford, 138.

Translation from Latin Neo-Moral.

27. †1530–40. *J. Palsgrave. Acolastus.*

1540. Thomas Berthelet. Ioannis Palsgravi Londoniensis, ecphrasis Anglica in comoediam Acolasti. ¶ The Comedye of Acolastus translated into oure englysshe tongue, . . . Interpreted by John Palsgraue.

This is a translation of the *Acolastus* (1530) of Wilhelm de Volder, known in learning as Gnaphaeus or Fullonius, of the Hague (Bahlmann, *Lat. Dr.* 39). It is arranged for school use, with marginal notes on grammar, &c. The original play is the most important of the group dealing with the Prodigal Son motive: cf. Herford, 152.

Drama of Catholic Controversy.

28. 1553. *Respublica.*

Printed by Collier, *Illustrations of Old English Literature* (1866), vol. i, and Brandl, 281, from sixteenth-century MS. of Mr. Hudson Gurney of Keswick Hall, Norfolk, with the heading 'A merye enterlude entitled Respublica, made in the yeare of our Lorde, 1553.'

The play is divided into Acts and Scenes, and is a 'Christmas devise' (prol. 6) by 'boyes' (prol. 39). The place-names are of London. The controversial tone is Catholic, and political, rather than theological. Brandl, lviii, finds the model in Lyndsay's *Satyre.* Except for the Prologue (the Poet) all the characters are abstractions. Avarice, *alias* Policy, is 'the vice of the plaie.'

Dramas of Protestant Controversy.

29. 1538. *John Bale. God's Promises.*

30. 1538. *John Bale. John Baptist.*

31. 1538. *John Bale. The Temptation.*

32. 1538. *John Bale. The Three Laws.*

33. ? 1539, 1561. *John Bale. King John.*
See s. v. Bale.

34. †1547–53. *R. Wever. Lusty Juventus.*

[1549–69.] W. Copland. An Enterlude called lusty Iuuentus. Lyuely describing the frailtie of youth: of natur prone to vyce: by grace and good counsayll, traynable to vertue.—At end of play, 'Finis, quod R. Wever.'

[1548–86.] A. Vele.

Copyright was entered on the Stationers' Register by John King in 1560–1. There are modern reprints in Hawkins, vol. i, and Hazlitt-Dodsley, vol. ii. The characters are abstractions with the Devil, a Messenger, and Little Bess a 'Curtisane.' The prayer is for a king and his council who rule, which points to the reign of Edward VI.

35. †1547–53. *T. R. Nice Wanton.*

1560. John King. A Preaty Interlude called, Nice wanton.—At end of play, 'Finis T. R.'

There are reprints in Hazlitt-Dodsley, vol. i, and Manly, vol. i. The characters are curiously heterogeneous: Messenger, Barnabas, Ismael, Dalila, Eulalia, Iniquitie, Baily Errand, Xantippe, Worldly Shame, Daniel. Brandl, lxxii, considers the play an adaptation of the *Rebelles* (1535) of George Van Langeveldt or Macropedius, of Utrecht (Bahlmann, *Lat. Dr.* 55). The rhyme 'queenes'—'things' in the final prayer shows an original date of composition under Edward VI.

36. †1547–53. *Somebody, Avarice and Minister.*

Fragment of unidentified edition amongst papers of the reign of Edward VI in Lambeth Library, reprinted by S. R. Maitland, *List of Early Printed Books at Lambeth* (1843), 280. Brandl, lix, considers this a politico-religious interlude of the school of Lyndsay.

Protestant Controversy : Translation.

37. †1561. *Henry Cheke. Freewill.*

[1558–63.] John Tisdale. A certayne Tragedie wrytten fyrst in Italian, by F. N. B. entituled, Freewyl, and translated into Englishe, by Henry Cheke.

The copyright of a book 'of frewil' was entered on the Stationers' Register on May 11, 1561 (Arber, i. 156). The original is the *Tragedia del Libero Arbitrio* (1546) of Francesco Nigri de Bassano. The translator cannot be, as stated in the *D. N. B.*, Henry, the son of Sir John Cheke, if the date of his birth is as there given (†1548).

Protestant Controversy : Pseudo-Interludes.

38. †1547–53. *Robin Conscience.*

Often described as an 'interlude,' but really a series of dialogues between Robin Conscience, his father Covetousness, his mother Newguise, and his sister Proud-beauty. Collier, ii. 315, describes it from a printed fragment in the Devonshire library, and inclines to ascribe it to the reign of Edward VI ; cf. Herford, 55. Hazlitt, iii. 225, prints the full text from a later edition.

39. 1549. *Ponet. Bishop of Rome.*

A tragoedie or Dialoge of the uniuste usurped primacie of the Bishop of Rome. A translation by John Ponet, Bishop of Winchester, from the Italian of Bernardino Ochino (1549); cf. Bale, i. 694 ; Herford, 33. Among the speakers are Edward VI and Somerset.

Lost Interludes.

See s. v. Skelton for the alleged *Nigramansir* (1504).

S. Jones, *Biographia Dramatica* (1812), ii. 328, describes 'A newe Interlude of Impacyente Poverte, newlye Imprinted. M. V. L. X.' The copyright of this play, which is in the Sir Thomas More list (cf. p. 200) and that in *Captain Cox*, cxviii, was transferred on the Stationers' Register from the late Sampson Awdeley to John Charlwood on Jan. 15, 1582.

Halliwell-Phillipps, *Dictionary of Old English Plays* (1860), quoting 'Coxeter's Notes,' is the authority for 'An Interlude of Welth and Helth, full of Sport and mery Pastyme,' n. d.

SUBJECT INDEX

[This index is almost wholly confined to the text, and only includes the principal passages dealing with each subject. I am sorry not to have been able to prepare a local or a nominal index. The want of the former may be in part met, so far as the miracle-plays are concerned, by the topographical list of representations in Appendix W.]

THE END